Economic Principles

A Contemporary Introduction

9e

William A. McEachern
University of Connecticut

SOUTH-WESTERN
CENGAGE Learning™

Australia • Brazil • Japan • Korea • Mexico • Singapore • Spain • United Kingdom • United States

SOUTH-WESTERN
CENGAGE Learning™

Economic Principles: A Contemporary Introduction, 9e

William A. McEachern

Vice President of Editorial, Business: Jack W. Calhoun

Publisher: Joe Sabatino

Acquisitions Editor: Steven Scoble

Sr. Developmental Editor: Susanna C. Smart

Editorial Assistant: Allyn Bissmeyer

Marketing Manager: John Carey

Associate Marketing Manager: Betty Jung

Content Project Manager: Corey Geissler

Sr. Frontlist Buyer, Manufacturing: Kevin Kluck

Marketing Communications Manager: Sarah Greber

Production Service: S4Carlisle Publishing Services

Art Director: Michelle Kunkler

Internal Designer: Albonetti Design

Cover Designer: Patti Hudepohl

Photo Credits:

B/W Image: Comstock Images

Cover Image: iStockphoto/Andrea Danti

Rights Acquisitions Specialists: John Hill & Deanna Ettinger

Library of Congress Control Number: 2010930339

International Edition:

ISBN-13: 978-0-538-45375-2

ISBN-10: 0-538-45375-3

Cengage Learning International Offices

Asia
www.cengageasia.com
tel: (65) 6410 1200

Australia/New Zealand
www.cengage.com.au
tel: (61) 3 9685 4111

Brazil
www.cengage.com.br
tel: (55) 11 3665 9900

India
www.cengage.co.in
tel: (91) 11 4364 1111

Latin America
www.cengage.com.mx
tel: (52) 55 1500 6000

UK/Europe/Middle East/Africa
www.cengage.co.uk
tel: (44) 0 1264 332 424

Represented in Canada by Nelson Education, Ltd.
tel: (416) 752 9100/(800) 668 0671
www.nelson.com

Cengage Learning is a leading provider of customized learning solutions with office locations around the globe, including Singapore, the United Kingdom, Australia, Mexico, Brazil, and Japan. Locate your local office at: **www.cengage.com/global**

For product information: **www.cengage.com/international**
Visit your local office: **www.cengage.com/global**
Visit our corporate website: **www. cengage.com**

Printed in Canada
1 2 3 4 5 6 7 14 13 12 11

About the Author

William A. McEachern started teaching large sections of economic principles when he joined the University of Connecticut in 1973. In 1980, he began offing teaching workshops around the country, and, in 1990, he created *The Teaching Economist*, a newsletter that focuses on making teaching more effective and more fun.

His research in public finance, public policy, and industrial organization has appeared in a variety of journals, including *Economic Inquiry, National Tax Journal, Journal of Industrial Economics, Quarterly Review of Economics and Finance, Southern Economic Journal, Econ Journal Watch, Kyklos,* and *Public Choice*. His books and monographs include *Managerial Control and Performance* (D.C. Heath), *School of Finance Reform* (CREUES), and *Tax-Exempt Property and Tax Capitalization in Metropolitan Areas* (CREUES). He has also contributed chapters to edited volumes such as *Rethinking Economic Principles* (Irwin), *Impact Evaluations of Vertical Restraint Cases* (Federal Trade Commission), and *Public Choice Economics* (University of Michigan Press).

Professor McEachern has advised federal, state, and local governments on policy matters and directed a bipartisan commission examining Connecticut's finances. He has been quoted in or written for publications such as the *Times* of London, *New York Times, Wall Street Journal, Christian Science Monitor, USA Today, Challenge Magazine, Connection,* CBS MarketWatch.com, and *Reader's Digest*. He has also appeared on Now with Bill Moyers, Voice of America, and National Public Radio.

In 1984, Professor McEachern won the University of Connecticut Alumni Association's Faculty Award for Distinguished Public Service and in 2000 won the Association's Faculty Excellence in Teaching Award. He is the only person in the university's history to receive both. He was born in Portsmouth, N.H., earned an undergraduate degree with honors from College of the Holy Cross, served three years as an Army Officer, and earned an M.A. and Ph.D. from the University of Virginia.

To Pat

Brief Contents

Contents

Preface

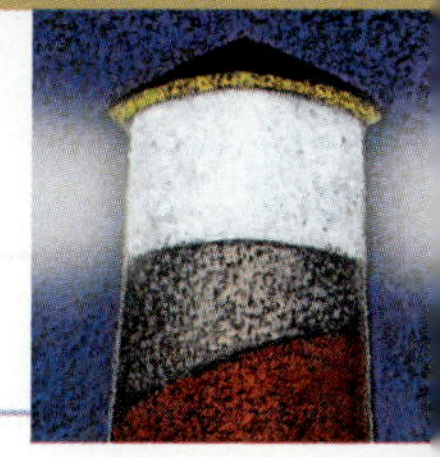

Economics has a short history but a long past. As a distinct discipline, economics has been studied for only a few hundred years, yet civilizations have confronted the economic problem of scarce resources and unlimited wants for millennia. Economics, the discipline, may be centuries old, but it's new every day, with fresh evidence that refines and extends economic theory. What could be newer than the financial crisis, the recession, and the policy responses to them? In this edition of *Economic Principles: A Contemporary Introduction*, I draw on more than three decades of teaching and research experience to convey the vitality, timeliness, and relevance of economics.

Lead by Example

Remember the last time you were in unfamiliar parts and had to ask for directions? Along with the directions came the standard comment, "You can't miss it!" So how come you missed it? Because the "landmark," so obvious to locals, was invisible to you, a stranger. Writing a principles textbook is much like giving directions. Familiarity is a must, but that very familiarity can cloud the author's ability to see the material through the fresh eyes of a new student. One could revert to a tell-all approach, but that will bury students in information. An alternative is to opt for the minimalist approach, writing abstractly about good *x* and good *y*, units of labor and units of capital, or the proverbial widget. But that shorthand turns economics into a foreign language.

Good directions rely on landmarks familiar to us all—a stoplight, a fork in the road, a white picket fence. Likewise, a good textbook builds bridges from the familiar to the new. That's what I try to do—*lead by example*. By beginning with examples that draw on common experience, I try to create graphic images that need little explanation, thereby eliciting from the reader that light of recognition, that "Aha!" I believe that the shortest distance between an economic principle and student comprehension is a lively example. Examples should convey the point quickly and directly. Having to explain an example is like having to explain a joke—the point gets lost. Throughout the book, I try to provide just enough intuition and institutional detail to get the point across. My emphasis is on economic ideas, not economic jargon.

Students show up the first day of class with at least 17 years of experience with economic choices, economic institutions, and economic events. Each grew up in a household—the most important economic institution in a market economy. As consumers, students are familiar with fast-food outlets, cineplexes, car dealerships, online retailers, and scores of stores at the mall. Most students have supplied labor to the job market—more than half had jobs in high school. Students also interact with government—they know about sales taxes, driver's licenses, speed limits, and public schools. And students have a growing familiarity with the rest of the world. Thus, students have abundant experience with economics. This rich lode of personal experience offers a perfect starting point. Rather than try to create for students a new world of economics—a new way of thinking, my approach is to build on student experience—on what Alfred Marshall called "the ordinary business of life."

This book starts with what students bring to the party. For example, to explain resource substitution, rather than rely on abstract units of labor and capital, I begin with washing a car, where the mix can vary from a drive-through car wash (much capital and little labor) to a Saturday morning charity car wash (much labor and little capital). Down-to-earth examples turn the abstract into the concrete to help students remember and learn. Because instructors can cover only a portion of a textbook in the classroom, textbook material should be self-contained and self-explanatory. This gives instructors the flexibility to emphasize in class topics of special interest.

What's New with the Ninth Edition

This edition builds on previous success with additional examples, more questions along the way, and frequent summaries as a chapter unfolds. By making the material both more natural and more personal, I try to engage students in a collaborative discussion. Chapters have been streamlined for a clearer, more intuitive presentation, with fresh examples, new or revised case studies (found at the end of the book), and additional exhibits to crystallize key points.

In terms of overarching themes, this revision emphasizes the recession and policy responses to it. These topics get extensive coverage in the macroeconomic chapters, but I now introduce the idea of macroeconomic fluctuations in Chapter 1. That way, I can bring the recession to the forefront in the introductory chapters (Chapters 1–4) as well as in the micro chapters (Chapters 5–18). There is no reason why micro topics need be insulated from macro effects. Throughout the book, I add timely examples from issues swirling around the recession.

It goes without saying that all data have been revised to reflect the most recent figures available. Time sensitive examples and discussions have also been updated. Here are other relevant revisions by chapter.

Introductory Chapters: 1–4

As with earlier editions, topics common to both macro- and microeconomics are covered in the first four chapters. Limiting introductory material to four chapters saves precious class time, particularly at those institutions where students can take macro and micro courses in either order (and so must cover introductory chapters twice). New or revised features in the introductory chapters include:

Ch. 1: *The Art and Science of Economic Analysis* This chapter provides more detail on the implications of rational self-interest, and adds an additional paragraph about macroeconomics. By elaborating a bit more about macroeconomics here, I can discuss how the recession affected particular micro decisions in other introductory chapters and in the micro chapters.

Ch. 2: *Economic Tools and Economic Systems* The case study on the opportunity cost of college notes that 40 percent of college students hold jobs during the academic year, and in the case study discussing the best and worst countries in which to do business, the pool of countries grows to 183.

Ch. 3: *Economic Decision Makers* I offer more detailed examples of home production. The case study on user-generated products includes more social networks such as Twitter. I discuss how the recession influenced household production. The case study on the information revolution and household production now references the impact of the recession on telecommuting.

Ch.4: *Demand, Supply, and Markets* I add a current example about how a plunge in copper prices affected quantity supplied. To explain how prices reflect scarcity, I discuss why the rental price of a truck from San Francisco to Austin is so much higher than the rental price of one going from Austin to San Francisco.

Microeconomic Chapters: 5–18

Behavioral economics gets more attention in this edition, including an introduction to this emerging field in Chapter 13, plus several case studies at the end of the book that reflect this research. More generally, my approach to microeconomics underscores the role of time and information in production and consumption. I also allow macro issues to affect the micro side. For example, a new case study for Chapter 12, the labor chapter, looks at how the General Motors and Chrysler bailouts affected union workers. And a new case study for Chapter 18, the income distribution chapter, looks at how the recession affected high-income households. The presentation also reflects the growing interest in the economic institutions that underpin impersonal market activity. More generally, I try to convey the idea that most microeconomic principles operate like gravity: Market forces exert pressure, whether or not individual economic actors understand them. At every opportunity, I try to turn the abstract into the concrete. New or revised features in the microeconomic chapters include:

Ch. 5: *Elasticity of Demand and Supply* To show the unintended consequences of public policy, I discuss a finding that smokers compensate for higher cigarette taxes by smoking each cigarette more intensively—that is, by sucking more nicotine from each cigarette.

Ch. 6: *Consumer Choice and Demand* The growing appeal of local produce has tripled the number of farmers' markets in the United States since 1995, showing how tastes change. In the case study on government subsidized health care I discuss how Medicare fraud has replaced illegal drugs as the top crime in Florida.

Ch. 7: *Production and Cost in the Firm* Diseconomies of scale are presented by discussing the world's largest cruise liner, which can accommodate 6,300 but is too large to visit some of the world's most popular destinations. In addition, the financial crisis of 2008 is presented, discussing how it resulted in part because some financial institutions had grown so large and complex that top executives couldn't accurately assess the risks of the financial products they were buying and selling.

Ch. 8: *Perfect Competition* I discuss a study of 732 firms in the United States, France, Germany, and the United Kingdom that finds that firms in competitive industries are more efficient than other firms. And I spell out the problems that arise with the competitive model when there are barriers to exit.

Ch. 9: *Monopoly* I discuss the impact of the recession on the jewelry business—another example of how the macro economy spills into the micro economy. I also mention that China has a world monopoly on the supply of pandas, and to enforce that monopoly—that is, to restrict supply—China requires that any offspring from the pandas rented to zoos around the world become China's property.

Ch.10: *Monopolistic Competition and Oligopoly* In the section on cartels, I cite research showing that cheating increases as the number of firms in the cartel grows. In the discussion of price wars, I describe the dollar-menu duel of cheeseburgers between the McDonald's McDouble and the Burger King Dollar Double.

Ch.11: *Resource Markets* The case study on the lumber industry as an example of derived demand now reflects the bottom falling out of the housing market—more macro leaking into micro. To help explain the shape of a resource supply curve, I note how a higher price for oil enables producers to drill deeper, explore more remote areas, and squeeze oil from tar sands that contain less of it.

Ch.12: *Labor Markets and Labor Unions* In the "Winner Take All" case study, I add more reasons why U.S. executive pay has increased so much. I expand the discussion of geographic wage differences, and provide a new case study about the federal bailout of GM and Chrysler and how it affected the United Auto Workers.

Ch. 13: *Capital, Interest, Entrepreneurship and Corporate Finance* I simplify the presentation of investment. A topic that gets more attention in this edition is entrepreneurship, reflected in the chapter title. I have added a major section discussing the sources of entrepreneurship along with examples of specific entrepreneurs and what they created.

Ch. 14: *Transaction Costs, Imperfect Information, and Behavioral Economics* In the previous edition, this chapter was titled "Transaction Costs, Imperfect Information, and Market Behavior." The substitution of "Behavioral Economics" for "Market Behavior" in the title reflects the coverage of behavioral economics in this edition. I have added a substantial section entitled "Behavioral Economics" that offers an overview of the subject and includes a case study that looks at why some economists are paying more attention to issues of self-control.

Ch.15: *Economic Regulation and Antitrust Policy* I note how critics charged that the Securities and Exchange Commission failed to uncover the massive fraud by Bernie Madoff, despite receiving many complaints about him, because the agency may have been captured by the industry it was supposed to be regulating.

Ch.16: *Public Goods and Public Choice* The case study on farm subsidies reflects the latest legislation. In the discussing the underground economy, I list names used in other countries to describe it, including the shady economy, informal economy, second economy, etc. The case study on campaign finance reform reflects the 2010 Supreme Court decision.

Ch. 17: *Externalities and the Environment* I add oil spills as a third source of water pollution and distinguish between spills on land and spills offshore. A new case study has been added about BP's spill in the Gulf of Mexico. This case study does more than explain events; it raises some fundamental questions about the definition of negative externalities.

Ch.18: *Income Distribution and Poverty* I point out that one reason for the increase in earnings inequality is that more jobs in the U.S. labor market pay workers for their productivity—using bonus pay, commissions, or piece-rate contracts. I cite research showing that one of the many problems with housing discrimination is that people stuck in neighborhoods where few have jobs cannot take advantage of the better job networking available in neighborhoods where more people are working. I add a new case study discussing how the recession affected high-income households.

Macroeconomic Chapters: 19–31

Rather than focus on the differences among competing schools of thought, I use the aggregate demand and aggregate supply model to underscore the fundamental distinction between the *active approach*, which views the economy as unstable and in need of government intervention when it gets off track, and the *passive approach*, which views the economy as essentially stable and self-correcting. Again, all macro data have been updated to reflect the most recent figures available. Equilibrium values for real GDP and the price level used in theoretical models throughout the macro chapters now match actual values prevailing in the U.S. economy. Wherever possible, I rely on student experience and intuition to help explain macroeconomic abstractions such as aggregate demand and aggregate supply. For example, to explain how employment can temporarily exceed its natural rate, I note how students, as the term draws to a close, can temporarily shift into high gear, studying for exams and finishing term papers. To reinforce the link between income and consumption, I point out how easy it is to figure out the relative income of a neighborhood just by driving through it. And to offer students a feel for the size of the federal budget, I note that if all 4.6 thousand tons of gold stored in Fort Knox could be sold at prevailing prices, the proceeds would run the federal government for only two weeks.

Incidentally, instructors who prefer to present macroeconomics first can easily do so by jumping from the final introductory chapter, Chapter 4, to the first macro chapter, Chapter 19. Macro chapters in this edition follow the same order as the previous edition with one exception: The chapter entitled "Productivity and Growth" slips from the second macro chapter to the fourth macro chapter. Because of the increased interest in economic fluctuations, I move up chapters entitled "Tracking the Economy" and "Unemployment and Inflation." New or revised features in the macroeconomics chapters include:

Ch. 19: *Introduction to Macroeconomics* In the previous edition, my "Brief History of the U.S. Economy" identified and discussed four eras. I have now added a fifth era, beginning with the recession compounded by the global financial crisis, and have added a section to describe this new era. To sharpen the focus, I summarize what happened to job totals and real GDP during each of the last three decades.

Ch. 20: *Tracking the U.S. Economy* A new case study describes *The State of the USA*, a Web site funded in part by the health care bill that will offer hundreds of statistics meant to challenge the dominance of GDP as the primary measure of economic progress. I add more background on how real GDP is computed each quarter, with staff members following an estimation process that dates back half a century. I provide similar background about how the CPI is computed.

Ch. 21: *Unemployment and Inflation* I work through the numbers to show that the decade between 2000 and 2010 was the worst for job growth since the Great Depression. I offer more detail about unemployment based on age, gender, ethnicity, and education. I provide two new cases studies: one on how the unemployment rate can rise even during a month of strong job growth (includes a discussion of those "marginally attached to the labor force"), and another on hyperinflation in Zimbabwe that draws in part on my visit there in 2008.

Ch. 22: *Productivity and Growth* I report the finding that countries whose colonizers established strong property rights hundreds of years ago have, on average, much higher per capita incomes today than countries whose colonizers did not. I summarize research about the effects of 9/11 on the vacancy rates of tall buildings in Chicago, and discuss labor productivity gains in TV journalism.

Ch. 23: *Aggregate Expenditure* I examine the impact on consumption and saving of declining net wealth among U.S. households between 2007 and 2009. In the section on the role of expectations on the consumption-saving decision, I note how the saving rate in China since the 1990s jumped on average from 7 percent to 25 percent because families there now have more responsibility for their own housing, health care, and education. In explaining the life-cycle hypothesis, I focus more on consumption and saving among the elderly.

Ch. 24: *Aggregate Expenditure and Aggregate Demand* The case study looking at the ripple effects of the 9/11 attacks now includes cost estimates for the U.S. economy. A new case study focuses on U.S. consumer spending and real GDP during the four worst quarters of the recession. I break consumption down into durable goods, nondurable goods, and services, and show that consumer services, which account for two-thirds of all consumption, held up well and kept the recession from being worse.

Ch. 25: *Aggregate Supply* I discuss the extension of unemployment benefits in some states to nearly two years. In the case study about high unemployment rates in Europe, I add material about the growing problem of long-term unemployment in the United States, and the difference between unemployment benefits in Western Europe and the United States, among other differences.

Ch. 26 *Fiscal Policy* Germane to the permanent-income hypothesis, I review the disappointing effects of the one-time tax rebate in early 2008. I added a substantial new section entitled "Fiscal Policy and the 2007–2009 Recession." This includes coverage of the financial crisis and its aftermath, the stimulus package, and government spending and real GDP. A new case study assessing the "Cash for Clunkers" program has been added for this chapter.

Ch. 27: *Federal Budgets and Public Policy* At various points throughout the chapter, the impact of the recession and stimulus program on the federal budget are discussed. The revision takes on more of an international flavor in light of growing sovereign debt burdens around the world. International comparisons add context to the U.S. levels of deficits and debt. I also add two new sections: "Trillion Dollar Deficits" and "Are Persistent Deficits Sustainable?"

Ch. 28: *Money and the Financial System* I add four sections on the following: "Subprime Mortgages and Mortgage-Backed Securities" "Incentive Problems and the Fiscal Crisis of 2008," "The Troubled Asset Relief Program," and "The Dodd-Frank Wall Street Reform and Consumer Protection Act." A new case study examines the medium of exchange used in the U.S. federal prison system, where cash is prohibited, and reinforces the fundamental properties of money in a way that students should find interesting.

Ch. 29: *Banking and the Money Supply* This chapter spells out the recent important changes in bank regulations. I look at the Fed's balance sheet, which takes on special significance in light of the dramatic changes in Fed assets and liabilities as the Fed tried to rescue America's financial institutions. A new case study looks at "payday lenders"—a decade ago there were no payday lenders in the country; now there are thousands.

Ch.30: *Monetary Theory and Policy* A substantial case study reviews the FOMC's use of the federal funds rate since 1996. I note that the velocity of money slowed during the recession as more people hoarded cash. I add a section describing "Other Fed Actions and Concerns" during the financial crisis, and note how economists are looking more at the Fed's balance sheet to understand monetary policy.

Ch. 31: *Macro Policy Debate: Active or Passive*? This revision reflects the rising use of fiscal policy and the growing debate about its costs and benefits. I note that the average lag between a recession's end and the official announcement that it has ended is about 15 months. I discuss the policy uncertainty created by several broad legislative actions, such as the stimulus bill, health care reform, and financial reform.

International Chapters: 32–34

This edition reflects the growing impact of the world economy on U.S. economic welfare. International issues are introduced early and discussed often. For example, the rest of the world is introduced in Chapter 1 and profiled in Chapter 3. Comparative advantage and the production possibilities frontier are discussed from a global perspective in Chapter 2. International coverage is woven throughout the text. By comparing the U.S. experience with that of other countries around the world, students gain a better perspective about such topics as unionization trends, antitrust laws, pollution, conservation, environmental laws, tax rates, the distribution of income, economic growth, productivity, unemployment, inflation, central bank independence, government spending, and federal debt. Exhibits show comparisons across countries of various economic measures—everything from the percentage of paper that gets recycled to public outlays relative to GDP. International references are scattered throughout the book, including a number of relevant case studies, located at the end of the text.

Again, every effort is made to give students a feel for the numbers. For example, to convey the importance of U.S. consumers in the world economy, I note that Americans represent less than 5 percent of the world's population, but they buy more than half the Rolls Royces and diamonds sold worldwide. New or revised features in the international chapters include:

Ch. 32 *International Trade* I discuss how the recession reduced the trade deficit as U.S. consumers cut back on all their purchases, including what they spent on foreign products. I now describe the terms of trade in a way that matches the slope of the production possibilities frontier in each country. I discuss how the national defense argument for trade restrictions has been extended to justify recent efforts to block China from buying American oil or steel producers.

Ch. 33: *International Finance* I describe how the recession shrank the U.S. trade deficit relative to GDP from 5.9 percent in 2007 to 3.5 percent in 2009, and identify some of those few countries with which the U.S. has a trade surplus. A case study notes how China seeks every trade advantage, especially for the 125 state-owned enterprises run directly by the central government. Between 2007 and 2010, China's holding of U.S. Treasury securities more than doubled from $400 billion to $900 billion.

Ch. 34: *Economic Development* I offer a brief summary of transitional economies and focus the chapter more on "Economic Development." A case study considers a new method of estimating economic growth in countries where data are poor or nonexistent by measuring differences over time in the intensity of night lights on the ground using a satellite camera high above the Earth. In the section entitled "Entrepreneurship," I highlight the role of McDonald's and other franchises that train a cadre of managers from poor countries and offer customers there an idea of what's possible in the way of service, cleanliness, and quality. To the section about how exporting subsidized food to developing countries has hurt poor farmers in those countries, I add a discussion of how sending used clothing from richer countries has hurt the local textile industry in recipient countries.

Student-Friendly Features

In some principles textbooks, chapters are broken up by boxed material, qualifying footnotes, and other distractions that disrupt the flow of the material. Students aren't sure when or if they should read such segregated elements. But this book has a natural flow. Each chapter opens with a few off-beat questions and then follows with a logical narrative. Students can thus read each chapter from the opening questions to the conclusion and summary. I also adhere to a "just-in-time" philosophy, introducing material just as it's needed to build an argument. Footnotes are used sparingly and then only to cite sources, not to qualify or extend material in the text.

This edition is more visual than its predecessors, with more exhibits to reinforce key findings. Exhibit titles convey the central points, and more exhibits now have summary captions. Captions have been edited for clarity and brevity. The point is to make the exhibits more self-contained. Students learn more if concepts are presented both in words and in exhibits. Additional summary paragraphs have been added throughout each chapter; these summaries begin with the bold-faced identifier "**To Review**". Economic jargon has been reduced. Although the number of terms defined in the margin has increased modestly, definitions have been pared to make them clearer and less like entries from a dictionary. In short, economic principles are now more transparent (a textbook should not be like some giant Easter egg hunt, where it's up to the student to figure out what the author is trying to say). Overall, the ninth edition is a cleaner presentation, a straighter shot into the student's brain.

Color is used systematically within graphs, charts, and tables to ensure that students can easily see what's going on. Throughout the book, demand curves are blue and supply curves are red. Color shading distinguishes key areas of many graphs, and color identifies outcomes in others. For example, economic profit and welfare gains are always shaded blue and economic loss and welfare losses are always shaded pink. In short, color is more than mere eye candy—it is coordinated consistently and with forethought to help students learn (a dyslexic student once told me she found the book's color guide quite helpful). Students benefit from these visual cues.

The McEachern TEXT *Web site (www.cengage.com/international).* The Web site designed to be used with this textbook provides chapter-by-chapter online study aids that include a glossary and Internet features, among others. Some of the highlights include:

Key Terms Glossary A convenient, online glossary enables students to use the point-and-click flashcard functionality of the glossary to test themselves on key terminology.

In-Text Web Feature To streamline navigation, the site links directly to Web sites discussed in the Internet-enhanced in-text e-Activities feature for each chapter. This application provides students with opportunities to interact with the material by performing real-world analyses.

CourseMate: Engaging, Affordable

Interested in a simple way to *complement* your text and course content with study and practice materials?

Cengage Learning's Economics CourseMate brings course concepts to life with interactive learning, study, and exam preparation tools that support the printed textbook. Watch student comprehension soar as your class works with the printed textbook and the textbook-specific website. Economics CourseMate goes beyond the book to deliver what you need!

Economic Principles: A Contemporary Introduction CourseMate includes:

- Interactive eBook
- Quizzes
- Flashcards
- Videos
- Graphing Tutorials
- News, Debates, and Data
- Engagement Tracker

Engagement Tracker

How do you assess your students' engagement in your course? How do you know your students have read the material or viewed the resources you've assigned? How can you tell if your students are struggling with a concept? With CourseMate, you can use the included Engagement Tracker to assess student preparation and engagement. Use the tracking tools to see progress for the class as a whole or for individual students. Identify students at risk early in the course. Uncover which concepts are most difficult for your class. Monitor time on task. Keep your students engaged.

Interactive Teaching and Learning Tools

CourseMate includes interactive teaching and learning tools: quizzes, flashcards, videos and more. These assets enable students to review for tests, prepare for class, and address the needs of students' varied learning styles. *Economic Principles, 9e* CourseMate also includes Economic Applications (news, policy debates, and data) and and Graphing Workshop.

Interactive eBook

In addition to interactive teaching and learning tools, CourseMate includes an interactive eBook. Students can take notes, highlight, search and interact with embedded media specific to their book. Use it as a supplement to the printed text, or as a substitute—the choice is up to your students with CourseMate.

Find out more at: www.cengage.com.

The Support Package

The teaching and learning support package that accompanies *Economic Principles: A Contemporary Introduction* provides instructors and students with focused, accurate, and innovative supplements to the textbook.

Study Guides Written by John Lunn of Hope College, study guides are available for the full textbook, as well as for the micro and macro "split" versions. Every chapter of each study guide corresponds to a chapter in the text and offers (1) an introduction; (2) a chapter outline, with definitions of all terms; (3) a discussion of the chapter's main points; (4) a *lagniappe*, or bonus, which supplements material in the chapter and includes a "Question to Think About"; (5) a list of key terms; (6) a variety of true-false, multiple-choice, and discussion questions; and (7) answers to all the questions.

Teaching Assistance Manual Written and revised by me, the *Teaching Assistance Manual* provides additional support beyond the *Instructor's Manual.* It is especially useful to new instructors, graduate assistants, and teachers interested in generating more class discussion. This manual offers (1) overviews and outlines of each chapter, (2) chapter objectives and quiz material, (3) material for class discussion, (4) topics warranting special attention, (5) supplementary examples, and (6) "What if?" discussion questions. Appendices provide guidance on (1) presenting material; (2) generating and sustaining class discussion; (3) preparing, administering, and grading quizzes; and (4) coping with the special problems confronting foreign graduate assistants.

Test Banks Thoroughly revised for currency and accuracy by Kenneth Slaysman, York College of Pennsylvania, the microeconomics and macroeconomics test banks contain over 6,600 questions in multiple-choice and true-false formats. All multiple-choice questions are rated by degree of difficulty, and are labeled with AACSB compliance tags.

ExamView—Computerized Testing Software *ExamView* is an easy-to-use test-creation software package available in versions compatible with Microsoft Windows and Apple Macintosh. It contains all the questions in the printed test banks. Instructors can add or edit questions, instructions, and answers; select questions by previewing them on the screen; and then choose them by number or at random. Instructors can also create and administer quizzes online, either over the Internet, through a local area network (LAN), or through a wide area network (WAN).

Microsoft PowerPoint Lecture Slides Lecture slides revised by Andreea Chiritescu of Eastern Illinois University, contain tables and graphs from the textbook, and are intended to enhance lectures and help integrate technology into the classroom.

Microsoft PowerPoint Figure Slides These PowerPoint slides contain key figures from the text. Instructors who prefer to prepare their own lecture slides can use these figures as an alternative to the text's PowerPoint lecture slides.

The Teaching Economist Since 1990, the author has edited *The Teaching Economist*, a newsletter aimed at making teaching more interesting and more fun. The newsletter discusses imaginative ways to present topics—for example, how to "sensationalize" economic concepts, useful resources on the Internet, economic applications from science fiction, recent research in teaching and learning, and more generally, ways to teach just for the fun of it. A regular feature of *The Teaching Economist*, "The Grapevine," offers teaching ideas suggested by colleagues from across the country. The latest issue—and back issues—of *The Teaching Economist* are available online at cengage.com/economics/mceachern/theteachingeconomist/index.html.

Aplia Started in 2000 by economist and instructor, Paul Romer, more students are currently using an Aplia Integrated Textbook Solution for principles of economics than are using all other web-based learning programs combined. Because the assignments in Aplia are automatically graded, you can assign homework more frequently to ensure your students are putting forth a full effort and getting the most out of your class. Assignments are closely tied to the text and each McEachern Aplia course has a digital edition of the textbook embedded right in the Aplia program. This digital text is now in the Aplia Text format, which gives students the same interactive experience they get on Web sites they use in their personal lives.

News Videos Video segments from news sources bring the real world to your classroom to illustrate how economics is an important part of daily life and how the text material applies to current events. Contact your Cengage Learning sales consultant for access.

WebTutor Toolbox WebTutor Toolbox offers basic online study tools including learning objectives, flashcards, and practice quizzes.

Acknowledgments

Many people contributed to this book's development. I gratefully acknowledge the insights, comments, and criticisms of those who have reviewed the book for this and previous editions or provided feedback on particular points. Their remarks changed my thinking on many points and improved the book.

Steve Abid,
Grand Rapids Community College
Basil Al-Hashimi,
Mesa Community College - Red Mountain
Polly Reynolds Allen,
University of Connecticut
Mary Allender,
University of Portland
Jeffrey Alstete,
Iona College
Hassan Y. Aly,
Ohio State University
Ted Amato,
University of North Carolina, Charlotte
Donna Anderson,
University of Wisconsin, La Crosse
Richard Anderson,
Texas A&M University
Kyriacos Aristotelous,
Otterbein College
James Aylesworth,
Lakeland Community College
Mohsen Bahmani Mohsen Bahmani-Oskooee,
University of Wisconsin, Milwaukee
Dale Bails,
Christian Brothers College
Benjamin Balak,
Rollins College
A. Paul Ballantyne,
University of Colorado at Colorado Springs
Andy Barnett,
Auburn University
Bharati Basu,
Central Michigan University
Klaus Becker,
Texas Tech University
Charles Bennett,
Gannon University
Trisha L. Bezmen,
Old Dominion University
Jay Bhattacharya,
Okaloosa Walton Community College
Gerald W. Bialka,
University of North Florida
William Bogart,
Case Western Reserve University
Andrew A. Bonacic
Adirondack College
Kenneth Boyer,
Michigan State University
David Brasfield,
Murray State University
Jurgen Brauer,
Augusta College
Taggert Brooks,
University of Wisconsin, La Crosse
Gardner Brown, Jr.,
University of Washington
Eric Brunner,
Morehead State University
Francine Butler,
Grand View College
Judy Butler,
Baylor University
Charles Callahan III,
SUNY College at Brockport
Giorgio Canarella,
California State University, Los Angeles
Shirley Cassing,
University of Pittsburgh
Shi-fan Chu,
University of Nevada–Reno
Ronald Cipcic,
Kalamazoo Valley Community College
Larry Clarke,
Brookhaven College
Rebecca Cline,
Middle Georgia College
Stephen Cobb,
Xavier University
Doug Conway,
Mesa Community College
Mary E. Cookingham,
Michigan State University
James P. Cover,
University of Alabama
James Cox,
DeKalb College
Jerry Crawford,
Arkansas State University
Thomas Creahan,
Morehead State University
Carl Davidson,
Michigan State University
Elynor Davis,
Georgia Southern University
Susan Davis,
SUNY College at Buffalo
A. Edward Day,
University of Central Florida
David Dean,
University of Richmond
Janet Deans,
Chestnut Hill College
Dennis Debrecht,
Carroll College
David Denslow,
University of Florida
Kruti R. Dholakia,
Grayson County College
Gary Dymski,
University of California–Riverside
John Edgren,
Eastern Michigan University
Ron D. Elkins,
Central Washington University
Donald Elliott, Jr.,
Southern Illinois University
G. Rod Erfani,
Transylvania University
Gisela Meyer Escoe,
University of Cincinnati
Mark Evans,
California State University, Bakersfield
Jamie Falcon,
University of Maryland Baltimore County
Gregory Falls,
Central Michigan University
Eleanor Fapohunda,
SUNY College at Farmingdale
Mohsen Fardmanesh,
Temple University
Paul Farnham,
Georgia State University
Rudy Fichtenbaum,
Wright State University

T. Windsor Fields, *James Madison University*
Rodney Fort, *Washington State University*
Richard Fowles, *University of Utah*
Roger Frantz, *San Diego State University*
Julie Gallaway, *Southwest Montana State University*
Gary Galles, *Pepperdine University*
Edward Gamber, *Lafayette College*
Adam Gifford, *California State University, Northridge*
J. P. Gilbert, *MiraCosta College*
Robert Gillette, *University of Kentucky*
Art Goldsmith, *Washington and Lee University*
Rae Jean Goodman, *U.S. Naval Academy*
Robert Gordon, *San Diego State University*
Fred Graham, *American University*
Philip Graves, *University of Colorado, Boulder*
Gary Greene, *Manatee Community College*
Harpal S. Grewal, *Claflin College*
Carolyn Grin, *Grand Rapids Community College*
Daniel Gropper, *Auburn University*
Simon Hakim, *Temple University*
Robert Halvorsen, *University of Washington*
Nathan Eric Hampton, *St. Cloud State University*
Mehdi Haririan, *Bloomsburg University*
William Hart, *Miami University*
Baban Hasnat, *SUNY College at Brockport*
Travis Lee Hayes, *Chattanooga State Technical Community College*
Julia Heath, *University of Memphis*
James Heisler, *Hope College*
James Henderson, *Baylor University*
Michael Heslop, *Northern Virginia Community College*
James R. Hill, *Central Michigan University*
Jane Smith Himarios, *University of Texas, Arlington*
Calvin Hoerneman, *Delta College*
Tracy Hofer, *University of Wisconsin, Stevens Point*
George E. Hoffer, *Virginia Commonwealth University*
Dennis Hoffman, *Arizona State University*
Bruce Horning, *Fordham University*
Calvin Hoy, *County College of Morris*
Jennifer Imazeki, *San Diego State University*
Beth Ingram, *University of Iowa*
Paul Isley, *Grand Valley State University*
Joyce Jacobsen, *Wesleyan University*
Nancy Jianakoplos, *Colorado State University*
Claude Michael Jonnard, *Fairleigh Dickinson University*
Nake Kamrany, *University of Southern California*
Bryce Kanago, *Miami University*
John Kane, *SUNY College at Oswego*
David Kennett, *Vassar College*
William Kern, *Western Michigan University*
Robert Kleinhenz, *California State University, Fullerton*
Faik Koray, *Louisiana State University*
Joseph Kotaska, *Monroe Community College*
Barry Kotlove, *Edmonds Community College*
Marie Kratochvil, *Nassau Community College*
Joseph Lammert, *Raymond Walters College*
Christopher Lee, *Saint Ambrose University, Davenport*
Jim Lee, *Fort Hays State University*
Dennis Leyden, *University of North Carolina, Greensboro*
Carl Liedholm, *Michigan State University*
Hyoung-Seok Lim, *Ohio State University*
C. Richard Long, *Georgia State University*
Ken Long, *New River Community College*
Michael Magura, *University of Toledo*
Thomas Maloy, *Muskegon Community College*
Gabriel Manrique, *Winona State University*
Barbara Marcus, *Davenport College*
Robert Margo, *Vanderbilt University*
Nelson Mark, *Ohio State University*
Richard Martin, *Agnes Scott College*
Peter Mavrokordatos, *Tarrant County College*
Wolfgang Mayer, *University of Cincinnati*
Bruce McCrea, *Lansing Community College*
John McDowell, *Arizona State University*
KimMarie McGoldrick, *University of Richmond*
David McKee, *Kent State University*
James McLain, *University of New Orleans*
Mark McNeil, *Irvine Valley College*
Michael A. McPherson, *University of North Texas*
Scott Eric Merryman, *University of Oregon*
Michael Metzger, *University of Central Oklahoma*
Art Meyer, *Lincoln Land Community College*
Carrie Meyer, *George Mason University*
Charles Meyrick, *Housatonic Community College*
Martin Milkman, *Murray State University*

Green R. Miller,
Morehead State University
Bruce D. Mills,
Troy State University, Montgomery
Milton Mitchell,
University of Wisconsin, Oshkosh
Shannon Mitchell,
Virginia Commonwealth University
Barry Morris,
University of North Alabama
Tina Mosleh,
Ohlone College
Kathryn Nantz,
Fairfield University
Paul Natke,
Central Michigan University
Rick Nelson,
Lansing Community College
Heather Newsome,
Baylor University
Farrokh Nourzad,
Marquette University
Maureen O'Brien,
University of Minnesota, Duluth
Norman P. Obst,
Michigan State University
Joan Q. Osborne,
Palo Alto College
Jeffrey Phillips,
Thomas College
Jeffrey D. Prager,
East Central College
Fernando Quijano,
Dickinson State University
Jaishankar Raman,
Valparaiso University
Reza Ramazani,
St. Michael's University
Carol Rankin,
Xavier University
Mitch Redlo,
Monroe Community College
Kevin Rogers,
Mississippi State University
Scanlon Romer,
Delta College
Duane Rosa,
West Texas A&M University
Robert Rossana,
Wayne State University
Mark Rush,
University of Florida
Richard Saba,
Auburn University
Simran Sahi,
University of Minnesota, Twin Cities
Richard Salvucci,
Trinity University
Rexford Santerre,
University of Connecticut
George D. Santopietro,
Radford University
Sue Lynn Sasser,
University of Central Oklahoma
Ward Sayre,
Kenyon College
Ted Scheinman,
Mt. Hood Community College
Peter Schwartz,
University of North Carolina, Charlotte
Carol A. Scotese,
Virginia Commonwealth University
Shahrokh Shahrokhi,
San Diego State University
Roger Sherman,
University of Houston
Michael Shields,
Central Michigan University
Alden Shiers,
California Polytechnic State University
Virginia Shingleton,
Valparaiso University
Frederica Shockley,
California State University, Chico
William Shughart II,
University of Mississippi
Paul Sicilian,
Grand Valley State University
Charles Sicotte,
Rock Valley College
Calvin Siebert,
University of Iowa
Gerald P. W. Simons,
Grand Valley State University
Brian W. Sloboda,
University of Phoenix
Phillip Smith,
DeKalb College
V. Kerry Smith,
Duke University
David Spencer,
Brigham Young University
Jane Speyrer,
University of New Orleans
Joanne Spitz,
University of Massachusetts
Mark Stegeman,
Virginia Polytechnic Institute
Houston Stokes,
University of Illinois, Chicago
Robert Stonebreaker,
Indiana University of Pennsylvania
Michael Stroup,
Stephen Austin State University
William Swift,
Pace University
James Swofford,
University of South Alabama
Linghui Tang,
Drexel University
Donna Thompson,
Brookdale Community College
John Tribble,
Russell Sage College
Lee J. Van Scyoc,
University of Wisconsin, Oshkosh
Percy Vera,
Sinclair Community College
Han X. Vo,
Winthrop University
Jin Wang,
University of Wisconsin, Stevens Point
Gregory Wassall,
Northeastern University
William Weber,
Eastern Illinois University
David Weinberg,
Xavier University
Bernard Weinrich,
St. Louis Community College
Donald Wells,
University of Arizona
Robert Whaples,
Wake Forest University
Mark Wheeler,
Western Michigan University
Michael White,
St. Cloud State University
Richard Winkelman,
Arizona State University
Stephan Woodbury,
Michigan State University
Kenneth Woodward,
Saddleback College
Patricia Wyatt,
Bossier Parish Community College
Peter Wyman,
Spokane Falls Community College
Mesghena Yasin,
Morehead State University
Edward Young,
University of Wisconsin, Eau Claire
Michael J. Youngblood,
Rock Valley College
William Zeis,
Bucks Community College

I also thank the many contributions and comments from the group of instructors who participated in the Online Survey of my book, or responded to our phone surveys:

Richard U. Agesa, *Marshall University*
John Beck, *Gonzaga University*
Randall Bennett, *Gonzaga University*
Andrew M. Bonacic, *Adirondack College*
Joseph Daniels, *Marquette University*
Maria Davis, *Indian River State College*
Mary Sue DePuy, *Arizona Western College*
Erwin F. Erhardt, , *III ,University of Cincinnati*
George Hoffer, *Virginia Commonwealth University*
Judy Hurtt, *East Central Community College*
E.M. Jankovic, *Fairfield University*
Sunita Kumari, *St. Petersburg College*
J. Franklin Lee, *Pitt Community College*
Harry Miley, *South Carolina State University*
Kaustav Misra, *Mississippi State University*
Phillip Mixon, *Troy University*
John Rapczak, *Community College of Rhode Island*
Richard Rouch, *Volunteer State Community College*
Jeff Wiltzius, *Indian River State College*
Sourushe Zandvakili, *University of Cincinnati*

To practice what I preach, I relied on the division of labor based on comparative advantage to help put together an attractive teaching package. John Lunn of Hope College authored the study guides. Robert Sandman of Wilmington College revised the instructor's manual. Kenneth Slaysman of York College of Pennsylvania reworked the test banks. And Andreea Chiritescu of Eastern Illinois University prepared the PowerPoint lecture slides. I thank them all for their help and for their imagination.

The talented professionals at South-Western Cengage provided invaluable editorial, administrative, and sales support. I owe a special debt to Susan Smart, senior developmental editor, who nurtured the manuscript through reviews, revisions, editing, and production. She also helped with Internet activities, photography selection, and coordinated the work of others who contributed to the publishing package. For the fresh look of the book, I owe a debt to Michelle Kunkler, art director, Lisa Albonetti, designer, and John Hill, photography manager. I am also grateful to the content project manager, Corey Geissler, and S4-Carlisle Publishing Services, who helped create the printed pages. Sharon Morgan has been valuable as the technology project manager. I would also like to thank Sarah Greber, senior marketing communications manager, who has been most helpful, especially with the publication of my newsletter, *The Teaching Economist*.

I am most grateful to Jack Calhoun, vice president and editorial director; Steve Scoble, senior acquisitions editor and problem solver; and John Carey, the senior marketing manager whose knowledge of the book dates back to the beginning. As good as the book may be, all our efforts would be wasted unless students get to read it. To that end, I greatly appreciate the dedicated service and sales force of South-Western Cengage, who have contributed in a substantial way to the book's success.

Finally, I owe an abiding debt to my wife, Pat, who provided abundant encouragement and support along the way and read the entire manuscript.

William A. McEachern

Economic Principles

A Contemporary Introduction

9e

The Art and Science of Economic Analysis

1

Siri Stafford/Getty Images

- Why are comic-strip and TV characters like Foxtrot, the Simpsons, and the Family Guy missing a finger on each hand?
- Why do the kids on South Park have hands that look like mittens? And where is Dilbert's mouth?
- Why does Japan have nearly 10 times more vending machines per capita than does Europe?
- In what way are people who pound on vending machines relying on theory?
- Why is a good theory like a California Closet?
- What's the big idea with economics?
- Finally, how can it be said that in economics "what goes around comes around"?

These and other questions are answered in this chapter, which introduces the art and science of economic analysis.

You have been reading and hearing about economic issues for years—unemployment, inflation, poverty, recessions, federal deficits, college tuition, airfares, stock prices, computer prices, gas prices. When explanations of such issues go into any depth, your eyes may glaze over and you may tune out, the same way you do when a weather forecaster tries to provide an in-depth analysis of high-pressure fronts colliding with moisture carried in from the coast.

What many people fail to realize is that economics is livelier than the dry accounts offered by the news media. Economics is about making choices, and you make economic choices every day—choices about whether to get a part-time job or focus on your studies, live in a dorm or off campus, take a course in accounting or one in history, get married or stay single, pack a lunch or buy a sandwich. You already know much more about economics than you realize. You bring to the subject a rich personal experience, an experience that will be tapped throughout the book to reinforce your understanding of the basic ideas.

Topics discussed in this chapter include:

- The economic problem
- Marginal analysis
- Rational self-interest
- Scientific method
- Normative versus positive analysis
- Pitfalls of economic thinking

The Economic Problem: Scarce Resources, Unlimited Wants

Would you like a new car, a nicer home, better meals, more free time, a more interesting social life, more spending money, more leisure, more sleep? Who wouldn't? But even if you can satisfy some of these desires, others keep popping up. *The problem is that, although your wants, or desires, are virtually unlimited, the resources available to satisfy these wants are scarce.* A resource is *scarce* when it is not freely available—that is, when its price exceeds zero. Because resources are scarce, you must choose from among your many wants, and whenever you choose, you must forgo satisfying some other wants. The problem of scarce resources but unlimited wants exists to a greater or lesser extent for each of the 6.9 billion people on earth. Everybody—cab driver, farmer, brain surgeon, dictator, shepherd, student, politician—faces the problem. For example, a cab driver uses time and other scarce resources, such as the taxi, knowledge of the city, driving skills, and gasoline, to earn income. That income, in turn, buys housing, groceries, clothing, trips to Disney World, and thousands of other goods and services that help satisfy some of the driver's unlimited wants. **Economics** examines how people use their scarce resources to satisfy their unlimited wants. Let's pick apart the definition, beginning with resources, then goods and services, and finally focus on the heart of the matter—economic choice, which arises from scarcity.

economics
The study of how people use their scarce resources to satisfy their unlimited wants

Resources

Resources are the inputs, or factors of production, used to produce the goods and services that people want. *Goods and services are scarce because resources are scarce.* Resources sort into four broad categories: labor, capital, natural resources, and entrepreneurial ability. **Labor** is human effort, both physical and mental. Labor includes the effort of the cab driver and the brain surgeon. Labor itself comes from a more fundamental resource: *time*. Without time we can accomplish nothing. We allocate our time to alternative uses: We can *sell* our time as labor, or we can *spend* our time doing other things, like sleeping, eating, studying, playing sports, going online, attending class, watching TV, or just relaxing with friends.

resources
The inputs, or factors of production, used to produce the goods and services that people want; resources consist of labor, capital, natural resources, and entrepreneurial ability

labor
The physical and mental effort used to produce goods and services

Capital includes all human creations used to produce goods and services. Economists often distinguish between physical capital and human capital. *Physical capital* consists

capital
The buildings, equipment, and human skills used to produce goods and services

of factories, tools, machines, computers, buildings, airports, highways, and other human creations used to produce goods and services. Physical capital includes the cab driver's taxi, the surgeon's scalpel, and the building where your economics class meets (or, if you are taking this course online, your computer and online connectors). *Human capital* consists of the knowledge and skill people acquire to increase their productivity, such as the cab driver's knowledge of city streets, the surgeon's knowledge of human anatomy, and your knowledge of economics.

Natural resources include all *gifts of nature*, such as bodies of water, trees, oil reserves, minerals, even animals. Natural resources can be divided into renewable resources and exhaustible resources. A *renewable resource* can be drawn on indefinitely if used conservatively. Thus, timber is a renewable resource if felled trees are replaced to regrow a steady supply. The air and rivers are renewable resources if they are allowed sufficient time to cleanse themselves of any pollutants. More generally, biological resources like fish, game, livestock, forests, rivers, groundwater, grasslands, and soil are renewable if managed properly. An *exhaustible resource*—such as oil or coal—does not renew itself and so is available in a limited amount. Once burned, each barrel of oil or ton of coal is gone forever. The world's oil and coal deposits are exhaustible.

A special kind of human skill called **entrepreneurial ability** is the talent required to dream up a new product or find a better way to produce an existing one. This special skill comes from an entrepreneur. An **entrepreneur** is a profit-seeking decision maker who starts with an idea, organizes an enterprise to bring that idea to life, and then assumes the risk of operation. An entrepreneur pays resource owners for the opportunity to employ their resources in the firm. Every firm in the world today, such as Ford, Microsoft, Google, and Dell, began as an idea in the mind of an entrepreneur.

Resource owners are paid **wages** for their labor, **interest** for the use of their capital, and **rent** for the use of their natural resources. Entrepreneurial ability is rewarded by **profit**, which equals the *revenue* from items sold minus the *cost* of the resources employed to make those items. The word *profit* comes from the Latin *proficere*, which means "to benefit." The entrepreneur benefits from what's left over after paying other resource suppliers. Sometimes the entrepreneur suffers a loss. Resource earnings are usually based on the *time* these resources are employed. Resource payments therefore have a time dimension, as in a wage of $10 *per hour*, interest of 6 percent *per year*, rent of $600 *per month*, or profit of $10,000 *per year*.

Goods and Services

Resources are combined in a variety of ways to produce goods and services. A farmer, a tractor, 50 acres of land, seeds, and fertilizer combine to grow the good: corn. One hundred musicians, musical instruments, chairs, a conductor, a musical score, and a music hall combine to produce the service: Beethoven's *Fifth Symphony*. Corn is a **good** because it is something you can see, feel, and touch; it requires scarce resources to produce; and it satisfies human wants. The book you are now holding, the chair you are sitting in, the clothes you are wearing, and your next meal are all goods. The performance of the *Fifth Symphony* is a **service** because it is intangible, yet it uses scarce resources to satisfy human wants. Lectures, movies, concerts, phone service, broadband connections, yoga lessons, dry cleaning, and haircuts are all services.

Because goods and services are produced using scarce resources, they are themselves scarce. *A good or service is scarce if the amount people desire exceeds the amount available at a zero price.* Because we cannot have all the goods and services we would like, we must continually choose among them. We must choose among more pleasant living quarters, better meals, nicer clothes, more reliable transportation, faster computers, and so on. Making choices in a world of **scarcity** means we must pass up some goods and

natural resources
All gifts of nature used to produce goods and services; includes renewable and exhaustible resources

entrepreneurial ability
The imagination required to develop a new product or process, the skill needed to organize production, and the willingness to take the risk of profit or loss

entrepreneur
A profit-seeking decision maker who starts with an idea, organizes an enterprise to bring that idea to life, and assumes the risk of the operation

wages
Payment to resource owners for their labor

interest
Payment to resource owners for the use of their capital

rent
Payment to resource owners for the use of their natural resources

profit
Reward for entrepreneurial ability; sales revenue minus resource cost

good
A tangible product used to satisfy human wants

service
An activity, or intangible product, used to satisfy human wants

scarcity
Occurs when the amount people desire exceeds the amount available at a zero price

services. But not everything is scarce. In fact some things we would prefer to have less of. For example, we would prefer to have less garbage, less spam email, and less pollution. Things we want none of even at a zero price are called *bads*, the opposite of goods.

A few goods and services seem *free* because the amount available at a zero price exceeds the amount people want. For example, air and seawater often seem free because we can breathe all the air we want and have all the seawater we can haul away. Yet, despite the old saying "The best things in life are free," most goods and services are scarce, not free, and even those that appear to be free come with strings attached. For example, *clean* air and *clean* seawater have become scarce. *Goods and services that are truly free are not the subject matter of economics. Without scarcity, there would be no economic problem and no need for prices.*

Sometimes we mistakenly think of certain goods as free because they involve no apparent cost to us. Napkins seem to be free at Starbucks. Nobody stops you from taking a fistful. Supplying napkins, however, costs the company millions each year and prices reflect that cost. Some restaurants make special efforts to keep napkin use down—such as packing them tightly into the dispenser or making you ask for them.

You may have heard the expression "There is no such thing as a free lunch." There is no free lunch because all goods and services involve a cost to someone. The lunch may seem free to you, but it draws scarce resources away from the production of other goods and services, and whoever provides a free lunch often expects something in return. A Russian proverb makes a similar point but with a bit more bite: "The only place you find free cheese is in a mousetrap." Albert Einstein once observed, "Sometimes one pays the most for things one gets for nothing."

Economic Decision Makers

There are four types of decision makers in the economy: households, firms, governments, and the rest of the world. Their interaction determines how an economy's resources are allocated. *Households* play the starring role. As consumers, households demand the goods and services produced. As resource owners, households supply labor, capital, natural resources, and entrepreneurial ability to firms, governments, and the rest of the world. *Firms, governments,* and *the rest of the world* demand the resources that households supply and then use these resources to supply the goods and services that households demand. The rest of the world includes foreign households, foreign firms, and foreign governments that supply resources and products to U.S. markets and demand resources and products from U.S. markets.

Markets are the means by which buyers and sellers carry out exchange. By bringing together the two sides of exchange, markets determine price, quantity, and quality. Markets are often physical places, such as supermarkets, department stores, shopping malls, or yard sales. But markets also include other mechanisms by which buyers and sellers communicate, such as classified ads, radio and television ads, telephones, bulletin boards, online sites, and face-to-face bargaining. These market mechanisms provide information about the quantity, quality, and price of products offered for sale. Goods and services are bought and sold in **product markets**. Resources are bought and sold in **resource markets**. The most important resource market is the labor, or job, market. Think about your own experience looking for a job, and you'll already have some idea of that market.

market
A set of arrangements by which buyers and sellers carry out exchange at mutually agreeable terms

product market
A market in which a good or service is bought and sold

resource market
A market in which a resource is bought and sold

A Simple Circular-Flow Model

Now that you have learned a bit about economic decision makers, consider how they interact. Such a picture is conveyed by the **circular-flow model**, which describes the flow of resources, products, income, and revenue among economic decision makers.

circular-flow model
A diagram that traces the flow of resources, products, income, and revenue among economic decision makers

EXHIBIT 1 The Simple Circular-Flow Model for Households and Firms

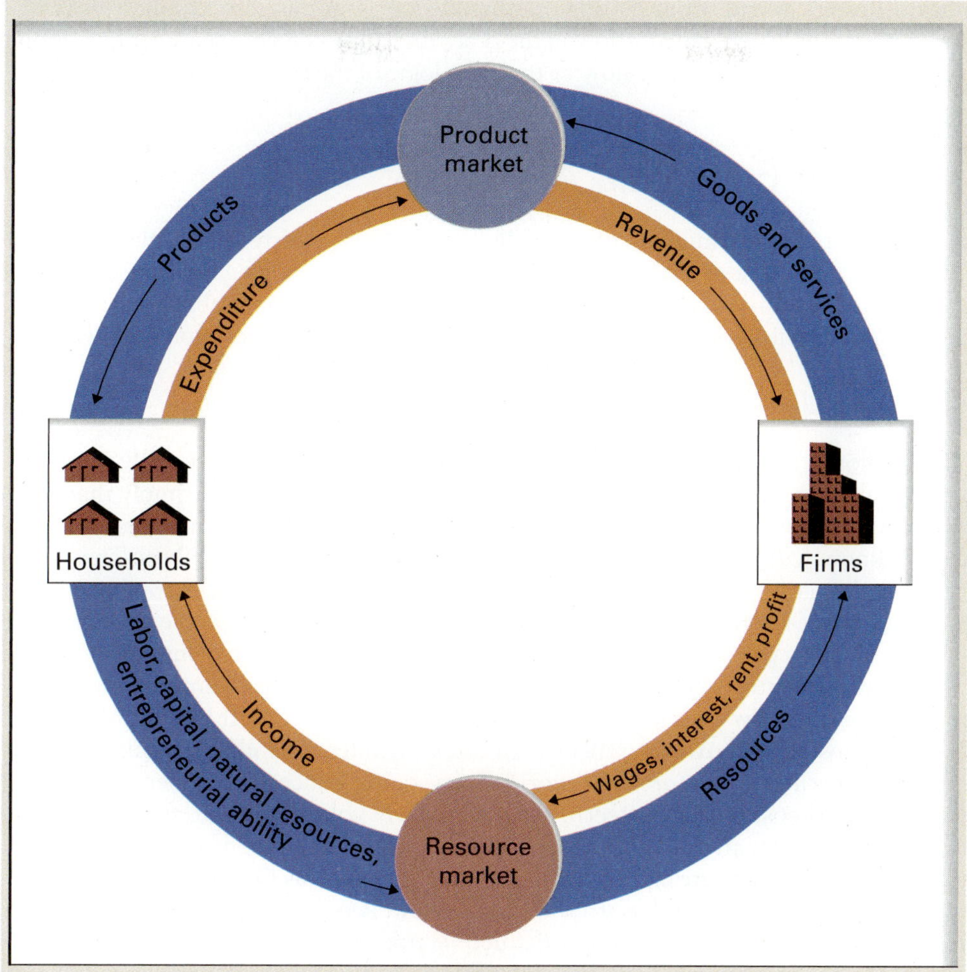

Households earn income by supplying resources to the resource market, as shown in the lower portion of the model. Firms demand these resources to produce goods and services, which they supply to the product market, as shown in the upper portion of the model. Households spend their income to demand these goods and services. This spending flows through the product market as revenue to firms.

The simple circular-flow model focuses on the primary interaction in a market economy—that between households and firms. Exhibit 1 shows households on the left and firms on the right; please take a look.

Households supply labor, capital, natural resources, and entrepreneurial ability to firms through resource markets, shown in the lower portion of the exhibit. In return, households demand goods and services from firms through product markets, shown on the upper portion of the exhibit. Viewed from the business end, firms demand labor, capital, natural resources, and entrepreneurial ability from households through resource markets, and firms supply goods and services to households through product markets.

The flows of resources and products are supported by the flows of income and expenditure—that is, by the flow of money. So let's add money. The demand and supply of resources come together in resource markets to determine what firms pay for resources. These resource prices—wages, interest, rent, and profit—flow as *income* to households. The demand and supply of products come together in product markets to determine what households pay for goods and services. These product prices of goods and services flow as *revenue* to firms. Resources and products flow in one direction—in this case, counterclockwise—and the corresponding payments flow in the other direction—clockwise. What goes around comes around. Take a little time now to trace the logic of the circular flows.

The Art of Economic Analysis

An economy results as millions of individuals attempt to satisfy their unlimited wants. Because their choices lie at the heart of the economic problem—coping with scarce resources but unlimited wants—these choices deserve a closer look. Learning about the forces that shape economic choice is the first step toward mastering the art of economic analysis.

Rational Self-Interest

rational self-interest
Each individual tries to maximize the expected benefit achieved with a given cost or to minimize the expected cost of achieving a given benefit

A key economic assumption is that individuals, in making choices, rationally select what they perceive to be in their best interests. By *rational,* economists mean simply that people try to make the best choices they can, given the available time and information. People may not know with certainty which alternative will turn out to be the best. They simply select the alternatives they *expect* will yield the most satisfaction and happiness. In general, **rational self-interest** means that each individual tries to maximize the expected benefit achieved with a given cost or to minimize the expected cost of achieving a given benefit.

Rational self-interest should not be viewed as blind materialism, pure selfishness, or greed. We all know people who are tuned to radio station WIIFM (What's In It For Me?). For most of us, however, self-interest often includes the welfare of our family, our friends, and perhaps the poor of the world. Even so, our concern for others is influenced by the personal cost of that concern. We may readily volunteer to drive a friend to the airport on Saturday afternoon but are less likely to offer a ride if the plane leaves at 6:00 A.M. When we donate clothes to an organization such as Goodwill Industries, they are more likely to be old and worn than brand new. People tend to give more to charities when their contributions are tax deductible and when contributions garner social approval in the community (as when contributor names are made public or when big donors get buildings named after them). TV stations are more likely to donate airtime for public-service announcements during the dead of night than during prime time (in fact, 80 percent of such announcements air between 11:00 P.M. and 7:00 A.M.[1]). In Asia some people burn money to soothe the passage of a departed loved one. But they burn fake money, not real money. The notion of self-interest does not rule out concern for others; it simply means that concern for others is influenced by the same economic forces that affect other economic choices. *The lower the personal cost of helping others, the more help we offer.* We don't like to think that our behavior reflects our self-interest, but it usually does. As Jane Austen wrote in *Pride and Prejudice*, "I have been a selfish being all my life, in practice, though not in principle."

Choice Requires Time and Information

Rational choice takes time and requires information, but time and information are scarce and therefore valuable. If you have any doubts about the time and information needed to make choices, talk to someone who recently purchased a home, a car, or a personal

1. Sally Goll Beatty, "Media and Agencies Brawl Over Do-Good Advertising," *Wall Street Journal,* 29 September 1997.

computer. Talk to a corporate official trying to decide whether to introduce a new product, sell online, build a new factory, or buy another firm. Or think back to your own experience in choosing a college. You probably talked to friends, relatives, teachers, and guidance counselors. You likely used school catalogs, college guides, and Web sites. You may have visited some campuses to meet the admissions staff and anyone else willing to talk. The decision took time and money, and it probably involved aggravation and anxiety.

Because information is costly to acquire, we are often willing to pay others to gather and digest it for us. College guidebooks, stock analysts, travel agents, real estate brokers, career counselors, restaurant critics, movie reviewers, specialized Web sites, and *Consumer Reports* magazine attest to our willingness to pay for information that improves our choices. As we'll see next, *rational decision makers continue to acquire information as long as the additional benefit expected from that information exceeds the additional cost of gathering it.*

Economic Analysis Is Marginal Analysis

Economic choice usually involves some adjustment to the existing situation, or status quo. Amazon.com must decide whether to add an additional line of products. The school superintendent must decide whether to hire another teacher. Your favorite jeans are on sale, and you must decide whether to buy another pair. You are wondering whether to carry an extra course next term. You just finished lunch and are deciding whether to order dessert.

Economic choice is based on a comparison of the *expected marginal benefit* and the *expected marginal cost* of the action under consideration. **Marginal** means incremental, additional, or extra. Marginal refers to a change in an economic variable, a change in the status quo. *A rational decision maker changes the status quo if the expected marginal benefit from the change exceeds the expected marginal cost.* For example, Amazon.com compares the marginal benefit expected from adding a new line of products (the additional sales revenue) with the marginal cost (the additional cost of the resources required). Likewise, you compare the marginal benefit you expect from eating dessert (the additional pleasure or satisfaction) with its marginal cost (the additional money, time, and calories).

marginal
Incremental, additional, or extra; used to describe a change in an economic variable

Typically, the change under consideration is small, but a marginal choice can involve a major economic adjustment, as in the decision to quit school and find a job. For a firm, a marginal choice might mean building a plant in Mexico or even filing for bankruptcy. By focusing on the effect of a marginal adjustment to the status quo, the economist is able to cut the analysis of economic choice down to a manageable size. Rather than confront a bewildering economic reality head-on, the economist begins with a marginal choice to see how this choice affects a particular market and shapes the economic system as a whole. Incidentally, to the noneconomist, *marginal* usually means relatively inferior, as in "a movie of marginal quality." Forget that meaning for this course and instead think of *marginal* as meaning incremental, additional, or extra.

Microeconomics and Macroeconomics

Although you have made thousands of economic choices, you probably seldom think about your own economic behavior. For example, why are you reading this book right now rather than doing something else? **Microeconomics** is the study of your economic behavior and the economic behavior of others who make choices about such matters as how much to study and how much to party, how much to borrow and how much to save, what to buy and what to sell. Microeconomics examines individual economic choices and how markets coordinate the choices of various decision makers. Microeconomics explains how price and quantity are determined in individual markets—the market for breakfast cereal, sports equipment, or used cars, for instance.

microeconomics
The study of the economic behavior in particular markets, such as that for computers or unskilled labor

You have probably given little thought to what influences your own economic choices. You have likely given even less thought to how your choices link up with those made by millions of others in the U.S. economy to determine economy-wide measures such as total production, employment, and economic growth. **Macroeconomics** studies the performance of the economy as a whole. Whereas microeconomics studies the individual pieces of the economic puzzle, as reflected in particular markets, macroeconomics puts all the pieces together to focus on the big picture.

macroeconomics
The study of the economic behavior of entire economies, as measured, for example, by total production and employment

The national economy usually grows over time, but along the way it sometimes stumbles, experiencing *recessions* in economic activity, as reflected by a decline in production, employment, and other aggregate measures. **Economic fluctuations** are the rise and fall of economic activity relative to the long-term growth trend of the economy. These fluctuations, or *business cycles,* vary in length and intensity, but they usually involve the entire nation and often other nations too. For example, the U.S. economy now produces more than four times as much as it did in 1960, despite experiencing eight recessions since then, including the painful recession of 2007–2009.

economic fluctuations
The rise and fall of economic activity relative to the long-term growth trend of the economy; also called business cycles

To Review: The art of economic analysis focuses on how people use their scarce resources in an attempt to satisfy their unlimited wants. Rational self-interest guides individual choice. Choice requires time and information, and involves a comparison of the expected marginal benefit and the expected marginal cost of alternative actions. Microeconomics looks at the individual pieces of the economic puzzle; macroeconomics fits the pieces together to form the big picture.

The Science of Economic Analysis

Economists use scientific analysis to develop theories, or models, that help explain economic behavior. An **economic theory**, or **economic model**, is a simplification of economic reality that *is used to make predictions about the real world.* A theory, or model, such as the circular-flow model, captures the important elements of the problem under study but need not spell out every detail and interrelation. In fact, adding more details may make a theory more unwieldy and, therefore, less useful. For example, a wristwatch is a model that tells time, but a watch festooned with extra features is harder to read at a glance and is therefore less useful as a time-telling model. The world is so complex that we must simplify it to make sense of things. Store mannequins simplify the human form (some even lack arms and heads). Comic strips and cartoons simplify characters—leaving out fingers or a mouth, for instance. You might think of economic theory as a stripped-down, or streamlined, version of economic reality.

economic theory, or economic model
A simplification of reality used to make predictions about cause and effect in the real world

A good theory helps us understand a messy and confusing world. Lacking a theory of how things work, our thinking can become cluttered with facts, one piled on another, as in a messy closet. You could think of a good theory as a closet organizer for the mind. A good theory offers a helpful guide to sorting, saving, and understanding information.

The Role of Theory

Most people don't understand the role of theory. Perhaps you have heard, "Oh, that's fine in theory, but in practice it's another matter." The implication is that the theory in question provides little aid in practical matters. People who say this fail to realize that they are merely substituting their own theory for a theory they either do not believe or do not understand. They are really saying, "I have my own theory that works better."

All of us employ theories, however poorly defined or understood. Someone who pounds on the Pepsi machine that just ate a quarter has a crude theory about how that machine works. One version of that theory might be "The quarter drops through a series of *whatchamacallits,* but sometimes it gets stuck. *If* I pound on the machine, *then* I can free up the quarter and send it on its way." Evidently, this theory is widespread enough that people continue to pound on machines that fail to perform (a real problem for the vending machine industry and one reason newer machines are fronted with glass). Yet, if you were to ask these mad pounders to explain their "theory" about how the machine works, they would look at you as if you were crazy.

The Scientific Method

To study economic problems, economists employ a process of theoretical investigation called the *scientific method,* which consists of four steps, as outlined in Exhibit 2.

Step One: Identify the Question and Define Relevant Variables

The scientific method begins with curiosity: Someone wants to answer a question. Thus, the first step is to identify the economic question and define the variables relevant to a solution. For example, the question might be "What is the relationship between the price of Pepsi and

EXHIBIT 2 The Scientific Method: Step by Step

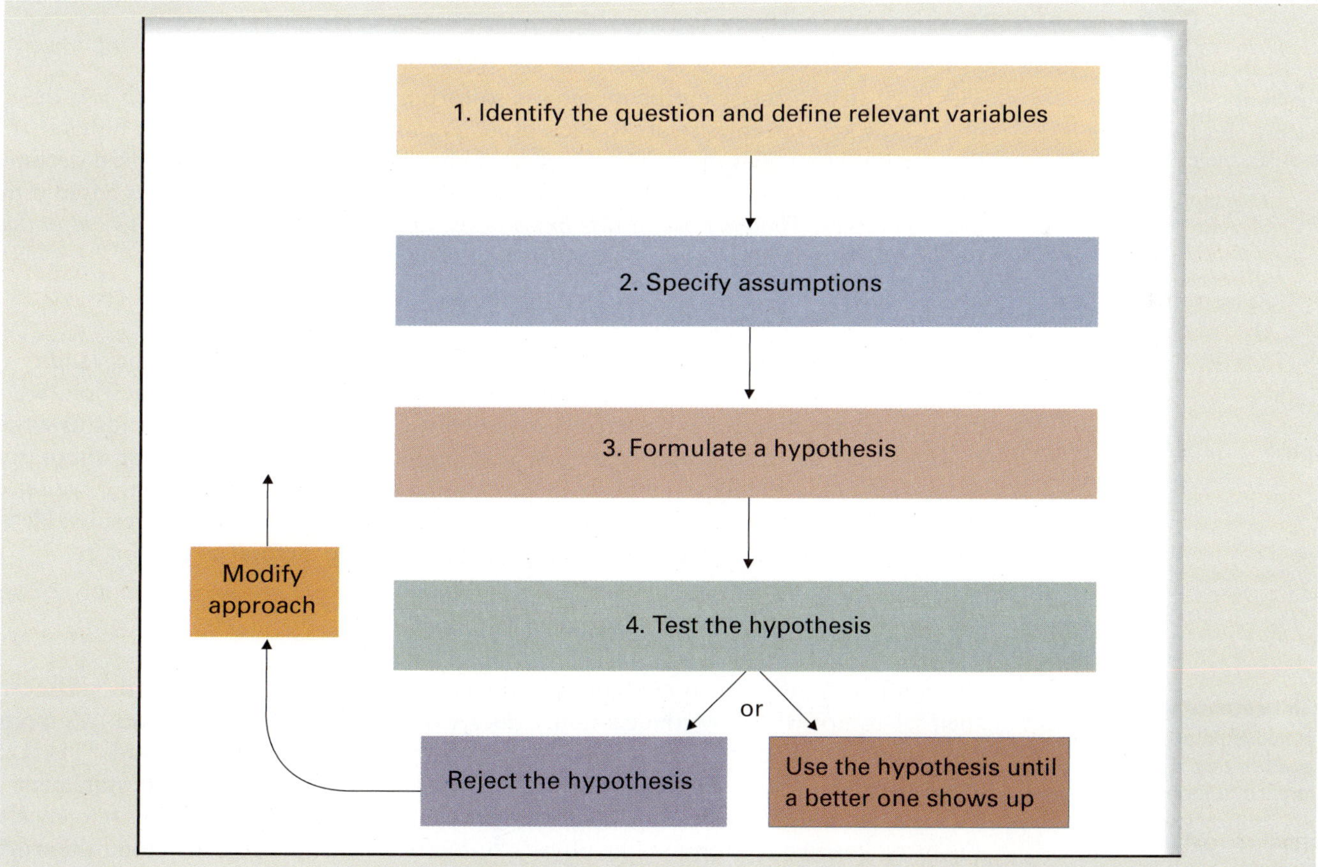

The steps of the scientific method are designed to develop and test hypotheses about how the world works. The objective is a theory that predicts outcomes more accurately than the best alternative theory. A hypothesis is rejected if it does not predict as accurately as the best alternative. A rejected hypothesis can be modified or reworked in light of the test results.

the quantity of Pepsi purchased?" In this case, the relevant variables are price and quantity. A **variable** is a measure that can take on different values at different times. The variables of concern become the elements of the theory, so they must be selected with care.

variable
A measure, such as price or quantity, that can take on different values at different times

Step Two: Specify Assumptions

The second step is to specify the assumptions under which the theory is to apply. One major category of assumptions is the **other-things-constant assumption**—in Latin, the *ceteris paribus* assumption. The idea is to identify the variables of interest and then focus exclusively on the relationships among them, assuming that nothing else important changes—that other things remain constant. Again, suppose we are interested in how the price of Pepsi influences the amount purchased. To isolate the relation between these two variables, we assume that there are no changes in other relevant variables such as consumer income, the average temperature, or the price of Coke.

other-things-constant assumption
The assumption, when focusing on the relation among key economic variables, that other variables remain unchanged; in Latin, *ceteris paribus*

We also make assumptions about how people behave; these are called **behavioral assumptions**. The primary behavioral assumption is rational self-interest. Earlier we assumed that each decision maker pursues self-interest rationally and makes choices accordingly. Rationality implies that each consumer buys the products expected to maximize his or her level of satisfaction. Rationality also implies that each firm supplies the products expected to maximize the firm's profit. These kinds of assumptions are called behavioral assumptions because they specify how we expect economic decision makers to behave—what makes them tick, so to speak.

behavioral assumption
An assumption that describes the expected behavior of economic decision makers, what motivates them

Step Three: Formulate a Hypothesis

The third step in the scientific method is to formulate a **hypothesis**, which is a theory about how key variables relate to each other. For example, one hypothesis holds that if the price of Pepsi goes up, other things constant, then the quantity purchased declines. The hypothesis becomes a prediction of what happens to the quantity purchased if the price increases. *The purpose of this hypothesis, like that of any theory, is to help make predictions about cause and effect in the real world.*

hypothesis
A theory about how key variables relate

Step Four: Test the Hypothesis

In the fourth step, by comparing its predictions with evidence, we test the validity of a hypothesis. To test a hypothesis, we must focus on the variables in question, while carefully controlling for other effects assumed not to change. The test leads us either to (1) reject the hypothesis, or theory, if it predicts worse than the best alternative theory or (2) use the hypothesis, or theory, until a better one comes along. If we reject the hypothesis, we can go back and modify our approach in light of the results. Please spend a moment now reviewing the steps of the scientific method in Exhibit 2.

Normative Versus Positive

Economists usually try to explain how the economy works. Sometimes they concern themselves not with how the economy *does* work but how it *should* work. Compare these two statements: "The U.S. unemployment rate is 9.7 percent." and "The U.S. unemployment rate should be lower." The first, called a **positive economic statement**, is an assertion about economic reality that can be supported or rejected by reference to the facts. Positive economics, like physics or biology, attempts to understand the world around us. The second, called a **normative economic statement**, reflects an opinion. And an opinion is merely that—it cannot be shown to be true or false by reference to the facts. Positive statements concern what *is;* normative statements concern what, in someone's opinion, *should be.* Positive statements need not necessarily be true, but

positive economic statement
A statement that can be proved or disproved by reference to facts

normative economic statement
A statement that reflects an opinion, which cannot be proved or disproved by reference to the facts

they must be subject to verification or refutation by reference to the facts. Theories are expressed as positive statements such as "If the price of Pepsi increases, then the quantity demanded decreases."

Most of the disagreement among economists involves normative debates—such as the appropriate role of government—rather than statements of positive analysis. To be sure, many theoretical issues remain unresolved, but economists generally agree on most fundamental theoretical principles—that is, about positive economic analysis. For example, in a survey of 464 U.S. economists, only 6.5 percent disagreed with the statement "A ceiling on rents reduces the quantity and quality of housing available." This is a positive statement because it can be shown to be consistent or inconsistent with the evidence. In contrast, there was much less agreement on normative statements such as "The distribution of income in the United States should be more equal." Half the economists surveyed "generally agreed," a quarter "generally disagreed," and a quarter "agreed with provisos."[2]

Normative statements, or value judgments, have a place in a policy debate such as the proper role of government, provided that statements of opinion are distinguished from statements of fact. In such policy debates, you are entitled to your own opinion, but you are not entitled to your own facts.

Economists Tell Stories

Despite economists' reliance on the scientific method for developing and evaluating theories, economic analysis is as much art as science. Formulating a question, isolating the key variables, specifying the assumptions, proposing a theory to answer the question, and devising a way to test the predictions all involve more than simply an understanding of economics and the scientific method. Carrying out these steps requires good intuition and the imagination of a storyteller. Economists explain their theories by telling stories about how they think the economy works. To tell a compelling story, an economist relies on case studies, anecdotes, parables, the personal experience of the listener, and supporting data. Throughout this book, you'll hear stories that bring you closer to the ideas under consideration. The stories, such as the one about the Pepsi machine, breathe life into economic theory and help you personalize abstract ideas. As another example, read the case study, "World of Business: A Yen for Vending Machines," at the end of the book on the popularity of vending machines in Japan.

This case study makes two points. First, producers combine resources in a way that conserves, or economizes on, the resource that is more costly—in this case, labor. Second, the customs and conventions of the marketplace can differ across countries, and this variance can result in different types of economic arrangements, such as the more extensive use of vending machines in Japan.

Predicting Average Behavior

The goal of an economic theory is to predict the impact of an economic event on economic choices and, in turn, the effect of these choices on particular markets or on the economy as a whole. Does this mean that economists try to predict the behavior of particular consumers or producers? Not necessarily, because a specific individual may behave in an unpredictable way. But the unpredictable actions of numerous individuals tend to cancel one another out, so the *average behavior* of groups can be predicted more accurately. For example, if the federal government cuts personal income taxes, certain

2. Richard M. Alston et al., "Is There a Consensus Among Economists in the 1990s?" *American Economic Review*, 82 (May 1992): 203–209, Table 1.

households may decide to save the entire tax cut. On average, however, household spending increases. Likewise, if Burger King cuts the price of Whoppers, the manager can better predict how much sales will increase than how a specific customer coming through the door will respond. *The random actions of individuals tend to offset one another, so the average behavior of a large group can be predicted more accurately than the behavior of a particular individual.* Consequently, economists tend to focus on the average, or typical, behavior of people in groups—for example, as average taxpayers or average Whopper consumers—rather than on the behavior of a specific individual.

Some Pitfalls of Faulty Economic Analysis

Economic analysis, like other forms of scientific inquiry, is subject to common mistakes in reasoning that can lead to faulty conclusions. Here are three sources of confusion.

The Fallacy That Association Is Causation

In the last two decades, the number of physicians specializing in cancer treatment increased sharply. At the same time, the incidence of some cancers increased. Can we conclude that physicians cause cancer? No. To assume that event A caused event B simply because the two are associated in time is to commit the **association-is-causation fallacy**, a common error. The fact that one event precedes another or that the two events occur simultaneously does not necessarily mean that one causes the other. Remember: Association is not necessarily causation.

association-is-causation fallacy
The incorrect idea that if two variables are associated in time, one must necessarily cause the other

The Fallacy of Composition

Perhaps you have been to a rock concert where everyone stands to get a better view. At some concerts, most people even stand on their chairs. But even standing on chairs does not improve the view if others do the same, unless you are quite tall. Likewise, arriving early to buy game tickets does not work if many have the same idea. These are examples of the **fallacy of composition**, which is an erroneous belief that what is true for the individual, or the part, is also true for the group, or the whole.

fallacy of composition
The incorrect belief that what is true for the individual, or part, must necessarily be true for the group, or the whole

The Mistake of Ignoring the Secondary Effects

In many cities, public officials have imposed rent controls on apartments. The primary effect of this policy, the effect policy makers focus on, is to keep rents from rising. Over time, however, fewer new apartments get built because renting them becomes less profitable. Moreover, existing rental units deteriorate because owners have plenty of customers anyway. Thus, the quantity and quality of housing may decline as a result of what appears to be a reasonable measure to keep rents from rising. The mistake was to ignore the **secondary effects**, or the unintended consequences, of the policy. Economic actions have secondary effects that often turn out to be more important than the primary effects. Secondary effects may develop more slowly and may not be immediately obvious, but good economic analysis tries to anticipate them and take them into account.

secondary effects
Unintended consequences of economic actions that may develop slowly over time as people react to events

If Economists Are So Smart, Why Aren't They Rich?

Why aren't economists rich? Well, some are, earning over $25,000 per appearance on the lecture circuit. Others top $2 million a year as consultants and expert witnesses.[3] Economists have been appointed to federal cabinet posts, such as secretaries of commerce,

3. As reported by George Anders, "An Economist's Courtroom Bonanza," *Wall Street Journal*, 19 March 2007.

defense, labor, state, and treasury, and to head the U.S. Federal Reserve System. Economics is the only social science and the only business discipline for which the prestigious Nobel Prize is awarded, and pronouncements by economists are reported in the media daily. *The Economist,* a widely respected news weekly from London, has argued that economic ideas have influenced policy "to a degree that would make other social scientists drool."[4]

The economics profession thrives because its models usually do a better job of making economic sense out of a confusing world than do alternative approaches. But not all economists are wealthy, nor is personal wealth the goal of the discipline. In a similar vein, not all doctors are healthy (some even smoke), not all carpenters live in perfectly built homes, not all marriage counselors are happily married, and not all child psychologists have well-adjusted children. Still, those who study economics do reap financial rewards, as discussed in the case study "The Information Economy: College Major and Annual Earnings" at the end of the book, which looks at the link between a college major and annual earnings.

Conclusion

This textbook describes how economic factors affect individual choices and how all these choices come together to shape the economic system. Economics is not the whole story, and economic factors are not always the most important. But economic considerations have important and predictable effects on individual choices, and these choices affect the way we live.

Sure, economics is a challenging discipline, but it is also an exciting and rewarding one. The good news is that you already know a lot about economics. To use this knowledge, however, you must cultivate the art and science of economic analysis. You must be able to simplify the world to formulate questions, isolate the relevant variables, and then tell a persuasive story about how these variables relate.

An economic relation can be expressed in words, represented as a table of quantities, described by a mathematical equation, or illustrated as a graph. The appendix to this chapter introduces graphs. You may find this unnecessary. If you are already familiar with relations among variables, slopes, tangents, and the like, you can probably just browse. But if you have little recent experience with graphs, you might benefit from a more careful reading with pencil and paper in hand.

The next chapter introduces key tools of economic analysis. Subsequent chapters use these tools to explore economic problems and to explain economic behavior that may otherwise seem puzzling. You must walk before you can run, however, and in the next chapter, you take your first wobbly steps.

Summary

1. Economics is the study of how people choose to use their scarce resources to produce, exchange, and consume goods and services in an attempt to satisfy unlimited wants. The economic problem arises from the conflict between scarce resources and unlimited wants. If wants were limited or if resources were not scarce, there would be no need to study economics.
2. Economic resources are combined in a variety of ways to produce goods and services. Major categories of resources include labor, capital, natural resources, and entrepreneurial ability. Because economic resources are scarce, only a limited number of goods and services can be produced with them. Therefore, goods and services are also scarce so choices must be made.

4. "The Puzzling Failure of Economics," *Economist,* 23 August 1997, p. 11.

3. Microeconomics focuses on choices made in households, firms, and governments and how these choices affect particular markets, such as the market for used cars. Choice is guided by rational self-interest. Choice typically requires time and information, both of which are scarce and valuable.
4. Whereas microeconomics examines the individual pieces of the puzzle, macroeconomics steps back to consider the big picture—the performance of the economy as a whole as reflected by such measures as total production, employment, the price level, and economic growth.
5. Economists use theories, or models, to help understand the effects of an economic change, such as a change in price or income, on individual choices and how these choices affect particular markets and the economy as a whole. Economists employ the scientific method to study an economic problem by (a) formulating the question and identifying relevant variables, (b) specifying the assumptions under which the theory operates, (c) developing a theory, or hypothesis, about how the variables relate, and (d) testing that theory by comparing its predictions with the evidence. A theory might not work perfectly, but it is useful as long as it predicts better than competing theories do.
6. Positive economics aims to discover how the economy works. Normative economics is concerned more with how, in someone's opinion, the economy should work. Those who are not careful can fall victim to the fallacy that association is causation, to the fallacy of composition, and to the mistake of ignoring secondary effects.

Key Concepts

Economics 2
Resources 2
Labor 2
Capital 2
Natural resources 3
Entrepreneurial ability 3
Entrepreneur 3
Wages 3
Interest 3
Rent 3
Profit 3
Good 3
Service 3
Scarcity 3
Market 4
Product market 4
Resource market 4
Circular-flow model 4
Rational self-interest 6
Marginal 7
Microeconomics 7
Macroeconomics 8
Economic fluctuations 8
Economic theory, or economic model 8
Variable 10
Other-things-constant assumption 10
Behavioral assumption 10
Hypothesis 10
Positive economic statement 10
Normative economic statement 10
Association-is-causation fallacy 12
Fallacy of composition 12
Secondary effects 12

Questions for Review

1. Definition of Economics What determines whether or not a resource is scarce? Why is the concept of scarcity important to the definition of economics?
2. Resources To which category of resources does each of the following belong?
   a. A taxi
   b. Computer software
   c. One hour of legal counsel
   d. A parking lot
   e. A forest
   f. The Mississippi River
   g. An individual introducing a new way to market products on the Internet
3. Goods and Services Explain why each of the following would *not* be considered "free" for the economy as a whole:
   a. Food vouchers
   b. U.S. aid to developing countries
   c. Corporate charitable contributions
   d. Noncable television programs
   e. Public high school education
4. Economic Decision Makers Which group of economic decision makers plays the leading role in the economic system? Which groups play supporting roles? In what sense are they supporting actors?
5. Micro Versus Macro Determine whether each of the following is primarily a microeconomic or a macroeconomic issue:
   a. What price to charge for an automobile
   b. Measuring the impact of tax policies on total consumer spending in the economy
   c. A household's decisions about what to buy
   d. A worker's decision regarding how much to work each week
   e. Designing a government policy to increase total employment
6. Micro Versus Macro Some economists believe that to really understand macroeconomics, you must first understand microeconomics. How does microeconomics relate to macroeconomics?

7. Normative Versus Positive Analysis Determine whether each of the following statements is normative or positive:
   a. The U.S. unemployment rate was below 10.0 percent in 2010.
   b. The inflation rate in the United States is too high.
   c. The U.S. government should increase the minimum wage.
   d. U.S. trade restrictions cost consumers $40 billion annually.
8. Role of Theory What good is economic theory if it can't predict the behavior of a specific individual?

Problems and Exercises

9. Rational Self-Interest Discuss the impact of rational self-interest on each of the following decisions:
   a. Whether to attend college full time or enter the workforce full time
   b. Whether to buy a new textbook or a used one
   c. Whether to attend a local college or an out-of-town college
10. Rational Self-Interest If behavior is governed by rational self-interest, why do people make charitable contributions of time and money?
11. Marginal Analysis The owner of a small pizzeria is deciding whether to increase the radius of delivery area by one mile. What considerations must be taken into account if such a decision is to increase profitability?
12. Time and Information It is often costly to obtain the information necessary to make good decisions. Yet your own interests can be best served by rationally weighing all options available to you. This requires informed decision making. Does this mean that making uninformed decisions is irrational? How do you determine how much information is the right amount?
13. Case Study: A Yen for Vending Machines (See page 697.) Do vending machines conserve on any resources other than labor? Does your answer offer any additional insight into the widespread use of vending machines in Japan?
14. Case Study: A Yen for Vending Machines (See page 697.) Suppose you had the choice of purchasing identically priced lunches from a vending machine or at a cafeteria. Which would you choose? Why?
15. Pitfalls of Economic Analysis Review the discussion of pitfalls in economic thinking in this chapter. Then identify the fallacy, or mistake in thinking, in each of the following statements:
    a. Raising taxes always increases government revenues.
    b. Whenever there is a recession, imports decrease. Therefore, to stop a recession, we should increase imports.
    c. Raising the tariff on imported steel helps the U.S. steel industry. Therefore, the entire economy is helped.
    d. Gold sells for about $1,000 per ounce. Therefore, the U.S. government could sell all the gold in Fort Knox at $1,000 per ounce and reduce the national debt.
16. Association Versus Causation Suppose I observe that communities with lots of doctors tend to have relatively high rates of illness. I conclude that doctors cause illness. What's wrong with this reasoning?
17. Case Study: College Major and Annual Earnings (See page 698.) Because some college majors pay nearly twice as much as others, why would students pursuing their rational self-interest choose a lower paying major?

Global Economic Watch Exercises

Login to www.cengagebrain.com and access the Global Economic Watch to do these exercises.

18. Global Economic Watch Go to the Global Economic Crisis Resource Center. Select Global Issues in Context. In the Basic Search box at the top of the page, enter the phrase "selfish." On the Results page, scroll down to the Magazines section. Choose the red link to View All. Scroll down to click on the link for the December 8, 2008, article "Going Green for Selfish Reasons." Are the companies described acting out of rational self-interest?
19. Global Economic Watch Go to the Global Economic Crisis Resource Center. Select Global Issues in Context. In the Basic Search box at the top of the page, enter either the term "microeconomic" or the term "macroeconomic." Choose one of the resources and write a summary in your own words. Especially emphasize how the resource is an example of microeconomics or macroeconomics.

Appendix

Understanding Graphs

Take out a pencil and a blank piece of paper. Go ahead. Put a point in the middle of the paper. This is your point of departure, called the **origin**. With your pencil at the origin, draw a straight line off to the right. This line is called the **horizontal axis**. The value of the variable *x* measured along the horizontal axis increases as you move to the right of the origin. Now mark off this line from 0 to 20, in increments of 5 units each. Returning to the origin, draw another line, this one straight north. This line is called the **vertical axis**. The value of the variable *y* measured along the vertical axis increases as you move north of the origin. Mark off this line from 0 to 20, in increments of 5 units each.

Within the space framed by the two axes, you can plot possible combinations of the variables measured along each axis. Each point identifies a value measured along the horizontal, or *x*, axis *and* a value measured along the vertical, or *y*, axis. For example, place point *a* in your graph to reflect the combination where *x* equals 5 units and *y* equals 15 units. Likewise, place point *b* in your graph to reflect 10 units of *x* and 5 units of *y*. Now compare your results with points shown in Exhibit 3.

EXHIBIT 3 Basics of a Graph

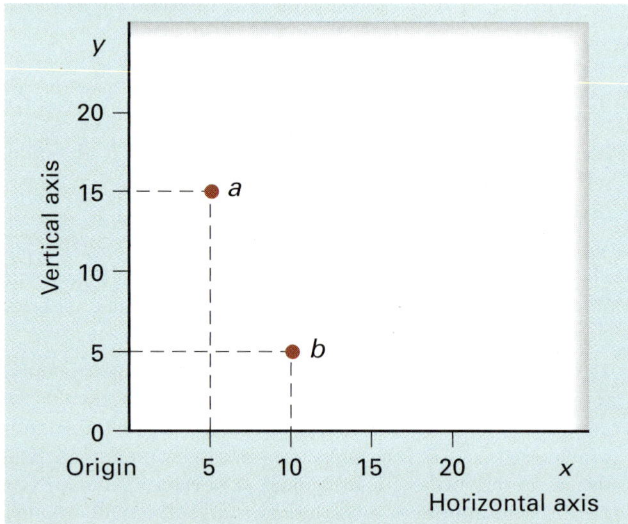

Any point on a graph represents a combination of particular values of two variables. Here point *a* represents the combination of 5 units of variable *x* (measured on the horizontal axis) and 15 units of variable *y* (measured on the vertical axis). Point *b* represents 10 units of *x* and 5 units of *y*.

A **graph** is a picture showing how variables relate, and a picture can be worth a thousand words. Take a look at Exhibit 4, which shows the U.S. annual unemployment rate since 1900. The year is measured along the horizontal axis and the unemployment rate is measured as a percentage along the vertical axis. Exhibit 4 is a *time-series graph,* which shows the value of a variable, in this case the percent of the labor force unemployed, over time. If you had to describe the information presented in Exhibit 4 in words, the explanation could take many words. The picture shows not only how one year compares to the next but also how one decade compares to another and how the unemployment rate trends over time. The sharply higher unemployment rate during the Great Depression of the 1930s is unmistakable. *Graphs convey information in a compact and efficient way.*

This appendix shows how graphs express a variety of possible relations among variables. Most graphs of interest in this book reflect the relationship between two economic variables, such as the unemployment rate and the year, the price of a product and the quantity demanded, or the price of production and the quantity supplied. Because we focus on just two variables at a time, we usually assume that other relevant variables remain constant.

One variable often depends on another. The time it takes you to drive home depends on your average speed. Your weight depends on how much you eat. The amount of Pepsi you buy depends on the price. A *functional relation* exists between two variables when the value of one variable *depends* on the value of another variable. The value of the **dependent variable** depends on the value of the **independent variable**. The task of the economist is to isolate economic relations and determine the direction of causality, if any. Recall that one of the pitfalls of economic

EXHIBIT 4 U.S. Unemployment Rate Since 1900

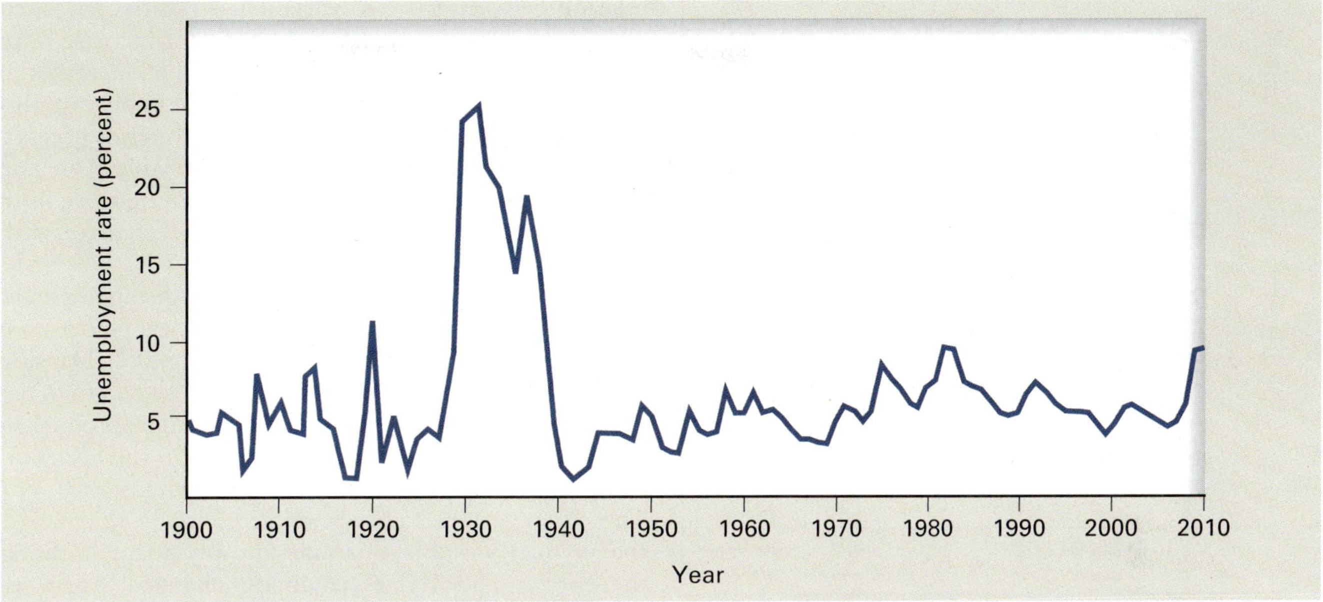

A time-series graph depicts the behavior of some economic variable over time. Shown here are U.S. unemployment rates since 1900.

Source: *Historical Statistics of the United States,* 1970; and *Economic Report of the President,* February 2010. The figure for 2010 is an estimate as of June of that year.

thinking is the erroneous belief that association is causation. We cannot conclude that, simply because two events relate in time, one causes the other. There may be no relation between the two events.

Drawing Graphs

Let's begin with a simple relation. Suppose you are planning to drive across country and want to figure out how far you will travel each day. You plan to average 50 miles per hour. Possible combinations of driving time and distance traveled per day appear in Exhibit 5. One column lists the hours driven per day, and the next column lists the number of miles traveled per day, assuming an average speed of 50 miles per hour. The distance traveled, the *dependent* variable, depends on the number of hours driven, the *independent* variable. Combinations of hours driven and distance traveled are shown as *a, b, c, d,* and *e*. Each combination is represented by a point in Exhibit 6. For example, point *a* shows that if you drive for 1 hour, you travel 50 miles. Point *b* indicates that if you drive for 2 hours, you travel 100 miles. By connecting the points, or possible combinations, we create a line running upward and to the right. This makes sense, because the longer you drive, the farther you travel. Assumed constant along this line is your average speed of 50 miles per hour.

EXHIBIT 5 Schedule Relating Distance Traveled to Hours Driven

	Hours Driven per Day	Distance Traveled per Day (miles)
a	1	50
b	2	100
c	3	150
d	4	200
e	5	250

The distance traveled per day depends on the number of hours driven per day, assuming an average speed of 50 miles per hour. This table shows combinations of hours driven and distance traveled. These combinations are shown as points in Exhibit 6.

Types of relations between variables include the following:

1. As one variable increases, the other increases—as in Exhibit 6; this is called a **positive, or direct, relation** between the variables.

EXHIBIT 6 Graph Relating Distance Traveled to Hours Driven

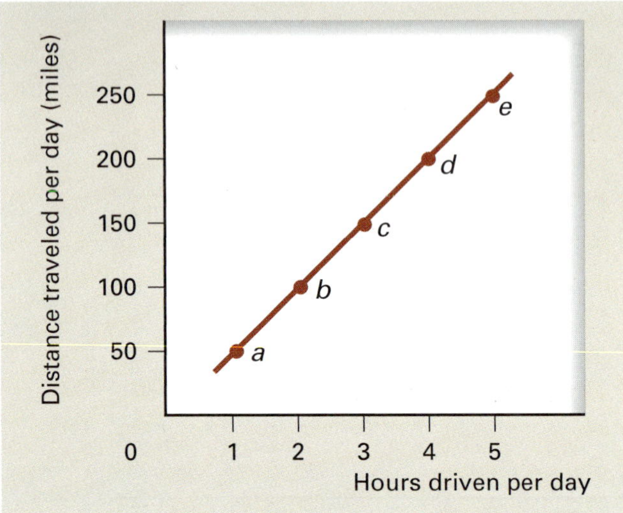

Points *a* through *e* depict different combinations of hours driven per day and the corresponding distances traveled. Connecting these points creates a graph.

2. As one variable increases, the other decreases; this is called a **negative**, or **inverse, relation.**
3. As one variable increases, the other remains unchanged; the two variables are said to be *independent,* or *unrelated.*

One of the advantages of graphs is that they easily convey the relation between variables. We do not need to examine the particular combinations of numbers; we need only focus on the shape of the curve.

The Slopes of Straight Lines

A more precise way to describe the shape of a curve is to measure its slope. The **slope of a line** indicates how much the vertical variable changes for a given increase in the horizontal variable. Specifically, the slope between any two points along any straight line is the vertical change between these two points divided by the horizontal increase, or

$$\text{Slope} = \frac{\text{Change in the vertical distance}}{\text{Increase in the horizontal distance}}$$

Each of the four panels in Exhibit 7 indicates a vertical change, given a 10-unit increase in the horizontal variable. In panel (a), the vertical distance increases by 5 units when the horizontal distance increases by 10 units. The slope of the line is therefore 5/10, or 0.5. Notice that the slope in this case is a positive number because the relation between the two variables is positive, or direct. This slope indicates that for every 1-unit increase in the horizontal variable, the vertical variable increases by 0.5 units. The slope, incidentally, does not imply causality; the increase in the horizontal variable does not necessarily *cause* the increase in the vertical variable. The slope simply measures the relation between an increase in the horizontal variable and the associated change in the vertical variable.

In panel (b) of Exhibit 7, the vertical distance declines by 7 units when the horizontal distance increases by 10 units, so the slope equals −7/10, or −0.7. The slope in this case is a negative number because the two variables have a negative, or inverse, relation. In panel (c), the vertical variable remains unchanged as the horizontal variable increases by 10, so the slope equals 0/10, or 0. These two variables are not related. Finally, in panel (d), the vertical variable can take on any value, although the horizontal variable remains unchanged. Again, the two variables are not related. In this case, any change in the vertical measure, for example a 10-unit change, is divided by 0, because the horizontal value does not change. Any change divided by 0 is mathematically undefined, but as the line tilts toward vertical, its slope gets incredibly large. For practical purposes, we will assume that the slope of this line is not undefined but infinitely large.

The Slope, Units of Measurement, and Marginal Analysis

The mathematical value of the slope depends on the units measured on the graph. For example, suppose copper tubing costs $1 a foot. Graphs depicting the relation between total cost and quantity purchased are shown in Exhibit 8. In panel (a), the total cost increases by $1 for each 1-foot increase in the amount of tubing purchased. Thus, the slope equals 1/1, or 1. If the cost per foot remains the same but units are measured not in *feet* but in *yards,* the relation between total cost and quantity purchased is as depicted in panel (b). Now total cost increases by $3 for each 1-*yard* increase in output, so the slope equals 3/1, or 3. Because different units are used to measure the copper tubing, the two panels reflect different slopes, even though the cost is $1 per foot in each panel. Keep in mind that *the slope depends in part on the units of measurement.*

EXHIBIT 7 Alternative Slopes for Straight Lines

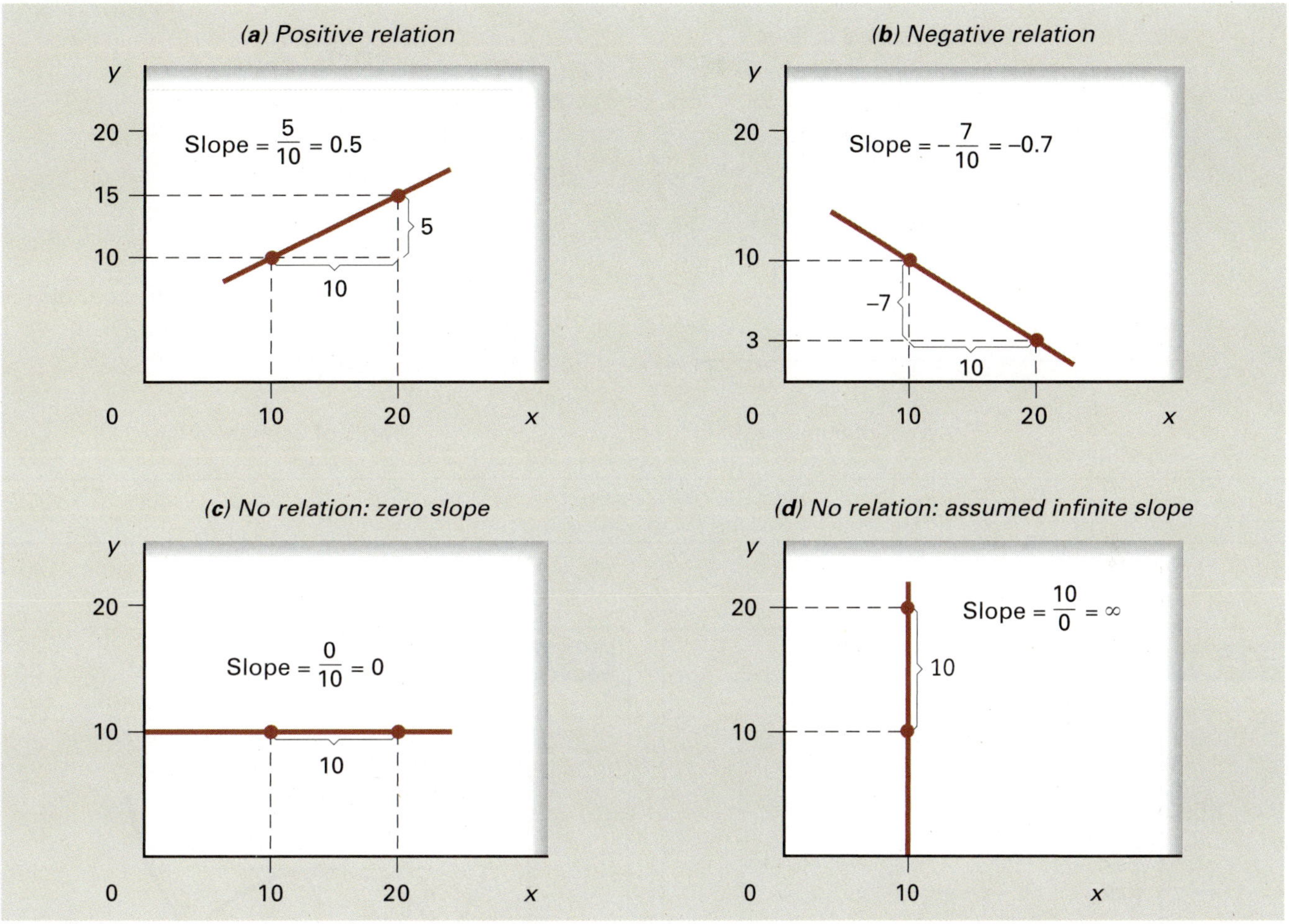

The slope of a line indicates how much the vertically measured variable changes for a given increase in the variable measured along the horizontal axis. Panel (a) shows a positive relation between two variables; the slope is 0.5, a positive number. Panel (b) depicts a negative, or inverse, relation. When the x variable increases, the y variable decreases; the slope is −0.7, a negative number. Panels (c) and (d) represent situations in which two variables are unrelated. In panel (c), the y variable always takes on the same value; the slope is 0. In panel (d), the x variable always takes on the same value; the slope is mathematically undefined but we simplify by assuming the slope is infinite.

Economic analysis usually involves *marginal analysis*, such as the marginal cost of one more unit of output. The slope is a convenient device for measuring marginal effects because it reflects the change in total cost, measured along the vertical axis, for each 1-unit change in output, measured along the horizontal axis. For example, in panel (a) of Exhibit 8, the marginal cost of another *foot* of copper tubing is $1, which also equals the slope of the line. In panel (b), the marginal cost of another *yard* of tubing is $3, which again is the slope of that line. Because of its applicability to marginal analysis, the slope has special relevance in economics.

The Slopes of Curved Lines

The slope of a straight line is the same everywhere along the line, but the slope of a curved line differs along the curve, as shown in Exhibit 9. To find the slope of a curved line at a particular point, draw a straight line that just touches the curve at that point but does not cut or cross the curve. Such a line is called a tangent to the curve at that point. The slope of the **tangent** gives the slope of the curve at that point. Look at line *A*, which is tangent to the curve at point *a*. As the horizontal value increases from 0 to 10, the vertical value drops along *A* from

EXHIBIT 8 Slope Depends on the Unit of Measure

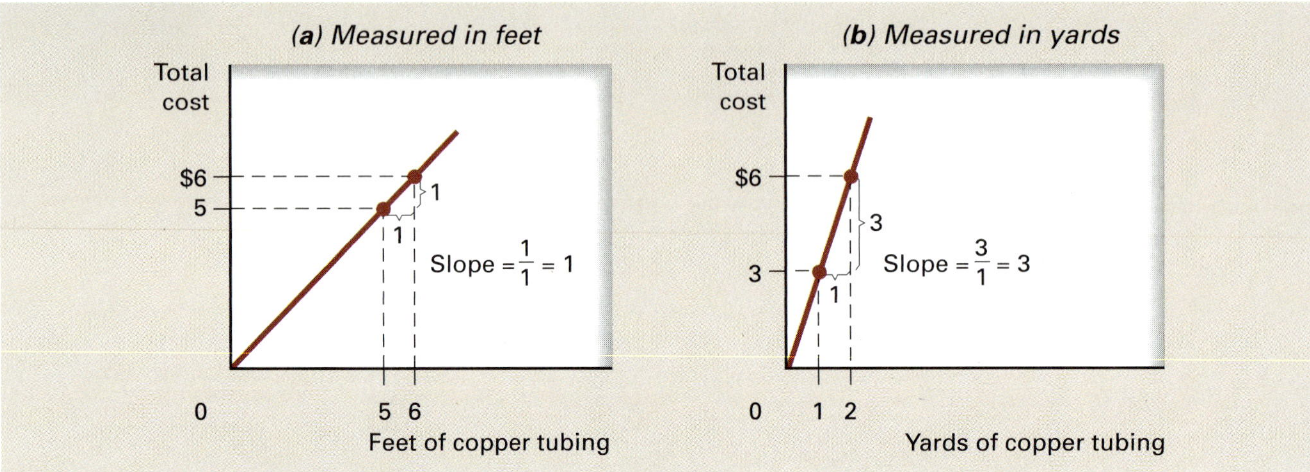

The value of the slope depends on the units of measure. In panel (a), output is measured in feet of copper tubing; in panel (b), output is measured in yards. Although the cost is $1 per foot in each panel, the slope is different in the two panels because copper tubing is measured using different units.

EXHIBIT 9 Slopes at Different Points on a Curved Line

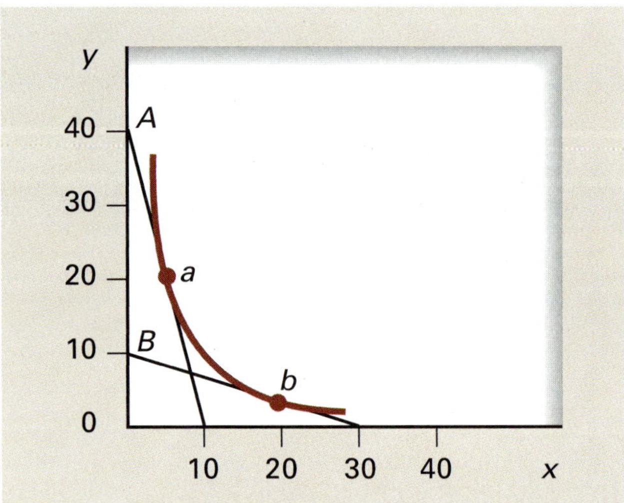

The slope of a curved line varies from point to point. At a given point, such as *a* or *b*, the slope of the curve is equal to the slope of the straight line that is tangent to the curve at the point.

EXHIBIT 10 Curves with Both Positive and Negative Slopes

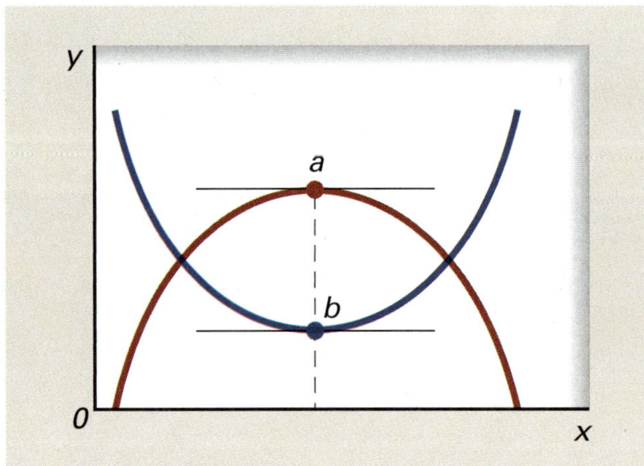

Some curves have both positive and negative slopes. The hill-shaped curve (in red) has a positive slope to the left of point *a*, a slope of 0 at point *a*, and a negative slope to the right of that point. The U-shaped curve (in blue) starts off with a negative slope, has a slope of 0 at point *b*, and has a positive slope to the right of that point.

40 to 0. Thus, the vertical change divided by the horizontal change equals −40/10, or −4, which is the slope of the curve at point *a*. This slope is negative because the vertical value decreases as the horizontal value increases. Line *B*, a line tangent to the curve at point *b*, has the slope −10/30, or −0.33. As you can see, the curve depicted in Exhibit 9 gets flatter as the horizontal variable increases, so the value of its slope approaches zero.

Other curves, of course, will reflect different slopes as well as different changes in the slope along the curve. Downward-sloping curves have negative slopes, and upward-sloping curves, positive slopes. Sometimes curves, such as those in Exhibit 10, are more complex, having both positive and negative ranges, depending on the horizontal value. In the hill-shaped curve, for small values of x, there is a positive relation between x and y, so the slope is positive. As the value of x increases, however, the slope declines and eventually becomes negative. We can divide the curve into two segments: (1) the segment between the origin and point a, where the slope is positive; and (2) the segment of the curve to the right of point a, where the slope is negative. The slope of the curve at point a is 0. The U-shaped curve in Exhibit 10 represents the opposite relation: x and y are negatively related until point b is reached; thereafter, they are positively related. The slope equals 0 at point b.

Line Shifts

Let's go back to the example of your cross-country trip, where we were trying to determine how many miles you would travel per day. Recall that we measured hours driven per day on the horizontal axis and miles traveled per day on the vertical axis, assuming an average speed of 50 miles per hour. That same relation is shown as line T in Exhibit 11. What happens if the average speed is 40 miles per hour? The entire relation between hours driven and distance traveled would change, as shown by the shift to the right of line T to T'. With a slower average speed, any distance traveled per day now requires more driving time. For example, 200 miles traveled requires 4 hours of driving when the average speed is 50 miles per hour (as shown by point d on curve T), but 200 miles takes 5 hours when your speed averages 40 miles per hour (as shown by point f on curve T'). Thus, *a change in the assumption about average speed changes the relationship between the two variables observed.* This changed relationship is expressed by a shift of the line that shows how the two variables relate.

That ends our once-over of graphs. Return to this appendix when you need a review.

EXHIBIT 11 **Shift of Line Relating Distance Traveled to Hours Driven**

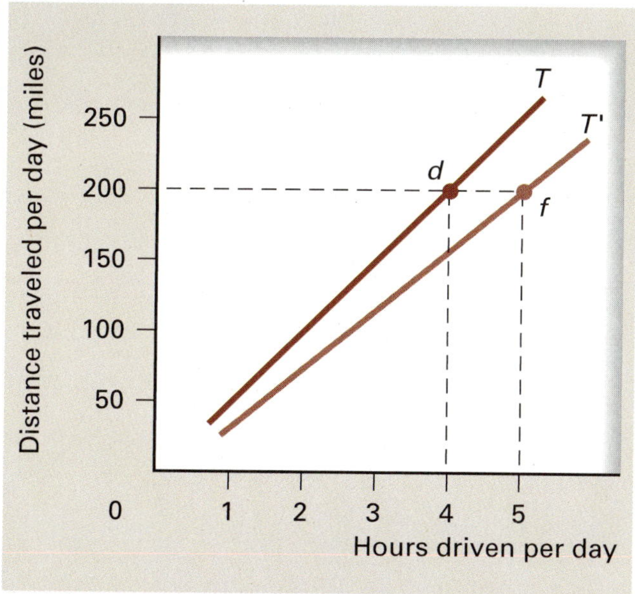

Line T appeared originally in Exhibit 6 to show the relation between hours driven and distance traveled per day, assuming an average speed of 50 miles per hour. If the average speed is only 40 miles per hour, the entire relation shifts to the right to T', indicating that any given distance traveled requires more driving time. For example, 200 miles traveled takes 4 hours of driving at 50 miles per hour but 5 hours at 40 miles per hour. This figure shows how a change in assumptions, in this case, the average speed assumed, can shift the entire relationship between two variables.

Appendix Questions

1. Understanding Graphs Look at Exhibit 4 and answer the following questions:
   a. In what year (approximately) was the unemployment rate the highest? In what year was it the lowest?
   b. In what decade, on average, was the unemployment rate highest? In what decade was it lowest?
   c. Between 1950 and 1980, did the unemployment rate generally increase, decrease, or remain about the same?
2. Drawing Graphs Sketch a graph to illustrate your idea of each of the following relationships. Be sure to label each axis appropriately. For each relationship, explain under what circumstances, if any, the curve could shift:
   a. The relationship between a person's age and height
   b. Average monthly temperature in your home town over the course of a year
   c. A person's income and the number of hamburgers consumed per month
   d. The amount of fertilizer added to an acre and the amount of corn grown on that land in one growing season
   e. An automobile's horsepower and its gasoline mileage (in miles per gallon)

3. SLOPE Suppose you are given the following data on wage rates and number of hours worked:

Point	Hourly Wage	Hours Worked per Week
a	$0	0
b	5	0
c	10	30
d	15	35
e	20	45
f	25	50

a. Construct and label a set of axes and plot these six points. Label each point *a*, *b*, *c*, and so on. Which variable do you think should be measured on the vertical axis, and which variable should be measured on the horizontal axis?
b. Connect the points. Describe the resulting curve. Does it make sense to you?
c. Compute the slope of the curve between points *a* and *b*. Between points *b* and *c*. Between points *c* and *d*. Between points *d* and *e*. Between points *e* and *f*. What happens to the slope as you move from point *a* to point *f*?

2

Economic Tools and Economic Systems

- Why are you reading this book right now rather than doing something else?
- What is college costing you?
- Why will you eventually major in one subject rather than continue to take courses in different ones?
- Why is fast food so fast?
- Why is there no sense crying over spilt milk?

These and other questions are addressed in this chapter, which introduces some tools of economic analysis—some tools of the trade.

Chapter 1 introduced the idea that scarcity forces us to make choices, but the chapter said little about how to make economic choices. This chapter develops a framework for evaluating economic alternatives. First, we consider the cost involved in selecting one alternative over others. Next, we develop tools to explore the choices available to individuals and to the economy as a whole. Finally, we examine the questions that different economies must answer—questions about what goods and services to produce, how to produce them, and for whom to produce them.

Topics discussed include:

- Opportunity cost
- Comparative advantage
- Specialization
- Division of labor
- Production possibilities frontier
- Economic systems
- Three economic questions
- Capitalism and command system

Choice and Opportunity Cost

Think about a choice you just made: the decision to begin reading this chapter right now rather than use your time to study for another course, play sports, watch TV, go online, get some sleep, hang with friends, or do something else. Suppose it's late and your best alternative to reading right now is getting some sleep. The cost of reading is passing up the opportunity of sleep. Because of scarcity, whenever you make a choice, you must pass up another opportunity; you must incur an *opportunity cost*.

Opportunity Cost

opportunity cost
The value of the best alternative forgone when an item or activity is chosen

What do we mean when we talk about the cost of something? Isn't it what we must give up—must forgo—to get that thing? The **opportunity cost** of the chosen item or activity is *the value of the best alternative that is forgone*. You can think of opportunity cost as the *opportunity lost*. Sometimes opportunity cost can be measured in terms of money, although, as we shall see, money is usually only part of opportunity cost.

How many times have you heard people say they did something because they "had nothing better to do"? They actually mean they had nothing else going on. Yet, according to the idea of opportunity cost, people *always* do what they do because they have nothing better to do. The choice selected seems, at the time, preferable to any other possible alternative. You are reading this chapter right now because you have nothing better to do. In fact, you are attending college for the same reason: College appears more attractive than your best alternative, as discussed in the case study "Bringing Theory to Life: The Opportunity Cost of College" at the end of the book.

Opportunity Cost Is Subjective

Like beauty, opportunity cost is in the eye of the beholder. It is subjective. Only the individual making the choice can identify the most attractive alternative. But the chooser seldom knows the actual value of what was passed up, because that alternative is "the road not taken." If you give up an evening of pizza and conversation with friends to work on a research paper, you will never know exactly what you gave up. You know only what you *expected*. Evidently, you expected the benefit of working on that paper to exceed the benefit of the best alternative. (Incidentally, focusing on the best alternative forgone makes all other alternatives irrelevant.)

Calculating Opportunity Cost Requires Time and Information

Economists assume that people rationally choose the most valued alternative. This does not mean you exhaustively assess the value of all possibilities. You assess alternatives as long as the expected marginal benefit of gathering more information about your options exceeds the expected marginal cost (even if you are not aware of making such conscious calculations). In other words, you do the best you can for yourself.

Because learning about alternatives is costly and time consuming, some choices are based on limited or even wrong information. Indeed, some choices may turn out badly (you went for a picnic but it rained; the movie you rented stunk; your new shoes pinch; your new exercise equipment gets no exercise; the stock you bought tanked). Regret about lost opportunities is captured in the common expression "coulda, woulda, shoulda." At the time you made the selection, however, you thought you were making the best use of all your scarce resources, including the time required to gather and evaluate information about your choices.

Time: The Ultimate Constraint

The Sultan of Brunei is among the richest people on earth, worth billions based on huge oil revenues that flow into his tiny country. He and his royal family (which has ruled since 1405) live in a palace with 1,788 rooms, 257 bathrooms, and a throne room the size of a football field. The family owns hundreds of cars, including dozens of Rolls-Royces; he can drive any of these or pilot one of his seven planes, including the 747 with gold-plated furniture. Supported by such wealth, the Sultan would appear to have overcome the economic problem of scarcity. Though he can buy just about whatever he wants, he lacks the time to enjoy his stuff. If he pursues one activity, he cannot at the same time do something else. Each activity involves an opportunity cost. Consequently, the Sultan must choose from among the competing uses of his scarcest resource, time. Although your alternatives are less exotic, you too face a time constraint, especially as the college term winds down.

Opportunity Cost Varies With Circumstance

Opportunity cost depends on your alternatives. This is why you are more likely to study on a Tuesday night than on a Saturday night. The opportunity cost of studying is lower on a Tuesday night, because your alternatives are less attractive than on a Saturday night, when more is going on. Suppose you go to a movie on Saturday night. Your opportunity cost is the value of your best alternative forgone, which might be attending a college game. For some of you, studying on Saturday night may rank well down the list of possibilities—perhaps ahead of reorganizing your closet but behind doing your laundry.

Opportunity cost is subjective, but in some cases, money paid for goods and services is a reasonable approximation. For example, the opportunity cost of the new DVD player you bought is the benefit from spending that $100 on the best forgone alternative. The money measure may leave out some important elements, however, particularly the value of the time involved. For example, watching the latest hit movie costs you not only the $10 admission price but also the time needed to get there, watch the movie, and return home.

Even religious practices are subject to opportunity cost. For example, about half the U.S. population attends religious services at least once a month. In some states, so-called blue laws prohibit retail activity on Sunday. Some states have repealed these laws in recent years, thus raising the opportunity cost of church attendance. Researchers have found that when a state repeals its blue laws, religious attendance declines as do church donations. These results do not seem to be linked to any decline in religiosity before the repeal.[1]

Sunk Cost and Choice

Suppose you have just finished grocery shopping and are wheeling your cart toward the checkout counters. How do you decide which line to join? Easy. You pick the one with the shortest expected wait. Suppose that barely moves for 10 minutes, when you notice that a cashier has opened a new line and invites you to check out. Do you switch to the open cashier, or do you think, "Since I've already spent 10 minutes in this line, I'm staying put"? The 10 minutes you waited represents a **sunk cost**, which is a cost that has already been incurred and cannot be recovered, regardless of what you do next.

sunk cost
A cost that has already been incurred, cannot be recovered, and thus is irrelevant for present and future economic decisions

1. See Jonathan Gruber and Daniel Hungerman, "The Church vs. the Mall: What Happens When Religion Faces Increased Secular Competition?" *Quarterly Journal of Economics,* 123 (May 2008): 831–862.

You should ignore sunk costs in making economic choices. Hence, you should switch. *Economic decision makers should consider only those costs that are affected by the choice. Sunk costs have already been incurred and are not affected by the choice, so they are irrelevant.* Likewise, you should walk out on a bad movie, even if you spent $10 to get in. Your $10 is gone, and sitting through that stinker only makes you worse off. The irrelevance of sunk costs is underscored by proverbs such as "Don't throw good money after bad," "Let bygones be bygones," "That's water over the dam," and "There's no sense crying over spilt milk." The milk has already spilled, so whatever you do now cannot change that. Or, as Tony Soprano would say, "Fuhgeddaboudit!"

Now that you have some idea about opportunity cost, let's see how it helps solve the economic problem.

Comparative Advantage, Specialization, and Exchange

Suppose you live in a dormitory. You and your roommate have such tight schedules that you each can spare only about an hour a week for mundane tasks like ironing shirts and typing papers (granted, in reality you may not iron shirts or type papers, but this example will help you understand some important principles). Each of you must turn in a typed three-page paper every week, and you each prefer ironed shirts when you have the time. Let's say it takes you a half hour to type a handwritten paper. Your roommate is from the hunt-and-peck school and takes about an hour. But your roommate is a talented ironer and can iron a shirt in 5 minutes flat (or should that be, iron it flat in 5 minutes?). You take twice as long, or 10 minutes, to iron a shirt.

During the hour set aside each week for typing and ironing, typing takes priority. If you each do your own typing and ironing, you type your paper in a half hour and iron three shirts in the remaining half hour. Your roommate spends the entire hour typing the paper, leaving no time for ironing. Thus, if you each do your own tasks, the combined output is two typed papers and three ironed shirts.

The Law of Comparative Advantage

Before long, you each realize that total output would increase if you did all the typing and your roommate did all the ironing. In the hour available for these tasks, you type both papers and your roommate irons 12 shirts. As a result of specialization, total output increases by 9 shirts! You strike a deal to exchange your typing for your roommate's ironing, so you each end up with a typed paper and 6 ironed shirts. Thus, *each of you is better off as a result of specialization and exchange.* By specializing in the task that you each do better, you rely on the **law of comparative advantage**, which states that the individual with the lower opportunity cost of producing a particular output should specialize in that output. You face a lower opportunity cost of typing than does your roommate, because in the time it takes to type a paper, you could iron 3 shirts whereas your roommate could iron 12 shirts. And if you face a lower opportunity cost of typing, your roommate must face a lower opportunity cost of ironing (try working that out).

law of comparative advantage
The individual, firm, region, or country with the lowest opportunity cost of producing a particular good should specialize in that good

Absolute Advantage Versus Comparative Advantage

The gains from specialization and exchange so far are obvious. A more interesting case is if you are faster at both tasks. Suppose the example changes only in one respect: Your roommate takes 12 minutes to iron a shirt compared with your 10 minutes. You now have an *absolute advantage* in both tasks, meaning each task takes you less time than it does your roommate. More generally, having an **absolute advantage** means making something using fewer resources than other producers require.

absolute advantage
The ability to make something using fewer resources than other producers use

Does your absolute advantage in both activities mean specialization is no longer a good idea? Recall that the law of comparative advantage states that the individual with *the lower opportunity cost* of producing a particular good should specialize in that good. You still take 30 minutes to type a paper and 10 minutes to iron a shirt, so your opportunity cost of typing the paper remains at three ironed shirts. Your roommate takes an hour to type a paper and 12 minutes to iron a shirt, so your roommate could iron five shirts in the time it takes to type a paper. Your opportunity cost of typing a paper is ironing three shirts; for your roommate, it's ironing five shirts. *Because your opportunity cost of typing is lower than your roommate's, you still have a comparative advantage in typing.* Consequently, your roommate must have a comparative advantage in ironing (again, try working this out to your satisfaction). Therefore, you should do all the typing and your roommate, all the ironing. Although you have an absolute advantage in both tasks, your **comparative advantage** calls for specializing in the task for which you have the lower opportunity cost—in this case, typing.

comparative advantage
The ability to make something at a lower opportunity cost than other producers face

If neither of you specialized, you could type one paper and iron three shirts. Your roommate could still type just the one paper. Your combined output would be two papers and three shirts. If you each specialized according to comparative advantage, in an hour you could type both papers and your roommate could iron five shirts. Thus, specialization increases total output by two ironed shirts. Even though you are better at both tasks than your roommate, you are comparatively better at typing. Put another way, your roommate, although worse at both tasks, is not quite as bad at ironing as at typing.

Don't think that this is just common sense. Common sense would lead you to do your own ironing and typing, because you are better at both. *Absolute advantage focuses on who uses the fewest resources, but comparative advantage focuses on what else those resources could produce—that is, on the opportunity cost of those resources.* Comparative advantage is the better guide to who should do what.

The law of comparative advantage applies not only to individuals but also to firms, regions of a country, and entire nations. Individuals, firms, regions, or countries with the lowest opportunity cost of producing a particular good should specialize in producing that good. Because of such factors as climate, workforce skills, natural resources, and capital stock, certain parts of the country and certain parts of the world have a comparative advantage in producing particular goods. From Washington State apples to Florida oranges, from software in India to hardware in Taiwan—*resources are allocated most efficiently across the country and around the world when production and trade conform to the law of comparative advantage.*

Specialization and Exchange

In the previous example, you and your roommate specialized and then exchanged output. No money was involved. In other words, you engaged in **barter**, where products are traded directly for other products. Barter works best in simple economies with little specialization and few traded goods. But for economies with greater specialization, *money* facilitates exchange. Money—coins, bills, checks, and debit cards—is a *medium of exchange* because it is the one thing that everyone accepts in return for goods and services.

barter
The direct exchange of one product for another without using money

Because of specialization and comparative advantage, most people consume little of what they produce and produce little of what they consume. Each individual specializes, then exchanges that product for money, which in turn is exchanged for other products. Did you make anything you are wearing? Probably not. Think about the degree of specialization that went into your cotton shirt. A farmer in a warm climate grew the cotton and sold it to someone who spun it into thread, who sold it to someone who wove it into fabric, who sold it to someone who sewed the shirt, who sold it to a wholesaler, who sold it to a retailer, who sold it to you. Many specialists in the chain of production created that shirt.

Evidence of specialization is all around us. Shops at the mall specialize in products ranging from luggage to lingerie. Restaurants range from subs to sushi. Or let your fingers do the walking through the help-wanted ads or *Yellow Pages,* where you will find thousands of specializations. Without moving a muscle, you can observe the division of labor within a single industry by watching the credits roll at the end of a movie. The credits list scores of specialists—from gaffer (lighting electrician) to assistant location scout. As an extreme example, more than 3,000 specialists helped create the movie *Avatar*.[2] Even a typical TV drama, such as *Grey's Anatomy* or *CSI: Miami*, requires hundreds of specialists.

Some specialties may seem odd. For example, professional mourners in Taiwan are sometimes hired by grieving families to scream, wail, and otherwise demonstrate the deep grief befitting a proper funeral. The sharp degree of specialization is perhaps most obvious online, where the pool of potential customers is so vast that individual sites become finely focused. For example, you can find sites specializing in musical bowls, tongue studs, toe rings, brass knuckles, mouth harps, ferret toys, and cat bandannas—just to name a few of the hundreds of thousands of specialty sites. You won't find such precise specialization at the mall. Adam Smith said the degree of specialization is limited by the extent of the market. Online sellers draw on the broadest customer base in the world to find a market niche.

Division of Labor and Gains From Specialization

Picture a visit to McDonald's: "Let's see, I'll have a Big Mac, an order of fries, and a chocolate shake." Less than a minute later your order is ready. It would take you much longer to make a homemade version of this meal. Why is the McDonald's meal faster, cheaper, and—for some people—tastier than one you could make yourself? Why is fast food so fast? McDonald's takes advantage of the gains resulting from the **division of labor.** Each worker, rather than preparing an entire meal, specializes in separate tasks. This division of labor allows the group to produce much more.

division of labor
Breaking down the production of a good into separate tasks

How is this increase in productivity possible? First, the manager can assign tasks according to *individual preferences and abilities*—that is, according to the law of comparative advantage. The worker with the friendly smile and pleasant personality can handle the customers up front; the one with the strong back but few social graces can handle the heavy lifting out back. Second, a worker who performs the same task again and again gets better at it (experience is a good teacher). The worker filling orders at the drive-through, for example, learns to deal with special problems that arise. As another example, consider the experience gained by someone screening bags at airport security. Experience helps the screener distinguish the harmful from the harmless. Third, specialization means no time is lost moving from one task to another. Finally, and perhaps most importantly, the **specialization of labor** allows for the introduction of more sophisticated production techniques—techniques that would not make sense on a smaller scale. For example, McDonald's large shake machine would be impractical in the home. *Specialized machines make each worker more productive.*

specialization of labor
Focusing work effort on a particular product or a single task

To summarize: The specialization of labor (a) takes advantage of individual preferences and natural abilities, (b) allows workers to develop more experience at a

2. As reported in Hendrik Hertzberg, "And the Oscar Goes To," *The New Yorker*, 15 & 22 February 2010, p. 46.

particular task, (c) reduces the need to shift between different tasks, and (d) permits the introduction of labor-saving machinery. Specialization and the division of labor occur not only among individuals but also among firms, regions, and indeed entire countries. The cotton shirt mentioned earlier might involve growing cotton in one country, turning it into cloth in another, making the shirt in a third, and selling it in a fourth.

We should also acknowledge the downside of specialization. Doing the same thing all day can become tedious. Consider, for example, the assembly line worker whose sole task is to tighten a particular bolt. Such a monotonous job could drive that worker bonkers or lead to repetitive motion injury. Thus, the gains from dividing production into individual tasks must be weighed against any problems caused by assigning workers to repetitive, tedious, and potentially harmful jobs. Fortunately, many routine tasks, particularly on assembly lines, can be turned over to robots.

The Economy's Production Possibilities

The focus to this point has been on how individuals choose to use their scarce resources to satisfy their unlimited wants or, more specifically, how they specialize based on comparative advantage. This emphasis on the individual has been appropriate because the economy is shaped by the choices of individual decision makers, whether they are consumers, producers, or public officials. Just as resources are scarce for the individual, they are also scarce for the economy as a whole (no fallacy of composition here). An economy has millions of different resources that can be combined in all kinds of ways to produce millions of different goods and services. This section steps back from the immense complexity of the real economy to develop another simple model, which explores the economy's production options.

Efficiency and the Production Possibilities Frontier, or PPF

Let's develop a model to get some idea of how much an economy can produce with the resources available. What are the economy's production capabilities? Here are the model's assumptions:

1. To simplify matters, output is limited to just two broad classes of products: consumer goods and capital goods.
2. The focus is on production during a given period—in this case, a year.
3. The economy's resources are fixed in both quantity and quality during that period.
4. Society's knowledge about how these resources combine to produce output—that is, the available *technology*—does not change during the year.
5. Also assumed fixed during the period are the "rules of the game" that facilitate production and exchange. These include such things as the legal system, property rights, tax laws, patent laws, and the manners, customs, and conventions of the market.

The point of these simplifying assumptions is to freeze in time the economy's resources, technology, and rules of the game so we can focus on the economy's production options. Otherwise, the production possibilities of the economy would be a moving target.

Given the resources, technology, and rules of the game available in the economy, the **production possibilities frontier,** or **PPF,** identifies possible combinations of the two types of goods that can be produced when all available resources are employed efficiently. *Resources are employed efficiently when there is no change that could increase the production of one good without decreasing the production of the other good.* **Efficiency** involves getting the most from available resources.

Production possibilities frontier (PPF)
A curve showing alternative combinations of goods that can be produced when available resources are used efficiently; a boundary line between inefficient and unattainable combinations

efficiency
The condition that exists when there is no way resources can be reallocated to increase the production of one good without decreasing the production of another; getting the most from available resources

The economy's PPF for consumer goods and capital goods is shown by the curve *AF* in Exhibit 1. Point *A* identifies the amount produced per year if all the economy's resources are used efficiently to produce consumer goods. Point *F* identifies the amount produced per year if all the economy's resources are used efficiently to produce capital goods. Points along the curve between *A* and *F* identify possible combinations of the two goods that can be produced when all the economy's resources are used efficiently.

Inefficient and Unattainable Production

Points inside the PPF, such as *I* in Exhibit 1, identify combinations that do not employ resources efficiently. Note that C yields more consumer goods and no fewer capital goods than *I*. And *E* yields more capital goods and no fewer consumer goods than *I*. Indeed, any point along the PPF between C and *E*, such as *D*, yields both more consumer goods and more capital goods than *I*. Hence, combination *I* is *inefficient*. By using resources more efficiently, the economy can produce more of at least one good without reducing the production of the other good. Points outside the PPF, such as *U* in Exhibit 1, identify *unattainable* combinations, given the availability of resources, technology, and rules of the game. Thus, *the PPF not only shows efficient combinations of production but also serves as the boundary*

EXHIBIT 1 The Economy's Production Possibilities Frontier

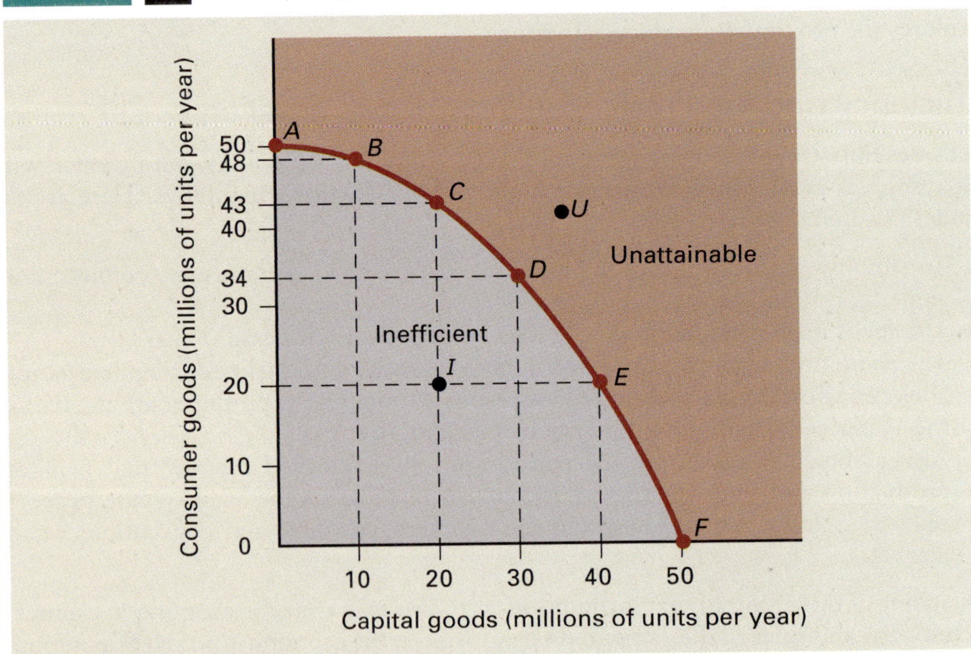

If the economy uses its available resources and technology efficiently to produce consumer goods and capital goods, that economy is on the production possibilities frontier, *AF*. The PPF is bowed out to reflect the law of increasing opportunity cost; the economy must sacrifice more and more units of consumer goods to produce an additional increment of capital goods. Note that more consumer goods must be given up in moving from *E* to *F* than in moving from *A* to *B*, although in each case the gain in capital goods is 10 million units. Points inside the PPF, such as *I*, represent inefficient use of resources. Points outside the PPF, such as *U*, represent unattainable combinations.

between inefficient combinations inside the frontier and unattainable combinations outside the frontier.

The Shape of the Production Possibilities Frontier

Any movement along the PPF involves producing less of one good to produce more of the other. Movements down along the curve indicate that the opportunity cost of more capital goods is fewer consumer goods. For example, moving from point *A* to point *B* *increases* capital production from none to 10 million units but *reduces* consumer units from 50 million to 48 million. Increasing capital goods to 10 million reduces consumer goods only a little. Capital production initially employs resources (such as heavy machinery used to build factories) that add few consumer units but are quite productive in making capital.

As shown by the dashed lines in Exhibit 1, each additional 10 million units of capital produced reduce consumer goods by successively larger amounts. The resources used to produce more capital are increasingly better suited to producing consumer goods. *The opportunity cost of making more capital goods increases, because resources in the economy are not all perfectly adaptable to the production of both types of goods.* The shape of the production possibilities frontier reflects the **law of increasing opportunity cost.** If the economy uses all resources efficiently, the law of increasing opportunity cost states that each additional increment of one good requires the economy to sacrifice successively larger and larger increments of the other good.

law of increasing opportunity cost
To produce more of one good, a successively larger amount of the other good must be sacrificed

The PPF derives its bowed-out shape from the law of increasing opportunity cost. For example, whereas the first 10 million units of capital have an opportunity cost of only 2 million consumer units, the final 10 million units of capital—that is, the increase from *E* to *F*—have an opportunity cost of 20 million consumer units. Notice that the slope of the PPF shows the opportunity cost of an increment of capital. As the economy moves down the curve, the curve becomes steeper, reflecting the higher opportunity cost of capital goods in terms of forgone consumer goods. The law of increasing opportunity cost also applies when shifting from capital goods to consumer goods. Incidentally, if resources were perfectly adaptable to the production of both consumer goods and capital goods, the PPF would be a straight line, reflecting a constant opportunity cost along the PPF.

What Can Shift the Production Possibilities Frontier?

Any production possibilities frontier assumes the economy's resources, technology, and rules of the game are fixed during the period under consideration. Over time, however, the PPF may shift if resources, technology, or the rules of the game change. **Economic growth** is an expansion in the economy's production possibilities as reflected by an outward shift of the PPF.

economic growth
An increase in the economy's ability to produce goods and services; reflected by an outward shift of the economy's production possibilities frontier

Changes in Resource Availability

If people decide to work longer hours, the PPF shifts outward, as shown in panel (a) of Exhibit 2. An increase in the size or health of the labor force, an increase in the skills of the labor force, or an increase in the availability of other resources, such as new oil discoveries, also shifts the PPF outward. In contrast, a decrease of resources shifts the PPF inward, as depicted in panel (b). For example, in 1990 Iraq invaded Kuwait, setting oil fields ablaze and destroying much of Kuwait's physical capital. In West Africa, the encroaching sands of the Sahara destroy thousands of square miles of farmland each year. And in northwest China, a rising tide of wind-blown sand has claimed grasslands, lakes, and forests, and swallowed entire villages, forcing tens of thousands of people to flee.

EXHIBIT 2 Shifts of the Economy's Production Possibilities Frontier

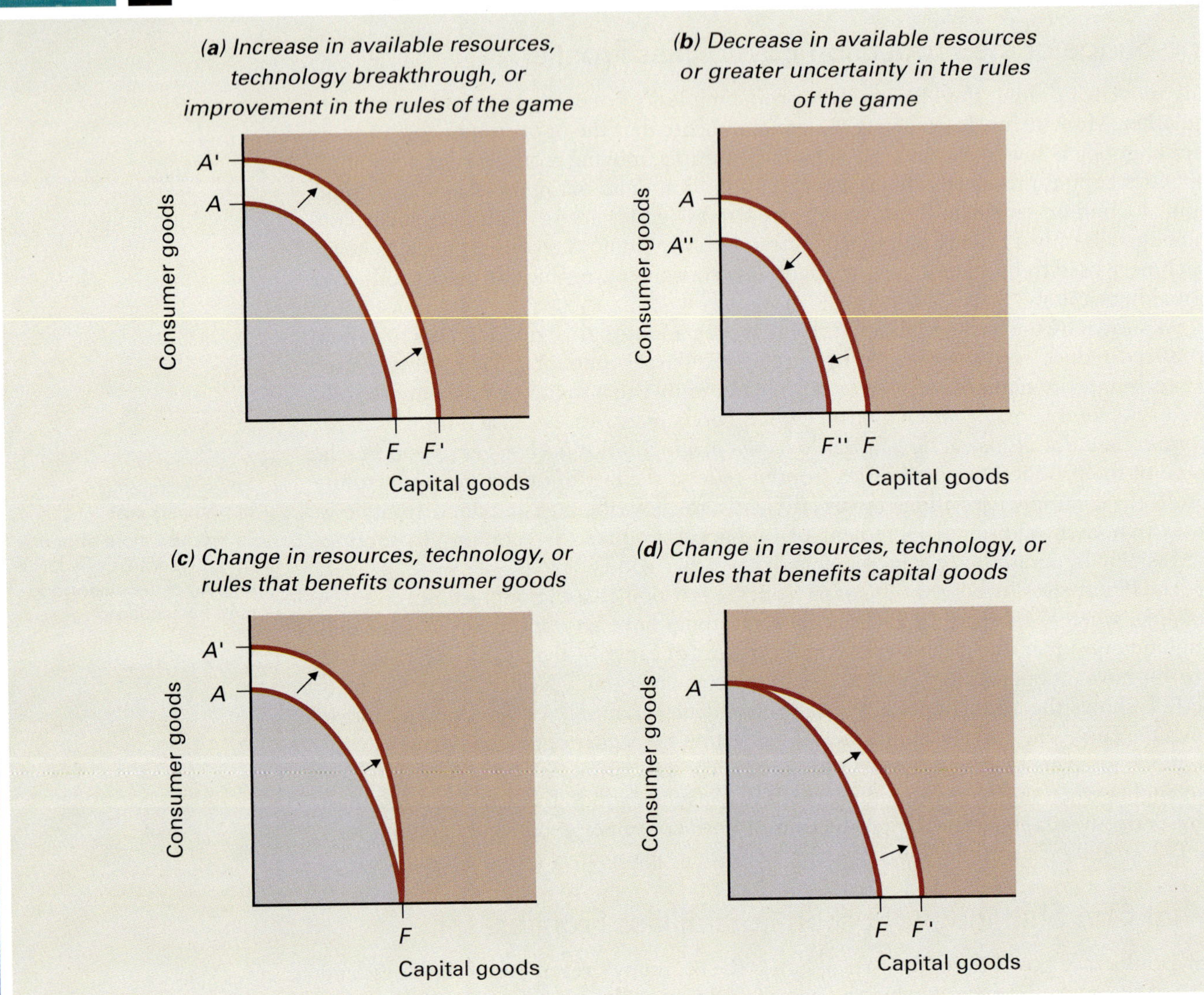

When the resources available to an economy change, the PPF shifts. If more resources become available, if technology improves, or if the rules of the game improve, the PPF shifts outward, as in panel (a), indicating that more output can be produced. A decrease in available resources or an upheaval in the rules causes the PPF to shift inward, as in panel (b). Panel (c) shows a change affecting consumer goods production. More consumer goods can now be produced at any given level of capital goods. Panel (d) shows a change affecting capital goods production.

The new PPFs in panels (a) and (b) appear to be parallel to the original ones, indicating that the resources that changed could produce both capital goods and consumer goods. For example, an increase in electrical power can enhance the production of both, as shown in panel (a). If a resource such as farmland benefits just consumer goods, then increased availability or productivity of that resource shifts the PPF more along the consumer goods axis, as shown in panel (c). Panel (d) shows the effect of an increase in a resource such as construction equipment that is suited only to capital goods.

Increases in the Capital Stock

An economy's PPF depends in part on the stock of human and physical capital. The more capital an economy produces one period, the more output can be produced the next period. Thus, producing more capital goods this period (for example, more machines in the case of physical capital or more education in the case of human capital) shifts the economy's PPF outward the next period.

Technological Change

A technological discovery that employs resources more efficiently could shift the economy's PPF outward. Some discoveries enhance the production of both consumer goods and capital goods, as shown in panel (a) of Exhibit 2. For example, the Internet has increased each firm's ability to find available resources. A technological discovery that benefits consumer goods only, such as more disease-resistant crops, is reflected by a rotation outward of the PPF along the consumer goods axis, as shown in panel (c). Note that point *F* remains unchanged because the breakthrough does not affect the production of capital goods. Panel (d) shows a technological advance in the production of capital goods, such as better software for designing heavy machinery.

Improvements in the Rules of the Game

The **rules of the game** are the formal and informal institutions that support the economy—the laws, customs, manners, conventions, and other institutional underpinnings that encourage people to pursue productive activity. A more stable political environment and more reliable property rights increase the incentive to work and to invest, and thus help the economy grow. For example, people have more incentive to work if taxes claim less of their paychecks. People have more incentive to invest if they are confident that their investment will not be appropriated by government, stolen by thieves, destroyed by civil unrest, or blown up by terrorists. Improvements in the rules of the game shift the economy's PPF outward. On the other hand, greater uncertainty about the rules of the game reduces the economy's productive capacity as reflected by an inward shift of the PPF. The case study "Public Policy: Rules of the Game and Economic Development" at the end of the book underscores the importance of the rules of the game.

What We Learn From the PPF

The PPF demonstrates several ideas introduced so far. The first is *efficiency:* The PPF describes efficient combinations of output, given the economy's resources, technology, and rules of the game. The second idea is *scarcity:* Given the resources, technology, and rules of the game, the economy can produce only so much output per period. The PPF slopes downward, because more of one good means less of the other good, thus demonstrating *opportunity cost*. The PPF's bowed-out shape reflects the *law of increasing opportunity cost*, which arises because some resources are not perfectly adaptable to the production of each type of good. And a shift outward in the PPF reflects *economic growth*.

Finally, because society must somehow select a specific combination of output—a single point—along the PPF, the PPF also underscores the need for *choice*. Selecting a particular combination determines not only consumer goods available this period, but also the capital stock available next period. One thing the PPF does not tell us is which combination to choose. The PPF tells us only about the costs, not the benefits, of the two goods. To make a selection, we need to know about both costs *and* benefits. How society goes about choosing a particular combination depends on the nature of the economic system, as you will see next.

Economic Systems

Each point along the economy's production possibilities frontier is an efficient combination of outputs. Whether the economy produces efficiently and how the economy selects the most preferred combination depends on the decision-making rules employed. But regardless of how decisions are made, each economy must answer three fundamental questions.

Three Questions Every Economic System Must Answer

economic system
The set of mechanisms and institutions that resolve the what, how, and for whom questions

What goods and services are to be produced? How are they to be produced? And for whom are they to be produced? An **economic system** is the set of mechanisms and institutions that resolve the *what, how,* and *for whom* questions. Some criteria used to distinguish among economic systems are (1) who owns the resources, (2) what decision-making process is used to allocate resources and products, and (3) what types of incentives guide economic decision makers.

What Goods and Services Are to Be Produced?

Most of us take for granted the incredible number of choices that go into deciding what gets produced—everything from which new kitchen appliances are introduced, which roads get built, to which of the 10,000 movie scripts purchased by U.S. studios each year get to be among the 500 movies made.[3] Although different economies resolve these and millions of other questions using different decision-making rules and mechanisms, all economies must somehow make such choices.

How Are Goods and Services to Be Produced?

The economic system must determine how output gets produced. Which resources should be used, and how should they be combined to make stuff? How much labor should be used and at what skill levels? What kinds of machines should be used? What new technology should be incorporated into the latest video games? Should the office complex be built in the city or closer to the interstate highway? Millions of individual decisions determine which resources are employed and how these resources are combined.

For Whom Are Goods and Services to Be Produced?

Who will actually consume the goods and services produced? The economic system must determine how to allocate the fruits of production among the population. Should everyone receive equal shares? Should the weak and the sick get more? Should those willing to wait in line get more? Should goods be allocated according to height? Weight? Religion? Age? Gender? Race? Looks? Strength? Political connections? The value of resources supplied? The question "For whom are goods and services to be produced?" is often referred to as the *distribution question.*

Although the three economic questions were discussed separately, they are closely related. The answer to one depends on the answers to the others. For example, an economy that distributes goods and services uniformly to all will, no doubt, answer the what-will-be-produced question differently than an economy that somehow allows more personal choice. As we have seen, laws about resource ownership and the role of

3. As reported in Ian Parker, "The Real McKee," *New Yorker*, 20 October 2003.

government determine the "rules of the game"—the set of conditions that shape individual incentives and constraints. Along a spectrum ranging from the freest to the most regimented types of economic systems, *pure capitalism* would be at one end and the *pure command system* at the other.

Pure Capitalism

Under **pure capitalism,** the rules of the game include the private ownership of resources and the market distribution of products. Owners have *property rights* to the use of their resources and are therefore free to supply those resources to the highest bidder. **Private property rights** allow individual owners to use resources or to charge others for their use. Any income derived from supplying labor, capital, natural resources, or entrepreneurial ability goes to the individual resources owners. Producers are free to make and sell whatever they think will be profitable. Consumers are free to buy whatever goods they can afford. All this voluntary buying and selling is coordinated by unrestricted markets, where buyers and sellers make their intentions known. Market prices guide resources to their most productive use and channel goods and services to the consumers who value them the most.

pure capitalism
An economic system characterized by the private ownership of resources and the use of prices to coordinate economic activity in unregulated markets

private property rights
An owner's right to use, rent, or sell resources or property

Under pure capitalism, markets answer the what, how, and for whom questions. That's why capitalism is also referred to as a *market system.* Markets transmit information about relative scarcity, provide individual incentives, and distribute income among resource suppliers. No individual or small group coordinates these activities. Rather, it is the voluntary choices of many buyers and sellers responding only to their individual incentives and constraints that direct resources and products to those who value them the most.

According to Adam Smith (1723–1790), market forces allocate resources as if by an "invisible hand"—an unseen force that harnesses the pursuit of self-interest to direct resources where they earn the greatest reward. According to Smith, *although each individual pursues his or her self-interest, the "invisible hand" of market forces promotes the general welfare.* Capitalism is sometimes called *laissez-faire;* translated from the French, this phrase means "to let do," or to let people do as they choose without government intervention. Thus, under capitalism, voluntary choices based on rational self-interest are made in unrestricted markets to answer the questions what, how, and for whom.

As we will see in later chapters, pure capitalism has its flaws. The most notable market failures are:

1. No central authority protects property rights, enforces contracts, and otherwise ensures that the rules of the game are followed.
2. People with no resources to sell could starve.
3. Some producers may try to monopolize markets by eliminating the competition.
4. The production or consumption of some goods involves side effects that can harm or benefit people not involved in the market transaction.
5. Private firms have no incentive to produce so-called *public goods,* such as national defense, because private firms cannot prevent nonpayers from enjoying the benefits of public goods.

Because of these limitations, countries have modified pure capitalism to allow some role for government. Even Adam Smith believed government should play a role. The United States is among the most market-oriented economies in the world today.

Pure Command System

In a **pure command system,** resources are directed and production is coordinated not by market forces but by the "command," or central plan, of government. In theory at least, instead of private property, there is public, or *communal,* ownership of property.

pure command system
An economic system characterized by the public ownership of resources and centralized planning

That's why central planning is sometimes called *communism*. Government planners, as representatives of all the people, answer the three questions through *central plans* spelling out how much steel, how many cars, and how much housing to produce. They also decide how to produce these goods and who gets them.

In theory, the pure command system incorporates individual choices into collective choices, which, in turn, are reflected in the central plans. In fact, command economies often have names that focus on collective choice, such as the People's Republic of China and the Democratic People's Republic of Korea (North Korea). In practice, the pure command system also has flaws, most notably:

1. Running an economy is so complicated that some resources are used inefficiently.
2. Because nobody in particular owns resources, each person has less incentive to employ them in their highest-valued use, so some resources are wasted.
3. Central plans may reflect more the preferences of central planners than those of society.
4. Because government is responsible for all production, the variety of products tends to be more limited than in a capitalist economy.
5. Each individual has less personal freedom in making economic choices.

Because of these limitations, countries have modified the pure command system to allow a role for markets. North Korea is perhaps the most centrally planned economy in the world today.

Mixed and Transitional Economies

mixed system
An economic system characterized by the private ownership of some resources and the public ownership of other resources; some markets are regulated by government

No country on earth exemplifies either type of economic system in its pure form. Economic systems have grown more alike over time, with the role of government increasing in capitalist economies and the role of markets increasing in command economies. The United States represents a **mixed system**, with government directly accounting for a little more than one-third of all economic activity. What's more, U.S. governments at all levels regulate the private sector in a variety of ways. For example, local zoning boards determine lot sizes, home sizes, and the types of industries allowed. Federal bodies regulate workplace safety, environmental quality, competitive fairness, food and drug quality, and many other activities.

Although both ends of the spectrum have moved toward the center, capitalism has gained the most converts in recent decades. Perhaps the benefits of markets are no better illustrated than where a country, as a result of war or political upheaval, became divided by ideology into a capitalist economy and a command economy, such as with Taiwan and China or South Korea and North Korea. In each case, the economies began with similar human and physical resources, but once they went their separate ways, economic growth diverged sharply, with the capitalist economies outperforming the command economies. For example, Taiwan's production per capita in 2010 was four times that of China's, and South Korea's production per capita was 15 times that of North Korea's.

Consider the experience of the pilgrims in 1620 while establishing Plymouth Colony. They first tried communal ownership of the land. That turned out badly. Crops were neglected and food shortages developed. After three years of near starvation, the system was changed so that each family was assigned a plot of land and granted the fruits of that plot. Yields increased sharply. The pilgrims learned that people take better care of what they own individually; common ownership often leads to common neglect.

Recognizing the incentive power of property rights and markets, some of the most die-hard central planners are now allowing a role for markets. For example, about one-fifth of the world's population lives in China, which grows more market oriented each day, even going so far as to give private property constitutional protection on a par with state property. In a poll of Chinese citizens, 74 percent agreed that "the free enterprise system is the best system on which to base the future of the world." Among Americans polled, 71 percent agreed with that statement.[4] Two decades ago, the former Soviet Union dissolved into 15 independent republics; most converted state-owned enterprises into private firms. From Moscow to Beijing, from Hungary to Mongolia, the transition to mixed economies now underway in former command economies will shape the world for decades to come.

Economies Based on Custom or Religion

Finally, some economic systems are molded largely by custom or religion. For example, caste systems in India and elsewhere restrict occupational choices. Charging interest is banned under Islamic law. Family relations also play significant roles in organizing and coordinating economic activity. Even in the United States, some occupations are still dominated by women, others by men, largely because of tradition. Your own pattern of consumption and choice of occupation may be influenced by some of these considerations.

Conclusion

Although economies can answer the three economic questions in a variety of ways, this book focuses primarily on the mixed market system, such as exists in the United States. This type of economy blends *private choice,* guided by the price system in competitive markets, with *public choice,* guided by democracy in political markets. The study of mixed market systems grows more relevant as former command economies try to develop markets. The next chapter focuses on the economic actors in a mixed economy and explains why and how government gets into the act.

Summary

1. Resources are scarce, but human wants are unlimited. Because you cannot satisfy all your wants, you must choose, and whenever you choose, you must forgo some option. Choice involves an opportunity cost. The opportunity cost of the selected option is the value of the best alternative forgone.

2. The law of comparative advantage says that the individual, firm, region, or country with the lowest opportunity cost of producing a particular good should specialize in that good. Specialization according to the law of comparative advantage promotes the most efficient use of resources.

3. The specialization of labor increases efficiency by (a) taking advantage of individual preferences and natural abilities, (b) allowing each worker to develop expertise and experience at a particular task, (c) reducing the need to shift between different tasks, and (d) allowing for the introduction of more specialized machines and large-scale production techniques.

4. The production possibilities frontier, or PPF, shows the productive capabilities of an economy when all resources are used efficiently. The frontier's bowed-out shape reflects the law of increasing opportunity cost, which arises because some resources are not perfectly adaptable to the production of different goods. Over time, the PPF can shift in or out as a result of changes in the availability of resources, in technology, or in the rules of the game. The PPF demonstrates several economic concepts, including efficiency, scarcity, opportunity cost, the law of increasing opportunity cost, economic growth, and the need for choice.

5. All economic systems, regardless of their decision-making processes, must answer three basic questions: What is to be produced? How is it to be produced? And for whom is it to be produced? Economies answer the questions differently, depending on who owns the resources and how economic activity is coordinated. Economies can be directed by market forces, by the central plans of government officials, or, in most cases, by a mix of the two.

4. As reported in "Capitalism, Comrade," *Wall Street Journal,* 18 January 2006.

Key Concepts

Opportunity cost 24
Sunk cost 25
Law of comparative advantage 26
Absolute advantage 27
Comparative advantage 27
Barter 27
Division of labor 28
Specialization of labor 28
Production possibilities frontier (PPF) 29
Efficiency 29
Law of increasing opportunity cost 31
Economic growth 31
Economic system 34
Pure capitalism 35
Private property rights 35
Pure command system 35
Mixed system 36

Questions for Review

1. Opportunity Cost Discuss the ways in which the following conditions might affect the opportunity cost of going to a movie tonight:
   a. You have a final exam tomorrow.
   b. School will be out for one month starting tomorrow.
   c. The same movie will be on TV next week.
   d. The Super Bowl is on TV.
2. Opportunity Cost Determine whether each of the following statements is true, false, or uncertain. Explain your answers:
   a. The opportunity cost of an activity is the total value of all the alternatives passed up.
   b. Opportunity cost is an objective measure of cost.
   c. When making choices, people carefully gather all available information about the costs and benefits of alternative choices.
   d. A decision maker seldom knows the actual value of a forgone alternative and therefore must make decisions based on expected values.
3. Comparative Advantage "You should never buy precooked frozen foods because the price you pay includes the labor costs of preparing food." Is this conclusion always valid, or can it be invalidated by the law of comparative advantage?
4. Specialization and Exchange Explain how the specialization of labor can lead to increased productivity.
5. Production Possibilities Under what conditions is it possible to increase production of one good without decreasing production of another good?
6. Production Possibilities Under what conditions would an economy be operating inside its PPF? On its PPF? Outside its PPF?
7. Shifting Production Possibilities In response to an influx of undocumented workers, Congress made it a federal offense to hire them. How do you think this measure affected the U.S. production possibilities frontier? Do you think all industries were affected equally?
8. Production Possibilities "If society decides to use its resources efficiently (that is, to produce *on* its production possibilities frontier), then future generations will be worse off because they will not be able to use these resources." If this assertion is true, full employment of resources may not be a good thing. Comment on the validity of this assertion.
9. Economic Questions What basic economic questions must be answered in a barter economy? In a primitive economy? In a capitalist economy? In a command economy?
10. Economic Systems What are the major differences between a pure capitalist system and a pure command system? Is the United States closer to a pure capitalist system or to a pure command system?

Problems and Exercises

11. Case Study: The Opportunity Cost of College (See page 700.) During the Vietnam War, colleges and universities were overflowing with students. Was this bumper crop of students caused by a greater expected return on a college education or by a change in the opportunity cost of attending college? Explain.
12. Sunk Cost and Choice Suppose you go to a restaurant and buy an expensive meal. Halfway through, despite feeling quite full, you decide to clean your plate. After all, you think, you paid for the meal, so you are going to eat all of it. What's wrong with this thinking?
13. Opportunity Cost You can either spend spring break working at home for $80 per day for five days or go to Florida for the week. If you stay home, your expenses will total about $100. If you go to Florida, the airfare, hotel, food, and miscellaneous expenses will total about $700. What's your opportunity cost of going to Florida?
14. Absolute and Comparative Advantage You have the following information concerning the production of wheat and cloth in the United States and the United Kingdom:

Labor Hours Required to Produce One Unit

	United Kingdom	United States
Wheat	2	1
Cloth	6	5

a. What is the opportunity cost of producing a unit of wheat in the United Kingdom? In the United States?
b. Which country has an absolute advantage in producing wheat? In producing cloth?
c. Which country has a comparative advantage in producing wheat? In producing cloth?
d. Which country should specialize in producing wheat? In producing cloth?

15. SPECIALIZATION Provide some examples of specialized markets or retail outlets. What makes the Web so conducive to specialization?

16. SHAPE OF THE PPF Suppose a production possibilities frontier includes the following combinations:

Cars	Washing Machines
0	1,000
100	600
200	0

a. Graph the PPF, assuming that it has no curved segments.
b. What is the cost of producing an additional car when 50 cars are being produced?
c. What is the cost of producing an additional car when 150 cars are being produced?
d. What is the cost of producing an additional washing machine when 50 cars are being produced? When 150 cars are being produced?
e. What do your answers tell you about opportunity costs?

17. PRODUCTION POSSIBILITIES Suppose an economy uses two resources (labor and capital) to produce two goods (wheat and cloth). Capital is relatively more useful in producing cloth, and labor is relatively more useful in producing wheat. If the supply of capital falls by 10 percent and the supply of labor increases by 10 percent, how will the PPF for wheat and cloth change?

18. PRODUCTION POSSIBILITIES There's no reason why a production possibilities frontier could not be used to represent the situation facing an individual. Imagine your own PPF. Right now—today—you have certain resources—your time, your skills, perhaps some capital. And you can produce various outputs. Suppose you can produce combinations of two outputs, call them studying and partying.

a. Draw your PPF for studying and partying. Be sure to label the axes of the diagram appropriately. Label the points where the PPF intersects the axes, as well as several other points along the frontier.
b. Explain what it would mean for you to move upward and to the left along your personal PPF. What kinds of adjustments would you have to make in your life to make such a movement along the frontier?
c. Under what circumstances would your personal PPF shift outward? Do you think the shift would be a "parallel" one? Why, or why not?

19. SHIFTING PRODUCTION POSSIBILITIES Determine whether each of the following would cause the economy's PPF to shift inward, outward, or not at all:

a. An increase in average length of annual vacations
b. An increase in immigration
c. A decrease in the average retirement age
d. The migration of skilled workers to other countries

20. Case Study: Rules of the Game and Economic Development (See page 701.) Why is the standard of living higher in countries where doing business is easier? Why do governments collect any taxes or impose any regulations at all?

21. ECONOMIC SYSTEMS The United States is best described as having a mixed economy. What are some elements of command in the U.S. economy? What are some elements of tradition?

Global Economic Watch Exercises

Login to www.cengagebrain.com and access the Global Economic Watch to do these exercises.

22. GLOBAL ECONOMIC WATCH Go to the Global Economic Crisis Resource Center. Select Global Issues in Context. In the Basic Search box at the top of the page, enter the phrase "Build Ontario's economy." On the Results page, scroll down to the Global Viewpoints section. Click on the link for the December 8, 2009, article "Build Ontario's economy on battle-tested financial sector." Use your understanding of opportunity cost to explain the idea that the Canadian province of Ontario has a comparative advantage in the financial sector.

23. GLOBAL ECONOMIC WATCH Go to the Global Economic Crisis Resource Center. Select Global Issues in Context. In the Basic Search box at the top of the page, enter the term "capitalism." Find one resource that supports capitalism and one that criticizes. Write a summary of the viewpoints in your own words.

Economic Decision Makers

3

©iStockphoto.com/Ramona d'Viola

- If we live in the age of specialization, then why haven't specialists taken over all production?
- For example, why do most of us still do our own laundry and perform dozens of other tasks for ourselves?
- In what sense has some production moved from the household to the firm and then back to the household?
- If the "invisible hand" of competitive markets is so efficient, why does government get into the act?

Answers to these and other questions are addressed in this chapter, which discusses the four economic decision makers: households, firms, governments, and the rest of the world.

To develop a better feel for how the economy works, you must get more acquainted with the key players. You already know more about them than you may realize. You grew up in a household. You have dealt with firms all your life, from Sony to Subway. You know much about governments, from taxes to public schools. And you have a growing awareness of the rest of the world, from online sites, to imports, to foreign travel. This chapter draws on your abundant personal experience with economic decision makers to consider their makeup and goals.

Topics discussed include:

- Evolution of the household
- Evolution of the firm
- Types of firms
- Market failures and government remedies
- Taxing and public spending
- International trade and finance

The Household

Households play the starring role in a market economy. Their demand for goods and services determines what gets produced. And their supply of labor, capital, natural resources, and entrepreneurial ability produces that output. As demanders of goods and services and suppliers of resources, households make all kinds of choices, such as what to buy, how much to save, where to live, and where to work. Although a household usually consists of several individuals, we will view each household as acting like a single decision maker.

The Evolution of the Household

In earlier times, when the economy was primarily agricultural, a farm household was largely self-sufficient. Each family member often specialized in a specific farm task—cooking meals, making clothes, tending livestock, planting crops, and so on. These early households produced what they consumed and consumed what they produced. With the introduction of new seed varieties, better fertilizers, and labor-saving machinery, farm productivity increased sharply. Fewer farmers were needed to grow enough food to feed a nation. At the same time, the growth of urban factories increased the demand for factory labor. As a result, many workers moved from farms to cities, where they became more specialized but less self-sufficient.

Households evolved in other ways. For example, in 1950, only about 15 percent of married women with young children were in the labor force. Since then, higher levels of education among women and a growing demand for their labor increased women's earnings, thus raising their opportunity cost of working in the home. This higher opportunity cost contributed to their growing labor force participation. Today about 70 percent of women with children under 18 are in the labor force.

The rise of two-earner households has affected the family as an economic unit. Households produce less for themselves and demand more from the market. For example, child-care services and fast-food restaurants have displaced some household production (Americans now consume about one-third of their calories away from home). The rise in two-earner families has reduced specialization within the household—a central feature of the farm family. Nonetheless, some production still occurs in the home, as we'll explore later.

Households Maximize Utility

There are more than 115 million U.S. households. All those who live together under one roof are considered part of the same household. What exactly do households attempt to accomplish in making decisions? Economists assume that people try to maximize their level of satisfaction, sense of well-being, happiness, and overall welfare. In short, households attempt to maximize **utility**. Households, like other economic decision makers, are viewed as rational, meaning that they try to act in their best interests and do not deliberately try to make themselves less happy. Utility maximization depends on each household's subjective goals, not on some objective standard. For example, some households maintain neat homes with well-groomed lawns; others pay little attention to their homes and use their lawns as junkyards.

utility
The satisfaction received from consumption; sense of well-being

Households as Resource Suppliers

Households use their limited resources—labor, capital, natural resources, and entrepreneurial ability—in an attempt to satisfy their unlimited wants. They can use these resources to produce goods and services in their homes. For example, they can cook, wash, sew, dust, iron, sweep, vacuum, mop, mow, paint, and fix a leaky faucet. They can also sell these resources in the resource market and use the income to buy goods and services in the product market. The most valuable resource sold by most households is labor.

Panel (a) of Exhibit 1 shows the sources of personal income received by U.S. households in 2009, when personal income totaled $12.0 trillion. As you can see, 60 percent of personal income came from wages and salaries. A distant second was transfer payments (to be discussed next), at 16 percent of personal income, followed by personal interest at 10 percent, and proprietors' income at 8 percent. *Proprietors* are people who work for themselves rather than for employers; farmers, plumbers, and doctors are often self-employed. Proprietors' income should also be considered a form of labor income. *Over two-thirds of personal income in the United States comes from labor earnings rather than from the ownership of other resources such as capital or natural resources.*

EXHIBIT 1 Where U.S. Personal Income Comes From and Where It Goes

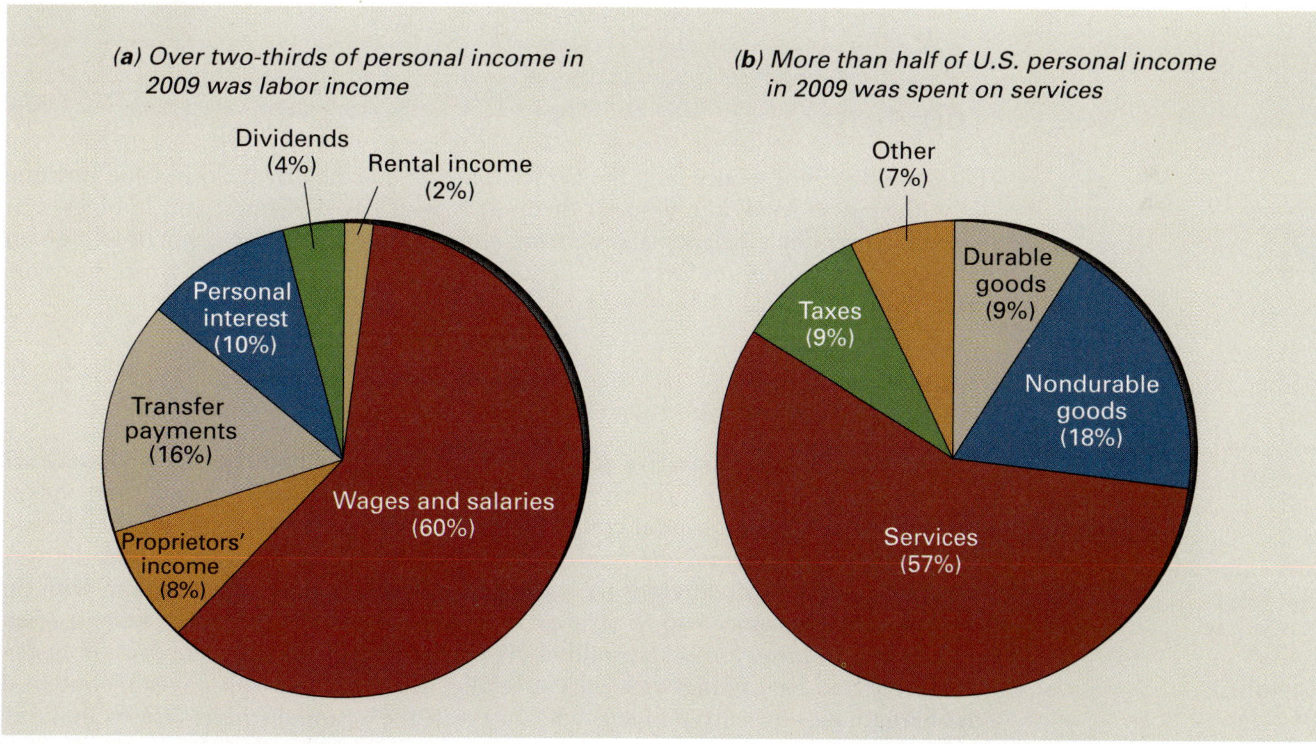

Source: Based on figures from *Survey of Current Business*, Bureau of Economic Analysis, March 2010, Tables 2.1 and 2.3.5. For the latest figures, go to http://www.bea.gov/scb/index.htm.

transfer payments
Cash or in-kind benefits given to individuals as outright grants from the government

Because of a limited education, disability, discrimination, poor health, the time demands of caring for small children, or just bad luck, some households have few resources that are valued in the market. Society has made the political decision that individuals in such circumstances should receive short-term public assistance. Consequently, the government gives some households **transfer payments**, which are outright grants. *Cash transfers* are monetary payments, such as welfare benefits, Social Security, unemployment compensation, and disability benefits. *In-kind transfers* provide for specific goods and services, such as food, health care, and housing.

Households as Demanders of Goods and Services

What happens to personal income once it comes into the household? Most goes to personal consumption, which sorts into three broad spending categories: (1) *durable goods*—that is, goods expected to last three or more years—such as an automobile or a refrigerator; (2) *nondurable goods,* such as food, clothing, and gasoline; and (3) *services,* such as haircuts, air travel, and medical care. As you can see from panel (b) of Exhibit 1, spending on durable goods in 2009 claimed 9 percent of U.S. personal income; nondurables, 18 percent; and services, 57 percent. Taxes claimed 9 percent, and all other categories, including savings, claimed just 7 percent. So more than half of all personal income went for services—the fastest growing sector, because many services, such as child care, are shifting from do-it-yourself home production to market purchases.

The Firm

Household members once built their own homes, made their own clothes and furniture, grew their own food, and amused themselves with books, games, and hobbies. Over time, however, the efficiency arising from comparative advantage resulted in a greater specialization among resource suppliers. This section takes a look at firms, beginning with their evolution.

The Evolution of the Firm

Specialization and comparative advantage explain why households are no longer self-sufficient. But why is a firm the natural result? For example, rather than make a woolen sweater from scratch, couldn't a consumer take advantage of specialization by negotiating with someone who produced the wool, another who spun the wool into yarn, and a third who knit the yarn into a sweater? Here's the problem with that model: If the consumer had to visit each of these specialists and reach an agreement, the resulting *transaction costs* could easily erase the gains from specialization. Instead of visiting and bargaining with each specialist, the consumer can pay someone to do the bargaining—an entrepreneur, who hires all the resources necessary to make the sweater. *An entrepreneur, by contracting for many sweaters rather than just one, is able to reduce the transaction costs per sweater.*

For about 200 years, profit-seeking entrepreneurs relied on "putting out" raw material, like wool and cotton, to rural households that turned it into finished products, like woolen goods made from yarn. The system developed in the British Isles, where workers' cottages served as tiny factories, especially during winter months, when farming chores were few (so the opportunity cost was low). This approach, which came to be known as the *cottage industry system,* still exists in some parts of the world. You might think of this system as partway between household self-sufficiency and the modern firm.

As the British economy expanded in the 18th century, entrepreneurs began organizing the stages of production under one roof. Technological developments, such as waterpower and later steam power, increased the productivity of each worker and helped shift employment from rural areas to urban factories. *Work, therefore, became organized in large, centrally powered factories that (1) promoted a more efficient division of labor, (2) allowed for the direct supervision of production, (3) reduced transportation costs, and (4) facilitated the use of machines far bigger than anything used in the home.* The development of large-scale factory production, known as the **Industrial Revolution**, began in Great Britain around 1750 and spread to the rest of Europe, North America, and Australia.

Industrial Revolution
Development of large-scale factory production that began in Great Britain around 1750 and spread to the rest of Europe, North America, and Australia

Production, then, evolved from self-sufficient rural households to the cottage industry system, where specialized production occurred in the household, to production in a firm. Today, entrepreneurs combine resources in firms such as factories, mills, offices, stores, and restaurants. **Firms** are economic units formed by profit-seeking entrepreneurs who combine labor, capital, and natural resources to produce goods and services. Just as we assume that households try to maximize utility, we assume that firms try to *maximize profit*. Profit, the entrepreneur's reward, equals sales revenue minus the cost of production, including the opportunity cost of the entrepreneur's time.

firms
Economic units formed by profit-seeking entrepreneurs who employ resources to produce goods and services for sale

Types of Firms

There are more than 30 million for-profit businesses in the United States. Two-thirds are small retail businesses, small service operations, part-time home-based businesses, and small farms. Each year more than a million new businesses start up and many fail. Firms are organized in one of three ways: as a sole proprietorship, as a partnership, or as a corporation.

Sole Proprietorships

The simplest form of business organization is the **sole proprietorship**, a single-owner firm. Examples include self-employed plumbers, farmers, and dentists. Most sole proprietorships consist of just the self-employed proprietor—there are no hired employees. To organize a sole proprietorship, the owner simply opens for business by, for example, taking out a classified ad announcing availability for plumbing services or whatever. The owner is in complete control. But he or she faces unlimited liability and could lose everything, including a home and other personal assets, to settle business debts or other claims against the business. Also, because the sole proprietor has no partners or other investors, raising enough money to get the business up and running and keep it going can be a challenge. One final disadvantage is that a sole proprietorship usually goes out of business when the proprietor dies or leaves the business. Still, a sole proprietorship is the most common type of business, accounting most recently for 71 percent of all U.S. businesses. Nonetheless, because this type of firm is typically small, proprietorships generate just a tiny portion of all U.S. business sales—only 4 percent. But keep in mind that many of the largest businesses in the world today began as an idea of a sole proprietor.

sole proprietorship
A firm with a single owner who has the right to all profits but who also bears unlimited liability for the firm's losses and debts

Partnerships

partnership
A firm with multiple owners who share the profits and bear unlimited liability for the firm's losses and debts

A more complicated form of business is the **partnership**, which involves two or more individuals who agree to combine their funds and efforts in return for a share of any profit or loss. Law, accounting, and medical partnerships typify this business form. Partners have strength in numbers and often find it easier than sole proprietors to raise enough funds to get the business going. But partners may not always agree. Also, each partner usually faces unlimited liability for any debts or claims against the partnership, so one partner could lose everything because of another's mistake. Finally, the death or departure of one partner can disrupt the firm's continuity and require a complete reorganization. The partnership is the least common form of U.S. business, making up only 10 percent of all firms and 13 percent of all business sales.

Corporations

corporation
A legal entity owned by stockholders whose liability is limited to the value of their stock ownership

By far the most influential form of business is the corporation. A **corporation** is a legal entity established through articles of incorporation. Shares of stock confer corporate ownership, thereby entitling stockholders to a claim on any profit. A major advantage of the corporate form is that many investors—hundreds, thousands, even millions—can pool their funds, so incorporating represents the easiest way to amass large sums to finance the business. Also, stockholders' liability for any loss is limited to the value of their stock, meaning stockholders enjoy *limited liability*. A final advantage of this form of organization is that the corporation has a life apart from its owners. The corporation survives even if ownership changes hands, and it can be taxed, sued, and even charged with a crime as if it were a person.

The corporate form has some disadvantages as well. A stockholder's ability to influence corporate policy is limited to voting for a board of directors, which oversees the operation of the firm. Each share of stock usually carries with it one vote. The typical stockholder of a large corporation owns only a tiny fraction of the shares and thus has little say. Whereas the income from sole proprietorships and partnerships is taxed only once, corporate income gets whacked twice—first as corporate profits and second as stockholder income, either as corporate dividends or as realized capital gains. A *realized capital gain* is any increase in the market price of a share that occurs between the time the share is purchased and the time it is sold.

A hybrid type of corporation has evolved to take advantage of the limited liability feature of the corporate structure while reducing the impact of double taxation. The *S corporation* provides owners with limited liability, but profits are taxed only once—as income on each shareholder's personal income tax return. To qualify as an S corporation, a firm must have no more than 100 stockholders and no foreign stockholders.

Corporations make up only 19 percent of all U.S. businesses, but because they tend to be much larger than the other two business forms, corporations account for 83 percent of all business sales. Exhibit 2 shows, by business type, the percentage of U.S. firms and the percentage of U.S. sales. *The sole proprietorship is the most important in sheer numbers, but the corporation is the most important in total sales.*

Cooperatives

cooperative
An organization consisting of people who pool their resources to buy and sell more efficiently than they could individually

A **cooperative**, or "co-op" for short, is a group of people who cooperate by pooling their resources to buy and sell more efficiently than they could independently. Cooperatives try to minimize costs and operate with limited liability of members. The government

EXHIBIT 2 Percent Distribution by Type of Firm Based on Number of Firms and Firm Sales

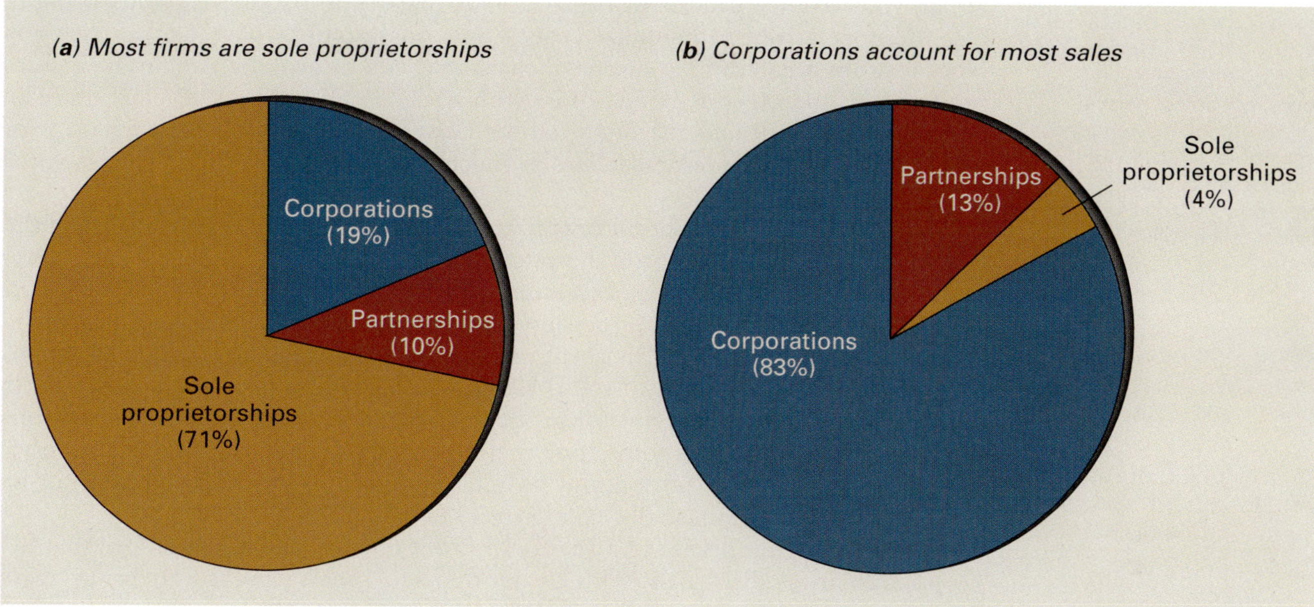

Source: U.S. Census Bureau, *Statistical Abstract of the United States: 2010*, U.S. Bureau of the Census, Table No. 728. For the latest figures, go to http://www.census.gov/compendia/statab/.

grants most cooperatives tax-exempt status. There are two types: consumer cooperatives and producer cooperatives.

Consumer Cooperatives

A *consumer cooperative* is a retail business owned and operated by some or all of its customers in order to reduce costs. Some cooperatives require members to pay an annual fee and others require them to work a certain number of hours each year. Members sometimes pay lower prices than other customers or may share in any revenues that exceed costs. In the United States, consumer cooperatives operate credit unions, electric-power facilities, health plans, apartment buildings, and grocery stores, among other businesses. Many college bookstores are cooperatives. For example, the UConn Co-op is owned by about 30,000 students, faculty, and staff. These members receive discounts on their purchases.

Producer Cooperatives

In a *producer cooperative,* producers join forces to buy supplies and equipment and to market their output. Each producer's objective is to reduce costs and increase profits. Federal legislation allows farmers to cooperate without violating antitrust laws. Firms in other industries could not do this legally. Farmers pool their funds to purchase machinery and supplies, provide storage and processing facilities, and transport products to market. Sunkist, for example, is a farm cooperative owned and operated by about 6,500 citrus growers in California and Arizona.

Not-for-Profit Organizations

not-for-profit organizations
Groups that do not pursue profit as a goal; they engage in charitable, educational, humanitarian, cultural, professional, or other activities, often with a social purpose

So far, you have learned about organizations that try to maximize profits or, in the case of cooperatives, to minimize costs. Some organizations have neither as a goal. **Not-for-profit organizations** engage in charitable, educational, humanitarian, cultural, professional, and other activities, often with a social purpose. Any revenue exceeding cost is plowed back into the organization. Government agencies do not have profit as a goal either, but governments are not included in this definition of not-for-profit organizations.

Like businesses, not-for-profit organizations evolved to help people accomplish their goals. Examples include nonprofit hospitals, private schools and colleges, religious organizations, the Red Cross, Greenpeace, charitable foundations, soup kitchens, orchestras, museums, labor unions, and professional organizations. There are about 1.5 million not-for-profit organizations in the United States. They employ about 12 million workers, or about 8 percent of the U.S. work force with not-for-profit hospitals the largest employers. But even not-for-profit organizations must somehow pay the bills. Revenue typically includes some combination of voluntary contributions and service charges, such as college tuition and hospital charges. In the United States, not-for-profit organizations are usually exempt from taxes.

Thus far we have discussed a variety of profit and nonprofit institutions that help people accomplish their goals. With greater frequency, some products are being created and improved by the users of those products; this is discussed further in the case study, "The Information Economy: User-Generated Products," at the end of the book.

Why Does Household Production Still Exist?

If firms are so efficient at reducing transaction and production costs, why don't they make everything? Why do households still perform some tasks, such as cooking and cleaning? *If a household's opportunity cost of performing a task is below the market price, then the household usually performs that task.* People with a lower opportunity cost of time do more for themselves. For example, janitors are more likely to mow their lawns than are physicians. Let's look at some reasons for household production.

No Skills or Special Resources Are Required

Some activities require so few skills or special resources that householders find it cheaper to do the jobs themselves. Sweeping the kitchen floor requires only a broom and some time so it's usually performed by household members. Sanding a wooden floor, however, involves special machinery and expertise, so this service is usually left to professionals. Similarly, although you wouldn't hire someone to brush your teeth, dental work is not for amateurs. *Households usually perform domestic chores that demand neither expertise nor special machinery.*

Household Production Avoids Taxes

Suppose you are deciding whether to pay someone $3,000 to paint your house or do it yourself. If the income tax rate is one-third, you must earn $4,500 before taxes to have the $3,000 after taxes to pay for the job. And the painter who charges you $3,000 nets only $2,000 after paying $1,000 in taxes. Thus, you must earn $4,500 so that the painter can take home $2,000. If you paint the house yourself, no taxes are involved. The tax-free nature of do-it-yourself activity favors household production over market transactions.

Household Production Reduces Transaction Costs

Getting estimates, hiring a contractor, negotiating terms, and monitoring job performance all take time and require information. Doing the job yourself reduces these transaction costs. Household production also allows for more personal control over the final product than is usually available through the market. For example, some people prefer home cooking, because they can prepare home-cooked meals to individual tastes.

Household production often grows during hard times. The economic recession of 2007–2009 prompted some families to shift from market purchases to household production to save money. For example, sales of hair clippers used for home haircuts increased 10 percent in 2008 and 11 percent in 2009.[1]

Technological Advances Increase Household Productivity

Technological breakthroughs are not confined to market production. Vacuum cleaners, washers and dryers, dishwashers, microwave ovens, and other modern appliances reduce the time and often the skill required to perform household tasks. Also, new technologies such as Blu-ray players, DVRs, HDTVs, broadband downloads, and computer games enhance home entertainment. Indeed, microchip-based technologies have shifted some production from the firm back to the household. See the case study, "The Information Economy: The Electronic Cottage," at the end of the book for further discussion.

The Government

You might think that production by households and firms could satisfy all consumer wants. Why must yet another economic decision maker get into the act? After all, governments play some role in every nation on earth.

The Role of Government

Sometimes the unrestrained operation of markets yields undesirable results. Too many of some goods and too few of other goods get produced. This section discusses the sources of **market failure** and how society's overall welfare may be improved through government intervention in the market.

market failure
A condition that arises when the unregulated operation of markets yields socially undesirable results

Establishing and Enforcing the Rules of the Game

Market efficiency depends on people like you using your resources to maximize your utility. But what if you were repeatedly robbed of your paycheck on your way home from work? Or what if, after you worked two weeks in a new job, your boss called you a sucker and said you wouldn't get paid? Why bother working? The market system would break down if you could not safeguard your private property or if you could not enforce contracts. Governments safeguard private property through police protection and enforce contracts through a judicial system. More generally, governments try to make sure that market participants abide by the rules of the game. These rules are established through government laws and regulations and also through the customs and conventions of the marketplace.

1. Mary Pilon, "Per Capita Savings: Home Barbering Grows in Recession," *Wall Street Journal*, 31 August 2009.

Promoting Competition

Although the "invisible hand" of competition usually promotes an efficient allocation of resources, some firms try to avoid competition through *collusion*, which is an agreement among firms to divide the market and fix the price. Or an individual firm may try to eliminate the competition by using unfair business practices. For example, to drive out local competitors, a large firm may temporarily sell at a price below cost. Government antitrust laws try to promote competition by prohibiting collusion and other anticompetitive practices.

Regulating Natural Monopolies

monopoly
A sole supplier of a product with no close substitutes

natural monopoly
One firm that can supply the entire market at a lower per-unit cost than could two or more firms

Competition usually keeps the product price below the price charged by a **monopoly**, a sole supplier to the market. In rare instances, however, a monopoly can produce and sell the product for less than could competing firms. For example, electricity is delivered more efficiently by a single firm that wires the community than by competing firms each stringing its own wires. When it is cheaper for one firm to serve the market than for two or more firms to do so, that one firm is called a **natural monopoly**. Since a natural monopoly faces no competition, it maximizes profit by charging a higher price than would be optimal from society's point of view. A lower price and greater output would improve social welfare. Therefore, the government usually regulates a natural monopoly, forcing it to lower its price and increase output.

Providing Public Goods

private good
A good, such as pizza, that is both rival in consumption and exclusive

public good
A good that, once produced, is available for all to consume, regardless of who pays and who doesn't; such a good is nonrival and nonexclusive, such as a safer community

So far this book has been talking about private goods, which have two important features. First, private goods are *rival* in consumption, meaning that the amount consumed by one person is unavailable for others to consume. For example, when you and some friends share a pizza, each slice they eat is one less available for you. Second, the supplier of a private good can easily exclude those who fail to pay. Only paying customers get pizza. Thus, private goods are said to be *exclusive*. So **private goods**, such as pizza, are both rival in consumption and exclusive. In contrast, **public goods** are *nonrival* in consumption. For example, your family's benefit from a safer neighborhood does not reduce your neighbor's benefit. What's more, once produced, public goods are available to all. Suppliers cannot easily prevent consumption by those who fail to pay. For example, reducing terrorism is *nonexclusive*. It benefits all in the community, regardless of who pays to reduce terrorism and who doesn't. Because public goods are *nonrival* and *nonexclusive*, private firms cannot sell them profitably. The government, however, has the authority to enforce tax collections for public goods. Thus, the government provides public goods and funds them with taxes.

Dealing With Externalities

externality
A cost or a benefit that affects neither the buyer nor seller, but instead affects people not involved in the market transaction

Market prices reflect the private costs and private benefits of producers and consumers. But sometimes production or consumption imposes costs or benefits on third parties—on those who are neither suppliers nor demanders in a market transaction. For example, a paper mill fouls the air breathed by nearby residents, but the price of paper usually fails to reflect such costs. Because these pollution costs are outside, or external to, the market, they are called *externalities*. An **externality** is a cost or a benefit that falls on a third party. A negative externality imposes an external cost, such as factory pollution, auto emissions, or traffic congestion. A positive externality confers an external benefit, such as getting a good education, getting inoculated against a disease (thus reducing the possibility of infecting others), or driving carefully. Because market prices usually do not reflect externalities, governments often use taxes, subsidies, and regulations to discourage negative externalities and encourage positive externalities. For example, a polluting factory may face taxes and regulations aimed at curbing that pollution. And because more educated people can read road signs and have options that pay better than crime, governments try to encourage education with free public schools, subsidized higher education, and by keeping people in school until their 16th birthdays.

A More Equal Distribution of Income

As mentioned earlier, some people, because of poor education, mental or physical disabilities, bad luck, or perhaps the need to care for small children, are unable to support themselves and their families. Because resource markets do not guarantee even a minimum level of income, transfer payments reflect society's willingness to provide a basic standard of living to all households. Most Americans agree that government should redistribute income to the poor (note the normative nature of this statement). Opinions differ about who should receive benefits, how much they should get, what form benefits should take, and how long benefits should last.

Full Employment, Price Stability, and Economic Growth

Perhaps the most important responsibility of government is fostering a healthy economy, which benefits just about everyone. The government—through its ability to tax, to spend, and to control the money supply—attempts to promote full employment, price stability, and economic growth. Pursuing these objectives by taxing and spending is called **fiscal policy**. Pursuing them by regulating the money supply is called **monetary policy**. Macroeconomics examines both policies.

fiscal policy
The use of government purchases, transfer payments, taxes, and borrowing to influence economy-wide variables such as inflation, employment, and economic growth

monetary policy
Regulation of the money supply to influence economy-wide variables such as inflation, employment, and economic growth

Government's Structure and Objectives

The United States has a *federal system* of government, meaning that responsibilities are shared across levels of government. State governments grant some powers to local governments and surrender some powers to the national, or federal, government. As the system has evolved, the federal government has primary responsibility for national security, economic stability, and market competition. State governments fund public higher education, prisons, and—with aid from the federal government—highways and welfare. Local governments provide primary and secondary education with aid from the state, plus police and fire protection. Here are some distinguishing features of government.

Difficulty in Defining Government Objectives

We assume that households try to maximize utility and firms try to maximize profit, but what about governments—or, more specifically, what about government decision makers? What do they try to maximize? One problem is that our federal system consists of not one but many governments—more than 89,500 separate jurisdictions in all, including 1 nation, 50 states, 3,033 counties, 35,991 cities and towns, 13,051 school districts, and 37,381 special districts. What's more, because the federal government relies on offsetting, or countervailing, powers across the executive, legislative, and judicial branches, government does not act as a single, consistent decision maker. Even within the federal executive branch, there are so many agencies and bureaus that at times they seem to work at cross-purposes. For example, at the same time as the U.S. Surgeon General required health warnings on cigarette packages, the U.S. Department of Agriculture pursued policies to benefit tobacco growers. Given this thicket of jurisdictions, branches, and bureaus, one useful theory of government behavior is that elected officials try to maximize the number of votes they get in the next election. So let's assume that elected officials are vote maximizers. In this theory, vote maximization guides the decisions of elected officials who, in turn, oversee government employees.

Voluntary Exchange Versus Coercion

Market exchange relies on the voluntary behavior of buyers and sellers. Don't like tofu? No problem—don't buy any. But in political markets, the situation is different. Any voting rule except unanimous consent must involve some government coercion. Public choices are enforced by the police power of the state. Those who don't pay their taxes could go to jail, even though they may object to some programs those taxes support, such as capital punishment or the war in Afghanistan.

No Market Prices

Another distinguishing feature of governments is that public output is usually offered at either a zero price or at some price below the cost of providing it. If you now pay in-state tuition at a public college or university, your tuition probably covers only about half the state's cost of providing your education. Because the revenue side of the government budget is usually separate from the expenditure side, there is no necessary link between the cost of a program and the benefit. In the private sector, the expected marginal benefit of a product is at least as great as marginal cost; otherwise, nobody would buy it.

The Size and Growth of Government

One way to track the impact of government over time is by measuring government outlays relative to the U.S. *gross domestic product,* or *GDP,* which is the total value of all final goods and services produced in the United States. In 1929, the year the Great Depression began, all government outlays, mostly by state and local governments, totaled about 10 percent of GDP. At the time, the federal government played a minor role. In fact, during the nation's first 150 years, federal outlays, except during war years, never exceeded 3 percent relative to GDP.

The Great Depression, World War II, a change in macroeconomic thinking, and extraordinary measures following the financial crisis of 2008 boosted the share of government outlays to 41 percent of GDP in 2010 with about two-thirds of that by the federal government. In comparison, government outlays relative to GDP were 41 percent in Japan, 44 percent in Canada, 48 percent in Germany, 51 percent in Italy, 53 percent in the United Kingdom, and 55 percent in France. Government outlays by the 28 largest industrial economies averaged 45 percent of GDP in 2010.[2] Thus, government outlays in the United States relative to GDP are below that of most other advanced economies.

Let's look briefly at the composition of federal outlays. Since 1960, defense spending has declined from over half of federal outlays to about one-fifth by 2011, as shown in Exhibit 3. Redistribution—Social Security, Medicare, and welfare programs—has been the mirror image of defense spending, jumping from only about one-fifth of federal outlays in 1960 to nearly half by 2011.

Sources of Government Revenue

Taxes provide the bulk of revenue at all levels of government. The federal government relies primarily on the individual income tax, state governments rely on income and sales taxes, and local governments rely on the property tax. Other revenue sources include

2. The Organization of Economic Cooperation and Development, *OECD Economic Outlook*, 87 (May 2010), Annex Table 25.

EXHIBIT 3 Redistribution Has Grown and Defense Has Declined as Share of Federal Outlays Since 1960

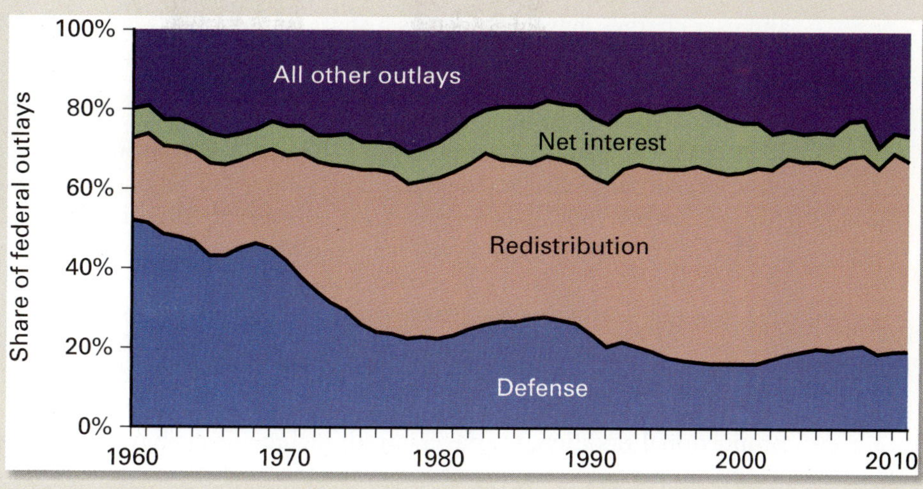

Source: Computed based on figures from the *Economic Report of the President,* February 2010, Table B-80. Figures for 2011 are estimates. For the latest figures, go to http://gpoaccess.gov/eop/.

EXHIBIT 4 Payroll Taxes Have Grown as a Share of Federal Revenue Since 1960

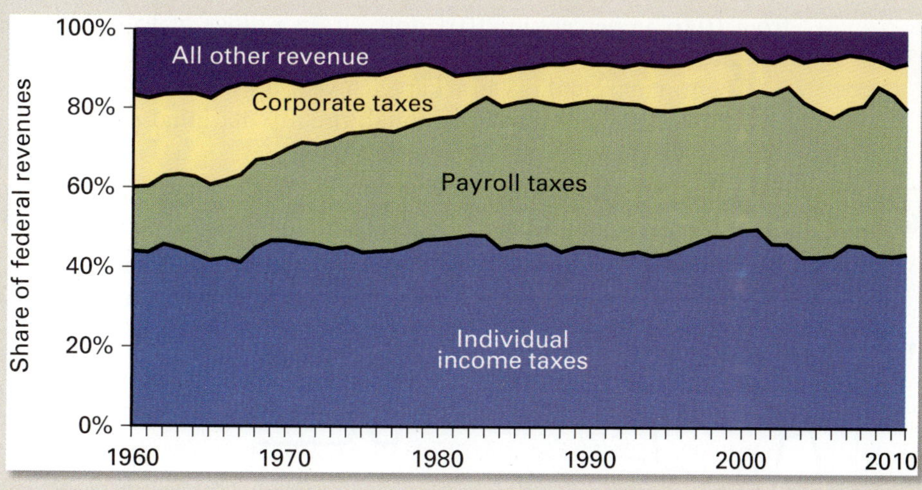

Source: Computed based on figures from the *Economic Report of the President,* February 2010, Tables B-81 and B-84. Figures for 2011 are projections. For the latest figures, go to http://www.gpoaccess.gov/eop/.

user charges, such as highway tolls, and borrowing. For additional revenue, some states also act as monopolies in certain markets, such as for lottery tickets and for liquor.

Exhibit 4 focuses on the composition of federal revenue since 1960. The share made up by the individual income tax has remained relatively steady, ranging from a low of 42 percent in the mid-1960s to a high of 50 percent in 2001, before settling down to 44 percent in 2011. The share from payroll taxes more than doubled from 15 percent

ability-to-pay tax principle
Those with a greater ability to pay, such as those earning higher incomes or those owning more property, should pay more taxes

benefits-received tax principle
Those who get more benefits from the government program should pay more taxes

tax incidence
The distribution of tax burden among taxpayers; who ultimately pays the tax

proportional taxation
The tax as a percentage of income remains constant as income increases; also called a flat tax

progressive taxation
The tax as a percentage of income increases as income increases

marginal tax rate
The percentage of each additional dollar of income that goes to the tax

in 1960 to 36 percent in 2011. *Payroll taxes* are deducted from paychecks to support Social Security and Medicare, which fund retirement income and medical care for the elderly. Corporate taxes and revenue from other sources, such as excise (sales) taxes and user charges, have declined as a share of federal revenue since 1960.

Tax Principles and Tax Incidence

The structure of a tax is often justified on the basis of one of two general principles. First, a tax could relate to the individual's ability to pay, so those with a greater ability pay more taxes. Income or property taxes often rely on this **ability-to-pay tax principle**. Alternatively, the **benefits-received tax principle** relates taxes to the benefits taxpayers receive from the government activity funded by the tax. For example, the tax on gasoline funds highway construction and maintenance, thereby linking tax payment to road use, since those who drive more, pay more gas taxes.

Tax incidence indicates who actually bears the burden of the tax. One way to evaluate tax incidence is by measuring the tax as a percentage of income. Under **proportional taxation**, taxpayers at all income levels pay the same percentage of their income in taxes. A proportional income tax is also called a flat tax, since the tax as a percentage of income remains constant, or flat, as income increases. Note that under proportional taxation, although taxes remain constant as a percentage of income, the dollar amount of taxes increases proportionately as income increases.

Under **progressive taxation**, the percentage of income paid in taxes increases as income increases. The **marginal tax rate** indicates the percentage of each additional dollar of income that goes to taxes. Because high marginal rates reduce the after-tax return from working or investing, high marginal rates can reduce people's incentives to work and invest. The six marginal rates applied to the U.S. personal income tax ranged from 10 to 35 percent in 2010, down from a range of 15 to 39.6 percent in 2000. The top rate was scheduled to return to 39.6 percent in 2011.

The top marginal tax bracket each year during the history of the personal income tax is shown by Exhibit 5. Although the top marginal rate is now lower than it was

EXHIBIT 5 Top Marginal Rate on Federal Personal Income Tax Since 1913

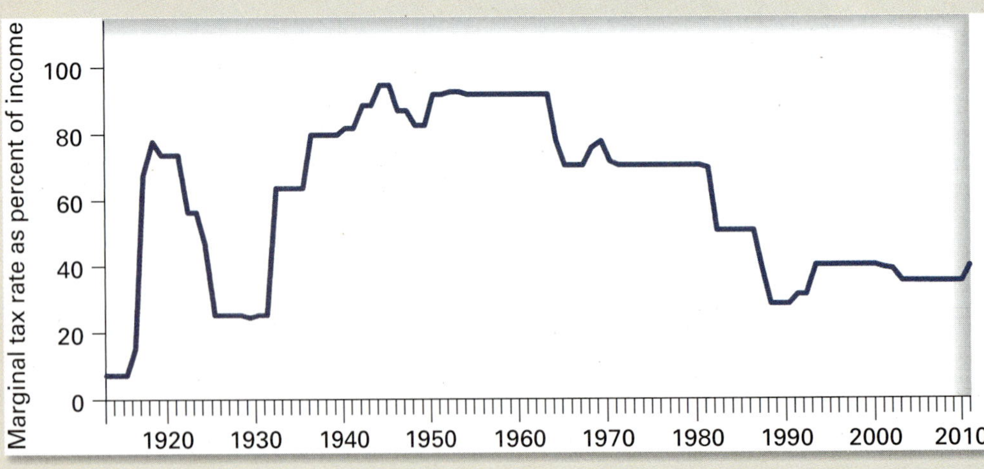

Source: U.S. Internal Revenue Service. For the latest figures on the personal income tax go to http://www.irs.gov/individuals/index.html.

during most other years, high-income households still pay most of the federal income tax collected. Nearly half of all U.S. households pay no federal income tax. According to the U.S. Internal Revenue Service, the top 1 percent of tax filers, based on income, paid 40.4 percent of all income taxes collected in 2007. Their average tax rate was 22.5 percent. And the top 10 percent of tax filers paid 71.2 percent of all income taxes collected. Their average tax rate was 18.9 percent. In contrast, the bottom 50 percent of tax filers paid only 2.9 percent of all income taxes collected. Their tax rate averaged only 3.0 percent. Whether we look at marginal tax rates or average tax rates, the U.S. income tax is progressive. High-income filers pay the overwhelming share of income taxes.

Finally, under **regressive taxation**, the percentage of income paid in taxes decreases as income increases, so the marginal tax rate declines as income increases. Most U.S. *payroll taxes* are regressive, because they impose a flat rate up to a certain level of income, above which the marginal rate drops to zero. For example, Social Security taxes were levied on the first $106,800 of workers' pay in 2010. Half the 12.4 percent tax is paid by employers and half by employees (the self-employed pay the entire 12.4 percent).

regressive taxation
The tax as a percentage of income decreases as income increases

Taxes often do more than fund public programs. Some taxes discourage certain activity. For example, a pollution tax can help clean the air. A tax on gasoline can encourage people to work at home, car pool, or use public transportation. Some taxes have unintended consequences. For example, in Egypt a property tax is not imposed until a building is complete. To avoid such taxes, builders never finish the job; multistory dwellings are usually missing the top floor. As another example of how taxes can distort the allocation of resources, property taxes in Amsterdam and Vietnam were originally based on the width of the building. As a result, buildings in those places are extremely narrow.

This discussion of revenue sources brings to a close, for now, our examination of the role of government in the U.S. economy. Government has a pervasive influence on the economy, and its role is discussed throughout the book.

The Rest of the World

So far, the focus has been on institutions within the United States—that is, on *domestic* households, firms, and governments. This focus is appropriate because our primary objective is to understand the workings of the U.S. economy, by far the largest in the world. But the rest of the world affects what U.S. households consume and what U.S. firms produce. For example, Japan and China supply all kinds of manufactured goods to America, thereby affecting U.S. prices, wages, and profits. Likewise, political events in the Persian Gulf can affect what Americans pay for oil. Foreign decision makers, therefore, influence the U.S. economy—what we produce and what we consume. The *rest of the world* consists of the households, firms, and governments in the other 200 or so sovereign nations throughout the world.

International Trade

In the previous chapter, you learned about comparative advantage and the gains from specialization. These gains explain why householders stopped doing everything for themselves and began to specialize. International trade arises for the same reasons. *International trade occurs because the opportunity cost of producing specific goods differs across countries.* Americans import raw materials like crude oil, bauxite (aluminum ore), and coffee beans and finished goods like cameras, DVD players, and cut diamonds. U.S. producers export sophisticated products like computer software, aircraft, and movies, as well as agricultural products like wheat, corn, and cotton.

Trade between the United States and the rest of the world has increased in recent decades. In 1970, U.S. exports of goods and services amounted to only 6 percent of the gross domestic product. That has increased to about 10 percent today. The top 10 destinations for U.S. exports in order of importance are Canada, Mexico, China, Japan, United Kingdom, Germany, Netherlands, South Korea, France, and Brazil.

merchandise trade balance
The value during a given period of a country's exported goods minus the value of its imported goods

The **merchandise trade balance** equals the value of exported goods minus the value of imported goods. Goods in this case are distinguished from services, which show up in another trade account. For the last quarter century, the United States has imported more goods than it has exported, resulting in a merchandise trade deficit. Just as a household must pay for its spending, so too must a nation. The merchandise trade deficit must be offset by a surplus in one or more of the other *balance-of-payments* accounts. A nation's **balance of payments** is the record of all economic transactions between its residents and residents of the rest of the world.

balance of payments
A record of all economic transactions during a given period between residents of one country and residents of the rest of the world

Exchange Rates

The lack of a common currency complicates trade between countries. How many U.S. dollars buy a Porsche? An American buyer cares only about the dollar cost; the German carmaker cares only about the *euros* received (the common currency of 16 European countries). To facilitate trade funded by different currencies, a market for foreign exchange has developed. **Foreign exchange** is foreign currency needed to carry out international transactions. The supply and demand for foreign exchange comes together in *foreign exchange markets* to determine the exchange rate. The *exchange rate* measures the price of one currency in terms of another. For example, the exchange rate between the euro and the dollar might indicate that one euro exchanges for $1.20. At that exchange rate, a Porsche selling for €100,000 costs $120,000. The exchange rate affects the prices of imports and exports and thus helps shape the flow of foreign trade.

foreign exchange
Foreign money needed to carry out international transactions

Trade Restrictions

Despite clear gains from international specialization and exchange, nearly all nations restrict trade to some extent. These restrictions can take the form of (1) **tariffs**, which are taxes on imports; (2) **quotas**, which are limits on the quantity of a particular good that can be imported or exported; and (3) other trade restrictions. If specialization according to comparative advantage is so beneficial, why do most countries restrict trade? Restrictions benefit certain domestic producers that lobby their governments for these benefits. For example, U.S. growers of sugarcane have benefited from legislation restricting imports, thereby raising U.S. sugar prices. These higher prices hurt domestic consumers, but consumers are usually unaware of this harm. Trade restrictions interfere with the free flow of products across borders and tend to hurt the overall economy.

tariff
A tax on imports

quota
A legal limit on the quantity of a particular product that can be imported or exported

Conclusion

This chapter examined the four economic decision makers: households, firms, governments, and the rest of the world. Domestic households are by far the most important, for they supply resources and demand goods and services.

If you were to stop reading right now, you would already know more economics than most people. But to understand market economies, you must learn how markets work. The next chapter introduces demand and supply.

Summary

1. Most household income arises from the sale of labor, and most household income is spent on personal consumption, primarily services.
2. Household members once built their own homes, made their own clothes and furniture, grew their own food, and supplied their own entertainment. Over time, however, the efficiency arising from comparative advantage resulted in a greater specialization among resource suppliers.
3. Firms bring together specialized resources and in the process reduce the transaction costs of bargaining with all these resource providers. U.S. firms can be organized in three different ways: as sole proprietorships, partnerships, or corporations. Because corporations are typically large, they account for the bulk of sales.
4. When private markets yield undesirable results, government may intervene to address these market failures. Government programs are designed to (a) protect private property and enforce contracts; (b) promote competition; (c) regulate natural monopolies; (d) provide public goods; (e) discourage negative externalities and encourage positive externalities; (f) promote a more even distribution of income; and (g) promote full employment, price stability, and economic growth.
5. In the United States, the federal government has primary responsibility for providing national defense, ensuring market competition, and promoting stability of the economy. State governments provide public higher education, prisons, and—with aid from the federal government—highways and welfare. And local governments provide police and fire protection, and, with help from the state, local schools.
6. The federal government relies primarily on the personal income tax, states rely on income and sales taxes, and localities rely on the property tax. A tax is often justified based on (a) the individual's ability to pay or (b) the benefits the taxpayer receives from the activities financed by the tax.
7. The rest of the world is also populated by households, firms, and governments. International trade creates gains that arise from comparative advantage. The balance of payments summarizes transactions between the residents of one country and the residents of the rest of the world. Although consumers gain from comparative advantage, nearly all countries impose trade restrictions to protect specific domestic industries.

Key Concepts

Utility 42
Transfer payments 44
Industrial Revolution 45
Firms 45
Sole proprietorship 45
Partnership 46
Corporation 46
Cooperative 46
Not-for-profit organizations 48
Market failure 49
Monopoly 50
Natural monopoly 50
Private good 50
Public good 50
Externality 50
Fiscal policy 51
Monetary policy 51
Ability-to-pay tax principle 54
Benefits-received tax principle 54
Tax incidence 54
Proportional taxation 54
Progressive taxation 54
Marginal tax rate 54
Regressive taxation 55
Merchandise trade balance 56
Balance of payments 56
Foreign exchange 56
Tariff 56
Quota 56

Questions for Review

1. **Households as Demanders of Goods and Services** Classify each of the following as a durable good, a nondurable good, or a service:
   a. A gallon of milk
   b. A lawn mower
   c. A DVD player
   d. A manicure
   e. A pair of shoes
   f. An eye exam
   g. A personal computer
   h. A neighborhood teenager mowing a lawn
2. Case Study: The Electronic Cottage (See page 704.) How has the development of personal computer hardware and software reversed some of the trends brought on by the Industrial Revolution?
3. **Evolution of the Firm** Explain how production after the Industrial Revolution differed from production under the cottage industry system.

4. Household Production What factors does a householder consider when deciding whether to produce a good or service at home or buy it in the marketplace?
5. Corporations How did the institution of the firm get a boost from the advent of the Industrial Revolution? What type of business organization existed before this?
6. Sole Proprietorships What are the disadvantages of the sole proprietorship form of business?
7. Cooperatives How do cooperatives differ from typical businesses?
8. Case Study: User-Generated Products (See page 703.) Why are users willing to help create certain products even though few, if any, users are paid for their efforts?
9. Government Often it is said that government is necessary when private markets fail to work effectively and fairly. Based on your reading of the text, discuss how private markets might break down.
10. Externalities Suppose there is an external cost, or negative externality, associated with production of a certain good. What's wrong with letting the market determine how much of this good will be produced?
11. Government Revenue What are the sources of government revenue in the United States? Which types of taxes are most important at each level of government? Which two taxes provide the most revenue to the federal government?
12. Objectives of the Economic Decision Makers In economic analysis, what are the assumed objectives of households, firms, and the government?
13. International Trade Why does international trade occur? What does it mean to run a deficit in the merchandise trade balance?
14. International Trade Distinguish between a tariff and a quota. Who benefits from and who is harmed by such restrictions on imports?

Problems and Exercises

15. Evolution of the Household Determine whether each of the following would increase or decrease the opportunity costs for mothers who choose not to work outside the home. Explain your answers.
    a. Higher levels of education for women
    b. Higher unemployment rates for women
    c. Higher average pay levels for women
    d. Lower demand for labor in industries that traditionally employ large numbers of women
16. Household Production Many households supplement their food budget by cultivating small vegetable gardens. Explain how each of the following might influence this kind of household production:
    a. Both husband and wife are professionals who earn high salaries.
    b. The household is located in a city rather than in a rural area.
    c. The household is located in a region where there is a high sales tax on food.
    d. The household is located in a region that has a high property tax rate.
17. Government Complete each of the following sentences:
    a. When the private operation of a market leads to overproduction or underproduction of some good, this is known as a(n) ________.
    b. Goods that are nonrival and nonexclusive are known as ________.
    c. ________ are cash or in-kind benefits given to individuals as outright grants from the government.
    d. A(n) ________ confers an external benefit on third parties that are not directly involved in a market transaction.
    e. ________ refers to the government's pursuit of full employment and price stability through variations in taxes and government spending.
18. Tax Rates Suppose taxes are related to income level as follows:

Income	Taxes
$1,000	$200
$2,000	$350
$3,000	$450

    a. What percentage of income is paid in taxes at each level?
    b. Is the tax rate progressive, proportional, or regressive?
    c. What is the marginal tax rate on the first $1,000 of income? The second $1,000? The third $1,000?

Global Economic Watch Exercises

Login to www.cengagebrain.com and access the Global Economic Watch to do these exercises.

19. GLOBAL ECONOMIC WATCH Go to the Global Economic Crisis Resource Center. Select Global Issues in Context. In the Basic Search box at the top of the page, enter the phrase "Not-So-Free Ride." On the Results page, scroll down to the Magazines section. Click on the link for the April 20, 2008, article "Not-So-Free Ride." Can you list negative externalities of driving in addition to the ones described in the article?

20. GLOBAL ECONOMIC WATCH Go to the Global Economic Crisis Resource Center. Global Issues in Context. In the Basic Search box at the top of the page, enter the terms "tax rate" and/or "tax rates." Find resources that are no more than three years old that describe tax rates in two foreign countries. Write an analysis of these tax rates in your own words.

Demand, Supply, and Markets

4

© Jason Moore/Alamy

- Why do roses cost more on Valentine's Day than during the rest of the year?
- Why do TV ads cost more during the Super Bowl ($3.0 million for 30 seconds in 2010) than during *Nick at Nite* reruns?
- Why do Miami hotels charge more in February than in August?
- Why do surgeons earn more than butchers?
- Why do basketball pros earn more than hockey pros?
- Why do economics majors earn more than most other majors?

Answers to these and most economic questions boil down to the workings of demand and supply—the subject of this chapter.

This chapter introduces demand and supply and shows how they interact in competitive markets. *Demand and supply are the most fundamental and the most powerful of all economic tools*—important enough to warrant a chapter. Indeed, some believe that if you program a computer to answer "demand and supply" to every economic question, you could put many economists out of work. An understanding of the two ideas will take you far in mastering the art and science of economic analysis. This chapter uses more graphs, so you may need to review the Chapter 1 appendix as a refresher.

Topics discussed include:

- Demand and quantity demanded
- Movement along a demand curve
- Shift of a demand curve
- Supply and quantity supplied
- Movement along a supply curve
- Shift of a supply curve
- Markets and equilibrium
- Disequilibrium

Demand

How many six packs of Pepsi will people buy each month at a price of $4? What if the price is $3? What if it's $5? The answers reveal the relationship between the price of a six pack and the quantity of Pepsi demanded. Such a relationship is called the *demand* for Pepsi. **Demand** indicates the quantity consumers are both *willing and able* to buy at each possible price during a given time period, other things constant. Because demand pertains to a specific period—a day, a week, a month—think of demand as the *amounts purchased per period* at each possible price. Also, notice the emphasis on *willing and able*. You may be *able* to buy a new Harley-Davidson Sportster Forty-Eight for $10,500 because you can afford one, but you may not be *willing* to buy one if motorcycles don't interest you.

demand
A relation between the price of a good and the quantity that consumers are willing and able to buy per period, other things constant

The Law of Demand

In 1962, Sam Walton opened his first store in Rogers, Arkansas, with a sign that read: "Wal-Mart Discount City. We sell for less." Wal-Mart now sells more than any other retailer in the world because prices there are among the lowest around. As a consumer, you understand why people buy more at a lower price. Sell for less, and the world will beat a path to your door. Wal-Mart, for example, sells on average over 20,000 pairs of shoes *an hour.* This relation between the price and the quantity demanded is an economic law. The **law of demand** says that quantity demanded varies inversely with price, other things constant. Thus, the higher the price, the smaller the quantity demanded; the lower the price, the greater the quantity demanded.

law of demand
The quantity of a good that consumers are willing and able to buy per period relates inversely, or negatively, to the price, other things constant

Demand, Wants, and Needs

Consumer demand and consumer wants are not the same. As we have seen, wants are unlimited. You may want a new Mercedes-Benz SL600 Roadster convertible, but the $139,100 price tag is likely beyond your budget (that is, the quantity you demand at that price is zero). Nor is demand the same as need. You may need a new muffler for your car, but a price of $300 is just too high for you right now. If, however, the price drops enough—say, to $200—then you become both willing and able to buy one.

The Substitution Effect of a Price Change

What explains the law of demand? Why, for example, is more demanded at a lower price? The explanation begins with unlimited wants confronting scarce resources. Many goods and services could satisfy particular wants. For example, you can satisfy your hunger with pizza, tacos, burgers, chicken, or hundreds of other foods. Similarly, you can satisfy your desire for warmth in the winter with warm clothing, a home-heating system, a trip to Hawaii, or in many other ways. Clearly, some alternatives have more appeal than others (a trip to Hawaii is more fun than warm clothing). In a world without scarcity, everything would be free, so you would always choose the most attractive alternative. Scarcity, however, is a reality, and the degree of scarcity of one good relative to another helps determine each good's relative price.

Notice that the definition of *demand* includes the other-things-constant assumption. Among the "other things" assumed to remain constant are the prices of other goods. For example, if the price of pizza declines while other prices remain constant, pizza becomes relatively cheaper. Consumers are more *willing* to purchase pizza when its relative price falls; they substitute pizza for other goods. This principle is called the **substitution effect of a price change**. On the other hand, an increase in the price of pizza, other things constant, increases the opportunity cost of pizza—that is, the amount of

substitution effect of a price change
When the price of a good falls, that good becomes cheaper compared to other goods so consumers tend to substitute that good for other goods

other goods you must give up to buy pizza. This higher opportunity cost causes consumers to substitute other goods for the now higher-priced pizza, thus reducing their quantity of pizza demanded. Remember that *it is the change in the relative price—the price of one good relative to the prices of other goods—that causes the substitution effect.* If all prices changed by the same percentage, there would be no change in relative prices and no substitution effect.

The Income Effect of a Price Change

A fall in the price of a good increases the quantity demanded for a second reason. Suppose you earn $30 a week from a part-time job, so $30 is your money income. **Money income** is simply the number of dollars received per period, in this case, $30 per week. Suppose you spend all that on pizza, buying three a week at $10 each. What if the price drops to $6? At the lower price, you can now afford five pizzas a week. Your money income remains at $30 per week, but the decrease in the price has increased your **real income**—that is, your income measured in terms of what it can buy. The price reduction, other things constant, increases the purchasing power of your income, thereby increasing your ability to buy pizza. The quantity of pizza you demand will likely increase because of this **income effect of a price change**. You may not increase your quantity demanded to five pizzas, but you could. If you decide to purchase four pizzas a week when the price drops to $6, you would still have $6 remaining to buy other stuff. Thus, the income effect of a lower price increases your real income and thereby increases your ability to purchase all goods, making you better off. The income effect is reflected in Wal-Mart's slogan, which trumpets low prices: "Save money. Live better." Because of the income effect, consumers typically increase their quantity demanded when the price declines.

money income
The number of dollars a person receives per period, such as $400 per week

real income
Income measured in terms of the goods and services it can buy; real income changes when the price changes

income effect of a price change
A fall in the price of a good increases consumers' real income, making consumers more able to purchase goods; for a normal good, the quantity demanded increases

Conversely, an increase in the price of a good, other things constant, reduces real income, thereby reducing your *ability* to purchase all goods. Because of the income effect, consumers typically reduce their quantity demanded when the price increases. Again, note that money income, not real income, is assumed to remain constant along a demand curve. A change in price changes your real income, so real income varies along a demand curve. The lower the price, the greater your real income.

The Demand Schedule and Demand Curve

Demand can be expressed as a *demand schedule* or as a *demand curve*. Panel (a) of Exhibit 1 shows a hypothetical demand schedule for pizza. In describing demand, we must specify the units measured and the period considered. In our example, the unit is a 12-inch regular pizza and the period is a week. The schedule lists possible prices, along with the quantity demanded at each price. At a price of $15, for example, consumers demand 8 million pizzas per week. As you can see, the lower the price, other things constant, the greater the quantity demanded. Consumers substitute pizza for other foods. And as the price falls, real income increases, causing consumers to increase the quantity of pizza they demand. If the price drops as low as $3, consumers demand 32 million per week.

The demand schedule in panel (a) appears as a **demand curve** in panel (b), with price measured on the vertical axis and the quantity demanded per week on the horizontal axis. Each price-quantity combination listed in the demand schedule in the left panel becomes a point in the right panel. Point *a*, for example, indicates that if the price is $15, consumers demand 8 million pizzas per week. Connecting points forms the demand curve for pizza, labeled *D*. (By the way, some demand curves are straight lines, some are curved lines, and some are even jagged lines, but they all are called demand *curves*.)

demand curve
A curve showing the relation between the price of a good and the quantity consumers are willing and able to buy per period, other things constant

EXHIBIT 1 The Demand Schedule and Demand Curve for Pizza

(a) Demand schedule

	Price per Pizza	Quantity Demanded per Week (millions)
a	$15	8
b	12	14
c	9	20
d	6	26
e	3	32

(b) Demand curve

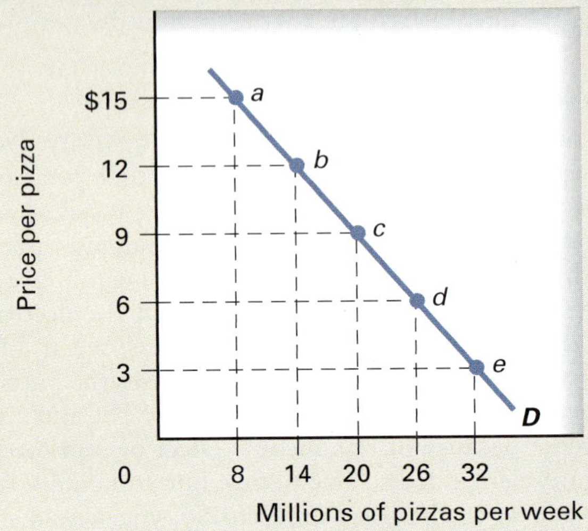

The market demand curve *D* shows the quantity of pizza demanded, at various prices, by all consumers. Price and quantity demanded are inversely related.

A demand curve slopes downward, reflecting the *law of demand:* Price and quantity demanded are inversely related, other things constant. Besides money income, also assumed constant along the demand curve are the prices of other goods. Thus, along the demand curve for pizza, the price of pizza changes *relative to the prices of other goods.* The demand curve shows the effect of a change in the *relative price* of pizza—that is, relative to other prices, which do not change.

Take care to distinguish between *demand* and *quantity demanded.* The *demand* for pizza is not a specific amount, but rather the *entire relationship* between price and quantity demanded—represented by the demand schedule or the demand curve. An individual point on the demand curve indicates the **quantity demanded** at a particular price. For example, at a price of $12, the quantity demanded is 14 million pizzas per week. If the price drops from $12 to, say, $9, this is shown in Exhibit 1 by *a movement along the demand curve*—in this case from point *b* to point *c*. Any movement along a demand curve reflects a *change in quantity demanded,* not a change in demand.

quantity demanded
The amount of a good consumers are willing and able to buy per period at a particular price, as reflected by a point on a demand curve

The law of demand applies to the millions of products sold in grocery stores, department stores, clothing stores, shoe stores, drugstores, music stores, bookstores, hardware stores, other retailers, travel agencies, and restaurants, as well as through mail-order catalogs, the *Yellow Pages,* classified ads, online sites, stock markets, real estate markets, job markets, flea markets, and all other markets. The law of demand applies even to choices that seem more personal than economic, such as whether or not to own a pet. For example, after New York City passed an anti-dog-litter law, law-abiding owners had to follow their dogs around the city with scoopers, plastic bags—whatever would do the job. Because the law in effect raised the personal cost of owning a dog, the quantity of dogs demanded decreased. Some dogs were abandoned, increasing strays in the city. The number of dogs left at animal shelters doubled. The law of demand predicts this inverse relation between cost, or price, and quantity demanded.

It is useful to distinguish between **individual demand**, which is the demand of an individual consumer, and **market demand**, which is the sum of the individual demands of all consumers in the market. In most markets, there are many consumers, sometimes millions. Unless otherwise noted, when we talk about demand, we are referring to market demand, as shown in Exhibit 1.

individual demand
The relation between the price of a good and the quantity purchased by an individual consumer per period, other things constant

market demand
The relation between the price of a good and the quantity purchased by all consumers in the market during a given period, other things constant; sum of the individual demands in the market

Shifts of the Demand Curve

A demand curve isolates the relation between the price of a good and quantity demanded when other factors that could affect demand remain unchanged. What are those other factors, and how do changes in them affect demand? Variables that can affect market demand are (1) the money income of consumers, (2) prices of other goods, (3) consumer expectations, (4) the number or composition of consumers in the market, and (5) consumer tastes. How do changes in each affect demand?

Changes in Consumer Income

Exhibit 2 shows the market demand curve *D* for pizza. This demand curve assumes a given level of money income. Suppose consumer income increases. Some consumers are then willing and able to buy more pizza at each price, so market demand increases. The demand curve shifts to the right from *D* to *D*′. For example, at a price of $12,

EXHIBIT 2 An Increase in the Market Demand for Pizza

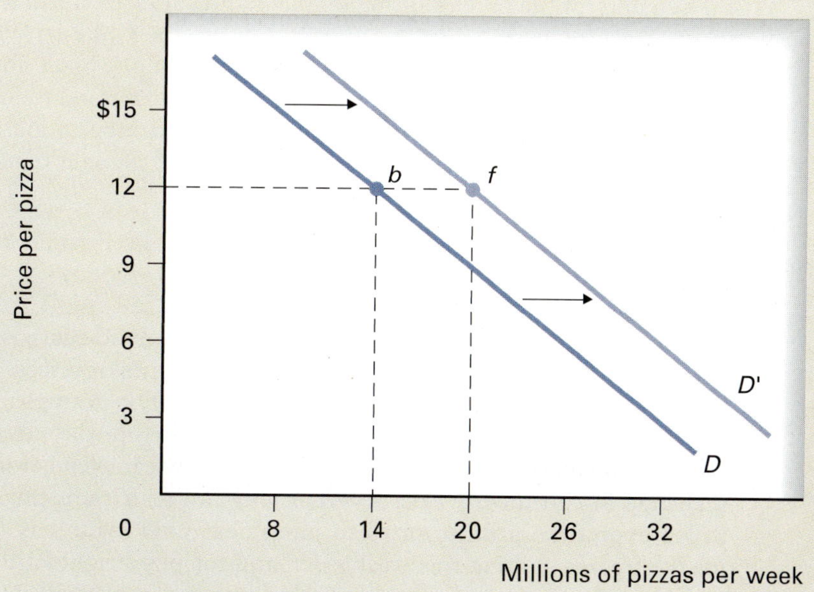

An increase in the demand for pizza is shown by a rightward shift of the demand curve, so the quantity demanded increases at each price. For example, the quantity of pizza demanded at a price of $12 increases from 14 million (point *b*) to 20 million (point *f*).

the amount of pizza demanded increases from 14 million to 20 million per week, as indicated by the movement from point *b* on demand curve *D* to point *f* on demand curve *D′*. In short, *an increase in demand—that is, a rightward shift of the demand curve—means that consumers are willing and able to buy more pizza at each price.*

Goods are classified into two broad categories, depending on how consumers respond to changes in money income. The demand for a **normal good** increases as money income increases. Because pizza is a normal good, its demand curve shifts rightward when money income increases. Most goods are normal. In contrast, demand for an **inferior good** actually decreases as money income increases, so the demand curve shifts leftward. Examples of inferior goods include bologna sandwiches, used furniture, and used clothes. As money income increases, consumers tend to switch from these inferior goods to normal goods (such as roast beef sandwiches, new furniture, and new clothes).

normal good
A good, such as new clothes, for which demand increases, or shifts rightward, as consumer income rises

inferior good
A good, such as used clothes, for which demand decreases, or shifts leftward, as consumer income rises

Changes in the Prices of Other Goods

Again, the prices of other goods are assumed to remain constant along a given demand curve. Now let's bring these other prices into play. Consumers have various ways of trying to satisfy any particular want. Consumers choose among substitutes based on relative prices. For example, pizza and tacos are substitutes, though not perfect ones. An increase in the price of tacos, other things constant, reduces the quantity of tacos demanded along a given taco demand curve. An increase in the price of tacos also increases the demand for pizza, shifting the demand curve for pizza to the right. Two goods are considered **substitutes** if an increase in the price of one shifts the demand for the other rightward and, conversely, if a decrease in the price of one shifts demand for the other leftward.

Goods used in combination are called **complements**. Examples include Coke and pizza, milk and cookies, computer software and hardware, and airline tickets and rental cars. Two goods are considered **complements** if an increase in the price of one decreases the demand for the other, shifting that demand curve leftward. For example, an increase in the price of pizza shifts the demand curve for Coke leftward. But most pairs of goods selected at random are *unrelated*—for example, pizza and housing, or milk and gasoline. Still, an increase in the price of an unrelated good reduces the consumers' real income and can reduce the demand for pizza and other goods. For example, a sharp increase in housing prices reduces the amount of income remaining for other goods, such as pizza.

substitutes
Goods, such as Coke and Pepsi, that relate in such a way that an increase in the price of one shifts the demand for the other rightward

complements
Goods, such as milk and cookies, that relate in such a way that an increase in the price of one shifts the demand for the other leftward

Changes in Consumer Expectations

Another factor assumed constant along a given demand curve is consumer expectations about factors that influence demand, such as incomes or prices. A change in consumers' *income expectations* can shift the demand curve. For example, a consumer who learns about a pay raise might increase demand well before the raise takes effect. A college senior who lands that first real job may buy a new car even before graduation. Likewise, a change in consumers' *price expectations* can shift the demand curve. For example, if you expect the price of pizza to jump next week, you may buy an extra one today for the freezer, shifting this week's demand for pizza rightward. Or if consumers come to believe that home prices will climb next year, some will increase their demand for housing now, shifting this year's demand for housing rightward. On the other hand, if housing prices are expected to fall next year, some consumers will postpone purchases, thereby shifting this year's housing demand leftward.

Changes in the Number or Composition of Consumers

As mentioned earlier, the market demand curve is the sum of the individual demand curves of all consumers in the market. If the number of consumers changes, the demand curve will shift. For example, if the population grows, the demand curve for pizza will shift rightward. Even if total population remains unchanged, demand could shift with a change in the composition of the population. For example, an increase over time in the teenage population could shift pizza demand rightward. A baby boom would shift rightward the demand for car seats and baby food. A growing Latino population would affect the demand for Latino foods.

Changes in Consumer Tastes

Do you like anchovies on your pizza? How about sauerkraut on your hot dogs? Are you into tattoos and body piercings? Is music to your ears more likely to be rock, country, hip-hop, reggae, R&B, jazz, funk, Latin, gospel, new age, or classical? Choices in food, body art, music, clothing, books, movies, TV—indeed, all consumer choices—are influenced by consumer tastes. **Tastes** are nothing more than your likes and dislikes as a consumer. What determines tastes? Your desires for food when hungry and drink when thirsty are largely biological. So too is your desire for comfort, rest, shelter, friendship, love, status, personal safety, and a pleasant environment. Your family background affects some of your tastes—your taste in food, for example, has been shaped by years of home cooking. Other influences include the surrounding culture, peer pressure, and religious convictions. So economists can say a little about the origin of tastes, but they claim no special expertise in understanding how tastes develop and change over time. Economists recognize, however, that tastes have an important impact on demand. For example, although pizza is popular, some people just don't like it and those who are lactose intolerant can't stomach the cheese topping. Thus, most people like pizza but some don't.

tastes
Consumer preferences; likes and dislikes in consumption; assumed to remain constant along a given demand curve

In our analysis of consumer demand, *we will assume that tastes are given and are relatively stable.* Tastes are assumed to remain constant along a given demand curve. A change in the tastes for a particular good would shift that good's demand curve. For example, a discovery that the tomato sauce and cheese combination on pizza promotes overall health could change consumer tastes, shifting the demand curve for pizza to the right. But because a change in tastes is so difficult to isolate from other economic changes, we should be reluctant to attribute a shift of the demand curve to a change in tastes. We try to rule out other possible reasons for a shift of the demand curve before accepting a change in tastes as the explanation.

That wraps up our look at changes in demand. Before we turn to supply, you should remember the distinction between a **movement along a given demand curve** and a **shift of a demand curve**. A change in *price,* other things constant, causes a *movement along a demand curve,* changing the quantity demanded. A change in one of the determinants of demand other than price causes a *shift of a demand curve,* changing demand.

movement along a demand curve
Change in quantity demanded resulting from a change in the price of the good, other things constant

shift of a demand curve
Movement of a demand curve right or left resulting from a change in one of the determinants of demand other than the price of the good

Supply

Just as demand is a relation between price and quantity demanded, supply is a relation between price and quantity supplied. **Supply** indicates how much producers are *willing* and *able* to offer for sale per period at each possible price, other things constant. The **law of supply** states that the quantity supplied is usually directly related to its price,

supply
A relation between the price of a good and the quantity that producers are willing and able to sell per period, other things constant

law of supply
The amount of a good that producers are willing and able to sell per period is usually directly related to its price, other things constant

other things constant. Thus, the lower the price, the smaller the quantity supplied; the higher the price, the greater the quantity supplied.

The Supply Schedule and Supply Curve

supply curve
A curve showing the relation between price of a good and the quantity producers are willing and able to sell per period other things constant

Exhibit 3 presents the market *supply schedule* and market **supply curve** *S* for pizza. Both show the quantities supplied per week at various possible prices by the thousands of pizza makers in the economy. As you can see, price and quantity supplied are directly, or positively, related. Producers offer more at a higher price than at a lower price, so the supply curve slopes upward.

There are two reasons why producers offer more for sale when the price rises. First, as the price increases, other things constant, a producer becomes more *willing* to supply the good. Prices act as signals to existing and potential suppliers about the rewards for producing various goods. A higher pizza price attracts resources from lower-valued uses. *A higher price makes producers more willing to increase quantity supplied.*

Higher prices also increase the producer's *ability* to supply the good. The law of increasing opportunity cost, as noted in Chapter 2, states that the opportunity cost of producing more of a particular good rises as output increases—that is, the *marginal cost* of production increases as output increases. Because producers face a higher marginal cost for additional output, they need to get a higher price for that output to be *able* to increase the quantity supplied. *A higher price makes producers more able to increase quantity supplied.* As a case in point, a higher price for gasoline increases oil companies' ability to extract oil from tar sands, to drill deeper, and to explore in less accessible areas, such as the remote jungles of the Amazon, the stormy waters of the North Sea, and the frozen tundra above the Arctic Circle. For example, at a market

EXHIBIT 3 The Supply Schedule and Supply Curve for Pizza

(a) Supply schedule

Price per Pizza	Quantity Supplied per Week (millions)
$15	28
12	24
9	20
6	16
3	12

(b) Supply curve

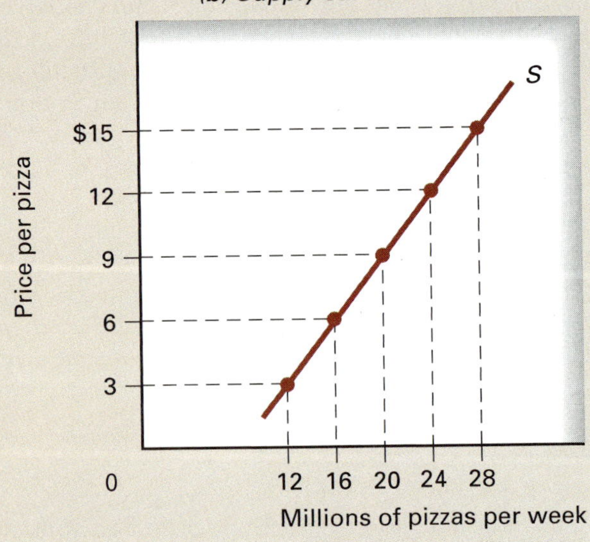

Market supply curve *S* shows the quantity of pizza supplied, at various prices, by all pizza makers. Price and quantity supplied are directly related.

price of $50 per barrel, extracting oil from tar sands is unprofitable, but at price of $55 per barrel, producers are able to supply millions of barrels per month from tar sands.

Thus, a higher price makes producers more *willing* and more *able* to increase quantity supplied. Producers are more *willing* because production becomes more attractive than other uses of the resources involved. Producers are more *able* because they can afford to cover the higher marginal cost that typically results from increasing output.

On the other hand, a lower price makes production less attractive, so suppliers are less willing and less able to offer the good. For example, a mining company "reacted quickly to steep copper price declines in 2008 by curbing production at its North American sites and implementing layoffs at its mines and corporate headquarters."[1]

As with demand, we distinguish between *supply* and *quantity supplied*. *Supply* is the entire relationship between prices and quantities supplied, as reflected by the supply schedule or supply curve. **Quantity supplied** refers to a particular amount offered for sale at a particular price, as reflected by a point on a given supply curve. We also distinguish between **individual supply**, the supply of an individual producer, and **market supply**, the sum of individual supplies of all producers in the market. Unless otherwise noted, the term *supply* refers to market supply.

quantity supplied
The amount offered for sale per period at a particular price, as reflected by a point on a given supply curve

individual supply
The relation between the price of a good and the quantity an individual producer is willing and able to sell per period, other things constant

market supply
The relation between the price of a good and the quantity all producers are willing and able to sell per period, other things constant

Shifts of the Supply Curve

The supply curve isolates the relation between the price of a good and the quantity supplied, other things constant. Assumed constant along a supply curve are the determinants of supply other than the price of the good, including (1) the state of technology, (2) the prices of resources, (3) the prices of other goods, (4) producer expectations, and (5) the number of producers in the market. Let's see how a change in each affects the supply curve.

Changes in Technology

Recall from Chapter 2 that the state of technology represents the economy's knowledge about how to combine resources efficiently. Along a given supply curve, technology is assumed to remain unchanged. If a better technology is discovered, production costs will fall; so suppliers will be more willing and able to supply the good at each price. For example, new techniques helped Marathon Oil cut drilling time for a new well from 56 days in 2006 to only 24 days in 2009.[2] Consequently, supply will increase, as reflected by a rightward shift of the supply curve. For example, suppose a new, high-tech oven that costs the same as existing ovens bakes pizza in half the time. Such a breakthrough would shift the market supply curve rightward, as from *S* to *S′* in Exhibit 4, where more is supplied at each possible price. For example, at a price of $12, the amount supplied increases from 24 million to 28 million pizzas, as shown in Exhibit 4 by the movement from point *g* to point *h*. In short, *an increase in supply—that is, a rightward shift of the supply curve—means that producers are willing and able to sell more pizza at each price.*

1. Andrew Johnson, "Freeport Outsourcing Will Cut 60 Valley Jobs," *Arizona Republic*, 23 February 2010.
2. Ben Casselman, "Oil Industry Boom—in North Dakota," *Wall Street Journal*, 26 February 2010.

EXHIBIT 4 An Increase in the Supply of Pizza

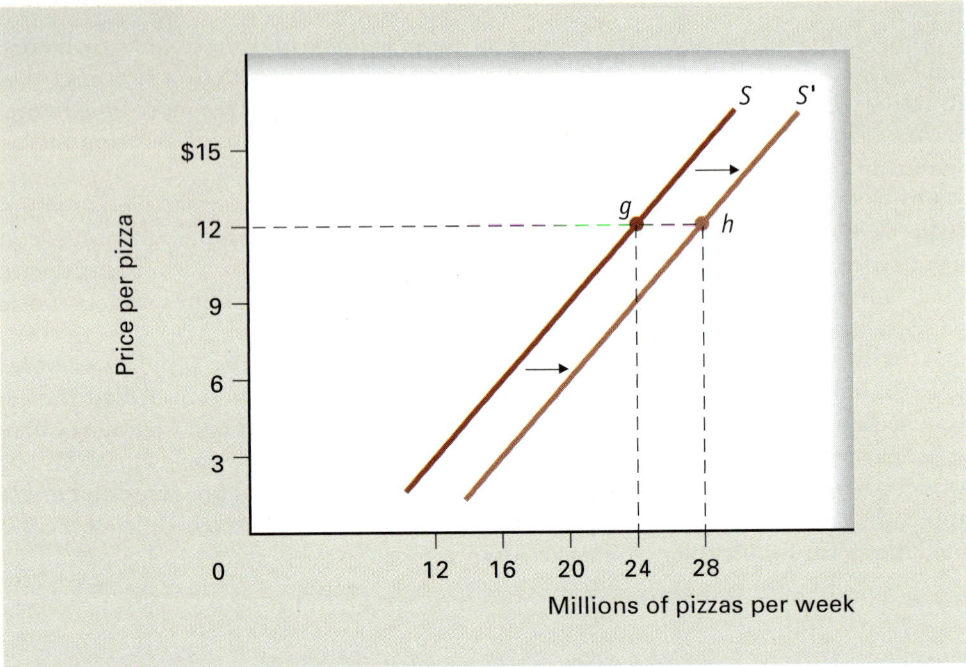

An increase in the supply of pizza is reflected by a rightward shift of the supply curve, from *S* to *S'*. Quantity supplied increases at each price level. For example, at a price of $12, the quantity of pizza supplied increases from 24 million pizzas (point *g*) to 28 million pizzas (point *h*).

Changes in the Prices of Resources

The prices of resources employed to make the good affect the cost of production and therefore the supply of the good. For example, suppose the price of mozzarella cheese falls. This reduces the cost of making pizza, so producers are more willing and better able to supply it. The supply curve for pizza shifts rightward, as shown in Exhibit 4. On the other hand, an increase in the price of a resource reduces supply, meaning a shift of the supply curve leftward. For example, a higher price of mozzarella increases the cost of making pizza. Higher production costs decrease supply, as reflected by a leftward shift of the supply curve.

Changes in the Prices of Other Goods

Nearly all resources have alternative uses. The labor, building, machinery, ingredients, and knowledge needed to run a pizza business could produce other goods instead. A drop in the price of one of these other goods, with the price of pizza unchanged, makes pizza production more attractive. For example, if the price of Italian bread declines, some bread makers become pizza makers so the supply of pizza increases, shifting the supply curve of pizza rightward as in Exhibit 4. On the other hand, if the price of Italian bread increases, supplying pizza becomes relatively less attractive compared to supplying Italian bread. As resources shift from pizza to bread, the supply of pizza decreases, or shifts to the left.

Changes in Producer Expectations

Changes in producer expectations can shift the supply curve. For example, a pizza maker expecting higher pizza prices in the future may expand his or her pizzeria now, thereby shifting the supply of pizza rightward. When a good can be easily stored (crude oil, for example, can be left in the ground), expecting higher prices in the future might prompt some producers to *reduce* their current supply while awaiting the higher price. Thus, an expectation of higher prices in the future could either increase or decrease current supply, depending on the good. More generally, any change affecting future profitability, such as a change in business taxes, could shift the supply curve now.

Changes in the Number of Producers

Because market supply sums the amounts supplied at each price by all producers, market supply depends on the number of producers in the market. If that number increases, supply will increase, shifting supply to the right. If the number of producers decreases, supply will decrease, shifting supply to the left. As an example of increased supply, the number of gourmet coffee bars has more than quadrupled in the United States since 1990 (think Starbucks), shifting the supply curve of gourmet coffee to the right.

movement along a supply curve
Change in quantity supplied resulting from a change in the price of the good, other things constant

shift of a supply curve
Movement of a supply curve left or right resulting from a change in one of the determinants of supply other than the price of the good

Finally, note again the distinction between a **movement along a supply curve** and a **shift of a supply curve**. A change in *price,* other things constant, causes *a movement along a supply curve,* changing the quantity supplied. A change in one of the determinants of supply other than price causes a *shift of a supply curve,* changing supply.

You are now ready to bring demand and supply together.

Demand and Supply Create a Market

Demanders and suppliers have different views of price. Demanders pay the price and suppliers receive it. Thus, a higher price is bad news for consumers but good news for producers. As the price rises, consumers reduce their quantity demanded along the demand curve and producers increase their quantity supplied along the supply curve. How is this conflict between producers and consumers resolved?

Markets

Markets sort out differences between demanders and suppliers. A *market,* as you know from Chapter 1, includes all the arrangements used to buy and sell a particular good or service. Markets reduce **transaction costs**—the costs of time and information required for exchange. For example, suppose you are looking for a summer job. One approach might be to go from employer to employer looking for openings. But this could have you running around for days or weeks. A more efficient strategy would be to pick up a copy of the local newspaper or go online and look for openings. Classified ads and Web sites, which are elements of the job market, reduce the transaction costs of bringing workers and employers together.

transaction costs
The costs of time and information required to carry out market exchange

The coordination that occurs through markets takes place not because of some central plan but because of Adam Smith's "invisible hand." For example, the auto dealers in your community tend to locate together, usually on the outskirts of town, where land is cheaper. The dealers congregate not because they all took an economics course or because they like one another's company but because grouped together they become a more attractive destination for car buyers. A dealer who makes the mistake of locating away from the others misses out on a lot of business. Similarly, stores locate together so that more shoppers will be drawn by the call of the mall. From Orlando theme parks to Broadway theaters to Las Vegas casinos, suppliers congregate to attract demanders. Some groupings can be quite specialized. For example, shops in Hong Kong that sell dress mannequins cluster along Austin Road. And diamond merchants in New York City congregate within a few blocks.

Market Equilibrium

To see how a market works, let's bring together market demand and market supply. Exhibit 5 shows the market for pizza, using schedules in panel (a) and curves in panel (b). Suppose the price initially is $12. At that price, producers supply 24 million

EXHIBIT 5 Equilibrium in the Pizza Market

(a) Market schedules

Price per Pizza	Quantity Demanded (Millions of Pizzas per Week)	Quantity Supplied (Millions of Pizzas per Week)	Surplus or Shortage (Millions of Pizzas per Week)	Effect on Price
$15	8	28	Surplus of 20	Falls
12	14	24	Surplus of 10	Falls
9	20	20	Equilibrium	Remains the same
6	26	16	Shortage of 10	Rises
3	32	12	Shortage of 20	Rises

(b) Market curves

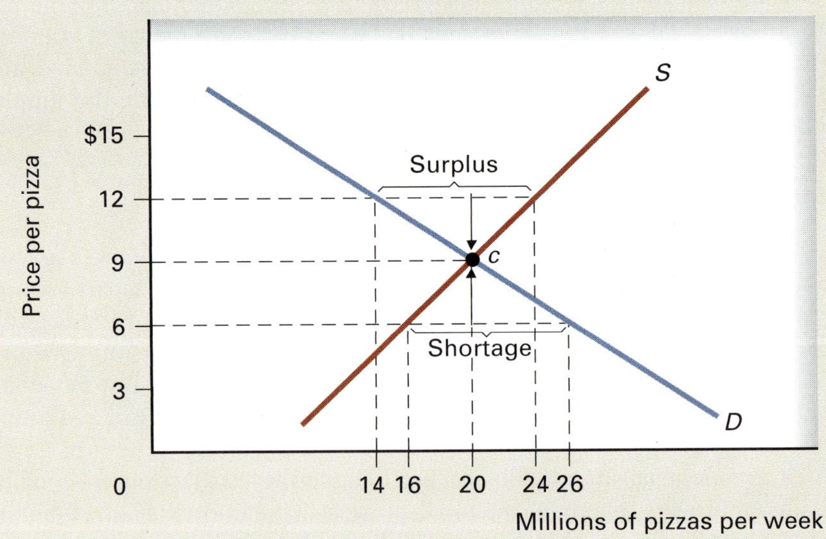

Market equilibrium occurs at the price where quantity demanded equals quantity supplied. This is shown at point c. Above the equilibrium price, quantity supplied exceeds quantity demanded. This creates a surplus, which puts downward pressure on the price. Below the equilibrium price, quantity demanded exceeds quantity supplied. The resulting shortage puts upward pressure on the price.

pizzas per week, but consumers demand only 14 million, resulting in an *excess quantity supplied,* or a **surplus**, of 10 million pizzas per week. Suppliers don't like getting stuck with unsold pizzas. Their desire to eliminate the surplus puts downward pressure on the price, as shown by the arrow pointing down in the graph. As the price falls, producers reduce their quantity supplied and consumers increase their quantity demanded. The price continues to fall as long as quantity supplied exceeds quantity demanded.

surplus
At a given price, the amount by which quantity supplied exceeds quantity demanded; a surplus usually forces the price down

Alternatively, suppose the price initially is $6. You can see from Exhibit 5 that at that price consumers demand 26 million pizzas but producers supply only 16 million, resulting in an *excess quantity demanded,* or a **shortage**, of 10 million pizzas per week. Producers quickly notice they have sold out and those customers still demanding pizzas are grumbling. Profit-maximizing producers and frustrated consumers create market pressure for a higher price, as shown by the arrow pointing up in the graph. As the price rises, producers increase their quantity supplied and consumers reduce their quantity demanded. The price continues to rise as long as quantity demanded exceeds quantity supplied.

shortage
At a given price, the amount by which quantity demanded exceeds quantity supplied; a shortage usually forces the price up

Thus, *a surplus creates downward pressure on the price, and a shortage creates upward pressure.* As long as quantity demanded differs from quantity supplied, this difference forces a price change. Note that a shortage or a surplus depends on the price. There is no such thing as a general shortage or a general surplus, only a shortage or a surplus at a particular price.

A market reaches equilibrium when the quantity demanded equals quantity supplied. In **equilibrium**, the independent plans of buyers and sellers exactly match, so market forces exert no pressure for change. In Exhibit 5, the demand and supply curves intersect at the *equilibrium point,* identified as point *c*. The *equilibrium price* is $9 per pizza, and the *equilibrium quantity* is 20 million per week. At that price and quantity, the market *clears*. Because there is no shortage or surplus, there is no pressure for the price to change. The demand and supply curves form an "x" at the intersection. The equilibrium point is found where "x" marks the spot.

equilibrium
The condition that exists in a market when the plans of buyers match those of sellers, so quantity demanded equals quantity supplied and the market clears

A market finds equilibrium through the independent actions of thousands, or even millions, of buyers and sellers. In one sense, the market is personal because each consumer and each producer makes a personal decision about how much to buy or sell at a given price. In another sense, the market is impersonal because it requires no conscious communication or coordination among consumers or producers. The price does all the talking. *Impersonal market forces synchronize the personal and independent decisions of many individual buyers and sellers to achieve equilibrium price and quantity.* Prices reflect relative scarcity. For example, to rent a 26-foot truck one-way from San Francisco to Austin, U-Haul recently charged $3,236. Its one-way charge for that same truck from Austin to San Francisco was just $399. Why the difference? Far more people wanted to move from San Francisco to Austin than vice versa, so U-Haul had to pay its own employees to drive the empty trucks back from Texas. Rental rates reflected that extra cost.

Changes in Equilibrium Price and Quantity

Equilibrium occurs when the intentions of demanders and suppliers exactly match. Once a market reaches equilibrium, that price and quantity prevail until something happens to demand or supply. A change in any determinant of demand or supply usually changes equilibrium price and quantity in a predictable way, as you'll see.

EXHIBIT 6 Effects of an Increase in Demand

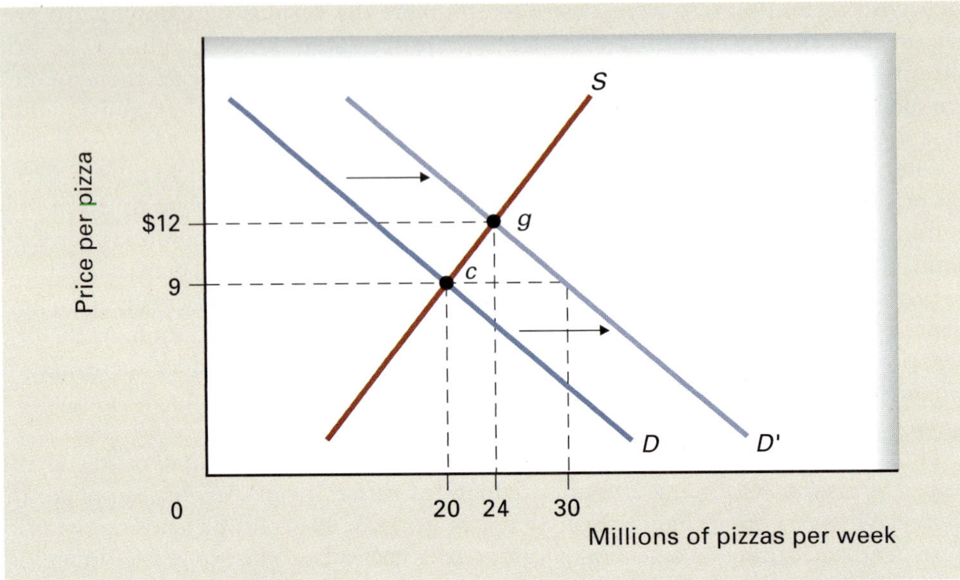

An increase in demand is shown by a shift of the demand curve rightward from *D* to *D′*. Quantity demanded exceeds quantity supplied at the original price of $9 per pizza, putting upward pressure on the price. As the price rises, quantity supplied increases along supply curve *S*, and quantity demanded decreases along demand curve *D′*. When the new equilibrium price of $12 is reached at point *g*, quantity demanded once again equals quantity supplied.

Shifts of the Demand Curve

In Exhibit 6, demand curve *D* and supply curve *S* intersect at point *c* to yield the initial equilibrium price of $9 and the initial equilibrium quantity of 20 million 12-inch regular pizzas per week. Now suppose that one of the determinants of demand changes in a way that increases demand, shifting the demand curve to the right from *D* to *D′*. Any of the following could shift the demand for pizza rightward: (1) an increase in the money income of consumers (because pizza is a normal good); (2) an increase in the price of a substitute, such as tacos, or a decrease in the price of a complement, such as Coke; (3) a change in consumer expectations that causes people to demand more pizzas now; (4) a growth in the number of pizza consumers; or (5) a change in consumer tastes—based, for example, on a discovery that the tomato sauce on pizza has antioxidant properties that improve overall health.

After the demand curve shifts rightward to *D′* in Exhibit 6, the amount demanded at the initial price of $9 is 30 million pizzas, which exceeds the amount supplied of 20 million by 10 million pizzas. This shortage puts upward pressure on the price. As the price increases, the quantity demanded decreases along the new demand curve *D′*, and the quantity supplied increases along the existing supply curve *S* until the two quantities are equal once again at equilibrium point *g*. The new equilibrium price is $12, and the new equilibrium quantity is 24 million pizzas per week. Thus, given an upward-sloping supply curve, an increase in demand increases both equilibrium price and quantity. A decrease in demand would lower both equilibrium price and quantity.

These results can be summarized as follows: *Given an upward-sloping supply curve, a rightward shift of the demand curve increases both equilibrium price and quantity and a leftward shift decreases both equilibrium price and quantity.*

Shifts of the Supply Curve

Let's now consider shifts of the supply curve. In Exhibit 7, as before, we begin with demand curve *D* and supply curve *S* intersecting at point *c* to yield an equilibrium price of $9 and an equilibrium quantity of 20 million pizzas per week. Suppose one of the determinants of supply changes, increasing supply from *S* to *S'*. Changes that could shift the supply curve rightward include (1) a technological breakthrough in pizza ovens; (2) a reduction in the price of a resource such as mozzarella cheese; (3) a decline in the price of another good such as Italian bread; (4) a change in expectations that encourages pizza makers to expand production now; or (5) an increase in the number of pizzerias.

After the supply curve shifts rightward in Exhibit 7, the amount supplied at the initial price of $9 increases from 20 million to 30 million, so producers now supply 10 million more pizzas than consumers demand. This surplus forces the price down. As the price falls, the quantity supplied declines along the new supply curve and the quantity demanded increases along the existing demand curve until a new equilibrium point *d* is established. The new equilibrium price is $6, and the new equilibrium quantity is 26 million pizzas per week. In short, an increase in supply reduces the price and increases the quantity. On the other hand, a decrease in supply increases the price but decreases the quantity. Thus, *given a downward-sloping demand curve, a rightward shift of the supply curve decreases price but increases quantity, and a leftward shift increases price but decreases quantity.*

EXHIBIT 7 Effects of an Increase in Supply

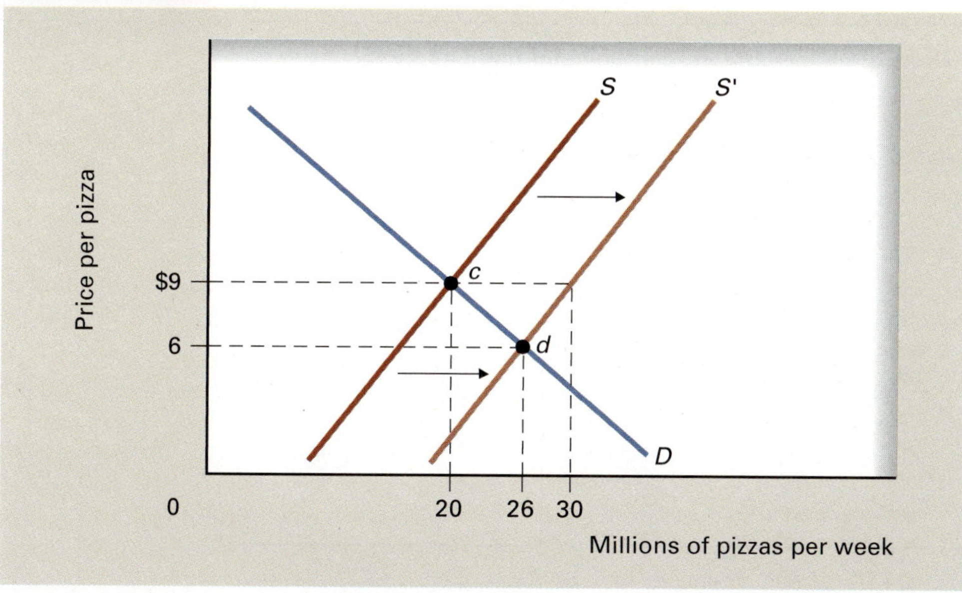

An increase in supply is shown by a shift of the supply curve rightward, from *S* to *S'*. Quantity supplied exceeds quantity demanded at the original price of $9 per pizza, putting downward pressure on the price. As the price falls, quantity supplied decreases along supply curve *S'*, and quantity demanded increases along demand curve *D*. When the new equilibrium price of $6 is reached at point *d*, quantity demanded once again equals quantity supplied.

Simultaneous Shifts of Demand and Supply Curves

As long as only one curve shifts, we can say for sure how equilibrium price and quantity will change. If both curves shift, however, the outcome is less obvious. For example, suppose both demand and supply increase, or shift rightward, as in Exhibit 8. Note that in panel (a), demand shifts more than supply, and in panel (b), supply shifts more than demand. In both panels, equilibrium quantity increases. The change in equilibrium price, however, depends on which curve shifts more. If demand shifts more, as in panel (a), equilibrium price increases. For example, between 1995 and 2005, the demand for housing increased more than the supply, so both price and quantity increased. But if supply shifts more, as in panel (b), equilibrium price decreases. For example, in the last decade, the supply of personal computers has increased more than the demand, so price has decreased and quantity increased.

Conversely, if both demand and supply decrease, or shift leftward, equilibrium quantity decreases. But, again, we cannot say what will happen to equilibrium price unless we examine relative shifts. (You can use Exhibit 8 to consider decreases in demand and supply by viewing D' and S' as the initial curves.) If demand shifts more, the price will fall. If supply shifts more, the price will rise.

If demand and supply shift in opposite directions, we can say what will happen to equilibrium price. Equilibrium price will increase if demand increases and supply decreases. Equilibrium price will decrease if demand decreases and supply increases. Without reference to particular shifts, however, we cannot say what will happen to equilibrium quantity.

These results are no doubt confusing, but Exhibit 9 summarizes the four possible combinations of changes. Using Exhibit 9 as a reference, please take the time right now to work through some changes in demand and supply to develop a feel for the results. Then, in the case study, "World of Business: The Market for Professional Basketball," evaluate changes in the market for professional basketball.

EXHIBIT 8 **Indeterminate Effect of an Increase in Both Demand and Supply**

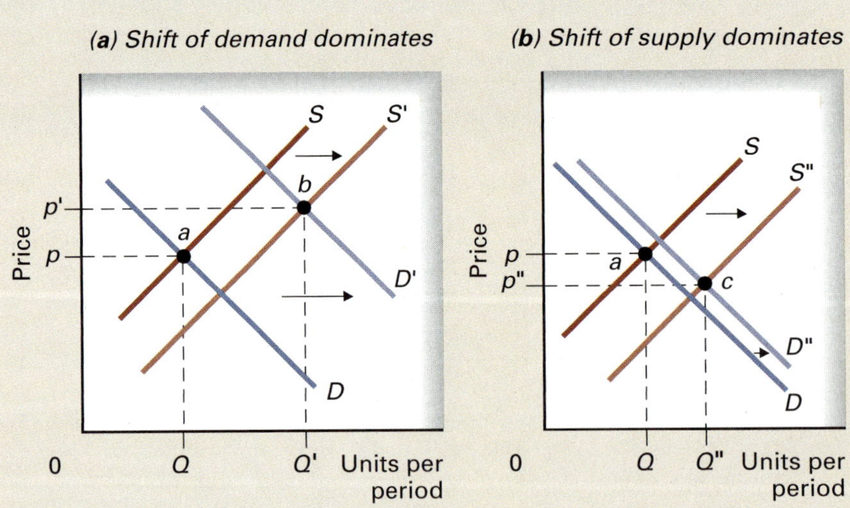

When both demand and supply increase, the equilibrium quantity also increases. The effect on price depends on which curve shifts more. In panel (a), the demand curve shifts more, so the price rises. In panel (b), the supply curve shifts more, so the price falls.

EXHIBIT 9 Effects of Shifts of Both Demand and Supply

Change in supply	Change in demand: Demand increases	Change in demand: Demand decreases
Supply increases	Equilibrium price change is indeterminate. Equilibrium quantity increases.	Equilibrium price falls. Equilibrium quantity change is indeterminate.
Supply decreases	Equilibrium price rises. Equilibrium quantity change is indeterminate.	Equilibrium price change is indeterminate. Equilibrium quantity decreases.

When the demand and supply curves shift in the same direction, equilibrium quantity also shifts in that direction. The effect on equilibrium price depends on which curve shifts more. If the curves shift in opposite directions, equilibrium price will move in the same direction as demand. The effect on equilibrium quantity depends on which curve shifts more.

Disequilibrium

A surplus exerts downward pressure on the price, and a shortage exerts upward pressure. Markets, however, don't always reach equilibrium quickly. During the time required to adjust, the market is said to be in disequilibrium. **Disequilibrium** is usually temporary as the market gropes for equilibrium. But sometimes, often as a result of government intervention, disequilibrium can last a while, perhaps decades, as we will see next.

disequilibrium
The condition that exists in a market when the plans of buyers do not match those of sellers; a temporary mismatch between quantity supplied and quantity demanded as the market seeks equilibrium

Price Floors

Sometimes public officials set prices above their equilibrium levels. For example, the federal government regulates some agriculture prices in an attempt to ensure farmers a higher and more stable income than they would otherwise earn. To achieve higher prices, the government sets a **price floor**, or a *minimum* selling price that is above the equilibrium price. Panel (a) of Exhibit 10 shows the effect of a $2.50 per gallon price floor for milk. At that price, farmers supply 24 million gallons per week, but consumers demand only 14 million gallons, yielding a surplus of 10 million gallons. This surplus milk will pile up on store shelves, eventually souring. To take it off the market, the government usually agrees to buy the surplus milk. The federal government, in fact, has spent billions buying and storing surplus agricultural products. Note, to have an impact, a price floor must be set *above* the equilibrium price. A price floor set at or

price floor
A minimum legal price below which a product cannot be sold; to have an impact, a price floor must be set above the equilibrium price

EXHIBIT 10 Price Floors and Price Ceilings

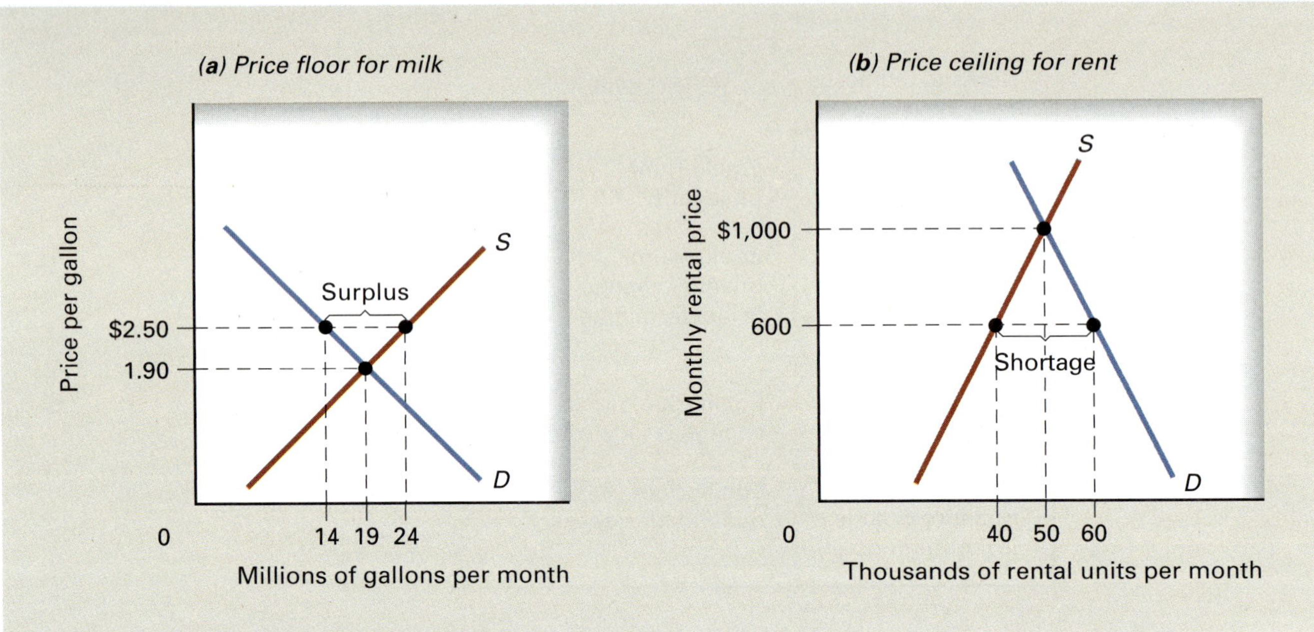

A price floor set above the equilibrium price results in a surplus, as shown in panel (a). A price floor set at or below the equilibrium price has no effect. A price ceiling set below the equilibrium price results in a shortage, as shown in panel (b). A price ceiling set at or above the equilibrium price has no effect.

below the equilibrium price wouldn't matter (how come?). Price floors distort markets and reduce economic welfare.

Price Ceilings

price ceiling
A maximum legal price above which a product cannot be sold; to have an impact, a price ceiling must be set below the equilibrium price

Sometimes public officials try to keep a price below the equilibrium level by setting a **price ceiling**, or a *maximum* selling price. Concern about the rising cost of rental housing in some cities prompted city officials to impose rent ceilings. Panel (b) of Exhibit 10 depicts the demand and supply of rental housing. The vertical axis shows monthly rent, and the horizontal axis shows the quantity of rental units. The equilibrium, or market-clearing, rent is $1,000 per month, and the equilibrium quantity is 50,000 housing units. Suppose city officials set a maximum rent of $600 per month. At that ceiling price, 60,000 rental units are demanded, but only 40,000 supplied, resulting in a housing shortage of 20,000 units. Because of the price ceiling, the rental price no longer rations housing to those who value it the most. Other devices emerge to ration housing, such as long waiting lists, personal connections, and the willingness to make under-the-table payments, such as "key fees," "finder's fees," high security deposits, and the like. To have an impact, a price ceiling must be set *below* the equilibrium price. A price ceiling set at or above the equilibrium level wouldn't matter. Price floors and ceilings distort markets and reduce economic welfare. Read the case study at the end of the book, "Bringing Theory to Life: Rent Ceilings in New York City," to take a closer look at rent ceilings in New York City.

Government intervention is not the only source of market disequilibrium. Sometimes, when new products are introduced or when demand suddenly changes, it takes a while to reach equilibrium. For example, popular toys, best-selling books, and chart-busting CDs sometimes sell out. On the other hand, some new products attract few customers and pile up unsold on store shelves, awaiting a "clearance sale."

Conclusion

Demand and supply are the building blocks of a market economy. Although a market usually involves the interaction of many buyers and sellers, few markets are consciously designed. Just as the law of gravity works whether or not we understand Newton's principles, market forces operate whether or not participants understand demand and supply. These forces arise naturally, much the way car dealers cluster on the outskirts of town to attract more customers.

Markets have their critics. Some observers may be troubled, for example, that an NBA star like Kevin Garnett earns a salary that could pay for 500 new schoolteachers, or that corporate executives, such as the head of Goldman Sachs, a financial firm, earns enough to pay for 1,000 new schoolteachers, or that U.S. consumers spend over $40 billion on their pets. On your next trip to the supermarket, notice how much shelf space goes to pet products—often an entire aisle. PetSmart, a chain store, sells over 12,000 different pet items. Veterinarians offer cancer treatment, cataract removal, root canals, even acupuncture. Kidney dialysis for a pet can cost over $75,000 per year.

In a market economy, consumers are kings and queens. Consumer sovereignty rules, deciding what gets produced. Those who don't like the market outcome usually look to government for a solution through price ceilings and price floors, regulations, income redistribution, and public finance more generally.

Summary

1. Demand is a relationship between the price of a product and the quantity consumers are willing and able to buy per period, other things constant. According to the law of demand, quantity demanded varies negatively, or inversely, with the price, so the demand curve slopes downward.
2. A demand curve slopes downward for two reasons. A price decrease makes consumers (a) more *willing* to substitute this good for other goods and (b) more *able* to buy the good because the lower price increases real income.
3. Assumed to remain constant along a demand curve are (a) money income, (b) prices of other goods, (c) consumer expectations, (d) the number or composition of consumers in the market, and (e) consumer tastes. A change in any of these could shift, or change, the demand curve.
4. Supply is a relationship between the price of a good and the quantity producers are willing and able to sell per period, other things constant. According to the law of supply, price and quantity supplied are usually positively, or directly, related, so the supply curve typically slopes upward.
5. The supply curve slopes upward because higher prices make producers (a) more *willing* to supply this good rather than supply other goods that use the same resources and (b) more *able* to cover the higher marginal cost associated with greater output rates.
6. Assumed to remain constant along a supply curve are (a) the state of technology; (b) the prices of resources used to produce the good; (c) the prices of other goods that could be produced with these resources; (d) supplier expectations; and (e) the number of producers in this market. A change in any of these could shift, or change, the supply curve.
7. Demand and supply come together in the market for the good. A market provides information about the price, quantity, and quality of the good. In doing so, a market reduces the transaction costs of exchange—the costs of time and information required for buyers and sellers to make a deal. The interaction of demand and supply guides resources and products to their highest-valued use.
8. Impersonal market forces reconcile the personal and independent plans of buyers and sellers. Market equilibrium, once established,

will continue unless there is a change in a determinant that shapes demand or supply. Disequilibrium is usually temporary while markets seek equilibrium, but sometimes disequilibrium lasts a while, such as when government regulates the price.

9. A price floor is the minimum legal price below which a particular good or service cannot be sold. The federal government imposes price floors on some agricultural products to help farmers achieve a higher and more stable income than would be possible with freer markets. If the floor price is set above the market clearing price, quantity supplied exceeds quantity demanded. Policy makers must figure out some way to prevent this surplus from pushing the price down.

10. A price ceiling is a maximum legal price above which a particular good or service cannot be sold. Governments sometimes impose price ceilings to reduce the price of some consumer goods such as rental housing. If the ceiling price is below the market clearing price, quantity demanded exceeds the quantity supplied, creating a shortage. Because the price system is not allowed to clear the market, other mechanisms arise to ration the product among demanders.

Key Concepts

Questions for Review

1. Law of Demand What is the law of demand? Give two examples of how you have observed the law of demand at work in the "real world." How is the law of demand related to the demand curve?

2. Changes in Demand What variables influence the demand for a normal good? Explain why a reduction in the price of a normal good does not increase the demand for that good.

3. Substitution and Income Effects Distinguish between the substitution effect and income effect of a price change. If a good's price increases, does each effect have a positive or a negative impact on the quantity demanded?

4. Demand Explain the effect of an increase in consumer income on the demand for a good.

5. Income Effects When moving along the demand curve, income must be assumed constant. Yet one factor that can cause a change in the quantity demanded is the "income effect." Reconcile these seemingly contradictory facts.

6. Demand If chocolate is found to have positive health benefits, would this lead to a shift of the demand curve or a movement along the demand curve?

7. Supply What is the law of supply? Give an example of how you have observed the law of supply at work. What is the relationship between the law of supply and the supply curve?

8. Changes in Supply What kinds of changes in underlying conditions can cause the supply curve to shift? Give some examples and explain the direction in which the curve shifts.

9. Supply If a severe frost destroys some of Florida's citrus crop, would this lead to a shift of the supply curve or a movement along the supply curve?

10. Markets How do markets coordinate the independent decisions of buyers and sellers?

11. Case Study: The Market for Professional Basketball (See page 705.) In what sense can we speak of a market for professional basketball? Who are the demanders and who are the suppliers? What are some examples of how changes in supply or demand conditions have affected this market?

Problems and Exercises

12. SHIFTING DEMAND Using demand and supply curves, show the effect of each of the following on the market for cigarettes:
    a. A cure for lung cancer is found.
    b. The price of cigars increases.
    c. Wages increase substantially in states that grow tobacco.
    d. A fertilizer that increases the yield per acre of tobacco is discovered.
    e. There is a sharp increase in the price of matches, lighters, and lighter fluid.
    f. More states pass laws restricting smoking in restaurants and public places.

13. SUBSTITUTES AND COMPLEMENTS For each of the following pair of goods, determine whether the goods are substitutes, complements, or unrelated:
    a. Peanut butter and jelly
    b. Private and public transportation
    c. Coke and Pepsi
    d. Alarm clocks and automobiles
    e. Golf clubs and golf balls

14. EQUILIBRIUM "If a price is not an equilibrium price, there is a tendency for it to move to its equilibrium level. Regardless of whether the price is too high or too low to begin with, the adjustment process will increase the quantity of the good purchased." Explain, using a demand and supply diagram.

15. EQUILIBRIUM Assume the market for corn is depicted as in the table that appears below.
    a. Complete the table below.
    b. What market pressure occurs when quantity demanded exceeds quantity supplied? Explain.
    c. What market pressure occurs when quantity supplied exceeds quantity demanded? Explain.
    d. What is the equilibrium price?
    e. What could change the equilibrium price?
    f. At each price in the first column of the table, how much is sold?

16. MARKET EQUILIBRIUM Determine whether each of the following statements is true, false, or uncertain. Then briefly explain each answer.
    a. In equilibrium, all sellers can find buyers.
    b. In equilibrium, there is no pressure on the market to produce or consume more than is being sold.
    c. At prices above equilibrium, the quantity exchanged exceeds the quantity demanded.
    d. At prices below equilibrium, the quantity exchanged is equal to the quantity supplied.

17. DEMAND AND SUPPLY How do you think each of the following affected the world price of oil? (Use demand and supply analysis.)
    a. Tax credits were offered for expenditures on home insulation.
    b. The Alaskan oil pipeline was completed.
    c. The ceiling on the price of oil was removed.
    d. Oil was discovered in the North Sea.
    e. Sport utility vehicles and minivans became popular.
    f. The use of nuclear power declined.

18. DEMAND AND SUPPLY What happens to the equilibrium price and quantity of ice cream in response to each of the following? Explain your answers.
    a. The price of dairy cow fodder increases.
    b. The price of beef decreases.
    c. Concerns arise about the fat content of ice cream. Simultaneously, the price of sugar (used to produce ice cream) increases.

19. EQUILIBRIUM Consider the following graph in which demand and supply are initially D and S, respectively. What are the equilibrium price and quantity? If demand increases to D', what are the new equilibrium price and quantity? What happens if the government does not allow the price to change when demand increases?

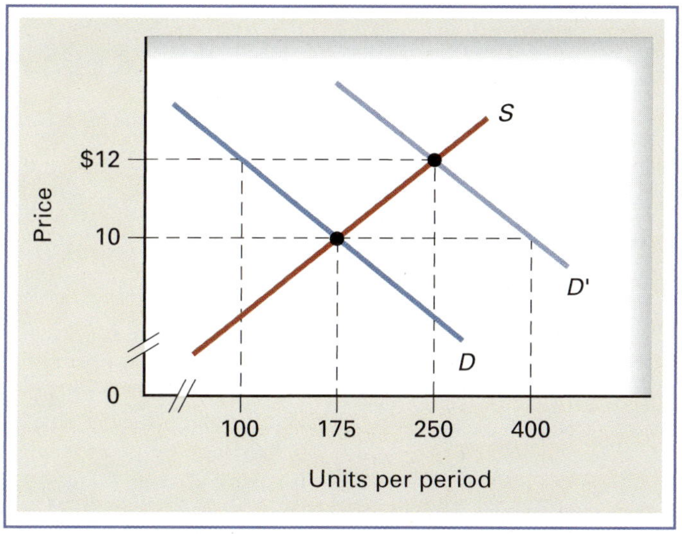

Price per Bushel ($)	Quantity Demanded (millions of bushels)	Quantity Supplied (millions of bushels)	Surplus/ Shortage	Will Price Rise or Fall?
1.80	320	200	______	______
2.00	300	230	______	______
2.20	270	270	______	______
2.40	230	300	______	______
2.60	200	330	______	______
2.80	180	350	______	______

20. Changes in Equilibrium What are the effects on the equilibrium price and quantity of steel if the wages of steelworkers rise and, simultaneously, the price of aluminum rises?

21. Price Floor There is considerable interest in whether the minimum wage rate contributes to teenage unemployment. Draw a demand and supply diagram for the unskilled labor market, and discuss the effects of a minimum wage. Who is helped and who is hurt by the minimum wage?

22. Case Study: Rent Ceilings in New York City (See page 706.) Suppose the demand and supply curves for rental housing units have the typical shapes and that the rental housing market is in equilibrium. Then, government establishes a rent ceiling below the equilibrium level.

    a. What happens to the quantity of housing available?
    b. What happens to the quality of housing and why?
    c. Who benefits from rent control?
    d. Who loses from rent control?
    e. How do landlords of rent-controlled apartments try to get tenants to leave?

Global Economic Watch Exercises

Login to www.cengagebrain.com and access the Global Economic Watch to do these exercises.

23. Global Economic Watch Go to the Global Economic Crisis Resource Center. Select Global Issues in Context. In the Basic Search box at the top of the page, enter the phrase "Law of Supply, Demand." On the Results page, go to the Global Viewpoints section. Click on the link for the November 21, 1984, article "Law of Supply, Demand Applies to Everyone." Did the article describe a surplus of supply or a shortage of supply?

24. Global Economic Watch Go to the Global Economic Crisis Resource Center. Select Global Issues in Context. Go to the menu at the top of the page and click on the tab for Browse Issues and Topics. Choose Business and Economy. Click on the link for Oil Prices. Find an article from the past 12 months. Compare and contrast the information about oil prices in the article from Problem 23 and in the current article. Use *demand*, *supply*, and *equilibrium* in your analysis.

Elasticity of Demand and Supply

5

Newscom

- What does the demand curve look like when price is no object?
- What does the supply curve look like for Cadillacs once owned by Elvis Presley?
- Why do higher cigarette taxes cut smoking by teenagers more than by other age groups?
- Why are consumers more sensitive to the price of Post Raisin Bran than to the price of cereal more generally?
- Why does an abundant harvest often spell trouble for farmers?

Answers to these and other questions are explored in this chapter, which takes a closer look at demand and supply.

As you learned in Chapter 1, macroeconomics concentrates on aggregate markets—on the big picture. But the big picture is a mosaic pieced together from individual decisions made by households, firms, governments, and the rest of the world. To understand how a market economy works, you must take a closer look at these individual choices, especially at the role of prices. In a market economy, prices tell producers and consumers about the relative scarcity of products and resources.

A downward-sloping demand curve and an upward-sloping supply curve form a powerful analytical tool. To use this tool wisely, you need to learn more about these curves. The more you know, the better you can predict the effects of a change in the price on quantity. Decision makers are willing to pay dearly for such knowledge. For example, Taco Bell would like to know what happens to sales if taco prices change. Governments would

like to know how a hike in cigarette taxes affects teenage smoking. Colleges would like to know how tuition increases affect enrollments. And subway officials would like to know how fare changes affect ridership. To answer such questions, you must learn how responsive consumers and producers are to price changes. This chapter introduces the idea of *elasticity*, a measure of *responsiveness*.

Topics discussed include:

- Price elasticity of demand
- Determinants of price elasticity
- Price elasticity and total revenue
- Price elasticity of supply
- Income elasticity of demand
- Cross-price elasticity of demand

Price Elasticity of Demand

Just before a recent Thanksgiving, Delta Airlines cut fares for some seats on more than 10,000 domestic flights. Was that a good idea? A firm's success or failure often depends on how much it knows about the demand for its product. For Delta's total revenue to increase, the gain in tickets sold would have to more than make up for the decline in ticket prices. Likewise, the operators of Taco Bell would like to know what happens to sales if the price drops from, say, \$1.10 to \$0.90 per taco. The law of demand tells us that a lower price increases quantity demanded, but by how much? How sensitive is quantity demanded to a change in price? After all, if quantity demanded increases enough, a price cut could be a profitable move for Taco Bell.

Calculating Price Elasticity of Demand

Let's get more specific about how sensitive changes in quantity demanded are to changes in price. Take a look at the demand curve in Exhibit 1. At the initial price of \$1.10 per taco, consumers demand 95,000 a day. If the price drops to \$0.90, quantity demanded increases to 105,000. Is such a response a little or a lot? The *price elasticity of demand* measures, in a standardized way, how responsive consumers are to a change in price. *Elasticity* is another word for *responsiveness*. In simplest terms, the **price elasticity of demand** measures the percentage change in quantity demanded divided by the percentage change in price, or:

price elasticity of demand
Measures how responsive quantity demanded is to a price change; the percentage change in quantity demanded divided by the percentage change in price

$$\text{Price elasticity of demand} = \frac{\text{Percentage change in quantity demanded}}{\text{Percentage change in price}}$$

So what's the price elasticity of demand when the price of tacos falls from \$1.10 to \$0.90—that is, what's the price elasticity of demand between points *a* and *b* in Exhibit 1? For price elasticity to be a clear and reliable measure, we should get the same result between points *a* and *b* as we get between points *b* and *a*. To ensure that consistency,

EXHIBIT 1 Demand Curve for Tacos

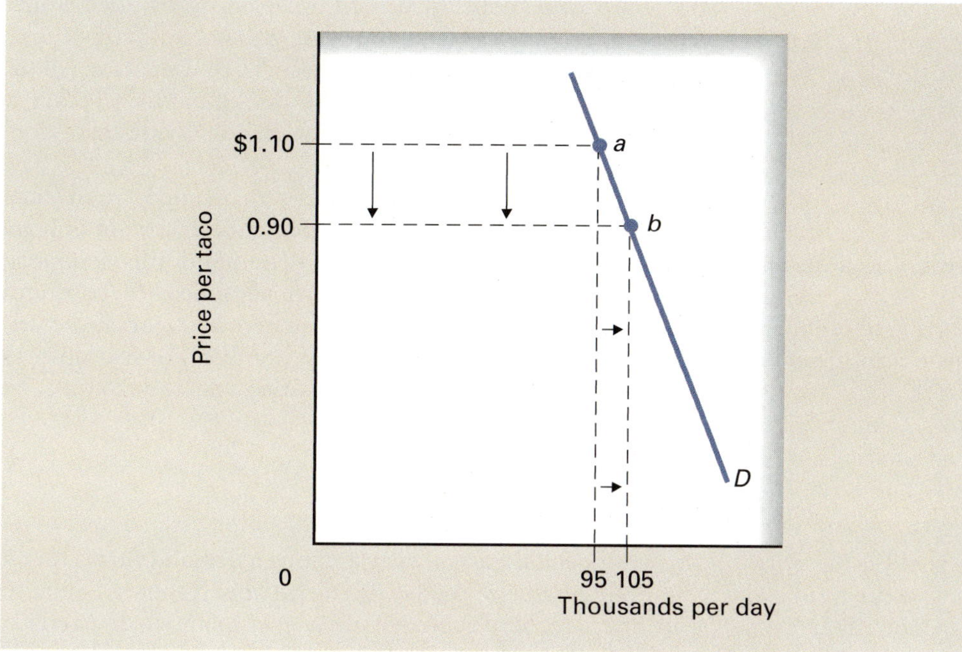

If the price of tacos drops from $1.10 to $0.90, the quantity demanded increases from 95,000 to 105,000.

we must take the average of the initial price and the new price and use that as the base for computing the percentage change in price. For example, in Exhibit 1, the base used to calculate the percentage change in price is the average of $1.10 and $0.90, which is $1.00. The percentage change in price is therefore the change in price, −$0.20, divided by $1.00, which works out to be −20 percent.

The same holds for changes in quantity demanded. In Exhibit 1, the base used for computing the percentage change in quantity demanded is the average of 95,000 and 105,000, which is 100,000. So the percentage increase in quantity demanded is the change in quantity demanded, 10,000, divided by 100,000, which works out to be 10 percent. So the resulting price elasticity of demand between points *a* and *b* (and between points *b* and *a*) is the percentage increase in quantity demanded, 10 percent, divided by the percentage decrease in price, −20 percent, which is −0.5 (=10%/−20%).

Let's generalize the **price elasticity formula.** If the price changes from p to p', other things constant, the quantity demanded changes from q to q'. The change in price can be represented as Δp and the change in quantity as Δq. The formula for calculating the price elasticity of demand E_D between the two points is the percentage change in quantity demanded divided by the percentage change in price, or:

price elasticity formula
Percentage change in quantity demanded divided by the percentage change in price; the average quantity and the average price are used as bases for computing percentage changes in quantity and in price

$$E_D = \frac{\Delta q}{(q+q')/2} \div \frac{\Delta p}{(p+p')/2}$$

Again, because the average quantity and average price are used as the bases for computing percentage change, the same elasticity results whether going from the higher price to the lower price or the other way around.

Elasticity expresses a relationship between two amounts: the percentage change in quantity demanded and the percentage change in price. Because the focus is on the *percentage change*, we don't need to be concerned with how output or price is measured. For example, suppose the good in question is apples. It makes no difference in the elasticity formula whether we measure apples in pounds, bushels, or even tons. All that matters is the percentage change in quantity demanded. Nor does it matter whether we measure price in U.S. dollars, Mexican pesos, Zambian kwacha, or Vietnamese dong. All that matters is the percentage change in price.

Finally, the law of demand states that price and quantity demanded are inversely related, so the change in price and the change in quantity demanded move in opposite directions. In the elasticity formula, the numerator and the denominator have opposite signs, leaving the price elasticity of demand with a negative sign. Because constantly referring to elasticity as a negative number gets old fast, from here on we treat the price elasticity of demand as an absolute value, or as a positive number. For example, the absolute value of the elasticity measured in Exhibit 1 is 0.5. Still, from time to time, you will be reminded that we are discussing absolute values.

Categories of Price Elasticity of Demand

As you'll see, the price elasticity of demand usually varies along a demand curve. Ranges of elasticity can be divided into three categories, depending on how responsive quantity demanded is to a change in price. If the percentage change in quantity demanded is less than the percentage change in price, the resulting elasticity has an absolute value between 0 and 1.0. That portion of the demand curve is said to be **inelastic**, meaning that quantity demanded is relatively unresponsive to a change in price. For example, the elasticity derived in Exhibit 1 between points *a* and *b* was 0.5, so that portion of the demand curve is inelastic. If the percentage change in quantity demanded just equals the percentage change in price, the resulting elasticity has an absolute value of 1.0, and that portion of a demand curve is **unit elastic**. Finally, if the percentage change in quantity demanded exceeds the percentage change in price, the resulting elasticity has an absolute value exceeding 1.0, and that portion of a demand curve is said to be **elastic**. In summary, *the price elasticity of demand is inelastic if its absolute value is between 0 and 1.0, unit elastic if equal to 1.0, and elastic if greater than 1.0.*

inelastic demand
A change in price has relatively little effect on quantity demanded; the percentage change in quantity demanded is less than the percentage change in price; the resulting price elasticity has an absolute value less than 1.0

unit-elastic demand
The percentage change in quantity demanded equals the percentage change in price; the resulting price elasticity has an absolute value of 1.0

elastic demand
A change in price has a relatively large effect on quantity demanded; the percentage change in quantity demanded exceeds the percentage change in price; the resulting price elasticity has an absolute value exceeding 1.0

Elasticity and Total Revenue

Knowledge of price elasticity of demand is especially valuable to producers, because it indicates the effect of a price change on total revenue. **Total revenue** (TR) is the price (p) multiplied by the quantity demanded (q) at that price, or $TR = p \times q$. What happens to total revenue when price decreases? Well, according to the law of demand, a lower price increases quantity demanded, which tends to increase total revenue. But, a lower price means producers get less for each unit sold, which tends to decrease total revenue. The overall impact of a lower price on total revenue therefore depends on the net result of these opposite effects. *If the positive effect of a greater quantity demanded more than offsets the negative effect of a lower price, then total revenue rises.* More specifically, if demand is elastic, the percentage increase in quantity demanded exceeds the percentage decrease in price, so total revenue increases. If demand is unit elastic, the percentage increase in quantity demanded just equals the percentage decrease in price, so total revenue remains unchanged. Finally, if demand is inelastic, the positive impact of an increase in quantity demanded on total revenue is more than offset by the negative impact of a decrease in price, so total revenue falls.

total revenue
Price multiplied by the quantity demanded at that price

Price Elasticity and the Linear Demand Curve

A look at elasticity along a particular type of demand curve, the linear demand curve, ties together the ideas discussed so far. A **linear demand curve** is simply a straight-line demand curve, as in panel (a) of Exhibit 2. Panel (b) shows the total revenue generated by each price-quantity combination along the demand curve in panel (a). Recall that total revenue equals price times quantity. Please take a moment to see how the demand curve and total revenue curve relate.

linear demand curve
A straight-line demand curve; such a demand curve has a constant slope but usually has a varying price elasticity

Because the demand curve is linear, its slope is constant, so a given decrease in price always causes the same unit increase in quantity demanded. For example, along the demand curve in Exhibit 2, a $10 drop in price always increases quantity demanded by

EXHIBIT 2 Demand, Price Elasticity, and Total Revenue

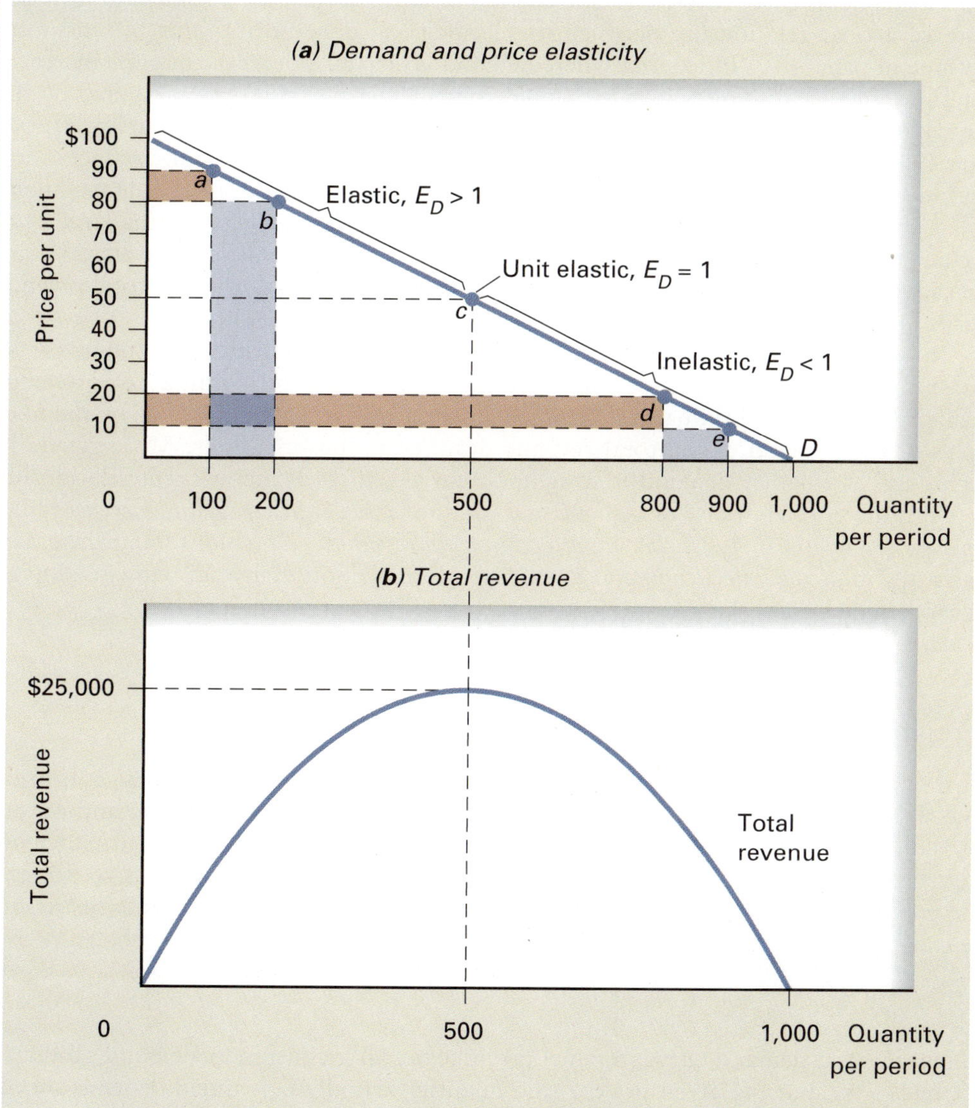

Where the demand curve is elastic, a lower price increases total revenue. Total revenue reaches a maximum at the rate of output where the demand curve is unit elastic. Where the demand curve is inelastic, further decreases in price reduce total revenue.

100 units. But the price elasticity of demand is larger on the higher-price end of the demand curve than on the lower-price end. Here's why. Consider a movement from point *a* to point *b* on the upper end of the demand curve in Exhibit 2. The \$10 price drop is a percentage change of 10/85, or 12 percent. The 100-unit increase in quantity demanded is a percentage change of 100/150, or 67 percent. Therefore, the price elasticity of demand between points *a* and *b* is 67%/12%, which equals 5.6. Between points *d* and *e* on the lower end, however, the \$10 price decrease is a percentage change of 10/15, or 67 percent, and the 100-unit quantity increase is a percentage change of 100/850, or only 12 percent. The price elasticity of demand is 12%/67%, or 0.2. In other words, *if the demand curve is linear, consumers are more responsive to a given price change when the initial price is high than when it's low.*

Demand becomes less elastic as we move down the curve. At a point halfway down the linear demand curve in Exhibit 2, the elasticity is 1.0. *This halfway point divides a linear demand curve into an elastic upper half and an inelastic lower half.* You can observe a clear relationship between the elasticity of demand in panel (a) and total revenue in panel (b). Notice that where demand is elastic, a decrease in price increases total revenue because the gain in revenue from selling more units (represented by the large blue rectangle) exceeds the loss in revenue from selling all units at the lower price (the small pink rectangle). But where demand is inelastic, a price decrease reduces total revenue because the gain in revenue from selling more units (the small blue rectangle) is less than the loss in revenue from selling all units at the lower price (the large pink rectangle). And where demand is unit elastic, the gain and loss of revenue exactly cancel each other out, so total revenue at that point remains constant (thus, total revenue peaks in the lower panel).

To review, total revenue increases as the price declines until the midpoint of the linear demand curve is reached, where total revenue peaks. In Exhibit 2, total revenue peaks at \$25,000 where quantity demanded equals 500 units. To the right of the midpoint of the demand curve, total revenue declines as the price falls. More generally, regardless of whether demand is straight or curved, there is a consistent relationship between the price elasticity of demand and total revenue: *A price decline increases total revenue if demand is elastic, has no effect on total revenue if demand is unit elastic, and decreases total revenue if demand is inelastic.* Finally, note that a downward-sloping linear demand curve has a constant slope but a varying elasticity, so *the slope of a demand curve is not the same as the price elasticity of demand.*

Constant-Elasticity Demand Curves

Again, price elasticity measures the responsiveness of consumers to a change in price. The shape of the demand curve for a firm's product is key in the pricing and output decision. This responsiveness varies along a linear demand curve unless the demand curve is horizontal or vertical, as in panels (a) and (b) of Exhibit 3. These two demand curves, along with the special demand curve in panel (c), are all called *constant-elasticity demand curves* because the elasticity does not change along the curves.

Perfectly Elastic Demand Curve

perfectly elastic demand curve
A horizontal line reflecting a situation in which any price increase would reduce quantity demanded to zero; the elasticity has an absolute value of infinity

The horizontal demand curve in panel (a) indicates that consumers demand all that is offered for sale at the given price *p* (the quantity actually demanded depends on the amount supplied at that price). If the price rises above *p*, however, quantity demanded drops to zero. This is a **perfectly elastic demand curve**, and its elasticity value is infinity, a number too large to be defined. You may think this an odd sort of demand curve: Consumers, as a result of a small increase in price, go from demanding as much as is

EXHIBIT 3 Constant-Elasticity Demand Curves

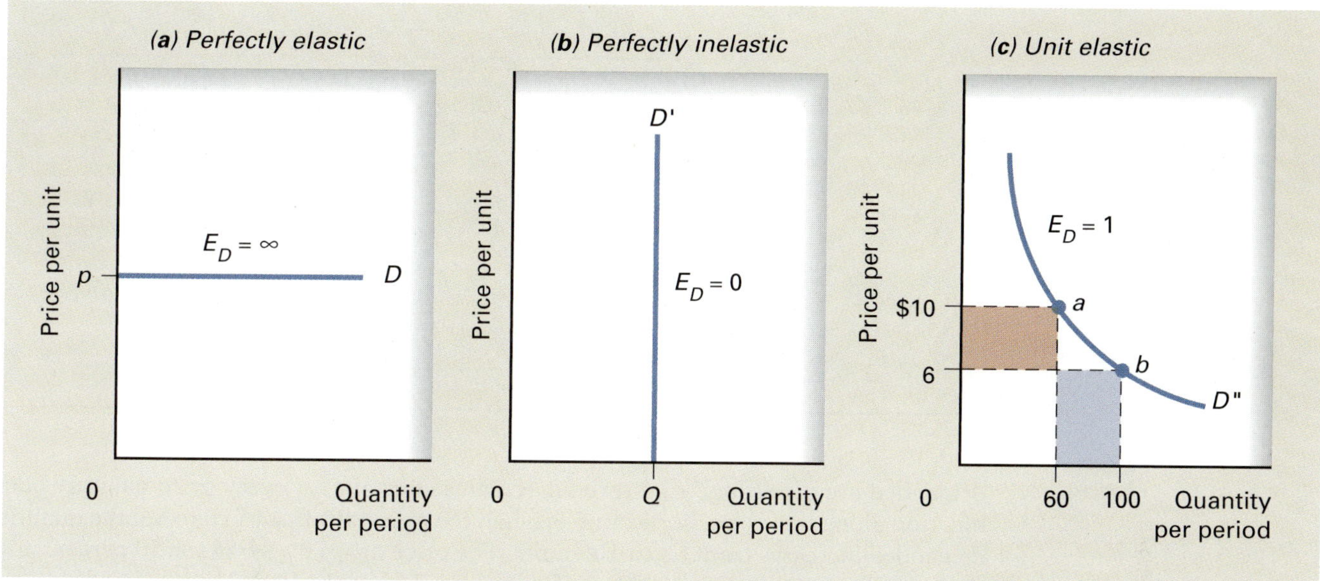

The three panels show constant-elasticity demand curves, so named because the elasticity value does not change along the demand curve. Along the perfectly elastic, or horizontal, demand curve of panel (a), consumers demand all that is offered for sale at price *p*, but demand nothing at a price above *p*. Along the perfectly inelastic, or vertical, demand curve of panel (b), consumers demand amount *Q* regardless of price. Along the unit-elastic demand curve of panel (c), total revenue is the same for each price-quantity combination.

supplied to demanding none of the good. Consumers are so sensitive to price changes that they tolerate no price increase. As you will see in a later chapter, this behavior reflects the demand for the output of any individual producer when many producers supply identical products at the market price of *p*.

Perfectly Inelastic Demand Curve

Along the vertical demand curve in panel (b) of Exhibit 3, quantity demanded does not vary when the price changes. This demand curve expresses consumer sentiment when "price is no object." For example, if you are extremely rich and need insulin to survive, price would be no object. No matter how high the price, you would continue to demand whatever it takes. And if the price of insulin should drop, you would not increase your quantity demanded. Another example of perfectly inelastic demand comes from Shakespeare's play *Richard III*. After his horse is slain in battle, the king, at the mercy of the enemy, cries out, "A horse! A horse! My kingdom for a horse!" The king is willing to pay a high price indeed—his kingdom—for a horse. On a less lofty level, Ben Franklin expressed a similar sentiment when he observed, "Necessity never made a good bargain." Because the percentage change in quantity demanded is zero for any given percentage change in price, the numerical value of the price elasticity is zero. A vertical demand curve is called a **perfectly inelastic demand curve**.

perfectly inelastic demand curve
A vertical line reflecting a situation in which any price change has no effect on the quantity demanded; the elasticity value is zero

unit-elastic demand curve
Everywhere along the demand curve, the percentage change in price causes an equal but offsetting percentage change in quantity demanded, so total revenue remains the same; the elasticity has an absolute value of 1.0

Unit-Elastic Demand Curve

Panel (c) in Exhibit 3 presents a demand curve that is unit elastic everywhere. Along a **unit-elastic demand curve**, any percentage change in price causes the exact opposite percentage change in quantity demanded. Because changes in price and in quantity

EXHIBIT 4 Summary of Price Elasticity of Demand

Effects of a 10 Percent Increase in Price

Absolute Value of Price Elasticity	Type of Demand	What Happens to Quantity Demanded	What Happens to Total Revenue
$E_D = 0$	Perfectly inelastic	No change	Increases by 10 percent
$0 < E_D < 1$	Inelastic	Drops by less than 10 percent	Increases by less than 10 percent
$E_D = 1$	Unit elastic	Drops by 10 percent	No change
$1 < E_D < \infty$	Elastic	Drops by more than 10 percent	Decreases
$E_D = \infty$	Perfectly elastic	Drops to 0	Drops to 0

demanded are offsetting, total revenue remains constant for every price-quantity combination along the curve. For example, when the price falls from $10 to $6, the quantity demanded increases from 60 to 100 units. The price drops by $4/$8, or 50 percent, and the quantity increases by 40/80, or 50 percent. The pink shaded rectangle shows the loss in total revenue from cutting the price; the blue shaded rectangle shows the gain in total revenue from selling more at the lower price. Because the demand curve is unit elastic, the revenue gained from selling more just offsets the revenue lost from lowering the price, so total revenue remains unchanged at $600.

constant-elasticity demand curve
The type of demand that exists when price elasticity is the same everywhere along the curve; the elasticity value is unchanged

Each demand curve in Exhibit 3 is called a **constant-elasticity demand curve** because the elasticity is the same all along the curve. In contrast, the downward-sloping linear demand curve examined earlier had a different elasticity value at each point along the curve. Exhibit 4 lists the absolute values for the five categories of price elasticity we have discussed, summarizing the effects of a 10 percent price increase on quantity demanded and on total revenue. Give this exhibit some thought now, and see if you can draw a demand curve for each category of elasticity.

Determinants of the Price Elasticity of Demand

So far we have explored the technical properties of demand elasticity and discussed why it varies along a downward-sloping demand curve. But we have yet to consider why elasticity is different for different goods. Several factors influence the price elasticity of demand.

Availability of Substitutes

As we saw in Chapter 4, your particular wants can be satisfied in a variety of ways. A rise in the price of pizza makes other food relatively cheaper. If close substitutes are available, an increase in the price of pizza prompts some consumers to buy substitutes. But if nothing else satisfies like pizza, the quantity of pizza demanded does not decline as much. *The greater the availability of substitutes and the more similar these substitutes are to the good in question, the greater that good's price elasticity of demand.*

The number and similarity of substitutes depend on how the good is defined. *The more narrow the definition, the more substitutes and, thus, the more elastic the demand.* For example, the demand for Post Raisin Bran is more elastic than the demand for raisin bran more generally because there are more substitutes for Post Raisin Bran, including Kellogg's Raisin Bran and Total Raisin Bran, than for raisin bran more generally. The demand for raisin bran, however, is more elastic than the demand for breakfast cereals more generally because the consumer has many substitutes for raisin bran, such as cereals made from corn, rice, wheat, or oats, and processed with or without honey, nuts, fruit, or chocolate. To give you some idea of the range of elasticities, the price elasticity of demand for Post Raisin Bran has been estimated to be −2.5 versus −0.9 for all breakfast cereals.[1]

Pro team owners worry that live TV broadcasts cut game attendance, especially now that more households enjoy large-screen HDTVs plus DVRs with playback and slow-motion capabilities. A study of attendance at Scottish Premier League soccer matches found that TV broadcasts cut pay-at-the-gate attendance by 30 percent.[2] This is why home teams black out TV coverage if a game is not sold out before a certain date.

Certain goods—some prescription drugs, for instance—have no close substitutes. The demand for such goods tends to be less elastic than for goods with close substitutes, such as Bayer aspirin. Much advertising is aimed at establishing in the consumer's mind the uniqueness of a particular product—an effort to convince consumers "to accept no substitutes." Why might a firm want to make the demand for its product less elastic?

Share of the Consumer's Budget Spent on the Good

Recall that a higher price reduces quantity demanded in part because a higher price reduces the real spending power of consumer income. Because spending on some goods claims a large share of the consumer's budget, a change in the price of such a good has a substantial impact on the consumer's *ability* to buy it. An increase in the price of housing, for example, reduces the ability to buy housing. The income effect of a higher price reduces the quantity demanded. In contrast, the income effect of an increase in the price of, say, paper towels is trivial because paper towels represent such a tiny share of any budget. *The more important the item is as a share of the consumer's budget, other things constant, the greater is the income effect of a change in price, so the more elastic is the demand for the item.* Hence, the quantity of housing demanded is more responsive to a given percentage change in price than is the quantity of paper towels demanded.

Length of Adjustment Period

Consumers can substitute lower-priced goods for higher-priced goods, but finding substitutes usually takes time. Suppose your college announces a sharp increase in room and board fees, effective next term. Some students will move off campus before that term begins; others may wait until the next academic year. Over time, the college may get fewer applicants and more incoming students will choose off-campus housing. The longer the adjustment period, the greater the consumers' ability to substitute away from relatively higher-priced products toward lower-priced substitutes. Thus, *the longer the period of adjustment, the more responsive the change in quantity demanded is to a given change in price.* Here's another example: Between 1973 and 1974, OPEC (Organization of the Petroleum Exporting Countries) raised gasoline prices 45 percent, but the quantity

1. See Jerry A. Hausman, "The Price Elasticity of Demand for Breakfast Cereal," in *The Economics of New Goods*, T. F. Bresnahan and J. J. Gordon, eds. (Chicago: University of Chicago Press, 1997).
2. Grant Allan and Graeme Roy, "Does Television Crowd Out Spectators?," *Journal of Sports Economics*, 5 (December 2008): 592–605.

EXHIBIT 5 Demand Becomes More Elastic Over Time

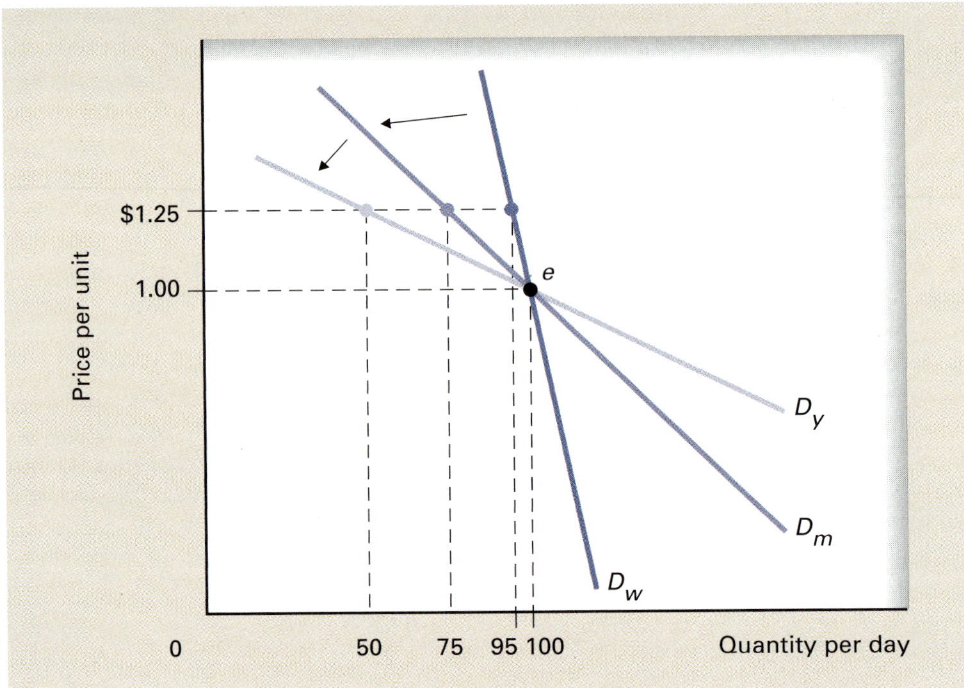

D_w is the demand curve one week after a price increase from $1.00 to $1.25. Along this curve, quantity demanded per day falls from 100 to 95. One month after the price increase, quantity demanded has fallen to 75 along D_m. One year after the price increase, quantity demanded has fallen to 50 along D_y. At any given price, D_y is more elastic than D_m, which is more elastic than D_w.

demanded initially decreased just 8 percent. As more time passed, however, people bought smaller cars and relied more on public transportation. They also bought more energy-efficient appliances and insulated their homes better. Thus, the percentage change in quantity demanded was greater the longer consumers adjusted to the price hike.

Exhibit 5 shows how demand becomes more elastic over time. Given an initial price of $1.00 at point *e*, let D_w be the demand curve one week after a price change; D_m, one month after; and D_y, one year after. Suppose the price increases to $1.25. The more time consumers have to respond to the price increase, the greater the reduction in quantity demanded. The demand curve D_w shows that one week after the price increase, the quantity demanded has not declined much—in this case, from 100 to 95 per day. The demand curve D_m indicates a reduction to 75 per day after one month, and demand curve D_y shows a reduction to 50 per day after one year. Notice that among these demand curves and over the range starting from point *e*, the flatter the demand curve, the more price elastic the demand. Here, elasticity seems linked to the slope because we begin from a common point—the price-quantity combination at point *e*.

Elasticity Estimates

Let's look at some estimates of the price elasticity of demand for particular goods and services. Remember, finding alternatives when the price increases takes time. Thus, when estimating price elasticity, economists often distinguish between a period during which

EXHIBIT 6 Selected Price Elasticities of Demand (Absolute Values)

Product	Short Run	Long Run
Cigarettes (among adults)	—	0.4
Electricity (residential)	0.1	1.9
Air travel	0.1	2.4
Medical care and hospitalization	0.3	0.9
Gasoline	0.4	1.5
Milk	0.4	—
Fish (cod)	0.5	—
Wine	0.7	1.2
Movies	0.9	3.7
Natural gas (residential)	1.4	2.1
Automobiles	1.9	2.2
Chevrolets	—	4.0

Sources: F. Chaloupka, "Rational Addictive Behavior and Cigarette Smoking," *Journal of Political Economy,* (August 1991); Hsaing-tai Cheng and Oral Capps, Jr., "Demand for Fish," *American Journal of Agricultural Economics,* (August 1998); J. Johnson et al., "Short-Run and Long-Run Elasticities for Canadian Consumption of Alcoholic Beverages," *Review of Economics and Statistics,* (February 1992); Douglas Young et al., "Alcohol Consumption, Measurement Error, and Beverage Prices," *Journal of Studies on Alcohol,* (March 2003); J. Griffin, *Energy Conservation in the OECD,* 1980–2000 (Balinger, 1979); and H. Houthakker and L. Taylor, *Consumer Demand in the United States: Analysis and Projections,* 2nd ed. (Harvard University Press, 1970).

consumers have little time to adjust—let's call it the *short run*—and a period during which consumers can more fully adjust to a price change—let's call it the *long run*. Exhibit 6 provides short-run and long-run price elasticity estimates for selected products.

The price elasticity of demand is greater in the long run because consumers have more time to adjust. For example, if the price of electricity rose today, consumers in the short run might cut back a bit in their use of electrical appliances, and those in homes with electric heat might lower the thermostat in winter. Over time, however, consumers would switch to more energy-efficient appliances, insulate their homes better, and perhaps switch from electric heat. So the demand for electricity is more elastic in the long run than in the short run, as shown in Exhibit 6. In fact, in every instance where estimates for both the short run and the long run are available, demand is more elastic in the long run than the short run. Notice also that the demand for Chevrolets is more elastic than the demand for automobiles more generally. Chevrolets have many more substitutes than do automobiles in general. There are no close substitutes for cigarettes, even in the long run, so the demand for cigarettes among adults is price inelastic. Elasticity measures are of more than just academic interest, as discussed in the case study, "Behavioral Economics: Deterring Young Smokers," found at the end of the book.

Price Elasticity of Supply

Prices signal both sides of the market about the relative scarcity of products. Higher prices discourage consumption but encourage production. Lower prices encourage consumption but discourage production. The price elasticity of demand measures how responsive consumers are to a price change. Likewise, the **price elasticity of supply** measures how responsive producers are to a price change. Supply elasticity is calculated in the same way as demand elasticity. In simplest terms, the price elasticity of supply

price elasticity of supply
A measure of the responsiveness of quantity supplied to a price change; the percentage change in quantity supplied divided by the percentage change in price

inelastic supply
A change in price has relatively little effect on quantity supplied; the percentage change in quantity supplied is less than the percentage change in price; the price elasticity of supply is less than 1.0

unit-elastic supply
The percentage change in quantity supplied equals the percentage change in price; the price elasticity of supply equals 1.0

elastic supply
A change in price has a relatively large effect on quantity supplied; the percentage change in quantity supplied exceeds the percentage change in price; the price elasticity of supply exceeds 1.0

equals the percentage change in quantity supplied divided by the percentage change in price. Because a higher price usually increases quantity supplied, the percentage change in price and the percentage change in quantity supplied move in the same direction, so the price elasticity of supply is usually a positive number.

Exhibit 7 depicts a typical upward-sloping supply curve. As you can see, if the price increases from p to p', the quantity supplied increases from q to q'. Price and quantity supplied move in the same direction. Let's look at the elasticity formula for the supply curve. The price elasticity of supply is:

$$E_S = \frac{\Delta q}{(q+q')/2} \div \frac{\Delta p}{(p+p')/2}$$

where Δq is the change in quantity supplied and Δp is the change in price. This is the same formula used to compute the price elasticity of demand except that q here is quantity supplied, not quantity demanded. The terminology for supply elasticity is the same as for demand elasticity: If supply elasticity is less than 1.0, supply is **inelastic**; if it equals 1.0, supply is **unit elastic**; and if it exceeds 1.0, supply is **elastic**.

Constant Elasticity Supply Curves

Again, price elasticity of supply measures the responsiveness of producers to a change in price. This responsiveness varies along a linear supply curve unless the curve is horizontal or vertical, as in panels (a) and (b) of Exhibit 8, or passes through the origin, as in panel (c). These three supply curves are called *constant-elasticity supply curves* because the elasticity does not change along the curves.

EXHIBIT 7 Price Elasticity of Supply

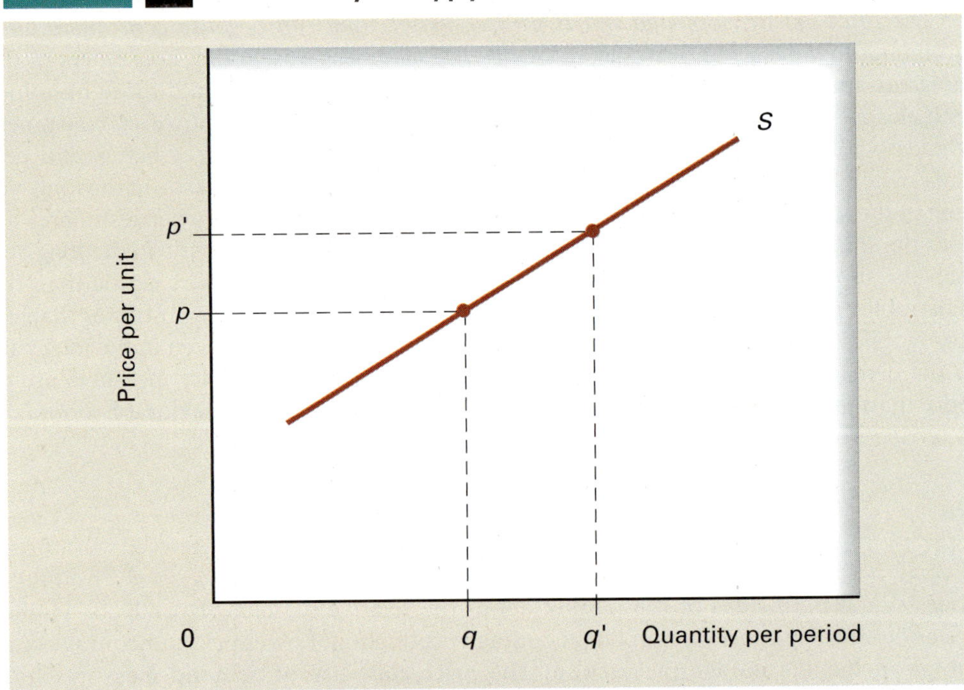

If the price increases from p to p', the quantity supplied increases from q to q'. Price and quantity supplied move in the same direction, so the price elasticity of supply is a positive number.

EXHIBIT 8 Constant-Elasticity Supply Curves

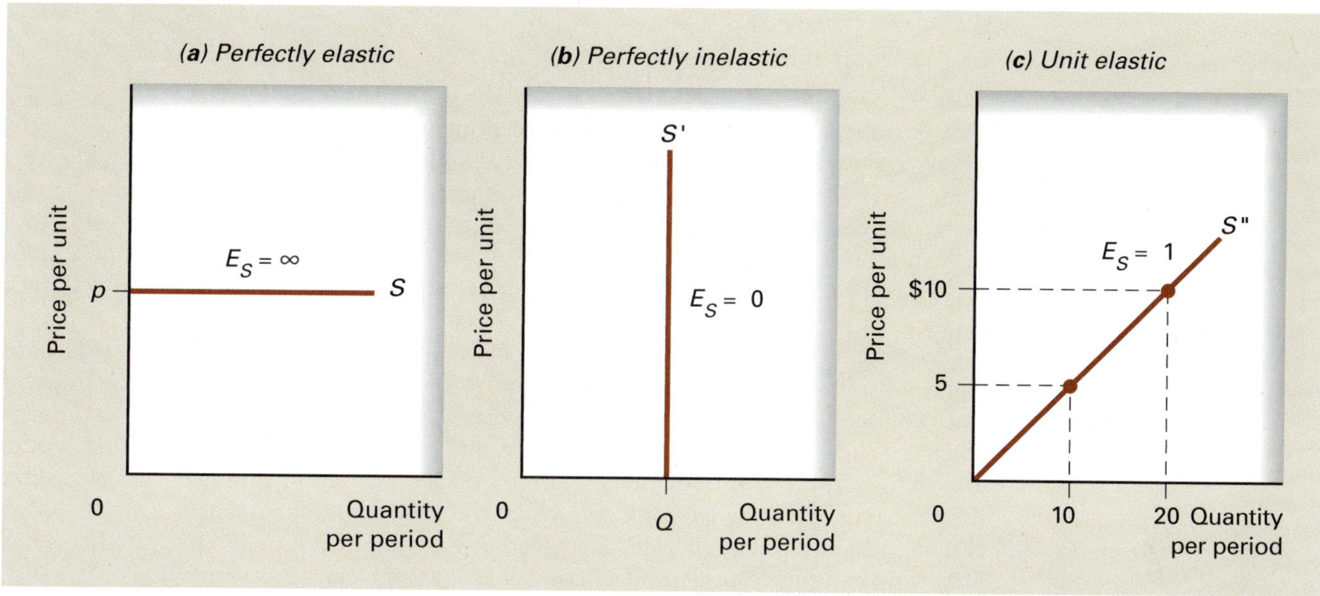

In each of the three panels is a constant-elasticity supply curve, so named because the elasticity value does not change along the curve. Supply curve *S* in panel (a) is perfectly elastic, or horizontal. Along *S*, firms supply any amount of output demanded at price *p*, but supply none at prices below *p*. Supply curve *S′* is perfectly inelastic, or vertical. *S′* shows that the quantity supplied is independent of the price. In panel (c), *S″*, a straight line from the origin, is a unit-elastic supply curve. Any percentage change in price results in the same percentage change in quantity supplied.

Perfectly Elastic Supply Curve

At one extreme is the horizontal supply curve, such as supply curve *S* in panel (a) of Exhibit 8. In this case, producers supply none of the good at a price below *p* but supply any amount at price *p* (the quantity actually supplied at price *p* depends on the amount demanded at that price). Because a tiny increase from a price just below *p* to a price of *p* results in an unlimited quantity supplied, this is called a **perfectly elastic supply curve,** which has a numerical value of infinity. As individual consumers, we typically face perfectly elastic supply curves. When we go to the supermarket, we usually can buy as much as we want at the prevailing price but none at a lower price. Obviously all consumers together cannot buy an unlimited amount at the prevailing price (recall the fallacy of composition from Chapter 1).

perfectly elastic supply curve
A horizontal line reflecting a situation in which any price decrease drops the quantity supplied to zero; the elasticity value is infinity

Perfectly Inelastic Supply Curve

The least responsive relationship is where there is no change in the quantity supplied regardless of the price, as shown by the vertical supply curve *S'* in panel (b) of Exhibit 8. Because the percentage change in quantity supplied is zero, regardless of the change in price, the price elasticity of supply is zero. This is a **perfectly inelastic supply curve.** Any good in fixed supply, such as Picasso paintings, 1995 Dom Perignon champagne, or Cadillacs once owned by Elvis Presley, has a perfectly inelastic supply curve.

Perfectly inelastic supply curve
A vertical line reflecting a situation in which a price change has no effect on the quantity supplied; the elasticity value is zero

Unit-Elastic Supply Curve

Any supply curve that is a straight line from the origin—such as *S*" in panel (c) of Exhibit 8—is a **unit-elastic supply curve.** This means a percentage change in price always generates an identical percentage change in quantity supplied. For example,

unit-elastic supply curve
A percentage change in price causes an identical percentage change in quantity supplied; depicted by a supply curve that is a straight line from the origin; the elasticity value equals 1.0

along S'' a doubling of the price results in a doubling of the quantity supplied. Note that unit elasticity is based not on the slope of the line but on the fact that the linear supply curve is a ray from the origin.

Determinants of Supply Elasticity

The elasticity of supply indicates how responsive producers are to a change in price. Their response depends on how easy it is to alter quantity supplied when the price changes. If the cost of supplying additional units rises sharply as output expands, then a higher price causes little increase in quantity supplied, so supply tends to be inelastic. But if the marginal cost rises slowly as output expands, the lure of a higher price prompts a large increase in quantity supplied. In this case, supply is more elastic.

One determinant of supply elasticity is the length of the adjustment period under consideration. Just as demand becomes more elastic over time as consumers adjust to price changes, supply also becomes more elastic over time as producers adjust to price changes. The longer the adjustment period under consideration, the more able producers are to adapt to a price change. Exhibit 9 presents different supply curves for each of three periods. S_w is the supply curve when the period of adjustment is a week. As you can see, a higher price generates little response in quantity supplied because firms have little time to adjust. This supply curve is inelastic between \$1.00 and \$1.25.

EXHIBIT 9 Supply Becomes More Elastic Over Time

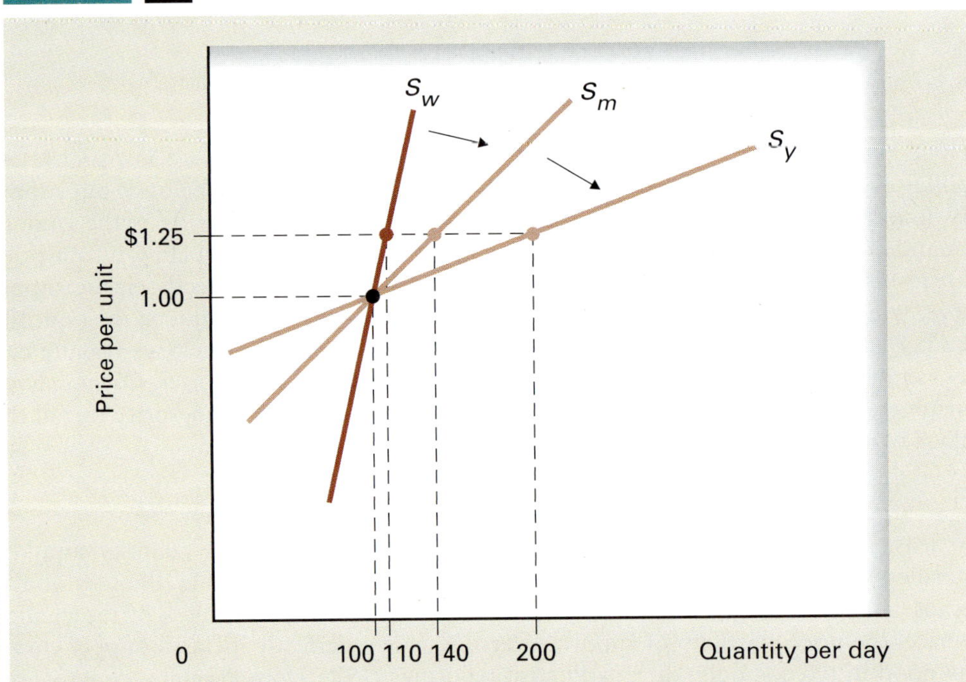

The supply curve one week after a price increase, S_w, is less elastic, at a given price, than the supply curve one month later, S_m, which is less elastic than the supply curve one year later, S_y. Given a price increase from \$1.00 to \$1.25, quantity supplied per day increases to 110 units after one week, to 140 units after one month, and to 200 units after one year.

S_m is the supply curve when the adjustment period under consideration is a month. Firms have more time to vary output. Thus, supply is more elastic when the adjustment period is a month than when it's a week. Supply is yet more elastic when the adjustment period is a year, as is shown by S_y. As the adjustment period lengthens, the supply response increases. For example, if the price of oil increases, oil producers in the short run can try to pump more from existing wells, but in the long run, a higher price stimulates more exploration. Research confirms the positive link between the price elasticity of supply and the length of the adjustment period. *The elasticity of supply is typically greater the longer the period of adjustment.*

The ability to increase quantity supplied in response to a higher price differs across industries. For example, oil was discovered on Alaska's north slope in 1967; but oil did not begin to flow south until a decade later. More generally, the response time is slower for suppliers of oil, electricity, and timber (where expansion may take years, if not decades) than for suppliers of window-washing services, lawn maintenance, and hot-dog vending (where expansion may take only days).

Other Elasticity Measures

Price elasticities of demand and supply are frequently used in economic analysis, but two other elasticity measures also provide valuable information.

Income Elasticity of Demand

What happens to the demand for new cars, fresh vegetables, or computer software if consumer income increases by, say, 10 percent? The answer is of great interest to producers because it helps them predict the effect of changing consumer income on quantity sold and on total revenue. The **income elasticity of demand** measures how responsive demand is to a change in consumer income. Specifically, *the income elasticity of demand measures the percentage change in demand divided by the percentage change in income that caused it.*

income elasticity of demand
The percentage change in demand divided by the percentage change in consumer income; the value is positive for normal goods and negative for inferior goods

As noted in Chapter 4, the demand for some products, such as used furniture and used clothing, actually declines, or shifts leftward, as income increases. Thus, the income elasticity of demand for such goods is negative. Goods with income elasticities less than zero are called *inferior goods*. But the demand for most goods increases, or shifts rightward, as income increases. These are called *normal goods* and have income elasticities greater than zero.

Let's take a closer look at normal goods. Suppose demand increases as income increases but by a smaller percentage than income increases. In such cases, the income elasticity is greater than 0 but less than 1. For example, people buy more food as their incomes rise, but the percentage increase in demand is less than the percentage increase in income. Normal goods with income elasticities less than 1 are called *income inelastic*. *Necessities* such as food, housing, and clothing often have income elasticities less than 1. Goods with income elasticity greater than 1 are called *income elastic*. *Luxuries* such as high-end cars, vintage wines, and meals at upscale restaurants have income elasticities greater than 1. By the way, the terms *inferior goods, necessities,* and *luxuries* are not value judgments about the merits of particular goods; these terms are simply convenient ways of classifying economic behavior.

Exhibit 10 presents income elasticity estimates for some goods and services. The figures indicate, for example, that as income increases, consumers spend proportionately

EXHIBIT 10 Selected Income Elasticities of Demand

Product	Income Elasticity	Product	Income Elasticity
Wine	5.03	Physicians' services	0.75
Private education	2.46	Coca-Cola	0.68
Automobiles	2.45	Beef	0.62
Owner-occupied housing	1.49	Food	0.51
Furniture	1.48	Coffee	0.51
Dental service	1.42	Cigarettes	0.50
Restaurant meals	1.40	Gasoline and oil	0.48
Spirits ("hard" liquor)	1.21	Rental housing	0.43
Shoes	1.10	Pork	0.18
Chicken	1.06	Beer	−0.09
Clothing	0.92	Flour	−0.36

Sources: Ivan Bloor, "Food for Thought," *Economic Review,* (September 1999); F. Gasmi et al., "Econometric Analysis of Collusive Behavior in a Soft-Drink Market," *Journal of Economics and Management Strategy,* (Summer 1992); X. M. Gao et al., "A Microeconomic Model Analysis of U.S. Consumer Demand for Alcoholic Beverages," *Applied Economics,* (January 1995); H. Houthakker and L. Taylor, *Consumer Demand in the United States: Analyses and Projections,* 2nd ed. (Harvard University Press, 1970); C. Huang et al., "The Demand for Coffee in the United States, 1963–77," *Quarterly Review of Economics and Business,* (Summer 1980); and G. Brester and M. Wohlgenant, "Estimating Interrelated Demands for Meats Using New Measures for Ground and Table Cut Beef," *American Journal of Agricultural Economics,* (November 1991).

more on wine, restaurant meals, and owner-occupied housing. Spending on food and rental housing also increases as income increases, but less than proportionately. Spending on beer declines as income increases. So as income rises, the demand for restaurant meals increases more in percentage terms than does the demand for food, and the demand for owner-occupied housing increases more in percentage terms than does the demand for rental housing. The demand for wine increases sharply, while the demand for beer declines. Flour also has negative income elasticity. According to these estimates, beer and flour are inferior goods.

As we have seen, the demand for food is income inelastic. The demand for food also tends to be price inelastic. This combination of income and price inelasticity creates special problems for farmers, as discussed in the case study, "Bringing Theory to Life: The Market for Food and the 'Farm Problem,'" found at the end of the book.

Cross-Price Elasticity of Demand

cross-price elasticity of demand
The percentage change in the demand of one good divided by the percentage change in the price of another good; it's positive for substitutes, negative for complements, and zero for unrelated goods

A firm that produces an entire line of products has a special interest in how a change in the price of one item affects the demand for another. For example, the Coca-Cola Company needs to know how changing the price of Cherry Coke affects sales of Classic Coke. The company also needs to know the relationship between the price of Coke and the demand for Pepsi and vice versa. Likewise, Apple needs to know how changing the price of one iPhone model affects the demand for the other iPhone models. The responsiveness of the demand for one good to changes in the price of another good is called the **cross-price elasticity of demand.** This is defined as the percentage change in the demand of one good divided by the percentage change in the price of another good. Its numerical value can be positive, negative, or zero, depending on whether the two goods in question are substitutes, complements, or unrelated, respectively.

Substitutes

If an increase in the price of one good leads to an increase in the demand for another good, their cross-price elasticity is positive and the two goods are *substitutes*. For example, an increase in the price of Coke, other things constant, shifts the demand for Pepsi rightward, so the two are substitutes. The cross-price elasticity between Coke and Pepsi has been estimated at about 0.7, indicating that a 10 percent increase in the price of one increases the demand for the other by 7 percent.[3]

Complements

If an increase in the price of one good leads to a decrease in the demand for another, their cross-price elasticity is negative and the goods are *complements*. For example, an increase in the price of gasoline, other things constant, shifts the demand for tires leftward because people drive less and replace their tires less frequently. Gasoline and tires have a negative cross-price elasticity and are complements.

To Review: The cross-price elasticity of demand is positive for substitutes and negative for complements. Most pairs of goods selected at random are unrelated, so their cross-price elasticity is zero, such as socks and sushi.

Conclusion

Because this chapter has been more quantitative than earlier ones, the mechanics may have overshadowed the intuitive appeal and neat simplicity of elasticity. *Elasticity measures the willingness and ability of buyers and sellers to alter their behavior in response to changes in their economic circumstances.* Firms try to estimate the price elasticity of demand for their products. Governments also have an ongoing interest in various elasticities. For example, state governments want to know the effect of an increase in the sales tax on total tax receipts, and local governments want to know how an increase in income affects the demand for real estate and thus the revenue generated by a given property tax rate. International groups are interested in elasticities; for example, OPEC is concerned about the price elasticity of demand for oil—in the short run and in the long run. Because a corporation often produces an entire line of products, it also has a special interest in cross-price elasticities. Some corporate economists estimate elasticities for a living. The appendix to this chapter shows how price elasticities of demand and supply shed light on who ultimately pays a tax.

3. F. Gasmi, J. J. Laffont, and Q. Vuong, "Econometric Analysis of Collusive Behavior in a Soft-Drink Market," *Journal of Economics and Management Strategy*, 1 (June 1992): 277–311.

Summary

1. The price elasticities of demand and supply show how responsive buyers and sellers are to changes in the price of a good. More elastic means more responsive.
2. When the percentage change in quantity demanded exceeds the percentage change in price, demand is price elastic. If demand is price elastic, a price increase reduces total revenue and a price decrease increases total revenue. When the percentage change in quantity demanded is less than the percentage change in price, demand is price inelastic. If demand is price inelastic, a higher price increases total revenue and a lower price reduces total revenue. When the percentage change in quantity demanded equals the percentage change in price, demand is unit elastic; a price change does not affect total revenue.
3. Along a straight-lined, downward-sloping demand curve, the elasticity of demand declines steadily as the price falls. A constant-elasticity demand curve, on the other hand, has the same elasticity everywhere.
4. Demand is more elastic (a) the greater the availability of substitutes; (b) the more narrowly the good is defined; (c) the larger the share of the consumer's budget spent on the good; and (d) the longer the time period consumers have to adjust to a change in price.
5. The price elasticity of supply measures the responsiveness of quantity supplied to price changes. This depends on how much the marginal cost of production changes as output changes. If marginal cost rises sharply as output expands, quantity supplied is less responsive to price increases and is thus less elastic. Also, the longer the time period producers have to adjust to price changes, the more elastic the supply.
6. Income elasticity of demand measures the responsiveness of demand to changes in consumer income. Income elasticity is positive for normal goods and negative for inferior goods.
7. The cross-price elasticity of demand measures the impact of a change in the price of one good on the demand for another good. Two goods are defined as substitutes, complements, or unrelated, depending on whether their cross-price elasticity of demand is positive, negative, or zero, respectively.

Key Concepts

Questions for Review

1. Categories of Price Elasticity of Demand For each of the following absolute values of price elasticity of demand, indicate whether demand is elastic, inelastic, perfectly elastic, perfectly inelastic, or unit elastic. In addition, determine what would happen to total revenue if a firm raised its price in each elasticity range identified.
   a. $E_D = 2.5$
   b. $E_D = 1.0$
   c. $E_D = \infty$
   d. $E_D = 0.8$
2. Elasticity and Total Revenue Explain the relationship between the price elasticity of demand and total revenue.
3. Price Elasticity and the Linear Demand Curve How is it possible for many price elasticities to be associated with a single demand curve?
4. Determinants of Price Elasticity Why is the price elasticity of demand for Coca-Cola greater than the price elasticity of demand for soft drinks generally?
5. Determinants of Price Elasticity Would the price elasticity of demand for electricity be more elastic over a shorter or a longer period of time?
6. Determinants of Price Elasticity What factors help determine the price elasticity of demand? What factors help determine the price elasticity of supply?
7. Cross-Price Elasticity Using demand and supply curves, predict the impact on the price and quantity demanded of Good 1 of an increase in the price of Good 2 if the two goods are substitutes. What if the two goods are complements?

8. Other Elasticity Measures Complete each of the following sentences:

   a. The income elasticity of demand measures, for a given price, the ________ in quantity demanded divided by the ________ income from which it resulted.

   b. If a decrease in the price of one good causes a decrease in demand for another good, the two goods are ________.

   c. If the value of the cross-price elasticity of demand between two goods is approximately zero, they are considered ________.

Problems and Exercises

9. Calculating Price Elasticity of Demand Suppose that 50 units of a good are demanded at a price of $1 per unit. A reduction in price to $0.20 results in an increase in quantity demanded to 70 units. Show that these data yield a price elasticity of 0.25. By what percentage would a 10 percent rise in the price reduce the quantity demanded, assuming price elasticity remains constant along the demand curve?

10. Price Elasticity and Total Revenue Fill in the blanks for each price-quantity combination listed in the following table. What relationship have you depicted?

P	Q	Price Elasticity	Total Revenue
$9	1	______	______
$8	2	______	______
$7	3	______	______
$6	4	______	______
$5	5	______	______
$4	6	______	______
$3	7	______	______
$2	8	______	______

11. Case Study: Deterring Young Smokers (See page 708.) Why is the price elasticity of demand for cigarettes among teenagers greater than it is among those 20 and over?

12. Income Elasticity of Demand Calculate the income elasticity of demand for each of the following goods:

	Quantity Demanded When Income Is $10,000	Quantity Demanded When Income Is $20,000
Good 1	10	25
Good 2	4	5
Good 3	3	2

13. Price Elasticity of Supply Calculate the price elasticity of supply for each of the following combinations of price and quantity supplied. In each case, determine whether supply is elastic, inelastic, perfectly elastic, perfectly inelastic, or unit elastic.

    a. Price falls from $2.25 to $1.75; quantity supplied falls from 600 units to 400 units.

    b. Price falls from $2.25 to $1.75; quantity supplied falls from 600 units to 500 units.

    c. Price falls from $2.25 to $1.75; quantity supplied remains at 600 units.

    d. Price increases from $1.75 to $2.25; quantity supplied increases from 466.67 units to 600 units.

Use the following diagram to answer the next two questions.

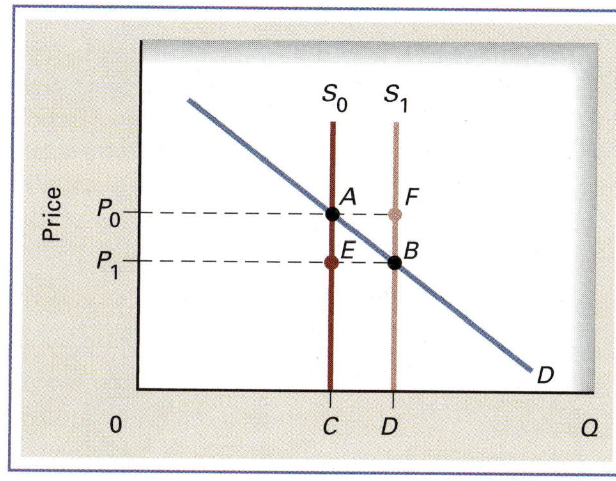

14. Case Study: The Market for Food and the "Farm Problem" (See page 709.) Interpret this diagram as showing the market demand and supply curves for agricultural products. Suppose that demand is inelastic over the relevant range of prices and supply increased from S_0 to S_1. What areas in the figure would you use to illustrate the net change in farmers' total revenue as a result of the increase in supply?

15. Case Study: The Market for Food and the "Farm Problem" (See page 709.) Again suppose that this diagram represents the market for agricultural products and that supply has increased from S_0 to S_1. To aid farmers, the federal government decides to stabilize the price at P_0 by buying up surplus farm products. Show on the diagram how much this would cost the government. By how much would farm income change compared to what it would have been without government intervention?

16. Cross-Price Elasticity Rank the following in order of increasing (from negative to positive) cross-price elasticity of demand with coffee. Explain your reasoning.

    Bleach

    Tea

    Cream

    Cola

Appendix

Price Elasticity and Tax Incidence

A contributing factor to the Revolutionary War was a British tax on tea imported by the American Colonies. The tea tax led to the Boston Tea Party, during which colonists dumped tea leaves into Boston Harbor. There was confusion about who would ultimately pay such a tax: Would it be paid by suppliers, demanders, or both? As you will see, tax incidence—that is, who pays a tax—depends on the price elasticities of demand and supply.

Demand Elasticity and Tax Incidence

Panel (a) of Exhibit 11 depicts the market for tea leaves, with demand *D* and supply *S*. Before the tax is imposed, the intersection of demand and supply yields a market price of \$1.00 per ounce and a market quantity of

EXHIBIT 11 Effects of Price Elasticity of Demand on Tax Incidence

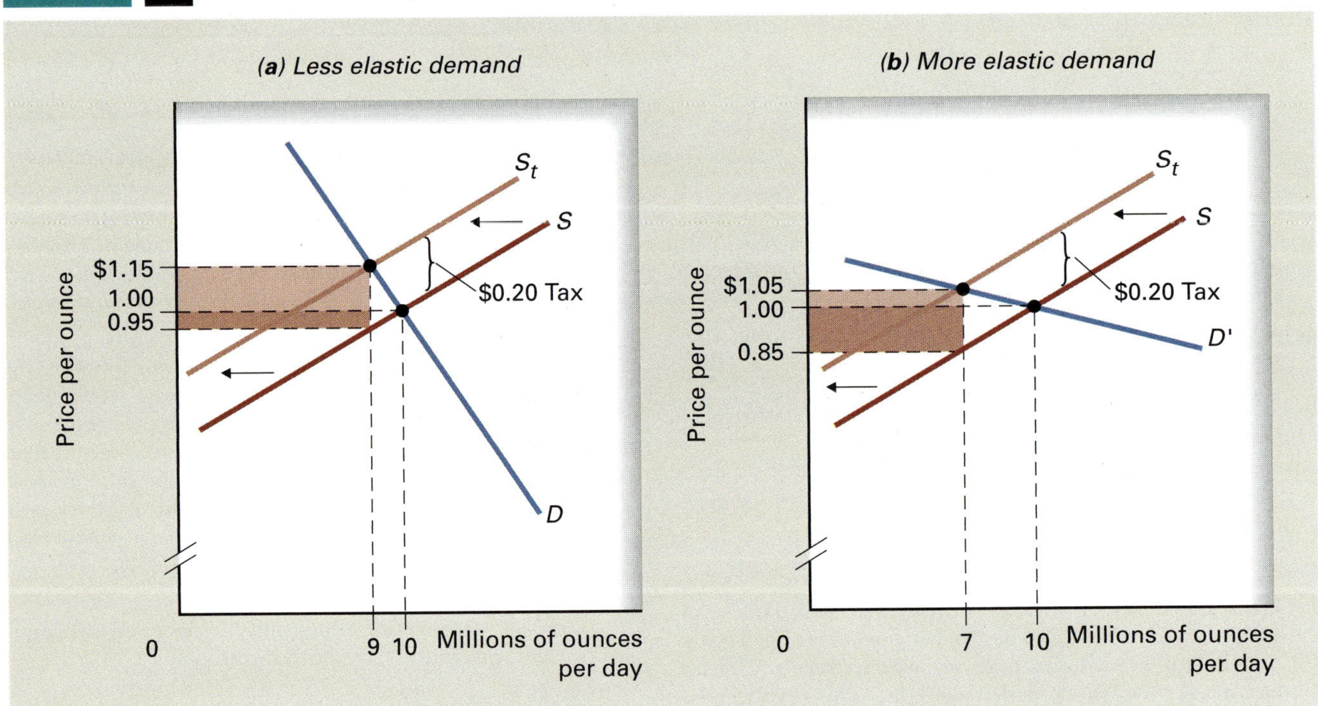

The imposition of a \$0.20-per-ounce tax on tea shifts the supply curve leftward from *S* to S_t. In panel (a), which has a less elastic demand curve, the market price rises from \$1.00 to \$1.15 per ounce and the market quantity falls from 10 million to 9 million ounces. In panel (b), which has a more elastic demand curve, the same tax leads to an increase in price from \$1.00 to \$1.05; market quantity falls from 10 million to 7 million ounces. The more elastic the demand curve, the more the tax is paid by producers in the form of a lower net-of-tax receipt.

10 million ounces per day. Now suppose a tax of $0.20 is imposed on each ounce sold. Recall that the supply curve represents the amount that producers are willing and able to supply at each price. Because the government now collects $0.20 in tax for each ounce sold, that amount must be added to the original supply curve to get a supply curve that includes the tax. Thus, the shift of the supply curve from S to S_t reflects the decrease in supply resulting from the tax. *The effect of a tax on tea is to decrease the supply by the amount of the tax.* The demand curve remains the same because nothing happened to demand; only the quantity demanded changes.

The result of the tax in panel (a) is to raise the equilibrium price from $1.00 to $1.15 and to decrease the equilibrium quantity from 10 million to 9 million ounces. As a result of the tax, consumers pay $1.15, or $0.15 more per ounce, and producers receive $0.95 after the tax, or $0.05 less per ounce. Thus, consumers pay $0.15 of the $0.20 tax as a higher price, and producers pay $0.05 as a lower receipt.

The shaded rectangle of panel (a) shows the total tax collected, which equals the tax per ounce of $0.20 times the 9 million ounces sold, for a total of $1.8 million in tax revenue per day. You can see that the original price line at $1 divides the shaded rectangle into two portions—an upper portion (light pink) showing the share of the tax paid by consumers through a higher price and a lower portion (dark pink) showing the tax paid by producers through a lower net-of-tax receipt.

The same situation is depicted in panel (b) of Exhibit 11, except that demand is more elastic than in the left panel. Consumers in panel (b) cut their quantity demanded more sharply in response to a price change, so producers cannot as easily pass the tax along at a higher price. The tax increases the price by $0.05, to $1.05, and the net-of-tax receipt to suppliers declines by $0.15 to $0.85. Total tax revenue equals $0.20 per ounce times 7 million ounces sold, or $1.4 million per day. Again, the upper portion of the shaded rectangle shows the share of the tax paid by consumers through a higher price, and the lower portion shows the share paid by producers through a lower net-of-tax receipt. The tax is the difference between the amount consumers pay and the amount producers receive.

More generally, as long as the supply curve slopes upward, the more price elastic the demand, the more tax producers pay as a lower net-of-tax receipt and the less consumers bear as a higher price. Also notice that the amount sold decreases more in panel (b) than in panel (a): Other things constant, the total tax revenue declines more when demand is more elastic. Because tax revenue falls as the price elasticity of demand increases, governments around the world tend to tax products with inelastic demand, such as cigarettes, liquor, gasoline, gambling, salt, coffee, and, yes, tea.

Supply Elasticity and Tax Incidence

The effect of the elasticity of supply on tax incidence is shown in Exhibit 12. The same demand curve appears in both panels, but the supply curve is more elastic in panel (a). Again we begin with an equilibrium price of $1.00 per ounce and an equilibrium quantity of 10 million ounces of tea leaves per day. Once the sales tax of $0.20 per ounce is imposed, supply decreases in both panels to reflect the tax. Notice that in panel (a), the price rises to $1.15, or $0.15 above the pretax price of $1.00, while in panel (b), the price increases by only $0.05. Thus, more of the tax is passed on to consumers in panel (a), where supply is more elastic. The more easily suppliers can cut production in response to a newly imposed tax, the more of the tax consumers pay. More generally, as long as the demand curve slopes downward, *the more elastic the supply, the less tax producers pay and the more consumers pay.*

We conclude that *the less elastic the demand and the more elastic the supply, the greater the share of the tax paid by consumers.* The side of the market that's more nimble (that is, more price elastic) in adjusting to a price increase is more able to stick the other side of the market with more of the tax.

EXHIBIT 12 Effects of Price Elasticity of Supply on Tax Incidence

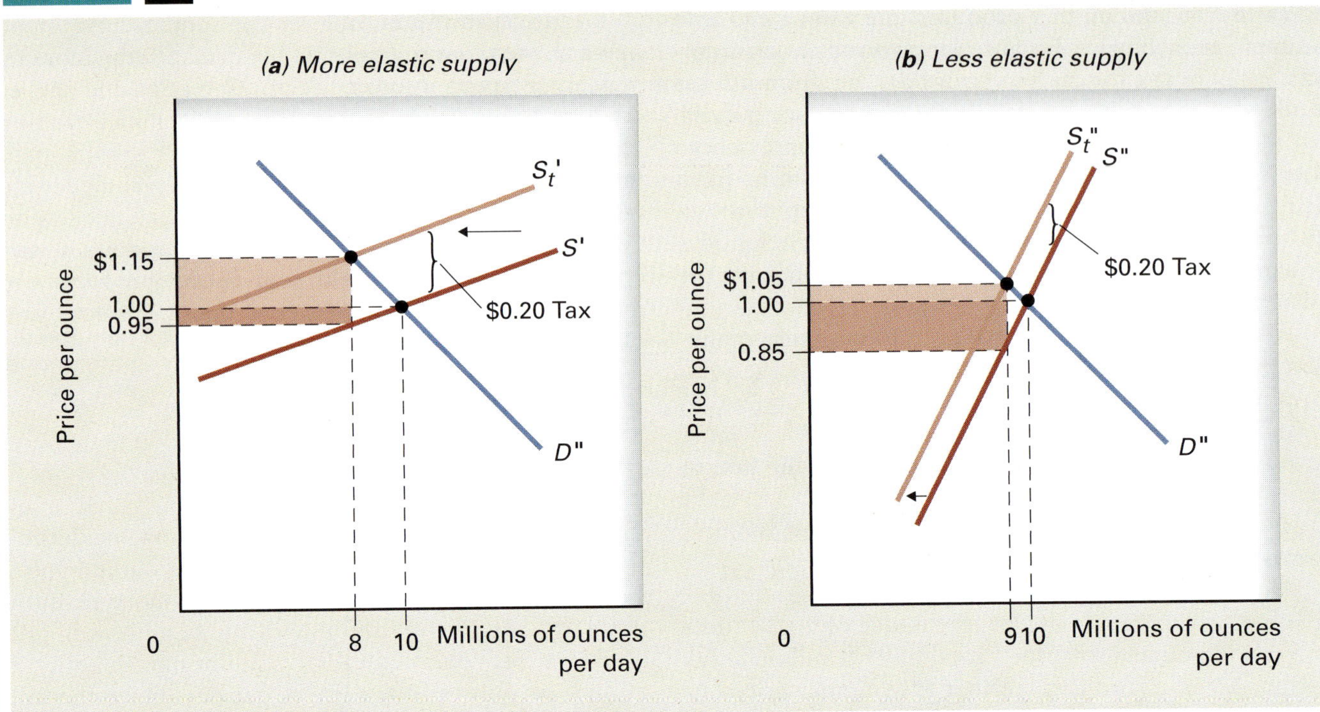

The imposition of a $0.20-per-ounce tax on tea shifts leftward both the more elastic supply curve in panel (a) and the less elastic supply curve of panel (b). In panel (a) the market price rises from $1.00 to $1.15 per ounce. In panel (b), the price rises only to $1.05 per ounce. Thus, the more elastic the supply curve, the more the tax is paid by consumers as a higher price.

Appendix Questions

1. The claim is often made that a tax on a specific good is simply passed on to consumers. Under what conditions of demand and supply elasticities does this occur? Under what conditions is little of the tax passed on to consumers?
2. Suppose a tax is imposed on a good with a perfectly elastic supply curve.
   a. Who pays the tax?
   b. Using demand and supply curves, show how much tax is collected.
   c. How would this tax revenue change if the supply curve becomes less elastic?
3. During the 1980s, the U.S. Congress imposed a high sales tax on yachts, figuring that the rich could afford to pay for this luxury. But so many jobs were lost in the boat-building industry that the measure was finally repealed. What did Congress get wrong in imposing this luxury tax?

Consumer Choice and Demand

6

Fuse/Jupiter Images

- Why are newspapers sold in vending machines that allow you to take more than one?
- How much do you eat when you can eat all you want?
- Why don't restaurants allow doggie bags with their all-you-can-eat specials?
- What cures cabin fever and spring fever?
- Why is water cheaper than diamonds even though water is essential to life while diamonds are simply bling?

To answer these and other questions, we take a closer look at consumer demand, a key building block in economics.

You have already learned two reasons why demand curves slope downward. The first is the *substitution effect* of a price change. When the price of a good falls, consumers substitute that now-cheaper good for other goods. The second is the *income effect* of a price change. When the price of a good falls, real incomes increase, boosting consumers' ability to buy more.

Demand is so important that it needs more attention. This chapter develops the law of demand based on the utility, or satisfaction, of consumption. As usual, the assumption is that you and other consumers try to maximize utility, or satisfaction. The point of this chapter is not to teach you how to maximize utility—that comes naturally. But learning the theory behind your behavior will help you understand the implications of that behavior, making predictions more accurate.

Topics discussed include:

- Total and marginal utility
- Law of diminishing marginal utility
- Measuring utility
- Utility-maximizing condition
- Consumer surplus
- Role of time in demand
- Time price of goods

Utility Analysis

Suppose you and a friend are dining out. After dinner, your friend asks how you liked your meal. You wouldn't say, "I liked mine twice as much as you liked yours." Nor would you say, "It deserves a rating of 86 on the Consumer Satisfaction Index." The utility, or satisfaction, you derive from that meal cannot be compared with another person's experience, nor can your utility be measured based on some uniform standard. But you might say something such as, "I liked it better than my last meal here" or "I liked it better than campus food." More generally, you can say whether one of your experiences is more satisfying than another. Even if you say nothing about your likes and dislikes, we can draw conclusions about your preferences by observing your behavior. For example, we can conclude that you prefer apples to oranges if, when the two are priced the same, you buy apples every time.

Tastes and Preferences

As introduced in Chapter 3, *utility* is the sense of pleasure, or satisfaction, that comes from consumption. Utility is subjective. The utility you derive from a particular good, service, or activity depends on your *tastes and preferences*—your likes and dislikes in consumption. Some things are extremely appealing to you and others are not. You may not understand, for example, why someone would pay good money for sharks' fin soup, calves' brains, polka music, or martial arts movies. Why are most baby carriages sold in the United States navy blue, whereas they are yellow in Italy and chartreuse in Germany? And why do Australians favor chicken-flavored potato chips and chicken-flavored salt?

As noted in Chapter 4, your desires for food and drink are largely biological, as is your desire for comfort, rest, shelter, friendship, love, status, personal safety, and a pleasant environment. Your family background shapes some of your tastes, such as food preferences. Other influences include your culture, peer pressure, and religious convictions. So economists can say something about the origin of tastes, but they claim no particular expertise. *Economists assume simply that tastes are given and are relatively stable—that is, different people may have different tastes, but an individual's tastes are not constantly in flux.* To be sure, tastes for some products do change over time. Here are four examples: (1) over the last two decades, hiking boots and work boots replaced running shoes as everyday footwear among many college students, (2) Americans began consuming leaner cuts of beef after a report linked the fat in red meat to a greater risk of cancer, (3) because of the decline in the popularity of baseball cards, the number of shops that sell and trade these cards fell from about

10,000 in the early 1990s to less than 1,600 by 2010; and (4) the increased appeal of locally grown produce has tripled the number of farmers markets in the United States since 1995.

Although some tastes do change over time, economists believe they are stable enough to allow us to examine relationships such as that between price and quantity demanded. If tastes were not relatively stable, then we could not reasonably make the other-things-constant assumption required for demand analysis. We could not even draw a demand curve.

The Law of Diminishing Marginal Utility

Suppose it's a hot summer day and you are extremely thirsty after running four miles. You pour yourself an 8-ounce glass of ice water. That first glass is wonderful, and it puts a serious dent in your thirst. The next glass is not quite as wonderful, but it is still pretty good. The third one is just fair; and the fourth glass you barely finish.

What can we say about the *utility,* or satisfaction, you get from water? Let's first distinguish between *total utility* and *marginal utility*. **Total utility** is the total satisfaction you derive from consumption. In this example, total utility is the total satisfaction you get from four glasses of water. **Marginal utility** is the change in total utility resulting from a one-unit change in consumption. For example, the marginal utility of a third glass of water is the change in total utility resulting from drinking that third glass.

total utility
The total satisfaction you derive from consumption; this could refer to either your total utility of consuming a particular good or your total utility from all consumption

marginal utility
The change in your total utility from a one-unit change in your consumption of a good

law of diminishing marginal utility
The more of a good a person consumes per period, the smaller the increase in total utility from consuming one more unit, other things constant

Your experience with water reflects an economic law—the **law of diminishing marginal utility**. This law states that the more of a good you consume per period, other things constant, the smaller the increase in your total utility from additional consumption—that is, the smaller the marginal utility of each additional unit consumed. The marginal utility you derive from each additional glass of water declines as you drink more. You enjoy the first glass a lot, but each additional glass provides less and less marginal utility. If forced to drink a fifth glass, you wouldn't like it; your marginal utility would be negative—you would experience *disutility*.

Diminishing marginal utility is a feature of all consumption. A second foot-long sub sandwich at one meal, for most people, would provide little or no marginal utility. You might still enjoy a second movie on Friday night, but a third would probably be too much to take. In fact, almost anything repeated enough could become torture, such as being forced to watch the same movie or listen to the same song over and over and over. Yes, variety is the spice of life.

A long, cold winter spent cooped up inside can cause "cabin fever." Each additional cold day brings more disutility. But the fever breaks with the arrival of the first warm day of spring, which is something special. That first warm, glorious day causes such delirious joy that this jump in marginal utility has its own fevered name—"spring fever." Spring fever is eventually "cured" by many warm days like the first. By the time August rolls around, you attach much less marginal utility to yet another warm day.

For some goods, the drop in marginal utility with additional consumption is greater. A second copy of the same daily newspaper would likely provide you no marginal utility (in fact, the design of newspaper vending machines relies on the fact that people will take no more than one).[1] Likewise, a second viewing of the same movie at one sitting usually yields no additional utility. More generally, expressions such as "Been there, done that" and "Same old, same old" convey the idea that, for many activities, things

1. This example appears in Marshall Jevons, *The Fatal Equilibrium* (Cambridge, Mass.: MIT Press, 1985).

start to get old fast. Restaurants depend on the law of diminishing marginal utility when they hold all-you-can-eat specials—and no doggie bags allowed, because the deal is all you can eat now, not now and over the next few days.

Measuring Utility

So far, the description of utility has used such words as *wonderful*, *good*, and *fair*. The analysis can't be pushed very far with such subjective language. To predict consumer behavior, we need to develop a consistent way of viewing utility.

Units of Utility

Let's go back to the water example. Although there really is no objective way of measuring utility, if pressed, you could be more specific about how much you enjoyed each glass of water. For example, you might say the second glass was half as good as the first, the third was half as good as the second, the fourth was half as good as the third, and you passed up a fifth glass because you expected no positive utility. To get a handle on this, let's assign arbitrary numbers to the utility you get from water, so the pattern reflects your expressed level of satisfaction. Let's say the first glass provides you with 40 units of utility, the second with 20, the third with 10, and the fourth with 5. A fifth glass, if you were forced to drink it, would cause negative utility, or disutility—in this case, say, −2 units. *Developing numerical values for utility allows us to be more specific about the utility of consumption.* If it would help, you could think of these units more playfully as thrills, kicks, or jollies—as in, getting your kicks from consumption.

By attaching a numerical measure to utility, we can compare the total utility a particular consumer gets from different goods as well as the marginal utility that a consumer gets from additional consumption. Thus, we can employ units of utility to evaluate a consumer's preferences. Note, however, that we cannot compare utility levels across consumers. *Each person has a uniquely subjective utility scale.*

The first column of Exhibit 1 lists possible quantities of water you might consume after running four miles on a hot day. The second column presents the total utility derived from that consumption, and the third column shows the marginal utility of each additional glass of water. Recall that marginal utility is the change in total utility from consuming an additional unit of the good. You can see from the second column that total utility increases with each of the first four glasses but by smaller and smaller amounts. The third column shows that the first glass of water yields 40 units of utility, the second glass yields an additional 20 units, and so on. Marginal utility declines

EXHIBIT 1 Utility Derived From Drinking Water After Running Four Miles

Amount Consumed (8-ounce glasses)	Total Utility	Marginal Utility
0	0	—
1	40	40
2	60	20
3	70	10
4	75	5
5	73	−2

after the first glass of water, becoming negative with the fifth glass. *At any level of consumption, marginal utilities sum to yield the total utility of that amount.* Total utility is graphed in panel (a) of Exhibit 2. Again, because of diminishing marginal utility, each additional glass of water adds less to total utility, so total utility increases for the first four glasses but at a decreasing rate. Panel (b) shows the law of diminishing marginal utility.

Utility Maximization in a World Without Scarcity

Economists assume that your purpose for drinking water, as with all consumption, is to *maximize your total utility.* So how much water do you consume? If the price of water is zero, you drink water as long as doing so increases total utility. Each of the first four glasses of water adds to your total utility. *If a good is free, you increase consumption as long as marginal utility is positive.* Let's broaden the analysis to a world of two goods—pizza and movie rentals. We continue to translate the satisfaction you receive from consumption into units of utility. Based on your tastes and preferences, suppose

EXHIBIT 2 Total Utility and Marginal Utility You Derive From Drinking Water After Running Four Miles

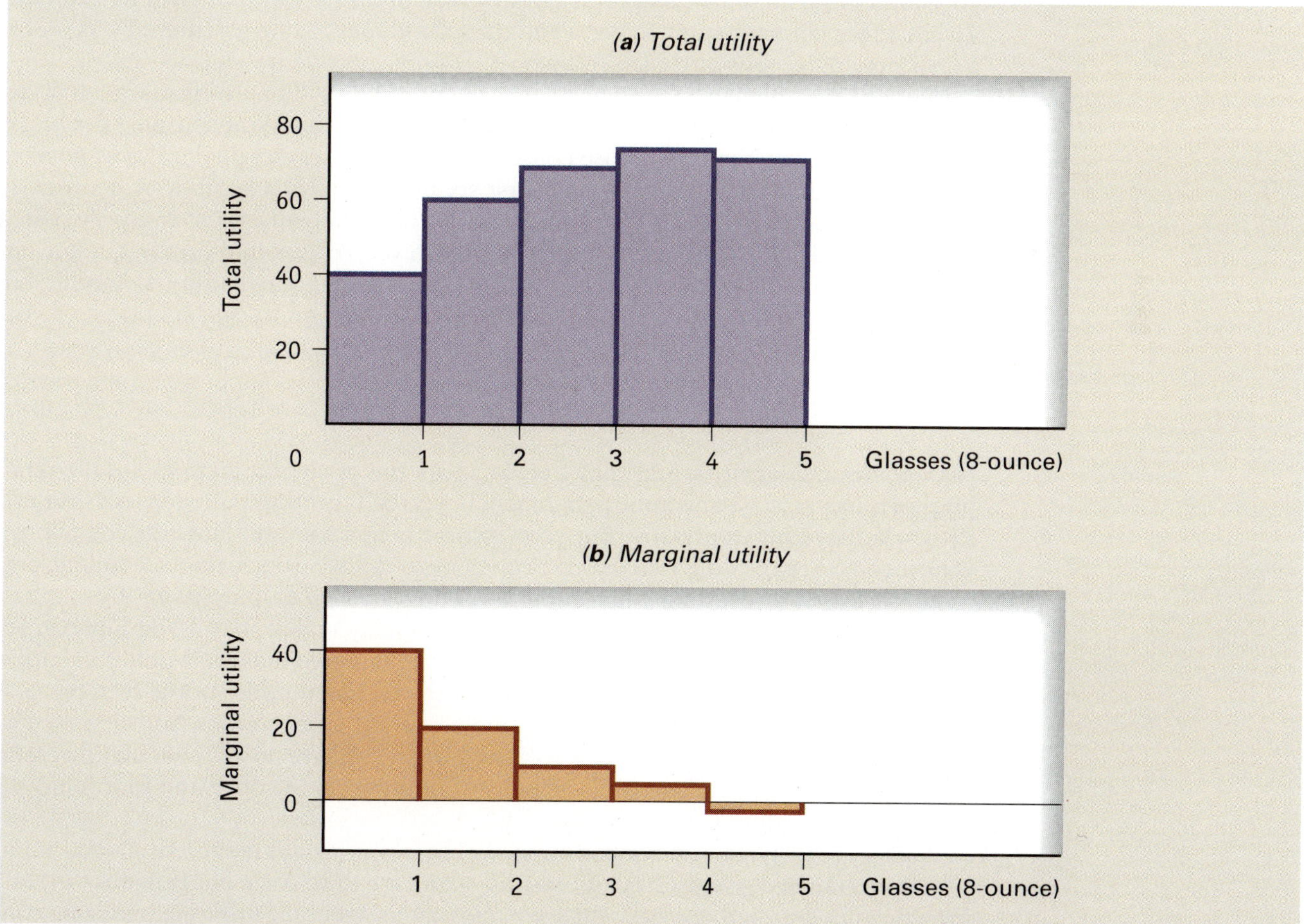

Total utility, shown in panel (a), increases with each of the first four glasses of water consumed but by smaller and smaller amounts. The fifth glass causes total utility to fall, implying that marginal utility is negative, as shown in panel (b).

EXHIBIT 3 Total and Marginal Utilities From Pizza and Movies

Pizza				Movie Rentals			
(1)	(2)	(3)	(4)	(5)	(6)	(7)	(8)
Consumed per Week	Total Utility	Marginal Utility	Marginal Utility per Dollar if p = \$8	Viewed per Week	Total Utility	Marginal Utility	Marginal Utility per Dollar if p = \$4
0	0	—	—	0	0	—	—
1	56	56	7	1	40	40	10
2	88	32	4	2	68	28	7
3	**112**	**24**	**3**	3	88	20	5
4	130	18	2¼	**4**	**100**	**12**	**3**
5	142	12	1½	5	108	8	2
6	150	8	1	6	114	6	1½

your total utility and marginal utility from consumption are as presented in Exhibit 3. The first four columns apply to pizza and the second four to movie rentals. Please spend a little time right now with each column.

Notice from columns (3) and (7) that each good shows diminishing marginal utility. Given this set of preferences, how much of each good would you consume per week? At a zero price, you would increase consumption as long as marginal utility is positive. Thus, you would consume at least the first six pizzas and first six movies because the sixth unit of each good yields positive marginal utility. Did you ever go to a party where the food and drinks were free to you? How much did you eat and drink? You ate and drank until you didn't want any more—that is, until the marginal utility of another bite and another sip fell to zero. Your consumption was determined not by prices or your income but simply by your tastes.

Utility Maximization in a World of Scarcity

Alas, goods are usually scarce, not free. Suppose the price of a pizza is \$8, the rental price of a movie is \$4, and your part-time job pays \$40 per week after taxes. Your utility is still based on your tastes, but your income is now limited. How do you allocate your income between the two goods to maximize utility? To get the ball rolling, suppose you start off spending your entire \$40 budget on pizza, purchasing five a week, which yields a total of 142 units of utility. You quickly realize that if you buy one less pizza, you free up enough income in your budget to rent two movies. Would total utility increase? Sure. You give up 12 units of utility, the marginal utility of the fifth pizza, to get 68 units of utility from the first two movies. Total utility zooms from 142 to 198. Then you notice that if you cut back to three pizzas, you give up 18 units of utility from the fourth pizza but gain a total of 32 units of utility from the third and fourth movies. This is another utility-increasing move.

Further reductions in pizza consumption, however, would reduce your total utility because you would give up 24 units of utility from the third pizza but gain only 14 units from the fifth and sixth movies. Thus, you quickly find that the utility-maximizing combination is three pizzas and four movies per week, for a total utility of 212. This means spending \$24 on pizza and \$16 on movies. *You are in equilibrium when consuming this combination because any affordable change would reduce your utility.*

Utility-Maximizing Conditions

Once a consumer is in equilibrium, there is no way to increase utility by reallocating the budget. Any change decreases utility. But, wait, there's more: In equilibrium, the last dollar spent on each good yields the same marginal utility. Let's see how this works. Column (4) shows the marginal utility of pizza divided by a price of $8. Column (8) shows the marginal utility of movies divided by a price of $4. The equilibrium combination of three pizzas and four movies exhausts the $40 budget and adds 3 units of utility for the last dollar spent on each good. **Consumer equilibrium** is achieved when the budget is exhausted and the last dollar spent on each good yields the same marginal utility. In equilibrium, the marginal utility of a pizza divided by its price equals the marginal utility of a movie divided by its price. In short, the consumer gets the same bang from the last buck spent on each good. This equality can be expressed as:

consumer equilibrium
The condition in which an individual consumer's budget is exhausted and the last dollar spent on each good yields the same marginal utility; therefore, utility is maximized

$$\frac{MU_p}{p_p} = \frac{MU_m}{p_m}$$

where MU_p is the marginal utility of pizza, p_p is the price of pizza, MU_m is the marginal utility of movies, and p_m is the rental price. The consumer reallocates spending until the last dollar spent on each product yields the same marginal utility. Although this example considers only two goods, the logic of utility maximization applies to any number of goods.

In equilibrium, higher-priced goods must yield more marginal utility than lower-priced goods—enough additional utility to compensate for their higher price. Because a pizza costs twice as much as a movies rental, the marginal utility of the final pizza purchased must, in equilibrium, be twice that of the final movie rented. Indeed, the marginal utility of the third pizza, 24, is twice that of the fourth movie, 12. Economists do not claim that you consciously equate the ratios of marginal utility to price, but they do claim that you act as if you made such calculations. Thus, you decide how much of each good to purchase by considering your tastes, market prices, and your income. Consumers maximize utility by equalizing the marginal utility from the last dollar spent on each good. This approach resolved what had been an economic puzzle, as discussed in the case study, "Bringing Theory to Life: Water, Water, Everywhere," at the end of the book.

Marginal Utility and the Law of Demand

How does utility analysis relate to your demand for pizza? The discussion so far yields a single point on your demand curve for pizza: At a price of $8, you demand three pizzas per week. This is based on income of $40 per week, a price of $4 per movie rental, and your tastes reflected by the utility tables in Exhibit 3. Knowing that three pizzas are demanded when the price is $8 offers no clue about the shape of your demand curve for pizza. To generate another point, let's see what happens to quantity demanded if the price of pizza changes, while keeping other things constant (such as tastes, income, and the price of movie rentals). Suppose the price of a pizza drops from $8 to $6.

Exhibit 4 is the same as Exhibit 3, except the price per pizza is $6. Your original choice was three pizzas and four movie rentals. At that combination and with the price of pizza now $6, the marginal utility per dollar spent on the third pizza is 4, while the marginal utility per dollar spent on the fourth movie remains at 3. The marginal utilities of the last dollar spent on each good are no longer equal. What's more, the original combination of three pizzas and four movies now leaves $6 unspent. So you could still buy your original combination but have $6 left to spend (this, incidentally, shows the income

EXHIBIT 4 Total and Marginal Utilities From Pizza and Movies After the Price of Pizza Decreases From $8 to $6

Pizza				Movie Rentals			
(1)	(2)	(3)	(4)	(5)	(6)	(7)	(8)
Consumed per Week	Total Utility	Marginal Utility	Marginal Utility per Dollar if p = $6	Viewed per Week	Total Utility	Marginal Utility	Marginal Utility per Dollar if p = $4
0	0	—	—	0	0	—	—
1	56	56	9⅓	1	40	40	10
2	88	32	5⅓	2	68	28	7
3	112	24	4	3	88	20	5
4	**130**	**18**	**3**	**4**	**100**	**12**	**3**
5	142	12	2	5	108	8	2
6	150	8	1⅓	6	114	6	1½

effect of the lower price). You can increase utility by adjusting your consumption. Take a moment now to see if you can figure out what the new equilibrium should be.

In light of your utility schedules in Exhibit 4, you would increase your consumption to four pizzas per week. This strategy exhausts your budget and equates the marginal utilities of the last dollar expended on each good. Your movie rentals remain unchanged. The marginal utility of the fourth pizza, 18, divided by the price of $6 yields 3 units of utility per dollar of expenditure, the same as you get from the fourth movie. You are in equilibrium once again. Total utility increases by the 18 units you derive from the fourth pizza. Thus, you are clearly better off as a result of the price decrease.

We now have a second point on your demand curve for pizza—if the price is $6, you demand four pizzas. The two points are presented as *a* and *b* in Exhibit 5. We could continue to change the price of pizza and thereby generate additional points on the demand curve, but you can get some idea of the demand curve's downward slope from these two points. The shape of the demand curve for pizza matches our expectations based on the law of demand: Price and quantity demanded are inversely related. (Try estimating your price elasticity of demand between points *a* and *b*. Hint: What does your total spending on pizza tell you?)

We have gone to some lengths to see how you (or any consumer) maximize utility. Given prices and your income, your tastes and preferences naturally guide you to the best bundle. You are not even conscious of your behavior. The urge to maximize utility is like the force of gravity—both work whether or not you understand them. Even animal behavior seems consistent with the law of demand. Wolves, for example, exhibit no territorial concerns when game is plentiful. But when game becomes scarce, wolves carefully mark their territory and defend it against intruders. Thus, wolves appear to value game more when it is scarce.

Now that you have some idea of utility, let's consider an application of utility analysis.

Consumer Surplus

In our earlier example, total utility increased when the price of pizza fell from $8 to $6. In this section, we take a closer look at how consumers benefit from a lower price. Suppose your demand for foot-long sub sandwiches is as shown in Exhibit 6. Recall that in constructing an individual's demand curve, we hold tastes, income, and the prices of other goods constant. Only the price of the good in question varies. At a price

EXHIBIT 5 Demand for Pizza Generated From Marginal Utility

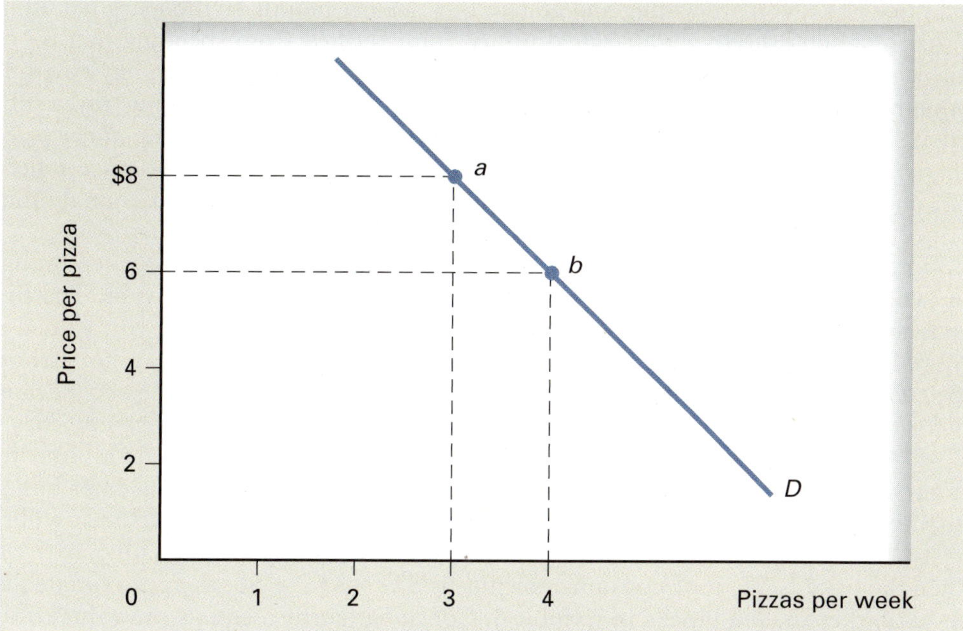

At a price of $8 per pizza, the consumer is in equilibrium when consuming three pizzas per week (point *a*). Marginal utility per dollar is the same for all goods consumed. If the price falls to $6, the consumer increases consumption to four pizzas (point *b*). Points *a* and *b* are two points on this consumer's demand curve for pizza.

EXHIBIT 6 Consumer Surplus From Sub Sandwiches

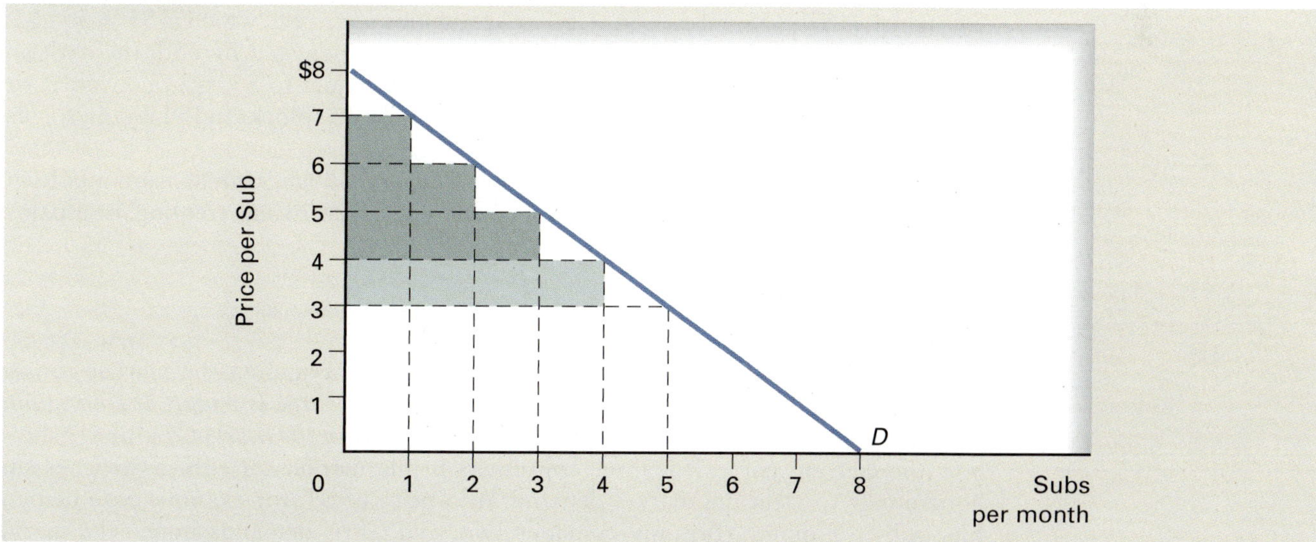

At a given quantity of sub sandwiches, the height of the demand curve shows the value of the last one purchased. The area under the demand curve for a specific quantity shows the total value a consumer attaches to that quantity. At a price of $4, the consumer purchases four subs. The first one is valued at $7, the second at $6, the third at $5, and the fourth at $4. The consumer values four at $22. Because the consumer pays $4 per sub, all four can be purchased for $16. The difference between what the consumer would have been willing to pay ($22) and what the consumer actually pays ($16) is called consumer surplus. When the price is $4, the consumer surplus is $6, as represented by the dark shaded area under the demand curve above $4. When the price of subs falls to $3, consumer surplus increases by $4, as reflected by the lighter shaded area.

of $8 or above, you find that the marginal utility of other goods that you could buy for $8 is higher than the marginal utility of a sub sandwich. Consequently, you buy no subs. At a price of $7, you are willing and able to buy one per month, so the marginal utility of that first sub exceeds the marginal utility you expected from spending that $7 on your best alternative—say, a movie ticket. A price of $6 prompts you to buy two subs a month. The second is worth at least $6 to you. At a price of $5, you buy three subs, and at $4, you buy four. *The value of the sub purchased must at least equal the price; otherwise, you wouldn't buy it.* Along the demand curve, therefore, the price reflects your **marginal valuation** of the good, or the dollar value to you of the marginal utility derived from consuming each additional unit.

Marginal valuation
The dollar value of the marginal utility derived from consuming each additional unit of a good

Notice that if the price is $4, you can purchase four subs for $4 each, even though you would have been willing to pay more for each of the first three subs. The first sandwich provides marginal utility that you valued at $7; the second you valued at $6; and the third you valued at $5. In fact, if you had to, rather than go without subs, you would have been willing to pay $7 for the first, $6 for the second, and $5 for the third. The dollar value of the total utility of the first four sandwiches is $7 + $6 + $5 + $4 = $22 per month. But when the price is $4, you get all four for a total of $16. Thus, a price of $4 confers a **consumer surplus**, or a consumer bonus, equal to the difference between the maximum amount you would have been willing to pay ($22) rather than go without subs altogether and what you actually pay ($16). When the price is $4, your consumer surplus is $22 – $16 = $6, as approximated by the six darker shaded blocks in Exhibit 6. Consumer surplus equals the value of the total utility you receive from consuming the sandwiches minus your total spending on them. *Consumer surplus is reflected by the area under the demand curve but above the price.*

consumer surplus
The difference between the most a consumer would pay for a given quantity of a good and what the consumer actually pays

If the price falls to $3, you buy five subs a month. Apparently, you feel that the marginal utility from the fifth one is worth at least $3. The lower price means that you get all five for $3 each, even though each except the fifth one is worth more to you than $3. Your consumer surplus when the price is $3 is the value of the total utility from the first five, which is $7 + $6 + $5 + $4 + $3 = $25, minus your cost, which is $3 × 5 = $15. Thus, your consumer surplus is $25 − $15 = $10, as indicated by both the dark and the light shaded blocks in Exhibit 6. So if the price declines to $3, your consumer surplus increases by $4, as reflected by the four lighter-shaded blocks in Exhibit 6. You can see how consumers benefit from lower prices.

Incidentally, in some cases your consumer surplus is huge, such as from a bottle of water if you are dying of thirst, a winter coat if you are at risk of freezing, or a pair of glasses if you can't see without them.

Market Demand and Consumer Surplus

Let's talk now about the market demand for a good, assuming the market consists of you and two other consumers. *The market demand curve is simply the horizontal sum of the individual demand curves for all consumers in the market.* Exhibit 7 shows how the demand curves for three consumers in the market for sub sandwiches sum horizontally to yield the market demand. At a price of $4, for example, you demand four subs per month, Brittany demands two, and Chris demands none. The market demand at a price of $4 is therefore six sandwiches. At a price of $2, you demand six per month, Brittany four, and Chris two, for a market demand of 12. *The market demand curve shows the total quantity demanded per period by all consumers at various prices.* Consumer surplus can be used to examine market demand as well as individual demand. *At a given price, consumer surplus for the market is the difference between the most consumers would pay for that quantity and the amount they do pay.*

EXHIBIT 7 **Summing Individual Demand Curves to Derive the Market Demand for Sub Sandwiches**

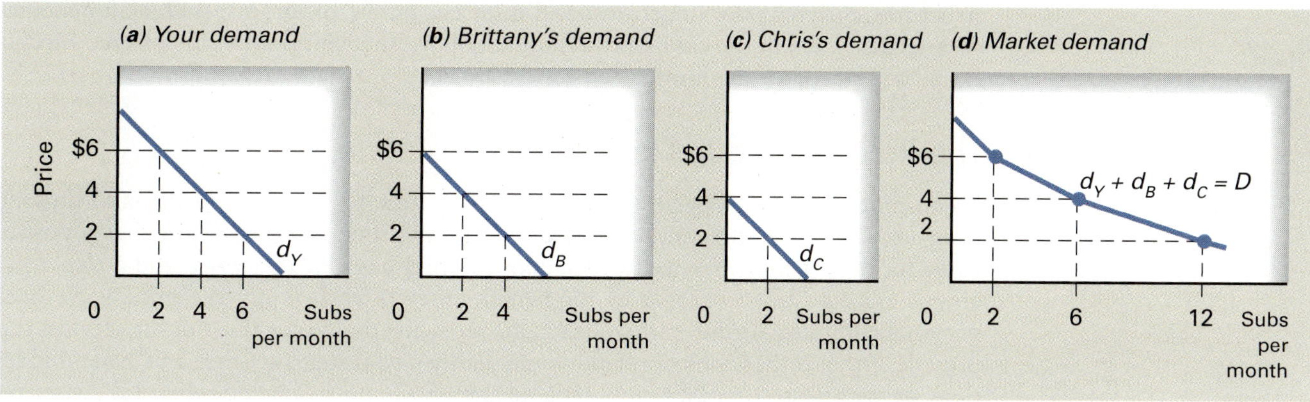

At a price of \$4 per sub, you demand 4 per month, Brittany demands 2, and Chris demands 0. Quantity demanded at a price of \$4 is 4 + 2 + 0 = 6 subs per month. At a lower price of \$2, you demand 6, Brittany demands 4, and Chris demands 2. Quantity demanded at a price of \$2 is 12 subs. The market demand curve *D* is the horizontal sum of individual demand curves d_Y, d_B, and d_C.

Instead of just three consumers in the market, suppose there are many. Exhibit 8 presents market demand for a good with millions of consumers. If the price is \$2 per unit, each person adjusts his or her quantity demanded until the marginal valuation of the final unit purchased equals \$2. But each consumer also gets to buy all other units for \$2 each. In Exhibit 8, the dark shading, bounded above by the demand curve and below by the price line at \$2, depicts the consumer surplus. The light shading shows the gain in consumer surplus if the price drops to \$1. Notice that if this good were given away, the consumer surplus would not be that much greater than when the price is \$1.

EXHIBIT 8 **Market Demand and Consumer Surplus**

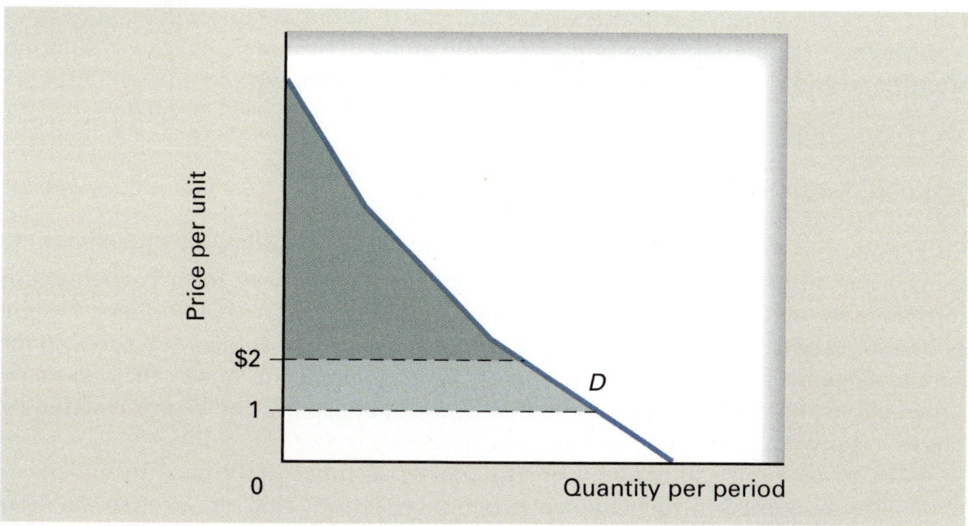

Consumer surplus at a price of \$2 is shown by the darker area. If the price falls to \$1, consumer surplus increases to include the lighter area. At a zero price, consumer surplus increases to include the entire area under the demand curve.

Consumer surplus is the net benefit consumers get from market exchange. It can be used to measure economic welfare and to compare the effects of different market structures, different tax structures, and different public programs, such as for medical care, as discussed in the case study, "Public Policy: The Marginal Value of Free Medical Care," at the end of the book.

The Role of Time in Demand

Because consumption does not occur instantly, time plays a role in demand analysis. Consumption takes time and, as Ben Franklin said, time is money—time has a positive value for most people. Consequently, consumption has a *money price* and a *time price*. Goods are demanded because of the benefits they offer. It is not the microwave oven, personal computer, airline trip, or headache medicine that you value but the services they provide. Other things constant, you would gladly pay more to get the same benefit in less time, as with faster ovens, computers, airline trips, and headache relief. Likewise, you are willing to pay more for seedless grapes, seedless oranges, and seedless watermelon.

Your willingness to pay a premium for time-saving goods and services depends on the opportunity cost of your time. Differences in the value of time among consumers help explain differences in the consumption patterns observed in the economy. For example, a retired couple has more leisure time than a working couple and may clip discount coupons and search the newspapers for bargains, sometimes even going from store to store for particular grocery items on sale that week. The working couple tends to ignore the coupons and sales, eats out more often, and shops more at convenience stores, where they pay more for the "convenience." The retired couple is more inclined to drive to a vacation destination, whereas the working couple flies.

Just inside the gates at Disneyland, Disney World, and Universal Studios are boards listing the waiting times of each attraction and ride. At that point, the dollar cost of admission has already been paid, so the marginal dollar cost of each ride and attraction is zero. The waiting times offer a menu of the marginal *time costs* of each ride or attraction. Incidentally, people willing to pay up to $55 an hour at Disney World and $60 an hour at Disneyland (plus the price of admission), until recently, could take VIP tours that bypass the lines. And at Universal Studios, you can still pay extra for a pass to the front of the line. How much would you pay to avoid the lines?

Differences in the opportunity cost of time among consumers shape consumption patterns and add another dimension to our analysis of demand.

Conclusion

This chapter has analyzed consumer choice by focusing on utility, or satisfaction. We assumed that utility could be measured in some systematic way for a particular consumer, even though utility measures could not be compared across consumers. The goal has been to explore utility maximization and predict how consumers react to a change in price. We judge a theory not by the realism of its assumptions but by the accuracy of its predictions. Based on this criterion, the theory of consumer choice presented in this chapter has proven to be quite useful.

Again, to maximize utility, you or any other consumer don't need to understand the material presented in this chapter. Economists assume that the urge to maximize utility is natural and instinctive. In this chapter, we simply tried to analyze that process. A more general approach to consumer choice, one that does not require a specific measure of utility, is developed in the appendix to this chapter.

Summary

1. Utility is the sense of pleasure or satisfaction that comes from consumption; it is the want-satisfying power of goods, services, and activities. The utility you get from consuming a particular good depends on your tastes. The law of diminishing marginal utility says that the more of a particular good you consume per period, other things constant, the smaller the gain in total utility from each additional unit consumed. The total utility derived from a good is the sum of the marginal utilities from each additional unit of the good. At some point, additional consumption could reduce total utility.
2. Utility is subjective. Each consumer makes a personal assessment of the want-satisfying power of consumption. By translating an individual's subjective measure of satisfaction into units of utility, we can predict the quantity demanded at a given price as well as the effect of a change in price on quantity demanded.
3. The consumer's objective is to maximize utility within the limits imposed by income and prices. In a world without scarcity, utility is maximized by consuming each good until its marginal utility reaches zero. In the real world—a world shaped by scarcity as reflected by prices—utility is maximized when the budget is exhausted and the marginal utility of the final unit consumed divided by that good's price is identical for each different good.
4. Utility analysis can be used to construct an individual consumer's demand curve. By observing the effects of a change in price on consumption, we can generate points that trace a demand curve.
5. Consumers typically receive a surplus, or a bonus, from consumption. Consumer surplus is the difference between the maximum amount consumers would pay for a given quantity of the good rather than go without it and the amount they actually pay. Consumer surplus increases as the price declines.
6. Consumption involves a money price and a time price. People are willing to pay a higher money price for products that save time.

Key Concepts

Total utility 107	Law of diminishing marginal utility 107	Marginal valuation 114
Marginal utility 107	Consumer equilibrium 111	Consumer surplus 114

Questions for Review

1. Law of Diminishing Marginal Utility Some restaurants offer "all you can eat" meals. How is this practice related to diminishing marginal utility? What restrictions must the restaurant impose on the customer to make a profit?
2. Law of Diminishing Marginal Utility Complete each of the following sentences:
   a. Your tastes determine the _______ you derive from consuming a particular good.
   b. _______ utility is the change in _______ utility resulting from a _______ change in the consumption of a good.
   c. As long as marginal utility is positive, total utility is _______.
   d. The law of diminishing marginal utility states that as an individual consumes more of a good during a given time period, other things constant, total utility _____.
3. Marginal Utility Is it possible for marginal utility to be negative while total utility is positive? If yes, under what circumstances is it possible?
4. Utility-Maximizing Conditions For a particular consumer, the marginal utility of cookies equals the marginal utility of candy. If the price of a cookie is less than the price of candy, is the consumer in equilibrium? Why or why not? If not, what should the consumer do to attain equilibrium?
5. Utility-Maximizing Conditions Suppose that marginal utility of Good $X = 100$, the price of X is \$10 per unit, and the price of Y is \$5 per unit. Assuming that the consumer is in equilibrium and is consuming both X and Y, what must the marginal utility of Y be?
6. Utility-Maximizing Conditions Suppose that the price of X is twice the price of Y. You are a utility maximizer who allocates your budget between the two goods. What must be true about the equilibrium relationship between the marginal utility levels of the last unit consumed of each good? What must be true about the equilibrium relationship between the marginal utility levels of the last dollar spent on each good?
7. Case Study: Water, Water Everywhere (See page 711.) What is the diamonds-water paradox, and how is it explained? Use the same reasoning to explain why bottled water costs so much more than tap water.
8. Consumer Surplus The height of the demand curve at a given quantity reflects the marginal valuation of the last unit of that good consumed. For a normal good, an increase in income shifts the demand curve to the right and therefore increases its height at any quantity. Does this mean that consumers get greater marginal utility from each unit of this good than they did before? Explain.

9. Consumer Surplus Suppose supply of a good is perfectly elastic at a price of $5. The market demand curve for this good is linear, with zero quantity demanded at a price of $25. Given that the slope of this linear demand curve is −0.25, draw a supply and demand graph to illustrate the consumer surplus that occurs when the market is in equilibrium.

10. Case Study: The Marginal Value of Free Medical Care (See page 712.) Medicare recipients pay a monthly premium for coverage, must meet an annual deductible, and have a co-payment for doctors' office visits. President George W. Bush introduced some coverage of prescription medications (prior to that, there was none). What impact would an increase in the monthly premium have on their consumer surplus? What would be the impact of a reduction in co-payments? What is the impact on consumer surplus of offering some coverage for prescription medication?

11. Role of Time in Demand In many amusement parks, you pay an admission fee to the park but you do not need to pay for individual rides. How do people choose which rides to go on?

Problems and Exercises

12. Utility Maximization The following tables illustrate Eileen's utilities from watching first-run movies in a theater and from renting movies from a video store. Suppose that she has a monthly movie budget of $36, each movie ticket costs $6, and each video rental costs $3.

Movies in a Theater

Q	TU	MU	MU/P
0	0	____	____
1	200	____	____
2	290	____	____
3	370	____	____
4	440	____	____
5	500	____	____
6	550	____	____
7	590	____	____

Movies from a Video Store

Q	TU	MU	MU/P
0	0	____	____
1	250	____	____
2	295	____	____
3	335	____	____
4	370	____	____
5	400	____	____
6	425	____	____

a. Complete the tables.
b. Do these tables show that Eileen's preferences obey the law of diminishing marginal utility? Explain your answer.
c. How much of each good does Eileen consume in equilibrium?
d. Suppose the prices of both types of movies drop to $1 while Eileen's movie budget shrinks to $10. How much of each good does she consume in equilibrium?

13. Utility Maximization Suppose that a consumer has a choice between two goods, X and Y. If the price of X is $2 and the price of Y is $3, how much of X and Y does the consumer purchase, given an income of $17? Use the following information about marginal utility:

Units	MU_X	MU_Y
1	10	5
2	8	4
3	2	3
4	2	2
5	1	2

14. The Law of Demand and Marginal Utility Daniel allocates his budget of $24 per week among three goods. Use the following table of marginal utilities for good A, good B, and good C to answer the questions below:

Q_A	MU_A	Q_B	MU_B	Q_C	MU_C
1	50	1	75	1	25
2	40	2	60	2	20
3	30	3	40	3	15
4	20	4	30	4	10
5	15	5	20	5	7.5

a. If the price of A is $2, the price of B is $3, and the price of C is $1, how much of each does Daniel purchase in equilibrium?
b. If the price of A rises to $4 while other prices and Daniel's budget remain unchanged, how much of each does he purchase in equilibrium?
c. Using the information from parts (a) and (b), draw the demand curve for good A. Be sure to indicate the price and quantity demanded for each point on the curve.

15. Consumer Surplus Suppose the linear demand curve for shirts slopes downward and that consumers buy 500 shirts per year when the price is $30 and 1,000 shirts per year when the price is $25.

a. Compared to the prices of $30 and $25, what can you say about the marginal valuation that consumers place on the 300th shirt, the 700th shirt, and the 1,200th shirt they might buy each year?
b. With diminishing marginal utility, are consumers deriving any consumer surplus if the price is $25 per shirt? Explain.
c. Use a market demand curve to illustrate the change in consumer surplus if the price drops from $30 to $25.

Global Economic Watch Exercises

Login to www.cengagebrain.com and access the Global Economic Watch to do these exercises.

16. Global Economic Watch Go to the Global Economic Crisis Resource Center. Select Global Issues in Context. In the Basic Search box at the top of the page, enter the phrase "applied economics." On the Results page, go to the Magazines section. Click on the link for the December 31, 2003, book review "How Economics Works." Think about the first paragraph of the book review. Do you expect to experience diminishing marginal utility in your economics course?
17. Global Economic Watch and Case Study: The Marginal Value of Free Medical Care (See page 712.) Go to the Global Economic Crisis Resource Center. Select Global Issues in Context. Go to the menu at the top of the page and click on the tab for Browse Issues and Topics. Choose Health and Medicine. Click on the link for Access to Health Care. At the bottom of the Overview section, select View Full Overview. Read about access to health care in three categories of countries: developing nations, the United States, and industrialized nations with national health insurance systems. Describe the consumer surplus of the average citizen in each category of country.

Appendix

Indifference Curves and Utility Maximization

The approach used in the body of the chapter required a numerical measure of utility to determine optimal consumption. Economists have developed a more general approach to consumer behavior, one that does not rely on a numerical measure of utility. All this approach requires is that consumers be able to indicate their preferences for various combinations of goods. For example, the consumer should be able to say whether combination *A* is preferred to combination *B*, combination *B* is preferred to combination *A*, or each combination is equally preferred. This approach discussed in this appendix is more general and more flexible than the one developed in the body of the chapter. But it's also a little more complicated.

EXHIBIT 9 An Indifference Curve

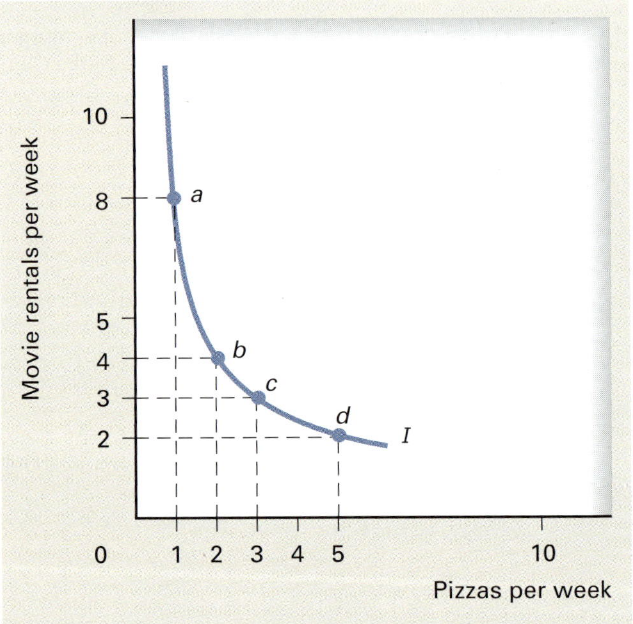

An indifference curve, such as *I*, shows all combinations of two goods that provide a particular consumer with the same total utility. Points *a* through *d* depict four such combinations. Indifference curves have negative slopes and are convex to the origin.

Consumer Preferences

An **indifference curve** shows all combinations of goods that provide the consumer with the same satisfaction, or the same utility. Thus, the consumer finds all combinations on a curve equally preferred. Because each bundle of goods yields the same level of utility, the consumer is *indifferent* about which combination is actually consumed. We can best understand the use of indifference curves through the following example.

In reality, consumers choose among thousands of goods and services, but to keep the analysis manageable, suppose only two are available: pizzas and movie rentals. In Exhibit 9, the horizontal axis measures the number of pizzas you buy per week, and the vertical axis measures the number of movies you rent per week. Point *a*, for example, consists of one pizza and eight movie rentals. Suppose you are given a choice of combination *a* or some combination with more pizza. The question is: Holding your total utility constant, how many movie rentals would you be willing to give up to get a second pizza? As you can see, in moving from point *a* to point *b*, you are willing to give up four movies to get a second pizza. Total utility is the same at points *a* and *b*. The marginal utility of that additional pizza is just sufficient to compensate you for the utility lost from decreasing your movie rentals by four. Thus, at point *b*, you are eating two pizzas and watching four movies a week.

In moving from point *b* to point *c*, again total utility is constant; you are now willing to give up only one movie for another pizza. At point *c*, your consumption bundle consists of three pizzas and three movies. Once at point *c*, you are willing to give up another movie only if you get two more pizzas in return. Combination *d*, therefore, consists of five pizzas and two movies.

Points *a*, *b*, *c*, and *d* connect to form indifference curve *I*, which represents possible combinations of pizza and movie rentals that would provide you the same total utility. Because points on the curve offer the same total utility, you are indifferent about which combination you choose—hence the name *indifference curve.* One sign of indifference is a willingness to allow someone else to choose for you. Expressions of indifference often include the phrases "Whatever" and "I could take it or leave it."

Note that we don't know, nor do we need to know, the value you attach to the utility reflected by the indifference curve—that is, no particular number is attached to the utility along *I*. *Combinations of goods along an indifference curve reflect some constant, though unspecified, level of utility.* So, unlike the approach adopted in the body of the chapter, indifference curves need not be measured in units of utility.

For you to remain indifferent among consumption alternatives, the increase in utility from eating more pizzas must just offset the decrease in utility from watching fewer movies. Thus, along an indifference curve, the quantity of pizza and the quantity of movies are inversely related. Because of this inverse relationship, *indifference curves slope downward to the right.*

Indifference curves are also *convex to the origin,* which means they are bowed inward toward the origin. The indifference curve gets flatter as you move down it. Here's why. Your willingness to substitute pizza for movies depends on how much of each you already consume. At combination *a,* for example, you watch eight movies and eat only one pizza a week. Because there are many movies relative to pizza, you are willing to give up four to get another pizza. Once you reach point *b,* your pizza consumption has doubled, so you are not quite so willing to give up movies to get a third pizza. In fact, you forgo just one movie to get another pizza. This moves you from point *b* to point *c.*

The **marginal rate of substitution**, or **MRS**, between pizza and movies indicates the number of movies that you are willing to give up to get one more pizza, neither gaining nor losing utility in the process. Because the MRS measures your willingness to trade movies for pizza, it depends on the amount of each good you are currently consuming. Mathematically, the MRS is equal to the absolute value of the slope of the indifference curve. Recall that the slope of any line is the vertical change between two points on the line divided by the corresponding horizontal change. For example, in moving from combination *a* to combination *b* in Exhibit 9, you are willing to give up four movies to get another pizza; the slope between these two points equals −4, so the MRS is 4. In the move from *b* to *c,* the slope is −1, so the MRS is 1. And from *c* to *d,* the slope is −½, so the MRS is ½.

The **law of diminishing marginal rate of substitution** says that as your consumption of pizza increases, the number of movies that you are willing to give up to get another pizza declines. This law applies to most pairs of goods. Because your marginal rate of substitution of movies for pizza declines as your pizza consumption increases, the indifference curve has a diminishing slope, meaning that it is convex when viewed from the origin. As you move down the indifference curve, your pizza consumption increases, so the marginal utility of additional pizza decreases. Conversely, the number of movies you rent decreases, so their marginal utility increases. Thus, in moving down the indifference curve, you require more pizza to offset the loss of each movie.

We have focused on a single indifference curve, which indicates some constant though unspecified level of utility. We can use the same approach to generate a series of indifference curves, called an **indifference map.** An indifference map is a graphical representation of a consumer's tastes. Each curve reflects a different level of utility. Part of such a map is shown in Exhibit 10, where indifference curves for a particular consumer, in this case you, are labeled I_1, I_2, I_3, and I_4. Each consumer has a unique indifference map based on his or her preferences.

Because both goods yield marginal utility, you, the consumer, prefer more of each, rather than less. Curves farther from the origin represent greater consumption levels and, therefore, higher levels of utility. The utility level along I_2 is higher than that along I_1. I_3 reflects a higher level of utility than I_2, and so on. We can show this best by drawing a line from the origin and following it to higher indifference curves. Such a line has been included in Exhibit 10. By following that line to higher and higher

EXHIBIT 10 An Indifference Map

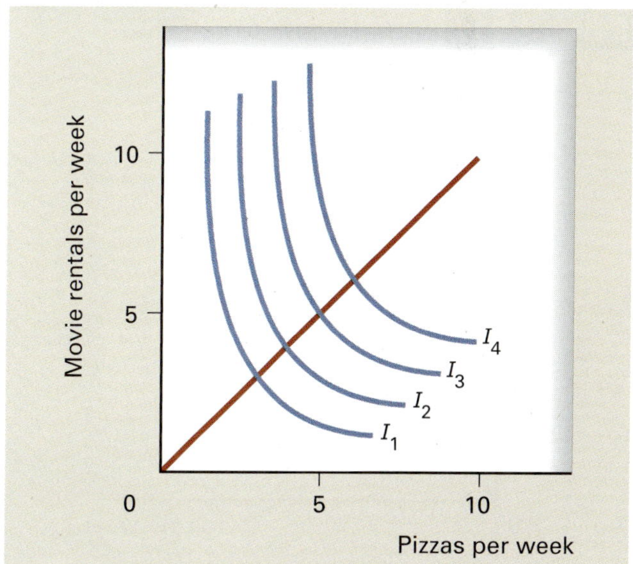

Indifference curves I_1 through I_4 are four examples from a particular consumer's indifference map. Indifference curves farther from the origin depict higher levels of utility. A line intersects each higher indifference curve, reflecting more of both goods.

indifference curves, you can see that the combination on each successive indifference curve reflects more of *both* goods. Because you value both goods, the greater amounts of each reflected on higher indifference curves represent higher levels of utility.

Indifference curves in a consumer's indifference map don't intersect. Exhibit 11 shows why. If indifference curves did cross, as at point *i*, then every point on indifference curve *I* and every point on curve *I′* would have to reflect the same level of utility as at point *i*. But because point *k* in Exhibit 11 is a combination with more pizza and more movies than point *j*, point *k* must represent a higher level of utility. This contradiction means that indifference curves cannot intersect.

Let's summarize the properties of indifference curves:

1. A particular indifference curve reflects a constant level of utility, so *the consumer is indifferent among all consumption combinations along a given curve.* Combinations are equally attractive.
2. If total utility is to remain constant, an increase in the consumption of one good must be offset by a decrease in the consumption of the other good, so *each indifference curve slopes downward to the right.*
3. Because of the law of diminishing marginal rate of substitution, *indifference curves bow in toward the origin.*
4. Higher indifference curves represent higher levels of utility.
5. Indifference curves do not intersect.

An indifference map is a graphical representation of a consumer's tastes for the two goods. Given a consumer's indifference map, how much of each good is consumed? To determine that, we must consider the relative prices of the goods and the consumer's income. In the next section, we focus on the consumer's budget.

The Budget Line

The **budget line** depicts all possible combinations of movies and pizzas, given their prices and your budget. Suppose, as in the body of this chapter, movies rent for $4, pizza sells for $8, and your budget is $40 per week. If you spend the entire $40 on movies, you can afford 10 per week. Alternatively, if you spend the entire $40 on pizzas, you can afford 5 per week. In Exhibit 12, your budget line meets the vertical axis at 10 movie rentals and meets the horizontal axis at 5 pizzas. We connect

EXHIBIT 11 Indifference Curves Do Not Intersect

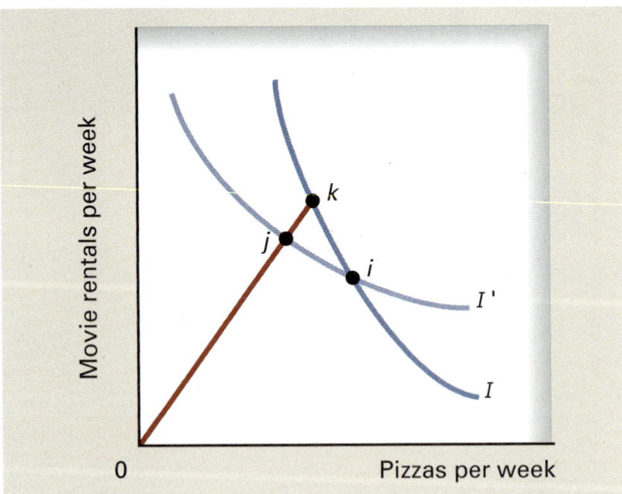

If indifference curves crossed, as at point *i*, then every point on indifference curve *I* and every point on indifference curve *I′* would have to reflect the same level of utility as at point *i*. But point *k* is a combination with more pizza and more movies than point *j*, so *k* must reflect a higher level of utility. This contradiction indicates that indifference curves cannot intersect.

EXHIBIT 12 A Budget Line

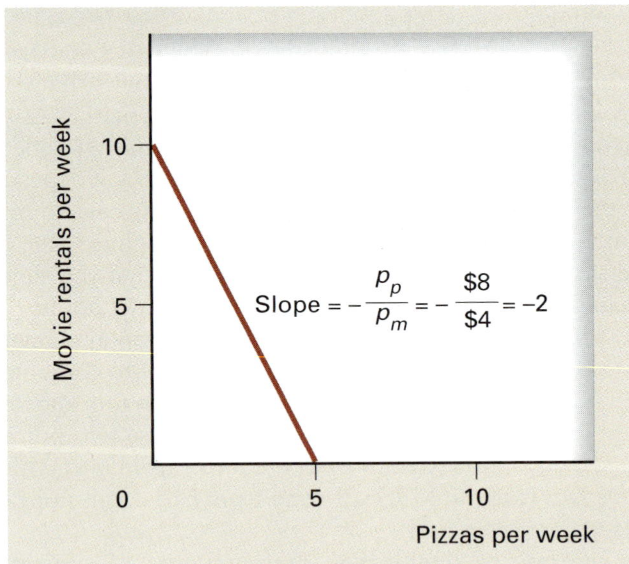

A budget line shows all combinations of pizza and movies that can be purchased at fixed prices with a given amount of income. If all income is spent on movies, 10 can be rented. If all income is spent on pizzas, 5 can be purchased. Points between the vertical intercept and the horizontal intercept show combinations of pizzas and movies. The slope of this budget line is −2, illustrating that the price of 1 pizza is 2 movies.

the intercepts to form the budget line. You can purchase any combination on your budget line, or your budget constraint. You might think of the budget line as your *consumption possibilities frontier.*

Let's find the slope of the budget line. At the point where the budget line meets the vertical axis, the maximum number of movies you can rent equals your income (I) divided by the movie rental price (p_m), or I/p_m. At the point where the budget line meets the horizontal axis, the maximum quantity of pizzas that you can purchase equals your income divided by the price of a pizza (p_p), or I/p_p. The slope of the budget line between the vertical intercept in Exhibit 12 and the horizontal intercept equals the vertical change, or $-I/p_m$, divided by the horizontal change, or I/p_p:

$$\text{Slope of budget line} = \frac{I/p_m}{I/p_p} - \frac{p_p}{p_m}$$

Note that the income term cancels out, so the slope of a budget line depends only on relative prices. In our example the slope is $-\$8/\$4$, which equals -2. The slope of the budget line indicates the cost of another pizza in terms of forgone movies. You must give up two movies for each additional pizza.

The indifference curve indicates what you are *willing* to buy. The budget line shows what you are *able* to buy. We must therefore bring together the indifference curve and the budget line to find out what quantities of each good you are both *willing* and *able* to buy.

EXHIBIT 13 Utility Maximization

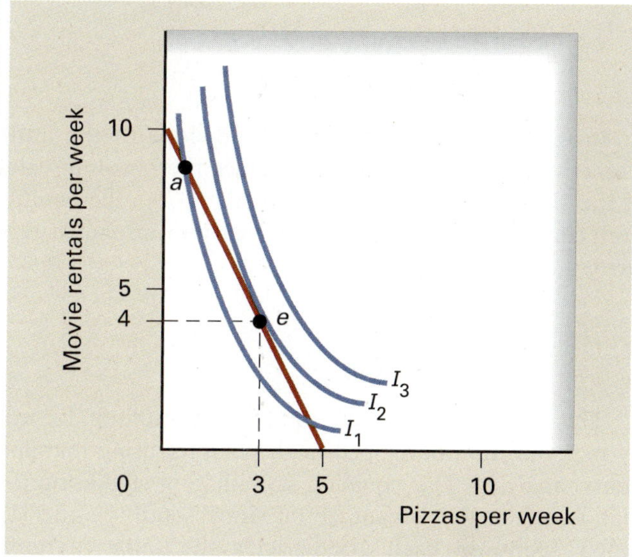

A consumer's utility is maximized at point e, where indifference curve I_2 is just tangent to the budget line.

Consumer Equilibrium at the Tangency

As always, the consumer's objective is to maximize utility. We know that indifference curves farther from the origin represent higher levels of utility. You, as a utility-maximizing consumer, select a combination along the budget line in Exhibit 13 that lies on the highest attainable indifference curve. Given prices and income, you maximize utility at the combination depicted by point *e* in Exhibit 13, where indifference curve I_2 just touches, or *is tangent to,* your budget line. At point *e,* you buy 3 pizzas at $8 each and rent 4 movies at $4 each, exhausting your budget of $40 per week. Other attainable combinations along the budget line reflect lower levels of utility. For example, point *a* is on the budget line, making it a combination you are *able* to purchase, but *a* is on a lower indifference curve, I_1. "Better" indifference curves, such as I_3, lie completely above the budget line and thus are unattainable.

Because you maximize utility at point *e,* that combination is an equilibrium outcome. Note that the indifference curve is tangent to the budget line at the equilibrium point. At the point of tangency, the slope of the indifference curve equals the slope of the budget line. Recall that the absolute value of the slope of the indifference curve is your marginal rate of substitution, and the absolute value of the slope of the budget line equals the price ratio. In equilibrium, therefore, your marginal rate of substitution between movies and pizza, MRS, must equal the ratio of the price of pizza to the price of movie rentals:

$$MRS = \frac{p_p}{p_m}$$

The marginal rate of substitution of pizza for movie rentals can also be found from the marginal utilities of pizza and movies presented in the chapter. Exhibit 3 indicated that, at the consumer equilibrium, the marginal utility you derived from the third pizza was 24 and the marginal utility you derived by the fourth movie was 12. Because the marginal utility of pizza (MU_p) is 24 and the marginal utility of movies (MU_m) is 12, in moving to that equilibrium, you were willing to give up two movies to get one more pizza. Thus, the marginal rate of substitution of pizza for movies equals the ratio of pizza's marginal utility (MU_p) to movie's marginal utility (MU_m), or

$$MRS = \frac{MU_p}{MU_m}$$

In fact, the absolute value of the slope of the indifference curve equals MU_p/MU_m. Since the absolute value of the slope of the budget line equals p_p/p_m, the equilibrium condition for the indifference curve approach can be written as

$$\frac{MU_p}{p_p} = \frac{MU_m}{p_m}$$

This equation is the same equilibrium condition for utility maximization developed in the chapter using marginal utility analysis. The equality says that in equilibrium—that is, when the consumer maximizes utility—the last dollar spent on each good yields the same marginal utility. If this equality did not hold, the consumer could increase utility by adjusting consumption until the equality occurs.

Effects of a Change in Price

What happens to quantity demanded when the price changes? The answer can be found by deriving the demand curve. We begin at point *e*, our initial equilibrium, in panel (a) of Exhibit 14. At point *e*, you eat 3 pizzas and watch 4 movies per week. Suppose that the price of pizzas falls from \$8 to \$6, other things constant. The price drop means that if the entire budget were spent on pizza, you could buy 6.67 (=\$40/\$6). Your money income remains at \$40 per week, but your real income has increased because of the lower pizza price. Because the rental price of movies has not changed, however, 10 remains the maximum number you can rent. Thus, the budget line's vertical intercept remains fixed at 10 movies, but the lower end of the budget line rotates to the right from 5 pizzas to 6.67 pizzas.

After the price of pizza changes, the new equilibrium occurs at *e*", where pizza purchases increase from 3 to 4 and, as it happens, movie rentals remains at 4. Thus, price and the quantity of pizza demanded are inversely related. The demand curve in panel (b) of Exhibit 14 shows how price and quantity demanded are related. Specifically, if the price of pizza falls from \$8 per unit to \$6 per unit, other things constant, your quantity demanded increases from 3 to 4. Because you are on a higher indifference curve at *e*", you are clearly better off after the price reduction (your consumer surplus has increased).

EXHIBIT 14 Effect of a Drop in the Price of Pizza

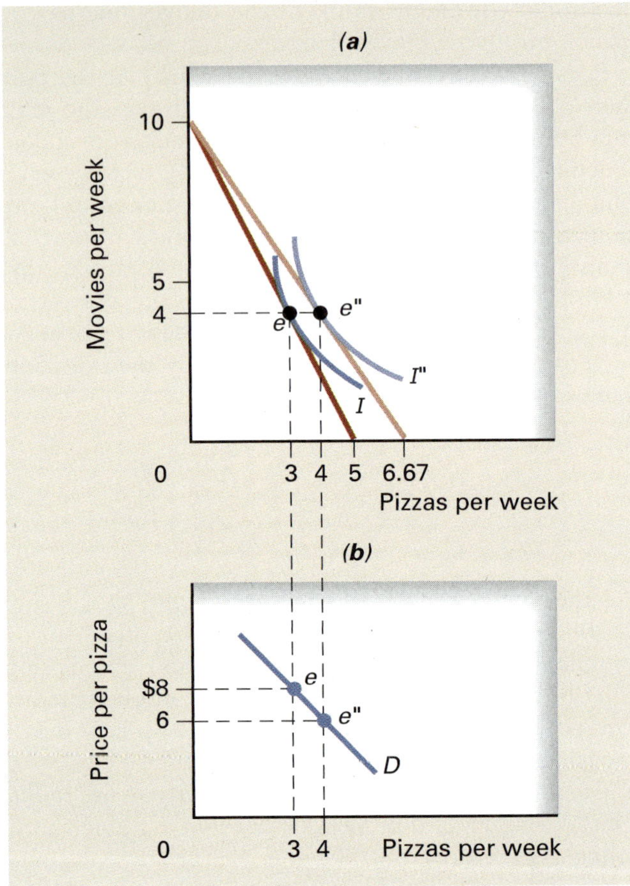

A reduction in the price of pizza rotates the budget line rightward in panel (a). The consumer is back in equilibrium at point *e*" along the new budget line. Panel (b) shows that a drop in the price of pizza from \$8 to \$6 increases quantity demanded from 3 to 4 pizzas. Price and quantity demanded are inversely related.

Income and Substitution Effects

The law of demand was initially explained in terms of an income effect and a substitution effect of a price change. You now have the tools to examine these two effects more precisely. Suppose the price of a pizza falls from \$8 to \$4, other things constant. You can now purchase a maximum of 10 pizzas with a budget of \$40 per week. As shown in Exhibit 15, the budget-line intercept rotates out from 5 to 10 pizzas. After the price change, the quantity of pizzas demanded increases from 3 to 5. The increase in utility shows how you benefit from the price decrease.

The increase in the quantity of pizzas demanded can be broken down into the substitution effect and the income effect of a price change. When the price of pizza falls, the

EXHIBIT 15 Substitution and Income Effects of a Drop in the Price of Pizza From $8 to $4

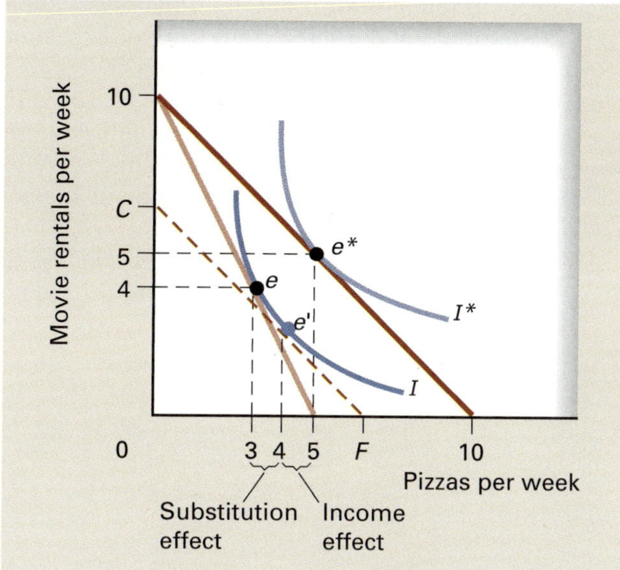

A reduction in the price of pizza moves the consumer from point *e* to point *e**. This movement can be decomposed into a substitution effect and an income effect. The substitution effect, shown from *e* to *e'*, reflects the consumer's reaction to a change in relative prices along the original indifference curve. The income effect, shown from *e'* to *e**, moves the consumer to a higher indifference curve at the new relative price ratio.

change in relative prices shows up through the change in the slope of the budget line. To derive the substitution effect, let's initially assume that you must maintain the same level of utility after the price change as before. In other words, let's suppose your utility level has not yet changed, but the relative prices you face have changed. We want to learn how you would adjust to the price change. A new budget line reflecting just the change in relative prices, not a change in utility, is shown by the dashed line, *CF,* in Exhibit 15. Given the new relative prices, you would increase the quantity of pizza demanded to the point on indifference curve *I* where the indifference curve is just tangent to the dashed budget line. That tangency keeps utility at the initial level but reflects the new relative prices. Thus, we adjust your budget line to correspond to the new relative prices, but we adjust your income level so that your utility remains unchanged.

You move down along indifference curve *I* to point *e'*, buying more pizza but renting fewer movies. These changes in quantity demanded reflect the *substitution effect* of lower pizza prices. The substitution effect always increases the quantity demanded of the good whose price has dropped. Because consumption bundle *e'* represents the same level of utility as consumption bundle *e*, you are neither better off nor worse off at point *e'*.

But at point *e'*, you have not spent your full budget. The drop in the price of pizza has increased the quantity of pizza you can buy, as shown by the expanded budget line that runs from 10 movie rentals to 10 pizzas. Your *real income* has increased because of the lower price of pizza. As a result, you are able to attain point *e** on indifference curve *I**. At this point, you buy 5 pizzas and rent 5 movies. Because prices remain constant during the move from *e'* to *e**, the change in consumption is due solely to a change in real income. Thus, the change in the quantity demanded from 4 to 5 pizzas reflects the *income effect* of the lower pizza price.

We can now distinguish between the substitution effect and the income effect of a drop in the price of pizza. The substitution effect is shown by the move from point *e* to point *e'* in response to a change in the relative price of pizza, with your utility held constant along *I*. The income effect is shown by the move from *e'* to *e** in response to an increase in your real income, with relative prices held constant.

The overall effect of a change in the price of pizza is the sum of the substitution effect and the income effect. In our example, the substitution effect accounts for a one-unit increase in the quantity of pizza demanded, as does the income effect. Thus, when the price falls from $8 to $4, the income and substitution effects combine to increase the quantity of pizza demanded by two units. The income effect is not always positive. For inferior goods, the income effect is negative; so as the price falls, the income effect can cause the consumption of one of the goods to fall, offsetting part or even all the substitution effect. Incidentally, notice that as a result of the increase in your real income, movie rentals increase as well—from 4 to 5 rentals per week in our example, though it is not always the case that the income effect is positive.

Conclusion

Indifference curve analysis does not require us to attach numerical values to particular levels of utility, as marginal utility theory does. The results of indifference curve analysis support the conclusions drawn from our simpler models: price and quantity demanded are inversely related. Indifference curves provide a logical way of viewing consumer choice, but consumers need not be aware of this approach to make rational choices. The purpose of the analysis in this chapter is to predict consumer behavior—not to advise consumers how to maximize utility. They already know that instinctively.

Appendix Questions

1. Consumer Preferences The absolute value of the slope of the indifference curve equals the marginal rate of substitution. If two goods were *perfect* substitutes, what would the indifference curves look like? Explain.

2. Effects of a Change in Price Chris has an income of $90 per month to allocate between Goods A and B. Initially the price of A is $3 and the price of B is $4.

   a. Draw Chris's budget line, indicating its slope if units of A are measured on the horizontal axis and units of B are on the vertical axis.

   b. Add an indifference curve to your graph and label the point of consumer equilibrium. Indicate Chris's consumption level of A and B. Explain why this is a consumer equilibrium. What can you say about Chris's total utility at this equilibrium?

   c. Now suppose the price of A rises to $4. Draw the new budget line, a new point of equilibrium, and the consumption level of Goods A and B. What is Chris's marginal rate of substitution at the new equilibrium point?

   d. Draw the demand curve for Good A, labeling the different price-quantity combinations determined in parts (b) and (c).

Production and Cost in the Firm

7

Ryan McVay/Getty Images

- Why do too many cooks spoil the broth?
- Why do movie theaters have so many screens?
- Why don't they add even more?
- If you go into business for yourself, how much must you earn just to break even?
- Why might your average fall even though your grades improved from the previous term?

Answers to these and other questions are discovered in this chapter, which introduces production and cost in the firm.

The previous chapter explored the consumer behavior shaping the demand curve. You were asked to think like a consumer, or demander. This chapter examines the producer behavior shaping the supply curve. You must now think like a producer, or supplier. You may feel more natural as a consumer (after all, you *are* one), but you already know a lot more about producers than you may realize. You have been around them all your life—Walmart, Starbucks, Google, Exxon, Amazon.com, Home Depot, McDonald's, Twitter, Facebook, Pizza Hut, Ford, the Gap, grocery stores, drugstores, convenience stores, bookstores, and hundreds more. So you already have some idea how businesses operate. They all have the same goal—they try to maximize profit, which is revenue minus cost. This chapter introduces the cost side of the profit equation.

Topics discussed include:

- Explicit and implicit costs
- Economic and normal profit
- Increasing and diminishing returns
- Short-run costs
- Long-run costs
- Economies and diseconomies of scale

Cost and Profit

With demand, we assume that consumers try to maximize utility, a goal that motivates their behavior. With supply, we assume that producers try to maximize *profit*, and this goal motivates their behavior. *Firms try to earn a profit by transforming resources into salable products.* Over time, firms that survive and grow are those that are more profitable. Unprofitable firms eventually fail. Each year, millions of new firms enter the marketplace and many leave. The firm's decision makers must choose what goods and services to produce and what resources to employ. They must make plans while confronting uncertainty about consumer demand, resource availability, and the intentions of other firms in the market. *The lure of profit is so strong, however, that eager entrepreneurs are always ready to pursue their dreams.*

Explicit and Implicit Costs

To hire a resource, a firm must pay at least the resource's *opportunity cost*—that is, at least what the resource could earn in its best alternative use. For most resources, a cash payment approximates the opportunity cost. For example, the $3 per pound that Domino's Pizza pays for cheese must at least equal the cheese producer's opportunity cost of supplying it. Firms do not make direct cash payments for resources they own. For example, a firm pays no rent to operate in a company-owned building. Similarly, small-business owners usually don't pay themselves an hourly wage. Yet these resources are not free. *Whether hired in resource markets or owned by the firm, all resources have an opportunity cost.* Company-owned buildings can be rented or sold; small-business owners can find other work.

A firm's **explicit costs** are its actual cash payments for resources: wages, rent, interest, insurance, taxes, and the like. In addition to these direct cash outlays, or explicit costs, the firm also incurs **implicit costs,** which are the opportunity costs of using resources owned by the firm or provided by the firm's owners. Examples include the use of a company-owned building, use of company funds, or the time of the firm's owners. Like explicit costs, implicit costs are opportunity costs. But unlike explicit costs, implicit costs require no cash payment and no entry in the firm's *accounting statement,* which records its revenues, explicit costs, and accounting profit.

explicit cost
Opportunity cost of resources employed by a firm that takes the form of cash payments

implicit cost
A firm's opportunity cost of using its own resources or those provided by its owners without a corresponding cash payment

Alternative Measures of Profit

An example may help clarify the distinction between explicit and implicit costs. Wanda Wheeler earns $50,000 a year as an aeronautical engineer with the Skyhigh Aircraft Corporation. On her way home from work one day, she gets an idea for a rounder, more friction-resistant airplane wheel. She decides to quit her job and start a business, which she calls Wheeler Dealer. To buy the necessary machines and equipment, she withdraws $20,000 from a savings account earning interest of $1,000 a year. She hires an assistant and starts producing the wheel using the spare bay in her condominium's parking garage, which she had been renting to a neighbor for $100 a month.

Sales are slow at first—people keep telling her she is just trying to reinvent the wheel—but her wheel eventually gets rolling. When Wanda reviews the firm's performance after the first year, she is pleased. As you can see in the top portion of Exhibit 1, company revenue in 2010 totaled $105,000. After paying her assistant and for materials and equipment, the firm shows an accounting profit of $64,000. **Accounting profit** equals total revenue minus explicit costs. Accountants use this profit to determine a firm's taxable income.

accounting profit
A firm's total revenue minus its explicit costs

But accounting profit ignores the opportunity cost of Wanda's own resources used in the firm. First is the opportunity cost of her time. Remember, she quit a $50,000-a-year job to work full time on her business, thereby forgoing that salary. Second is the $1,000 in annual interest she passes up by funding the operation with her own savings. And third, by using the spare bay in the garage for the business, she forgoes $1,200 per year in rental income. The forgone salary, interest, and rental income are implicit costs because she no longer earns income from the best alternative uses of these resources.

Economic profit equals total revenue minus all costs, both implicit and explicit; *economic profit takes into account the opportunity cost of all resources used in production.* In Exhibit 1, accounting profit of $64,000 less implicit costs of $52,200 yields an economic profit of $11,800. Economic profit is what Wanda Wheeler earns as an entrepreneur—an amount over and above what her resources could earn in their best alternative use. What would happen to the accounting statement if Wanda decided to pay herself a salary of $50,000 per year? Explicit costs would increase by $50,000, and implicit costs would decrease by $50,000. Thus, accounting profit would decrease by $50,000, but economic profit would not change because it already reflects both implicit and explicit costs.

economic profit
A firm's total revenue minus its explicit and implicit costs

There is one other profit measure to consider. The accounting profit just sufficient to ensure that *all* resources used by the firm earn their opportunity cost is called a **normal profit.** Wheeler Dealer earns a normal profit when accounting profit equals implicit costs—the sum of the salary Wanda gave up at her regular job ($50,000), the interest she gave up by using her own savings ($1,000), and the rent she gave up on her garage ($1,200). Thus, if the accounting profit is $52,200 per year—the opportunity cost of resources Wanda supplies to the firm—the company earns a normal profit. *Any*

normal profit
The accounting profit earned when all resources earn their opportunity cost

EXHIBIT 1 Wheeler Dealer Accounts, 2010

Total revenue		$105,000
Less explicit costs:		
Assistant's salary	−$21,000	
Material and equipment	−$20,000	
Equals accounting profit		$64,000
Less implicit costs:		
Wanda's forgone salary	−$50,000	
Forgone interest on savings	−$1,000	
Forgone garage rental	−$1,200	
Equals economic profit		$11,800

accounting profit in excess of a normal profit is economic profit. If accounting profit is large enough, it can be divided into normal profit and economic profit. The $64,000 in accounting profit earned by Wanda's firm consists of (1) a normal profit of $52,200, which covers her implicit costs—the opportunity cost of resources she supplies the firm, and (2) an economic profit of $11,800, which is over and above what these resources, including Wanda's time, could earn in their best alternative use.

As long as economic profit is positive, Wanda is better off running her own firm than working for Skyhigh Aircraft. If total revenue had been only $50,000, an accounting profit of only $9,000 would cover less than one-fifth of her salary, to say nothing of her forgone rent and interest. Because Wanda would not have covered her implicit costs, she would not be earning even a normal profit and would be better off back in her old job.

To understand profit maximization, you must develop a feel for both revenue and cost. In this chapter, you begin learning about the cost of production, starting with the relationship between inputs and outputs.

Production in the Short Run

We shift now from a discussion of profit, which is why firms exist, to a discussion of how firms operate. Suppose a new McDonald's just opened in your neighborhood and business is booming far beyond expectations. The manager responds to the unexpected demand by quickly hiring more workers. But cars are still backed up into the street waiting for a parking space. The solution is to add a drive-through window, but such an expansion takes time.

Fixed and Variable Resources

variable resource
Any resource that can be varied in the short run to increase or decrease production

fixed resource
Any resource that cannot be varied in the short run

short run
A period during which at least one of a firm's resources is fixed

long run
A period during which all resources under the firm's control are variable

Some resources, such as labor, are called **variable resources** because they can be varied quickly to change the output rate. But adjustments in other resources take more time. Resources that cannot be altered easily—the size of the building, for example—are called **fixed resources**. When considering the time required to change the quantity of resources employed, economists distinguish between the short run and the long run. In the **short run**, at least one resource is fixed. In the **long run**, no resource is fixed.

Output can be changed in the short run by adjusting variable resources, but the size, or *scale*, of the firm is fixed in the short run. In the long run, all resources can be varied. The length of the long run differs from industry to industry because the nature of production differs. For example, the size of a McDonald's outlet can be increased more quickly than can the size of an auto plant. Thus, the long run for that McDonald's is shorter than the long run for an automaker.

The Law of Diminishing Marginal Returns

Let's focus on the short-run link between resource use and the rate of output by considering a hypothetical moving company called Smoother Mover. Suppose the company's fixed resources, such as a warehouse, are already in place and that labor is the only variable resource. Exhibit 2 relates the amount of labor employed to the amount of output produced. Labor is measured in worker-days, which is one worker for one day, and output is measured in tons of furniture moved per day. The first column shows the amount of labor employed, which ranges from 0 to 8 worker-days. The second column

EXHIBIT 2 **The Short-Run Relationship Between Units of Labor and Tons of Furniture Moved**

Units of the Variable Resource (worker-days)	Total Product (tons moved per day)	Marginal Product (tons moved per day)
0	0	–
1	2	2
2	5	3
3	9	4
4	12	3
5	14	2
6	15	1
7	15	0
8	14	−1

Marginal product increases as the firm hires each of the first three workers, reflecting increasing marginal returns. Then marginal product declines, reflecting diminishing marginal returns. Adding more workers may, at some point, actually reduce total product (as occurs here with an eighth worker) because workers start getting in each other's way.

shows the tons of furniture moved per day, or the **total product,** at each level of employment. The relationship between the amount of resources employed and total product is called the firm's **production function.** The third column shows the **marginal product** of each worker—that is, the change in total product resulting from an additional unit of labor, assuming other resources remain unchanged. Spend a little time now getting acquainted with the three columns.

total product
A firm's total output

production function
The relationship between the amount of resources employed and a firm's total product

marginal product
The change in total product that occurs when the use of a particular resource increases by one unit, all other resources constant

Increasing Marginal Returns

Without labor, nothing gets moved, so total product is 0. If one worker is hired, that worker must do all the driving, packing, crating, and moving. Some of the larger items, such as couches and major appliances, cannot easily be moved by a single worker. Still, in our example one worker moves 2 tons of furniture per day. When a second worker is hired, some division of labor occurs, and two together can move the big stuff more easily, so production more than doubles to 5 tons per day. The marginal product of the second worker is 3 tons per day. Adding a third worker allows for a finer division of labor. For example, one can pack fragile items while the other two do the heavy lifting. Total product is 9 tons per day, 4 tons more than with two workers. Because the marginal product increases, the firm experiences **increasing marginal returns** from labor as each of the first three workers is hired.

increasing marginal returns
The marginal product of a variable resource increases as each additional unit of that resource is employed

Diminishing Marginal Returns

A fourth worker's marginal product is less than that of a third worker. Hiring still more workers increases total product by successively smaller amounts, so the marginal product declines after three workers. With that fourth worker, the **law of diminishing marginal returns** takes hold. This law states that as more of a variable resource is combined with a given amount of another resource, marginal product eventually declines. *The law of diminishing marginal returns is the most important feature of production in the short run.* As more and more labor is hired, marginal product could even turn negative, so total product would decline. For example, when Smoother Mover hires an eighth worker, workers start getting in each other's way, and they take up valuable space in the moving van. As a result, an eighth worker actually subtracts from total

law of diminishing marginal returns
As more of a variable resource is added to a given amount of another resource, marginal product eventually declines and could become negative

output, yielding a negative marginal product. Likewise, a McDonald's outlet can hire only so many workers before congestion and confusion in the work area cut total product ("too many cooks spoil the broth").

The Total and Marginal Product Curves

Exhibit 3 illustrates the relationship between total product and marginal product, using data from Exhibit 2. Note that because of increasing marginal returns, marginal product in panel (b) increases with each of the first three workers. With marginal product increasing, total product in panel (a) increases at an increasing rate (although this is hard to see in Exhibit 3). But once decreasing marginal returns set in, which begins with the fourth worker, marginal product declines. Total product continues to increase but at a decreasing rate. As long as marginal product is positive, total product increases. Where marginal product turns negative, total product starts to fall. Exhibit 3 summarizes all this by sorting production into three ranges: increasing marginal returns, diminishing but positive marginal returns, and negative marginal returns. These ranges for marginal product correspond with total product that increases at an increasing rate, increases at a decreasing rate, and declines.

Costs in the Short Run

Now that we have examined the relationship between the amount of resources used and the rate of output, let's consider how the cost of production varies as output varies. There are two kinds of costs in the short run: fixed and variable. Fixed cost pays for fixed resources and variable cost pays for variable resources. A firm must pay a **fixed cost** even if no output is produced. For example, in the steel industry, giant ovens must remain hot even when the plant isn't making steel. Otherwise, bricks inside would disintegrate. And a huge vacuum that sucks out pollutants must run continuously because turning its motors off and on can damage them.[1] Similarly, even if Smoother Mover hires no labor and moves no furniture, it incurs property taxes, insurance, vehicle registration, plus any opportunity cost for warehouse and equipment. By definition, fixed cost is just that: fixed—it does not vary with output in the short run. Suppose the *fixed cost* for Smoother Mover is $200 per day.

fixed cost
Any production cost that is independent of the firm's rate of output

Variable cost, as the name implies, is the cost of variable resources—in this case, labor. When no labor is employed, output is zero, as is variable cost. As workers are hired, output increases, as does variable cost. Variable cost depends on the amount of labor employed and on the wage. If the wage is $100 per day, *variable cost* equals the number of workers hired times $100.

variable cost
Any production cost that changes as the rate of output changes

Total Cost and Marginal Cost in the Short Run

Exhibit 4 offers cost data for Smoother Mover. The table lists the cost of production associated with alternative rates of output. Column (1) shows possible rates of output in the short run, measured in tons of furniture moved per day.

Total Cost

Column (2) shows the fixed cost (*FC*) at each rate of output. Note that fixed cost, by definition, remains constant at $200 per day regardless of output. Column (3) shows the labor needed to produce each rate of output based on the productivity figures reported in the previous two exhibits. For example, moving 2 tons a day requires one

1. Robert Guy Matthews, "Fixed Costs Chafe Steel Mills," *Wall Street Journal*, 10 June 2009.

EXHIBIT 3 The Total and Marginal Product of Labor

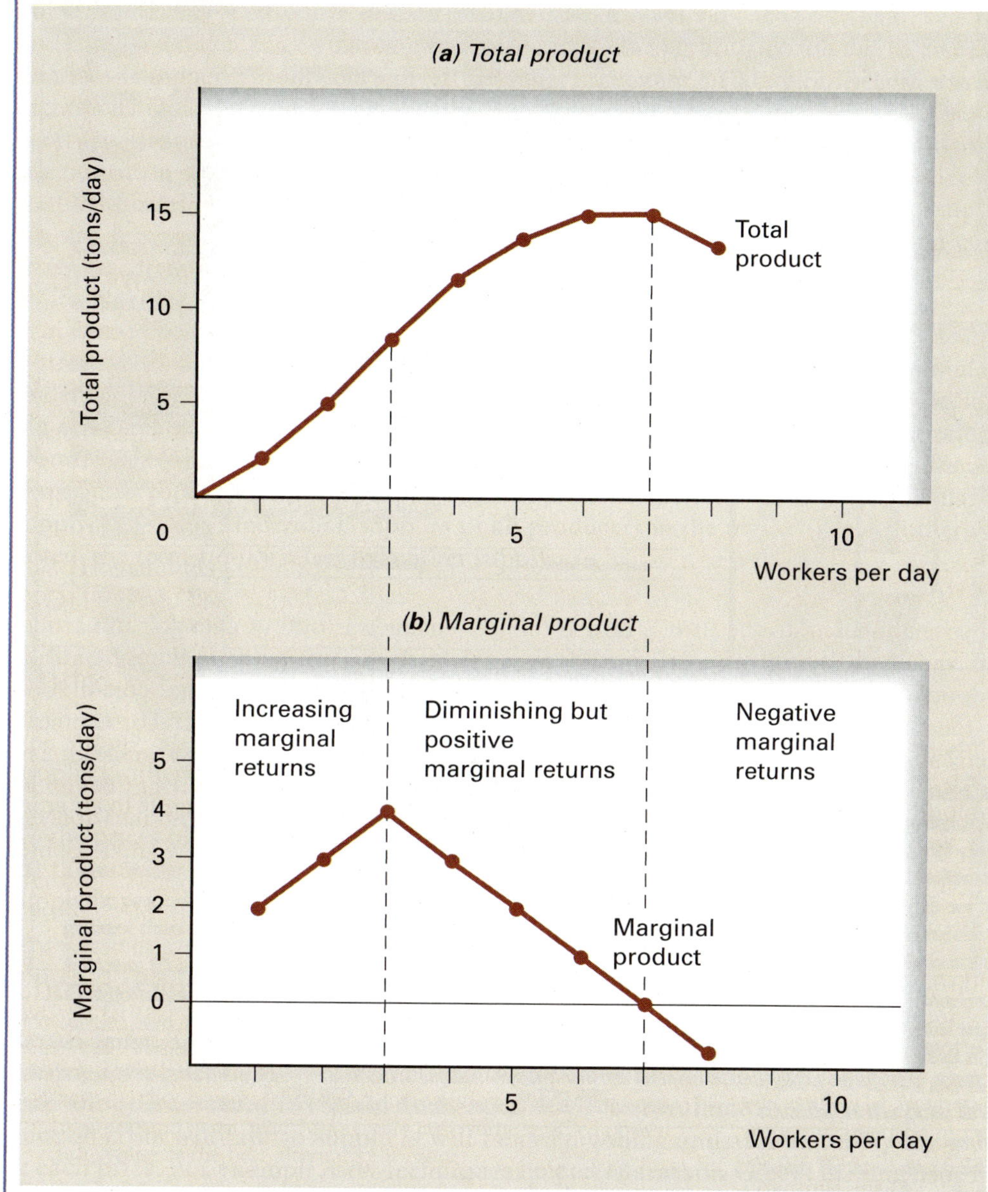

When marginal product is rising, total product increases by increasing amounts. When marginal product is falling but still positive, total product increases by decreasing amounts. When marginal product equals 0, total product is at a maximum. When marginal product is negative, total product is falling.

worker, 5 tons requires two workers, and so on. Only the first six workers are listed because additional workers would add nothing to output and so would not be hired. Column (4) lists variable cost (*VC*) per day, which equals $100 times the number of workers employed. For example, the variable cost of moving 9 tons of furniture per day is $300 because this output rate requires three workers. Column (5) lists the **total cost** (*TC*), the sum of fixed cost and variable cost: $TC = FC + VC$. As you can see, when output is zero, variable cost is zero, so total cost consists entirely of the fixed cost of $200. Incidentally, because total cost is the opportunity cost of all resources used by the firm, total cost includes a normal profit but not an economic profit. Think about that.

total cost
The sum of fixed cost and variable cost, or $TC = FC + VC$

EXHIBIT 4 Short-Run Total and Marginal Cost Data for Smoother Mover

(1) Tons Moved per Day (q)	(2) Fixed Cost (FC)	(3) Workers per Day	(4) Variable Cost (VC)	(5) Total Cost ($TC = FC + VC$)	(6) Marginal Cost $MC = \Delta TC/\Delta q$
0	$200	0	$0	$200	—
2	200	1	100	300	$50.00
5	200	2	200	400	33.33
9	200	3	300	500	25.00
12	200	4	400	600	33.33
14	200	5	500	700	50.00
15	200	6	600	800	100.00

Because of increasing marginal returns from the first three workers, marginal cost declines at first, as shown in column (6). Because of diminishing marginal returns beginning with the fourth worker, marginal cost starts increasing.

Marginal Cost

marginal cost
The change in total cost resulting from a one-unit change in output; the change in total cost divided by the change in output, or $MC = \Delta TC/\Delta q$

Of special interest to the firm is how total cost changes as output changes. In particular, what is the marginal cost of producing another unit? The **marginal cost** (MC) of production listed in column (6) of Exhibit 4 is simply the change in total cost divided by the change in output, or $MC = \Delta TC/\Delta q$, where Δ means "change in." For example, increasing output from 0 to 2 tons increases total cost by $100 (=$300−$200). The marginal cost of each of the first 2 tons is the change in total cost, $100, divided by the change in output, 2 tons, or $100/2, which equals $50. The marginal cost of each of the next 3 tons is $100/3, or $33.33.

Notice in column (6) that marginal cost first decreases, then increases. *Changes in marginal cost reflect changes in the marginal productivity of the variable resource.* Because of increasing marginal returns, the second worker produces more than the first and the third worker produces more than the second. This greater productivity results in a falling marginal cost for the first 9 tons moved. Beginning with the fourth worker, the firm experiences diminishing marginal returns from labor, so the marginal cost of output increases. *When the firm experiences increasing marginal returns, the marginal cost of output falls; when the firm experiences diminishing marginal returns, the marginal cost of output increases.* Thus, marginal cost in Exhibit 4 first falls and then rises, because marginal returns from labor first increase and then diminish.

Total and Marginal Cost Curves

Exhibit 5 shows cost curves for the data in Exhibit 4. Because fixed cost does not vary with output, the fixed cost curve is a horizontal line at the $200 level in panel (a). Variable cost is zero when output is zero, so the *variable cost curve* starts from the origin. The *total cost curve* sums the fixed cost curve and the variable cost curve. Because a constant fixed cost is added to variable cost, the total cost curve is simply the variable cost curve shifted vertically by the fixed cost.

In panel (b) of Exhibit 5, marginal cost declines until the ninth unit of output and then increases, reflecting labor's increasing and then diminishing marginal returns. There is a relationship between the two panels because the change in total cost resulting from a one-unit change in production equals the marginal cost. With each successive unit of output, total cost increases by the marginal cost of that unit. Thus, *the slope of the total*

EXHIBIT 5 Total and Marginal Cost Curves for Smoother Mover

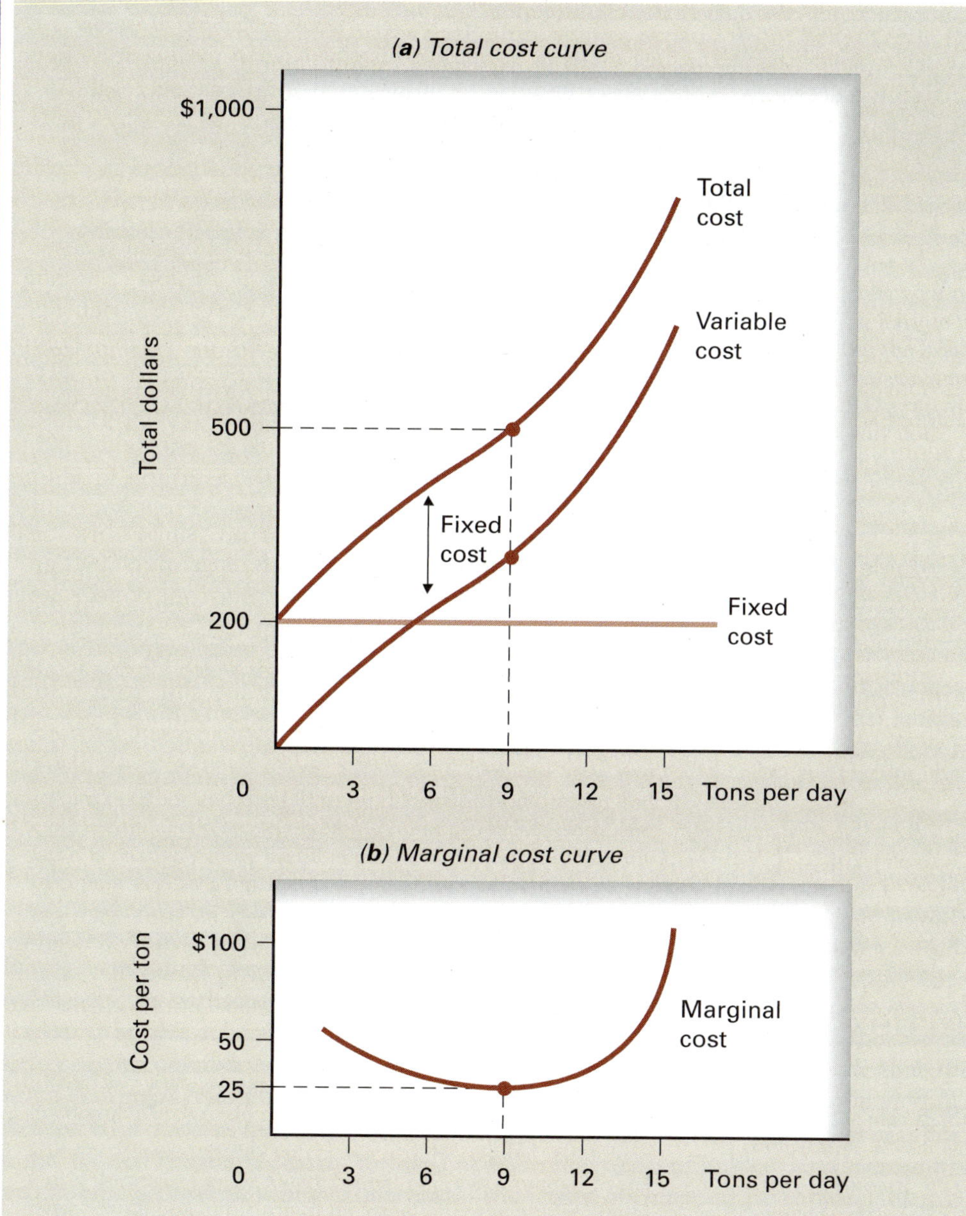

In panel (a), fixed cost is $200 at all levels of output. Variable cost starts from the origin and increases slowly at first as output increases. When the variable resource generates diminishing marginal returns, variable cost begins to increase more rapidly. Total cost is the vertical sum of fixed cost and variable cost. In panel (b), marginal cost first declines, reflecting increasing marginal returns from the variable resource (labor in this example) and then increases, reflecting diminishing marginal returns.

cost curve at each rate of output equals the marginal cost at that rate of output. The total cost curve can be divided into two sections, based on what happens to marginal cost:

1. Because of increasing marginal returns from labor, marginal cost at first declines, so total cost initially increases by successively smaller amounts and the total cost curve becomes less steep.

2. Because of diminishing marginal returns from labor, marginal cost starts increasing after the ninth unit of output, so total cost increases by successively larger amounts and the total cost curve becomes steeper.

Keep in mind that economic analysis is marginal analysis. Marginal cost is the key to economic decisions. Marginal cost indicates how much total cost increases if one more unit is produced or how much total cost drops if production declines by one unit.

Average Cost in the Short Run

average variable cost
Variable cost divided by output, or $AVC = VC/q$

average total cost
Total cost divided by output, or $ATC = TC/q$; the sum of average fixed cost and average variable cost, or $ATC = AFC + AVC$

Although marginal cost is of most interest, the average cost per unit of output is also useful. We can distinguish between average variable cost and average total cost. These measures appear in columns (5) and (6) of Exhibit 6. Column (5) lists **average variable cost,** or *AVC*, which equals variable cost divided by output, or $AVC = VC/q$. The final column lists **average total cost,** or *ATC*, which equals total cost divided by output, or $ATC = TC/q$. Each measure of average cost first declines as output expands and then increases.

The Relationship Between Marginal Cost and Average Cost

To understand the relationship between marginal cost and average cost, let's begin with an example of college grades. Think about how your grades each term affect your grade point average (GPA). Suppose you do well your first term, starting your college career with a 3.4 (out of 4.0). Your grades for the second term drop to 2.8, reducing your GPA to 3.1. You slip again in the third term to a 2.2, lowering your GPA to 2.8. Your fourth-term grades improve a bit to 2.4, but your GPA continues to slide to 2.7. In the fifth term, your grades improve to 2.7, leaving your GPA unchanged at 2.7. And in the sixth term, you get 3.3, pulling your GPA up to 2.8. Notice that when your term grades are below your GPA, your GPA falls. Even when your term performance improves, your GPA does not improve until your term grades *exceed* your GPA. Your term grades first pull down your GPA and then eventually pull it up.

Let's now take a look at the relationship between marginal cost and average cost. In Exhibit 6, marginal cost has the same relationship to average cost as your term grades have to your GPA. You can observe this marginal-average relationship in columns

EXHIBIT 6 Short-Run Total, Marginal, and Average Cost Data for Smoother Mover

(1) Tons Moved per Day (*q*)	(2) Variable Cost (*VC*)	(3) Total Cost ($TC = FC + VC$)	(4) Marginal Cost ($MC = \Delta TC/\Delta q$)	(5) Average Variable Cost ($AVC = VC/q$)	(6) Average Total Cost ($ATC = TC/q$)
0	$0	$200	0	—	∞
2	100	300	$50.00	$50.00	$150.00
5	200	400	33.33	40.00	80.00
9	300	500	25.00	33.33	55.55
12	400	600	33.33	33.33	50.00
14	500	700	50.00	35.71	50.00
15	600	800	100.00	40.00	53.33

Marginal cost first falls then increases because of increasing then diminishing marginal returns from labor. As long as marginal cost is below average cost, average cost declines. Once marginal cost exceeds average cost, average cost increases. Columns (4), (5), and (6) show the relation between marginal and average costs.

(4) and (5). Because of increasing marginal returns from the first three workers, marginal cost falls for the first 9 tons of furniture moved. Because marginal cost is below average cost, marginal cost pulls down average cost. Marginal cost equals average variable cost when output is 12 tons, and marginal cost exceeds average variable cost when output exceeds 12 tons, so marginal cost pulls up average variable cost.

Exhibit 7 shows the same marginal cost curve first presented in Exhibit 5, along with average cost curves based on data in Exhibit 6. At low rates of output, marginal cost declines as output expands because of increasing marginal returns from labor. As long as marginal cost is below average cost, marginal cost pulls down average cost as output expands. At higher rates of output, marginal cost increases because of diminishing marginal returns from labor. Once marginal cost exceeds average cost, marginal cost pulls up average cost. The fact that marginal cost first pulls average cost down and then pulls it up explains why the average cost curves have U shapes. The shapes of the average variable cost curve and the average total cost curve are determined by the shape of the marginal cost curve, so each is shaped by increasing, then diminishing, marginal returns.

Notice also that the rising marginal cost curve intersects both the average variable cost curve and the average total cost curve where these average curves reach their minimum. This occurs because the marginal pulls down the average where the marginal is below the average and pulls up the average where the marginal is above the average. One more thing: The distance between the average variable cost curve and the average total cost curve is *average fixed cost*, which gets smaller as the rate of output increases. (Why does average fixed cost get smaller?)

EXHIBIT 7 Average and Marginal Cost Curves for Smoother Mover

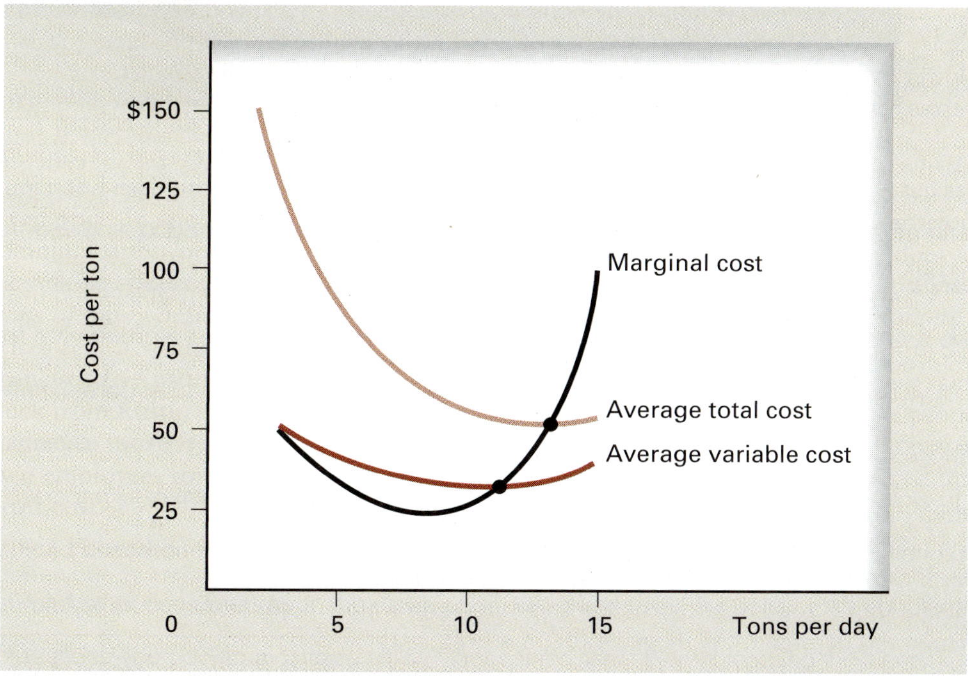

Average variable cost and average total cost curves first decline, reach low points, and then rise. Overall, they have U shapes. When marginal cost is below average variable cost, average variable cost is falling. When marginal cost equals average variable cost, average variable cost is at its minimum. When marginal cost is above average variable cost, average variable cost is increasing. The same relationship holds between marginal cost and average total cost.

The law of diminishing marginal returns determines the shapes of short-run cost curves. When the marginal product of labor increases, the marginal cost of output falls. Once diminishing marginal returns take hold, the marginal cost of output rises. Thus, marginal cost first falls and then rises. And the marginal cost curve dictates the shapes of the average cost curves. When marginal cost is less than average cost, average cost declines. When marginal cost is above average cost, average cost increases. Got it? If not, please reread this paragraph.

Costs in the Long Run

So far, the analysis has focused on how costs vary as the rate of output expands in the short run for a firm of a given size. In the long run, all inputs that are under the firm's control can be varied, so there is no fixed cost. The long run is not just a succession of short runs. The long run is best thought of as a *planning horizon*. In the long run, the choice of input combinations is flexible. But once the size of the plant has been selected and the concrete has been poured, the firm has fixed costs and is operating in the short run. Firms plan for the long run, but they produce in the short run. We turn now to long-run costs.

Economies of Scale

economies of scale
Forces that reduce a firm's average cost as the scale of operation increases in the long run

Like short-run average cost curves, a firm's long-run average cost curve is U-shaped. Recall that the shape of the short-run average total cost curve is determined primarily by increasing and diminishing marginal returns from the variable resource. A different principle shapes the long-run cost curve. If a firm experiences **economies of scale**, long-run average cost falls as output expands. Consider some sources of economies of scale. *A larger size often allows for larger, more specialized machines and greater specialization of labor.* For example, compare the household-size kitchen of a small restaurant with the kitchen at a McDonald's. At low rates of output, the smaller kitchen produces meals at a lower average cost than does McDonald's. But if production in the smaller kitchen increases beyond, say, 100 meals per day, a kitchen on the scale of McDonald's would make meals at a lower average cost. Thus, because of economies of scale, the long-run average cost for a restaurant may fall as size increases. As an example, the idea for McDonald's snack wrap started when a franchisee suggested that the company find more uses for the strips of chicken served with dipping sauce. Selling more chicken allowed each restaurant to cook new batches more frequently, which meant customers got a fresher product.[2]

A larger scale of operation allows a firm to use larger, more efficient machines and to assign workers to more specialized tasks. Production techniques such as the assembly line can be introduced only if the rate of output is sufficiently large. Typically, as the scale of a firm increases, capital substitutes for labor and complex machines substitute for simpler machines.

Diseconomies of Scale

diseconomies of scale
Forces that may eventually increase a firm's average cost as the scale of operation increases in the long run

Often another force, called **diseconomies of scale**, may eventually take over as a firm expands its plant size, increasing long-run average cost as output expands. For example, Oasis of the Sea, the world's largest cruise liner, can accommodate 6,300 guests, but the ship is too large to visit some of the world's most popular destinations, such as Venice and Bermuda.[3] More generally in a firm, as the amount and variety of resources employed increase, so does the *task of coordinating all these inputs*. As the workforce grows, additional layers of management are needed to monitor production. In the thicket of bureaucracy that develops, communications may get mangled. Top executives have

2. As reported by Janet Adamy, "For McDonald's It's a Wrap," *Wall Street Journal*, 30 January 2007.
3. Sarah Nassauer, "What It Takes to Keep a City Afloat," *Wall Street Journal*, 3 March 2010.

more difficulty keeping in touch with the factory floor because information is distorted as it moves up and down the chain of command. Indeed, in large organizations, rumors may become a primary source of information, reducing efficiency and increasing average cost.

The crisis of 2008 resulted in part because some financial institutions had grown so large and complex that top executives couldn't accurately assess the risks of the financial products they were buying and selling. One could argue that such firms were experiencing diseconomies of scale. For example, "Former Citigroup CEO Charles Prince apologized for his firm's role in the financial crisis, suggesting bank executives were wholly unaware of the risks posed by collateralized debt securities on the firm's books."[4]

Note that *diseconomies of scale result from a larger firm size, whereas diminishing marginal returns result from using more variable resources in a firm of a given size.*

The Long-Run Average Cost Curve

Because of the special nature of technology in the industry, suppose a firm must choose from among three possible plant sizes: small, medium, and large. Exhibit 8 presents this simple case. The average total cost curves for the three sizes are *SS'*, *MM'*, and *LL'*. Which size should the firm build to minimize average cost? The appropriate size, *or scale*, for the firm depends on how much output the firm wants to produce. For example, if *q* is the desired output, average cost is lowest with a small plant size. If the desired output is *q'*, the medium plant size offers the lowest average cost. With the medium plant, the firm experiences economies of scale. With the large plant, the firm experiences diseconomies of scale.

EXHIBIT 8 **Short-Run Average Total Cost Curves Form the Long-Run Average Cost Curve, or Planning Curve**

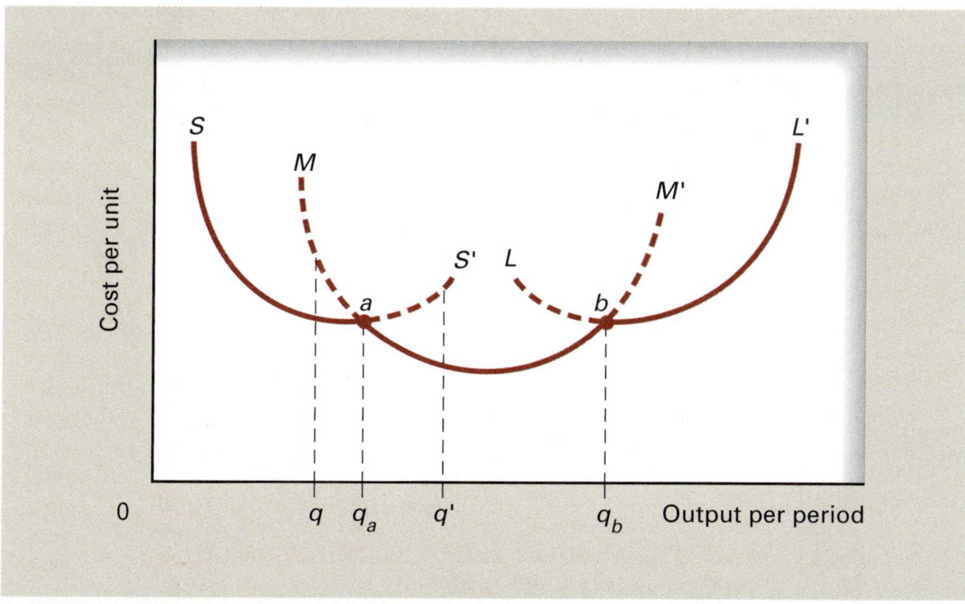

Curves *SS'*, *MM'*, and *LL'* show short-run average total costs for small, medium, and large plants, respectively. For output less than q_a, average cost is lowest when the plant is small. Between q_a and q_b, average cost is lowest with a medium-size plant. If output exceeds q_b, the large plant offers the lowest average cost. The long-run average-cost curve connects these low cost segments of each curve and is identified as *SabL'*.

4. As reported by Michael Crittenden, "Citi's Prince: I'm Sorry," *Wall Street Journal*, 8 April 2010. For more evidence see David Wessel, *In Fed We Trust*, (Crown Business, 2009); Michael Lewis, *The Big Short*, (Norton, 2010); and Roger Lowenstein, *The End of Wall Street*, (Penguin Press, 2010).

More generally in Exhibit 8, for output less than q_a, average cost is lowest when the plant is small. For output between q_a and q_b, average cost is lowest for the medium plant. And for output that exceeds q_b average cost is lowest when the plant is large. The **long-run average cost curve**, or *LRAC* curve, sometimes called the firm's *planning curve,* connects portions of the three short-run average cost curves that are lowest for each output rate. In Exhibit 8, that curve consists of the line segments connecting *S, a, b,* and *L'*. So even though the firm experiences diseconomies of scale with the largest plant size, the large firm is the one to build if the firm needs to produce more than q_b.

long-run average cost curve
A curve that indicates the lowest average cost of production at each rate of output when the size, or scale, of the firm varies; also called the planning curve

Now suppose there are many possible plant sizes. Exhibit 9 presents a sample of short-run cost curves shown in pink. The long-run average cost curve, shown in red, is formed by connecting the points on the various short-run average cost curves that represent the lowest per-unit cost for each rate of output. Each of the short-run average cost curves is tangent to the long-run average cost curve, or *planning curve*. If we could display enough short-run cost curves, we would have a different plant size for each rate of output. *These points of tangency represent the least-cost way of producing each particular rate of output, given resource prices and the technology*. For example, the short-run average total cost curve ATC_1 is tangent to the long-run average cost curve at point *a,* where \$11 is the lowest average cost of producing output *q*. Note, however, that other output rates along ATC_1 have a lower average cost. For example, the average cost of producing *q'* is only \$10, as identified at point *b*. Point *b* depicts the lowest average cost along ATC_1. So, while the point of tangency reflects the least-cost way of producing a particular rate of output, that tangency point does not reflect the minimum average cost for this particular plant size.

If the firm decides to produce *q'*, which size plant should it choose to minimize the average cost of production? Output rate *q'* could be produced at point *b,* which represents the minimum average cost along ATC_1. But average cost is lower with a larger plant. With the plant size associated with ATC_2, the average cost of producing *q'* would

EXHIBIT 9 Many Short-Run Average Total Cost Curves Form a Firm's Long-Run Average Cost Curve, or Planning Curve

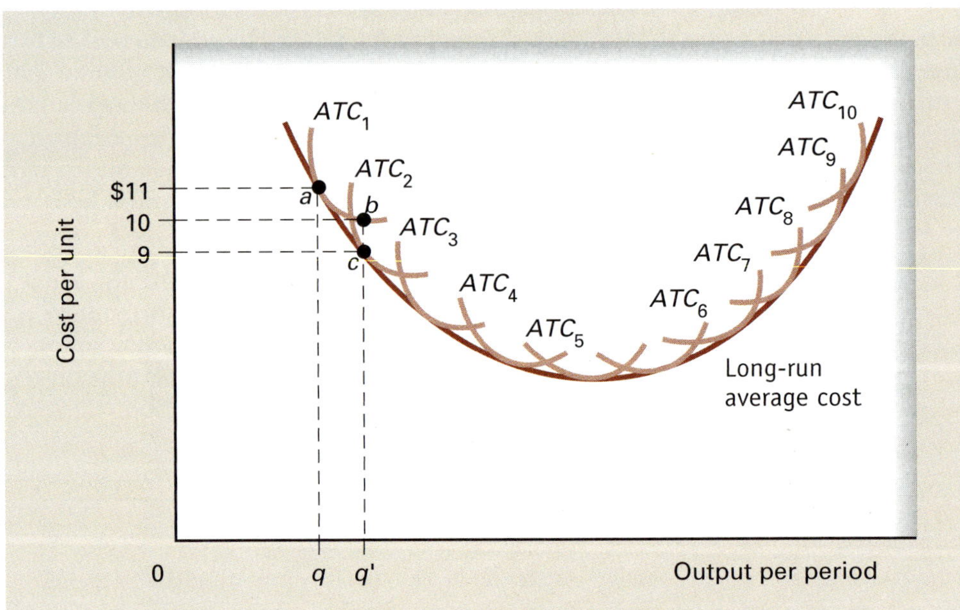

With many possible plant sizes, the long-run average cost curve is the envelope of portions of the short-run average cost curves. Each short-run curve is tangent to the long-run average cost curve. Each point of tangency represents the least-cost way of producing that rate of output.

be minimized at $9 per unit at point *c*. *Each point of tangency between a short-run average cost curve and the long-run average cost curve represents the least-cost way of producing that particular rate of output.*

In the long run, a firm can vary the inputs under its control. Some resources, however, are not under the firm's control, and the inability to vary them may contribute to diseconomies of scale. Let's consider economies and diseconomies of scale at movie theaters in the case study, "Bringing Theory to Life: Scale Economies and Diseconomies at the Movies," at the end of the book.

It is possible for average cost to neither increase nor decrease with changes in firm size. If neither economies of scale nor diseconomies of scale are apparent over some range of output, a firm experiences **constant long-run average cost.** Perhaps economies and diseconomies of scale exist simultaneously in the firm but have offsetting effects. Exhibit 10 presents a firm's long-run average cost curve, or LRAC curve, which is divided into output segments reflecting economies of scale, constant long-run average costs, and diseconomies of scale. Output must reach quantity A for the firm to achieve the **minimum efficient scale,** which is the lowest rate of output at which long-run average cost is at a minimum.

constant long-run average cost
A cost that occurs when, over some range of output, long-run average cost neither increases nor decreases with changes in firm size

minimum efficient scale
The lowest rate of output at which a firm takes full advantage of economies of scale

Economies and Diseconomies of Scale at the Firm Level

Our discussion so far has referred to a particular plant—a movie theater or a restaurant, for example. But a firm could also be a collection of plants, such as the hundreds of movie theaters in a chain or the thousands of McDonald's restaurants. More generally, we can distinguish between economies and diseconomies of scale at the *plant level*—that is, at a particular location—and at the *firm level,* where the firm is a collection of plants.

EXHIBIT 10 A Firm's Long-Run Average Cost Curve

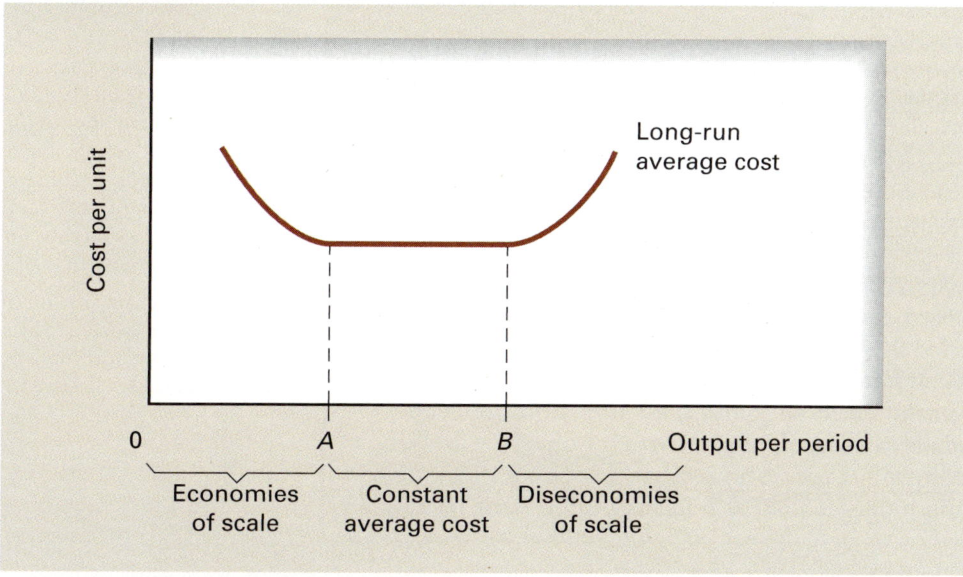

Up to output level *A*, long-run average cost falls as the firm experiences economies of scale. Output level *A* is the minimum efficient scale—the lowest rate of output at which the firm takes full advantage of economies of scale. Between *A* and *B*, the average cost is constant. Beyond output level *B*, long-run average cost increases as the firm experiences diseconomies of scale.

The case study, "World of Business: Scale Economies and Diseconomies at McDonald's" at the end of the book, explores issues of multiplant scale economies and diseconomies.

Other large firms do what they can to reduce diseconomies of scale at the firm level. For example, IBM undertook a massive restructuring program to decentralize into six smaller decision-making groups. Some big corporations have even spun off parts of their operation to form new corporations. For example, Hewlett-Packard split off Agilent Technologies, AT&T created Lucent Technologies, and Time Warner spun off AOL.

Conclusion

By considering the relationship between production and cost, we have developed the foundation for a theory of firm behavior. Despite what may appear to be a tangle of short-run and long-run cost curves, *only two relationships between resources and output underlie all the curves. In the short run, it's increasing and diminishing returns from the variable resource. In the long run, it's economies and diseconomies of scale.* If you understand the sources of these two phenomena, you grasp the central points of the chapter. Our examination of production and cost in the short run and long run lays the groundwork for a firm's supply curve, to be covered in the next chapter. But before that, the appendix develops a more sophisticated approach to production and cost.

Summary

1. Explicit costs are opportunity costs of resources employed by a firm that take the form of cash payments. Implicit costs are the opportunity costs of using resources owned by the firm. A firm earns a normal profit when total revenue covers all implicit and explicit costs. Economic profit equals total revenue minus both explicit and implicit costs.
2. Resources that can be varied quickly to increase or decrease output are called variable resources. In the short run, at least one resource is fixed. In the long run, all resources are variable.
3. A firm may initially experience increased marginal returns as it takes advantage of increased specialization of the variable resource. But the law of diminishing marginal returns indicates that the firm eventually reaches a point where adding more units of the variable resource yields an ever-smaller marginal product.
4. The law of diminishing marginal returns from the variable resource is the most important feature of production in the short run and explains why marginal cost and average cost eventually increase as output expands.
5. In the long run, all inputs under the firm's control are variable, so there is no fixed cost. The firm's long-run average cost curve, also called its planning curve, is an envelope formed by a series of short-run average total cost curves. The long run is best thought of as a planning horizon.
6. A firm's long-run average cost curve, like its short-run average cost curves, is U-shaped. As output expands, average cost at first declines because of economies of scale—a larger plant size allows for bigger and more specialized machinery and a more extensive division of labor. Eventually, average cost stops falling. Average cost may be constant over some range. If output expands still further, the plant may experience diseconomies of scale as the cost of coordinating resources grows. Economies and diseconomies of scale can occur at the plant level and at the firm level.
7. In the long run, a firm selects the most efficient size for the desired rate of output. Once that size is chosen, some resources become fixed, so the firm is back operating in the short run. Thus, the firm plans for the long run but produces in the short run.

Key Concepts

Explicit cost 128
Implicit cost 128
Accounting profit 129
Economic profit 129
Normal profit 129
Variable resource 130
Fixed resource 130
Short run 130
Long run 130
Total product 131
Production function 131
Marginal product 131
Increasing marginal returns 131
Law of diminishing marginal returns 131

Fixed cost 132
Variable cost 132
Total cost 133
Marginal cost 134
Average variable cost 136
Average total cost 136
Economies of scale 138
Diseconomies of scale 138
Long-run average cost curve 140
Constant long-run average cost 141
Minimum efficient scale 141

Questions for Review

1. Explicit and Implicit Costs Amos McCoy is currently raising corn on his 100-acre farm and earning an accounting profit of $100 per acre. However, if he raised soybeans, he could earn $200 per acre. Is he currently earning an economic profit? Why or why not?

2. Explicit and Implicit Costs Determine whether each of the following is an explicit cost or an implicit cost:
   a. Payments for labor purchased in the labor market
   b. A firm's use of a warehouse that it owns and could rent to another firm
   c. Rent paid for the use of a warehouse not owned by the firm
   d. The wages that owners could earn if they did not work for themselves

3. Alternative Measures of Profit Calculate the accounting profit or loss as well as the economic profit or loss in each of the following situations:
   a. A firm with total revenues of $150 million, explicit costs of $90 million, and implicit costs of $40 million
   b. A firm with total revenues of $125 million, explicit costs of $100 million, and implicit costs of $30 million
   c. A firm with total revenues of $100 million, explicit costs of $90 million, and implicit costs of $20 million
   d. A firm with total revenues of $250,000, explicit costs of $275,000, and implicit costs of $50,000

4. Alternative Measures of Profit Why is it reasonable to think of normal profit as a type of cost to the firm?

5. Short Run Versus Long Run What distinguishes a firm's short-run period from its long-run period?

6. Law of Diminishing Marginal Returns As a farmer, you must decide how many times during the year to plant a new crop. Also, you must decide how far apart to space the plants. Will diminishing returns be a factor in your decision making? If so, how will it affect your decisions?

7. Marginal Cost What is the difference between fixed cost and variable cost? Does each type of cost affect short-run marginal cost? If yes, explain how each affects marginal cost. If no, explain why each does or does not affect marginal cost.

8. Marginal Cost Explain why the marginal cost of production *must* increase if the marginal product of the variable resource is decreasing.

9. Costs in the Short Run What effect would each of the following have on a firm's short-run marginal cost curve and its fixed cost curve?
   a. An increase in the wage rate
   b. A decrease in property taxes
   c. A rise in the purchase price of new capital
   d. A rise in energy prices

10. Costs in the Short Run Identify each of the curves in the following graph:

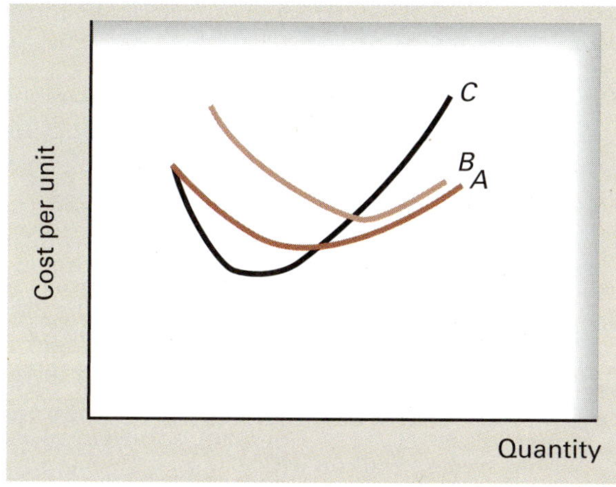

11. Marginal Cost and Average Cost Explain why the marginal cost curve must intersect the average total cost curve and the average variable cost curve at their minimum points. Why do the average total cost and average variable cost curves get closer to one another as output increases?

12. Marginal Cost and Average Cost In Exhibit 7 in this chapter, the output level where average total cost is at a minimum is greater than the output level where average variable cost is at a minimum. Why?

13. Long-Run Average Cost Curve What types of changes could shift the long-run average cost curve? How would these changes also affect the short-run average total cost curve?

14. Long-Run Average Cost Curve Explain the shape of the long-run average cost curve. What does "minimum efficient scale" mean?

15. Case Study: Scale Economies and Diseconomies at the Movies (See page 714.) The case study notes that the concession stand accounts for well over half the profits at most theaters. Given this, what are the benefits of the staggered movie times allowed by multiple screens? What is the benefit to a multiscreen theater of locating at a shopping mall?

16. Case Study: Scale Economies and Diseconomies at McDonald's (See page 715.) How does having a menu that is uniform around the country provide McDonald's with economies of scale? How is menu planning made more complex by expanding into other countries?

Problems and Exercises

17. **Production in the Short Run** Complete the following table. At what point does diminishing marginal returns set in?

Units of the Variable Resource	Total Product	Marginal Product
0	0	___
1	10	___
2	22	___
3	___	9
4	___	4
5	34	___

18. **Total Cost and Marginal Cost** Complete the following table, assuming that each unit of labor costs $75 per day.

Quantity of Labor per Day	Output per Day	Fixed Cost	Variable Cost	Total Cost	Marginal Cost
0	___	$300	$___	$___	$___
1	5	___	75	___	15
2	11	___	150	450	12.5
3	15	___	___	525	___
4	18	___	300	600	25
5	20	___	___	___	37.5

a. Graph the fixed cost, variable cost, and total cost curves for these data.
b. What is the marginal product of the third unit of labor?
c. What is average total cost when output is 18 units per day?

19. **Total Cost and Marginal Cost** Complete the following table, where *L* is units of labor, *Q* is units of output, and *MP* is the marginal product of labor.

L	*Q*	*MP*	*VC*	*TC*	*MC*	*ATC*
0	0	___	$ 0	$ 12	___	___
1	6	___	$ 3	$15	___	___
2	15	___	$ 6	___	___	___
3	21	___	$ 9	___	___	___
4	24	___	$ 12	___	___	___
5	26	___	$ 15	___	___	___

a. At what level of labor input do the marginal returns from labor begin to diminish?
b. What is the average variable cost when $Q = 24$?
c. What is this firm's fixed cost?
d. What is the wage rate per day?

20. **Relationship Between Marginal Cost and Average Cost** Assume that labor and capital are the only inputs used by a firm. Capital is fixed at 5 units, which cost $100 each. Workers can be hired for $200 each. Complete the following table to show average variable cost (*AVC*), average total cost (*ATC*), and marginal cost (*MC*).

Quantity of Labor	Total Output	*AVC*	*ATC*	*MC*
0	0	___	___	___
1	100	___	___	___
2	250	___	___	___
3	350	___	___	___
4	400	___	___	___
5	425	___	___	___

21. **Long-Run Costs** Suppose the firm has only three possible scales of production as shown below:

a. Which scale of production is most efficient when $Q = 65$?
b. Which scale of production is most efficient when $Q = 75$?
c. Trace out the long-run average cost curve on the diagram.

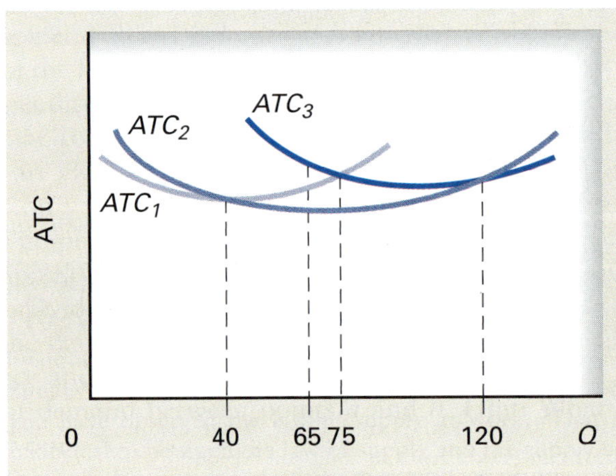

Appendix

A Closer Look at Production and Cost

This appendix develops a model for determining how a profit-maximizing firm combines resources to produce a particular rate of output. The quantity of output that can be produced with a given amount of resources depends on the existing *state of technology*, which is the prevailing knowledge of how resources can be combined. Let's begin by considering the technological possibilities available to the firm.

EXHIBIT 11 A Firm's Production Function Using Labor and Capital: Production per Month

Units of Capital Employed per Month	Units of Labor Employed per Month						
	1	2	3	4	5	6	7
1	40	90	150	200	240	270	290
2	90	140	200	250	290	315	335
3	150	195	260	310	345	370	390
4	200	250	310	350	385	415	440
5	240	290	345	385	420	450	475
6	270	320	375	415	450	475	495
7	290	330	390	435	470	495	510

The Production Function and Efficiency

The ways in which resources can be combined to produce output are summarized by a firm's production function. The *production function* identifies the most that can be produced per time period using various combinations of resources, for a given state of technology. The production function can be presented as an equation, a graph, or a table.

The production function summarized in Exhibit 11 reflects, for a hypothetical firm, the output resulting from various combinations of resources. This firm uses only two resources: capital and labor. The amount of capital used is listed down the left side of the table and the amount of labor across the top. For example, if 1 unit of capital is combined with 7 units of labor, the firm can produce 290 units of output per month. The firm produces the maximum possible output given the combination of resources used; that same output could not be produced with fewer resources. Thus, we say that production is **technologically efficient**.

We can examine the effects of adding labor to capital by starting with any level of capital and reading across the table. For example, when the firm uses 1 unit of capital and 1 unit of labor, it produces 40 units of output per month. If the amount of labor increases by 1 unit and the amount of capital remains constant, output increases to 90 units, so the marginal product of labor is 50 units. If the amount of labor employed increases from 2 to 3 units, other things constant, output goes to 150 units, yielding a marginal product of 60 units. By reading across the table, you find that the marginal product of labor first rises, showing increasing marginal returns from labor, and then declines, showing diminishing marginal returns. Similarly, by holding the amount of labor constant and following down the column, you find that the marginal product of capital also reflects first increasing marginal returns and then diminishing marginal returns.

Isoquants

Notice from the tabular presentation of the production function in Exhibit 11 that different combinations of resources yield the same rate of output. For example, several combinations of labor and capital yield 290 units of output per month (try to find the four combinations). Some of the information provided in Exhibit 11 can be presented more clearly in graphical form. In Exhibit 12, labor is measured along the horizontal axis and capital along the vertical axis. Combinations that yield 290 units of output are presented in Exhibit 12 as points *a*, *b*, *c*, and *d*. These points can be connected to form an *isoquant*, Q_1, a curve that shows the possible combinations of the two inputs that produce 290 units of output per month. Likewise, Q_2 shows combinations of inputs that yield 415 units of output, and Q_3, 475 units of output. (The isoquant colors match the corresponding entries in the production function table in Exhibit 11.)

An **isoquant**, such as Q_1 in Exhibit 12, is a curve that shows all the technologically efficient combinations of two resources, such as labor and capital, that produce a certain rate of output. *Iso* is from the Greek word meaning "equal," and *quant* is short for "quantity"; so *isoquant* means "equal quantity." Along a particular isoquant, such as Q_1, the output remains constant—in this case, 290 units per month—but the quantities of inputs vary. To produce a particular rate of output, the firm can use resource combinations ranging from much capital and little labor to little capital and much labor. For example, a paving contractor can put in a new driveway with 10 workers using shovels, wheelbarrows, and hand rollers. The same job can also be done with only two workers, a road grader, and a paving machine. A charity car wash is labor intensive, involving many workers per car, plus buckets, sponges, and hose. In contrast, a professional car wash is fully automated, requiring only one worker to turn on the machine and collect the money. An isoquant depicts alternative combinations of resources that produce the same output. Although we have included only three isoquants in Exhibit 12, there is a different isoquant for every amount listed in Exhibit 11. Indeed, there is a different isoquant for every amount the firm could possibly produce. Let's consider some properties of isoquants:

1. Isoquants farther from the origin represent greater output rates.

EXHIBIT 12 A Firm's Isoquants

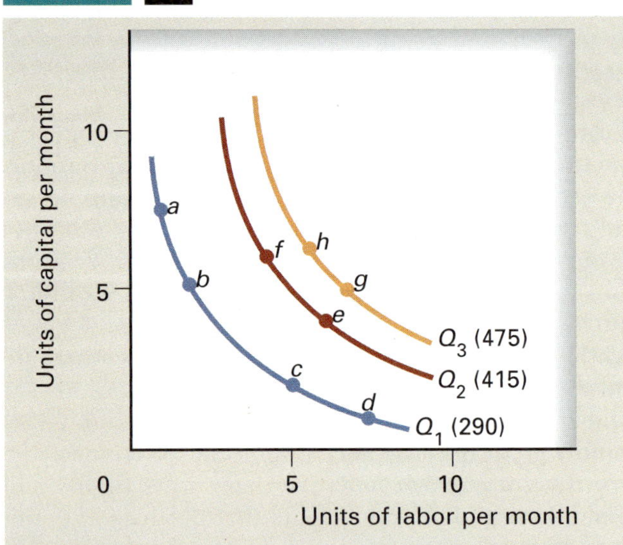

Isoquant Q_1 shows all technologically efficient combinations of labor and capital that can be used to produce 290 units of output. Isoquant Q_2 reflects 415 units, and Q_3 reflects 475 units. Each isoquant has a negative slope and is convex to the origin.

2. Isoquants have negative slopes because along a given isoquant, the quantity of labor employed inversely relates to the quantity of capital employed.
3. Isoquants do not intersect because each isoquant refers to a specific rate of output. An intersection would indicate that the same combination of resources could, with equal efficiency, produce two different rates of output.
4. *Isoquants are usually convex to the origin*, which means that any isoquant becomes flatter as you move down along the curve.

The slope of an isoquant measures the ability of additional units of one resource—in this case, labor—to substitute in production for another resource—in this case, capital. As noted already, the isoquant has a negative slope. The absolute value of the slope of an isoquant is the **marginal rate of technical substitution**, or **MRTS**, between two resources. The MRTS is the rate at which labor substitutes for capital without affecting output. When much capital and little labor are used, the marginal productivity of capital is relatively small and the marginal productivity of labor is relatively great. One unit of labor substitutes for a relatively large amount of capital. For example, in moving from point *a* to *b* along isoquant Q_1 in Exhibit 12, one unit of labor substitutes for two units of capital, so the MRTS between points *a* and *b* equals 2. But as more labor and less capital are employed, the marginal product of labor declines and the marginal product of capital increases, so it takes more labor to make up for a one-unit reduction in capital. For example, in moving from point *c* to point *d*, two units of labor substitute for one unit of capital; thus, the MRTS between points *c* and *d* equals ½.

The extent to which one input substitutes for another, as measured by the marginal rate of technical substitution, is linked to the marginal productivity of each input. For example, between points *a* and *b*, one unit of labor replaces two units of capital, yet output remains constant. So labor's marginal product, MP_L—that is, the additional output resulting from an additional unit of labor—must be twice as large as capital's marginal product, MP_C. In fact, *anywhere along the isoquant, the marginal rate of technical substitution of labor for capital equals the marginal product of labor divided by the marginal product of capital, which also equals the absolute value of the slope of the isoquant*, or:

$$|\text{Slope of isoquant}| = MRTS = MP_L/MP_C$$

where the vertical lines on either side of "Slope of isoquant" indicate the absolute value. For example, the slope between points *a* and *b* equals −2 and has an absolute value of 2, which equals both the marginal rate of substitution of labor for capital and the ratio of marginal productivities. Between points b and c, three units of labor substitute for three units of capital, while output remains constant at 290. Thus, the slope between b and c is $-3/3$, for an absolute value of 1. Note that the absolute value of the isoquant's slope declines as we move down the curve because larger increases in labor are required to offset each one-unit decline in capital. Put another way, as less capital is employed, its marginal product increases, and as more labor is employed, its marginal product decreases.

If labor and capital were perfect substitutes in production, the rate at which labor substituted for capital would remain fixed along the isoquant, so the isoquant would be a downward-sloping straight line. Because most resources are *not* perfect substitutes, however, the rate at which one substitutes for another changes along an isoquant. As we move down along an isoquant, more labor is required to offset each one-unit decline in capital, so the isoquant becomes flatter and is convex to the origin.

Isocost Lines

Isoquants graphically illustrate a firm's production function for all quantities of output the firm could possibly produce. We turn now to the question of what combination of resources to employ to minimize the cost of producing a given rate of output. The answer, as we'll see, depends on the cost of resources.

Suppose a unit of labor costs the firm \$1,500 per month, and a unit of capital costs \$2,500 per month. The total cost (TC) of production per month is

$$\begin{aligned} TC &= (w \times L) + (r \times C) \\ &= \$1{,}500L + \$2{,}500C \end{aligned}$$

where w is the monthly wage rate, L is the quantity of labor employed, r is the monthly cost of capital, and C is the quantity of capital employed. An **isocost line** identifies all combinations of capital and labor the firm can hire for a given total cost. Again, *iso* is Greek for "equal," so an isocost line is a line representing resource combinations of equal cost. In Exhibit 13, for example, the line $TC = \$15{,}000$ identifies all combinations of labor and capital that cost the firm \$15,000 per month. The entire \$15,000 could pay for either 6 units of capital or 10 units of labor per month. Or the firm could employ any other combination of the two resources along the isocost line.

Recall that the slope of any line is the vertical change between two points on the line divided by the corresponding horizontal change. At the point where the isocost line meets the vertical axis, the quantity of capital that can be purchased equals the total cost divided by the monthly cost of a unit of capital, or TC/r. At the point where the isocost line meets the horizontal axis, the quantity of labor that can be hired equals the firm's total cost divided by the monthly wage, or TC/w. The slope of any isocost line in Exhibit 13 can be calculated by considering a movement from the vertical intercept to the horizontal intercept. That is, we divide the vertical change ($-TC/r$) by the horizontal change (TC/w), as follows:

$$\text{Slope of isocost line} = -\frac{TC/r}{TC/w} = \frac{-w}{r}$$

The slope of the isocost line is the negative of the price of labor divided by the price of capital, or $-w/r$, which indicates the relative prices of the inputs. In our example, the absolute value of the slope of the isocost line equals w/r, or

$$\begin{aligned} |\text{Slope of isocost line}| &= w/r \\ &= \$1{,}500/\$2{,}500 \\ &= 0.6 \end{aligned}$$

The monthly wage is 0.6, or six-tenths, of the monthly cost of a unit of capital, so hiring one more unit of labor, without changing total cost, implies that the firm must employ 0.6 fewer units of capital.

A firm is not confined to a particular isocost line. This is why Exhibit 13 includes three of them, each corresponding to a different total budget. In fact, there is a different isocost line for every possible budget. *These isocost*

EXHIBIT 13 A Firm's Isocost Lines

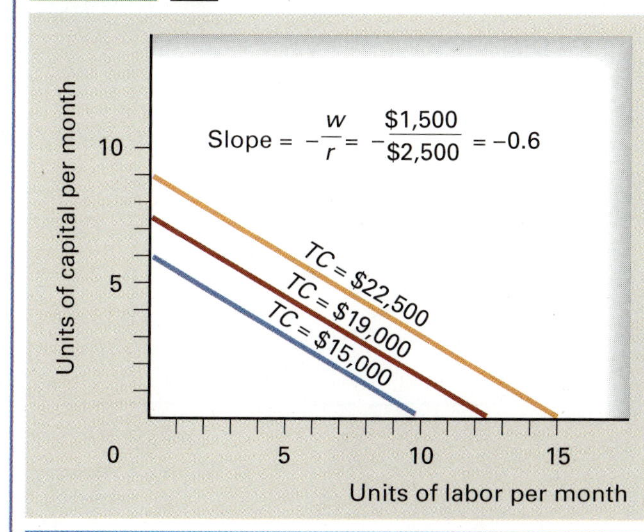

Each isocost line shows combinations of labor and capital that can be purchased for a given amount of total cost. The slope of each equals the negative of the monthly wage rate divided by the rental cost of capital per month. Higher costs are represented by isocost lines farther from the origin.

lines are parallel because each reflects the same relative resource prices. Resource prices in our example are assumed to be constant regardless of the amount of each resource the firm employs.

The Choice of Input Combinations

Exhibit 14 brings together the isoquants and the isocost line. Suppose the firm has decided to produce 415 units of output and wants to minimize the cost of doing so. The firm could select point *f*, where 6 units of capital combine with 4 units of labor to produce 415 units. This combination, however, would cost $21,000 at prevailing prices. Because the profit-maximizing firm wants to produce its chosen output at the minimum cost, it tries to find the isocost line closest to the origin that still touches the isoquant. The isoquant for 415 units of output is tangent to the isocost line at point *e*. This resource combination costs $19,000. From the point of tangency, any movement in either direction along an isoquant increases the cost. So *the tangency between the isocost line and the isoquant shows the minimum cost required to produce a given output.*

Look at what's going on at the point of tangency. At point *e* in Exhibit 14, the isoquant and the isocost line have the same slope. As mentioned already, the absolute value of the slope of an isoquant equals the *marginal rate of technical substitution* between labor and capital, and the absolute value of the slope of the isocost line equals the *ratio of the input prices.* So when a firm produces output in the least costly way, the marginal rate of technical substitution must equal the ratio of the resource prices, or:

$$\text{MRTS} = w/r = \$1{,}500/\$2{,}500 = 0.6$$

This equality shows that the firm adjusts resource use so that the rate at which one input substitutes for another in production—that is, the marginal rate of technical substitution—equals the rate at which one resource exchanges for another in resource markets, which is w/r. If this equality does not hold, the firm could adjust its input mix to produce the same output for less.

EXHIBIT 14 A Firm's Optimal Combination of Inputs

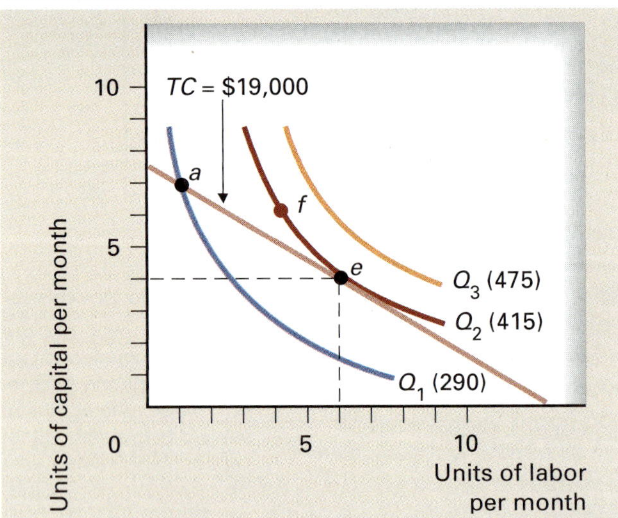

At point **e**, isoquant Q_2 is tangent to the isocost line. The optimal combination of inputs is 6 units of labor and 4 units of capital. The most that can be produced for $19,000 is 415 units. Another way of looking at this is that point **e** identifies the least costly way of producing 415 units.

The Expansion Path

Imagine a set of isoquants representing each possible rate of output. Given the relative cost of resources, we could then draw isocost lines to determine the optimal combination of resources for producing each rate of output. The points of tangency in Exhibit 15 show the least-cost input combinations for producing several output rates. For example, output rate Q_2 can be produced most cheaply using *C* units of capital and *L* units of labor. The line formed by connecting these tangency points is the firm's **expansion path.** The expansion path need not be a straight line, although it generally slopes upward, indicating that the firm expands the use of both resources in the long run as output increases. Note that we have assumed that the prices of inputs remain constant as the firm varies output along the expansion path, so the isocost lines at the points of tangency are parallel—that is, they have the same slope.

The expansion path indicates the lowest long-run total cost for each rate of output. For example, the firm can produce output rate Q_2 for TC_2, output rate Q_3 for TC_3, and so on. Similarly, the firm's long-run average cost curve indicates, at each rate of output, the total cost divided by the rate of output. The firm's expansion path and the firm's long-run average cost curve represent alternative ways of portraying costs in the long run, given resource prices and technology.

We can use Exhibit 15 to distinguish between short-run and long-run adjustments in output. Let's begin with the firm producing Q_2 at point *b*, which requires *C* units of capital and *L* units of labor. Now suppose that in the short run, the firm wants to increase output to Q_3. If capital is fixed in the short run, the only way to produce Q_3 is by increasing the quantity of labor employed to L', which requires moving to point *h* in Exhibit 15. Point *h* is not

EXHIBIT 15 **A Firm's Expansion Path**

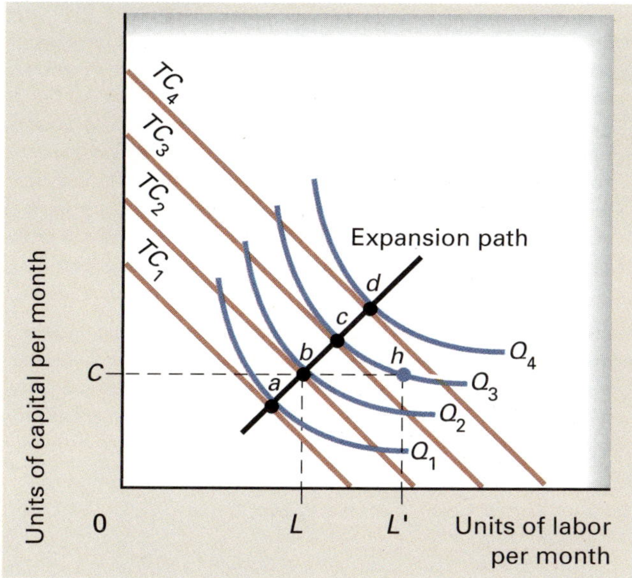

Points of tangency between isoquants and isocost lines identify the least costly resource combination of producing each particular quantity of output. Connecting these tangency points traces out the firm's expansion path, which usually slopes up to the right, indicating that more of both goods is needed to increase output.

the cheapest way to produce Q_3 in the long run because it is not a tangency point. In the long run, all resources are variable, and if the firm wishes to produce Q_3, it should minimize total cost by adjusting from point *h* to point *c*.

One final point: If the relative prices of resources change, the least-cost resource combination also changes, so the firm's expansion path changes. For example, if the price of labor increases, capital becomes cheaper relative to labor. Efficient production therefore calls for less labor and more capital. With the cost of labor higher, the firm's total cost for each rate of output rises. Such a cost increase would also be reflected by an upward shift of the average total cost curve.

Summary

A firm's *production function* specifies the relationship between resource use and output, given prevailing technology. An *isoquant* is a curve that illustrates the possible combinations of resources that produce a particular rate of output. An *isocost* line presents the combinations of resources the firm can employ, given resource prices and the firm's total budget. For a given rate of output—that is, for a given isoquant—the firm minimizes total cost by choosing the lowest isocost line that just touches, or is tangent to, the isoquant. The least-cost combination of resources depends on the productivity of resources and their relative cost. Economists believe that although firm owners may not understand the material in this appendix, they must act as if they do to maximize profit.

Appendix Questions

1. Choice of Input Combinations Suppose that a firm's cost per unit of labor is $100 per day and its cost per unit of capital is $400 per day.
   a. Draw the isocost line for a total cost per day of $2,000. Label the axes.
   b. If the firm is producing efficiently, what is the marginal rate of technical substitution between labor and capital?
   c. Demonstrate your answer to part (b) using isocost lines and isoquant curves.
2. The Expansion Path How are the expansion path and the long-run average cost curve related?

Perfect Competition

8

- What do wheat and Google have in common?
- Why might a firm continue to operate even when it's losing money?
- Why do many firms fail to earn an economic profit?
- How can it be said that the more competitive the industry, the less individual firms compete with each other?
- What's the difference between making stuff right and making the right stuff?
- And what's so perfect about perfect competition?

Answers to these and other questions are provided in this chapter, which examines the first of four market structures—perfect competition

The previous chapter developed cost curves for an individual firm in the short run and in the long run. In light of these costs, how much should a firm produce and what price should it charge? To discover the firm's profit-maximizing output and price, we revisit an old friend—demand. Demand and supply, together, guide the firm to maximize any profit or minimize any loss. In the next few chapters, we examine how firms respond to their economic environments in deciding what to supply, in what quantities, and at what price. We continue to assume that firms try to maximize profit.

Topics discussed include:

- Market structure
- Price takers
- Marginal revenue
- Golden rule of profit maximization
- Loss minimization
- Short-run supply curve
- Long-run supply curve
- Competition and efficiency
- Producer surplus
- Gains from exchange

An Introduction to Perfect Competition

market structure
Important features of a market, such as the number of firms, product uniformity across firms, firm's ease of entry and exit, and forms of competition

Market structure describes the important features of a market, such as the number of suppliers (are there many or few?), the product's degree of uniformity (do firms in the market supply identical products, or are there differences across firms?), the ease of entry into and exit from the market (can firms come and go easily or are entry and exit blocked?), and the forms of competition among firms (do firms compete based on price alone or do they also compete through advertising and product differences?). The various features will become clearer as we examine each of the four market structures in the next few chapters. *A firm's decisions about how much to produce or what price to charge depend on the structure of the market.*

Before we get started, a few words about terminology. An *industry* consists of all firms that supply output to a particular *market*, such as the auto market, the shoe market, or the wheat market. The terms *industry* and *market* are used interchangeably throughout this chapter.

Perfectly Competitive Market Structure

perfect competition
A market structure with many fully informed buyers and sellers of a standardized product and no obstacles to entry or exit of firms in the long run

commodity
A standardized product, a product that does not differ across producers, such as bushels of wheat or an ounce of gold

We begin with **perfect competition**, in some ways the most basic of market structures. A *perfectly competitive* market is characterized by (1) many buyers and sellers—so many that each buys or sells only a tiny fraction of the total amount in the market; (2) firms sell a **commodity**, which is a standardized product, such as a bushel of wheat, an ounce of gold, or a share of Google stock; such a product does not differ across suppliers; (3) buyers and sellers are fully informed about the price and availability of all resources and products; and (4) firms and resources are freely mobile—that is, over time they can easily enter or leave the industry without facing obstacles like patents, licenses, and high capital costs.

If these conditions exist in a market, an individual buyer or seller has no control over the price. Price is determined by market demand and supply. Once the market establishes the price, any firm is free to supply whatever quantity maximizes profit. *A perfectly competitive firm is so small relative to the market that the firm's supply decision does not affect the market price.* Examples of perfectly competitive markets include those for most agricultural products, such as wheat, corn, and livestock; markets for basic metals, such as gold, silver, and copper; markets for widely traded stock, such as Google, Bank of America, and General Electric; and markets for foreign exchange, such as yen, euros, and pesos. Again, there are so many buyers and sellers that the actions of any one cannot influence the market price. For example, about 65,000 farmers in the United States raise hogs, and tens of millions of U.S. households buy pork products. The model of perfect competition allows us to make a number of predictions that hold up pretty well when compared to the real world. Perfect competition is also an important benchmark for evaluating the efficiency of other types of markets. Let's look at demand under perfect competition.

Demand Under Perfect Competition

Suppose the market in question is the world market for wheat and the firm in question is a wheat farm in Kansas. In the world market for wheat, there are hundreds of thousands of farms, so any one supplies only a tiny fraction of market output. For example, the thousands of wheat farmers in Kansas together produce less than 3 percent of the world's supply of wheat. In Exhibit 1, the market price of wheat of $5 per bushel is determined in panel (a) by the intersection of the market demand curve *D* and the market

EXHIBIT 1 Market Equilibrium and a Firm's Demand Curve in Perfect Competition

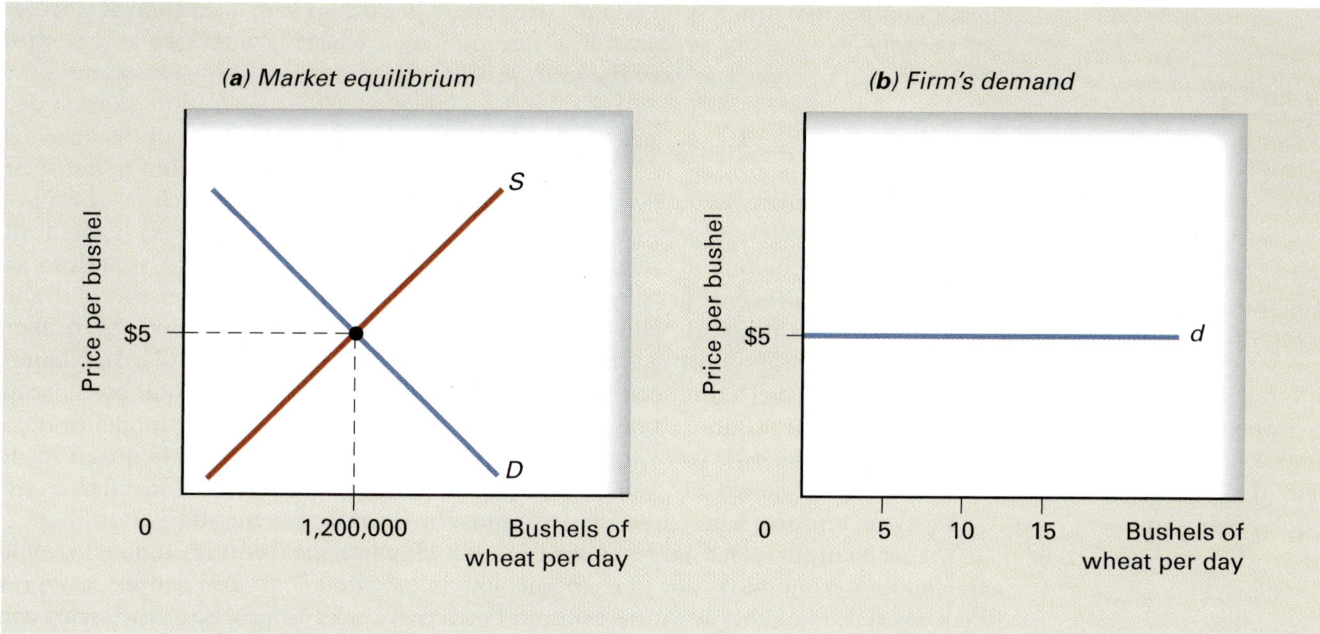

In panel (a), the market price of $5 is determined by the intersection of the market demand and market supply curves. A perfectly competitive firm can sell any amount at that price. The demand curve facing the perfectly competitive firm is horizontal at the market price, as shown by demand curve *d* in panel (b).

supply curve *S*. Once the market determines the price, any farmer can sell all he or she wants to at that market price.

Each farm is so small relative to the market that each has no impact on the market price. Because all farmers produce an identical product—bushels of wheat, in this case—anyone who charges more than the market price sells no wheat. For example, a farmer charging $5.05 per bushel would find no buyers. Of course, any farmer is free to charge less than the market price, but why do that when all wheat can be sold at the market price? Farmers aren't stupid (if they are, they don't last long). *The demand curve facing an individual farmer is, therefore, a horizontal line drawn at the market price.* In our example, the demand curve facing an individual farmer, identified as *d* in panel (b), is drawn at the market price of $5 per bushel. Thus, each farmer faces a horizontal, or a *perfectly elastic,* demand curve for wheat. A perfectly competitive firm is called a **price taker** because that firm must "take," or accept, the market price—as in "take it or leave it."

price taker
A firm that faces a given market price and whose quantity supplied has no effect on that price; a perfectly competitive firm that decides to produce must accept, or "take," the market price

It has been said, "In perfect competition there is no competition." Ironically, two neighboring wheat farmers in perfect competition are not really rivals. They both can sell all they want at the market price. The amount one sells has no effect on the market price or on the amount the other can sell.

Short-Run Profit Maximization

Each firm tries to maximize economic profit. Firms that ignore this strategy don't survive for long. Economic profit equals total revenue minus total cost, including both explicit and implicit costs. Implicit cost, remember, is the opportunity cost of resources owned by the firm and includes a normal profit. Economic profit is any profit above normal profit. How do firms maximize profit? You have already learned that a perfectly competitive firm has no control over price. What that firm does control is its rate of output—its quantity supplied. The question each wheat farmer asks is this: *How much should I produce to earn the most profit?*

Total Revenue Minus Total Cost

The firm maximizes economic profit by finding the quantity at which total revenue exceeds total cost by the greatest amount. The firm's total revenue is simply its output times the price. Column (1) in Exhibit 2 shows the farmer's output possibilities measured in bushels of wheat per day. Column (2) shows the market price of $5 per bushel, a price that does not vary with the farmer's output. Column (3) shows the farmer's total revenue, which is output times price, or column (1) times column (2). And column (4) shows the farmer's total cost of supplying each quantity shown. Total cost already includes a normal profit, so total cost includes all opportunity costs. Although the table does not distinguish between fixed and variable costs, fixed cost must equal $15 per day because total cost is $15 when output is zero. The presence of fixed cost tells us that at least one resource is fixed, so the farm must be operating in the short run.

At each output rate, total revenue in column (3) minus total cost in column (4) yields the farmer's economic profit or economic loss in column (7). As you can see, total revenue exceeds total cost at rates of output between 7 and 14 bushels, so the farm earns an *economic profit* at those output rates. Economic profit is maximized at $12 per day when the farm produces 12 bushels of wheat per day (the $12 and 12 bushels combination here is just a coincidence).

These results are graphed in panel (a) of Exhibit 3, which shows the total revenue and total cost curves. As output increases by 1 bushel, total revenue increases

EXHIBIT 2 Maximizing Short-Run Profit for a Perfectly Competitive Firm

(1) Bushels of Wheat per Day (q)	(2) Marginal Revenue (Price) (p)	(3) Total Revenue ($TR = q \times p$)	(4) Total Cost (TC)	(5) Marginal Cost ($MC = \Delta TC/\Delta q$)	(6) Average Total Cost ($ATC = TC/q$)	(7) Economic Profit or Loss = $TR - TC$
0	—	$ 0	$15.00	—	—	$-15.00
1	$ 5	5	19.75	$ 4.75	$19.75	-14.75
2	5	10	23.50	3.75	11.75	-13.50
3	5	15	26.50	3.00	8.83	-11.50
4	5	20	29.00	2.50	7.25	-9.00
5	5	25	31.00	2.00	6.20	-6.00
6	5	30	32.50	1.50	5.42	-2.50
7	5	35	33.75	1.25	4.82	1.25
8	5	40	35.25	1.50	4.41	4.75
9	5	45	37.25	2.00	4.14	7.75
10	5	50	40.00	2.75	4.00	10.00
11	5	55	43.25	3.25	3.93	11.75
12	**5**	**60**	**48.00**	**4.75**	**4.00**	**12.00**
13	5	65	54.50	6.50	4.19	10.50
14	5	70	64.00	9.50	4.57	6.00
15	5	75	77.50	13.50	5.17	-2.50
16	5	80	96.00	18.50	6.00	-16.00

EXHIBIT 3 Short-Run Profit Maximization for a Perfectly Competitive Firm

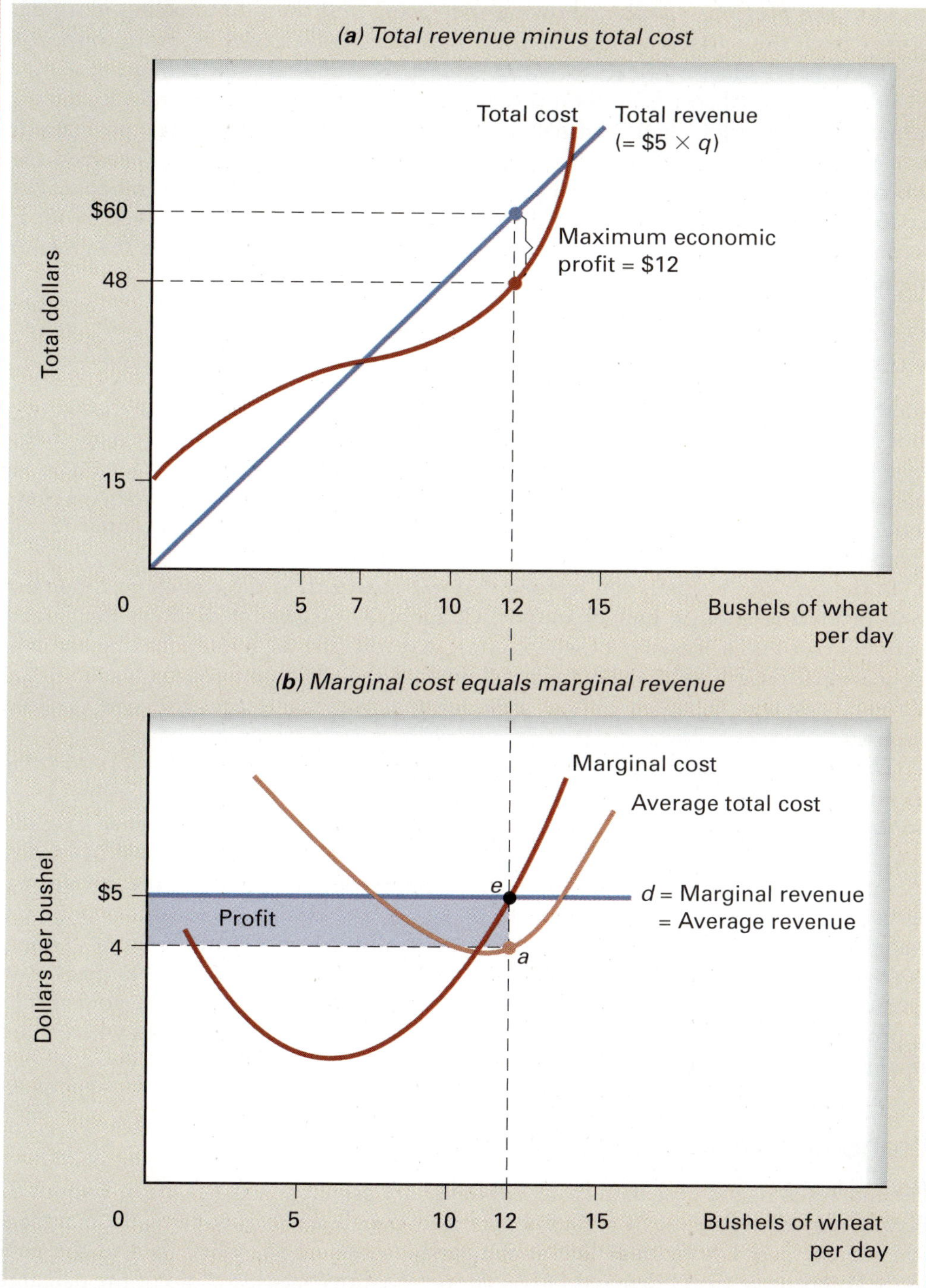

In panel (a), the total revenue curve for a perfectly competitive firm is a straight line with a slope of 5, the market price. Total cost increases with output, first at a decreasing rate and then at an increasing rate. Economic profit is maximized where total revenue exceeds total cost by the greatest amount, which occurs at 12 bushels of wheat per day. In panel (b), marginal revenue is a horizontal line at the market price of $5. Economic profit is maximized at 12 bushels of wheat per day, where marginal revenue equals marginal cost (point *e*). That profit equals 12 bushels multiplied by the amount by which the market price of $5 exceeds the average total cost of $4. Economic profit is identified by the shaded rectangle.

by $5, so the farm's total revenue curve is a straight line emanating from the origin, with a slope of 5. The short-run total cost curve has the backward S shape introduced in the previous chapter, showing increasing and then diminishing marginal returns from the variable resource. Total cost always increases as more output is produced.

Subtracting total cost from total revenue is one way to find the profit-maximizing output. For output less than 7 bushels and greater than 14 bushels, total cost exceeds total revenue. The economic loss is measured by the vertical distance between the two curves. Between 7 and 14 bushels per day, total revenue exceeds total cost. The economic profit, again, is measured by the distance between the two curves. *Profit is maximized at the rate of output where total revenue exceeds total cost by the greatest amount.* Profit is greatest when 12 bushels are produced per day.

Marginal Revenue Equals Marginal Cost

marginal revenue (MR)
The firm's change in total revenue from selling an additional unit; a perfectly competitive firm's marginal revenue is also the market price

Another way to find the profit-maximizing rate of output is to focus on marginal revenue and marginal cost. **Marginal revenue**, or **MR**, is the change in total revenue from selling another unit of output. In perfect competition, each firm is a price taker, so selling one more unit increases total revenue by the market price. Thus, *in perfect competition, marginal revenue is the market price*—in this example, $5. Column (2) of Exhibit 2 presents the farm's marginal revenue for each bushel of wheat.

In the previous chapter, you learned that *marginal cost* is the change in total cost from producing another unit of output. Column (5) of Exhibit 2 shows the farm's marginal cost for each bushel of wheat. Marginal cost first declines, reflecting increasing marginal returns in the short run as more of the variable resource is employed. Marginal cost then increases, reflecting diminishing marginal returns from the variable resource.

The firm increases production as long as each additional unit adds more to total revenue than to total cost—that is, as long as marginal revenue exceeds marginal cost. Comparing columns (2) and (5) in Exhibit 2, we see that marginal revenue exceeds marginal cost for each of the first 12 bushels of wheat. The marginal cost of bushel 13, however, is $6.50, compared with its marginal revenue of $5. Therefore, producing bushel 13 would reduce economic profit by $1.50. The farmer, as a profit maximizer, limits output to 12 bushels per day. More generally, a firm expands output as long as marginal revenue exceeds marginal cost and stops expanding before marginal cost exceeds marginal revenue. A shorthand expression for this approach is the **golden rule of profit maximization**, which says that a profit-maximizing firm produces where marginal revenue equals marginal cost.

golden rule of profit maximization
To maximize profit or minimize loss, a firm should produce the quantity at which marginal revenue equals marginal cost; this rule holds for all market structures

Economic Profit in the Short Run

Per-unit revenue and cost data from Exhibit 2 are graphed in panel (b) of Exhibit 3. Because marginal revenue in perfect competition equals the market price, the marginal revenue curve is a horizontal line at the market price of $5, which is also the perfectly competitive firm's demand curve. At any quantity measured along the demand curve, marginal revenue is the price. Because the perfectly competitive firm can sell any amount for the same price per unit, marginal revenue is also **average revenue**, or **AR**. Average revenue equals total revenue divided by quantity, or $AR = TR/q$. Regardless of the output rate, therefore, the following equality holds along a perfectly competitive firm's demand curve:

average revenue
Total revenue divided by quantity, or $AR = TR/q$; in all market structures, average revenue equals the market price

$$\text{Market price} = \text{Marginal revenue} = \text{Average revenue}$$

The marginal cost curve intersects the marginal revenue curve at point *e*, where output is about 12 bushels per day. At lower rates of output, marginal revenue exceeds marginal cost, so the farm could increase profit by expanding output. At higher rates of output, marginal cost exceeds marginal revenue, so the farm could increase profit by reducing output. Profit itself appears as the shaded rectangle. The height of that rectangle, *ae*, equals the price (or average revenue) of $5 minus the average total cost of $4. Price minus average total cost yields an average profit of $1 per bushel. Profit per day, $12, equals the average profit per bushel, $1 (denoted by *ae*), times the 12 bushels produced.

Note that with the total cost and total revenue curves, we measure economic profit by the vertical *distance* between the two curves, as shown in panel (a). But with the per-unit curves of panel (b), we measure economic profit by an *area*—that is, by multiplying the average profit of $1 per bushel times the 12 bushels sold.

Minimizing Short-Run Losses

A firm in perfect competition has no control over the market price. Sometimes that price may be so low that a firm loses money no matter how much it produces. Such a firm can either continue to produce at a loss or temporarily shut down. But even if the firm shuts down, it cannot, *in the short run*, go out of business or produce something else. The short run is by definition a period too short to allow existing firms to leave the industry. In a sense, firms are stuck in their industry in the short run.

Fixed Cost and Minimizing Losses

When facing a loss, should a firm temporarily shut down? Intuition suggests the firm should. But keep in mind that the firm faces two types of costs in the short run: fixed cost, such as property taxes and fire insurance, which must be paid even if the firm produces nothing, and variable cost, such as labor, which depends on the amount produced. A firm that shuts down in the short run must still pay its fixed cost. But, by producing, a firm's revenue may cover variable cost and a portion of fixed cost. *A firm produces rather than shuts down if total revenue exceeds the variable cost of production.* After all, if total revenue exceeds variable cost, that excess covers at least a portion of fixed cost.

Let's look at the same cost data presented in Exhibit 2, but now suppose the market price of wheat is only $3 a bushel, not $5. This new situation is presented in Exhibit 4. Because of the lower price, total cost in column (4) exceeds total revenue in column (3) at all output rates. Each quantity thus yields a loss, as indicated by column (8). If the firm produces nothing, it loses the fixed cost of $15 per day. But, by producing anywhere from 6 to 12 bushels, the firm can cut that loss. From column (8), you can see that the loss is minimized at $10 per day where 10 bushels are produced. Compared to shutting down, producing 10 bushels adds $5 more to total revenue than to total cost. That $5 pays some of the firm's fixed cost.

Panel (a) of Exhibit 5 presents the firm's total cost and total revenue curves for data in Exhibit 4. The total cost curve remains as in Exhibit 3. Because the price is $3, the total revenue curve now has a slope of 3, so it's flatter than at a price of $5. The total revenue curve now lies below the total cost curve for all output rates. The vertical distance between the two curves measures the loss at each output rate. If the farmer produces nothing, the loss is the fixed cost of $15 per day. The vertical distance between the two curves is minimized at 10 bushels, where the loss is $10 per day.

EXHIBIT 4 Minimizing Short-Run Losses for a Perfectly Competitive Firm

(1) Bushels of Wheat per Day (q)	(2) Marginal Revenue (Price) (p)	(3) Total Revenue (TR = q × p)	(4) Total Cost (TC)	(5) Marginal Cost (MC = ΔTC/Δq)	(6) Average Total Cost (ATC = TC/q)	(7) Average Variable Cost (AVC = VC/q)	(8) Economic Profit or Loss = TR – TC
0	—	$ 0	$15.00	—	—	—	$-15.00
1	$3	3	19.75	$ 4.75	$19.75	$4.75	-16.75
2	3	6	23.50	3.75	11.75	4.25	-17.50
3	3	9	26.50	3.00	8.83	3.83	-17.50
4	3	12	29.00	2.50	7.25	3.50	-17.00
5	3	15	31.00	2.00	6.20	3.20	-16.00
6	3	18	32.50	1.50	5.42	2.92	-14.50
7	3	21	33.75	1.25	4.82	2.68	-12.75
8	3	24	35.25	1.50	4.41	2.53	-11.25
9	3	27	37.25	2.00	4.14	2.47	-10.25
10	**3**	**30**	**40.00**	**2.75**	**4.00**	**2.50**	**-10.00**
11	3	33	43.25	3.25	3.93	2.57	-10.25
12	3	36	48.00	4.75	4.00	2.75	-12.00
13	3	39	54.50	6.50	4.19	3.04	-15.50
14	3	42	64.00	9.50	4.57	3.50	-22.00
15	3	45	77.50	13.50	5.17	4.17	-32.50
16	3	48	96.00	18.50	6.00	5.06	-48.00

Marginal Revenue Equals Marginal Cost

We get the same result using marginal analysis. The per-unit data from Exhibit 4 are graphed in panel (b) of Exhibit 5. First we find the rate of output where marginal revenue equals marginal cost. Marginal revenue equals marginal cost at an output of 10 bushels per day. At that output, the market price of $3 exceeds the average variable cost of $2.50. Because price exceeds average variable cost, total revenue covers variable cost plus a portion of fixed cost. Specifically, $2.50 of the price pays the average variable cost, and the remaining $0.50 helps pay some of average fixed cost (average fixed cost equals average total cost of $4.00 minus average variable cost of $2.50). This still leaves a loss of $1 per bushel, which when multiplied by 10 bushels yields an economic loss of $10 per day, identified in panel (b) by the pink-shaded rectangle. *The bottom line is that the firm produces rather than shuts down if there is some rate of output where the price at least covers average variable cost.* (Why is the farmer in the short run better off operating at a loss rather than shutting down?)

Shutting Down in the Short Run

If total revenue exceeds variable costs, the farmer produces in the short run. You may have read or heard of firms reporting a loss; most continue to operate. In fact, many new firms lose money during the first few years of operations. Still, they hang on because they hope to be profitable eventually (for example, the TV network UPN lost more than $1 billion during its first 11 years before merging with the WB network to form the CW network). But *if average variable cost exceeds the price at all rates of output, the firm shuts down.* After all, why produce if doing so only increases the loss? For example, a wheat price of $2 would fall below the average variable cost at all rates

EXHIBIT 5 Short-Run Loss Minimization for a Perfectly Competitive Firm

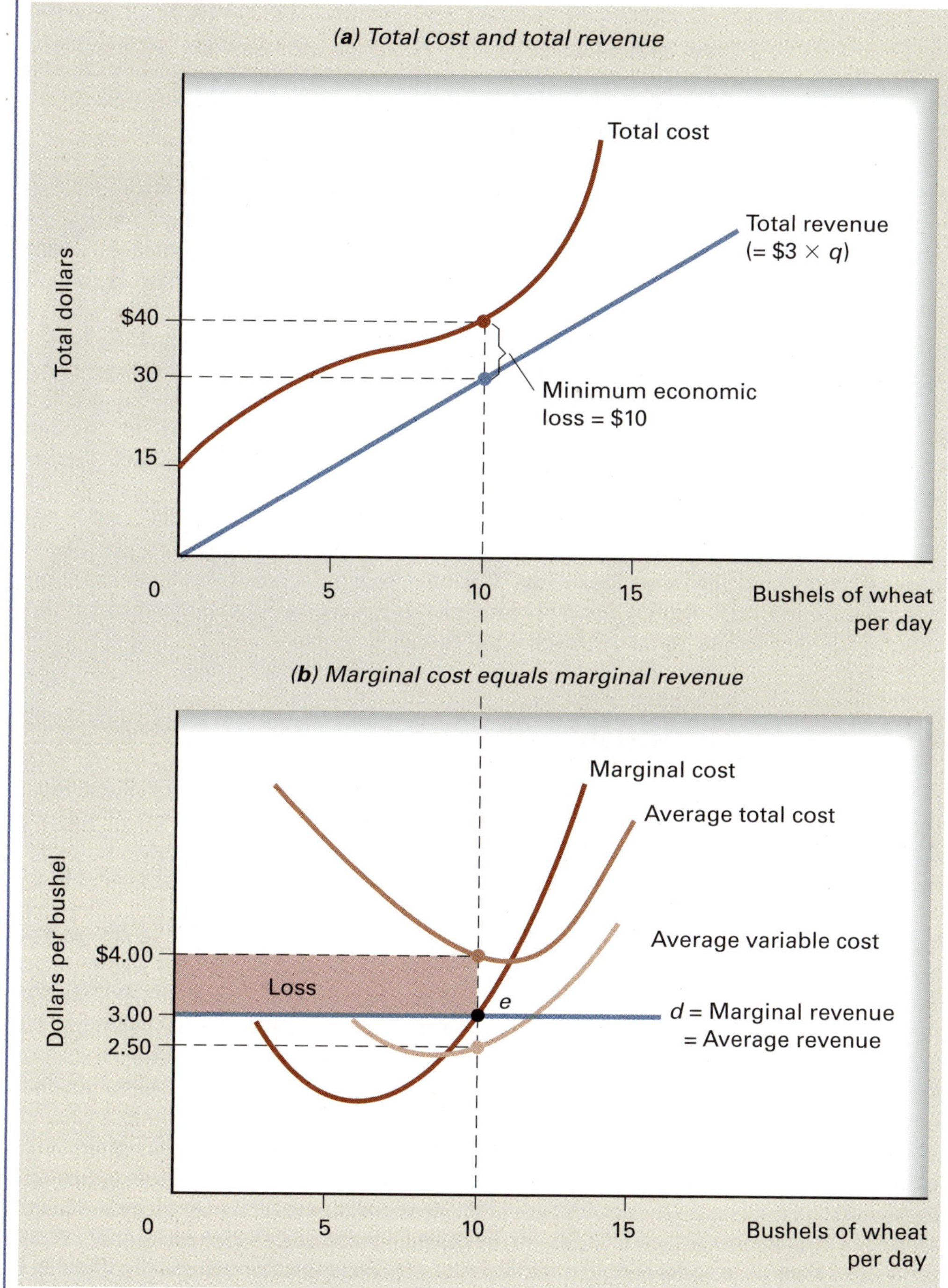

Because total cost always exceeds total revenue in panel (a), the firm suffers a loss no matter how much is produced. The loss is minimized where output is 10 bushels per day. Panel (b) shows that marginal revenue equals marginal cost at point *e*. The loss is equal to output of 10 multiplied by the difference between average total cost ($4) and price ($3). Because price exceeds average variable cost ($2.50), the firm is better off continuing to produce in the short run, since revenue covers some fixed cost.

of output. Faced with such a low price, a farmer would shut down and lose just fixed cost, rather than produce and lose both fixed cost plus some variable cost.

From column (7) of Exhibit 4, you can also see that the lowest price at which the farmer would just cover average variable cost is \$2.47 per bushel, when output is 9 bushels per day. At this price, the farmer is indifferent between producing and shutting down, because either way the loss is the \$15 per day in fixed cost. Any price above \$2.47 allows the farmer, by producing, to also cover some fixed cost.

Shutting down is not the same as going out of business. In the short run, even a firm that shuts down keeps productive capacity intact—paying rent, insurance, and property taxes, keeping water pipes from freezing in the winter, and so on. For example, Dairy Queen shuts down for the winter in cooler climates, a business serving a college community may close during term breaks, an auto plant responds to slack sales by temporarily halting production, and Yahoo recently shut down for a week to save money. A firm that shuts down does not escape fixed cost. When demand picks up again, production resumes. If the market outlook remains grim, the firm may decide to leave the market, but that's a long-run decision. The short run is defined as a period during which some costs are fixed, so a firm cannot escape those costs in the short run, no matter what it does. *Fixed cost is sunk cost in the short run, whether the firm produces or shuts down.*

Likewise, a concert promoter may cancel an event because of poor ticket sales even though the hall has already been rented. And a movie producer may pull the plug on a nearly completed film that looks like a turkey to avoid sinking millions more into advertising and distribution. Concert promoters and movie producers want to cut their losses. They don't want to throw more good money after bad.

The Firm and Industry Short-Run Supply Curves

If average variable cost exceeds price at all output rates, the firm shuts down in the short run. But if price exceeds average variable cost, the firm produces the quantity at which marginal revenue equals marginal cost. As we'll see, a firm changes the rate of output if the market price changes.

The Short-Run Firm Supply Curve

The relationship between price and quantity is summarized in Exhibit 6. Points 1, 2, 3, 4, and 5 identify where the marginal cost curve intersects alternative marginal revenue, or demand, curves. At a price as low as p_1, the firm shuts down rather than produce at point 1 because that price is below average variable cost. So the loss-minimizing output rate at price p_1 is zero, as identified by q_1. At price p_2, the price just equals average variable cost, so the firm is indifferent between producing q_2 and shutting down; either way the firm loses fixed cost. Point 2 is called the *shutdown point*. If the price is p_3, the firm produces q_3 to minimize its loss (see if you can identify that loss in the diagram). At p_4, the firm produces q_4 to earn a normal profit, because price equals average total cost. Point 4 is called the *break-even point*. If the price rises to p_5, the firm earns short-run economic profit by producing q_5 (see if you can identify that economic profit in the diagram).

At prices below p_2, the firm shuts down in the short run. The quantity supplied when the price is p_2 or higher is determined by the intersection of the firm's marginal cost curve and its demand, or marginal revenue, curve. As long as the price covers average variable cost, the firm supplies the quantity at which the upward-sloping marginal cost curve intersects the marginal revenue, or demand, curve. Thus, that portion of the

EXHIBIT 6 Summary of a Perfectly Competitive Firm's Short-Run Output Decisions

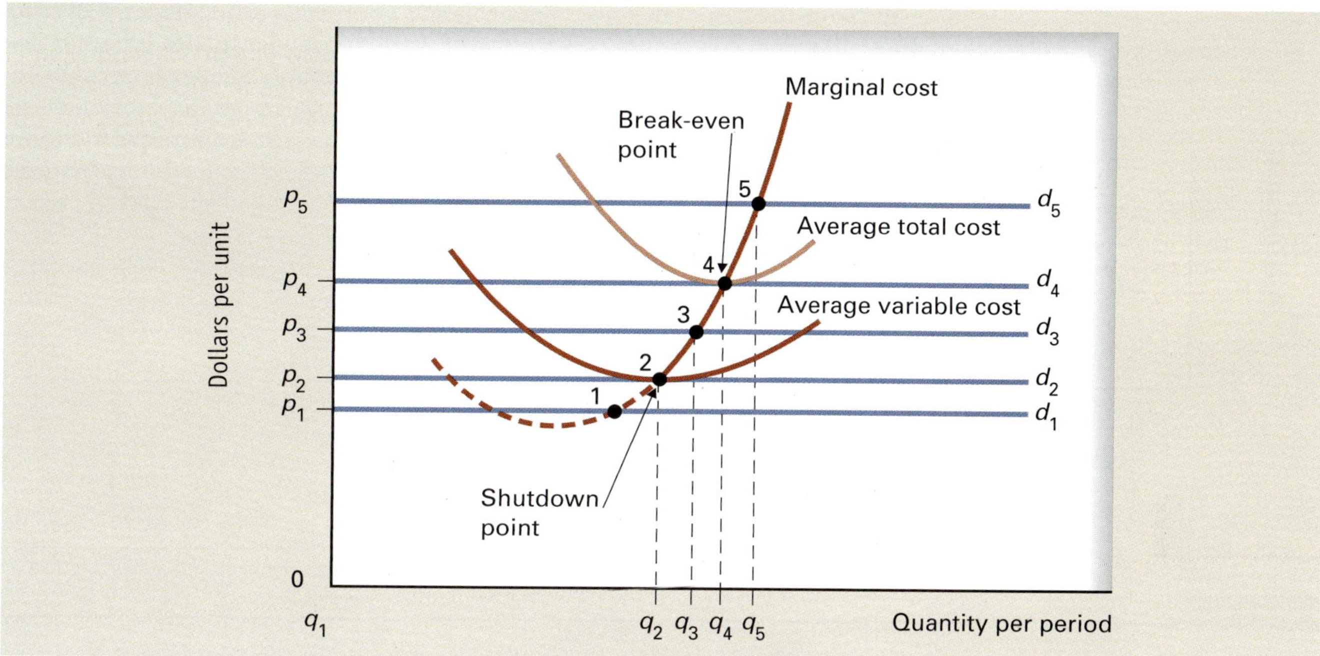

At price p_1, the firm produces nothing because p_1 is less than the firm's average variable cost. At price p_2, the firm is indifferent between shutting down or producing q_2 units of output, because in either case, the firm suffers a loss equal to its fixed cost. At p_3, it produces q_3 units and suffers a loss that is less than its fixed cost. At p_4, the firm produces q_4 and just breaks even, earning a normal profit, because p_4 equals average total cost. Finally, at p_5, the firm produces q_5 and earns an economic profit. The firm's short-run supply curve is that portion of its marginal cost curve at or rising above the minimum point of average variable cost (point 2).

firm's marginal cost curve that intersects and rises above the lowest point on its average variable cost curve becomes the **short-run firm supply curve**. In Exhibit 6, the short-run supply curve is the upward-sloping portion of the marginal cost curve, beginning at point 2, the shutdown point. The solid portion of the short-run supply curve indicates the quantity the firm offers for sale at each price.

short-run firm supply curve
A curve that shows how much a firm supplies at each price in the short run; in perfect competition, that portion of a firm's marginal cost curve that intersects and rises above the low point on its average variable cost curve

The Short-Run Industry Supply Curve

Exhibit 7 presents examples of how supply curves for three firms with identical marginal cost curves can be summed *horizontally* to form the short-run industry supply curve (in perfect competition, there are many more firms). The **short-run industry supply curve** is the horizontal sum of all firms' short-run supply curves. At a price below *p*, no output is supplied. At price *p*, each of the three firms supplies 10 units, so the market supplies 30 units. At *p*′, which is above *p*, each firm supplies 20 units, so the market supplies 60 units.

short-run industry supply curve
A curve that indicates the quantity supplied by the industry at each price in the short run; in perfect competition, the horizontal sum of each firm's short-run supply curve

Firm Supply and Market Equilibrium

Exhibit 8 shows the relationship between the short-run profit-maximizing output of the individual firm and market equilibrium price and quantity. Suppose there are 100,000 identical wheat farmers in this industry. Their individual supply curves (represented by

EXHIBIT 7 Aggregating Individual Supply Curves of Perfectly Competitive Firms to Form the Market Supply Curve

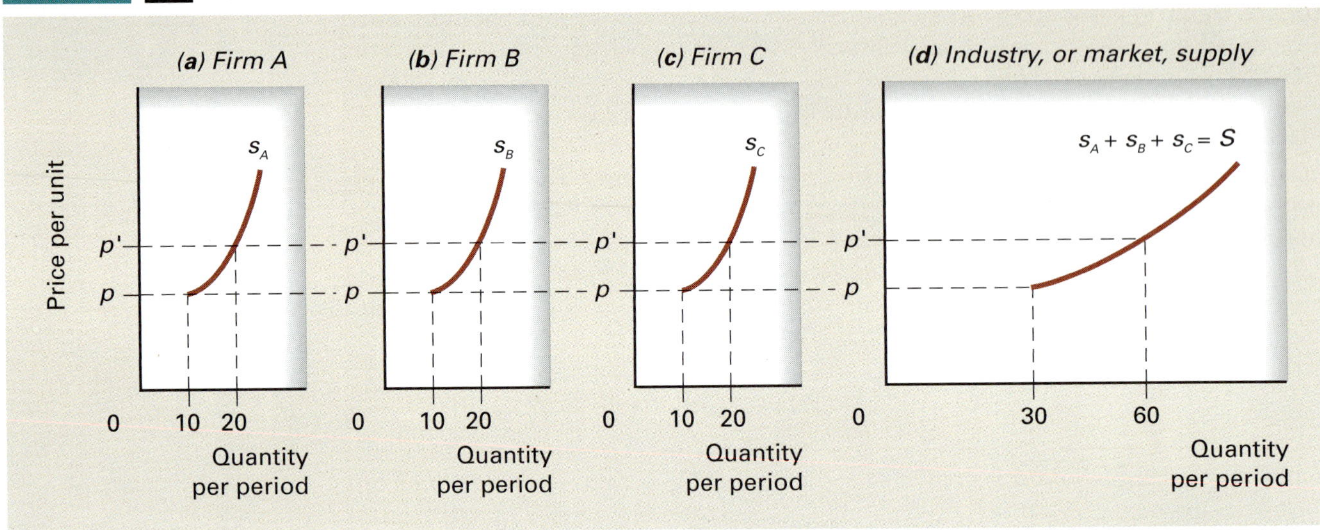

At price p, each firm supplies 10 units of output and the market supplies 30 units. In general, the market supply curve in panel (d) is the horizontal sum of the individual firm supply curves s_A, s_B, and s_C.

EXHIBIT 8 Short-Run Profit Maximization and Market Equilibrium in Perfect Competition

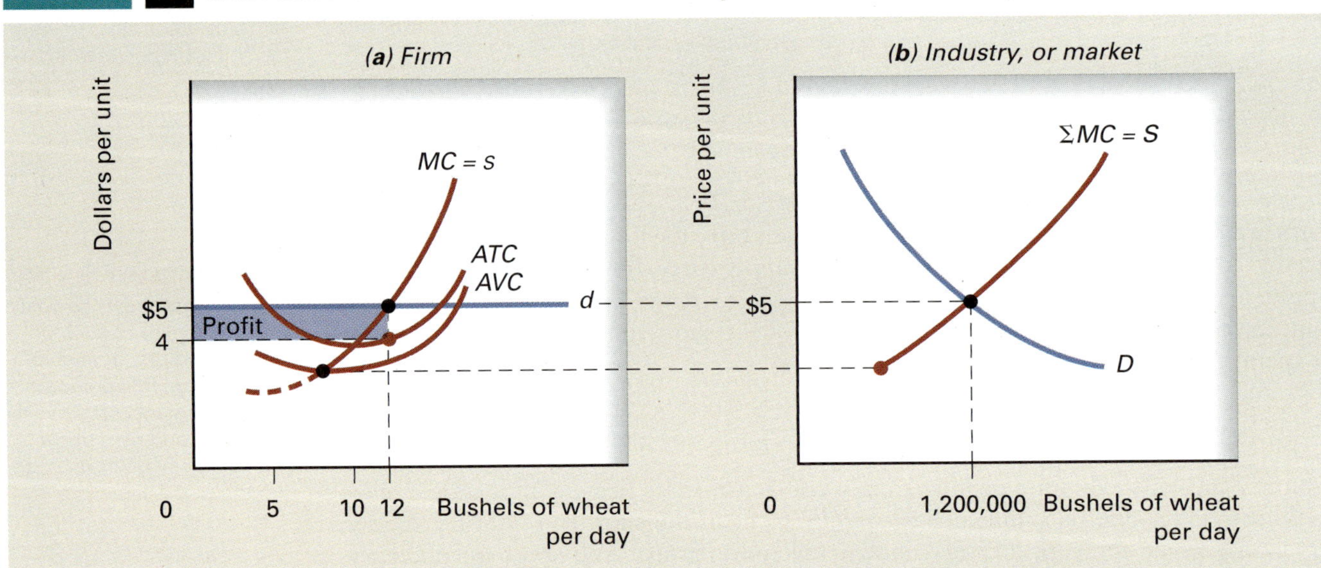

The market supply curve S in panel (b) is the horizontal sum of the supply curves of all 100,000 firms in this perfectly competitive industry. The intersection of S with the market demand curve D determines the market price of \$5. That price, in turn, determines the height of the perfectly elastic demand curve facing the individual firm in panel (a). That firm produces 12 bushels per day (where marginal cost equals marginal revenue of \$5) and earns economic profit in the short run of \$1 per bushel, or \$12 in total per day.

the portions of the marginal cost curve at or rising above the average variable cost) are summed horizontally to yield the market, or industry, supply curve. The market supply curve appears in panel (b), where it intersects the market demand curve to determine the market price of \$5 per bushel. At that price, each farmer supplies 12 bushels per day, as shown in panel (a), which sums to 1,200,000 bushels for the market, as shown in panel (b). Each farmer in the short run earns an economic profit of $12 per day, represented by the shaded rectangle in panel (a).

To Review: A perfectly competitive firm supplies the short-run quantity that maximizes profit or minimizes loss. When confronting a loss, a firm either produces an output that minimizes that loss or shuts down temporarily. Given the conditions for perfect competition, the market converges toward the equilibrium price and quantity. But how is that equilibrium actually reached? In the real world, markets operate based on customs and conventions, which vary across markets. For example, the rules acceptable on the New York Stock Exchange are not the same as those followed in the market for fresh fish. The case study, "World of Business: Auction Markets" at the end of the book, discusses one mechanism for reaching equilibrium—auctions.

Perfect Competition in the Long Run

In the short run, the quantity of variable resources can change, but other resources, which mostly determine firm size, are fixed. In the long run, however, a firm has time to enter and leave and to adjust its size—that is, to adjust its *scale* of operations. In the long run, there is no distinction between fixed and variable cost because all resources under the firm's control are variable.

Short-run economic profit encourages new firms to enter the market in the long run and may prompt existing firms to get bigger. Economic profit attracts resources from industries where firms are losing money or earning only a normal profit. This expansion in the number and size of firms shifts the industry supply curve rightward in the long run, driving down the price. New firms continue to enter a profitable industry and existing firms continue to expand as long as economic profit is greater than zero. Entry and expansion stop only when the resulting increase in supply drives down the price enough to erase economic profit. In the case of wheat farming, economic profit attracts new wheat farmers and may encourage existing wheat farmers to expand. *Short-run economic profit attracts new entrants in the long run and may cause existing firms to expand. Market supply thereby increases, driving down the market price until economic profit disappears.*

On the other hand, a short-run loss forces some firms to leave the industry in the long run or to reduce their scale of operation. In the long run, departures and reductions in scale shift the market supply curve to the left, thereby increasing the market price until remaining firms just break even—that is, earn a normal profit.

Zero Economic Profit in the Long Run

In the long run, firms in perfect competition earn just a normal profit, which means zero economic profit. Exhibit 9 shows a firm and the market in long-run equilibrium. Market supply adjusts as firms enter or leave or change their size. *This long-run adjustment continues until the market supply curve intersects the market demand curve at a price that corresponds to the lowest point on each firm's long-run average cost curve, or LRAC curve.* Because the long run is a period during which all resources under a firm's control are variable, a *firm in the long run is forced by competition to adjust its scale until average cost is minimized.* A firm that fails to minimize average cost will not survive in the long run. At point *e* in panel (a) of Exhibit 9, the firm is in equilibrium, producing *q* units per period and earning just a normal profit. At point *e*, price, marginal cost, short-run average total cost, and long-run average cost are all equal. No

EXHIBIT 9 Long-Run Equilibrium for a Firm and Industry in Perfect Competition

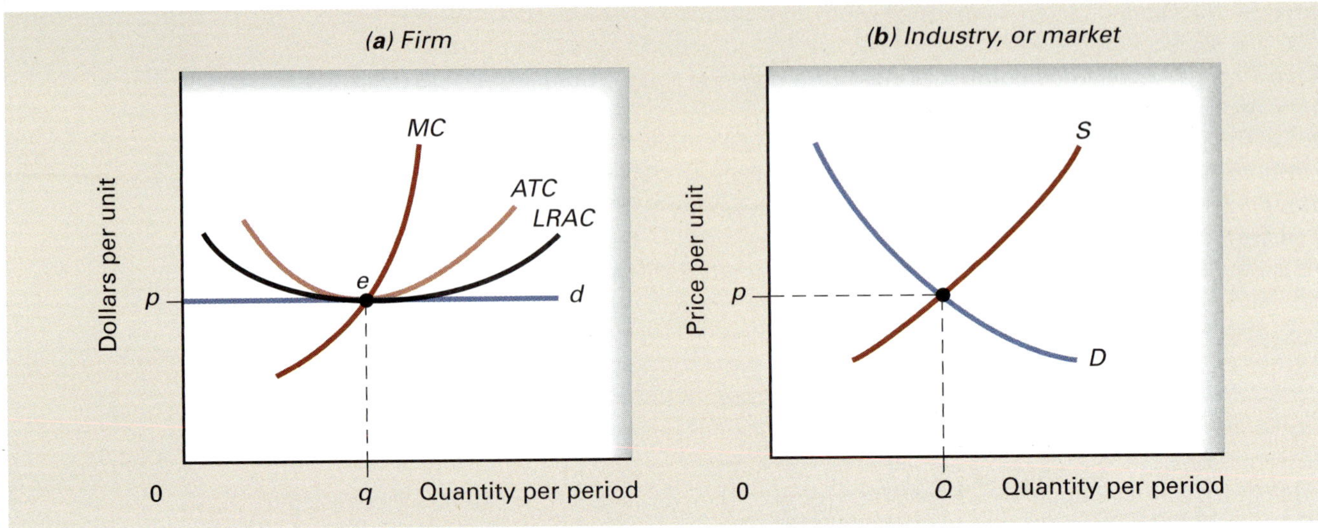

In long-run equilibrium, the firm produces *q* units of output per period and earns a normal profit. At point *e*, price, marginal cost, marginal revenue, short-run average total cost, and long-run average cost are all equal. There is no reason for new firms to enter the market or for existing firms to leave. As long as the market demand and supply curves remain unchanged, the industry will continue to produce a total of *Q* units of output at price *p*.

firm in the market has any reason to change its output, and no outside firm has any incentive to enter this industry, because firms in this market are earning normal, but not economic, profit. In other words, all resources employed in this industry earn their opportunity costs.

The Long-Run Adjustment to a Change in Demand

To explore the long-run adjustment process, let's consider how a firm and an industry respond to an increase in market demand. Suppose that the costs facing each firm do not depend on the number of firms in the industry (an assumption explained soon).

Effects of an Increase in Demand

Exhibit 10 shows a perfectly competitive firm and industry in long-run equilibrium, with the market supply curve intersecting the market demand curve at point a in panel (b). The market-clearing price is p, and the market quantity is Q_a. The firm, shown in panel (a), supplies q units at that market price, earning a normal profit. This representative firm produces where price, or marginal revenue, equals marginal cost, short-run average total cost, and long-run average cost. (Remember, a normal profit is included in the firm's average cost curves.)

Now suppose market demand increases, as reflected by a rightward shift of the market demand curve, from D to D' in panel (b), causing the market price to increase in the short run to p'. Each firm responds to the higher price by expanding output along its short-run supply, or marginal cost, curve until its quantity supplied increases to q', shown in panel (a) of Exhibit 10. At that output, the firm's marginal cost curve intersects the new marginal revenue curve, which is also the firm's new demand curve, d'. Note that in the short run, each firm now earns an economic profit, shown by the

EXHIBIT 10 Long-Run Adjustment in Perfect Competition to an Increase in Demand

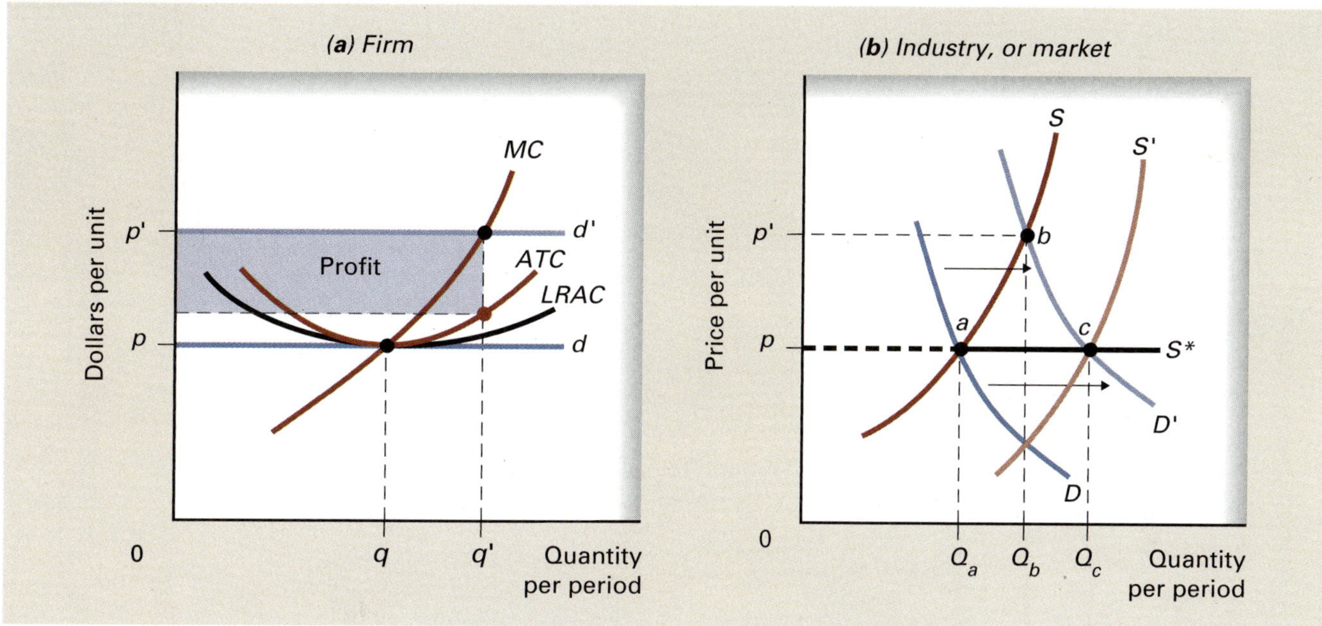

An increase in market demand from *D* to *D′* in panel (b) moves the short-run market equilibrium point from *a* to *b*. Output increases to Q_b, and price rises to *p′*. The price rise shifts up the individual firm's demand curve from *d* to *d′* in panel (a). The firm responds to the higher price by increasing output to *q′* and earns economic profit identified by the shaded rectangle. Economic profit attracts new firms to the industry in the long run. Market supply shifts right to *S′* in panel (b), pushing the market price back down to *p*. In panel (a), the firm's demand curve shifts back down to *d*, erasing economic profit. The short-run adjustment is from point *a* to point *b* in panel (b), but the long-run adjustment is from point *a* to point *c*.

shaded rectangle. Because all firms increase their quantity supplied, industry quantity supplied increases to Q_b in panel (b).

Economic profit attracts new firms in the long run. Their entry shifts the market supply curve to the right, which forces the price down. Firms continue to enter as long as they can earn economic profit. The market supply curve eventually shifts out to *S′*, where it intersects *D′* at point *c*, returning the price to its initial equilibrium level, *p*. The firm's demand curve drops from *d′* back down to *d*. As a result, each firm reduces output from *q′* back to *q*, and once again, each earns just a normal profit. Notice that although industry output increases from Q_a to Q_c, each firm's output returns to *q*. In this example, the additional output comes entirely from new firms drawn to the industry rather than from more output by existing firms (existing firms don't expand in this example because an increase in scale would increase average cost).

New firms are attracted to the industry by short-run economic profits resulting from the increase in demand. But this new entry shifts out market supply, forcing the market price down until economic profit disappears. In panel (b) of Exhibit 10, the short-run adjustment to increased demand is from point *a* to point *b;* the long-run adjustment moves to point *c*.

Effects of a Decrease in Demand

Next, let's trace the effects of a decrease of demand on the long-run market adjustment. The initial long-run equilibrium in Exhibit 11 is the same as in Exhibit 10. Market demand and supply curves intersect at point *a* in panel (b), yielding an equilibrium

EXHIBIT 11 Long-Run Adjustment in Perfect Competition to a Decrease in Demand

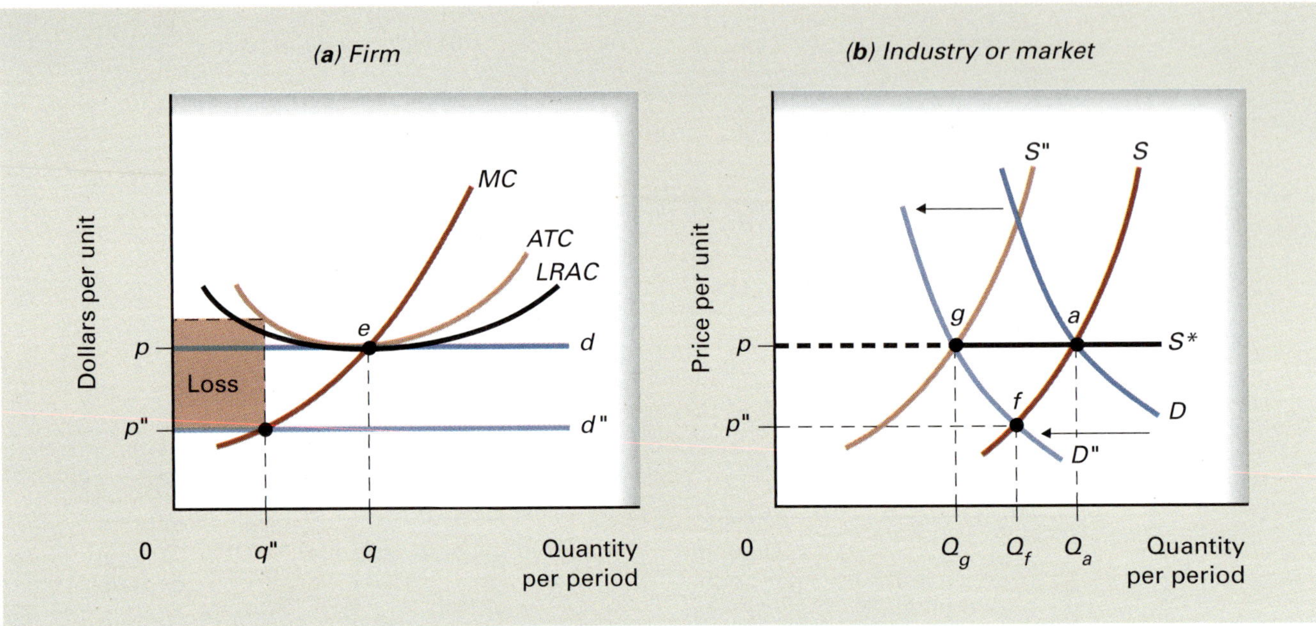

A decrease of demand to *D*″ in panel (b) disturbs the long-run equilibrium at point *a*. The price drops to *p*″ in the short run; output falls to Q_f. In panel (a), the firm's demand curve shifts down to *d*″. Each firm cuts output to *q*″ and suffers a loss. As firms leave the industry in the long run, the market supply curve shifts left to *S*″. Market price rises to *p* as output falls further to Q_g. At price *p*, the remaining firms once again earn a normal profit. Thus, the short-run adjustment is from point *a* to point *f* in panel (b); the long-run adjustment is from point *a* to point *g*.

price *p* and an equilibrium quantity Q_a. As shown in panel (a), each firm earns a normal profit in the long run by producing output rate *q*, where price, or marginal revenue, equals marginal cost, short-run average total cost, and long-run average cost.

Now suppose that market demand declines, as reflected in panel (b) by a leftward shift of the market demand curve, from *D* back to *D*″. In the short run, this forces the market price down to *p*″. With the market price lower, the demand curve facing each individual firm drops from *d* to *d*″. Each firm responds in the short run by reducing quantity supplied to *q*″ where the firm's marginal cost equals its now-lower marginal revenue, or price. Market output falls to Q_f. Because the lower market price is below average total cost, each firm operates at a loss. This loss is shown by the shaded rectangle in Exhibit 11. Note, the price must still be above the average variable cost, because the firm's short-run supply curve, *MC*, is defined as that portion of the firm's marginal cost curve at or above its average variable cost curve.

A short-run loss forces some firms out of business in the long run. As firms exit, market supply decreases, or shifts leftward, so the price increases along market demand curve *D*″. Firms continue to leave until the market supply curve decreases to *S*″, where it intersects *D*″ at point *g*. Market output has fallen to Q_g, and price has returned to *p*. With the price back up to *p*, remaining firms once again earn a normal profit. When the dust settles, each remaining firm produces *q*, the initial equilibrium quantity. But, because some firms have left the industry, market output has fallen from Q_a to Q_g. Again, note that the adjustment involves the departure of firms from the industry rather than a reduction in the scale of firms, as a reduction in scale would increase each firm's long-run average cost.

The Long-Run Industry Supply Curve

Thus far, we have looked at a perfectly competitive firm's and industry's response to changes in demand, distinguishing between a short-run adjustment and a long-run adjustment. In the short run, a firm alters quantity supplied by moving up or down its marginal cost curves (that portion at or above average variable cost) until marginal cost equals marginal revenue, or price. If the price is too low to cover minimum average variable cost, a firm shuts down in the short run. Short-run economic profit (or loss) prompts some firms in the long run to enter (or leave) the industry or to adjust firm size until remaining firms earn just a normal profit.

In Exhibits 10 and 11, we began with an initial long-run equilibrium point; then, in response to a shift of the demand curve, we found a new long-run equilibrium point. In each case, the price changed in the short run but not in the long run. Market output increased in Exhibit 10 and decreased in Exhibit 11. Connecting these long-run equilibrium points yields the *long-run industry supply curve,* labeled S^* in Exhibits 10 and 11. The **long-run industry supply curve** shows the relationship between price and quantity supplied once firms fully adjust to any short-term economic profit or loss resulting from a change in demand.

long-run industry supply curve
A curve that shows the relationship between price and quantity supplied by the industry once firms adjust in the long run to any change in market demand

Constant-Cost Industries

The industry we have examined thus far is called **constant-cost industry** because each firm's long-run average cost curve does not shift up or down as industry output changes. In a **constant-cost industry**, each firm's per-unit costs are independent of the number of firms in the industry. *The long-run supply curve for a constant-cost industry is horizontal,* as is depicted by S^* in Exhibits 10 and 11. A constant-cost industry uses such a small portion of the resources available that increasing industry output does not bid up resource prices. For example, output in the pencil industry can expand without bidding up the prices of wood, graphite, and rubber, because the pencil industry uses such a tiny share of the market supply of these resources.

constant-cost industry
An industry that can expand or contract without affecting the long-run per-unit cost of production; the long-run industry supply curve is horizontal

Increasing-Cost Industries

The firms in some industries encounter higher average costs as industry output expands in the long run. Firms in these **increasing-cost industries** find that expanding output bids up the prices of some resources or otherwise increases per-unit production costs, and these higher costs shift up each firm's cost curves. For example, a market expansion of oil production could bid up the prices of drilling rigs and the wages of petroleum engineers and geologists, raising per-unit production costs for each oil producer. Likewise, more housing construction could bid up what developers must pay for land, carpenters, lumber, and other building materials.

increasing-cost industry
An industry that faces higher per-unit production costs as industry output expands in the long run; the long-run industry supply curve slopes upward

To illustrate the equilibrium adjustment process for an increasing-cost industry, we begin again in long-run equilibrium in Exhibit 12, with the firm shown in panel (a) and the industry in panel (b). Market demand curve D in panel (b) intersects short-run market supply curve S at equilibrium point a to yield market price p_a and market quantity Q_a. When the price is p_a, the demand (and marginal revenue) curve facing each firm is d_a as shown in panel (a). The firm supplies quantity q, where the price, or marginal revenue, equals marginal cost. At that output, average total cost equals the price, so the firm earns no economic profit in this long-run equilibrium.

Suppose an increase in the demand for this product shifts the market demand curve in panel (b) to the right from D to D'. The new demand curve intersects the

EXHIBIT 12 Long-Run Adjustment for an Increasing-Cost Industry in Perfect Competition

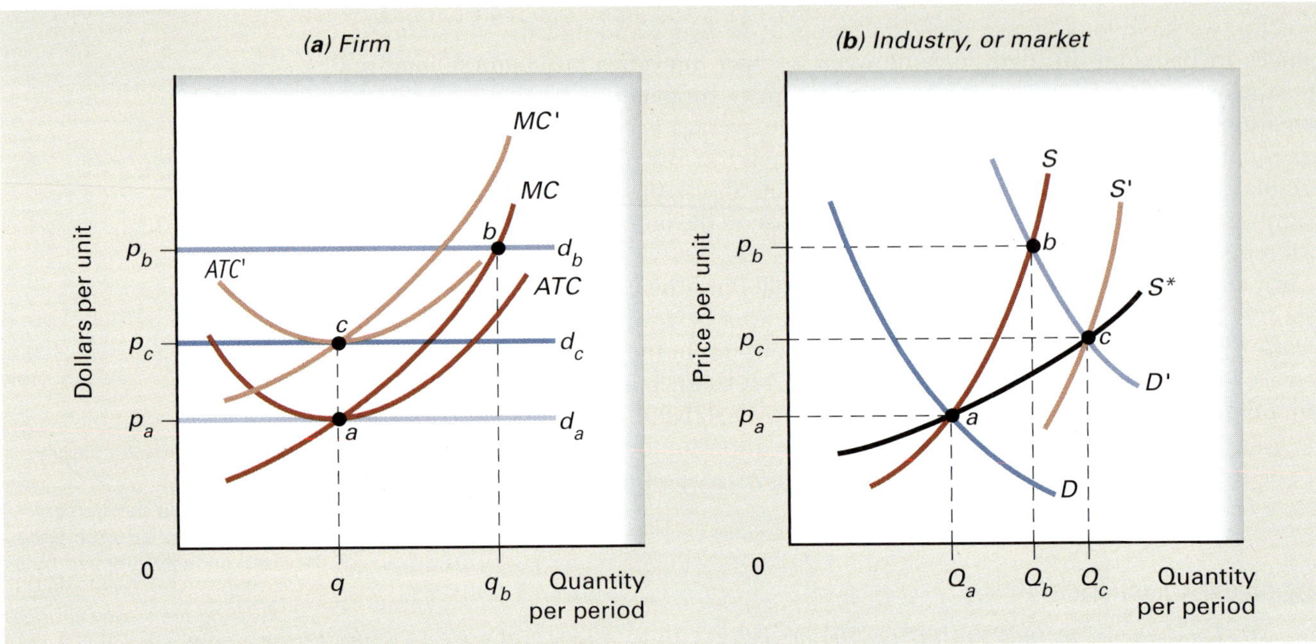

An increase in demand to D' in panel (b) disturbs the initial equilibrium at point *a*. Short-run equilibrium is established at point *b*, where D' intersects the short-run market supply curve *S*. At the higher price p_b, the firm's demand curve shifts up to d_b, and its output increases to q_b in panel (a). At point *b*, the firm is now earning economic profit, which attracts new firms. As new firms enter, input prices get bid up, so each firm's marginal and average cost curves rise. New firms increase the short-run market supply curve from *S* to S'. The intersection of the new market supply curve, S', with D' determines the market price, p_c. At p_c, individual firms are earning a normal profit. Point *c* shows the long-run equilibrium combination of price and quantity. By connecting long-run equilibrium points *a* and *c* in panel (b), we obtain the upward-sloping long-run market supply curve S^* for this increasing-cost industry.

short-run market supply curve *S* at point *b*, yielding the market price p_b and market quantity Q_b. With this price increase, each firm's demand curve shifts from d_a up to d_b. The firm's new short-run equilibrium occurs at point *b* in panel (a), where the marginal cost curve intersects the new demand curve, which is also the marginal revenue curve. Each firm produces output q_b. In the short run, each firm earns an economic profit equal to q_b times the difference between price p_b and the average total cost at that rate of output. So far, the sequence of events is the same as for a constant-cost industry.

Economic profit attracts new firms. Because this is an increasing-cost industry, new entrants drive up the cost of production, raising each firm's marginal and average cost curves. In panel (a) of Exhibit 12, *MC* and *ATC* shift up to MC' and ATC'. (We assume for simplicity that new average cost curves are vertical shifts of the initial ones, so the minimum efficient plant size remains the same.)

The entry of new firms also shifts the short-run industry supply curve to the right in panel (b), thus reducing the market price along D'. *New firms enter the industry until the combination of a higher production cost and a lower price squeezes economic profit to zero.* This long-run equilibrium occurs when the entry of new firms has shifted the short-run industry supply curve out to S', which lowers the price until it equals the minimum on each firm's new average total cost curve. The market price does not fall back to the initial equilibrium level because each firm's average total cost curve has increased, or shifted up, with the expansion of industry output. The intersection of the new short-run market supply curve, S', and the new market demand curve, D', determines the new long-run market equilibrium point, *c*. Points *a* and *c* in panel (b) are both on the *upward-sloping* long-run supply curve S^* for this increasing-cost industry.

In constant-cost industries, each firm's costs depend simply on the scale of its plant and its rate of output. For increasing-cost industries, each firm's costs depend also on the number of firms in the market. By bidding up the price of resources, long-run expansion in an increasing-cost industry increases each firm's marginal and average costs. The long-run supply curve slopes upward, like S^* in Exhibit 12.

To Review: Firms in perfect competition can earn an economic profit, a normal profit, or an economic loss in the short run. But in the long run, the entry or exit of firms and adjustments in each firm's size squeeze economic profit to zero. Competitive firms earn only a normal profit in the long run. This is true whether the industry in question experiences constant costs or increasing costs in the long run. Notice that, regardless of the nature of costs in the industry, the market supply curve is more elastic in the long run than in the short run. In the long run, firms can adjust all their resources, so they are better able to respond to changes in price. One final point: Firms in an industry could theoretically experience a lower average cost as industry output expands in the long run, resulting in a downward-sloping long-run industry supply curve. But such an outcome is considered so rare that we do not examine it.

As mentioned at the outset, perfect competition provides a useful benchmark for evaluating the efficiency of markets. Let's examine the qualities of perfect competition that make it so useful.

Perfect Competition and Efficiency

How does perfect competition stack up as an efficient user of resources? Two concepts of efficiency are used to judge market performance. The first, called *productive efficiency,* refers to producing output at the least possible cost. The second, called *allocative efficiency,* refers to producing the output that consumers value the most. *Perfect competition guarantees both productive efficiency and allocative efficiency in the long run.*

Productive Efficiency: Making Stuff Right

Productive efficiency occurs when the firm produces at the minimum point on its long-run average cost curve, so the market price equals the minimum average cost. The entry and exit of firms and any adjustment in the scale of each firm ensure that each firm produces at the minimum of its long-run average cost curve. Firms that do not reach minimum long-run average cost must, to avoid continued losses, either adjust their scale or leave the industry. Thus, *perfect competition produces output at minimum average cost in the long run.*

productive efficiency
The condition that exists when production uses the least-cost combination of inputs; minimum average cost in the long run

Allocative Efficiency: Making the Right Stuff

Just because *production* occurs at the least possible cost does not mean that the *allocation* of resources is the most efficient one possible. The products may not be the ones consumers want. This situation is akin to that of the airline pilot who informs passengers that there's good news and bad news: "The good news is that we're making record time. The bad news is that we're lost!" Likewise, firms may be producing goods efficiently but producing the wrong goods—that is, making stuff right but making the wrong stuff.

allocative efficiency
The condition that exists when firms produce the output most preferred by consumers; marginal benefit equals marginal cost

Allocative efficiency occurs when firms produce the output that consumers value most. How do we know that perfect competition guarantees allocative efficiency? The answer lies with the market demand and supply curves. Recall that the demand curve reflects the marginal value that consumers attach to each unit of the good, so the market price is the amount people are willing and able to pay for the final unit they consume. We also know that, in both the short run and the long run, the equilibrium price in perfect competition equals the marginal cost of supplying the last unit sold. Marginal cost measures the opportunity cost of resources employed to produce that last unit sold. Thus, the demand and supply curves intersect at the combination of price and quantity at which *the marginal value, or the marginal benefit, that consumers attach to the final unit purchased, just equals the opportunity cost of the resources employed to produce that unit.*

As long as marginal benefit equals marginal cost, the last unit produced is valued by consumers as much as, or more than, any other good those resources could have produced. There is no way to reallocate resources to increase the total value of all output in the economy. Thus, there is no way to reallocate resources to increase the total utility or total benefit consumers reap from production. *When the marginal benefit that consumers derive from a good equals the marginal cost of producing that good, that market is said to be allocatively efficient.*

$$\text{Marginal benefit} = \text{Marginal cost}$$

Firms not only are making stuff right, they are making the right stuff.

What's so Perfect About Perfect Competition?

If the marginal cost of supplying a good just equals the marginal benefit to consumers, does this mean that market exchange confers no net benefits to participants? No. Market exchange usually benefits both consumers and producers. Recall that consumers enjoy a surplus from market exchange because the most they would be willing and able to pay for each unit of the good usually exceeds what they actually do pay. Exhibit 13 depicts a market in short-run equilibrium. The *consumer surplus* in this exhibit is represented by blue shading, which is the area below the demand curve but above the market-clearing price of $10.

Producers in the short run also usually derive a net benefit, or a surplus, from market exchange, because what they receive for their output exceeds the least they would accept to supply that quantity in the short run. Recall that the short-run market supply curve is the sum of each firm's marginal cost curve at or above its minimum average variable cost. Point *m* in Exhibit 13 is the minimum point on the market supply curve; it indicates that at a price of $5, quantity supplied is 100,000 units. At prices below $5, quantity supplied would be zero because firms could not cover average variable cost. A price of $5 just covers average variable cost.

If the market price rises to $6, quantity supplied increases until marginal cost equals $6. Market output increases from 100,000 to 120,000 units. Total revenue in this market increases from $500,000 to $720,000. Part of the higher revenue covers the higher marginal cost of production. But the rest provides a bonus to producers. After all, suppliers would have offered the first 100,000 units for only $5 each. If the price is $6, firms get to supply these 100,000 units for $6 each. Producer surplus at a price of $6 is the gold-shaded area between the prices of $5 and $6.

EXHIBIT 13 Consumer Surplus and Producer Surplus for Perfectly Competitive Market

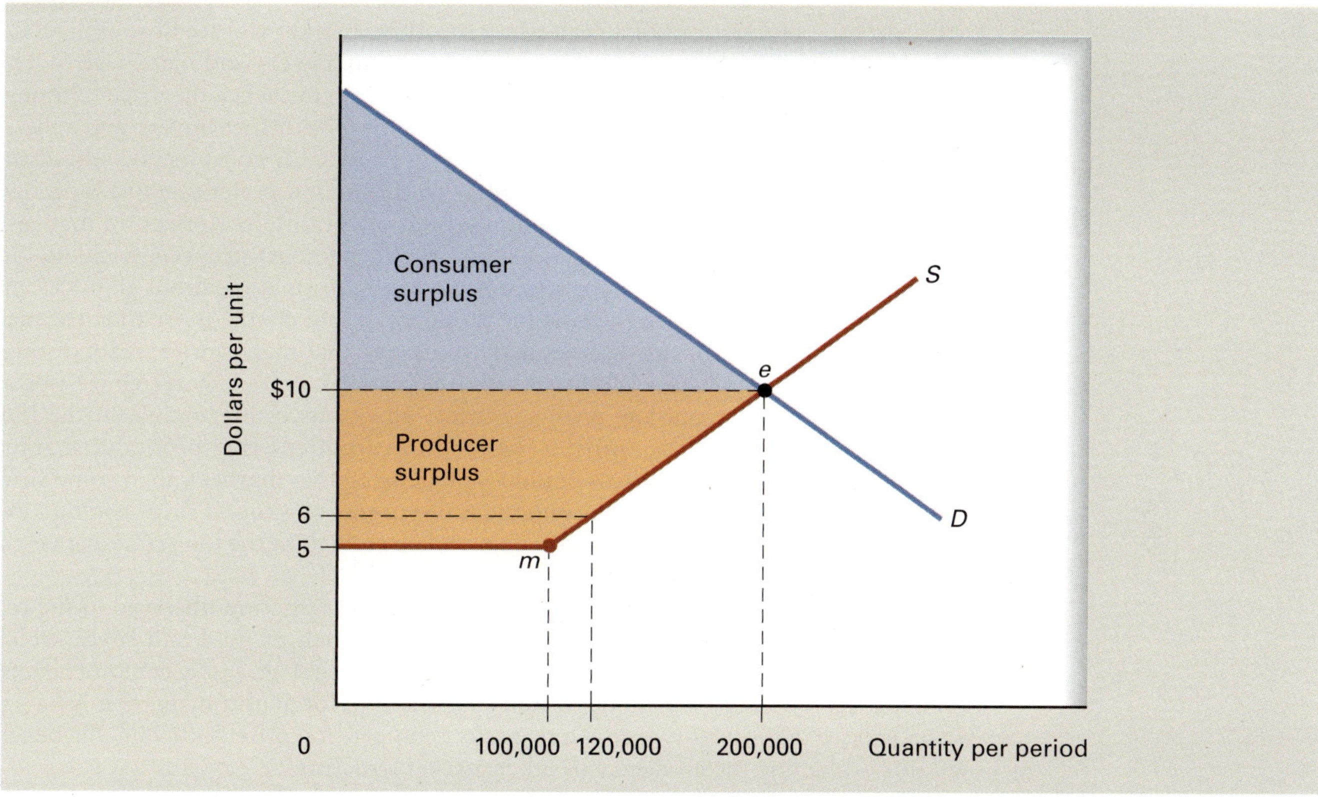

Consumer surplus is represented by the area above the market-clearing price of $10 per unit and below the demand curve; it appears as the blue triangle. Producer surplus is represented by the area above the short-run market supply curve and below the market-clearing price of $10 per unit; it appears as the gold area. At a price of $5 per unit, there would be no producer surplus. At a price of $6 per unit, producer surplus would be the gold shaded area between $5 and $6. A price of $5 just covers each firm's average variable cost.

In the short run, **producer surplus** equals the total revenue producers are paid minus their variable cost of production. In Exhibit 13, the market-clearing price is $10 per unit, and producer surplus is depicted by the gold-shaded area between a price of $5 and the market price of $10. The most the firm can lose in the short run is to shut down. Any price that exceeds average variable cost, which is $5 in this example, reduces that short-run loss, and generates a producer surplus. A high enough price could yield economic profit.

producer surplus
A bonus for producers in the short run; the amount by which total revenue from production exceeds variable cost

The combination of consumer surplus and producer surplus shows the gains from voluntary exchange. Productive and allocative efficiency in the short run occurs at equilibrium point *e*, which also is the combination of price and quantity that maximizes the sum of consumer surplus and producer surplus, thus maximizing social welfare. **Social welfare** is the overall well-being of people in the economy. Even though marginal cost equals marginal benefit for the final unit produced and consumed, both producers and consumers usually derive a surplus, or a bonus, from market exchange.

social welfare
The overall well-being of people in the economy; maximized when the marginal cost of production equals the marginal benefit to consumers

The gains from market exchange have been examined in an experimental setting, as discussed in the case study, "Information Economy: Experimental Economics," at the end of the book.

Conclusion

Let's review the assumptions of a perfectly competitive market and see how each relates to ideas developed in this chapter. *First,* there are many buyers and many sellers. This assumption ensures that no individual buyer or seller can influence the price (although recent experiments show that competition occurs even with few buyers and sellers). *Second,* firms produce a commodity, or a uniform product. If consumers could distinguish between the products of different suppliers, they might prefer one firm's product even at a higher price, so different producers could sell at different prices. In that case, not every firm would be a price taker—that is, each firm's demand curve would no longer be horizontal. *Third,* market participants have full information about all prices and all production processes. Otherwise, some producers could charge more than the market price, and some uninformed consumers would pay that higher price. Also, through ignorance, some firms might select outdated technology or fail to recognize opportunities for short-run economic profits. *Fourth,* all resources are mobile in the long run, with nothing preventing firms in the long run from entering profitable markets or leaving losing markets. If firms couldn't enter profitable markets, then some firms already in that market could earn economic profit in the long run. If firms couldn't exit losing markets, then market supply couldn't decline enough in the long run to erase the economic losses of remaining firms.

Perfect competition is not the most common market structure observed in the real world. The markets for agricultural products, metals such as gold and silver, widely traded stocks, and foreign exchange come close to being perfect. But even if not a single example could be found, the model would still be useful for analyzing market behavior. As you will see in the next two chapters, perfect competition provides a valuable benchmark for evaluating the efficiency of other market structures.

Summary

1. Market structure describes important features of the economic environment in which firms operate. These features include the number of buyers and sellers in the market, the ease or difficulty of entering and leaving the market, differences in the product across firms, and the forms of competition among firms.
2. A perfectly competitive market is characterized by (a) a large number of buyers and sellers, each too small to influence the market price; (b) firms in the market supply a commodity, which is a product undifferentiated across producers; (c) buyers and sellers possess full information about the availability and prices of all resources, goods, and technologies; and (d) firms and resources are freely mobile in the long run.
3. The market price in perfect competition is determined by the intersection of the market demand and market supply curves. Each firm then faces a demand curve that is a horizontal line at the market price. The firm's demand curve also indicates the average revenue and marginal revenue received at each rate of output. Firms in perfect competition are said to be price takers because no firm can influence the market price. Each firm can vary only the amount it supplies at that price.
4. For a firm to produce in the short run, rather than shut down, the market price must at least cover the firm's average variable cost. If price is below average variable cost, the firm shuts down. That portion of the marginal cost curve at or rising above the average variable cost curve becomes the perfectly competitive firm's short-run supply curve. The horizontal sum of each firm's supply curve forms the market supply curve. As long as price covers average variable cost, each perfectly competitive firm maximizes profit or minimizes loss by producing where marginal revenue equals marginal cost.
5. Because firms are not free to enter or leave the market in the short run, economic profit or loss is possible. In the long run, however, firms enter or leave the market and otherwise adjust their scale of operation until any economic profit or loss is eliminated.
6. Competition drives each firm in the long run to produce at the lowest point on its long-run average cost curve. At this rate of output, marginal revenue equals marginal cost and each also equals the price and average cost. Firms that fail to produce at this least-cost combination do not survive in the long run.
7. In the short run, a firm's change in quantity supplied is shown by moving up or down its marginal cost, or supply, curve. In the long run, firms enter or leave the market and existing firms may change their scale of operation until firms still in the industry

earn just a normal profit. As the industry expands or contracts in the long run, the long-run industry supply curve has a shape that reflects either constant costs or increasing costs.

8. Perfectly competitive markets exhibit both productive efficiency (because output is produced using the most efficient combination of resources available) and allocative efficiency (because the goods produced are those most valued by consumers). In equilibrium, a perfectly competitive market allocates goods so that the marginal cost of the final unit produced equals the marginal value that consumers attach to that final unit. In the long run, market pressure minimizes the average cost of production. Voluntary exchange in competitive markets maximizes the sum of consumer surplus and producer surplus, thus maximizing social welfare.

Key Concepts

Market structure 152
Perfect competition 152
Commodity 152
Price taker 153
Marginal revenue (MR) 156
Golden rule of profit maximization 156
Average revenue 156
Short-run firm supply curve 161
Short-run industry supply curve 161
Long-run industry supply curve 167
Constant-cost industry 167
Increasing-cost industry 167
Productive efficiency 169
Allocative efficiency 170
Producer surplus 171
Social welfare 171

Questions for Review

1. Market Structure Define *market structure*. What factors are considered in determining the market structure of a particular industry?
2. Demand Under Perfect Competition What type of demand curve does a perfectly competitive firm face? Why?
3. Total Revenue Look back at Exhibit 3, panel (a) in this chapter. Explain why the total revenue curve is a straight line from the origin, whereas the slope of the total cost curve changes.
4. Profit in the Short Run Look back at Exhibit 3, panel (b), in this chapter. Why doesn't the firm choose the output that maximizes average profit (i.e., the output where average cost is the lowest)?
5. The Short-Run Firm Supply Curve An individual competitive firm's short-run supply curve is the portion of its marginal cost curve that equals or rises above the average variable cost. Explain why.
6. Case Study: Auction Markets (See page 716.) Which of the characteristics of the perfectly competitive market structure are found in FloraHolland Aalsmeer?
7. Long-Run Industry Supply Why does the long-run industry supply curve for an increasing-cost industry slope upward? What increases costs in an increasing-cost industry?
8. Perfect Competition and Efficiency Define productive efficiency and allocative efficiency. What conditions must be met to achieve them?
9. Case Study: Experimental Economics (See page 717.) In Professor Vernon Smith's experiment, which "buyers" ended up with a surplus at the market-clearing price of $2? Which "sellers" had a surplus? Which "buyers" or "sellers" did not engage in transactions?

Problems and Exercises

10. Short-Run Profit Maximization A perfectly competitive firm has the following fixed and variable costs in the short run. The market price for the firm's product is $150.

Output	FC	VC	TC	TR	Profit/Loss
0	$100	$0	___	___	___
1	$100	$100	___	___	___
2	$100	$180	___	___	___
3	$100	$300	___	___	___
4	$100	$440	___	___	___
5	$100	$600	___	___	___
6	$100	$780	___	___	___

a. Complete the table.
b. At what output rate does the firm maximize profit or minimize loss?
c. What is the firm's marginal revenue at each positive rate of output? Its average revenue?
d. What can you say about the relationship between marginal revenue and marginal cost for output rates below the profit-maximizing (or loss-minimizing) rate? For output rates above the profit-maximizing (or loss-minimizing) rate?

11. THE SHORT-RUN FIRM SUPPLY CURVE Use the following data to answer the questions below:

Q	VC	MC	AVC
1	$10	___	___
2	$16	___	___
3	$20	___	___
4	$25	___	___
5	$31	___	___
6	$38	___	___
7	$46	___	___
8	$55	___	___
9	$65	___	___

a. Calculate the marginal cost and average variable cost for each level of production.
b. How much would the firm produce if it could sell its product for $5? For $7? For $10?
c. Explain your answers.
d. Assuming that its fixed cost is $3, calculate the firm's profit at each of the production levels determined in part (b).

12. THE SHORT-RUN FIRM SUPPLY CURVE Each of the following situations could exist for a perfectly competitive firm in the short run. In each case, indicate whether the firm should produce in the short run or shut down in the short run, or whether additional information is needed to determine what it should do in the short run.

a. Total cost exceeds total revenue at all output levels.
b. Total variable cost exceeds total revenue at all output levels.
c. Total revenue exceeds total fixed cost at all output levels.
d. Marginal revenue exceeds marginal cost at the current output level.
e. Price exceeds average total cost at all output levels.
f. Average variable cost exceeds price at all output levels.
g. Average total cost exceeds price at all output levels.

13. PERFECT COMPETITION IN THE LONG RUN Draw the short- and long-run cost curves for a competitive firm in long-run equilibrium. Indicate the long-run equilibrium price and quantity.

a. Discuss the firm's short-run response to a reduction in the price of a variable resource.
b. Assuming that this is a constant-cost industry, describe the process by which the industry returns to long-run equilibrium following a change in market demand.

14. THE LONG-RUN INDUSTRY SUPPLY CURVE A normal good is being produced in a constant-cost, perfectly competitive industry. Initially, each firm is in long-run equilibrium.

a. Graphically illustrate and explain the short-run adjustments for the market and the firm to a decrease in consumer incomes. Be sure to discuss any changes in output levels, prices, profits, and the number of firms.
b. Next, show on your graph and explain the long-run adjustment to the income change. Be sure to discuss any changes in output levels, prices, profits, and the number of firms.

15. THE LONG-RUN INDUSTRY SUPPLY CURVE The following graph shows possible long-run market supply curves for a perfectly competitive industry. Determine which supply curve indicates a constant-cost industry and which an increasing-cost industry.

a. Explain the difference between a constant-cost industry and an increasing-cost industry.
b. Distinguish between the long-run impact of an increase in market demand in a constant-cost industry and the impact in an increasing-cost industry.

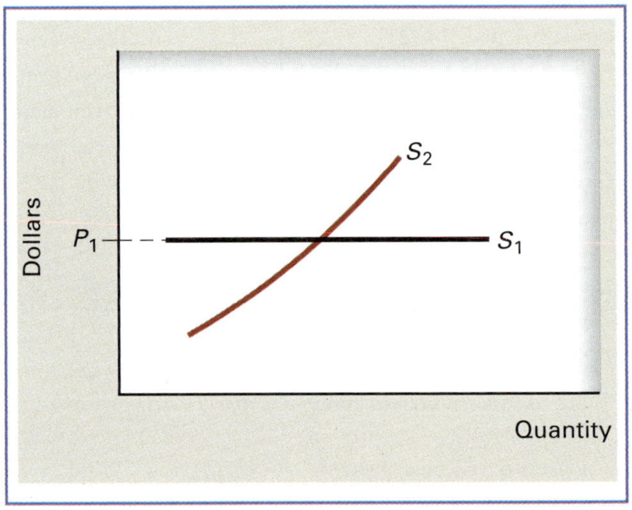

16. WHAT'S SO PERFECT ABOUT PERFECT COMPETITION Use the following data to answer the questions.

Quantity	Marginal Cost	Marginal Benefit
0	—	—
1	$ 2	$10
2	$ 3	$ 9
3	$ 4	$ 8
4	$ 5	$ 7
5	$ 6	$ 6
6	$ 8	$ 5
7	$10	$ 4
8	$12	$ 3

a. For the product shown, assume that the minimum point of each firm's average variable cost curve is at $2. Construct a demand and supply diagram for the product and indicate the equilibrium price and quantity.
b. On the graph, label the area of consumer surplus as *f*. Label the area of producer surplus as *g*.
c. If the equilibrium price were $2, what would be the amount of producer surplus?

Global Economic Watch Exercises

Login to www.cengagebrain.com and access the Global Economic Watch to do these exercises.

17. Global Economic Watch Go to the Global Economic Crisis Resource Center. Select Global Issues in Context. In the Basic Search box at the top of the page, enter the phrase "Green Shoots." On the Results page, go to the Magazines section. Click on the link for the March 13, 2010, article "Green Shoots; Agribusiness in India." As you read the article, concentrate on the fourth paragraph, which describes the traditional market structure for Indian agriculture. How well does the description fit the four characteristics of perfect competition?

18. Global Economic Watch Go to the Global Economic Crisis Resource Center. Select Global Issues in Context. In the Basic Search box at the top of the page, enter the term "perfect competition." Find three or four resources that discuss the economic definition of *perfect competition*. Writing in your own words, analyze whether the authors support or dispute the idea that perfect competition is realistic and applicable.

Monopoly

9

AP Photo/Rick Rycroft

- How can a firm monopolize a market?
- Why aren't most markets monopolized?
- Why don't most monopolies last?
- Why don't monopolies charge the highest possible price?
- How has China monopolized the world market for pandas?
- Why is the head of Starbucks worried about his coffee becoming a commodity?
- Do student and senior discounts come from corporate generosity?
- Why are there so many different airfares for the same flight?

These and other questions are answered in this chapter, which looks at our second market structure—monopoly.

Monopoly is from the Greek, meaning "one seller." In some parts of the United States, monopolists sell electricity, cable TV service, and local phone service. Monopolists also sell postage stamps, hot dogs at sports arenas, some patented products, some prescription drugs, and other goods and services with no close substitutes. You have probably heard about the evils of monopoly. You may have even played the board game *Monopoly* on a rainy day. Now we sort out fact from fiction.

Like perfect competition, pure monopoly is not as common as other market structures. But by understanding monopoly, you grow more familiar with market structures that lie between the extremes of perfect competition and pure monopoly. This chapter examines the sources of monopoly power, how a monopolist maximizes profit, differences

between monopoly and perfect competition, and why a monopolist sometimes charges different prices for the same product.

Topics include:

- Barriers to entry
- Price elasticity and marginal revenue
- Profit maximization and loss minimization
- Monopoly and resource allocation
- Welfare cost of monopoly
- Price discrimination
- The monopolist's dream

Barriers to Entry

barrier to entry
Any impediment that prevents new firms from entering an industry and competing on an equal basis with existing firms

As noted in Chapter 3, a *monopoly* is the sole supplier of a product with no close substitutes. Why do some markets come to be dominated by a single supplier? A monopolized market is characterized by **barriers to entry**, which are restrictions on the entry of new firms into an industry. Because of barriers, new firms cannot profitably enter that market. Let's examine three types of entry barriers: legal restrictions, economies of scale, and control of an essential resource.

Legal Restrictions

One way to prevent new firms from entering a market is to make entry illegal. Patents, licenses, and other legal restrictions imposed by the government provide some producers with legal protection against competition.

Patents and Invention Incentives

patent
A legal barrier to entry that grants the holder the exclusive right to sell a product for 20 years from the date the patent application is filed

innovation
The process of turning an invention into a marketable product

In the United States, a **patent** awards an inventor the exclusive right to produce a good or service for 20 years from the date the patent is filed with the patent office. Originally enacted in 1790, patent laws encourage inventors to invest the time and money required to discover and develop new products and processes. If others could simply copy successful products, inventors would be less interested in incurring the upfront costs of invention. Abraham Lincoln said that "the patent system added the fuel of interest to the fire of genius." The 20-year clock starts ticking as soon as the application is filed, thus providing a stimulus to turn inventions into marketable products, a process called **innovation**.

Licenses and Other Entry Restrictions

Governments often confer monopoly status by awarding an individual firm the exclusive right to supply a particular good or service. Federal licenses give certain firms the right to broadcast radio and TV signals. State licenses authorize suppliers of medical care, haircuts, and legal advice. A license may not grant a monopoly, but it does block entry and often gives firms the power to charge prices above the competitive level. Thus, a license can serve as an effective barrier against new competitors. Governments also grant monopoly rights to sell hot dogs at civic auditoriums, collect garbage, provide bus and taxi service, and supply other services ranging from electricity to cable TV. Sometimes the government itself may claim that right by outlawing competitors. For example, many state governments sell liquor and lottery tickets, and the U.S. Postal Service has the exclusive right to deliver first-class mail to your mailbox.

Economies of Scale

A monopoly sometimes occurs naturally when a firm experiences *economies of scale,* as reflected by the downward-sloping, long-run average cost curve shown in Exhibit 1. In such instances, a single firm can supply market demand at a lower average cost per unit than could two or more firms, each producing less. Put another way, market demand is not great enough to allow more than one firm to achieve sufficient economies of scale. Thus, a single firm emerges from the competitive process as the only low-cost supplier in the market. For example, even though electricity *production* has become more competitive, electricity *transmission* still exhibits economies of scale. Once wires are strung throughout a community, the cost of linking an additional household to the power grid is relatively small. Consequently, the average cost of delivering electricity declines as more and more households are wired into an existing system.

A monopoly that emerges from the nature of costs is called a *natural monopoly,* to distinguish it from the artificial monopolies created by government patents, licenses, and other legal barriers to entry. A new entrant cannot sell enough to experience the economies of scale achieved by an established natural monopolist. Therefore,

EXHIBIT 1 **Economies of Scale as a Barrier to Entry**

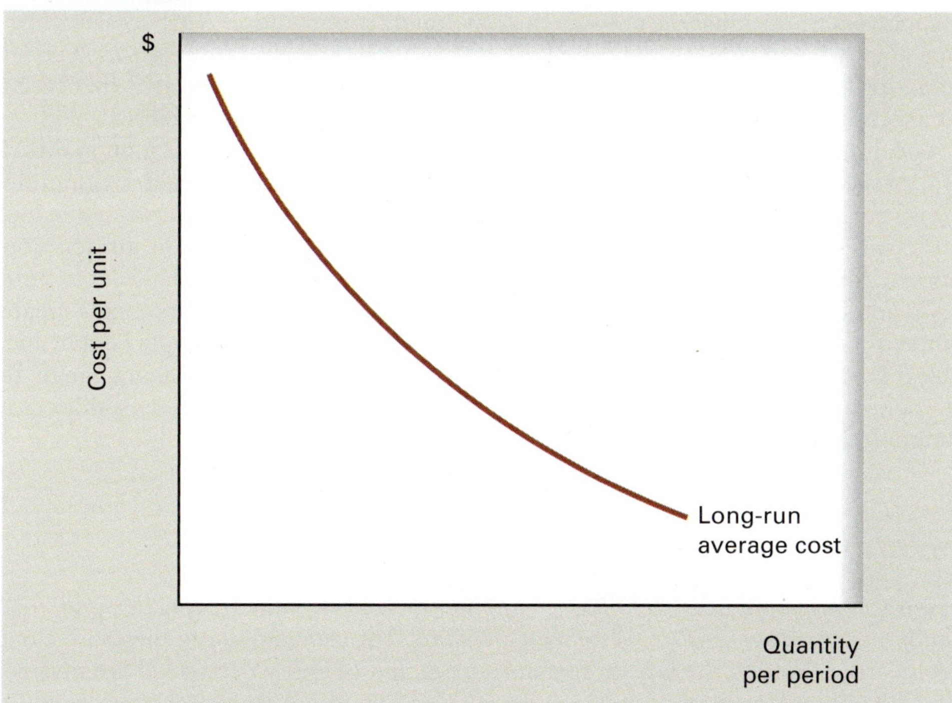

A monopoly sometimes emerges naturally when a firm experiences economies of scale as reflected by a downward-sloping, long-run average cost curve. One firm can satisfy market demand at a lower average cost per unit than could two or more firms each operating at smaller rates of output.

market entry is naturally blocked. A later chapter gets into the regulation of natural monopolies.

Control of Essential Resources

Sometimes the source of monopoly power is a firm's control over some resource critical to production. Here are some examples. Alcoa was the sole U.S. maker of aluminum from the late 19th century until World War II. Its monopoly power initially stemmed from production patents that expired in 1909, but for the next three decades, it controlled the supply of bauxite, the key raw material in making aluminum. Professional sports leagues try to block the formation of competing leagues by signing the best athletes to long-term contracts and by seeking the exclusive use of sports stadiums and arenas. China is a monopoly supplier of pandas to the world's zoos. The National Zoo in Washington, D.C., for example, rents its pair of pandas from China for $1 million a year. Other zoos have similar arrangements. To limit the supply, China stipulates that any offspring becomes China's property.[1] For example, in 2010 a male offspring of the Washington pair was shipped back to China. Finally, for decades, the world's diamond trade was controlled primarily by De Beers Consolidated Mines, which mined diamonds and also bought most of the world's supply of rough diamonds, as discussed in the case study, "World of Business: Is a Diamond Forever?" at the end of the book.

Monopoly profits often spring from supplying something that other producers can't match. For example, Starbucks over the years has built up a unique "experience" for the customer, including baristas who know customer orders by heart and a comfortable atmosphere that encourages patrons to relax and linger. That uniqueness has given Starbucks the market power to grow and to charge a premium price that has rocketed the company's stock price more than 25-fold since 1992. But a recent memo from the company chairman to employees warned that the pressure to grow could "commoditize" Starbucks, making it more vulnerable to competition from other coffee shops and even from fast-food chains. Once a product loses its uniqueness—in this case, by going from a special experience to just another cup of coffee—the supplier loses market power and profitability.[2]

Local monopolies are more common than national or international monopolies. In rural areas, monopolies may include the only grocery store, movie theater, restaurant, or gas station for miles around. These are natural monopolies for products sold in local markets. But long-lasting monopolies are rare because economic profit attracts competitors. Also, over time, technological change tends to break down barriers to entry. For example, the development of wireless transmission of long-distance calls created competitors to AT&T. Wireless transmission is also erasing the monopoly held by local cable TV providers and even local phone service. Likewise, text messaging, email, the Internet, and firms such as FedEx and UPS now compete with the U.S. Postal Service's monopoly, as described in a case study at the end of the book.

Revenue for the Monopolist

Because a monopoly, by definition, supplies the entire market, the demand for a monopolist's output is also the market demand. The demand curve therefore slopes downward, reflecting the law of demand—price and quantity demanded are inversely related. Let's look at demand, average revenue, and marginal revenue for a monopolist.

1. D'Vera Cohn, "Zoos Find Pandas Don't Make the Cash to Cover the Keep," *Washington Post*, 7 August 2005.
2. The company memo is discussed in Janet Adamy, "Starbucks Chairman Says Trouble May Be Brewing," *Wall Street Journal*, 24 February 2007.

Demand, Average Revenue, and Marginal Revenue

Suppose De Beers controls the diamond market. Exhibit 2 shows the demand curve for high-quality 1-carat diamonds. De Beers, for example, can sell three diamonds a day at $7,000 each. That price-quantity combination yields total revenue of $21,000 (=$7,000 × 3). Total revenue divided by quantity is the *average revenue per diamond,* which also is $7,000. Thus, the monopolist's price equals the average revenue per unit. To sell a fourth diamond, De Beers must lower the price to $6,750. Total revenue from selling four diamonds is $27,000 (=$6,750 × 4), and average revenue is $6,750. All along the demand curve, price equals average revenue. Therefore, *the demand curve is also the monopolist's average revenue curve,* just as the perfectly competitive firm's demand curve is that firm's average revenue curve.

What's the marginal revenue from selling a fourth diamond? When De Beers drops the price from $7,000 to $6,750, total revenue increases from $21,000 to $27,000. Thus, *marginal revenue*—the change in total revenue from selling one more diamond—is $6,000, which is less than the price, or average revenue, of $6,750. *For a monopolist, marginal revenue is less than the price, or average revenue.* Recall that for a perfectly competitive firm, marginal revenue equals the price, or average revenue, because that firm can sell all it supplies at the market price.

The Gains and Loss From Selling One More Unit

A closer look at Exhibit 2 reveals why a monopolist's marginal revenue is less than the price. By selling another diamond, De Beers gains the revenue from that sale. For example, De Beers gets $6,750 from the fourth diamond, as shown by the blue-shaded vertical

EXHIBIT 2 **A Monopolist's Gain and Loss in Total Revenue from Selling a Fourth Unit**

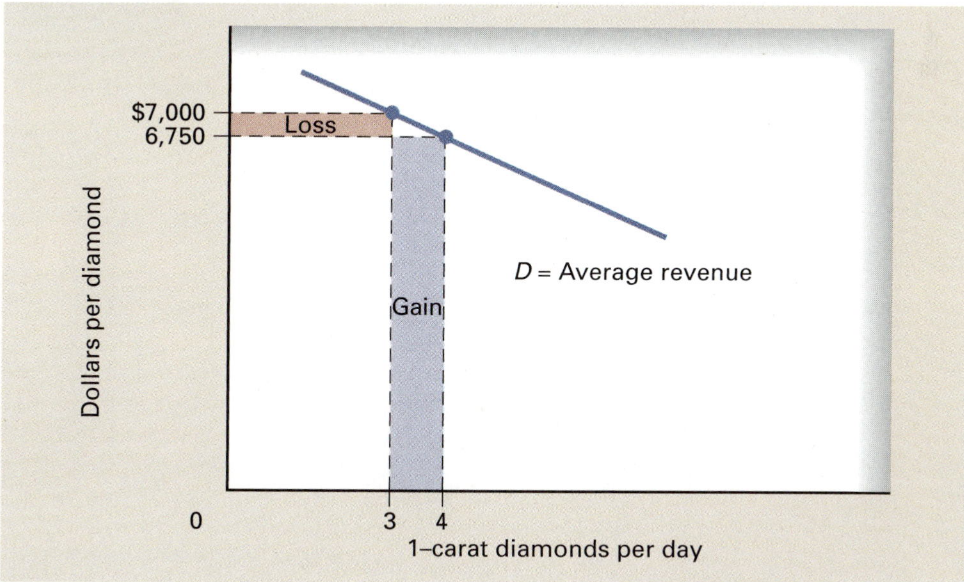

If De Beers increases quantity supplied from 3 to 4 diamonds per day, the gain in revenue from the fourth diamond is $6,750. But the monopolist loses $750 from selling the first 3 diamonds for $6,750 each instead of $7,000 each. Marginal revenue from the fourth diamond equals the gain minus the loss, or $6,750 − $750 = $6,000. Thus, the marginal revenue of $6,000 is less than the price of $6,750.

rectangle marked "Gain." But to sell that fourth unit, De Beers must sell all four diamonds for $6,750 each. Thus, to sell a fourth diamond, De Beers must sacrifice $250 on each of the first three diamonds, which could have been sold for $7,000 each. This loss in revenue from the first three units totals $750 (=$250 × 3) and is identified in Exhibit 2 by the pink-shaded horizontal rectangle marked "Loss." The net change in total revenue from selling the fourth diamond—that is, the marginal revenue from the fourth diamond—equals the *gain* minus the *loss*, which equals $6,750 minus $750, or $6,000. So marginal revenue equals the gain minus the loss, or the price minus the revenue forgone by selling all units for a lower price. Because a monopolist's marginal revenue equals the price minus the loss, you can see why the marginal revenue is less than the price.

Incidentally, this analysis assumes that all units are sold at the market price; for example, the four diamonds are sold for $6,750 each. Although this is usually true, later in the chapter you learn how some monopolists try to increase profit by charging different customers different prices.

Revenue Schedules

Let's flesh out more fully the revenue schedules behind the demand curve of Exhibit 2. Column (1) of Exhibit 3 lists the quantity of diamonds demanded per day, and column (2) lists the corresponding price, or average revenue. Together, the two columns are the demand schedule for 1-carat diamonds. The price in column (2) times the quantity in column (1) yields the monopolist's *total revenue* schedule in column (3). So $TR = p \times Q$. As De Beers sells more, total revenue increases until quantity reaches 15 diamonds.

EXHIBIT 3 Revenue for De Beers, a Monopolist

(1) 1-Carat Diamonds per Day (Q)	(2) Price (average revenue) (p)	(3) Total Revenue ($TR = p \times Q$)	(4) Marginal Revenue ($MR = \Delta TR/\Delta Q$)
0	$7,750	0	—
1	7,500	$ 7,500	$7,500
2	7,250	14,500	7,000
3	7,000	21,000	6,500
4	6,750	27,000	6,000
5	6,500	32,500	5,500
6	6,250	37,500	5,000
7	6,000	42,000	4,500
8	5,750	46,000	4,000
9	5,500	49,500	3,500
10	5,250	52,500	3,000
11	5,000	55,000	2,500
12	4,750	57,000	2,000
13	4,500	58,500	1,500
14	4,250	59,500	1,000
15	4,000	60,000	500
16	3,750	60,000	0
17	3,500	59,500	−500

To sell more, the monopolist must lower the price on all units sold. Because the revenue lost from selling all units at a lower price must be subtracted from the revenue gained from selling another unit, marginal revenue is less than the price. At some point, marginal revenue turns negative, as shown here when the price is reduced to $3,500.

Marginal revenue, the change in total revenue from selling one more diamond, appears in column (4). In shorthand, $MR = \Delta TR/\Delta Q$, or the change in total revenue divided by the change in quantity. Note in Exhibit 3 that after the first unit, marginal revenue is less than price. As the price declines, the gap between price and marginal revenue widens. As the price declines, the *loss* from selling all diamonds for less increases (because quantity increases) and the *gain* from selling another diamond decreases (because the price falls).

Revenue Curves

The schedules in Exhibit 3 are graphed in Exhibit 4, which shows the demand and marginal revenue curves in panel (a) and the total revenue curve in panel (b). Recall that total revenue equals price times quantity. Note that *the marginal revenue curve is below the demand curve and that total revenue reaches a maximum where marginal revenue is zero*. Please take a minute now to study these relationships—they are important.

Again, along the demand curve, price equals average revenue, so the demand curve is also the monopolist's average revenue curve. In Chapter 5 you learned that the price elasticity for a straight-line demand curve declines as you move down the curve. When demand is elastic—that is, when the percentage increase in quantity demanded more than offsets the percentage decrease in price—a decrease in price increases total revenue. Therefore, *where demand is elastic, marginal revenue is positive, and total revenue increases as the price falls.* On the other hand, where demand is inelastic—that is, where the percentage increase in quantity demanded is less than the percentage decrease in price—a decrease in price reduces total revenue. In other words, the loss in revenue from selling all diamonds for the lower price overwhelms the gain in revenue from selling more diamonds. Therefore, *where demand is inelastic, marginal revenue is negative, and total revenue decreases as the price falls.*

From Exhibit 4, you can see that marginal revenue turns negative if the price drops below \$3,750, indicating inelastic demand below that price. *A profit-maximizing monopolist would never expand output to the inelastic range of demand because doing so would reduce total revenue.* It would make no sense to sell more if total revenue drops in the process. Also note that demand is unit elastic at the price of \$3,750. At that price, marginal revenue is zero and total revenue reaches a maximum.

The Firm's Costs and Profit Maximization

In perfect competition, each firm's choice is confined to *quantity* because the market has already determined the price. The perfect competitor is a *price taker. The monopolist, however, can choose either the price or the quantity, but choosing one determines the other—they come in pairs.* For example, if De Beers decides to sell 10 diamonds a day, consumers would demand that many only at a price of \$5,250 per diamond. Alternatively, if De Beers decides to sell diamonds for \$6,000 each, consumers would demand 7 a day. Because the monopolist can choose any price-quantity combination on the demand curve, we say the monopolist is a *price maker.* More generally, any firm that has some control over what price to charge is a **price maker**.

price maker
A firm with some power to set the price because the demand curve for its output slopes downward; a firm with market power

Profit Maximization

Exhibit 5 repeats revenue schedules from Exhibits 3 and 4 and also includes a short-run cost schedule similar to those already introduced in the two previous chapters. Please take a little time now to become familiar with this table. Then ask yourself this question: Which price-quantity combination should De Beers select to maximize profit? As

EXHIBIT 4 Monopoly Demand, Marginal Revenue, and Total Revenue

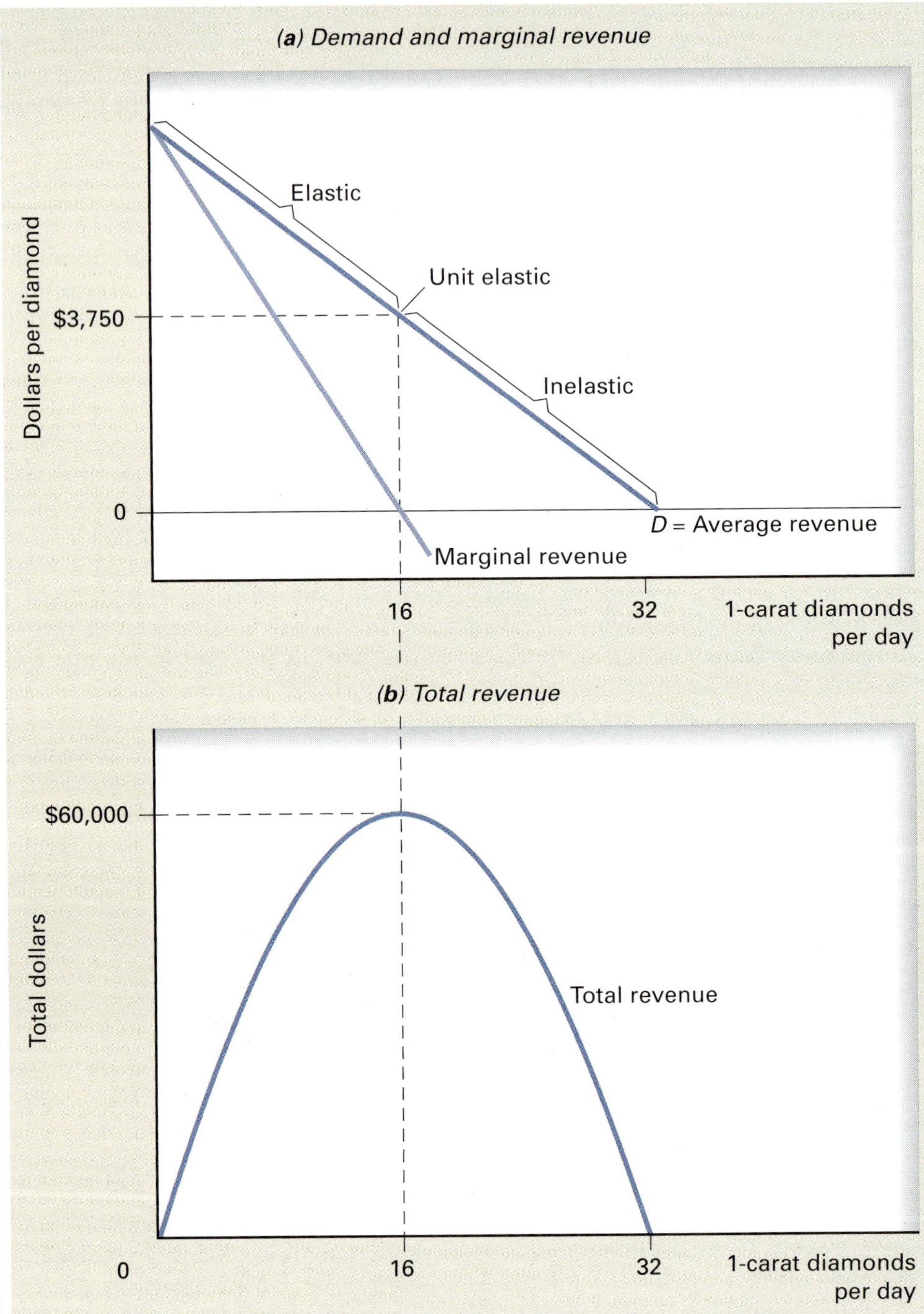

Where demand is price elastic, marginal revenue is positive, so total revenue increases as the price falls. Where demand is price inelastic, marginal revenue is negative, so total revenue decreases as the price falls. Where demand is unit elastic, marginal revenue is zero, so total revenue is at a maximum, neither increasing nor decreasing.

EXHIBIT 5 Short-Run Costs and Revenue for a Monopolist

(1) Diamonds per Day (Q)	(2) Price (p)	(3) Total Revenue (TR = p × Q)	(4) Marginal Revenue (MR = ΔTR/ΔQ)	(5) Total Cost (TC)	(6) Marginal Cost (MC = ΔTC/ΔQ)	(7) Average Total Cost (ATC = TC/Q)	(8) Total Profit or Loss (=TR − TC)
0	$7,750	0	___	$ 15,000	___	___	$−15,000
1	7,500	$ 7,500	$7,500	19,750	$ 4,750	$19,750	−12,250
2	7,250	14,500	7,000	23,500	3,750	11,750	−9,000
3	7,000	21,000	6,500	26,500	3,000	8,833	−5,500
4	6,750	27,000	6,000	29,000	2,500	7,250	−2,000
5	6,500	32,500	5,500	31,000	2,000	6,200	1,500
6	6,250	37,500	5,000	32,500	1,500	5,417	5,000
7	6,000	42,000	4,500	33,750	1,250	4,821	8,250
8	5,750	46,000	4,000	35,250	1,500	4,406	10,750
9	5,500	49,500	3,500	37,250	2,000	4,139	12,250
10	**5,250**	**52,500**	**3,000**	**40,000**	**2,750**	**4,000**	**12,500**
11	5,000	55,000	2,500	43,250	3,250	3,932	11,750
12	4,750	57,000	2,000	48,000	4,750	4,000	9,000
13	4,500	58,500	1,500	54,500	6,500	4,192	4,000
14	4,250	59,500	1,000	64,000	9,500	4,571	−4,500
15	4,000	60,000	500	77,500	13,500	5,167	−17,500
16	3,750	60,000	0	96,000	18,500	6,000	−36,000
17	3,500	59,500	−500	121,000	25,000	7,118	−61,500

was the case with perfect competition, the monopolist can approach profit maximization in two ways—the total approach and the marginal approach.

Total Revenue Minus Total Cost

The profit-maximizing monopolist employs the same decision rule as the competitive firm. *The monopolist supplies the quantity at which total revenue exceeds total cost by the greatest amount.* Economic profit appears in column (8) of Exhibit 5. As you can see, maximum profit is $12,500 per day, which occurs at 10 diamonds per day. At that quantity, total revenue is $52,500 and total cost is $40,000.

Marginal Revenue Equals Marginal Cost

De Beers, as a profit-maximizing monopolist, increases output if it adds more to total revenue than to total cost. So De Beers expands output as long as marginal revenue, shown in column (4) of Exhibit 5, exceeds marginal cost, shown in column (6). But De Beers stops short of producing where marginal cost exceeds marginal revenue. Again, profit is maximized at $12,500 when 10 diamonds per day are sold. For the 10th diamond, marginal revenue is $3,000 and marginal cost is $2,750. As you can see, if output exceeds 10 diamonds per day, marginal cost exceeds marginal revenue. An 11th diamond's marginal cost of $3,250 exceeds its marginal revenue of $2,500. For simplicity, we say that *the profit-maximizing output occurs where marginal revenue equals marginal cost,* which, you will recall, is the golden rule of profit maximization.

Graphical Solution

The revenue and cost schedules in Exhibit 5 are graphed in Exhibit 6, with per-unit cost and revenue curves in panel (a) and total cost and revenue curves in panel (b). The intersection of the two marginal curves at point *e* in panel (a) indicates that profit is

EXHIBIT 6 Monopoly Costs and Revenue

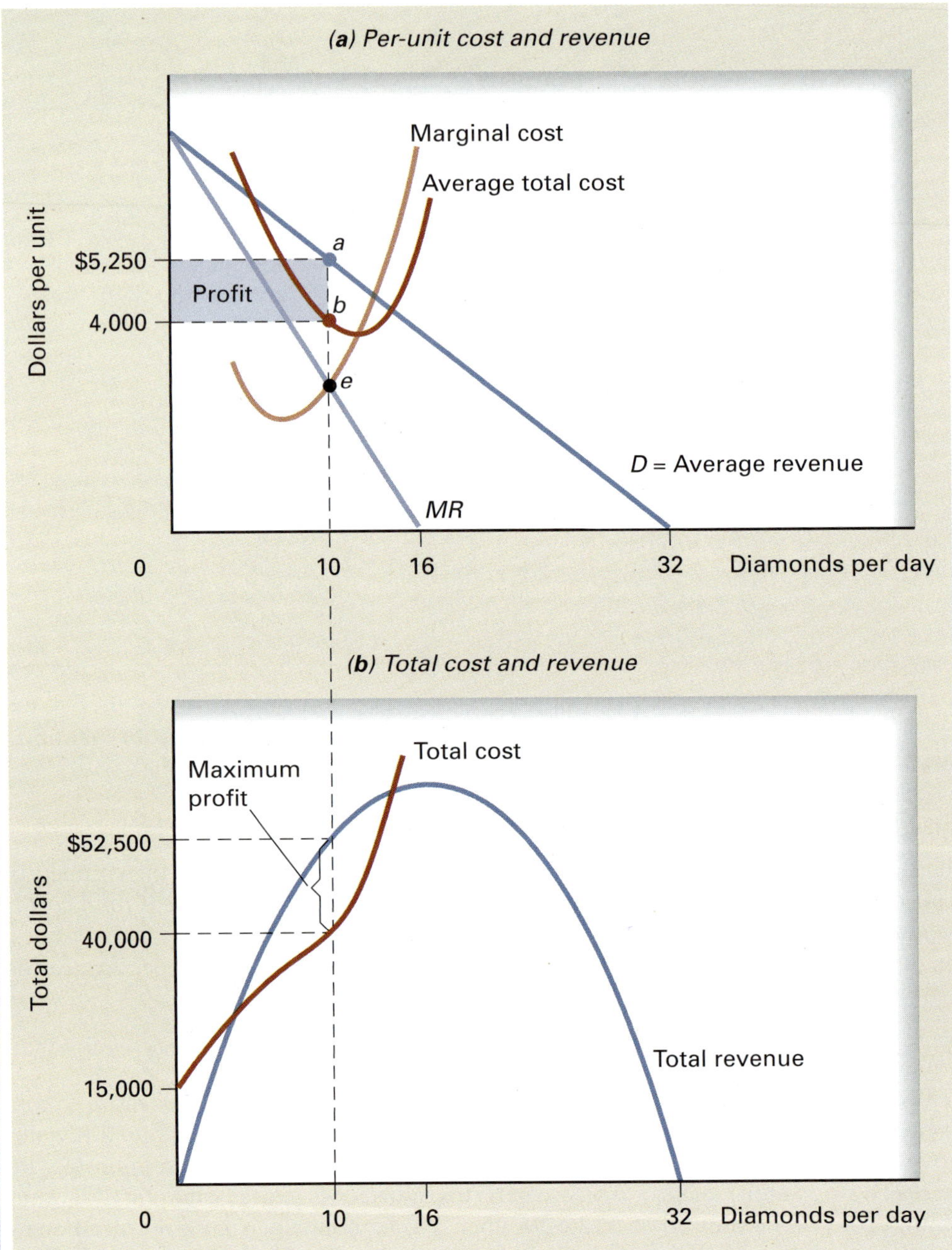

Profit is maximized by producing where marginal cost equals marginal revenue, which is point *e* in panel (a). A profit-maximizing monopolist supplies 10 diamonds per day and charges $5,250 per diamond. Total profit, shown by the blue rectangle in panel (a), is $12,500, the profit per unit multiplied by the number of units sold. In panel (b), profit is maximized by producing where total revenue exceeds total cost by the greatest amount, which occurs at an output rate of 10 diamonds per day. Maximum profit is total revenue ($52,500) minus total cost ($40,000), or $12,500. In panel (a) profit is measured by an area and in panel (b) by a vertical distance. That's because panel (a) measures cost, revenue, and profit per unit of output while panel (b) measures them as totals.

maximized when 10 diamonds are sold. At that quantity, we move up to the demand curve to find the profit-maximizing price of $5,250. Average total cost of $4,000 is identified by point *b*. The average profit per diamond equals the price of $5,250 minus the average total cost of $4,000. Economic profit is the average profit per unit of $1,250 multiplied by the 10 diamonds sold, for a total profit of $12,500 per day, as identified by the blue-shaded rectangle. *So the profit-maximizing rate of output is found where the marginal cost curve intersects the marginal revenue curve.*

In panel (b), the firm's profit or loss is measured by the vertical distance between the total revenue and total cost curves. De Beers expands output if the increase in total revenue from selling another diamond exceeds the increase in total cost. *The profit-maximizing firm produces where total revenue exceeds total cost by the greatest amount.* Again, profit is maximized where De Beers sells 10 diamonds per day. Total profit in panel (b) is measured by the *vertical distance* between the two total curves; in panel (a), total profit is measured by the shaded *area* formed by multiplying average profit per unit by the number of units sold.

One common myth about monopolies is that they charge the highest price possible. But the monopolist is interested in maximizing profit, not price. What the monopolist can charge is limited by consumer demand. De Beers, for example, could charge $7,500, but selling only one diamond would result in a big loss. Indeed, De Beers could charge $7,750 or more but would sell no diamonds. So charging the highest possible price is not consistent with maximizing profit. A monopolist may be able to set the price, but the quantity demanded at that price is determined by consumers. *Even the most powerful monopolist must obey the law of demand.*

Short-Run Losses and the Shutdown Decision

A monopolist is not assured an economic profit. Although a monopolist is the sole supplier of a good with no close substitutes, the demand for that good may not generate economic profit in either the short run or the long run. After all, many new products are protected from direct competition by patents, yet most of the 200,000, or so, U.S. patents issued each year never turn into profitable products. And even a monopolist that is initially profitable may eventually suffer losses because of rising costs, falling demand, or market entry of similar products. For example, Coleco, the original mass producer of Cabbage Patch dolls, went bankrupt after that craze died down. And Cuisinart, the company that introduced the food processor, soon faced many imitators and filed for bankruptcy (though the name lives on). In the short run, the loss-minimizing monopolist, like the loss-minimizing perfect competitor, must decide whether to produce or to shut down. *If the price covers average variable cost, the monopolist produces, at least in the short run. If not, the monopolist shuts down, at least in the short run.*

Exhibit 7 brings average variable cost back into the picture. Recall from Chapter 7 that average variable cost and average fixed cost sum to average total cost. Loss minimization occurs in Exhibit 7 at point *e*, where the marginal revenue curve intersects the marginal cost curve. At the equilibrium rate of output, *Q*, price *p* is found on the demand curve at point *b*. That price exceeds average variable cost, at point *c*, but is below average total cost, at point *a*. Because price covers average variable cost and a portion of average fixed cost, this monopolist loses less by producing *Q* than by shutting down. The loss, identified by the shaded rectangle, is the average loss per unit, *ab*, times the quantity sold, *Q*. The firm shuts down in the short run if the average variable cost curve is above the demand curve, or average revenue curve, at all output rates.

Recall that a perfectly competitive firm's supply curve is that portion of the marginal cost curve at or above the average variable cost curve. The intersection of a monopolist's marginal revenue and marginal cost curves identifies the profit-maximizing (or loss-minimizing) quantity, but the price is found up on the demand curve. Because

EXHIBIT 7 The Monopolist Minimizes Losses in the Short Run

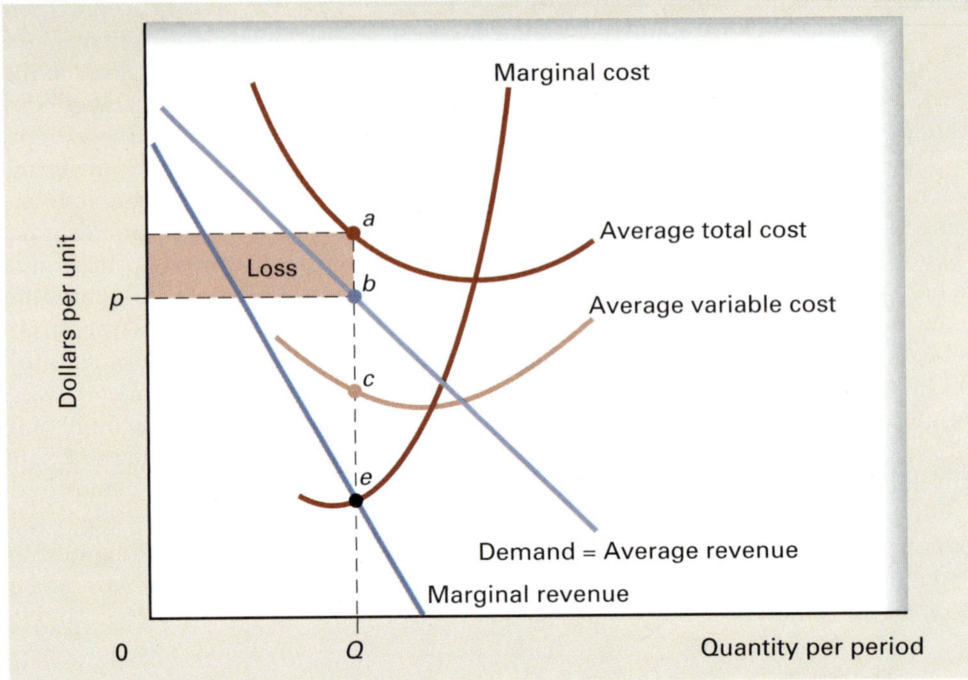

Marginal revenue equals marginal cost at point *e*. At quantity *Q*, price *p* (at point *b*) is less than average total cost (at point *a*), so the monopolist suffers a loss, identified by the pink rectangle. But the monopolist continues to produce rather than shut down in the short run because price exceeds average variable cost (at point *c*).

the equilibrium quantity can be found along a monopolist's marginal cost curve, but the equilibrium price appears on the demand curve, no single curve traces points showing unique combinations of both the price and quantity supplied. Because no curve reflects combinations of price and quantity supplied, *there is no monopolist supply curve.*

Long-Run Profit Maximization

For perfectly competitive firms, the distinction between the short run and the long run is important because entry and exit of firms can occur in the long run, erasing any economic profit or loss. For the monopolist, the distinction between the short run and long run is less relevant. *If a monopoly is insulated from competition by high barriers that block new entry, economic profit can persist into the long run.* Yet short-run profit is no guarantee of long-run profit. For example, suppose the monopoly relies on a patent. Patents last only so long and even while a product is under patent, the monopolist often must defend it in court (patent litigation has nearly doubled in the last decade). On the other hand, a monopolist may be able to erase a loss (most firms lose money initially) or increase profit in the long run by adjusting the scale of the firm or by advertising to increase demand. A monopolist unable to erase a loss will, in the long run, leave the market.

Monopoly and the Allocation of Resources

If monopolists are no greedier than perfect competitors (because both maximize profit), if monopolists do not charge the highest possible price (because the highest price would reduce quantity demanded to zero), and if monopolists are not guaranteed a profit (because demand for the product may be weak), then what's the problem with monopoly? To get a handle on the problem, let's compare monopoly with the benchmark established in the previous chapter—perfect competition.

Price and Output Under Perfect Competition

Let's begin with the long-run equilibrium price and output in a perfectly competitive market. Suppose the long-run market supply curve in perfect competition is horizontal, as shown by S_c in Exhibit 8. Because this is a constant-cost industry, the horizontal long-run supply curve also shows marginal cost and average total cost at each quantity. Equilibrium in perfect competition occurs at point *c*, where the market demand and market supply curves intersect to yield price p_c and quantity Q_c. Remember, the demand curve reflects the marginal benefit of each unit purchased. In competitive equilibrium, the marginal benefit of the final unit sold equals the marginal cost to society of producing that final unit. As noted in the previous chapter, when the marginal benefit that consumers derive from a good equals the marginal cost of producing that good, that market is said to be efficient and to maximize social welfare. There is no way of reallocating resources to increase the total value of output or to increase social welfare. Because consumers are able to purchase Q_c units at price p_c, they enjoy a net benefit from consumption, or a consumer surplus, measured by the entire shaded triangle, acp_c.

Price and Output Under Monopoly

With only one firm in the industry, the industry demand curve *D* in Exhibit 8 becomes the monopolist's demand curve, so the price the monopolist charges determines the market quantity. Because the monopolist's demand curve slopes downward, the marginal

EXHIBIT 8 Perfect Competition and Monopoly Compared

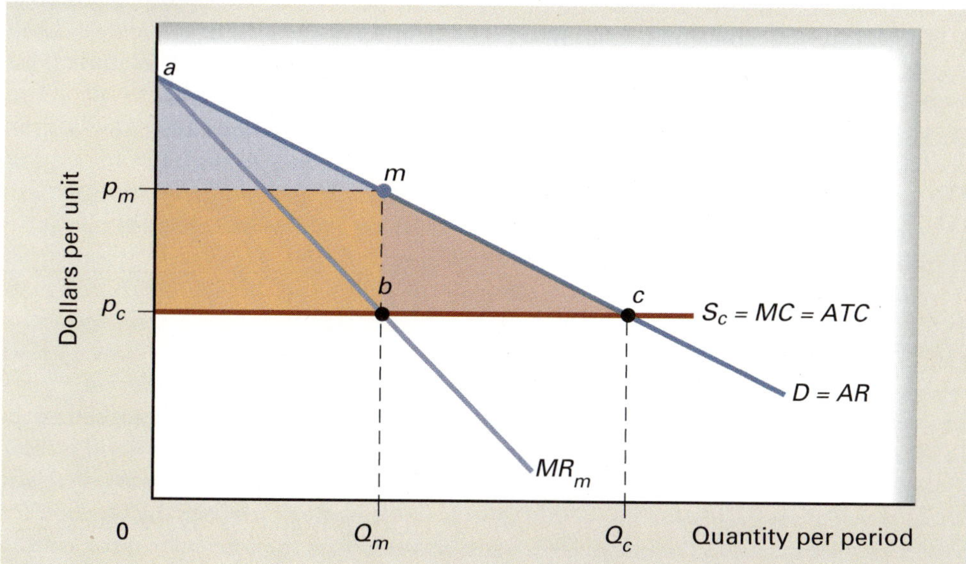

A perfectly competitive industry would produce output Q_C, determined by the intersection of the market demand curve *D* and the market supply curve S_C. The price would be p_C. A monopoly that could produce output at the same minimum average cost as a perfectly competitive industry would produce output Q_m, determined at point *b*, where marginal cost intersects marginal revenue. The monopolist would charge price p_m. Thus, given the same costs, output is lower and price is higher under monopoly than under perfect competition.

revenue curve also slopes downward and is beneath the demand curve, as is indicated by MR_m in Exhibit 8. Suppose the monopolist can produce at the same constant cost in the long run as can firms in the perfectly competitive industry. The monopolist maximizes profit by equating marginal revenue with marginal cost, which occurs at point *b*, yielding equilibrium price p_m and market output Q_m. Again, the price shows the consumers' marginal benefit for unit Q_m. This marginal benefit, identified at point *m*, exceeds the monopolist's marginal cost, identified at point *b*. Because marginal benefit exceeds marginal cost, society would be better off if output expanded beyond Q_m. *The monopolist restricts quantity below what would maximize social welfare.* Even though the monopolist restricts output, consumers still derive some benefit, just not as much as with perfect competition. Consumer surplus is shown by the smaller triangle, amp_m.

Allocative and Distributive Effects

Consider the allocative and distributive effects of monopoly versus perfect competition. In Exhibit 8, consumer surplus under perfect competition is the large triangle, acp_c. Under monopoly, consumer surplus shrinks to the smaller triangle amp_m, which in this example is only one-fourth as large (how do we know that?). The monopolist earns economic profit equal to the shaded rectangle. By comparing the situation under perfect competition with that under monopoly, you can see that the monopolist's economic profit comes entirely from what was consumer surplus under perfect competition. Because the profit rectangle reflects a transfer from consumer surplus to monopoly profit, this amount is not lost to society and so is not considered a welfare loss.

deadweight loss of monopoly
Net loss to society when a firm with market power restricts output and increases the price

Notice, however, that consumer surplus has been reduced by more than the profit rectangle. Consumers also lose the triangle *mcb*, which is part of the consumer surplus with perfect competition. The *mcb* triangle is called the **deadweight loss of monopoly** because it is a loss to consumers but a gain to nobody. This loss results from *the allocative inefficiency arising from the higher price and reduced output of a monopoly*. Again, society would be better off if output exceeded the monopolist's profit-maximizing quantity, because the marginal benefit of more output exceeds its marginal cost. Under monopoly, the price, or marginal benefit, always exceeds marginal cost. Empirical estimates of the annual deadweight loss of monopoly in the United States have ranged from about 1 percent to about 5 percent of national income. Applied to national income data for 2010, these estimates imply a deadweight loss of monopoly ranging from about \$475 to \$2,400 per capita—not a trivial amount.

Problems Estimating the Deadweight Loss of Monopoly

The actual cost of monopoly could differ from the deadweight loss described so far. These costs could be lower or higher. Here's the reasoning.

Why the Deadweight Loss of Monopoly Might Be Lower

If economies of scale are substantial enough, a monopolist might be able to produce output at a lower cost per unit than could competitive firms. Therefore, the price, or at least the cost of production, could be lower under monopoly than under competition. The deadweight loss shown in Exhibit 8 may also overstate the true cost of monopoly because monopolists might, in response to public scrutiny and political pressure, keep prices below the profit-maximizing level. Although monopolists would like to earn as much profit as possible, they realize that if the public outcry over high prices and high profit grows loud enough, some sort of government intervention could reduce or even erase that profit. For example, the prices and profit of drug companies, which individually are monopoly suppliers of patented medicines, come under scrutiny from time to time by elected officials who propose regulating drug prices or taxing "windfall profits." Drug firms might try to avoid such treatment by keeping prices below the level that would maximize profit. Finally, a monopolist might keep the price below the profit-maximizing level to avoid attracting competitors to the market. For example, some observers claim that Alcoa, when it was the only U.S. producer of aluminum, kept prices low enough to discourage new entry by potential rivals.

Why the Deadweight Loss Might Be Higher

Another line of reasoning suggests that the deadweight loss of monopoly might be greater than shown in our simple diagram. *If resources must be devoted to securing and maintaining a monopoly position, monopolies may impose a greater welfare loss than simple models suggest.* For example, radio and TV broadcasting rights confer on the recipient the use of a particular band of the scarce broadcast spectrum. In the past, these rights have been given away by government agencies to the applicants deemed most deserving. Because these rights are so valuable, numerous applicants have spent millions on lawyers' fees, lobbying expenses, and other costs to make themselves appear the most deserving. The efforts devoted to securing and maintaining a monopoly position are largely a social waste because they use up scarce resources but add not one unit to output. Activities undertaken by individuals or firms to influence public policy to directly or indirectly redistribute income to themselves are referred to as **rent seeking.**

rent seeking
Activities undertaken by individuals or firms to influence public policy in a way that increases their incomes

The monopolist, insulated from the rigors of competition in the marketplace, might also grow fat and lazy—and become inefficient. Because some monopolies could still earn an economic profit even if the firm is inefficient, corporate executives might waste resources by creating a more comfortable life for themselves. Long lunches, afternoon golf, plush offices, corporate jets, and excessive employee benefits might make company life more pleasant, but they increase production costs and raise prices.

Monopolists have also been criticized for being slow to adopt the latest production techniques, being reluctant to develop new products, and generally lacking innovation. Because monopolists are largely insulated from the rigors of competition, they might take it easy. It's been said "The best of all monopoly profits is a quiet life."

The case study, "Public Policy: The Mail Monopoly" at the end of the book, discusses the performance of one of the nation's oldest monopolies, the U.S. Postal Service.

Not all economists believe that monopolies manage their resources with any less vigilance than perfect competitors do. Some argue that because monopolists are protected from rivals, they are in a good position to capture the fruits of any innovation and therefore are more innovative than competitive firms are. Others believe that if a monopolist strays from the path of profit maximization, its share price will drop enough to attract someone who will buy a controlling interest and shape up the company. This market for corporate control is said to keep monopolists on their toes.

Price Discrimination

In the model developed so far, to sell more output, a monopolist must lower the price. In reality, a monopolist can sometimes increase profit by charging higher prices to those who value the product more. This practice of charging different prices to different

price discrimination
Increasing profit by charging different groups of consumers different prices for the same product

groups of consumers is called **price discrimination.** For example, children, students, and senior citizens often pay lower admission prices to ball games, movies, amusement parks, and other events. You may believe that firms do this out of some sense of fairness to certain groups, but the primary goal is to boost profits. Let's see how and why.

Conditions for Price Discrimination

To practice price discrimination, a firm's product must meet certain conditions. First, the demand curve for the firm's product must slope downward, indicating that the firm is a price maker—the producer has some market power, some ability to set the price. Second, there must be at least two groups of consumers for the product, each with a different price elasticity of demand. Third, the firm must be able, at little cost, to charge each group a different price for essentially the same product. Finally, the firm must be able to prevent those who pay the lower price from reselling the product to those facing the higher price.

A Model of Price Discrimination

Exhibit 9 shows the effects of price discrimination. Consumers are sorted into two groups with different demand elasticities. For simplicity, let's assume that the firm produces at a constant long-run average and marginal cost of $1.00. *At a given price,* the price elasticity of demand in panel (b) is greater than that in panel (a). Think of panel (b) as reflecting the demand of college students, senior citizens, or some other group more sensitive to the price. *This firm maximizes profit by finding the price in each market that equates marginal revenue with marginal cost.* For example, consumers with a lower price elasticity pay $3.00, and those with a higher price elasticity pay $1.50.

EXHIBIT 9 Price Discrimination with Two Groups of Consumers

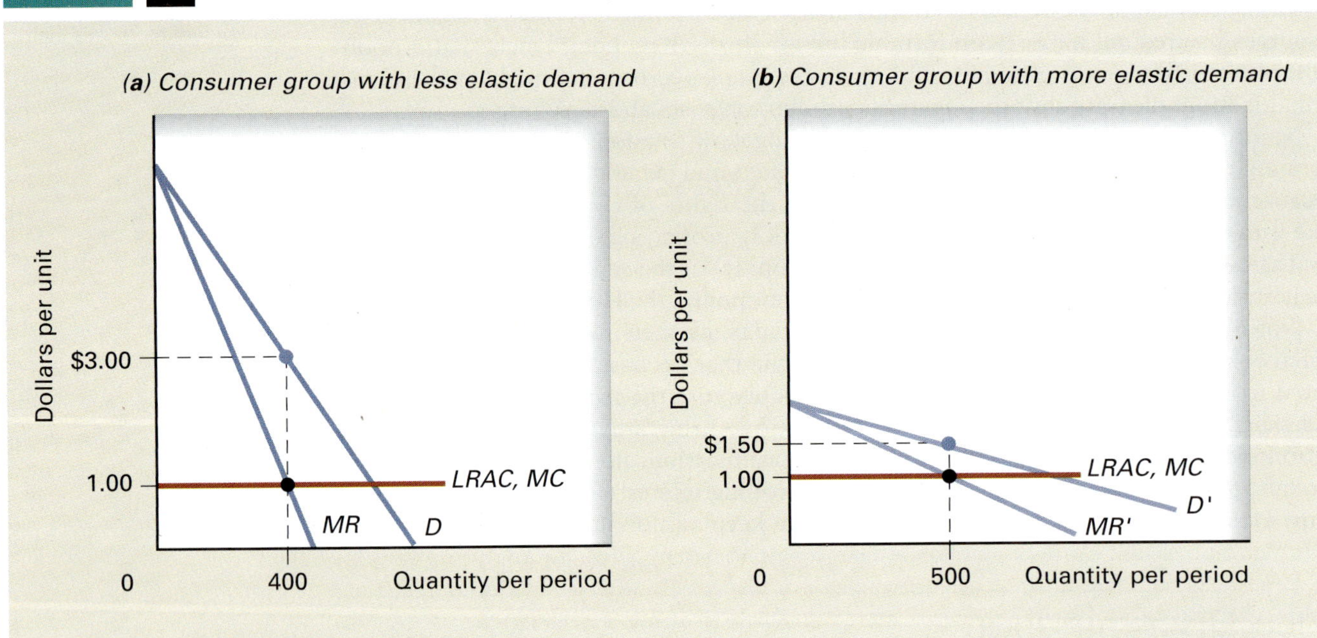

A monopolist facing two groups of consumers with different demand elasticities may be able to practice price discrimination to increase profit or reduce any loss. With marginal cost the same in both markets, the firm charges a higher price to the group in panel (a), which has less elastic demand than the group in panel (b).

Profit maximization means charging a lower price to the group with the more elastic demand. Despite the price difference, the firm gets the same marginal revenue of $1.00 from the last unit sold to each group. Note that charging both groups $3.00 would erase any profit from that right-hand group of consumers, who would be priced out of the market. Charging both groups $1.50 would lead to negative marginal revenue from the left-hand group, which would reduce profit. No single price could generate the profit achieved through price discrimination.

Examples of Price Discrimination

Let's look at some examples of price discrimination. Because businesspeople face unpredictable yet urgent demands for travel, and because their employers pay such expenses, businesspeople tend to be less sensitive to price than are householders. In other words, businesspeople have a less elastic demand for travel than do householders, so airlines try to maximize profits by charging businesses more than households. Business-class tickets cost much more than coach-class tickets. Business seats offer more room than coach seats, and the food is a little better, but the difference in ticket prices far exceeds differences in the airline's cost of providing each service. Even within a class of tickets, airlines charge different rates based on how far in advance tickets are purchased. Householders usually plan their trips well in advance and often spend the weekend. But business travel is more unpredictable, more urgent, and seldom involves a weekend stay. The airlines sort out the two groups by limiting discount fares to travelers who buy tickets well in advance. More generally, airlines use computer models to price discriminate depending on the circumstances. Still, an airline's ability to charge a higher price for a particular seat is limited by competition from other airlines.

Here are other examples of price discrimination: IBM wanted to charge business users of its laser printer more than home users. To distinguish between the two groups, IBM decided to slow down the home printer to 5 pages a minute (versus 10 for the business model). To do this, they added an extra chip that inserted pauses between pages.[3] Thus, IBM could sell the home model for less than the business model without cutting into sales of its business model. Intel offered two versions of the same computer chip; the cheaper version was the expensive version with some extra work done to reduce its speed. And Adobe stripped some features from its Photoshop CD to offer a cheaper version, Photoshop Elements.

Major amusement parks, such as Disney World and Universal Studios, distinguish between local residents and out-of-towners when it comes to the price of admission. Out-of-towners typically spend substantial amounts on airlines and lodging just to be there, so they are less sensitive to the admission price than are local residents. The problem is how to charge a lower price to locals. The parks do this by making discount coupons available at local businesses, such as dry cleaners, which vacationers are less likely to visit. The Las Vegas monorail sorts out the locals from the visitors by charging $1 for those presenting a Nevada driver's license and $5 for those without one.

Perfect Price Discrimination: The Monopolist's Dream

The demand curve shows the marginal value of each unit consumed, which is also the maximum amount consumers would pay for each unit. If the monopolist could charge a different price for each unit sold—a price reflected by the height of the demand curve—the firm's marginal revenue from selling one more unit would equal the price of that unit. Thus, the demand curve would become the firm's marginal

3. Carl Shapiro and Hal Varian, *Information Rules: A Strategic Guide to the Network Economy* (Boston: Harvard Business School Press, 1999), p. 59.

EXHIBIT 10 Perfect Price Discrimination

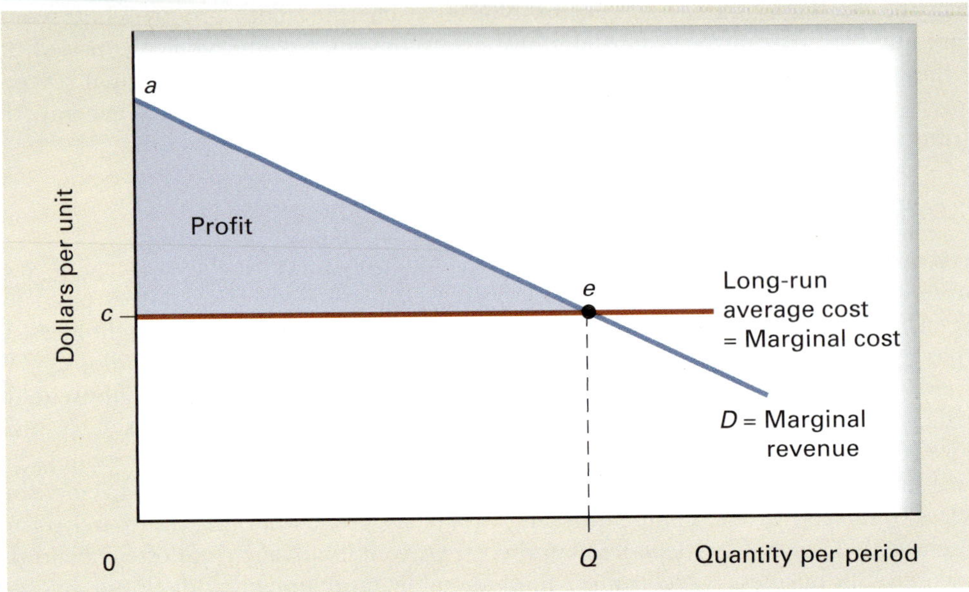

If a monopolist can charge a different price for each unit sold, it may be able to practice perfect price discrimination. By setting the price of each unit equal to the maximum amount consumers are willing to pay for that unit (shown by the height of the demand curve), the monopolist can earn a profit equal to the area of the shaded triangle. Consumer surplus is zero. Ironically, this outcome is efficient because the monopolist has no incentive to restrict output, so there is no deadweight loss.

perfectly discriminating monopolist
A monopolist who charges a different price for each unit sold; also called the monopolist's dream

revenue curve. A **perfectly discriminating monopolist** would charge a different price for each unit sold.

In Exhibit 10, again for simplicity, the monopolist is assumed to produce at a constant average and marginal cost in the long run. A perfectly discriminating monopolist, like any producer, would maximize profit by producing the quantity at which marginal revenue equals marginal cost. Because the demand curve is now the marginal revenue curve, the profit-maximizing quantity occurs where the demand, or marginal revenue, curve intersects the marginal cost curve, identified at point *e* in Exhibit 10. Price discrimination is a way of increasing profit. The area of the shaded triangle *aec* shows the perfectly discriminating monopolist's economic profit.

By charging a different price for each unit sold, the perfectly discriminating monopolist is able to convert every dollar of consumer surplus into economic profit. Although this practice seems unfair to consumers, perfect price discrimination gets high marks based on allocative efficiency. Because such a monopolist does not have to lower the price to all customers to sell more, there is no reason to restrict output. In fact, because this is a constant-cost industry, Q is the same quantity produced in perfect competition (though in perfect competition, the triangle *aec* would be consumer surplus, not economic profit). As in the perfectly competitive outcome, the marginal benefit of the final unit produced and consumed just equals its marginal cost. And although perfect price discrimination yields no consumer surplus, the total benefit consumers derive from consuming this good just equals their total cost. Note also that because the monopolist does not restrict output, *there is no deadweight loss*. Thus, perfect price discrimination enhances social welfare when compared with monopoly output in the absence of price discrimination. But the monopolist reaps all net gains from production, while consumers just break even on the deal because their total benefit equals their total cost.

The pricing of cell phone service reflects a firm's effort to capture more consumer surplus as profit. Pricing alternatives include (1) a per-minute price with no basic fee, (2) a flat rate for the month plus a price per minute, and (3) a flat rate for unlimited calls. These alternatives allow the company to charge those who use fewer minutes more per minute than those who call more. Such suppliers are trying to convert some consumer surplus into profit.

Conclusion

Pure monopoly, like perfect competition, is not that common. Perhaps the best examples are firms producing patented items that provide unique benefits, such as certain prescription drugs, but patents eventually expire so generic substitutes become available. Some firms may enjoy monopoly power in the short run, but the lure of economic profit encourages rivals to hurdle seemingly high entry barriers in the long run. Changing technology also works against monopoly in the long run. For example, the railroad monopoly was erased by the interstate highway system. AT&T's monopoly on long-distance phone service crumbled as wireless technology replaced copper wire. The U.S. Postal Service's monopoly on first-class mail is being eroded by fax machines, texting, Twittering, email, e-payments, and private firms offering overnight delivery. De Beers has lost its grip on the diamond market. And cable TV is losing its local monopoly to technological breakthroughs in fiber-optics technology, wireless broadband, and the Internet.

Although perfect competition and pure monopoly are rare, our examination of them yields a framework to help understand market structures that lie between the two extremes. Many firms have some degree of monopoly power—that is, they face downward-sloping demand curves. The next chapter discusses the two market structures that lie in the gray region between perfect competition and monopoly.

Summary

1. A monopolist sells a product with no close substitutes. Short-run economic profit earned by a monopolist can persist in the long run only if the entry of new firms is blocked. Three barriers to entry are (a) legal restrictions, such as patents and operating licenses; (b) economies of scale over a broad range of output; and (c) control over a key resource.
2. Because a monopolist is the sole supplier of a product with no close substitutes, a monopolist's demand curve is also the market demand curve. Because a monopolist that does not price discriminate can sell more only by lowering the price for all units sold, marginal revenue is less than the price. Where demand is price elastic, marginal revenue is positive and total revenue increases as the price falls. Where demand is price inelastic, marginal revenue is negative and total revenue decreases as the price falls. A monopolist never voluntarily produces where demand is inelastic because raising the price and reducing output would increase total revenue.
3. If the monopolist can at least cover variable cost, profit is maximized or loss is minimized in the short run by finding the output rate that equates marginal revenue with marginal cost. At the profit-maximizing quantity, the price is found on the demand curve.
4. In the short run, a monopolist, like a perfect competitor, can earn economic profit but will shut down unless price at least covers average variable cost. In the long run, a monopolist, unlike a perfect competitor, can continue to earn economic profit as long as entry of potential competitors is blocked.
5. If costs are similar, a monopolist charges a higher price and supplies less output than does a perfectly competitive industry. Monopoly usually results in a deadweight loss when compared with perfect competition because the loss of consumer surplus exceeds the gains in monopoly profit.
6. To increase profit through price discrimination, the monopolist must have at least two identifiable groups of customers, each with a different price elasticity of demand at a given price, and must be able to prevent customers charged the lower price from reselling to those facing the higher price.
7. A perfect price discriminator charges a different price for each unit sold, thereby converting all consumer surplus into economic profit. Perfect price discrimination seems unfair because the monopolist reaps maximum profit and consumers get no consumer surplus. Yet perfect price discrimination is as efficient as perfect competition because the monopolist has no incentive to restrict output, so there is no deadweight loss.

Key Concepts

Questions for Review

1. Barriers to Entry Complete each of the following sentences:
   a. A U.S. _______ awards inventors the exclusive right to production for 20 years.
   b. Patents and licenses are examples of government-imposed ______ that prevent entry into an industry.
   c. When economies of scale make it possible for a single firm to satisfy market demand at a lower cost per unit than could two or more firms, the single firm is considered a _______.
   d. A potential barrier to entry is a firm's control of a(n) ______ critical to production in the industry.
2. Barriers to Entry Explain how economies of scale can be a barrier to entry.
3. Case Study: Is a Diamond Forever? (See page 718.) How did the De Beers cartel try to maintain control of the price in the diamond market? How has this control been undermined?
4. Revenue for the Monopolist How does the demand curve faced by a monopolist differ from the demand curve faced by a perfectly competitive firm?
5. Revenue for the Monopolist Why is it impossible for a profit-maximizing monopolist to choose any price *and* any quantity it wishes?
6. Revenue Schedules Explain why the marginal revenue curve for a monopolist lies below its demand curve, rather than coinciding with the demand curve, as is the case for a perfectly competitive firm. Is it ever possible for a monopolist's marginal revenue curve to coincide with its demand curve?
7. Revenue Curves Why would a monopoly firm never knowingly produce on the inelastic portion of its demand curve?
8. Profit Maximization Review the following graph showing the short-run situation of a monopolist. What output level does the firm choose in the short run? Why?

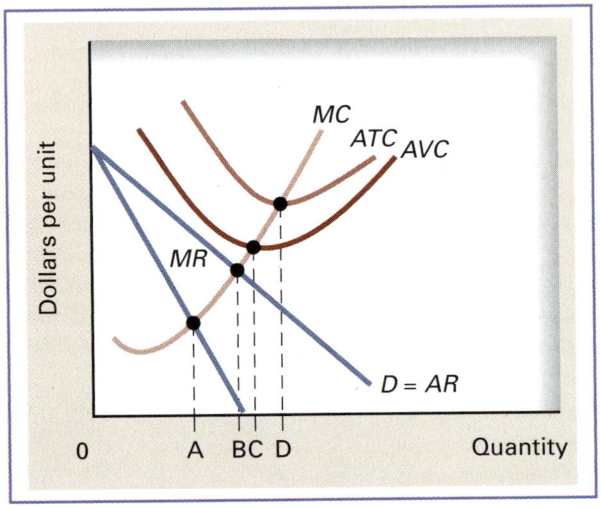

9. Allocative and Distributive Effects Why is society worse off under monopoly than under perfect competition, even if both market structures face the same constant long-run average cost curve?
10. Welfare Cost of Monopoly Explain why the welfare loss of a monopoly may be smaller or larger than the loss shown in Exhibit 8 in this chapter.
11. Case Study: The Mail Monopoly (See page 720.) Can the U.S. Postal Service be considered a monopoly in first-class mail? Why or why not? What has happened to the price elasticity of demand for first-class mail in recent years?
12. Conditions for Price Discrimination List three conditions that must be met for a monopolist to price discriminate successfully?
13. Price Discrimination Explain how it may be profitable for South Korean manufacturers to sell new autos at a lower price in the United States than in South Korea, even with transportation costs included.
14. Perfect Price Discrimination Why is the perfectly discriminating monopolist's marginal revenue curve identical to the demand curve it faces?

Problems and Exercises

15. SHORT-RUN PROFIT MAXIMIZATION Answer the following questions on the basis of the monopolist's situation illustrated in the following graph.
    a. At what output rate and price does the monopolist operate?
    b. In equilibrium, approximately what is the firm's total cost and total revenue?
    c. What is the firm's economic profit or loss in equilibrium?

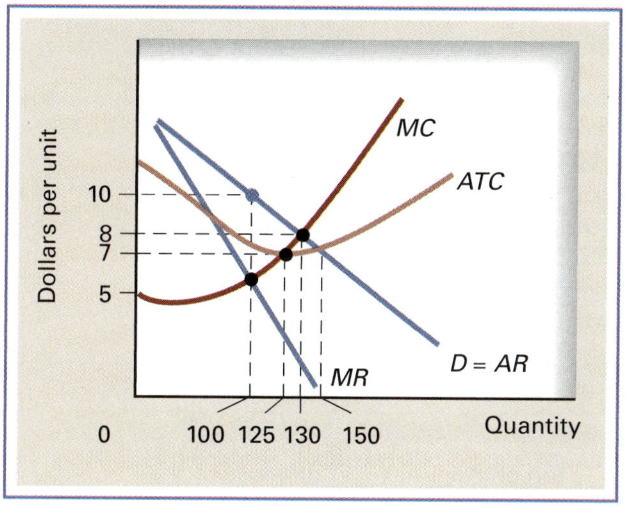

16. MONOPOLY Suppose that a certain manufacturer has a monopoly on the sorority and fraternity ring business (a constant-cost industry) because it has persuaded the "Greeks" to give it exclusive rights to their insignia.
    a. Using demand and cost curves, draw a diagram depicting the firm's profit-maximizing price and output level.
    b. Why is marginal revenue less than price for this firm?
    c. On your diagram, show the deadweight loss that occurs because the output level is determined by a monopoly rather than by a competitive market.
    d. What would happen if the Greeks decided to charge the manufacturer a royalty fee of $3 per ring?

Global Economic Watch Exercises

Login to www.cengagebrain.com and access the Global Economic Watch to do these exercises.

17. GLOBAL ECONOMIC WATCH Go to the Global Economic Crisis Resource Center. Select Global Issues in Context. In the Basic Search box at the top of the page, enter the phrase "Google monopoly." On the Results page, go to the Global Viewpoints section. Click on the link for the February 19, 2010, article "Is Google Gaining a Monopoly on the World's Information?" Does Google enjoy a barrier to entry? What is the source of that barrier, if any?

18. GLOBAL ECONOMIC WATCH Go to the Global Economic Crisis Resource Center. Select Global Issues in Context. In the Basic Search box at the top of the page, enter the term "price discrimination." Write a paragraph about one example of an organization practicing price discrimination.

10

Monopolistic Competition and Oligopoly

© Jeff Greenberg/Alamy

- Why is Perrier water sold in green, tear-shaped bottles?
- Why are some shampoos sold only in salons?
- Why do some pizza makers deliver?
- Which market structure is like a golf tournament and which is like a tennis match?
- Why do airlines engage in airfare warfare?
- Why was the oil cartel, OPEC, created, and why has it met with only spotty success?
- Why is there a witness protection program?

To answer these and other questions, we turn in this chapter to the vast gray area that lies between perfect competition and monopoly.

Perfect competition and monopoly are extreme market structures. Under perfect competition, many suppliers offer an identical product and, in the long run, entry and exit erase economic profit. A monopolist supplies a product with no close substitutes in a market where natural and artificial barriers keep out would-be competitors, so a monopolist can earn economic profit in the long run. These polar market structures are logically appealing and offer a useful description of some industries observed in the economy.

But most firms fit into neither market structure. Some markets have many sellers producing goods that vary slightly, such as the many convenience stores that abound. Other markets consist of just a few sellers that in some industries produce essentially identical products, or commodities (such as oil), and in other industries produce differentiated goods (such as automobiles). This chapter examines the two remaining market structures that together include most firms in the economy.

Topics discussed include:

- Monopolistic competition
- Product differentiation
- Excess capacity
- Oligopoly
- Collusion
- Prisoner's dilemma

Monopolistic Competition

monopolistic competition
A market structure with many firms selling products that are substitutes but different enough that each firm's demand curve slopes downward; firm entry is relatively easy

As the expression *monopolistic competition* suggests, this market structure contains elements of both monopoly and competition. **Monopolistic competition** describes a market in which many producers offer products that are substitutes but are not viewed as identical by consumers. Because the products of different suppliers differ slightly—for example, some convenience stores are closer to you than others—the demand curve for each is not horizontal but slopes downward. Each supplier has some power over the price it can charge. Thus, the firms that populate this market are not *price takers,* as they would be under perfect competition, but are *price makers.* Because barriers to entry are low, firms in monopolistic competition can, in the long run, enter or leave the market with ease. Consequently, there are enough sellers that they behave competitively. There are also enough sellers that each tends to get lost in the crowd. For example, in a large metropolitan area, an individual restaurant, gas station, drugstore, dry cleaner, or convenience store tends to act *independently.* In other market structures, there may be only two or three sellers in each market, so they keep an eye on one another; they act *interdependently.* You will see the relevance of this distinction later in the chapter.

Product Differentiation

In perfect competition, the product is a commodity, meaning it's identical across producers, such as a bushel of wheat. In monopolistic competition, the product differs somewhat among sellers, as with the difference between one rock radio station and another, or one convenience store and another. Sellers differentiate their products in four basic ways.

Physical Differences

The most obvious way products differ is in their physical appearance and their qualities. Packaging is also designed to make a product stand out in a crowded field, such as a distinctive bottle of water (Perrier) and instant soup in a cup (Cup-a-Soup). Physical differences are seemingly endless: size, weight, color, taste, texture, and so on. Shampoos, for example, differ in color, scent, thickness, lathering ability, and bottle design. Particular brands aim at consumers with dandruff and those with normal, dry, or oily hair.

Location

The number and variety of locations where a product is available are other ways of differentiation—*spatial differentiation.* Some products seem to be available everywhere, including online; finding other products requires some search and travel. If you live in a metropolitan area, you are no doubt accustomed to the many convenience stores that populate the region. Each wants to be closest to you when you need milk, bread, or nachos—thus, the proliferation of stores. As the name says, these mini–grocery stores are selling *convenience*. Their prices are higher and selections more limited than at regular grocery stores, but they are usually closer to customers, don't have long lines, and some are open 24/7.

Services

Products also differ in terms of their accompanying services. For example, some products are delivered to your door, such as Domino's pizza and Amazon books; some products are delivered to your computer or wirelessly, like software and e-books; others products are cash and carry. Some products are demonstrated by a well-trained sales staff; others are mostly self-service. Some products include online support and toll-free help lines; others come with no help at all. Some sellers provide money-back guarantees; others say "no refunds." The quality and range of accompanying services often differentiate otherwise close substitutes.

Product Image

A final way products differ is in the image the producer tries to foster in the customer's mind. Producers try to create and maintain brand loyalty through product promotion and advertising. For example, suppliers of sportswear, clothing, watches, and cosmetics often pay for endorsements from athletes, fashion models, and other celebrities. Some producers emphasize the care and attention to detail in each item. For example, Hastens, a small, family-owned Swedish bedding company, underscores the months of labor required to craft each bed by hand—as a way to justify the $60,000 price tag. Some producers try to demonstrate high quality based on where products are sold, such as shampoo sold only in salons. Some products tout their all-natural ingredients, such as Ben & Jerry's ice cream, Tom's of Maine toothpaste, and Nantucket Nectars, or appeal to environmental concerns by focusing on recycled packaging, such as the Starbucks coffee cup insulating sleeve "made from 60% post-consumer recycled fiber." More generally, firms advertise to increase sales and profits. Research has found that each dollar of online advertising increased the firm's sales more than ten-fold.[1]

Short-Run Profit Maximization or Loss Minimization

Because each monopolistic competitor offers a product that differs somewhat from what others supply, each has some control over the price charged. This *market power* means that each firm's demand curve slopes downward. Because many firms offer close but not identical products, any firm that raises its price can expect to lose some customers to rivals. By way of comparison, a price hike by an individual firm would cost a monopolist fewer customers but would cost a perfect competitor *all* customers. Therefore, a monopolistic competitor faces a demand curve that tends to be more elastic than a monopolist's but less elastic than a perfect competitor's.

Recall that the availability of substitutes for a given product affects its price elasticity of demand. The price elasticity of the monopolistic competitor's demand depends on (1) the number of rival firms that produce similar products and (2) the firm's ability to differentiate its product from those of its rivals. *A firm's demand curve is more elastic the more substitutes there are and the less differentiated its product is.*

1. Randall Lewis and David Reiley, "Does Retail Advertising Work? Measuring the Effects of Advertising on Sales Via a Controlled Experiment on Yahoo!," Paper Presented at the American Economics Association Annual Meeting, 3 January 2010.

EXHIBIT 1 Monopolistic Competitor in the Short Run

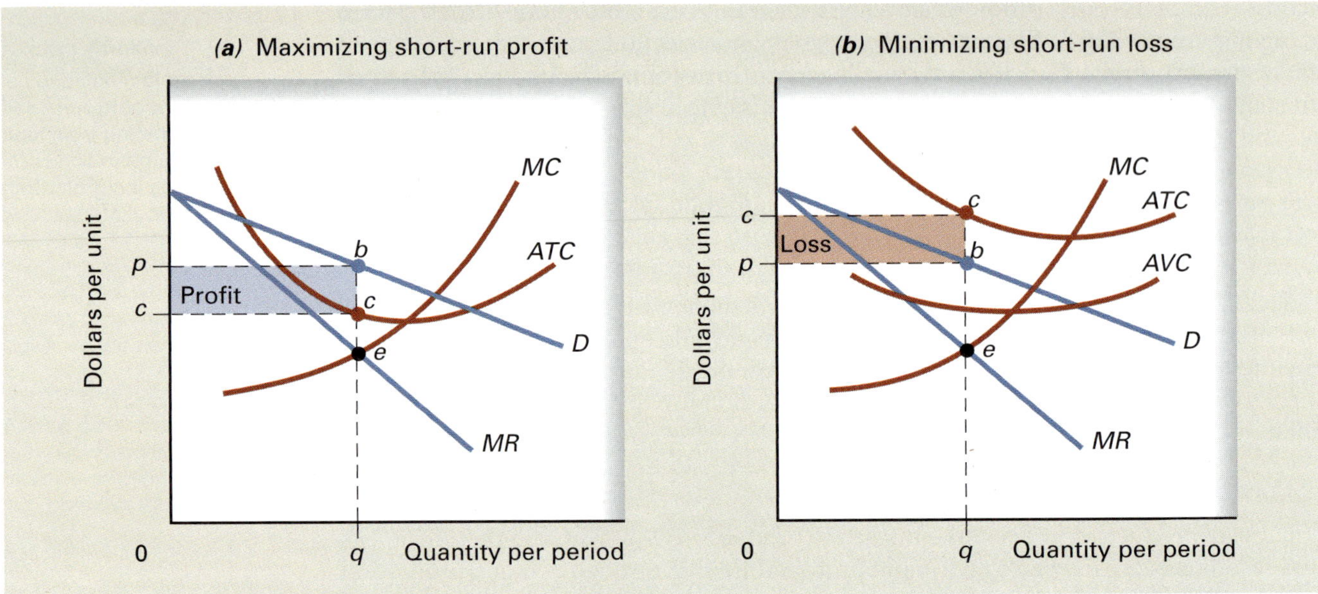

The monopolistically competitive firm produces the level of output at which marginal revenue equals marginal cost (point *e*) and charges the price indicated by point *b* on the downward-sloping demand curve. In panel (a), the firm produces *q* units, sells them at price *p*, and earns a short-run economic profit equal to $(p - c)$ multiplied by *q*, shown by the blue rectangle. In panel (b), the average total cost exceeds the price at the output where marginal revenue equals marginal cost. Thus, the firm suffers a short-run loss equal to $(c - p)$ multiplied by *q*, shown by the pink rectangle.

Marginal Revenue Equals Marginal Cost

From our study of monopoly, we know that a downward-sloping demand curve means the marginal revenue curve also slopes downward and lies beneath the demand curve. Exhibit 1 depicts demand and marginal revenue curves for a monopolistic competitor. The exhibit also presents average and marginal cost curves. Remember that the forces that determine the cost of production are largely independent of the forces that shape demand, so there is nothing special about a monopolistic competitor's cost curves. In the short run, a firm that can at least cover its variable cost increases output as long as marginal revenue exceeds marginal cost. A monopolistic competitor maximizes profit just as a monopolist does: *the profit-maximizing quantity occurs where marginal revenue equals marginal cost; the profit-maximizing price for that quantity is found up on the demand curve.* Exhibit 1 shows the price and quantity combinations that maximize short-run profit in panel (a), and minimize short-run loss in panel (b). In each panel, the marginal cost and marginal revenue curves intersect at point *e*, yielding equilibrium output *q*, equilibrium price *p*, and average total cost *c*.

Maximizing Profit or Minimizing Loss in the Short Run

Recall that the short run is a period too brief to allow firms to enter or leave the market. The demand and cost conditions shown in panel (a) of Exhibit 1 indicate that this firm earns economic profit in the short run. At the firm's profit-maximizing quantity, average total cost, *c*, is below the price, *p*. Price minus average total cost is the firm's profit per unit, which, when multiplied by the quantity, yields economic profit, shown by the blue rectangle. Again, the profit-maximizing quantity is found where marginal revenue equals marginal cost; price is found up on the demand curve at that quantity. Thus, a monopolistic competitor, like a monopolist, has no supply curve—that is, *there is no curve that uniquely relates prices and corresponding quantities supplied.*

The monopolistic competitor, like monopolists and perfect competitors, is not guaranteed an economic profit or even a normal profit. The firm's demand and cost curves could be as shown in panel (b), where the average total cost curve lies entirely above the demand curve, so no quantity allows the firm to escape a loss. In such a situation, the firm must decide whether to produce at a loss or to shut down in the short run. The rule here is the same as with perfect competition and monopoly: as long as price exceeds average variable cost, the firm in the short run loses less by producing than by shutting down. If no price covers average variable cost, the firm shuts down. Recall that the halt in production may be only temporary; shutting down is not the same as going out of business. Firms that expect economic losses to persist may, in the long run, leave the industry.

Short-run profit maximization in monopolistic competition is quite similar to that under monopoly. But the stories differ in the long run, as we'll see next.

Zero Economic Profit in the Long Run

Low barriers to entry in monopolistic competition mean that short-run economic profit attracts new entrants in the long run. Because new entrants offer similar products, they draw customers away from other firms in the market, thereby reducing the demand facing other firms. Entry continues in the long run until economic profit disappears. *Because market entry is easy, monopolistically competitive firms earn zero economic profit in the long run.*

On the other side of the ledger, economic losses drive some firms out of business in the long run. As firms leave the industry, their customers switch to the remaining firms, increasing the demand for those products. Firms continue to leave in the long run until the remaining firms have enough customers to earn normal profit, but not economic profit.

Exhibit 2 shows long-run equilibrium for a typical monopolistic competitor. In the long run, entry and exit shifts each firm's demand curve until economic profit disappears—that is, until price equals average total cost. In Exhibit 2, the marginal revenue curve intersects the marginal cost curve at point *a*. At the equilibrium quantity, *q*, the average total cost curve is tangent to the demand curve at point *b*. Because average total cost equals the price, the firm earns no economic profit but does earn a normal profit (how do we know this?). At all other quantities, the firm's average total cost curve lies above the demand curve, so the firm would lose money by reducing or expanding production.

Thus, because entry is easy in monopolistic competition, short-run economic profit attracts new entrants in the long run. The demand curve facing each monopolistic competitor shifts left until economic profit disappears. A short-run economic loss prompts some firms to leave the industry in the long run until remaining firms earn just a normal profit. In summary: *Monopolistic competition is like monopoly in the sense that firms in each industry face demand curves that slope downward. Monopolistic competition is like perfect competition in the sense that easy entry and exit eliminate economic profit or economic loss in the long run.*

One way to understand how firm entry erases short-run economic profit is to consider the evolution of an industry, as discussed in the case study, "World of Business: Fast Forward to Creative Destruction" at the end of the book.

EXHIBIT 2 Long-Run Equilibrium in Monopolistic Competition

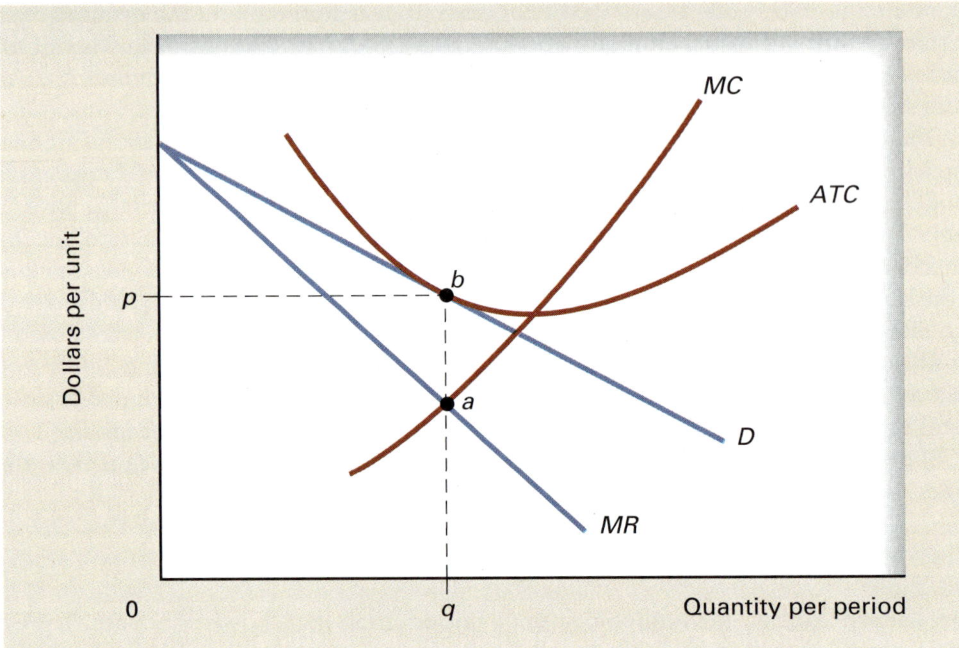

If existing firms earn economic profit in the short run, new firms will enter the industry in the long run. This entry reduces the demand facing each firm. In the long run, each firm's demand curve shifts leftward until marginal revenue equals marginal cost (point *a*) and the demand curve is tangent to the average total cost curve (point *b*). Economic profit is zero at output *q*. With zero economic profit, no more firms will enter, so the industry is in long-run equilibrium. The same long-run outcome occurs if firms suffer a short-run loss. Firms leave until remaining firms earn just a normal profit.

Monopolistic Competition and Perfect Competition Compared

How does monopolistic competition compare with perfect competition in terms of efficiency? In the long run, neither earns economic profit, so what's the difference? The difference traces to the demand curves facing individual firms in each of the two market structures. Exhibit 3 presents the long-run equilibrium price and quantity for a typical firm in each market structure, assuming each firm has identical cost curves. In each case, the marginal cost curve intersects the marginal revenue curve at the quantity where the average total cost curve is tangent to the firm's demand curve.

A perfect competitor's demand curve is a horizontal line drawn at the market price, as shown in panel (a). This demand curve is tangent to the lowest point of the firm's long-run average total cost curve. Thus, a perfect competitor in the long run produces at the lowest possible average cost. In panel (b), a monopolistic competitor faces a downward-sloping demand curve because its product differs somewhat from those of other suppliers. In the long run, the monopolistic competitor produces less than required to achieve the lowest possible average cost. Thus, the price and average cost in monopolistic competition, identified as p' in panel (b), exceed the price and average cost in perfect competition, identified as p in panel (a). *If firms have the same cost curves, the monopolistic competitor produces less and charges more than the perfect competitor does in the long run, though neither earns economic profit.*

Firms in monopolistic competition are not producing at minimum average cost. They are said to have **excess capacity**, because production falls short of the quantity that

excess capacity
The difference between a firm's profit-maximizing quantity and the quantity that minimizes average cost; firms with excess capacity could reduce average cost by increasing quantity

EXHIBIT 3 Perfect Competition Versus Monopolistic Competition in Long-Run Equilibrium

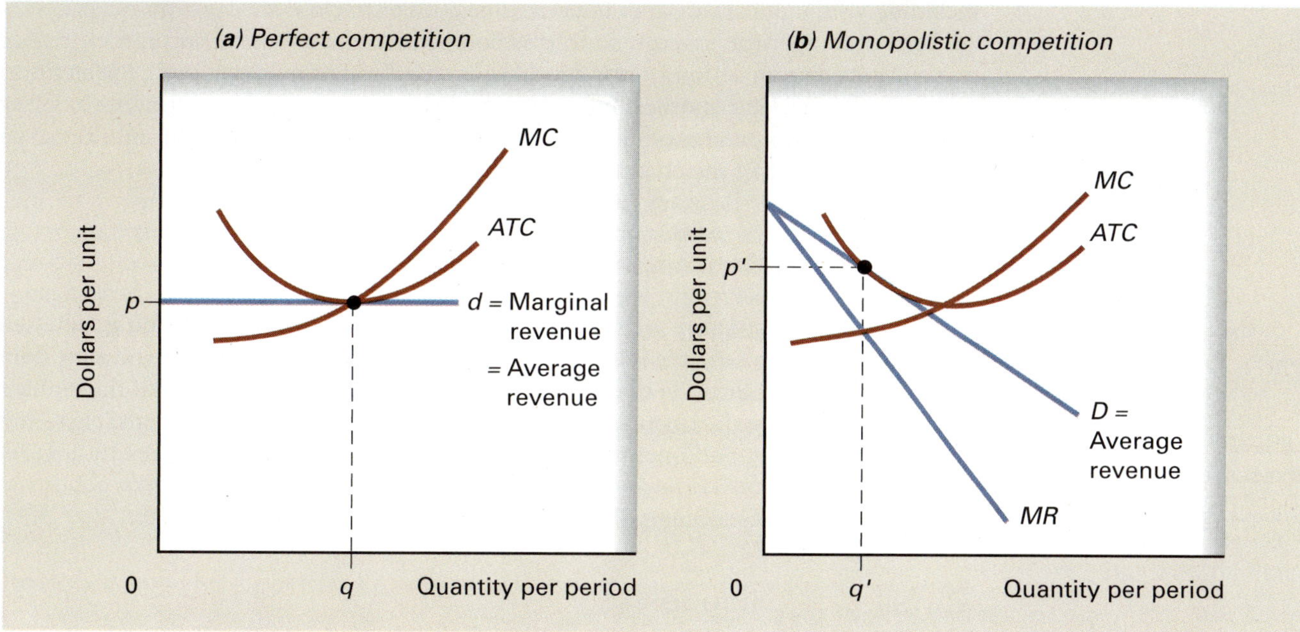

Cost curves are assumed to be the same in each panel. The perfectly competitive firm of panel (a) faces a demand curve that is horizontal at market price p. Long-run equilibrium occurs at output q, where the demand curve is tangent to the average total cost curve at its lowest point. The monopolistically competitive firm of panel (b) is in long-run equilibrium at output q', where demand is tangent to the average total cost curve. Because the demand curve slopes downward in panel (b), however, the tangency does not occur at the minimum point of average total cost. Thus, the monopolistically competitive firm produces less output and charges a higher price than does a perfectly competitive firm with the same cost curves. Neither firm earns economic profit in the long run. The firm in monopolistic competition has excess capacity, meaning that it could reduce average cost by increasing its rate of output.

would achieve the lowest average cost. Excess capacity means that each producer could easily serve more customers and, in the process, lower average cost. *The marginal value of increased output would exceed its marginal cost, so greater output would increase social welfare.* Such excess capacity exists with gas stations, drugstores, convenience stores, restaurants, motels, bookstores, flower shops, and firms in other monopolistic competitive industries. A specific example is the funeral business. Industry analysts argue that the nation's 22,000 funeral directors could efficiently handle 4 million funerals a year, but only about 2.4 million people die. So the industry operates at only 60 percent of capacity, resulting in a higher average cost per funeral because valuable resources remain idle much of the time.

One other difference between perfect competition and monopolistic competition does not show up in Exhibit 3. Although the cost curves drawn in each panel of the exhibit are identical, firms in monopolistic competition spend more to differentiate their products than do firms in perfect competition, where products are identical. This higher cost of product differentiation shifts up the average cost curve.

Some economists have argued that monopolistic competition results in too many suppliers and in artificial product differentiation. The counterargument is that consumers are willing to pay a higher price for a wider selection. According to this latter view, consumers benefit from more choice among gas stations, restaurants, convenience stores, clothing stores, video stores, drugstores, textbooks, hiking boots, and many other goods and services. For example, what if half of the restaurants in your area were to close just so the remaining ones could reduce their excess capacity? Some consumers, including you, might be disappointed if a local favorite closed.

Perfect competitors and monopolistic competitors are so numerous in their respective markets that an action by any one of them has little or no effect on the behavior of others in the market. Another important market structure on the continuum between perfect competition and monopoly has just a few firms. We explore this market structure in the balance of the chapter.

An Introduction to Oligopoly

oligopoly
A market structure characterized by so few firms that each behaves interdependently

The final market structure we examine is *oligopoly*, a Greek word meaning "few sellers." When you think of "big business," you are thinking of **oligopoly**, an industry dominated by just a few firms. Perhaps three or four account for more than half the industry supply. Many industries, including steel, automobiles, oil, breakfast cereals, cigarettes, personal computers, and operating systems software, are *oligopolistic*. Because an oligopoly has only a few firms, each one must consider the effect of its own actions on competitors' behavior. Oligopolists are therefore said to be *interdependent*.

Varieties of Oligopoly

undifferentiated oligopoly
An oligopoly that sells a commodity, or a product that does not differ across suppliers, such as an ingot of steel or a barrel of oil

differentiated oligopoly
An oligopoly that sells products that differ across suppliers, such as automobiles or breakfast cereal

In some oligopolies, such as steel or oil, the product is identical, or undifferentiated, across producers. Thus, an **undifferentiated oligopoly** sells a commodity, such as an ingot of steel or a barrel of oil. But in other oligopolies, such as automobiles or breakfast cereals, the product is differentiated across producers. A **differentiated oligopoly** sells products that differ across producers, such as a Toyota Camry versus a Honda Accord.

The more similar the products, the greater the interdependence among firms in the industry. For example, because steel ingots are essentially identical, steel producers are quite sensitive to each other's pricing. A small rise in one producer's price sends customers to rivals. But with differentiated oligopoly, such as the auto industry, producers are not quite as sensitive about each other's prices. As with monopolistic competitors, oligopolists differentiate their products through (1) physical qualities, (2) sales locations, (3) services offered with the product, and (4) the image of the product established in the consumer's mind.

Because of interdependence, the behavior of any particular firm is difficult to predict. *Each firm knows that any changes in its product's quality, price, output, or advertising policy may prompt a reaction from its rivals. And each firm may react if another firm alters any of these features.* Monopolistic competition is like a professional golf tournament, where each player strives for a personal best. Oligopoly is more like a tennis match, where each player's actions depend on how and where the opponent hits the ball. Here's another analogy to help you understand the effects of interdependence: Did you ever find yourself in an awkward effort to get around someone coming toward you on a sidewalk? You each end up turning this way and that in a brief, clumsy encounter. You each are trying to figure out which way the other will turn. But since neither can read the other's mind, neither can work out the problem independently. The solution is for one of you to put your head down and just walk. The other can then easily adjust.

Why have some industries evolved into oligopolies, dominated by only a few firms? Although the reasons are not always clear, *an oligopoly can often be traced to some form of barrier to entry, such as economies of scale, legal restrictions, brand names built up by years of advertising, or control over an essential resource.* In the previous chapter, we examined barriers to entry as they applied to monopoly. Those same principles apply to oligopoly.

Economies of Scale

Perhaps the most important barrier to entry is economies of scale. Recall that the minimum efficient scale is the lowest output at which the firm takes full advantage of economies of scale. If a firm's minimum efficient scale is relatively large compared to industry output, then only a few firms are needed to satisfy industry demand. For example, an automobile plant of minimum efficient scale could make enough cars to supply nearly 10 percent of the U.S. market. If there were 100 auto plants, each would supply such a tiny portion of the market that the average cost per car would be higher than if only 10 plants manufacture autos. In the automobile industry, economies of scale create a barrier to entry. To compete with existing producers, a new entrant must sell enough automobiles to reach a competitive scale of operation.

Exhibit 4 presents the long-run average cost curve for a typical firm in the industry. If a new entrant can sell only *S* cars, the average cost per unit, c_a, far exceeds the average cost, c_b, of a manufacturer that sells enough cars to reach the minimum efficient size, *M*. If autos sell for less than c_a, a potential entrant can expect to lose money, and this prospect discourages entry. For example, John Delorean tried to break into the auto industry in the early 1980s with a modern design featured in the *Back to the Future* movies. But his company managed to build and sell only 8,583 Deloreans before going bankrupt. If an auto plant costs $1 billion to build, just paying for the plant would have cost over $100,000 per Delorean.

EXHIBIT 4 Economies of Scale as a Barrier to Entry

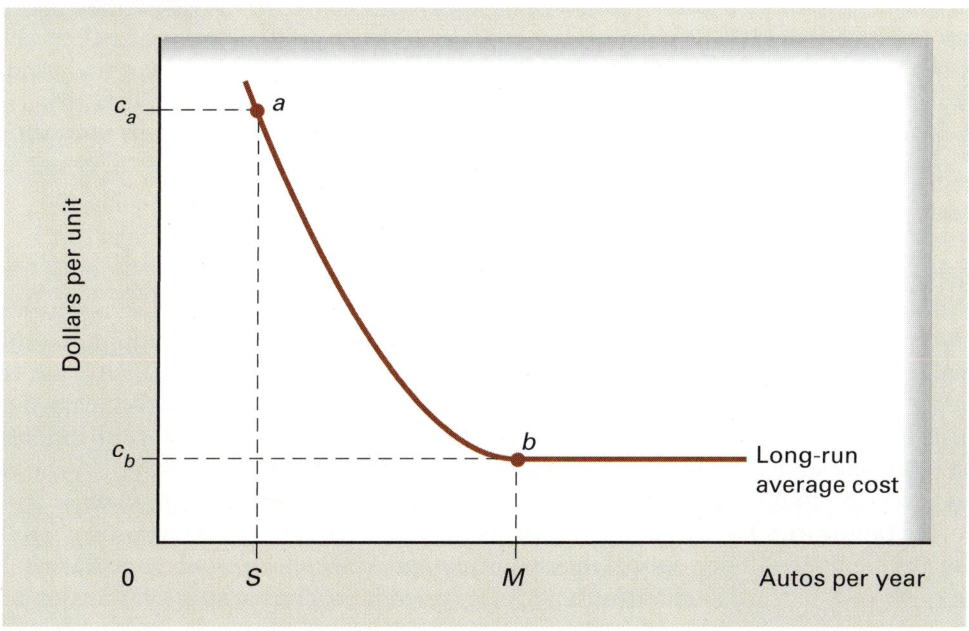

At point *b*, an existing firm can produce *M* or more automobiles at an average cost of c_b. A new entrant able to sell only *S* automobiles would incur a much higher average cost of c_a at point *a*. If automobile prices are below c_a, a new entrant would suffer a loss. In this case, economies of scale serve as a barrier to entry, insulating firms that have achieved minimum efficient scale from new competitors.

The High Cost of Entry

Potential entrants into oligopolistic industries could face another problem. The total investment needed to reach the minimum efficient size is often gigantic. A new auto plant or new semiconductor plant can cost over $3 billion. The average cost of developing and testing a new drug exceeds $800 million (only 1 in 25 drug candidates identified by the industry ever makes it to market).[2] Advertising a new product enough to compete with established brands may also require enormous outlays.

High start-up costs and well-established brand names create huge barriers to entry, especially because the market for new products is so uncertain (four out of five new consumer products don't survive). An unsuccessful product could cripple an upstart firm. The prospect of such a loss discourages many potential entrants. That's why most new products come from established firms. For example, Colgate-Palmolive spent $100 million introducing Total toothpaste, as did McDonald's in its failed attempt to sell the Arch Deluxe. Unilever lost $160 million when its new detergent, Power, washed out.

Firms often spend millions and sometimes billions trying to differentiate their products. Some of these outlays offer consumers useful information and wider choice. But some spending seems to offer neither. For example, Pepsi and Coke spend billions on messages such as "It's the Cola" or "Open Happiness." Regardless, *product differentiation expenditures create a barrier to entry.*

Crowding Out the Competition

Oligopolies compete with existing rivals and try to block new entry by offering a variety of products. Entrenched producers may flood the market with new products in part to crowd out other new entries. For example, a few cereal makers offer more than a dozen products each. Many of these variations offer little that is new. One study of 25,500 new products introduced during one year found only 7 percent offered new or added benefits.[3] *Multiple products from the same brand dominate shelf space and attempt to crowd out new entrants.*

This does not mean that small producers can't survive. Brenda Jensen, for example, handcrafts two-pound wheels of cheese in her small business that produces only about 12,000 pounds a year. She survives because her cheese sells for $20 to $40 a pound at boutique retailers.[4]

Models of Oligopoly

Because oligopolists are interdependent, analyzing their behavior is complicated. No single model or single approach explains oligopoly behavior completely. At one extreme, oligopolists may try to coordinate their behavior so they act collectively as a single monopolist, forming a cartel, such as OPEC. At the other extreme, oligopolists may compete so fiercely that price wars erupt, such as those that break out among airlines, tobacco companies, computer chip makers, and wireless service providers.

Several theories have been developed to explain oligopoly behavior. We will study three of the better-known approaches: collusion, price leadership, and game theory. As

2. As reported in "Little Big Pharma," *Wall Street Journal*, 6 December 2006.
3. The study was carried out by Market Intelligence Service and was reported in "Market Makers," *The Economist*, 14 March 1998.
4. Pervaiz Shallwani, "From Corporate to Camembert: Cheesemaking Lures Newcomers," *Wall Street Journal*, 7 November 2008.

you will see, each has some relevance in explaining observed behavior, although none is entirely satisfactory as a general theory of oligopoly. Thus, *there is no general theory of oligopoly but rather a set of theories, each based on the diversity of observed behavior in an interdependent market.*

Collusion and Cartels

In an oligopolistic market, there are just a few firms so, to decrease competition and increase profit, these firms may try to *collude,* or conspire to rig the market. **Collusion** is an agreement among firms in the industry to divide the market and fix the price. A **cartel** is a group of firms that agree to collude so they can act as a monopoly to increase economic profit. Cartels are more likely among sellers of a commodity, like oil or steel. *Colluding firms, compared with competing firms, usually produce less, charge more, block new firms, and earn more profit. Consumers pay higher prices, and potential entrants are denied the opportunity to compete.*

collusion
An agreement among firms to increase economic profit by dividing the market and fixing the price

cartel
A group of firms that agree to coordinate their production and pricing decisions to reap monopoly profit

Collusion and cartels are illegal in the United States. Still, monopoly profit can be so tempting that some U.S. firms break the law. For example, top executives at Archer Daniels Midland were convicted of conspiring with four Asian competitors to rig the $650 million world market for lysine, an amino acid used in animal feed. Some other countries are more tolerant of cartels and a few even promote cartels, as with the 12 member-nations of OPEC. If OPEC ever met in the United States, its representatives could be arrested for price fixing. Cartels can operate worldwide because there are no international laws against them.

Suppose all firms in an industry formed a cartel. The market demand curve, D, appears in Exhibit 5. What price maximizes the cartel's profit, and how is output allocated among participating firms? The first task of the cartel is to determine its marginal cost of production. Because a cartel acts like a monopoly that runs many plants, the marginal cost curve for the cartel in Exhibit 5 is the horizontal sum of each firm's marginal cost curve. The cartel's marginal cost curve intersects the market's marginal revenue curve to determine output that maximizes the cartel's profit. This intersection yields quantity Q. The cartel's price, p, is read off the demand curve at that quantity.

So far, so good. To maximize cartel profit, output Q must be allocated among cartel members so that each member's marginal cost equals c. Any other allocation would lower cartel profit. Thus, *for cartel profit to be maximized, output must be allocated so that the marginal cost for the final unit produced by each firm is identical.* Let's look at why this is easier said than done.

Differences in Average Cost

If all firms have identical average cost curves, output and profit would be easily allocated across firms (each firm would produce the same amount), but if costs differ, as they usually do, problems arise. The greater the difference in average costs across firms, the greater the differences in economic profit among them. If cartel members try to equalize each firm's total profit, a high-cost firm would need to sell more than would a low-cost firm. But this allocation scheme would violate the cartel's profit-maximizing condition. Thus, *if average costs differ across firms, the output allocation that maximizes cartel profit yields unequal profit across cartel members.* Firms earning less profit could drop out of the cartel, thereby undermining it. Usually, the allocation of output is the result of haggling among cartel members. Firms that are more influential or more adept at bargaining get a larger share of output and profit. Allocation schemes are sometimes based on geography or on the historical division of output among firms. OPEC, for example, allocates output in proportion to each member country's share of

EXHIBIT 5 Cartel as a Monopolist

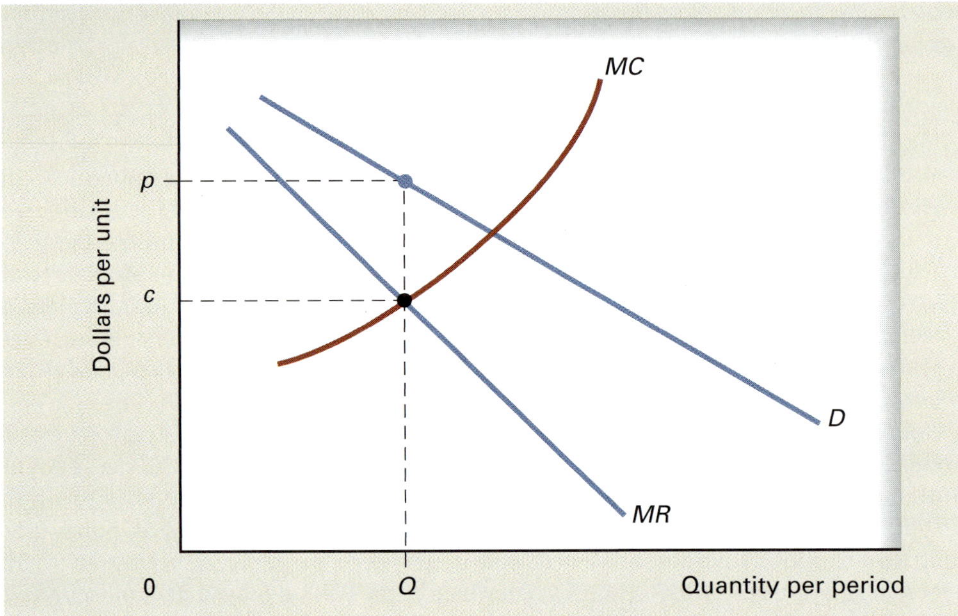

A cartel acts like a monopolist. Here, *D* is the market demand curve, *MR* the associated marginal revenue curve, and *MC* the horizontal sum of the marginal cost curves of cartel members (assuming all firms in the market join the cartel). Cartel profits are maximized when the industry produces quantity *Q* and charges price *p*.

estimated oil reserves. Cartel members of Norway's cement market base output on each firm's share of industry capacity.[5]

Number of Firms in the Cartel

The more firms in an industry, the more difficult it is to negotiate an acceptable allocation of output among them. *Consensus becomes harder to achieve as the number of firms grows.* And the more firms in the industry, the more likely that some will become dissatisfied and bolt from the cartel.

New Entry Into the Industry

If a cartel can't prevent new entry into the market, new firms will eventually force prices down, squeeze economic profit, and disrupt the cartel. The profit of the cartel attracts entry, entry increases market supply, and increased supply forces the price down. A cartel's success therefore depends on barriers that block the entry of new firms.

Cheating

Perhaps the biggest problem in keeping the cartel together is the powerful temptation to cheat on the agreement. Because oligopolists usually operate with excess capacity, some cheat on the price. By offering a price slightly below the fixed price,

5. Lars-Hendrik Roller and Frode Steen, "On the Workings of a Cartel: Evidence from the Norwegian Cement Industry," *American Economic Review* 96 (March 2006), p. 322.

any cartel member can usually increase sales and profit. Even if cartel members keep an eagle eye on each firm's price, one firm can increase sales by offering extra services, secret rebates, or other concessions. Research suggests that cheating increases as the number of firms in the cartel grows.[6] Cartels collapse once cheating becomes widespread.

OPEC's Spotty History

The problems of establishing and maintaining a cartel are reflected in the spotty history of OPEC. Many members are poor countries that rely on oil as their major source of revenue, so they argue over the price and their market share. OPEC members also cheat on the cartel. In 1980, the price of oil exceeded $85 a barrel (measured in 2010 dollars). During the 1990s, the price averaged around $32 a barrel and dipped as low as $10 a barrel. Prices topped $145 in 2008, but fell back to $45 by the end of that year. Like other cartels, OPEC has difficulty with new entry. The high prices resulting from OPEC's early success attracted new oil supplies from non-OPEC members operating in the North Sea, Mexico, and Siberia. The high price also made extraction from Canadian oil sands economical. As a result of new exploration and other oil sources, about 60 percent of the world's oil now comes from non-OPEC sources.

To Review: In those countries where cartels are legal, establishing and maintaining an effective cartel is more difficult if (1) the product is differentiated among firms, (2) average costs differ among firms, (3) there are many firms in the industry, (4) entry barriers are low, or (5) cheating on the cartel agreement becomes widespread. Efforts to cartelize the world supply of a number of products, including bauxite, copper, tin, and coffee, have failed so far. Russia is trying to form a natural gas cartel with other gas exporters, but obstacles abound.

Price Leadership

An informal, or *tacit,* form of collusion occurs if there is a **price leader** who sets the price for the rest of the industry. Typically, a dominant firm sets the market price, and other firms follow that lead, thereby avoiding price competition. The price leader also initiates any price changes, and, again, others follow. The steel industry was an example of the price-leadership form of oligopoly. Typically, U.S. Steel, the largest firm in the industry, would set the price for various products. Public pressure on U.S. Steel not to raise prices eventually shifted the price-leadership role onto less prominent producers, resulting in a rotation of leadership among firms. Although the rotating price leadership reduced price conformity, price leadership kept prices high.

price leader
A firm whose price is matched by other firms in the market as a form of tacit collusion

Like other forms of collusion, price leadership faces obstacles. Most importantly, the practice violates U.S. antitrust laws. Second, the greater the product differentiation among sellers, the less effective price leadership is as a means of collusion. Third, there is no guarantee that other firms will follow the leader. Firms that fail to follow a price increase take business away from firms that do. Fourth, unless there are barriers to entry, a profitable price attracts new entrants, which could destabilize the price-leadership agreement. And finally, as with formal cartels, some firms are tempted to cheat on the agreement to boost sales and profit.

6. John List, "The Economics of Open Air Markets," NBER Working Paper 15420 (October 2009).

Game Theory

game theory
An approach that analyzes oligopolistic behavior as a series of strategic moves and countermoves by rival firms

prisoner's dilemma
A game that shows why players have difficulty cooperating even though they would benefit from cooperation

How do firms act when they recognize their interdependence but either cannot or do not collude? Because oligopoly involves interdependence among a few firms, we can think of interacting firms as players in a game. **Game theory** examines oligopolistic behavior as a series of strategic moves and countermoves among rival firms. This approach analyzes the behavior of decision makers, or players, whose choices affect one another. Game theory is not really a separate model of oligopoly but a general approach, an approach that focuses on each player's incentives to cooperate—say, through cartels or price leaders—or to compete, in ways to be discussed now.

To get some feel for game theory, let's work through the **prisoner's dilemma**, the most widely examined game. The game originally considered a situation in which two thieves, let's call them Ben and Jerry, are caught near the crime scene and brought to police headquarters, where they are interrogated in separate rooms. The police know the two guys did it but can't prove it, so they need a confession. Each thief faces a choice of confessing, thereby "squealing" on the other, or "clamming up," thereby denying any knowledge of the crime. If one confesses, turning state's evidence, he is granted immunity from prosecution and goes free, while the other guy gets 10 years. If both clam up, each gets only a 1-year sentence on a technicality. If both confess, each gets 5 years.

strategy
In game theory, the operational plan pursued by a player

payoff matrix
In game theory, a table listing the payoffs that each player can expect from each move based on the actions of the other player

What will Ben and Jerry do? The answer depends on the assumptions about their behavior—that is, what *strategy* each pursues. A **strategy** reflects a player's game plan. In this game, suppose each player tries to save his own skin—each tries to minimize his time in jail, regardless of what happens to the other (after all, there is no honor among thieves). Exhibit 6 shows the *payoff matrix* for the prisoner's dilemma. A **payoff matrix** is a table listing the rewards (or, in this case, the penalties) that Ben and Jerry can expect based on the strategy each pursues.

Ben's choices are shown down the left margin and Jerry's across the top. Each prisoner can either confess or clam up. The numbers in the matrix indicate the prison time in years each can expect based on the corresponding strategies. Ben's numbers are in red and Jerry's in blue. Take a moment now to see how the matrix works. Notice that the sentence each player receives depends on the strategy he chooses *and* on the strategy the other player chooses.

EXHIBIT 6 The Prisoner's Dilemma Payoff Matrix (years in jail)

Ben \ Jerry	Confess	Clam up
Confess	Ben 5 / Jerry 5	Ben 0 / Jerry 10
Clam up	Ben 10 / Jerry 0	Ben 1 / Jerry 1

This matrix shows the years each prisoner can expect to spend in jail based on his actions and the actions of the other prisoner. Ben's payoff is in red and Jerry's in blue.

What strategies are rational assuming that each player tries to minimize jail time? For example, put yourself in Ben's shoes. You know that Jerry, who is being questioned in another room, will either confess or clam up. If Jerry confesses, the left column of Exhibit 6 shows the penalties. If you confess too, you both get 5 years in jail, but if you clam up, you get 10 years and Jerry "walks." So, if you think Jerry will confess, you should too.

What if you believe Jerry will clam up? The right-hand column shows the two possible outcomes. If you confess, you do no time, but if you clam up too, you each get 1 year in jail. Thus, if you think Jerry will clam up, you're better off confessing. In short, whatever Jerry does, Ben is better off confessing. The same holds for Jerry. He's better off confessing, regardless of what Ben does. So each has an incentive to confess and each gets 5 years in jail. This is called the **dominant-strategy equilibrium** of the game because each player's action does not depend on what he thinks the other player will do.

dominant-strategy equilibrium
In game theory, the outcome achieved when each player's choice does not depend on what the other player does

But notice that if each crook could just hang tough and clam up, both would be better off. After all, if both confess, each gets 5 years, but if both clam up, the police can't prove otherwise, so each gets only 1 year in jail. If each could trust the other to clam up, they both would be better off. But there is no way for the two to communicate or to coordinate their actions. That's why police investigators keep suspects apart, that's why organized crime threatens "squealers" with death, and that's why the witness protection program tries to shield "squealers."

Price-Setting Game

The prisoner's dilemma applies to a broad range of economic phenomena including pricing policy and advertising strategy. For example, consider the market for gasoline in a rural community with only two gas stations, Texaco and Exxon. Here the oligopoly consists of two sellers, or a **duopoly**. Suppose customers are indifferent between the brands and focus only on the price. Each station posts its daily price early in the morning before learning about the other station's price. To keep things simple, suppose only two prices are possible—a low price or a high price. If both charge the low price, they split the market and each earns a profit of $500 per day. If both charge the high price, they also split the market, but profit jumps to $700 each. If one charges the high price but the other the low one, the low-price station gets most of the business, earning a profit of $1,000, leaving the high-price station with only $200.

duopoly
A market with only two producers; a special type of oligopoly market structure

Exhibit 7 shows the payoff matrix, with Texaco's strategy down the left margin and Exxon's across the top. Texaco's profit appears in red, and Exxon's in blue. Suppose you are running the Texaco station and are trying to decide what to charge. If Exxon charges the low price, you earn $500 charging the low price but only $200 charging the high price. So you earn more charging the low price. If, instead, Exxon charges the high price, you earn $1,000 charging the low price and $700 charging the high price. Again, you earn more charging the low price. Exxon faces the same incentives. Thus, each charges the low price, regardless of what the other does.

The prisoner's dilemma outcome is an equilibrium because each player maximizes profit, given the price chosen by the other. Neither gas station can increase profit by changing its price, given the price chosen by the other firm. A situation in which a player chooses its best strategy given the strategies chosen by other firms is called a **Nash equilibrium**, named after Nobel Prize winner and former Princeton professor John Nash. He inspired the award-winning movie *A Beautiful Mind* starring Russell Crowe as Nash.

Nash equilibrium
A situation in which a firm, or a player in game theory, chooses the best strategy given the strategies chosen by others; no participant can improve his or her outcome by changing strategies even after learning of the strategies selected by other participants

In this prisoner's dilemma, each charges the low price, earning $500 a day, although each would earn $700 charging the high price. Think of yourself as a member of the oil cartel discussed earlier, where the cartel determines the price and sets production quotas

EXHIBIT 7 Price-Setting Payoff Matrix (profit per day)

Texaco \ Exxon	Low price	High price
Low price	$500 / $500	$1,000 / $200
High price	$200 / $1,000	$700 / $700

This matrix shows the daily profit each gas station can expect to earn based on the price each charges. Texaco's price is in red and Exxon's is in blue.

for each member. If you think other firms in the cartel will stick with their quotas, you can increase your profit by cutting your price and thereby increasing quantity sold. If you think the other firms will cheat on the cartel by cutting the price, then you should too—otherwise, you will get your clock cleaned by those cheaters. Either way, your incentive as a cartel member is to cheat on the quota. All members have an incentive to cheat, although all would earn more by sticking with the agreement that maximizes joint profit. Cheating is a Nash equilibrium, unless the cartel has real teeth to keep members in line—that is, unless cartel members have the strategy imposed on them.

This incentive to cut prices suggests why price wars sometimes break out among oligopolists. Even in industries with just two or three firms, competition often locks these rivals in a steel-cage death match for survival. For example, in 2010, McDonald's and Burger King were each selling two beef patties with one slice of cheese on a bun for $1—a dollar-menu duel between the McDouble and the BK Dollar Double.[7] A bitter price war with Dell cut Hewlett-Packard's earnings on each $500 personal computer sold to a razor-thin $1.75.[8] Early profits in the animated movie business attracted entry, which over time cut profit and led to some bankruptcies. And just before a recent Thanksgiving weekend, a price war erupted in airfares. American Airlines first announced holiday discounts. Delta responded with cuts of up to 50 percent. Within hours, American, United, and other major carriers said they would match Delta's reductions. All these airlines were losing money at the time. So go the price wars.

Cola War Game

As a final example of a prisoner's dilemma, consider the marketing strategies of Coke and Pepsi. Suppose each is putting together a promotional budget for the coming year, not knowing the other's plans. The choice boils down to adopting either a moderate budget or a big budget—one that involves multiple Super Bowl ads, showy in-store displays, and other marketing efforts aimed mostly at attracting customers from each other. If each adopts a big budget, their costly efforts will, for the most part, cancel each other out and limit each company's profit to $2 billion a year. If each adopts a moderate

7. See Dollar Menu news at http://www.mcdonalds.com/content/usa/eat/features/mcdouble.html.
8. David Bank, "H-P Posts 10% Increase in Revenue," *Wall Street Journal,* 20 November 2003.

promotional budget, the money saved boosts profit for each to $3 billion a year. And if one adopts a big budget but the other does not, the heavy promoter captures a bigger market share and earns $4 billion, while the other loses market share and earns only $1 billion. What to do, what to do?

Exhibit 8 shows the payoff matrix for the two strategies, with Pepsi's choices listed down the left margin and Coke's across the top. In each cell of the matrix, Pepsi's profit appears in red, and Coke's in blue. Let's look at Pepsi's decision. If Coke adopts a big promotional budget, Pepsi earns $2 billion by doing the same but only $1 billion by adopting a moderate budget. Thus, if Coke adopts a big budget, so should Pepsi. If Coke adopts a moderate budget, Pepsi earns $4 billion with a big budget and $3 billion with a moderate one. Again, Pepsi earns more with a big budget. Coke faces the same incentives, so both adopt big budgets, earning $2 billion each in profit, even though each would have earned $3 billion with a moderate budget.

One-Shot Versus Repeated Games

The outcome of a game often depends on whether it is a *one-shot game* or a *repeated game*. The classic prisoner's dilemma is a one-shot game. If the game is to be played just once, the strategy of confessing makes you better off regardless of what the other player does. Your choice won't influence the other player's behavior. But if the same players repeat the prisoner's dilemma, as would likely occur with the price-setting game, the cola war game, and the OPEC cartel, other possibilities unfold. In a repeated-game setting, each player has a chance to establish a reputation for cooperation and thereby may be able to encourage other players to do the same. After all, the cooperative solution—whether that involves clamming up, maintaining a high price, or adopting a moderate marketing budget—makes both players better off than if both fail to cooperate.

Experiments have shown that the strategy with the highest payoff in repeated games turns out to be the simplest—**tit-for-tat**. You begin by cooperating in the first round. On every round thereafter, you cooperate if the other player cooperated in the previous round, and you cheat if your opponent cheated in the previous round. In short, in any given round, you do whatever your opponent did in the previous round. The tit-for-tat strategy offers the other player immediate rewards for cooperation and immediate punishment for cheating. Some cartels seem to exhibit tit-for-tat strategies.

tit-for-tat
In game theory, a strategy in repeated games when a player in one round of the game mimics the other player's behavior in the previous round; an optimal strategy for getting the other player to cooperate

EXHIBIT 8 Cola War Payoff Matrix (annual profit in billions)

Pepsi \ Coke	Big budget	Moderate budget
Big budget	Pepsi $2 / Coke $2	Pepsi $4 / Coke $1
Moderate budget	Pepsi $1 / Coke $4	Pepsi $3 / Coke $3

This matrix shows the annual profit each soft-drink company can expect to earn based on the promotional budget each adopts. Pepsi's profit is in red and Coke's is in blue.

Coordination Game

coordination game
A type of game in which a Nash equilibrium occurs when each player chooses the same strategy; neither player can do better than matching the other player's strategy

In the **coordination game,** a Nash equilibrium occurs when each player chooses the same strategy. For example, you are driving on a country road and have to decide whether to drive on the right or the left side. Suppose you decide to drive on your left. If the driver coming from the opposite direction drives on his or her left, you pass each other without incident, so the cost to each of you is zero. But if the other player drives on the right-hand side, the probability of a crash increases. If, instead, you choose to drive on the right-hand side, you encounter no problems if the oncoming driver does the same, but face a greater likelihood of crashing if the other driver chooses the left-hand side. In this game, cost is minimized when both players choose the same strategy. And each strategy is a Nash equilibrium because no player can improve on that outcome, given the other player's choice. So if you choose the left-hand side and the other player chooses his or her left-hand side, then you can do no better and would do worse choosing the right-hand side.

To Review: Our discussion has given you some idea of game theory by focusing mostly on the prisoner's dilemma. Other games can be more complicated and involve more strategic interaction. Because firms are interdependent, oligopoly gives rise to all kinds of behavior and many approaches. Each approach helps explain certain behavior observed in oligopolistic markets. The *cartel,* or *collusion,* model shows why oligopolists might want to cooperate in fixing the market price; but that model also explains why a cartel is hard to establish and maintain. The *price-leadership* model explains why and how firms may charge the same price without explicitly establishing a formal cartel. Finally, *game theory,* expressed here mostly by the prisoner's dilemma, shows how difficult a cooperative solution might be even though cooperation benefits all players. Game theory is more of an approach to oligopoly rather than a distinct model.

Comparison of Oligopoly and Perfect Competition

As we have seen, each approach explains a piece of the oligopoly puzzle. But each has limitations, and none provides a complete picture of oligopoly behavior. Because there is no typical, or representative, model of oligopoly, "the" oligopoly model cannot be compared with the competitive model. We might, however, imagine an experiment in which we took the many firms that populate a competitive industry and, through a series of giant mergers, combined them to form, say, four firms. We would thereby transform the industry from perfect competition to oligopoly. How would firms in this industry behave before and after the massive merger?

Price Is Usually Higher Under Oligopoly

With fewer competitors after the merger, remaining firms would become more interdependent. Oligopoly models presented in this chapter suggest why firms may try to coordinate their pricing policies. *If oligopolists engaged in some sort of implicit or explicit collusion, industry output would be smaller and the price would be higher than under perfect competition.* Even if oligopolists did not collude but simply operated with excess capacity, the price would be higher and the quantity lower with oligopoly than with perfect competition. The price could become lower under oligopoly compared with perfect competition if a price war broke out among oligopolists. Two rivals, Intel and Advanced Micro Devices, together account for the entire market for a specific type of computer chip, yet these two are always at each other's throat, thereby keeping prices and profits down. Behavior also depends on whether there are barriers to entry. The lower the barriers to entry into the oligopoly, the more oligopolists act like perfect competitors.

Higher Profits Under Oligopoly

In the long run, easy entry prevents perfect competitors from earning more than a normal profit. With oligopoly, however, there may be barriers to entry, such as economies of scale or a way to differentiate a product such as with brand names, which allow firms in the industry to earn long-run economic profit. *With barriers to entry, we should expect profit in the long run to be higher under oligopoly than under perfect competition.* Profit rates do in fact appear to be higher in industries where a few firms account for a high proportion of industry sales. Some economists view these higher profit rates as troubling evidence of market power. But not all economists share this view. Some note that the largest firms in oligopolistic industries tend to earn the highest rate of profit. Thus, the higher profit rates observed in oligopolistic industries do not necessarily stem from market power per se. Rather, these higher profit rates stem from the greater efficiency arising from economies of scale in these large firms. An individual firm can also achieve greater market power and higher profit by differentiating its product, as discussed in the case study, "World of Business: Timely Fashions Boost Profit for Zara" at the end of the book.

Conclusion

Firms in monopolistic competition and in oligopoly face a downward-sloping demand curve for their products. With monopolistic competition, there are so many firms in the market that each tends to get lost in the crowd. Each behaves independently. But with oligopoly, there are so few firms in the market that each must consider the impact that its pricing, output, and marketing decisions will have on other firms. Each oligopolist behaves interdependently, and this makes oligopoly difficult to analyze. As a result, there are different models and approaches to oligopoly, three of which were discussed in this chapter.

The analytical results derived in this chapter are not as clear-cut as for the polar cases of perfect competition and monopoly. Still, we can draw some general conclusions using perfect competition as a guide. In the long run, perfect competitors operate at minimum average cost, while other types of firms usually operate with excess capacity. Therefore, given identical cost curves, monopolists, monopolistic competitors, and oligopolists tend to charge higher prices than perfect competitors do, especially in the long run. In the long run, monopolistic competitors, like perfect competitors, earn only a normal profit because entry barriers are low. Monopolists and oligopolists can earn economic profit in the long run if new entry is restricted. In a later chapter, we examine government policies aimed at increasing competition. *Regardless of the market structure, however, profit maximization prompts firms to produce where marginal revenue equals marginal cost.*

This chapter has moved us from the extremes of perfect competition and monopoly to the gray area inhabited by most firms. Exhibit 9 compares features and examples of the four market structures. Please take a moment now to review these key distinctions. Some of these issues are revisited later when we explore the government's role in promoting market competition.

EXHIBIT 9 Comparison of Market Structures

	Perfect Competition	Monopoly	Monopolistic Competition	Oligopoly
Number of firms	Most	One	Many	Few
Control over price	None	Complete	Limited	Some
Product differences	None	Only one supplier	Some	None or some
Barriers to entry	None	Insurmountable	Low	Substantial
Examples	Wheat	Local electricity	Convenience stores	Automobiles

Summary

1. Whereas the output of a monopolist has no close substitutes, a monopolistic competitor must contend with many rivals. But because of differences among the products offered by different firms, each monopolistic competitor faces a downward-sloping demand curve.
2. Sellers in monopolistic competition and in oligopoly differentiate their products through (a) physical qualities, (b) sales locations, (c) services offered with the product, and (d) the product image.
3. In the short run, monopolistic competitors that can at least cover their average variable costs maximize profits or minimize losses by producing that quantity where marginal revenue equals marginal cost. In the long run, easy entry and exit of firms means that a monopolistic competitor earns only a normal profit, which occurs where its average total cost curve is tangent to the downward-sloping demand curve for its product.
4. An oligopoly is an industry dominated by a few sellers. In undifferentiated oligopolies, such as steel or oil, the product is a commodity—meaning that it does not differ across firms. In differentiated oligopolies, such as automobiles or breakfast cereals, the product differs across firms.
5. Because an oligopoly consists of just a few firms, each may react to another firm's changes in quality, price, output, services, or advertising. Because of this interdependence, the behavior of oligopolists is difficult to analyze and predict. No single approach characterizes all oligopolistic markets.
6. In this chapter, we considered three approaches to oligopoly behavior: (a) collusion, in which firms form a cartel to act collectively like a monopolist; (b) price leadership, in which one firm, usually the biggest one, sets the price for the industry and other firms follow the leader; and (c) game theory, which analyzes oligopolistic behavior as a series of strategic moves by rival firms.
7. The prisoner's dilemma game shows why each player has difficulty cooperating even though all players would be better off if they did. In a variety of decisions such as what price to charge and how much to spend on marketing, rival firms could increase profit by cooperating. Yet each faces incentives that encourage noncooperation.

Key Concepts

Monopolistic competition 200
Excess capacity 204
Oligopoly 206
Undifferentiated oligopoly 206
Differentiated oligopoly 206
Collusion 209
Cartel 209
Price leader 211
Game theory 212
Prisoner's dilemma 212
Strategy 212
Payoff matrix 212
Dominant-strategy equilibrium 212
Duopoly 213
Nash equilibrium 213
Tit-for-tat 215
Coordination game 216

Questions for Review

1. CHARACTERISTICS OF MONOPOLISTIC COMPETITION Why does the demand curve facing a monopolistically competitive firm slope downward in the long run, even after the entry of new firms?
2. PRODUCT DIFFERENTIATION What are four ways in which a firm can differentiate its product? What role can advertising play in product differentiation? How can advertising become a barrier to entry?
3. ZERO ECONOMIC PROFIT IN THE LONG RUN In the long run, a monopolistically competitive firm earns zero economic profit, which is exactly what would occur if the industry were perfectly competitive. Assuming that the cost curves for each firm are the same whether the industry is perfectly or monopolistically competitive, answer the following questions.
   a. Why don't perfectly and monopolistically competitive industries produce the same equilibrium quantity in the long run?
   b. Why is a monopolistically competitive industry said to be economically inefficient?
   c. What benefits might cause consumers to prefer the monopolistically competitive result to the perfectly competitive result?
4. VARIETIES OF OLIGOPOLY Do the firms in an oligopoly act independently or interdependently? Explain your answer.
5. COLLUSION AND CARTELS Why would each of the following induce some members of OPEC to cheat on their cartel agreement?
   a. Newly joined cartel members are less-developed countries.
   b. The number of cartel members doubles from 12 to 24.
   c. International debts of some members grow.
   d. Expectations grow that some members will cheat.
6. PRICE LEADERSHIP Why might a price-leadership model of oligopoly not be an effective means of collusion in an oligopoly?
7. MARKET STRUCTURES Determine whether each of the following is a characteristic of perfect competition, monopolistic competition, oligopoly, and/or monopoly:
   a. A large number of sellers
   b. Product is a commodity
   c. Advertising by firms
   d. Barriers to entry
   e. Firms are price makers

Problems and Exercises

8. SHORT-RUN PROFIT MAXIMIZATION A monopolistically competitive firm faces the following demand and cost structure in the short run:

Output	Price	FC	VC	TC	TR	Profit/Loss
0	$100	$100	$0	___	___	___
1	90	___	50	___	___	___
2	80	___	90	___	___	___
3	70	___	150	___	___	___
4	60	___	230	___	___	___
5	50	___	330	___	___	___
6	40	___	450	___	___	___
7	30	___	590	___	___	___

   a. Complete the table.
   b. What is the highest profit or lowest loss available to this firm?
   c. Should this firm operate or shut down in the short run? Why?
   d. What is the relationship between marginal revenue and marginal cost as the firm increases output?
9. Case Study: Fast Forward to Creative Destruction (See page 721.) Use a cost-and-revenue graph to illustrate and explain the initial short-run profits in the video rental business in monopolistic competition. Then, use a second graph to illustrate the long-run situation. Explain fully.
10. MONOPOLISTIC COMPETITION AND PERFECT COMPETITION COMPARED Illustrated to the right are the marginal cost and average total cost curves for a small firm that is in long-run equilibrium.
    a. Locate the long-run equilibrium price and quantity if the firm is perfectly competitive.
    b. Label the price and quantity p_1 and q_1.
    c. Draw in a demand and marginal revenue curve to illustrate long-run equilibrium if the firm is monopolistically competitive. Label the price and quantity p_2 and q_2.
    d. How do the monopolistically competitive firm's price and output compare to those of the perfectly competitive firm?
    e. How do long-run profits compare for the two types of firms?

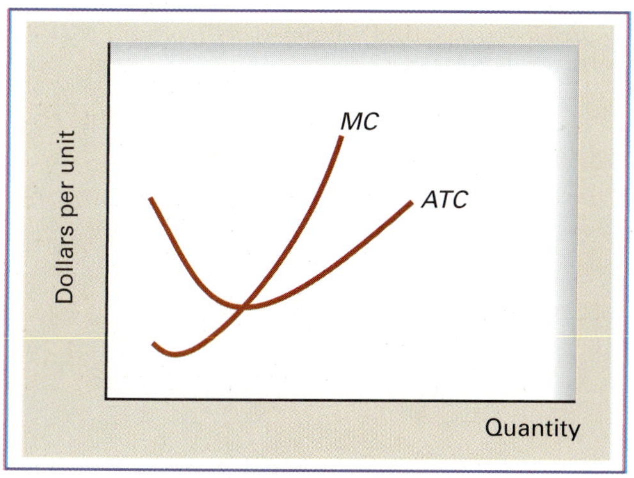

11. COLLUSION AND CARTELS Use revenue and cost curves to illustrate and explain the sense in which a cartel behaves like a monopolist.

12. GAME THEORY Suppose there are only two automobile companies, Ford and Chevrolet. Ford believes that Chevrolet will match any price it sets, but Chevrolet too is interested in maximizing profit. Use the following price and profit data to answer the following questions.

Ford's Selling Price in $	Chevrolet's Selling Price in $	Ford's Profits in $ (millions)	Chevrolet's Profits in $ (millions)
4,000	4,000	8	8
4,000	8,000	12	6
4,000	12,000	14	2
8,000	4,000	6	12
8,000	8,000	10	10
8,000	12,000	12	6
12,000	4,000	2	14
12,000	8,000	6	12
12,000	12,000	7	7

a. What price will Ford charge?
b. What price will Chevrolet charge once Ford has set its price?
c. What is Ford's profit after Chevrolet's response?
d. If the two firms collaborated to maximize joint profits, what prices would they set?
e. Given your answer to part (d), how could undetected cheating on price cause the cheating firm's profit to rise?

13. GAME THEORY While grading a final exam, an economics professor discovers that two students have virtually identical answers. She is convinced the two cheated but cannot prove it. The professor speaks with each student separately and offers the following deal: Sign a statement admitting to cheating. If both students sign the statement, each will receive an "F" for the course. If only one signs, he is allowed to withdraw from the course while the other student is expelled. If neither signs, both receive a "C" because the professor does not have sufficient evidence to prove cheating.

a. Draw the payoff matrix.
b. Which outcome do you expect? Why?

14. Case Study: Timely Fashions Boost Profits for Zara (See page 722.) Firms earn economic profit by offering a differentiated product. How does Zara differentiate its clothing?

Global Economic Watch Exercises

Login to www.cengagebrain.com and access the Global Economic Watch to do these exercises.

15. GLOBAL ECONOMIC WATCH Go to the Global Economic Crisis Resource Center. Select Global Issues in Context. In the Basic Search box at the top of the page, enter the phrase "product and service differentiation." On the Results page, go to the News section. Click on the link for the April 1, 2010, article "Study Results from University of Adelaide Broaden Understanding of Research Policy." According to the article, are innovation-related activities enough to create product and service differentiation?

16. GLOBAL ECONOMIC WATCH Go to the Global Economic Crisis Resource Center. Select Global Issues in Context. In the Basic Search box at the top of the page, enter the term "game theory." Write a paragraph about one example of game theory being used to analyze economic behavior.

Resource Markets

11

Comstock © 2010 Jupiterimages Corporation

- Why do surgeons earn twice as much as general practitioners?
- Why do truck drivers in the United States earn at least 20 times more than bicycle-rickshaw drivers in India?
- Why does prime Iowa corn acreage cost more than scrubland in the high plains of Montana?
- Why are buildings taller in downtown Chicago than those in the suburbs?

To answer these and other questions, we turn to the demand and supply of resources.

You say you've been through this demand-and-supply drill already? True. But the earlier focus was on the product market—that is, on the market for final goods and services. Goods and services are produced by resources—labor, capital, natural resources, and entrepreneurial ability. Demand and supply in resource markets determine the price and quantity of resources. And the ownership of resources determines the distribution of earnings throughout the economy.

Because your earnings depend on the market value of your resources, you should find a study of resource markets particularly relevant to your future. Certainly one consideration in your career choice is the expected earnings associated with alternative careers. The next three chapters examine how demand and supply interact to establish market prices for various resources.

Topics discussed in this chapter include:

- Demand and supply of resources
- Opportunity cost and economic rent
- Marginal revenue product
- Marginal resource cost
- Changes in resource demand

The Once-Over

Just to prove you already know more about resource markets than you may think, try answering the questions that arise in the following examples of resource demand and supply.

Resource Demand

Let's begin with the demand for labor. The manager of Walmart estimates that hiring another sales clerk would increase total revenue by $500 per week but increase total cost by $400 per week. Should Walmart hire another sales clerk? Sure, because profit would increase by $100 per week. *As long as the additional revenue from employing another worker exceeds the additional cost, the firm should hire that worker.*

What about capital? Suppose that you run a lawn service during the summer, getting an average of $50 per lawn. You have all the business you can handle. You mow about 15 lawns a week, for total revenue of $750 a week. You are thinking of upgrading to a larger, faster mower called the Lawn Monster, but it would cost you an extra $500 per week. The bigger mower would cut your time per lawn in half, enabling you to mow 30 lawns per week, so your total revenue would double to $1,500. Should you make the switch? Because the additional revenue of $750 exceeds the additional cost of $500, you should move up to the Monster.

What about natural resources? A neighbor offers Farmer Jones the chance to lease 100 acres of farmland. Jones figures that farming the extra land would cost $70 per acre but would yield $60 per acre in additional revenue. Should Jones lease the extra land? What do you think? Because the additional cost of farming that land would exceed the additional revenue, the answer is no.

These examples show that a *producer demands another unit of a resource as long as its marginal revenue exceeds its marginal cost.*

Resource Supply

You likely also understand the logic behind resource supply. Suppose you are trying to decide between two jobs that are identical in all ways except that one pays more than the other. Is there any question which one you'll take? If the working conditions are equally attractive, you would choose the higher-paying job. Now let's say your choice is between two jobs that pay the same. One has normal 9 to 5 hours, but the other starts at 5 A.M., an hour when your body tends to reject conscious activity. Which would you choose? You would pick the one that suits your tastes.

People supply their resources to the highest-paying alternative, other things constant. Because other things are not always constant, people must be paid more for jobs less suited to their tastes. Your utility depends on both monetary and nonmonetary aspects of the job. Generally, people must be paid more for jobs that are dirty, dangerous, dull, exhausting, illegal, low status, have no future, have no benefits, and involve inconvenient hours than for jobs that are clean, safe, interesting, energizing, legal, high status, have bright prospects, have good benefits, and involve convenient hours.

The Demand and Supply of Resources

In the market for goods and services—that is, in the product market—households are the demanders and firms are suppliers. Households demand the goods and services that maximize utility, and firms supply the goods and services that maximize profit. In the

EXHIBIT 1 Resource Market for Carpenters

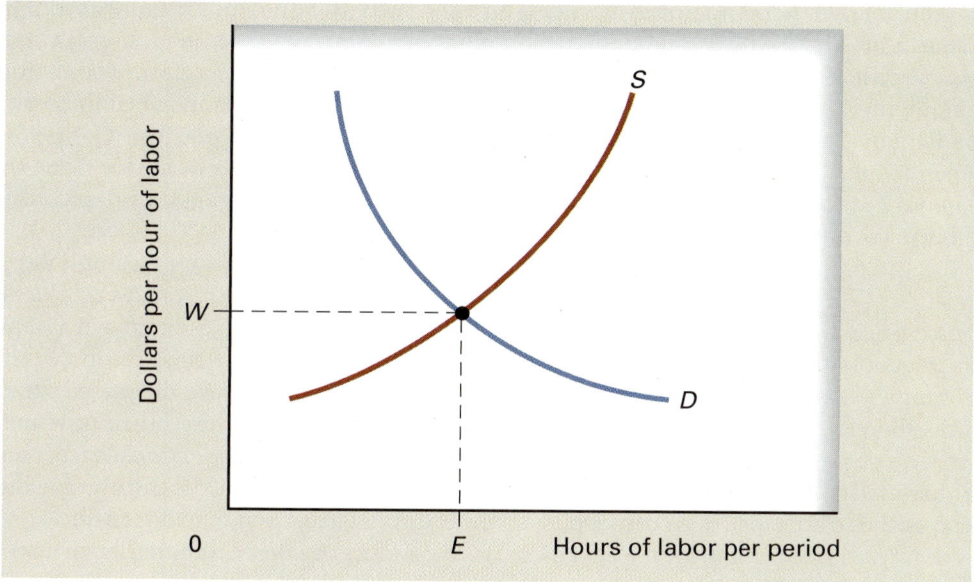

The intersection of the upward-sloping supply curve of carpenters with the downward-sloping demand curve determines the equilibrium wage, *W*, and the level of employment, *E*.

resource market, roles are reversed: Firms are demanders and households are suppliers. Firms demand the resources that maximize profit, and households supply the resources that maximize utility. *Any differences between the profit-maximizing goals of firms and the utility-maximizing goals of households are sorted out through voluntary exchange in markets.*

Exhibit 1 presents the market for a particular resource—in this case, carpenters. As you can see, the demand curve slopes downward and the supply curve slopes upward. *Like the demand and supply for final goods and services, the demand and supply for resources depend on the willingness and ability of buyers and sellers to engage in market exchange.* This market converges to the equilibrium wage, or the market price, for this type of labor.

The Market Demand for Resources

Why do firms employ resources? Resources produce goods and services, which firms try to sell for a profit. A firm values not the resource itself but the resource's ability to produce goods and services. Because the value of any resource depends on the value of what it produces, the demand for a resource is said to be a **derived demand**—arising from the demand for the final product. For example, a carpenter's pay derives from the demand for the carpenter's output, such as a kitchen cabinet or a new deck. A professional baseball player's pay derives from the demand for ballgames. A truck driver's pay derives from the demand for transporting goods. The derived nature of resource demand helps explain why professional baseball players usually earn more than professional hockey players, why brain surgeons earn more than tree surgeons, and why drivers of big rigs earn more than drivers of delivery vans. Derived demand also explains

derived demand
Demand that arises from the demand for the product the resource produces

why, in the face of an industry-wide slump in box office sales, Hollywood stars like Tom Cruise, Brad Pitt, and Cameron Diaz accepted pay cuts.[1]

The market demand for a particular resource is the sum of demands for that resource in all its different uses. For example, the market demand for carpenters adds together the demands for carpenters in residential and commercial construction, remodeling, cabinetmaking, and so on. Similarly, the market demand for timber sums the demand for this resource as lumber, railway ties, furniture, pencils, toothpicks, paper products, firewood, and so on. The demand curve for a resource, like the demand for the goods produced by that resource, slopes downward, as depicted in Exhibit 1.

As the price of a resource falls, producers are more willing and able to employ that resource. Consider first the producer's greater *willingness* to hire resources as the resource price falls. In developing the demand curve for a particular resource, we assume the prices of other resources remain constant. So if the price of a particular resource falls, it becomes cheaper compared with other resources that could produce the same output. Firms therefore are more willing to hire this resource rather than hire other, now relatively more costly, resources. Thus, we observe *substitution in production*—carpenters for masons, coal for oil, security alarms for security guards, and backhoes for grave diggers, as the relative prices of carpenters, coal, security alarms, and backhoes fall.

A lower price for a resource also increases a producer's *ability* to hire that resource. For example, if the wage of carpenters falls, home builders can hire more carpenters for the same total cost. The lower resource price means the firm is *more able* to employ the resource. Another key resource in residential construction is lumber. The case study, "World of Business: Lumber Prices and Housing Markets" at the end of the book, discusses the derived demand for lumber.

The Market Supply of Resources

The market supply curve for a resource sums all the individual supply curves for that resource. Resource suppliers are more *willing* and more *able* to increase quantity supplied as the resource price increases, so the market supply curve slopes upward, as in Exhibit 1. Resource suppliers are more *willing* because a higher resource price, other things constant, means more goods and services can be purchased with the earnings from each unit of the resource supplied. Resource prices are signals about the rewards for supplying resources. A high resource price tells the resource owner, "The market will reward you more for what you supply." Higher prices draw resources from lower-valued uses, including leisure. For example, as the wage for carpenters increases, the quantity of labor supplied increases. Some carpenters give up leisure to work more.

The second reason a resource supply curve slopes upward is that resource owners are more *able* to increase the quantity supplied as the resource price increases. For example, a higher carpenter's wage means more apprentices can afford to undergo the extensive training to become carpenters. A higher wage *enables* resource suppliers to increase their quantity supplied. Similarly, a higher timber price enables loggers to harvest trees in less accessible forests, a higher gold price enables miners to extract the metal from lower grade ore, and a higher oil price enables producers to drill deeper, to explore more remote parts of the world, and to squeeze oil from tar sands that contain less oil.

1. John Hiscock, "Hollywood Stars Meet the Real World," *The Independent*, 16 July 2006.

Temporary and Permanent Resource Price Differences

People have a strong interest in selling their resources to the highest bidder, other things constant. *Resources tend to flow to their highest-valued use.* If, for example, carpenters can earn more building homes than making furniture, and if the two activities are otherwise equally attractive, they shift into home building until wages in the two uses are equal. Because resource owners seek the highest pay, *other things constant*, earnings should tend toward equality for different uses of the same type of resource. For example, suppose carpenters who build homes earn $25 per hour, which is $5 more than carpenters who make furniture. This difference is shown in Exhibit 2 by an initial wage of $25 per hour in panel (a) and an initial wage of $20 per hour in panel (b). This gap encourages some carpenters to move from furniture making into home building, pulling up the wage in furniture making and driving down the wage in home building. Carpenters migrate into home building until wages equalize. In Exhibit 2, labor supply shifts leftward for furniture making and rightward for home building until the wage reaches $24 in both markets. Note that 2,000 hours of

EXHIBIT 2 Market for Carpenters in Alternative Uses

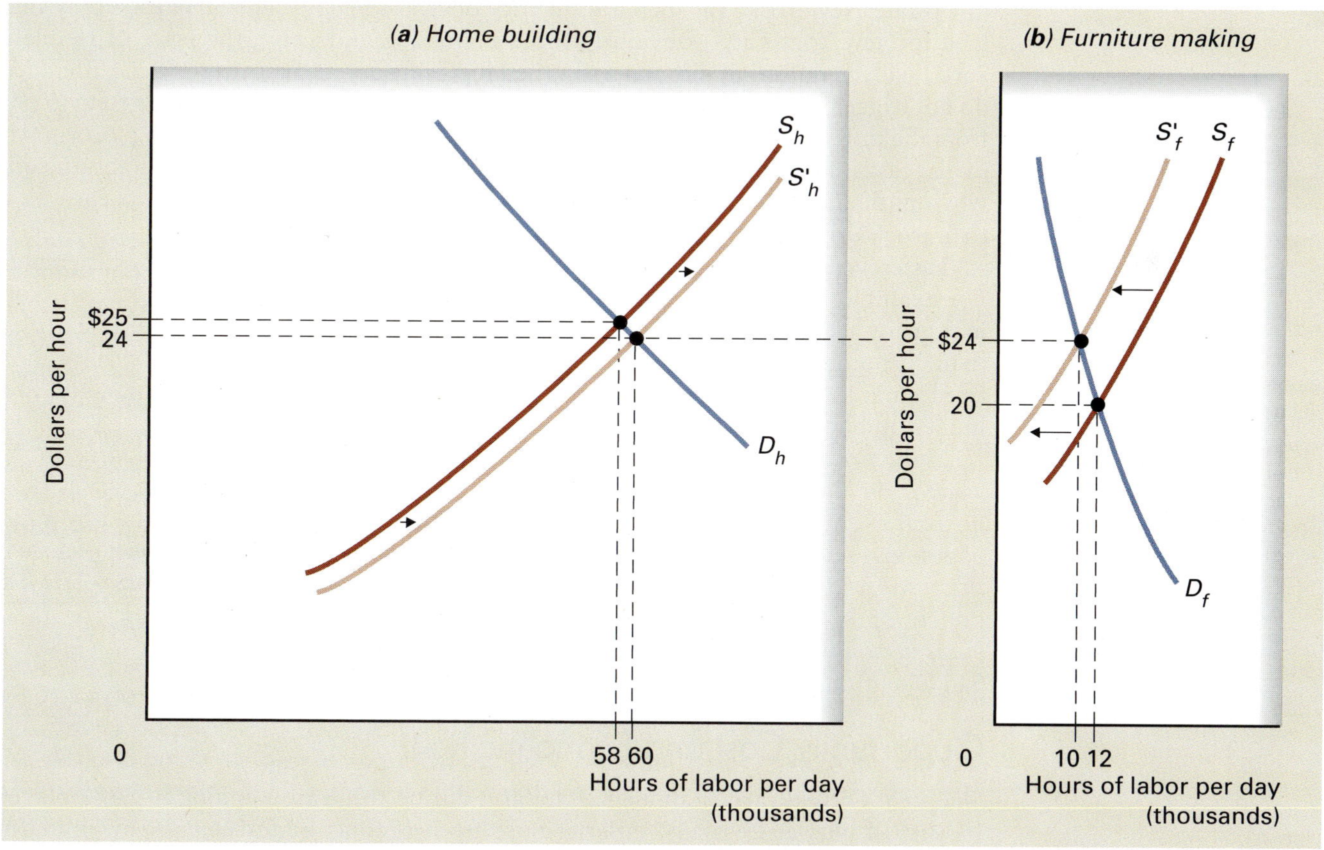

Suppose initially the hourly wage of carpenters is $25 in the home-building market but only $20 in the furniture-making market, and suppose also that carpenters view the jobs as equally attractive, aside from the wage. This differential prompts some carpenters to shift from furniture making to home building until the wage is identical in the two markets. In panel (b), the reduction of labor supplied to furniture making increases the market wage from $20 to $24. In panel (a), the increase of labor supplied to home building reduces the market wage from $25 to $24. note that 2,000 carpenter-hours per day shift from furniture making to home building.

labor per day shift from furniture making to home building. *As long as the nonmonetary benefits of supplying resources to alternative uses are identical and as long as resources are freely mobile, resources adjust across uses until they earn the same in different uses.*

Sometimes earnings appear to differ for seemingly similar resources. For example, corporate economists on average earn more than academic economists, and land in the city goes for more than land in the country. As you will now see, these differences also reflect the workings of demand and supply.

Temporary Differences in Resource Prices

Resource prices might differ temporarily across markets because adjustment takes time. As you have seen, however, a difference between the prices of similar resources prompts resource owners and firms to make adjustments that drive resource prices toward equality, as with the carpenters in Exhibit 2. The process may take years, but when resource markets are free to adjust, price differences trigger the reallocation of resources, which equalizes earnings for similar resources.

Permanent Differences in Resource Prices

Not all resource price differences cause reallocation. For example, for the price of a square yard of land along New York's Fifth Avenue you could buy several acres of land in Upstate New York. Yet such a difference does not prompt upstaters to supply their land to New York City—obviously that's impossible. Likewise, the price of farmland varies widely, reflecting differences in the land's fertility and location. Such differences do not trigger shifts of resource supply. Similarly, certain wage differentials stem in part from the different costs of acquiring the education and training needed to perform particular tasks. This difference explains why brain surgeons earn more than tree surgeons, why ophthalmologists earn more than optometrists, and why airline pilots earn more than truck drivers.

Differences in the nonmonetary aspects of similar jobs also lead to pay differences. For example, other things constant, most people would require higher pay to work in a grimy factory than in a pleasant office. Similarly, academic economists earn less than corporate economists, in part because academic economists typically have more freedom in their daily schedules, their attire, their choices of research topics, and even in their public statements.

Some price differences are temporary because they spark shifts of resource supply away from lower-paid uses and toward higher-paid uses. Other price differences cause no such shifts and are permanent. Permanent price differences are explained by *a lack of resource mobility* (urban land vs. rural land), *differences in the inherent quality of the resource* (fertile land vs. scrubland), *differences in the time and money involved in developing the necessary skills* (certified public accountant vs. file clerk), or *differences in nonmonetary aspects of the job* (lifeguard at Malibu Beach vs. prison guard at San Quentin).

Opportunity Cost and Economic Rent

Shaquille O'Neal earned about $20 million during the season ending in 2010 playing basketball plus at least $10 million more from product endorsements, including his Nike sneakers. But he would probably have been willing to play basketball and endorse products for less. The question is, how much less? What was his best alternative? Suppose his best alternative was to become a full-time rap artist, something he did on the side (as of 2010, he had released six rap albums). Suppose, as a full-time rapper, he could earn $1 million a year, including endorsements. And suppose, aside from the pay gap, he was indifferent between basketball and rap, so the nonmonetary aspects of the two jobs even out. Thus, he had to be paid at least $1 million a year to remain in basketball, and this represents his opportunity cost. *Opportunity cost is what that resource could earn in its best alternative use.*

The amount O'Neal earned in excess of his opportunity cost is called *economic rent.* **Economic rent** is that portion of a resource's earnings that exceeds the amount necessary to keep the resource in its present use. Economic rent is, as the saying goes, "pure gravy." In O'Neal's case, economic rent was $29 million in 2010. Economic rent is producer surplus earned by resource suppliers. The *division* of earnings between opportunity cost and economic rent depends on the resource owner's elasticity of supply. *In general, the less elastic the resource supply, the greater the economic rent as a proportion of total earnings.* To develop a feel for the difference between opportunity cost and economic rent, let's consider three resource markets.

economic rent
Portion of a resource's total earnings that exceeds its opportunity cost; earnings greater than the amount required to keep the resource in its present use

Resource Market A: All Earnings Are Economic Rent

If the supply of a resource to a particular market is perfectly inelastic, that resource has no alternative use. Thus, there is no opportunity cost, and all earnings are economic rent. For example, scrubland in the high plains of Montana has no use other than for grazing cattle. The supply of this land is depicted by the red vertical line in panel (a) of Exhibit 3, which indicates that the 10 million acres have no alternative use. Because supply is fixed, the rent paid to graze cattle on this land has no effect on the quantity of land supplied for cattle grazing. *The land's opportunity cost is zero, so all earnings are economic rent, shown by the blue-shaded area.* Here, fixed supply determines the equilibrium quantity of the resource, but demand determines the equilibrium price.

Resource Market B: All Earnings Are Opportunity Cost

At the other extreme is the market in which a resource can earn as much in its best alternative use as in its present use. This situation is illustrated by the perfectly elastic supply curve in panel (b) of Exhibit 3, which shows the market for janitors in the local school system. Here, janitors earn $10 an hour and supply 1,000 hours of labor per day. If the school system paid less than $10 per hour, janitors could find jobs elsewhere, perhaps in nearby factories, where the wage is $10 per hour. *All earnings reflect opportunity cost.* There is no economic rent in the market for janitors. In this resource market, the horizontal supply curve determines the equilibrium wage, but demand determines the equilibrium quantity.

Resource Market C: Earnings Include Both Economic Rent and Opportunity Cost

If the supply curve slopes upward, most resource suppliers earn economic rent in addition to their opportunity cost. For example, if the market wage for semiskilled work in your college community increases from $10 to $20 per hour, the quantity of labor supplied would increase, as would the economic rent earned by these workers. This market occurs in panel (c) of Exhibit 3, where the pink shading identifies opportunity cost and the blue shading, economic rent. If the wage increases from $10 to $20 per hour, the quantity supplied increases by 5,000 hours per day. For those who had been willing to work for $10 per hour, the difference between $10 and $20 is economic rent. *When resource supply slopes upward, as it usually does, earnings consist of both opportunity cost and economic rent.* In the case of an upward-sloping supply curve and a downward-sloping demand curve, both demand and supply determine equilibrium price and quantity.

EXHIBIT 3 Opportunity Cost and Economic Rent

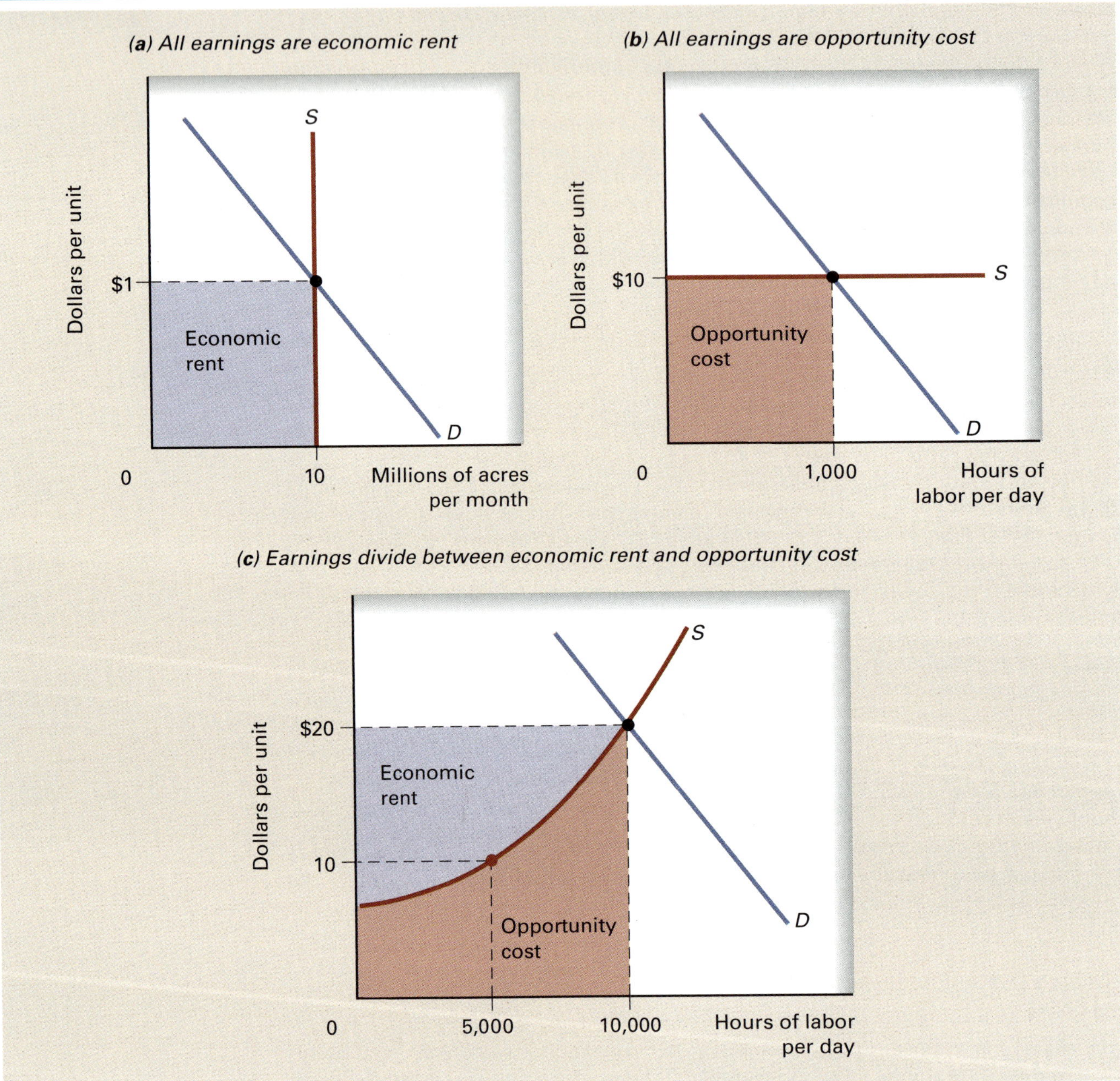

In panel (a), the resource supply curve is vertical, indicating that the resource has no alternative use. The price is demand-determined, and all earnings are economic rent. In panel (b), the resource supply curve is horizontal at $10 per hour, indicating that the resource can also earn that much in its best alternative use. Employment is demand-determined, and all earnings are opportunity cost. Panel (c) shows an upward-sloping resource supply curve. Earnings are partly opportunity cost and partly economic rent. Both demand and supply determine the equilibrium price and quantity.

Note that specialized resources tend to earn a higher proportion of economic rent than do resources with alternative uses. Thus, Shaquille O'Neal earned a greater *proportion* of his income as economic rent than did the janitor who cleaned the team's locker room. O'Neal would have taken a huge pay cut if he didn't play professional basketball, but the janitor could probably have found another job that paid about the same.

To Review: Given a resource demand curve that slopes downward, when the resource supply curve is vertical (perfectly inelastic), all earnings are economic rent; when that supply curve is horizontal (perfectly elastic), all earnings are opportunity cost; and when that supply curve slopes upward (an elasticity greater than zero but less than infinity), earnings divide between economic rent and opportunity cost. Remember, *the opportunity cost of a resource is what that resource could earn in its best alternative use. Economic rent is earnings in excess of opportunity cost.* Economic rent to a resource holder is like economic profit to the firm.

This completes our introduction to resource demand and supply. In the balance of the chapter, we take a closer look at resource demand. The determinants of resource demand are largely the same whether we are talking about labor, capital, or natural resources. The supply of different resources, however, has certain peculiarities depending on the resource, so the supply of resources is taken up in the next chapter.

A Closer Look at Resource Demand

Although production usually involves many resources, we cut the analysis down to size by focusing on a single resource, assuming that employment of other resources remains constant. As usual, we assume that firms try to maximize profit and households try to maximize utility.

The Firm's Demand for a Resource

You may recall that when production costs were introduced in Chapter 7, we considered a moving company, where labor was the only variable resource in the short run. We examined the relationship between the quantity of labor employed and the amount of furniture moved per day. The same approach is used in Exhibit 4, where only one resource varies. Column (1) lists possible employment levels of the variable resource, here measured as workers per day. Column (2) lists the amount produced, or total product, and column (3) lists the marginal product. The *marginal product* of labor is the change in total product from employing one more unit of labor.

With only one worker, total product is 10 units as is the marginal product. The marginal product of a second worker is 9 units. Notice in this example that diminishing marginal returns set in immediately—that is, right after the first worker.

Although labor is the variable resource here, we could examine the marginal product of any resource. For example, we could consider the number of lawns cut per week by varying the quantity of capital. We might start off with very little capital—imagine cutting grass with scissors—and then move up to a push mower, a power mower, and the Lawn Monster. By holding labor constant and varying the quantity of capital employed, we could compute the marginal product of capital. Likewise, we could compute the marginal product of natural resources by examining crop production for varying amounts of farmland, holding other inputs constant.

Marginal Revenue Product

The important question is: what happens to the firm's *revenue* when additional workers are hired? The first three columns of Exhibit 4 show how output changes with more workers. The *marginal revenue product* of labor indicates how much total revenue

EXHIBIT 4 Marginal Revenue Product When a Firm Sells in a Competitive Market

(1) Workers per Day	(2) Total Product	(3) Marginal Product	(4) Product Price	(5) Total Revenue (5) = (2) × (4)	(6) Marginal Revenue Product (6) = (3) × (4)
0	0	—	$ 20	$ 0	—
1	10	10	20	200	$ 200
2	19	9	20	380	180
3	27	8	20	540	160
4	34	7	20	680	140
5	40	6	20	800	120
6	45	5	20	900	100
7	49	4	20	980	80
8	52	3	20	1040	60

Because of diminishing marginal returns, the marginal product of labor declines as more labor is employed, as shown in column (3). Because this firm sells in a competitive market, it can sell all it wants at the market price of $20 per unit of output, as shown in column (4). The marginal product of labor in column (3) times the product price of $20 in column (4) yields the marginal revenue product of labor in column (6). Labor's marginal revenue product is the change in total revenue as a result of hiring another unit of labor.

marginal revenue product
The change in total revenue when an additional unit of a resource is employed, other things constant

changes as more labor is employed, other things constant. The **marginal revenue product** of any resource is the change in the firm's total revenue resulting from employing an additional unit of the resource, other things constant. You could think of the marginal revenue product as the firm's "marginal benefit" from hiring one more unit of the resource. *Marginal revenue product depends on how much additional output the resource produces and at what price that output is sold.*

Selling Output in Competitive Markets

The calculation of marginal revenue product is simplest when the firm sells in a perfectly competitive market, which is the assumption underlying Exhibit 4. An individual firm in perfect competition can sell as much as it wants at the market price. The marginal revenue product, listed in column (6) of Exhibit 4, is the change in total revenue from hiring an additional unit of the resource. For the perfectly competitive firm, the marginal revenue product is simply the marginal product of the resource multiplied by the product price of $20. Notice that because of diminishing returns, the marginal revenue product falls steadily as the firm employs more of the resource.

Selling Output With Some Market Power

If the firm has some power in the product market—that is, some ability to set the price—the demand curve for that firm's output slopes downward. To sell more, the firm must lower its price. Exhibit 5 reproduces the first two columns of Exhibit 4. But column (3) now shows the price at which that output can be sold. Total output multiplied by the price yields the firm's total revenue, which appears in column (4).

The marginal revenue product of labor, which is the change in total revenue from adding another worker, appears in column (5). For example, the first worker produced 10 units per day, which sell for $40 each, yielding total revenue and marginal revenue

EXHIBIT 5 The Marginal Revenue Product When a Firm Sells with Market Power

(1) Workers per Day	(2) Total Product	(3) Product Price	(4) Total Revenue (4) = (2) × (3)	(5) Marginal Revenue Product
0	0	—	—	—
1	10	$ 40	$ 400	$ 400
2	19	35	665	265
3	27	31	837	172
4	34	28	952	115
5	40	25	1000	48
6	45	23	1035	35
7	49	21	1029	−6
8	52	19	988	−41

To sell more, this firm must lower the price, as indicated in column (3). Total revenue in column (4) equals total product in column (2) times the product price in column (3). Labor's marginal revenue product in column (5) equals the change in total revenue from hiring another worker. The marginal revenue product declines both because of diminishing marginal returns from labor and because the product price must fall to sell more.

of $400. Hiring the second worker adds 9 more units to total product, but to sell 9 more units, the firm must lower the price from $40 to $35. Total revenue increases to $665, which means the marginal revenue product from hiring a second worker is $265. For firms selling with some market power, the marginal revenue product curve slopes downward both because of diminishing marginal returns and because additional output can be sold only if the price falls. A profit-maximizing firm is willing and able to pay as much as the marginal revenue product for an additional unit of the resource. Thus, *the marginal revenue product curve can be thought of as the firm's demand curve for that resource.* You could think of the marginal revenue product curve as the marginal benefit to the firm of hiring each additional unit of the resource.

To Review: Whether a firm sells its product in a competitive market or sells with some market power, the marginal revenue product of a resource is the change in total revenue resulting from a 1-unit change in that resource, other things constant. The marginal revenue product curve of a resource is also the demand curve for that resource—it shows the most a firm would be willing and able to pay for each additional unit of the resource. For firms selling in competitive markets, the marginal revenue product curve slopes downward only because of diminishing marginal returns to the resource. For firms selling with some market power, the marginal revenue product curve slopes downward both because of diminishing marginal returns and because additional output can be sold only if the price falls. *For all types of firms, the marginal revenue product is the change in total revenue resulting from hiring an additional unit of the resource.*

Marginal Resource Cost

If we know a firm's marginal revenue product, can we determine how much labor that firm should employ to maximize profit? Not yet, because we also need to know how much labor costs the firm. Specifically, what is the **marginal resource cost**—what does another unit of labor cost the firm? The typical firm hires such a tiny fraction of the

marginal resource cost
The change in total cost when an additional unit of a resource is hired, other things constant

market supply that the firm's hiring decision has no effect on the market price of the resource. Thus, each firm usually faces a given market price for the resource and decides only on how much to hire at that price.

For example, panel (a) of Exhibit 6 shows the market for factory workers, measured as workers per day. The intersection of market demand and market supply determines the market wage of $100 per day. Panel (b) shows the situation for the firm. The market wage becomes the firm's marginal resource cost of labor. The *marginal resource cost* curve is the horizontal line drawn at the $100 level in panel (b); this is the labor supply curve to the firm. Panel (b) also shows the marginal revenue product curve, or resource demand curve, based on the schedule presented in Exhibit 4. The marginal revenue product curve indicates the additional revenue the firm gets from adding another worker.

Resource Employment to Maximize Profit or Minimize Loss

Given a marginal resource cost of $100 per worker per day, how much labor should the firm employ to maximize profit? *The firm hires more labor as long as doing so adds more to revenue than to cost—that is, as long as labor's marginal revenue product exceeds its marginal resource cost. The firm stops adding labor once the two are equal.* If marginal resource cost is a constant $100 per worker, the firm hires six workers per day because the marginal revenue product from hiring a sixth worker equals $100. Thus, the firm hires additional workers until

$$\text{Marginal revenue product} = \text{Marginal resource cost}$$

EXHIBIT 6 Market Equilibrium for a Resource and the Firm's Employment Decision

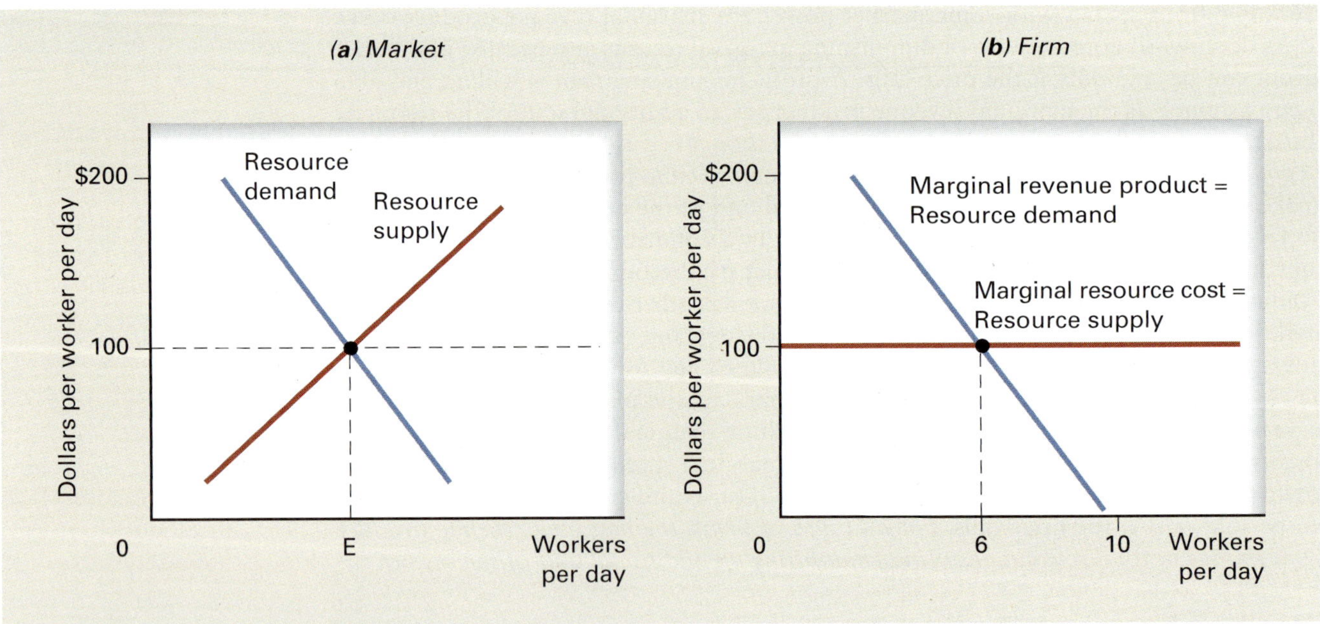

Market demand and supply of a resource, in panel (a), determine that resource's market wage and quantity. In panel (b), an individual firm can employ as much as it wants at the market wage, so that wage becomes the firm's marginal resource cost. The marginal resource cost curve also is the supply curve of that resource to the firm. In panel (b), a resource's marginal revenue product is the firm's demand curve for that resource. The firm maximizes profit (or minimizes its loss) by hiring a resource up to the point where the resource's marginal revenue product equals its marginal resource cost, which is six workers per day in this example.

This equality holds for all types of resources employed, whether the firm sells in perfectly competitive markets or sells with some market power. Profit maximization occurs where labor's marginal revenue product equals the market wage. Based on data presented so far, we can't yet determine the firm's actual profit because we don't yet know about the firm's other costs. We do know, however, that in Exhibit 6, a seventh worker would add $100 to cost but would add less than that to revenue, so hiring a seventh worker would reduce the firm's profit (or increase its loss).

Whether a firm sells in competitive markets or with some market power, the profit-maximizing level of employment occurs where the marginal revenue product of labor equals its marginal resource cost. Similarly, profit-maximizing employment of other resources, such as natural resources and capital, occurs where their respective marginal revenue products equal their marginal resource costs. Each unit of a resource must "pull its own weight"—that is, each unit must bring in additional revenue that at least covers the additional cost.

Optimal Input and Optimal Output Decisions Are Equivalent

In earlier chapters, you learned how to find the profit-maximizing level of output. Maximum profit (or minimum loss) occurs where the marginal revenue from *output* equals its marginal cost. Likewise, maximum profit (or minimum loss) occurs where the marginal revenue from an *input* equals its marginal resource cost. The two are equivalent ways of deriving the same principle of profit maximization. For example, in Exhibit 6, the firm maximizes profit by hiring six workers when the market wage is $100 per day. Exhibit 4 indicates that a sixth worker adds 5 units to output, which sell for $20 each, yielding labor's marginal revenue product of $100. The *marginal revenue* of that output is the change in total revenue from selling another unit of output, which is $20. The *marginal cost* of that output is the change in total cost, $100, divided by the change in output, 5 units; so the marginal cost of output is $100/5, or $20. Thus, *in equilibrium, the marginal revenue of output equals its marginal cost.* Now that you have some idea of how to derive the demand for a resource, let's discuss what could shift the resource demand curve.

Changes in Resource Demand

As we have seen, a resource's marginal revenue product depends on the resource's marginal product and the price at which that product is sold. Two things can change a resource's marginal product: (1) a change in the amount of other resources employed and (2) a change in technology. Only one thing can change the price of the product: a change in demand for the product. Let's consider first changes that could affect marginal product, then changes that could affect demand for the product.

Change in Other Resources Employed

Although our focus so far has been on a single input, in reality the marginal product of any resource depends on the quantity and quality of other resources used in production. Sometimes resources are *substitutes*. For example, coal substitutes for oil in generating electricity. And ATMs substitute for tellers in handling bank transactions. If two resources are **substitutes**, an increase in the price of one increases the demand for the other. An increase in the price of oil increases the demand for coal, and an increase in the market wage of tellers increases the demand for ATMs.

Sometimes resources are *complements*—trucks and truck drivers, for example. If two resources are **complements**, a decrease in the price of one leads to an increase in the

resource substitutes
Resources that substitute in production; an increase in the price of one resource increases the demand for the other

resource complements
Resources that enhance one another's productivity; a decrease in the price of one resource increases the demand for the other

demand for the other. If the price of tractor-trailers decreases, the quantity demanded increases, which increases the demand for truck drivers. More generally, any increase in the quantity and quality of a complementary resource, such as trucks, raises the marginal productivity of the resource in question, such as truck drivers, and so increases the demand for that resource. A bigger and better truck makes the driver more productive. One big reason a truck driver in the United States earns much more than a bicycle-rickshaw driver in India is the truck.

Changes in Technology

Technological improvements can boost the productivity of some resources but make other resources obsolete. The introduction of computer-controlled machines increased the demand for computer-trained machinists but reduced the demand for machinists without computer skills. The development of synthetic fibers, such as rayon and Orlon, increased the demand for acrylics and polyesters but reduced the demand for natural fibers, such as cotton and wool. Breakthroughs in fiber-optic and satellite telecommunications increased the demand for fiberglass and satellites and reduced the demand for copper wire.

Computer programs are changing job prospects in fields such as law, medicine, accounting, and architecture. For example, Quicken's WillMaker software has written more wills than any lawyer alive. In medicine, software such as Skyscape's 5-Minute Clinical Consult is a handheld program that helps doctors diagnose more than a thousand medical and surgical conditions. In accounting, software such as TurboTax completes tax forms with ease. And in architecture, three-dimensional modeling programs such as 3D Home Architect help configure all aspects of a structure. As software and hardware get cheaper, better, and easier to use, the demand for some professional services declines.

Changes in the Demand for the Final Product

Because the demand for a resource is *derived* from the demand for the final output, any change in the demand for output affects resource demand. For example, an increase in the demand for video games increases their market price and thereby increases the marginal revenue product of game programmers.

To Review: The demand for a resource depends on its marginal revenue product, which is the change in total revenue resulting from employing one more unit of the resource. Any change that increases a resource's marginal revenue product increases resource demand.

The Optimal Use of More Than One Resource

As long as marginal revenue product exceeds marginal resource cost, a firm can increase profit or reduce a loss by employing more of that resource. Again, the firm hires more of a resource until the marginal revenue product just equals the marginal resource cost. This principle holds for each resource employed. The opening paragraph asked why buildings in downtown Chicago are taller than those in the suburbs. Land and capital, to a large extent, substitute in the production of building space. Because land is more expensive downtown than in the suburbs, builders downtown substitute capital for land, building up instead of out. Hence, buildings are taller closer to the center of the city and are tallest in cities where land is most expensive. Buildings in Chicago and New York City are taller than those in Salt Lake City and Tucson, for example.

The high price of land in metropolitan areas has other implications for the efficient use of resources. For example, in New York City, as in many large cities, food carts seem to be on every corner. New York City has more than 3,000 of them. Why are they so popular? Consider the resources needed to supply sidewalk food: land, labor, capital, food, and perhaps a tiny morsel of entrepreneurial ability. Which of these do you suppose is most expensive in New York City? Retail space along Madison Avenue's Golden Mile can rent for an average $800 a year per square foot (even after the drop that followed the financial crisis of 2008). Because operating a food cart requires about 6 square yards (or 54 square feet), renting that space could cost as much as $43,000 a year. Aside from the necessary public permits, however, space on the public sidewalk is free to vendors. Profit-maximizing street vendors substitute public sidewalks for costly commercial space. (Incidentally, does free public space mean sidewalk vendors earn long-run economic profit?)

Government policy can affect resource allocation in other ways, as discussed in the case study, "Public Policy: The McMinimum Wage" at the end of the book.

Conclusion

A firm hires each resource until the marginal revenue product of that resource equals its marginal cost. The objective of profit maximization ensures that to produce any given level of output, firms employ the least-cost combination of resources and thereby use the economy's resources most efficiently. Although our focus has been on the marginal productivity of each resource, we should keep in mind that an orchestra of resources combines to produce output, so the marginal productivity of a particular resource depends in part on the amount and quality of other resources employed.

Summary

1. Firms demand resources to maximize profit. Households supply resources to maximize utility. The profit-maximizing goals of firms and the utility-maximizing goals of households are reconciled through voluntary exchange in resource markets.
2. Because the value of any resource depends on what it produces, the demand for a resource is a derived demand—arising from the demand for the final product. Resource demand curves slope downward because firms are more willing and able to increase quantity demanded as the price of a resource declines. Resource supply curves slope upward because resource owners are more willing and able to increase quantity supplied as their reward for doing so increases.
3. Some differences in the market prices of similar resources trigger the reallocation of resources to equalize those prices. Other price differences do not cause a shift of resources among uses because of a lack of resource mobility, differences in the inherent quality of the resources, differences in the time and money involved in developing necessary skills, and differences in nonmonetary aspects of jobs.
4. Resource earnings divide between (a) opportunity cost and (b) economic rent—that portion of earnings that exceeds opportunity cost. If a resource has no other use, earnings consist entirely of economic rent. If a resource has other uses that pay just as well, earnings consist entirely of opportunity cost. Most resources earn both economic rent and opportunity cost.
5. A firm's demand curve for a resource is the resource's marginal revenue product curve, which shows the change in total revenue from employing one more unit of the resource, other things constant. If a firm sells output in a competitive market, the marginal revenue product curve slopes downward because of diminishing marginal returns. If a firm has some power in the product market, the marginal revenue product curve slopes downward both because of diminishing marginal returns and because the price must fall to sell more.
6. The demand curve for a resource shifts to the right if (a) its marginal productivity increases, (b) the output price increases, (c) the price of a substitute resource increases, or (d) the price of a complement resource decreases.
7. Marginal resource cost is the change in total cost resulting from employing one more unit of the resource, other things constant. A firm maximizes profit by employing each resource up to the point where its marginal revenue product equals its marginal resource cost. This is the flip side of the profit-maximizing output decision that equates marginal revenue with marginal cost.

Key Concepts

Derived demand 223
Economic rent 227
Marginal revenue product 230
Marginal resource cost 231
Resource substitutes 233
Resource complements 233

Questions for Review

1. Resource Demand and Supply Answer each of the following questions about the labor market:
   a. Which economic decision makers determine the demand for labor? What is their goal, and what decision criteria do they use in trying to reach that goal?
   b. Which economic decision makers determine the supply of labor? What is their goal and what decision criteria do they use in trying to reach that goal?
   c. In what sense is the demand for labor a derived demand?
2. Case Study: Lumber Prices and Housing Markets (See page 723.) Between 2001 and 2009, how was the demand for lumber affected by the demand for housing? In what sense is the demand for lumber a derived demand?
3. Market Supply for Resources Explain why the market supply curve of a resource slopes upward.
4. Resource Price Differences Distinguish between how the market reacts to a temporary difference in prices for the same resource and how the market reacts to a permanent difference. Why do the reactions differ?
5. Opportunity Cost and Economic Rent On-the-job experience typically enhances a person's productivity in that particular job. If the person's salary increases to reflect increased experience but the additional experience has no relevance for other jobs, does this higher salary reflect an increase in opportunity cost or in economic rent?
6. Firm's Demand for a Resource How does the law of diminishing marginal returns affect a firm's demand for labor?
7. Shifts of Resource Demand Many countries are predominantly agricultural. How would changes in the supply of fertilizer affect the marginal product, and thus the income, of farmers in such countries?
8. Optimal Use of More Than One Resource Explain the rule for determining optimal resource use when a firm employs more than one resource.

Problems and Exercises

9. Opportunity Cost and Economic Rent Define economic rent. In the graph below, assume that the market demand curve for labor is initially D_1.

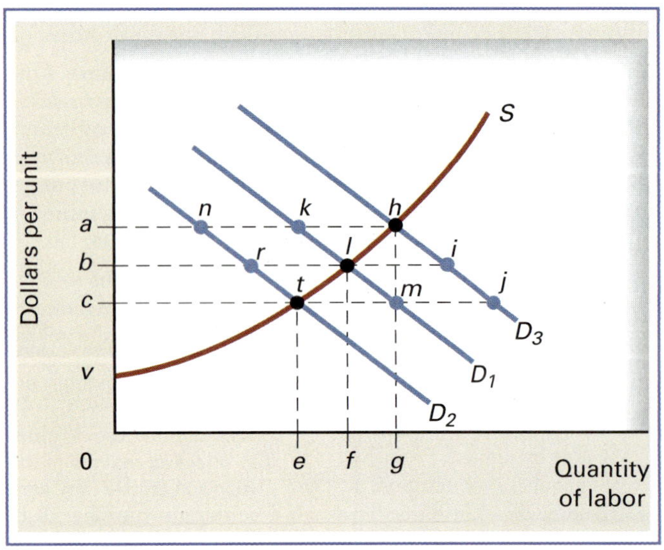

   a. What are the equilibrium wage rate and employment level? What is the economic rent?
   b. Next assume that the price of a substitute resource increases, other things constant. What happens to demand for labor? What are the new equilibrium wage rate and employment level? What happens to economic rent?
   c. Suppose instead that demand for the final product drops, other things constant. Using labor demand curve D_1 as your starting point, what happens to the demand for labor? What are the new equilibrium wage rate and employment level? Does the amount of economic rent change?

10. Firm's Demand for a Resource Use the following data to answer the questions below. Assume a perfectly competitive product market.

Units of Labor	Units of Output
0	0
1	7
2	13
3	18
4	22
5	25

a. Calculate the marginal revenue product for each additional unit of labor if output sells for $3 per unit.
b. Draw the demand curve for labor based on the above data and the $3-per-unit product price.
c. If the wage rate is $15 per hour, how much labor will be hired?
d. Using your answer to part (c), compare the firm's total revenue to the total amount paid for labor. Who gets the difference?
e. What would happen to your answers to parts (b) and (c) if the price of output increased to $5 per unit, other things constant?

11. Selling Output as a Price Taker If a competitive firm hires another full-time worker, total output increases from 100 units to 110 units per week. Suppose the market price of output is $25 per unit. What is the maximum weekly wage at which the firm would hire that additional worker?

12. Shifts of Resource Demand A local pizzeria hires college students to make pizza, wait on tables, take phone orders, and deliver pizzas. For each situation described, determine whether the demand for student employees by the restaurant would increase, decrease, or remain unchanged. Explain each answer.
    a. The demand for pizza increases.
    b. Another pizzeria opens up next door.
    c. An increase in the minimum wage raises the cost of hiring student employees.
    d. The restaurant buys a computer system for taking phone orders.

13. Case Study: The McMinimum Wage (See page 723.) Describe some ways that an employer might adjust to an increase in the minimum wage.

Global Economic Watch Exercises

Login to www.cengagebrain.com and access the Global Economic Watch to do these exercises.

14. Global Economic Watch Go to the Global Economic Crisis Resource Center. Select Global Issues in Context. In the Basic Search box at the top of the page, enter the phrase "minimum wage face-off." Click on the link for the May 11, 2010, editorial "The Minimum Wage Face-Off." According to the editorial, what is one advantage and one disadvantage of raising the Nigerian minimum wage?

15. Global Economic Watch Go to the Global Economic Crisis Resource Center. Select Global Issues in Context. In the Basic Search box at the top of the page, enter the term "housing market." Write a paragraph about the recent housing market in a foreign country. How are resource costs affecting housing prices? Alternatively, how is housing demand affecting resource prices?

Labor Markets and Labor Unions

12

AP Photo/Robert Caplin

- How do you divide your time between work and leisure?
- Why do some people work *less* if the wage increases enough?
- For example, why do unknown rock bands play hours for peanuts, while famous bands play much less for much more?
- Why are butchers more likely than surgeons to mow their own lawns?
- What determines the wage structure in the economy?
- What else besides the wage affects your labor supply?
- In what sense have labor unions become the victims of their own success?

This chapter digs deeper into labor markets and wage determination.

You can be sure of one thing: demand and supply play a central role in all this. You have already considered the demand for resources. Demand depends on a resource's marginal revenue product. The first half of this chapter focuses on the supply of labor, then brings demand and supply together to arrive at the market wage. The second half considers the role of labor unions.

We examine the economic impact of unions and review recent trends in union membership.

Topics discussed include:

- Theory of time allocation
- Backward-bending labor supply curve
- Nonwage factors in labor supply
- Why wages differ
- Unions and collective bargaining
- Union wages and employment
- Trends in union membership

Labor Supply

As a resource supplier, you have a labor supply curve for each of the many possible uses of your labor. To some markets, your quantity supplied is zero over the realistic range of wages. The qualifier "over the realistic range" is added because, for a high enough wage (say, $1 million per hour), you might supply labor to just about *any* activity. In most labor markets, your quantity supplied may be zero either because you are *willing* but *unable* to perform the job (professional golfer, airline pilot, novelist) or because you are *able* but *unwilling* to do so (soldier of fortune, prison guard, P.E. instructor). You have as many individual supply curves as there are labor markets, just as you have as many individual demand curves as there are markets for goods and services. Your labor supply to each market depends, among other things, on your abilities, your taste for the job, and the opportunity cost of your time. Your supply to a particular labor market assumes that wages in other markets are constant, just as your demand for a particular product assumes that other prices are constant.

Labor Supply and Utility Maximization

Recall the definition of economics: *the study of how people use their scarce resources in an attempt to satisfy their unlimited wants*—that is, how people use their scarce resources to maximize their utility. Two sources of utility are of special interest in this chapter: the consumption of goods and services and the enjoyment of leisure. The utility derived from consumption serves as the foundation of demand. Another valuable source of utility is leisure—time spent relaxing with friends, sleeping, eating, watching TV, gaming, reading for pleasure, and in other recreation. Leisure is a normal good that, like other goods, is subject to the law of diminishing marginal utility. Thus, the more leisure time you have, the less you value an additional hour of it. Sometimes you may have so much leisure that you "have time on your hands" and are "just killing time." As that sage of the comic page Garfield the cat once lamented, "Spare time would be more fun if I had less to spare." Or as Shakespeare wrote, "If all the year were playing holidays, to sport would be as tedious as to work." Leisure's diminishing marginal utility explains why some of the "idle rich" may grow bored in their idleness.

Three Uses of Time

market work
Time sold as labor

nonmarket work
Time spent getting an education or on do-it-yourself production for personal consumption

leisure
Time spent on nonwork activities

Some of you are at a point in your careers when you have few resources other than your time. Time is the raw material of life. You can use your time in three ways. First, you can undertake **market work**—selling your time in the labor market. In return for a wage, you surrender control of your time to the employer. Second, you can undertake **nonmarket work**—using time to produce your own goods and services. Nonmarket work includes the time you spend doing your laundry, making a sandwich, or cleaning up after yourself. Nonmarket work also includes the time spent acquiring skills and education that enhance your productivity. Although studying and attending class may provide little immediate utility, you expect that the knowledge and perspective so gained will enrich your future. Third, you can spend time in **leisure**—using your time in nonwork pursuits.

Work and Utility

Unless you are among the fortunate few, work is not a pure source of utility, as it's often boring, uncomfortable, and aggravating. In short, time spent working can be "a real pain," a source of *disutility*—the opposite of utility. And work is subject *to increasing marginal disutility*—the more you work, the greater the marginal disutility of working another hour. In the extreme, you get burned out from overwork. You may work nonetheless, because your earnings buy goods and services. You expect the utility from these products to more than offset the disutility of work. Thus, the *net utility of work*—the utility of the additional consumption possibilities from earnings minus the disutility of the work itself—usually makes some amount of work an attractive use of your time. In the case of market work, your income buys goods and services. In the case of nonmarket work, either you produce goods and services directly, as in making yourself a sandwich, or you invest your time in education with an expectation of higher future earnings and higher future consumption possibilities.

Utility Maximization

Within the limits of a 24-hour day, seven days a week, you balance your time among market work, nonmarket work, and leisure to maximize utility. As a rational consumer, *you attempt to maximize utility by allocating your time so that the expected marginal utility of the last unit of time spent in each activity is identical.* Thus, in the course of a week or a month, the expected marginal utility of the last hour of leisure equals the expected net marginal utility of the last hour of market work, which equals the expected net marginal utility of the last hour of nonmarket work. In the case of time devoted to acquiring more human capital, you must consider the marginal utility expected from the future increase in earnings that result from your enhanced productivity.

Maybe at this point you are saying, "Wait a minute. I don't know what you're talking about. I don't allocate my time like that. I just sort of bump along, doing what feels good." Economists do not claim that you are even aware of making these marginal calculations. But as a rational decision maker, you allocate your scarce time trying to satisfy your unlimited wants, or trying to maximize utility. And utility maximization, or "doing what feels good," implies that you act *as if* you allocated your time to derive the same expected net marginal utility from the last unit of time spent in each alternative use.

You probably have settled into a rough plan for meals, work, entertainment, study, sleep, and so on—a plan that fits your immediate objectives. This plan is probably in constant flux as you make expected and unexpected adjustments in your use of time. For example, last weekend you may have failed to crack a book, despite good intentions. This morning you may have overslept because you were up late. Over a week, a month, or a year, however, your use of time is roughly in line with an allocation that maximizes utility as you perceive it at the time. Put another way, if you could alter your use of time to increase your utility, you would do so. Nobody's stopping you! You may emphasize immediate gratification over long-term goals, but, hey, that's your choice and you bear the consequences. *This time-allocation process ensures that at the margin, the expected net utilities from the last unit of time spent in each activity are equal.*

Because information is costly and because the future is uncertain, you sometimes make mistakes. You don't always get what you expect. Some mistakes are minor, such as going to a movie that turns out to be a waste of time. But other mistakes can be costly. For example, some people are now studying for a field that will grow crowded by the time they graduate, or some people may be acquiring skills that new technology will soon make obsolete.

Implications

The theory of time allocation described thus far has several implications for individual choice. First, consider the choices among market work, nonmarket work, and leisure. The higher your market wage, other things constant, the higher your opportunity cost of leisure and nonmarket work. For example, those who earn a high wage spend less time in nonmarket work, other things constant. Surgeons are less likely to mow their lawns than are butchers. And among those earning the same wage, those more productive in nonmarket work—handy around the house, good cooks—do more for themselves. Conversely, those who are all thumbs around the house and have trouble boiling water hire more household services and eat out more.

By the same logic, the higher the expected earnings right out of high school, other things constant, the higher the opportunity cost of attending college. Most young, successful movie stars do not go to college, and many even drop out of high school, as noted earlier. Promising athletes often turn professional as soon as they can. But the vast majority of people, including female basketball stars, do not face such a high opportunity cost of higher education. As one poor soul lamented, "Since my wife left me, my kids joined a cult, my job is history, and my dog died, I think now might be a good time to go back for an MBA."

Wages and Individual Labor Supply

To breathe life into the time-allocation problem, consider your choices for the summer. If you can afford to, you can take the summer off, spending it entirely on leisure, perhaps as a fitting reward for a rough academic year. Or you can get a job. Or you can undertake nonmarket work, such as cleaning the garage, painting the house, or attending summer school. As a rational decision maker, you select the mix of leisure, market work, and nonmarket work that you expect will maximize your utility. And the optimal combination is likely to involve allocating time to each activity. For example, even if you work, you might still take one or two summer courses.

Suppose the only summer job available is some form of unskilled labor, such as working in a fast-food restaurant or for the municipal parks department. For simplicity, let's assume that you view all such jobs as equally attractive (or unattractive) in terms of their nonmonetary aspects, such as working conditions, working hours, and so on. (These nonmonetary aspects are discussed in the next section.) If there is no difference among these unskilled jobs, the most important question for you in deciding how much market labor to supply is: What's the market wage?

Suppose the wage is $7 per hour, not even the legal minimum. Rather than working for a wage that low, you might decide to work around the house, attend summer school, take a really long nap, travel across the country to find yourself, or perhaps pursue some combination of these. In any case, you supply no market labor at such a low wage. The market wage must rise to $8 before you supply any market labor. Suppose at a wage of $8, you supply 20 hours per week, perhaps taking fewer summer courses and shorter naps.

As the wage increases, your opportunity cost of time spent in other activities rises, so you substitute market work for other uses of your time. You decide to work 30 hours per week at a wage of $9 per hour, 40 hours at $10, 48 hours at $11, and 55 hours at $12. At a wage of $13 you go to 60 hours per week; you are starting to earn serious money—$780 a week. If the wage hits $14 per hour, you decide to cut back to 58 hours per week. Despite the cutback, your weekly pay rises to $812, which is more than when the wage was $13. Finally, if the wage hits $15, you cut back to 55 per week, earning $825. To explain why you may eventually reduce the quantity of labor supplied, let's consider the impact of wage increases on your time allocation.

Substitution and Income Effects

A higher wage has two effects on your use of time. First, because each hour of work now buys more goods and services, a higher wage increases the opportunity cost of leisure and nonmarket work. Thus, as the wage increases, you substitute market work for other activities. This is the **substitution effect of a wage increase.** Second, a higher wage means a higher income for a given number of hours. This higher income increases your demand for all normal goods. Because leisure is a normal good, a higher income increases your demand for leisure, thereby reducing your allocation of time to market work. The **income effect of a wage increase** tends to reduce the quantity of labor supplied to market work. As the Greek philosopher Aristotle observed, "The end of labor is to gain leisure."

substitution effect of a wage increase
A higher wage encourages more work because other activities now have a higher opportunity cost

income effect of a wage increase
A higher wage raises a worker's income, increasing the demand for all normal goods, including leisure, so the quantity of labor supplied to market work decreases

As the wage increases, the substitution effect causes you to work more, but the income effect causes you to work less and demand more leisure. In our example, the substitution effect exceeds the income effect for wages up to $13 per hour, resulting in more labor supplied as the wage increases. When the wage reaches $14, however, the income effect exceeds the substitution effect, causing you to reduce the quantity of labor supplied.

Backward-Bending Labor Supply Curve

The labor supply curve just described appears in Exhibit 1. As you can see, this slopes upward until the wage reaches $13 per hour; then the curve bends backward. The **backward-bending supply curve** gets its shape because the income effect of a higher wage eventually dominates the substitution effect, reducing the quantity of labor supplied as the wage increases. We see evidence of a backward-bending supply curve particularly among high-wage individuals, who reduce their work and consume more leisure as their wage increases. For example, entertainers typically perform less as they become more successful. Unknown musicians play for hours for hardly any money; famous musicians play much less for much more. But the backward-bending supply curve may also apply to ordinary workers, such as you during the summer or to New York City taxi drivers, who reduced their hours after an increase in taxi fares.[1] The income effect of rising real wages helps explain the decline in the U.S. workweek from an average of 60 hours in 1900 to about 40 hours in 1960 to about 34 hours today.

backward-bending supply curve of labor
As the wage rises, the quantity of labor supplied may eventually decline; the income effect of a higher wage increases the demand for leisure, which reduces the quantity of labor supplied enough to more than offset the substitution effect of a higher wage

Flexibility of Hours Worked

The model we have been discussing assumes that workers have some control over how much they work. Opportunities for part-time work and overtime allow workers to put together their preferred quantity of hours. Workers also have some control over the timing and length of their vacations. More generally, individuals usually have some control over how long to stay in school, when to enter or leave the workforce, and when to retire. Thus, most people actually have more control over the number of hours worked than you might think.

Nonwage Determinants of Labor Supply

The supply of labor to a particular market depends on a variety of factors other than the wage, just as the demand for a particular good depends on factors other than the price. As we have already seen, the supply of labor to a particular market depends on wages in other labor markets. What nonwage factors shape a college student's labor supply for the summer?

1. Orley Ashenfelter, Kirk Doran, and Bruce Schaller, "A Shred of Credible Evidence on the Long Run Elasticity of Labor Supply," NBER Working Paper 15746, (February 2010).

EXHIBIT 1 Your Labor Supply Curve for the Summer

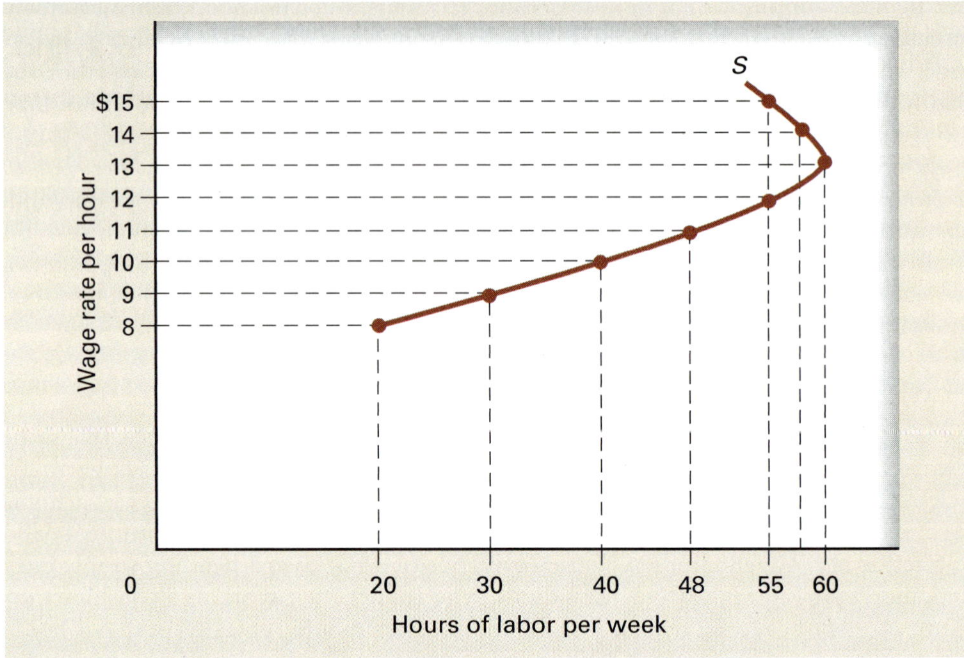

When the substitution effect of a wage increase outweighs the income effect, the quantity of labor you supply increases with the wage. Above some wage, shown here at $13 per hour, the income effect dominates. Above that wage, your supply curve bends backward. Further increases in the wage reduce the quantity of labor you supply.

Other Sources of Income

Although some jobs are rewarding in a variety of nonmonetary ways, the main reason people work is to earn money. Thus, your willingness to supply labor depends on income from other sources, including from family, savings, student loans, and scholarships. A student who receives a generous scholarship, for example, faces less pressure to work in the summer or during the college term. More generally, wealthy people have less incentive to work. For example, multimillion-dollar lottery winners often quit their jobs. And those who inherit a large sum are more likely to retire early.[2]

Nonmonetary Factors

Labor is a special kind of resource. Unlike capital or natural resources, which can be supplied regardless of the whereabouts of the resource owner, the supplier of labor must be where the work is performed. Because individuals must usually be physically present to supply labor, such *nonmonetary factors* as the difficulty of the job, the quality of the work environment, and the status of the position become important to labor suppliers. For example, deckhands on crab boats in the icy waters off Alaska can earn over $10,000 for five days of work, but the job is dangerous, winter temperatures seldom exceed zero, and daily shifts allow only three hours of sleep.

2. As found in research by Jeffrey Brown, Courtney Coile, and Scott Weisbenner, "The Effect of Inheritance Receipt on Retirement," *Review of Economics and Statistics*, 92 (May 2010): 425–434.

Consider the different working conditions you might encounter. A campus job that lets you study on the job is more attractive than one with no study time. Some jobs offer flexible hours; other work schedules are rigid. Is the workplace air-conditioned, or do you have to sweat it out? The more attractive the working conditions, the more labor you supply to that market, other things constant. Finally, some jobs convey more status than others. For example, the president of the United States earns less than one-tenth that of corporate heads, but there is no shortage of applicants for the job. Similarly, U.S. Supreme Court justices typically took a huge pay cut to accept the job.

The Value of Job Experience

All else equal, you are more inclined to take a position that provides valuable job experience. Serving as the assistant treasurer for a local business during the summer provides better job experience and looks better on a résumé than serving mystery meat at the college cafeteria. Some people are willing to accept relatively low wages now for the promise of higher wages in the future. For example, new lawyers are eager to fill clerkships for judges, though the pay is low and the hours long, because these positions offer experience and contacts future employers value. Likewise, athletes who play in the minor leagues for little pay believe that experience will give them a shot at the major leagues. Thus, *the more a job enhances future earning possibilities, the greater the supply of labor, other things constant.* Consequently, the pay in such jobs is usually lower than for jobs that impart less valuable experience. Sometimes the pay is zero, as with some internships.

Taste for Work

Just as the taste for goods and services differs among consumers, the taste for work also differs among labor suppliers. Some people prefer physical labor and hate office work. Some become surgeons; others can't stand the sight of blood. Some become airline pilots; others are afraid to fly. Teenagers prefer jobs at Starbucks and Gap to those at McDonald's and Burger King. Many struggling writers, artists, actors, and dancers could earn more elsewhere, but prefer the creative process and the chance, albeit slim, of becoming rich and famous in the arts (for example, the 120,000 members of the Screen Actors Guild average less than $10,000 a year from acting). Some people have such strong preferences for certain jobs that they expect no pay, such as auxiliary police officers or volunteer firefighters.

As with the taste for goods and services, economists do not try to explain how work preferences develop. They simply argue that your preferences are relatively stable and you supply more labor to jobs you like. Based on taste, workers seek jobs in a way that tends to minimize the disutility of work. This is not to say that everyone ends up in his or her most preferred position. The transaction costs of job information and of changing jobs may prevent some matchups that might otherwise seem desirable. But in the long run, people tend to find jobs that suit them. We are not likely to find tour guides who hate to travel, zookeepers who are allergic to animals, or garage mechanics who hate getting their hands dirty.

Market Supply of Labor

In the previous section, we considered those factors, both monetary and nonmonetary, that influence individual labor supply. *The supply of labor to a particular market is the horizontal sum of all the individual supply curves.* The horizontal sum at each particular wage is found by adding the quantities supplied by each worker. If an individual supply curve of labor bends backward, does this mean that the market supply curve for

EXHIBIT 2 Deriving the Market Labor Supply Curve From Individual Labor Supply Curves

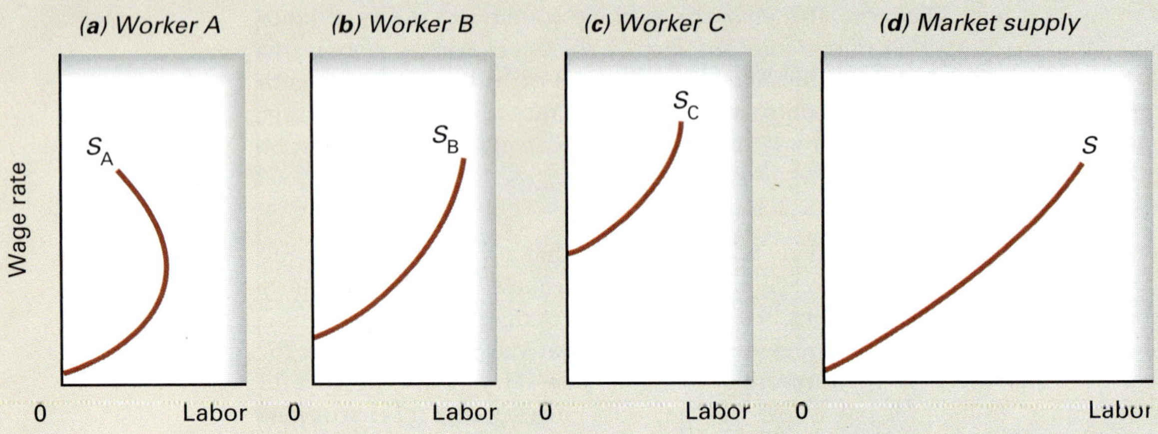

The individual labor supply curve in panel (a) bends backward. The market supply curve, however, may still slope upward over the relevant range of wages.

labor also bends backward? Not necessarily. Because different individuals have different opportunity costs and different tastes for work, the bend in the supply curve occurs at different wages for different individuals. And, for some individuals, the labor supply curve may not bend backward over the realistic range of wages. Exhibit 2 shows how just three individual labor supply curves sum to yield a market supply curve that slopes upward.

Why Wages Differ

Just as both blades of scissors contribute equally to cutting paper, both labor demand and labor supply determine the market wage. Exhibit 3 shows average hourly wages for more than 130 million U.S. workers. Workers are sorted into 22 occupations from the highest to the lowest wage as of May 2009. Management earns the highest wage, at \$49.47 an hour. The lowest is the \$10.04 an hour averaged by workers preparing and serving food. Wage differences across labor markets trace to differences in labor demand and in labor supply, as you will see. The previous chapter discussed the elements that influence the demand for resources and examined labor in particular. In brief, *a profit-maximizing firm hires labor up to the point where labor's marginal revenue product equals its marginal resource cost*—that is, where the last unit employed increases total revenue enough to cover the added cost. Because we have already discussed what affects the demand for labor—namely, labor's marginal revenue product—let's focus more on labor supply.

Differences in Training, Education, Age, and Experience

Some jobs pay more because they require a long and expensive training period, which reduces market supply because few are willing to incur the time and expense required. But such training increases labor productivity, thereby increasing demand for the skills. Reduced supply and increased demand both raise the market wage. For example,

EXHIBIT 3 Average Hourly Wage by Occupation in the United States

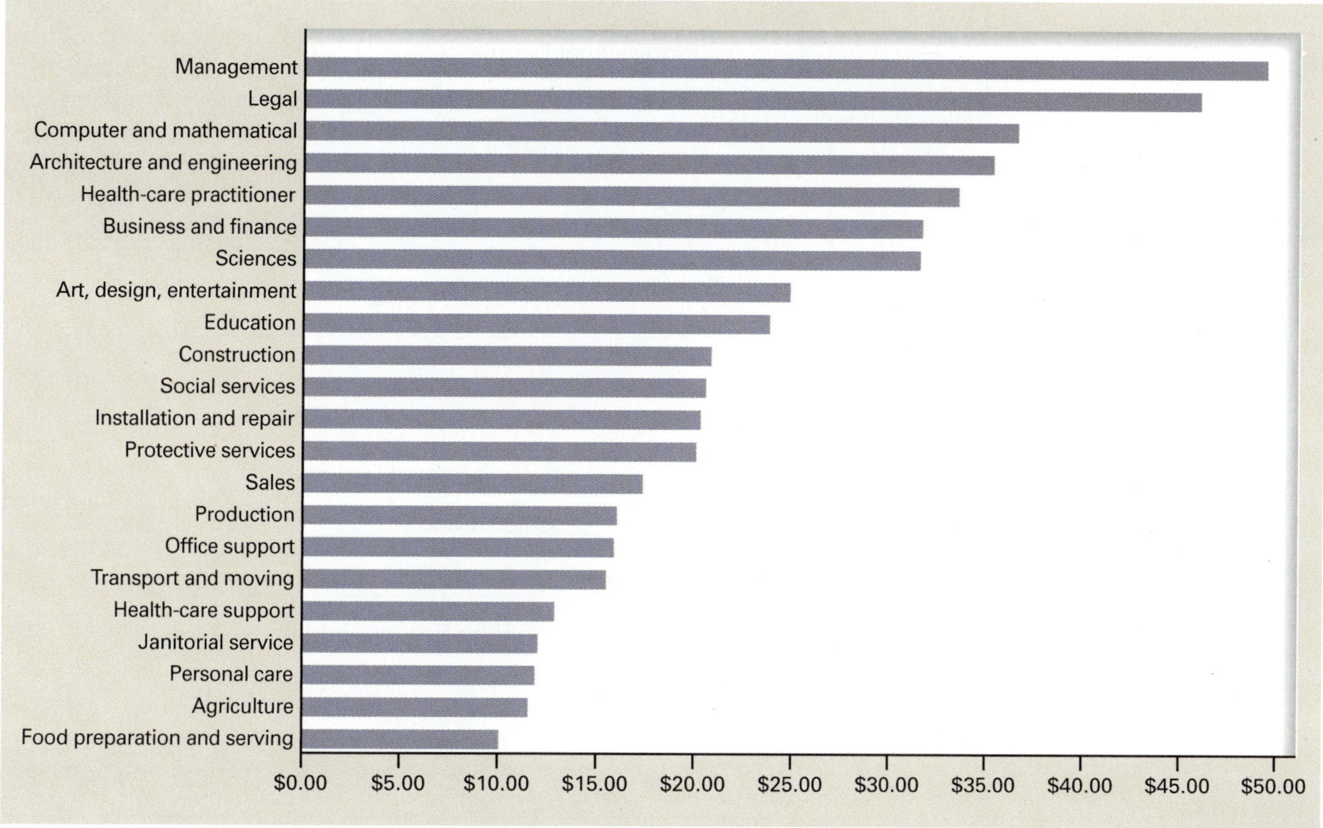

Source: Developed from "Occupational Employment and Wages, May 2009," Bureau of Labor Statistics, U.S. Department of Labor News Release, Table 1, 14 May 2010, also available at http://www.bls.gov/news.release/pdf/ocwage.pdf. Wages are as of May 2009.

certified public accountants (CPAs) earn more than file clerks because the extensive training of CPAs limits the supply to this field and because this training increases the productivity of CPAs compared to file clerks.

Exhibit 4 shows how education and experience affect earnings. Age groups are indicated on the horizontal axis and average annual earnings on the vertical axis. To standardize things, pay is for the highest level of education achieved. The relationship between income and education is clear. At every age, those with more education earn more. For example, among those ages 55–64, workers with professional degrees earned more than twice those with bachelor's degrees and more than five times those without high school diplomas.

Age itself also has an important effect on income. Earnings tend to increase as workers acquire job experience and get promoted. Among educated workers, experience pays more. For example, among those with professional degrees, workers in the 55–64 age group earned on average 70 percent more than those in the 25–34 age group. But among those without high school diplomas, workers in the 55–64 age group earned on average only 14 percent more than those in the 25–34 age group. Differences in earnings reflect the normal workings of resource markets, whereby workers are rewarded according to their marginal productivity.

EXHIBIT 4 Age, Education, and Pay

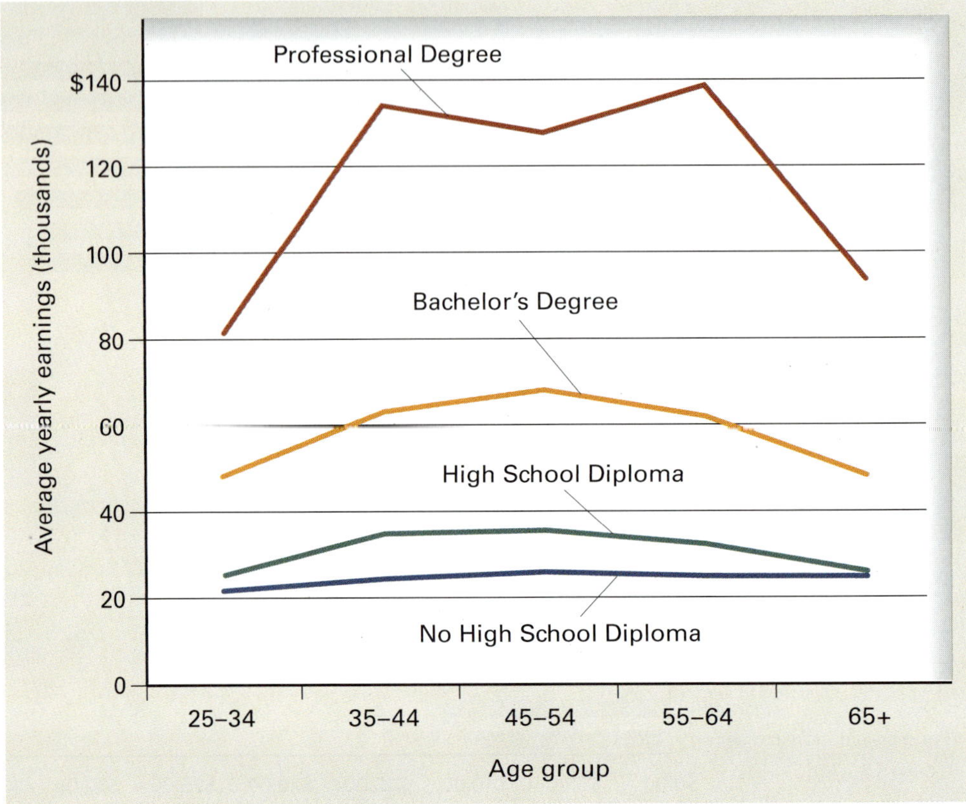

For every age group, workers with more education earn more. The premium paid for years of experience increases more for those with more education.

Source: U.S. Census Bureau. Figures are average earnings in 2008 based on the highest degree earned.

Differences in Ability

Because they are more able and more talented, some people earn more than others with the same training and education. For example, two lawyers may have identical educations, but earnings differ because of differences in underlying ability. Most executives have extensive training and business experience, but only a few get to run large corporations. In professional basketball, some players earn up to 50 times more than others. From lawyers to executives to professional athletes, pay differences reflect differing abilities and different marginal productivities. The case study, "World of Business: Winner-Take-All Labor Markets" at the end of the book, examines why the premium awarded greater marginal productivity has grown in recent decades.

Differences in Risk

Research indicates that jobs with a higher probability of injury or death, such as coal mining, usually pay more, other things constant. Russians working at the partially disabled nuclear power plant, Chernobyl, earned 10 times the national average, but workers there face continued health risk from radiation exposure. Sex workers in Mexico earn 23 percent more for unprotected sex.[3] Truck drivers for American contractors in Iraq earn over $100,000 a year, but the job is dangerous. Workers also earn more, other things constant, in seasonal jobs such as construction, where the risk of unemployment is greater.

Geographic Differences

People have a strong incentive to sell their resources in the market where they earn the most. For example, the National Basketball Association attracts talent from around the world. About 20 percent come from abroad. Likewise, thousands of foreign-trained physicians migrate to the United States each year for the high pay. The same goes for nurses (a nurse from the Philippines can earn six times more in the United States). The flow of labor is not all one way: Some Americans seek their fortune abroad, with American basketball players going to Europe and baseball players to Japan. Workers often face migration hurdles. Any reduction in these hurdles would reduce wage differentials across countries.

Discrimination

Sometimes wage differences stem from racial or gender discrimination in the job market. Although such discrimination is illegal, history shows that certain groups—including African Americans, Hispanics, and women—have systematically earned less than others of equal ability. This is discussed in a later chapter.

To Review: Wage differences trace to training, education, age, experience, ability, risk of injury, risk of job loss, geography, and racial and gender discrimination. Other things equal, members of organized labor earn more than nonmembers. The balance of this chapter discusses the effects of labor unions on labor markets.

Unions and Collective Bargaining

Few aspects of labor markets make news more than labor unions. Labor negotiations, strikes, picket lines, confrontations between workers and employers—all fit TV's "action news" format. Despite media attention, only about one in eight U.S. workers is a union member and nearly all union agreements are reached without a strike. But labor unions are more important than their current membership indicates. Let's examine the tools that unions use to seek higher pay and better benefits for their members.

Types of Unions

A **labor union** is a group of workers who join together to improve their terms of employment. Labor unions in the United States date back to the early days of national independence, when workers in a particular craft—such as carpenters, shoemakers, or printers—formed a local group to seek higher wages and better working conditions. A **craft union** is limited to workers with a particular skill, or craft. Each craft union kept its individual identity but combined forces with other craft unions to form a national organization in 1886, the *American Federation of Labor* (*AFL*). The Clayton Act of 1914 exempted labor unions from antitrust laws, meaning that *unions at competing companies could legally join forces*. Unions were also tax exempt. Membership jumped

labor union
A group of workers who organize to improve their terms of employment

craft union
A union whose members have a particular skill or work at a particular craft, such as plumbers or carpenters

3. See Paul Gertler et al., "Risky Business: The Market for Unprotected Commercial Sex," *Journal of Political Economy*, 113 (June 2005): 518–550.

during World War I but fell by half between 1920 and 1933, as the government retreated from its support of union efforts.

The *Congress of Industrial Organizations* (*CIO*) was formed in 1935 to serve as a national organization of unions in mass-production industries, such as autos or steel. Whereas the AFL organized workers in particular crafts, such as plumbers or carpenters, the CIO consisted of unions whose membership embraced all workers in a particular industry. These **industrial unions** included unskilled, semiskilled, and skilled workers in an industry, such as all autoworkers or all steelworkers.

industrial union
A union consisting of both skilled and unskilled workers from a particular industry, such as all autoworkers or all steelworkers

collective bargaining
The process by which union and management negotiate a labor agreement

mediator
An impartial observer who helps resolve differences between union and management

binding arbitration
Negotiation in which union and management must accept an impartial observer's resolution of a dispute

strike
A union's attempt to withhold labor from a firm to halt production

Collective Bargaining, Mediation, and Arbitration

Collective bargaining is the process by which representatives of union and management negotiate a mutually agreeable contract specifying wages, employee benefits, and working conditions. A tentative agreement, once reached, goes to the membership for a vote. If accepted by the membership, the agreement holds for the years of the contract. If the agreement is rejected, the union can return to the bargaining table to continue negotiations. If negotiations reach an impasse and the public interest is involved, government officials may ask an independent mediator to step in. A **mediator** is an impartial observer who listens to each side separately and then suggests a resolution. If each side still remains open to a settlement, the mediator brings them together to work out a contract, but the mediator has no power to impose a settlement. In certain critical sectors, such as police and fire protection, where a strike could harm the public interest, differences are sometimes settled through **binding arbitration.** A neutral third party evaluates each position and issues a ruling that both sides must accept. Some disputes skip the mediation and arbitration steps and go directly from impasse to strike.

The Strike

A major source of union power is a **strike,** which is a union's attempt to withhold labor to stop production, thereby hoping to force the firm into accepting the union's position. But strikes are also risky for workers, who earn no pay or benefits during the strike and could lose their jobs. Union funds and, in some states, unemployment benefits, may aid strikers some, but incomes still fall substantially. *Although neither party usually wants a strike, both sides, rather than concede on key points, usually act as if they could endure one.* Unions usually picket to prevent or discourage so-called strikebreakers, or "scabs," from crossing the picket lines to work. But the targeted firm, by hiring temporary workers and nonstriking union workers, can sometimes continue production.

Some industries are more vulnerable to strikes—industries that deal in perishable goods, such as strawberries, and industries where picket lines can turn away lots of customers, such as Broadway theaters. But in other industries, advances in technology have reduced the effectiveness of strikes, as petroleum and chemical workers learned when strikers found that skeleton crews of supervisors could run computer-controlled refineries for a long time.

Union Wages and Employment

Samuel Gompers, the AFL's founder and long-time head, was once asked what unions want. "More!" he roared. Union members, like everyone else, have unlimited wants. But because resources are scarce, choices must be made. A menu of union desires includes higher wages, more benefits, greater job security, better working conditions, and so on. To keep the analysis manageable, let's focus on a single objective, higher wages, and consider three ways unions might increase wages: (1) by forming an inclusive, or industrial, union; (2) by forming an exclusive, or craft, union; and (3) by increasing the demand for union labor.

Inclusive, or Industrial, Unions: Negotiating a Higher Industry Wage

The market demand and supply curves for a particular type of labor are labeled *D* and *S* in panel (a) of Exhibit 5. In the absence of a union, the market wage is *W* and industry employment is *E*. At the market wage, each firm faces a horizontal, or perfectly elastic, supply of labor, as depicted by *s* in panel (b) of Exhibit 5. Thus, each firm can hire as much labor as it wants at the market wage of *W*. The firm hires workers up to the point where labor's marginal revenue product equals its marginal resource cost, resulting in *e* units of labor in panel (b). As we saw earlier, in equilibrium, labor is paid a wage just equal to its marginal revenue product.

With the *inclusive, or industrial,* approach, the union tries to negotiate industry-wide wages for each class of labor. Suppose the union negotiates a wage above the market-clearing level. Specifically, suppose the negotiated wage is *W′* in panel (a), meaning that no labor is supplied at a lower wage. In effect, the market supply of labor is perfectly elastic at the union wage out to point *a*. To the right of point *a*, however, the wage floor no longer applies; *aS* becomes the relevant portion of the labor supply curve. For an industry facing a wage floor of *W′*, the entire labor supply curve becomes *W′aS*, which has a kink where the wage floor joins the upward-sloping portion of the original labor supply curve.

EXHIBIT 5 Effects of Labor Union's Wage Floor

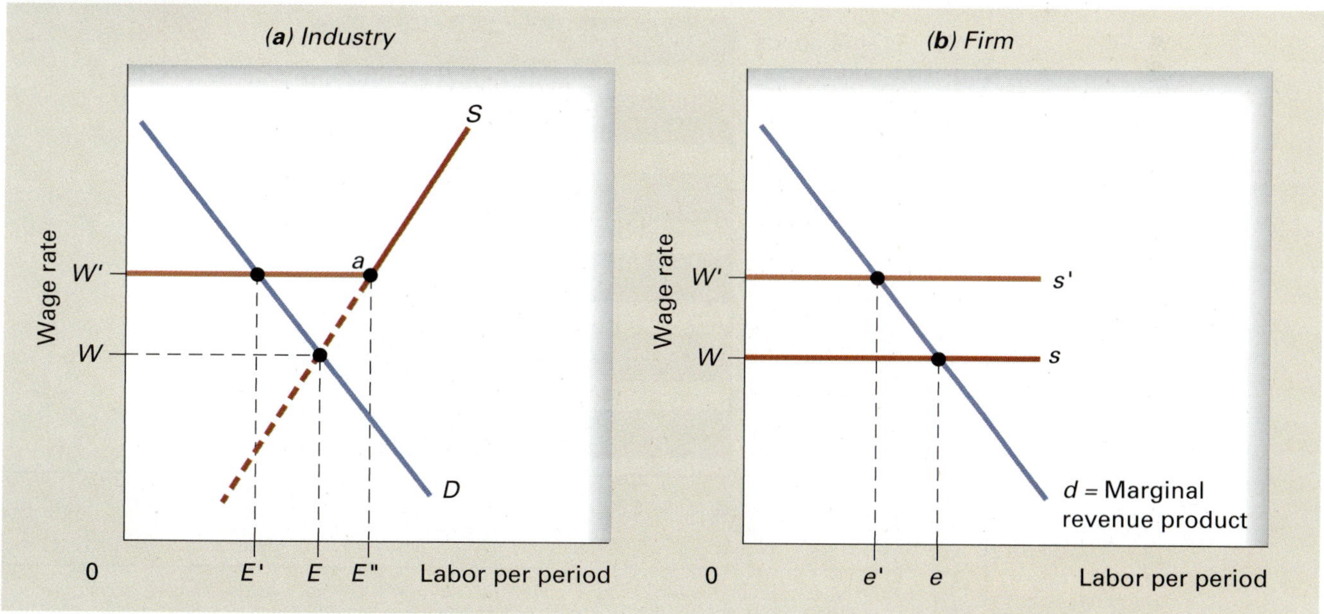

Without a labor union, the market wage is *W* in panel (a). At that wage, each firm can hire as much labor as it wants. The individual firm in panel (b) hires more labor until the marginal revenue product equals the market wage, *W*. Each firm hires *e* units of labor, and industry employment is *E*. If a union negotiates a wage *W′*, which is above the market wage *W*, the supply curve facing the firm shifts up from *s* to *s′*. Each firm hires less labor, *e′*, so industry employment falls to *E′*. At the union wage there is now an excess quantity of labor supplied equal to *E″–E′*.

Once this wage floor is negotiated for the industry, each firm in the industry faces a horizontal supply curve of labor at the collectively bargained wage, W'. Because the union wage is higher than the market-clearing wage, each firm hires less labor. Consequently, the higher wage leads to a reduction in employment; the quantity of labor demanded by the industry drops from E to E' in panel (a). At wage W' workers in the industry would like to supply, E'', which exceeds the quantity of labor demanded, E'. Ordinarily this excess quantity supplied would force the wage down. But because union members agree *collectively* to the union wage, individual workers can't work for less, nor can employers hire them for less. *With the inclusive, or industrial, union, which negotiates with the entire industry, the wage is higher and employment lower than they would be in the absence of a union.*

The union must somehow ration the limited jobs available, such as by awarding them based on worker seniority, personal connections within the union, or lottery. Those who can't find union jobs must turn to the nonunion sector. *This increases the supply of labor in the nonunion sector, which drives down the nonunion wage.* So wages are relatively higher in the union sector first, because unions bargain for a wage that exceeds the market-clearing wage, and second, because those unable to find union jobs crowd into the nonunion sector. Studies show that union wages average about 15 percent above the wages of similarly qualified nonunion workers. Exhibit 6 compares median

EXHIBIT 6 **Median Weekly Earnings Are Higher for Union Than Nonunion Workers**

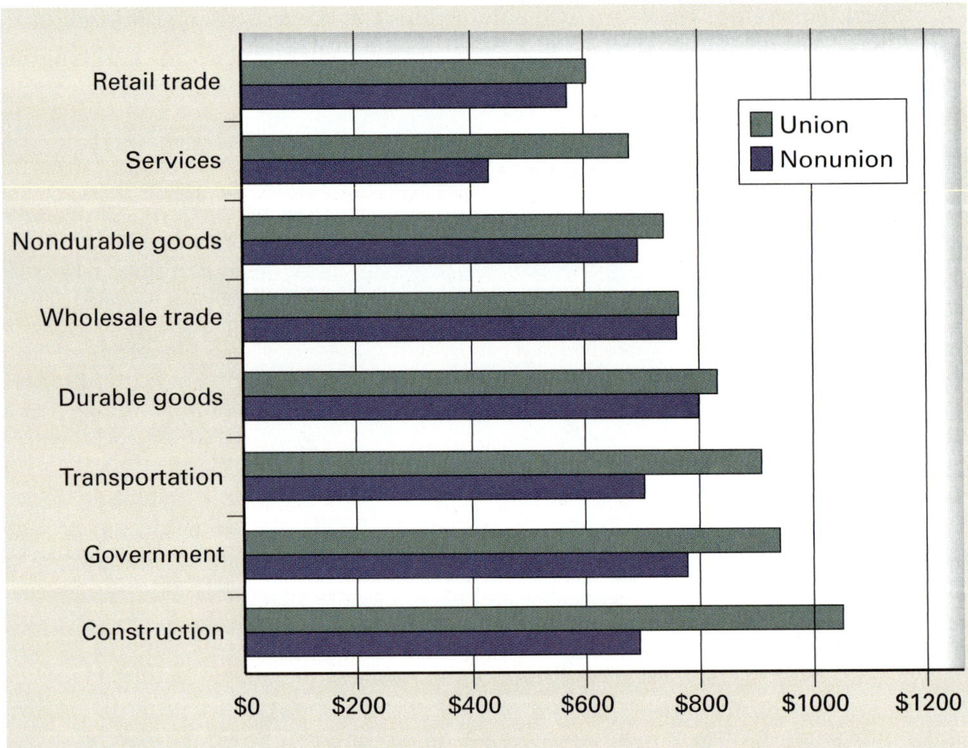

Unions are more successful at raising wages in less competitive markets, such as government, transportation, and construction. In more competitive markets, such as retail trade, employers cannot easily pass along higher union wages as higher product prices. Nonunion firms can enter the industry, pay workers market wages, which are below union wages, and attract customers by selling the product for less.

Source: U.S. Bureau of Labor Statistics, "Union Members," 22 January 2010, Table 4, at http://www.bls.gov/news.release/union2.t04.htm. Figures are for full-time workers in 2009.

weekly earnings of union and nonunion workers. Note that unions are less successful at raising wages in more competitive sectors. For example, unions have less impact on manufacturing and retail trade, where product markets tend to be competitive. Unions have greater success in services, government, transportation, and construction—sectors that tend to be less competitive. When there is more competition in the product market, employers cannot easily pass along higher union wages as higher product prices. New, nonunion, firms can enter the industry, pay market wages, and sell the product for less.

Exclusive, or Craft, Unions: Reducing Labor Supply

One way to increase wages while avoiding an excess quantity of labor supplied is to somehow reduce the supply of labor, shown in Exhibit 7 as a leftward shift of the labor supply curve in panel (a). This supply reduction increases the wage and reduces employment. Successful supply restrictions of this type require that the union first limit its membership and second force all employers in the industry to hire only union members. The union can restrict membership with higher initiation fees, longer apprenticeship periods, tougher qualification exams, more restrictive licensing requirements, and so on. But even if unions restrict membership, they still have difficulty unionizing all firms in the industry.

Whereas wage setting is more typical of industrial unions, such as autos or steel, restricting supply is more typical of craft unions, such as unions of carpenters, plumbers, or bricklayers. Professional groups—doctors, lawyers, and accountants, for instance—also impose entry restrictions through education, examination, and licensing requirements. These restrictions, usually defended as protecting the public, are often little more than self-serving attempts to increase wages by restricting labor supply.

EXHIBIT 7 Effect of Reducing Labor Supply or Increasing Labor Demand

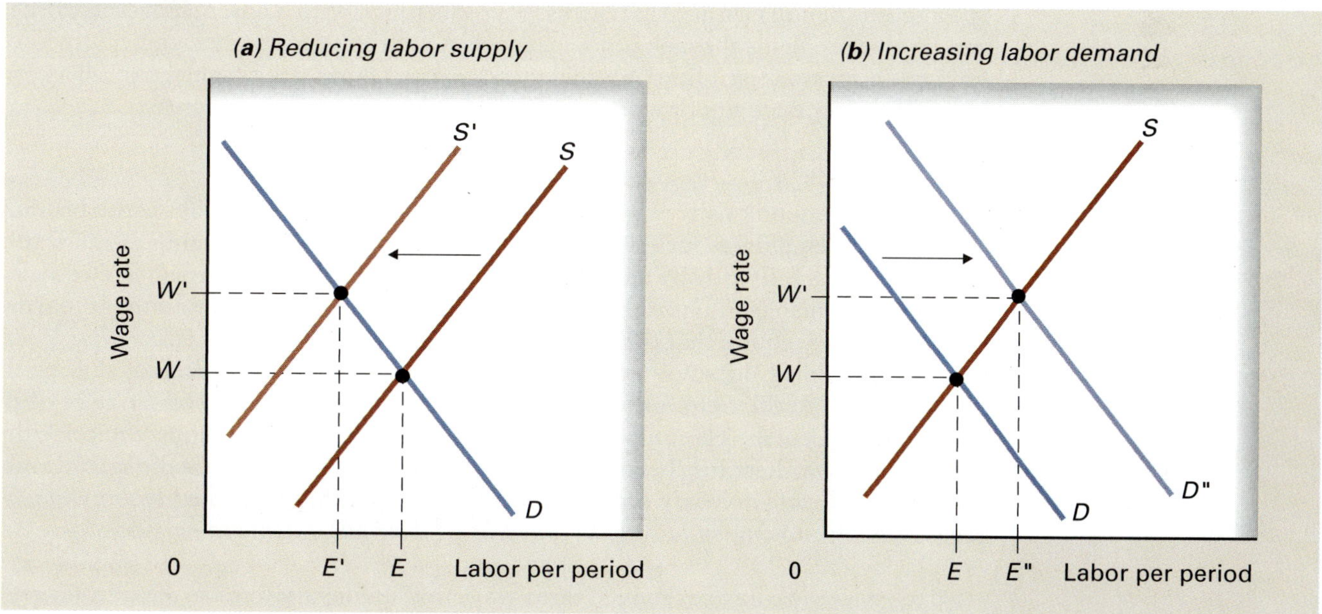

If a union can successfully restrict labor supply in an industry, the supply curve shifts to the left from S to S', as in panel (a). The wage rises from W to W', but at the cost of reducing employment from E to E'. If a union can increase the demand for union labor, as in panel (b), the demand curve shifts right from D to D'', raising the wage and increasing employment.

Increasing Demand for Union Labor

A third way to increase wages is to increase the demand for union labor by somehow shifting the labor demand curve outward as from D to D'' in panel (b) of Exhibit 7. This is an attractive alternative *because it increases both the wage and employment*, so there is no need to restrict labor supply or to ration jobs among union members. Here are some ways unions try to increase the demand for union labor.

Increase Demand for Union-Made Goods

The demand for union labor may be increased through a direct appeal to consumers to buy only union-made products. Because the demand for labor is a derived demand, increasing the demand for union-made products increases the demand for union labor.

Restrict Supply of Nonunion-Made Goods

Another way to increase the demand for union labor is to restrict the supply of products that compete with union-made products. This approach also relies on the derived nature of labor demand. The United Auto Workers, for example, has supported restrictions on imported cars. Fewer imported cars means greater demand for cars produced by U.S. workers, who are mostly union members. This strategy became less effective when foreign automakers, such as Toyota, established nonunion plants in the United States.

Increase Productivity of Union Labor

Some observers claim union representation improves labor-management relations. According to this theory, unions increase worker productivity by minimizing conflicts, resolving differences, and at times even straightening out workers who goof off. In the absence of a union, a dissatisfied worker may simply quit, increasing job turnover. Turnover is costly to the firm because the departing worker leaves with company-specific, on-the-job training that increases productivity. With a union, however, workers can resolve problems through union channels. Quit rates are in fact significantly lower among union workers (although this could also be due to the higher pay). If unions increase the productivity of workers, the demand for union labor increases.

Featherbedding

featherbedding
Union efforts to force employers to hire more workers than demanded at a particular wage

Yet another way unions try to increase jobs for union members is by **featherbedding,** which makes employers hire more labor than they demand. For example, union rules require that each Broadway theater have a permanent "house" carpenter, electrician, and property manager. Once the play opens, these workers show up only on payday. The union may require that the box office be staffed by three people.

Featherbedding does not create an increase in demand, in the sense of shifting the demand curve to the right. Instead, it forces an employer to a point to the right of the labor demand curve. The union tries to limit a firm to an all-or-none choice: Either hire so many workers for the job, or we'll strike. Thus, with featherbedding, *the union attempts to dictate not only the wage but also the quantity that must be hired at that wage, thereby moving employers to the right of their labor demand curve.*

To Review: We have examined three ways that unions try to raise members' wages: (1) by negotiating a wage floor above the equilibrium wage for the industry then somehow rationing the limited jobs among union members, (2) by restricting the supply of labor, and (3) by increasing the demand for union labor. Unions try to increase the demand for union labor in four ways: (1) through a direct public appeal to buy only union-made products, (2) by restricting the supply of products made by nonunion labor, (3) by reducing labor turnover and thereby increasing labor's marginal productivity, and (4) through featherbedding, which forces employers to hire more union workers than they want or need.

Trends in Union Membership

In 1955, about 35 percent of U.S. workers belonged to unions. Since then, union membership as a fraction of the workforce has declined steadily. By 2009, only 12 percent of U.S. workers belonged to unions, about the same rate as in 1900. Government workers are much more unionized than other workers—37 percent of government workers are unionized versus just 7 percent of private sector workers; most union members are now government workers. A typical union member is a schoolteacher. Compared with other industrialized countries, the United States ranks relatively low in the extent of unionization, though rates abroad have been declining as well.

The bar graph in Exhibit 8 indicates U.S. union membership rates by age and gender in 2009. The rates for men, shown by the green bars, are higher than the rates for women, in part because women work more in the service sector, where union membership is

EXHIBIT 8 Unionization Rates by Age and Gender

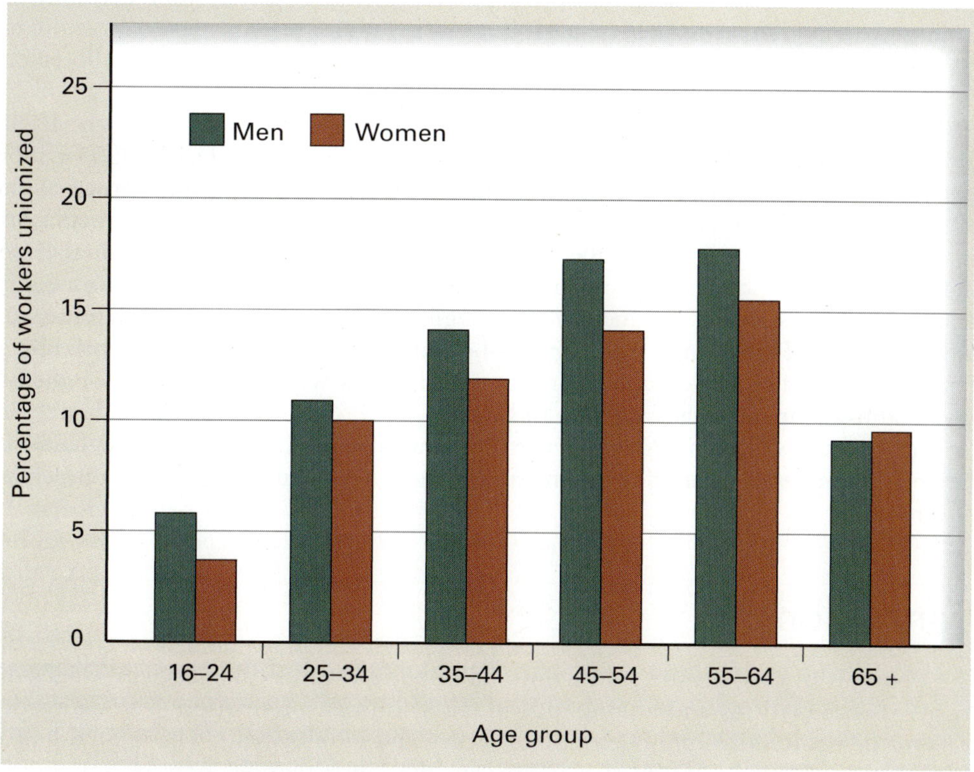

Unionization rates for men, shown by the green bars, are higher than the rates for women, in part because men work more in manufacturing and women work more in the service sector, where union membership is lower. The highest membership rates are for middle-aged men.

Source: U.S. Bureau of Labor Statistics, "Union Members," 22 January 2010, Table 1, at http://www.bls.gov/news.release/union2.t01.htm. Figures show union membership in 2009 as a percentage of all U.S. wage and salary workers.

right-to-work states
States where workers in unionized companies do not have to join the union or pay union dues

lower. The highest membership rates are for middle-aged males. Although the exhibit does not show it, black workers have a higher union membership rate than white workers (14 percent vs. 12 percent), in part because African Americans are employed more by government and by heavy industries such as autos and steel, where union representation is higher. Union membership is below average among Asians and those of Hispanic origin (10 percent each).

Union membership rates also vary across states. New York had the highest unionization rate at 25 percent and North Carolina, the lowest at 3 percent. Unionization rates in right-to-work states average only half the rates in other states. In **right-to-work states,** workers in unionized companies do not have to join the union or pay union dues. Over the years, the number of right-to-work states has increased and this has hurt the union movement.

The decline in union membership rates is also due to structural changes in the U.S. economy. Unions have long been more important in the industrial sector than in the service sector. But employment in the industrial sector, which includes manufacturing, mining, and construction, has declined in recent decades as a share of all jobs. What's more, union jobs are a dwindling share of jobs in the industrial sector. For example, in the last three decades, U.S. manufacturing jobs have declined from 20 million to 16 million. But the union share of those jobs dropped from 8 million to only 2 million. Nonunion jobs in manufacturing increased.

Another factor in the decline of the union movement is a growth in market competition, particularly from imports. Increased competition from nonunion employers, both foreign and domestic, has reduced the ability of unionized firms to pass on higher labor costs as higher prices. And fewer union members mean fewer voters who belong to unions, so unions have lost political clout.

Finally, the near disappearance of the strike has cut union power. During the 1970s, an average of about 300 strikes a year in the United States involved 1,000 or more workers. Since 2000, there were only about 20 such strikes a year on average. Worse still for organized labor, many recent strikes have ended badly for union workers; companies such as Caterpillar, Continental Airlines, Hormel Foods, International Paper, and Phelps Dodge Copper hired replacement workers. Union members are now less inclined to strike because of the increased willingness of employers to hire strikebreakers and the increased willingness of workers—both union and nonunion—to work during a strike. Strikes also cut company profits, which hurts workers whose pay is tied to profits, thus dampening the incentive to strike.

The case study, "Public Policy: Federal Bailout of GM, Chrysler, and the UAW" at the end of the book, examines the impact of the United Auto Workers on American automakers.

Conclusion

The first half of this chapter focused on labor supply and explained why wages differ across occupations and among individuals within an occupation. The interaction of labor demand and supply determines wages and employment. The second half of the chapter explored the effect of unions on the labor market. At one time unions dominated some key industries. But as global competition intensifies, employers have a harder time passing higher union labor costs along to consumers. Both in the United States and in other industrial economies, union members represent a dwindling segment of the labor force. Now only 7 percent of private sector workers are union members.

Summary

1. The labor demand curve shows the relationship between the wage and the quantity of labor that producers are willing and able to hire, other things constant. The labor supply curve shows the relationship between the wage and the quantity of labor that workers are willing and able to supply, other things constant. The intersection of labor demand and labor supply determines the market wage and market employment.
2. People allocate their time to maximize utility. There are three uses of time: market work, nonmarket work, and leisure. A person attempts to maximize utility by allocating time so that the expected marginal utility of the last unit of time spent in each activity is identical.
3. The higher the wage, other things constant, the more goods and services can be purchased with that wage, so a higher wage encourages people to substitute market work for other uses of their time. But a higher wage also increases income for a given amount of work, increasing the demand for all normal goods, including leisure. The net effect of a higher wage on the quantity of labor supplied depends on both the substitution effect and the income effect.
4. The supply of labor depends on factors other than the wage, including (a) other sources of income, (b) job amenities, (c) the value of job experience, and (d) worker tastes.
5. Market wages differ because of (a) differences in training and education; (b) differences in the skill and ability of workers; (c) risk differences, both in terms of the workers' safety and the chances of getting laid off; (d) geographic differences; (e) racial and gender discrimination; and (f) union membership.
6. Labor unions and employers try to negotiate a labor contract through collective bargaining. A major source of union power has been the threat of a strike, which is an attempt to withhold labor from the firm.
7. Inclusive, or industrial, unions attempt to establish a wage floor that exceeds the competitive, or market-clearing, wage. A union wage above the market-clearing level creates an excess quantity of labor supplied, so the union must somehow ration the limited jobs available among its members. Exclusive, or craft, unions try to raise union wages by restricting the supply of labor. Another way to raise union wages is to increase the demand for union labor.
8. Union membership as a percentage of the labor force has been falling for half a century. Reasons for the decline include right-to-work laws, growing global competition, a shift in employment from goods to services, a greater willingness to hire replacements for striking workers, a greater willingness of union members and others to work during strikes, and less political support for the labor movement.

Key Concepts

Market work 240
Nonmarket work 240
Leisure 240
Substitution effect of a wage increase 243
Income effect of a wage increase 243
Backward-bending supply curve of labor 243
Labor union 249
Craft union 249
Industrial union 250
Collective bargaining 250
Mediator 250
Binding arbitration 250
Strike 250
Featherbedding 254
Right-to-work states 256

Questions for Review

1. Uses of Time Describe the three possible uses of an individual's time, and give an example of each.
2. Work and Utility Explain the concept of the "net utility of work." How is it useful in developing the labor supply curve?
3. Utility Maximization How does a rational consumer allocate time among competing uses?
4. Substitution and Income Effects Suppose that the substitution effect of an increase in the wage rate exactly offsets the income effect as the hourly wage increases from $12 to $13. What would the supply of labor curve look like over this range of wages? Why?
5. Substitution and Income Effects Suppose that the cost of living increases, thereby reducing the purchasing power of your income. If your money wage doesn't increase, you may work *more* hours because of this cost-of-living increase. Is this response predominantly an income effect or a substitution effect? Explain.
6. Nonwage Determinants of Labor Supply Suppose that two jobs are exactly the same except that one is performed in an air-conditioned workplace. How could you measure the value workers attach to such a job amenity?
7. Why Wages Differ Why might permanent wage differences occur between different markets for labor or within the same labor market?

8. Case Study: Winner-Take-All Labor Markets (See page 725.) What characterizes a winner-take-all labor market? Offer some reasons why corporate heads now earn relatively more than they did in 1980.

9. MEDIATION AND ARBITRATION Distinguish between mediation and binding arbitration. Under what circumstances do firms and unions use these tools? What is the role of a strike in the bargaining process?

10. THE STRIKE Why might firms in industries with high fixed costs be inclined to prevent strikes or end strikes quickly?

11. INDUSTRIAL UNIONS Why are unions more effective at raising wages in oligopolistic industries than in competitive industries?

12. CRAFT UNIONS Both industrial unions and craft unions attempt to raise their members' wages, but each goes about it differently. Explain the difference in approaches and describe the impact these differences have on excess quantity of labor supplied.

13. Case Study: Federal Bailout of GM, Chrysler, and the UAW (See page 726.) How would the UAW benefit for increased demand for GM and Chrysler vehicles?

Problems and Exercises

14. MARKET SUPPLY OF LABOR The following table shows the hours per week supplied to a particular market by three individuals at various wage rates. Calculate the total hours per week (Q_T) supplied to the market.

Hourly Wage	Hours per Week			
	Q_1	Q_2	Q_3	Q_T
$15	20	0	0	___
16	25	0	0	___
17	35	10	0	___
18	45	25	10	___
19	42	40	30	___
20	38	37	45	___

Which individuals, if any, have backward-bending supply curves in the wage range shown? Does the market supply curve bend backward in the wage range shown in the table?

15. INDUSTRIAL UNIONS Review the logic underlying Exhibit 5. Then determine the effect, on the industry and a typical firm, of an increase in the demand for industry output. Show your conclusions on a graph. Does the magnitude of the increase in demand make a difference?

Global Economic Watch Exercises

Login to www.cengagebrain.com and access the Global Economic Watch to do these exercises.

16. GLOBAL ECONOMIC WATCH Go to the Global Economic Crisis Resource Center. Select Global Issues in Context. In the Basic Search box at the top of the page, enter the phrase "nonmarket work." On the Results page, go to the News Section. Click on the link for the January 7, 2008, article "Research on Marriage and Family Described by Scientists at University of California." According to the article, what are some differences between work by boys and girls in Indonesia?

17. GLOBAL ECONOMIC WATCH Go to the Global Economic Crisis Resource Center. Select Global Issues in Context. In the Basic Search box at the top of the page, enter the term "union strike." Find a website with a date within the two most recent years. Analyze the union situation described.

Capital, Interest, Entrepreneurship, and Corporate Finance

13

AP Photo/Paul Sakuma

- Why is a movie rental or download only half the price of a movie ticket?
- Why do you burn your mouth eating pizza?
- What's seed money and why can't Farmer Jones grow a thing without it?
- What's the harm in pirated software, music, and DVDs?
- Why are state lottery jackpots worth much less than the advertised millions?
- Who is and is not an entrepreneur?

These and other questions are answered in this chapter, which examines how businesses get started and how they are financed.

So far, our discussion of resources has focused primarily on labor markets. This emphasis is appropriate because labor generates most income—more than two-thirds of the total. The rewards to labor, however, depend in part on the amount and quality of the other resources employed, particularly capital. A farmer plowing a field with a tractor is more productive than one scraping the soil with a stick. This chapter first looks at the role of capital in production—its cost and its expected return. Secondly, we consider the role the entrepreneur plays in driving the economy forward. Finally, we explore the sources of corporate finance.

Topics include:

- Production, saving, and time
- Consumption, saving, and time
- Optimal investment
- Loanable funds market
- Present value and discounting
- Role of the entrepreneur
- Corporate finance
- Stocks, bonds, and retained earnings

The Role of Time in Production and Consumption

Time is important in both production and consumption. In this section, we first consider the role of time in the production decision, then show why firms borrow household savings. Next, we consider the role of time in the consumption decision and show why households are rewarded to save, or to defer consumption. By bringing together borrowers and savers, we find the market interest rate.

Production, Saving, and Time

Suppose Jones is a primitive farmer in a simple economy. Isolated from any neighbors or markets, he literally scratches out a living on a plot of land, using only some crude sticks. While his crop is growing, none of it is available for current consumption. Because production takes time, to survive, Jones must rely on food saved from prior harvests. The longer the growing season, the more he must save. Thus, even in this simple example, it is clear that *production cannot occur without savings*.

With his current resources, consisting of land, labor, seed corn, fertilizer, and some crude sticks, Jones grows about 100 bushels of corn a year. He soon realizes that if he had a plow—a type of investment good, or capital—his productivity would increase. Making a plow in such a primitive setting, however, is time consuming and would keep him away from his fields for a year. Thus, the plow has an opportunity cost of 100 bushels of corn. He could not survive this drop in production without enough saved from previous harvests.

The question is: Should he invest his time in the plow? The answer depends on the cost and benefit of the plow. We already know that the plow's opportunity cost is 100 bushels—the forgone output. The benefit depends on how much the plow increases crop production and how long it lasts. Jones figures that the plow would boost annual yield by 50 bushels and would last his lifetime. In making the investment decision, he compares the current cost to the future benefit. Suppose he decides that adding 50 bushels a year outweighs the one-time cost of 100 bushels to make the plow.

In making the plow, Jones engages in *roundabout production.* Rather than working the soil with his crude sticks, he produces capital to increase his productivity. More roundabout production in an economy means more capital, so more goods can be produced in the future. Advanced industrial economies are characterized by much roundabout production and thus abundant capital accumulation.

You can see why production cannot occur without savings. *Production requires savings because both direct and roundabout production take time—time during which goods and services are not available from current production.* Now let's modernize the example by introducing the ability to borrow. Many farmers visit the bank each spring to borrow enough "seed money" to get by until the harvest. Likewise, other businesses often borrow at least a portion of the start-up funds needed to get going. Thus, in a modern economy, producers need not rely just on their own savings. Banks and other financial institutions serve as *intermediaries* between savers and borrowers. Financial markets for stocks and bonds also help channel savings to producers.

Let's take a look at the incentive to save.

Consumption, Saving, and Time

Did you ever burn the roof of your mouth eating a slice of pizza? Have you done this more than once? Why do you persist in such self-mutilation? You persist because that bite of pizza is worth more to you now than the same bite a minute from now. In fact, you are willing to risk burning your mouth rather than wait until the pizza has lost its destructive properties. In a small way, this reflects the fact that you and other consumers value *present* consumption more than *future* consumption. Not pie in the sky; pie now. You and other consumers are said to have a **positive rate of time preference.**

positive rate of time preference
Consumers value present consumption more than future consumption

Because you value present consumption more than future consumption, you are willing to pay more to consume now rather than wait. And prices often reflect this greater willingness to pay. Consider the movies. You pay about twice as much for a movie ticket than to rent the DVD or download it three months later. The same is true for books. By waiting for the paperback, you can save more than half the hardback price. Photo developers, dry cleaners, fast-food restaurants, furniture stores promising same-day delivery, cable news networks, and other suppliers tout the speed of their services, knowing that consumers prefer earlier availability. Thus, *impatience* is one explanation for a positive rate of time preference. Another is *uncertainty*. If you wait, something might prevent you from consuming the good. A T-shirt slogan captures this point best: "Life is uncertain. Eat dessert first."

Because people value present consumption more than future consumption, they must be rewarded to postpone consumption—to delay gratification. By saving a portion of their incomes in financial institutions such as banks, people forgo present consumption for a greater ability to consume in the future. Interest is the reward for postponing consumption. The **interest rate** is the annual reward for saving as a percentage of the amount saved. For example, if the interest rate is 5 percent, the reward, or interest, is $5 per year for each $100 saved. The higher the interest rate, other things constant, the more consumers are rewarded for saving, so the more they save. You will learn more about this later in the chapter.

interest rate
Interest per year as a percentage of the amount saved or borrowed

Optimal Investment

In a market economy characterized by specialization and exchange, Farmer Jones no longer needs to produce his own capital, nor need he rely on his own savings. He can purchase capital with borrowed funds. More generally, firms invest now in the expectation of a future return. Because the return is in the future, a would-be investor must estimate how much a particular investment will yield this year, next year, the year after, and in all years during the productive life of the investment. *Firms buy new capital goods only if they expect this investment to yield a higher return than other possible uses of their funds.*

To understand the investment decision in a modern economy, let's switch from the farm to a golf course to consider another simple example. The operators of the Hacker Haven Golf Course are thinking about buying some solar-powered golf carts. The model under consideration, called the Weekend Warrior, sells for $5,000, requires no maintenance or operating expenses, and is expected to last indefinitely. *The expected rate of return of each cart equals the expected annual earnings divided by the cart's purchase price.* More generally, the **expected rate of return on capital** is the expected annual earnings divided by capital's purchase price. The first cart is expected to generate rental income of $1,000 per year. This income, divided by the cost of the cart, yields an expected rate of return on the investment of $1,000/$5,000, or 20 percent per year. Additional carts will be used less. A second is expected to generate $750 per year in rental income, yielding a rate of return of $750/$5,000, or 15 percent; a third cart, $500 per year, or 10 percent; and a fourth cart, $250 per year, or 5 percent. They don't expect a fifth cart to get rented at all, so it has a zero expected rate of return.

expected rate of return on capital
The expected annual earnings divided by capital's purchase price

Should the operators of Hacker Haven invest in golf carts, and if so, how many? Suppose they plan to borrow the money to buy the carts. The number of carts they purchase depends on the interest rate they must pay for borrowing. If the market interest rate exceeds 20 percent, the cost of borrowing would exceed the expected rate of return for even the first cart, so the club would buy no carts. What if the operators have enough cash on hand to buy the carts? Suppose the market interest rate also reflects what club owners could earn on savings. If the interest rate earned on savings exceeded 20 percent, course owners would earn more saving their money than buying golf carts. *The market interest rate is the opportunity cost of investing in capital.*

What if the market rate is 8 percent per year? At that rate, the first three carts, all with expected returns exceeding 8 percent, would each yield more than the market rate. A fourth cart would lose money, because its expected rate of return is only 5 percent. Exhibit 1 measures the interest rate along the vertical axis and the amount invested in golf carts along the horizontal axis. The step-like relationship shows the expected rate of return earned on additional dollars invested in golf carts. This relationship also indicates the amount invested in golf carts at each interest rate, so you can view this step-like relationship as Hacker Haven's demand curve for this type of investment. For example, the first cart costs $5,000 and earns a rate of return of 20 percent. A firm should reject any investment with an expected rate of return that falls below the market rate of interest.

The horizontal line at 8 percent indicates the market interest rate, which is Hacker Haven's opportunity cost of investing. The course operators' objective is to choose an investment strategy that maximizes profit. Profit is maximized when $15,000 is invested in the carts—that is, when three carts are purchased. The expected return from a fourth cart is 5 percent, which is below the opportunity cost of funds. Therefore, investing in four or more carts would reduce total profit.

EXHIBIT 1 Expected Rate of Return on Golf Carts and the Opportunity Cost of Funds

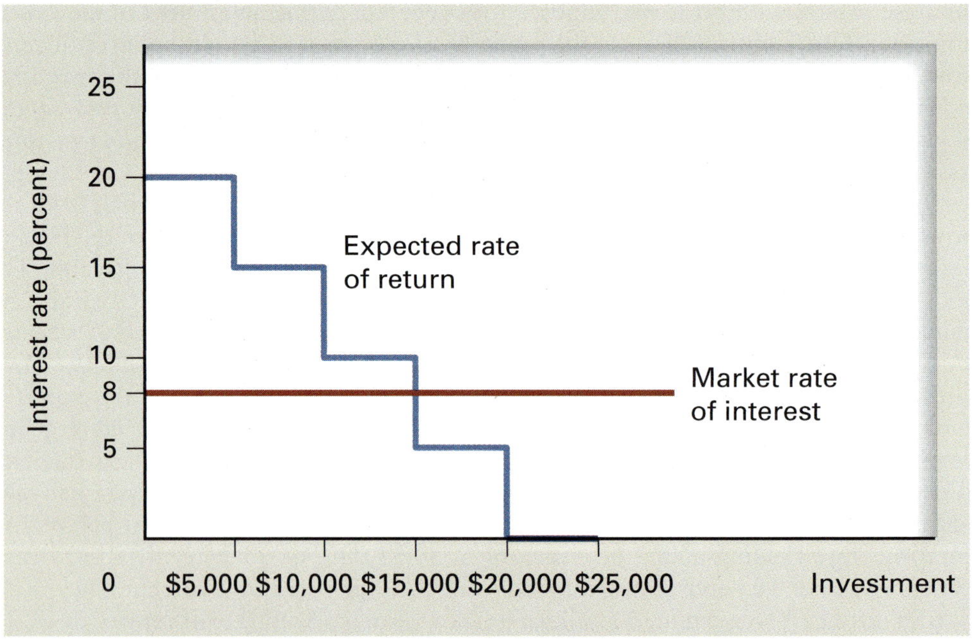

An individual firm invests in any project with an expected rate of return that exceeds the market interest rate. At an interest rate of 8 percent, Hacker Haven invests $15,000 in three golf carts.

So far, we have looked at the investment decision for a single golf course, but there are over 16,000 golf courses in the United States. The industry demand for golf carts shows the relationship between the amount all courses invest and the expected rate of return. Like the step-like relationship in Exhibit 1, the investment demand curve for the golf industry slopes downward. The lower the market rate of interest, the more invested in golf carts.

Let's move beyond golf carts and consider the investment decisions of all industries: publishing, software, farming, fast food, sporting goods, and thousands more. Individual industries have downward-sloping demand curves for investment. More is invested when the opportunity cost of borrowing is lower, other things constant. A downward-sloping investment demand curve for the entire economy can be derived, with some qualifications, from a horizontal summation of all industries' downward-sloping investment demand curves.

We have now discussed investing in physical capital. Whether the firm borrows money or draws on savings, the market interest rate represents the opportunity cost of investment. A less tangible form of capital, intellectual capital, is discussed in the case study, "The Information Economy: The Value of a Good Idea—Intellectual Property" at the end of the book.

The Market for Loanable Funds

You earlier learned why producers are willing to pay interest to borrow money: *Money provides a command over resources, making both direct production and roundabout production possible.* The simple principles developed for Farmer Jones and Hacker Haven can be generalized to other producers. The major demanders of loans are entrepreneurs who borrow to start firms and to invest in physical capital, such as machines, trucks, and buildings, and in intellectual capital, such as patents, copyrights, and trademarks. At any time, a firm has a variety of investment opportunities. The firm ranks these from highest to lowest, based on the expected rates of return. The firm increases investment until the expected rate of return just equals the market interest rate. With other inputs held constant, the demand curve for investment slopes downward.

But entrepreneurs are not the only demanders of loans. As we have seen, households value present consumption more than future consumption; they are willing to pay extra to consume now rather than later. One way to ensure that goods and services are available now is to borrow for present consumption, as reflected by home mortgages, car loans, and credit card purchases. Some people also borrow to invest in their human capital, as reflected by college loans. The household's demand curve for loans, like the firm's demand for loans, slopes downward, indicating that consumers are more willing and able to borrow at lower interest rates, other things constant. The government sector and the rest of the world are also demanders of loans.

Demand for Loanable Funds

The **demand for loanable funds** curve shows the negative relationship between the market interest rate and the quantity of loans demanded, other things constant. This curve is based on the expected rate of return these borrowed funds yield when invested in capital. Each firm has a downward-sloping demand curve for loanable funds, reflecting a declining rate of return on investment. With some qualifications, the demand for loanable funds of each firm can be summed horizontally to yield the market demand for loanable funds, shown as *D* in Exhibit 2. Factors assumed constant along this demand curve include the expected rate of inflation, the prices of other resources, the level of technology, the customs and conventions of the market, and the tax laws.

demand for loanable funds
The negative relationship between the market interest rate and the quantity of loanable funds demanded, other things constant

Supply of Loanable Funds

Banks are willing to pay interest on savings because they can, in turn, lend these savings to those who need credit, such as farmers, golf courses, construction companies, home buyers, college students, and entrepreneurs looking to start a new business or buy new capital. Banks and other financial institutions play the role of *financial intermediaries* in what is known as the market for loanable funds. The higher the interest rate, other things constant, the greater the reward for saving. As people save more, the quantity of loanable funds increases. The **supply of loanable funds** curve shows the positive relationship between the market interest rate and the quantity of savings supplied, other things constant, as reflected by the usual upward-sloping supply curve shown as *S* in Exhibit 2. In recent years, a lot of savings have come from abroad, especially China. Factors assumed constant along this supply curve include the expected rate of inflation and people's retirement plans.

supply of loanable funds
The positive relationship between the market interest rate and the quantity of loanable funds supplied, other things constant

Market Interest Rate

The **loanable funds market** brings together borrowers, or demanders of loanable funds, and savers, or suppliers of loanable funds, to determine the market interest rate. The demand and supply of loanable funds come together, as in Exhibit 2, to determine the market interest rate. In this case, the equilibrium interest rate of 8 percent is the only one that exactly matches the wishes of borrowers and savers. The equilibrium quantity of loanable funds is $1.0 trillion per year. Any change in the demand or supply of loanable funds changes the market interest rate. For example, a major technological breakthrough that increases the

loanable funds market
The market in which savers (suppliers of loanable funds) and borrowers (demanders of loanable funds) come together to determine the market interest rate and the quantity of loanable funds exchanged

EXHIBIT 2 Market for Loanable Funds

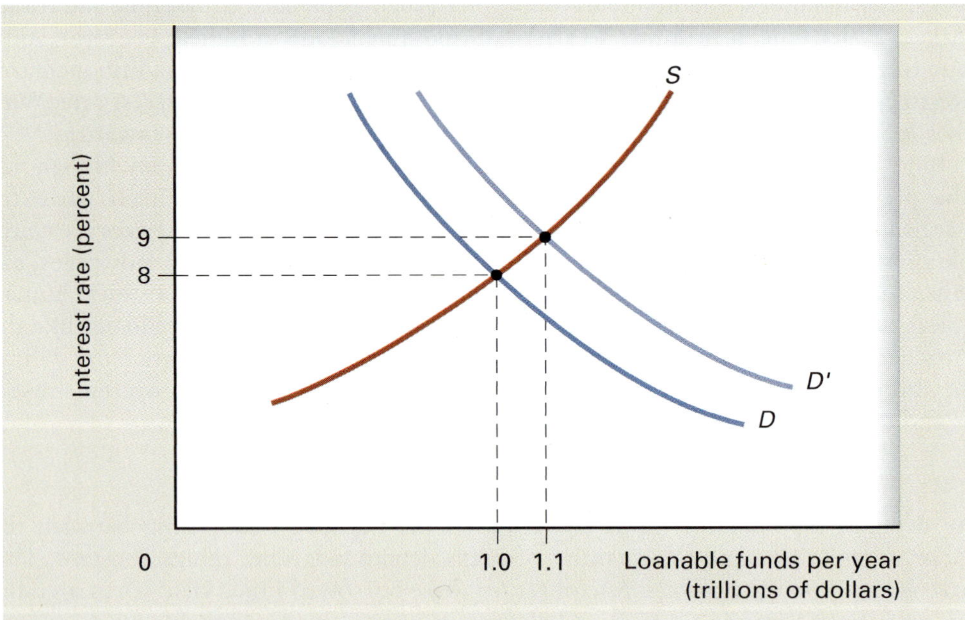

Because of the declining expected rate of return on capital, the quantity of loanable funds demanded is inversely related to the interest rate. The market rate of interest, 8 percent, is found where the demand curve for loanable funds intersects the supply curve of loanable funds. An increase in the demand for loanable funds from D to D′ raises the market interest rate from 8 percent to 9 percent and increases the equilibrium quantity of loanable funds from $1.0 trillion to $1.1 trillion.

productivity of capital increases its expected rate of return, shifting the demand curve for loanable funds rightward, as shown in the movement from D to D'. Such an increase in the demand for loanable funds would raise the equilibrium interest rate to 9 percent and increase the market quantity of loanable funds to $1.1 trillion per year.

Why Interest Rates Differ

So far, we have been talking about *the* market interest rate, implying that only one rate prevails in the loanable funds market. At any particular time, however, a range of interest rates coexist in the economy. Exhibit 3 shows interest rates for loans in various markets. The interest rate for home mortgages is relatively low because this loan is backed up by the home itself. The so-called **prime rate** is the interest rate lenders charge their most trustworthy business borrowers. The highest is the rate charged on credit card balances, which is nearly triple the rate on mortgages. Let's see why interest rates differ.

prime rate
The interest rate lenders charge their most trustworthy business borrowers

Risk

Some borrowers are more likely than others to *default* on their loans—that is, not to pay them back. Before a bank lends money, it usually requires a borrower to put up **collateral,** which is an asset pledged by the borrower that can be sold to pay off the loan in the event

collateral
An asset pledged by the borrower that can be sold to pay off the loan in the event the borrower defaults

EXHIBIT 3 Interest Rates Charged for Different Types of Loans

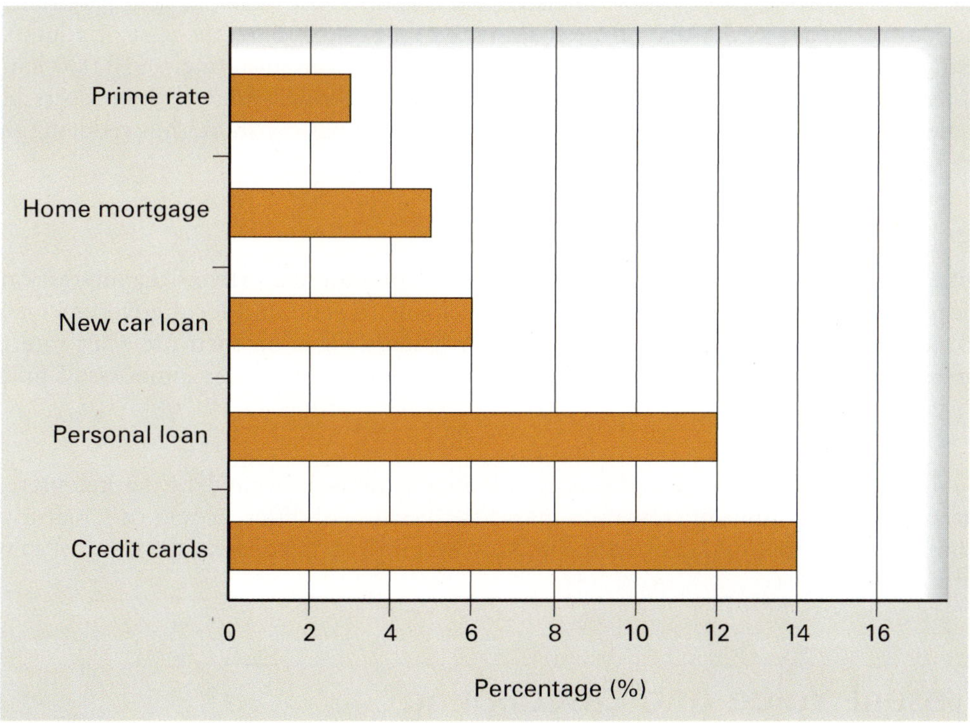

Interest rates are higher for riskier loans. Rates for home mortgages and new cars are relatively low because these loans are backed up by the home or car as collateral. Personal loans and credit card balances face the highest rates, because these loans are riskier—that is, the likelihood borrowers fail to repay the loans is greater and the borrower offers no collateral.

Source: Federal Reserve Board; Bankrate.com; and Moneycentral.msn.com. Rates are as of April 2010.

of a default. With business loans, any valuable asset—land, buildings, machinery—the firm owns can serve as collateral. With a home mortgage, the home itself becomes collateral. And with a car loan, the car becomes collateral. The more valuable the collateral backing up the loan, other things constant, the lower the interest rate charged on that loan. For example, the interest rate charged on car loans is usually higher than on home loans. A car loses its value more quickly than a home does, and a car can be driven away by a defaulting borrower, whereas a home usually increases in value and stays put (home prices declined during the recent economic crisis, creating trouble for both borrowers and banks, but that was unusual). So a car typically offers worse collateral than a home—hence, the interest charged on a car loan is higher. Interest rates are higher still for personal loans and credit cards, because such borrowers usually provide no collateral.

Duration of the Loan

The future is uncertain, and the further into the future a loan is to be repaid, the more uncertain that repayment becomes. Bad things can happen over time. Thus, as the duration of a loan increases, lenders require a higher interest rate to compensate for the greater risk. The **term structure of interest rates** is the relationship between the duration of a loan and the interest rate charged. *The interest rate usually increases with the duration of the loan, other things constant.*

term structure of interest rates
The relationship between the duration of a loan and the interest rate charged; typically interest rates increase with the duration of the loan, because longer loans are considered more risky

Administration Costs

The costs of executing the loan agreement, monitoring the loan, and collecting payments are called the *administration costs* of the loan. These costs, as a proportion of the loan, decrease as the size of the loan increases. For example, the cost of administering a $100,000 loan is less than 10 times the cost of administering a $10,000 loan. Consequently, that portion of the interest charge reflecting administration costs becomes smaller as the size of the loan increases, other things constant, thus reducing the interest rate for larger loans.

Tax Treatment

Differences in the tax treatment of different types of loans also affects the interest rate charged. For example, the interest earned on loans to state and local governments is not subject to federal income taxes. Because lenders focus on their after-tax rate of interest, state and local governments pay a lower interest rate than otherwise similar borrowers pay.

To Review: The demand and supply of loanable funds determine the market interest rate. At any given time, interest rates may differ because of differences in risk, maturity, administrative costs, and tax treatment. Now we move on to consider the value of some future benefit.

Present Value and Discounting

Because you value present consumption more than future consumption, present and future consumption cannot be compared directly. Someone who "eats like there's no tomorrow" apparently values present consumption much more than consumption tomorrow. A way of standardizing the discussion is to measure all consumption in terms of its present value. **Present value** is the current value of a payment or payments to be received in the

present value
The value today of income to be received in the future

future. For example, how much would you pay now to receive $100 one year from now? Put another way, what is the *present value* to you of receiving $100 one year from now?

Present Value of Payment One Year Hence

Suppose the market interest rate is 8 percent and you can either lend or borrow at that rate. One way to determine how much you would pay for the opportunity to receive $100 one year from now is to ask how much you would have to save now, at the market interest rate, to end up with $100 one year from now. Here's the problem we are trying to solve: What amount of money, if saved at an interest rate of, say, 8 percent, would accumulate to $100 one year from now? We can calculate the answer with a simple formula:

$$\text{Present value} \times 1.08 = \$100$$

or:

$$\text{Present value} = \frac{100}{1.08} = \$92.59$$

Thus, if the interest rate is 8 percent, $92.59 is the present value of receiving $100 one year from now; it is the most you would pay today to receive $100 one year from now. Rather than pay more than $92.59, you could simply deposit your $92.59, earn the market interest rate of 8 percent, and end up with $100 a year from now (ignoring taxes). Dividing the future payment by 1 plus the prevailing interest rate to express it in today's dollars is called **discounting.**

discounting
Converting future dollar amounts into present value

The present value of $100 to be received one year from now depends on the interest rate. The more that present consumption is preferred to future consumption, the more must be offered savers to defer consumption. *The higher the interest rate, the more any future payment is discounted and the lower its present value.* Put another way, the higher the interest rate, the less you need to save now to yield a given amount in the future. For example, if the interest rate is 10 percent, the present value of receiving $100 one year from now is $100/1.10, which equals $90.91.

On the other hand, the less present consumption is preferred to future consumption, the less savers need to be paid to defer consumption, so the lower the interest rate. The lower the interest rate, the less the future income is discounted and the greater its present value. A lower interest rate means that you must save more now to yield a given amount in the future. As a general rule, the present value of receiving an amount one year from now is:

$$\text{Present value} = \frac{\text{Amount received one year from now}}{1 + \text{interest rate}}$$

For example, when the interest rate is 5 percent, the present value of receiving $100 one year from now is:

$$\text{Present value} = \frac{\$100}{1 + 0.05} = \frac{\$100}{1.05} = \$95.24$$

Present Value for Payments in Later Years

Now consider the present value of receiving $100 two years from now. What amount of money, if deposited at the market interest rate of 5 percent, would total $100 after two years? After one year, the value would be the present value times 1.05, which would then earn the market interest rate during the second year. After two years, the deposit would have accumulated to the present value times 1.05 times 1.05. Thus, we have the equation:

$$\text{Present value} \times 1.05 \times 1.05 = \text{Present value} \times (1.05)^2 = \$100$$

Solving for the present value yields:

$$\text{Present value} = \frac{\$100}{(1.05)^2} = \frac{\$100}{1.1025} = \$90.70$$

If the $100 were to be received three years from now, we would discount the payment over three years:

$$\text{Present value} = \frac{\$100}{(1.05)^3} = \$86.38$$

If the interest rate is i, the present value of M dollars received t years from now is:

$$\text{Present value} = \frac{M}{(1 + i)^t}$$

Because $(1 + i)$ is greater than 1, the more times it is multiplied by itself (as determined by t), the larger the denominator and the smaller the present value. Thus, *the present value of a given payment is smaller the further into the future that payment is to be received.*

Present Value of an Income Stream

So far, we have figured out the present value of a single sum to be received in the future. Most investments, however, yield a stream of income over time. In cases where the income is received for a period of years, the present value of each receipt can be computed individually and the results summed to yield the present value of the entire income stream. For example, the present value of receiving $100 next year and $150 the year after is simply the present value of the first year's receipt plus the present value of the second year's receipt. If the interest rate is 5 percent:

$$\text{Present value} = \frac{\$100}{1.05} + \frac{\$150}{(1.05)^2} = \$231.29$$

Present Value of an Annuity

annuity
A given sum of money received each year for a specified number of years

A given sum of money received each year for a specified number of years is called an **annuity**. Such an income stream is called a *perpetuity* if it continues indefinitely. The present value of receiving a certain amount forever seems like it should be a very large sum indeed. But because future income is valued less the more distant into the future it is to be received, the present value of receiving a particular amount forever is not much more than that of receiving it for, say, 20 years.

To determine the present value of receiving $100 a year forever, we need only ask how much money must be deposited in a savings account to yield $100 in interest each year. If the interest rate is 8 percent, a deposit of $1,250 will earn $100 per year. Thus, the present value of receiving $100 a year indefinitely when the interest rate is 8 percent is $1,250. More generally, the present value of receiving a sum each year forever equals the amount received each year divided by the interest rate.

$$\text{Present value of receiving } M \text{ dollars each year forever} = \frac{M}{i}$$

The concept of present value is useful for investment decisions. What about your decision to invest in human capital—to go to college? A chart in the previous chapter showed that those with at least a college degree earned nearly twice as much as those with just a high school diploma. We could compute the present value of an education by discounting earnings based on that level of education, then summing total earnings over your working life. Even without doing the calculations, we can say with reasonable certainty that the present value of at least a college education will be nearly twice that of just a high school education. To develop an appreciation for present value and discounting, read the case study, "Bringing Theory to Life: The Million-Dollar Lottery?" at the end of the book, to put the payoff from state lotteries in perspective.

This discussion of present value and discounting concludes our treatment of capital and interest. We now turn to a special factor of production, entrepreneurial ability, or entrepreneurship.

Entrepreneurship

In a market economy, people are free to risk their time and savings to start a business. If the business succeeds, they are rewarded with profit. If it fails, they could lose their life's savings. Chances of success are not great—most new businesses don't last five years. But many survive, some thrive, and a few make their founders rich. Despite the high failure rate, the profit motive and the drive to create something of lasting value, to make a mark in the world, attract many would-be entrepreneurs.

Role of the Entrepreneur

An entrepreneur comes up with an idea, turns that idea into a marketable product, accepts the risk of success or failure, and claims any resulting profit or loss. That idea might be a new product, a better version of an existing product, or a more efficient way of making something already available. Because each of those activities often involves long and costly development, such ventures are risky. Entrepreneurs must have the confidence to accept that risk and must inspire confidence in others needed to succeed, such as resource suppliers, lenders, investors, and consumers.

Because there is no formal market for entrepreneurship, entrepreneurs become their own bosses—that is, they hire themselves. In addition to entrepreneurship, or entrepreneurial ability, some supply other resources to the firm. Imagine an entrepreneur who comes up with a good idea, borrows start-up money from a bank, and hires a manager to line up all the other resources required to bring that idea to life. The entrepreneur promises to pay resource suppliers at least their opportunity cost; otherwise, they would go elsewhere. This entrepreneur, by hiring a manager and by agreeing to pay all resources, supplies nothing other than entrepreneurship. Yet the entrepreneur has acquired the right to control these resources in return for the promise to pay at least the market rate. Despite what may seem like limited involvement, this entrepreneur owns the firm, and the firm consists of a bundle of contracts or agreements between the entrepreneur and resource suppliers. At the end of the week or month or year, the entrepreneur can claim as profit whatever is left after paying all other resources. The entrepreneur is the *residual claimant*, the one who gets to keep what's left over and who is responsible for covering any loss.

What distinguishes the role of the entrepreneur is not the management of resources in the firm, but the power to choose who manages those resources. An entrepreneur who decides to manage the firm, and many do, would still delegate some decisions to employees. Therefore, don't think that an entrepreneur must manage the firm. *An entrepreneur must simply have the authority to hire and fire the manager.*

In reality, an entrepreneur seldom has the limited role described above. An entrepreneur often manages the business, at least in the beginning, and usually supplies at least some of the financial capital required to get the business off the ground, because banks may be reluctant to lend to a risky startup.

Entrepreneurs Drive the Economy Forward

Entrepreneurs create new or better products, new production methods, or new ways of doing business. These are sources of technological progress and economic growth in the economy. Successful entrepreneurs initiate creative change, thereby earning a profit and driving the economy forward.

New Products

Some entrepreneurs come up with new products, opening up markets that had not before existed. For example, Levi Strauss and his partner Jacob Davis in 1873 won a patent for fastening blue denim with small metal studs to create the most popular clothing in the world, now called Levi's jeans. As another example, Dean Kamen developed the Segway® Human Transporter, a personal transport device, which went on the market in 2001 as an alternative to walking or riding a bicycle.

Improve Existing Products

Some entrepreneurs begin with an existing product and make it better. For example, Howard Schultz took the simple cup of coffee and turned it into a $20 billion corporation by offering higher quality and greater variety in a more inviting setting. Founded by Schultz in 1985, Starbucks now employs more than 140,000 people at about 9,000 locations around the world. Guy Laliberte founded Cirque du Soleil in 1984 as a modern update on the circus. By 2010 he had created 21 different shows, some staying put and some touring. For his creative efforts, he accumulated an estimated net worth of $2.5 billion as of 2010.[1]

New Production Methods

Some entrepreneurs combine resources more efficiently to reduce costs. They use less costly materials, employ newer technology, and generally make better use of resources. Henry Ford, for example, introduced the assembly line, where automobiles move along a conveyer and the workers stay put. Ford didn't invent the automobile, but his assembly line made owning one affordable for millions of Americans. Similarly, Ray Croc didn't invent the hamburger or the hamburger stand, but he applied the principles of mass production to make McDonald's hamburgers quickly and cheaply, first across the nation then around the world.

1. Joan Acocella, "Night at the Circus," *The New Yorker*, 7 June 2010, p. 82.

New Ways of Doing Business

Some entrepreneurs step outside existing business models to create new ways of doing business. For example, Michael Dell began in 1984 with $1,000 and an idea to sell personal computers directly to customers rather than through retailers. His made-to-order computers sold by phone and now over the Internet make Dell one of the world's largest computer sellers, with sales exceeding $150 million *a day.* Mary Kay Ash did the same for skin care products and cosmetics, selling more than $2 billion a year directly to consumers around the world through independent Mary Kay consultants.

Who Are Not Entrepreneurs?

Some people may carry out a particular function of an entrepreneur. For example, they may dream up a new product or process, they may manage resources, or they may assume the risk of success or failure. But carrying out just one of these roles does not usually make for an entrepreneur. One way of appreciating the role of an entrepreneur is to identify those who are not serving that role.

Corporate Inventors

Inventors are considered entrepreneurs if they bear the risk of success or failure. But most inventors are hired hands. Corporations such as Pfizer, Dupont, and Apple employ thousands of scientists and engineers to improve existing products, develop new ones, and devise more efficient ways to make things. These corporate inventors still get paid even in years when their creative juices slow to a trickle. Because these hired inventors take no more risk than most other employees, they are not considered entrepreneurs.

Exhibit 4 shows the sources of invention since 1990 as measured by the number of U.S. patents awarded. Patents increased 76 percent between 1990 and 2008. But the share of

EXHIBIT 4 Source of U.S. Patents

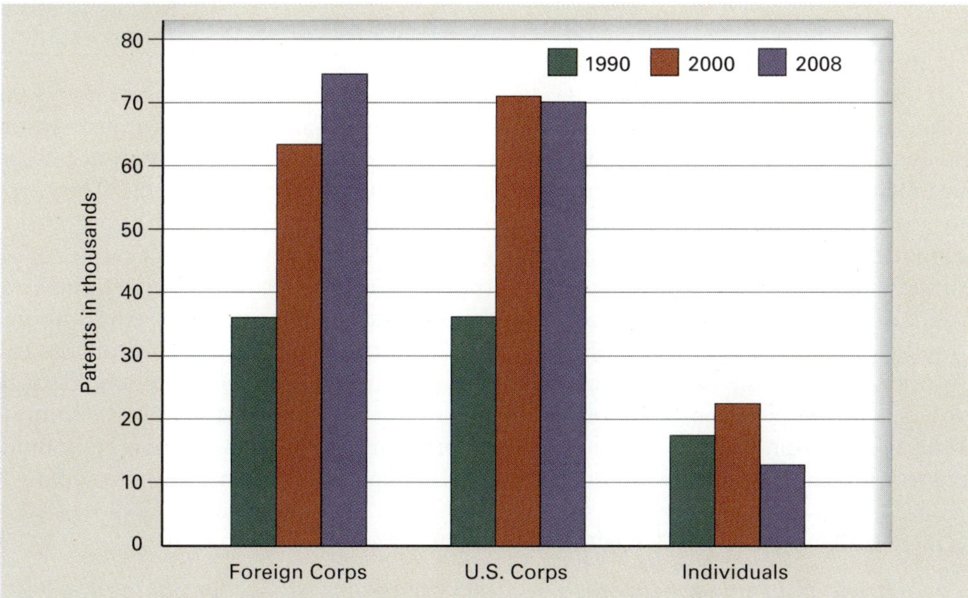

Source: U.S. Bureau of the Census, *Statistical Abstract of the United States: 2010*, Table 754.

patents awarded to individual inventors fell from 19 percent in 1990 to only 8 percent in 2008. Individual inventors usually are considered entrepreneurs, even those who sell their ideas for others to develop and market. These inventors take on risks in a way that inventors who work for corporations do not. So self-employed inventors usually are considered entrepreneurs.

Managers

Most entrepreneurs do more than simply sell their good ideas for others to run with. They try to bring their ideas to the market by going into business. But, as already noted, founding a business does not necessarily mean the entrepreneur must manage it. For example, Dean Kamen, inventor of the Segway, created a company to make and market his invention. He hired a manager to run the company because he was too busy inventing things (besides the Segway, Kamen holds patents for a water purifier, a mobile dialysis system, the first insulin pump, and an all-terrain electric wheelchair, among other things). Even though he doesn't manage the business himself, he is still an entrepreneur because he has the power to hire and fire the manager. The manager is a well-paid and important employee, but he is not an entrepreneur.

Stockholders

More than half of all households in the United States own corporate stock, either directly or indirectly, and thus take on the risk of a corporation's success or failure. Does this risk-bearing make the stockholder an entrepreneur? No. Entrepreneurs do more than assume the risk of success or failure. They begin with a bright idea and usually figure out how to profit from that idea. An individual stockholder, on the other hand, typically has little say in a firm's operation (and most like it that way).

To Review: The entrepreneur is a prime mover in a market economy—a visionary, someone who can see what others can't. By coming up with new products, making existing products better, finding better ways to make things, of finding new ways of doing business, the entrepreneur drives the economy forward. This concludes our discussion of entrepreneurs. You now have sufficient background to consider how firms, especially corporations, are financed.

Corporate Finance

During the Industrial Revolution, labor-saving machinery and improved transportation and communication networks made large-scale production more profitable, but building huge factories filled with heavy machinery required substantial investments. The corporate structure became the easiest way to finance such outlays, and by 1920, corporations accounted for most employment and output in the U.S. economy. Back in Chapter 3, you learned about the pros and cons of the corporate form of business. Thus far, however, little has been said about corporate finance. As noted in Chapter 3, a corporation is a legal entity, distinct from its shareholders. The corporation may own property, earn a profit, sue or be sued, incur debt, even be found guilty of a crime. Stockholders, the owners of the corporation, are liable only to the extent of their investment in the firm. Use of the abbreviation Inc. or Corp. in the company name serves as a warning to potential creditors that stockholders will not accept personal liability for debts of the company.

Corporate Stock and Retained Earnings

Corporations fund investment in three ways: by issuing stock, by retaining some of their profits, and by borrowing. Corporations issue and sell stock to raise money for operations and for new plants and equipment. Suppose the founder of a new firm has met with early success, but finds that to remain competitive, the firm needs to achieve economies of scale, which means the firm must grow fast. To fund that growth, the entrepreneur decides to incorporate. The newly incorporated company issues 1,000,000 shares of stock. The entrepreneur takes 100,000 shares as *owner's equity* in the corporation. The rest are sold to the public for $50 per share, which raises $45 million for the company. The entrepreneur, in effect, has already paid for his or her shares with the "sweat equity" required to come up with the idea, found the company, and get it rolling. The initial sale of stock to the public is called an **initial public offering,** or **IPO.** A *share* of **corporate stock** is a claim on the net income and assets of a corporation, as well as the right to vote on corporate directors and on other important matters. A person who buys 1 percent of the 1,000,000 shares issued thereby owns 1 percent of the corporation, is entitled to 1 percent of any profit, and gets to cast 1 percent of the votes on important corporate decisions.

initial public offering (IPO)
The initial sale of corporate stock to the public

corporate stock
Certificate reflecting part ownership of a corporation

Corporations must pay corporate income taxes on any profit. After-tax profit is either paid as **dividends** to shareholders or reinvested in the corporation. Reinvested profit, or **retained earnings,** helps the firm grow. Stockholders usually expect dividends, but the corporation is not required to pay dividends, and most new firms don't. Once shares are issued, their price tends to fluctuate directly with the firm's profit prospects. People buy stock because the firm is expected to eventually pay dividends and because they hope the share price will appreciate, or increase, over time.

dividends
After-tax corporate profit paid to stockholders rather than retained by the firm and reinvested

retained earnings
After-tax corporate profit reinvested in the firm rather than paid to stockholders as dividends

Corporate Bonds

Again, a corporation can acquire funds by issuing stock, by retaining earnings, or by borrowing. To borrow money, the corporation can go to a bank for a loan or it can issue and sell bonds. A **bond** is the corporation's promise to pay back the holder a fixed sum of money on the designated *maturity date* plus make interest payments until that date. For example, a corporation might sell for $1,000 a bond that promises to make an annual interest payment of, say, $80 for 20 years and to repay the $1,000 at the end of 20 years.

bond
Certificate reflecting a firm's promise to pay the lender periodic interest and to repay the borrowed sum of money on the designated maturity date

The payment stream for bonds is more predictable than that for stocks. Unless this corporation goes bankrupt, it must pay bondholders as promised. In contrast, stockholders are last in line when resource suppliers get paid, so bondholders get paid before stockholders. Investors usually consider bonds less risky than stocks, although bonds involve risks as well. Risks include corporate bankruptcy and higher market interest rates. For example, suppose you buy a bond that pays 8 percent interest. Soon after that purchase, the market interest rate increases, so newly issued bonds pay 10 percent interest. Your 8 percent bond is less attractive than the new bonds, so the market value of your bond declines. The value of your bond declines until bond buyers are indifferent between buying your 8 percent bond and buying a 10 percent bond.

Securities Exchanges

Once stocks and bonds have been issued and sold, owners of these securities are free to resell them on *securities exchanges*. In the United States, the *Securities and Exchange Commission (SEC)* is the federal body that regulates securities markets. The largest securities market is the New York Stock Exchange (now NYSE Euronext), which trades the securities of about 2,800 major corporations, including about 500 non-U.S. companies. Altogether approximately 10,000 corporations trade on various U.S. exchanges. These are called publicly traded companies, to be distinguished from privately owned companies. Although privately owned companies, such as sole proprietors and partnerships, make up the overwhelming share of U.S. businesses in terms of numbers, corporations account for the overwhelming share of employment and sales.

Nearly all the securities traded each business day are *secondhand securities* in the sense that they have already been issued by the corporation. So the bulk of daily transactions do not finance firms in need of investment funds. Most money from daily trading goes from a securities buyer to a securities seller. *Institutional investors,* such as banks, insurance companies, and mutual funds, account for most of the trading volume on major exchanges. By providing a *secondary market* for securities, exchanges enhance the *liquidity* of securities—that is, the exchanges make the securities more readily sold for cash and thus more attractive to own. Of growing importance in securities exchanges are *hedge funds*, which often follow complex strategies to invest for institutions and wealthy clients.

The secondary markets for stocks also determine the current market value of the corporation. The market value of a firm at any given time can be found by multiplying the share price by the number of shares issued. Because the share price fluctuates throughout the trading day, so does the value of the corporation. In theory, the share price reflects the present value of the discounted stream of expected profit. Just to give you some idea, Exxon Mobil, the top-valued U.S. corporation, had a market value of $280 billion at the close of the trading day on June 4, 2010. The 2,300 U.S. corporations traded on the New York Stock Exchange had a combined market value of more than $10 trillion.

Securities prices give corporate management some indication of the wisdom of raising investment funds through retained earnings, new stock issues, or new bond issues. The greater a corporation's expected profit, other things constant, the higher the value of shares on the stock market and the lower the interest rate that would have to be paid on new bond issues. Securities markets usually promote the survival of the fittest by allocating investment funds to those firms able to make the most profitable use of them. *Thus, securities markets allocate funds more readily to successful firms than to firms in financial difficulty.* Some firms may be in such poor shape that they can't issue new securities.

One final point: When economists talk about investing, they have in mind purchases of new capital, such as new machines and new buildings. When the media talk about investing, they usually mean buying stocks and bonds. To an economist, Farmer Jones is investing only when he buys new farm machinery, not when he buys stocks. As noted already, the overwhelming share of stock transactions are in secondary markets, so the money goes from buyers to sellers, and does not go toward new capital purchases. Regardless, secondary markets make shares more readily convertible into cash and thus more attractive to own.

Conclusion

This chapter introduced you to capital, interest, entrepreneurship, and corporate finance. Capital is a more complicated resource than this chapter has conveyed. For example, the demand curve for investment is a moving target, not the stable relationship drawn in Exhibit 1. An accurate depiction of the investment demand curve calls for knowledge of the marginal product of capital and the price of output in the future. But capital's productivity changes with breakthroughs in technology and with changes in the employment of other resources. The future price of the product can also vary widely. Consider, for example, the dilemma of a firm contemplating an investment in oil-drilling rigs in recent years, when the price of crude oil fluctuated between $10 and $145 per barrel, as it has over the last two decades.

Summary

1. Production cannot occur without savings, because both direct production and roundabout production require time—time during which the resources required for production must be paid. Because people value present consumption more than future consumption, they must be rewarded to defer consumption. Interest is the reward to savers for forgoing present consumption and the cost to borrowers for being able to spend now.

2. Choosing the profit-maximizing level of capital is complicated because capital purchased today yields a stream of benefits for years into the future. The expected rate of return on capital equals the expected annual earnings of that capital divided by that capital's purchase price. The profit-maximizing firm invests up to the point where the expected rate of return on capital equals the market rate of interest. The market interest rate is the opportunity cost of investing.

3. The demand and supply of loanable funds determine the market interest rate. At any given time, interest rates may differ because of differences in risk, maturity, administrative costs, and tax treatment.

4. The current value of future payments is the present value. The process of translating future payments into present value is called discounting. The present value of a given payment is smaller the further into the future that payment is to be received. A given sum of money received each year for a specified number of years is called an annuity. The present value of receiving a sum each year forever is the amount received each year divided by the market interest rate.

5. An entrepreneur is a profit-seeker who comes up with an idea, tries to turn that idea into a marketable product, and accepts the risk of success or failure. The entrepreneur need not supply any resource other than entrepreneurial ability, though many manage the firm and provide some start-up funds. By developing new products, improving existing ones, employing better production methods, and finding new ways of doing business, successful entrepreneurs earn a profit and drive the economy forward.

6. Corporations fund new investment from three main sources: new stock issues, retained earnings, and borrowing (either directly from financial institutions or by issuing bonds). Once new stocks and bonds are issued, they can then be bought and sold on securities markets. The value of corporate stocks and bonds tends to vary directly with the firm's profit prospects. More profitable firms have better access to funds needed for expansion.

Key Concepts

Positive rate of time preference 261
Interest rate 261
Expected rate of return on capital 261
Demand for loanable funds 263
Supply of loanable funds 264
Loanable funds market 264
Prime rate 265
Collateral 265
Term structure of interest rates 266
Present value 266
Discounting 267
Annuity 268
Initial public offering (IPO) 273
Corporate stock 273
Dividends 273
Retained earnings 273
Bond 273

Questions for Review

1. Role of Time Complete the following sentences with a word or a phrase:
    a. If Bryan values present consumption more than future consumption, he has a __________.
    b. The reward to households for forgoing present consumption is ______.
    c. Producing capital goods rather than producing final goods is known as ___________.

2. Consumption, Saving, and Time Explain why the supply of loanable funds curve slopes upward to the right.

3. Case Study: The Value of a Good Idea—Intellectual Property (See page 727.) Many who use pirated software and illegal downloads of music and movies believe their actions are harmless. Identify some downsides for individuals and the economy of violating intellectual property rights.

4. Why Interest Rates Differ At any given time, a range of interest rates prevails in the economy. What are some factors that contribute to differences among interest rates?

5. Present Value of an Annuity Why is $10,000 a close approximation of the price of an annuity that pays $1,000 each year for 30 years at 10 percent annual interest?

6. Present Value of an Annuity Suppose you are hired by your state government to determine the profitability of a lottery offering a grand prize of $10 million paid out in equal annual

installments over 20 years. Show *how* to calculate the cost to the state of paying out such a prize. Assume payments are made at the end of each year.

7. Case Study: The Million-Dollar Lottery? (See page 729.) In many states with lotteries, people can take their winnings in a single, discounted, lump-sum payment or in a series of annual payments for 20 or 30 years. What factors should a winner consider in determining how to take the money?
8. ENTREPRENEURSHIP What entrepreneurial idea do you have? How would your idea contribute to the economy?
9. CORPORATE FINANCE Describe the three ways in which corporations acquire funds for investment.
10. SECURITIES EXCHANGES What role do securities exchanges play in financing corporations?

Problems and Exercises

11. OPTIMAL INVESTMENT Review Exhibit 1 in this chapter. If the operators of the golf course revised their revenue estimates so that each cart is expected to earn $250 less, how many carts would they buy at an interest rate of 8 percent? How many would they buy if the interest rate is 3 percent?
12. MARKET FOR LOANABLE FUNDS Using the demand-supply for loanable funds diagram, show the effect on the market interest rate of each of the following:
    a. An increase in the purchase price of capital
    b. An increase in the productivity of capital
    c. A shift in preferences toward present consumption and away from future consumption
13. PRESENT VALUE Calculate the present value of each of the following future payments. (For some of these problems you may wish to use the online calculator available at http://www.moneychimp.com/articles/finworks/ fmpresval.htm.)
    a. A $10,000 lump sum received 1 year from now if the market interest rate is 8 percent
    b. A $10,000 lump sum received 2 years from now if the market interest rate is 10 percent
    c. A $1,000 lump sum received 3 years from now if the market interest rate is 5 percent
    d. A $25,000 lump sum received 1 year from now if the market interest rate is 12 percent
    e. A $25,000 lump sum received 1 year from now if the market interest rate is 10 percent
    f. A perpetuity of $500 per year if the market interest rate is 6 percent
14. PRESENT VALUE OF AN INCOME STREAM Suppose the market interest rate is 10 percent. Would you be willing to lend $10,000 if you were guaranteed to receive $1,000 at the end of each of the next 12 years plus a $5,000 payment 15 years from now? Why or why not?

Global Economic Watch Exercises

Login to www.cengagebrain.com and access the Global Economic Watch to do these exercises.

15. GLOBAL ECONOMIC WATCH Go to the Global Economic Crisis Resource Center. Select Global Issues in Context. In the Basic Search box at the top of the page, enter the phrase "Whose Concept Was It, Anyway." On the Results page, go to the Global Viewpoints Section. Click on the link for the July 11, 2010, column "Whose Concept Was It Anyway?." Which outcome would benefit the economy more, Jane Wyler having a patent on all reusable dry-cleaning bags or Rick Siegel developing a cheaper reusable bag?
16. GLOBAL ECONOMIC WATCH Go to the Global Economic Crisis Resource Center. Select Global Issues in Context. In the Basic Search box at the top of the page, enter the term "initial public offering." Read about an IPO within the two most recent years. How much money was raised? For what will the money be used?

Transaction Costs, Imperfect Information, and Behavioral Economics

14

PhotoLink/Getty Images

- Why do some firms, such as Domino's Pizza, specialize in a single product, while other firms, such as General Electric, make hundreds of different products?
- Why stop at hundreds? Why not thousands? In fact, why doesn't a giant firm make everything?
- Why is proper spelling important on your résumé?
- Why is buying a used car such a gamble?
- Why do some winners of online auctions end up losers?
- What have economists learned from psychologists about the limits of rational self-interest?

Answers to these and other seemingly unrelated questions are addressed in this chapter, which digs deeper into assumptions about firms, the information required for competitive markets, and why some people make choices that seem inconsistent with their self-interest.

In the first third of this chapter, we step inside the firm to reconsider some simplifying assumptions about how firms work. We ask: Why do firms exist? How do they decide what to make themselves and what to buy from other firms? These steps toward realism move us beyond the simple depiction of the firm employed to this point. In the second third of this chapter, we challenge some simplifying assumptions about the information available to market participants. We ask: How does the lack of certain information affect behavior and shape market outcomes? And in the final third of the chapter, we consider why some economists are drawing on findings from psychology to enrich models of economic behavior. Specifically, we consider why many people eat too much, drink too much, smoke too much, and do other things that appear to be at odds with their rational self-interest.

Overall, this chapter should help you develop a more realistic view of how the economy works.

Topics discussed include:

- Transaction costs
- Vertical integration
- Bounded rationality
- Economies of scope
- Optimal search
- Winner's curse
- Asymmetric information
- Adverse selection
- Principal-agent problem
- Moral hazard
- Signaling and screening
- Behavioral economics

Rationale for the Firm and its Scope of Operation

The competitive model assumes that all participants in the market know everything they need to about the price and availability of all inputs, outputs, and production processes. The firm is assumed to be headed by a brilliant decision maker with a computer-like ability to calculate all the relevant marginal products. This individual knows everything necessary to solve complex production and pricing problems. The irony is that if the marginal products of all inputs could be measured easily and if prices for all inputs could be easily determined, there would be little reason for production to take place in firms. In a world characterized by perfect competition, perfect information, constant returns to scale, and costless exchange, the consumer could bypass the firm to deal directly with resource suppliers, purchasing inputs in the appropriate amounts. Someone who wanted a table could buy timber, have it milled, hire a carpenter, hire a painter, and end up with a finished product. The consumer could carry out transactions directly with each resource supplier.

The Firm Reduces Transaction Costs

So why is production carried out within firms? About 75 years ago, in a classic article, Nobel Prize winner Ronald Coase asked the question, "Why do firms exist?"[1] Why do people organize in the hierarchical structure of the firm and coordinate their decisions through a manager rather than simply rely on market exchange? His answer would not surprise today's students of economics: *Organizing activities through the hierarchy of the firm is usually more efficient than market exchange because production requires the coordination of many transactions among many resource suppliers.* In short, firms are superior to markets when production is complicated.

Consider again the example of purchasing a table by contracting directly with all the different resource suppliers—from the logger to the painter who applied the finishing varnish. Using resource markets directly involves (1) the cost of determining what

1. "The Nature of the Firm," *Economica*, 4 (November 1937): 386–405.

inputs are needed and how they should be combined and (2) the cost of reaching an agreement with each resource supplier *over and above* the direct costs of the timber, nails, machinery, paint, and labor required to make the table. Where inputs are easily identified, measured, priced, and hired, production can be carried out through a price-guided "do-it-yourself" approach using the market. For example, getting your house painted is a relatively simple task: You can buy the paint and brushes and hire painters by the hour. You become your own painting contractor, hiring inputs in the market and combining them to do the job. Likewise you could talk about different approaches to a European vacation. One traveler plans every aspect of a trip—booking flights, reserving hotel rooms, planning excursions, transportation, meals, and so on. A second traveler buys a packaged tour that includes everything. And a third traveler buys a land package covering hotels and excursions, but books all the flights.

Where the costs of identifying the appropriate inputs and negotiating for each specific contribution are high, the consumer minimizes transaction costs by purchasing the finished product from a firm. For example, although some people serve as their own contractor when painting a house, fewer do so when building a house; most buy a home already built or hire a building contractor. *The more complicated the task, the greater the ability to economize on transaction costs through specialization and centralized control.* For example, attempting to buy a new car by contracting with the thousands of suppliers required to assemble one would be time consuming, costly, and impossible for most anyone. What type of skilled labor should be hired and at what wages? How much steel, aluminum, plastic, glass, paint, and other materials should be purchased? How should resources be combined and in what proportions? Anyone without a detailed knowledge of auto production couldn't do it. (General Motors and Ford, for example, each deals with more than 20,000 suppliers.) That's why consumers buy assembled cars rather than contract separately with each resource supplier.

At the margin, some activities could go either way, with some consumers using firms and some hiring resources directly in markets. The choice depends on each consumer's skill and opportunity cost of time. For example, some people may not want to be troubled with hiring all the inputs to get their house painted. Instead, they simply hire a firm for an agreed-on price—they hire a painting contractor. As you will see later in the chapter, however, hiring a contractor may give rise to other problems of quality control.

The Boundaries of the Firm

So far, the chapter has explained why firms exist: *Firms minimize the transaction costs and the production costs of economic activity.* The next question is: What are the efficient boundaries of the firm? The theory of the firm described in earlier chapters is largely silent on the boundaries of the firm—that is, on the appropriate degree of vertical integration. **Vertical integration** is the expansion of a firm into stages of production earlier or later than those in which it specializes. For example, a steel company may decide (1) to integrate backward to mine iron ore and even mine the coal used to smelt iron ore or (2) to integrate forward to fashion raw steel into various components. A large manufacturer employs an amazing variety of production processes, but on average about half of the cost of production goes to purchase inputs from other firms. For example, General Motors and Ford each spends over $50 billion a year on parts, materials, and services. The total exceeds the annual output of some countries.

vertical integration
The expansion of a firm into stages of production earlier or later than those in which it specializes, such as a steel maker that also mines iron ore

Outsourcing occurs when a firm buys products, such as auto parts, or services, such as data processing, from outside suppliers. How does the firm determine which activities to undertake and which to purchase from other firms? A firm relies on the division of labor and the law of comparative advantage to focus on what it does best, what it

outsourcing
A firm buys inputs from outside suppliers

core competency
Area of specialty; the product or phase of production a firm supplies with greatest efficiency

considers its **core competency**. Should Dell manufacture its own computer chips or buy them from another firm? The answer depends on the benefits and costs of internal production versus market purchases. The point bears repeating: *Internal production and market purchases are alternative ways of organizing transactions.* The choice depends on which is a more efficient way of carrying out the transaction in question. Keep in mind that market prices coordinate transactions *between* firms, whereas managers coordinate activities *within* firms. The market coordinates resources by meshing the independent plans of separate decision makers, but a firm coordinates resources through the conscious direction of the manager.

The usual assumption is that transactions are organized by market exchange unless markets pose problems. Market exchange allows each firm to benefit from specialization and comparative advantage. For example, Apple can specialize in making computers and buy chips from Intel, a specialist. At this point, it might be useful to discuss specific criteria firms consider when deciding whether to purchase a particular input from the market.

Bounded Rationality of the Manager

bounded rationality
The notion that there is a limit to the information that a firm's manager can comprehend and act on

To direct and coordinate activity in a conscious way in the firm, a manager must understand how all the pieces of the puzzle fit together. As the firm takes on more and more activities, however, the manager may start losing track of details, so the quality of managerial decisions suffers. The more tasks the firm takes on, the longer the lines of communication between the manager and the production workers who must implement the decision. One constraint on vertical integration is the manager's **bounded rationality**, which limits the amount of information a manager can comprehend about the firm's operation. As the firm takes on more and more functions, coordination and communication become more difficult. The firm can experience diseconomies similar to those it experiences when it expands output beyond the efficient scale of production. The solution is for the firm to reduce its functions to those where it has a comparative advantage.

Incidentally, outsourcing is growing on college campuses. The number of college bookstores run by outside companies has more than doubled since 1992. Barnes & Noble, for example, runs over 600 college bookstores. But college outsourcing has moved beyond bookstores to dozens of activities including food service, custodial service, real estate management, laundry, parking, printing, and security. The growing consensus is that colleges should focus on their core competency, teaching and research, leaving other functions to specialists in each area.

Minimum Efficient Scale

As noted when firm costs were introduced, the *minimum efficient scale* is the minimum rate of output at which economies of scale are fully exploited. For example, suppose that minimum efficient scale in the production of personal computers is 1 million per month, as shown by the firm's long-run average cost curve in panel (a) of Exhibit 1. Suppose this also turns out to be the amount that maximizes profit. Because the computer chip is an important component in a personal computer, should the PC maker integrate backward into chip production? What if the minimum efficient scale in chip production is 5 million per month? As you can see in panel (b) of Exhibit 1, the average cost of producing 1 million chips is much higher than the average cost at the minimum efficient scale of chip production. The PC manufacturer therefore minimizes costs by buying chips from a chip maker of optimal size. More generally, *other things constant, a firm should buy an input if the market price is below what it would cost the firm to make.*

EXHIBIT 1 Minimum Efficient Scale and Vertical Integration

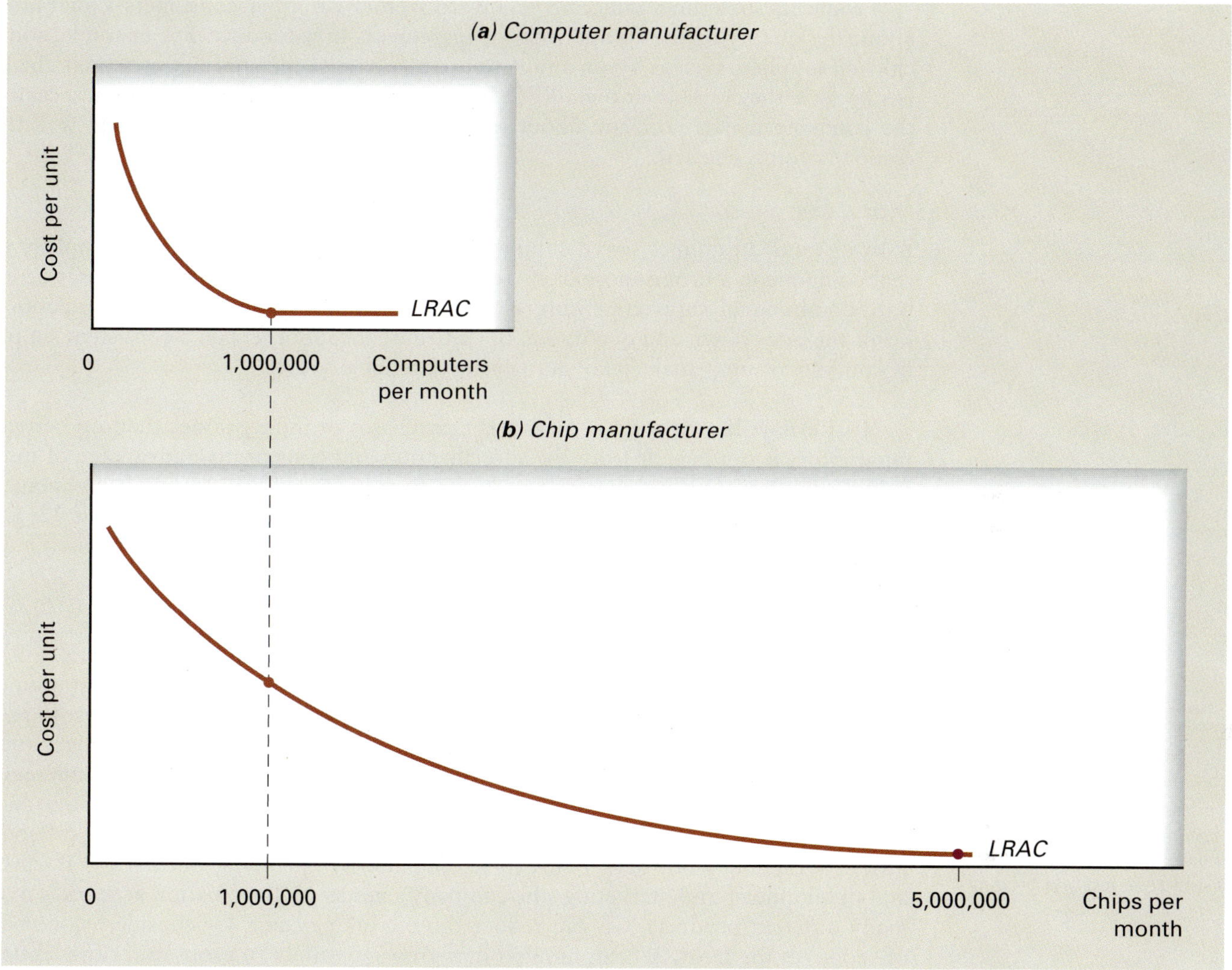

The manufacturer in panel (a) is producing at the minimum efficient scale of 1,000,000 computers per month. That output requires 1,000,000 computer chips. If the computer manufacturer produced its own chips, the cost would be much higher than if it buys them from a chip maker operating on a much larger scale. As panel (b) shows, economies of scale in chip production are far from exhausted when 1,000,000 chips a month are produced.

Easily Observable Quality

If an input is well defined and its quality is easily determined at the time of purchase, that input is more likely to be purchased in the market than produced internally, other things constant. For example, a flour mill typically buys wheat in the market rather than grow its own, as the quality of the wheat can be easily assessed upon inspection. In contrast, the quality of certain inputs can be determined only during production. Firms whose reputations depend on the operation of a key component are likely to produce the component, especially if the quality varies widely across producers over time and can't be easily observed by inspection. For example, suppose that the manufacturer of a sensitive measuring instrument requires a crucial gauge, the quality of which can be observed only as the gauge is assembled. If the firm produces the gauge itself, it can closely monitor quality.

Producers sometimes integrate backward so they can offer consumers a guarantee about the quality of the components or ingredients in a product. For example, some chicken suppliers such as Tyson and Perdue can advertise the upbringing of their chickens because they raise their own. KFC, however, omits this family background because the company makes no claim about raising them, focusing instead on how well the company cooks chicken.

Many Suppliers

A firm wants an uninterrupted supply of components. If there are many suppliers of that component, a firm is more likely to buy it than make it, other things constant. Not only do abundant suppliers ensure a dependable source of components, competition keeps the price down and quality up. But a firm that cannot rely on a consistent supply of components may make its own to ensure a reliable source.

To Review: If a firm relies on market purchases of inputs rather than on vertical integration, it can benefit from the specialization and comparative advantage of individual suppliers. Other things constant, the firm is more likely to buy a component rather than produce it if (1) buying the component is cheaper than making it, (2) the component is well defined and its quality easily observable, and (3) there are many suppliers of the component.

Economies of Scope

economies of scope
Average costs decline as a firm makes a range of different products rather than specialize in just one product

So far we have considered issues affecting the optimal degree of vertical integration in producing a particular product. Even with outsourcing, the focus is on how best to produce a particular product, such as an automobile or a computer. But some firms branch into product lines that do not have a vertical relationship. **Economies of scope** exist when it's cheaper to produce two or more different items in one firm than to produce them in separate firms. For example, General Electric produces hundreds of different products ranging from light bulbs to jet engines. By spreading outlays for research and development and marketing (the company's motto is "Imagination at work") over many different products, GE can reduce those costs per unit. Or consider economies of scope on the farm. A farm family often grows a variety of crops and raises different farm animals—animals that recycle damaged crops and food scraps into meat and fertilizer. With economies of *scale*, the average cost per unit of output falls as the *scale* of the firm increases; *with economies of scope, average costs per unit fall as the firm supplies more types of products—that is, as the scope of the firm increases.* The cost of some fixed resources, such as specialized knowledge, can be spread across product lines.

Our focus has been on why firms exist, why they often integrate vertically, why they outsource, and why they sometimes produce a range of products. These steps toward realism move us beyond the simple picture of the firm created earlier. The next section challenges some simplifying assumptions about the amount of information available to market participants.

Market Behavior With Imperfect Information

For the most part, our analysis of market behavior has assumed that market participants have full information about products and resources. For consumers, full information involves knowledge about a product's price, quality, and availability. For firms, full information includes knowledge about the marginal productivity of various resources, about the appropriate technology for combining them, and about the demand for the firm's product. In reality, *reliable information is often costly for both consumers and producers.* This section examines the impact of less-than-perfect information on market behavior.

Optimal Search With Imperfect Information

Suppose you want to buy a new computer. You need information about the quality and features of each model and the prices at various retail outlets and online sites. To learn more about your choices, you may talk with friends and experts, read promotional brochures and computer publications, and visit online sites. Once you narrow your choice to one or two models, you may visit the mall, or let your fingers do the walking through the *Yellow Pages,* computer catalogs, online search engines, newspaper ads, and the like. Searching for the lowest price for a particular model involves a cost, primarily the opportunity cost of your time. This cost obviously varies from individual to individual and from item to item. Some people actually enjoy shopping, as you will see later in the chapter, but this "shop 'til you drop" attitude does not necessarily carry over to all purchases. *For most of us, the process of gathering consumer information can be considered nonmarket work.*

Marginal Cost of Search

In your quest for product information, you gather the easy and obvious information first. You may check on the price and availability at the few electronics stores at the mall. But as your search widens, the *marginal cost* of information increases, both because you may have to travel greater distances to check prices and services and because the opportunity cost of your time increases as you spend more time acquiring information. Consequently, the marginal cost curve for information slopes upward, as is shown in Exhibit 2. Note that a certain amount of information, I_f, is common knowledge and is freely available, so its marginal cost is zero.

Marginal Benefit of Search

The *marginal benefit* of acquiring additional information is a better quality for a given price or a lower price for a given quality. The marginal benefit is relatively large at first, but as you gather more information and grow more acquainted with the market, additional information yields less and less marginal benefit. For example, the likelihood of uncovering valuable information, such as an added feature or a lower price, at the second store or Web site visited is greater than the likelihood of finding this information at the twentieth store or Web site visited. Thus, the marginal benefit curve for additional information slopes downward, as is shown in Exhibit 2.

Optimal Search

Market participants continue to gather information as long as the marginal benefit of additional information exceeds its marginal cost. *Optimal search occurs where the marginal benefit just equals the marginal cost,* which in Exhibit 2 is where the two marginal curves intersect. Notice that at search levels exceeding the equilibrium amount, the marginal benefit of additional information is still positive but below marginal cost. Notice also that at some point the value of additional information reaches zero, as identified by I_p on the horizontal axis. This level of information could be identified as *full information.* The high marginal cost of acquiring I_p, however, makes it impractical to become fully informed. Thus, firms and consumers, by gathering the optimal amount

EXHIBIT 2 **Optimal Search With Imperfect Information**

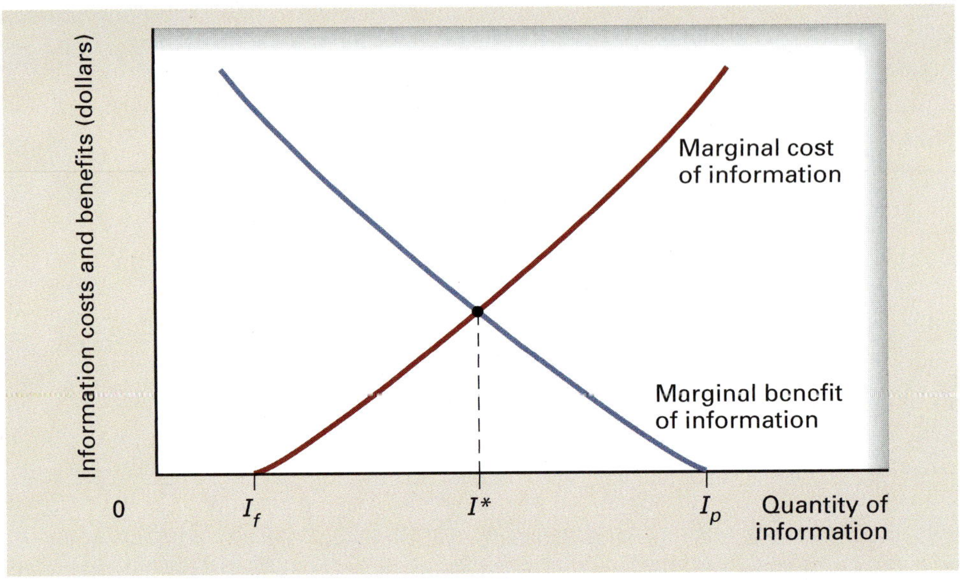

When information is not free, additional information is acquired as long as its marginal benefit exceeds its marginal cost. Equilibrium, or optimal search, occurs where marginal benefit equals marginal cost. I^* is the optimal quantity of information.

of information, I^*, have less-than-full information about the price, availability, and quality of products and resources.

Implications

This search model was developed by Nobel laureate George Stigler, who showed that the price of a product can differ among sellers because some consumers are unaware of lower prices elsewhere.[2] Thus, *search costs result in price dispersion, or different prices for the same product.* Some sellers call attention to price dispersions by claiming to have the lowest prices around and by promising to match any competitor's price—for example, Walmart makes such a promise. *Search costs also lead to quality differences across sellers, even for identically priced products, because consumers find the expected marginal cost of finding a higher quality product outweighs the expected marginal benefit.*

There are other implications of Stigler's search model. The more expensive the item, the greater the price dispersion in dollar terms, so the greater the expected marginal benefit from shopping around. You are more likely to shop around for a new car than for a new toothbrush. Also, as earnings increase, so does the opportunity cost of time, resulting in less searching and more price dispersion. On the other hand, any technological change that reduces the marginal cost of information lowers the marginal cost curve in Exhibit 2, increasing the optimal amount of information and reducing price dispersion. For example, some online sites, like mySimon.com, identify the lowest prices for books, airfares, automobiles, computers, and dozens of other products. And

2. George Stigler, "The Economics of Information," *Journal of Political Economy*, 69 (June 1961): 213–225.

some online sellers, like Buy.com, maintain the lowest prices on the Web as a way of attracting customers who undertake such searches. As a result of more readily available price information, consumers have become much more price-sensitive.[3] Thus, by reducing search costs, the Internet reduces price dispersion.

Here's another example of how information technology can improve market performance and enhance social welfare. Between 1997 and 2001, mobile phone service was introduced throughout a state in India with a large fishing industry. Researchers found that the adoption of mobile phones by fishermen and wholesalers sharply reduced price dispersions, in the process increasing both consumer and producer welfare.[4]

The Winner's Curse

In 1996, the federal government auctioned off leases to valuable space on the scarce radio spectrum. The space was to be used for cell phones, wireless networks, and portable fax machines. The bidding was carried out in the face of much uncertainty about what were then new markets. Bidders had little experience with the potential value of such leases. At the time, 89 companies made winning bids for 493 licenses totaling $10.2 billion. But by 1998, it became clear that many of the winning bidders couldn't pay, and many went bankrupt.[5] The auction eventually collected only half the amount of the winning bids. In auctions for products of uncertain value, such as wireless communications licenses, why do so many "winners" end up losers?

When bids were submitted, the true value of space on the radio spectrum could only be estimated. Suppose the average bid for a license was $10 million, with some higher and others lower. Suppose also that the winning bid was $20 million. The winning bid was not the average bid, which may have been the most reliable estimate of the true value, but the highest bid, which was the most optimistic estimate. Winners of such bids are said to experience the **winner's curse** because they often lose money after winning the bid, paying the price of being overly optimistic. (It will be interesting to see if similar problems result from the 2008 wireless spectrum auction, which raised $19.6 billion.)

winner's curse
The plight of the winning bidder who overestimates an asset's true value

The winner's curse applies to all cases of bidding in which the true value is unknown at the outset. For example, online auctions, such as eBay, often sell items of unknown value. Movie companies often bid up the price of screenplays to what some argue are unrealistic levels (only about 5 percent of screenplays studios purchase ever become movies). Likewise, publishers get into bidding wars over book manuscripts and even book proposals that are little more than titles. Team owners bid and often overpay for athletes who become free agents. And research shows that professional basketball players improve their performance in the year before signing a multiyear contract, but performance declines after that.[6] NBC lost money on the 2008 summer Olympics in Beijing and the 2010 winter Olympics in Vancouver; at the time of the bid for broadcast rights, the Olympic cities had not even been selected.

With perfect information about market value, potential buyers would never bid more than that market value. But *when competitive bidding is coupled with imperfect information, the winning bidder often ends up an overly optimistic loser.*

3. Glenn Ellison and Sara Ellison, "Search, Obfuscation, and Price Elasticities on the Internet." *Econometrica*, 77 (March 2009): 427–452.
4. Robert Jensen, "The Digital Provide: Information (Technology), Market Performance, and Welfare in the South Indian Fisheries Sector," *Quarterly Journal of Economics*, 122 (August 2007): 879–924.
5. Scott Ritter, "FCC Says Several Bidders to Return Wireless Licenses," *Wall Street Journal*, 18 June 1998.
6. Kevin Stiroh, "Playing for Keeps: Pay and Performance in the NBA," *Economic Inquiry*, 45 (January 2007): 145–161.

Asymmetric Information in Product Markets

We have considered the effects of costly information and limited information on market behavior. But the issue becomes more complicated when one side of the market knows more than the other side does, a problem of **asymmetric information**. There are two types of information that a market participant may want but lack: information about a product's *characteristics* and information about *actions* taken by the other party to the transaction. This section examines several examples of asymmetric information in the product market and the effects on market efficiency.

asymmetric information
One side of the market has better information about the product than does the other side

Hidden Characteristics: Adverse Selection

When one side of the market knows more than the other side about important product characteristics, the asymmetric information problem involves **hidden characteristics.** For example, the seller of a used car normally has abundant personal experience with important *characteristics* of that car, such as any accidents, breakdowns, gas mileage, maintenance record, performance in bad weather, and so on. A prospective buyer can only guess at these characteristics based on the car's appearance, ratings in *Consumer Reports*, and perhaps a test drive. The buyer cannot really know how well the car performs without driving it under varying traffic and weather conditions.

hidden characteristics
One side of the market knows more than the other side about product characteristics that are important to the other side

To simplify the problem, suppose there are only two types of used cars for sale: good ones and bad ones, or "lemons." A buyer who is certain about a car's type would be willing to pay $10,000 for a good used car but only $4,000 for a lemon. Again, only the seller knows which type is for sale. Prospective buyers believe that half the used cars on the market are good ones and half are lemons and are willing to pay, say, $7,000 for a car of unknown quality (the average expected value of cars on the market). Would $7,000 become the market price of used cars?

So far, the analysis has ignored the actions of potential sellers, who know which type of car they have. Because sellers of good cars can get only $7,000 for cars they know to be worth $10,000 on average, many will keep their cars or will sell them only to friends or relatives. But sellers of lemons will find $7,000 an attractive price for a car they know to be worth only $4,000. As a result, the proportion of good cars on the market will fall and the proportion of lemons will rise, reducing the average value of used cars on the market. As buyers come to realize that the mix has shifted toward lemons, they will reduce what they are willing to pay for cars of unknown quality. As the market price of used cars falls, potential sellers of good cars become even more reluctant to sell at such a low price, so the proportion of lemons increases, leading to still lower prices. The process could continue until few good cars are for sale on the open market. More generally, *when sellers have better information about a product's quality than buyers do, lower-quality products dominate the market.*

When those on the informed side of the market self-select in a way that harms the uninformed side of the market, the problem is one of **adverse selection.** In our example, car sellers, the informed side, self-select—that is, they decide whether or not to offer their cars for sale—in a way that increases the proportion of lemons for sale. Because of adverse selection, those still willing to buy on the open market often get stuck with lemons. There is empirical support for adverse selection in used car markets. For example, one researcher found that owners of lemons try to sell them to ill-informed buyers while owners of good cars hold onto theirs.[7]

adverse selection
Those on the informed side of the market self-select in a way that harms those on the uninformed side of the market

7. George Seldon, "The Market for Used Cars: New Evidence of the Lemons Phenomenon," *Applied Economics*, 41 (Issue 22, 2009): 2867–2885.

Hidden Actions: The Principal-Agent Problem

A second type of problem occurs when one side of a transaction can pursue an unobservable *action* that affects the other side. Whenever one side of an economic relationship can take a relevant action that the other side cannot observe, the situation is described as one of **hidden actions.** In this age of specialization, there are many tasks we do not perform for ourselves because others do them better and because others have a lower opportunity cost of time. Suppose your car isn't working and you have no clue what's wrong. The mechanic you hire may have other objectives, such as minimizing on-the-job effort or maximizing the garage's profit. But the mechanic's actions are hidden from you. Although your car's problem may be only a loose connection wire, the mechanic could inflate the bill by charging you for work not needed or not performed. This asymmetric information problem occurs because one side of a transaction can pursue *hidden actions* that affect the other side. When buyers have difficulty monitoring and evaluating the quality of goods or services purchased, some suppliers may substitute poor-quality resources or exercise less diligence in providing the service.

hidden actions
One side of an economic relationship can do something that the other side cannot observe

The problem that arises from hidden actions is called the **principal-agent problem,** which describes a relationship in which one party, known as the **principal,** contracts with another party, known as the **agent,** in the expectation that the agent will act on behalf of the principal. *The problem arises when the goals of the agent are incompatible with those of the principal* **and** *when the agent can pursue hidden actions.* For example, you are the *principal* and the garage mechanic is your *agent.* You could also confront a principal-agent problem when you deal with a doctor, lawyer, stockbroker, plumber, building contractor, or real estate agent, to name a few. For example, real estate agents are usually better informed than their clients about the housing market. Research suggests that agents exploit this asymmetry by encouraging their clients to sell their homes too cheaply and too quickly.[8]

principal-agent problem
The agent's objectives differ from those of the principal's, and one side can pursue hidden actions

principal
A person or firm who hires an agent to act on behalf of that person or firm

agent
A person or firm who is supposed to act on behalf of the principal

Any employer-employee relationship could become a principal-agent problem, with the employer as the principal and the employee as the agent. Again, the problem arises because the agent's objectives are not the same as the principal's *and* because the agent's actions are hidden. Not all principal-agent relationships pose a problem. For example, when you hire someone to cut your hair or your lawn, there are no hidden actions so you can judge the results for yourself.

Asymmetric Information in Insurance Markets

Asymmetric information also creates problems in insurance markets. For example, from an insurer's point of view, the ideal candidate for health insurance is someone who leads a long, healthy life, then dies peacefully while sleeping. But many people are poor risks for health insurers because of hidden characteristics (bad genes) or hidden actions (smoking and drinking excessively, getting exercise only on trips to the refrigerator, and thinking a balanced meal consists of some beef jerky and a six-pack of beer). In the insurance market, it is the buyers, not the sellers, who have more information about the characteristics and actions that predict their likely need for insurance in the future.

If the insurance company has no way of distinguishing among applicants, it must charge those who are good health risks the same price as those who are poor ones. This price is attractive to poor risks but not to good ones, some of whom will not buy insurance. The insured group becomes less healthy on average, so rates must rise, making

8. Steven Levitt and Chad Syverson, "Market Distortions When Agents Are Better Informed: The Value of Information in Real Estate Transactions," *Review of Economics and Statistics*, 90 (November 2008): 599–611.

insurance even less attractive to healthy people. *Because of adverse selection, insurance buyers tend to be less healthy than the population as a whole.* Adverse selection was used as an argument for the health care reform introduced in 2010.

The insurance problem is compounded by the fact that once people buy insurance, their behavior may change in a way that increases the probability that a claim will be made. For example, those with health insurance may take less care of their health, and those with theft insurance may take less care of their valuables. This incentive problem is referred to as *moral hazard.* **Moral hazard** occurs when an individual's behavior changes in a way that increases the likelihood of an unfavorable outcome. More generally, *moral hazard is a principal-agent problem because it occurs when those on one side of a transaction have an incentive to shirk their responsibilities because the other side is unable to observe them.* The responsibility could be to repair a car, maintain one's health, or safeguard one's valuables. Both the mechanic and the insurance buyer may take advantage of the ignorant party. In the car-repair example, the mechanic is the agent; in the insurance example, the policy buyer is the principal. Thus, moral hazard arises when someone can undertake hidden action; this could be either the agent or the principal, depending on the situation.

moral hazard
A situation in which one party, as a result of a contract, has an incentive to alter their behavior in a way that harms the other party to the contract

Moral hazard was a frequent topic of debate each time the federal government decided to bail out or not bail out a company or industry during the 2008 global financial crisis. For example, if an investment bank was rescued after its past risky behavior, would such a bank be more inclined to take similar risks in the future? Some observers believe the answer is yes.

Coping With Asymmetric Information

There are ways of reducing the consequences of asymmetric information. An incentive structure or an information-revealing system can be developed to reduce the problems associated with the lopsided availability of information. For example, all states now have "lemon laws" that offer compensation to buyers of new or used cars that turn out to be lemons. Used-car dealers may also offer warranties to reduce the buyer's risk of getting stuck with a lemon. Most garages provide written estimates before a job is done, and many return the defective parts to the customer as evidence that the repair was necessary and was carried out. People often get multiple estimates for major repairs.

Insurance companies deal with adverse selection and moral hazard in a variety of ways. Prior to recent federal legislation, most required applicants to undergo a physical exam and to answer questions about their medical history and lifestyle (false information could block benefits). Preexisting medical conditions were not usually covered. To avoid adverse selection, an insurer often covers all those in a group, such as all company employees, not just those who would otherwise self-select. Insurers reduce moral hazard by making the policyholder pay, say, the first $250 of a claim as a "deductible" and by requiring the policyholder to copay a percentage of a claim. Also, as more claims are filed, insurance premiums go up and the policy could be canceled. Property insurers reduce premiums for those who install security systems, smoke alarms, sprinkler systems, and who take other safety precautions.

Asymmetric Information in Labor Markets

Our market analysis for particular kinds of labor typically assumes that workers are more or less interchangeable. In equilibrium, each worker in a particular labor market is assumed to be paid the same wage, a wage equal to the marginal revenue product of the last unit of labor hired. But what if ability differs across workers? Differences in ability present no particular problem as long as these differences can be readily observed by the employer. If the productivity of each worker is easily quantified through measures such as crates of oranges picked, quantity of garments sewn, or number of cars sold, these can and do serve as the basis for pay. And such incentives seem to affect output. For example, when the British National Health Service changed the pay basis of dentists from "contact hours" with patients to the number of cavities filled, dentists found more cavities and filled them in only a third of the time they took under the contact-hour pay scheme.[9]

Because production often requires a team effort, the employer may not be able to attribute specific outputs to particular workers. When information about each worker's marginal productivity is hard to come by, employers usually pay workers by the hour. Sometimes the pay combines an hourly rate and incentive pay linked to a measure of productivity. For example, a sales representative typically earns a base salary plus a commission tied to sales. At times, the task of evaluating performance is left to customers. Workers who provide personal services, such as waiters, barbers, beauticians, pizza deliverers, and bellhops, rely partly or mostly on tips. These services are "personal" and visible, so customers are usually in the best position to judge the quality and timeliness of service and to tip accordingly.

Adverse Selection in Labor Markets

A job applicant's true abilities—motivation, work habits, skills, ability to get along with others, and the like—are, to a large extent, *hidden characteristics*. In a labor market with hidden characteristics, employers might be better off offering a higher wage. The higher the wage, the more attractive the job is to more-qualified workers. Paying a higher wage also encourages those who are hired not to goof off or otherwise jeopardize an attractive job. Paying above-market wages to attract and retain more-productive workers is called paying **efficiency wages,** something that Henry Ford did.

efficiency wage theory
The idea that offering high wages attracts a more talented labor pool and encourages those hired to perform well to keep their jobs

Signaling and Screening

The person on the side of the market with hidden characteristics and hidden actions has an incentive to say the right thing. For example, a job applicant might say, "Hire me because I am hardworking, reliable, prompt, highly motivated, and just an all-around great employee." Or a manufacturer might say, "At Ford, quality is job one." But such claims appear self-serving and thus are not necessarily believable. To cut through this fog, both sides of the market try to develop credible ways of communicating reliable information about qualifications.

Signaling is the attempt by the informed side of the market to communicate information that the other side would find valuable. Consider signaling in the job market. Because some jobs require abilities that are unobservable on a résumé or in an interview, job applicants offer proxy measures, such as years of education, college grades, and letters of recommendation. A proxy measure is called a *signal*, which is an observable indicator of some hidden characteristic. A signal is sent by the informed side of the market to the uninformed side and is useful as long as less-qualified applicants face more difficulty sending the same signal.

signaling
Using a proxy measure to communicate information about unobservable characteristics; the signal is more effective if more-productive workers find it easier to send than do less-productive workers

To identify the best workers, employers try to *screen* applicants. **Screening** is the attempt by the uninformed side of the market to uncover the relevant but hidden characteristics of the informed party. An initial screen might check each résumé for spelling and typographical errors. Although not important in themselves, such errors suggest a lack of attention to detail—which could reduce labor productivity. The uninformed party must

screening
The process used by employers to select the most qualified workers based on observable characteristics, such as a job applicant's level of education and course grades

9. John Pencavel, "Piecework and On-the-Job Screening," *Working Paper*, Stanford University, (June 1975).

identify signals that less-productive individuals have more difficulty sending. A signal that can be sent with equal ease by all workers, regardless of their productivity, does not provide a useful way of screening applicants. But if, for example, more-productive workers find it easier to graduate from college than do less-productive workers, a college degree is a measure worth using to screen workers. In this case, education may be valuable, not so much because of its direct effect on a worker's productivity, but simply because it enables employers to distinguish between types of workers. In fact, the actual pay increase from a fourth year of college that results in graduation is several times the pay increase from just a third year of college. This finding is consistent with the screening theory of education.

To Review: Because the potential productivity of job applicants cannot be measured directly, an employer must rely on proxy measures to screen applicants. *The most valuable proxy is a signal that can be sent more easily by more-productive workers and also is a good predictor of future productivity.* The problems of adverse selection, signaling, and screening are discussed in the case study of how McDonald's selects franchisees, "World of Business: Reputation of a Big Mac" at the end of the book.

Behavioral Economics

Traditional economics assumes that people act rationally to maximize their overall well-being. People know what they want, they try to make the most of what they have, they make choices that are fairly consistent given the circumstances, and they follow through with those choices. In short, *the traditional economic approach assumes that people pursue their rational self-interest.* And according to Adam Smith, the pursuit of self-interest promotes the general good, so the market system works in a reinforcing and beneficial cycle. In the extreme, this standard approach views the economy as populated by calculating, unemotional maximizers who make choices consistent with rational self-interest and then follow through on those choices.

Viewing people as robot-like maximizers is a simplification that can be defended on the grounds that this approach is easy to spell out in a theoretical model and it yields clear, testable implications about how people behave. Much empirical work backs up this version of human nature. And even if people don't actually make such complex calculations, they act as if they do. For example, they act as if they can maximize utility by equating the relevant marginal utilities.

On the other hand, psychologists have come to believe that people are prone to mistakes, are fickle and inconsistent, and often do not get the best deal when making choices. Psychologists investigate the biases, faulty assumptions, and errors that affect how people make decisions in all aspects of life. In recent decades, some economists have begun to rely on findings from psychology to look at instances where people do not act according to traditional economic theory. The convergence of economics and psychology eventually created a new field of study referred to as behavioral economics, a field pursued by a small but growing band of economists. **Behavioral economics** borrows insights from psychology to help explain some economic decisions. This approach questions some assumptions of traditional economics, particularly the assumptions of (1) unbounded rationality and (2) unbounded willpower.

behavioral economics
An approach that borrows insights from psychology to help explain economic choices

Unbounded Rationality

Nobel Prize winner Herbert Simon was an early critic of the idea that people have unlimited information-processing capabilities. He introduced the term "bounded rationality" to describe a more realistic conception of human problem-solving ability, a term introduced earlier in this chapter to help explain optimal firm size. Because we have only so much brainpower and only so much time, we cannot be expected to solve complex production or consumption problems optimally. When faced with lots of information that we aren't sure how to process, most of us rely on simple rules of thumb for guidance. The simplest rule of thumb in the face of a difficult decision is to do nothing.

Psychologists find that people are prone to inertia, even when doing nothing may cost them money. In the face of uncertainty, doing nothing or doing little also means that people are inclined to accept default rules. For example, employees have a strong tendency to stick to whatever savings option an employer presented to them as the default option, even when they are free to choose better options. Many accept the default option even when that option is not to save at all, and thereby miss out on any free money available through a company-match. Inertia is also why, once a decision is made, or made for them, the chooser tends to stick with that option even when circumstances change. In short, we humans try to avoid making some decisions even when the consequences of no decision are costly. In that regard, we do not seem to be pursuing our self-interest.

Unbounded Willpower

A second assumption of traditional economics is that people, once they make a decision, have unbounded willpower—that is, they have complete self-control. But we humans, even when we know what's best for us, often lack the discipline to follow through. Most of us have, despite our best intentions, ended up eating, drinking, or spending too much, and exercising, saving, or studying too little. For example, nearly two-thirds of American adults are overweight. The case study, "Behavioral Economics: Self-Control: Just Don't Do It!" at the end of the book, looks at issues of self-control.

Conclusion

The firm has evolved through a natural selection process as the form of organization that minimizes both transaction and production costs. Ways of organizing production that are more efficient will be selected by the economic system for survival. Attributes that yield an economic profit will thrive, and those that do not will fall away. The form of organization selected may not be optimal in the sense that it cannot be improved, but it is the most efficient of those that have been tried. If there is a way to organize production that is more efficient, some entrepreneur will stumble on it one day and will be rewarded with greater profit. The improvement may not always be the result of conscious design. Once a more efficient way of organizing production is uncovered, others will imitate it.

In conventional demand-and-supply analysis, trades occur in impersonal markets, and the buyer has no special concern about who is on the sell side. But with asymmetric information, the mix and characteristics of the other side of the market become important. When the problem of adverse selection is severe enough, some markets may cease to function. Market participants try to overcome the limitations of asymmetric information by signaling, screening, and trying to be quite explicit and transparent about the terms of the transaction.

Behavioral economists have borrowed insights from psychology to help explain some economic choices that seem inconsistent with rational self-interest. Psychologists argue that because people have trouble with complex choices, they tend to do nothing or go with whatever default option is presented. And people often lack the self-control to put up with near-term costs for long-term benefits.

Summary

1. According to Ronald Coase, firms arise when production is more efficient using the hierarchy of the firm than using market transactions. Because production requires elaborate coordination of many resources, all this activity can usually be carried out more efficiently under the direction of a firm's manager than by having a consumer negotiate detailed performance contracts with many resource suppliers.
2. The extent to which a firm integrates vertically depends on the transaction costs and the production costs of economic activity. Other things constant, the firm is more likely to buy a component rather than produce it if (a) it's cheaper to buy it than make it, (b) the item is well defined and its quality easily determined, and (c) there are many suppliers of the component.
3. Economics of scope exist when it is cheaper to produce two or more different products in one firm than to produce them in separate firms.
4. A buyer searches for product information as long as the marginal benefit of search exceeds its marginal cost. Because information is costly, product prices may differ across suppliers of otherwise identical products. A new technology, such as the Internet, that reduces search costs will increase the amount of search and reduce price differences for a given product.
5. Asymmetric information occurs when one side of the market is better informed about a product than the other side is. The uninformed side may not know about hidden characteristics or about hidden actions. Because of adverse selection, those on the uninformed side of the market may find they are dealing with exactly the wrong people.
6. When the productivity of job applicants cannot be directly observed, an employer may try to screen them based on some signal, such as the level of education or college grades, that more-productive workers can send more easily than can less-productive workers.
7. Standard economics assumes that people are rational in pursuing their self-interest. They have computer-like abilities to make marginal calculations and have sufficient willpower to follow through on decisions that involve near term costs for long-term gains. Psychologists question the ability of humans to make complex decisions and to follow through on choices that involve near-term costs. Behavioral economics borrows insights from psychology to help explain some economic decisions that otherwise seem inconsistent with rational self-interest.

Key Concepts

Vertical integration 279
Outsourcing 279
Core competency 280
Bounded rationality 280
Economies of scope 282
Winner's curse 285
Asymmetric information 286
Hidden characteristics 286
Adverse selection 286
Hidden actions 287
Principal-agent problem 287
Principal 287
Agent 287
Moral hazard 288
Efficiency wage theory 289
Signaling 289
Screening 289
Behavioral economics 290

Questions for Review

1. Rationale for the Firm Explain Ronald Coase's theory of why firms exist. Why isn't all production consolidated in one large firm?
2. Boundaries of the Firm Define vertical integration. What factors should a firm consider when determining what degree of vertical integration to undertake?
3. Boundaries of the Firm Ashland Oil buys its crude oil in the market. Larger oil refiners, such as Texaco, drill for their own crude oil. Why do some oil companies drill for their own crude oil and others buy crude oil in the market?
4. Boundaries of the Firm In the movement to downsize government, advocates often recommend turning over some government services to private firms hired by the government. What are the potential benefits and costs of such outsourcing? Prepare your answer by reviewing. The Outsourcing Institute's "Top 10 Reasons Companies Outsource" at http://www.horizontech.net/toptenreasons.htm.
5. Economies of Scope Distinguish between economies of scale and economies of scope. Why do some firms produce multiple product lines, while others produce only one?
6. Search with Imperfect Information Fifty years ago, people shopped by mail using catalogs from large mail-order houses. In the last few years, catalog shopping has again become a widely used method of buying. Online shopping is also growing. What reasons can you suggest for the growth in these forms of shopping?
7. Asymmetric Information Define asymmetric information. Distinguish between hidden characteristics and hidden actions. Which type of asymmetric information contributes to the principal-agent problem?

8. THE PRINCIPAL-AGENT PROBLEM Discuss the nature of the principal-agent problem. Determine which is the principal and which is the agent in each of the following relationships:
   a. A firm that produces goods for export and the export management company that helps market its goods overseas
   b. The management of a firm and its stockholders
   c. A homeowner and the plumber hired to make repairs
   d. A dentist and a patient
   e. An employee-pension management firm and the company using its services

9. ADVERSE SELECTION AND MORAL HAZARD Describe the problems faced by health insurance companies as a result of adverse selection and moral hazard. How do insurance companies try to reduce these problems?

10. SIGNALING Give an example of signaling in each of the following situations:
    a. Choosing a doctor
    b. Applying to graduate school
    c. Filling out a form for a dating service

11. SIGNALING AND SCREENING What roles do signaling and screening play in a labor market with asymmetric information?

12. Case Study: The Reputation of a Big Mac (See page 730.) Explain how the time and financial requirements involved in obtaining a McDonald's franchise relate to the hidden-characteristics problem. Why would existing franchise owners have an interest in the maintenance of high application standards for new franchise owners?

Problems and Exercises

13. BEHAVIORAL ECONOMICS A management consultant advised a small business owner to fully analyze all transaction costs, delineate the boundaries of the business, and develop an equation to calculate exactly economies of scope. The owner replied that there were not enough hours in the day to gather all this information and so the owner would just keep running the business in the same way as usual. What assumption from traditional economics is in dispute here?

14. SEARCH WITH IMPERFECT INFORMATION The following questions concern the accompanying graph.

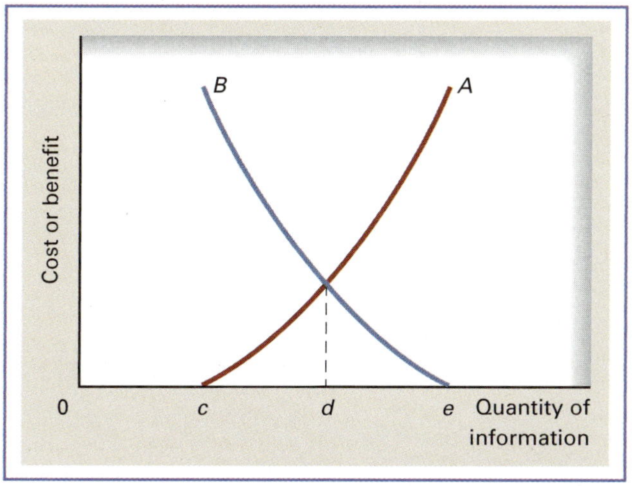

    a. Identify the two curves shown on the graph, and explain their upward or downward slopes.
    b. Why does curve *A* intersect the horizontal axis?
    c. What is the significance of quantity *d*?
    d. What does *e* represent?
    e. How would the optimal quantity of information change if the marginal benefit of information increased—that is, if the marginal benefit curve shifted upward?

15. SEARCH WITH IMPERFECT INFORMATION Determine the effect of each of the following on the optimal level of search.
    a. The consumer's wage increases.
    b. One seller guarantees to offer the lowest price on the market.
    c. The technology of gathering and transmitting market information improves.

Global Economic Watch Exercises

Login to www.cengagebrain.com and access the Global Economic Watch to do these exercises.

16. GLOBAL ECONOMIC WATCH Go to the Global Economic Crisis Resource Center. Select Global Issues in Context. In the Basic Search box at the top of the page, enter the phrase "behavioral economics." On the Results page, go to the Global Viewpoints Section. Click on the link for the July 15, 2010, editorial "Economics Behaving Badly." The authors stated, "Behavioral economics should complement, not substitute for, more substantive economic interventions." Use one of the examples from the editorial to explain this statement.

17. GLOBAL ECONOMIC WATCH Go to the Global Economic Crisis Resource Center. Select Global Issues in Context. In the Basic Search box at the top of the page, enter the term "moral hazard." Choose an article published in the most recent two years. Explain how the article illustrates the concept of moral hazard.

15 Economic Regulation and Antitrust Policy

JIM BRYANT/UPI/Landov

- If the "invisible hand" of competition yields such desirable results for the economy, why does the government need to regulate business?
- Is monopoly ever better than competition?
- Who benefits most when government regulates monopoly?
- Why did the U.S. government haul Microsoft into court, and what about recent regulator interest in Apple and in Google?
- Is the U.S. economy becoming more competitive or less competitive?

Answers to these and other questions are addressed in this chapter, which discusses government regulation of business.

Businesspeople praise competition but they love monopoly. They praise competition because it harnesses the diverse and often conflicting objectives of various market participants and channels them into the efficient production of goods and services. Competition does this as if by "an invisible hand." Businesspeople love monopoly because it provides the surest path to economic profit in the long run—and, after all, profit is the name of the game for any business. The fruits of monopoly are so tempting that a firm might try to eliminate competitors or conspire with them to raise prices. As Adam Smith observed more than two centuries ago, "People of the same trade seldom meet together, even for merriment or diversion, but the conversation ends in a conspiracy against the public, or in some contrivance to raise prices."

The tendency of firms to seek monopolistic advantage is understandable, but monopoly usually harms consumers and other producers. Public policy can play a role by promoting competition in those markets where competition seems desirable and by

reducing the harmful effects of monopoly in those markets where the output can be most efficiently supplied by one or just a few firms.

Topics discussed include:

- Regulating natural monopolies
- Theories of economic regulation
- Deregulation
- Antitrust policy
- Per se illegality
- Rule of reason
- Merger waves
- Competitive trends

Types of Government Regulation

market power
The ability of a firm to raise its price without losing all its customers to rival firms

social regulation
Government regulations aimed at improving health and safety

economic regulation
Government regulation of natural monopoly, where, because of economies of scale, average production cost is lowest when a single firm supplies the market

antitrust policy
Government regulation aimed at preventing monopoly and fostering competition in markets where competition is desirable

You'll recall that a monopolist supplies a product with no close substitutes, so a monopolist can usually charge a higher price than would prevail with competition. When only a few firms serve a market, those firms are sometimes able to coordinate their actions, either explicitly or implicitly, to act like a monopolist. The ability of a firm to raise the price without losing all its sales to rivals is called **market power**. Any firm facing a downward-sloping demand curve has some control over the price and thus some market power. The presumption is that a monopoly, or a group of firms acting as a monopoly, restricts output to charge a higher price than competing firms would charge. With output restricted, the marginal benefit of the final unit sold exceeds its marginal cost, so expanding output would increase social welfare. *By failing to expand output to the point where marginal benefit equals marginal cost, firms with market power produce less of the good than would be socially optimal.*

Other distortions have also been associated with monopolies. For example, some critics argue that because a monopoly is insulated from competition, it is not as innovative as aggressive competitors would be. Worse still, because of their size and economic importance, monopolies may influence public choices to protect and enhance their monopoly power.

Three kinds of government policies are designed to alter or control firm behavior: social regulation, economic regulation, and antitrust policy. **Social regulation** tries to improve health and safety, such as control over unsafe working conditions and dangerous products. Health care reform is another example of social regulation; the 2010 health care act was the broadest social legislation since the Great Depression. Social regulation can have far-reaching economic consequences, but that's not the focus of this chapter. **Economic regulation** aims to control the price, output, the entry of new firms, and the quality of service *in industries in which monopoly appears inevitable or even desirable.* Government controls over *natural monopolies,* such as local electricity transmission, local phone service, and a subway system, are examples of economic regulation. Several other industries, such as land and air transportation, have also been regulated in the past. Federal, state, and local governments carry out economic regulation. **Antitrust policy** outlaws attempts to monopolize, or cartelize, markets in which competition is desirable. Antitrust policy is pursued in the courts by government attorneys and by individual firms that charge other firms with violating antitrust laws. Economic regulation and antitrust policy are examined in this chapter. Let's turn first to economic regulation—specifically, the regulation of natural monopolies.

Regulating a Natural Monopoly

Because of economies of scale, a natural monopoly has a long-run average cost curve that slopes downward over the range of market demand. This means that the lowest average cost is achieved when one firm serves the entire market. For example, a subway system is a natural monopoly. If two competing systems tunnel parallel routes throughout a city, the average cost per trip would be higher than if a single system provided this service.

Unregulated Profit Maximization

Exhibit 1 shows the demand and cost conditions for a natural monopoly, in this case a metropolitan subway system. A natural monopoly usually faces huge initial capital costs, such as those associated with digging a subway system, building a natural gas pipeline, launching a communications satellite, or wiring a city for electricity or cable TV. Once capital is in place, average cost falls as output increases, so the average cost curve slopes downward over a broad range of output. In this situation, average cost is lowest when a single firm supplies the market.

An unregulated monopolist, like any other firm, chooses the price-quantity combination that maximizes profit. In Exhibit 1, the monopolist—in this case, the operator of a subway system—maximizes profit by producing where marginal revenue equals marginal cost—that is, where 50 million riders per month pay $4 per trip. The monopolist reaps the profit identified by the blue-shaded rectangle. The *abc* triangle, which is the area below the demand curve and above the $4 price, measures the consumer surplus—consumers' net gain from riding the subway. The problem with letting the monopolist maximize profit is that the resulting price-output combination is inefficient in terms of social welfare. Consumers pay a price that far exceeds the marginal cost of providing the service. *The marginal value of additional output exceeds its marginal cost, so social welfare would increase if output expanded.*

Government can increase social welfare by forcing the monopolist to lower the price and expand output. To accomplish this, government can either operate the monopoly itself, as it does with most urban transit systems, or government can *regulate* a privately owned monopoly, as it does with some urban transit systems, local phone services, cable TV service, and electricity transmission. Government-owned or government-regulated monopolies are called **public utilities**. Here we focus on government regulation, though the issues discussed are similar if the government owns the monopoly.

public utilities
Government-owned or government-regulated monopolies

Setting Price Equal to Marginal Cost

Many facets of a natural monopoly have been regulated, but the price-output combination gets the most attention. Suppose government regulators require the monopolist to produce the level of output that is efficient—that is, where the price, which also measures the marginal benefit to consumers, equals the marginal cost of the good. This price-output combination is depicted in Exhibit 1 as point *e*, where the demand curve, or the marginal benefit curve, intersects the marginal cost curve, yielding a price of $0.50 per trip and quantity of 105 million trips per month. Consumers clearly prefer this price to the $4 charged by the unregulated monopolist. The consumer surplus from riding the subway jumps from triangle *abc* without regulation to triangle *aef* with regulation.

EXHIBIT 1 Regulating a Natural Monopoly

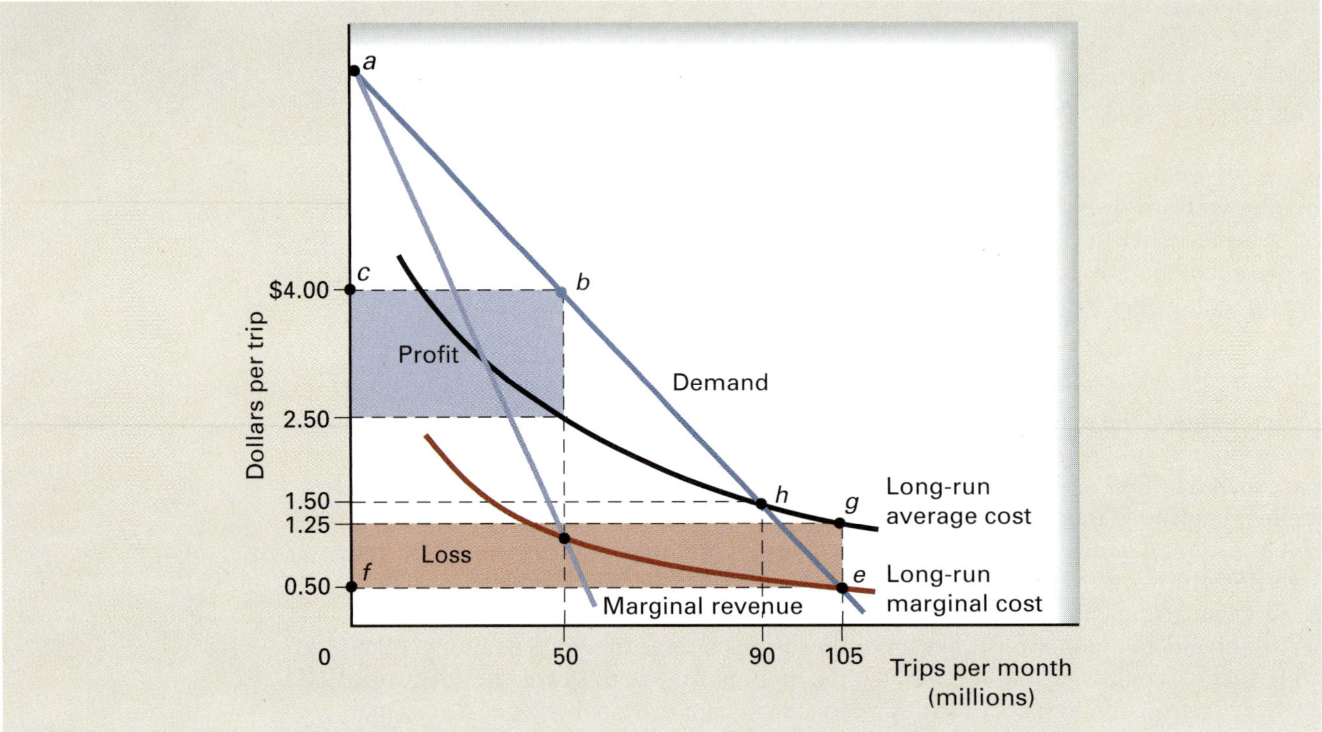

With a natural monopoly, the long-run average cost curve slopes downward where it intersects the market demand curve. The unregulated firm maximizes profit by producing where marginal revenue equals marginal cost, in this case, 50 million trips per month at a price of $4.00 per trip. This outcome is inefficient because price, or marginal benefit, exceeds marginal cost. To achieve the efficient output rate, regulators could set the price at $0.50 per trip. The subway would sell 105 million trips per month, which would be an efficient outcome. But at that price, the subway would lose money and would require a subsidy to keep going. As an alternative, regulators could set the price at $1.50 per trip. The subway would sell 90 million trips per month and would just break even (because price equals average cost). Social welfare could still be increased by expanding output as long as the price, or marginal benefit, exceeds marginal cost, but that would result in an economic loss.

Notice, however, that the monopolist now has a problem. The average cost of supplying each of the 105 million trips per month is $1.25, identified by point *g* on the average cost curve. This is more than double the regulated price of $0.50. Rather than earning a profit, the monopolist suffers a loss—in this case, $0.75 per trip, for a total loss of $79 million a month, identified by the pink-shaded rectangle. *Forcing a natural monopolist to produce where price, or marginal benefit, equals marginal cost results in an economic loss to this monopolist.* In the long run, the monopolist would go out of business rather than endure such a loss.

Subsidizing the Natural Monopolist

How can regulators encourage the monopolist to stay in business yet still produce where price equals marginal cost? The government can cover the loss—*subsidize* the firm so it earns a normal profit. Bus and subway fares are typically set below the average cost of providing the service, with the difference made up by a government subsidies. For example, government subsidies pay more than 40 percent of the Washington, DC, Metro subway system. Amtrak gets a federal subsidy covering about a third of its operating budget. One drawback with the subsidy solution is that, to provide the subsidy, the government must raise taxes or forgo public spending in some other area. Thus, the subsidy has an opportunity cost and could easily result in inefficiencies elsewhere in the economy.

Setting Price Equal to Average Cost

Although some public utilities are subsidized, most are not. Instead, regulators try to establish a price that provides the monopolist with a "fair return." Recall that the average cost curve includes a normal profit. Thus, *setting price equal to average cost* provides a normal, or "fair," profit for the monopolist. In Exhibit 1, the demand curve intersects the average cost curve at point *h*, yielding a price of \$1.50 per trip and a quantity of 90 million trips a month. This price-output combination allows the monopolist to stay in business without a subsidy.

Setting price equal to average total cost enhances social welfare compared to the unregulated situation. The monopolist would prefer an economic profit but accepts a normal profit to stay in business. After all, a normal profit is the most this firm could expect if resources were redirected to their best alternative uses. But note that the marginal benefit of the 90 millionth trip exceeds its marginal cost. Therefore, expanding output beyond 90 million trips per month would increase social welfare.

The Regulatory Dilemma

Setting price equal to marginal cost yields the *socially optimal* allocation of resources because *the consumers' marginal benefit from the last unit sold equals the marginal cost of producing that last unit.* In our example, setting the price at \$0.50 equates marginal benefit and marginal cost, but the monopolist faces losses unless government provides a subsidy. These losses disappear if price equals average cost, which in our example is \$1.50. The higher price ensures a normal profit, but output falls 15 million trips short of the socially optimal level.

Thus, the dilemma facing the regulator is whether to set price equal to marginal cost, which is socially optimal but requires a government subsidy, or to set a break-even price even though output falls short of the socially optimal level. There is no right answer. Compared with the unregulated profit-maximizing price of \$4, both reduce the price, increase output, erase economic profit, increase consumer surplus, and increase social welfare. Although Exhibit 1 lays out the options neatly, regulators usually face a cloudier picture. Demand and cost curves can only be estimated, and the regulated firm may withhold or distort information. For example, a natural monopoly may overstate costs so it can charge more.

Alternative Theories of Economic Regulation

Why do governments regulate certain industries? Why not let market forces allocate resources? There are two views of government regulation. The first has been implicit in the discussion so far—namely, economic regulation is in the *public interest.* Economic regulation promotes social welfare by keeping prices down when one or just a few firms serve a market. A second, darker, view is that economic regulation is not in the public interest but is in the *special interest* of producers. According to this view, *well-organized producer groups expect to profit from economic regulation and persuade public officials to impose restrictions that existing producers find attractive, such as limiting entry into the industry or preventing competition among existing firms.* Individual producers have more to gain or to lose from regulation than do individual consumers. Producers typically are also better organized and more focused than consumers and are therefore better able to bring about regulations that favor producers.

Producers' Special Interest in Economic Regulation

To understand how and why producer interests could influence public regulation, think back to the last time you got a haircut. Most states regulate the training and licensing of barbers and beauticians. If any new regulation affecting the profession is proposed, who do you suppose has more interest in that legislation, you or someone who cuts hair for a living? *Producers have an intense interest in matters that affect their livelihood, so they try to shape such legislation.* Those who cut hair for a living often try to restrict entry by requiring thousands of hours of instruction. At any public hearings on haircut regulations, industry officials provide self-serving testimony, while consumers largely ignore the whole thing.

As a consumer, you do not specialize in getting haircuts. You purchase haircuts, cold cuts, hardware, software, underwear, and thousands of other goods and services. You have no *special interest* in haircuts. Some economists argue that because consumers ignore such matters, regulators often favor producer interests. Well-organized producer groups, as squeaky wheels in the legislative machinery, get the most grease in the form of favorable regulations. Such regulations are usually introduced under the guise of advancing consumer interests or protecting the public. Producer groups may argue that unbridled competition in their industry would hurt consumers. For example, the alleged problem of "cutthroat" competition among taxi drivers led to regulations that eliminated price competition and restricted the number of taxis in most large metropolitan areas. New York City has 10,000 fewer taxis now than it did 70 years ago (Mexico City has many more taxis per resident). As a result, taxis in New York City are harder to find and fares are higher. To operate a cab in New York City, someone must purchase a "medallion." The purchase price reflects the market value to taxi owners of regulations that restrict entry and set fares above the competitive level. The average price of a taxi medallion increased from $27,000 in 1968 to more than $700,000 in 2010. Regulation gives medallion owners an abiding interest in blocking entry. If market entry and taxi fares were deregulated, cabs would become more plentiful, fares would fall to competitive levels, and medallions would become worthless.

Regulation may be introduced under the guise of quality control, such as keeping "quacks" out of certain professions. But entry restrictions usually reduce competition and increase prices. The special-interest theory may be valid even when the initial intent of the legislation was in the consumer interest. Over time, the regulatory machinery may shift toward the special interests of producers, who, in effect, "capture" the regulating agency. This **capture theory of regulation** was discussed by George Stigler, the Nobel laureate mentioned in the previous chapter. He argued that "as a general rule, regulation is acquired by the industry and is designed and operated for its benefit."[1]

capture theory of regulation
Producers' political power and strong stake in the regulatory outcome lead them, in effect, to "capture" the regulating agency and prevail on it to serve producer interests

Critics charge that the Securities and Exchange Commission failed to uncover the massive fraud by Bernie Madoff, despite numerous complaints to the agency, because it was captured by the industry it was supposed to regulate. For example, SEC lawyers didn't want to ruffle feathers because they hoped to land high-paying jobs in the securities industry after building contacts and experience in Washington.[2] The case study, "Public Policy: Airline Regulation and Deregulation" at the end of the book, discusses the regulation and, more recently, deregulation of another industry—airlines.

1. George Stigler, "The Theory of Economic Regulation," *Bell Journal of Economics and Management Science*, 3 (Spring 1971): 3.
2. See Erin Arvedlund, *Too Good to Be True: The Rise and Fall of Bernie Madoff*, (Penguin Group, 2009): 199.

Recall the alternative views of regulation: one holds that regulation is in the public, or consumer, interest; the other holds that regulation is in the special, or producer, interest. In the airline industry, regulation initially appeared more in accord with producer interests, and producer groups fought deregulation, which benefited consumers.

To Review: Economic regulation tries to reduce the harmful consequences of monopolistic behavior in those markets where the output can be most efficiently supplied by one or a few firms. We now turn to antitrust policy, which tries to promote competition in those markets where competition seems desirable.

Antitrust Law and Enforcement

Although competition typically ensures the most efficient use of the nation's resources, an individual competitor would rather be a monopolist. If left alone, a firm might try to create a monopoly by driving competitors out of business, by merging with competitors, or by colluding with competitors. *Antitrust policy* reflects the government's attempt to reduce anticompetitive behavior and promote a market structure that leads to greater competition. *Antitrust policy attempts to promote socially desirable market performance.*

Origins of Antitrust Policy

Economic developments in the last half of the 19th century created bigger firms serving wider markets. Perhaps the two most important developments were (1) technological breakthroughs that led to a larger optimal plant size in manufacturing and (2) the rise of the railroad from 9,000 miles of track in 1850 to 167,000 miles by 1890, which reduced transport costs. *Economies of scale and cheaper transport costs extended the geographical size of markets,* so firms grew larger to serve this bigger market.

Sharp declines in the national economy in 1873 and in 1883, however, panicked large manufacturers. Because their heavy fixed costs required large-scale production, they cut prices in an attempt to stimulate sales. Price wars erupted, creating economic turmoil. Firms desperately sought ways to stabilize their markets. One solution was for competing firms to form a **trust** by transferring their voting stock to a single board of trustees, which would vote in the interest of the industry. Early trusts were formed in the sugar, tobacco, and oil industries. Although the impact of these early trusts is still debated today, they allegedly pursued anticompetitive practices to develop and maintain a monopoly advantage. Gradually the word **trust** came to mean any firm or group of firms that tried to monopolize a market.

trust
Any firm or group of firms that tries to monopolize a market

Sherman Antitrust Act of 1890

In the presidential election of 1888, the major political parties put antitrust planks in their platforms. This consensus culminated in the **Sherman Antitrust Act of 1890,** the first national legislation in the world against monopoly. The law prohibited trusts, restraint of trade, and monopolization, but the law's vague language allowed room for much anticompetitive activity.

Sherman Antitrust Act of 1890
First national legislation in the world against monopoly; prohibited trusts, restraint of trade, and monopolization, but the law was vague and, by itself, ineffective

Clayton Act of 1914

The **Clayton Act of 1914** was passed to outlaw certain practices not prohibited by the Sherman Act and to help government stop a monopoly before it develops. For example, the Clayton Act outlaws price discrimination when this practice creates a

Clayton Act of 1914
Beefed up the Sherman Act; outlawed certain anticompetitive practices not prohibited by the Sherman Act, including price discrimination, tying contracts, exclusive dealing, interlocking directorates, and buying the corporate stock of a competitor

monopoly. You'll recall that *price discrimination* charges different customers different prices for the same good. The act also prohibits *tying contracts* and *exclusive dealing* if they substantially lessen competition. **Tying contracts** require the buyer of one good to purchase another good as part of the deal. For example, a seller of a patented machine might require customers to buy other supplies. **Exclusive dealing** means a customer must agree not to buy any of the product from other suppliers. For example, a manufacturer might sell computer chips to a computer maker only if the computer maker agrees not to buy chips from other manufacturers. Another prohibition of the act is **interlocking directorates,** whereby the same individual serves on the boards of directors of competing firms. For example, in 2009 two individuals serving on the boards of both Apple and Google were forced to resign from one.[3] Finally, acquiring the corporate stock of a competing firm is outlawed if this would substantially lessen competition.

tying contract
A seller of one good requires a buyer to purchase other goods as part of the deal

exclusive dealing
A supplier prohibits its customers from buying from other suppliers of the product

interlocking directorate
A person serves on the boards of directors of two or more competing firms

Federal Trade Commission Act of 1914

The **Federal Trade Commission (FTC) Act of 1914** established a federal body to help enforce antitrust laws. The president appoints the five commissioners, who are assisted by a staff of economists and lawyers. The Sherman, Clayton, and FTC acts provide the framework for U.S. antitrust laws. Subsequent amendments and court decisions have clarified and embellished these laws. A loophole in the Clayton Act was closed in 1950 with the passage of the *Celler-Kefauver Anti-Merger Act,* which prevents one firm from buying the *physical assets* of another firm if the effect is to reduce competition. This law can block both **horizontal mergers,** or the merging of firms that produce the same product, such as Coke and Pepsi, and **vertical mergers,** or the merging of firms where one supplies inputs to the other or demands output from the other, such as Microsoft software going into Dell hardware.

Federal Trade Commission (FTC) Act of 1914
Established a federal body to help enforce antitrust laws; run by commissioners assisted by economists and lawyers

horizontal merger
A merger in which one firm combines with another that produces the same type of product

vertical merger
A merger in which one firm combines with another from which it had purchased inputs or to which it had sold output

Antitrust Enforcement

Any law's effectiveness depends on the vigor and vigilance of enforcement. The pattern of antitrust enforcement goes something like this. Either the Antitrust Division of the U.S. Justice Department or the FTC charges a firm or group of firms with breaking the law. Federal agencies are usually acting on a complaint by a customer or a competitor. At that point, those charged with wrongdoing may be able, without admitting guilt, to sign a **consent decree,** whereby they agree not to do whatever they had been charged with. If the accused contests the charges, evidence from both sides is presented in a court trial, and a judge decides. Some decisions may be appealed all the way to the Supreme Court, and in such cases the courts may render new interpretations of existing laws.

consent decree
The accused party, without admitting guilt, agrees not to do whatever it was charged with if the government drops the charges

Per Se Illegality and the Rule of Reason

The courts have interpreted antitrust laws in essentially two different ways. One set of practices has been declared **per se illegal**—that is, illegal regardless of the economic rationale or consequences. For example, under the Sherman Act, all agreements among competing firms to fix prices, restrict output, or otherwise restrain competition are viewed as per se illegal. To prove guilt under a per se rule, the government need only show that the offending practice took place. Thus, the government need only examine the firm's *behavior*.

per se illegal
In antitrust law, business practices deemed illegal regardless of their economic rationale or their consequences

3. Miguel Helft, "Google and Apple Eliminate Another Tie," *New York Times*, 13 October 2009.

Another set of practices falls under the **rule of reason**. Here the courts take into account the facts surrounding the particular offense—namely, the reasons why the offending practice was adopted and its effect on competition. The rule of reason was first set forth in 1911, when the Supreme Court held that Standard Oil had illegally monopolized the petroleum refining industry. Standard Oil allegedly had come to dominate 90 percent of the market by acquiring more than 120 competitors and by practicing **predatory pricing** to drive remaining rivals out of business—for example, by temporarily selling below marginal cost or dropping the price only in certain markets. In finding Standard Oil guilty, the Court focused on both the company's *behavior* and the *market structure* that resulted from that behavior. Based on this approach, the Court found that the company had behaved *unreasonably* and ruled that the monopoly should be broken up.

rule of reason
Before ruling on the legality of certain business practices, a court examines why they were undertaken and what effect they have on competition

predatory pricing
Pricing tactics employed by a dominant firm to drive competitors out of business, such as temporarily selling below marginal cost or dropping the price only in certain markets

But in 1920, the rule of reason led the Supreme Court to find U.S. Steel not guilty of monopolization. In that case, the Court ruled that not every contract or combination in restraint of trade is illegal—only those that "unreasonably" restrained trade violated antitrust laws. The Court said that *mere size is not an offense*. Although U.S. Steel clearly possessed market power, the company, in the Court's view, had not violated antitrust laws because it had not unreasonably used that power. The Court switched positions in 1945, ruling that although Alcoa's conduct might be reasonable and legal, its mere possession of market power—Alcoa controlled 90 percent of the aluminum ingot market—violated antitrust laws per se. Here the Court was using *market structure* rather than firm *behavior* as the test of legality.

Mergers and Public Policy

Some firms have pursued rapid growth by merging with other firms or by acquiring other firms. Much of what the Antitrust Division in the U.S. Justice Department and the FTC's Bureau of Competition do is approve or reject proposed mergers and acquisitions. As a guiding rule, regulators challenge any merger that would "create, enhance, or entrench market power." In determining possible harmful effects that a merger might have on competition, regulators sometimes consider its impact on the share of sales accounted for by the largest firms in the industry. If a few firms account for a relatively large share of sales, the industry is said to be *concentrated*. As a measure of sales concentration, the Justice Department and FTC often use the **Herfindahl-Hirschman Index, or HHI**, which is found by squaring the percentage of market share of each firm in the market and then summing these squares. For example, if the industry consists of 100 firms of equal size, the HHI is 100 [$= 100 \times (1)^2$]. If the industry is a pure monopoly, its index is 10,000 [$= (100)^2$], the largest possible value. *The more firms in the industry and the more equal their size, the smaller the HHI*. This index gives greater weight to firms with larger market shares, as can be seen in Exhibit 2. Each industry has 44 firms, but, for ease of exposition, only the market share of the top 4 firms differs across industries. Note that the index for Industry III is nearly triple that for each of the two other industries. Please take a minute now to work through the logic of the exhibit.

Herfindahl-Hirschman Index, or HHI
A measure of market concentration that squares each firm's percentage share of the market then sums these squares

The Justice Department and FTC guidelines sort all mergers into one of two categories: *horizontal mergers*, which involve firms in the same market, and *nonhorizontal mergers*, which include all other types of mergers. Of greatest interest for antitrust purposes are horizontal mergers, such as a merger between competing oil companies like Shell and Chevron. The government challenges any merger in an industry that meets two conditions: (1) the HHI exceeds 2,500 and (2) the merger increases the index by more than 200 points. Mergers in an industry with an index of less than 1,500 are

EXHIBIT 2 **Herfindahl-Hirschman Index (HHI) Based on Market Share in Three Industries**

	Industry I		Industry II		Industry III	
Firm	Market Share (percent)	Market Share Squared	Market Share (percent)	Market Share Squared	Market Share (percent)	Market Share Squared
A	23	529	15	225	57	3,249
B	18	324	15	225	1	1
C	13	169	15	225	1	1
D	6	36	15	225	1	1
Remaining 40 firms	1 each	40	1 each	40	1 each	40
HHI		1,098		940		3,292

Each of the three industries shown has 44 firms. The HHI is found by squaring each firm's market share then summing the squares. Under each industry, each firm's market share is shown in the left column and the square of the market share is shown in the right column. For ease of exposition, only the market share of the top four firms differs across industries. The remaining 40 firms have 1 percent market share each. The HHI for Industry III is nearly triple that for each of the other two industries.

seldom challenged.[4] Other factors, such as the ease of entry into the market, the stability of market shares, and gains in efficiency, are considered for indexes between 1,500 and 2,500. For example, regulators are less likely to challenge a merger in an industry where market share fluctuates a lot.

Merger Waves

There have been four merger waves in this country over the last 125 years, as outlined in Exhibit 3. Between 1887 and 1904 some of the twentieth century's largest firms, including U.S. Steel and Standard Oil, were formed. Mergers during this first wave tended to be horizontal. For example, the firm that is today the United States Steel Corporation was created in 1901 through a billion-dollar merger that involved dozens of individual steel producers and two-thirds of the industry's production capacity. This merger wave was a reaction to technological progress in transportation, communication, and manufacturing. Simply put, it became easier and cheaper to run a corporation that stretched across the nation, so firms merged to reach national markets. During this first wave, similar merger activity occurred in Canada, Great Britain, and elsewhere, creating dominant firms, some of which still exist. The U.S. merger wave cooled with the severe national recession of 1904 and with the first stirrings of antitrust laws with real bite.

Because antitrust laws began to restrain *horizontal* mergers, *vertical* mergers became more common during the second merger wave, between 1916 and 1929. A vertical merger is one between a firm that either supplies the other firm inputs or demands the other firm's outputs—the merger of firms at different stages of the production process. For example, a copper refiner merges with a fabricator of copper piping. The stock

4. Merger guidelines were under revision in 2010. See the proposed guidelines at http://www.ftc.gov/os/2010/04/100420hmg.pdf.

EXHIBIT 3 U.S. Merger Waves in the Past Century

Wave	Years	Dominant Type of Merger	Examples	Stimulus
First	1887–1904	Horizontal	U.S. Steel, Standard Oil	Span national markets
Second	1916–1929	Vertical	Copper refiner with fabricator	Stock market boom
Third	1948–1969	Conglomerate	Litton Industries	Diversification
Fourth	1982–present	Horizontal and vertical	Banking, telecommunications, health services, insurance	Span national and global markets, stock market boom

market boom of the 1920s fueled this second wave, and the stock market crash of 1929 stopped it cold.

The Great Depression and World War II cooled mergers for two decades, but the third merger wave got under way after the war. More than 200 of the 1,000 largest firms in 1950 disappeared by the early 1960s as a result of the third merger wave, which stretched between 1948 and 1969. In that span, many large firms were absorbed by other, usually larger, firms. The third merger wave peaked during 1964 to 1969, when **conglomerate mergers**, which join firms in different industries, accounted for four-fifths of all mergers. For example, Litton Industries combined firms that made calculators, appliances, electrical equipment, and machine tools. Merging firms were looking to diversify their product mix and perhaps achieve some *economies of scope*—meaning, to reduce average costs by producing a variety of goods.

conglomerate merger
A merger of firms in different industries

The fourth merger wave began in 1982 and involved both horizontal and vertical mergers. Some large conglomerate mergers from the third wave were dissolved during the fourth wave, as the core firm sold off unrelated operations. About one-third of mergers in the 1980s resulted from *hostile takeovers,* where one firm would buy control of another against the wishes of the target firm's management. Hostile takeovers dwindled to less than one-tenth of mergers during the 1990s and later.

Merger activity gained momentum during the latter half of the 1990s, with the dollar value of each new merger topping the previous record. Most mergers during this period were financed by the exchange of corporate stock and were spurred on by a booming stock market (like the mergers of the 1920s). The dissolution of the Soviet Union ended the Cold War and boosted capitalism around the world. Companies merged to achieve a stronger competitive position in global markets. The largest mergers in history took place since the late 1990s, with the biggest action in banking, radio and television, insurance, telecommunications, and health services. The fourth merger wave continues, as the global economic slump of 2008 and 2009 forced firms in some industries, especially banking and finance, to merge in order to survive. But not all mergers work out. For example, Daimler-Benz bought Chrysler for $36 billion in 1998. After nearly a decade of disappointing results, the merged company had to pay $650 million in 2007 to unload 80 percent of its Chrysler division (Chrysler stayed in business in 2009 only after filing for bankruptcy then getting billions in aid from the federal government for the newly reorganized company).

In recent years, there have been fewer objections to mergers on antitrust grounds either from academics or regulatory officials. The government shifted from rules that restrict big mergers to a more flexible approach that allows big companies to merge. For example, after several months of review, the U.S. Justice Department concluded that Whirlpool's acquisition of Maytag would not reduce competition substantially and could achieve efficiencies and cost savings. What's more, growing competition from Asia would prevent the merged company from raising prices.

Antitrust officials ask "will the merger hurt competition?" Most, apparently, do not. Regulators ultimately have challenged only about 2 percent of all mergers proposed in recent years, though just the threat of a legal challenge has probably deterred many potentially anticompetitive mergers and acquisitions.

Competitive Trends in the U.S. Economy

For years, there has been concern about the sheer size of some firms because of the real or potential power they might exercise in the economy. One way to measure the power of the largest corporations is to calculate the share of the nation's corporate assets controlled by the 100 largest manufacturing firms. They now control about half of all manufacturing assets in the United States, up from 40 percent after World War II. We should recognize, however, that size alone is not the same as market power. A very big firm, such as a large chip maker, may face stiff competition from another large chip maker foreign or domestic. On the other hand, the only movie theater in an isolated community may be able to raise its price with less concern about competition.

Competition Over Time

More important than the size of the largest firms in the nation is the market structure of each industry. Various studies have examined the level of competition by industry and changes in competition over the years. All began with some measure of market share, such as the HHI. Among the most comprehensive is the research of William G. Shepherd, who relied on a variety of sources to determine the competitiveness of each industry in the U.S. economy.[5] He sorted industries into four groups: (1) pure monopoly, in which a single firm controlled the entire market and was able to block entry; (2) dominant firm, in which a single firm had more than half the market share and no close rival; (3) tight oligopoly, in which the top four firms supplied more than 60 percent of market output, with stable market shares and evidence of cooperation; and (4) effective competition, in which firms in the industry exhibited low concentration, low entry barriers, and little or no collusion.

Exhibit 4 presents Shepherd's breakdown of U.S. industries into the four categories for 1939, 1958, and 2000. Between 1939 and 1958, the table shows a modest growth in competition, with the share of those industries rated as "effectively competitive" increasing from 52 percent to 56 percent of all industries. Between 1958 and 2000, however, the share of effectively competitive industries jumped from 56 percent to 77 percent.

According to Shepherd, the growth in competition from 1958 to 2000 can be traced to three sources: (1)*competition from imports,* (2) *deregulation,* and (3) *antitrust*

5. William G. Shepherd, "Causes of Increased Competition in the U.S. Economy, 1939–1980," *Review of Economics and Statistics*, 64 (November 1982); and William G. Shepherd and Joanna M. Shepherd, *The Economics of Industrial Organization*, 5th ed. (Waveland, 2004).

EXHIBIT 4 Competitive Trends in the U.S. Economy: 1939 to 2000

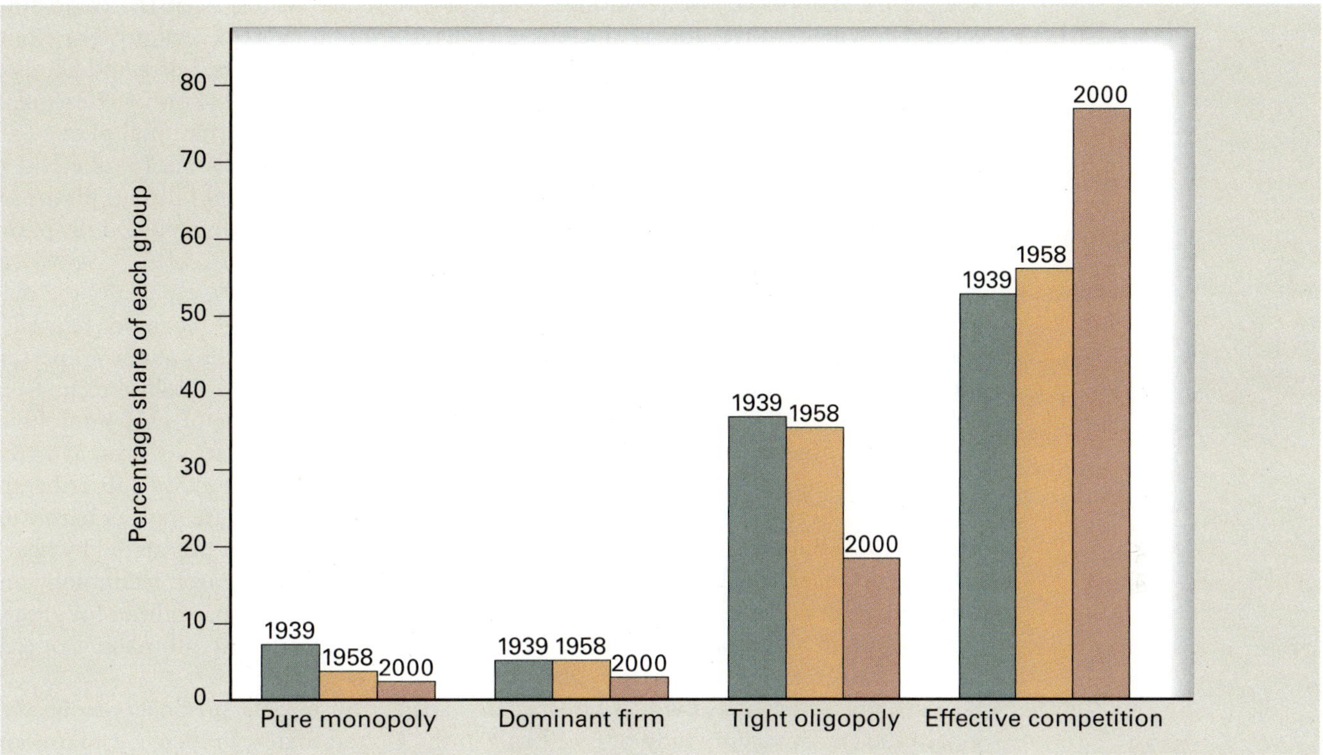

Sources: William G. Shepherd, "Causes of Increased Competition in the U.S. Economy, 1939–1980," *Review of Economics and Statistics*, 64 (November 1982); and William G. Shepherd and Joanna M. Shepherd, *The Economics of Industrial Organization*, 5th ed. (Long Grove, Illinois: Waveland Press, 2004), p. 15.

policy. Foreign imports between 1958 and 2000 increased competition in more than a dozen industries, including autos, tires, and steel. The growth in imports accounted for one-sixth of the overall increase in competition. Imports were attractive to consumers because of their higher quality and lower price. Finding themselves at a cost and technological disadvantage, U.S. producers initially sought protection from foreign competitors through trade barriers, such as quotas and tariffs.

Shepherd argues that deregulation accounted for one-fifth of the increase in competition. Trucking, airlines, securities trading, banking, and telecommunications were among the industries deregulated between 1958 and 2000. We have already discussed some of the effects of deregulation in airlines, particularly in reducing barriers to entry and in eliminating uniform pricing schedules.

Although it is difficult to attribute an increase in competition to specific antitrust cases, Shepherd credits antitrust policy with two-fifths of the growth in competition between 1958 and 2000. To summarize: According to Shepherd, the three primary reasons for increased competition were international trade, deregulation, and antitrust policy. One-sixth of the growth in competition between 1958 and 2000 came from imports, one-fifth from deregulation, and two-fifths, the largest share, from antitrust policy. In light of the important role that Shepherd accords antitrust policy, the case study, "Public Policy: MIcrosoft on Trial" at the end of the book, looks at the most significant antitrust case of the last two decades.

Recent Competitive Trends

Shepherd's analysis of competition extended to 2000. What has been the trend since then? Growing world trade has increased competition in the U.S. economy. For example, the share of the U.S. auto market controlled by General Motors, Ford, and Chrysler fell from 80 percent in 1970 to 45 percent by 2010. And federal action to deregulate international phone service forced down the average price of international phone calls from $0.88 a minute in 1997 to well under $0.10 a minute by 2010. In an effort to reduce international phone rates, federal officials even subpoenaed Filipino phone executives who were attending a conference in Hawaii, alleging they colluded on phone rates to the United States.

Technological change is boosting competition in many markets, especially the market for media. For example, the prime-time audience share of the three major television networks (NBC, CBS, and ABC) dropped from 90 percent in 1980 to under 30 percent today as FOX became a fourth major network, and as cable and satellite technology delivered hundreds of networks and channels. About 90 percent of U.S. households have either cable or satellite television. And the 14,000 radio stations now available is double the number in 1970 (satellite radio alone has about 20 million subscribers).

Despite Microsoft's dominance in operating systems, the software market barely existed in 1980 but now flourishes in a technology-rich environment populated by nearly 10,000 producers, with Microsoft scrambling to catch up with search technology and with social networking. And the Internet has opened far-ranging possibilities for greater competition in a number of industries, from online stock trading to all manner of electronic commerce and information distribution.

Let's not forget that competition benefits society by forcing producers to become more efficient. A recent study of 732 firms in the United States, France, Germany, and the United Kingdom found that firms in competitive industries are more efficient than other firms.[6]

Problems With Antitrust Policy

There is growing doubt about the economic value of the lengthy antitrust cases pursued in the past. A case against Exxon, for example, was in the courts for 17 years before the company was cleared of charges in 1992. Another case began in 1969 when IBM, with nearly 70 percent of domestic sales of electronic data-processing equipment, was accused of monopolizing that market. In 1982, the government dropped the case, noting that the threat of monopoly had diminished enough that the case was "without merit." As noted already, the U.S. case against Microsoft took nearly six years to resolve; the case dragged on in state courts five more years.

Competition May Not Require That Many Firms

Joseph Schumpeter argued half a century ago that competition should be viewed as a dynamic process, one of "creative destruction." Firms are continually in flux—introducing new products, phasing out old ones, trying to compete for the consumer's dollar in a variety of ways. In light of this, antitrust policy should not necessarily aim at increasing the *number* of firms in each industry. In some cases, firms grow large because they are better than rivals at offering what consumers want. Accordingly, firm size should not be the primary concern. Moreover, as noted in the chapter on perfect competition, economists have shown through market experiments that most of the

6. Nicholas Bloom and John Van Reenan, "Measuring and Explaining Management Practices Across Firms and Countries," *Quarterly Journal of Economics*, 122 (November 2007): 1351–1408.

desirable properties of perfect competition can be achieved with relatively few firms.[7] For example, the two leading chip makers, Intel and Advanced Micro Devices, have been locked in a price war for years, as each fights for market share. Likewise, Boeing, the only U.S. maker of commercial jets, competes fiercely with Europe's Airbus for every new contract. And it was not that long ago that Google was the upstart among Internet search engines. Now it dominates 65 percent of that market, but may face a fierce competitor as Microsoft and Yahoo join forces. And all three are laggards to Facebook and Twitter in social networking.

Antitrust Abuses

Parties that can show injury from firms that violate antitrust laws can sue the offending company and recover three times the damages sustained. These so-called *treble damage* suits increased after World War II. More than 1,000 are filed each year. Courts have been relatively generous to those claiming to have been wronged. Even foreign firms have started suing in U.S. courts. And, in an unusual twist, foreign firms are now suing other foreign firms using U.S courts, laws, and lawyers. But studies show that such suits can be used to intimidate an aggressive competitor or to convert a contract dispute between, say, a firm and its supplier into treble damage payoffs. The result can have a chilling effect on competition. Many economists now believe that the anticompetitive costs from this abuse of treble damage suits may exceed any competitive benefits of these laws.

Growth of International Markets

Finally, a standard approach to measuring the market power of a firm is its share of the market. With greater international trade, however, the local or even national market share becomes less relevant. General Motors may still dominate U.S. auto manufacturing, accounting for 42 percent of national sales by U.S. firms in 2010. But when Japanese and European producers are included, GM's share of the U.S. auto market falls to only about 20 percent of all sales. GM's share of world production has declined steadily since the mid-1950s. After 77 years as the world's largest automaker, GM was surpassed by Toyota in 2008. GM and Chrylser's very survival came into question in 2009 as the two car makers sought and received federal aid. *Where markets are open to foreign competition, antitrust enforcement that focuses on domestic producers makes less economic sense.*

In response to the global nature of markets, antitrust policy is starting to take an international approach. The U.S. government has signed cooperative agreements with some other governments, including Japan and the European Union, to promote antitrust enforcement and reduce conflicting decisions. For example, investigators from the United States, the European Union, and Japan simultaneously raided car-parts manufacturers in a price fixing probe.[8] Through the International Competition Network, more than 100 nations discuss antitrust procedures and policies. Such discussions have thrown light on anticompetitive regulations in place around the world. Many countries for decades have sheltered firms in some politically powerful industries. For example, until recently, regulations in India restricted entry into the hotel business. As a result, there were fewer hotel rooms in all of India, a country with more than a billion people, than in New York City, with less than 1 percent that population.

7. See, for example, Vernon Smith, "Markets as Economizers of Information: Experimental Examination of the 'Hayek Hypothesis,'" *Economic Inquiry*, 20 (April 1982): 165–179; and Douglas Davis and Charles Holt, *Experimental Economics* (Princeton, N.J.: Princeton University Press, 1993).

8. Jeff Bennett and Peppi Kiviniemi, "Car-Parts Makers Raided in Price-Fixing Probe," *Wall Street Journal*, 26 February 2010.

Bailing Out Troubled Industries

Finally, the collapse of housing prices in 2007 and 2008 caused mortgage defaults and led to rising unemployment. The federal government responded by aiding affected industries, especially financial institutions and two of the big three automakers. The intent was to promote financial stability and keep the economy from sinking further. But the long-term effect of such market intervention on competition remains to be seen.

Conclusion

Competition has been growing in recent decades because of changing technology, greater international trade, industry deregulation, and antitrust policy. Consumers benefit as firms compete by offering lower prices, better products, and new services to keep existing customers and attract new ones. Competition also ensures that the economy's resources find their most efficient uses. Through the process of creative destruction, competition promotes the survival of the fittest. Market forces continuously pressure firms to innovate—that is, to develop new and better products, services, methods of doing business, and technologies.

Summary

1. In this chapter, we examined two forms of government regulation of business: (a) economic regulation, such as the regulation of natural monopolies, and (b) antitrust policy, which promotes competition and prohibits efforts to monopolize, or to cartelize, an industry.
2. Governments regulate natural monopolies so that output is greater and prices lower than if the monopolist was allowed to maximize profits. One problem with regulation is that the price that maximizes social welfare results in an economic loss, whereas the price that allows the firm to earn a normal profit does not maximize social welfare.
3. There are two views of economic regulation. The first is that economic regulation is in the public, or consumer, interest because it controls natural monopolies where production by one or just a few firms is most efficient. A second view is that regulation is more in the special interest of producers who use regulations to fix prices, block entry, and increase profits.
4. Regulations in effect for 40 years in the airline industry restricted entry and fixed prices. Deregulation in 1978 stimulated new entry, unleashed price competition, and reduced prices overall. Price wars in the industry are now common, and benefit consumers.
5. Antitrust laws are aimed at promoting competition and prohibiting efforts to cartelize, or monopolize, an industry. The Sherman, Clayton, and FTC acts provide the legal and institutional framework for antitrust enforcement, a framework that subsequent amendments and court cases have clarified and embellished.
6. Competition in U.S. industries has been increasing since World War II. Four sources of increased competition are greater international trade, deregulation, antitrust policy, and technological change.

Key Concepts

Market power 296
Social regulation 296
Economic regulation 296
Antitrust policy 296
Public utilities 297
Capture theory of regulation 300
Trust 301
Sherman Antitrust Act of 1890 301
Clayton Act of 1914 301
Tying contract 302
Exclusive dealing 302
Interlocking directorate 302
Federal Trade Commission (FTC) act of 1914 302
Horizontal merger 302
Vertical merger 302
Consent decree 302
Per se illegal 302
Rule of reason 303
Predatory pricing 303
Herfindahl-Hirschman Index, or HHI 303
Conglomerate merger 305

Questions for Review

1. Business Behavior and Public Policy Define market power, and then discuss the rationale for government regulation of firms with market power.
2. Government Regulation What three types of government policies are used to alter or control firm behavior? Determine which type of regulation is used for each of the following:
    a. Preventing a merger that the government believes would lessen competition
    b. The activities of the Food and Drug Administration
    c. Regulation of fares charged by a municipal bus company
    d. Occupational safety and health regulations that affect working conditions
3. Regulating Natural Monopolies What is the "regulatory dilemma?" That is, what trade-offs do regulators have to consider when deciding how to control a natural monopoly?
4. Theories of Regulation Why do producers have more interest in government regulations than consumers do?
    a. Compare and contrast the public-interest and special-interest theories of economic regulation. What is the capture theory of regulation?
    b. Which of these theories best describes the case of airline deregulation? Which best explains the government's case against Microsoft?
5. Case Study: Airline Regulation and Deregulation (See page 732.) Consumers now treat air travel like a commodity and meals on some airlines are nonexistent. Does this mean that consumers have suffered because of airline deregulation?
6. Antitrust Law and Enforcement Discuss the difference between per se illegality and the rule of reason.
7. Antitrust Activity "The existence of only two or three big U.S. auto manufacturers is evidence that the market structure is anticompetitive and that antitrust laws are being broken." Evaluate this assertion.
8. Mergers and Public Policy Under what circumstances, and why, would the government be opposed to a merger of two firms? How does the Justice Department decide which mergers to challenge?
9. Competitive Trends in the U.S. Economy William Shepherd's study of U.S. industries showed a clear increase in competition in the U.S. economy between 1958 and 2000. How did Shepherd explain this trend?

Problems and Exercises

10. Regulating Natural Monopolies The following graph represents a natural monopoly.

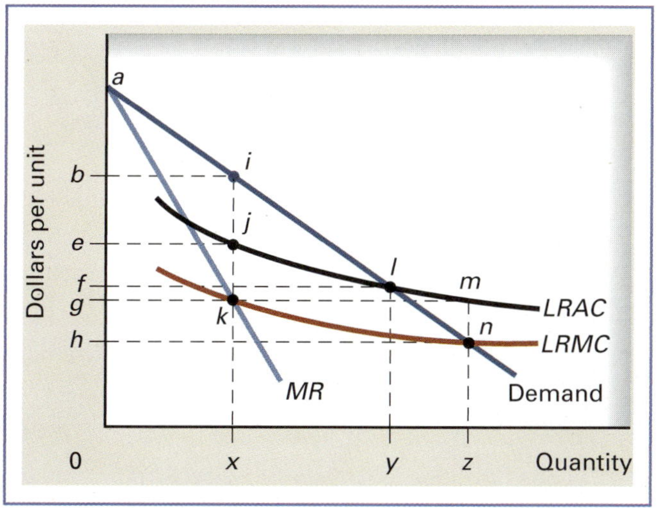

    a. Why is this firm considered a natural monopoly?
    b. If the firm is unregulated, what price and output would maximize its profit? What would be its profit or loss?
    c. If a regulatory commission establishes a price with the goal of achieving allocative efficiency, what would be the price and output? What would be the firm's profit or loss?
    d. If a regulatory commission establishes a price with the goal of allowing the firm a "fair return," what would be the price and output? What would be the firm's profit or loss?
    e. Which one of the prices in parts b, c, and d maximizes consumer surplus? What problem, if any, occurs at this price?
11. Origins of Antitrust Policy Identify the type of anticompetitive behavior illustrated by each of the following:
    a. A university requires buyers of season tickets for its basketball games to buy season tickets for its football games as well.
    b. Dairies that bid on contracts to supply milk to school districts collude to increase what they charge.
    c. The same individual serves on the boards of directors of General Motors and Ford.
    d. A large retailer sells merchandise below cost in certain regions to drive competitors out of business.
    e. A producer of carbonated soft drinks sells to a retailer only if the retailer agrees not to buy from the producer's major competitor.

12. MERGERS AND PUBLIC POLICY Calculate the Herfindahl-Hirschman Index (HHI) for each of the following industries. Which industry is the most concentrated?
    a. An industry with five firms that have the following market shares: 50 percent, 30 percent, 10 percent, 5 percent, and 5 percent
    b. An industry with five firms that have the following market shares: 60 percent, 20 percent, 10 percent, 5 percent, and 5 percent
    c. An industry with five firms, each of which has a 20 percent market share

13. Case Study: Microsoft on Trial (See page 733.) What was the government's argument in the Microsoft trial and what was the company's defense? Which side prevailed?

Global Economic Watch Exercises

Login to www.cengagebrain.com and access the Global Economic Watch to do these exercises.

14. GLOBAL ECONOMIC WATCH Go to the Global Economic Crisis Resource Center. Select Global Issues in Context. In the Basic Search box at the top of the page, enter the phrase "law on antitrust." On the Results page, go to the News Section. Click on the link for the July 27, 2009, article "Obama Aide Is Aiming to Tighten Law on Antitrust." What does this article reveal about the role of politics in setting antitrust policy?

15. GLOBAL ECONOMIC WATCH Go to the Global Economic Crisis Resource Center. Select Global Issues in Context. In the Basic Search box at the top of the page, enter the term "regulation." Choose one article and analyze whether it is in favor of or opposed to government regulation. Summarize the article's arguments.

Public Goods and Public Choice

16

Joe Raedle/Getty Images

- How do public goods differ from private goods?
- Why do most people remain largely ignorant about what's happening in the public sector?
- Why is it so difficult to interest the public in the public interest?
- Why is voter turnout so low?
- Why do some politicians express concern for average Americans, but vote for special interests?
- Why are incumbents more likely than challengers to support campaign spending limits?

Answers to these and related questions are discussed in this chapter, which focuses on the public sector—both the rationale for public goods and public choices about those goods.

The effects of government are all around us. Stitched into the clothes you put on this morning are government-required labels providing washing instructions. Government subsidies affect the price of your Cheerios and the milk and sugar you put on them. Governments regulate the motor vehicle you get around in as well the speed and the sobriety of the driver. Taxpayers subsidize your education in a variety of ways. Yes, government plays a major role in the economy. The federal government alone spends about $3,700,000,000,000—about $3.7 *trillion*. Spending by governments at all levels tops $5.0 trillion.

The role of government has been discussed throughout this book. For the most part, we assumed that government makes optimal adjustments to the shortcomings of the private sector—that is, when confronted with market failure, government adopts and implements the appropriate program to address the problem. But, just as there are limits to the market's effectiveness, there are limits to government's effectiveness.

In this chapter, we look at the pros and cons of government activity. We begin with public goods, discuss the decision-making process, and then examine the limitations of that process.

Topics discussed include:

- Private versus public goods
- Representative democracy
- Rational ignorance
- Special-interest legislation
- Rent seeking
- The underground economy
- Bureaucratic behavior
- Private versus public production

Public Goods

Throughout most of this book, we have been talking about *private goods*, such as pizzas and haircuts ("goods" in this chapter usually mean goods and services). As noted in Chapter 3, private goods have two important features. First, they are *rival* in consumption, meaning that the amount consumed by one person is unavailable for others to consume. For example, when you and friends share a pizza, each slice others eat is one less available for you (which is why you tend to eat a little faster when sharing). A second key feature of private goods is that suppliers can easily *exclude* those who don't pay. Only paying customers get pizzas. Thus, private goods are said to be *rival* and *exclusive*.

Private Goods, Public Goods, and In Between

In contrast to private goods, *public goods*, such as national defense, the national weather service, the Centers for Disease Control, or a local mosquito-control program, are *nonrival* in consumption. One person's consumption does not diminish the amount available to others. Once produced, such goods are available to all in equal amount; the good can be supplied to an additional consumer for zero marginal cost. But once a public good is produced, suppliers cannot easily deny it to those who don't pay. There are no vending machines for public goods. For example, if a firm sprays a neighborhood for mosquitoes, all those in the neighborhood benefit. The firm can't easily exclude those who fail to pay. Thus, the mosquito spraying is *nonexclusive*—it benefits all those in the neighborhood. Some people figure, "Since I can enjoy the benefits without paying, why bother paying?" As a consequence, for-profit firms can't profitably sell public goods. In this case of market failure, the government comes to the rescue by providing public goods and paying for them through enforced taxation. Sometimes nonprofit agencies also provide public goods, funding them through contributions and other revenue sources.

But the economy consists of more than just the polar cases of private and public goods. Some goods are *nonrival* but *exclusive*. For example, additional households can watch a TV show without affecting the reception of other viewers. It's not as if there is only so much TV signal to go around. Television signals are nonrival in consumption. Yet the program's producers, should they choose to, could charge each household for reception, as with cable TV, so the TV signal is nonrival but exclusive. A good that is nonrival but exclusive is called a *natural monopoly*, a term already introduced. Along the same lines, short of the point of congestion, additional people can benefit from a subway system, golf course, swimming pool, rock concert, or highway without diminishing the benefit to other users. These goods, when not congested, are nonrival. Yet producers can, with relative ease, exclude anyone who doesn't pay the subway fare, greens fee, pool admission, ticket price, or road toll. These uncongested goods are both nonrival and exclusive and are therefore natural monopolies. Once congestion sets in, however, these goods become rival—space is scarce on a stuffed subway car, on a backed-up golf course, in a crowded swimming pool, at a jam-packed concert, or on a bumper-to-bumper highway. Once congestion sets in, these natural monopolies morph into private goods—both rival and exclusive.

Some other goods are *rival* but *nonexclusive*. The fish in the ocean are rival in the sense that every fish caught is no longer available for others to catch; the same goes for migratory game, like geese. But ocean fish and migratory game are nonexclusive in that it would be costly if not impossible for someone to block access to these goods. A good that is rival but nonexclusive is called an **open-access good**. Problems that arise with open-access goods will be examined in the next chapter.

open-access good
A good such as ocean fish that is rival in consumption but nonpayers cannot be excluded easily

Exhibit 1 sorts out the four categories of goods. Across the top, goods are classified as either *rival* or *nonrival,* and along the left margin, goods are classified as either *exclusive* or *nonexclusive*. Private goods are usually provided by the private sector. Natural monopolies are sometimes provided by the private sector, as with a private golf course, and sometimes provided by government, as with a municipal golf course. Open-access goods are usually regulated by government, as you will see in the next chapter. And public goods are usually provided by government.

Optimal Provision of Public Goods

Because private goods are rival in consumption, the market demand for a private good at a given price is the sum of the quantities demanded by each consumer. For example, the market quantity of pizza demanded when the price is $10 is the quantity demanded by Alan plus the quantity demanded by Maria plus the quantity demanded by all other

EXHIBIT 1 Categories of Goods

	Rival	Nonrival
Exclusive	1. Private Goods —*Pizza* —*Crowded Subway*	2. Natural Monopolies —*Cable TV* —*Uncrowded Subway*
Nonexclusive	3. Open-Access Goods —*Ocean fish* —*Migratory birds*	4. Public Goods —*National defense* —*Mosquito control*

consumers in the market. The market demand curve for a private good is the *horizontal* sum of individual demand curves, an idea developed in Exhibit 7 of Chapter 6. The efficient quantity of a private good occurs where the market demand curve intersects the market supply curve.

But a public good is nonrival in consumption, so that good, once produced, is available in that amount to all consumers. For example, the market demand for a given level of mosquito control reflects the marginal benefit that Alan gets from that amount plus the marginal benefit that Maria gets plus the marginal benefit that all others in the community get from that amount of the good. Therefore, the market demand curve for a public good is the *vertical* sum of each consumer's demand for the public good. To arrive at the efficient level of the public good, we find where the market demand curve intersects the marginal cost curve—that is, where the sum of the marginal valuations equals the marginal cost.

Suppose the public good in question is mosquito control in a neighborhood, which, for simplicity, has only two households, one headed by Alan and the other by Maria. Alan spends more time in the yard than does Maria and thus values a mosquito-free environment more than she does. Their individual demand curves are shown in Exhibit 2 as D_a and D_m, reflecting the marginal benefits that Alan and Maria enjoy at each rate of output. Quantity is measured here as hours of mosquito spraying per week. By vertically summing marginal valuations at each rate of output, we derive the neighborhood demand curve, *D*, for mosquito spraying. For example, when the town

EXHIBIT 2 Market for Public Goods

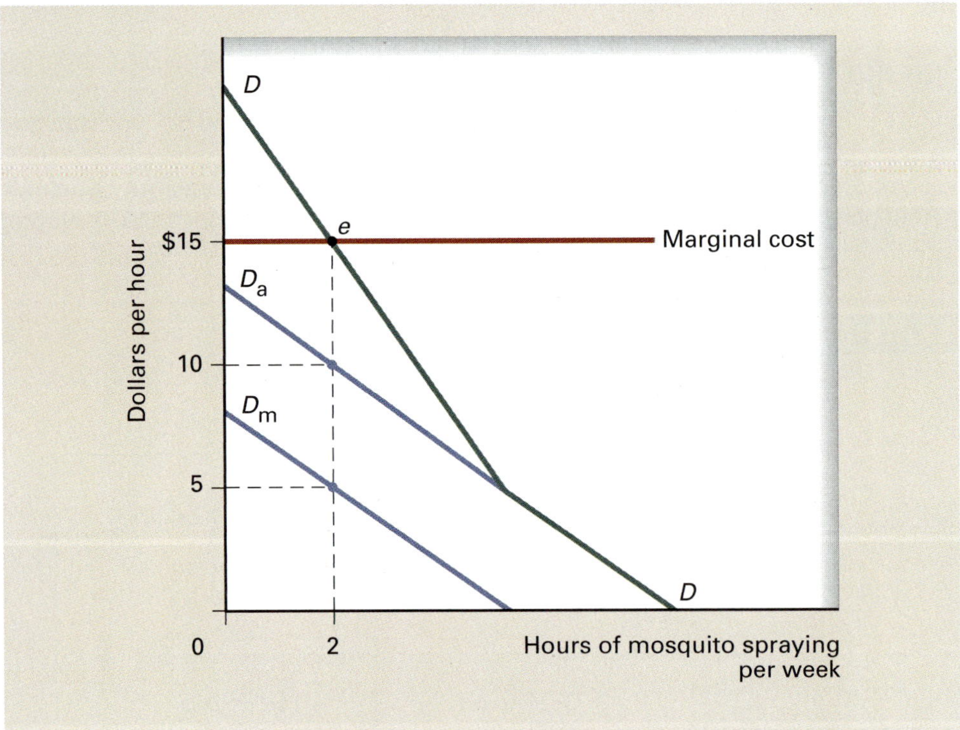

Because public goods, once produced, are available to all in identical amounts, the demand for a public good is the vertical sum of each individual's demand. Thus, the market demand for mosquito spraying is the vertical sum of Maria's demand, D_m, and Alan's demand, D_a. The efficient level of provision is found where the marginal cost of mosquito spraying equals its marginal benefit. This occurs at point *e*, where the marginal cost curve intersects the market demand curve, *D*.

sprays two hours a week, Maria values the second hour at $5 and Alan values it at $10. To get the market demand for the second hour of spraying, we simply add each resident's marginal benefit to get $15, as identified by point *e*.

How much mosquito spraying should the government provide? Suppose the marginal cost of spraying is a constant $15 an hour, as shown in Exhibit 2. The efficient level of output is found where the marginal benefit to the neighborhood equals the marginal cost, which occurs where the neighborhood demand curve intersects the marginal cost curve. In our example, these curves intersect where quantity is two hours per week.

Paying for Public Goods

Suppose the government pays for the mosquito spray through taxes. The efficient approach would be to impose a tax on each resident equal to his or her marginal valuation. Simple enough, but there are at least two problems with this. First, once people realize their taxes are based on government estimates of how much they value the good, some people tend to understate their true valuation. Why admit you really value the good if, as a result, you get socked with a higher tax bill? After all, people in the neighborhood can enjoy mosquito abatement whether or not they pay for it. So taxpayers tend to understate their true valuation of public goods. This creates the **free-rider problem,** which occurs because some people try to benefit from the public good without paying for it.

free-rider problem
Because nobody can be easily excluded from consuming a public good, some people may try to reap the benefits of the good without paying for it

But even if the government has accurate information about everyone's marginal valuations, some households have a greater ability to pay taxes than others. In our example, Alan values mosquito control more because he spends more time in the yard than does Maria. What if Alan is around more because he can't find a job? Should his taxes be double those of Maria, who has, say, a high-paying job? *Taxing people according to their marginal valuations of the public good may be efficient, but it may not be fair if the ability to pay differs.*

Once the public good is produced, only that quantity is available, such as two hours of mosquito spraying per week. With private goods, each consumer can buy any quantity he or she demands and each can purchase a different amount. Thus, *public goods are more complicated than private goods in terms of what goods should be provided, in what quantities, and who should pay*. These decisions are thrashed out through public choices, which we explore in the balance of this chapter.

Public Choice in Representative Democracy

Government decisions about public goods and taxes are *public choices*. In a democracy, public choices usually require approval by a majority of voters. About 60 percent of the world's 200 independent nations are democracies. Thus, issues raised in this section about majority rule apply to most of the world, including all of Western Europe and nearly all of the Americas.

Median-Voter Model

As it turns out, we can usually explain the outcome of majority rule by focusing on the preferences of the median voter. The *median voter* is the one whose preferences lie in the middle of all voters' preferences. For example, if the issue is the size of the government budget, half the voters prefer a larger budget than the median voter and half prefer a smaller one. The **median-voter model** predicts that under certain conditions, the preference of the median, or middle, voter will dominate other choices. Here's an example. Suppose you and two roommates have just moved into an apartment, and the three of

median-voter model
Under certain conditions, the preferences of the median, or middle, voter will dominate the preferences of all other voters

you must decide on furnishings. You agree to share common expenses equally and to make choices by majority rule. The issue at hand is whether to buy a TV and, if so, of what size. You each have a different preference. Your studious roommate considers a TV an annoying distraction and would rather go without; otherwise, the smaller, the better. Your other roommate, an avid TV watcher, prefers a 48-inch screen but would settle for a smaller one rather than go without. A 27-inch screen is your first choice, but you would prefer the 48-inch screen rather than go without. What to do, what to do?

You all agree to make the decision by voting on two alternatives at a time, then pairing the winner against the remaining alternative until one choice dominates the others. When the 27-inch screen is paired with the no-TV option, the 27-inch screen gets both your vote and the TV fan's vote. When the 27-inch screen is then paired with the 48-inch screen, the 27-inch screen wins again, this time because your studious roommate sides with you.

Majority voting in effect delegates the public choice to the person whose preference is the median for the group. As the median voter in this example, you get your way. You have the votes for any choice between no TV and a 48 incher. Similarly, *the median voter in an electorate often determines public choices. Political candidates try to get elected by appealing to the median voter.* This is why candidates focus their rhetoric on "hard-working Americans," "middle-class America," or "American families." They are targeting median voters. This is one reason why candidates often seem so much alike. Note that under majority rule, only the median voter gets his or her way. Other voters must go along with the median choice. Thus, other voters usually end up paying for what they consider to be either too much or too little of the public good. On the contrary, in private markets each individual gets whatever amount he or she is willing and able to buy.

People vote directly on issues at New England town meetings and on the occasional referendum, but *direct democracy* is not the most common form of public choice. When you consider the thousands of choices made in the public sector—from the number of teachers to hire to what software to use for municipal records—it becomes clear that direct democracy for all public choices through referenda would be unwieldy and impractical. Rather than make decisions by direct referenda, voters elect *representatives*, who, at least in theory, make public choices that reflect their constituents' views. More than 500,000 elected officials serve in the United States. Under certain conditions, the resulting public choices reflect the preferences of the median voter. Some complications of representative democracy are explored next.

Special Interest and Rational Ignorance

We assume that consumers maximize utility and firms maximize profit, but what about governments? As noted in Chapter 3, there is no common agreement about what, if anything, governments try to maximize or, more precisely, what elected officials try to maximize. One theory that stems from the rational self-interest assumption of economic behavior is that elected officials try to *maximize their political support.*

To maximize political support, elected officials may cater to special interests rather than serve the interest of the public. The possibility arises because of the asymmetry between special interest and public interest, an idea introduced in the previous chapter. Consider only one of the thousands of decisions elected representatives make: funding an obscure federal program that subsidizes U.S. wool production. Under the wool-subsidy program, the federal government guarantees that a floor price is paid to sheep farmers for each pound of wool they produce, a subsidy that has cost taxpayers over $75 million since 2000. During deliberations to renew the program, the only person to testify before Congress was a representative of the National Wool Growers Association, who claimed that the subsidy was vital to the nation's economic welfare. Why didn't a single taxpayer challenge the subsidy?

Households consume so many different public and private goods and services that they have neither the time nor the incentive to understand the effects of public choices on every product. What's more, voters realize that each of them has but a tiny possibility of influencing public choices. And even if an individual voter is somehow able to affect the outcome, the impact on that voter is likely to be small. For example, if a taxpayer could have successfully staged a grassroots campaign in 2000 to eliminate the wool subsidy, the average taxpayer would have saved about 50 cents in federal income taxes since then. Therefore, unless voters have a *special* interest in the legislation, they adopt a stance of **rational ignorance,** which means that they remain largely oblivious to most public choices. The cost to the typical voter of acquiring information about each public choice and acting on it usually exceeds any expected benefit. It's not easy to interest the public in the public interest. Or as Joseph Pulitzer, who funded the Pulitzer Prize, said, "What is everybody's business is nobody's business—except the journalist's."

rational ignorance
A stance adopted by voters when they realize that the cost of understanding and voting on a particular issue exceeds the benefit expected from doing so

In contrast, consumers have much more incentive to gather and act on information about market decisions because they benefit directly and immediately from such information. *Because information and the time required to acquire and digest it are scarce, consumers concentrate on private choices rather than public choices. The payoff in making better private choices is usually more immediate, more direct, and more substantial.* For example, a consumer in the market for a new car has an incentive to examine the performance records of different models, test-drive a few, and check prices at dealerships and online. That same person has less incentive to examine the performance records of candidates for public office because that single voter has virtually no chance of deciding the election. What's more, because candidates aim to please the median voter anyway, they often take positions that are similar.

Distribution of Benefits and Costs

Let's turn now to a different topic—how the benefits and costs of public choices are spread across the population. Depending on the issue, particular legislation may benefit only a small group or much of the population. Likewise, the costs of that legislation may be imposed only on a small group or on much of the population. The combinations of benefits and costs yield four possible categories of distributions: (1) widespread benefits and widespread costs, (2) concentrated benefits and widespread costs, (3) widespread benefits and concentrated costs, and (4) concentrated costs and concentrated benefits.

Traditional public-goods legislation, such as for national defense, a justice system, or cancer research, involve widespread benefits and widespread costs—nearly everyone benefits and nearly everyone pays. Traditional public-goods legislation usually has a positive impact on the economy because total benefits exceed total costs.

traditional public-goods legislation
Legislation that involves widespread costs and widespread benefits—nearly everyone pays and nearly everyone benefits

With **special-interest legislation,** benefits are concentrated but costs widespread. For example, as you'll see shortly, price supports for dairy products have benefited a small group—dairy farmers. To benefit dairy farmers, a special interest, the program spread costs across nearly all taxpayers and consumers. Legislation that caters to special interests usually harms the economy, on net, because total costs often exceed total benefits. Special-interest legislation benefitting a narrow geographical interest is called **pork-barrel spending.** To boost their reelection prospects, members of Congress "bring home the bacon" by delivering pork-barrel programs for their constituents. For example, a recent federal budget appropriated $50,000 for a tattoo removal program in San Luis Obispo, California; $150,000 to restore the Augusta Historic Theater in Georgia; and $2 million for a statue of a Roman god in Birmingham, Alabama.[1]

special-interest legislation
Legislation with concentrated benefits but widespread costs

pork-barrel spending
Special-interest legislation with narrow geographical benefits but funded by all taxpayers

1. Robert Novak, "Senate Sneaks Preserve Pork," *New York Post,* 19 April 2007.

populist legislation
Legislation with widespread benefits but concentrated costs

Populist legislation involves widespread benefits but concentrated costs. Populist legislation usually has a tough time getting approved because the widespread group that benefits typically remains rationally ignorant about the proposed legislation, so these voters provide little political support. But the concentrated group who would get whacked by the taxes object strenuously. Most economists agree that tort-reform legislation, for example, would benefit the economy as a whole by limiting product liability lawsuits, reducing insurance costs, and bringing some goods to the market that, because of liability suits, have all but disappeared, such as personal aircraft. But trial lawyers, the group that would be most harmed by such limits, have successfully blocked reforms for years. Because the small group that bears the cost is savvy about the impact of such proposals but those who would reap the benefits remain rationally ignorant, populist legislation has little chance of approval. The only way such measures get approved is if some political entrepreneur raises enough visibility about the issue to gather public attention and votes. For example, a candidate for governor may run against high electric bills. The key is to somehow get the issue on voters' radar screens.

competing-interest legislation
Legislation that confers concentrated benefits on one group by imposing concentrated costs on another group

Finally, **competing-interest legislation** involves both concentrated benefits and concentrated costs, such as labor unions versus employers, or steel makers versus steel-using industries. These are fierce political battles because both sides have a heavy stake in the outcome.

Exhibit 3 arrays the four categories of distributions. Across the top, benefits of legislation are either *widespread* or *concentrated,* and along the left margin, costs are either *widespread* or *concentrated*. Box 1 shows *traditional public-goods legislation,* such as national defense, with both widespread benefits and widespread costs. Box 2 shows *special-interest legislation,* such as farm subsidies, with concentrated benefits but widespread costs. Box 3 shows *populist legislation,* such as tort reform, with widespread benefits but concentrated costs. And Box 4 shows *competing-interest legislation,* such as labor union issues, with both concentrated benefits and concentrated costs.

The case study, "Public Policy: Farm Subsidies" at the end of the book, considers a special-interest program—farm price supports.

EXHIBIT 3 Categories of Legislation Based on the Distribution of Costs and Benefits

Distribution of Costs	Distribution of Benefits: Widespread	Distribution of Benefits: Concentrated
Widespread	1. Traditional Public Goods *—National defense*	2. Special Interest *—Farm subsidies*
Concentrated	3. Populist *—Tort reform*	4. Competing Interest *—Labor union issues*

Rent Seeking

An important feature of representative democracy is the incentive and political power it offers interest groups to increase their wealth, either from direct government transfers or from favorable public expenditures and regulations. Special-interest groups, such as dairy farmers, trial lawyers, and other producers, seek from government some special advantage or some outright transfer or subsidy. Such benefits are often called *rents* because they exceed what the producer would require to supply the product. Thus, rents represents earnings that exceed opportunity cost. The activity that interest groups undertake to secure these special favors from government is called *rent seeking,* a term already introduced.

The government frequently bestows some special advantage on a producer or group of producers, and abundant resources are expended to acquire these advantages. For example, *political action committees,* known more popularly as *PACs,* contribute millions to congressional campaigns. Seven of the top ten spending PACs in 2009–2010 were labor unions.

To the extent that special-interest groups engage in rent seeking, they shift resources from productive endeavors that create output and income to activities that focus more on transferring income to their special interests. *Resources employed to persuade government to redistribute income and wealth to special interests are unproductive because they do nothing to increase total output and usually end up reducing it.* Often many firms compete for the same government advantage, thereby wasting still more resources. If the advantage conferred by government on some special-interest group requires higher income taxes, the earnings people expect from working and investing fall, so they may work less and invest less. If this happens, productive activity declines.

As a firm's profitability relies more and more on decisions made in Washington, resources are diverted from productive activity to rent seeking, or lobbying efforts. One firm may thrive because it secured some special government advantage at a critical time; another firm may fail because its managers were more concerned with productive efficiency than with rent seeking.

Special-interest groups have little incentive to make the economy more efficient. In fact, they usually support legislation that transfers wealth to them even if the economy's overall efficiency suffers. For example, suppose lawyers are able to change product liability laws in a way that boosts their annual incomes by a total of $1 billion, or about $1,800 for each of the 550,000 lawyers in private practice. Suppose, too, that this measure drives up the insurance premiums of producers, raising the total cost of production by, say, $2 billion per year. Lawyers themselves have to bear part of this higher cost, but because their personal consumption accounts for only about 1 percent of total spending in the economy, they bear only about 1 percent of the $2 billion in higher costs, or about $20 million. This amounts to $36 per lawyer per year. Thus, the legislation is a good deal for lawyers because their annual incomes grow about $1,800 each but their annual costs increase only about $36 each, resulting in the net average gain of $1,764 per lawyer in private practice. Much special-interest legislation leads to a net reduction in social welfare. For example, some of the nation's best minds are now occupied devising schemes to avoid taxes or divert income to favored groups at the expense of market efficiency.

There are hundreds of special-interest groups representing farmers, physicians, lawyers, teachers, manufacturers, barbers, and so on. One way special interests try to gain access to the political process is through campaign contributions. The tricky issue of campaign finance reform is discussed in the case study, "Public Policy: Campaign Finance Reform" at the end of the book.

The Underground Economy

underground economy
An expression used to describe market activity that goes unreported either because it is illegal or because those involved want to evade taxes

A government subsidy promotes production. Conversely, a tax discourages production. Perhaps it would be more accurate to say that when government taxes productive activity, less production gets *reported*. If you ever worked as a waitress or waiter, did you faithfully report all your tip income to the Internal Revenue Service? If not, your unreported income became part of the underground economy. The **underground economy** describes all market activity that goes unreported either to evade taxes or because the activity itself is illegal. Income arising in the underground economy ranges from unreported tips to the earnings of drug dealers.

Taxing productive activity has two effects. First, resource owners may supply less of the taxed resource because the after-tax earnings decline. Second, to evade taxes, some people shift from the formal, reported economy to an underground, "off the books" economy. Thus, when the government taxes market exchange and the income it generates, less market activity and less income get reported. The underground economy is known by a variety of other names in different countries, including the shady economy, informal economy, second economy, cash economy, hidden economy, unrecorded economy, parallel economy, off-the-books economy, and black economy.

We should take care to distinguish between tax *avoidance* and tax *evasion*. Tax avoidance is a *legal* attempt to arrange one's economic affairs to pay the least tax possible, such as buying municipal bonds because they yield interest free of federal income taxes. Tax evasion, on the other hand, is *illegal;* it takes the form of either failing to file a tax return or filing a fraudulent return by understating income or overstating deductions. Research around the world indicates that the underground economy grows more when (1) government regulations increase, (2) tax rates increase, and (3) government corruption is more widespread.[2]

The U.S. Commerce Department estimates that official figures capture only about 90 percent of U.S. income. And an Internal Revenue Service survey estimates that only about 90 percent of taxable income gets reported on tax returns. These studies suggest an underground economy of about $1.5 trillion in 2010.

Those who pursue rent-seeking activity and those involved in the underground economy view government from opposite sides. Rent seekers want government to become actively involved in transferring wealth to them, but those in the underground economy want to avoid government contact. *Subsidies and other advantages bestowed by government draw some people closer to government; taxes and regulations drive some others underground.*

Bureaucracy and Representative Democracy

bureaus
Government agencies charged with implementing legislation and financed by appropriations from legislative bodies

Elected representatives approve legislation, but the task of implementing that legislation is typically left to **bureaus**, which are government agencies whose activities are financed by appropriations from legislative bodies.

Ownership and Funding of Bureaus

We can get a better feel for government bureaus by comparing them to corporations. Stockholders own a corporation and share any profit or loss. Stockholders also get to vote on important corporate matters based on the number of shares owned. Corporate shares can be bought and sold in the stock market: ownership is *transferable* to whomever buys

2. For a summary of these studies, see Simon Johnson et al., "Regulatory Discretion and the Unofficial Economy," *American Economic Review*, 88 (May 1998): 387–392.

the shares. Taxpayers are in a sense the "owners" of government bureaus. If the bureau earns a "profit," taxes may decline; if the bureau operates at a "loss," as most do, this loss must be made up by taxes. Each taxpayer has just one vote, regardless of the taxes he or she pays. Ownership in the bureau is surrendered only if the taxpayer dies or moves out of the jurisdiction, but ownership is not transferable—it cannot be bought or sold directly.

Whereas corporations cover their costs if enough people buy their products, bureaus are usually financed by government appropriation, most of which comes from taxpayers. Bureaus do not have to meet a market test. Some bureaus get revenue through user charges, such as admission fees to state parks or tuition at state colleges, but even these bureaus typically rely on taxes for part of their revenue. Because of these differences in the forms of ownership and in the sources of funding, bureaus have different incentives than do for-profit firms, so they are likely to behave differently, as we'll see next.

Ownership and Organizational Behavior

A central assumption of economics is that people behave rationally and respond to economic incentives. The more tightly compensation is linked to individual incentives, the more people behave in accordance with those incentives. For example, if a letter carrier's pay is based on customer satisfaction, the carrier will make a greater effort to deliver mail promptly and intact.

A private firm receives a steady stream of consumer feedback. If the price is too high or too low to clear the market, surpluses or shortages become obvious. Not only is consumer feedback abundant, but the firm's owners have a profit incentive to act on that information to satisfy consumer wants. The promise of profits also creates incentives to produce output at the least cost. Thus, the firm's owners stand to gain from any improvement in customer satisfaction for a given cost or any reduction in cost for a given level of consumer satisfaction.

Because public goods and services are not sold in markets, government bureaus receive less consumer feedback and have less incentive to act on any feedback they do receive. There are usually no prices and no obvious shortages or surpluses. For example, how would you know whether there was a shortage or a surplus of police protection in your community? Not only do bureaus receive less consumer feedback than firms do, bureaus have less incentive to act on the information available. If a corporation is run poorly, someone could buy most of the shares, improve performance, then profit from a higher share price. But because the ownership of bureaus is not transferable, there is less incentive to eliminate waste and inefficiency.

Voters could pressure their elected representatives to make bureaus more responsive. But this discipline is rather crude. Most voters remain rationally ignorant about government performance in part because each voter has little impact on the outcome and each stands to gain so little from any increase in efficiency. For example, suppose that you are one of a million taxpayers in a city and you learn that by having FedEx Offices do all public copying, the city could save $1 million a year. If, through letters to the editor and calls to local officials, you somehow convince the city to adopt this cost-saving measure, you, as a typical taxpayer, would save yourself about a dollar a year in taxes.

Voters can leave a jurisdiction if they believe government is inefficient. This mechanism, whereby people "vote with their feet," does promote some efficiency and consumer satisfaction at the state and local levels, but it's also crude. What if you like some public programs but not others? Moreover, voters dissatisfied with the biggest spender and taxer, the federal government, cannot easily vote with their feet. If you were to move abroad, you, as a U.S. citizen, must still pay U.S. federal taxes on your worldwide income even if you did not earn a dime from U.S. sources (most other countries tax only the domestic income of those living abroad).

Because of differences between public and private organizations—in the owners' ability both to transfer ownership and to appropriate profits—we expect bureaus to be less concerned with satisfying consumer demand or with minimizing costs than private firms are. A variety of empirical studies compares costs for products that are provided by both public bureaus and private firms, such as garbage collection. Of those studies that show a difference, most find private firms are more efficient.

Bureaucratic Objectives

Assuming that bureaus are not simply at the beck and call of the legislature—that is, assuming that bureaucrats have some autonomy—what sort of objectives do *they* pursue? The traditional view is that bureaucrats are "public servants," who try to serve the public as best they can. No doubt some public employees do just that, but is this a realistic assumption for bureaucrats more generally? Why should we assume self-sacrificing behavior by public-sector employees when we make no such assumption about private-sector employees?

One widely discussed theory of bureaucratic behavior claims that bureaus try to *maximize their budget*, for along with a bigger budget come size, prestige, amenities, staff, and pay—all features that are valued by bureaucrats.[3] According to this view, bureaus are monopoly suppliers of their output to elected officials. Rather than charge a price per unit, bureaus offer the entire amount as a package deal in return for the requested appropriation. This theory assumes that the elected officials have only limited ability to dig into the budget and cut particular items. If elected officials do try to cut the bureau's budget, the bureau may threaten to make those cuts as painful to constituents as possible. For example, if city officials attempt to slow the growth of the school budget, school bureaucrats, rather than increase teaching loads or reducing pay raises, may threaten to eliminate kindergarten, abolish the high school football team, or disband the school band. If such threats force elected officials to back off, the government budget turns out to be larger than the public would prefer. *Budget maximization results in a larger budget than that desired by the median voter.* The key to this argument is that bureaus are monopoly suppliers of public goods and elected officials have only limited ability to cut that budget. If taxpayers have alternatives in the private sector or if elected officials can dig into the budget, the monopoly power of the bureau is diminished.

Private Versus Public Production

Simply because some goods and services are *financed* by the government does not mean that they must be *produced* by the government. Elected officials may contract directly with private firms to produce public output. For example, city officials may contract with a private firm to collect garbage for the city. In some jurisdictions, for-profit firms now provide everything from fire protection to prisons. Elected officials may also use a combination of bureaus and firms to produce the desired output. For example, the Pentagon, a giant bureau, hires and trains military personnel, yet contracts with private firms to develop and produce various weapon systems. State governments typically hire private contractors to build highways but employ state workers to maintain them. The mix of firms and bureaus varies over time and across jurisdictions, but the trend is toward increased *privatization*, or production by the private sector, of public goods and services.

When governments produce public goods and services, they are using *the internal organization of the government*—the bureaucracy—to supply the product. When governments contract with private firms to produce public goods and services, they are using *the market* to supply the product. While private firms have more incentives to be efficient than bureaus do, public officials sometimes prefer dealing with bureaus. Public

3. William A. Niskanen Jr., in *Bureaucracy and Representative Government* (Aldine-Atherton, 1971).

officials may have more control over the bureau than over a private firm. Bureaus may also offer public officials more opportunities to appoint friends and political supporters to government jobs.

In situations where it would be difficult to specify a contract for the public good in question, a bureau may be more responsive to public concerns than a for-profit firm would be. Suppose the service provided by social workers is put out for bid. The firm that wins the bid may be tempted to skimp on quality, particularly if quality can be determined only by direct observation at the time the service is provided. The governments would have difficulty monitoring the quality provided by a private contractor. The services of social workers might be better provided by a government bureau. Because profit is not its goal, a bureau may be less inclined to minimize cost by reducing quality. For example, one study found that privately operated juvenile correction facilities in Florida had lower costs but experienced higher rates of recidivism than state-operated juvenile correction facilities. The lower costs of privately operated facilities were more than offset by the increased recidivism, making state operation the better choice.[4]

Conclusion

Governments attempt to address market failures in the private economy. But simply turning problems of perceived market failure over to government may not always be the best solution, because government has limitations and failings of its own. Participation in markets is based on voluntary exchange. Governments, however, have the legal power to enforce public choices. We should employ at least as high a standard in judging the performance of government, where allocations have the force of law, as we do in judging the private market, where allocations are decided by voluntary exchange between consenting parties. In other words, we should scrutinize a system that is compulsory at least as much as we scrutinize a system that is voluntary. After all, nobody is forcing you to buy tofu, but if you refuse to pay taxes to fund public programs you hate, you could go to prison.

Summary

1. Private goods are rival and exclusive, such as a pizza. Public goods are nonrival and nonexclusive, such as national defense. Goods that are in between public and private goods include natural monopolies, which are nonrival but exclusive, such as cable TV, and open-access goods, which are rival but nonexclusive, such as ocean fish. Because private-sector producers cannot easily exclude nonpayers from consuming a public good, public goods are typically provided by government, which has the power to enforce tax collections.
2. Public choice based on majority rule usually reflects the preferences of the median voter. Other voters often must "buy" either more or less of the public good than they would prefer.
3. Producers have an abiding interest in any legislation that affects their livelihood. Consumers, however, purchase thousands of different goods and services and thus have no special interest in legislation affecting any particular product. Most consumers adopt a stance of rational ignorance, because the expected costs of keeping up with special-interest issues usually outweigh the expected benefits.
4. The intense interest that producer groups have in relevant legislation, coupled with the rational ignorance of voters regarding most issues, leave government vulnerable to rent seeking by special interests. Elected officials trying to maximize their political support sometimes serve special interests at the expense of the public interest.
5. Bureaus differ from firms in the amount of consumer feedback they receive, in their incentives to minimize costs, and in the transferability of their ownership. Because of these differences, bureaus may not be as efficient or as sensitive to consumer preferences as for-profit firms are.

4. Patrick Bayer and David Pozen, "The Effectiveness of Juvenile Correction Facilities: Public Versus Private Management," *Journal of Law and Economics*, 48 (October 2005): 549–589.

Key Concepts

Questions for Review

1. Private and Public Goods Distinguish among private goods, natural monopolies, open-access goods, and public goods. Provide examples of each.
2. Free Rider Does the free-rider problem arise from the characteristics of consumption rivalry, excludability, or both?
3. Median-Voter Model In a single-issue majority vote, such as the TV example in this chapter, does the median voter always get his or her most preferred outcome?
4. Representative Democracy Major political parties typically offer "middle of the road" platforms rather than take extreme positions. Is this consistent with the concepts of the median voter and rational ignorance discussed in this chapter?
5. Distribution of Costs and Benefits Why are consumer interest groups usually less effective than producer lobbies in influencing legislation?
6. Distribution of Costs and Benefits Which groups typically bear the costs and which groups enjoy the benefits of (a) traditional public goods, (b) special-interest legislation, and (c) competing-interest legislation?
7. Case Study: Farm Subsidies (See page 734.) "Subsidizing the price of milk or other agricultural products is not very expensive considering how many consumers there are in the United States. Therefore, there is little harmful effect from such subsidies." Evaluate this statement.
8. Case Study: Farm Subsidies (See page 734.) Subsidy programs are likely to have a number of secondary effects in addition to the direct effect on dairy prices. What impact do you suppose farm subsidies are likely to have on the following?
   a. Housing prices
   b. Technological change in the dairy industry
   c. The price of dairy product substitutes
9. Rent Seeking Explain how rent seeking can lead to a drop in production of goods and services. What role might the underground economy play in lessening the drop in productive activities?
10. The Underground Economy What is the underground economy? What is the impact on the underground economy of instituting a tax on a certain productive activity?
11. Bureaucracy and Representative Democracy How do the incentives and feedback for government bureaus differ from those for profit-making firms?
12. Bureaucracy and Representative Democracy A firm is described as combining managerial coordination with market exchange in order to produce its good or service. Does similar behavior occur in government bureaus? Explain.
13. Case Study: Campaign Finance Reform (See page 736.) The motivation behind campaign finance reform was to limit the influence of special interests. In what sense could that legislation have the opposite effect?

Problems and Exercises

14. Optimal Provision of Public Goods Using at least two individual consumers, show how the market demand curve is derived from individual demand curves (a) for a private good and (b) for a public good. Once you have derived the market demand curve in each case, introduce a market supply curve and then show the optimal level of production.
15. Distribution of Costs and Benefits Suppose that the government decides to guarantee an above-market price for a good by buying up any surplus at that above-market price. Using a conventional supply-demand diagram, illustrate the following gains and losses from such a price support:
    a. The loss of consumer surplus
    b. The gain of producer surplus in the short run
    c. The cost of running the government program (assuming no storage costs)
    d. What is the total cost of the program to consumers?
    e. Are the costs and benefits of the support program widespread or concentrated?

Global Economic Watch Exercises

Login to www.cengagebrain.com and access the Global Economic Watch to do these exercises.

16. Global Economic Watch Go to the Global Economic Crisis Resource Center. Select Global Issues in Context. In the Basic Search box at the top of the page, enter the phrase "public goods." On the Results page, go to the Global Viewpoints Section. Click on the link for the July 2003 editorial "Global Public Goods and Health." What is a global public good?

17. Global Economic Watch Go to the Global Economic Crisis Resource Center. Select Global Issues in Context. In the Basic Search box at the top of the page, enter one of the following terms: "underground economy," "shadow economy," or "informal economy." Choose one article about a foreign country and write an analysis of the underground economy there.

Externalities and the Environment

17

REUTERS/Sean Gardner/Landov

- Why do people fish until the fish are gone?
- Why might environmentalists buy rights to pollute the air and water?
- How did barbed wire tame the Wild West?
- In what sense was the biggest environmental disaster in U.S. history not a negative externality?
- And how does someone else's antitheft device affect the chances that your car will get stolen?

These and other questions are answered in this chapter, which looks at externalities and the environment.

The rivers in Jakarta, Indonesia, are dead—killed by acid, alcohol, and oil. Coral reefs in the South Pacific are being ripped apart by dynamite fishing. BP's drilling accident could affect the Gulf of Mexico for years. The tropical rainforest is shrinking because of slash-and-burn claims on the land's resources. The build-up of greenhouse gases threatens to warm the oceans and near-surface air. Some streams in Colorado are still considered toxic from gold mining that ended more than a century ago. These environmental problems are all negative externalities, which result from the actions of producers or consumers that affect many others. Markets can allocate resources efficiently only as long as property rights are well defined and can be easily enforced. But property rights to clean water, air, and soil, to fish in the ocean, to peace and quiet, and to scenic vistas are hard to establish and enforce. This lack of property rights to some resources results in externalities.

Externalities may be either negative, such as air and water pollution, or positive, such as the general improvement in the civic climate that results from better education.

This chapter discusses externalities and explores how public policies can reduce negative externalities and increase positive externalities.

Topics discussed include:

- Exhaustible resources
- Renewable resources
- Common-pool problem
- Private property rights
- Optimal pollution
- Marginal social cost
- Marginal social benefit
- Coase theorem
- Markets for pollution rights
- Environmental protection

Externalities and the Common-Pool Problem

exhaustible resource
A resource in fixed supply, such as crude oil or coal

Let's begin by distinguishing between exhaustible resources and renewable resources. An **exhaustible resource** such as oil or coal does not renew itself and so is available in a finite amount. Technology may improve the ability to extract and utilize these resources, but each gallon of oil burned is gone forever. Sooner or later, all oil wells will run dry. The world's oil reserves are *exhaustible*.

Renewable Resources

renewable resource
A resource that regenerates itself and so can be used indefinitely if used conservatively, such as a properly managed forest

A resource is **renewable** if, when used conservatively, it can be drawn on indefinitely. Thus, timber is a **renewable resource** if trees are cut at sustainable rates and replaced with seedlings. The atmosphere and rivers are renewable resources to the extent that they can absorb and neutralize a certain level of pollutants. More generally, biological resources like fish, game, forests, rivers, grasslands, and agricultural soil are renewable if managed appropriately.

common-pool problem
Unrestricted access to a renewable resource results in overuse

Some renewable resources are also open-access resources, an idea introduced in the previous chapter. An open-access resource is rival in consumption, but exclusion is costly. Fish caught in the ocean, for example, are not available for others to catch, so fish are rival in consumption. Yet it would be difficult, if not impossible, for a person or a firm to "own" fish still swimming in open waters and to prevent others from catching them, so ocean fish are nonexclusive. An open-access good is often subject to the **common-pool problem,** which results because people harvest a resource as long as the marginal benefit exceeds marginal cost. For example, people will fish the oceans as long as the marginal benefit of catching more fish exceeds the marginal cost. Practically speaking, unless otherwise checked, people will fish until the oceans become "fished out." Open-access goods are overfished, overhunted, overharvested, and overused. Because the atmosphere is an open-access resource, it's used as a dump for unwanted gases. Air pollution is a negative externality imposed on society by polluters. The problem is that people exploit any resource as long as their personal marginal benefit exceeds their personal marginal cost. As we'll see, personal marginal cost ignores the costs imposed on others.

In a market system, specific individuals usually own the rights to resources and therefore have a strong interest in using those resources efficiently. *Private property rights*, a term introduced in Chapter 2, allow individuals to use resources or to charge others for their use. Private property rights are defined and enforced by government, by informal social actions, and by ethical norms. As Robert Frost wrote, "Good fences make good neighbors."[1] But because defining and enforcing property rights to open-access resources, such as the air, are quite costly or even impossible, these resources usually are not owned as private property.

Pollution and other negative externalities arise because there are no practical, enforceable, private property rights to open-access resources, such as the air. Market prices usually fail to include the costs that negative externalities impose on society. For example, the price you pay for a gallon of gasoline does not reflect the costs imposed by the greenhouse gases, sootier air, oil spills, and the greater traffic congestion your driving creates. Electric rates do not reflect the negative externalities, or external costs, caused by fossil-fueled power plants. Note that externalities are unintended side effects of actions that are themselves useful and purposeful. Electricity producers, for example, did not go into business to pollute.

Resolving the Common-Pool Problem

Users of the atmosphere, waterways, wildlife, or other open-access resources tend to ignore the impact of their use on the resource's renewal ability. As quality and quantity diminish from overuse, the resource grows scarcer and could disappear. For example, Georges Bank, located off the New England coast, long one of the world's most productive fishing grounds, became so depleted by overfishing that by the 1990s the catch was down 85 percent from peak years. Tuna, once abundant in the Mediterranean, now faces extinction there. The United Nations reports that 11 of the world's 15 primary fishing grounds are seriously depleted.

By imposing restrictions on resource use, government regulations may reduce the common-pool problem. Output restrictions or taxes could force people to use the resource at a rate that is socially optimal. For example, in the face of the tendency to overfish and to catch fish before they are sufficiently mature, the U.S. government has imposed a variety of restrictions on the fishing industry. The laws limit the total catch, the size of fish, the length of the fishing season, the equipment used, and other aspects of the business.

More generally, when imposing and enforcing private property rights would be too costly, government regulations may improve allocative efficiency. For example, stop signs and traffic lights allocate the scarce space at intersections, minimum size restrictions control lobster fishing, hunting seasons control the stock of game, and enforced study hours may calm the din in the college dormitory.

But not all regulations are equally efficient. For example, fishing authorities sometimes limit the total industry catch and allow all firms to fish until that limit is reached. Consequently, when the fishing season opens, there is a mad scramble to catch as much as possible before the industry limit is reached. Because time is of the essence, fishing boats make no effort to fish selectively. And the catch reaches processors all at once, creating congestion throughout the supply chain. Also, each firm has an incentive to expand its fishing fleet to catch more in those precious few weeks. Thus, large fleets of technologically efficient fishing vessels operate for a few weeks until the limit is reached and then sit in port for the rest of the year. Each operator is acting rationally, but the collective effect of the regulation is grossly inefficient in terms of social welfare. Consider the complicated and sometimes confounding fishing regulations in Iceland:

> *The Icelandic government realized that it would have to curb the capacity of its own fleet. But the fishermen compensated by buying more trawlers. Then the*

1. From the poem "Mending Wall" in Robert Frost, *You Come Too* (Holt, Rinehart, and Winston, 1967): 64.

government restricted the size of the fleet and the number of days at sea; the fishermen responded by buying larger, more efficient gear. The cod stocks continued to decline. In 1984, the government introduced quotas on species per vessel per season. This was a controversial and often wasteful system. A groundfish hauled up from 50 fathoms [300 feet] is killed by the change in pressure. But if it is a cod and the cod quota has been used up, it is thrown overboard. Or if the price of cod is low that week and cod happens to come in the haddock net, the fishermen will throw them overboard because they do not want to use up their cod quota when they are not getting a good price.[2]

Ocean fish remain a common-pool resource because firms have not yet been able to establish and enforce rights to particular schools of fish. But advances in technology may some day allow the creation of private property rights to ocean fish, migrating birds, and other open-access resources. Establishing property rights to cattle on the Great Plains once seemed impossible, but the invention of barbed wire allowed ranchers to fence the range. Patented in 1867, barbed wire was advertized as "The finest fence in the world. Light as air. Stronger than whiskey. Cheaper than dirt." In a sense, barbed wire tamed the Wild West.

Optimal Level of Pollution

Though the science is not yet fully resolved, fossil fuel used to power the likes of automobiles and electricity generators produces carbon dioxide, which mixes with other greenhouse gases that may contribute to climate change. Electricity production from fossil fuels, therefore, involves the external cost of using the atmosphere as a gas dump. This section considers a way to analyze such externalities.

External Costs With Fixed Technology

Suppose *D* in Exhibit 1 depicts the demand for electricity. Recall that a demand curve reflects consumers' marginal benefit of each unit. The lower horizontal line reflects the marginal private cost of electricity using fossil fuels. If producers base their pricing and output decisions on their marginal private costs, the equilibrium quantity per month is 50 million kilowatt-hours and the equilibrium price is $0.10 per kilowatt-hour. At that price and quantity, identified by point *a,* the marginal private cost of production just equals the marginal benefit enjoyed by consumers of electricity.

Electricity production involves not only the private cost of the resources employed but also the external cost of using the atmosphere as a dump for greenhouse gases. Suppose that the marginal external cost imposed on the environment by the generation of electricity is $0.04 per kilowatt-hour. If the only way to cut emissions is to reduce electricity production, then the relationship between electricity production and pollution is fixed; the pollution in this case occurs with **fixed-production technology**.

fixed-production technology
Occurs when the relationship between the output rate and the generation of an externality is fixed; the only way to reduce the externality is to reduce the output

marginal social cost
The sum of the marginal private cost and the marginal external cost of production or consumption

The vertical distance between the marginal private cost curve and the marginal social cost curve in Exhibit 1 shows the marginal external cost of $0.04 per kilowatt-hour. The **marginal social cost** includes both the marginal private cost and the marginal external cost that production imposes on society. Because the marginal external cost here is assumed to be a constant $0.04 per kilowatt-hour, the two cost curves are parallel. Notice that at the private-sector equilibrium output level of 50 million kilowatt-hours, the marginal social cost, identified at point *b*, exceeds society's marginal benefit of

2. Mark Kurlansky, *Cod: A Biography of the Fish That Changed the World* (New York: Walker., 1997), p. 172.

EXHIBIT 1 Negative Externalities: The Market for Electricity in the Midwest

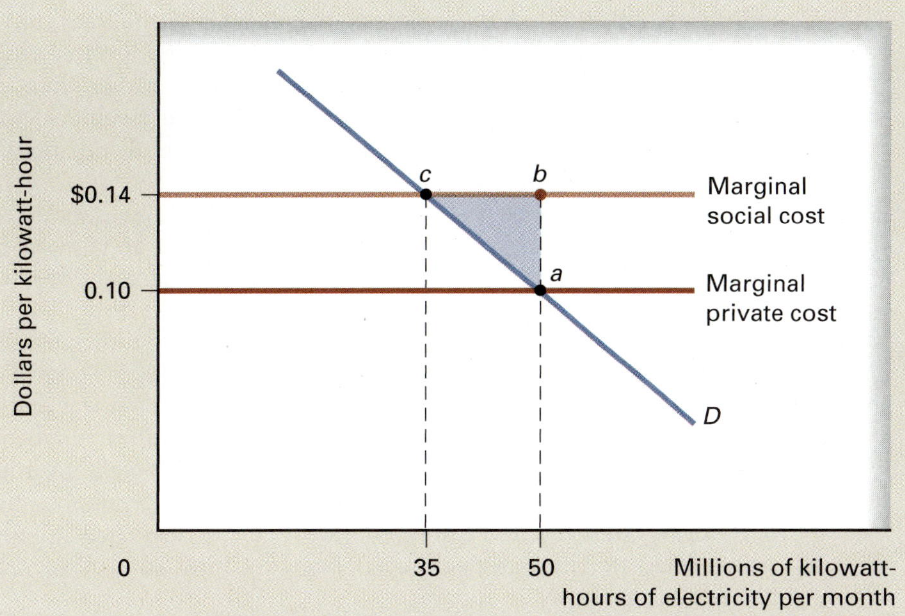

If producers base their output on marginal private cost, 50 million kilowatt-hours of electricity are produced per month. The marginal external cost of electricity is the cost of pollution imposed on society. The marginal social cost curve includes both the marginal private cost and the marginal external cost. If producers base their output decisions on marginal social cost, only 35 million kilowatt-hours are produced, which is the optimal output. The total social gain from basing production on marginal social cost is reflected by the blue-shaded triangle.

electricity, identified on the demand curve at point *a*. The 50-millionth kilowatt-hour of electricity costs society $0.14 but yields only $0.10 of marginal benefit. Because the marginal social cost exceeds the marginal benefit, too much electricity is produced.

The efficient quantity of 35 million kilowatt-hours is found where the demand, or marginal benefit, curve intersects the marginal social cost curve. This intersection is identified at point *c*. How could output be restricted to the socially efficient amount? If regulators knew the demand and marginal cost curves, they could simply limit production to 35 million kilowatt-hours, the efficient quantity. Or, on each kilowatt-hour produced, they could impose a tax equal to the marginal external cost of $0.04. Such a pollution tax would lift the marginal private cost curve up to the marginal social cost curve. Thus, the tax would bring private costs in line with social costs.

With a tax of $0.04 per kilowatt-hour, the equilibrium combination of price and output moves from point *a* to point *c*. The price rises from $0.10 to $0.14 per kilowatt-hour, and output falls to 35 million kilowatt-hours. Setting the tax equal to the marginal external cost results in the efficient level of output. At point *c*, the marginal social cost of production equals the marginal benefit. Notice that greenhouse gas emissions are not eliminated at point *c*, but the utilities no longer generate electricity for which marginal social cost exceeds marginal benefit. The social gain from reducing production to the socially optimal level is shown by the blue-shaded triangle in Exhibit 1. This triangle also measures the social cost of allowing firms to ignore the external cost of production. Although Exhibit 1 offers a tidy solution, the external costs of greenhouse gases often cannot be easily calculated or taxed. At times, government intervention may result in more or less production than the optimal solution requires.

External Costs With Variable Technology

variable technology
Occurs when the amount of externality generated at a given rate of output can be reduced by altering the production process

The previous example assumes that the only way to reduce greenhouse gases is to reduce output. But power companies, particularly in the long run, can usually change their resource mix to reduce emissions for any given level of electricity. If pollution can be reduced by altering the production process rather than by simply adjusting the quantity, these externalities are said to be produced under conditions of **variable technology.** With variable technology, the idea is to find the optimal level of pollution for a given quantity of electricity.

Let's look at Exhibit 2. The horizontal axis measures greenhouse gas emissions for a given level of electricity production. Emissions can be reduced by adopting cleaner production technology. Yet the production of cleaner air, like the production of other goods, is subject to diminishing returns. Cutting emissions of the most offensive greenhouse gases may involve simply changing the fuel mix, but further reductions call for more sophisticated and more expensive processes. Thus, the marginal social cost of reducing greenhouse gases increases, as shown by the upward-sloping marginal social cost curve in Exhibit 2.

marginal social benefit
The sum of the marginal private benefit and the marginal external benefit of production or consumption

The **marginal social benefit** curve reflects the additional benefit society derives from greenhouse gas reductions. When emissions are high, an improvement can save lives and thus is valued by society more than when emissions are low. Cleaner air, like other goods, has a declining marginal benefit to society (though the total benefit still increases). The marginal social benefit curve from cleaner air therefore slopes downward, as shown in Exhibit 2.

EXHIBIT 2 The Optimal Reduction in Greenhouse Gas Emissions

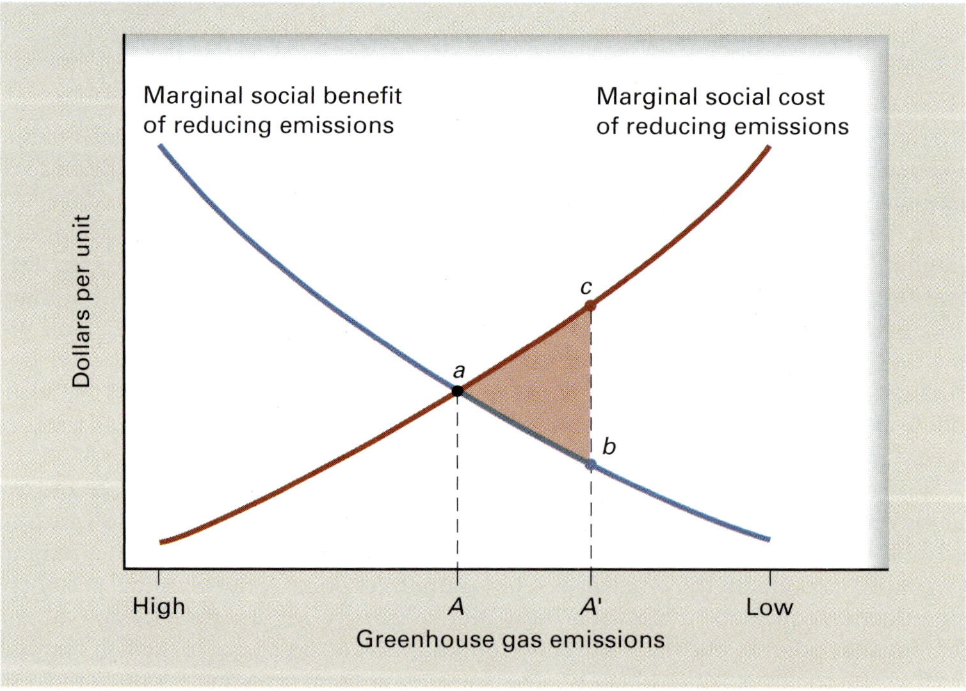

The optimal level of greenhouse gas emissions is found at point *a*, where the marginal social benefit of reducing such emissions equals the marginal social cost. If some lower level of emissions were dictated by the government, such as *A'*, the marginal social cost would exceed the marginal social benefit, and social waste would result. The total social waste resulting from a lower than optimal level of emissions is shown by the pink-shaded triangle.

The optimal level of air quality for a given quantity of electricity is found at point *a*, where the marginal social benefit of cleaner air equals the marginal social cost. In this example, the optimal level of greenhouse gas emissions is *A*. If firms made their production decisions based simply on their private cost—that is, if the emission cost is external to the firm—then firms would have little incentive to search for production methods that reduce greenhouse gas emission, so too much production would result.

What if government regulators decree that greenhouse gas emission levels should be no greater than *A*'? For example, suppose a law establishes *A*' as the maximum acceptable level of emissions. The marginal social cost, identified as *c*, of achieving that level of air quality exceeds the marginal social benefit, identified as *b*. The total social waste associated with imposing a greater-than-optimal level of air quality is shown by the pink-shaded triangle, *abc*. This area is the total amount by which the additional social costs of cleaner air (associated with a move from *A* to *A*') exceed the additional social benefits. Improving air quality benefits society only as long as the marginal social benefit of cleaner air exceeds its marginal social cost.

What would happen to the optimal level of emissions if either the marginal cost curve or the marginal benefit curve shifted? For example, suppose some technological breakthrough reduces the marginal cost of cutting greenhouse gas emissions. As shown in panel (a) of Exhibit 3, the marginal social cost curve of reducing emissions would shift downward to *MSC*', leading to cleaner air as reflected by the movement from *A* to *A*'. *The simple logic is that the lower the marginal cost of reducing greenhouse gases, other things constant, the cleaner the air.*

An increase in the marginal benefit of air quality would have a similar effect. For example, suppose research indicates that the effects of a one degree increase in the Earth's average surface temperature would be much more devastating than previously believed. This finding would increase the perceived benefits of reducing greenhouse gases. Thus, the marginal benefit of cleaner air would increase, as reflected in panel

EXHIBIT 3 Effect of Changes in Costs or Benefits of Reducing Greenhouse Gas Emissions

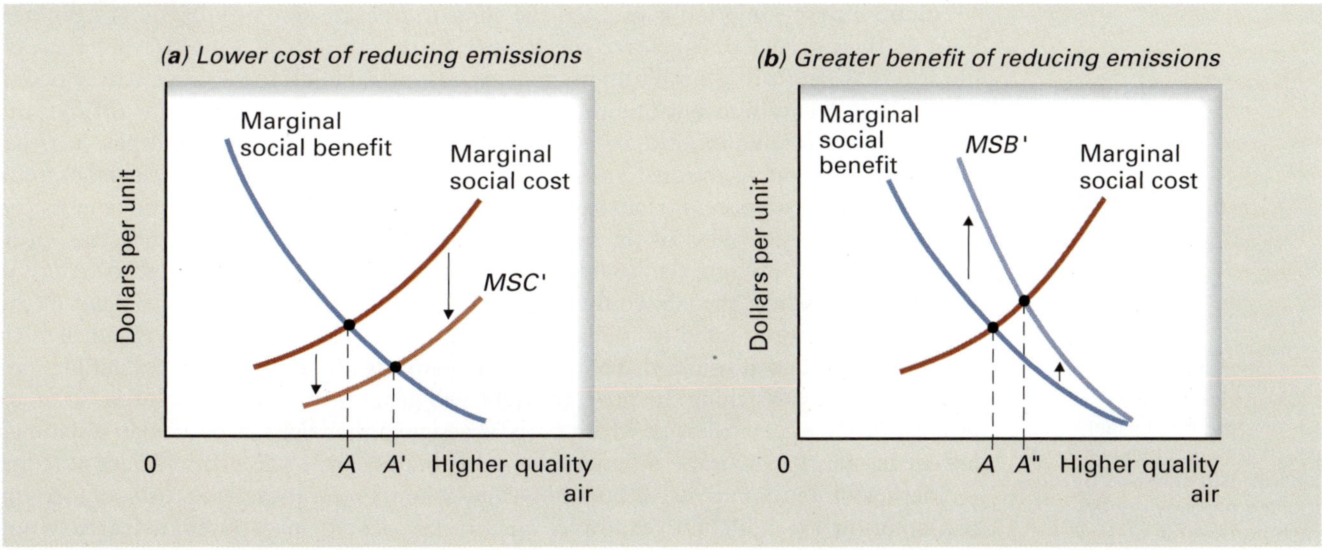

Either a reduction in the marginal social cost of cleaner air, as shown in panel (a), or an increase in the marginal social benefit of cleaner air, as shown in panel (b), increases the optimal level of air quality.

(b) of Exhibit 3 by an upward shift of the marginal social benefit curve to *MSB'*. As a result, air quality would improve, moving from A to A" in panel (b) of Exhibit 3. *The greater the marginal benefit of reducing greenhouse gases, other things constant, the cleaner the air.* As another example, recent research indicates that deaths from heart and lung disease would decrease 0.7 percent in large U.S. cities if suspended particulates in the air decrease by just 1/100,000th of a gram per cubic meter of air.[3] This finding increases the perceived benefits of cleaner air, leading to an increase in the optimal quality of air.

The atmosphere has the ability to cleanse itself of some emissions, but the destruction of the tropical rainforest has reduced this ability, as discussed in the case study, "Public Policy: The Lungs of the Planet," located at the back of the book.

The Coase Theorem

The traditional analysis of externalities assumes that market failures arise because people ignore the external effects of their actions. For example, suppose a manufacturer of heavy machinery is next door to a research laboratory that tests delicate equipment. The vibrations caused by the manufacturing process throw off the delicate equipment next door. Professor Ronald Coase, who won the Nobel Prize in 1991, would argue that the negative externality in this case is not necessarily imposed by the heavy machinery—rather, it arises from the incompatible activities of the two firms. The externality is the result of both vibrations created by the factory *and* the location of the testing lab next door. Solutions might include modifying the factory, moving the factory, making the test equipment more shock resistant, or moving the testing lab.

According to Coase, the efficient solution depends on which party can avoid the externality at the lower cost. Suppose it would cost $2 million for the factory to reduce vibrations enough for the lab to function normally. On the other hand, if the factory makes no changes, the lab can't insulate its testing equipment enough to operate accurately, so the lab would have to relocate at a cost of $1 million. Based on this information, the least-cost solution would be for the testing lab to relocate at a cost of $1 million. Coase argues that, as long as transaction costs are low, the parties will reach the efficient solution if one party is assigned the property right. And here's Coase's special insight: *This efficient solution will be achieved regardless of which party gets the property right.*

Suppose the testing lab is granted the right to operate free of vibrations from next door, so the testing lab can force the factory to reduce its vibration. Rather than cut vibrations at a cost of $2 million, the factory can pay the lab to relocate. Any payment greater than $1 million but less than $2 million makes both sides better off, because the lab would receive more than its moving cost and the factory would pay less than its cost of reducing vibrations. Thus, the lab will move, which is the efficient outcome.

Alternatively, suppose the factory is granted the right to generate vibrations in its production process, regardless of the impact on the testing lab. For the factory, this means business as usual. Because the minimum payment the factory would accept to reduce vibrations is $2 million, the lab would rather relocate at a cost of $1 million. Thus, whether property rights are granted to the lab or to the factory, the lab will move, which is the efficient, or least-cost, solution. The **Coase theorem** says that as long as bargaining costs are small, merely assigning the property right will generate an efficient solution to an externality problem regardless of which party is assigned that right. A particular assignment determines which side bears the externality costs but does not affect the efficient outcome.

Coase theorem
As long as bargaining costs are low, an efficient solution to the problem of externalities is achieved by assigning property rights to one party or the other, it doesn't matter which

Inefficient outcomes do occur, however, when the transaction costs of arriving at a solution are high. For example, an airport located in a populated area would

3. Jonathan M. Samet et al., "Fine Particulate Air Pollution and Mortality in 20 U.S. Cities, 1987–1994," 343 *New England Journal of Medicine*, (14 December 2000): 1742–1749.

have difficulty negotiating noise levels with all the affected residents. Or peasants contemplating clearing a portion of the tropical rainforest would be unable to negotiate with the millions, and perhaps, billions, of people ultimately affected by that decision. *When the number of parties involved in the transaction is large, Coase's solution of assigning property rights may not be enough.*

Markets for Pollution Rights

According to the Coase theorem, the assignment of property rights is often sufficient to resolve the market failure typically associated with externalities. Additional government intervention is not necessary. If pollution can be easily monitored and polluters easily identified, the government may be able to achieve an efficient solution to the problem of pollution simply by assigning the right to pollute. To see how this could work, let's look at an example. Firms that dump into a river evidently value the ability to discharge waste in this way. For them, the river provides a zero cost outlet for by products that otherwise would have to be disposed of at greater cost. The river provides a disposal service, and the demand curve for that service slopes downward, just like the demand for other resources.

The demand for the river as a discharge system is presented as *D* in Exhibit 4. The horizontal axis measures the tons of discharge dumped into the river per day, and the vertical axis measures firms' marginal benefit of disposing of each ton of waste in this way. The demand curve thus measures the marginal value to firms of using the river as a disposal service. With no restrictions on river pollution—that is, if all firms were free

EXHIBIT 4 Optimal Allocation of Pollution Rights

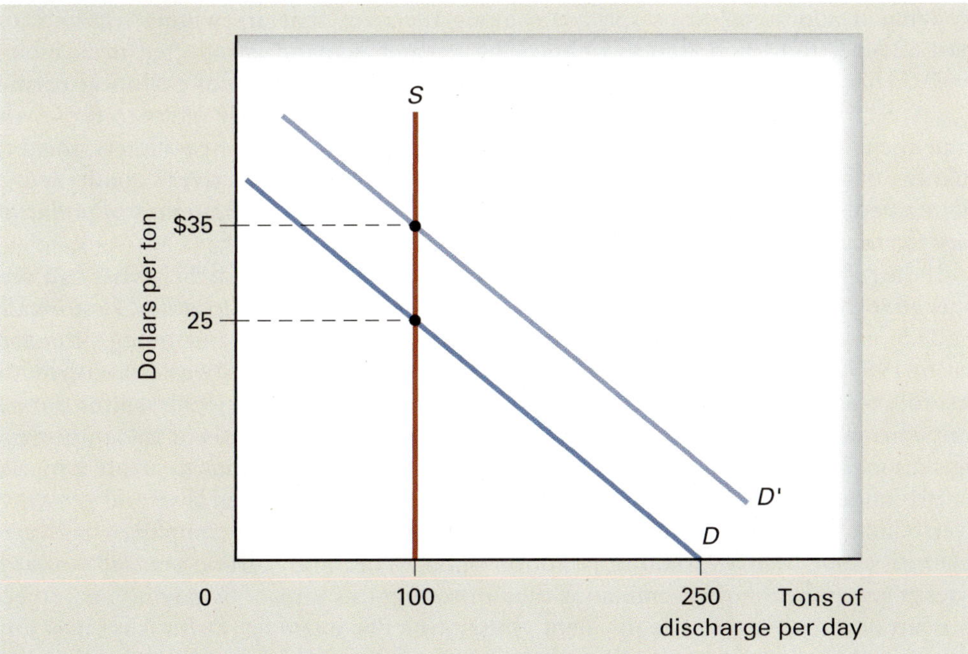

Suppose the demand for a river as a discharge service is *D*. In the absence of any environmental controls, polluters dump 250 tons per day, where the marginal benefit of discharge is zero. If regulatory authorities establish 100 tons as the maximum daily level of discharge and then sell the rights, the market for these pollution rights clears at $25 per ton. If the demand for pollution rights increases to *D*′, the market-clearing price of pollution rights rises to $35 per ton.

to dump waste into the river—dumping would continue as long as it provided firms some marginal benefit. This marginal benefit falls to zero in Exhibit 4 when 250 tons per day are discharged. At that point the marginal private cost of dumping, which is zero, equals the marginal private benefit.

The river, like the atmosphere, the soil, and the sea can absorb and neutralize a certain amount of discharge per day without deteriorating in quality. What if voters make the public choice that the river should remain clean enough for swimming and fishing? Suppose engineers determine this level of water quality can be maintained as long as no more than 100 tons are discharged per day. Thus, the "supply" of the discharge service provided by the river is fixed at 100 tons per day, shown by the vertical supply curve, *S*, in Exhibit 4.

If government regulators can easily identify polluters and monitor their behavior, authorities can allocate permits to discharge 100 tons per day. If polluters are simply given these permits (that is, if the price of permits is zero), there will be an excess demand for them, because the quantity supplied is 100 tons but the quantity demanded at a price of zero would be 250 tons. An alternative is to sell permits for 100 tons of pollution at the market-clearing price. The intersection of supply curve *S* and demand curve *D* yields a permit price of $25 per ton, which is the marginal value of discharging the 100th ton into the river each day. To most permit buyers, the marginal value of a permit exceeds $25 per ton.

The beauty of this system is that producers who value the discharge rights the most ultimately end up with them. Producers who attach a marginal value below $25 per ton apparently have cheaper ways of resolving their waste problems, including changing production techniques. And if conservation groups, such as the Sierra Club, want a cleaner river than the government's standard, such as water clean enough to drink, they can purchase pollution permits but not exercise them.

What if additional firms spring up along the river that are willing to pay more than $25 per ton for pollution rights? This greater demand is reflected in Exhibit 4 by *D*'. This increase of demand would bid up the market price of pollution permits to, say, $35 per ton. Some existing permit holders would sell their rights to those who value them more. Regardless of the comings and goings of would-be polluters, the total quantity of discharge rights is restricted to 100 tons per day, so the river's quality will be maintained. Thus, *the value of pollution permits, but not the total amount of pollution, may fluctuate over time.*

If the right to pollute could be granted, monitored, and enforced, then what had been a negative externality problem could be solved through market allocation. Historically, the U.S. government had relied on setting discharge standards and fining offenders. But in 1989, a pollution rights market for fluorocarbon emissions was established and was followed in 1990 by a market for sulfur dioxide. During the 1990s, sulfur dioxide emissions in the nation fell by more than half, exceeding the goals of the authorizing legislation. The "cap-and-trade" proposal by President Obama aims to create a market for greenhouse gas emissions. So the market for pollution rights is alive and growing.[4] Even China is now experimenting with this approach. Some companies and even celebrities have used a variant of pollution rights to become "carbon neutral"—that is, by estimating their carbon emissions then offsetting this impact by paying for projects to neutralize, or "sop up," equivalent emissions.[5] For example, Delta Air Lines until recently allowed online ticket buyers to pay an extra $5.50 for domestic flights or

4. For a discussion of the market for sulfur dioxide emissions, see Paul Joskow, Richard Schmalensee, and Elizabeth Bailey, "The Market for Sulfur-Dioxide Emissions," *American Economic Review*, 88 (September 1998): 669–685.

5. See Andrew Revkin, "Carbon-Neutral Is Hip, But Is It Green," *New York Times*, 29 April 2007.

$11 for international flights for tree plantings to help offset flight emissions. And the band Coldplay funded the planting of 10,000 mango trees in India to help sop up emissions related to the release of a new CD.[6]

Pollution Rights and Public Choice

Unfortunately, legislation dealing with pollution is affected by the same problems of representative democracy that trouble other public policy questions. Big polluters have a special interest in government proposals relating to pollution, and they fight measures to reduce pollution. But members of the public remain rationally ignorant about pollution legislation. So pollution regulations may be less in accord with the public interest than with the special interests of polluters. To win their cooperation, a portion of pollution permits are often *given* to existing firms or offered at below-market prices. For example, under the sulfur dioxide program, the nation's 101 dirtiest power plants were granted credits equal to between 30 and 50 percent of the pollution they emitted before the program began. Because they received something of value, polluters were less inclined to oppose the legislation. Once permits were granted, some recipients found it profitable to sell their permits to other firms that valued them more. Thus, a market emerged that led to an efficient allocation of pollution permits. According to some analysts, the sulfur dioxide program saves up to $3 billion annually compared with the old system. More generally, a system of marketable pollution rights can reduce the cost of pollution abatement by as much as 75 percent.

Before 1990, **command-and-control environmental regulations** were the norm—an approach that required polluters, such as electric utilities, to introduce particular technologies to reduce emissions by specific amounts. These regulations were based on engineering standards and did not recognize unique circumstances across generating plants, such as plant design, ability to introduce scrubbers, and the ease of switching to low-sulfur fuels. But the market for pollution rights reflects an **economic efficiency approach** that offers each electric utility the flexibility to reduce emissions in the most cost-effective manner, given its unique operation. Firms with the lowest costs of emission control have an incentive to implement the largest reduction in emissions and then sell unused pollution permits to those with greater control costs.

command-and-control environmental regulations
An approach that required polluters to adopt particular technologies to reduce emissions by specific amounts; inflexible regulations based on engineering standards that ignore each firm's unique ways of reducing pollution

economic efficiency approach
An approach that offers each polluter the flexibility to reduce emissions as cost-effectively as possible, given its unique cost conditions; the market for pollution rights is an example

Now that you know something about the theory of externalities, let's turn to an important application of the theory—environmental protection.

Environmental Protection

Federal efforts to address the common-pool problems of air, water, and soil pollution are coordinated by the Environmental Protection Agency (EPA). Four federal laws and subsequent amendments underpin U.S. efforts to protect the environment: (1) the Clean Air Act of 1970, (2) the Clean Water Act of 1972, (3) the Resource Conservation and Recovery Act of 1976 (which governs solid waste disposal), and (4) the Superfund law of 1980 (legislation focusing on toxic waste dumps). When the EPA was created in 1970, it began with about 4,000 employees and a budget of $1.2 billion (in 2011 dollars). By 2011, it had about 18,000 employees and a $10.0 billion budget.

According to EPA estimates, compliance with pollution-control regulations cost U.S. producers and consumers about $300 billion in 2011, an amount equivalent to 2 percent of gross domestic product, the market value of all final goods and services produced in

6. Michael Hill, "Can Planting a Tree Absolve Your Eco-Sins?" *Arizona Republic*, 28 May 2007.

the economy. We can divide pollution control spending into three categories: spending for air pollution abatement, spending for water pollution abatement, and spending for solid waste disposal. About 40 percent of the pollution control expenditures in the United States goes toward cleaner air, another 40 percent goes toward cleaner water, and 20 percent goes toward disposing of solid waste. (These figures are from a typical year, and do not include cleanup costs after the drilling accident in the Gulf of Mexico.) In this section, we consider, in turn, air pollution, water pollution, Superfund activities, and disposing of solid waste.

Air Pollution

In the Clean Air Act of 1970 and in subsequent amendments, Congress set national standards for the amount of pollution that could be released into the atmosphere. Congress thereby recognized the atmosphere as an economic resource, which, like other resources, has alternative uses. The air can be used as a source of life-giving oxygen, as a prism for viewing breathtaking vistas, or as a dump for carrying away unwanted soot and gases. The 1970 act gave Americans the right to breathe air of a certain quality and at the same time gave producers the right to emit particular amounts of specified pollutants. Research shows that people value clean air and are willing to pay more to live in communities with less pollution.[7]

Smog is the most visible form of air pollution. Automobile emissions account for 40 percent of smog. Another 40 percent comes from consumer-oriented products, such as paint thinner, fluorocarbon sprays, dry-cleaning solvents, and baker's yeast by products. Surprisingly, only 15 percent of smog comes from manufacturing. The 1970 Clean Air Act mandated a reduction of 90 percent in auto emissions, leaving it to the auto industry to achieve this target. At the time, automakers said the target was impossible. Between 1970 and 1990, however, average emissions of lead fell 97 percent, carbon monoxide emissions fell 41 percent, and sulfur dioxide emissions fell 25 percent. In fact, an EPA study concluded that because auto emissions and industrial smoke have been reduced so much, *air pollution on average is now greater indoors than outdoors*. For example, in the Los Angeles area, a smog alert, meaning the air reached dangerous levels, occurred on a weekly basis during the 1980s, but the city did not experience a smog alert between 2003 and the heavy forest-fire season of 2008. U.S. air quality is now considered good compared to the air quality in much of the world. For example, no U.S. city ranks among the world's worst in sulfur dioxide. Despite recent improvements in air quality, the United States is still a major source of fossil-fuel carbon dioxide emissions, a major greenhouse gas. As you can see from Exhibit 5, which shows the world's 25 worst nations in annual fossil-fuel carbon dioxide emissions per capita, the United States ranks fourth worst with 5.2 tons per capita.

There have been efforts to address greenhouse gases on an international scale. A report by the Intergovernmental Panel on Climate Change, a group sponsored by the United Nations, was approved in May 2007 by more than 120 nations.[8] The study says, to fight climate change, the world must cut emissions of carbon dioxide and other greenhouse gases by (1) sharply improving energy efficiency in buildings, vehicles, and machines; (2) shifting from fossil fuels to nuclear, wind, solar, and other renewable energy sources; (3) preserving forests as absorbers of carbon dioxide, or as "carbon sinks"; and (4) capping agricultural emissions. The United States and China, which account for more than 40 percent of the world's emissions, approved the report but

7. Kenneth Chay and Michael Greenstone, "Does Air Quality Matter? Evidence from the Housing Market," *Journal of Political Economy*, 113 (April 2005): 376–424.
8. For panel reports, go to http://www.ipcc.ch/.

EXHIBIT 5 **Fossil-Fuel Carbon Dioxide Emissions per Capita: The 25 Worst Nations**

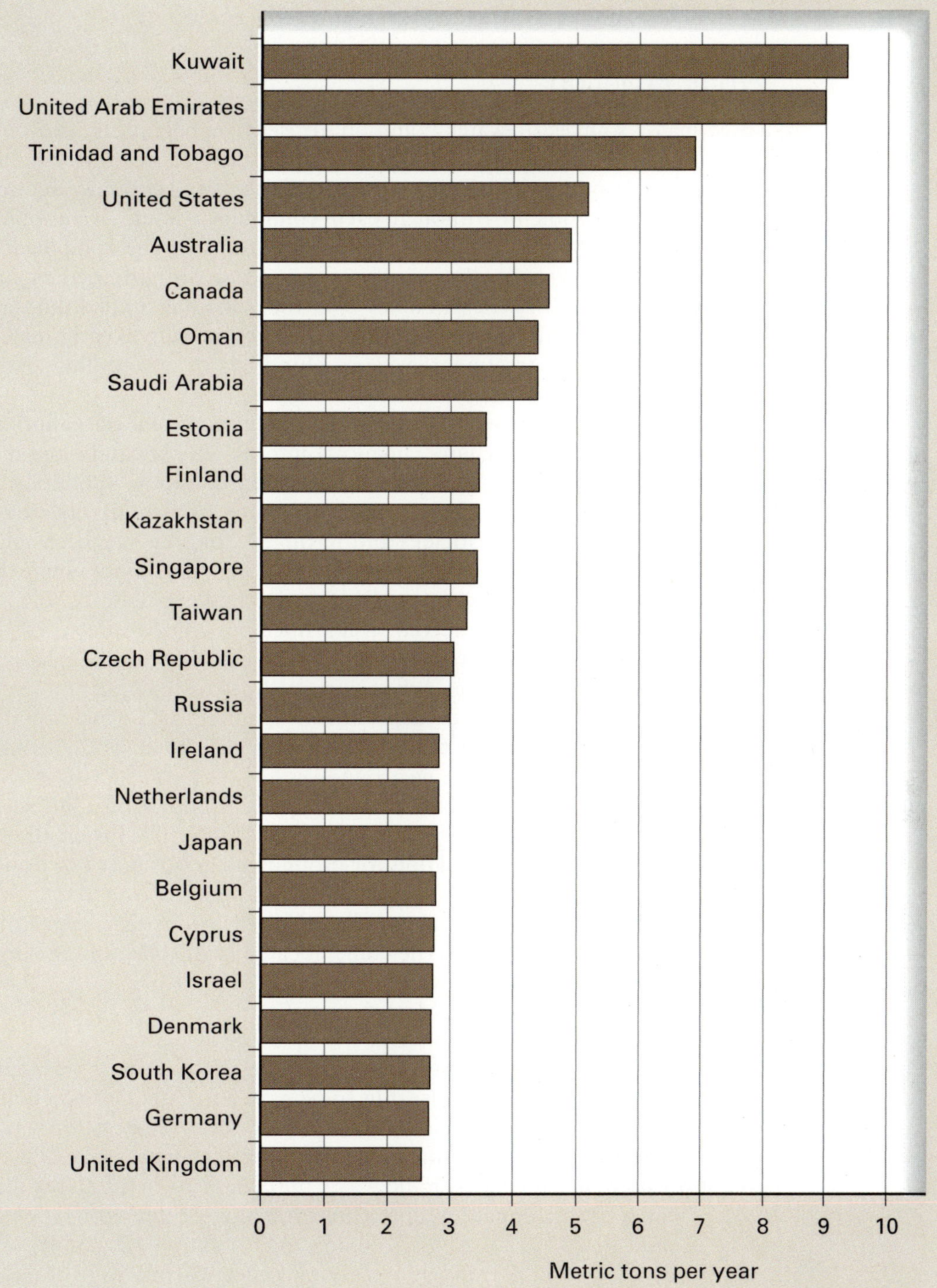

Sources: Figures are for 2006 and were estimated by Tom Boden, Gregg Marland, and Bob Andres at the Oak Ridge National Laboratory and can be found at http://cdiac.ornl.gov/trends/emis/top2006.cap. Excluded are nations with fewer than one million people.

offered no indication that they would reverse their opposition to mandatory emission reductions. The report said that such reforms would require lifestyle changes, increased prices for some basics including gasoline and electricity, and greater investment in research and development.

Water Pollution

Three major sources of water pollution are sewage, chemicals, and oil. For decades, U.S. cities had an economic incentive to dump their sewage directly into waterways rather than clean it up first. Water current or tides would carry off the waste to become someone else's problem. Although each community found it rational, based on a narrow view of the situation, to dump into waterways, the combined effect of these local choices was water pollution, a negative externality imposed by one community on other communities. Federal money over the years has funded thousands of sewage treatment plants, which cut water pollution substantially. Nearly all U.S. cities now have modern sewage treatment systems. Hundreds of once-polluted waterways have been cleaned up enough for swimming and fishing.

Chemicals are a second source of water pollution. Chemical pollution may conjure up an image of a pipe spewing chemicals into a river, but only about 10 percent of chemical pollution in the water comes from point pollution—pollution from factories and other industrial sites. About two-thirds come from nonpoint pollution—mostly runoff from agricultural pesticides and fertilizer. Congress has been reluctant to limit the use of pesticides, although pesticides pollute water and contaminate food. Industrial America seems an easier target than Old MacDonald's farm. In 1970, Congress shifted control of pesticides from the U.S. Department of Agriculture to the newly created Environmental Protection Agency (EPA). But the EPA already had its hands full administering the Clean Water Act, so it turned pesticide regulation over to the states. Most states gave the job to their departments of agriculture, which usually promote the interests of farmers, not restrict what farmers can do. The EPA now reports that in most states pesticides have fouled some groundwater.[9]

A third source of water pollution is oil. The cleanup of oil spills on land are overseen by the EPA. About 600,000 underground storage tanks for oil and chemicals pose a potential threat of contamination for groundwater, the source of drinking water for half of Americans. The cleanup of offshore oil spills is overseen by the U.S. Coast Guard. The most notable offshore spill in U.S. history is discussed in the case study, "Public Policy: BP's Oil Spill in the Gulf," located at the back of the book.

Hazardous Waste and the Superfund

The U.S. synthetic chemical industry has flourished in the last 50 years, and over 50,000 chemicals are now in common use. But some have harmful effects on humans and other living creatures. These chemicals can pose risks at every stage of their production, use, and disposal. New Jersey manufactures more toxic chemicals than any other state and, not surprisingly, has the worst toxic waste burden. Prior to 1980, the disposal of toxic waste created get-rich-quick opportunities for anyone who could rent or buy a few acres of land to open a toxic waste dump. As an extreme example, one site in New Jersey took in 71 million gallons of hazardous chemicals during a three-year period.[10]

Before 1980, once a company paid someone to haul away its hazardous waste, that company was no longer responsible. The Comprehensive Environmental Response,

9. John Cushman, "E.P.A. and States Found to Be Lax on Pollution Law," *New York Times,* 7 June 1998.
10. Jason Zweig, "Real-Life Horror Story," *Forbes,* 12 December 1988.

Compensation, and Liability Act of 1980, known more popularly as the Superfund law, requires any company that generates, stores, or transports hazardous wastes to pay to clean up any wastes that are improperly disposed of. A producer or hauler who is the source of even one barrel of pollution dumped at a site can be held liable for cleaning up the entire site.

The Superfund law gave the federal government authority over sites contaminated with toxins. But to get an offending company to comply, the EPA frequently must sue. The process is slow, and nearly half the budget goes to lawyers, consultants, and administrators rather than to site cleanups. The law did not require that benefits of a cleanup exceed costs or even that such comparisons be attempted. Although billions have been spent so far, a recent EPA study concluded that the health hazards of Superfund sites have been vastly exaggerated. Chemicals in the ground usually move slowly, sometimes taking years to travel a few feet, so any possible health threat is confined to the site itself. People know when they live near toxic waste sites, and they can exert political pressure to get something done, whereas people exposed to polluted air, water, and pesticide residue may develop health problems but never make the connection to their environment. Thus, people see less reason to press public officials for cleaner air and water (though the threat of climate change has focused more attention on greenhouse gas emissions). Toxic waste sites, because of their greater political urgency and media appeal (witness the movies on the subject), tend to receive more attention than air or water pollution. And with the federal government picking up the tab, localities demand all the cleanup they can get. But research indicates that Superfund cleanups have little or no impact on residential property values, property rental rates, the housing supply, total population, or the types of individuals living near the sites.[11] In short, Superfund cleanups seem to be much to do about not much.

Solid Waste: "Paper or Plastic?"

Throughout most of human history, households tossed their trash outside as fodder for pigs and goats. New York City, like other cities, had no trash collections, so domestic waste was thrown into the street, where it mixed with mud and manure (until recently, many residents of Beijing and other parts of China did the same thing).[12] Decades of such accumulation explain why the oldest Manhattan streets are anywhere from 3 to 15 feet above their original levels. Until the last century, people buried their trash near their homes or took it to a local dump. Most localities now forbid trash burning.

U.S. households generate about 4 pounds of garbage per resident per day—more than twice the 1960 level and the most in the world. Much of the solid waste consists of packaging. The question is, how do we dispose of the more than 200 million tons of household garbage generated in this country each year? Advanced economies produce and buy more than less developed economies, so there is more to throw away. And because of higher incomes in advanced economies, the opportunity cost of time is higher, so Americans tend to discard items rather than repair or recycle them. For example, it's cheaper to buy a new toaster for $20 than to pay $40 an hour to fix a broken one, assuming you can even find a repair service. (Look up "Appliance Repair, Small" in the *Yellow Pages* and see if you can find even one such service in your area.)

About 70 percent of the nation's garbage is bulldozed and covered with soil in landfills. Although a well-managed landfill poses few environmental concerns, at one time, communities dumped all kinds of toxins in them—stuff that could leach into the soil, contaminating wells and aquifers. So landfills got a bad reputation. Now, the

11. Michael Greenstone and Justin Gallagher, "Does Hazardous Waste Matter? Evidence from the Housing Market and Superfund Programs," *Quarterly Journal of Economics*, 123 (August 2008): 951–1003.
12. Laurence Brahm, "Hygiene? It's a Load of Rubbish," *South China Morning Post*, 1 November 2005.

prevailing attitude with landfills is Nimby! (Not in my backyard!). We all want our garbage picked up but nobody wants it put down anywhere nearby.

As the cost of solid waste disposal increases, some state and local governments are economizing, charging households by the pound for trash pickups, and requiring more recycling and returnable bottles. **Recycling** is the process of converting waste products into reusable materials. Nearly half of U.S. households participate in curbside recycling programs. Still, according to the EPA, only about 15 percent of U.S. garbage gets recycled; about 15 percent is incinerated and, as noted already, the remaining 70 percent goes into landfills. Of the recycled material, three-quarters consists of corrugated boxes, newspapers, office paper, and other paper products. Some paper is shipped to Korea, Taiwan, and China, where it becomes packaging material for U.S. imports such as Blu-ray players and computer components. Exhibit 6 ranks the world's top 25 recyclers of paper and cardboard among major economies. Ireland heads the list, recycling 78 percent. The United States is in a five-way tie for 18th, recycling 50 percent (but more than double that of 1985). Poorer countries recycle much less—Mexico, for example, only 7 percent.

recycling
The process of converting waste products into reusable material

Most of the 15 percent of garbage that is incinerated gets burned in trash-to-energy plants, which generate electricity using the heat from incineration. Until recently, such plants looked like the wave of the future, but less favorable tax treatment and environmental concerns over incinerator locations (Nimby strikes again!) have taken the steam out of the trash-to-energy movement.

To repeat, only 30 percent of U.S. garbage is recycled or incinerated, and about 70 percent goes to landfills. In contrast, the Japanese recycle or incinerate 73 percent, sending only 27 percent to landfills. Japanese households sort their trash into as many as 21 categories. Because land is scarcer in Japan—we know this because it costs relatively more—it is not surprising that the Japanese deposit a smaller share of their garbage in landfills.

Some recycling is clearly economical—such as aluminum cans, which are a relatively cheap source of aluminum compared to producing raw aluminum. About two out of three aluminum cans now get recycled, though only 11 states require returnable deposits on such cans. Still, returnable deposit laws increase recycling. Incentives matter. Even if you decide to discard your empties, chances are that someone down the line with a lower opportunity cost than you will find them and claim the deposits. For example, researchers found an average of 47 bottles and cans along a one-block path of city park each day prior to the enactment of deposit law, but one year after the law was introduced, they found an average of only two bottles and cans each day along the same path.[13]

Recycling paper and cardboard is also economical and occurred long before the environmental movement. Such old standbys as paper drives, drop-off bins, and redemption centers collect more tonnage than curbside programs. Most recycling results from salvaging scrap material from business and industry, a practice that dates back decades.

Governments have tried to stimulate demand for recycled material—for example, by requiring newspapers to use a minimum percentage of recycled newsprint. Other recycled products are not in such demand. In fact, some recycled products have become worthless and must be hauled to landfills. Recycling imposes its own environmental cost. Curbside recycling requires fleets of trucks that pollute the air. Newsprint must first be de-inked, creating a sludge that must be disposed of. But greater environmental awareness has made consumers more receptive to more efficient packaging. For example, liquid laundry detergent now comes in a concentrated "ultra" form, which cuts volume in half, and Unilever's brand All Small & Mighty cuts volume by two-thirds. Labels for all kinds of products proudly identify the recycled content of the packaging.

13. J. Trinkaus, "A Bottle Law: An Informal Look," *Perceptual and Motor Skills*, 59 (December 1984): 806.

EXHIBIT 6 Paper and Cardboard Recycling: Top 25 Among Advanced Economies

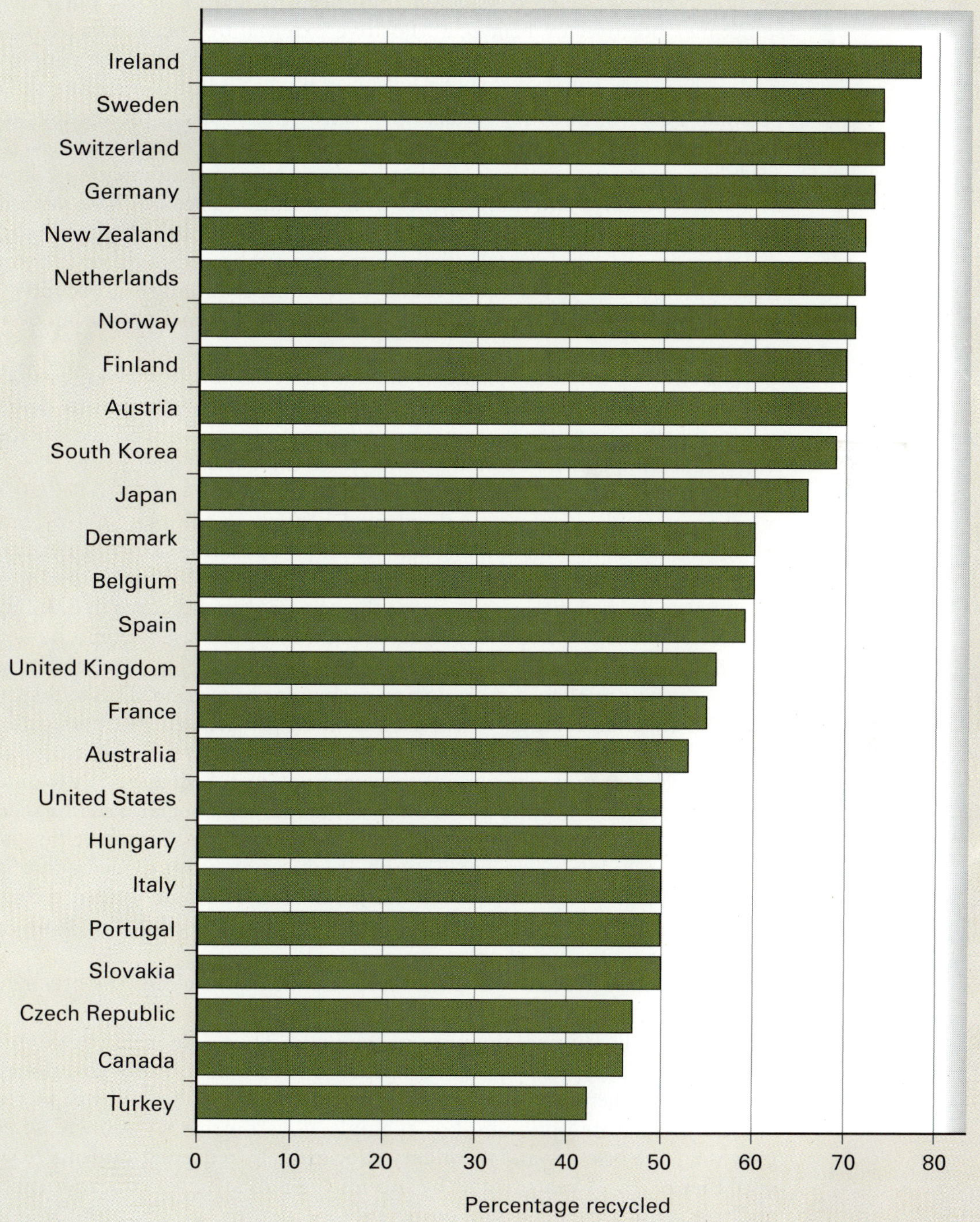

Sources: Figures are rankings among members of the Organization of Economic Cooperation and Development as reported in *OECD Environmental Data 2006/2007*, Table 4A, p. 25. This can be found at http://www.oecd.org/dataoecd/60/59/38106368.pdf. Figures are for 2005, except for South Korea, Germany, Sweden, and the U.K., which are for 2004, and for Japan and Turkey, which are for 2003.

Positive Externalities

To this point, we have considered only negative externalities. But externalities are sometimes positive, or beneficial. Positive externalities occur when consumption or production benefits other consumers or other firms. For example, people who get inoculated against a disease reduce their own likelihood of contracting the disease (the personal benefit), but they reduce the risk of transmitting the disease to others (the external benefit). Parents who don't get their children vaccinated risk triggering an epidemic, so the vaccination decision is not simply a private matter. Likewise, society as a whole receives external benefits from education because those with more education become better citizens, can read road signs, are better able to support themselves and their families, and are less likely to require public assistance or to resort to violent crime for income. Researchers found that more schooling significantly reduces the probability of incarceration.[14] Thus, your education benefits you but it also benefits others.

The effect of external benefits is illustrated in Exhibit 7, which presents the demand and supply of education. The demand curve, *D*, represents the private demand for education, which reflects the marginal private benefit for those who acquire the education. More education is demanded at a lower price than at a higher price.

The benefit of education, however, spills over to others in society. If we add this positive externality, or marginal external benefit, to the marginal private benefit of education, we get the marginal social benefit of education. *The marginal social benefit includes all the benefits society derives from education, both private and external.* The marginal social benefit curve is above the private demand curve in Exhibit 7. If education were a strictly private decision, the amount purchased would be determined by the intersection of the private demand curve *D* with supply curve *S*. The supply curve reflects the marginal cost of producing each unit of the good. This intersection at point *e* yields education level *E*, where the marginal private benefit of education equals its marginal cost, as reflected by the supply curve. But at level *E*, the marginal social benefit, identified as point *b*, exceeds the marginal cost. Social welfare would increase if education expands beyond *E*. As long as the marginal social benefit exceeds the marginal cost, social welfare increases as education expands. Social welfare is maximized at point *e*' in Exhibit 7, where *E*' units of education are provided—that is, where the marginal social benefit equals the marginal cost. The blue-shaded triangle identifies the increase in social welfare that results from increasing education from *E*, the private optimum, to *E*', the social optimum.

Thus, society is better off if the level of education exceeds the private equilibrium. With positive externalities, decisions based on private marginal benefits result in less than the socially optimal quantity of the good. Thus, like negative externalities, positive externalities typically point to market failure, which is why government often gets into the act. When there are external benefits, public policy aims to increase quantity beyond the private optimum. For example, governments try to increase education by providing free primary and secondary education, by requiring students to stay in school until they reach 16 years of age, by subsidizing public higher education, and by offering tax breaks for some education costs.

Another source of externalities stems from precautions people take to avoid becoming crime victims, such as LoJack, a device used to track and recover a stolen vehicle. Because the device is completely undetectable by a potential thief, the more

14. Lance Lochner and Enrico Moretti, "The Effects of Education on Crime: Evidence from Prison Inmates," *American Economic Review*, 94 (March 2004): 155–189.

EXHIBIT 7 Education and Positive Externalities

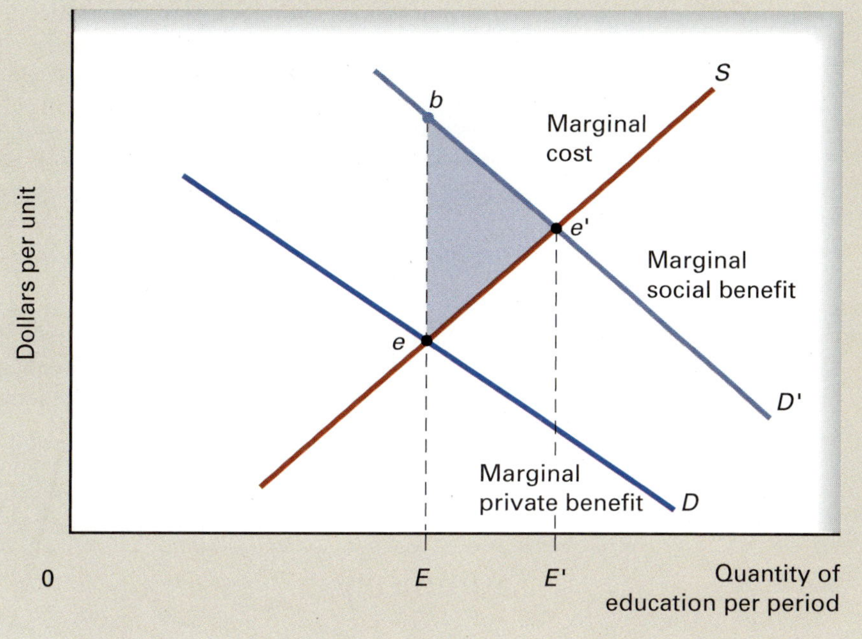

In the absence of government intervention, the equilibrium quantity of education is *E*, where the marginal private benefit of education equals the marginal cost as reflected by the supply curve. Education also confers a positive externality on the rest of society, so the social benefit exceeds the private benefit. At quantity *E*, the marginal social benefit, point *b*, exceeds the marginal cost, point *e*, so more education increases social welfare. In this situation, government tries to increase education to *E'*, where the marginal social benefit equals the marginal cost.

LoJacks installed, the more nervous thieves get and the fewer vehicles stolen in general. Thus, car owners without LoJack get a positive externality when others install the device. Researchers estimated that a 1 percent increase in LoJack installations cuts car thefts in general by at least 20 percent.[15] On the other hand, the use of The Club, a very visible lock for the steering wheel, generates a negative externality, because it increases the likelihood that vehicles without The Club will get stolen. In terms of social welfare, there are not enough LoJacks installed and too many Clubs.

Conclusion

About 6.9 billion people live on the planet, and over 72 million are added each year. World population is projected to reach 9.3 billion by 2050, according to the U.S. Census Bureau, with most of this growth occurring in countries where most people barely eke out a living. Population pressure coupled with a lack of incentives to conserve open-access resources results in deforestation, dwindling fish stocks, and polluted air, land, and water.

Ironically, because of the tighter pollution controls in industrial countries, these countries are less polluted than developing countries, where there is more pollution

15. Ian Ayres and Steven Levitt, "Measuring Positive Externalities for Unobservable Victim Precautions: An Empirical Analysis of Lojack," *Quarterly Journal of Economics*," 113 (February 1998): 43–77.

from what little industry there is. Most developing countries have such profound economic problems that environmental quality is not a priority. For example, when India's Supreme Court tried to close some polluting factories in New Delhi, thousands of workers torched buses, threw stones, and blocked major roads, demanding the factories stay open. Although New Delhi's pollution masks any trace of a blue sky, workers believe their jobs are more important. Here's one account of New Delhi's air quality:

> *In the heat of the afternoons, a yellow-white mixture hung above the city, raining acidic soot into the dust and exhaust fumes. At night the mixture condenses into a dry, choking fog that envelops the headlights of passing cars, and creeps its stink into even the tightest houses. The residents could do little to keep the poison out of their lungs or the lungs of their children, and if they were poor, they could not even try.*[16]

Market prices can direct the allocation of resources only as long as property rights are well defined. Pollution arises not so much from the greed of producers and consumers as from the fact that open-access resources are subject to the common-pool problem.

Summary

1. An exhaustible resource is available in fixed supply, such as crude oil or coal. A renewable resource can regenerate itself if used conservatively, such as a properly managed forest. Some renewable resources suffer from a common-pool problem because unrestricted access leads to overuse.
2. Production that generates negative externalities results in too much output. Production that generates positive externalities results in too little output. Public policy should tax or otherwise limit production that generates negative externalities and should subsidize or otherwise promote production that generates positive externalities.
3. The optimal amount of environmental quality occurs where the marginal social benefit of an improvement equals its marginal social cost. An upward shift of the marginal benefit curve of environmental quality or a downward shift of its marginal cost curve increases the optimal level of environmental quality.
4. The world's tropical rainforests recycle greenhouse gases into oxygen and wood. Because rainforests are open-access resources, settlers and loggers cut them down to make a living. This destruction reduces the environment's ability to cleanse itself of greenhouse gases, which may contribute to climate change.
5. The Coase theorem argues that as long as bargaining costs are low, assigning property rights to one party leads to an efficient solution to the externality problem. The market for pollution permits reflects the Coase theorem in action.
6. Aside from greenhouse gases, America's air and waterways are getting cleaner. The air is cleaner because of stricter emissions standards for motor vehicles, and waterways are cleaner because of billions spent on sewage treatment plants. Toxic waste sites do not pose as great a health threat as other forms of pollution such as smog and pesticide residue, but toxic waste sites often get more media and political attention.

Key Concepts

Exhaustible resource 330
Renewable resource 330
Common-pool problem 330
Fixed-production technology 332
Marginal social cost 332
Variable technology 334
Marginal social benefit 334
Coase theorem 336
Command-and-control environmental regulations 339
Economic efficiency approach 339
Recycling 344

16. William Langewiesche, "The Shipbreakers," *Atlantic Monthly* (August 2000): 42.

Questions for Review

1. EXTERNALITIES Complete each of the following sentences:
   a. Resources that are available only in a fixed amount are _______ resources.
   b. The possibility that a open-access resource is used until the marginal value of additional use equals zero is known as the _______.
   c. Resources for which periodic use can be continued indefinitely are known as _______ resources.
2. RESOLVING THE COMMON-POOL PROBLEM Why have authorities found it so difficult to regulate the fishing catch in the open ocean to allow for a sustainable yield?
3. OPTIMAL LEVEL OF POLLUTION Explain the difference between fixed-production technology and variable technology. Should the government set a goal of reducing the marginal social cost of pollution to zero in industries with fixed-production technology? Should they do so in industries with variable technology?
4. Case Study: The Lungs of the Planet (See page 737.) Why does a solution to the overharvesting of timber in the tropical rainforests require some form of international cooperation? Would this be a sufficient solution to the deforestation problem?
5. THE COASE THEOREM Suppose a firm pollutes a stream that has a recreational value only when pollution is below a certain level. If transaction costs are low, why does the assignment of property rights to the stream lead to the same (efficient) level of pollution whether the firm or recreational users own the stream?
6. THE COASE THEOREM Ronald Coase points out that a market failure does not arise simply because people ignore the external cost of their actions. What other condition is necessary? What did Coase consider to be an efficient solution to a negative externality?
7. Four federal laws and subsequent amendments underpin U.S. environmental protection. Identify these laws.
8. Case Study: BP's Oil Spill in the Gulf (See page 738.) Should the government require deepwater oil companies to spend whatever it takes to reduce the chance of future spills to zero?
9. POSITIVE EXTERNALITIES The value of a home depends in part on how attractive other homes and yards in the neighborhood are. How do local zoning ordinances try to promote land uses that generate external benefits for neighbors?

Problems and Exercises

10. EXTERNAL COSTS WITH FIXED-PRODUCTION TECHNOLOGY Review the situation illustrated in Exhibit 1 in this chapter. If the government sets the price of electricity at the socially optimal level, why is the net gain equal to triangle *abc*, even though consumers now pay a higher price for electricity? What would the net gain be if the government set the price above the optimal level?
11. NEGATIVE EXTERNALITIES Suppose you wish to reduce a negative externality by imposing a tax on the activity that creates that externality. When the amount of the externality produced per unit of output increases as output increases, the correct tax can be determined by using a demand-supply diagram; show this. Assume that the marginal private cost curve slopes upward.
12. EXTERNAL COSTS Use the data in the table falls in this page to answer the following questions.
    a. What is the external cost per unit of production?
    b. What level is produced if there is no regulation of the externality?
    c. What level should be produced to achieve economic efficiency?
    d. Calculate the dollar value of the net gain to society from correcting the externality.

Quantity	Marginal Private Benefit (demand) ($)	Marginal Private Cost (supply) ($)	Marginal Social Cost ($)
0	—	0	0
1	10	2	4
2	9	3	5
3	8	4	6
4	7	5	7
5	6	6	8
6	5	7	9
7	4	8	10
8	3	9	11
9	2	10	12
10	1	11	13

13. External Costs with Variable Technology Think of an industry that pollutes the water and has access to variable technology for reducing that pollution. Graphically illustrate and explain the impact of each of the following, other things constant, on the optimal level of water quality:
    a. New evidence is discovered about a greater risk of cancer from water pollution.
    b. The cost of pollution-control equipment increases.
    c. A technological improvement reduces the cost of pollution control.

14. Market for Pollution Rights The following graph shows the market for pollution rights.

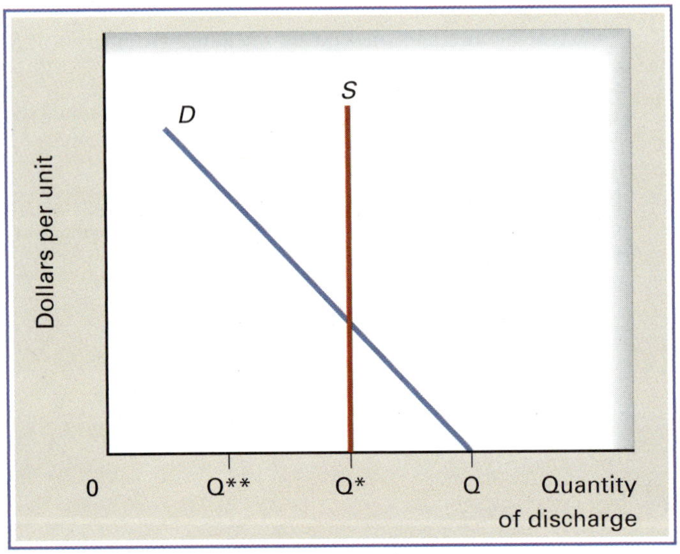

    a. If there are no restrictions on pollution, what amount is discharged?
    b. What is the quantity supplied and the quantity demanded if the government restricts the amount of discharge to Q* but gives the permits away?
    c. Where is market equilibrium if the government sells the permits? Illustrate this on the graph.
    d. What happens to market equilibrium if the government reduces the amount of discharge permitted to Q**? Illustrate this on the graph.

Global Economic Watch Exercises

Login to www.cengagebrain.com and access the Global Economic Watch to do these exercises.

15. Global Economic Watch and Case Study: The Lungs of the Planet (See page 737.) Go to the Global Economic Crisis Resource Center. Select Global Issues in Context. In the Basic Search box at the top of the page, enter the phrase "carbon ranching." On the Results page, go to the Global Viewpoints Section. Click on the link for the June 16, 2007, editorial "Home on the Rainforest." Is the program described an example of command-and-control environmental regulation or of the economic efficiency approach?

16. Global Economic Watch Go to the Global Economic Crisis Resource Center. Select Global Issues in Context. Go to the menu at the top of the page and click on the tab for Browse Issues and Topics. Choose Environment and Climate Change. Choose one of the topics listed and read the overview for that topic. Analyze the marginal social benefit and marginal social cost involved in your chosen topic.

Income Distribution and Poverty

18

- Why are some people poor even in the most productive economy on Earth?
- Who are the poor, how did they get that way, and how long do they stay poor?
- What's been the trend in U.S. poverty?
- What's been the impact of the changing family structure on poverty?
- What public programs aim to reduce poverty, and how well have they worked?
- Why was someone fined more than $200,000 for speeding 25 miles over the limit?
- And which group will likely get little sympathy for being hit hard by the recent recession?

Answers to these and related questions are addressed in this chapter, which discusses income distribution and poverty in America.

To establish a reference point, we first consider the distribution of income in the United States, paying special attention to trends in recent decades. We then examine the "social safety net"—government programs aimed at helping poor people. We also consider the impact of the changing family structure on poverty, focusing in particular on the increase in households headed by women.

We close by examining recent welfare reforms.

Topics discussed include:

- Distribution of income
- Official poverty level
- Public policy and poverty
- The feminization of poverty
- Poverty and discrimination
- Welfare reforms

The Distribution of Household Income

In a market economy, income depends primarily on earnings, which depend on the productivity of one's resources. The problem with allocating income according to productivity is that some people have few resources to sell. People with mental or physical disabilities, a poor education, those facing discrimination, bad luck, or the demands of caring for small children, and the elderly may be less productive and unable to earn a living.

Income Distribution by Quintiles

As a starting point, let's consider the distribution of income in the economy and see how it has changed over time, focusing on the household as the economic unit. After sorting U.S. households based on income into five groups of equal size, or *quintiles,* we can examine the percentage of total income received by each quintile. Such a division is presented in Exhibit 1 since 1980. Take a moment to look over this exhibit. Notice that households in the lowest, or poorest, fifth of the population received only 4.3 percent of the income in 1980, whereas households in the highest, or richest, fifth received 43.7 percent of the income. The U.S. Census Bureau measures income after cash transfer payments are received but before taxes are paid or in-kind transfers are received (from food vouchers, Medicare, Medicaid, public housing, and employer-provided benefits).

EXHIBIT 1 Share of Aggregate Household Income by Quintile

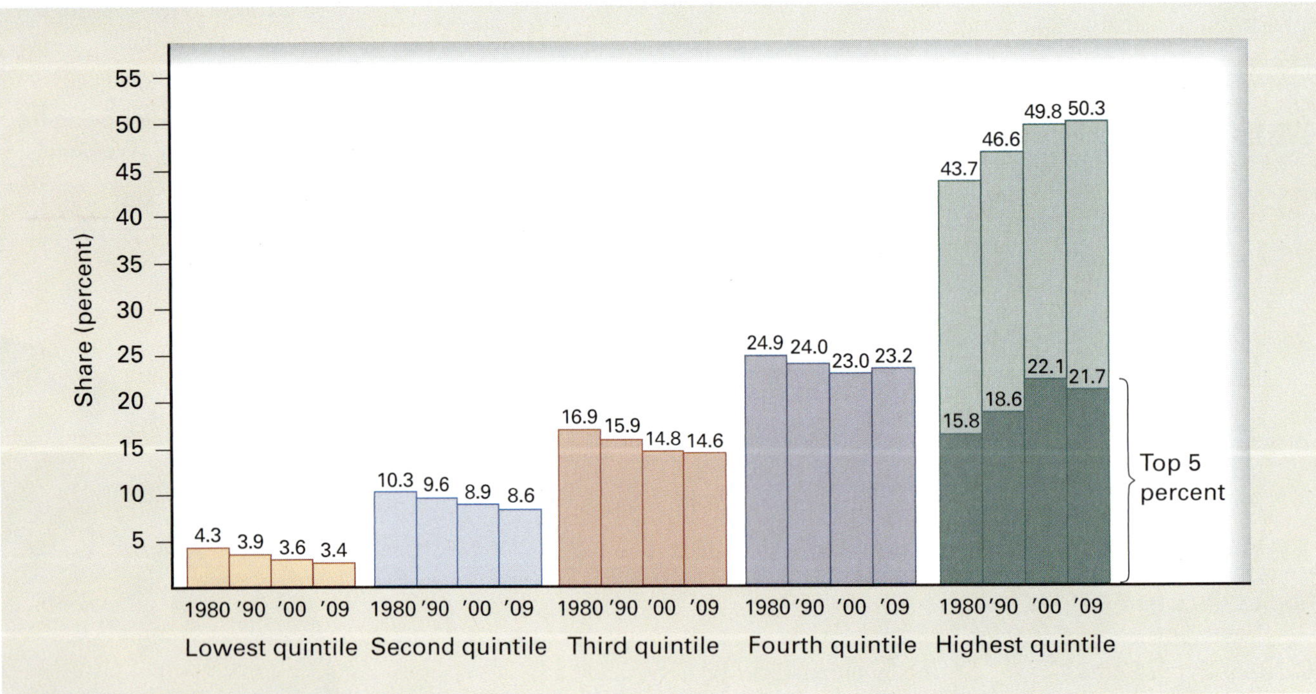

Source: Developed from data found in U.S. Census Bureau, *Income, Poverty, and Health Insurance Coverage in the United States: 2009*, Current Population Reports P-60-238, September 2010, Table 3 found at http://www.census.gov/prod/2010pubs/p60-238.pdf and http://www.census.gov/hhes/www/income/histinc/h02ar.html.

In recent decades, the share of income going to the top fifth has increased, and the share going to the bottom fifth has declined. The richest fifth's share of income increased from 43.7 percent in 1980 to 50.3 percent in 2009. A primary contributor to the larger share of income going to the highest group has been the growth of two-earner households in that top group. Three out of four households in the top quintile have two or more people working. A primary contributor to the smaller share going to the lowest group has been the growth of single-parent households in the bottom group. Only about one in three households in the bottom quintile has anybody working, and only about one in seven has anybody working full time.

Also shown in Exhibit 1 is the share of income going to the top 5 percent of households; that share has grown since 1980, accounting for nearly all the growth of the top 20 percent of households. Because of substantial reductions in the top marginal tax rates in 1981 and 1986, high-income people had less incentive to engage in tax avoidance, so their reported income increased, boosting the share of reported income going to the richest 5 percent of households.

The Lorenz Curve

We have just examined the distribution of income using a bar chart. Another way to picture that distribution is with a Lorenz curve. A **Lorenz curve** shows the percentage of total income received by any given percentage of households when incomes are arrayed from smallest to largest. As shown in Exhibit 2, the cumulative percentage of households is measured along the horizontal axis, and the cumulative percentage of income is measured along the vertical axis. Any given distribution of income can be compared to an equal distribution of income among households. If income were evenly distributed, each 20 percent of households would also receive 20 percent of the total income, and the Lorenz curve would be a straight line with a slope equal to 1.0, as shown by the "equal distribution" line in Exhibit 2.

lorenz curve
A curve showing the percentage of total income received by a given percentage of recipients whose incomes are arrayed from smallest to largest

As the distribution becomes more uneven, the Lorenz curve pulls down to the right, away from the line of equal distribution. The Lorenz curves in Exhibit 2 were calculated for 1980 and 2009 based on the data in Exhibit 1. As a reference, point *a* on the 1980 Lorenz curve indicates that in that year, the bottom 80 percent of families received 56.3 percent of the income, and the top 20 percent received 43.7 percent of the income. The Lorenz curve for 2009 is farther from the line of equal distribution than is the Lorenz curve for 1980, showing that income among households has become more unevenly distributed. Point *b* on the 2009 curve shows that the bottom 80 percent received 49.7 percent of the income and the top 20 percent received 50.3 percent of the income.

Why Incomes Differ

Income differences across households stem in part from differences in the *number* of workers in each household. Thus, *one reason household incomes differ is that the number of household members who are working differs.* For example, among households in the bottom 20 percent based on income, only one in seven includes a full-time, year-round worker. Consider the link between median income and the number of workers. The **median income** of all households is the middle income when incomes are ranked from lowest to highest. In any given year, half the households are above the median income and half are below it. The median income for households with two earners is 91 percent higher than for households with only one earner and is more than four times higher than for households with no earners.

median income
The middle income when all incomes are ranked from smallest to largest

EXHIBIT 2 **Lorenz Curves Show That Income Was Less Evenly Distributed Across U.S. Households in 2009 Than It Was in 1980**

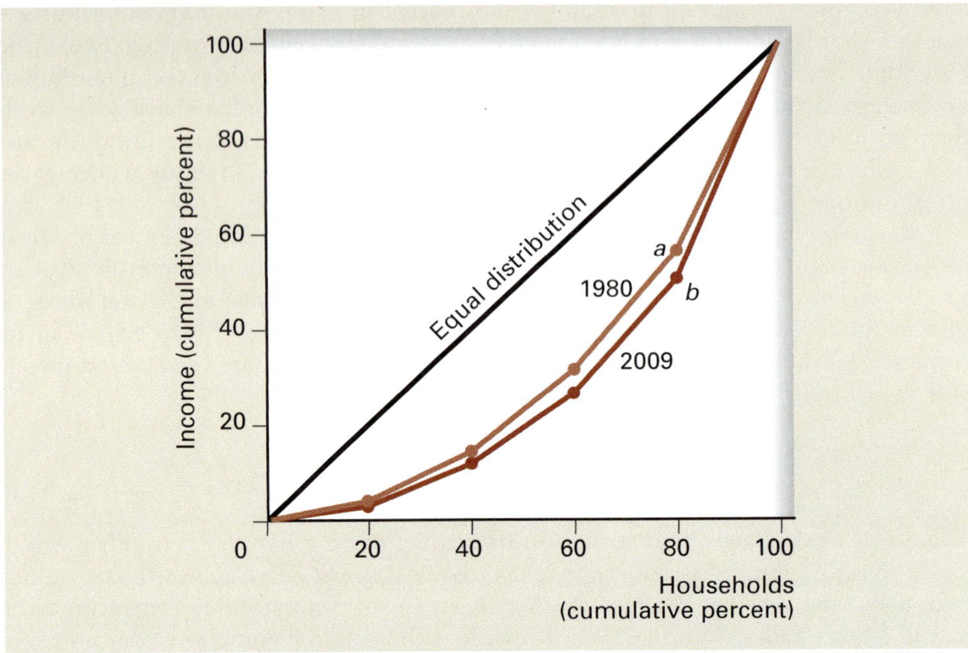

The Lorenz curve is a convenient way of showing the percentage of total income received by any given percentage of households when households are arrayed from smallest to largest based on income. For example, point *a* shows that in 1980, the bottom 80 percent of households received 56.3 percent of all income. Point *b* shows that in 2009, the share of all income going to the bottom 80 percent of households was lower than in 1980. If income were evenly distributed across households, the Lorenz curve would be a straight line.

Incomes also differ for all the reasons labor earnings differ, such as differences in education, ability, job experience, and so on. At every age, those with more education earn more, on average. As noted a few chapters back, those with a professional degree earn at least five times more than those without a high school diploma. Age itself also has an important effect on income. As workers mature, they acquire valuable job experience, get promoted, and earn more.

Differences in earnings based on age and education reflect a normal *life cycle* pattern of income. In fact, most income differences across households reflect the normal workings of resource markets, whereby workers are rewarded according to their productivity. Because of these lifetime patterns, it is not necessarily the same households that remain rich or poor over time. Indeed, one study of income mobility found that more than three-quarters of people in the bottom 20 percent in one particular year had moved into the top 40 percent for at least one year during the following 16 years.[1]

Despite this income mobility over time, we can still characterize rich and poor households at a point in time. *A high-income household usually consists of a well-educated couple with both spouses employed. A low-income household is usually one person living alone or is a family headed by a single parent who is young, female, poorly educated, and not working.* Low incomes are a matter of public concern, especially when children are involved, as we see in the next section.

1. W. Michael Cox and Richard Arm, "By Our Own Bootstraps," *Federal Reserve Bank of Dallas: 1995 Annual Report*.

A College Education Pays More

Also contributing to the dominance of the top group is an increased pay advantage for those with college educations. In the last two decades, the median wage (adjusted for inflation) for people with only high school diplomas declined 6 percent, while the median wage for college graduates rose 12 percent. The **median wage** is the middle wage when wages are ranked from lowest to highest. Why have more-educated workers done better? First, trends such as industry deregulation, declining unionization, and freer international trade and migration have reduced the pay for workers with less education. Labor unions, for example, raised the wages of many workers who would have otherwise ended up in the bottom half of the income distribution. But the share of the workforce that is unionized declined from 26 percent in 1973 to only 12 percent in 2009. More generally, an increasing fraction of jobs in the U.S. labor market explicitly pay workers for their productivity using bonus pay, commissions, or piece-rate contracts. Research suggests that productivity pay has increased earnings inequality.[2]

median wage
The middle wage when wages of all workers are ranked from lowest to highest

Second, new computer-based information technologies have reduced the demand for low-skilled clerical workers, because their jobs became computerized. Computers also offered more timely and accurate information to management, allowing for organizational innovations that made managers and other professionals more productive.[3] So computers reduced the demand for workers with low skills, such as clerical staff and bank tellers, and increased the demand for those who use computers to boost labor productivity, such as managers and accountants.

Third, the supply of less-educated workers increased more than the supply of more-educated workers, thus increasing the rewards of education. For example, compared to average residents, recent U.S. immigrants tend to be less educated, including an estimated 12 million illegal immigrants, more than half from Mexico. The Hispanic population more than doubled between the 1980 census and 2000 census, and the percentage of foreign-born Hispanics increased. Among males age 25 and older, only 57 percent of Hispanics had at least a high school education in 2000, compared with 85 percent of whites and 79 percent of blacks. More generally, the foreign-born share of the U.S. population more than doubled from 5 percent in 1970 to over 12 percent today, the largest share since the 1930s. Thus, immigration has increased the supply of relatively poorly educated workers, which has depressed wages of the less educated generally.

Finally, marriage trends have reinforced the income gap, as discussed in the case study, "Public Policy: Marital Sorting and Income Inequality," at the end of the book.

So economic forces, immigration, and marriage trends have hurt those at the low end of the income distribution and have benefited those at the high end, and this helps explain the growing disparity in household income.

Income in the United States is less evenly distributed than in other developed countries throughout the world, such as Canada, France, Great Britain, Italy, and Australia, but is more evenly distributed than in most developing countries, such as Brazil, Chile, Mexico, Nigeria, and the Philippines.

Problems With Distribution Benchmarks

One problem with assessing income distributions is that there is no objective standard for evaluating them. The usual assumption is that a more equal distribution of income is more desirable, but is equal distribution most preferred? If not, then how uneven

2. Thomas Lamieux et al., "Performance Pay and Wage Inequality," *Quarterly Journal of Economics*, 124 (February 2009): 1–49.
3. Lex Borghans and Bas ter Weel, "The Diffusion of Computers and the Distribution of Wages," *European Economic Review*, 51 (April 2007): 715–748.

should it be? For example, among major league baseball players, well over half the pay goes to 20 percent of the players. Professional basketball pay skews even more, with top NBA players earning up to 50 times more than the bottom players. Does this mean the economy, as a whole, is in some sense "fairer" than these professional sports?

A second problem is that because Exhibits 1 and 2 measure money income after cash transfers but before taxes, they neglect the effects of taxes and in-kind transfers, such as food vouchers and free medical care for poor families. The tax system as a whole is progressive, meaning that families with higher incomes pay a larger fraction of their incomes in taxes. In-kind transfers benefit the lowest income groups the most. Consequently, if Exhibit 1 incorporated the effects of taxes and in-kind transfers, the share of income going to the lower groups would increase, the share going to the higher groups would decrease, and income would become more evenly distributed.

Third, focusing on the share of income going to each income quintile overlooks the fact that household size differs across quintiles. Most households in the bottom quintile consist of one person living alone. Only one in 16 households in the top quintile consists of one person living alone. Fourth, Exhibits 1 and 2 include only *reported* income. If people receive payment "under the table" to evade taxes, or if they earn money through illegal activities, their actual income will exceed their reported income. The omission of unreported income distorts the data if unreported income as a percentage of total family income differs across income levels.

Finally, Exhibits 1 and 2 focus on the distribution of *income*, but a better measure of household welfare would be the distribution of *spending*. Available evidence indicates that *spending by quintiles is much more evenly distributed than income by quintiles*.

Redistribution Programs

Because poverty is such a relative concept, how do we measure it objectively, and how do we ensure that the measure can be applied with equal relevance over time? The federal government has developed a method for calculating an official poverty level, which serves as a benchmark for poverty analysis in the United States.

Official Poverty Level

U.S. official poverty level
Benchmark level of income computed by the federal government to track poverty over time; initially based on three times the cost of a nutritionally adequate diet

To derive the **U.S. official poverty level**, the U.S. Department of Agriculture in 1959 first estimated the cost of a nutritionally adequate diet. Then, based on the assumption that the poor spend about one-third of their income on food, the official poverty level was calculated by multiplying this food cost by three. The U.S. Census Bureau tracks the official poverty level, making adjustments for family size and for inflation. For example, the official poverty level of money income for a family of four was $22,050 in 2009; a family of four below that income threshold was regarded as living in poverty. Poverty levels in 2009 ranged from $10,830 for a person living alone to $40,750 for a family of nine. The poverty definition is based on pretax money income, including cash transfers, but it excludes the value of noncash transfers such as food vouchers, Medicaid, subsidized housing, or employer-provided health insurance.

Each year since 1959, the Census Bureau has conducted a survey comparing each family's cash income to the annual poverty level applicable to that family. Results of this survey are presented in Exhibit 3, which indicates both the millions of people living below the official poverty level and the percentage of the U.S. population below that level. Periods of U.S. recession are also shown (a recession is usually defined as two or more successive quarters of declining output in the economy). Note that poverty increased during recessions.

EXHIBIT 3 **Number and Percentage of U.S. Population in Poverty**

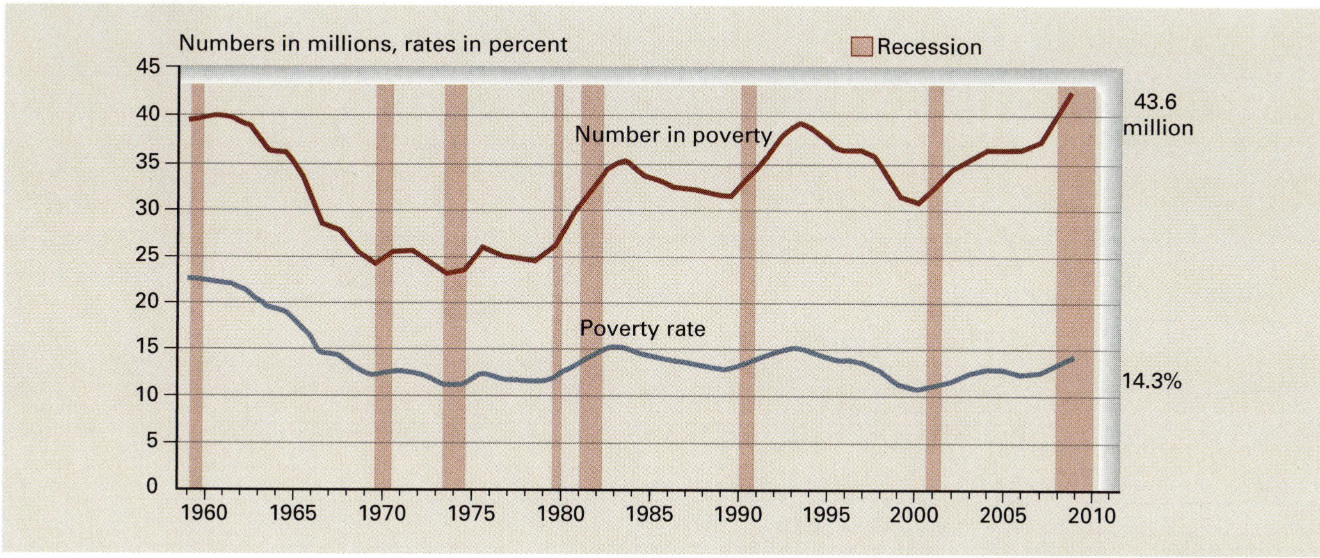

Source: U.S. Census Bureau, *Income, Poverty, and Health Insurance Coverage in the United States: 2009*, Current Population Reports, P60-238(RV), September 2010, Figure 3, p. 13, http://www.census.gov/prod/2010pubs/p60-238.pdf.

The biggest decline in poverty occurred before 1970; *the poverty rate dropped from 22.4 percent in 1959 to 12.1 percent in 1969*. During that period, the number of poor people decreased from about 40 million to 24 million. The poverty rate has not shown huge fluctuations since that initial drop. After declining from 1994 to 2000, the poverty rate and the number of poor people drifted higher over the next five years because of the national recession in 2001. The recession of 2007–2009 increased the number of people in poverty to 43.6 million in 2009 and the poverty rate to 14.3 percent, or one in seven U.S. residents.

Poverty is a relative term. If we examined the distribution of income across countries, we would find huge gaps between rich and poor nations. The U.S. official poverty level of income is much greater than the average income for three-fourths of the world's population. The U.S. poverty level for a family of four in 2009 works out to be a $15.10 per person per day. Most nations employ a much lower poverty threshold. About 40 percent of the world's population lives on $2 a day or less.[4]

Programs to Help the Poor

What should society's response to poverty be? The best predictor of poverty is whether someone has a job. Adults with full-time jobs in 2009 had a poverty rate of 2.7 percent; adults who did not work during the year had a rate of 22.7 percent. One way government can try to reduce poverty, therefore, is to promote a healthy economy. The stronger the economy, the greater the job opportunities, and the more likely people find work. Perhaps the best indicator of whether or not jobs are readily available is the *unemployment rate*, which shows the percentage of the labor force out of work. The *lower* the unemployment rate, the *higher* the likelihood that someone who wants

4. As reported in Daryl Collins et al., *Portfolios of the Poor: How the World's Poor Live on $2 a Day*, (Princeton University Press, 2009).

EXHIBIT 4 U.S. Poverty Rates and Unemployment Rates Are Related Over Time

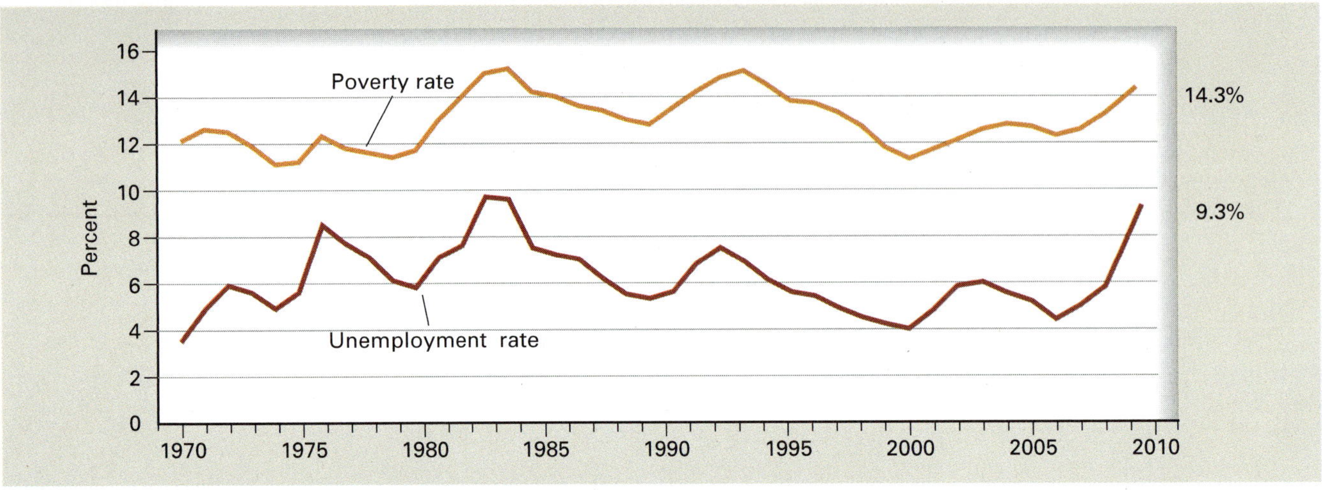

Source: U.S. Census Bureau and U.S. Bureau of Labor Statistics.

a job can find one. Thus, the lower the unemployment rate, the lower the poverty rate. Exhibit 4 shows poverty rates and unemployment rates in the United States each year since 1969. As you can see, the poverty rate, shown by the top line, tends to rise when the unemployment rate increases and to fall when the unemployment rate declines.

Thus, the government's first line of defense in fighting poverty is promoting a healthy economy. Yet even when the unemployment rate is low, some people are still poor. Although some antipoverty programs involve direct market intervention, such as minimum-wage laws, the most visible antipoverty programs redistribute income after the market has made an initial distribution. Since the mid-1960s, social welfare expenditures at all levels of government have increased significantly. We can divide these programs into two broad categories: social insurance and income assistance.

social insurance
Government programs designed to help make up for lost income of people who worked but are now retired, unemployed, or unable to work because of disability or work-related injury

Social Security
Supplements retirement income to those with a record of contributing to the program during their working years; by far the largest government redistribution program

Medicare
Social insurance program providing health insurance for short-term medical care to older Americans, regardless of income

Social Insurance

Social insurance programs are designed to help make up for the lost income of people who worked but are now retired, temporarily unemployed, or unable to work because of disability or work-related injury. The major social insurance program is **Social Security,** established during the Great Depression to supplement retirement income of those with a work history and a record of contributing to the program. **Medicare,** another social insurance program, provides health insurance for short-term medical care, mostly to those ages 65 and older, regardless of income. There are over 47 million Social Security and Medicare beneficiaries. Other social insurance programs include *unemployment insurance*, which supports those who have lost jobs, and *workers' compensation*, which supports workers injured on the job; both programs require that beneficiaries have a history of employment.

The social insurance system deducts "insurance premiums" from workers' pay to provide benefits to other retired, disabled, and unemployed individuals. These programs protect some families from poverty, particularly the elderly, but they are aimed more at those with a work history. Still, the social insurance system tends to redistribute income from rich to poor and from young to old. Most current Social Security beneficiaries will receive far more in benefits than they ever paid into the program, especially those with a brief work history or a record of low wages.

Income Assistance

Income assistance programs—what we usually call welfare programs—provide cash and in-kind assistance to the poor. Unlike social insurance, income assistance programs do not require recipients to have a work history or to have paid into the program. Income assistance programs are means tested. Those with sufficient means are not eligible. In a **means-tested program,** a household's income and assets must be below a certain level to qualify for benefits. The federal government funds about two-thirds of welfare spending, and state and local governments fund about one-third.

The two primary *cash transfer* programs are **Temporary Assistance for Needy Families (TANF),** which provides cash to poor families with dependent children, and **Supplemental Security Income (SSI),** which provides cash to the elderly poor and the disabled. Cash transfers vary inversely with family income from other sources. In 1997, TANF replaced Aid for Families with Dependent Children (AFDC), which began during the Great Depression and originally supported widows with young children. Whereas AFDC was a federal *entitlement* program, meaning that anyone who met the criteria was *entitled* to benefits, TANF is under the control of each state and carries no federal entitlement. The federal government gives each state a fixed grant to help fund TANF programs.

The SSI program provides support for the elderly and disabled poor. It is the fastest-growing cash transfer program with outlays exceeding $100 billion in 2010. SSI coverage has been broadened to include people addicted to drugs and alcohol, children with learning disabilities, and, in some cases, the homeless. The federal portion of this program is uniform across states, but states can supplement federal aid. For example, benefit levels in California average twice those in Alabama. Most states also offer modest *General Assistance* aid to those who are poor but do not qualify for TANF or SSI. The federal government also provides an **earned-income tax credit,** which supplements wages of the working poor. For example, a low-income family with three children would not only pay no federal income tax but would receive a cash transfer of up to $5,700 in 2010. More than 20 million tax filers received such transfers in 2010, when outlays of more than $40 billion for the program were double federal spending for TANF. The earned income tax credit lifts millions of families out of poverty. Twenty-three states and the District of Columbia also offer earned-income tax credits on top of the federal plan.

In addition to cash transfers, a variety of *in-kind transfer* programs provide health care, food vouchers, and housing assistance to the poor. **Medicaid** pays for medical care for those with low incomes who are aged, blind, disabled, or are in families with dependent children. *Medicaid is by far the largest welfare program, costing more than all cash and other in-kind transfer programs combined.* It has grown more than any other poverty program, quadrupling in the last decade and accounting for nearly a quarter of the typical state's budget (though states receive federal grants covering half or more of their Medicaid budget). The qualifying level of income is set by each state, and some states are stricter than others. Therefore, the proportion of poor people covered by Medicaid varies across states. More than 57 million, or more than one in six U.S. residents, received Medicaid benefits at a total cost of over $400 billion in 2010 (about 10 million Medicaid beneficiaries also receive Medicare). For many elderly, Medicaid covers long-term nursing care, which can cost taxpayers up to $100,000 a year per recipient.

The Supplemental Nutrition Assistance Program, or **SNAP,** provides vouchers that the poor can redeem for food. Forty million people received vouchers in an average month of 2010, and the monthly benefit averaged $290 per household. SNAP outlays exceeded $60 billion in 2010. Still, many of those eligible for food vouchers do not apply for them. *Housing assistance* programs include direct assistance for rental payments and subsidized low-income housing for over 10 million people. Federal spending alone came to about $58 billion in 2010. Other in-kind transfer programs for the poor include support for day care, school lunches, extra food for pregnant women, energy

income assistance programs
Welfare programs that provide money and in-kind assistance to the poor; benefits do not depend on prior contributions

means-tested program
A program in which, to be eligible, an individual's income and assets must not exceed specified levels

Temporary Assistance for Needy Families (TANF)
An income assistance program funded largely by the federal government but run by the states to provide cash transfer payments to poor families with dependent children

Supplemental Security Income (SSI)
An income assistance program that provides cash transfers to the elderly poor and the disabled; a uniform federal payment is supplemented by transfers that vary across states

earned-income tax credit
A federal program that supplements the wages of the working poor

Medicaid
An in-kind transfer program that provides medical care for poor people; by far the most costly welfare program

SNAP
An in-kind transfer program that offers low-income households vouchers redeemable for food; benefit levels vary inversely with household income

EXHIBIT 5 Federal Redistribution Outlays Each Year by Category

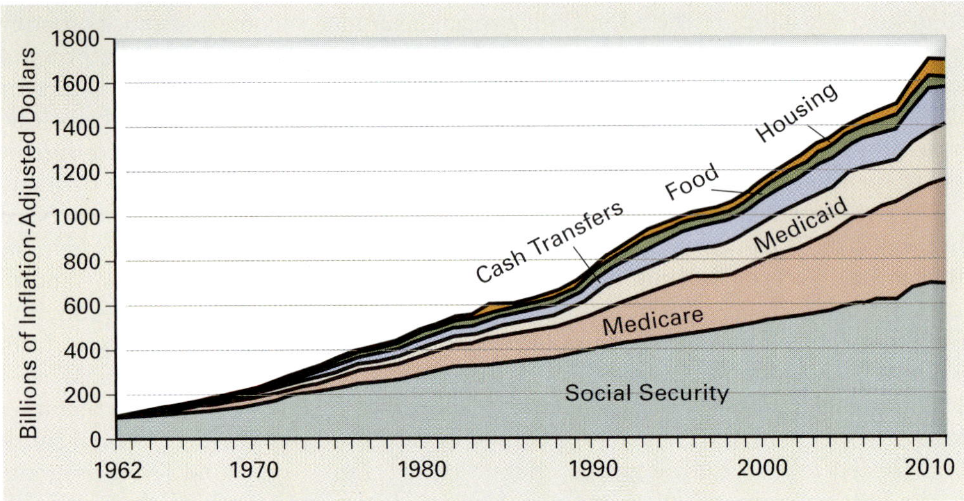

Source: Developed from figures in *Historical Tables, Budget of the United States, Fiscal Year 2011* at http://www.whitehouse.gov/omb/budget/Overview. Figures are in constant purchasing power using the 2008 GDP Price Index. Data for 2010 and 2011 are estimates based on the proposed federal budget for 2011. Cash transfers were projected to decline in 2011, which is why the total levels off that year.

assistance, and education and training, such as Head Start. *In all, the federal government funds more than 80 means-tested programs.*

Here's an overview: Federal redistribution programs totaled about $1.8 trillion in 2010, more than twice the amount spent on national defense. Adding in state and local outlays pushes the total to $2.4 trillion. Exhibit 5 shows the growth in federal redistribution programs since 1962. To eliminate the effects of inflation, figures are expressed in dollars of constant purchasing power. Overall, redistribution outlays have grown at an annual average of 6 percent since 1962, even after netting out the effects of inflation. Social Security and Medicare, programs that mostly benefit the elderly, make up the greatest share throughout the period. Next is Medicaid, which, as noted earlier, exceeds outlays for cash transfers and other in-kind transfers combined. Although more than half the federal welfare budget goes for health care, about 50 million U.S. residents still lacked health insurance in 2009, or about one in six. Health care coverage is expected to increase after the adoption of federal health care reform in 2010.

Some countries also have far more extensive redistribution programs than does the United States, basing a variety of public policies on income. The heir to a sausage fortune who was caught speeding 50 miles per hour in a 25 mile-an-hour zone paid a $204,000 fine.[5]

Who Are the Poor?

Who are the poor, and how has their composition changed over time? We will slice poverty statistics in several ways to examine the makeup of the group. Keep in mind that we are relying on official poverty estimates, which ignore the value of in-kind transfers, so, to that extent, official estimates overstate poverty.

5. Lisa Moore, "Sticking It to the Scofflaw," *U.S. News & World Report*, March 18, 2007.

Poverty and Age

Earlier we looked at poverty among the U.S. population. Here we focus on poverty and age. Exhibit 6 presents the poverty rates for three age groups since 1959: people less than 18 years old, those between 18 and 64, and those 65 and older. As you can see, poverty rates for each group declined between 1959 and 1968. The rate among those under 18 trended upward between the mid-1970s and the early 1980s. The rate then remained around 20 percent for a dozen years, declined during the 1990s, before rising to 20.7 percent by 2009.

In 1959, the elderly were the poorest group, with a poverty rate of 35 percent. Poverty among the elderly declined to 8.9 percent by 2009, the lowest rate on record and below the rate of 12.9 percent for people 18 to 64 years of age. The decline in poverty among the elderly stems from the tremendous growth in spending for Social Security and Medicare. In real terms—that is, after adjusting for the effects of inflation—those two programs have grown more than twelvefold since 1959 (Medicare didn't even exist until 1965). *Although not welfare programs in a strict sense, Social Security and Medicare have been hugely successful in reducing poverty among the elderly.*

Poverty and Public Choice

In a democracy, public policies depend very much on the political influence of the interest groups involved. In recent years, the elderly have become a powerful political force. The voter participation rate of those 65 and over is higher than that of any other age group. For example, people 65 years of age and older vote at triple the rate of those between 18 and 24 and four times that of welfare recipients. The political muscle of

EXHIBIT 6 U.S. Poverty Rates by Age

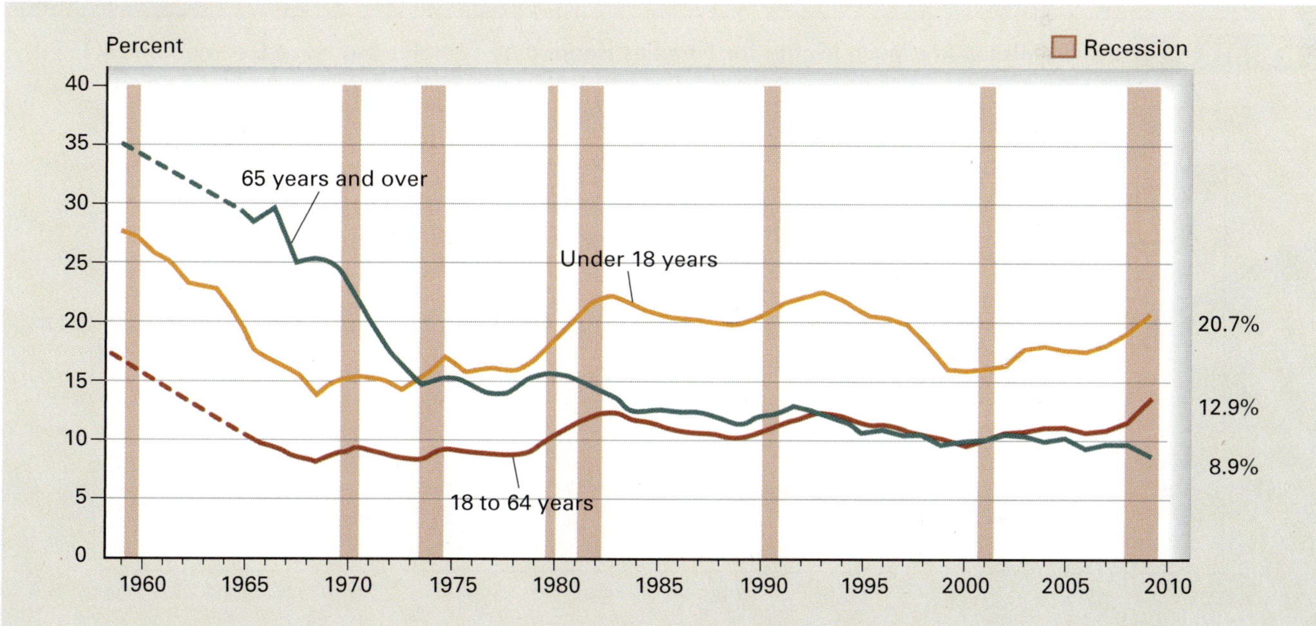

Source: U.S. Census Bureau, *Poverty in the United States: 2009*, Current Population Reports, P60-238(RV), September 2010, Figure 4, http://www.census.gov/prod/2009pubs/p60-236.pdf.

the elderly has been flexed whenever a question of Social Security or Medicare benefits is considered.

Unlike most interest groups, the elderly make up a group we all expect to join one day. The elderly are supported by at least five constituencies: (1) the elderly themselves; (2) people under 65 who are concerned about the current benefits of their parents or other elderly relatives; (3) people under 65 who are concerned about their own benefits in the future; (4) people who earn their living by caring for the elderly, such as doctors, nurses, and nursing-home operators; and (5) candidates for office who want to harvest the votes that seniors deliver. So the elderly have a broad constituency, and this pays off in terms of redistribution of wealth to the elderly and in the reduction of poverty among this group. The poverty rate among those 65 and over in 2009 was less than half that among those under 18.

The Feminization of Poverty

Another way to look at poverty is based on the status of the household head. Exhibit 7 compares poverty rates among families headed by females with no husband present with poverty rates for other families. Two trends are unmistakable. First, poverty rates among families headed by females are much higher than rates among other families—about four times higher. Second, poverty rates among female-headed families have trended down since the early 1990s, falling from 39.7 percent in 1991 to 32.5 percent in 2009.

The exhibit compares poverty among female householders to other families. What it doesn't show is the growth in the number of people in female-headed households. The number of people in families headed by women increased 177 percent between 1965 and 2009, while the number in all other families grew just 25 percent. The percentage of births to unmarried mothers is five times greater today than in the 1960s. In 1960,

EXHIBIT 7 Poverty Rates Are Much Higher for Families Headed by Females but Have Declined Since 1990

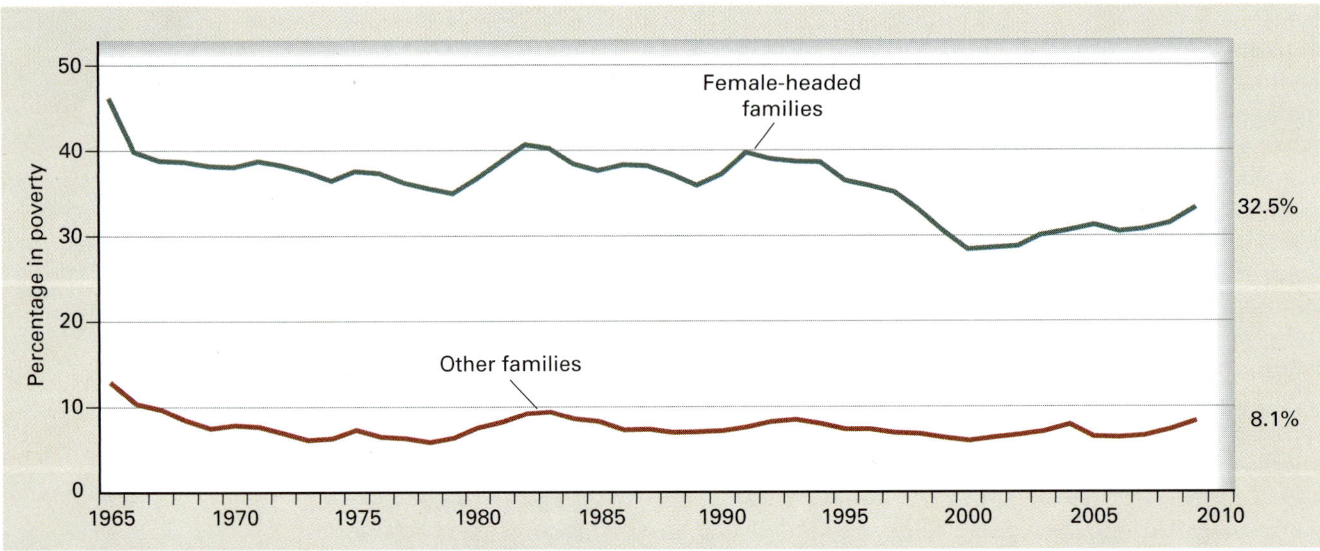

Source: Developed from data in U.S. Census Bureau, *Income, Poverty, and Health Insurance Coverage in the United States: 2009*, Current Population Reports, P60-236(RV), September 2010, Table B-1, http://www.census.gov/prod/2010pubs/p60-236.pdf.

only 1 in 200 children lived with a single parent who had never married. Today, 1 in 10 children lives with a single parent who has never married.

The United States has the highest teenage pregnancy rate in the developed world—twice the rate of Great Britain and 15 times that of Japan. Most recently, more than 85 percent of teen mothers were unmarried when they gave birth. Because fathers in such cases typically provide little support, children born outside marriage are likely to be poorer than other children. *The growth in the number of poor families since 1965 results overwhelmingly from a growth in the number of female householders.* The number of jobs in the U.S. economy more than doubled in the last four decades. Families with a female householder were in the worst position to take advantage of this job growth. *Children of female householders are five times more likely to live in poverty than are other children. Young, single motherhood is a recipe for poverty.* Often the young mother drops out of school, which reduces her future earning possibilities when and if she seeks work outside the home. Even a strong economy is little help to households with nobody in the labor force. Worse yet, young, single mothers-to-be are less likely to seek adequate medical care; the result is a higher proportion of premature, underweight babies. This is one reason why the U.S. infant mortality rate exceeds that of some other industrialized countries. Compared to two-parent families, children in one-parent families are twice as likely to drop out of school, and girls from one-parent families are twice as likely to become single mothers themselves.

Because of a lack of education and limited job skills, most single mothers go on welfare. Before recently imposed lifetime limits on welfare, the average never-married mother had been on welfare for a decade, twice as long as divorced mothers on welfare. Of all teenagers who gave birth, the proportion unmarried was 13 percent in 1950, 30 percent in 1970, 67 percent in 1990, and 87 percent in 2008.[6]

Poverty has therefore become increasingly feminized, mostly because female householders have become more common. Children from mothers who finished high school, married before having a child, and gave birth after age 20 are 10 times less likely to be poor than children from mothers who fail to do these things.[7] Because the number of female householders has grown more rapidly among African Americans, the feminization of poverty has been more dramatic in those households. Seventy-two percent of all births to non-Hispanic black mothers in 2008 were to unmarried women, compared with 52 percent among women of Hispanic origin, 29 percent among non-Hispanic whites, and 17 percent among Asians and Pacific Islanders.[8] But we should be careful in drawing conclusions about the role of race or ethnicity per se, because black and Hispanic households are poorer on average than other households. Low income alone could account for much of the difference in birth rates. In other words, a better comparison would adjust for income differences across groups, but such data are not available.

Exhibit 8 shows poverty rates for each of the 50 states. States with a deeper shade of red have higher poverty rates. States with no shading have lower rates. As you can see, poverty rates are higher across the bottom half of the United States. Poverty rates tend to be higher in states where births to single mothers make up a larger percentage of all births. For example, Louisiana and Mississippi have the highest poverty rates and among the highest rates of births to unmarried mothers. Nearly half of all births in these states are to unmarried mothers.

6. "Births: Preliminary Data for 2008," *National Vital Statistics Report* 58, No. 16 (April 2010), Table 7 at http://www.cdc.gov/nchs/data/nvsr/nvsr58/nvsr58_16.pdf.
7. James Q. Wilson, "Human Remedies for Social Disorder," *Public Interest* (Spring 1998): 27.
8. "Births: Preliminary Data for 2008," *National Vital Statistics Report* 58, No. 16 (April 2010), Table 1, found at http://www.cdc.gov/nchs/data/nvsr/nvsr58/nvsr58_16.pdf.

EXHIBIT 8 Percent of Population Living in Poverty by State

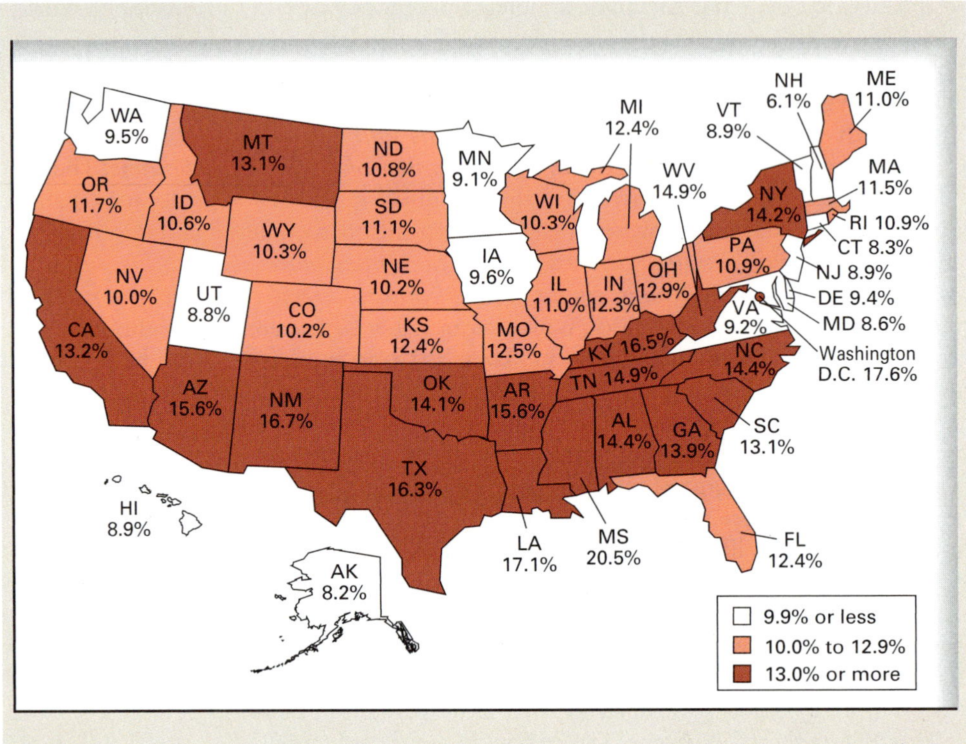

Source: *Poverty in the United States: 2008*, U.S. Census Bureau, September 2009, at http://www.census.gov/hhes/www/poverty/poverty08/state.pdf. Rates are averaged for 2006, 2007, and 2008 to provide more reliable figures.

Poverty and Discrimination

To what extent has racial discrimination limited job opportunities and increased poverty among minorities? Discrimination can occur in many ways: in school funding, in housing, in employment, in career advancement. Also, discrimination in one area can affect opportunities in another. For example, housing discrimination can reduce job opportunities if a black family cannot move within commuting distance of the best jobs, or cannot take advantage of the job networking available in neighborhoods where more people are working.[9] Job-market discrimination can take many forms. An employer may fail to hire a black job applicant because the applicant lacks training. But this lack of training can arise from discrimination in the schools, in union apprenticeship programs, or in training programs run by other employers. For example, evidence suggests that black workers receive less on-the-job training than otherwise similar white workers.

After adjusting for a variety of factors that could affect the wage, such as education and work experience, research shows that white workers earn more than black workers. The gap between the two narrowed between 1940 and 1976 to the point where black

9. Researchers have found that individuals living in the same city block are more likely to work together than those living in nearby blocks. See Patrick Bayer, Stephen L. Ross, and Giorgio Topa, "Place of Work and Place of Residence: Informal Hiring Networks and Labor Market Outcomes," *Journal of Political Economy*, 116 (December 2008): 1150–1197.

workers earned only 7 percent less than white workers; then it widened somewhat.[10] Since 1993, the gap has again narrowed. Could explanations besides job discrimination account for the wage gap? Though the data adjust for *years* of schooling, some research suggests that black workers received a lower *quality* of schooling than white workers. For example, black students were less likely to use computers in school. Inner-city schools often have more problems with classroom discipline, which takes time and attention away from instruction. And schools serving the poorest students experience the highest rates of teacher absences.[11] Such quality differences could account for at least a portion of the remaining gap in standardized wages.

Evidence of discrimination comes from studies where otherwise similar white and black candidates are sent to seek jobs, rent apartments, or apply for mortgages. For example, white and black job applicants with similar qualifications and résumés applied for the same job. These studies find that employers are less likely to interview or offer a job to minority applicants. Minority applicants also tend to be treated less favorably by real estate agents and lenders. One study concluded that one quarter of the wage gap between blacks and whites was the result of discrimination.[12]

Affirmative Action

The Equal Employment Opportunity Commission, established by the Civil Rights Act of 1964, monitors cases involving unequal pay for equal work and unequal access to promotion. All companies doing business with the federal government had to set numerical hiring, promotion, and training goals to ensure that these firms did not discriminate in hiring on the basis of race, sex, religion, or national origin. Black employment increased in those firms required to file affirmative action plans.[13] The fraction of the black labor force employed in white-collar jobs increased from 16.5 percent in 1960 to 40.5 percent in 1981—an increase that greatly exceeded the growth of white-collar jobs in the labor force as a whole. Research also suggests that civil rights legislation played a role in narrowing the black-white earnings gap between 1960 and the mid-1970s.[14]

Attention focused on hiring practices and equality of opportunity at the state and local levels as well, as governments introduced so-called *set-aside* programs to guarantee minorities a share of contracts. But a 1995 U.S. Supreme Court decision challenged affirmative action programs, ruling that Congress must meet a rigorous legal standard to justify any contracting or hiring practice based on race, especially programs that reserve jobs for minorities and women. Programs must be shown to be in response to injustices created by past discrimination, said the Court.

In summary, evidence suggests that black workers earn less than white workers after adjustment for other factors that could affect wages, such as education and job experience. Part of this wage gap may also reflect differences in the quality of education, differences that could themselves be the result of discrimination.[15] Keep in mind that

10. M. Boozer, A. Krueger, and S. Wolken, "Race and School Quality Since *Brown v. Board of Education*," *Brookings Papers on Economic Activity: Microeconomics* (1992): 269–326.
11. Charles Clotfelter et al., "Are Teacher Absences Worth Worrying About in the United States?" *Education Finance and Policy*, 4 (Spring 2009): 115–149.
12. Kerwin Kofi Charles and Jonathan Guryan, "Prejudice and Wages: An Empirical Assessment of Becker's *The Economics of Discrimination*," *Journal of Political Economy*, 116 (October 2008): 773–809.
13. James Smith and Finis Welch, "Black Economic Progress After Myrdal," *Journal of Economic Literature*, 27 (June 1989): 519–563.
14. David Card and Alan Krueger, "Trends in Relative Black-White Earnings Revisited," *American Economic Review*, 83 (May 1993): 85–91.
15. Huoying Wu, "Can the Human Capital Approach Explain Life-Cycle Wage Differentials Between Races and Sexes," *Economic Inquiry*, 45 (January 2007): 24–39.

unemployment rates are higher among blacks than among whites and are higher still among black teenagers, the group most in need of job skills and job experience. *But we should also note that black families are not a homogeneous group. In fact, the distribution of income is more uneven among black families than among the population as a whole.*

On the upside, there is a growing middle class among black households. Since 1970, the number of black doctors, nurses, college professors, and newspaper reporters has more than tripled; the number of black engineers, computer programmers, accountants, managers, and administrators has quadrupled; the number of black elected officials has increased fivefold; and the number of black lawyers has increased more than sixfold. In Georgia, for example, the number of black lawyers increased from just 54 in 1970 to more than 2,000 today. Two of the most admired Americans are African American—President Barack Obama and talk show host Oprah Winfrey.

Unintended Consequences of Income Assistance

On the plus side, antipoverty programs increase the consumption possibilities of poor families, and that's a good thing, especially because children are the largest poverty group. But programs to assist the poor have secondary effects that limit their ability to reduce poverty over time. Here we consider some unintended consequences.

Society, through government, tries to provide families with an adequate standard of living, but society also wants to ensure that only the needy receive benefits. As we have seen, income assistance consists of a combination of cash and in-kind transfer programs. Because these programs are designed to help the poor and only the poor, benefits decrease as income from other sources increases. With transfers declining sharply as earned income increases, welfare recipients face a high marginal tax rate on earned income. An increase in earnings may reduce benefits from TANF, Medicaid, SNAP (food vouchers), housing assistance, energy assistance, and others among the 80 means-tested programs. With a loss in support from each program as earned income increases, working may lead to little or no increase in total income. Over certain income ranges, a welfare recipient may lose more than $1 in welfare benefits for each additional $1 in earnings. Thus, the *marginal tax rate* on earned income could exceed 100 percent!

Holding even a part-time job involves some costs—for clothing, transportation, and child care, for instance—not to mention the loss of free time. Such a system of perverse incentives can frustrate people trying to work their way off welfare. *The high marginal tax rate discourages employment and self-sufficiency.* In many cases, welfare benefits exceed the income resulting from full-time employment.

The longer people stay out of the labor force, the more their job skills deteriorate, so when they do look for work, their productivity is lower than when they were last employed. This reduces their expected wage, making work even less attractive. Some economists argue that in this way, welfare benefits can lead to long-term dependency. While welfare seems to be a rational choice in the short run, it has unfavorable long-term consequences for the family, for society, and for the economy.

Welfare programs can cause other disincentives. For example, children may be eligible for Supplemental Security Income if they have a learning disability. According to one firsthand account, some low-income parents encouraged poor performance in school so their children could qualify for this program.[16]

16. Jacqueline Goldwyn Kingon, "Education Life: A View from the Trenches," *New York Times*, 8 April 2001.

A serious concern is whether children on welfare are more likely to end up on welfare as adults. Is there a cycle of dependency? Why might we expect one? Children in welfare households may learn the ropes about the welfare system and may come to view welfare as a normal way of life rather than as a temporary bridge over a rough patch. Research indicates that daughters from welfare families are more likely than daughters from other families to participate in the welfare system themselves and are more likely to have premarital births.[17] It is difficult to say whether welfare "causes" the link between mother and daughter, because the same factors that contribute to a mother's welfare status can also contribute to her daughter's welfare status. Evidence of a link is weaker when it comes to sons from welfare families.

Welfare Reform

There has been much dissatisfaction with the welfare system among both those who pay for the programs and direct beneficiaries. Welfare reforms introduced more than a decade ago have been aimed at reducing long-term dependency.

Recent Reforms

Some analysts believe that one way to reduce poverty is to provide welfare recipients with job skills and make them find jobs. Even before the 1996 federal reform of welfare, to be discussed shortly, some sort of "workfare" component for welfare recipients operated in most states. In these states, as a condition of receiving welfare, the head of the household had to participate in education and training programs, search for work, or take some paid or unpaid position. The idea was to expose people on welfare to the job market. Evidence from various states indicates that programs involving mandatory job searches, short-term unpaid work, and training could operate at low cost and could increase employment. The government saved money because those in welfare-to-work programs left welfare rolls sooner.

Reforms at the state level set the stage for federal reforms. By far the biggest reform in the welfare system in the last 70 years came with the 1996 legislation that replaced Aid to Families with Dependent Children (AFDC) with Temporary Assistance for Needy Families (TANF). Whereas the AFDC program set eligibility rules and left federal costs open-ended through matching grants to the states, TANF offers a fixed grant to the states to run their welfare programs. States ended AFDC and began TANF by July 1, 1997. Under the new system, states have much more control over their own welfare programs. But concerns about welfare dependency fostered some special provisions. The act imposes a five-year lifetime limit on cash transfers and requires states to move a certain percentage of people from welfare to work.

Aside from the time limits and work participation rates imposed by the federal government, states are free to set benefit levels and experiment however they choose. For example, about half the states impose time limits shorter than five years. Some observers fear that states now have an incentive to keep welfare costs down by cutting benefits. To avoid becoming destinations for poor people—that is, to avoid becoming "welfare magnets"—states may be tempted to offer relatively low benefits.

17. Robert Moffitt, "Welfare Reform: The U.S. Experience," *From Welfare to Work,* Paper Presented at the Economic Council of Sweden Conference, 7 May 2007.

EXHIBIT 9 Welfare Recipients as a Percentage of the U.S. Population Declined Sharply after Welfare Reform

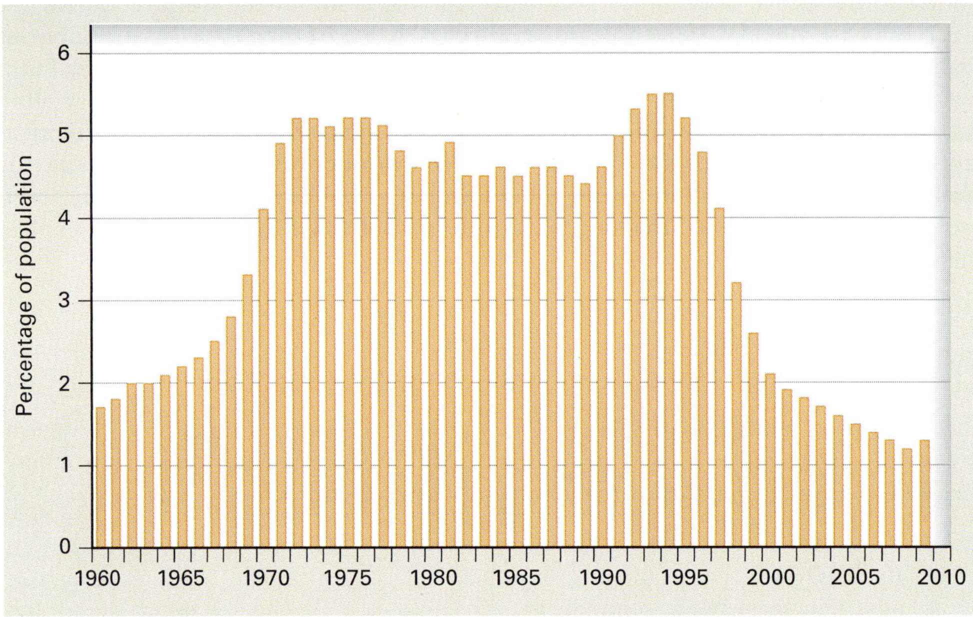

Source: Developed from data from the U.S. Department of Health and Human Services. Figures are for AFDC recipients before 1997 and TANF recipients for 1997 and later. Figures found at http://www.acf.hhs.gov/programs/ofa/data-reports/caseload/2009/2009_recipient_tan.htm.

The fear is that states will undercut benefits in what has been called a "race to the bottom."

Welfare Rolls Have Declined

Work requirements and time limits have resulted in substantial declines in the welfare caseload. The number of welfare recipients peaked in January 1994 at 14.2 million, mostly single women with children. By September 2009, the rolls had fallen to 4.1 million—71 percent below the peak. Exhibit 9 shows since 1960 the percentage of the U.S. population on welfare. Note the sharp decline in recent years. As a share of the U.S. population, welfare recipients fell from 5.5 percent in 1994 to 1.3 percent in 2009, only a tiny bit above the 1.2 rate for 2008, which was the lowest rate in the last half century.

A major result of welfare reform has been a substantial increase in employment among mothers who head families, especially those who have never married. About two-thirds found work during the period immediately after reform, and many more got jobs in the next year or two. This is a remarkable improvement from historical employment rates of women on welfare of about 10 percent. Their incomes went up on average, and they tended to hang onto their jobs. New York City officials reported that 85 percent of those getting off welfare did so because they had found work.

Because the welfare rolls have declined but federal grants have not, welfare spending per recipient increased significantly. Most states combined tough new eligibility rules with an expanded menu of welfare services. States have made large investments in work-related services such as job placement, transportation, and especially child care. Most of those going to work can continue to receive food vouchers, child care, and Medicaid. The earned-income tax credit also helps low-income workers—boosting pay up to $5,700 in 2009. Twenty-three states have added their own earned-income tax credits.

Despite the good news, some poor people are still having a hard time, particularly because of the recent downturn in the economy. Because many on welfare are poorly educated and have few job skills, wages for some remain low, and part-time work is common. Still, welfare reform has been quite successful in getting people off welfare and into jobs.

Check out the case study, "Public Policy: The Rich Got Poorer During the Recession" at the end of the book, which looks at how another income class has been affected by the recent recession, a group that won't get much sympathy.

Conclusion

Government redistribution programs have been most successful at reducing poverty among the elderly. But poverty rates among children increased because of the growth in the number of female householders. We might ask why transfer programs have reduced poverty rates more among the elderly than among female householders. Transfer programs do not encourage people to get old; that process occurs naturally and is independent of the level of transfers. But the level and availability of transfer programs at the margin could influence some young unmarried women as they are deciding whether or not to have a child and may, at the margin, influence a married mother's decision to get divorced.

Most transfers in the economy are not from the government but are in-kind transfers within the family, from parents to children. Thus, any change in a family's capacity to earn income has serious consequences for dependent children. *Family structure is a primary determinant of family income.* About one in five children in the United States lives in poverty. Children are the innocent victims of the changing family structure. Recent welfare reforms have succeeded in reducing welfare roles and increasing employment among single mothers.

Summary

1. Money income in the United States has become less evenly distributed since 1980. The poverty rate has dropped most among the elderly, thanks to Social Security and Medicare.
2. Young, single motherhood is a recipe for poverty. Often the young mother drops out of school, which reduces her future earning possibilities when and if she seeks work outside the home. Growth in the number of female householders in the last four decades increased poverty among children, though the overall poverty rate among households headed by females has declined since peaking in 1993. More unmarried mothers are working than ever.
3. The wage gap between black and white workers narrowed between 1940 and 1976, widened until the early 1990s, and has been narrowing again since 1993. Affirmative action programs and gains in education seem to have increased employment opportunities among black workers.
4. One undesirable effect of income assistance is a high marginal tax rate on earned income, which discourages employment and encourages welfare dependency. Worse still, welfare dependency could be passed on to the next generation. Research suggests that daughters from welfare families are more likely than daughters from other families to participate in the welfare system themselves and are more likely to have premarital births.
5. Welfare reforms introduced by the states set the stage for federal welfare reforms aimed at breaking the cycle of poverty and promoting the transition from welfare to work. The states began experimenting with different systems to encourage more personal responsibility. As a result of state reforms and federal welfare reform, welfare rolls dropped by more than two-thirds since 1994.

Key Concepts

Lorenz curve 353
Median income 353
Median wage 355
U.S. official poverty level 356
Social insurance 358
Social Security 358
Medicare 358
Income assistance programs 359
Means-tested program 359
Temporary Assistance for Needy Families (TANF) 359
Supplemental Security Income (SSI) 359
Earned-income tax credit 359
Medicaid 359
SNAP 359

Questions for Review

1. Distribution of Household Income Look back at Exhibit 1 in this chapter. How would you explain the shift of the U.S. income distribution in the last two decades?
2. Lorenz Curve What is a Lorenz curve? What does the Lorenz curve in Exhibit 2 illustrate?
3. Case Study: Marital Sorting and Income Inequality (See page 740.) How have marriage trends widened the gap between low-income and high-income households?
4. Official Poverty Level Although the poverty rate among single mothers has decreased since 1960, the number of poor children from such families has more than doubled. Explain.
5. Income Differences List some reasons why household incomes differ. Which factors are the most important?
6. Official Poverty Level How does the U.S. Department of Agriculture calculate the official poverty level? What government assistance programs does the Census Bureau consider when calculating household income? What programs are ignored?
7. Programs to Help the Poor Distinguish between social insurance programs and income assistance programs. Identify key examples of each.
8. Poverty and Age Poverty among the elderly fell dramatically between 1959 and 1974 and has continued to decline. However, poverty among that portion of the U.S. population that is less than 18 years old is no lower today than in the 1970s. Why have the experiences of these two age groups differed?
9. Poverty and Public Choice Why is it difficult to pass legislation to reduce the growth in Social Security or Medicare benefits?
10. Poverty and Discrimination Which types of discrimination may cause an earnings gap between white and black workers? Consider discrimination in schooling, for example. How would researchers detect such discrimination?
11. Disincentives How does the implicit tax on earned income (in the form of lost benefits from government assistance programs as earned income increases) affect work incentives? How do some people avoid the implicit tax?
12. Welfare Reform What has happened to the number of people on welfare since 1994? What explains the change over time?
13. Case Study: The Rich Got Poorer During the Recession (See page 741.) List the ill effects that the 2007–2009 recession had on high-income households and therefore on the economy.

Global Economic Watch Exercises

Login to www.cengagebrain.com and access the Global Economic Watch to do these exercises.

14. Global Economic Watch Go to the Global Economic Crisis Resource Center. Select Global Issues in Context. In the Basic Search box at the top of the page, enter the word "poverty." On the Results page, click on the link to View Full Overview. What is the difference between absolute and relative poverty?
15. Global Economic Watch Go to the Global Economic Crisis Resource Center. Select Global Issues in Context. In the Basic Search box at the top of the page, enter the words "poverty discrimination." Find an article about the effects of poverty and discrimination in a foreign country. Has discrimination increased poverty in that country?

Introduction to Macroeconomics

19

© Fabian Gonzales/Alamy

- What's the big idea with macroeconomics?
- Why is its focus the national economy?
- How do we measure the economy's performance over time?
- Which has more impact on your standard of living, the economy's short-term ups-and-downs or its long-term growth trend?
- What's the difference between demand-side economics and supply-side economics?
- How has the economic role of government evolved during the last century?

Answers to these and related questions are provided in this chapter, which introduces macroeconomics.

Macroeconomics looks at the big picture—not the demand for iPhones but the demand for everything produced in the economy; not the price of gasoline but the average price of all goods and services produced in the economy; not consumption by the Martinez household but consumption by all households; not investment by Google but investment by all firms in the economy.

Macroeconomists develop and test theories about how the economy as a whole works—theories that can help predict the impact of economic policies and events. Macroeconomists are concerned not only with what determines such big-picture indicators as production, employment, and the price level but also with understanding how and why they change over time. Macroeconomists are especially interested in what makes an economy grow, because a growing economy creates more jobs and more goods and services—in short, more growth means a rising standard of living. What determines the economy's ability to use resources productively, to adapt, to grow? This chapter begins exploring such questions.

Topics discussed include:

- The national economy
- Economic fluctuations
- Aggregate demand
- Aggregate supply
- Equilibrium price level and aggregate output
- Brief history of the U.S. economy
- Demand-side economics
- Stagflation
- Supply-side economics
- Recession of 2007–2009

The National Economy

economy
The structure of economic activity in a community, a region, a country, a group of countries, or the world

Macroeconomics concerns the overall performance of the *economy*. The term **economy** describes the structure of economic life, or economic activity, in a community, a region, a country, a group of countries, or the world. We could talk about the Chicago economy, the Illinois economy, the Midwest economy, the U.S. economy, the North American economy, or the world economy. We measure an economy's size in different ways, such as the amount produced, the number of people working, or their total income. The most common yardstick is *gross product*, which measures the market value of final goods and services produced in a particular geographical region during a given period, usually one year.

gross domestic product (GDP)
The market value of all final goods and services produced in the nation during a particular period, usually a year

gross world product
The market value of all final goods and services produced in the world during a given period, usually a year

If the focus is the Illinois economy, we consider the *gross state product*. If the focus is the U.S. economy, we consider the **gross domestic product**, or **GDP**, which measures the market value of all final goods and services produced in the United States during a given period, usually a year. GDP adds up production of the economy's incredible variety of goods and services, from trail bikes to pedicures. We can use the gross domestic product to compare different economies at the same time or to track the same economy over time. We could also consider the **gross world product**, which measures the value of all final goods and services produced in the world during a given period, usually a year. But the focus of macroeconomics is usually the national economy.

What's Special About the National Economy?

The national economy deserves special attention. Here's why. If you were to drive west on Interstate 10 in Texas, you would hardly notice crossing into New Mexico. But if, instead, you took the Juarez exit south into Mexico, you would be stopped at the border, asked for identification, and possibly searched. You would become quite aware of crossing an international border. Like most countries, the United States and Mexico usually allow people and goods to move more freely *within* their borders than *across* their borders.

The differences between the United States and Mexico are far greater than the differences between Texas and New Mexico. For example, each country has its own standard of living and currency, its own culture and language, its own communication and transportation system, its own system of government, and its own "rules of the game"—that is, its own laws, regulations, customs, manners, and ways of doing business both within and across its borders.

Macroeconomics typically focuses on the performance of the national economy, including how the national economy interacts with other national economies around the world. The U.S. economy is the largest and most complex in world history, with about 115 million households, more than 30 million for-profit businesses, and 89,500 separate government jurisdictions. The world economy includes about 200 sovereign nations, ranging from tiny Liechtenstein, with only 35,000 people, to China, with 1.4 billion people. These numbers offer snapshots, but the economy is a motion picture, a work in progress—too complex to capture in snapshots. This is why we use theoretical models to focus on key relationships. To help you get your mind around the economy, let's begin with a simple analogy.

The Human Body and the U.S. Economy

Consider the similarities and differences between the human body and the economy. The body consists of millions of cells, each performing particular functions yet each linked to the entire body. Similarly, the U.S. economy is composed of millions of decision makers, each acting with some independence yet each connected with the economy as a whole. The economy, like the body, is continually renewing itself, with new households, new businesses, a changing cast of public officials, and new foreign competitors and customers. Blood circulates throughout the body, facilitating the exchange of oxygen and vital nutrients among cells. Similarly, *money* circulates throughout the economy, facilitating the exchange of resources and products among individual economic units. In fact, blood and money are each called a *medium of exchange*. In Chapter 1 we saw that the movement of money, products, and resources throughout the economy follows a *circular flow*, as does the movement of blood, oxygen, and nutrients throughout the body.

Flow and Stock Variables

Just as the same blood recirculates as a medium of exchange in the body, the same dollars recirculate as a medium of exchange in the economy to finance transactions. The dollars you spend on bagels are spent by the baker on butter and then spent by the dairy farmer on work boots. Dollars *flow* through the economy. To measure a flow, we use a **flow variable**, which is an amount per unit of time, such as your average spending per week or your heartbeats per minute. In contrast, a **stock variable** is an amount measured at a particular point in time, such as the amount of money you have with you right now or your weight this morning.

flow variable
A measure of something over an interval of time, such as your income per week

stock variable
A measure of something at a particular point in time, such as the amount of money you have with you right now

Testing New Theories

Physicians and other natural scientists test their theories using controlled experiments. Macroeconomists, however, have no laboratories and little ability to run economy-wide experiments of any kind. Granted, they can study different economies around the world, but each economy is unique, so comparisons are tricky. Controlled experiments also provide the natural sciences with something seldom available to economists—the chance, or serendipitous, discovery (such as penicillin). Macroeconomists studying the U.S. economy have only one patient, so they can't introduce particular policies in a variety of alternative settings. You can't squeeze economies into a test tube. Cries of "Eureka!" are seldom heard from macroeconomists.

Knowledge and Performance

Throughout history, little was known about the human body, yet many people still enjoyed good health. For example, the fact that blood circulates in the body was not established until 1638; it took scientists another 150 years to figure out why. Similarly, over the millennia, various complex economies developed and flourished, although at the time there was little understanding about how an economy worked.

The economy is much like the body: As long as it functions smoothly, policy makers need not understand how it works. But if a problem develops—severe unemployment, high inflation, or sluggish growth, for example—we must know how a healthy economy works before we can consider whether anything can be done about it. We need not know every detail of the economy, just as we need not know every detail of the body. But we must understand essential relationships among key variables. For example, does the economy work well on its own, or does it often perform poorly? If it performs poorly, are there remedies? Can we be sure that a proposed remedy would not do more harm than good? When doctors didn't understand how the human body worked, their attempted "cures" were often worse than the diseases. Much of the history of medicine describes misguided efforts to deal with maladies. Even today, medical care is based on less scientific evidence than you might think. According to one study, only one in seven medical interventions is supported by reliable scientific evidence.[1] For example, acetaminophen (e.g., Tylenol) is a popular pain reliever, but nobody really knows how it works. According to an old saying, "Nature heals and the doctor collects the fee." Or as Voltaire wrote, "The art of medicine consists of amusing the patient while nature cures the disease."

Likewise, policy makers may adopt the wrong prescription because of a flawed theory about how the economy works. At one time, for example, a nation's economic vitality was thought to spring from the stock of precious metals accumulated in the public treasury. This theory spawned a policy called **mercantilism**, which held that, as a way of accumulating gold and silver, a nation should try to export more than it imports. To achieve this, nations restricted imports by such barriers as tariffs and quotas. But these restrictions led to retaliations by other countries, reducing international trade and the gains from specialization. Another flawed economic theory prompted President Herbert Hoover to introduce a major tax *increase* during the Great Depression. Economists have since learned that such a policy does more harm than good. Debates about the effectiveness of government policies were widespread as officials reacted to the crushing recession of 2007–2009.

mercantilism
The incorrect theory that a nation's economic objective should be to accumulate precious metals in the public treasury; this theory prompted trade barriers to cut imports, but other countries retaliated, reducing trade and the gains from specialization

We turn now to the performance of the U.S. economy.

Economic Fluctuations and Growth

The U.S. economy and other industrial market economies historically have experienced alternating periods of expansion and contraction in economic activity. As noted in Chapter 1, *economic fluctuations* are the rise and fall of economic activity relative to the long-term growth trend of the economy. These fluctuations, or *business cycles,* vary in length and intensity, yet some features appear common to all. The ups and downs usually involve the entire nation and often many other economies around the world, and they affect nearly all dimensions of economic activity, not just production and employment.

U.S. Economic Fluctuations

Perhaps the easiest way to understand the business cycle is to examine its components. During the 1920s and 1930s, Wesley C. Mitchell, director of the National Bureau of Economic Research (NBER), analyzed business cycles, noting that the economy has two phases: *expansions* and *contractions*. During an **expansion**, the economy grows as reflected by rising output, employment, income, and other aggregate measures. During a **contraction**, the economy declines as reflected by falling output, employment,

expansion
A period during which the economy grows as reflected by rising output, employment, income, and other aggregate measures

contraction
A period during which the economy declines as reflected by falling output, employment, income, and other aggregate measures

1. As reported by Sherwin Nuland, "Medical Fads: Bran, Midwives and Leeches," *New York Times*, 25 January 1995.

income, and other aggregate measures. Prior to World War II, a contraction might be so sharp as to be called a **depression**, which is a severe and prolonged reduction in the nation's economic activity as occurred during the 1930s. A milder contraction is called a **recession**, which is a period of decline in economic activity lasting more than a few months, as reflected by falling output employment, income, and other aggregate measures. The U.S. economy experienced both recessions and depressions before World War II. Since then, there have been recessions but no depressions, so things have improved.

Despite these ups and downs, the U.S. economy has grown dramatically over the long term. Although economic activity is measured in a variety of ways, if we had to settle on a single indicator, output best captures what's going on. The economy now produces over 13 times more output than it did in 1929. Output is measured by real GDP, the value of final goods and services after stripping away changes due to **inflation**, which is an increase in the economy's average price level. Production increased because of (1) increases in the amount and quality of resources, especially labor and capital; (2) better technology; and (3) improvements in the *rules of the game* that facilitate production and exchange, such as property rights, patent laws, the legal system, and market practices.

Exhibit 1 shows the long-term growth trend in economic activity as an upward-sloping straight line. Economic fluctuations reflect movements around this growth trend.

depression
A severe and prolonged reduction in economic activity as occurred during the 1930s

recession
A period of decline in economic activity lasting more than a few months, as reflected by falling output, employment, income, and other aggregate measures

inflation
An increase in the economy's average price level

EXHIBIT 1 Hypothetical Business Cycles

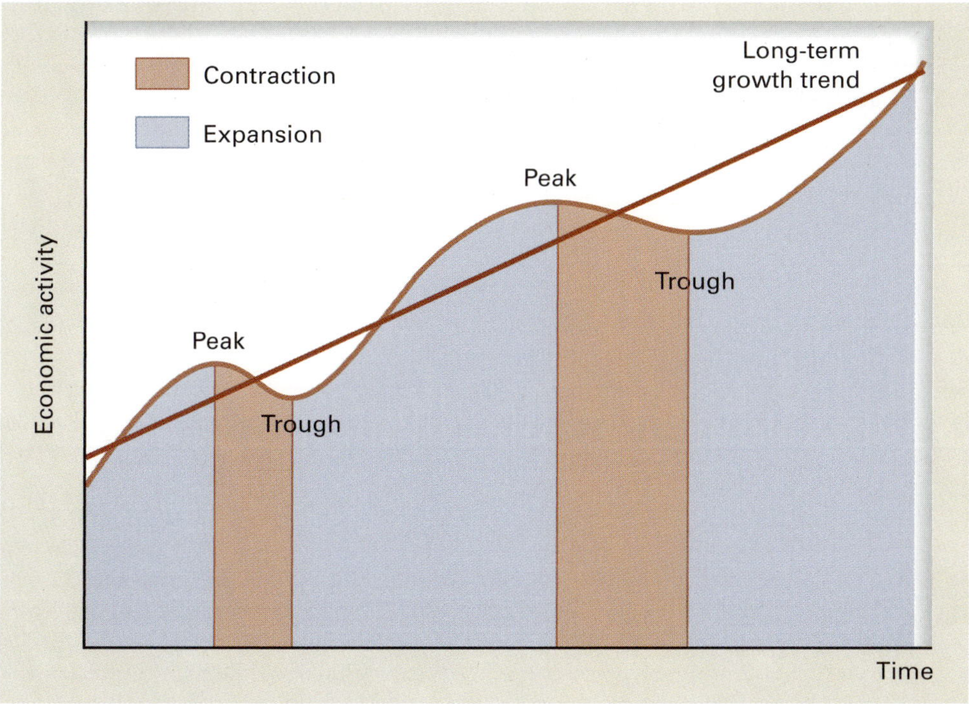

Business cycles reflect movements of economic activity around a trend line that shows long-term growth. An expansion (shaded in blue) begins when the economy starts to grow and continues until the economy reaches a peak. After an expansion has peaked, a contraction (shaded in pink) begins and continues until the economy reaches a trough.

A contraction begins after the previous expansion has reached a *peak*, or high point, and continues until the economy reaches a *trough*, or low point. The period between a peak and trough is a *contraction*, and the period between a trough and subsequent peak is an *expansion*. Note that expansions last longer than contractions, but the length of the full cycle varies.

Analysts at NBER have tracked the U.S. economy back to 1854. Since then, the nation has experienced 33 peak-to-trough-to-peak cycles. No two have been exactly alike. During the 22 business cycles prior to 1945, expansions averaged 29 months and contractions 21 months. During the 11 cycles since 1945, expansions stretched twice as long to 57 months, and recessions fell by half to 11 months. Thus, since 1945 expansions are longer and recessions are shorter. Both developments have been hugely beneficial for economic growth and the U.S. standard of living. The longest expansion on record lasted 10 years, from March 1991 to March 2001. The longest contraction lasted five and a half years from 1873 to 1879.

Exhibit 2 shows annual percentage changes in real GDP since 1929. Years of declining real GDP are shown as red bars and years of increasing real GDP as blue bars. The big decline during the Great Depression of the early 1930s and the sharp jump during World War II stand in stark contrast. Growth since 1929 has averaged 3.3 percent a year.

The intensity of U.S. economic fluctuations varies across regions. A recession hits hardest those regions that produce capital goods, such as heavy machinery, and durable goods, such as appliances, furniture, and automobiles. The demand for these goods falls more during hard times than does the demand for other goods and services, such as breakfast cereal, gasoline, and haircuts.

Because of seasonal fluctuations and random disturbances, the economy does not move smoothly through phases of the business cycle. Economists can't always distinguish a temporary drop in economic activity from the beginning of a downturn.

EXHIBIT 2 Annual Percentage Change in U.S. Real GDP Since 1929

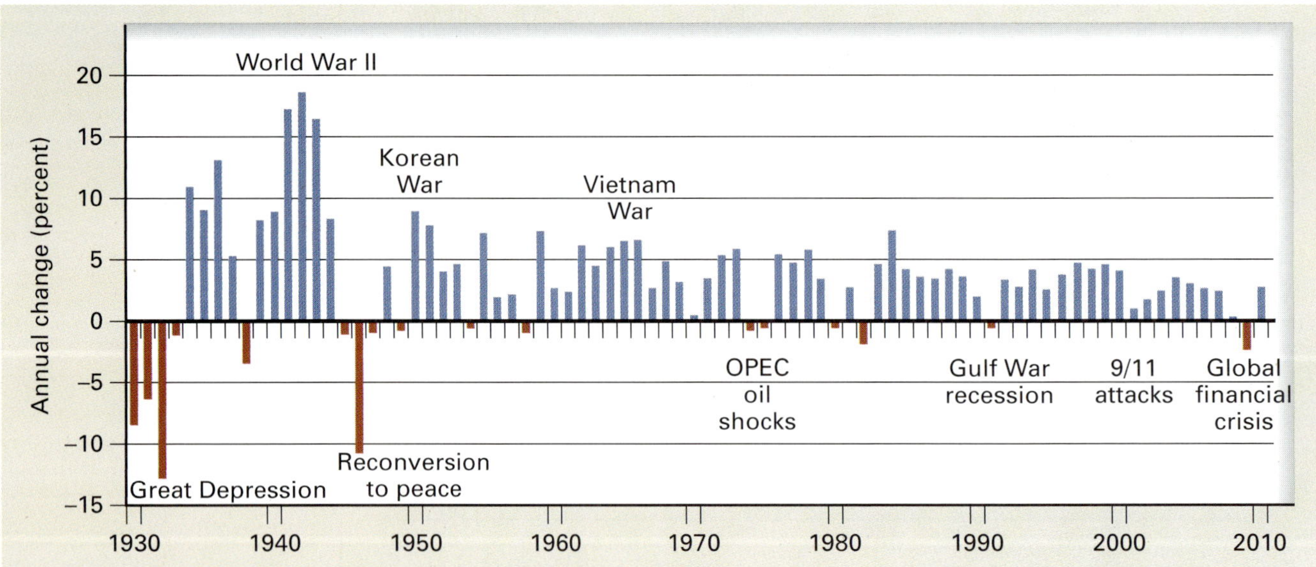

Years of declining real GDP are shown as red bars and years of growth as blue bars. Note that the year-to-year swings in output became less pronounced after World War II.

Source: Bureau of Economic Analysis, U.S. Dept. of Commerce. For the latest data, go to http://bea.gov/national/index.htm#gdp. Figure for 2010 is a projection from *OECD Economic Outlook*, 87 (May 2010), Table 1.

A drop in economic activity may result from a temporary slowdown, such as a snowstorm or a poor growing season. Turning points—peaks and troughs—are thus identified by the NBER only after the fact. Because a recession means economic activity declines for more than a few months (two quarters, or six months, is sometimes used as a rule of thumb), and because the official announcement that a recession has begun is not made until months after that, we sometimes don't know for sure when a recession starts until a year later (as was the case with the recession that began in December 2007). Likewise, a recession's end is sometimes not announced until a year or more after it's over (for example, the recent recession ended in June 2009, but the official announcement of that fact did not come until 15 months later).

As noted, fluctuations usually involve the entire nation. Indeed, major economies around the world often move together. For example, the Great Depression was a worldwide calamity. The unemployment rate in Germany reached 34 percent, which helped bring Adolf Hitler to power. Recession also spanned most of the globe as a result of the financial crisis of 2008. The case study, "World of Business: The Global Economy" at the end of the book, compares the year-to-year output changes in the United States with those in another major economy, the United Kingdom, during the last three decades.

Leading Economic Indicators

Certain events foreshadow a turning point in economic activity. Months before a recession is fully under way, changes in leading economic indicators point to the coming storm. In the early stages of a recession, business slows down, orders for machinery and computers slip, and the stock market, anticipating lower profits, turns down. Consumer confidence in the economy also begins to sag, so households spend less, especially on big-ticket items like homes and automobiles. Unsold goods start piling up. All these signs are called **leading economic indicators** because they usually predict, or *lead to,* a downturn. Likewise, upturns in leading indicators point to an economic recovery. But leading indicators cannot predict precisely *when* a turning point will occur, or even *whether* one will occur. Sometimes leading indicators sound a false alarm.

Some economic indicators measure what's going on in the economy right now. **Coincident economic indicators** are those measures that reflect expansions, contractions, peaks, and troughs as they occur. Coincident indicators include total employment, personal income, and industrial production. And some economic indicators measure what has already happened. **Lagging economic indicators** follow, or trail, changes in overall economic activity. Lagging indicators, which look at the economy through the rearview mirror, include interest rates, the unemployment rate, and how long people remain unemployed.

Our introduction to business cycles has been largely mechanical, focusing on the history and measurement of these fluctuations. We have not discussed why economies fluctuate, in part because such a discussion requires firmer footing in macroeconomic theory and in part because the causes remain in dispute. In the next section, we begin to build a macroeconomic framework by introducing a key model of analysis.

leading economic indicators
Variables that predict, or *lead to,* a recession or recovery; examples include consumer confidence, stock market prices, business investment, and big-ticket purchases, such as automobiles and homes

coincident economic indicators
Variables that reflect peaks and troughs in economic activity as they occur; examples include employment, personal income, and industrial production

lagging economic indicators
Variables that follow, or trail, changes in overall economic activity; examples include the interest rate and the average duration of unemployment

Aggregate Demand and Aggregate Supply

The economy is so complex that we need to simplify matters, or to abstract from the millions of relationships to isolate the important ones. We must step back from all the individual economic transactions to survey the resulting mosaic.

Aggregate Output and the Price Level

Let's begin with something you already know. Picture a pizza. Now picture food more generally. Food, of course, includes not just pizza but thousands of other items. Although food is more general than pizza, you probably have no difficulty picturing food. Now make the leap from food to all goods and services produced in the economy—food, housing, clothing, entertainment, transportation, health care, and so on. Economists call this **aggregate output**. Because *aggregate* means total, aggregate output is the total amount of goods and services produced in the economy during a given period. Because output is measured per period, it's a flow measure. The best measure of aggregate output is *real GDP*, which you'll soon learn more about.

aggregate output
A composite measure of all final goods and services produced in an economy during a given period; real GDP

aggregate demand
The relationship between the economy's price level and aggregate output demanded, with other things constant

price level
A composite measure reflecting the prices of all goods and services in the economy relative to prices in a base year

Just as we can talk about the demand for pizza, or the demand for food, we can talk about the demand for aggregate output. **Aggregate demand** is the relationship between the average price of aggregate output in the economy and the quantity of aggregate output demanded. The average price of aggregate output is called the economy's **price level**. You are more familiar than you may think with these aggregate measures. Headlines refer to the growth of aggregate output—as in "Growth Slows in Second Quarter." News accounts also report on changes in the "cost of living," reflecting movements in the economy's price level—as in "Prices Jump in June."

In a later chapter, you learn how the economy's price level is computed. All you need to know now is that the price level in any year is an *index number*, or a reference number, comparing average prices that year with average prices in some base, or reference, year. If we say that the price level is higher, we mean compared with where it was. In Chapter 4, we talked about the price of a particular product, such as pizza, *relative to the prices of other products*. Now we talk about the *average price* of all goods and services produced in the economy *relative to the price level in some base year*.

The price level in the *base year* is standardized to a benchmark value of 100, and price levels in other years are expressed relative to the base-year price level. For example, in 2009, the U.S. price level, or price index, was 109.8, indicating that the price level that year was 9.8 percent higher than its value of 100 in the base year of 2005. The price level, or price index, is used not only to compare prices over time but also to compare real aggregate output over time. Economists use the *price index* to eliminate year-to-year changes in GDP due solely to changes in the price level. What's left is the change in real output—the change in the amount of goods and services produced. After adjusting GDP for price level changes, we end up with what is called the **real gross domestic product**, or **real GDP**. So the price index (1) shows how the economy's price level changes over time and (2) is used to figure out real GDP each year. You'll get a better idea of these two roles as we discuss the U.S. economy.

real gross domestic product (real GDP)
The economy's aggregate output measured in dollars of constant purchasing power

Aggregate Demand Curve

In Chapter 4, you learned about the demand for a particular product, such as pizza. Now let's talk about the demand for our composite measure of output—aggregate output, or real GDP. The **aggregate demand curve** shows the relationship between the price level in the economy and real GDP demanded, other things constant. Exhibit 3 shows a hypothetical aggregate demand curve, *AD*. The vertical axis measures an index of the economy's price level relative to a 2005 base-year price level of 100. The horizontal axis shows real GDP, which measures output in dollars of constant purchasing power (here we use 2005 prices).

aggregate demand curve
A curve representing the relationship between the economy's price level and real GDP demanded per period, with other things constant

The aggregate demand curve in Exhibit 3 reflects an inverse relationship between the price level in the economy and real GDP demanded. Aggregate demand sums demands

EXHIBIT 3 Aggregate Demand Curve

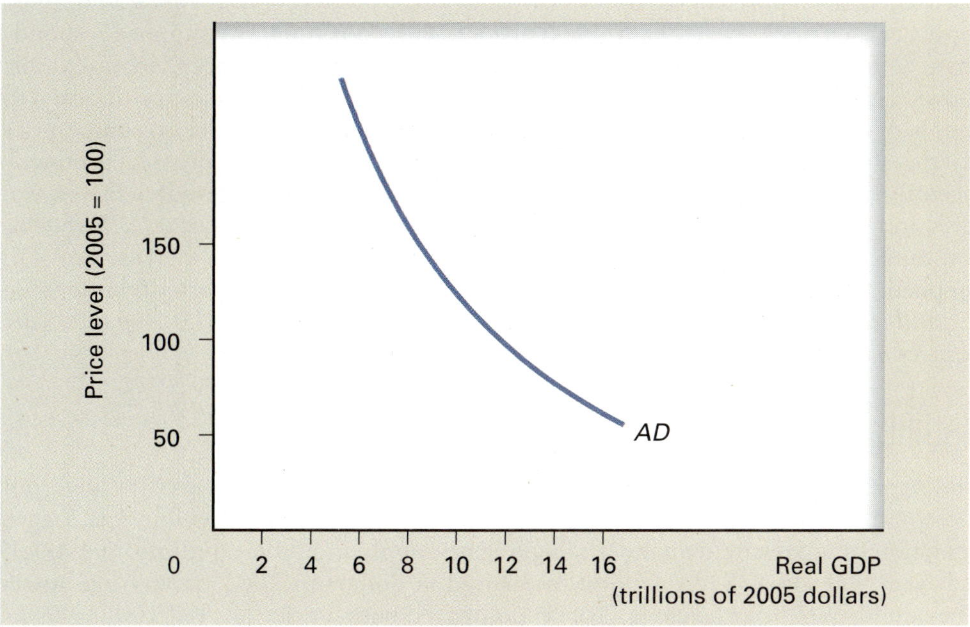

The quantity of aggregate output demanded is inversely related to the price level, other things constant. This inverse relationship is reflected by the aggregate demand curve *AD*.

of the four economic decision makers: households, firms, governments, and the rest of the world. As the price level increases, other things constant, households demand less housing and furniture, firms demand fewer trucks and tools, governments demand less computer software and military hardware, and the rest of the world demands less U.S. grain and U.S. aircraft.

The reasons behind this inverse relationship get a closer look in later chapters, but here's a quick summary. Real GDP demanded depends in part on household *wealth*. Some wealth is usually held in bank accounts and in currency. An increase in the price level, other things constant, decreases the purchasing power of bank accounts and currency. Households are therefore poorer when the price level increases, so the quantity of real GDP they demand decreases. Conversely, a reduction in the price level increases the purchasing power of bank accounts and currency. Because households are richer as the price level decreases, the quantity of real GDP they demand increases.

Factors held constant along a given aggregate demand curve include the price levels in other countries as well as the exchange rates between the U.S. dollar and foreign currencies. When the U.S. price level increases, U.S. products become more expensive relative to foreign products. Consequently, households, firms, and governments both here and abroad decrease the quantity of U.S. products demanded. On the other hand, a lower U.S. price level makes U.S. products cheaper relative to foreign products, so the quantity of U.S. products demanded increases.

Consider the demand for a particular product versus aggregate demand. If the price of a particular product, such as pizza, increases, quantity demanded declines in part because pizza becomes more costly compared to substitutes. If the economy's price level increases, the quantity of U.S. real GDP demanded declines in part because U.S. products become more costly compared to foreign products.

Aggregate Supply Curve

aggregate supply curve
A curve representing the relationship between the economy's price level and real GDP supplied per period, with other things constant

The **aggregate supply curve** shows how much U.S. producers are willing and able to supply at each price level, other things constant. How does quantity supplied respond to changes in the price level? The upward-sloping aggregate supply curve, *AS*, in Exhibit 4 shows a positive relationship between the price level and the quantity of real GDP supplied. Assumed constant along an aggregate supply curve are (1) resource prices, (2) the state of technology, and (3) the rules of the game that provide production incentives, such as patents and business practices. With regard to resource prices, wage rates are typically assumed to be constant along the aggregate supply curve. With wages constant, firms find a higher price level more profitable, so they increase real GDP supplied. *As long as the prices firms receive for their products rise faster than their cost of production, firms find it profitable to expand output, so real GDP supplied varies directly with the economy's price level.*

Equilibrium

The aggregate demand curve intersects the aggregate supply curve to determine the equilibrium levels of price and real GDP in the economy. Exhibit 4 is a rough depiction of aggregate demand and aggregate supply in 2009. Equilibrium real GDP that year was about $13.0 trillion (measured in dollars of 2005 purchasing power). The equilibrium price level was 109.8 (compared with a price level of 100 in the base year of 2005). At any other price level, quantity demanded would not match quantity supplied.

EXHIBIT 4 Aggregate Demand and Aggregate Supply in 2009

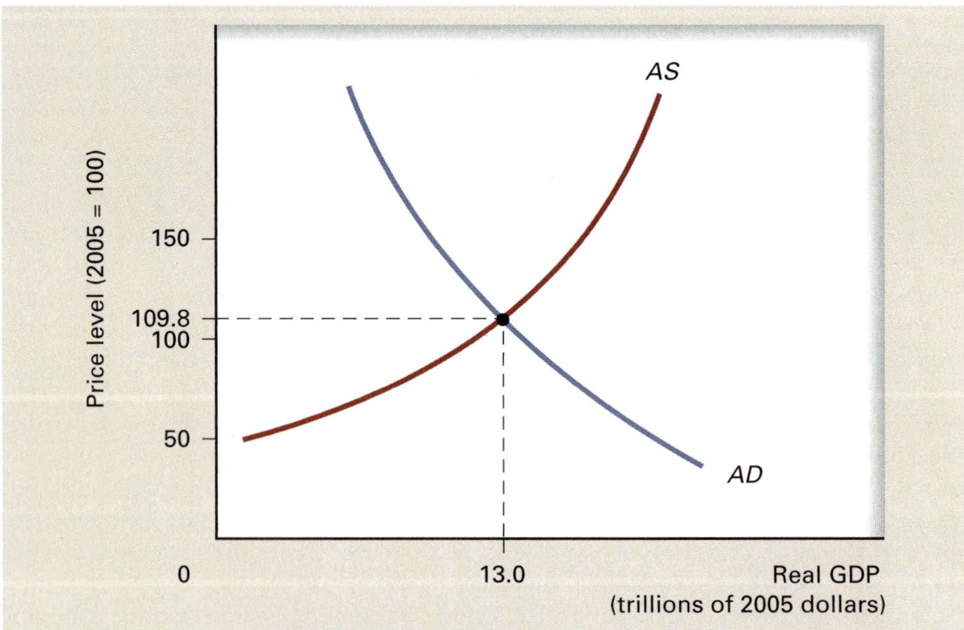

The total output of the economy and its price level are determined at the intersection of the aggregate demand and aggregate supply curves. This point reflects real GDP and the price level for 2009, using 2005 as the base year.

Incidentally, although employment is not measured directly along the horizontal axis, firms usually must hire more workers to produce more output. So higher levels of real GDP can be beneficial because (1) more goods and services become available in the economy, and (2) more people are usually employed. Perhaps the best way to understand aggregate demand and aggregate supply is to apply these tools to the U.S. economy. The following section simplifies U.S. economic history to review changes in the price and output levels over time.

Brief History of the U.S. Economy

The history of the U.S. economy can be divided roughly into five economic eras: (1) before and during the Great Depression, (2) after the Great Depression to the early 1970s, (3) from the early 1970s to the early 1980s, (4) from the early 1980s to 2007, and (5) the recession of 2007–2009 and beyond. The first era suffered from recessions and depressions, culminating in the Great Depression of the 1930s. These depressions were often accompanied by a falling price level. The second era was one of generally strong economic growth, with only moderate increases in the price level. The third era saw both high unemployment and high inflation at the same time, a troubling combination. The fourth era was more like the second, with good economic growth on average and only moderate increases in the price level. And the fifth era brought us the worst recession since the Great Depression. It remains to be seen whether the recession turns out to be just a temporary setback or has long-term consequences.

1. The Great Depression and Before

Before World War II, the U.S. economy alternated between hard times and prosperity. As noted earlier, the longest contraction on record occurred between 1873 and 1879, when 80 railroads went bankrupt and most of the nation's steel industry shut down. During the 1890s, the economy contracted about half the time, and the unemployment rate topped 18 percent. In October 1929, the stock market crash began what was to become the deepest, though not the longest, economic contraction in our nation's history, the Great Depression of the 1930s.

In terms of aggregate demand and aggregate supply, the Great Depression can be viewed as a shift to the left of the aggregate demand curve, as shown in Exhibit 5. AD_{1929} is the aggregate demand curve in 1929, before the onset of the depression. Real GDP in 1929 was \$977 billion (measured in dollars of 2005 purchasing power), and the price level was 10.6 (relative to a 2005 base-year price level of 100). By 1933, aggregate demand shifted leftward, decreasing to AD_{1933}. Why did aggregate demand decline? Though economists still debate the exact causes, most agree that the stock market crash of 1929 was the trigger. From there, grim business expectations cut investment, consumer spending fell, banks failed, the nation's money supply dropped by one-third, and world trade was severely restricted by high tariffs. All this contributed to a big decline in aggregate demand. The aggregate supply curve probably also shifted somewhat during this period, but the drop in aggregate demand was the dominant force.

Because of the decline in aggregate demand, both the price level and real GDP dropped. Real GDP fell 27 percent, from \$977 billion in 1929 to \$716 billion in 1933, and the price level fell 26 percent, from 10.6 to 7.9. As real GDP declined, unemployment soared from only 3 percent of the labor force in 1929 to 25 percent in 1933, the highest U.S. rate ever recorded.

EXHIBIT 5 The Decrease in Aggregate Demand From 1929 to 1933

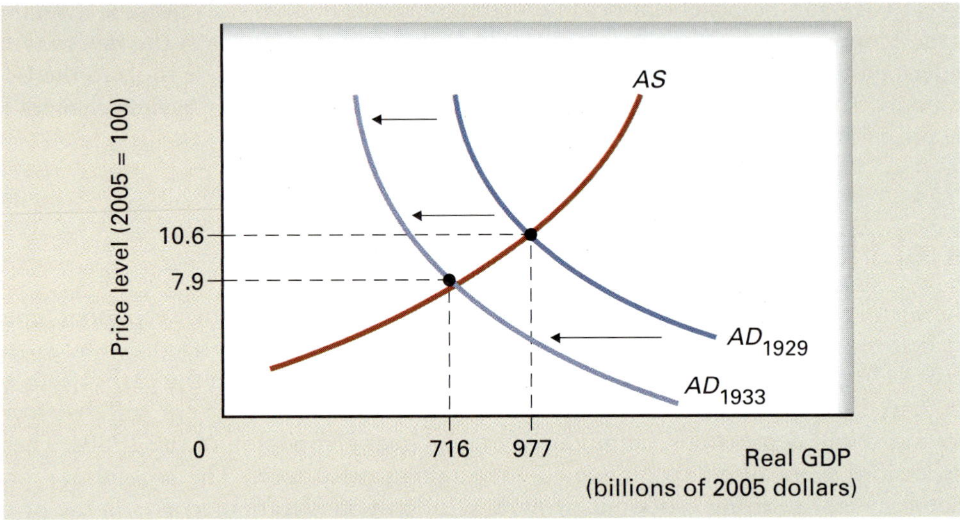

The Great Depression of the 1930s can be represented by a shift to the left of the aggregate demand curve, from AD_{1929} to AD_{1933}. In the resulting depression, real GDP fell from $977 billion to $716 billion, and the price level dropped from 10.6 to 7.9, measured relative to a price level of 100 in the base year 2005.

Before the Great Depression, macroeconomic policy was based primarily on the *laissez-faire* philosophy of Adam Smith. Smith, you may recall, argued in his famous book, *The Wealth of Nations*, that if people are allowed to pursue their self-interest in free markets, resources would be guided as if by an "invisible hand" to produce the most efficient and most valued level of aggregate output. Although the U.S. economy suffered many sharp contractions even before the Great Depression, most economists of the day viewed these as a natural phase of the economy—unfortunate for those who lost jobs and savings but ultimately therapeutic and *self-correcting*.

2. The Age of Keynes: After the Great Depression to the Early 1970s

The Great Depression was so deep that it stimulated new thinking about how the economy worked (or didn't work). In 1936, John Maynard Keynes (1883–1946) published *The General Theory of Employment, Interest, and Money,* the most famous economics book of the 20th century. In it, he argued that aggregate demand was inherently unstable, in part because investment decisions were often guided by the unpredictable "animal spirits" of business expectations. If businesses grew pessimistic about the economy, they would invest less, which would reduce aggregate demand, output, and employment. For example, investment dropped more than 80 percent between 1929 and 1933. Keynes saw no natural market forces operating to ensure that the economy, even if allowed a reasonable time to adjust, would get output and employment growing again.

Keynes proposed that the government jolt the economy out of its depression by increasing aggregate demand. He recommended an expansionary fiscal policy to help offset contractions. The government could achieve this stimulus either directly by increasing its own spending, or indirectly by cutting taxes to stimulate consumption and investment. But either action would likely create a federal budget deficit. A **federal budget deficit** is a flow variable that measures, for a particular period, the amount by which federal outlays exceed federal revenues.

federal budget deficit
A flow variable measuring the amount by which federal government outlays exceed federal government revenues in a particular period, usually a year

To understand what Keynes had in mind, imagine federal budget policies that would increase aggregate demand in Exhibit 5, shifting the aggregate demand curve to the right, back to its original position. Such a shift would raise real GDP, which would increase employment. According to the Keynesian prescription, the miracle drug of fiscal policy—changes in government spending and taxes—could compensate for what he viewed as the instability of private-sector spending, especially investment. If demand in the private sector declined, Keynes said the government should pick up the slack. We can think of the Keynesian approach as **demand-side economics** because it focused on how changes in aggregate demand might promote full employment. Keynes argued that government stimulus could shock the economy out of its depression. Once investment returned to normal levels, and the economy started growing on its own, the government's shock treatment would no longer be necessary.

demand-side economics
Macroeconomic policy that focuses on shifting the aggregate demand curve as a way of promoting full employment and price stability

The U.S. economy bounced back beginning in 1933, growing four years in a row (see Exhibit 2 again). The outbreak of World War II boosted employment to fight for the country and to make tanks, ships, aircraft, and the like. Federal government spending increased from 7 percent of GDP in 1940 to 46 percent in 1944. The explosion of output and sharp drop in unemployment seemed to confirm the powerful role government spending could play in the economy. The increase in government spending, with no significant increase in tax rates, created large federal deficits during the war.

Immediately after the war, memories of the Great Depression were still vivid. Trying to avoid another depression, Congress approved the *Employment Act of 1946,* which imposed a clear responsibility on the federal government to promote "maximum employment, production, and purchasing power." The act also required the president to appoint a *Council of Economic Advisers,* a three-member team of economists to provide economic advice and report on the economy.

The economy seemed to prosper during the 1950s largely without added stimulus from fiscal policy. The 1960s, however, proved to be the *golden age of Keynesian economics,* a period when fiscal policy makers thought they could "fine-tune" the economy for top performance—just as a mechanic fine-tunes a racecar. During the early 1960s, nearly all advanced economies around the world enjoyed low unemployment and healthy growth with only modest inflation.

The U.S. economy was on such a roll that toward the end of the 1960s some economists believed the business cycle was history. As a sign of the times, the name of a federal publication, *Business Cycle Developments,* was changed to *Business Conditions Digest.* In the early 1970s, however, the business cycle returned with a fury. Worse yet, the problems of recession were compounded by higher inflation, which increased during the recessions of 1973–1975 and 1980. Prior to that, high inflation was limited primarily to periods of expansion—that is, to boom times. Confidence in demand-side policies was shaken, and the expression "fine-tuning" dropped from the economic vocabulary. What ended the golden age of Keynesian economics?

3. Stagflation: 1973 to 1980

During the late 1960s, federal spending increased on both the war in Vietnam and social programs at home. This combined stimulus increased aggregate demand enough that in 1968 the *inflation rate,* the annual percentage increase in the price level, rose to 4.4 percent, after averaging only 2.0 percent during the previous decade. Inflation climbed to 4.9 percent in 1969 and to 5.3 percent in 1970. These rates were so alarming at the time that in 1971, President Richard Nixon imposed ceilings on prices and wages. Those ceilings were eliminated in 1973, about the time that crop failures around the world caused grain prices to soar. To compound these problems, the Organization of Petroleum Exporting Countries (OPEC) cut its supply of oil to world markets, so oil prices jumped. Crop failures plus the OPEC action reduced aggregate supply, shown in Exhibit 6 by the leftward shift of the aggregate supply curve from AS_{1973} to AS_{1975}. This resulted in **stagflation**, meaning a *stag*nation, or a contraction, in the economy's aggregate output and in*flation*, or increase, in the economy's price level. Real GDP declined between 1973 and 1975, and unemployment climbed from 4.9 percent to 8.5 percent. During the same two-year period, the price level jumped by 20 percent.

stagflation
A contraction, or *stag*nation, of a nation's output accompanied by in*flation* in the price level

Stagflation hit again five years later, stoked again by more OPEC cutbacks. Between 1979 and 1980, real GDP declined but the price level increased by 9.1 percent. Macroeconomics has not been the same since. Because stagflation was on the supply side, not on the demand side, the demand-management prescriptions of Keynes seemed ineffective. Increasing aggregate demand might reduce unemployment but would worsen inflation.

4. Relatively Normal Times: 1980 to 2007

Increasing aggregate supply seemed an appropriate way to combat stagflation, for such a move would both lower the price level and increase output and employment. Attention thus turned from aggregate demand to aggregate supply. A key idea behind **supply-side economics** was that the federal government, by lowering tax rates, would increase after-tax wages, which would provide incentives to increase the supply of labor

supply-side economics
Macroeconomic policy that focuses on a rightward shift of the aggregate supply curve through tax cuts or other changes to increase production incentives

EXHIBIT 6 Stagflation From 1973 to 1975

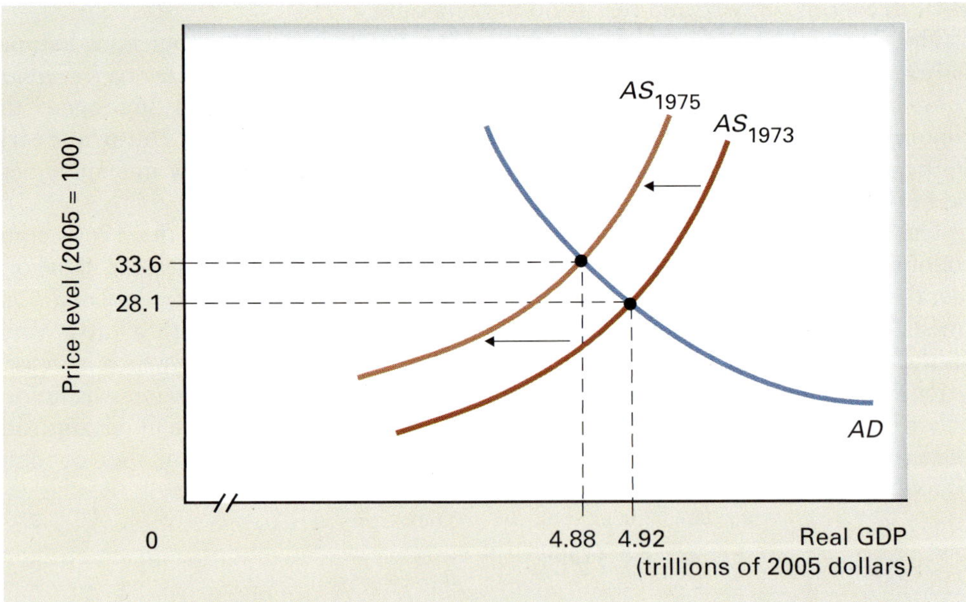

The stagflation of the mid-1970s can be represented as a leftward shift of the aggregate supply curve from AS_{1973} to AS_{1975}. Aggregate output fell from $4.92 trillion in 1973 to $4.88 trillion in 1975, for a decline of about $40 billion (*stagnation*). The price level rose from 28.1 to 33.6, for a growth of 20 percent (in*flation*).

and other resources. According to advocates of the supply-side approach, the resulting increase in aggregate supply would achieve the happy result of expanding real GDP and reducing the price level. You can get the idea behind supply-side economics in Exhibit 6 by picturing the aggregate supply curve as shifting back to the right from AS_{1975} to AS_{1973}. Such a move would increase real GDP while lowering the price level. But this was easier said than done.

In 1981, to provide economic incentives to increase aggregate supply, President Ronald Reagan and Congress cut personal income tax rates by an average of 23 percent to be phased in over three years. They believed that lower tax rates would increase aggregate supply, thereby expanding output and employment. They hoped that higher tax revenue from a larger economy would more than make up for the revenue lost by the cut in tax rates. In other words, the tax cutters hoped that the government's smaller share of a bigger pie would exceed what had been its larger share of a smaller pie.

But even before the tax cut took effect, recession hit, contracting output and pushing the unemployment rate up to 10 percent. Once the recession ended in late 1982, the economy began to grow, and this growth continued for the rest of the decade. Between 1980 and 1990 employment grew 20 percent and real GDP grew 38 percent, an indication that each worker was producing more. But the growth in federal spending exceeded the growth in federal tax revenues during this period, so federal budget deficits increased. Deficits worsened with the onset of a recession in 1990–1991, which was brought on by the first war in the Persian Gulf. Annual deficits accumulated as a growing federal debt. The **federal debt** is a stock variable that measures the net accumulation of prior federal deficits. But robust economic growth during the 1990s boosted employment by 15 percent and real GDP by 40 percent, again an indication that output per worker was growing nicely. The expanding economy combined with a booming stock market to increase tax revenue enough to yield a federal budget surplus by the end of the 1990s. By early 2001, the U.S. economic expansion had lasted ten years to become the longest on record. Then the economy slipped into a short recession aggravated by the terrorist attacks of September 2001. The recession lasted only eight months, but the recovery was slow and uneven. President George W. Bush pushed through tax cuts "to get the economy moving again." But the tax cuts and spending programs increased the federal budget deficit, which exceeded $400 billion in 2004. Still, the employment grew 7 percent between 2000 and 2007, and real GDP grew 18 percent. That growth helped cut the budget deficit to $161 billion by 2007. In fact, during the quarter century between 1982 and 2007, employment grew 47 percent and real GDP grew 126 percent, quite an impressive performance and the envy of the world. Then things went bad.

federal debt
A stock variable that measures the net accumulation of annual federal deficits

5. The Recession of 2007–2009 and Beyond

By late 2007, the expansion, which began in late 2001, had lasted six years, about average for expansions since World War II. So it was not that surprising when the expansion peaked in December 2007; then the recession began, this time precipitated by declining home prices and rising foreclosures, as more borrowers failed to make their mortgage payments. With home prices falling, fewer were getting built, meaning fewer jobs in residential construction, furnishings, and other industries that rely on the housing sector. During the first eight months of the recession, U.S. job losses averaged 151,000 a month, in line with monthly losses during the prior two recessions. In early 2008, Washington tried to stimulate aggregate demand with a $117 billion tax rebate, but the result was disappointing. The softer economy and tax cuts nearly triple the federal deficit from $161 billion in 2007 to $459 billion in 2008; at the time this deficit seemed huge.

Fears about the effect of rising home foreclosures on the banking system fed into a full-scale global financial panic in September 2008, triggered by the collapse of Lehman Brothers, a Wall Street investment bank. Banks grew reluctant to lend, so credit dried up—a major problem for an economy that relies a lot on credit. Businesses cut investments sharply. Consumers cut their spending in the face of sliding home prices, mounting job losses, and a collapsing stock market. You could picture all this as a leftward shift of the aggregate demand curve. These events unfolded against the backdrop of a presidential election. Is it any wonder that voters went for "hope and change"?

After the collapse of Lehman Brothers and the freezing up of financial flows around the world, policy makers were emboldened to enact some extraordinary measures to shore up confidence in financial institutions, open up the flow of credit, and stimulate consumer spending. These included two huge programs: (1) the $700 billion Troubled Asset Relief Program, or TARP, aimed at stabilizing financial institutions, and (2) the $787 billion American Recovery and Reinvestment Act, or the stimulus bill, aimed at increasing aggregate demand (the estimated cost would rise to $862 billion). The effects of these programs are still being debated today and will be discussed in later chapters. One point to underscore now is just how extraordinary these measures were. What we know for sure is that these rescue programs tripled the federal deficit from $460 in 2008 to $1.4 trillion in 2009. That grew to $1.5 trillion in 2010.

We also know that during the 12 months following the failure of Lehman Brothers, job losses averaged 565,000 a month, nearly four times the average during the two prior recessions and during the first eight months of 2008. Job losses on that scale had not been experienced since the Great Depression. Altogether, employment fell by 8.4 million between December 2007 and December 2009, a drop of 6.1 percent. Despite the sizable job losses, real GDP didn't fall that much. Because those who still had jobs were more productive, output dropped only about 2 percent between 2007 and 2009, and the price level hardly budged. The recession ended in June 2009. By the third quarter of 2009, real GDP was growing again, though the unemployment rate remained stubbornly high deep into 2010. Events during the recession of 2007–2009 traumatized the economy. Lasting 18 months, this was the longest of the 11 recessions since World War II. This recession will be discussed in the course of these chapters.

Focusing on the ups and downs of the economy can miss the point that the U.S. economy over the long run has been an incredible creator of jobs and output—the most productive economy in the world. To underscore that point, read the case study, "Public Policy: U.S. Economic Growth Since 1929" at the end of the book.

Conclusion

Because macroeconomists have no test subjects and cannot rely on luck, they hone their craft by developing models of the economy and then searching for evidence to support or reject these models. In this sense, macroeconomics is retrospective, always looking at recent developments for hints about which model works best. The macroeconomist is like a traveler who can see only the road behind and must find the way ahead using a collection of poorly drawn maps. The traveler must continually check each map (or model) against the landmarks to see whether one map is more consistent with the terrain than the others. Each new batch of information about the economy causes macroeconomists to shuffle through their "maps" to check their models.

Macroeconomics often emphasizes what can go wrong with the economy. Sagging output, high unemployment, and rising inflation capture much of the attention, and we'll examine those problems in the next two chapters. But perhaps the most important performance measure is economic growth, and we'll devote a chapter to that after you learn more about real GDP, unemployment, and inflation.

Summary

1. Macroeconomics focuses on the national economy. A standard measure of performance is the growth of real gross domestic product, or real GDP, the value of final goods and services produced in the nation during the year.
2. The economy has two phases: periods of expansion and periods of contraction. No two business cycles are the same. Before 1945, expansions averaged 29 months and contractions 21 months. Since 1945, expansions have averaged 57 months and contractions 11 months. Despite the Great Depression and later recessions, the economy's output has grown thirteenfold since 1929 and employment has grown faster than the population.
3. The aggregate demand curve slopes downward, reflecting a negative, or inverse, relationship between the price level and real GDP demanded. The aggregate supply curve slopes upward, reflecting a positive, or direct, relationship between the price level and real GDP supplied. The intersection of the two curves determines the economy's real GDP and price level.
4. The Great Depression and earlier depressions prompted John Maynard Keynes to argue that the economy is unstable, largely because business investment is erratic. Keynes did not believe that contractions were self-correcting. He argued that whenever aggregate demand sagged, the federal government should spend more or tax less to stimulate aggregate demand. His demand-side policies dominated macroeconomic thinking between World War II and the late 1960s.
5. During the 1970s, higher oil prices and global crop failures reduced aggregate supply. The result was stagflation, the troublesome combination of declining real GDP and rising inflation. Demand-side policies appeared less effective in an economy suffering from a reduction in aggregate supply, because stimulating aggregate demand would worsen inflation.
6. Supply-side tax cuts in the early 1980s were aimed at increasing aggregate supply, thereby increasing output while dampening inflation. Output and employment grew nicely during the 1980s, but federal spending increased faster than federal tax revenue, resulting in a budget deficit that grew into the early 1990s. Output and employment also grew nicely during the 1990s. The expanding economy increased federal revenues enough to create a federal budget surplus by the end of the decade. But after the longest expansion on record, the economy experienced an eight-month recession in 2001. The economy started growing again, and the expansion lasted until the end of 2007.
7. After peaking in December 2007, the economy entered a recession because of falling home prices and rising foreclosure rates. The collapse of a Wall Street bank in September 2008 panicked financial markets around the world, cutting investment and consumption. Job losses were the highest since the Great Depression. Massive federal programs aimed at stabilizing the economy resulted in gigantic federal deficits. Economic growth returned in the second half of 2009, but the unemployment rate remained stubbornly high deep into 2010.

Key Concepts

Questions for Review

1. The National Economy Why do economists pay more attention to national economies (for example, the U.S. or Canadian economies) than to state or provincial economies (such as California or Ontario)?
2. The Human Body and the U.S. Economy Based on your own experiences, extend the list of analogies between the human body and the economy as outlined in this chapter. Then, determine which variables in your list are stocks and which are flows.
3. Stocks and Flows Differentiate between stock and flow variables. Give an example of each.
4. Economic Fluctuations Describe the various components of fluctuations in economic activity over time. Because economic activity fluctuates, how is long-term growth possible?

5. Economic Fluctuations Why doesn't the National Bureau of Economic Research identify the turning points in economic activity until months or even a year after they occur?

6. Case Study: The Global Economy (See page 742.) How are economic fluctuations linked among national economies? Could a recession in the United States trigger a recession abroad?

7. Leading Economic Indicators Define *leading economic indicators* and give some examples. You may wish to take a look at the Conference Board's index of leading economic indicators at http://www.conference-board.org/data/.

8. Aggregate Demand and Aggregate Supply Why does a decrease of the aggregate demand curve result in less employment, given an aggregate supply curve?

9. Aggregate Demand and Aggregate Supply Is it possible for the price level to fall while production and employment both rise? If it is possible, how could this happen? If it is not possible, explain why not.

10. Aggregate Demand Curve Describe the relationship illustrated by the aggregate demand curve. Why does this relationship exist?

11. Demand-Side Economics What is the relationship between demand-side economics and the federal budget deficit?

12. Stagflation What were some of the causes of the stagflations of 1973 and 1979? In what ways were these episodes of stagflation different from the Great Depression of the 1930s?

13. Recession of 2007–2009 How did the recession of 2007–2009 affect the economy?

14. Case Study: U.S. Economic Growth Since 1929 (See page 743.) The price level grew slightly faster than real GDP between 1947 and 2009. Does this mean that the rising price level masked an actual decline in output? Why or why not?

Problems and Exercises

15. Aggregate Demand and Supply Review the information on demand and supply curves in Chapter 4. How do the aggregate demand and aggregate supply curves presented in this chapter differ from the market curves of Chapter 4?

16. Aggregate Demand and Supply Determine whether each of the following would cause a shift of the aggregate demand curve, a shift of the aggregate supply curve, neither, or both. Which curve shifts, and in which direction? What happens to aggregate output and the price level in each case?

    a. The price level changes
    b. Consumer confidence declines
    c. The supply of resources increases
    d. The wage rate increases

17. Supply-Side Economics One supply-side measure introduced by the Reagan administration was a cut in income tax rates. Use an aggregate demand/aggregate supply diagram to show what effect was intended. What might happen if such a tax cut also shifted the aggregate demand curve?

Global Economic Watch Exercises

Login to www.cengagebrain.com and access the Global Economic Watch to do these exercises.

18. Global Economic Watch Go to the Global Economic Crisis Resource Center. Select Global Issues in Context. In the Basic Search box at the top of the page, enter the phrase "growth imperative." On the Results page, go to the News Section. Click on the link for the July 31, 2010, article "The Growth Imperative." What did the author David Brooks suggest as remedies for the poor condition of the U.S. business cycle?

19. Global Economic Watch Go to the Global Economic Crisis Resource Center. Select Global Issues in Context. In the Basic Search box at the top of the page, enter the phrase "leading indicators." Find an article no more than two years old about U.S. leading indicators. Find a similar article no more than two years old about leading indicators in a foreign country. Compare and contrast what the leading indicators in the two countries are forecasting.

Tracking the U.S. Economy

20

©iStockphoto.com/hfng

- How do we keep track of the most complex economy in world history?
- What's gross about the gross domestic product?
- What's domestic about it?
- If you make yourself a tuna sandwich, how much does your effort add to the gross domestic product?
- Because prices change over time, how can we compare the economy's production in one year with that in other years?

Answers to these and other questions are addressed in this chapter, which introduces an economic scorecard for a $14 trillion U.S. economy. That scorecard is the national income accounting system, which reduces a huge network of economic activity to a few aggregate measures.

As you will see, aggregate output is measured either by the spending on that output or by the income derived from producing it. We examine each approach and learn why they are equivalent. The major components and important equalities built into the national income accounts are offered here as another way of understanding how the economy works—not as a foreign language to be mastered before the next exam. The emphasis is more on economic intuition than on accounting precision. The body of the chapter provides the background you need for later chapters.

Some details about the national income accounts are offered in the appendix.

Topics discussed in this chapter include:

- National income accounts
- Expenditure approach to GDP
- Income approach to GDP
- Circular flow of income and expenditure
- Leakages and injections
- Limitations of national income accounting
- Consumer price index
- GDP price index

The Product of a Nation

How do we measure the economy's performance? During much of the 17th and 18th centuries, when the dominant economic policy was mercantilism, many thought that economic prosperity was best measured by the *stock* of precious metals a nation accumulated in the public treasury. Mercantilism led to restrictions on international trade, with the unintended consequence of reducing the gains from comparative advantage. In the latter half of the 18th century, François Quesnay became the first to measure economic activity as a *flow*. In 1758 he published his *Tableau Économique*, which described the *circular flow* of output and income through different sectors of the economy. His insight was likely inspired by his knowledge of blood's circular flow in the body—Quesnay was court physician to King Louis XV of France.

Rough measures of national income were developed in England two centuries ago, but detailed calculations built up from microeconomic data were refined in the United States during the Great Depression. The resulting *national income accounting system* organizes huge quantities of data collected from a variety of sources across America. These data were summarized, assembled into a coherent framework, and reported by the federal government. The conception and implementation of these accounts have been hailed as one of the greatest achievements of the 20th century. The U.S. national income accounts are the most widely copied and most highly regarded in the world and earned their developer, Simon Kuznets, the Nobel Prize in 1971 for "giving quantitative precision to economic entities."

National Income Accounts

How do the national income accounts keep track of the economy's incredible variety of goods and services, from hiking boots to Pilates classes? The *gross domestic product*, or GDP, measures the market value of all final goods and services produced during a year by resources located in the United States, regardless of who owns the resources. For example, GDP includes production in the United States by foreign firms, such as a Toyota plant in Kentucky, but excludes foreign production by U.S. firms, such as a Ford plant in Mexico.

GDP estimates are computed each quarter by the Bureau of Economic Analysis in Washington, D.C. On computation day, staff members follow a process that dates back half a century. The office is in "lockup." Communications with the outside are shut down—no cell phones, land lines, or Internet connections. Office drapes are drawn. Only certain people are allowed in and out. To estimate GDP, they review more than 10,000 streams of data describing economic activity. Nobody speaks the final GDP estimate aloud for fear that it could be overheard and exploited in securities markets. Once they estimate GDP and its components, they write a press release, make hundreds of copies, then lock all but one in a safe for distribution to the media the next morning at 8:30 A.M. Eastern Time. The single copy not locked away is delivered to the head of the president's Council of Economic Advisors, who could give the president a heads-up.

The national income accounts are based on the simple fact that *one person's spending is another person's income*. GDP can be measured either by total spending on U.S. production or by total income received from that production. The **expenditure approach** adds up spending on all final goods and services produced during the year. The **income approach** adds up earnings during the year by those who produce all that output. In the *double-entry bookkeeping system* used to track the economy, spending on aggregate output is recorded on one side of the ledger and income from producing that aggregate output is recorded on the other side.

expenditure approach to GDP
Calculating GDP by adding up spending on all final goods and services produced in the nation during the year

income approach to GDP
Calculating GDP by adding up all earnings from resources used to produce output in the nation during the year

Gross domestic product includes only **final goods and services,** which are goods and services sold to the final, or end, user. A toothbrush, a pair of contact lenses, and a bus ride are examples of final goods and services. Whether a sale is to the final user depends on who buys the product. When you buy chicken for dinner, that's reflected in GDP. When KFC buys chicken, however, that's not counted in GDP because KFC is not the final consumer. Only after the chicken is cooked and sold by KFC is the transaction counted in GDP.

final goods and services
Goods and services sold to final, or end, users

Intermediate goods and services are those purchased for additional processing and resale, like KFC's chicken. This change may be imperceptible, as when a grocer buys canned goods to restock shelves. Or the intermediate goods can be dramatically altered, as when a painter transforms a $100 canvas and $30 in oils into a work of art that sells for $5,000. Sales of intermediate goods and services are excluded from GDP to avoid the problem of **double counting,** which is counting an item's value more than once. For example, suppose the grocer buys a can of tuna for $1.00 and sells it for $1.50. If GDP counted both the intermediate transaction of $1.00 and the final transaction of $1.50, the recorded value of $2.50 would exceed its final value by $1.00. Hence, GDP counts only the market value of the final sale. As another example, in a recent year Walmart paid $287 billion for products it sold for $375 billion. If GDP counted both Walmart's intermediate transactions and final transactions, Walmart's impact on GDP would be $287 billion too high. GDP also ignores most of the secondhand value of used goods, such as existing homes, used cars, and used textbooks. These goods were counted in GDP when they were produced. But just as the services provided by the grocer and by Walmart are captured in GDP, so are the services provided by real estate agents, used-car dealers, and used-book sellers.

intermediate goods and services
Goods and services purchased by firms for further reprocessing and resale

double counting
The mistake of including both the value of intermediate products and the value of final products in calculating gross domestic product; counting the same production more than once

GDP Based on the Expenditure Approach

As noted already, one way to measure GDP is to add up spending on all final goods and services produced in the economy during the year. The easiest way to understand the spending approach is to sort aggregate expenditure into its components: consumption, investment, government purchases, and net exports. **Consumption,** or more specifically, *personal consumption expenditures,* consists of purchases of final goods and services by households during the year. Consumption is the largest spending category, averaging 70 percent of U.S. GDP during this past decade. Along with *services* like dry cleaning, haircuts, and air travel, consumption includes *nondurable goods,* like soap and soup,

consumption
Household purchases of final goods and services, except for new residences, which count as investment

and *durable goods*, like furniture and kitchen appliances. Durable goods are expected to last at least three years.

investment
The purchase of new plants, new equipment, new buildings, and new residences, plus net additions to inventories

physical capital
Manufactured items used to produce goods and services; includes new plants and new equipment

residential construction
Building new homes or dwelling places

inventories
Producers' stocks of finished and in-process goods

Investment, or more specifically, *gross private domestic investment*, consists of spending on new capital goods and on net additions to inventories. The most important investment is **physical capital,** such as new buildings and new machinery. Investment also includes new **residential construction.** Although it fluctuates from year to year, investment averaged 16 percent of U.S. GDP this past decade. More generally, investment consists of spending on current production that is not used for current consumption. A net increase to inventories also counts as investment because it represents current production not used for current consumption. **Inventories** are stocks of goods in process, such as computer parts, and stocks of finished goods, such as new computers awaiting sale. Inventories help manufacturers cope with unexpected changes in the supply of their resources or in the demand for their products.

Although investment includes purchasing a new residence, it excludes purchases of *existing* buildings and machines and purchases of financial assets, such as stocks and bonds. Existing buildings and machines were counted in GDP when they were produced. Stocks and bonds are not investments themselves but simply indications of ownership.

government purchases
Spending for goods and services by all levels of government; government outlays minus transfer payments

Government purchases, or more specifically, *government consumption and gross investment,* include government spending for goods and services—from clearing snowy roads to clearing court dockets, from buying library books to paying librarians. Government purchases averaged 19 percent of U.S. GDP during the last decade. Government purchases, and therefore GDP, exclude transfer payments, such as Social Security, welfare benefits, and unemployment insurance. Such payments are not true purchases by the government or true earnings by the recipients.

net exports
The value of a country's exports minus the value of its imports

The final spending component, net exports, reflects international trade in goods and services. Goods, or *merchandise* traded, include physical items such as bananas and HDTVs (stuff you can load on a ship). Services, or so-called *invisibles,* include intangible items, such as European tours and online customer service from India. Foreign purchases of U.S. goods and services are counted as part of U.S. GDP. But U.S. purchases of foreign goods and services are subtracted from U.S. GDP. **Net exports** equal the value of U.S. exports of goods and services minus the value of U.S. imports of goods and services. U.S. imports have exceeded U.S. exports nearly every year since the 1960s, meaning U.S. net exports have been negative. During the last decade, net exports averaged a negative 5 percent of GDP.

aggregate expenditure
Total spending on final goods and services in an economy during a given period, usually a year

With the expenditure approach, the nation's **aggregate expenditure** sums consumption, C; investment, I; government purchases, G; and net exports, which is the value of exports, X, minus the value of imports, M, or $(X - M)$. Summing these yields aggregate expenditure, or GDP:

$$C + I + G + (X - M) = \text{Aggregate expenditure} = \text{GDP}$$

GDP Based on the Income Approach

aggregate income
All earnings of resource suppliers in an economy during a given period, usually a year

The expenditure approach sums, or aggregates, spending on production. The income approach sums, or aggregates, income arising from that production. Again, double-entry bookkeeping ensures that the value of aggregate output equals the aggregate income paid for resources used to produce that output: the wages, interest, rent, and profit arising from production. The price of a Hershey Bar reflects the income earned by resource suppliers along the way. **Aggregate income** equals the sum of all the income earned by resource suppliers in the economy. Thus, we can say that

$$\text{Aggregate expenditure} = \text{GDP} = \text{Aggregate income}$$

EXHIBIT 1 Computing Value Added for a New Desk

Stage of Production	(1) Sale Value	(2) Cost of Intermediate Goods	(3) Value Added (3) = (1) − (2)
Logger	$ 20	—	$20
Miller	50	$ 20	30
Manufacturer	120	50	70
Retailer	200	120	80
		Market value of final good	$200

The value added at each stage of production is the sale price at that stage minus the cost of intermediate goods, or column (1) minus column (2). The values added at each stage sum to the market value of the final good, shown at the bottom of column (3).

A product usually goes through several stages involving different firms on its way to the consumer. A wooden desk, for example, starts as raw timber, which is typically cut by one firm, milled by another, made into a desk by a third, and retailed by a fourth. We avoid double counting either by including only the market value of the desk when sold to the final user or by *summing the value added at each stage of production*. The **value added** by each firm equals that firm's selling price minus payments for inputs from other firms. The value added at each stage is the income earned by resource suppliers at that stage. *The value added at all stages sums to the market value of the final good, and the value added for all final goods sums to GDP based on the income approach.* For example, suppose you buy a wooden desk for $200. This final market value gets added directly into GDP. Consider the history of that desk. Suppose the tree that gave its life for your studies was cut into a log and sold to a miller for $20, who converted the log to lumber that sold for $50 to a desk maker, who made the desk and sold it for $120 to a retailer, who sold it to you for $200.

value added
At each stage of production, the selling price of a product minus the cost of intermediate goods purchased from other firms

Column (1) of Exhibit 1 lists the selling price at each stage of production. If all these transactions were added up, the sum of $390 would exceed the $200 market value of the desk. To avoid double counting, we include only the value added at each stage, listed in column (3) as the difference between the purchase price and the selling price at that stage. Again, *the value added at each stage equals the income earned by those who supply their resources at that stage*. For example, the $80 in value added by the retailer consists of income to resource suppliers at that stage, from the salesperson to the janitor who cleans the showroom to the trucker who provides "free delivery" of your desk. The value added at all stages totals $200, which is both the final market value of the desk and the total income earned by all resource suppliers along the way.

To reinforce your understanding of the equality of income and spending, let's return to something introduced in the first chapter, the circular-flow model.

Circular Flow of Income and Expenditure

The model in Exhibit 2 outlines the circular flow of income and spending in the economy for not only households and firms, as was the case in Chapter 1, but governments and the rest of the world. The main stream flows clockwise around the circle, first as income from firms to households (in the lower half of the circle), and then as spending from households back to firms (in the upper half of the circle). For each flow of money, there is an equal and opposite flow of products or resources. Here we follow the money.

EXHIBIT 2 Circular Flow of Income and Expenditure

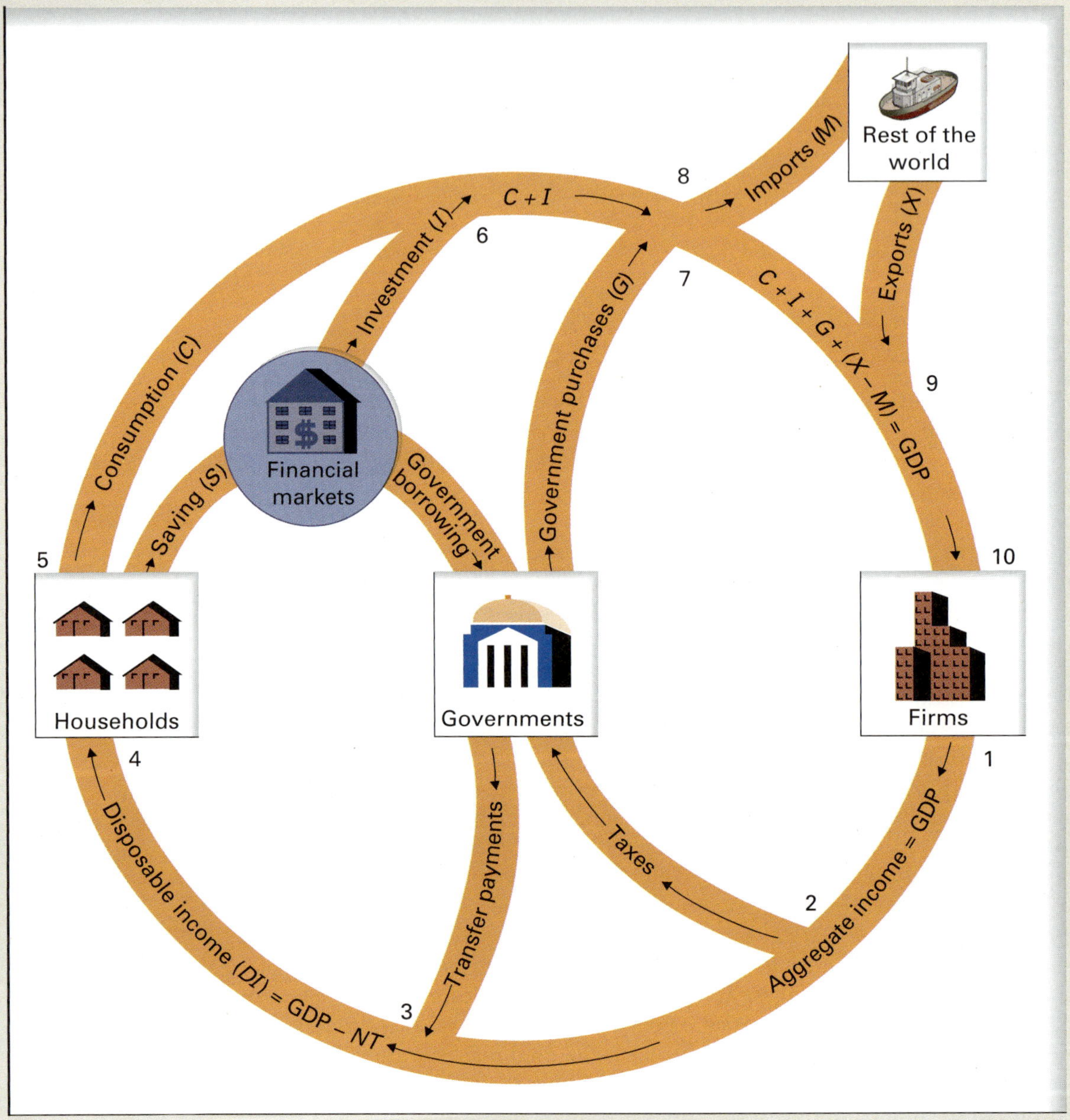

The circular-flow model captures important relationships in the economy. The bottom half depicts the income arising from production. At juncture (1), GDP equals aggregate income. Taxes leak from the flow at (2), but transfer payments enter the flow at (3). Taxes minus transfers equals net taxes, *NT*. Aggregate income minus net taxes equals disposable income, ***DI***, which flows to households at juncture (4). The top half of the model shows the flow of expenditure. At (5), households either spend disposable income or save it. Consumption enters the spending flow directly. Saving leaks from the spending flow into financial markets, where it is channeled to borrowers. At (6), investment enters the spending flow. At (7), government purchases enter the spending flow. At (8), imports leak from the spending flow, and at (9), exports enter the spending flow. Consumption plus investment plus government purchases plus net exports add up to the aggregate expenditure on GDP received by firms at (10).

Income Half of the Circular Flow

To develop a circular flow of income and spending, we must make some simplifying assumptions. Specifically, by assuming that physical capital does not wear out (i.e., no capital depreciation) and that firms pay out all profits to firm owners (i.e., firms retain no earnings), we can say that *GDP equals aggregate income*. The circular flow is a continuous process, but the logic of the model is clearest if we begin at juncture (1) in Exhibit 2, where U.S. firms make production decisions. After all, production must occur before output can be sold and income earned. As Henry Ford explained, "It is not the employer who pays the wages—the employer only handles the money. It is the product that pays wages." Households supply their labor, capital, natural resources, and entrepreneurial ability to make products that sell to pay wages, interest, rent, and profit. Production of aggregate output, or GDP, gives rise to an equal amount of aggregate income.

Thus, at juncture (1), aggregate output equals aggregate income. But not all that income is available to spend. At juncture (2), governments collect taxes. Some of these tax dollars return as transfer payments to the income stream at juncture (3). By subtracting taxes and adding transfers, we transform aggregate income into **disposable income, DI**, which flows to households at juncture (4). Disposable income is take-home pay, which households can spend or save.

disposable income (DI)
The income households have available to spend or to save after paying taxes and receiving transfer payments

The bottom half of this circular flow is the *income half* because it focuses on the income arising from production. Aggregate income is the total income from producing GDP, and disposable income is the income remaining after taxes are subtracted and transfers added. To simplify the discussion, we define **net taxes, NT**, as taxes minus transfer payments. So *disposable income equals GDP minus net taxes*. Put another way, we can say that aggregate income equals disposable income plus net taxes:

net taxes (NT)
Taxes minus transfer payments

$$\text{GDP} = \text{Aggregate income} = DI + NT$$

At juncture (4), firms have produced output and have paid resource suppliers; governments have collected taxes and made transfer payments. With the resulting disposable income in hand, households now decide how much to spend and how much to save. Because firms have already produced the output and have paid resource suppliers, firms wait to see how much consumers want to spend. Any unsold production gets added to firm inventories.

Expenditure Half of the Circular Flow

Disposable income splits at juncture (5). Part is spent on consumption, C, and the rest is saved, S. Thus,

$$DI = C + S$$

Consumption remains in the circular flow and is the biggest aggregate expenditure, about 70 percent of the total. Household saving flows to **financial markets**, which consist of banks and other financial institutions that link savers to borrowers. For simplicity, Exhibit 2 shows households as the only savers, though governments, firms, and the rest of the world could save as well (for example, savings from China finance U.S. borrowers). The primary borrowers are firms and governments, but households borrow too, particularly for new homes, and the rest of the world also borrows. In reality, financial markets should be connected to all four economic decision makers, but we have simplified the flows to keep the model from looking like a plate of spaghetti.

financial markets
Banks and other financial institutions that facilitate the flow of funds from savers to borrowers

In our simplified model, firms pay resource suppliers an amount equal to the entire value of output. With nothing left for investment, firms must borrow to finance purchases of physical capital plus any increases in their inventories. Households also borrow to purchase new homes. Therefore, investment, I, consists of spending on new capital by firms, including inventory changes, plus spending on residential construction. Investment enters the circular flow at juncture (6), so aggregate spending at that point totals $C + I$.

Governments must also borrow whenever they incur deficits, that is, whenever their total *outlays*—transfer payments plus purchases of goods and services—exceed their revenues. Government purchases of goods and services, represented by G, enter the spending stream in the upper half of the circular flow at juncture (7). Remember that G *excludes* transfer payments, which already entered the stream as income at juncture (3).

Some spending by households, firms, and governments goes for imports. Because spending on imports flows to foreign producers, spending on imports, M, leaks from the circular flow at juncture (8). But the rest of the world buys U.S. products, so foreign spending on U.S. exports, X, enters the spending flow at juncture (9). Net exports, the impact of the *rest of the world* on aggregate expenditure, equal exports minus imports, $X - M$, which can be positive, negative, or zero. In recent decades, net exports have been negative.

The upper half of the circular flow, the *expenditure half*, tracks the four components of aggregate expenditure: consumption, C; investment, I; government purchases, G; and net exports, $X - M$. Aggregate expenditure flows into firms at juncture (10). Aggregate expenditure equals the market value of aggregate output, or GDP. In short,

$$C + I + G + (X - M) = \text{Aggregate expenditure} = \text{GDP}$$

Leakages Equal Injections

Let's step back now to view the big picture. In the upper half of the circular flow, aggregate expenditure is total spending on U.S. output. In the lower half, aggregate income is the income arising from that spending. This is the first accounting identity. Aggregate expenditure (spending by each sector) equals aggregate income (disposable income plus net taxes), or

$$C + I + G + (X - M) = DI + NT$$

Because disposable income equals consumption plus saving, we can substitute $C + S$ for DI in the above equation to yield

$$C + I + G + (X - M) = C + S + NT$$

After subtracting C from both sides and adding M to both sides, the equation reduces to

$$I + G + X = S + NT + M$$

injection
Any spending other than by households or any income other than from resource earnings; includes investment, government purchases, exports, and transfer payments

leakage
Any diversion of income from the domestic spending stream; includes saving, taxes, and imports

Note that **injections** into the main stream occur at various points around the circular flow. Investment, I, government purchases, G, and exports, X, are *injections* of spending into the circular flow. At the same time, some of the circular flow leaks from the main stream. Saving, S, net taxes, NT, and imports, M, are **leakages** from the circular flow. As you can see from the equation, *injections into the circular flow equal leakages from the flow.* This injections-leakages equality demonstrates a second accounting identity based on double-entry bookkeeping.

Limitations of National Income Accounting

Imagine the difficulty of developing an accounting system that must capture such a complex and dynamic economy. In the interest of clarity and simplicity, certain features get neglected. In this section, we examine some limitations of the national income accounting system, beginning with production not captured by GDP.

Some Production Is Not Included in GDP

With some minor exceptions, GDP includes only those products that are sold in markets. This ignores all do-it-yourself production—child care, meal preparation, house cleaning, family laundry, and home maintenance and repair. Thus, an economy in which householders are largely self-sufficient has a lower GDP than an otherwise similar economy in which households specialize and sell products to one another. During the 1950s, more than 80 percent of American mothers with small children remained at home caring for the family, but all this care added not one cent to GDP. Today most mothers with small children are in the workforce, where their labor gets counted in GDP. Meals, child care, and the like are now often purchased in markets and thus get reflected in GDP. In less developed economies, more economic activity is do-it-yourself.

GDP also ignores off-the-books production. The term **underground economy** describes market activity that goes unreported because either it's illegal or because people want to evade taxes on otherwise legal activity. Although there is no official measure of the underground economy, most economists agree that it is substantial. A federal study suggests the equivalent of 10 percent of U.S. GDP is underground production; this would have amounted to about $1.5 trillion in 2011.

underground economy
Market transactions that go unreported either because they are illegal or because people involved want to evade taxes

For some economic activity, income must be *imputed*, or assigned a value, because market exchange does not occur. For example, included in GDP is an *imputed rental income* from home ownership, even though no rent is actually paid or received. Also included in GDP is an imputed dollar amount for (1) wages paid *in kind*, such as employers' payments for employees' medical insurance, and (2) food produced by farm families for their own consumption. *GDP therefore includes some economic production that does not involve market exchange.*

Leisure, Quality, and Variety

The average U.S. workweek is much shorter now than it was a century ago, so people work less to produce today's output. People also retire earlier and live longer after retirement. As a result of a shorter work week and earlier retirement, more leisure is available. But leisure is not reflected in GDP because it is not directly bought and sold in a market. The quality and variety of products available have also improved on average over the years because of technological advances and greater competition. For example, the magazine *Consumer Reports* finds a consistent improvement in the quality of the automobile over time. Yet most of these improvements are not reflected in GDP. Recording systems, computers, tires, running shoes, cell phones, and hundreds of other products have gotten better over the years. Also, new products are being introduced all the time, such as smartphones, e-readers, and energy drinks. *The gross domestic product fails to capture changes in the availability of leisure time and often fails to reflect changes in the quality of products or in the availability of new products.*

What's Gross About Gross Domestic Product?

In the course of producing GDP, some capital wears out, such as the delivery truck that finally dies, and some capital becomes obsolete, such as an aging computer that can't run the latest software. A new truck that logs 100,000 miles its first year has been subject to wear and tear, and therefore has a diminished value as a resource. A truer picture of the *net* production that actually occurs during a year is found by subtracting this

depreciation
The value of capital stock used up to produce GDP or that becomes obsolete during the year

net domestic product
Gross domestic product minus depreciation

capital *depreciation* from GDP. **Depreciation** measures the value of the capital stock that is used up or becomes obsolete in the production process. Gross domestic product is called "gross" because it fails to take into account this depreciation. **Net domestic product** equals gross domestic product minus depreciation, the capital stock used up in the production process.

We now have two measures of investment. *Gross investment* is the value of all investment during a year and is used in computing GDP. *Net investment* equals gross investment minus depreciation. The economy's production possibilities depend on what happens to net investment. If net investment is positive—that is, if gross investment exceeds depreciation—the economy's capital stock increases, so its contribution to output increases as well. If net investment is zero, the capital stock remains constant, as does its contribution to output. And if net investment is negative, the capital stock declines, as does its contribution to output.

As the names imply, *gross* domestic product reflects gross investment and *net* domestic product reflects net investment. But estimating depreciation involves some guesswork. For example, what is the appropriate measure of depreciation for the roller coasters at Six Flags, the metal display shelves at Walmart, or the parking lots at the Mall of America in Minnesota?

GDP Does Not Reflect All Costs

Some production and consumption degrades the quality of our environment. Trucks and automobiles pump pollution into the atmosphere, which may contribute to climate change. Housing developments displace scenic open space and forests. Paper mills foul the lungs and burn the eyes. Oil spills foul the coastline. These negative externalities—costs that fall on those not directly involved in the transactions—are mostly ignored in GDP calculations, even though they diminish the quality of life now and in the future. To the extent that growth in GDP generates negative externalities, a rising GDP may not be as attractive as it would first appear.

Although the national income accounts reflect the depreciation of buildings, machinery, vehicles, and other manufactured capital, this accounting ignores the depletion of natural resources, such as standing timber, oil reserves, fish stocks, and soil fertility. So national income accounts reflect depreciation of the physical capital stock but not the natural capital stock. For example, intensive farming may raise productivity and boost GDP temporarily, but this depletes soil fertility. Worse still, some production may speed the extinction of certain plants and animals. The U.S. Commerce Department is now in the process of developing so-called *green accounting*, or *green GDP*, trying to register the impact of production on air pollution, water pollution, soil depletion, and the loss of other natural resources.

GDP and Economic Welfare

In computing GDP, the market price of output is the measure of its value. Therefore, each dollar spent on handguns or cigarettes is counted in GDP the same as each dollar spent on baby formula or fitness programs. Positive economic analysis tries to avoid making value judgments about *how* people spend their money. Because GDP, as a number, provides no information about its composition, some economists question whether GDP is the best measure of the nation's economic welfare. One challenge to the dominance of GDP as a measure of national progress may come not from another single measure but from hundreds of measures compiled by a nonprofit group called The

State of the USA. This is discussed at the end of the book in the case study, "Public Policy: GDP and the State of the USA."

Despite the limitations of official GDP estimates, GDP offers a useful snapshot of the U.S. economy at a point in time. Inflation, however, clouds comparability over time. In the next section, we discuss how to adjust GDP for changes in the economy's price level.

Accounting for Price Changes

As noted earlier, the national income accounts are based on the market values of final goods and services produced in a particular year. Initially, gross domestic product measures the value of output in *nominal dollars*—that is, in the dollar values at the time production occurs. When GDP is based on nominal dollars, the national income accounts measure the *nominal value* of national output. Thus, **nominal GDP** is based on the prices prevailing when production takes place. National income accounts based on nominal dollars allow for comparisons among income or expenditure components in a particular year. Because the economy's average price level changes over time, however, nominal-dollar comparisons across years can be misleading. For example, between 1979 and 1980, nominal GDP increased by about 9 percent. That sounds impressive, but the economy's average price level rose more than 9 percent. So the growth in nominal GDP came entirely from inflation. Real GDP, or GDP measured in terms of the goods and services produced, in fact declined. If nominal GDP increases in a given year, part of this increase may simply reflect inflation—pure hot air. To make meaningful comparisons of GDP across years, we must take out the hot air, or *deflate* nominal GDP. We focus on *real* changes in production by eliminating changes due solely to inflation.

nominal GDP
GDP based on prices prevailing at the time of production

Price Indexes

To compare the price level over time, let's first establish a point of reference, a base year to which prices in other years can be compared. An *index number* compares the value of some variable in a particular year to its value in a base year, or reference year. Think about the simplest of index numbers. Suppose bread is the only good produced in an economy. As a reference point, let's look at its price in some specific year. The year selected is called the **base year**; prices in other years are expressed relative to the base-year price.

base year
The year with which other years are compared when constructing an index; the index equals 100 in the base year

Suppose the base year is 2009, when a loaf of bread in our simple economy sold for \$1.25. Let's say the price of bread increased to \$1.30 in 2010 and to \$1.40 in 2011. We construct a **price index** by dividing each year's price by the price in the base year and then multiplying by 100, as shown in Exhibit 3. For 2009, the base year, we divide the base price of bread by itself, \$1.25/\$1.25, or 1, so the price index in 2009 equals $1 \times 100 = 100$. *The price index in the base period is always 100*. The price index in 2010 is \$1.30/\$1.25, or 1.04, which when multiplied by 100 equals 104. In 2011, the index is \$1.40/\$1.25, or 1.12, which when multiplied by 100 equals 112. Thus, the index is 4 percent higher in 2010 than in the base year and 12 percent higher in 2011 than in the base year. The price index permits comparisons across years. For example, what if you were provided the indexes for 2010 and 2011 and asked what happened to the price level between the two years? By dividing the 2011 price index by the 2010 price index, 112/104, you find that the price level rose 7.7 percent.

price index
A number that shows the average price of products; changes in a price index over time show changes in the economy's average price level

EXHIBIT 3 Hypothetical Example of a Price Index (base year = 2009)

Year	(1) Price of Bread in Current Year	(2) Price of Bread in Base Year	(3) Price Index (3) = [(1)/(2)] × 100
2009	$1.25	$1.25	100
2010	1.30	1.25	104
2011	1.40	1.25	112

The price index equals the price in the current year divided by the price in the base year, all multiplied by 100.

This section has shown how to develop a price index assuming we already know the price level each year. Determining the price level is a bit more involved, as we'll now see.

Consumer Price Index

consumer price index, or CPI
A measure of inflation based on the cost of a fixed market basket of goods and services

The price index most familiar to you is the **consumer price index**, or **CPI**, which measures changes over time in the cost of buying a "market basket" of goods and services purchased by a typical family. For simplicity, suppose a typical family's market basket for the year includes 365 packages of Twinkies, 500 gallons of heating oil, and 12 months of cable TV. Prices in the base year are listed in column (2) of Exhibit 4. The total cost of each product in the base year is found by multiplying price by quantity, as shown in column (3). The cost of the market basket in the base year is shown at the bottom of column (3) to be $1,184.85.

Prices in the current year are listed in column (4). Notice that not all prices changed by the same percentage since the base year. The price of fuel oil increased by 50 percent, but the price of Twinkies declined. The cost of that same basket in the current year is $1,398.35, shown as the sum of column (5). To compute the consumer price index for the current year, we simply divide the cost in the current year by the cost of that same basket in the base year, $1,398.35/$1,184.85, and then multiply by 100. This yields a price index of 118. We could say that between the base period and the current year, the "cost of living" increased by 18 percent, although not all prices increased by the same percentage.

EXHIBIT 4 Hypothetical Market Basket Used to Develop the Consumer Price Index

Product	(1) Quantity in Market Basket	(2) Prices in Base Year	(3) Cost of Basket in Base Year (3) = (1) × (2)	(4) Prices in Current Year	(5) Cost of Basket in Current Year (5) = (1) × (4)
Twinkies	365 packages	$ 0.89/package	$324.85	$ 0.79	$288.35
Fuel Oil	500 gallons	1.00/gallon	500.00	1.50	750.00
Cable TV	12 months	30.00/month	360.00	30.00	360.00
			$1,184.85		$1,398.35

The cost of a market basket in the current year, shown at the bottom of column (5), sums the quantities of each item in the basket, shown in column (1), times the price of each item in the current year, shown in column (4).

The federal government uses the 36 months of 1982, 1983, and 1984 as the base period for calculating the CPI for a market basket consisting of hundreds of goods and services. The CPI is reported monthly based on prices collected from about 23,000 sellers across the country in 87 metropolitan areas. In reality, each household consumes a unique market basket, so we could theoretically develop about 115 million CPIs—one for each household.

Problems With the CPI

There is no perfect way to measure changes in the price level. As we have already seen, the quality and variety of some products are improving all the time, so some price increases may be as much a reflection of improved quality as of inflation. Thus, there is a *quality bias* in the CPI, because it assumes that the quality of the market basket remains relatively constant over time. *To the extent that the CPI ignores quality improvements, it overstates the true extent of inflation.* Those who come up with the CPI each month try to make some quality adjustments, as discussed in the case study, "Public Policy: Price Check on Aisle 2" at the end of the book.

But the CPI tends to overstate inflation for another reason. Recall that the CPI holds constant over time the kind and amount of goods and services in the typical market basket. Because not all items in the market basket experience the same rate of price change, relative prices change over time. A rational household would respond to changes in relative prices by buying less of the more expensive products and more of the cheaper products. The CPI allows for some substitution within narrow categories (for example shoppers in Chicago can switch among choices of ground beef based on price), but consumers can't easily switch across categories because the point of the CPI is to look at price changes over time for a given market basket. Because the CPI holds the market basket constant for long periods, the CPI is slow to incorporate consumer responses to changes in relative prices. *The CPI calculations, by not allowing households to shift away from goods that have become more costly, overestimates the true extent of inflation experienced by the typical household.*

The CPI has also failed to keep up with the consumer shift toward discount stores such as Walmart, Target, and Home Depot. Government statisticians consider goods sold by discounters as different from goods sold by regular retailers. Hence, the discounter's lower price does not necessarily translate into a reduction in the cost of living, but simply as a different consumer purchase decision.

Finally, the CPI overstates inflation because it includes an item in the market basket only after the product becomes widely used. By that time, the major price drops have already taken place. For example, the first portable video recorder and camera, the Ampex VR-3000 Backpack, weighed over 40 pounds and sold for $65,000. Now for less than $200 you can buy a high definition video camera that fits in your pocket. The CPI captured little of the major price drops. The same is true for all kinds of new products, such as the cell phone, which began as big as a brick and priced north of $1,000. Only after the price of cell phones fell far enough for wide adoption, did they make the CPI basket.

Experts conclude the CPI has overestimated inflation by about 1 percent per year. This problem is of more than academic concern because changes in the CPI determine changes in tax brackets and in an array of payments, including wage agreements that include a cost-of-living adjustment, Social Security benefits totaling more than $500 billion annually, welfare benefits, even alimony. In fact, about 30 percent of federal outlays are tied to changes in the CPI. A 1 percent correction in the upward bias of the CPI would save the federal budget nearly $200 billion annually by 2015.

Overstating the CPI also distorts other measures, such as wages, that use the CPI to adjust for inflation. For example, based on the official CPI, the average real wage in the U.S. economy fell by a total of about 2 percent in the last two decades. But if the CPI overstated inflation by 1 percent per year, as researchers now believe, then the average real wage, instead of dropping by 2 percent, actually increased by about 20 percent. The Bureau of Labor Statistics, the group that estimates the CPI, is now working on these problems and has introduced an experimental version of the CPI that would reduce measured inflation. One experiment uses scanner data at supermarkets to find out how consumers respond, for example, to a rise in the price of romaine lettuce relative to iceberg lettuce, two products assumed to be reasonable substitutes.

The GDP Price Index

GDP price index
A comprehensive inflation measure of all goods and services included in the gross domestic product

A price index is a weighted sum of various prices. Whereas the CPI focuses on just a sample of consumer purchases, a more complex and more comprehensive price index, the **GDP price index,** measures the average price of all goods and services produced in the economy. To calculate the GDP price index, we use the formula

$$\text{GDP price index} = \frac{\text{Nominal GDP} \times 100}{\text{Real GDP}}$$

where nominal GDP is the dollar value of GDP in a particular year measured in prices of that same year, and real GDP is the dollar value of GDP in a particular year measured in base-year prices. The challenge is finding real GDP in a particular year. Any measure of real GDP is constructed as the weighted sum of thousands of different goods and services produced in the economy. The question is what weights, or prices, to use. Prior to 1995, the Bureau of Economic Analysis (BEA) used prices for a particular base year (most recently 1987) to estimate real GDP. In this case, the quantity of each output in a particular year was valued by using the 1987 price of each output. So real GDP in, say, 1994 was the sum of 1994 output valued at 1987 prices.

Moving From Fixed Weights to Chain Weights

chain-weighted system
An inflation measure that adjusts the weights from year to year in calculating a price index, thereby reducing the bias caused by a fixed-price weighting system

Estimating real GDP by using prices from a base year yields an accurate measure of real GDP as long as the year in question is close to the base year. But BEA used prices that prevailed in 1987 to value production from 1929 to 1995. In early 1996, BEA switched from a fixed-price weighting system to a **chain-weighted system,** using a complicated process that changes price weights from year to year. All you need to know is that the chain-weighted real GDP adjusts the weights more or less continuously from year to year, reducing the bias caused by a fixed-price weighting system.

Even though the chain-type index adjusts the weights from year to year, any index, by definition, must still use some year as an anchor, or reference point—that is, any index must answer the question, "Compared to what?" To provide such a reference point, BEA measures U.S. real GDP and its components in *chained (2005) dollars.* Exhibit 5 presents nominal-dollar estimates of GDP as well as chained (2005) dollar estimates of real GDP. The blue line indicates nominal-dollar GDP since 1959. The red line indicates real GDP since 1959, or GDP measured in chained (2005) dollars. The two lines intersect in 2005, because that's when real GDP equaled nominal GDP. Nominal GDP is below real GDP in years prior to 2005 because real GDP is based on chained (2005) prices, which on average are higher than prices prior to 2005. Nominal GDP reflects growth in real GDP and in the price level. Chained-dollar GDP reflects growth only in real GDP. So nominal-dollar GDP grows faster than chained-dollar GDP.

EXHIBIT 5 U.S. Gross Domestic Product in Nominal Dollars and Chained (2005) Dollars

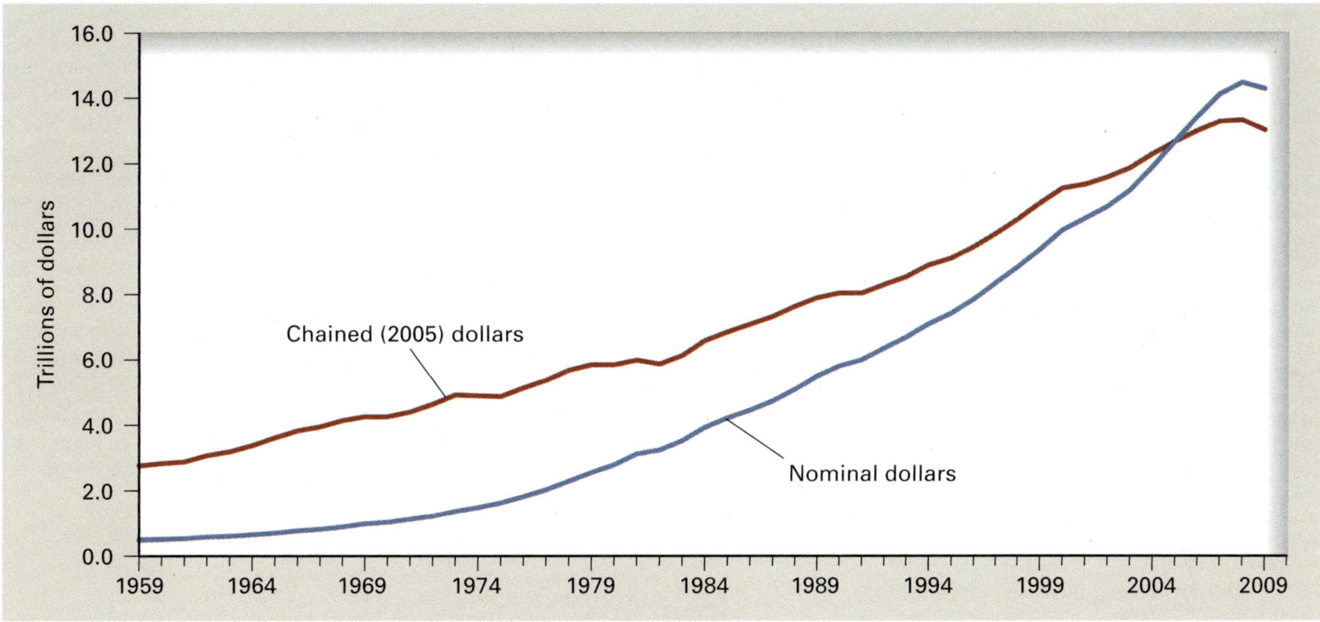

Real GDP, the red line, shows the value of output measured in chained (2005) dollars. The blue line measures GDP in nominal dollars of each year shown. The two lines intersect in 2005, when real GDP equaled nominal GDP. Year-to-year changes in nominal-dollar GDP reflect changes in both real GDP and in the price level. Year-to-year changes in chained-dollar GDP reflect changes in real GDP only. Nominal-dollar GDP grows faster than chained-dollar GDP. Prior to 2005, nominal-dollar prices are less than chained-dollar prices, so nominal-dollar GDP is less than chained-dollar GDP.

Source: Based on annual estimates from the Bureau of Economic Analysis, U.S. Department of Commerce. For the latest data, go to http://bea.gov/national/index.htm#gdp.

Conclusion

This chapter discussed how GDP is measured and how it's adjusted for changes in the price level over time. The national income accounts have limitations, but they offer a reasonably accurate picture of the economy at a point in time as well as year-to-year movements in the economy. Subsequent chapters will refer to the distinction between real and nominal values.

The national income accounts are published in much greater detail than this chapter indicates. The appendix provides some flavor of the additional detail available.

Summary

1. Gross domestic product, or GDP, measures the market value of all final goods and services produced during the year by resources located in the United States, regardless of who owns those resources.
2. The expenditure approach to GDP adds up the market value of all final goods and services produced in the economy during the year. The income approach to GDP adds up all the income generated as a result of that production.
3. The circular-flow model summarizes the flow of income and spending through the economy. The aggregate income from producing GDP equals the aggregate expenditure from purchasing that GDP. Thus, aggregate income equals aggregate expenditure. Saving, net taxes, and imports leak from the circular flow. These leakages equal the injections into the circular flow from investment, government purchases, and exports. Thus, leakages from the circular flow equal injections into the circular flow.
4. GDP reflects market production in a given period, usually a year. Most household production and the underground economy are not captured by GDP. Improvements in the quality and variety of products also are not fully reflected in GDP. Nor are changes in leisure captured in GDP. In other ways GDP may overstate the value of production. GDP fails to subtract for the depreciation of the capital stock or for the depletion of natural resources and fails to account for most negative externalities arising from production.
5. Nominal GDP in a particular year values output based on market prices when the output was produced. To determine real GDP, nominal GDP must be adjusted for price changes. The consumer price index, or CPI, tracks prices for a basket of goods and services over time. The GDP price index tracks price changes for all output. No adjustment for price changes is perfect, but current approaches offer a reasonably good estimate of real GDP both at a point in time and over time.

Key Concepts

Questions for Review

1. National Income Accounting Identify the component of aggregate expenditure to which each of the following belongs:
   a. A U.S. resident's purchase of a new automobile manufactured in Japan
   b. A household's purchase of one hour of legal advice
   c. Construction of a new house
   d. An increase in semiconductor inventories over last year's level
   e. A city government's acquisition of 10 new police cars
2. National Income Accounting Define gross domestic product. Determine which of the following would be included in the 2011 U.S. gross domestic product:
   a. Profits earned by Ford Motor Company in 2011 on automobile production in Ireland
   b. Automobile parts manufactured in the United States in 2011 but not used until 2012
   c. Social Security benefits paid by the U.S. government in 2011

d. Ground beef purchased and used by McDonald's in 2011
e. Ground beef purchased and consumed by a private U.S. household in 2011
f. Goods and services purchased in the United States in 2011 by a Canadian tourist

3. National Income Accounting Explain why intermediate goods and services usually are not included directly in GDP. Are there any circumstances under which they would be included directly?

4. Leakages and Injections What are the leakages from and injections into the circular flow? How are leakages and injections related in the circular flow?

5. Investment In national income accounting, one component of investment is net changes in inventories. Last year's inventories are subtracted from this year's inventories to obtain a net change. Explain why net inventory increases are counted as part of GDP. Also, discuss why it is not sufficient to measure the level of inventories only for the current year. (Remember the difference between stocks and flows.)

6. Limitations of National Income Accounting Explain why each of the following should be taken into account when GDP data are used to compare the "level of well-being" in different countries:

   a. Population levels
   b. The distribution of income
   c. The amount of production that takes place outside of markets
   d. The length of the average work week
   e. The level of environmental pollution

7. Nominal GDP Which of the following is a necessary condition—something that must occur—for nominal GDP to rise? Explain your answers.

   a. Actual production must increase.
   b. The price level must increase.
   c. Real GDP must increase.
   d. Both the price level and actual production must increase.
   e. Either the price level or real GDP must increase.

8. Price Indexes E-readers and HDTVs have not been part of the U.S. economy for very long. Both goods have been decreasing in price and improving in quality. What problems does this pose for people responsible for calculating a price index?

9. GDP and Depreciation What is gross about gross domestic product? Could an economy enjoy a constant—or growing—GDP while not replacing worn-out capital?

10. Consumer Price Index One form of the CPI that has been advocated by lobbying groups is a "CPI for the elderly." The Bureau of Labor Statistics currently produces only indexes for "all urban households" and "urban wage earners and clerical workers." Should the BLS produce such an index for the elderly?

11. GDP Price Index The health expenditure component of the GDP price index has been rising steadily. How might this index be biased by quality and substitution effects? Are there any substitutes for health care?

12. Case Study: GDP and the State of the USA (See page 745.) Is The State of the USA designed to replace GDP as the primary measure of economic performance?

13. Case Study: Price Check on Aisle 2 (See page 746.) What is the hedonic method and why is it sometimes used to track changes in the consumer price index?

Problems and Exercises

14. Income Approach to GDP How does the income approach to measuring GDP differ from the expenditure approach? Explain the meaning of *value added* and its importance in the income approach. Consider the following data for the selling price at each stage in the production of a 5-pound bag of flour sold by your local grocer. Use the value-added approach to calculate the final market value of the flour.

Stage of Production	Sale Price
Farmer	$0.30
Miller	0.50
Wholesaler	1.00
Grocer	1.50

15. Expenditure Approach to GDP Given the following annual information about a hypothetical country, answer questions a through d.

	Billions of Dollars
Personal consumption expenditures	$200
Personal taxes	50
Exports	30
Depreciation	10
Government purchases	50
Gross private domestic investment	40
Imports	40
Government transfer payments	20

a. What is the value of GDP?
b. What is the value of net domestic product?
c. What is the value of net investment?
d. What is the value of net exports?

16. INVESTMENT Given the following data, answer questions a through c.

	Billions of Dollars
New residential construction	$500
Purchases of existing homes	250
Sales value of newly issued stocks and bonds	600
New physical capital	800
Depreciation	200
Household purchases of new furniture	50
Net change in firms' inventories	100
Production of new intermediate goods	700

a. What is the value of gross private domestic investment?
b. What is the value of net investment?
c. Are any intermediate goods counted in gross investment?

17. CONSUMER PRICE INDEX Calculate a new consumer price index for the data in Exhibit 4 in this chapter. Assume that current-year prices of Twinkies, fuel oil, and cable TV are $0.95/package, $1.25/gallon, and $15.00/month, respectively. Calculate the current year's cost of the market basket and the value of the current year's price index. What is this year's percentage change in the price level compared to the base year?

18. CONSUMER PRICE INDEX Given the following data, what was the value of the consumer price index in the base year? Calculate the annual rate of consumer price inflation in 2012 in each of the following situations:

a. The CPI equals 200 in 2011 and 240 in 2012.
b. The CPI equals 150 in 2011 and 175 in 2012.
c. The CPI equals 325 in 2011 and 340 in 2012.
d. The CPI equals 325 in 2011 and 315 in 2012.

Global Economic Watch Exercises

Login to www.cengagebrain.com and access the Global Economic Watch to do these exercises.

19. GLOBAL ECONOMIC WATCH Go to the Global Economic Crisis Resource Center. Select Global Issues in Context. In the Basic Search box at the top of the page, enter the phrase "G.D.P. R.I.P." On the Results page, go to the Global Viewpoints Section. Click on the link for the August 10, 2009, article "G.D.P. R.I.P." What does the author mean by "gross domestic transactions"?

20. GLOBAL ECONOMIC WATCH Go to the Global Economic Crisis Resource Center. Select Global Issues in Context. In the Basic Search box at the top of the page, enter the phrase "price index." Write a summary of an article about a price index in a foreign country.

Appendix

National Income Accounts

This chapter has focused on gross domestic product, or GDP, the measure of output of most interest in subsequent chapters. Other economic aggregates also convey useful information and get media attention. One of these, *net domestic product*, has already been introduced. Exhibit 6 shows that net domestic product equals gross domestic product minus depreciation. In this appendix we examine other aggregate measures.

National Income

So far, we have been talking about the value of production from resources located in the United States, regardless of who owns them. Sometimes we want to know how much American resource suppliers earn for their labor, capital, natural resources, and entrepreneurial ability. **National income** captures all income earned by American-owned resources, whether located in the United States or abroad. To get the net value of production from American-owned resources, we add income earned by American resources abroad and subtract income earned by resources in the United States owned by those outside the country. We also account for any statistical discrepancy created by noise in the accounting system.

National income therefore equals net domestic product plus net earnings from American resources abroad minus the statistical discrepancy. Exhibit 6 shows how to go from net domestic product to national income. We have now moved from gross domestic product to net domestic product to national income. Next we peel back another layer from the onion to arrive at personal income, the income people actually receive.

Personal and Disposable Income

Some of the income received this year was not earned this year and some of the income earned this year was not received this year by those who earned it. By adding to national income the income received but not earned and subtracting the income earned but not received, we move from national income to the income *received* by individuals, which is called **personal income,** a widely reported measure of economic welfare. The federal government estimates and reports personal income monthly.

The adjustment from national income to personal income is shown in Exhibit 7. Income *earned but not received* in the current period includes the employer's share of Social Security taxes, taxes on production (e.g., sales and property taxes) net of subsidies, corporate income taxes, and undistributed corporate profits, which are profits the firm retains rather than pays out as dividends. Income *received but not earned* in the current

EXHIBIT 6 Deriving Net Domestic Product and National Income in 2009 (trillions)

Gross domestic product (GDP)	$ 14.26
Minus depreciation	−1.86
Net domestic product	12.40
Plus net earnings of American resources abroad	+0.11
Statistical discrepancy	−0.23
National income	$ 12.28

Source: Figures are nominal estimates for 2009 from the Bureau of Economic Analysis, U.S. Department of Commerce. For the latest figures, go to http://bea.gov/national/index.htm.

EXHIBIT 7 Deriving Personal Income and Disposable Income in 2009 (trillions)

National income	$ 12.28
Income received but not earned minus income earned but not received	−0.26
Personal income	12.02
Minus personal taxes and nontax charges	−1.10
Disposable income	$ 10.92

Source: Figures are nominal estimates for 2009 from the Bureau of Economic Analysis, U.S. Department of Commerce. For the latest figures, go to http://bea.gov/national/index.htm.

period includes government transfer payments, receipts from private pension plans, and interest paid by government and by consumers.

Although business taxes have been considered so far, we have not yet discussed personal taxes, which consist mainly of federal, state, and local personal income taxes and the employee's share of the Social Security tax. Subtracting personal taxes and other government charges from personal income yields *disposable income,* which is the amount available to spend or save—the amount that can be "disposed of" by the household. Think of disposable income as take-home pay. Exhibit 7 shows that personal income minus personal taxes and other government charges yields disposable income.

EXHIBIT 8 **Expenditure and Income Statement for the U.S. Economy in 2009 (trillions)**

Aggregate Expenditure	
Consumption (*C*)	$ 10.09
Gross investment (*I*)	1.63
Government purchases (*G*)	2.93
Net exports (*X* − *M*)	−0.39
GDP	$ 14.26

Aggregate Income	
Depreciation	$1.86
Net taxes on production	1.10
Statistical discrepancy	0.23
Compensation of employees	7.77
Proprietors' income	1.04
Corporate profits	1.31
Net interest	0.68
Rental income of persons	0.27
GDP	$ 14.26

Source: Figures are nominal estimates for 2009 from the Bureau of Economic Analysis, U.S. Department of Commerce. For the latest figures, go to http://bea.gov/national/index.htm.

Summary of National Income Accounts

Let's summarize the income side of national income accounts. We begin with *gross domestic product,* or *GDP,* the market value of all final goods and services produced during the year by resources located in the United States. We subtract depreciation from GDP to yield the *net domestic product.* To net domestic product we add net earnings from American resources abroad and allow for any statistical discrepancy to yield *national income.* We obtain *personal income* by subtracting from national income all income earned this year but not received this year (for example, undistributed corporate profits) and by adding all income received this year but not earned this year (for example, transfer payments). By subtracting personal taxes and other government charges from personal income, we arrive at the bottom line: *disposable income,* the amount people can either spend or save.

Summary Income Statement of the Economy

Exhibit 8 presents an annual income statement for the entire economy. The upper portion lists aggregate expenditure, which consists of consumption, gross investment, government purchases, and net exports. Because imports exceeded exports, net exports are negative. The aggregate income from this expenditure is allocated as shown in the lower portion of Exhibit 8. Some spending goes to cover depreciation, net taxes on production, and the statistical discrepancy; and so it's not received as income by anyone. What remains are five income sources: employee compensation, proprietors' income, corporate profits, net interest, and rental income of persons. *Employee compensation,* by far the largest income source, includes both money wages and employer contributions to cover Social Security taxes, medical insurance, and other fringe benefits. *Proprietors' income* includes the earnings of unincorporated businesses. *Corporate profits* are the net revenues received by incorporated businesses but before subtracting corporate income taxes. *Net interest* is the interest received by individuals, excluding interest paid by consumers to businesses and interest paid by government.

Each family that owns a home is viewed as a tiny firm that rents that home to itself. Because homeowners do not, in fact, rent homes to themselves, an imputed rental value is based on an estimate of market rent. *Rental income of persons* consists primarily of the imputed rental value of owner-occupied housing minus the cost of owning that property (such as property taxes, insurance, depreciation, and interest paid on the mortgage). From the totals in Exhibit 8, you can see that aggregate spending in the economy equals the income generated by that spending, thus satisfying the accounting identity.

Appendix Questions

1. NATIONAL INCOME ACCOUNTING Use the following data to answer the questions below:

	Billions of Dollars ($)
Net investment	110
Depreciation	30
Exports	50
Imports	30
Government purchases	150
Consumption	400
Production taxes (net of subsidies)	35
Income earned but not received	60
Income received but not earned	70
Personal income taxes	50
Employee compensation	455
Corporate profits	60
Rental income	20
Net interest	30
Proprietor's income	40
Net earnings of U.S. resources abroad	40

   a. Calculate GDP using the income and the expenditure methods.
   b. Calculate gross investment.
   c. Calculate net domestic product, national income, personal income, and disposable income.

2. NATIONAL INCOME ACCOUNTING According to Exhibit 8 in this chapter, GDP can be calculated either by adding expenditures on final goods or by adding the allocations of these expenditures to the resources used to produce these goods. Why do you suppose the portion of final goods expenditures that goes to pay for intermediate goods or raw materials is excluded from the income method of calculation?

Unemployment and Inflation

21

© David Young-Wolff/Photo Edit

- Who among the following would be counted as unemployed: a college student who is not working, a bank teller displaced by an automatic teller machine, Kristen Stewart between movies, or baseball slugger Alex Rodriquez in the off-season?
- What type of unemployment might be healthy for the economy?
- What's so bad about inflation?
- Why is anticipated inflation less of a problem than unanticipated inflation?

These and other questions are answered in this chapter, where we explore two macroeconomic problems: unemployment and inflation.

To be sure, unemployment and inflation are not the only problems an economy could face. Sluggish growth and widespread poverty are others. But low unemployment and low inflation go a long way toward reducing other economic problems. Although unemployment and inflation are often related, each is introduced separately. The causes of each and the relationship between the two will become clearer as you learn more about how the economy works.

This chapter shows that not all unemployment or all inflation harms the economy. Even in a healthy economy, a certain amount of unemployment reflects the voluntary choices of workers and employers seeking their best options. And low inflation that is fully anticipated creates fewer distortions than does unanticipated inflation.

Topics discussed include:

- Measuring unemployment
- Frictional, structural, seasonal, and cyclical unemployment
- Full employment
- Sources and consequences of inflation
- Relative price changes
- Nominal and real interest rates

Unemployment

"They scampered about looking for work. . . . They swarmed on the highways. The movement changed them; the highways, the camps along the road, the fear of hunger and the hunger itself, changed them. The children without dinner changed them, the endless moving changed them."[1] There is no question, as John Steinbeck writes in *The Grapes of Wrath*, a novel set in the Great Depression, that a long stretch of unemployment profoundly affects the jobless and their families. The most obvious loss is a steady paycheck, but the unemployed often lose self-esteem and part of their identity as well. Losing a job often means losing the social connections to coworkers. According to psychologists, in terms of stressful events, the loss of a good job ranks only slightly below a divorce or the death of a loved one. Moreover, unemployment appears to be linked to a greater incidence of crime and to a variety of afflictions, including heart disease, suicide, and clinical depression.[2] No matter how often people complain about their jobs, they rely on those same jobs not only for their livelihood but for part of their personal identity. When strangers meet, one of the first questions asked is "what do you do for a living?" Alfred Marshall wrote that your job is often the main object of your thoughts and intellectual development.

In addition to the personal costs, unemployment imposes a cost on the economy as a whole because fewer goods and services are produced. When those who are willing and able to work can't find jobs, their labor is lost forever. *This lost output coupled with the economic and psychological cost of unemployment on the individual and the family are the true costs of unemployment.* As we begin our analysis, keep in mind that the national unemployment rate reflects millions of individuals with their own stories. As President Harry Truman once remarked, "It's a recession when your neighbor loses his job; it's a depression when you lose your own." For some lucky people, unemployment is a brief vacation between jobs. For some others, a long stretch can have a lasting effect on family stability, economic welfare, self-esteem, and personal identity.

Measuring Unemployment

The unemployment rate is the most widely reported measure of the nation's economic health. What does the unemployment rate measure? What are the sources of unemployment? How has unemployment changed over time? These are some of the questions explored in this section. Let's first see how to measure unemployment.

We begin with the U.S. *civilian noninstitutional adult population*, which consists of all civilians 16 years of age and older, except those in prison, in mental facilities, or in homes for the aged. The adjective *civilian* means the definition excludes those in the military. From here on, references to the *adult population* mean the civilian noninstitutional adult population. The **labor force** consists of the people in the adult population who are either working or looking for work. *Those who want a job but can't find one are unemployed.* The Bureau of Labor Statistics interviews 60,000 households monthly (which translates into about 110,000 individuals) and counts people as unemployed if they have no job but want one and have looked for work at least once during the preceding four weeks. Thus, the college student, the displaced bank teller, Kristen Stewart,

labor force
Those 16 years of age and older who are either working or looking for work

1. John Steinbeck, *The Grapes of Wrath* (Viking, 1939): 293.
2. For a study linking a higher incidence of suicides to recessions, see Christopher Ruhm, "Are Recessions Good for Your Health," *Quarterly Journal of Economics*, 115 (May 2000): 617–650. Clinical depression is also higher among the unemployed, as demonstrated in Frederick Zimmerman and Wayne Katon, "Socioeconomic Status, Depression Disparities, and Financial Strain: What Lies Behind the Income-Depression Relationship," *Health Economics*, 14 (December 2004): 1197–1215.

and Alex Rodriguez would all be counted as unemployed if they want a job and looked for work in the previous month. The **unemployment rate** measures the percentage of those in the labor force who are unemployed. Hence, the unemployment rate, which is reported monthly, equals the number unemployed—that is, people without jobs who are looking for work—divided by the number in the labor force.

unemployment rate
The number unemployed as a percentage of the labor force

Only a fraction of adults who are not working are considered unemployed. The others may have retired, are students, are caring for children at home, or simply don't want to work. Others may be unable to work because of long-term illness or disability. Some may have become so discouraged by a long, unfruitful job search that they have given up in frustration. These **discouraged workers** have, in effect, dropped out of the labor force, so they are not counted as unemployed. Finally, about one-third of those working part time would prefer to work full time, yet all part-timers are counted as employed. Because the official unemployment rate does not include discouraged workers and counts all part-time workers as employed, it may underestimate the true extent of unemployment in the economy. Later we consider some reasons why the unemployment rate may exaggerate the true extent of unemployment.

discouraged workers
Those who drop out of the labor force in frustration because they can't find work

These definitions are illustrated in Exhibit 1, where circles represent the various groups, and the number (in millions) of individuals in each category and subcategory is shown in parentheses. The circle on the left depicts the entire U.S. labor force in April 2010, including both employed and unemployed people. The circle on the right represents those in the adult population who, for whatever reason, are not working. These two circles combined show the adult population. The overlapping area identifies the

EXHIBIT 1 **The Adult Population Sums the Employed, the Unemployed, and Those Not in the Labor Force: April 2010 (in millions)**

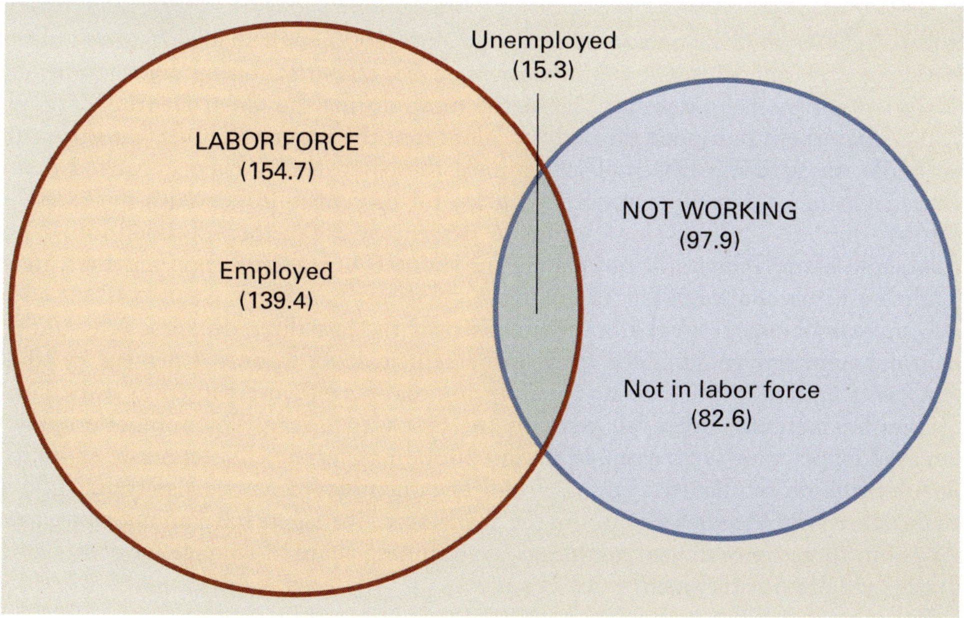

The labor force, depicted by the left circle, consists of those employed plus those unemployed. Those not working, depicted by the right circle, consists of those not in the labor force and those unemployed. The adult population sums the employed, the unemployed, and those not in the labor force.

Source: Figures are for April 2010 from the U.S. Bureau of Labor Statistics. For the latest data, go to http://www.bls.gov/news.release/empsit.toc.htm.

number of *unemployed* workers—that is, people in the labor force who are not working. The unemployment rate is found by dividing the number unemployed by the number in the labor force. In April 2010, 15.3 million people were unemployed in a labor force of 154.7 million, yielding an unemployment rate of 9.9 percent.

Labor Force Participation Rate

labor force participation rate
The labor force as a percentage of the adult population

The productive capability of any economy depends in part on the proportion of adults in the labor force, measured as the *labor force participation rate*. In Exhibit 1, the U.S. adult population equals those in the labor force (154.7 million) plus those not in the labor force (82.6 million)—a total of 237.3 million people. The **labor force participation rate** therefore equals the number in the labor force divided by the adult population, or 65 percent (= 154.7 million/237.3 million). So, on average, about two out of three adults are in the labor force. The labor force participation rate increased from 60 percent in 1970 to 67 percent in 1990, and has remained relatively steady since then.

One striking development since World War II has been the convergence in the labor force participation rates of men and women. In 1950, only 34 percent of adult women were in the labor force. Today 59 percent are, with the greatest increase among younger women. The labor force participation rate among men has declined from 86 percent in 1950 to 72 percent today, primarily because of earlier retirement. The participation rate is higher among white males than black males but higher among black females than white females. Finally, the participation rate climbs with education—from 43 percent for those without a high school diploma to 76 percent among those with a college degree.

Unemployment Over Time

Exhibit 2 shows the U.S. unemployment rate since 1900, with shaded bars to indicate periods of recession or depression. As you can see, rates rise during contractions and fall during expansions. Most striking is the jump during the Great Depression of the 1930s, when the rate topped 25 percent. Note that the rate trended upward from the end of World War II in the mid-1940s until the early 1980s; then it backed down, from a high of 10 percent in 1982 to a low of 4 percent in 2000. With the recession of 2001, the rate gradually increased to 6 percent by 2003, then declined into 2007. But the global financial crisis of 2008 and sharp U.S. recession boosted the rate to 10 percent by the end of 2009.

Let's examine some of the broad trends over the last three decades. Why did the unemployment rate trend down from 10 percent in 1982 to only 4 percent in 2000? First, the overall economy was on a roll during that period, interrupted by only a brief recession in the early 1990s triggered by the first war in Iraq. The number employed increased by 37 million between 1982 and 2000, making the U.S. economy an incredible job machine and the envy of the world. The unemployment rate also trended down because there were fewer teenagers in the workforce. Teenagers have an unemployment rate about three times that of adults, so the declining share of teenage workers helped cut the overall unemployment rate.

But job growth between 2000 and 2010 was hobbled by a recession in 2001 and a much sharper one in 2007–2009. Employment during the decade increased by only about 4 million, not nearly enough to absorb the 13 million people joining the labor force. As a result, the number unemployed swelled from 6 million in 2000 to 15 million in 2010, and the unemployment rate climbed from only 4 percent to 10 percent. This was the worst decade of employment growth since the Great Depression.

EXHIBIT 2 The U.S. Unemployment Rate Since 1900

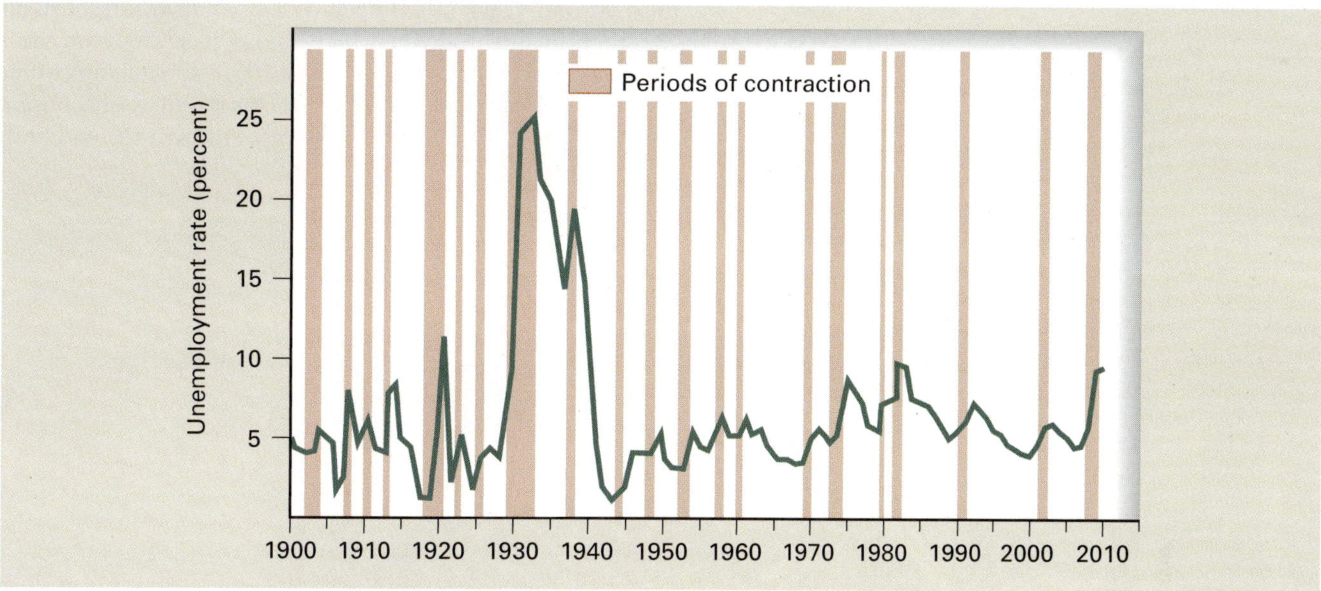

Since 1900, the unemployment rate has fluctuated widely, rising during contractions and falling during expansions. During the Great Depression of the 1930s, the rate spiked to 25 percent.

Sources: U.S. Census Bureau, *Historical Statistics of the United States: Colonial Times to 1970* (Washington, D.C. U.S. Government Printing Office, 1975); *Economic Report of the President,* February 2010; and U.S. Bureau of Labor Statistics. Figure for 2010 is estimated based on figures through June 2010, seasonally adjusted. For the latest unemployment rate, go to http://www.bls.gov/news.release/empsit.toc.htm.

Unemployment Among Various Groups

The unemployment rate says nothing about who is unemployed or for how long. The overall rate masks wide differences in the labor force based on education, race, gender, and age. For example, when the U.S. unemployment rate in April 2010 was 9.9 percent, the rate among workers 25 years of age or older who were high school dropouts was 14.7 percent; this was triple the rate among workers 25 or older who were college graduates. So education provides some insurance against unemployment. Unemployment also differs based on race and ethnicity; the rate was 9.0 percent among white workers, 16.5 percent among African Americans, 12.5 percent among those of Hispanic ethnicity, and 6.8 percent among Asian workers. Finally, the unemployment rate was 10.1 percent among males 20 and older, 8.2 percent among females 20 and older, and 25.4 percent among workers 16 to 19 years of age. Why is the unemployment rate among teenage workers so much higher than other workers? Teenagers enter the labor force with little education or job experience, so they take unskilled jobs and are first laid off if the economy slows down (last hired, first fired). Teenagers also move in and out of the labor force more frequently as they juggle school demands. Even those who have left school often shop around more than workers 20 and older, quitting one job in search of a better one.

Unemployment rates for different groups appear in Exhibit 3. Each panel shows the rate by race and by gender since 1972. Panel (a) shows the rates for workers 20 and older, and panel (b) the rates for 16- to 19-year-old workers. Periods of recession are shaded pink. As you can see, rates are higher among black workers than among white workers, and rates are higher among teenage workers than among those 20 and older. During recessions, rates climbed for all groups. Rates peaked during the recession of 1982 and then trended down. After the recession of the early 1990s, unemployment rates continued downward, with the rate among black workers falling in 2000 to the lowest on record. Rates rose again beginning with the recession of 2001, peaking at 6.0 percent in 2003. The rate then declined over the next four years, but jumped because of the sharp recession of 2007–2009. Exhibit 3 shows that the unemployment rate among black men was more than double that among white men. Notice that since the early 1990s the unemployment rate trended higher for a while even after each recession ended. This paradox of economic recovery with a higher unemployment rate is discussed in the case study, at the end of the book, "Public Policy: 'Hiring Picks Up, But Jobless Rate Rises.'"

EXHIBIT 3 Unemployment Rates for Various Groups

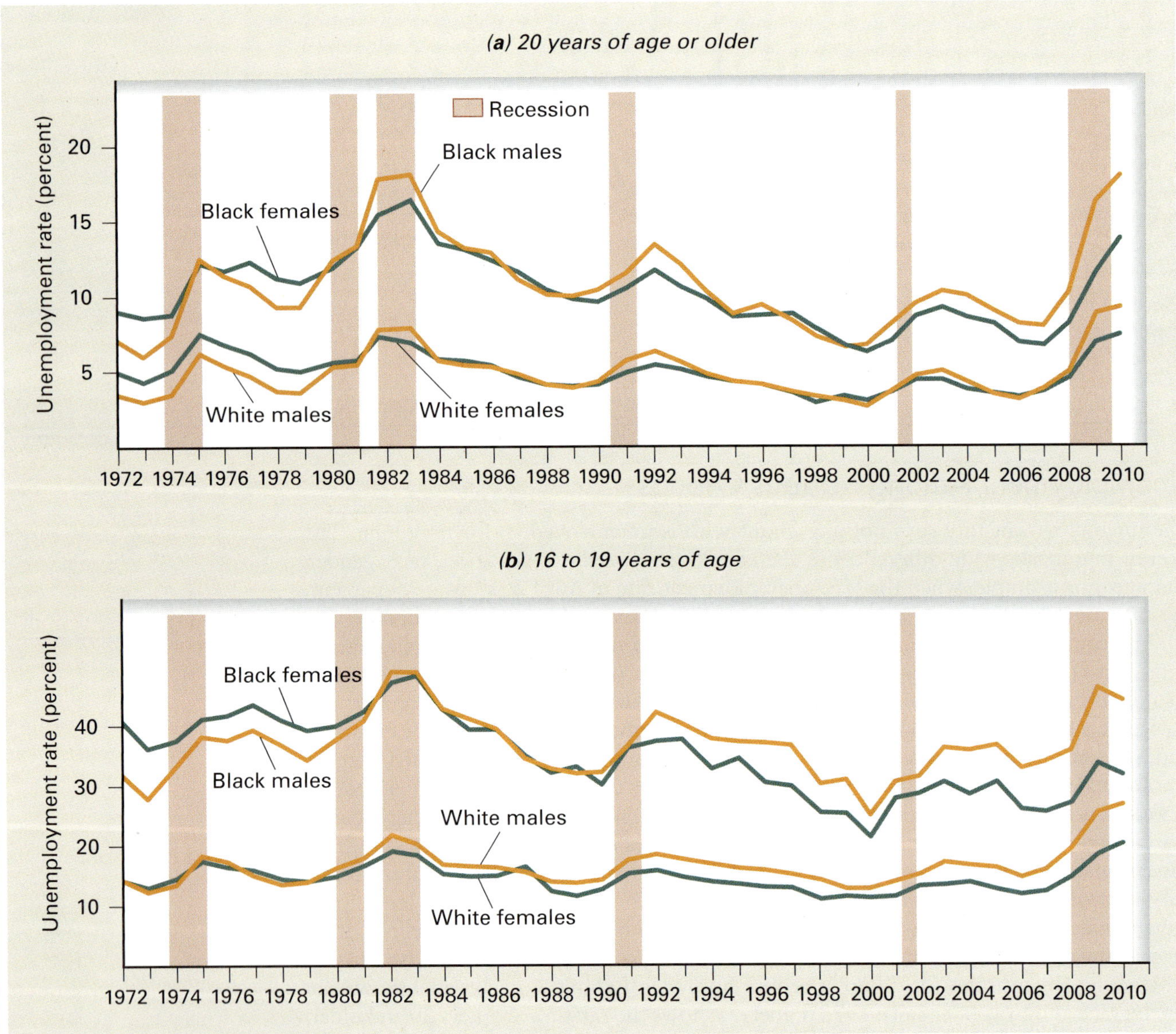

Different groups face different unemployment rates. The unemployment rate is higher for black workers than for white and higher for teenagers than for those 20 and older.

Source: *Economic Report of the President,* February 2010, Table B-43; and U.S. Bureau of Labor Statistics. Figures for 2010 are estimated based on figures through May 2010, seasonally adjusted. For the latest data, go to http://www.bls.gov/news.release/empsit.toc.htm.

Unemployment Varies Across Occupations and Regions

The unemployment rate varies by occupation. Professional and technical workers experience lower unemployment rates than blue-collar workers. Construction workers at times face high rates because that occupation is both seasonal and subject to wide swings over the business cycle.

Partly because certain occupations dominate labor markets in certain regions, unemployment rates also vary by region. For example, because of pressure on blue-collar jobs in smokestack industries such as autos and steel, in April 2010 unemployment rates in Illinois, Michigan, and Ohio were nearly triple those in the upper Midwest farm states of Nebraska, North Dakota, and South Dakota. Even within a state, unemployment can vary widely. For example, the California city of El Centro had nearly triple the unemployment rate of Santa Barbara.

Exhibit 4 shows unemployment rates for 27 major metropolitan areas in April 2010. As you can see, Detroit had the highest unemployment rate, at 14.8 percent. This

EXHIBIT 4 Unemployment Rates Differ Across U.S. Metropolitan Areas

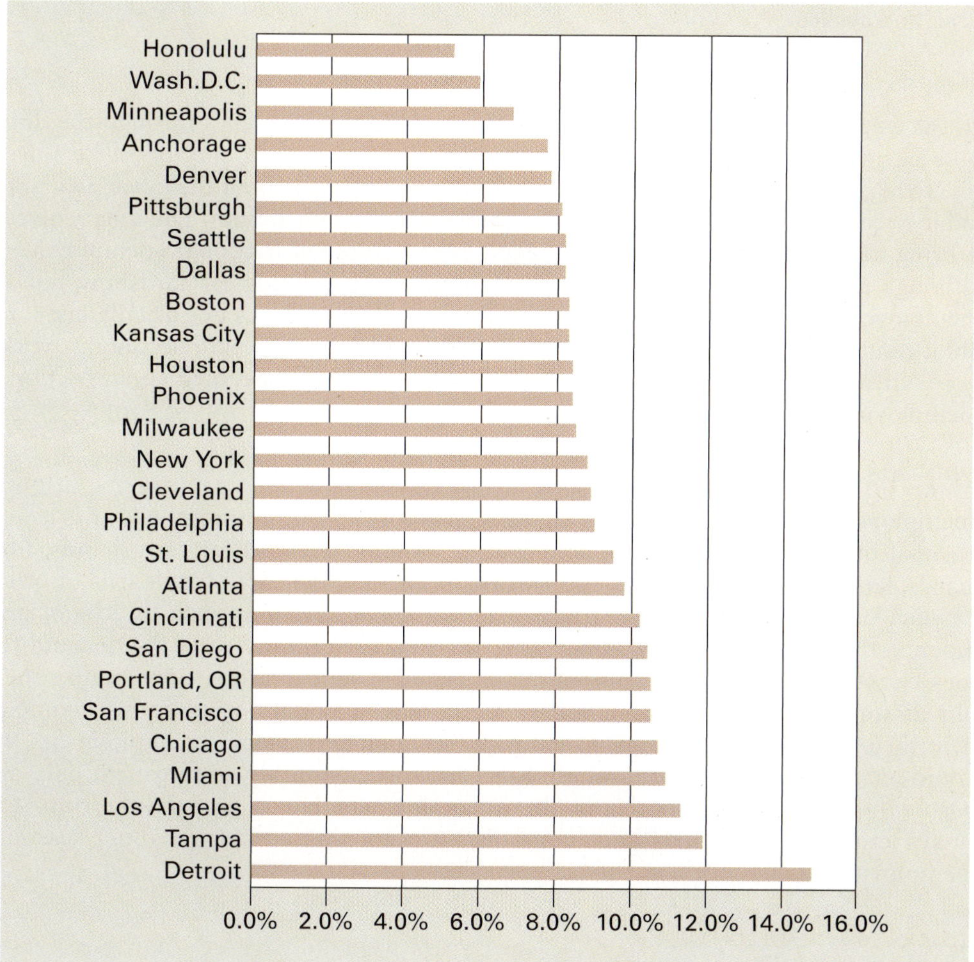

Source: Based on figures for April 2010 from the U.S. Bureau of Labor Statistics. For the latest figures, go to http://www.bls.gov/lau/home.htm.

was nearly triple the rate for the city with the lowest rate, Honolulu, at 5.2 percent. The point is that *the national unemployment rate masks differences across the country and even across an individual state*. Still, most cities in Exhibit 4 had rates between 8.0 percent and 11.0 percent.

Sources of Unemployment

Pick up any metropolitan newspaper and thumb through the classifieds. The help-wanted section may include thousands of jobs, from accountants to X-ray technicians. Online job sites such as Monster.com list hundreds of thousands of openings. Why, when millions are unemployed, are so many jobs available? To understand this, we must think about all the reasons why people are unemployed. They may be looking for a first job, or they may be reentering the labor force after an absence. They may have quit or been fired from their last job. Sixty-one percent of those unemployed in April 2010 lost their previous job, 6 percent quit, 8 percent entered the labor market for the first time, and 25 percent reentered the labor market. *Thus, 39 percent were unemployed either because they quit jobs or because they were just joining or rejoining the labor force.*

More generally, there are four sources of unemployment: frictional, seasonal, structural, and cyclical.

Frictional Unemployment

Just as employers do not always hire the first applicant who comes through the door, job seekers do not always accept the first offer. Both employers and job seekers need time to explore the job market. Employers need time to learn about the talent available, and job seekers need time to learn about employment opportunities. The time required to bring together employers and job seekers is the source of **frictional unemployment**. Although unemployment often creates economic and psychological hardships, not all unemployment is necessarily bad. Frictional unemployment does not usually last long and it results in a better match between workers and jobs, so the entire economy works more efficiently. Policy makers and economists are not that concerned about frictional unemployment.

frictional unemployment
Unemployment that occurs because job seekers and employers need time to find each other

Seasonal Unemployment

Unemployment caused by seasonal changes in labor demand during the year is called **seasonal unemployment.** During cold winter months, demand for farm hands, lifeguards, landscapers, and construction workers shrinks, as it does for dozens of other seasonal occupations. Likewise, tourism in winter destinations such as Miami and Phoenix melts in the heat of summer. The Christmas season increases the demand for sales clerks, postal workers, and Santa Clauses. Those in seasonal jobs realize their jobs disappear in the off-season. Some even choose seasonal occupations to complement their lifestyles or academic schedules. To eliminate seasonal unemployment, we would have to outlaw winter and abolish Christmas. Monthly employment data are *seasonally adjusted* to smooth out the unemployment bulges that result from seasonal factors. Policy makers and economists are not that concerned about seasonal unemployment.

seasonal unemployment
Unemployment caused by seasonal changes in the demand for certain kinds of labor

Structural Unemployment

A third reason why job vacancies and unemployment coexist is that unemployed workers often do not have the skills in demand or do not live where their skills are demanded. For example, the Lincoln Electric Company in Ohio took a long time filling 200 openings because few among the thousands who applied could operate computer-controlled machines. Unemployment arising from a mismatch of skills or geographic location is called **structural unemployment.** *Structural unemployment occurs because changes in tastes, technology, taxes, and competition reduce the demand for certain skills and increase the demand for other skills.* In our dynamic economy, some workers, such as coal miners in West Virginia, are stuck with skills no longer demanded. Likewise, golf carts replaced caddies, ATMs replaced bank tellers, and office technology is replacing clerical staff. For example, because of e-mail, voice mail, PCs, PDAs, BlackBerries, smart phones, and other wireless devices, the number of secretaries, typists, and administrative assistants in the United States has fallen by more than half over the past two decades. Structural unemployment may also arise from a change in tastes and preferences. For example, because Americans smoke less, some tobacco farmers had to look for other work. And because Americans buy fewer newspapers, employment in that industry has declined.

structural unemployment
Unemployment because (1) the skills demanded by employers do not match those of the unemployed, or (2) the unemployed do not live where the jobs are

Whereas most frictional unemployment is short term and voluntary, structural unemployment poses more of a problem because workers must either develop the skills demanded in the local job market or look elsewhere. Moving is not easy. Most people prefer to remain near friends and relatives. Those laid off from good jobs hang around in hopes of getting rehired. Married couples with one spouse still employed may not want to give up that job to look for two jobs elsewhere. Finally, available jobs may be in regions where the living cost is much higher. So those structurally unemployed often stay put. Some federal retraining programs aim to reduce structural unemployment.

Cyclical Unemployment

As output declines during recessions, firms reduce their demand for nearly all resources, including labor. **Cyclical unemployment** increases during recessions and decreases during expansions. Between 1932 and 1934, when unemployment averaged about 24 percent, there was clearly much cyclical unemployment. Between 1942 and 1945, when unemployment averaged less than 2 percent, there was no cyclical unemployment. Cyclical unemployment means the economy is operating inside its production possibilities frontier. Government policies that stimulate aggregate demand aim to reduce cyclical unemployment.

cyclical unemployment
Unemployment that fluctuates with the business cycle, increasing during contractions and decreasing during expansions

Duration of Unemployment

A given unemployment rate tells us little about how long people have been unemployed. In April 2010, with the unemployment rate at 9.9 percent, the average duration of unemployment was 33 weeks, the longest since the Great Depression. Some people were unemployed longer than others: 18 percent were unemployed less than 5 weeks; 20 percent 5–14 weeks; 16 percent 15–26 weeks, and 46 percent 27 weeks or longer. Those out 27 weeks or longer are called the **long-term unemployed,** and are of special concern to policy makers. Thus, nearly half of those out of work in April 2010 were long-term unemployed.

long-term unemployed
Those out of work for 27 weeks or longer

The Meaning of Full Employment

In a dynamic economy such as ours, changes in product demand and in technology continually alter the supply and demand for particular types of labor. Thus, even in a healthy economy, there is some frictional, structural, and seasonal unemployment. The economy is viewed as operating at *full employment* if there is no cyclical unemployment. When economists talk about "full employment," they do not mean zero unemployment but low unemployment, with estimates ranging from 4 to 6 percent.

full employment
Employment level when there is no cyclical unemployment

Even when the economy is at **full employment,** there is some frictional, structural, and seasonal unemployment. Even after the recession of 2007–2009, 39 percent of those unemployed in April 2010 had quit their previous job or were new entrants or reentrants into the labor force. We can't expect people to find jobs overnight. Many in this group would be considered frictionally unemployed.

Unemployment Compensation

As noted at the outset, unemployment often involves an economic and psychological hardship. For a variety of reasons, however, the burden of unemployment on the individual and the family may not be as severe today as it was during the Great Depression. Today, many households have two or more workers in the labor force, so if one loses a job, another may still have one—a job that could provide health insurance and other benefits for the family. *Having more than one family member in the labor force cushions the shock of unemployment.*

unemployment benefits
Cash transfers to those who lose their jobs and actively seek employment

Moreover, unlike the experience during the Great Depression, most who lose their jobs now collect unemployment benefits. In response to the Great Depression, Congress passed the Social Security Act of 1935, which provided unemployment insurance financed by a tax on employers. Unemployed workers who meet certain qualifications can receive **unemployment benefits** for up to six months, provided they actively look for work. During recessions, benefits usually extend beyond six months in states with especially high unemployment. During and following the recession of 2007–2009, the extension of benefits was nationwide, and many states offered benefits for up to two years. Benefits go primarily to people who have lost jobs. Those just entering or reentering the labor force are not covered, nor are those who quit their last job or those fired for just cause, such as excessive absenteeism or theft. Because of these restrictions, about two-thirds of those unemployed in April 2010 received benefits.

Unemployment benefits replace on average about half of a person's take-home pay, with a higher percentage for those whose jobs paid less. Benefits averaged about $310 per week in 2010. Because these benefits reduce the opportunity cost of remaining unemployed, they may reduce the incentives to find work. For example, if faced with a choice of washing dishes for $350 per week or collecting $250 per week in unemployment benefits, which would you choose? Evidence suggests that those collecting unemployment benefits remain out of work weeks longer than those without benefits. Many leave the labor force once their benefits are exhausted.[3] So although unemployment insurance provides a safety net, it may reduce the urgency of finding work, thereby increasing unemployment. On the plus side, because beneficiaries need not take the first job that comes along, unemployment insurance allows for a higher quality job search. As a result of a higher quality search, there is a better match between job skills and job requirements, and this promotes economic efficiency.

International Comparisons of Unemployment

How do U.S. unemployment rates compare with those around the world? Exhibit 5 shows rates since 1980 for the United States, Japan, and the average of four major European economies (France, Germany, Italy, and the United Kingdom). Over the last two decades and prior to the recent recession, unemployment trended down in the

3. See David Card, Raj Chetty, and Andrea Weber, "Cash-On-Hand and Competing Models of Intertemporal Behavior: New Evidence from the Labor Markets," *Quarterly Journal of Economics*, 122 (November 2007): 1511–1560.

EXHIBIT 5 During the Last Quarter Century, the U.S. Unemployment Rate Fell, Europe's Remained High, and Japan's Rose

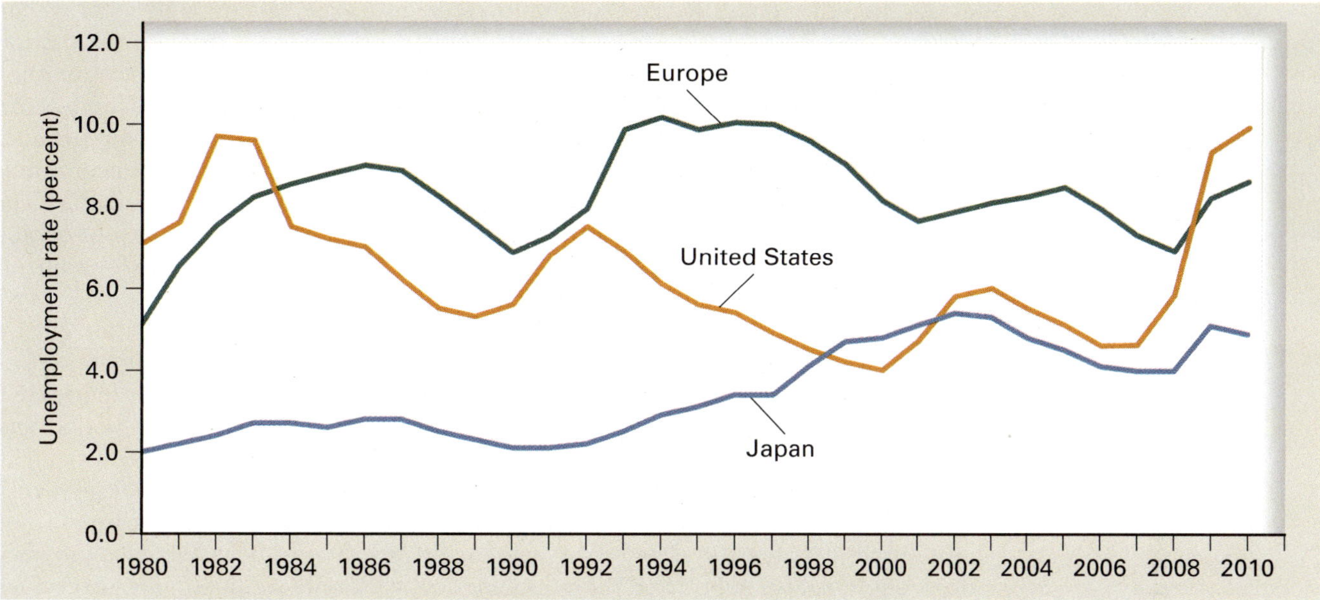

Source: Based on standardized rates in *OECD Economic Outlook 87* (May 2010) and *Economic Report of the President*, February 2010. Figures for Europe are the averages for France, Germany, Italy, and the United Kingdom. Figures for 2010 are projections based on reported rates through the first third of the year. For the latest international data, go to http://www.bls.gov/fls/home.htm.

United States, trended up in Japan, and remained high in Europe. At the beginning of the period, the United States had the highest rate among the three economies. After trending lower between the early 1980s and late 2007, the U.S. rate spiked above that of Western Europe because of the 2007–2009 recession. The rate in Japan remained relatively low.

The unemployment rate in Europe averaged 8.3 percent over the last three decades versus a U.S. average of 6.2 percent. Why have rates averaged higher in Europe? The ratio of unemployment benefits to average pay is higher in Europe than in the United States, and unemployment benefits last longer there, sometimes years. So those collecting unemployment benefits have less incentive to find work. What's more, government regulations have made European employers more reluctant to hire new workers because firing them is difficult.

Historically, unemployment has been low in Japan because many firms there offered job security for life. Thus, some employees who do little or no work are still carried on company payrolls. Both labor laws and social norms limit layoffs in Japan. Unemployment has increased there since the early 1990s because more firms went bankrupt.

Problems With Official Unemployment Figures

Official unemployment statistics are not problem free. Not counting discouraged workers and others marginally attached to the labor force as unemployed understates unemployment. Official employment data also ignore the problem of **underemployment,** which arises because people are counted as employed even if they can find only part-time work or are vastly overqualified for their jobs, as when someone with a

underemployment
Workers are overqualified for their jobs or work fewer hours than they would prefer

Ph.D. in literature can find only a clerk's position. Counting overqualified and part-time workers as employed tends to understate the actual amount of unemployment.

On the other hand, because unemployment insurance benefits and most welfare programs require recipients to seek work, some people may go through the motions of looking for a job just to qualify for these benefits. If they do not in fact want a job, counting them as unemployed overstates actual unemployment. Likewise, some people who would prefer to work part time can find only full-time jobs, and some forced to work overtime and weekends would prefer to work less. To the extent that people must work more than they would prefer, the official unemployment rate overstates the actual rate. Finally, people in the underground economy may not admit they have jobs because they are breaking the law. For example, someone working off the books or someone selling illegal drugs would not admit to being employed.

On net, however, because discouraged workers and others marginally attached to the labor force aren't counted as unemployed and because underemployed workers are counted as employed, most experts agree that official U.S. unemployment figures tend to underestimate unemployment. Still, the size of this underestimation may not be huge, even in the wake of a recession. For example, counting discouraged workers as unemployed would have raised the unemployment rate in April 2010 from 9.9 percent to 10.6 percent. Adding in others who were marginally attached to the labor force would have raised the rate to 11.3 percent. There are no estimates of what the unemployment rate would be if we subtracted those looking for work only to qualify for government benefits.

Despite these qualifications and limitations, the U.S. unemployment rate is a useful measure of trends across demographic groups, across regions, and over time.

We turn next to inflation.

Inflation

As noted already, *inflation* is a sustained increase in the economy's average price level. At the end of the book, the case study, "Bringing Theory to Life: Hyperinflation in Zimbabwe," underscores the problem of high inflation.

We have already discussed inflation in different contexts. If the price level bounces around—moving up one month, falling back the next month—any particular increase in the price level would not necessarily be called inflation in a meaningful sense. We typically measure inflation on an annual basis. The annual *inflation rate* is the percentage increase in the average price level from one year to the next. For example, between April 2009 and April 2010, the U.S. *consumer price index* increased 2.2 percent. Extremely high inflation, as in Zimbabwe, is called **hyperinflation.** A sustained *decrease* in the average price level is called **deflation,** as occurred in the United States during the Great Depression and in 2009. Japan, Hong Kong, and Taiwan have also experienced deflation in recent years. And a reduction in the rate of inflation is called **disinflation,** as occurred in the United States from 1981 to 1986, 1991 to 1994, and 2000 to 2002.

hyperinflation
A very high rate of inflation

deflation
A sustained decrease in the price level

disinflation
A reduction in the rate of inflation

In this section, we first consider two sources of inflation. Then, we examine the extent and consequences of inflation in the United States and around the world.

Two Sources of Inflation

Inflation is a sustained increase in the economy's price level; it results from an increase in aggregate demand, a decrease in aggregate supply, or both. Panel (a) of Exhibit 6 shows that an increase in aggregate demand raises the economy's price level from

EXHIBIT 6 Inflation Caused by Shifts of Aggregate Demand and Aggregate Supply Curves

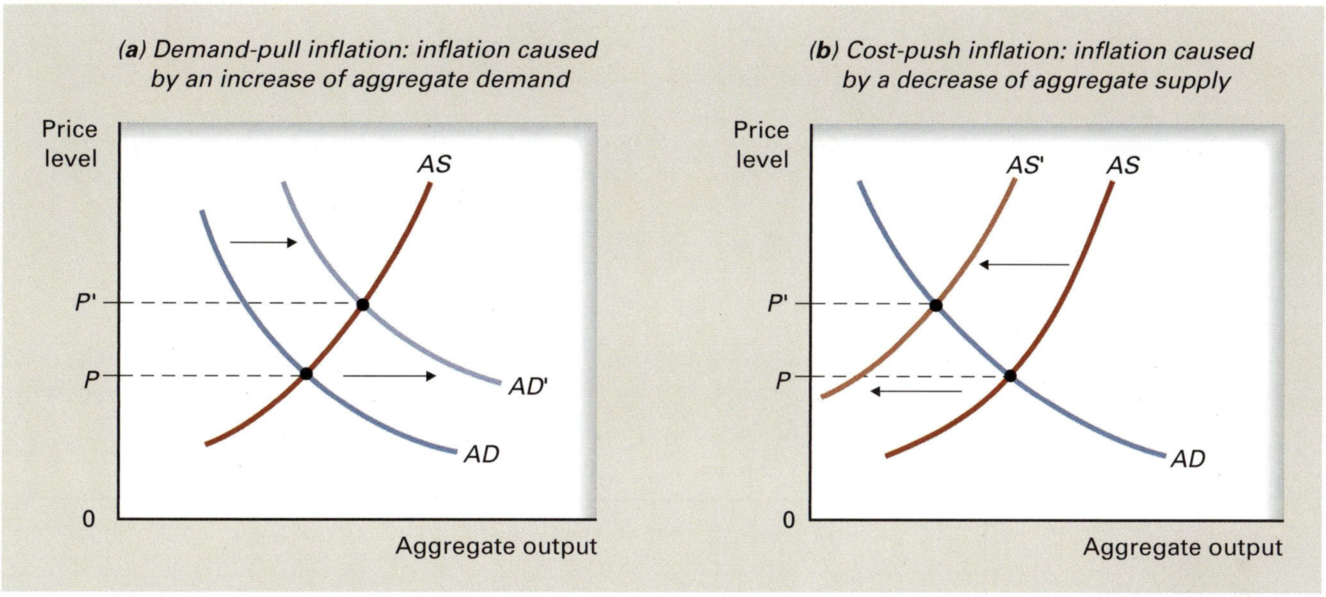

Panel (a) illustrates demand-pull inflation. An outward shift of the aggregate demand to *AD'* "pulls" the price level up from *P* to *P'*. Panel (b) shows cost-push inflation. A decrease of aggregate supply to *AS'* "pushes" the price level up from *P* to *P'*.

P to *P'*. In such cases, a shift to the right of the aggregate demand curve *pulls up* the price level. Inflation resulting from increases in aggregate demand is called **demand-pull inflation.** To generate continuous demand-pull inflation, the aggregate demand curve would have to keep shifting out along a given aggregate supply curve. Rising U.S. inflation during the late 1960s came from demand-pull inflation, when federal spending for the Vietnam War and expanded social programs boosted aggregate demand.

demand-pull inflation
A sustained rise in the price level caused by a rightward shift of the aggregate demand curve

Alternatively, inflation can arise from reductions in aggregate supply, as shown in panel (b) of Exhibit 6, where a leftward shift of the aggregate supply curve raises the price level. For example, crop failures and OPEC price hikes reduced aggregate supply during 1974 and 1975, thereby raising the price level in the economy. Inflation stemming from decreases in aggregate supply is called **cost-push inflation,** suggesting that increases in the cost of production *push up* the price level. Prices increase and real GDP decreases, a combination identified earlier as *stagflation.* Again, to generate sustained and continuous cost-push inflation, the aggregate supply curve would have to keep shifting left along a given aggregate demand curve.

cost-push inflation
A sustained rise in the price level caused by a leftward shift of the aggregate supply curve

A Historical Look at Inflation and the Price Level

The consumer price index is the inflation measure you most often encounter, so it gets the most attention here. As you learned in the previous chapter, the *consumer price index*, or *CPI*, measures the cost of a market basket of consumer goods and services over time. Exhibit 7 shows prices in the United States since 1913, using the consumer price index. Panel (a) shows the price *level*, measured by an index relative to the base period of 1982 to 1984. As you can see, the price level was lower in 1940 than in 1920. Since 1940, however, it has risen steadily, especially during the 1970s.

EXHIBIT 7 Consumer Price Index Since 1913

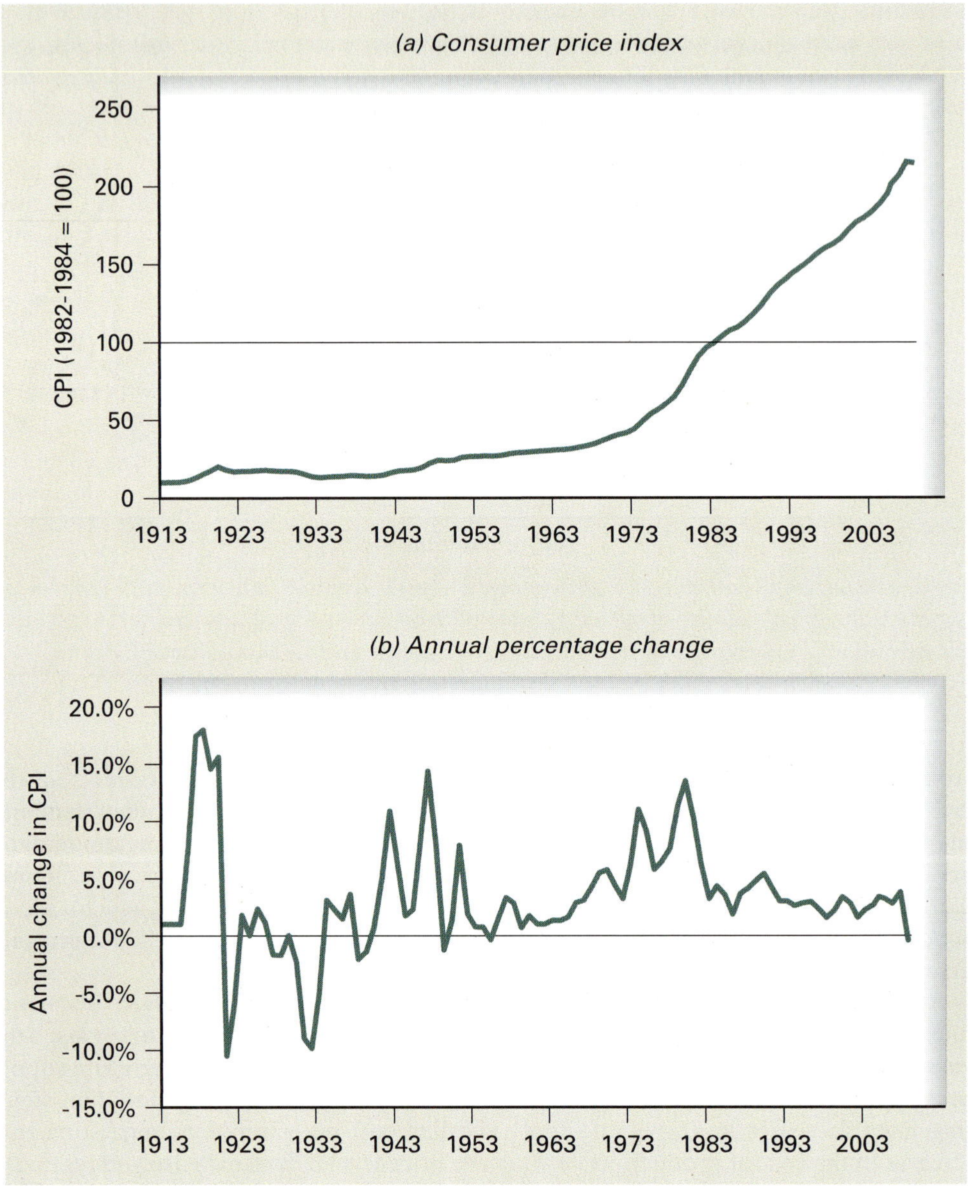

Panel (a) shows that, despite fluctuations, the price level, as measured by the consumer price index, was lower in 1940 than in 1920. The price level began rising in the 1940s. Panel (b) shows the annual rate of change in the price level.

Source: The CPI home page of the U.S. Bureau of Labor Statistics is at http://www.bls.gov/cpi/home.htm. Go there for the latest figures.

People are concerned less about the price level and more about year-to-year changes in that level. The lower panel shows the annual *rate of change* in the CPI, or the annual rate of *inflation* or *deflation*. The 1970s was not the only period of high inflation. Inflation exceeded 10 percent from 1916 to 1919 and in 1947—periods associated with world wars. Prior to the 1950s, high inflation was war related and was usually followed by deflation. Such an inflation-deflation cycle stretches back over the last two centuries. In fact, between the Revolutionary War and World War II, the price level fell in about as many years as it rose. At the end of World War II, the price level was about where it stood at the end of the Civil War.

So fluctuations in the price level are nothing new. But prior to World War II, years of inflation and deflation balanced out over the long run. Therefore, people had good reason to believe the dollar would retain its purchasing power over the long term. Since the end of World War II, however, the CPI has increased by an average of 3.7 percent per year. That may not sound like much, but it translates into nearly a tenfold increase in the consumer price index since 1947. *Inflation erodes confidence in the value of the dollar over the long term.*

Anticipated Versus Unanticipated Inflation

What is the effect of inflation on the economy? *Unanticipated inflation* creates more problems than *anticipated inflation.* To the extent that inflation is higher or lower than anticipated, it arbitrarily creates winners and losers. For example, suppose inflation is expected to be 3 percent next year, and you and your employer agree to a 4 percent increase in your nominal, or money, wage. You both expect your *real* wage—that is, your wage measured in dollars of constant purchasing power—to increase by 1 percent. If inflation turns out to be 3 percent, as expected, you and your employer are both satisfied. If inflation turns out to be 5 percent, your real wage will fall by 1 percent, so you are a loser and your employer a winner. If inflation turns out to be only 1 percent, your real wage increased by 3 percent, so you are a winner and your employer a loser.

More generally, if inflation is higher than expected, the losers are those who agreed to sell at a price that anticipated lower inflation and the winners are those who agreed to pay that price. If inflation is lower than expected, the situation is reversed: The losers are those who agreed to pay a price that anticipated higher inflation, and the winners are those who agreed to sell at that price. *The arbitrary gains and losses arising from unanticipated inflation is one reason inflation is so unpopular.* Inflation just doesn't seem fair.

The Transaction Costs of Variable Inflation

During long periods of price stability, people correctly believe they can predict future prices and can therefore plan accordingly. If inflation changes unexpectedly, however, the future is cloudier, so planning gets harder. Uncertainty about inflation undermines money's ability to link the present with the future. U.S. firms dealing with the rest of the world face an added burden. They must not only anticipate U.S. inflation, they must also guess how the value of the dollar will change relative to foreign currencies. Inflation uncertainty and the resulting exchange-rate uncertainty complicate international transactions. In this more uncertain environment, managers must shift attention from production decisions to anticipating the effects of inflation and exchange-rate changes on the firm's finances. Market transactions, particularly long-term contracts, become more complicated as inflation becomes more unpredictable. Some economists believe that the high and variable U.S. inflation during the 1970s and early 1980s cut economic growth during those periods.

Inflation Obscures Relative Price Changes

Even with no inflation, some prices would increase and some would decrease, reflecting normal activity in particular markets. For example, since the mid-1980s the U.S. price level has doubled, yet the prices of flat screen TVs, computers, long-distance phone service, and many other products have declined sharply. Because the prices of various goods change by different amounts, *relative prices* change. Consider price changes over a longer period. In the last hundred years, consumer prices overall increased about 2,000 percent, but the price of a hotel room in New York City jumped 7,500 percent, while the price of a three-minute phone call from New York to Chicago dropped 99 percent. Whereas the economy's price level describes the exchange rate between a market basket and *money*, relative prices describe the exchange rate among goods—that is, how much one good costs compared to another.

Inflation does not necessarily cause a change in relative prices, but it can obscure that change. During periods of volatile inflation, there is greater uncertainty about the price of one good relative to another—that is, about relative prices. But relative price changes are important signals for allocating the economy's resources efficiently. If all prices moved together, suppliers could link the selling prices of their goods to the overall inflation rate. Because prices usually do not move in unison, however, tying a particular product's price to the overall inflation rate may result in a price that is too high or too low based on market conditions. The same is true of agreements to link wages with inflation. If the price of an employer's product grows more slowly than the rate of inflation in the economy, the employer may be hard-pressed to increase wages by the rate of inflation. Consider the problem confronting oil refiners who signed labor contracts agreeing to pay their workers cost-of-living wage increases. In some years, those employers had to increase wages at a time when the price of oil was falling like a rock.

Inflation Across Metropolitan Areas

Inflation rates differ across regions mostly because of differences in housing prices, which rise or fall faster in some places than in others. But most prices, such as for automobiles, refrigerators, or jeans, do not differ that much across regions. The federal government tracks separate CPIs for each of 27 U.S. metropolitan areas. Based on these CPIs from 2005 to 2009, the average annual inflation rate is presented in Exhibit 8. Annual inflation between 2005 and 2009 averaged from a low of 1.9 percent in Detroit to a high of 3.8 percent in Honolulu. Most cities averaged between 2.0 percent and 3.0 percent. Again, the metropolitan inflation rate is heavily influenced by what's happening in the local housing market. We can conclude that the housing market in Honolulu was hotter than in Detroit.

International Comparisons of Inflation

Exhibit 9 shows annual inflation based on the CPI for the past three decades in the United States, Japan, and Europe, represented here as the average of four major nations (France, Germany, Italy, and the United Kingdom). All three economies show a similar trend, with declining inflation, or disinflation, during the first half of the 1980s, rising inflation during the second half of the 1980s to a peak in the early 1990s, and then another trend lower. The overall trend since 1980 has been toward lower inflation. Inflation rates in Europe were similar to those in the United States. Rates in Japan were consistently lower, even dipping into deflation in recent years. In the United States and Japan, the price level declined in 2009 due to slack demand from the global recession. Inflation since 1980 averaged 3.8 percent in Europe, 3.4 percent in the United States, and 0.9 percent in Japan.

The quantity and quality of data going into the price index varies across countries. Governments in less-developed countries sample fewer products and measure prices only in the capital city. Whereas hundreds of items are sampled to determine the U.S. consumer price index, as few as 30 might be sampled in some developing countries.

EXHIBIT 8 Average Annual Inflation from 2005 to 2009 Differed Across U.S. Metropolitan Areas

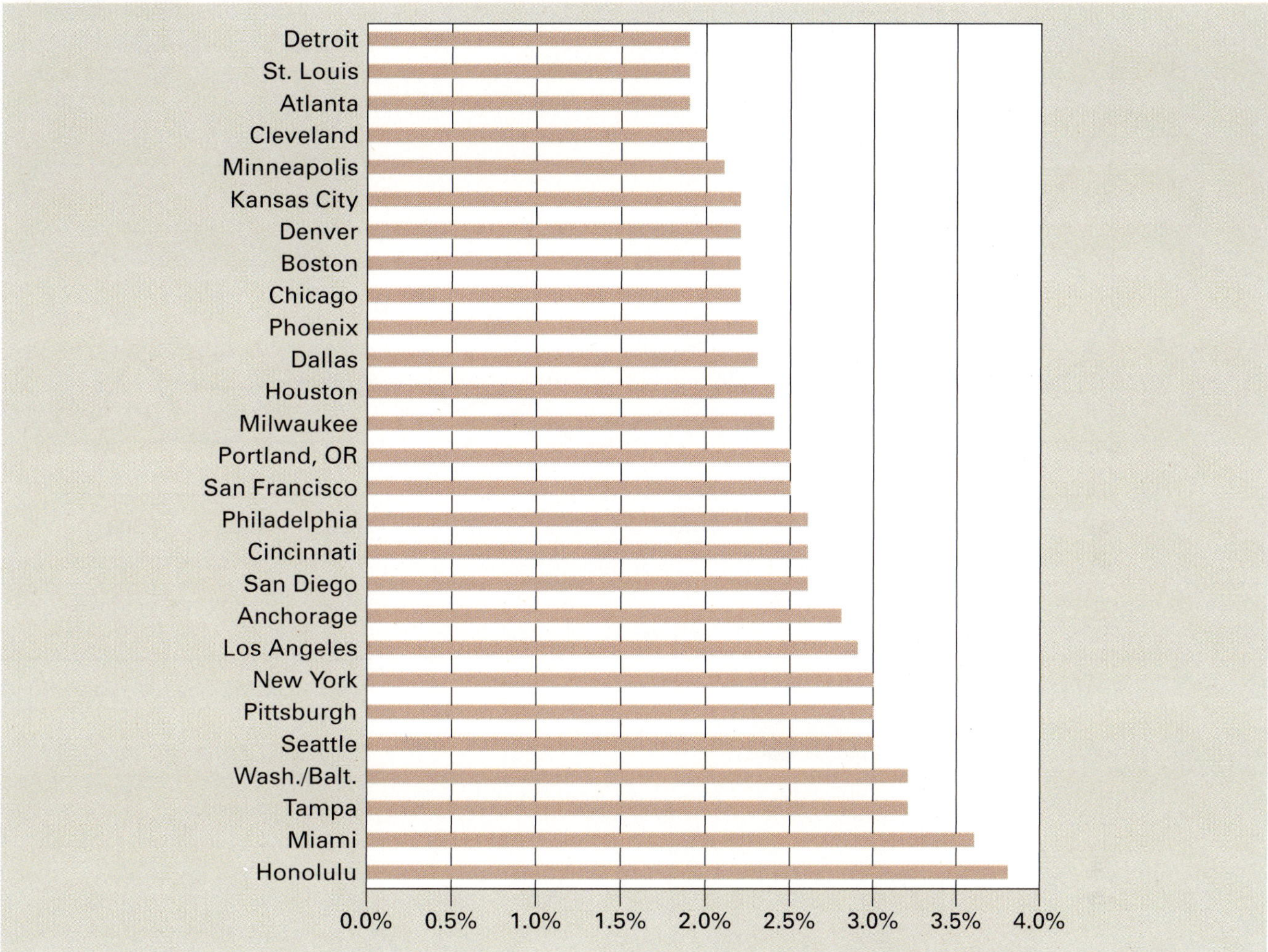

Source: Annual averages for 2005 to 2009 based on CPI estimates from the U.S. Bureau of Labor Statistics. For the latest figures go to http://www.bls.gov/cpi/home.htm and find "Regional Resources."

Inflation and Interest Rates

No discussion of inflation would be complete without some mention of the interest rate. **Interest** is the dollar amount paid by borrowers to lenders. Lenders must be rewarded for forgoing present consumption, and borrowers are willing to pay a premium to spend now. The **interest rate** is the amount paid per year as a percentage of the amount borrowed. For example, an interest rate of five percent means $5 per year on a $100 loan. The greater the interest rate, other things constant, the greater the reward for lending money. The amount of money people are willing to lend, called *loanable funds*, increases as the interest rate rises, other things constant. The supply curve for loanable funds therefore slopes upward, as indicated by curve *S* in Exhibit 10.

interest
The dollar amount paid by borrowers to lenders

interest rate
Interest per year as a percentage of the amount loaned

These funds are demanded by households, firms, and governments to finance homes, buildings, machinery, college, and other major purchases. The lower the interest rate,

EXHIBIT 9 Inflation Rates in Major Economies Have Trended Lower Over the Past Three Decades

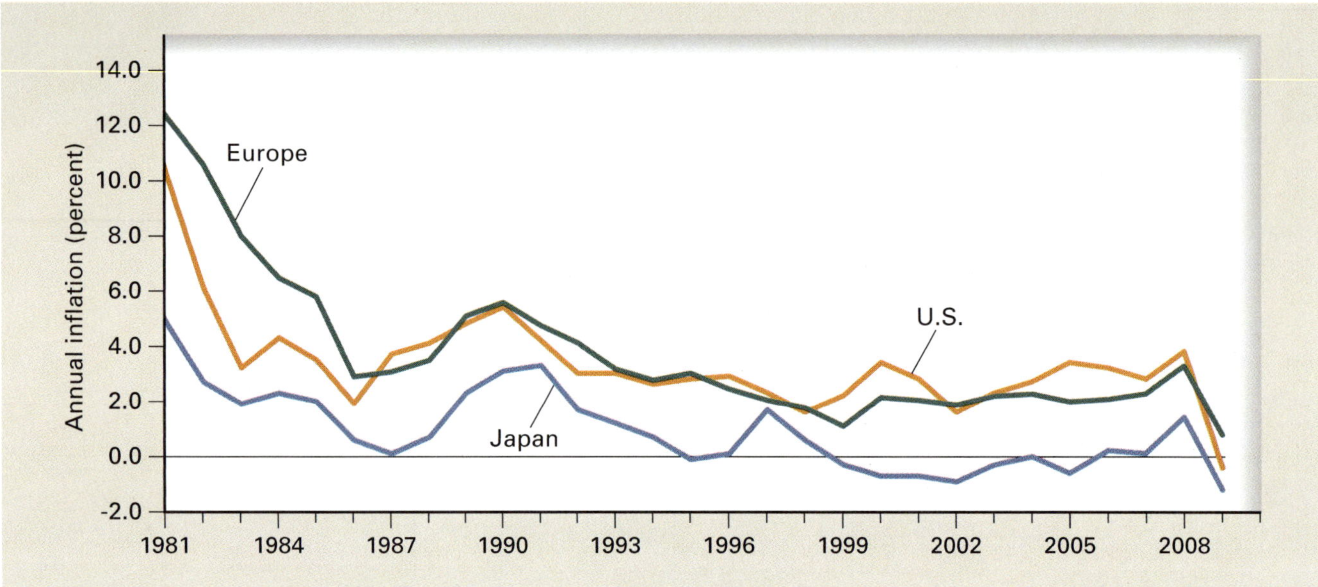

Source: Developed from CPI inflation reported in *OECD Economic Outlook* 87 (May 2010). Figures for Europe are the averages for France, Germany, Italy, and the United Kingdom. For the latest data, go to http://www.bls.gov/fls/home.htm.

EXHIBIT 10 The Market for Loanable Funds

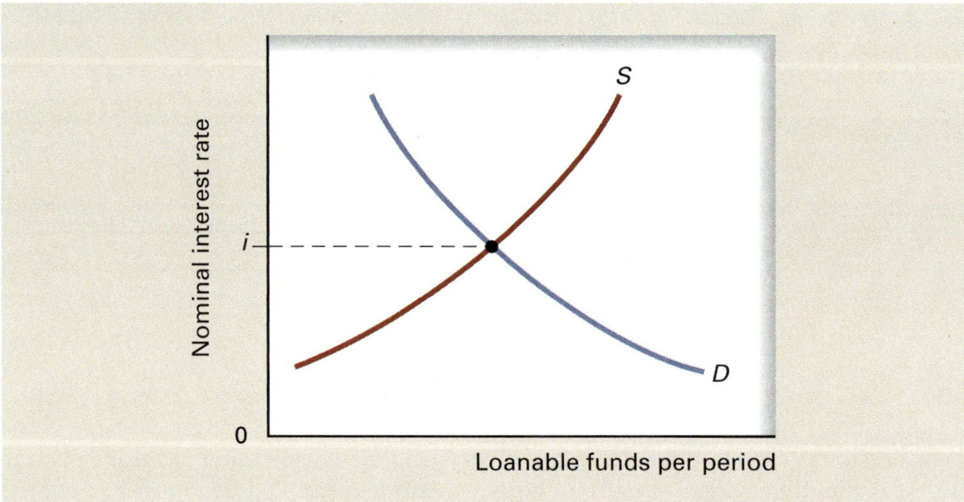

The upward-sloping supply curve, *S*, shows that more loanable funds are supplied at higher interest rates. The downward-sloping demand curve, *D*, shows that the quantity of loanable funds demanded is greater at lower interest rates. The two curves intersect to determine the market interest rate, *i*.

other things constant, the cheaper the cost of borrowing. So the quantity of loanable funds demanded increases as the interest rate decreases, other things constant. That is, the interest rate and the quantity of loanable funds demanded are inversely related. The demand curve therefore slopes downward, as indicated by curve D in Exhibit 10. The downward-sloping demand curve and the upward-sloping supply curve intersect to yield the equilibrium nominal rate of interest, i.

The **nominal interest rate** measures interest in terms of the current dollars paid. The nominal rate is the one that appears on the loan agreement; it is the rate discussed in the news media and is often of political significance. The **real interest rate** equals the nominal rate minus the inflation rate:

nominal interest rate
The interest rate expressed in dollars of current value (that is, not adjusted for inflation) as a percentage of the amount loaned; the interest rate specified on the loan agreement

real interest rate
The interest rate expressed in dollars of constant purchasing power as a percentage of the amount loaned; the nominal interest rate minus the inflation rate

$$\text{Real interest rate} = \text{Nominal interest rate} - \text{Inflation rate}$$

For example, if the nominal interest rate is 5 percent and the inflation rate is 3 percent, the real interest rate is 2 percent. With no inflation, the nominal rate and the real rate would be identical. But with inflation, the nominal rate exceeds the real rate. If inflation is unexpectedly high—higher, for example, than the nominal rate—then the real interest rate would be negative. In this case, the nominal interest earned for lending money would not even cover the loss of spending power caused by inflation. Lenders would lose purchasing power. This is why lenders and borrowers are concerned more about the real rate than the nominal rate. The real interest rate, however, is known only after the fact—that is, only after inflation actually occurs.

Because the future is uncertain, lenders and borrowers must form expectations about inflation, and they base their willingness to lend and borrow on these expectations. The higher the *expected* inflation, the higher the nominal rate of interest that lenders require and that borrowers are willing to pay. Lenders and borrowers base their decisions on the *expected* real interest rate, which equals the nominal rate minus the expected inflation rate.

Although the discussion has implied that there is only one market rate of interest, there are many rates. Rates differ depending on such factors as the duration of the loan, tax treatment of interest, and the risk the loan will not be repaid.

Why Is Inflation Unpopular?

Whenever the price level increases, spending must increase just to buy the same amount of goods and services. If you think of inflation only in terms of spending, you consider only the problem of paying those higher prices. But if you think of inflation in terms of the higher money income that results, you see that higher prices mean higher receipts for resource suppliers, including higher wages for workers. When viewed from the income side, inflation is not so bad.

If every higher price is received by some resource supplier, why are people so troubled by inflation? People view their higher incomes as well-deserved rewards for their labor, but they see inflation as a penalty that unjustly robs them of purchasing power. Most people do not stop to realize that unless they are producing more with each hour of labor, higher wages *must* result in higher prices. Prices and wages are simply two sides of the same coin. To the extent that nominal wages on average keep up with inflation, workers retain their purchasing power.

Presidents Ford and Carter could not control inflation and were turned out of office. Inflation slowed significantly during President Reagan's first term, and he won reelection easily, even though the unemployment rate was higher during his first term than during President Carter's tenure. During the 1988 election, George H. W. Bush won in part by reminding voters what inflation was in 1980, the last time a Democrat was president. But he lost his bid at reelection in part because inflation spiked to 6.0 percent in 1990, the highest in nearly a decade. Inflation remained under 3.0 percent during President Clinton's first term, and he was reelected easily. In the elections of 2000, 2004, and 2008, inflation was low enough as not to be an issue in those presidential elections.

Although inflation affects everyone to some extent, it hits hardest those whose incomes are fixed in nominal terms. For example, pensions are often fixed amounts and are eroded by inflation. And retirees who rely on fixed nominal interest income also see their incomes shrunk by inflation. But the benefits paid by the largest pension program, Social Security, are adjusted annually for changes in the CPI. Thus, Social Security recipients get a cost-of-living adjustment, or a **COLA**.

COLA
Cost-of-living adjustment; an increase in a transfer payment or wage that is tied to the increase in the price level

To Review: anticipated inflation is less of a problem than unanticipated inflation. Unanticipated inflation arbitrarily redistributes income and wealth from one group to another, reduces the ability to make long-term plans, and forces people to focus more on money and prices. The more unpredictable inflation becomes the harder it is to negotiate long-term contracts. Productivity suffers because people must spend more time coping with inflation, leaving less time for production.

Conclusion

This chapter has focused on unemployment and inflation. Although we have discussed them separately, they are related in ways that will unfold in later chapters. Politicians sometimes add the unemployment rate to the inflation rate to come up with what they refer to as the "misery index." In 1980, for example, an unemployment rate of 7.1 percent combined with a CPI increase of 13.5 percent to yield a misery index of 20.6—a number that helps explain why President Carter was not reelected. By 1984 the misery index dropped to 11.8, and by 1988 to 9.6; Republicans retained the White House in both elections. In 1992, the index climbed slightly to 10.4 percent, spelling trouble for President George H. W. Bush. And in 1996, the index fell back to 8.4 percent, helping President Clinton's reelection. During the election of 2000, the misery index was down to 7.7, which should have helped Al Gore, the candidate of the incumbent party. But during the campaign, Gore distanced himself from President Clinton and thus was not able to capitalize on the strong economy. In the 2004 election, the misery index remained about the same as in 2000, which helps explain why challenger John Kerry had difficulty making much of an issue of the economy. And a misery index of 10.4 the month before the 2008 election helped defeat the incumbent party and put Barack Obama in office.

Summary

1. The unemployment rate is the number of people looking for work divided by the number in the labor force. The unemployment rate masks differences among particular groups and across regions. The rate is lowest among white adults and highest among black teenagers.
2. There are four sources of unemployment. Frictional unemployment arises because employers and qualified job seekers need time to find one another. Seasonal unemployment stems from the effects of weather and the seasons on certain industries, such as construction and agriculture. Structural unemployment arises because changes in tastes, technology, taxes, and competition reduce the demand for certain skills and increase the demand for other skills. And cyclical unemployment results from fluctuations in economic activity caused by the business cycle. Policy makers and economists are less concerned with frictional and seasonal unemployment. Full employment occurs when cyclical unemployment is zero.

3. Unemployment often creates both an economic and a psychological hardship. For some, this burden is reduced by an employed spouse and by unemployment insurance. Unemployment insurance provides a safety net for some and that's good, but it may also reduce incentives to find work, as is the case in Europe, and that's an unintended consequence.
4. Inflation is a sustained rise in the average price level. An increase in aggregate demand can cause demand-pull inflation. A decrease in aggregate supply can cause cost-push inflation. Prior to World War II, both inflation and deflation were common, but since then the price level has increased nearly every year.
5. Anticipated inflation causes fewer distortions in the economy than unanticipated inflation. Unanticipated inflation arbitrarily creates winners and losers, and forces people to spend more time and energy coping with the effects of inflation. The negative effects of high and variable inflation on productivity can be observed in countries that have experienced hyperinflation, such as Zimbabwe.
6. Because not all prices change by the same amount during inflationary periods, people have trouble keeping track of the changes in relative prices. Unexpected inflation makes long-term planning more difficult and more risky.
7. The intersection of the demand and supply curves for loanable funds yields the market interest rate. The real interest rate is the nominal interest rate minus the inflation rate. Borrowers and lenders base decisions on the expected real interest rate.

Key Concepts

Questions for Review

1. Labor Force Refer to Exhibit 1 in the chapter to determine whether each of the following statements is true or false.
   a. Some people who are officially unemployed are not in the labor force.
   b. Some people in the labor force are not working.
   c. Everyone who is not unemployed is in the labor force.
   d. Some people who are not working are not unemployed.
2. Unemployment in Various Groups Does the overall unemployment rate provide an accurate picture of the impact of unemployment on all U.S. population groups?
3. Case Study: "Hiring Picks Up, But Jobless Rate Rises" (See page 747.) Imagine that during an expansion the U.S. economy adds 300,000 jobs. In addition, because of the improving economic conditions, the labor force increases by 200,000. Would the unemployment rate go up or down?
4. The Meaning of Full Employment When the economy is at full employment, is the unemployment rate at zero percent? Why or why not? How would a more generous unemployment insurance system affect the full employment figure?
5. International Comparisons of Unemployment How has the U.S. unemployment rate compared with rates in other major economies? Can you offer any reasons why rates on average have differed across major economies during the last three decades?
6. Official Unemployment Figures Explain why most experts believe that official U.S. data underestimate the actual rate of unemployment. What factors could make the official rate overstate the actual unemployment rate?
7. Case Study: Hyperinflation in Zimbabwe (See page 748.) In countries such as Zimbabwe, which had problems with high inflation, the increased use of another country's currency (such as the U.S. dollar or South African rand) became common. Why do you suppose this occurred?
8. Sources of Inflation What are the two sources of inflation? How would you illustrate them graphically?
9. Anticipated Versus Unanticipated Inflation If actual inflation exceeds anticipated inflation, who will lose purchasing power and who will gain?
10. Inflation and Relative Price Changes What does the consumer price index measure? Does the index measure changes in relative prices? Why, or why not?
11. Inflation and Interest Rates Explain as carefully as you can why borrowers would be willing to pay a higher interest rate if they expected the inflation rate to increase in the future.
12. Inflation Why is a relatively constant and predictable inflation rate less harmful to an economy than a rate that fluctuates unpredictably?
13. Inflation Why do people dislike inflation?

Problems and Exercises

14. MEASURING UNEMPLOYMENT Determine the impact on each of the following if 2 million formerly unemployed workers decide to return to school full time and stop looking for work:
    a. The labor force participation rate
    b. The size of the labor force
    c. The unemployment rate
15. MEASURING UNEMPLOYMENT Suppose that the U.S. noninstitutional adult population is 230 million and the labor force participation rate is 67 percent.
    a. What would be the size of the U.S. labor force?
    b. If 85 million adults are not working, what is the unemployment rate?
16. TYPES OF UNEMPLOYMENT Determine whether each of the following would be considered frictional, structural, seasonal, or cyclical unemployment:
    a. A UPS employee who was hired for the Christmas season is laid off after Christmas.
    b. A worker is laid off due to reduced aggregate demand in the economy.
    c. A worker in a DVD rental store becomes unemployed as video-on-demand cable service becomes more popular.
    d. A new college graduate is looking for employment.
17. INFLATION Here are some recent data on the U.S. consumer price index:

Year	CPI	Year	CPI	Year	CPI
1992	140.3	1998	163.0	2004	188.9
1993	144.5	1999	166.6	2005	195.3
1994	148.2	2000	172.2	2006	201.6
1995	152.4	2001	177.1	2007	207.3
1996	156.9	2002	179.9	2008	215.3
1997	160.5	2003	184.0	2009	214.5

    Compute the inflation rate for each year 1993–2009 and determine which years were years of inflation. In which years did deflation occur? In which years did disinflation occur? Was there hyperinflation in any year?
18. SOURCES OF INFLATION Using the concepts of aggregate supply and aggregate demand, explain why inflation usually increases during wartime.
19. INFLATION AND INTEREST RATES Using a demand-supply diagram for loanable funds (like Exhibit 10), show what happens to the nominal interest rate and the equilibrium quantity of loans when both borrowers and lenders increase their estimates of the expected inflation rate from 5 percent to 10 percent.

Global Economic Watch Exercises

Login to www.cengagebrain.com and access the Global Economic Watch to do these exercises.

20. GLOBAL ECONOMIC WATCH and Case Study: Hyperinflation in Zimbabwe (See page 748.) Go to the Global Economic Crisis Resource Center. Select Global Issues in Context. In the Basic Search box at the top of the page, enter the word "hyperinflation." On the Results page, go to the Magazines Section. Click on the link for the February 2, 2009, article "What Currency Crisis?" At the time of publication of the article, what was the price in Zimbabwean dollars of a loaf of bread?
21. GLOBAL ECONOMIC WATCH Go to the Global Economic Crisis Resource Center. Select Global Issues in Context. Go to the menu at the top of the page and click on the tab for Browse Issues and Topics. Choose Business and Economy. Click on the link for Unemployment and Joblessness. Find an article from the past three years about unemployment in a foreign country. What is the trend? Is there any information about the causes of and solutions to unemployment in that country?

Productivity and Growth

22

- Why is the standard of living so much higher in some countries than in others?
- How does an economy increase its living standard?
- Why is the long-term growth rate more important than short-term fluctuations in economic activity?
- What's labor productivity, why did it slow for a while, and why did it pick up again?
- What's been the impact of computers and the Internet on labor productivity?

Answers to these and other questions are addressed in this chapter, which focuses on arguably the most important criteria for judging an economy's performance—productivity and growth.

The single most important determinant of a nation's standard of living in the long run is the productivity of its resources. Even seemingly low growth in productivity, if sustained for years, can have a substantial effect on the average living standard—that is, on the average availability of goods and services per capita. Growing productivity is therefore critical to a rising standard of living and has kept the U.S. economy a world leader.

Economic growth is a complicated process, one that even experts do not yet fully understand. Since before Adam Smith inquired into the sources of the *Wealth of Nations*, economists have puzzled over what makes some economies prosper while others founder. Because a market economy is not the product of conscious design, it does not reveal its secrets readily, nor can it be easily manipulated in pursuit of growth. We can't simply push here and pull there to achieve the desired result. Changing the economy

is not like remodeling a home by knocking out a wall to expand the kitchen. Because we have no clear blueprint of the economy, we cannot make changes to specifications.

Still, there is much economists do know. In this chapter, we first develop a few simple models to examine productivity and growth. Then, we use these models to help explain why some nations are rich and some poor. U.S. performance gets special attention, particularly compared with other major economies around the world. We close with some controversies of technology and growth.

Topics include:

- Labor productivity
- The production function
- U.S. productivity and growth
- Technological change and unemployment
- Research and development
- Industrial Policy
- Convergence
- Income and Happiness

Theory of Productivity and Growth

Two centuries ago, 90 percent of the American workforce was in agriculture, where the hours were long and rewards unpredictable. Other workers had it no better, toiling from sunrise to sunset for a wage that bought just the bare necessities. People had little intellectual stimulation and little contact with the outside world. A skilled worker's home in 1800 was described as follows: "Sand sprinkled on the floor did duty as a carpet. . . . What a stove was he did not know. Coal he had never seen. Matches he had never heard of. . . . He rarely tasted fresh meat. . . . If the food of a [skilled worker] would now be thought coarse, his clothes would be thought abominable."[1]

Over the last two centuries, there has been an incredible increase in the U.S. *standard of living* as measured by the amount of goods and services available on average per person. An economy's standard of living grows over the long run because of (1) increases in the amount and quality of resources, especially labor and capital, (2) better technology, and (3) improvements in the *rules of the game* that facilitate production and exchange, such as tax laws, property rights, patent laws, the legal system, and the manners, customs, and conventions of the market. Perhaps the easiest way to introduce economic growth is by beginning with something you have already read about, the production possibilities frontier.

Growth and the Production Possibilities Frontier

The *production possibilities frontier,* or *PPF,* first introduced in Chapter 2, shows what the economy can produce if available resources are used efficiently. Let's briefly review the assumptions made in developing the frontier shown in Exhibit 1. During the period under consideration, usually a year, the quantity of resources in the economy

1. E. L. Bogart, *The Economic History of the United States* (Longmans Green, 1912), pp. 157–158.

EXHIBIT 1 **Economic Growth Shown by Shifts Outward of the Production Possibilities Frontier**

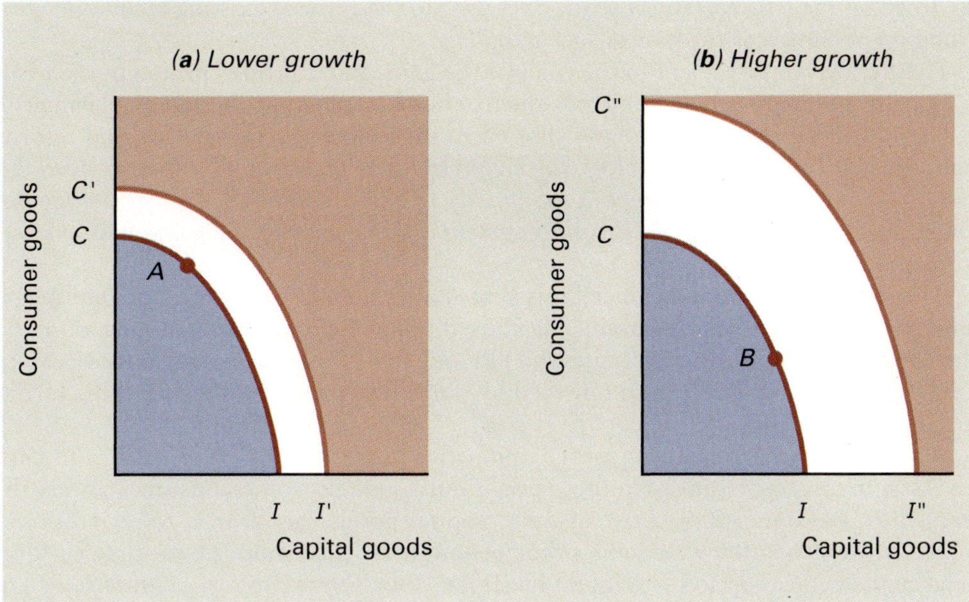

An economy that produces more capital goods will grow more, as reflected by a shift outward of the production possibilities frontier. More capital goods are produced in panel (b) than in panel (a), so the PPF shifts out more in panel (b).

and the level of technology are assumed to be fixed. Also assumed fixed during the period are the rules of the game that facilitate production and exchange. We classify all production into two broad categories—in this case, consumer goods and capital goods. Capital goods are used to produce other goods. For example, the economy can bake pizzas and make pizza ovens. Pizzas are consumer goods, and ovens are capital goods.

When resources are employed efficiently, the production possibilities frontier *CI* in each panel of Exhibit 1 shows the possible combinations of consumer goods and capital goods that can be produced in a given year. Point *C* depicts the quantity of consumer goods produced if all the economy's resources are employed efficiently to produce them. Point *I* depicts the same for capital goods. Points inside the frontier are inefficient combinations, and points outside the frontier are unattainable combinations, given the resources, technology, and rules of the game. The production possibilities frontier is bowed out because resources are not perfectly adaptable to the production of both goods; some resources are specialized.

Economic growth is shown by an outward shift of the production possibilities frontier, as reflected in each panel of Exhibit 1. What can cause growth? An increase in resources, such as a growth in the labor supply or in the capital stock, shifts the frontier outward. Labor supply can increase either because of population growth or because the existing population works more. The capital stock increases if the economy produces more capital this year. The more capital produced this year, the more the economy grows, as reflected by an outward shift of the production frontier.

Breakthroughs in technology also shift out the frontier by making more efficient use of resources. Technological change often improves the quality of capital, but it can enhance the productivity of any resource. And technological change can free up resources for other uses. For example, the development of synthetic dyes in the 19th century freed up millions of acres of agricultural land that had been growing dye crops such as madder (red) and indigo (blue). The development of fiber-optic cable and cellular technology freed up the world's largest stock of copper in the form of existing telephone wires strung on poles across the nation.

Finally, any improvement in the rules of the game that nurtures production and exchange promotes growth and expands the frontier. For example, the economy can grow as a result of improved patent laws that encourage more inventions[2] or legal reforms that reduce transaction costs. Thus, *the economy grows because of a greater availability of resources, an improvement in the quality of resources, technological change that makes better use of resources, or improvements in the rules of the game that enhance production.*

The amount of capital produced this year shapes the PPF next year. For example, in panel (a) of Exhibit 1, the economy has chosen point *A* from possible points along *CI*. The capital produced this year shifts the PPF out to *C′I′* next year. But if more capital goods are produced this year, as reflected by point *B* in panel (b), the PPF shifts farther out next year, to *C″I″*.

An economy that produces more capital this year is said to *invest* more in capital. As you can see, to invest more, people must give up some consumer goods this year. Thus, the opportunity cost of more capital goods this year is fewer consumer goods. More generally, we can say that people must *save* more now—that is, forgo some current consumption—to invest in capital. *Investment cannot occur without saving.* Economies that save more can invest more, as we'll see later. But let's get back to production.

What Is Productivity?

Production *is a process that transforms resources into goods and services.* Resources coupled with technology produce output. Productivity measures how efficiently resources are employed. In simplest terms, the greater the productivity, the more can be produced from a given amount of resources, and the farther out the production possibilities frontier. Economies that use resources more efficiently create a higher standard of living, meaning that more goods and services are produced per capita.

productivity
The ratio of a specific measure of output, such as real GDP, to a specific measure of input, such as labor; in this case productivity measures real GDP per hour of labor

labor productivity
Output per unit of labor; measured as real GDP divided by the hours of labor employed to produce that output

Productivity is defined as the ratio of total output to a specific measure of input. Productivity usually reflects an average, expressing total output divided by the amount of a particular kind of resource employed to produce that output. For example, **labor productivity** is the output per unit of labor and measures total output divided by the hours of labor employed to produce that output.

We can talk about the productivity of any resource, such as labor, capital, or natural resources. When agriculture accounted for most output in the economy, land productivity, such as bushels of grain per acre, was a key measure of economic welfare. Where soil was rocky and barren, people were poorer than where soil was fertile and fruitful. Even today, soil productivity determines the standard of living in some economies. Industrialization and trade, however, have liberated many from dependence on soil fertility. Today, some of the world's most productive economies have little land or have land of poor fertility. For example, Japan has a high living standard even though its population, which is 40 percent that of the United States, lives on a land area only 4 percent the size of the United States.

2. For evidence how the greater protection of intellectual property stimulates technological change, see Sunil Kanwar and Robert Evenson, "Does Intellectual Property Protection Spur Technological Change?" *Oxford Economic Papers*, 55 (April 2003): 235–264.

Labor Productivity

Labor is the resource most commonly used to measure productivity. Why labor? First, labor accounts for most production cost—about 70 percent on average. Second, labor is more easily measured than other inputs, whether we speak of hours per week or full-time workers per year. Statistics about employment and hours worked are more readily available and more reliable than those about other resources.

But the resource most responsible for increasing labor productivity is capital. As introduced in Chapter 1, the two broad categories are human capital and physical capital. *Human capital* is the accumulated knowledge, skill, and experience of the labor force. As workers acquire more human capital, their productivity and their incomes grow. That's why surgeons earn more than butchers and accountants earn more than file clerks. You are reading this book right now to enhance your human capital. *Physical capital* includes the machines, buildings, roads, airports, communication networks, and other human creations used to produce goods and services. Think about digging a ditch with bare hands versus using a shovel. Now switch the shovel for a backhoe. More physical capital obviously makes diggers more productive. Or consider picking oranges with bare hands versus using a picking machine that combs the trees with steel bristles. In less than 15 minutes the machine can pick 18 tons of oranges from 100 trees, catch the fruit, and drop it into storage carts. Without the machine, that would take four workers all day.[3] The operator of the picking machine is at least 128 times more productive than an orange picker using hands only.

In poorer countries labor is cheap and capital dear, so producers substitute labor for capital. For example, in India a beverage truck makes its rounds festooned with workers so as to minimize the time the truck, the valuable resource, spends at each stop. In the United States, where labor is more costly (compared with capital), the truck makes its rounds with just the driver. As another example, in Haiti, the poorest country in the Western Hemisphere, a ferry service could not afford to build a dock, so it hired workers to carry passengers through the water to and from the ferry on their shoulders.[4]

As an economy accumulates more capital per worker, labor productivity increases and the standard of living grows. The most productive combination of all is human capital combined with physical capital. For example, one certified public accountant with a computer and specialized software can sort out a company's finances more quickly and more accurately than could a thousand high-school-educated file clerks using just pencils and paper.

Per-Worker Production Function

We can express the relationship between the amount of capital per worker and the output per worker as an economy's **per-worker production function.** Exhibit 2 shows the amount of capital per worker, measured along the horizontal axis, and average output per worker, or labor productivity, measured along the vertical axis, other things constant—including the amount of labor, the level of technology, and rules of the game. Any point on the production function, *PF*, shows the average output per worker on the vertical axis for each level of capital per worker on the horizontal axis. For example, with k units of capital per worker, the average output per worker in the economy is y. The curve slopes

per-worker production function
The relationship between the amount of capital per worker in the economy and average output per worker

3. Eduardo Porter, "In Florida Groves, Cheap Labor Means Machines," *New York Times*, 22 March 2004.
4. This example was noted by Tyler Cowen, "The Ricardo Effect in Haiti," 23 February 2004, http://www.marginalrevolution.com.

EXHIBIT 2 Per-Worker Production Function

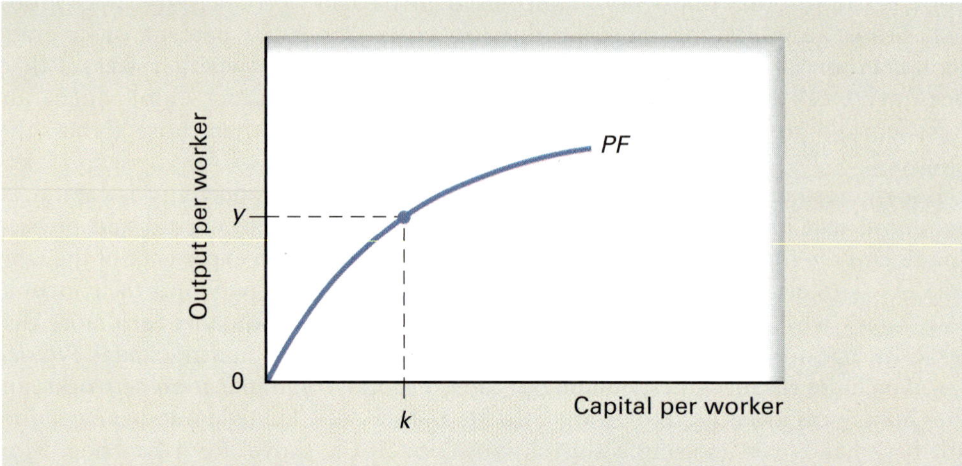

The per-worker production function, *PF*, shows a direct relationship between the amount of capital per worker, *k*, and the output per worker, *y*. The bowed shape of *PF* reflects the law of diminishing marginal returns from capital, which holds that as more capital is added to a given number of workers, output per worker increases but at a diminishing rate and eventually could turn negative.

upward from left to right because an increase in capital per worker helps each worker produce more output. For example, bigger trucks make truck drivers more productive.

capital deepening
An increase in the amount of capital per worker; one source of rising labor productivity

An increase in the amount of capital per worker is called **capital deepening** and is one source of rising productivity. *Capital deepening contributes to labor productivity and economic growth.* As the quantity of capital per worker increases, output per worker increases but at a diminishing rate, as reflected by the shape of the per-worker production function. The diminishing slope of this curve reflects the *law of diminishing marginal returns from capital*, which says that beyond some level of capital per worker, increases in capital add less and less to output per worker. For example, increasing the size of trucks beyond some point has diminishing returns as trucks become too large to negotiate some public roads. Thus, given the amount of labor, the level of technology, and the rules of the game, additional gains from more capital per worker eventually diminish and could turn negative.

Technological Change

Held constant along a per-worker production function is the level of technology in the economy. Technological change usually improves the *quality* of capital and represents another source of increased productivity. For example, a tractor is more productive than a horse-drawn plow, a word processor more productive than a typewriter, and an Excel spreadsheet more productive than pencil and paper. Better technology is reflected in Exhibit 3 by an upward rotation in the per-worker production function from *PF* to *PF*'. As a result of a technological breakthrough, more is produced at each level of capital per worker. For example, if there are *k* units of capital per worker, a major breakthrough in technology increases the output per worker in the economy from *y* to *y*'.

Simon Kuznets, who won a Nobel Prize in part for his analysis of economic growth, claimed that technological change and the ability to apply such breakthroughs to all aspects of production are the driving forces behind economic growth in market economies. Kuznets argued that changes in the *quantities* of labor and capital account for only one-tenth of the increase in economic growth. Nine-tenths came from improvements in the *quality* of these inputs. As technological breakthroughs become *embodied* in new capital, resources are combined more efficiently, increasing total output. *From the wheel to the assembly-line robot, capital embodies the fruits of discovery and drives economic growth.*

Thus, two kinds of changes in capital improve worker productivity: (1) an increase in the *quantity* of capital per worker, as reflected by a movement along the per-worker production function, and (2) an improvement in the *quality* of capital per worker, as reflected by technological change that rotates the curve upward. More capital per worker and better capital per worker result in more output per worker, which, over time, translates into more output per capita, meaning a higher standard of living.

Rules of the Game

Perhaps the most elusive ingredients for productivity and growth are the **rules of the game**, the formal and informal institutions that promote economic activity: the laws, customs, manners, conventions, and other institutional elements that encourage people to undertake productive activity. A stable political environment and system of well-defined property rights are important. Less investment occurs if potential investors believe their capital could be seized by the government, stolen by thieves, destroyed by civil unrest, or blown up by terrorists. For example, countries whose colonizers established strong property rights hundreds of years ago have, on average, much higher incomes today than countries whose colonizers did not.[5] Improvements in the rules of the game could result in more output for each level of capital per worker, thus reflected by a rotation up in the per-worker production function as shown in Exhibit 3.

rules of the game
The formal and informal institutions that promote economic activity; the laws, customs, manners, conventions, and other institutional elements that determine transaction costs and thereby affect people's incentive to undertake production and exchange

EXHIBIT 3 **Impact of a Technological Breakthrough on the Per-Worker Production Function**

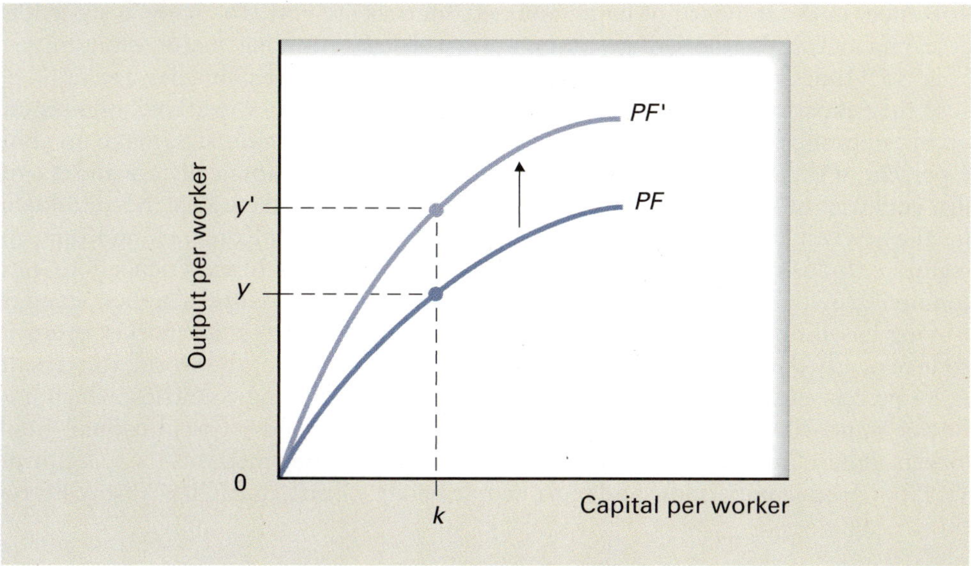

A technological breakthrough increases output per worker at each level of capital per worker. Better technology makes workers more productive. This is shown by a rotation upward in the per-worker production function from *PF* to *PF'*. An improvement in the rules of the game would have a similar effect.

5. Daron Acemoglu, Simon Johnson, and James A. Robinson, "The Colonial Origins of Comparative Development," *American Economic Review*, 91(December 2001): 1369–1401.

We tend to think that laws are the backbone of market exchange, but we should not underestimate the role of manners, customs, and conventions. According to the 18th century British philosopher Edmund Burke, "Manners are of more importance than law. . . . The law touches us but here and there and now and then. Manners are what vex or soothe, corrupt or purify, exalt or debase, barbarize or refine us, by a constant, steady, uniform and insensible operation like that of the air we breathe in."[6] The Russian proverb, "Custom is stronger than law," makes a similar point.

Simply put, a more stable political climate could benefit productivity just like a technological improvement. Conversely, events that foster instability can harm an economy's productivity and rotate the per-worker production function downward. The terrorist attack on the World Trade Center and Pentagon was such a destabilizing event. According to Albert Abadie, a Harvard economist, the attack affected "the spinal cord of any favorable business environment"—the ability of business and workers "to meet and communicate effectively without incurring risks."[7] The 9/11 attacks increased the vacancy rates of tall buildings even in cities besides New York, such as Chicago's Sears Tower, making that capital less productive.[8] As other examples, a greater threat to airport security adds to the time and cost of flying. Shops in countries plagued by suicide bombers must hire security guards to deter such horror, and this increases the cost of doing business. And the mortgage meltdown of 2007–2009 reduced the trust that one bank had in another, thereby freezing up credit markets and increasing the cost of borrowing.

Now that you have some idea about the theory of productivity and growth, let's look at them in practice, beginning with the vast difference in performance among economies around the world. Then we turn to the United States.

Productivity and Growth in Practice

Differences in the standard of living among countries are vast. To give you some idea, per capita output in the United States, a world leader among major economies, is about 155 times that of the world's poorest countries. Poor countries are poor because they experience low labor productivity. We can sort the world's economies into two broad groups. **Industrial market countries**, or *developed countries*, make up about 16 percent of the world's population. They consist of the economically advanced capitalist countries of Western Europe, North America, Australia, New Zealand, and Japan, plus the newly industrialized Asian countries of Taiwan, South Korea, Hong Kong, and Singapore. Industrial market countries were usually the first to experience long-term economic growth during the 19th century, and today have the world's highest standard of living based on abundant human and physical capital. Industrial market countries produce nearly three-quarters of the world's output. The rest of the world, the remaining 84 percent of the world's population, consists of **developing countries**, which have a lower standard of living because they have less human and physical capital. Many workers in developing countries are farmers. Because farming methods there are primitive, labor productivity is low and most people barely subsist, much like Americans two centuries ago.

industrial market countries
Economically advanced capitalist countries of Western Europe, North America, Australia, New Zealand, and Japan, plus the newly industrialized Asian economies of Taiwan, South Korea, Hong Kong, and Singapore

developing countries
Countries with a low living standard because of less human and physical capital per worker

6. Edmund Burke, *Letters to Parliament*, 2nd ed. (London, 1796): 105.
7. As quoted in Greg Ip and John McKinnon, "Economy Likely Won't See Gain from War Against Terrorism," *Wall Street Journal*, 25 September 2001.
8. Alberto Abadie and Sofia Dermisi, "Is Terrorism Eroding Agglomeration Economies in Central Business Districts? Lessons from the Office Real Estate Market in Downtown Chicago," *Journal of Urban Economics*, 64 (September 2008): 451–463.

Education and Economic Development

Another important source of productivity is human capital—the skill, experience, and education of workers. If knowledge is lacking, other resources may not be used efficiently. *Education makes workers aware of the latest production techniques and more receptive to new approaches and methods.* Exhibit 4 shows the percentage of the population ages 25 to 64 who have at least a degree beyond high school. Figures are presented for the United States and six other industrial market economies, together called the *Group of Seven*, or *G-7* (sometimes Russia is added to form the G-8, but Russia is not yet an industrial market economy and has a per capita income less than half of any G-7 country). In 1998, 35 percent of the U.S. adult population had at least a degree beyond high school, ranking second behind Canada. The U.S. percentage grew to 40 by 2007, though America slipped to third behind Canada and Japan.

But a focus on younger adults, those ages 25 to 34, indicates that more countries are passing the United States. Whereas 40 percent of Americans ages 25 to 34 had at least a degree beyond high school in 2007, 54 percent of Canadians did, as well as 54 percent of the Japanese, and 41 percent of the French. And outside of the largest economies, a half dozen other industrial economies exceeded the U.S. percentage.

Not shown in Exhibit 4 are developing countries, which have far lower education levels. For example, while the literacy rate exceeds 95 percent in industrial market economies, more than half the adults in the world's poorest countries can't read or write.

EXHIBIT 4 **Percent of Adult Population With at Least a Post-High School Degree: 1998 and 2007**

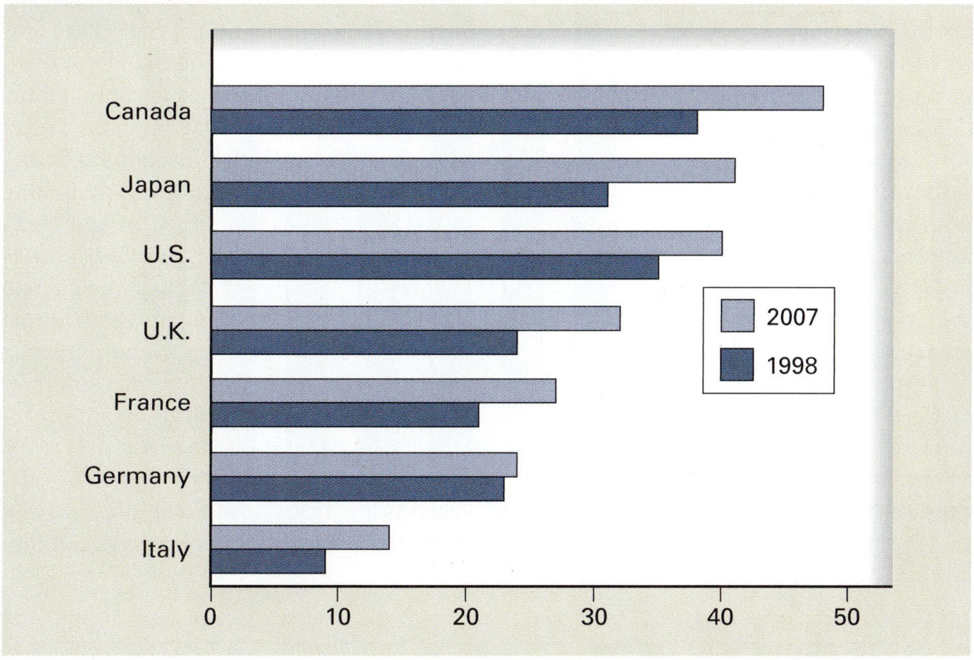

The share of the U.S. population ages 25 to 64 with at least a degree beyond high school increased from 35 percent in 1998 to 40 percent in 2007. The United States slipped from second among major industrial market economies in 1998 to third in 2007.

Source: Based on figures in *Education at a Glance: 2009*, OECD at http://www.oecd.org.

U.S. Labor Productivity

What has been the record of labor productivity in the United States? Exhibit 5 offers a long-run perspective, showing growth in real output per work hour for the last 140 years. Annual productivity growth is averaged by decade. The huge dip during the Great Depression and the strong rebound during World War II are unmistakable. Growth slowed during the 1970s and 1980s but recovered since 1990. Labor productivity has grown an average of 2.1 percent per year since 1870. This may not impress you, but because of the power of compounding, output per hour has jumped 1,735 percent during the period. To put this in perspective, if a roofer in 1870 could shingle one roof in a day, today's roofer could shingle more than 18 roofs in a day.

Over long periods, small differences in productivity can make huge differences in the economy's ability to produce and therefore in the standard of living. For example, if productivity grew only 1.0 percent per year instead of 2.1 percent, output per work hour since 1870 would have increased by only 303 percent, not 1,735 percent. On the

EXHIBIT 5 Long-Term Trend in U.S. Labor Productivity Growth: Annual Average by Decade

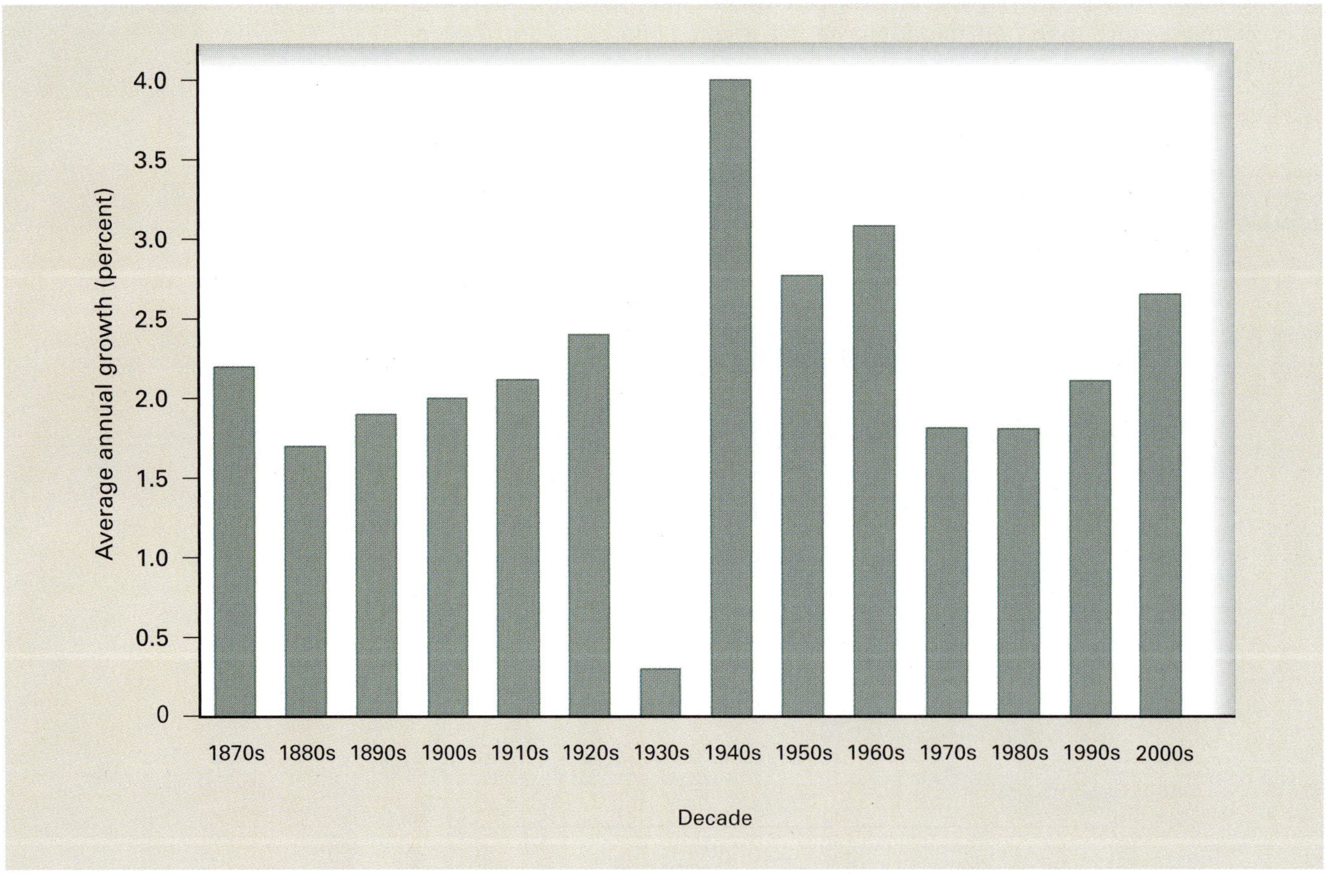

Annual productivity growth, measured as the growth in real output per work hour, is averaged by decade. For the entire period since 1870, labor productivity grew an average of 2.1 percent per year. Note the big dip during the Great Depression of the 1930s and the big bounce back during World War II. Productivity growth slowed during the 1970s and 1980s but recovered during the 1990s and 2000s.

Sources: Angus Maddison, *Phases of Capitalist Development* (New York: Oxford University Press, 1982) and U.S. Bureau of Labor Statistics. Average for the "2000s" decade goes through first half of 2010. For the latest data, go to http://www.bls.gov/lpc/.

other hand, if productivity grew 2.6 percent per year (the average since 1996), output per work hour since 1870 would have jumped 3,536 percent! The wheels of progress seem to grind slowly but they grind very fine, and the cumulative effect is powerful.

So far, we have averaged productivity growth for all workers. Productivity has grown more in some industries than in others. In ocean shipping, for example, cargo carried per worker hour is about 100 times greater now than in 1900, for an average annual growth of 4.3 percent. On the other hand, those making wooden office furniture are only about three times more productive today than in 1900, for an average annual growth in productivity of only 1.3 percent. Consider productivity gains in TV journalism. Not long ago, a TV reporter covering a story would need a camera operator, a sound technician, and a broadcast editor. Now, because of technological advances in the size, quality, and ease of equipment, TV reporters set up their own cameras on the scene, shoot their own footage, and do their own editing. One person can do what used to take four to accomplish.

Slowdown and Rebound in Productivity Growth

You can see in Exhibit 5 that productivity growth slowed to 1.8 percent per year during the 1970s and 1980s, and has recovered since 1990. By breaking the data down into intervals other than decades, we can get a better feel for years since World War II. Exhibit 6 offers average annual growth for four periods. Labor productivity growth averaged 2.9 percent per year between 1948 and 1973; these could be called the golden

EXHIBIT 6 **U.S. Labor Productivity Growth Slowed During 1974 to 1982 and Then Rebounded**

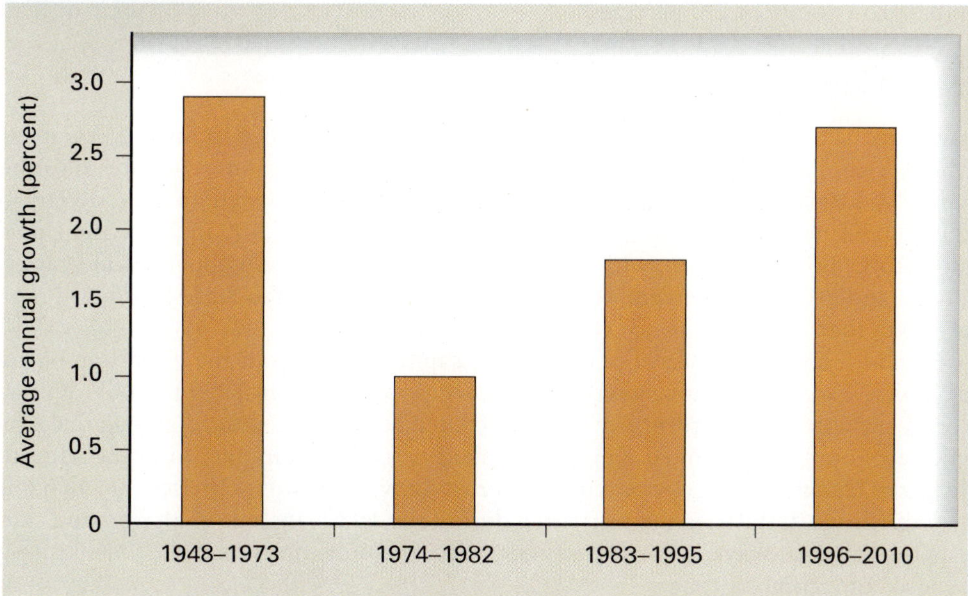

The growth in labor productivity declined from an average of 2.9 percent per year between 1948 and 1973 to only 1.0 percent between 1974 and 1982. A jump in the price of oil contributed to three recessions during that stretch, and new environmental and workplace regulations, though necessary and beneficial, slowed down productivity growth temporarily. The information revolution powered by the computer chip and the Internet has boosted productivity in recent years.

Source: Averages based on annual estimates from the U.S. Bureau of Labor Statistics. For the latest data go to http://www.bls.gov/lpc/home.htm. Average for 1996–2010 is through the first half of 2010.

years of productivity growth. But, between 1974 and 1982, productivity growth slowed to only a third of that, averaging just 1.0 percent. Why the slowdown? First, oil prices jumped from 1973 to 1974 and again from 1979 to 1980 as a result of OPEC actions, boosting inflation and contributing to stagflation and three recessions. Second, legislation in the early 1970s necessary to protect the environment and improve workplace safety slowed the growth of labor productivity.

Fortunately, productivity rebounded off the 1974–1982 low, averaging 1.8 percent from 1983 to 1995 and 2.7 percent from 1996 to 2010. Why the rebound? The information revolution powered by the computer chip started paying off, as discussed in the case study, "The Information Economy: Computers, the Internet, and Productivity Growth" at the end of the book.

Higher labor productivity growth can easily make up for output lost from most recessions. For example, if over the next 10 years the U.S. labor productivity grows an average of 2.7 percent per year (the average from 1996 to 2010) instead of 1.8 percent (the average from 1983 to 1995), that higher growth would add $1.5 trillion to GDP in the 10th year—more than enough to make up for the output lost during the worst recession since the Great Depression. *This cumulative power of productivity growth is why economists pay so much attention to long-term growth.*

Output per Capita

As noted earlier, the best measure of an economy's standard of living is output per capita. *Output per capita*, or GDP divided by the population, indicates how much an economy produces on average per resident. Exhibit 7 presents real GDP per capita for the United States since 1959. Notice the general upward trend, interrupted by eight recessions, indicated by the pink bars. Real GDP per capita nearly tripled for an average annual growth rate of 2.0 percent.

International Comparisons

How does U.S. output per capita compare with that of other industrial countries? Exhibit 8 compares GDP per capita in 2009 for the United States and the six other leading industrial nations. Local currencies have been converted to U.S. dollars of 2009 purchasing power. With nominal GDP per capita of $46,400 in 2009, the United States stood alone at the top, with a per capita income 21 percent above second-ranked Canada and at least 32 percent above the rest. Thus, the United States produced more per capita than any other major economy.

Exhibit 8 looks at the *level* of output per capita. What about the *growth* in output per capita? Exhibit 9 shows growth in real GDP per capita from 1979 to 2009. With an average growth of 1.8 percent per year, the United States ranked third among the seven major economies. The United Kingdom ranked first, thanks in part to Prime Minister Margaret Thatcher, who converted some crusty government enterprises into dynamic for-profit firms. Industries she *privatized* during the 1980s include coal, iron and steel, gas, electricity, railways, trucking, airlines, telecommunications, and the water supply. She also cut income tax rates.

To Review: U.S. labor productivity growth has averaged 2.1 percent per year since 1870. Productivity growth slowed between 1974 and 1982, because of spikes in energy prices and implementation of necessary but costly new environmental and workplace regulations. Since 1982 labor productivity growth has picked up, especially since 1996, due primarily to breakthroughs in information technology. Among the seven major

EXHIBIT 7 **U.S. Real GDP per Capita has Nearly Tripled Since 1959**

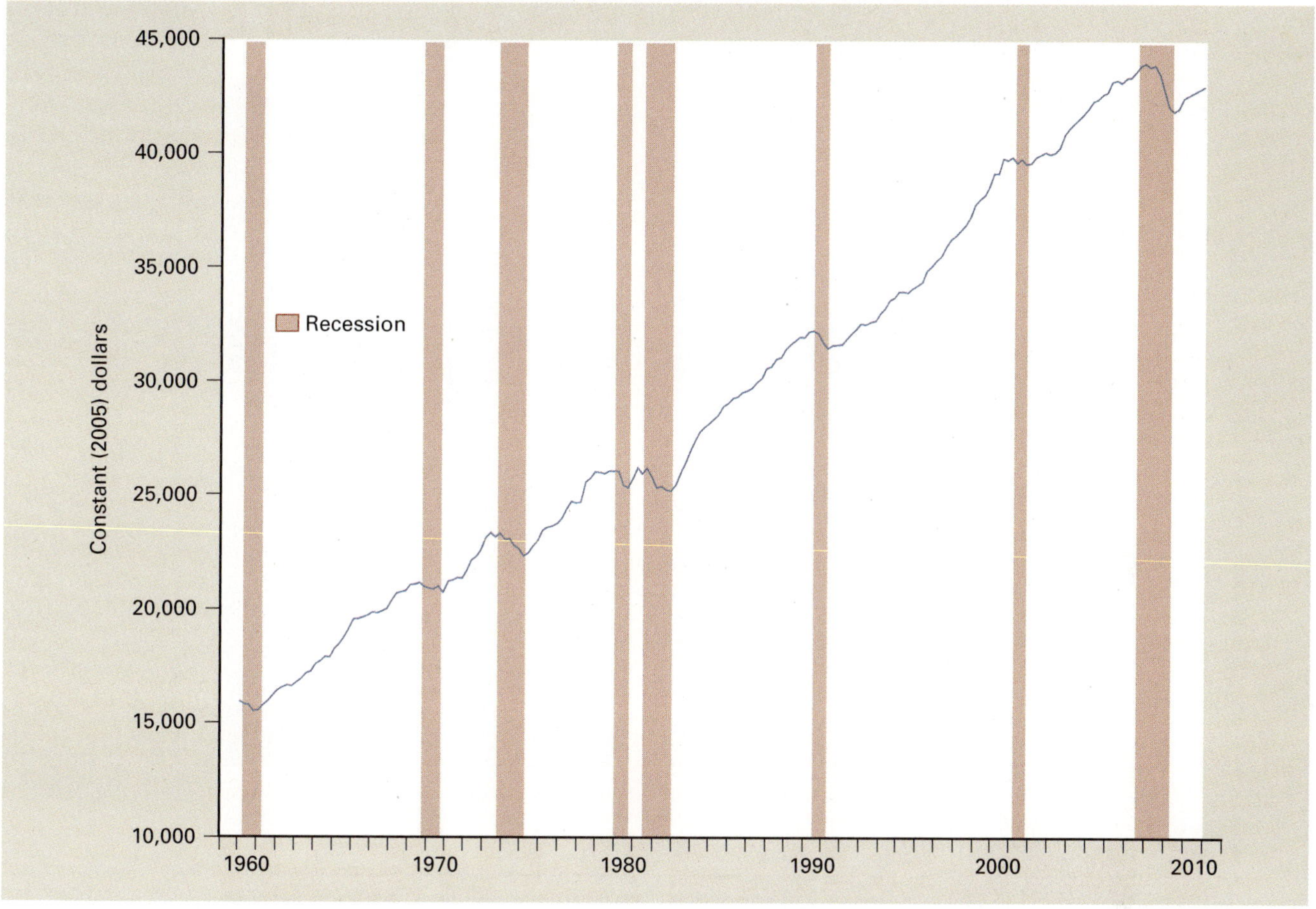

Despite eight recessions since 1959, real GDP per capita has nearly tripled. Periods of recession are indicated by the pink shaded bars.

Source: *Survey of Current Business,* 90 (May 2010), Chart D. For the latest data, go to http://www.bea.gov/scb/index.htm. Select the most recent month, go to the "National Data" section toward the end of the page, and then select "Charts."

economies, the United States experienced the third fastest growth in real GDP per capita income between 1979 and 2009, and in 2009 boasted the highest GDP per capita among major economies.

Other Issues of Technology and Growth

In this section we consider some other issues of technology and growth, beginning with the question whether technological change creates unemployment.

Does Technological Change Lead to Unemployment?

Because technological change usually reduces the labor needed to produce a given amount of output, some observers fear technological change increases unemployment. True, technological change can create dislocations as displaced workers try to find jobs

EXHIBIT 8 U.S. GDP per Capita in 2009 was Highest of Major Economies

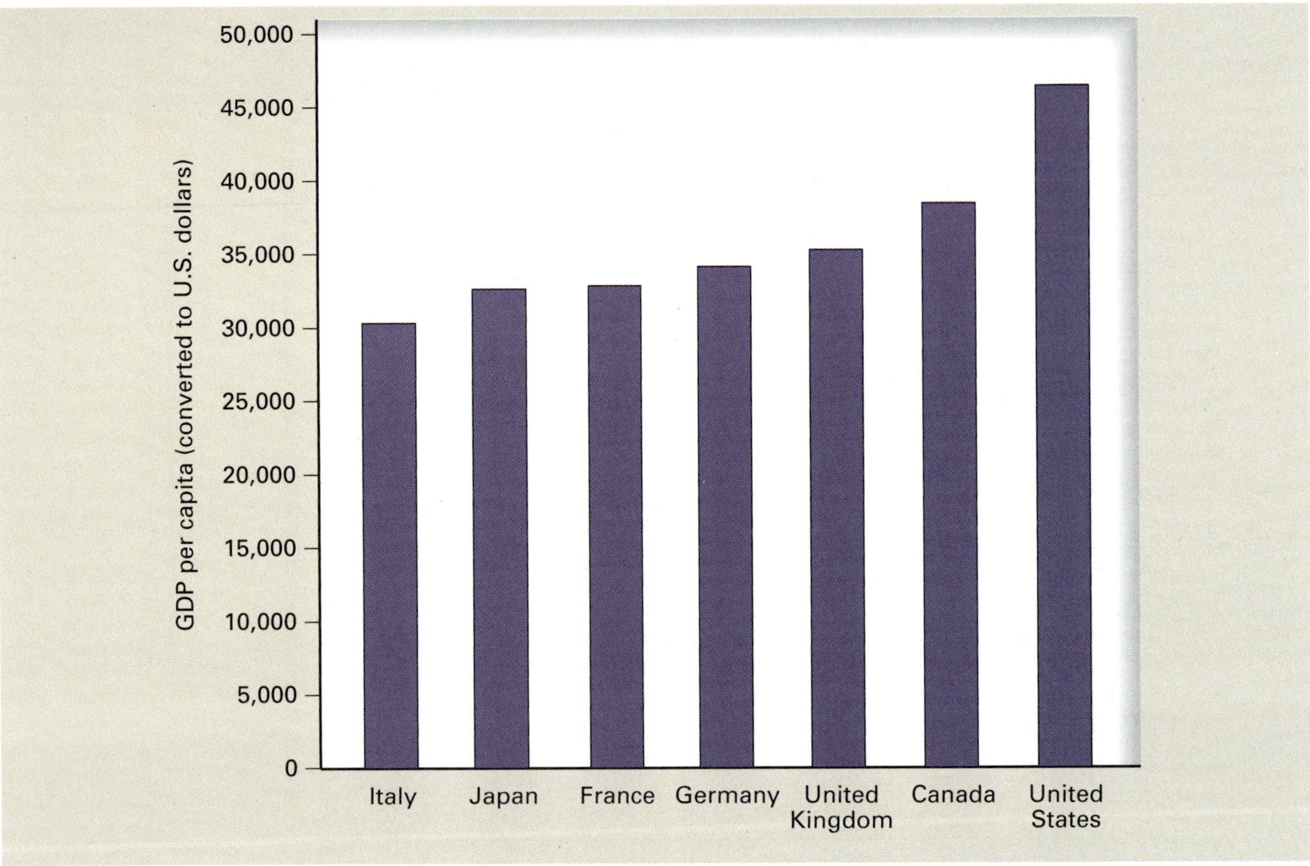

Source: Based on 2009 dollar estimates from the OECD at http://www.oecd.org/home/ and *The World Factbook:* at https://www.cia.gov/library/publications/the-world-factbook/index.html. Estimates have been adjusted across countries using the purchasing power of the local currency in 2009.

elsewhere. But technological change can also create new products and job opportunities and make existing products more affordable. For example, the assembly line cut the cost of automobiles, making them more affordable for the average household. This increased the quantity of automobiles demanded, boosting production and employment. Even in industries where machines displace some workers, those who keep their jobs become more productive, so they earn more. And *because human wants are unlimited, displaced workers usually find jobs producing other goods and services demanded in a growing economy.*

Although job data from the 19th century are sketchy, there is no evidence that the unemployment rate is any higher today than it was in 1870. Since then, worker productivity has increased over 1,700 percent, and the length of the average workweek has been cut nearly in half. Although technological change may displace some workers in the short run, long-run benefits include higher real incomes and more leisure—in short, a higher standard of living.

EXHIBIT 9 U.S. Real GDP per Capita Outgrew Most Other Major Economies Between 1979 and 2009

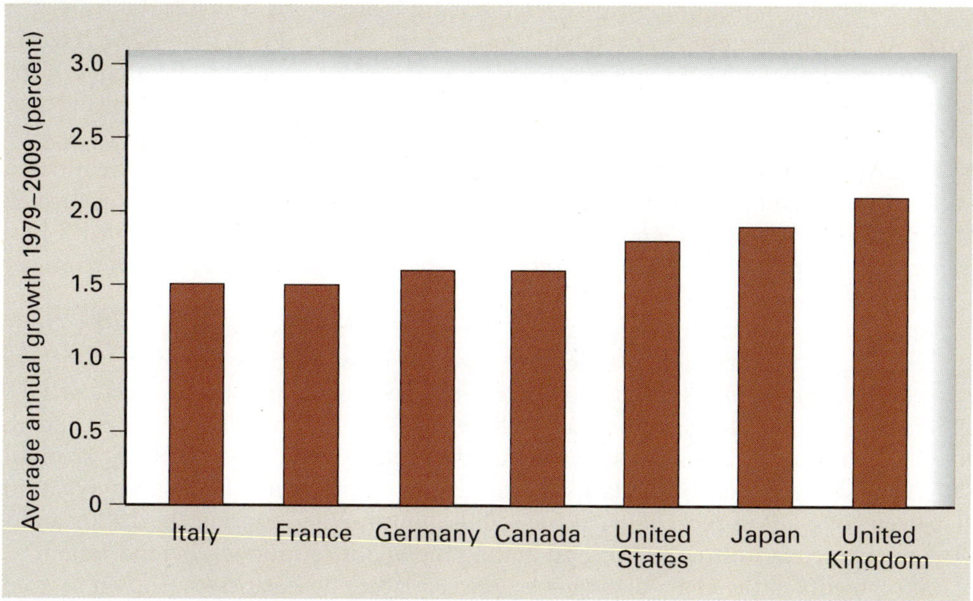

Source: Based on annual figures from 1979 to 2009 from the U.S. Bureau of Labor Statistics at ftp://ftp.bls.gov/pub/special.requests/ForeignLabor/flsgdp.txt. Figures were converted into U.S. dollars based on the purchasing power of local currency. The German growth rate prior to 1991, is for West Germany. For the latest data, go to http://www.stats.bls.gov/fls/.

If technological change causes unemployment, then the recent spurt in productivity growth should have increased unemployment compared to the slow-growth years from 1974 to 1982. But the unemployment rate, the percentage of the workforce looking for jobs, averaged 7.2 percent during 1974 to 1982, compared to only 5.6 percent from 1996 to 2010. And if technological change causes unemployment, then unemployment rates should be lower in economies where the latest technology has not yet been adopted, such as in developing countries. But unemployment is much worse there, and those fortunate enough to find work earn little because they are not very productive.

Again, there is no question that technological change sometimes creates job dislocations and hardships in the short run, as workers scramble to adjust to a changing world. Some workers with specialized skills made obsolete by technology may be unable to find jobs that pay as well as the ones they lost. These dislocations are one price of progress. Over time, however, most displaced workers find other jobs, often in new industries created by technological change. In a typical year of expansion, the U.S. economy eliminates about 10 million jobs but creates nearly 12 million new ones. Out with the old, in with the new.

Research and Development

As noted several times already, a prime contributor to labor productivity growth has been an improvement in the quality of human and physical capital. Human capital has benefited from better education and more job training. Better technology embodied in physical capital has also helped labor productivity. For example, because of extensive investments in cellular transmission, new satellites, and fiber-optic technology, labor productivity in the telecommunications industry has increased by an average of 5.5 percent per year during the past three decades.

basic research
The search for knowledge without regard to how that knowledge will be used

applied research
Research that seeks answers to particular questions or to apply scientific discoveries to develop specific products

Improvements in technology arise from scientific discovery, which is the fruit of research. We can distinguish between basic research and applied research. **Basic research**, the search for knowledge without regard to how that knowledge will be used, is a first step toward technological advancement. In terms of economic growth, however, scientific discoveries are meaningless until they are implemented, which requires applied research. **Applied research** seeks to answer particular questions or to apply scientific discoveries to the development of specific products. Because technological breakthroughs may or may not have commercial possibilities, the payoff is less immediate with basic research than with applied research. *Yet basic research yields a higher return to society as a whole than does applied research.*

Because technological change is the fruit of research and development (R&D), investment in R&D improves productivity through technological discovery. One way to track R&D spending is to measure it relative to gross domestic product, or GDP. Exhibit 10 shows R&D spending as a share of GDP for the United States and the six other major economies for the 1980s, 1990s, and 2007. Overall R&D spending in the United States during the last quarter century has remained constant, averaging 2.7 percent of GDP in the 1980s, in the 1990s, and in 2007. During the 1990s and in 2007, the United States ranked second among the major economies, behind Japan.

Bar segments in the chart distinguish between R&D by businesses (shown as green segments) and R&D by governments and nonprofit institutions (shown as orange segments). Business R&D is more likely to target applied research and innovations. R&D spending by governments and nonprofits, such as universities, may generate basic knowledge that has applications in the long run (for example, the Internet sprang from R&D spending on national defense). R&D by U.S. businesses averaged about 1.9 percent of GDP in all three periods. Again, only Japan had higher business R&D than the United States in the 1990s and in 2007. In short, the United States devotes more resources to R&D than most other advanced economies, and this helps America maintain a higher standard of living.

Industrial Policy

Policy makers have debated whether government should become more involved in shaping an economy's technological future. One concern is that technologies of the future will require huge sums to develop, sums that an individual firm cannot easily raise and put at risk. Another concern is that some technological breakthroughs spill over to other firms and other industries, but the firm that develops the breakthrough may not be in a position to reap benefits from these spillover effects, so individual firms may underinvest in such research. One possible solution is more government involvement in economic planning.

industrial policy
The view that government—using taxes, subsidies, and regulations—should nurture the industries and technologies of the future, thereby giving these domestic industries an advantage over foreign competition

Industrial policy is the idea that government, using taxes, subsidies, regulations, and coordination of the private sector, could help nurture the industries and technologies of the future to give domestic industries an advantage over foreign competitors. The idea is to secure a leading role for domestic industry in the world economy. One example of European industrial policy is Airbus Industrie, a four-nation aircraft consortium. With an estimated $20 billion in government aid, the aircraft maker has become Boeing's main rival. When Airbus seeks aircraft orders around the world, it can draw on government backing to promise favorable terms, such as landing rights at key European airports and an easing of regulatory constraints. U.S. producers get less government backing.

EXHIBIT 10 **R&D Spending as a Percentage of GDP for Major Economies During the 1980s, 1990s, and 2007**

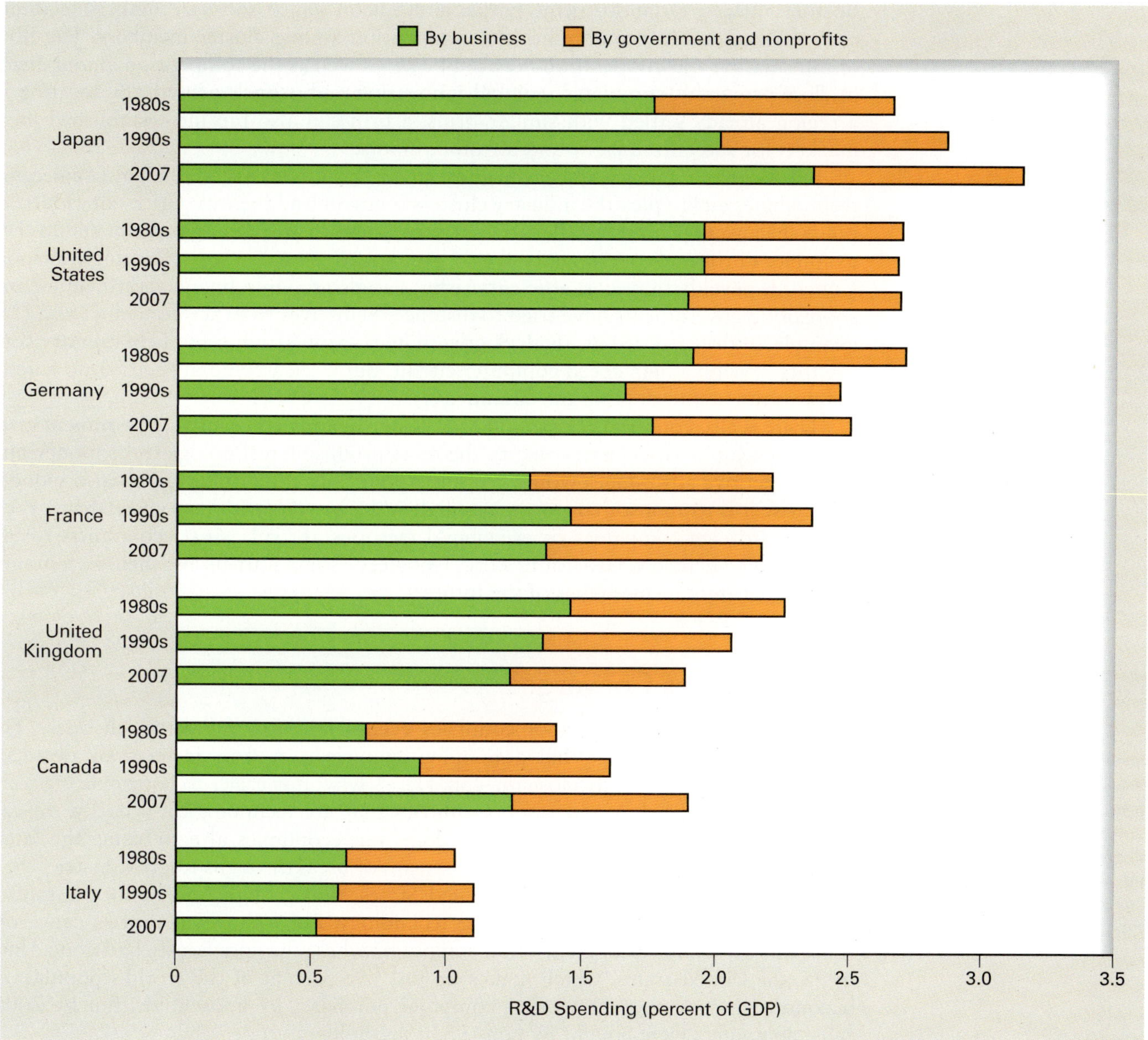

Source: Based on estimates developed by the OECD at www.oecd.org.

For decades, U.S. industrial policy was aimed at creating the world's most advanced military production capacity. With the demise of the Soviet Union, however, defense technologies became less important, but wars in Iraq and Afghanistan have shifted some attention back to military applications. Some argue that U.S. industrial policy should shift from a military to a civilian focus. Many state governments are also trying to identify what industries to support. Economists have long recognized that firms in some industries gain a performance advantage by *clustering*—that is, by locating in a region already thick with firms in the same industry or in related industries. Clusters such as Hollywood studios, Wall Street brokers, Broadway theaters, Las Vegas casinos, Boston colleges, Orlando theme parks, and Silicon Valley software makers facilitate communication and promote healthy competition among cluster members. The flow of information and cooperation between firms, as well as the competition among firms in close proximity, stimulates regional innovation and propels growth. By locating in a region already settled with similar firms, a firm can also tap into established local markets for specialized labor and for other inputs.

But skeptics wonder whether the government should be trusted to identify emerging technologies and to pick the industry clusters that will lead the way. Critics of industrial policy believe that markets allocate scarce resources better than governments do. For example, European governments' costly attempt to develop the supersonic transport Concorde never became cost efficient. Airbus has also run into financial difficulties, and sponsoring governments have tried to distance themselves from the company. As a U.S. example, in the early 1980s, the U.S. government spent $1 billion to help military contractors develop a high-speed computer circuit. But Intel, a company getting no federal aid, was the first to develop the circuit.

There is also concern that an industrial policy would evolve into a government giveaway program. Rather than going to the most promising technologies, the money and the competitive advantages would go to the politically connected. Critics also wonder how wise it is to sponsor corporate research when beneficiaries may share their expertise with foreign companies or even build factories abroad. Most economists would prefer to let Microsoft, General Electric, Google, or some start-up bet their own money on the important technologies of the future.

Do Economies Converge?

convergence
A theory predicting that the standard of living in economies around the world will grow more similar over time, with poorer countries eventually catching up with richer ones

If given enough time, will poor countries eventually catch up with rich ones? The **convergence** theory argues that developing countries can grow faster than advanced ones and should eventually close the gap. Here's why: It is easier to copy existing technology than to develop new ones. Countries that are technologically backward can grow faster by adopting existing technology. But economies already using the latest technology must come up with a steady stream of breakthroughs to grow faster.

Leading countries, such as the United States, find growth limited by the rate of creation of new knowledge and better technology. But follower countries can grow more quickly by, for example, adding computers where they previously had none. Until 1995, the United States, which makes up just five percent of the world's population, accounted for most of the world's computer purchases by households. But by 2000, most computers were bought by non-U.S. households.

What's the evidence on convergence? Some poor countries have begun to catch up with richer ones. For example, the newly industrialized Asian economies of Hong Kong, Singapore, South Korea, and Taiwan, by adopting the latest technology and investing in human resources, are closing the gap with the world leaders. Real output per capita in South Korea has grown three times faster than the average for the seven major economies. These *Asian Tigers* have graduated from developing economies to industrial market economies. But these are the exceptions. According to research by the World Bank, among the nations that comprise the poorest third of the world's population, consumption per capita has grown only about 1.0 percent per year over the past two decades compared with a 2.5 percent growth in the rest of the world, so the standard of living in the poorest third of the world has grown somewhat in absolute terms but has fallen further behind in relative terms. Worse yet, a billion people seem trapped in poor economies that are going nowhere.

One reason per capita consumption has grown so slowly in the poorest economies is that birthrates there are double those in richer countries, so poor economies must produce still more just to keep up with a growing population. Another reason why convergence has not begun, particularly for the poorest third of the world, is the vast difference in the quality of human capital across countries. Whereas technology is indeed portable, the knowledge, skill, and training needed to take advantage of that technology are not. Countries with a high level of human capital can make up for other shortcomings. For example, much of the capital stock in Japan and Germany was destroyed during World War II. But the two countries retained enough of their well-educated and highly skilled labor force to rejoin elite industrial market economies in little more than a generation. But some countries, such as those in Africa, simply lack the human capital needed to identify and absorb new technology. As noted already, such poor economies tend to have low education levels and low literacy rates. What's more, some countries lack the stable macroeconomic environment and the established institutions needed to nurture economic growth. Many developing countries have serious deficiencies in their infrastructures, lacking, for example, the reliable source of electricity to power new technologies. For example, in Northern Nigeria, near the Sahara, 90 percent of the villages have no electricity. Some of the poorest nations have been ravaged by civil war for years. And simply communicating can be challenging in some developing countries. In Nigeria, for example, more than 400 languages are spoken by 250 distinct ethnic groups. (To learn more about the challenges facing the poorest nations, read the final chapter of this book, entitled "Economic Development.")

Some argue that the focus should be less on a nation's production and income and more on the happiness of the population. The link between income and happiness is discussed in the case study, "Public Policy: Income and Happiness," at the end of the book.

Conclusion

Productivity and growth depend on the supply and quality of resources, the level of technology, and the rules of the game that nurture production and exchange. These elements tend to be correlated with one another. An economy with an unskilled and poorly educated workforce usually is deficient in physical capital, in technology, and in the institutional support that promotes production and exchange. Similarly, an economy with a high-quality workforce likely excels in the other sources of productivity and growth.

We should distinguish between an economy's standard of living, as measured by output per capita, and improvements in that standard of living, as measured by the growth in output per capita. Growth in output per capita can occur when labor productivity increases or when the number of workers in the economy grows faster than the population. *In the long run, productivity growth and the growth in workers relative to the growth in population will determine whether or not the United States continues to enjoy one of the world's highest standard of living.*

Summary

1. If the population is continually increasing, an economy must produce more goods and services simply to maintain its standard of living, as measured by output per capita. If output grows faster than the population, the standard of living rises.
2. An economy's standard of living grows over the long run because of (a) increases in the amount and quality of resources, especially labor and capital, (b) better technology, and (c) improvements in the rules of the game that facilitate production and exchange, such as tax laws, property rights, patent laws, the legal system, and customs of the market.
3. The per-worker production function shows the relationship between the amount of capital per worker in the economy and the output per worker. As capital per worker increases, so does output per worker but at a decreasing rate. Technological change and improvements in the rules of the game shift the per-worker production function upward, so more is produced for each ratio of capital per worker.
4. Since 1870, U.S. labor productivity growth has averaged 2.1 percent per year. The *quality* of labor and capital is much more important than the *quantity* of these resources. Labor productivity growth slowed between 1974 and 1982, in part because of spikes in energy prices and implementation of costly but necessary environmental and workplace regulations. Since 1983 productivity growth has picked up, especially since 1996, due primarily to information technology.
5. Among the seven major industrial market economies, the United States has experienced the third highest growth rate in real GDP per capita over the last quarter of a century and most recently produced the highest real GDP per capita.
6. Technological change sometimes costs jobs and imposes hardships in the short run, as workers scramble to adapt to a changing world. Over time, however, most displaced workers find other jobs, sometimes in new industries created by technological change. There is no evidence that, in the long run, technological change increases unemployment in the economy.
7. Some governments use industrial policy in an effort to nurture the industries and technologies of the future, giving domestic industries an advantage over foreign competitors. But critics are wary of the government's ability to pick the winning technologies.
8. Convergence is a theory predicting that the standard of living around the world will grow more alike, as poorer countries catch up with richer ones. Some Asian countries that had been poor are catching up with the leaders, but many poor countries around the world have failed to close the gap.

Key Concepts

Productivity 436
Labor productivity 436
Per-worker production function 437
Capital deepening 438
Rules of the game 439
Industrial market countries 440
Developing countries 440
Basic research 448
Applied research 448
Industrial policy 448
Convergence 450

Questions for Review

1. Productivity As discussed in the text, per capita GDP in many developing countries depends on the fertility of land there. However, many richer economies have little land or land of poor quality. How can a country with little land or unproductive land become rich?
2. Labor Productivity What two kinds of changes in the capital stock can improve labor productivity? How can each type be illustrated with a per-worker production function? What determines the slope of the per-worker production function?
3. Slowdown in Labor Productivity Growth What slowed the rate of growth in labor productivity during the 1974–1982 period?
4. Output per Capita Explain how output per capita can grow faster than labor productivity. Is it possible for labor productivity to grow faster than output per capita?
5. Technology and Productivity What measures can government take to promote the development of practical technologies?
6. Basic and Applied Research What is the difference between basic research and applied research? Relate this to the human genome project—research aimed at developing a complete map of human chromosomes, showing the location of every gene.
7. Rules of the Game How do "rules of the game" affect productivity and growth? What types of "rules" should a government set to encourage growth?
8. Case Study: Computers, the Internet, and Productivity Growth (See page 749.) How has the increased use of computers affected U.S. productivity in recent years? Is the contribution of computers expected to increase or decrease in the near future? Explain.
9. International Productivity Comparisons How does output per capita in the United States compare with output per

capita in other major industrial economies? How has this comparison changed over time?

10. Industrial Policy Define industrial policy. What are some arguments in favor of industrial policy?

11. Technological Change and Unemployment Explain how technological change can lead to unemployment in certain industries. How can it increase employment?

12. Convergence Explain the convergence theory. Under what circumstances is convergence unlikely to occur?

13. Productivity What factors might contribute to a low *level* of productivity in an economy? Regardless of the level of labor productivity, what impact does slow *growth* in labor productivity have on the economy's standard of living?

14. Case Study: Income and Happiness (See page 750.) How would you explain the finding that people in high-income economies seem happier than people in low-income economies, but, over generations, Americans do not seem to become happier even though the nation grows richer?

Problems and Exercises

15. Growth and the PPF Use the production possibilities frontier (PPF) to demonstrate economic growth.
    a. With consumption goods on one axis and capital goods on the other, show how the combination of goods selected this period affects the PPF in the next period.
    b. Extend this comparison by choosing a different point on this period's PPF and determining whether that combination leads to more or less growth over the next period.

16. Long-Term Productivity Growth Suppose that two nations start out in 2011 with identical levels of output per work hour—say, $100 per hour. In the first nation, labor productivity grows by one percent per year. In the second, it grows by two percent per year. Use a calculator or a spreadsheet to determine how much output per hour each nation will be producing 20 years later, assuming that labor productivity growth rates do not change. Then, determine how much each will be producing per hour 100 years later. What do your results tell you about the effects of small differences in productivity growth rates?

17. Technological Change and Unemployment What are some examples, other than those given in the chapter, of technological change that has caused unemployment? And what are some examples of new technologies that have created jobs? How do you think you might measure the net impact of technological change on overall employment and GDP in the United States?

18. Shifts in the PPF Terrorist attacks foster instability and may affect productivity over the short and long term. Do you think the September 11, 2001, terrorist attacks on the World Trade Center and the Pentagon affected short- or long-term productivity in the United States? Explain your response and show any movements in the PPF.

Global Economic Watch Exercises

Login to www.cengagebrain.com and access the Global Economic Watch to do these exercises.

19. Global Economic Watch Go to the Global Economic Crisis Resource Center. Select Global Issues in Context. In the Basic Search box at the top of the page, enter the word "productivity." On the Results page, go to the Global Viewpoints Section. Click on the link for the May 15, 2009, article "Will Productivity Pull Us Out?" Traditionally, why do Canada and Europe experience slower productivity growth after a recession than does the U.S.?

20. Global Economic Watch Go to the Global Economic Crisis Resource Center. Select Global Issues in Context. In the Basic Search box at the top of the page, enter the phrase "economic convergence." Choose one article. Does it support the concept of economic convergence or not? Explain why.

Aggregate Expenditure

23

- When driving through a neighborhood new to you, how can you guess the income of the residents?
- How would your spending change if your summer job pays more than you expected?
- What's the most predictable and useful relationship in macroeconomics?
- Why are consumer confidence and business confidence in the economy so important?
- Why did Americans spend less and save more after the financial crisis of 2008?

Answers to these and other questions are addressed in this chapter, which focuses on the makeup of aggregate expenditure.

Consumption is the most important, accounting for about two-thirds of all spending. But in this short chapter, we also examine investment, government purchases, and net exports. We discuss how each relates to income in the economy. Let's see where this leads. In the next chapter, we combine these spending components to derive the aggregate demand curve. After that, we develop the aggregate supply curve and see how the two curves interact to determine the economy's equilibrium levels of price and output.

Topics in the current chapter include:

- Consumption and income
- Marginal propensities to consume and to save
- Changes in consumption and in saving
- Investment
- Government purchases
- Net exports
- Composition of spending

Consumption

What if a college friend invites you home for the weekend? On your first visit, you would get some idea of the family's standard of living. Is their house a mansion, a dump, or in between? Do they drive a new BMW or take the bus? The simple fact is that consumption tends to reflect income. Although some people can temporarily live beyond their means and others still have the first nickel they ever earned, in general, consumption depends on income. *The positive and stable relationship between consumption and income, both for the household and for the economy as a whole, is the main point of this chapter.*

A key decision in the circular-flow model developed three chapters back was how much households spent and how much they saved. Consumption depends primarily on income. Although this relationship seems obvious, the link between consumption and income is fundamental to understanding how the economy works. Let's look at this link in the U.S. economy over time.

A First Look at Consumption and Income

Exhibit 1 shows consumer spending, or consumption, in the United States since 1959 as the red line and *disposable income* as the blue line. Disposable income, remember, is the income actually available for consumption and saving. Data have been adjusted for

EXHIBIT 1 Disposable Income, Consumption, and Saving in the United States

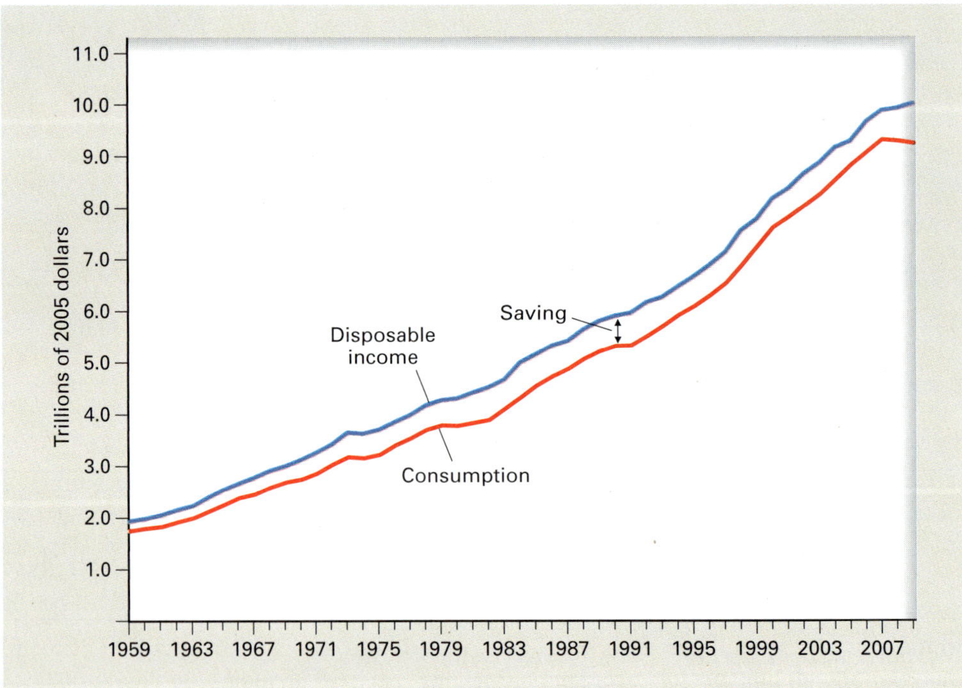

There is a clear and direct relationship between consumption, shown by the red line, and disposable income, shown by the blue line. Disposable income minus consumption equals saving, shown by the vertical distance between disposable income and consumption.

Source: Based on annual estimates from the Bureau of Economic Analysis, U.S. Department of Commerce. For the latest data, go to http://bea.gov/.

inflation so that dollars are of constant purchasing power—in this case, 2005 dollars. Notice that consumer spending and disposable income move together over time. Both increased nearly every year, and the relationship between the two appears relatively stable. Specifically, consumer spending has averaged about 90 percent of disposable income. Disposable income minus consumption equals saving. In Exhibit 1, saving is measured by the vertical distance between the two lines. Saving has averaged about 10 percent of disposable income. Exhibit 1 reflects the flow each year of disposable income, consumption, and saving.

Another way to graph the relationship between consumption and income over time is shown in Exhibit 2, where consumption is measured along the vertical axis and disposable income along the horizontal axis. Notice that each axis measures the same units: trillions of 2005 dollars. Each year is depicted by a point that reflects two flow values: disposable income and consumption. For example, the combination for 1985, identified by the red point, shows that when disposable income (measured along the horizontal axis) was $5.1 trillion, consumption (measured along the vertical axis) was $4.5 trillion.

EXHIBIT 2 U.S. Consumption Depends on Disposable Income

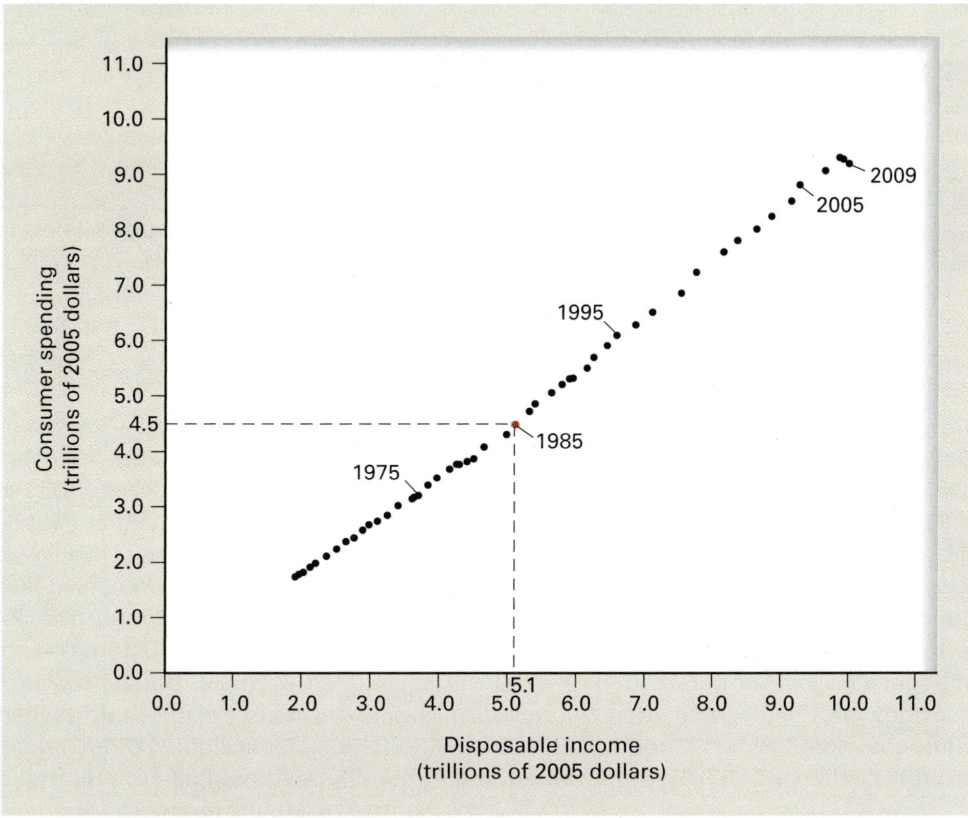

Consumption is on the vertical axis and disposable income on the horizontal axis. Notice that each axis measures trillions of 2005 dollars. For example, in 1985, identified by the red point, consumption was $4.5 trillion and disposable income $5.1 trillion. There is a clear and direct relationship over time between disposable income and consumption. As disposable income increases, so does consumption.

Source: Based on estimates from the Bureau of Economic Analysis, U.S. Department of Commerce. For the latest data, go to http://bea.gov/.

As you can see, there is a clear and direct relationship between consumption and disposable income, a relationship that should come as no surprise after Exhibit 1. You need little imagination to see that by connecting the dots in Exhibit 2, you could trace a line relating consumption to income. This relationship has special significance in macroeconomics.

The Consumption Function

consumption function
The relationship in the economy between consumption and income, other things constant

After examining the link between consumption and income, we found it to be quite stable. Based on their disposable income, households decide how much to consume and how much to save. So consumption depends on disposable income. *Consumption is the dependent variable and disposable income, the independent variable.* Because consumption depends on income, we say that consumption is a *function* of income. Exhibit 3 presents for the economy a hypothetical **consumption function,** which shows that consumption increases with disposable income, assuming other determinants of consumption remain constant. Again, both consumption and disposable income are in real terms, or in inflation-adjusted dollars. Notice that this hypothetical consumption function reflects the historical relationship between consumption and income shown in Exhibit 2.

EXHIBIT 3 The Consumption Function

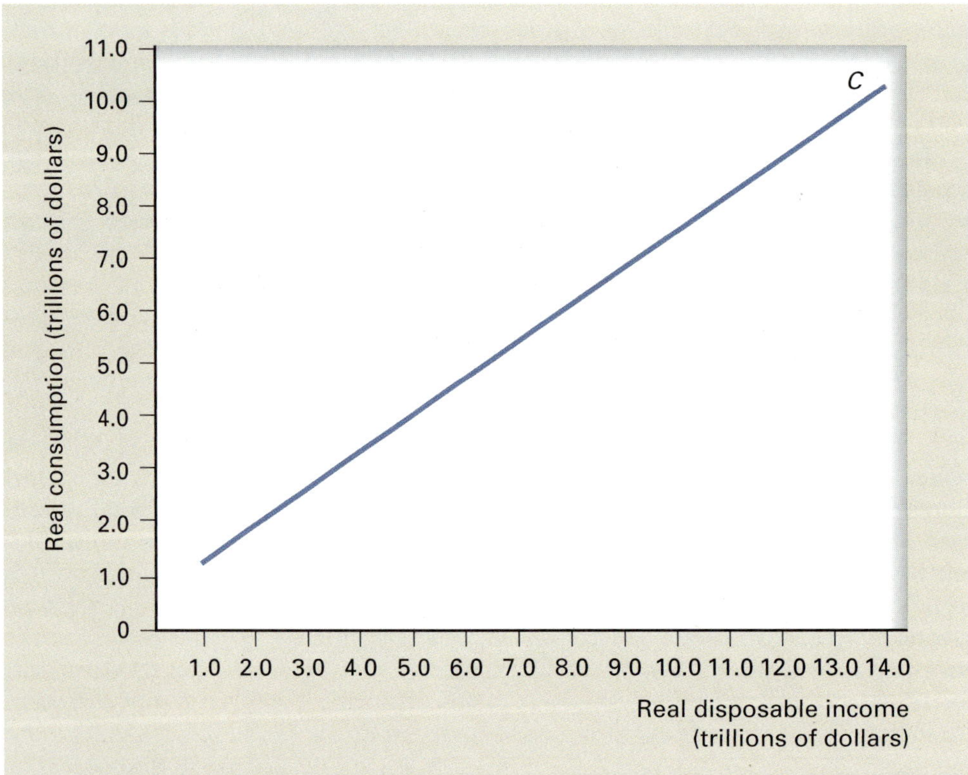

The consumption function, *C*, shows the relationship between consumption and disposable income, other things constant.

Marginal Propensities to Consume and to Save

In Chapter 1, you learned that economic analysis focuses on activity at the margin. For example, what happens to consumption if income changes by a certain amount? Suppose U.S. households receive another billion dollars in disposable income. Some is spent on consumption, and the rest is saved. The fraction of the additional income that is spent is called the marginal propensity to consume. More precisely, the **marginal propensity to consume**, or **MPC**, equals the change in consumption divided by the change in income. Likewise, the fraction of that additional income that is saved is called the marginal propensity to save. More precisely, the **marginal propensity to save**, or **MPS**, equals the change in saving divided by the change in income.

marginal propensity to consume (MPC)
The fraction of a change in income that is spent on consumption; the change in consumption divided by the change in income that caused it

marginal propensity to save (MPS)
The fraction of a change in income that is saved; the change in saving divided by the change in income that caused it

For example, if U.S. income increases from $14.0 trillion to $14.5 trillion, consumption increases by $0.4 trillion and saving by $0.1 trillion. The marginal propensity to consume equals the change in consumption divided by the change in income. In this case, the change in consumption is $0.4 trillion and the change in income is $0.5 trillion, so the marginal propensity to consume is 0.4/0.5, or 4/5. Income not spent is saved. Saving increases by $0.1 trillion as a result of the $0.5 trillion increase in income, so the marginal propensity to save equals 0.1/0.5, or 1/5. Because disposable income is either spent or saved, the marginal propensity to consume plus the marginal propensity to save must sum to 1. In our example, $4/5 + 1/5 = 1$. We can say more generally that $MPC + MPS = 1$.

MPC, MPS, and the Slope of the Consumption and Saving Functions

You may recall from the appendix to Chapter 1 that the slope of a straight line is the vertical distance between any two points divided by the horizontal distance between those same two points. Consider, for example, the slope between points *a* and *b* on the consumption function in panel (a) of Exhibit 4, where the delta symbol (Δ) means "change in." The horizontal distance between these points shows the change in disposable income, denoted as ΔDI—in this case, $0.5 trillion. The vertical distance shows the change in consumption, denoted as ΔC—in this case, $0.4 trillion. The slope equals the vertical distance divided by the horizontal distance, or 0.4/0.5, which equals the marginal propensity to consume of 4/5.

Thus, the marginal propensity to consume is measured graphically by the slope of the consumption function. After all, the slope is nothing more than the increase in consumption divided by the increase in income. Because the slope of any straight line is constant everywhere along the line, the MPC for any linear, or straight-line, consumption function is constant at all incomes. We assume here for convenience that the consumption function is a straight line, though it need not be.

Panel (b) of Exhibit 4 presents the **saving function**, *S*, which relates saving to income. The slope between any two points on the saving function measures the change in saving divided by the change in income. For example, between points *c* and *d* in panel (b) of Exhibit 4, the change in income is $0.5 trillion and the resulting change in saving is $0.1 trillion. The slope between these two points therefore equals 0.1/0.5, or 1/5, which by definition equals the marginal propensity to save. Because the marginal propensity to consume and the marginal propensity to save are simply different sides of the same coin, from here on we focus more on the marginal propensity to consume.

saving function
The relationship between saving and income, other things constant

EXHIBIT 4 Marginal Propensities to Consume and to Save

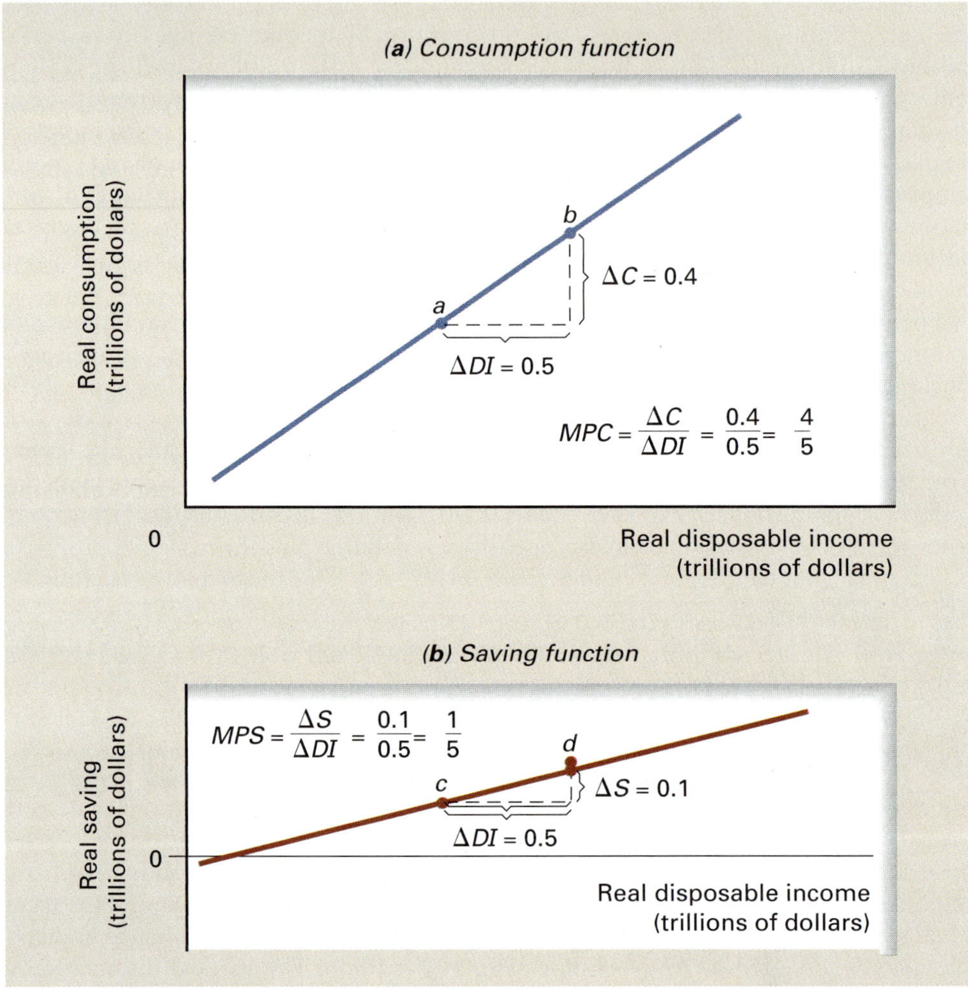

The slope of the consumption function equals the marginal propensity to consume. For the straight-line consumption function in panel (a), the slope is the same at all levels of income and is given by the change in consumption divided by the change in disposable income that causes it. Thus, the marginal propensity to consume equals $\Delta C/\Delta DI$, or $0.4/0.5 = 4/5$. The slope of the saving function in panel (b) equals the marginal propensity to save, $\Delta S/\Delta DI$, or $0.1/0.5 = 1/5$. Both consumption and disposable income are in real terms.

Nonincome Determinants of Consumption

Along a given consumption function, consumer spending depends on disposable income in the economy, other things constant. Now let's see what factors are held constant and how changes in them could shift the entire consumption function up or down.

Net Wealth and Consumption

net wealth
The value of assets minus liabilities

Given the economy's income, an important influence on consumption is each household's **net wealth**—that is, the value of all assets that each household owns minus any liabilities, or debts. Net wealth is a *stock* variable. Consumption and income are *flow* variables. Your family's assets may include a home, furnishings, automobiles, bank accounts, corporate stock and bonds, cash, and the value of any pensions. Your family's liabilities, or debts, may include a mortgage, car loans, student loans, credit card balances, and the like.

Net wealth is assumed to be constant along a given consumption function. A decrease in net wealth would make consumers less inclined to spend and more inclined to save at each income level. To see why, suppose prices fall sharply on the stock market. Stockholders are poorer than they were, so they spend less. For example, the stock market crash of 2008 and that combined with the slide in home prices cut the net wealth of U.S. households from \$64.5 trillion in 2007 to \$54.5 trillion in 2009.[1] As a result, people spent less and saved more at each income level. Consumption as a share of disposable income fell from 95 percent in 2007 to 92 percent in 2009. Our original consumption function is depicted as line *C* in Exhibit 5. If net wealth declines, the consumption function shifts from *C* down to *C*', because households now spend less and save more at every income level.

Conversely, suppose stock prices increase sharply. This increase in net wealth increases the desire to spend. For example, stock prices surged in 1999, increasing stockholders' net wealth. Consumers spent 93 percent of disposable income that year compared with an average of about 90 percent during the first half of the decade. Purchases of homes and cars soared. Because of an increase in net wealth, the

EXHIBIT 5 Shifts of the Consumption Function

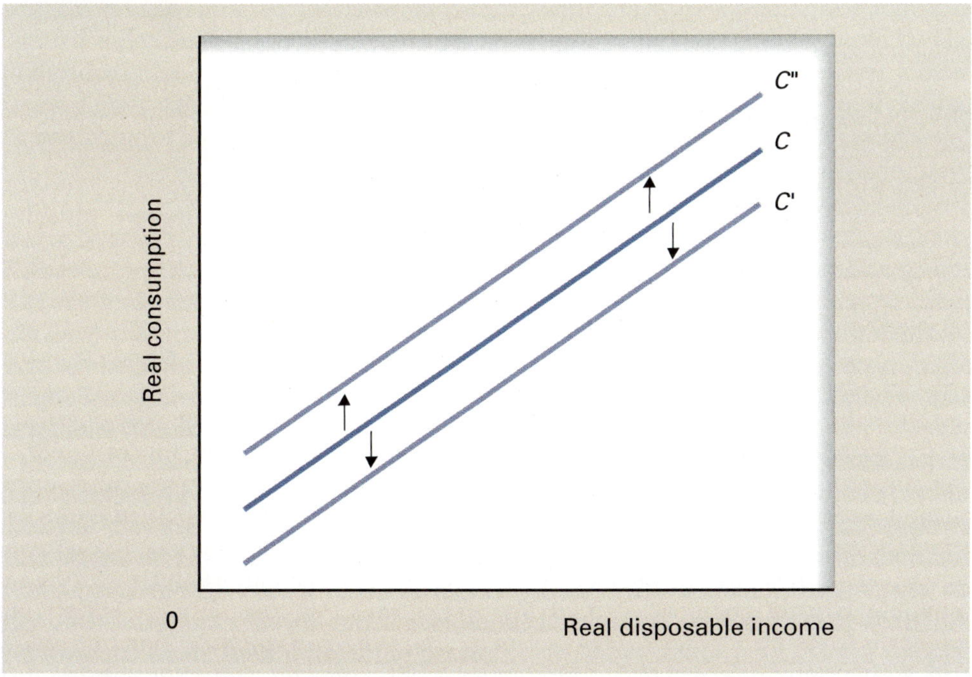

A downward shift of the consumption function, such as from *C* to *C'*, can be caused by a decrease in net wealth, an increase in the price level, an unfavorable change in consumer expectations, or an increase in the interest rate. An upward shift, such as from *C* to *C"*, can be caused by an increase in net wealth, a decrease in the price level, a favorable change in expectations, or a decrease in the interest rate.

1. Figures are from *Flow of Funds Accounts of the United States: 2005 to 2009*, Board of Governors of the Federal Reserve System, Washington, D.C. (March 11, 2010), Table B.100 at http://www.federalreserve.gov/RELEASES/z1/Current/annuals/a2005–2009.

consumption function shifts from C up to C', reflecting households' desire to spend more at each income level. Research by the Federal Reserve indicates that consumer spending eventually rises or falls between three to five cents for every dollar rise or fall in the value of stock market holdings.

Again, it is a change in net wealth, not a change in disposable income, that shifts the consumption function. A change in disposable income, other things constant, means a movement along a given consumption function, not a shift of that function. Be mindful of the difference between a movement along the consumption function, which results from a change in income, and a shift of the consumption function, which results from a change in one of the nonincome determinants of consumption, such as net wealth.

The Price Level

Another variable that affects the consumption function is the price level prevailing in the economy. As we have seen, net wealth is an important determinant of consumption. The greater the net wealth, other things constant, the greater the consumption at each income level. Some household wealth is held as money, such as cash and bank accounts. When the price level changes, so does the real value of cash and bank accounts.

For example, suppose your wealth consists of a $20,000 bank account. If the economy's price level increases by 5 percent, your bank account buys about 5 percent less in real terms. You feel poorer because you are poorer. To rebuild the real value of your money holdings to some desired comfort level, you decide to spend less and save more. *An increase in the price level reduces the purchasing power of money holdings, causing households to consume less and save more at each income level.* So the consumption function would shift downward from C to C', as shown in Exhibit 5.

Conversely, should the price level fall, as it did frequently before World War II, in 2009, and recently in Japan, Hong Kong, and Taiwan, the real value of money holdings increases. Households would be wealthier, so they decide to consume more and save less at each income level. For example, if the price level declined by 5 percent, your $20,000 bank account would then buy about 5 percent more in real terms. A drop in the price level would shift the consumption function from C up to C'. *At each income level, a change in the price level influences consumption by affecting the real value of money holdings.*

The Interest Rate

Interest is the reward savers earn for deferring consumption and the cost borrowers pay for current spending power. When graphing the consumption function, we assume a given interest rate in the economy. If the interest rate increases, other things constant, savers or lenders are rewarded more, and borrowers are charged more. The higher the interest rate, the less is spent on those items typically purchased on credit, such as cars. Thus, at a higher interest rate, households save more, borrow less, and spend less. Greater saving at each income level means less consumption. Simply put, *a higher interest rate, other things constant, shifts the consumption function downward.* Conversely, *a lower interest rate, other things constant, shifts the consumption function upward.*

Expectations

Expectations influence economic behavior in a variety of ways. For example, suppose as a college senior you land a good job that starts after graduation. Your consumption probably jumps long before the job actually begins because you expect an increase in your income. You might buy a car, for example. On the other hand, a worker who gets a layoff notice to take effect at the end of the year likely reduces consumption immediately, well before the actual layoff. More generally, if people grow more concerned about their job security, they reduce consumption at each income level.

A change in expectations about price levels or interest rates also affects consumption. For example, a change that leads householders to expect higher car prices or higher interest rates in the future prompts some to buy a new car now. On the other hand, a change leading householders to expect lower car prices or lower interest rates in the future causes some to defer a car purchase. Thus, expectations affect spending, and a change in expectations can shift the consumption function. This is why economic forecasters monitor consumer confidence so closely.

Sometimes people find they need to save more for the future. For example, each Chinese household now is more personally responsible for housing, education, and health care—items that in the past were more of a government responsibility. This increased the need to accumulate personal savings. As a consequence, the average saving rate as a percentage of income among urban households in China jumped from 7 percent in 1995 to 25 percent in 2005.[2]

To Review: Keep in mind the distinction between *a movement along a given consumption function*, which results from a change in income, and a *shift of the consumption function,* which results from a change in one of the factors assumed to remain constant along the consumption function. We conclude our introduction to consumption with the case study at the end of the book, "Bringing Theory to Life: The Life-Cycle Hypothesis," which discusses consumption and saving patterns over a lifetime.

We turn next to the second component of aggregate expenditure—investment. Keep in mind that our initial goal is to understand the relationship between total spending and income.

Investment

The second component of aggregate expenditure is investment, or, more precisely, *gross private domestic investment.* Again, by *investment* we do not mean buying stocks, bonds, or other financial assets. Investment consists of spending on (1) new factories, office buildings, malls, and new equipment, such as computers; (2) new housing; and (3) net increases to inventories. People invest now in the expectation of a future return. Because the return is in the future, a would-be investor must estimate how much a particular investment will yield this year, next year, the year after, and in all years during the productive life of the investment. *Firms buy new capital goods only if they expect this investment to yield a higher return than other possible uses of their funds.*

Investment Demand Curve

The market interest rate is the opportunity cost of investing in capital. More is invested when the opportunity cost of borrowing is lower, other things constant. A downward-sloping investment demand curve for the entire economy can be derived, with some qualifications, from a horizontal summation of each firm's downward-sloping investment demand curves. The economy's *investment demand curve* is depicted as *D* in Exhibit 6, which shows the inverse relationship between the quantity of investment demanded and the market interest rate, other things—including business expectations—held constant. For example, in Exhibit 6, when the market

2. Marcos Chamon and Eswar S. Prasad. "Why Are Saving Rates of Urban Households in China Rising?" *American Economic Journal: Macroeconomics*, 2 (January 2010): 93–130.

EXHIBIT 6 Investment Demand Curve for the Economy

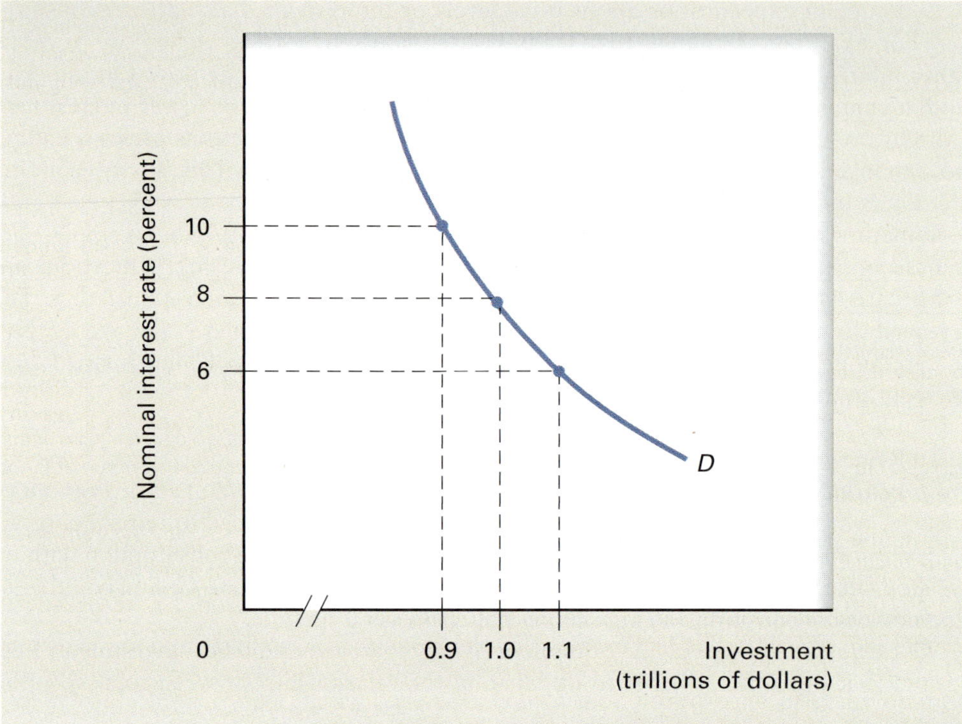

The investment demand curve for the economy sums the investment demanded by each firm at each interest rate. At lower interest rates, more investment projects become profitable for individual firms, so total investment in the economy increases.

rate is 8 percent, the quantity of investment demanded is $1.0 trillion. If the interest rate rises to 10 percent, investment declines to $0.9 trillion, and if the rate falls to 6 percent, investment increases to $1.1 trillion. Assumed constant along the investment demand curve are business expectations about the economy. If firms grow more optimistic about profit prospects, the demand for investment increases, so the investment demand curve shifts to the right.

Investment and Disposable Income

To integrate the discussion of investment with our earlier analysis of consumption, we need to know if and how investment varies with income in the economy. Whereas we were able to present evidence relating consumption to income over time, the link between investment and income is weaker. Investment in a particular year shows little relation to income that year. *Investment depends more on interest rates and on business expectations than on the prevailing income level.* One reason investment is less related to income is that some investments, such as a new power plant, take years to build. And investment, once in place, is expected to last for years, sometimes decades. The investment decision is thus said to be *forward looking*, based more on expected profit than on current income.

investment function
The relationship between the amount businesses plan to invest and the economy's income, other things constant

autonomous
A term that means "independent"; for example, autonomous investment is independent of income

So how does the amount firms plan to invest relate to income? The simplest **investment function** assumes that *investment* is unrelated to disposable income. Investment is assumed to be **autonomous** with respect to disposable income. For example, suppose

EXHIBIT 7 Investment Function

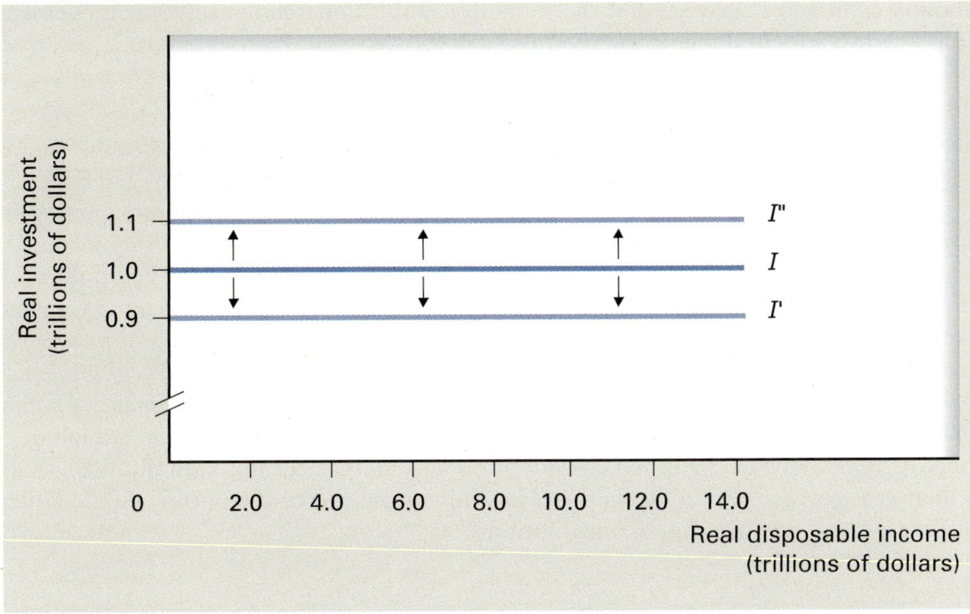

Investment is assumed to be independent of income, as shown by the horizontal lines. Thus, investment is assumed to be autonomous. An increase in the interest rate or less favorable business expectations would decrease investment at every level of income, as shown by the downward shift from *I* to *I*'. A decrease in the interest rate or more upbeat business expectations would increase investment at every level of income, as shown by the upward shift from *I* to *I*".

that, given current business expectations and a market interest rate of 8 percent, firms plan to invest $1.0 trillion per year, regardless of the economy's income level. Exhibit 7 measures disposable income on the horizontal axis and investment on the vertical axis. Investment of $1.0 trillion is shown by the flat investment function, *I*. As you can see, along *I*, investment does not vary even though disposable income does.

Nonincome Determinants of Investment

The investment function isolates the relationship between income in the economy and *investment*—the amount firms plan to invest, other things constant. We have already introduced two determinants that are assumed to be constant: the interest rate and business expectations. Now let's look at how changes in each factor would affect investment.

Market Interest Rate

Exhibit 6 shows that if the market interest rate is 8 percent, investment is $1.0 trillion. This investment is also shown as *I* in Exhibit 7. If the interest rate increases because of, say, a change in the nation's monetary policy (as happened in 2005 and 2006), the cost of borrowing increases, which increases the opportunity cost of investment. For example, if the interest rate increases from 8 percent to 10 percent, investment drops from $1.0 trillion to $0.9 trillion. This decrease is reflected in Exhibit 7 by a shift of the investment function from *I* down to *I*'. Conversely, if the market interest rate decreases because of, say, a change in the nation's monetary policy (as happened in 2007 and 2008), the cost of borrowing decreases, which reduces the opportunity cost of investment. For example, a drop in the rate of interest from 8 percent to 6 percent, other things remaining constant, reduces the cost of borrowing and increases investment from \$1.0 trillion to \$1.1 trillion, as reflected by the upward shift of the investment function from *I* to *I'*. Notice that the shifts in Exhibit 7 match interest rate movements along the investment demand curve in Exhibit 6.

Business Expectations

Investment depends primarily on business expectations, or on what Keynes called the "animal spirits" of business. Suppose investment initially is \$1.0 trillion, as depicted by *I* in Exhibit 7. If firms now become more pessimistic about their profit prospects, perhaps expecting the worst, as in 2008 during the global financial crisis, investment decreases at every income, as reflected in Exhibit 7 by a shift of the investment function from *I* down to *I'*. On the other hand, if profit expectations become rosier, as they did in 2010, firms become more willing to invest, thereby increasing the investment function from *I* up to *I'*. *Examples of factors that could affect business expectations, and thus investment plans, include wars, technological change, tax changes, and destabilizing events such as terrorist attacks or financial panics.* Changes in business expectations would shift the investment demand curve in Exhibit 6.

Now that we have examined consumption and investment individually, take a look at their year-to-year variability in the case study at the end of the book, "Public Policy: Investment Varies More than Consumption."

Government

The third component of aggregate expenditure is government purchases of goods and services. Federal, state, and local governments buy thousands of goods and services, ranging from weapon systems to traffic lights to education. During the most recent decade, government purchases in the United States accounted for 19 percent of GDP, most of that by state and local governments.

Government Purchase Function

government purchase function
The relationship between government purchases and the economy's income, other things constant

The **government purchase function** relates government purchases to income in the economy, other things constant. Decisions about government purchases are largely under the control of public officials, such as the decision to build an interstate highway, boost military spending, or hire more teachers. These spending decisions do not depend directly on income in the economy. We therefore assume that *government purchases* are autonomous, or independent of income. Such a function would relate to income as a flat line similar to the investment function shown in Exhibit 7. An increase in government purchases would result in an upward shift of the government purchase function. And a decrease in government purchases would result in a downward shift of the government purchase function.

Net Taxes

As noted earlier, government purchases represent only one of the two components of government outlays; the other is *transfer payments,* such as for Social Security, welfare benefits, and unemployment insurance. Transfer payments, which make up about a third of government outlays, are outright grants from governments to households and are thus not considered part of aggregate expenditure. Transfer payments vary inversely with income—as income increases, transfer payments decline.

To fund government outlays, governments impose taxes. Taxes vary directly with income; as income increases, so do taxes. *Net taxes* equal taxes minus transfers. Because taxes tend to increase with income but transfers tend to decrease with income, for simplicity, let's assume that net taxes do not vary with income. Thus, we assume for now that *net taxes* are *autonomous,* or independent of income.

Net taxes affect aggregate spending indirectly by changing disposable income, which in turn changes consumption. We saw from the discussion of circular flow that by subtracting net taxes, we transform real GDP into *disposable income*. Disposable income is take-home pay—the income households can spend or save. We examine the impact of net taxes in the next few chapters.

Net Exports

The rest of the world affects aggregate expenditure through imports and exports and has a growing influence on the U.S. economy. The United States, with only one-twentieth of the world's population, accounts for about one-eighth of the world's imports and one-ninth of the world's exports.

Net Exports and Income

How do imports and exports relate to the economy's income? When incomes rise, Americans spend more on all normal goods, including imports. Higher incomes lead to more spending on Persian rugs, French wine, Korean DVD players, German cars, Chinese toys, European vacations, African safaris, and thousands of other foreign goods and services.

How do U.S. exports relate to the economy's income? U.S. exports depend on the income of foreigners, not on U.S. income. U.S. disposable income does not affect Europe's purchases of U.S. DVDs or Africa's purchases of U.S. grain. The **net export function** shows the relationship between net exports and U.S. income, other things constant. Because our exports are insensitive to U.S. income but our imports tend to increase with income, *net exports,* which equal the value of exports minus the value of imports, tend to decline as U.S. incomes increase. Such an inverse relationship is developed graphically in the appendix to this chapter. For simplicity, we assume now that net exports are *autonomous,* or independent of income.

net export function
The relationship between net exports and the economy's income, other things constant

If exports exceed imports, net exports are positive; if imports exceed exports, net exports are negative; and if exports equal imports, net exports are zero. U.S. net exports have been negative nearly every year during the past three decades, so let's suppose net exports are autonomous and equal to $-\$0.4$ trillion, or $-\$400$ billion, as shown by the net export function $X - M$ in Exhibit 8.

Nonincome Determinants of Net Exports

Factors assumed constant along the net export function include the U.S. price level, price levels in other countries, interest rates here and abroad, foreign income levels, and the exchange rate between the dollar and foreign currencies. Consider the effects of a change in one of these factors. Suppose the value of the dollar increases relative to foreign currencies such as those of Europe, as happened in 2010. With the dollar worth more on world markets, foreign products become cheaper for Americans, and U.S. products become more costly for foreigners. A rise in the dollar's exchange value increases imports and decreases exports, thus reducing net exports, shown in Exhibit 8 by a parallel drop in the net export line from $X - M$ down to $X' - M'$, a decline from $-\$400$ billion to $-\$420$ billion.

EXHIBIT 8 Net Export Function

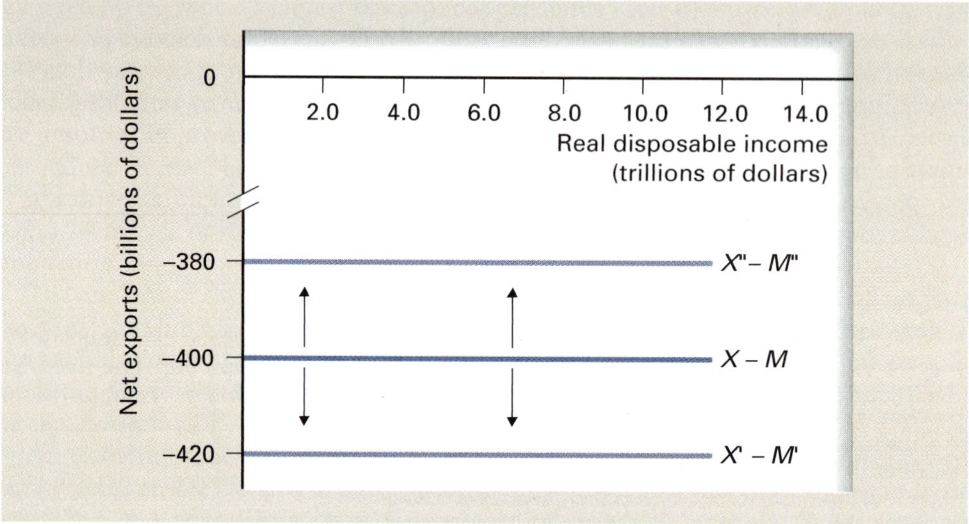

Net exports here are assumed to be independent of disposable income, as shown by the horizontal lines. $X - M$ is the net export function when autonomous net exports equal −\$400 billion. An increase in the value of the dollar relative to other currencies would decrease net exports at each level of income, as shown by the shift down to $X' - M'$. A decrease in the value of the dollar would increase net exports at each level of income, as shown by the shift up to $X'' - M''$.

A decline in the value of the dollar, as occurred in 2002 and 2003, has the opposite effect, increasing exports and decreasing imports. An increase in autonomous net exports is shown in our example by a parallel increase in the net export function, from $X - M$ up to $X'' - M''$, reflecting an increase in autonomous net exports from −\$400 billion to −\$380 billion. A country sometimes tries to devalue its currency in an attempt to increase its net exports and thereby increase employment. The effect of changes in net exports on aggregate spending are taken up in the next chapter.

Composition of Aggregate Expenditure

Now that we have examined each component of aggregate spending, let's get a better idea of spending over time. Exhibit 9 shows the composition of spending in the United States since 1959. As you can see, consumption's share of GDP appears stable from year to year, but the long-term trend shows an increase from an average of 62 percent during the 1960s to 70 percent during the most recent decade. Investment fluctuates more year to year but with no long-term trend up or down; investment averaged 16 percent of GDP in the most recent decade. But, as you can see in the exhibit, investment's share of GDP dropped sharply during the recession of 2007–2009.

Government purchases declined from an average of 22 percent of GDP during the 1960s to an average of 19 percent during the last decade, due primarily to decreases in defense spending since the 1960s. Remember, government purchases do not include transfer payments, which have grown more. Net exports averaged close to zero in the 1960s but were negative nearly every year since then, averaging a minus 5 percent of GDP during the last decade. Negative net exports mean that the sum of consumption, investment, and government purchases exceeds GDP, the amount produced in the U.S. economy.

EXHIBIT 9 U.S. Spending Components as Percentages of GDP Since 1959

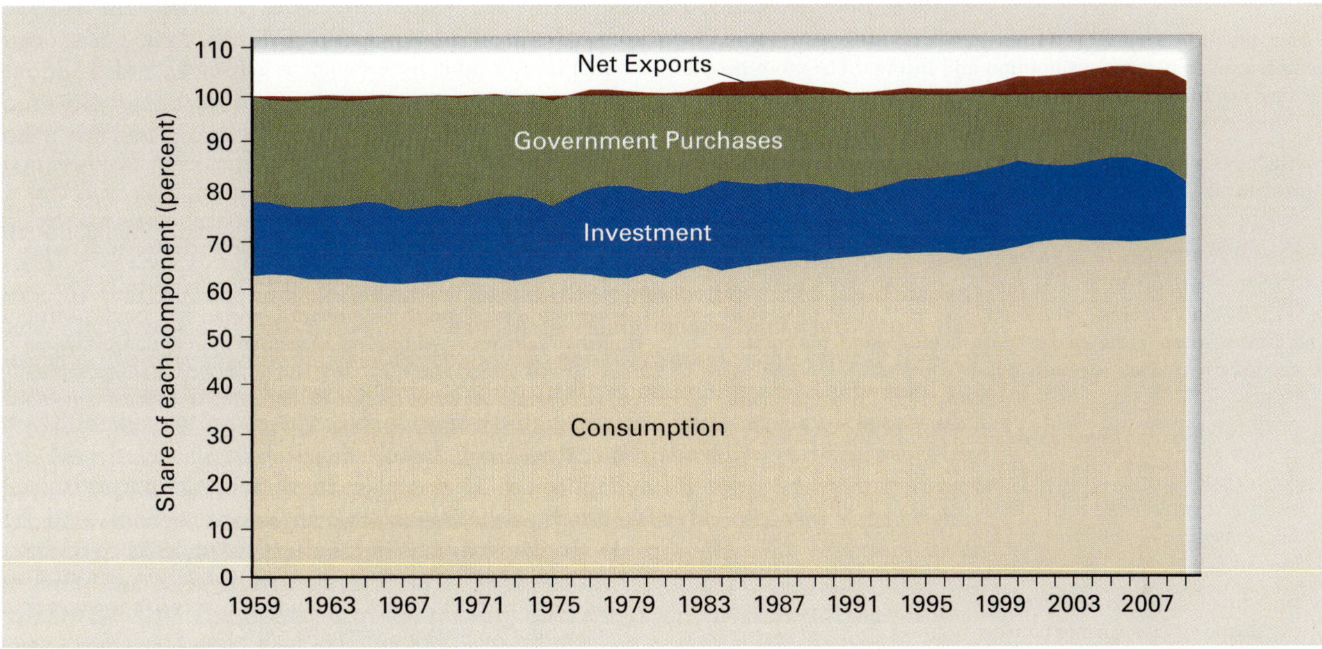

The composition of U.S. GDP has not changed that much since 1959. Consumption's share edged up from an average of 62 percent during the 1960s to 70 percent during the last decade. Investment has fluctuated from year to year but with no clear long-term trend up or down. Government purchases declined slightly from an average of 22 percent of GDP during the 1960s to an average of 19 percent in the last decade. And net exports have become more negative, expressed in red by that portion exceeding 100 percent of GDP.

Source: Bureau of Economic Analysis, U.S. Dept. of Commerce. For the latest data, go to http://bea.gov/national/nipaweb/index.asp and select Table 1.1.1.

Americans are spending more than they make, and they are covering the difference by borrowing from abroad. U.S. spending exceeds U.S. GDP by the amount shown as negative net exports. Because the spending components must sum to GDP, *negative* net exports are expressed in Exhibit 9 by the red portion of spending that exceeds 100 percent of GDP.

In summary: During the last five decades, consumption's share of total spending increased and government purchases decreased. Investment's share bounced around and net exports' share turned negative, meaning that imports exceeded exports.

Conclusion

This chapter has focused on the relationship between spending and income. We considered the four components of aggregate expenditure: consumption, investment, government purchases, and net exports. Consumption increases with income. Investment relates more to interest rates and business expectations than it does to income. Government purchases also tend to be autonomous, or independent of income. And net exports are assumed, for now, to be affected more by such factors as the exchange rate than by U.S. income. The appendix to this chapter develops a more realistic but also more complicated picture by showing how net exports decline as income increases. In the next chapter, we see how aggregate spending depends on income and how this link helps shape the aggregate demand curve.

Summary

1. The most predictable and most useful relationship in macroeconomics is between consumption and income. The more people have to spend, the more they spend on consumption, other things constant.
2. The consumption function shows the link between consumption and income in the economy. The slope of the consumption function reflects the marginal propensity to consume, which is the change in consumption divided by the change in income. The slope of the saving function reflects the marginal propensity to save, which is the change in saving divided by the change in income.
3. Certain factors can cause consumers to change spending at each income level. An increase in net wealth reduces the need to save, thus increasing consumption at every income. A higher price level reduces the value of money holdings, and this lowers net wealth, thus reducing consumption at every income. An increase in the interest rate makes saving more rewarding and borrowing more costly, thus increasing saving and decreasing consumption at every income. Expectations about future incomes, prices, and interest rates also influence consumption.
4. Investment depends on the market interest rate and on business expectations. Investment fluctuates from year to year but averaged 16 percent of GDP during the last decade. We'll assume for now that investment in the economy is unrelated to income.
5. Government purchases, which exclude transfer payments, averaged 19 percent of GDP during the last decade. Government purchases are based on the public choices of elected officials and are assumed to be autonomous, or independent of the economy's income level. Net taxes, or taxes minus transfer payments, are also assumed for now to be unrelated to income.
6. Net exports equal the value of exports minus the value of imports. U.S. exports depend on foreign income, not on U.S. income. Imports increase with U.S. income. So net exports decline as income increases. For simplicity, however, we initially assume that net exports are autonomous, or unrelated to domestic income.
7. Consumption's share of total spending increased from 62 percent during the 1960s to 70 percent during the most recent decade. The share reflected by government purchases fell from 22 percent to 19 percent. Investment's share bounced around but averaged 16 percent of GDP during the most recent decade. Net exports' share averaged close to zero during the 1960s, but after that turned negative, meaning that imports exceeded exports, averaging a minus 5 percent during the most recent decade.

Key Concepts

Questions for Review

1. Consumption Function How would an increase in each of the following affect the consumption function? How would it affect the saving function?
   a. Net taxes
   b. The interest rate
   c. Consumer optimism, or confidence
   d. The price level
   e. Consumers' net wealth
   f. Disposable income
2. Consumption Function A number of factors can cause the consumption function to shift. What, if anything, happens to the saving function when the consumption function shifts? Explain.
3. Case Study: The Life-Cycle Hypothesis (See page 751.) According to the life-cycle hypothesis, what is the typical pattern of saving for an individual over his or her lifetime? What impact does this behavior have on an individual's lifetime consumption pattern? What impact does the behavior have on the saving rate in the overall economy?
4. Investment Why would the following investment expenditures increase as the interest rate declines?
   a. Purchases of a new plant and equipment
   b. Construction of new housing
   c. Increase inventories
5. Nonincome Determinants of Investment What are some factors assumed to be constant along the investment function? What kinds of changes in each factor could cause investment spending to increase at each level of real disposable income?
6. Case Study: Investment Varies More than Consumption (See page 752.) Why do economic forecasters pay special attention to investment plans? Take a look at the Conference

Board's index of leading economic indicators at http://www.conference-board.org/. Which of those indicators might affect investment?

7. GOVERNMENT SPENDING How do changes in disposable income affect government purchases and the government purchase function? How do changes in net taxes affect the consumption function?

8. NET EXPORTS What factors are assumed constant along the net export function? What would be the impact on net exports of a change in real disposable income?

Problems and Exercises

9. CONSUMPTION Use the following data to answer the questions below:

Real Disposable Income billions ($)	Consumption Expenditures billions ($)	Saving billions ($)
100	150	______
200	200	______
300	250	______
400	300	______

a. Graph the consumption function, with consumption spending on the vertical axis and disposable income on the horizontal axis.
b. If the consumption function is a straight line, what is its slope?
c. Fill in the saving column at each level of income. If the saving function is a straight line, what is its slope?

10. MPC AND MPS If consumption increases by $12 billion when disposable income increases by $15 billion, what is the value of the MPC? What is the relationship between the MPC and the MPS? If the MPC increases, what must happen to the MPS? How is the MPC related to the consumption function? How is the MPS related to the saving function?

11. CONSUMPTION AND SAVING Suppose that consumption equals $500 billion when disposable income is $0 and that each increase of $100 billion in disposable income causes consumption to increase by $70 billion. Draw a graph of the saving function using this information.

Global Economic Watch Exercises

Login to www.cengagebrain.com and access the Global Economic Watch to do these exercises.

12. GLOBAL ECONOMIC WATCH Go to the Global Economic Crisis Resource Center. Select Global Issues in Context. In the Basic Search box at the top of the page, enter the phrase "pity poor Japan." On the Results page, go to the Global Viewpoints Section. Click on the link for the August 2, 2010, article "Crisis? What Crisis?" What is the possible upside to decreases in Japanese consumption spending? How does this analysis connect with what you learned about measures of quality of life in the chapter on tracking the U.S. economy?

13. GLOBAL ECONOMIC WATCH Go to the Global Economic Crisis Resource Center. Select Global Issues in Context. In the Basic Search box at the top of the page, enter the phrase "capital investment." Use quotation marks before and after the phrase to ensure finding articles about the economic concept of investment. Choose one article from the past two years. Does it describe growing or shrinking investment in an economy? How will that investment trend affect economic growth?

Appendix

Variable Net Exports

In this appendix, we examine the relationship between net exports and U.S. income. We first look at exports and imports separately and then consider exports minus imports, or net exports.

Net Exports and Income

As noted earlier in the chapter, the amount of U.S. output purchased by foreigners depends not on U.S. income but on the income of foreigners. We therefore assume that U.S. exports do not vary with U.S. income. Specifically, suppose the rest of the world spends \$0.9 trillion, or \$900 billion, per year on U.S. exports of goods and services. The export function, X, is as shown in panel (a) of Exhibit 10. But when income increases, Americans spend more on all goods and services, including imports. Thus, the relationship between imports and income is positive, as expressed by the upward-sloping import function, M, in panel (b) of Exhibit 10. If Americans spend 10 percent of their disposable income on imports, when disposable income is \$9.0 trillion, imports are \$0.9 trillion.

So far, we have considered imports and exports as separate functions of income. What matters in terms of total spending on U.S. products are exports, X, minus imports, M, or net exports, $X - M$. Because money spent on imports goes to foreign producers, not U.S. producers, imports get subtracted from the circular flow of spending. By subtracting the import function depicted in panel (b) from the export function in panel (a), we derive the *net export function,* depicted as $X - M$ in panel (c) of Exhibit 10.

Because exports in panel (a) equal \$0.9 trillion at all levels of income, net exports equal zero when U.S. disposable income is \$9.0 trillion. At incomes less than \$9.0 trillion, net exports are positive because exports exceed imports. At incomes greater than \$9.0 trillion, net exports are negative because imports exceed exports. As a case in point, U.S. recessions in 1991, 2001, and 2009 reduced the trade deficits those years as imports declined. As the economy recovered, the trade deficit increased.

EXHIBIT 10 Imports, Exports, and Net Exports (in trillions of dollars)

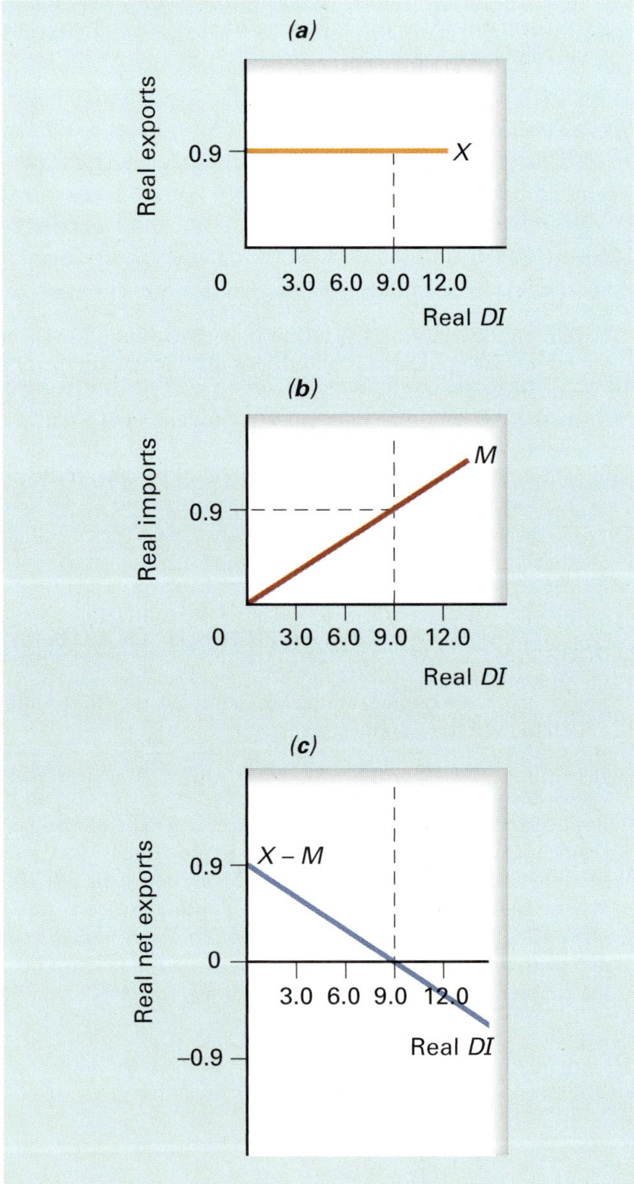

Exports are independent of income, as shown in panel (a). Imports are positively related to income, as shown in panel (b). Net exports equal exports minus imports. Net exports are negatively related to income, as shown in panel (c). Net exports are zero when disposable income is \$9.0 trillion.

Shifts of Net Exports

The net export function, $X - M$, shows the relationship between net exports and disposable income, other things constant. Suppose the value of the dollar increases relative to foreign currencies, as happened in 2010. With the dollar worth more, foreign products become cheaper for Americans, and U.S. products become more expensive for foreigners. The impact of a rising dollar is to decrease exports but increase imports at each income level, thus decreasing net exports. This relationship is shown in Exhibit 11 by the shift from $X - M$ down to $X' - M'$. A decline in the dollar's value, as occurred in 2003 and 2004, has the opposite effect, increasing exports and decreasing imports, as reflected in Exhibit 11 by an upward shift of the net export function from $X - M$ to $X'' - M''$.

In summary, in this appendix we assumed that imports relate positively to income, while exports are independent of domestic income. Therefore, net exports, which equal exports minus imports, vary inversely with income. The net export function shifts downward if the value of the dollar rises and shifts upward if the value of the dollar falls.

Appendix Question

1. (REST OF THE WORLD) Using a graph of net exports ($X - M$) against disposable income, show the effects of the following. Explain each of your answers.
    a. An increase in foreign disposable income
    b. An increase in U.S. disposable income
    c. An increase in the U.S. interest rate
    d. An increase in the value of the dollar against foreign currencies

EXHIBIT 11 Shifts of Net Exports (in trillions of dollars)

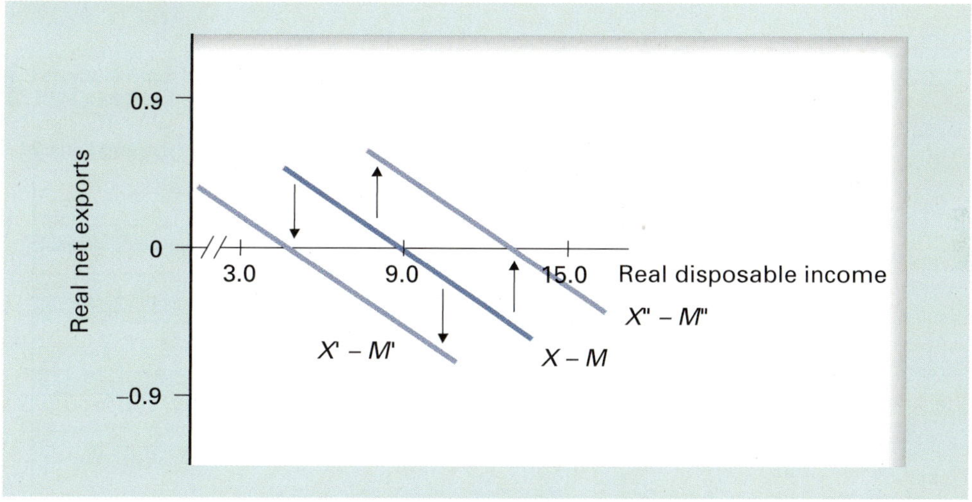

A rise in the value of the dollar, other things constant, will decrease exports and increase imports, thereby decreasing net exports, as shown by the shift from $X - M$ down to $X' - M'$. A decrease in the value of the dollar will increase exports and decrease imports, causing net exports to rise, as shown by the shift from $X - M$ up to $X'' - M''$.

Aggregate Expenditure and Aggregate Demand

24

AP Photo/Adam Nadel

- Now that we have considered consumption, investment, government purchases, and net exports, how do they combine to yield total spending in the economy?
- How is spending linked to income?
- How does a change in spending affect the economy? For example, did the grounding of all commercial airlines following the 9/11 attacks affect other sectors of the economy?
- And what was the impact of the financial crisis of 2008 on consumption?

Answers to these and other questions are covered in this chapter, which develops the aggregate demand curve.

Your economic success depends in part on the overall performance of the economy. When the economy grows, job opportunities expand, so your chances of finding a good job increase. When the economy contracts, job opportunities shrink, and so do your job prospects. Thus, you have a personal stake in the economy's success.

The previous chapter discussed how each spending component relates to income in the economy. In this chapter, these components add up to show how total spending, or aggregate expenditure, relates to income. We then see how a change in the economy's price level affects aggregate expenditure. All this is aimed at getting to the economy's aggregate demand curve. Appendix A shows what happens when imports increase with income, and Appendix B develops the algebra behind all this. Aggregate supply will be developed in the next chapter. The effects of government spending and taxing will be explored in the chapter after that.

Topics discussed include:

- Aggregate expenditure line
- Real GDP demanded
- Changes in aggregate expenditure
- Simple spending multiplier
- Changes in the price level
- Aggregate demand curve

Aggregate Expenditure and Income

In the previous chapter, the big idea was that consumption depends on income; a link that is the most stable in all of macroeconomics. In this section, we build on that connection to learn how total spending in the economy changes with income. If we try to confront the economy head-on, it soon becomes a bewildering maze, which is why we make progress by starting with simple models. We continue to assume, as we did in developing the circular-flow model, that there is no capital depreciation and no business saving. Thus, we can say that *each dollar of spending translates directly into a dollar of income*. Therefore, gross domestic product, or GDP, equals aggregate income.

The Components of Aggregate Expenditure

When income increases, consumption increases. As noted in the previous chapter, the marginal propensity to consume indicates the fraction of each additional dollar of income that is spent on consumption. For example, if the marginal propensity to consume is 4/5 (four-fifths), spending increases by \$4 for every \$5 increase in income. The consumption function shows how much consumption increases with income.

For simplicity, we continue to assume that the other spending components do not vary with income; thus, investment, government purchases, and net exports are autonomous, or independent of the economy's income level. Specifically, we'll assume that investment and government purchases each equals \$1.0 trillion for the year in question and net exports are a negative \$0.4 trillion. We'll also assume that government purchases equal net taxes, so the government budget is balanced. We first want to see how a balanced budget works before we consider the effects of budget deficits or surpluses.

If we stack up the consumption function, the investment function, the government purchase function, and the net export function, we get the aggregate expenditure line presented in Exhibit 1 as $C + I + G + (X - M)$. Real GDP is measured on the horizontal axis, and aggregate expenditure is measured on the vertical axis. The **aggregate expenditure line** shows how much households, firms, governments, and the rest of the world plan to spend on U.S. output at each level of real GDP, or real income. Again, the only spending component that varies with real GDP is consumption. Since only consumption varies with income, the slope of the aggregate expenditure line equals the marginal propensity to consume.

aggregate expenditure line
A relationship tracing, for a given price level, spending at each level of income, or real GDP; the total of $C + I + G + (X - M)$ at each level of income, or real GDP

Real GDP Demanded

Let's begin developing the aggregate demand curve by asking how much aggregate output would be demanded at a given price level. By finding the quantity demanded at a given price level, we'll end up identifying a single point on the aggregate demand

EXHIBIT 1 Deriving the Real GDP Demanded for a Given Price Level

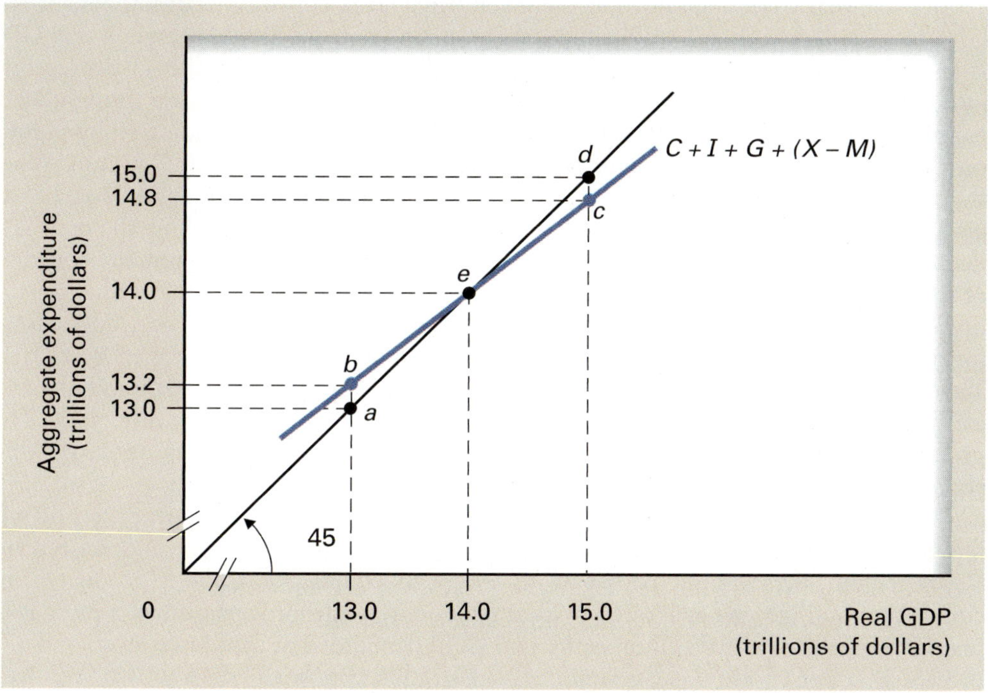

Real GDP demanded for a given price level is found where aggregate expenditure equals aggregate output—that is, where spending equals the amount produced, or real GDP. This occurs at point *e*, where the aggregate expenditure line intersects the 45-degree line.

curve. We begin by considering the relationship between aggregate spending in the economy and aggregate income. To get us started, suppose that the price level in the economy is 110, or 10 percent higher than in the base-year price level. We want to find out how much is spent at various levels of real income, or real GDP. By *real* GDP, we mean GDP measured in terms of real goods and services produced. Exhibit 1 combines the relationships introduced in the previous chapter—consumption, saving, investment, government purchases, net taxes, and net exports. Although the entries are hypothetical, they bear some relation to levels observed in the U.S. economy. For example, real GDP in the U.S. economy was a little less than $14 trillion in 2010, and the price level was about 110, or 10 percent higher than the chained (2005) base-year index of 100.

Real GDP, measured along the horizontal axis in Exhibit 1, can be viewed in two ways—as the value of *aggregate output* and as the *aggregate income* generated by that output. Because real GDP or aggregate income is measured on the horizontal axis, and aggregate expenditure is measured on the vertical axis, this graph is often called the **income-expenditure model.** To gain perspective on the relationship between income and expenditure, we use a handy analytical tool: the 45-degree ray from the origin. The special feature of this line is that any point along it is the same distance from each axis. Thus, the 45-degree line identifies all points where spending equals real GDP. *Aggregate output demanded at a given price level occurs where aggregate expenditure, measured along the vertical axis, equals real GDP, measured along the horizontal axis.* In Exhibit 1, this occurs at point *e*, where the aggregate expenditure line intersects the 45-degree line. At point *e*, the amount people spend equals the amount produced. We conclude that, at the given price level of 110, the quantity of real GDP demanded equals $14.0 trillion.

income-expenditure model
A relationship that shows how much people plan to spend at each income level; this model identifies, for a given price level, where the amount people plan to spend equals the amount produced in the economy

What if Spending Exceeds Real GDP?

To find the real GDP demanded at the given price level, consider what happens if real GDP is initially less than $14.0 trillion. As you can see from Exhibit 1, when real GDP is less than $14.0 trillion, the aggregate expenditure line is above the 45-degree line, indicating that spending exceeds the amount produced (give this a little thought). For example, if real GDP is $13.0 trillion, spending is $13.2 trillion, as indicated by point *b* on the aggregate expenditure line, so spending exceeds output by $0.2 trillion. When the amount people want to spend exceeds the amount produced, something has to give. Ordinarily what gives is the price, but remember that we are seeking the real GDP demanded for a given price level, so the price level is assumed to remain constant, at least for now. What gives in this model are *inventories*. Unplanned reductions in inventories cover the $0.2 trillion shortfall in output. Because firms can't draw down inventories indefinitely, *inventory reductions* prompt firms to produce more output. That increases employment and consumer income, leading to more spending. As long as spending exceeds output, firms increase production to make up the difference. This process of more output, more income, and more spending continues until spending equals real GDP, an equality achieved at point *e* in Exhibit 1.

When output reaches $14.0 trillion, spending exactly matches output, so no unintended inventory adjustments occur. More importantly, when output reaches $14.0 trillion, the amount people want to spend equals the amount produced and equals the total income generated by that production. Earlier we assumed a price level of 110. Therefore, $14.0 trillion is the real GDP demanded at that price level.

What if Real GDP Exceeds Spending?

To reinforce the logic of the model, consider what happens when the amount produced exceeds the amount people want to spend. Notice in Exhibit 1 that, to the right of point *e*, spending falls short of production. For example, suppose real GDP is $15.0 trillion. Spending, as indicated by point *c* on the aggregate expenditure line, is $0.2 trillion less than real GDP, indicated by point *d* on the 45-degree line. Because real GDP exceeds spending, unsold goods accumulate. This swells inventories by $0.2 trillion more than firms planned on. Rather than allow inventories to pile up indefinitely, firms cut production, which reduces employment and income. As an example of such behavior, a recent news account read, "General Motors will idle two assembly plants in a move to trim inventories in the wake of slowing sales." *Unplanned inventory buildups* cause firms to cut production until the amount they produce equals aggregate spending, which occurs, again, where real GDP is $14.0 trillion. Given the price level, real GDP demanded is found where the amount people spend equals the amount produced. *For a given price level, there is only one point along the aggregate expenditure line at which spending equals real GDP.*

We have now discussed the forces that determine real GDP demanded for a given price level. In the next section, we examine changes that can alter spending plans.

The Simple Spending Multiplier

We just used the aggregate expenditure line to find real GDP demanded for a particular price level. In this section, we continue to assume that the price level stays the same as we trace the effects of other changes that could affect spending plans. Like a

EXHIBIT 2 **Effect of an Increase in Investment on Real GDP Demanded**

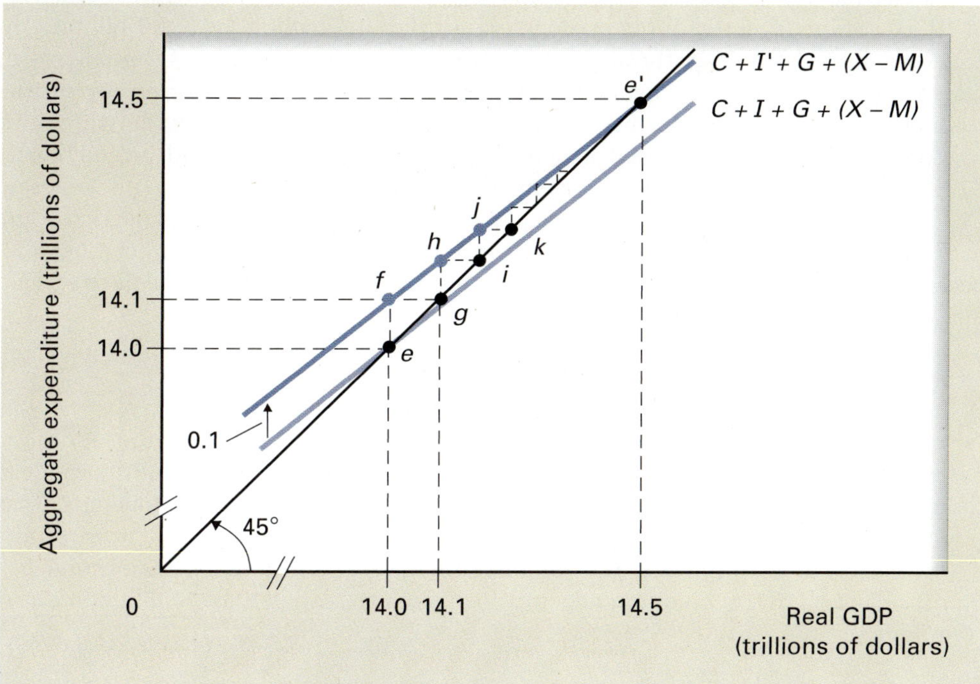

The economy is initially at point *e*, where spending and real GDP equal $14.0 trillion. A $0.1 trillion increase in investment shifts the aggregate expenditure line up vertically by $0.1 trillion from $C + I + G + (X - M)$ to $C + I' + G + (X - M)$. Real GDP increases until it equals spending at point *e*′. As a result of the $0.1 trillion increase in investment, real GDP demanded increases by $0.5 trillion, to $14.5 trillion. This analysis assumes a given price level.

stone thrown into a still pond, the effects of any change in spending ripple through the economy, generating changes in aggregate output that exceed the initial change in spending.

An Increase in Spending

We begin at point *e* in Exhibit 2, where spending equals real GDP at $14.0 trillion. Now let's consider the effect of an increase in one of the components of spending. Suppose that firms become more optimistic about profit prospects and decide to increase their investment from $1.0 trillion to $1.1 trillion per year at each level of real GDP. Exhibit 2 reflects this change by an upward shift of the aggregate expenditure line by $0.1 trillion, from $C + I + G + (X - M)$ to $C + I' + G + (X - M)$.

What happens to real GDP demanded? An instinctive response is to say that real GDP demanded increases by $0.1 trillion as well. In this case, however, instinct is a poor guide. As you can see, the new spending line intersects the 45-degree line at point *e*′, where real GDP demanded is $14.5 trillion. How can a $0.1 trillion increase in spending increase real GDP demanded by $0.5 trillion? What's going on?

The idea of the circular flow is central to an understanding of the adjustment process. As noted earlier, real GDP can be thought of as both the value of production and the income arising from that production. Recall that production yields income, which generates spending. We can think of each trip around the circular flow as a "round" of income and spending.

Round One

An upward shift of the aggregate expenditure line means that, at the initial real GDP of $14.0 trillion, spending now exceeds output by $0.1 trillion, or $100 billion. This is shown in Exhibit 2 as the distance between point *e* and point *f*. Initially, firms match this increased investment spending by an unplanned reduction in inventories. John Deere, for example, satisfies the increased demand for tractors by drawing down tractor inventories. But reduced inventories prompt firms to expand production by $100 billion, as shown by the movement from point *f* to point *g*. This generates $100 billion more income. The movement from point *e* to point *g* shows the first round in the multiplier process. The income-generating process does not stop there, however, because those who earn this additional income spend some of it and save the rest, leading to round two of spending and income.

Round Two

Given a marginal propensity to consume of 0.8, those who earn the additional $100 billion spend $80 billion on toasters, backpacks, gasoline, restaurant meals, and thousands of other goods and services. They save the other $20 billion. The move from point *g* to point *h* in Exhibit 2 shows this $80 billion spending increase. Firms respond by increasing their output by $80 billion, shown by the movement from point *h* to point *i*. Thus, the $100 billion in new income increases real GDP by $80 billion during round two.

Round Three and Beyond

We know that four-fifths of the $80 billion earned during round two gets spent during round three and one-fifth gets saved. Thus, $64 billion is spent during round three on still more goods and services, as reflected by the movement from point *i* to point *j*. The remaining $16 billion gets saved. The added spending causes firms to increase output by $64 billion, as shown by the movement from point *j* to point *k*. Round three's additional production generated $64 billion more income, which sets up subsequent rounds of spending, output, and income. *As long as spending exceeds output, production increases, thereby creating more income, which generates still more spending.*

Exhibit 3 summarizes the multiplier process, showing the first three rounds, round 10, and the cumulative effect of all rounds. The new spending from each round

EXHIBIT 3 Tracking the Rounds of Spending Following a $100 Billion Increase in Investment (billions of dollars)

Round	New Spending This Round	Cumulative New Spending	New Saving This Round	Cumulative New Saving
1	100	100	—	—
2	80	180	20	20
3	64	244	16	36
⋮	⋮	⋮	⋮	⋮
10	13.4	446.3	3.35	86.6
⋮	⋮	⋮	⋮	⋮
∞	0	500	0	100

is shown in the second column, and the accumulation of new spending appears in the third column. For example, the cumulative new spending as of the third round totals $244 billion—the sum of the first three rounds of spending ($100 billion + $80 billion + $64 billion). The new saving from each round appears in the fourth column, and the accumulation of new saving appears in the final column. All this develops with the price level assumed to remain unchanged.

Using the Simple Spending Multiplier

In our model, consumers spend four-fifths of the change in income each round, with each fresh round equal to the change in spending from the previous round times the marginal propensity to consume, or the MPC. This goes on round after round, leaving less and less to fuel more spending and income. At some point, the new rounds of income and spending become so small that they disappear and the process stops. The question is, by how much does total spending increase? We can get some idea of the total by working through a limited number of rounds. For example, as shown in Exhibit 3, total new spending after 10 rounds sums to $446.3 billion. But calculating the exact total for all rounds would require us to work through an infinite number of rounds—an impossible task.

Fortunately, we can borrow a shortcut from mathematicians, who have shown that the sum of an infinite number of rounds, each of which is MPC times the previous round, equals $1/(1 - MPC)$ times the initial change. Translated, the cumulative spending change equals $1/(1 - MPC)$, which, in our example, was 1/0.2, or 5, times the initial increase in spending, which was $100 billion. In short, the increase in investment eventually boosts real GDP demanded by 5 times $100 billion, or $500 billion—and again, all this happens with the price level assumed to remain unchanged.

The simple spending multiplier is the factor by which real GDP demanded changes for a given initial change in spending.

simple spending multiplier
The ratio of a change in real GDP demanded to the initial change in spending that brought it about; the numerical value of the simple spending multiplier is $1/(1 - MPC)$; called "simple" because only consumption varies with income

$$\text{Simple spending multiplier} = \frac{1}{1 - \text{MPC}}$$

The simple spending multiplier provides a shortcut to the total change in real GDP demanded. This multiplier depends on the MPC. The larger the MPC, the larger the simple spending multiplier. That makes sense—the more people spend from each dollar of fresh income, the more total spending increases. For example, if the MPC was 0.9 instead of 0.8, the denominator of the multiplier formula would equal 1.0 minus 0.9, or 0.1, so the multiplier would be 1/0.1, or 10. With an MPC of 0.9, a $0.1 trillion investment increase would boost real GDP demanded by $1.0 trillion. On the other hand, an MPC of 0.75 would yield a denominator of 0.25 and a multiplier of 4. So a $0.1 trillion investment increase would raise real GDP demanded by $0.4 trillion.

Let's return to Exhibit 2. The $0.1 trillion rise in autonomous investment raised real GDP demanded from $14.0 trillion to $14.5 trillion. Note that real GDP demanded would have increased by the same amount if consumers had decided to spend $0.1 trillion more at each income level—that is, if the consumption function, rather than the investment function, had shifted up by $0.1 trillion. Real GDP demanded likewise would have increased if government purchases or net exports increased $0.1 trillion. *The change in aggregate output demanded depends on how much the aggregate expenditure line shifts, not on which spending component causes the shift.*

In our example, investment increased by $0.1 trillion in the year in question. *If this greater investment is not sustained the following year, real GDP demanded would fall back*. For example, if investment returns to its initial level, other things constant, real GDP demanded would return to $14.0 trillion. Finally, recall from the previous chapter that the MPC and the MPS sum to 1, so 1 minus the MPC equals the MPS. With this information, we can define the simple spending multiplier in terms of the MPS as follows:

$$\text{Simple spending multiplier} = \frac{1}{1 - MPC} = \frac{1}{MPS}$$

We can see that the smaller the MPS, the less leaks from the spending stream as saving. Because less is saved, more gets spent each round, so the spending multiplier is greater. Incidentally, this spending multiplier is called "simple" because consumption is the only spending component that varies with income.

As an example of how a decline in aggregate expenditure can ripple through the economy, the case study, "Public Policy: The Ripple Effect on the Economy of 9/11" at the end of the book, considers what happened to air travel in the wake of the 9/11 attacks.

The Aggregate Demand Curve

In this chapter, we have used the aggregate expenditure line to find real GDP demanded *for a given price level*. But what happens if the price level changes? As you will see, for each price level, there is a unique aggregate expenditure line, which yields a unique real GDP demanded. By altering the price level, we find a different real GDP demanded. By pairing a price level with the real GDP demanded at that price level, we can derive the aggregate demand curve.

A Higher Price Level

What is the effect of a higher price level on spending and, in turn, on real GDP demanded? Recall that consumers hold many assets that are fixed in dollar terms, such as currency and bank accounts. A higher price level decreases the real value of these money holdings. This cuts consumer wealth, making people less willing to spend at each income level. For reasons that will be explained in a later chapter, a higher price level also tends to increase the market interest rate, and a higher interest rate reduces investment. Finally, a higher U.S. price level, other things constant, means that foreign goods become relatively cheaper for U.S. consumers, and U.S. goods become more expensive abroad. So imports rise and exports fall, decreasing net exports. Therefore, *a higher price level reduces consumption, investment, and net exports, which all reduce aggregate spending*. This decrease in spending reduces real GDP demanded.

Exhibit 4 represents two different ways of expressing the effects of a change in the price level on real GDP demanded. Panel (a) offers the income-expenditure model, and panel (b) offers the aggregate demand curve, showing the inverse relationship between the price level and real GDP demanded. The idea is to find the real GDP demanded for a given price level in panel (a), and then show that price-quantity combination as a point on the aggregate demand curve in panel (b). The two panels measure real GDP on the horizontal axes. At the initial price level of 110 in panel (a), the aggregate expenditure line, now denoted simply as *AE*, intersects the 45-degree line at point *e* to yield real GDP demanded of $14.0 trillion. Panel (b) shows more directly the link between real GDP demanded and the price level. As you can see, when the price level is 110, real GDP demanded is $14.0 trillion. This combination is identified by point *e* on the aggregate demand curve.

EXHIBIT 4 Changing the Price Level to Find the Aggregate Demand Curve

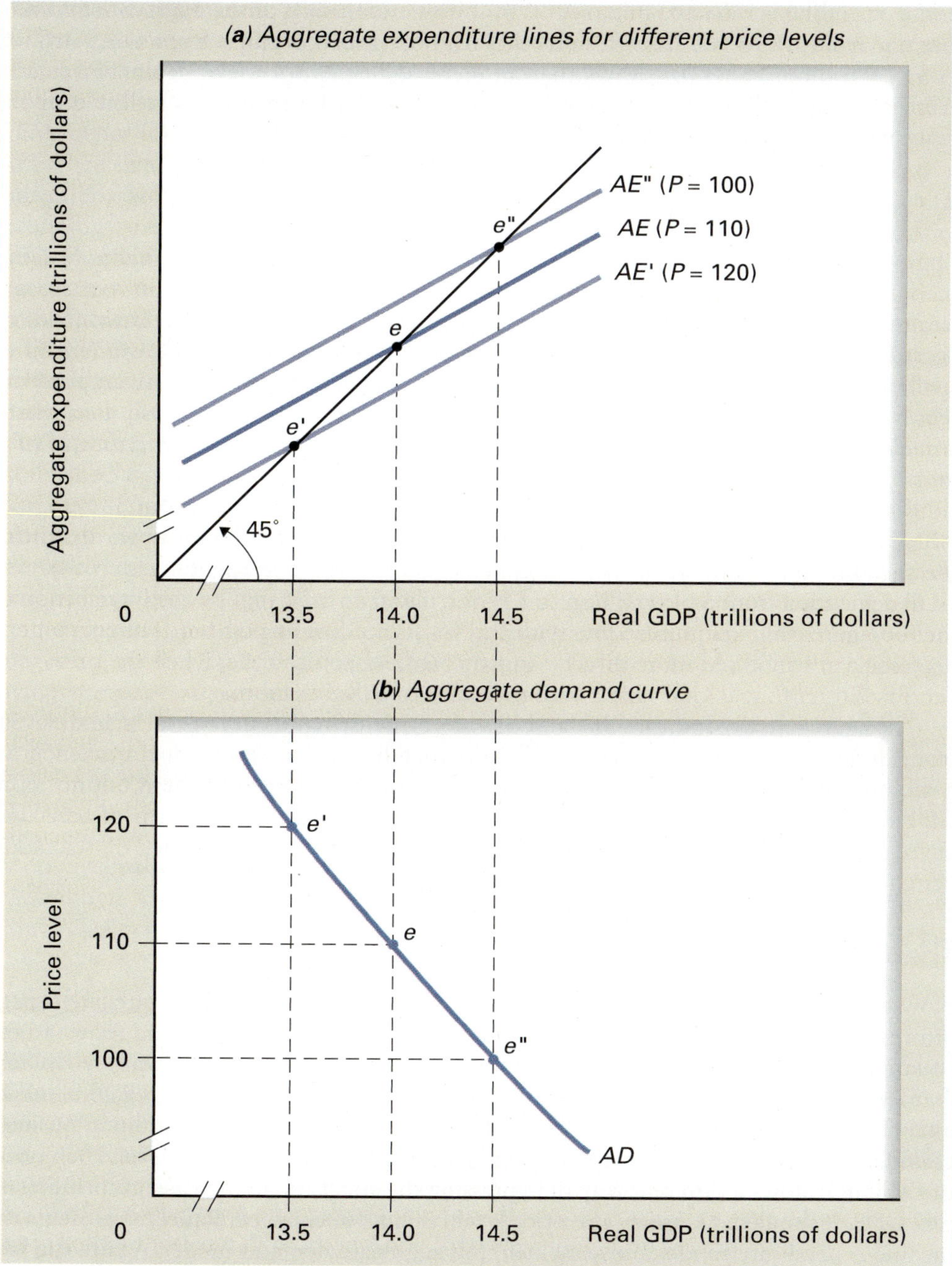

At the initial price level of 110, the aggregate expenditure line is *AE*, which identifies real GDP demanded of \$14.0 trillion. This combination of a price level of 110 and a real GDP demanded of \$14.0 trillion determines one combination (point e) on the aggregate demand curve in panel (b). At the higher price level of 120, the aggregate expenditure line shifts down to *AE′*, and real GDP demanded falls to \$13.5 trillion. This price-quantity combination is identified as point *e′* in panel (b). At the lower price level of 100, the aggregate expenditure line shifts up to *AE″*, which increases real GDP demanded. This combination is plotted as point *e″* in panel (b). Connecting points *e*, *e′*, and *e″* in panel (b) yields the downward-sloping aggregate demand curve AD, which shows the inverse relation between the price level and real GDP demanded.

What if the price level increases from 110 to, say, 120? As you've just learned, an increase in the price level reduces consumption, investment, and net exports. This reduction in spending is reflected in panel (a) by a downward shift of the aggregate expenditure line from *AE* to *AE'*. As a result, real GDP demanded declines from $14.0 trillion to $13.5 trillion. Panel (b) shows that an increase in the price level from 110 to 120 decreases real GDP demanded from $14.0 trillion to $13.5 trillion, as reflected by the movement from point *e* to point *e'*.

A Lower Price Level

The opposite occurs if the price level falls. At a lower price level, the value of bank accounts, currency, and other money holdings increases. Consumers on average are wealthier and thus spend more at each income level. A lower price level also tends to decrease the market interest rate, which increases investment. Finally, a lower U.S. price level, other things constant, makes U.S. products cheaper abroad and foreign products relatively more expensive here, so exports increase and imports decrease. *Because of a decline in the price level, consumption, investment, and net exports increase at each income level.*

Refer again to Exhibit 4 and suppose the price level declines from 110 to, say, 100. This increases spending at each income level, as reflected by an upward shift of the spending line from *AE* to *AE"* in panel (a). An increase in spending increases real GDP demanded from $14.0 trillion to $14.5 trillion, as indicated by the intersection of the top aggregate expenditure line with the 45-degree line at point *e"*. This same price decrease can be viewed more directly in panel (b). As you can see, when the price level decreases to 100, real GDP demanded increases to $14.5 trillion.

The aggregate expenditure line and the aggregate demand curve present real output from different perspectives. The aggregate expenditure line shows, for a given price level, how spending relates to income, or the amount produced in the economy. Real GDP demanded is found where spending equals income, or the amount produced. The aggregate demand curve shows, for various price levels, the quantities of real GDP demanded.

The Multiplier and Shifts in Aggregate Demand

Now that you have some idea how changes in the price level shift the aggregate expenditure line to generate the aggregate demand curve, let's reverse course and return to the situation where the price level is assumed to remain constant. What we want to do now is trace through the effects of a shift of a spending component on aggregate demand, assuming the price level does not change. For example, suppose that a jump in business confidence spurs a $0.1 trillion increase in investment at each real GDP level. Each panel of Exhibit 5 shows a different way of expressing the effects of an increase in spending on real GDP demanded, assuming the price level remains unchanged. Panel (a) presents the income-expenditure model and panel (b), the aggregate demand model. Again, the two panels measure real GDP on the horizontal axes. At a price level of 110 in panel (a), the aggregate expenditure line, $C + I + G + (X - M)$, intersects the 45-degree line at point *e* to yield $14.0 trillion in real GDP demanded. Panel (b) shows more directly the link between real GDP demanded and the price level. As you can see, when the price level is 110, real GDP demanded is $14.0 trillion, identified as point *e* on the aggregate demand curve.

Exhibit 5 shows how a shift of the aggregate expenditure line relates to a shift of the aggregate demand curve, given a constant price level. In panel (a), a $0.1 trillion increase in investment shifts the aggregate expenditure line up by $0.1 trillion. Because of the multiplier effect, real GDP demanded climbs from $14.0 trillion to $14.5 trillion. Panel (b) shows

EXHIBIT 5 **A Shift of the Aggregate Expenditure Line That Shifts the Aggregate Demand Curve**

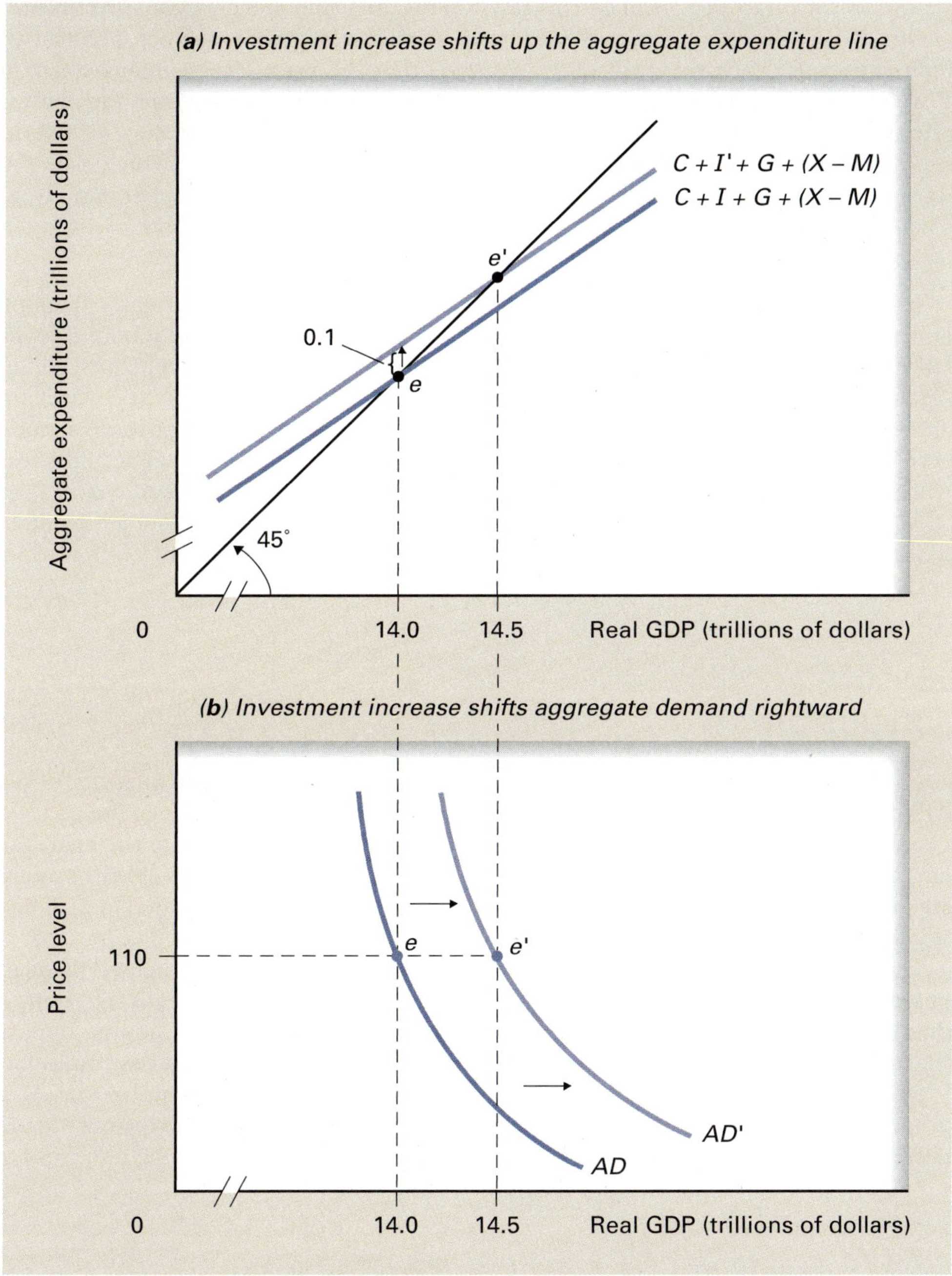

A shift of the aggregate expenditure line at a given price level shifts the aggregate demand curve. In panel (a), an increase in investment of \$0.1 trillion, with the price level constant at 110, causes the aggregate expenditure line to increase from $C + I + G + (X - M)$ to $C + I' + G + (X - M)$. As a result, real GDP demanded increases from \$14.0 trillion to \$14.5 trillion. In panel (b), the aggregate demand curve has shifted from *AD* out to *AD'*. At the prevailing price level of 110, real GDP demanded has increased by \$0.5 trillion.

the effect of the increase in spending on the aggregate demand curve, which shifts to the right, from *AD* to *AD′*. At the prevailing price level of 110, real GDP demanded increases from $14.0 trillion to $14.5 trillion as a result of the $0.1 trillion increase in investment.

Our discussion of the simple spending multiplier exaggerates the actual effect we might expect. For one thing, we have assumed that the price level remains constant. As we shall see in the next chapter, incorporating aggregate supply into the analysis reduces the multiplier because of the resulting price change. Moreover, as income increases, there are leakages from the circular flow in addition to saving, such as higher income taxes and additional imports; these leakages reduce the multiplier. Finally, although we have presented the process in a timeless framework, the spending multiplier takes time to work through rounds—perhaps a year or more.

To Review: For a given price level, the aggregate expenditure line relates spending plans to income, or real GDP. Real GDP demanded is found where the amount people plan to spend equals the amount produced. A change in the price level shifts the aggregate expenditure line, changing real GDP demanded. Changes in the price level and consequent changes in real GDP demanded generate points along an aggregate demand curve. But at a given price level, changes in spending plans, such as changes in investment, consumption, or government purchases, shift the aggregate demand curve.

At the end of the book, the case study, "Bringing Theory to Life: Consumer Spending on Services During the Recession," considers how the financial panic of 2008 affected consumption and GDP.

Conclusion

Three ideas central to this chapter are (1) certain forces determine the quantity of real GDP demanded at a given price level, (2) changes in the price level change the quantity of real GDP demanded and these price-quantity combinations generate the aggregate demand curve, and (3) at a given price level, changes in spending plans shift the aggregate demand curve. The simple multiplier provides a crude but exaggerated idea of how a change in spending plans affects real GDP demanded.

This chapter focused on aggregate spending. A simplifying assumption used throughout was that imports do not vary with income. Appendix A adds more realism by considering what happens when imports increase with income. Because spending on imports leak from the circular flow, this more realistic approach reduces the spending multiplier.

So far, we have derived real GDP demanded using intuition, examples, and graphs. With the various approaches, we find that for each price level there is a specific quantity of real GDP demanded, other things constant. Appendix B uses algebra to show the same results.

Summary

1. The aggregate expenditure line indicates, for a given price level, spending at each income level. At a given price level, real GDP demanded is found where the amount that people plan to spend equals the amount produced.
2. The spending multiplier indicates the multiple by which a change in the amount people plan to spend changes real GDP demanded. The simple spending multiplier developed in this chapter is $1/(1 - MPC)$. The larger the MPC, the more is spent and the less is saved, so the larger the simple spending multiplier. This multiplier is called "simple" because only consumption changes with changes in income.
3. A higher price level causes a downward shift of the aggregate expenditure line, leading to a lower real GDP demanded. A lower price level causes an upward shift of the aggregate expenditure line, increasing real GDP demanded. By tracing the impact of price changes on real GDP demanded, we can derive an aggregate demand curve.
4. The aggregate expenditure line and the aggregate demand curve portray real output from different perspectives. The aggregate expenditure line shows, for a given price level, how much people plan to spend at each income level. Real GDP demanded is found where spending equals income, or real GDP. The aggregate demand curve shows, for various price levels, the quantities of real GDP demanded. At a given price level, a change in spending plans shifts the aggregate demand curve.

Key Concepts

Aggregate expenditure line 476

Income-expenditure model 477

Simple spending multiplier 481

Questions for Review

1. Aggregate Expenditure What are the components of aggregate expenditure? In the model developed in this chapter, which components vary with changes in the level of real GDP? What determines the slope of the aggregate expenditure line?
2. Real GDP Demanded In your own words, explain the logic of the income-expenditure model. What determines the amount of real GDP demanded?
3. Real GDP Demanded What equalities hold at the level of real GDP demanded? When determining real GDP demanded, what do we assume about the price level? What do we assume about inventories?
4. When Output and Spending Differ What role do inventories play in determining real GDP demanded? In answering this question, suppose initially that firms are either producing more than people plan to spend, or producing less than people plan to spend.
5. Simple Spending Multiplier "A rise in investment in an economy leads to a rise in spending." Use the spending multiplier to verify this statement.
6. Case Study: The Ripple Effect on the Economy of 9/11 (See page 753.) How do events, such as the World Trade Center and Pentagon attacks described in the case study "The Ripple Effect on the Economy of 9/11" affect the aggregate expenditure line and the aggregate demand curve? Explain fully.
7. The Aggregate Demand Curve What is the effect of a lower price level, other things constant, on the aggregate expenditure line and real GDP demanded? How does the multiplier interact with the price change to determine the new real GDP demanded?

Problems and Exercises

8. Simple Spending Multiplier For each of the following values for the MPC, determine the size of the simple spending multiplier and the total change in real GDP demanded following a $10 billion decrease in spending:

   a. $MPC = 0.9$
   b. $MPC = 0.75$
   c. $MPC = 0.6$

9. Simple Spending Multiplier Suppose that the MPC is 0.8 and that $14 trillion of real GDP is currently being demanded. The government wants to increase real GDP demanded to $15 trillion at the given price level. By how much would it have to increase government purchases to achieve this goal?

10. Simple Spending Multiplier Suppose that the MPC is 0.8, while investment, government purchases, and net exports sum to $500 billion. Suppose also that the government budget is in balance.

    a. What is the sum of saving and net taxes when desired spending equals real GDP? Explain.
    b. What is the value of the multiplier?
    c. Explain why the multiplier is related to the slope of the consumption function.

11. Investment and the Multiplier This chapter assumes that investment is autonomous. What would happen to the size of the multiplier if investment increases as real GDP increases? Explain.

12. Shifts of Aggregate Demand Assume the simple spending multiplier equals 10. Determine the size and direction of any changes of the aggregate expenditure line, real GDP demanded, and the aggregate demand curve for each of the following changes in spending:

    a. Spending rises by $8 billion at each income level.
    b. Spending falls by $5 billion at each income level.
    c. Spending rises by $20 billion at each income level.

13. Case Study: Consumer Spending on Services During the Recession (See page 755.) What are the components of consumption discussed in this case study? How did each component change in the recession of 2008-2009?

Appendix A

Variable Net Exports Revisited

This chapter has assumed that net exports do not vary with income. A more realistic approach has net exports varying inversely with income. Such a model was developed in the appendix to the previous chapter. The resulting net export function, $X - M$, is presented in panel (a) of Exhibit 6. Recall that the higher the income level in the economy, the more is spent on imports, and this lowers net exports. (If this is not clear, review the appendix to the previous chapter.) Panel (b) of Exhibit 6 shows what happens when variable net exports are added to

EXHIBIT 6 Net Exports and the Aggregate Expenditure Line

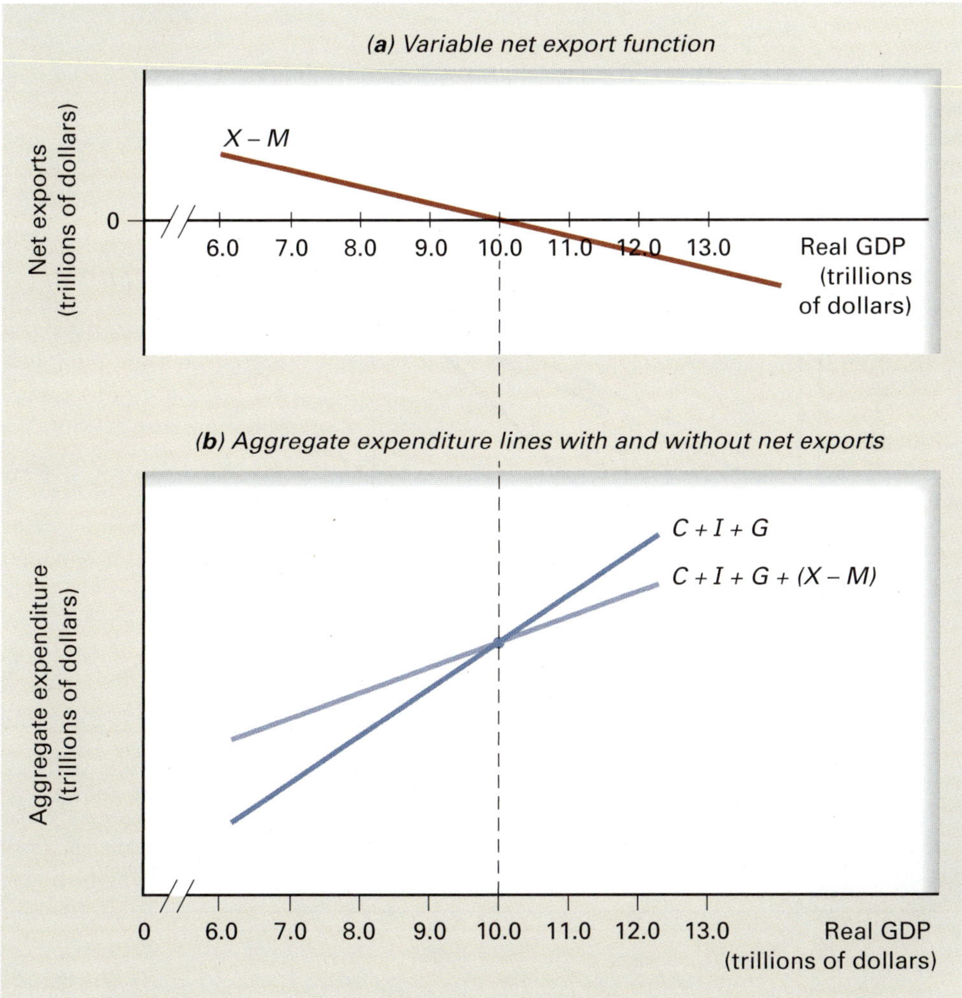

In panel (a), net exports, $X - M$, equal exports minus imports. Net exports are added to consumption, investment, and government purchases in panel (b) to yield $C + I + G + (X - M)$. The addition of net exports has the effect of rotating the spending line about the point where net exports are zero, which occurs in this example where real GDP is \$10.0 trillion.

consumption, government purchases, and investment. We add the variable net export function to $C + I + G$ to get $C + I + G + (X - M)$. Perhaps the easiest way to see how introducing net exports affects spending is to begin where real GDP equals \$10.0 trillion. Because net exports equal zero when real GDP equals \$10.0 trillion, the addition of net exports has no effect on spending. So the $C + I + G$ and $C + I + G + (X - M)$ lines intersect where real GDP equals \$10.0 trillion. At real GDP levels less than \$10.0 trillion, net exports are positive, so the $C + I + G + (X - M)$ line is above the $C + I + G$ line. At real GDP levels greater than \$10.0 trillion, net exports are negative, so the $C + I + G + (X - M)$ line is below the $C + I + G$ line. *Because variable net exports and real GDP are inversely related, the addition of variable net exports has the effect of flattening out, or reducing the slope of, the aggregate expenditure line.*

Net Exports and the Spending Multiplier

The inclusion of variable net exports makes the model more realistic but more complicated, and it requires a reformulation of the spending multiplier. If net exports are autonomous, or independent of income, only the marginal propensity to consume determines how much gets spent and how much gets saved as income changes. The inclusion of variable net exports means that, as income increases, U.S. residents spend more on imports. The *marginal propensity to import*, or *MPM*, is the fraction of each additional dollar of disposable income spent on imported products. Imports leak from the circular flow. Thus, two leakages now increase with income: saving and imports.

EXHIBIT 7 Effect of a Shift of Autonomous Spending on Real GDP Demanded

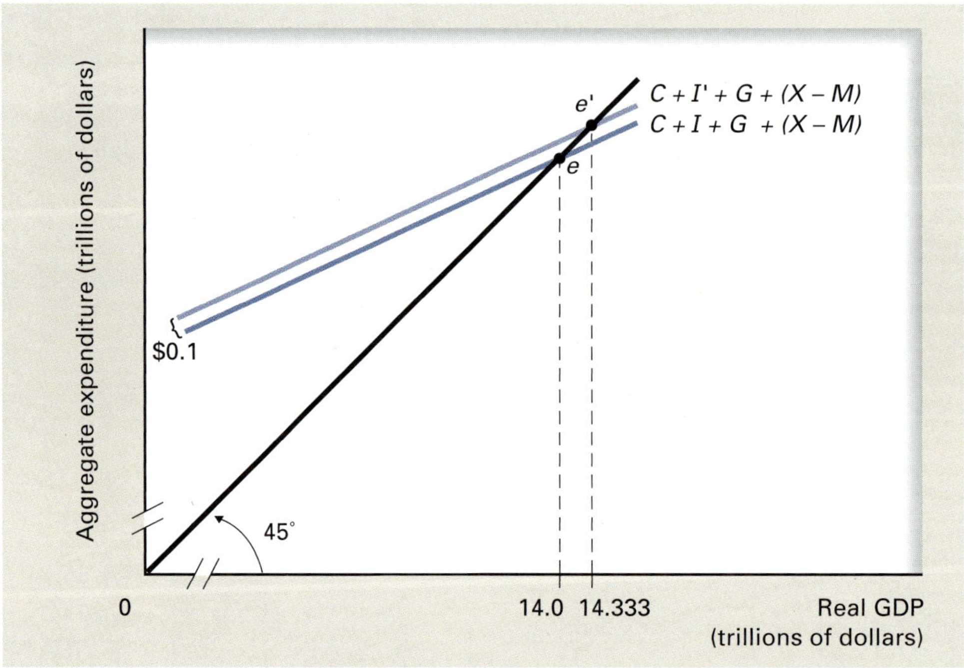

An increase in investment, other things constant, shifts the spending line up from $C + I + G + (X - M)$ to $C + I' + G + (X - M)$, increasing the quantity of real GDP demanded.

This additional leakage changes the value of the multiplier from $1/MPS$ to:

$$\text{Spending multiplier with variable net exports} = \frac{1}{MPS + MPM}$$

The larger the marginal propensity to import, the greater the leakage during each round of spending and the smaller the resulting spending multiplier. Suppose the MPM equals 1/10, or 0.1. If the marginal propensity to save is 0.2 and the marginal propensity to import is 0.1, then only $0.70 of each additional dollar of disposable income gets spent on output produced in the United States. We can compute the new multiplier as follows:

$$\text{Spending multiplier with variable net exports} = \frac{1}{MPS + MPM} = \frac{1}{0.2 + 0.1} = \frac{1}{0.3} = 3.33$$

Thus, the inclusion of net exports reduces the spending multiplier in our hypothetical example from 5 to 3.33. Because some of each additional dollar of income goes toward imports, less is spent on U.S. products, so any given shift of the aggregate expenditure line has less of an impact on real GDP demanded.

A Change in Autonomous Spending

Given the net export function described in the previous section, what is the real GDP demanded, and how does income change when there is a change in autonomous spending? To answer these questions, let's begin in Exhibit 7 with an aggregate expenditure line of $C + I + G + (X - M)$, where net exports vary inversely with income. This aggregate expenditure line intersects the 45-degree line at point *e*, determining real GDP demanded of $14.0 trillion. Suppose now that investment increases by $0.1 trillion at every income, with the price level unchanged. This shifts the entire aggregate expenditure line up by $0.1 trillion, from $C + I + G + (X - M)$ to $C + I' + G + (X - M)$, as shown in Exhibit 7. Output demanded increases from $14.0 trillion to $14.333 trillion, representing an increase of $0.333 trillion, or $333 billion, which is $0.1 trillion times the spending multiplier with variable exports of 3.33. The derivation of the output level and the size of the multiplier are explained in Appendix B.

Appendix A Question

1. **Net Exports and the Spending Multiplier** Suppose that the marginal propensity to consume (MPC) is 0.8 and the marginal propensity to import (MPM) is 0.05.
   a. What is the value of the spending multiplier?
   b. By how much would the real GDP demanded change if investment increased by $100 billion?
   c. Using your answer to part (b), calculate the change in net exports caused by the change in aggregate output.

Appendix B

The Algebra of Income and Expenditure

This appendix explains the algebra behind real GDP demanded. You should see some similarity between this and the circular-flow explanation of national income accounts.

The Aggregate Expenditure Line

We first determine where spending equals output and then derive the relevant spending multipliers, assuming a given price level. Initially, let's assume net exports are autonomous, or independent of the income. Then we'll incorporate variable net exports into the framework.

Real GDP demanded for a given price level occurs where spending equals income, or real GDP. Spending is equal to the sum of consumption, C, investment, I, government purchases, G, and net exports, $X - M$. We can write the equality as

$$Y = C + I + G + (X - M)$$

where Y equals income, or real GDP. To find where real GDP equals spending, we begin with the heart of the income-expenditure model: the consumption function. The consumption function used throughout this chapter is a straight line; the equation for that line can be written as

$$C = 2.0 + 0.8\,(Y - 1.0)$$

The marginal propensity to consume is 0.8, Y is income, or real GDP, and 1.0 is autonomous net taxes in trillions of dollars. Thus $(Y - 1.0)$ is real GDP minus net taxes, which equals disposable income. The consumption function can be simplified to

$$C = 1.2 + 0.8Y$$

Consumption at each real GDP level, therefore, equals \$1.2 trillion (which could be called autonomous consumption—that is, consumption that does not vary with income), plus 0.8 times income, which is the marginal propensity to consume times income.

The second component of spending is investment, I, which we have assumed is autonomous and equal to \$1.0 trillion. The third component of spending is autonomous government purchases, G, which we assumed to be \$1.0 trillion. Net exports, $X - M$, the final spending component, we assumed to be −\$0.4 trillion at all levels of income. Substituting the numerical values for each spending component in spending, we get

$$Y = 1.2 + 0.8Y + 1.0 + 1.0 - 0.4$$

Notice there is only one variable in this expression: Y. If we rewrite the expression to

$$Y - 0.8Y = 1.2 + 1.0 + 1.0 - 0.4$$
$$0.2Y = 2.8$$

we can solve for real GDP demanded:

$$Y = 2.8/0.2$$
$$Y = \$14.0 \text{ trillion}$$

A More General Form of Income and Expenditure

The advantage of algebra is that it allows us to derive the equilibrium quantity of real GDP demanded in a more general way. Let's begin with a consumption function of the general form

$$C = a + b\,(Y - NT)$$

where b is the marginal propensity to consume and NT is net taxes. Consumption can be rearranged as

$$C = a - bNT + bY$$

where $a - bNT$ is *autonomous* consumption (the portion of consumption that is independent of income) and bY is *induced* consumption (the portion of consumption generated by higher income in the economy). Real GDP demanded equals the sum of consumption, C, investment, I, government purchases, G, and net exports, $X - M$, or

$$\text{Income} = \text{Expenditure}$$
$$Y = a - bNT + bY + I + G + (X - M)$$

Again, by rearranging terms and isolating Y on the left side of the equation, we get

$$Y = \frac{1}{1 - b}(a - bNT + I + G + X - M)$$

The $(a - bNT + I + G + X - M)$ term represents autonomous spending—that is, the amount of spending that is independent of income. And $(1 - b)$ equals 1 minus the MPC. In the chapter, we showed that $1/(1 - MPC)$ equals the simple spending multiplier. One way of viewing what's going on is to keep in mind that autonomous spending is *multiplied* through the economy to arrive at real GDP demanded.

The formula that yields real GDP demanded can be used to derive the spending multiplier. We can increase autonomous spending by, say, \$1, to see what happens to real GDP demanded.

$$Y' = \frac{1}{1 - b}(a - bNT + I + G + X - M + \$1)$$

The difference between this expression and the initial one (that is, between Y' and Y) is $\$1/(1 - b)$. Because b equals the MPC, the simple multiplier equals $1/(1 - b)$. Thus, the change in equilibrium income equals the change in autonomous spending times the multiplier.

Varying Net Exports

Here we explore the algebra behind variable net exports, first introduced in the appendix to the previous chapter. We begin with the equality

$$Y = C + I + G + (X - M)$$

Exports are assumed to equal \$0.9 trillion at each income level. Imports increase as disposable income increases, with a marginal propensity to import of 0.1. Therefore, net exports equal

$$X - M = 0.9 - 0.1\,(Y - 1.0)$$

After incorporating the values for C, I, and G presented earlier, we can express the equality as

$$Y = 1.2 + 0.8Y + 1.0 + 1.0 + 0.9 - 0.1\,(Y - 1.0)$$

which reduces to $0.3Y = \$4.2$ trillion, or $Y = \$14.0$ trillion.

Algebra can be used to generalize these results. If m represents the marginal propensity to import, net exports become $X - m(Y - NT)$. Real GDP demanded can be found by solving for Y in the expression

$$Y = a + b(Y - NT) + I + G + X - m(Y - NT)$$

which yields

$$Y = \frac{1}{1 - b + m}(a - bNT + I + G + X + mNT)$$

The expression in parentheses represents autonomous spending. In the denominator, $1 - b$ is the marginal propensity to save and m is the marginal propensity to import. Appendix A demonstrated that $1/(MPS + MPM)$ equals the spending multiplier when variable net exports are included. Thus, real GDP demanded equals the spending multiplier times autonomous spending. And an increase in autonomous spending times the multiplier gives us the resulting increase in real GDP demanded.

Appendix B Question

1. Suppose that $C = 100 + 0.75(Y - 100)$, $I = 50$, $G = 30$, and $X - M = -100$, all in billions of dollars. What is the simple spending multiplier? What is real GDP demanded? What would happen to real GDP demanded if government purchases increased to \$40 billion?

Aggregate Supply

25

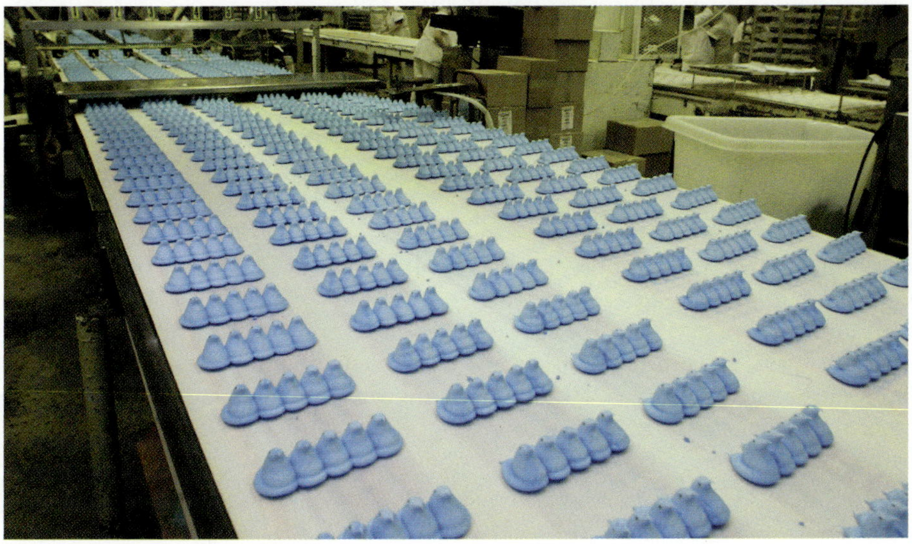

DON EMMERT/AFP/GETTY IMAGES/Newscom

- What is your normal capacity for academic work, and when do you exceed that effort?
- If the economy is already operating at full employment, how can it produce more?
- What valuable piece of information do employers and workers lack when they negotiate wages?
- Why do employers and workers fail to agree on pay cuts that could save jobs?
- How might a long stretch of high unemployment reduce the economy's ability to produce in the future?

These and other questions are answered in this chapter, which develops the aggregate supply curve in the short run and in the long run.

Up to this point, we have focused on aggregate demand. We have not yet examined aggregate supply in any detail, a much debated topic. The debate involves the shape of the aggregate supply curve and the reasons for that shape. This chapter develops a single, coherent approach to aggregate supply. Although the focus continues to be on economic aggregates, you should keep in mind that aggregate supply reflects billions of production decisions made by millions of individual resource suppliers and firms in the economy. Each firm operates in its own little world, dealing with its own suppliers and customers, and keeping a watchful eye on existing and potential competitors.

Yet each firm recognizes that success also depends on the performance of the economy as a whole. The theory of aggregate supply described here must be consistent with both the microeconomic behavior of individual suppliers and the macroeconomic behavior of the economy.

Topics discussed include:

- Expected price level and long-term contracts
- Potential output
- Short-run aggregate supply
- Long-run aggregate supply
- Expansionary gap
- Recessionary gap
- Changes in aggregate supply

Aggregate Supply in the Short Run

Aggregate supply is the relationship between the economy's price level and the amount of output firms are willing and able to supply, with other things constant. Assumed constant along a given aggregate supply curve are resource prices, the state of technology, and the set of formal and informal institutions that structure production incentives, such as the system of property rights, patent laws, tax systems, respect for laws, and the customs and conventions of the marketplace. The greater the supply of resources, the better the technology, and the more effective the production incentives provided by the economic institutions, the greater the aggregate supply. Let's begin with the key resource—labor.

Labor and Aggregate Supply

Labor is the most important resource, accounting for about 70 percent of production cost. The supply of labor in an economy depends on the size and abilities of the adult population and their preferences for work versus leisure. Along a given labor supply curve—that is, for a given adult population with given abilities and preferences for work and leisure—the quantity of labor supplied depends on the wage. The higher the wage, other things constant, the more labor supplied.

So far, so good. But things start getting complicated once we recognize that the purchasing power of any given nominal wage depends on the economy's price level. *The higher the price level, the less any given money wage purchases, so the less attractive that wage is to workers.* Consider wages and the price level over time. Suppose a worker in 1970 was offered a job paying $20,000 per year. That salary may not impress you today, but its real purchasing power back then would exceed $80,000 in today's dollars. Because the price level matters, we must distinguish between the **nominal wage**, or money wage, which measures the wage in dollars of the year in question (such as 1970), and the **real wage**, which measures the wage in constant dollars—that is, dollars measured by the goods and services they buy. A higher real wage means workers can buy more goods and services.

nominal wage
The wage measured in dollars of the year in question; the dollar amount on a paycheck

real wage
The wage measured in dollars of constant purchasing power; the wage measured in terms of the quantity of goods and services it buys

Both workers and employers care more about the real wage than about the nominal wage. The problem is that nobody knows for sure how the price level will change during the life of the wage agreement, so labor contracts must be negotiated in terms of nominal wages, not real wages. Some resource prices, such as wages set by long-term contracts, remain in force for extended periods, often for two or three years. Workers as well as other resource suppliers must therefore negotiate based on the *expected* price level.

Even where there are no explicit labor contracts, there is often an implicit agreement that the wage, once negotiated, will not change for a while. For example, in many firms the standard practice is to revise wages annually. So wage agreements may be either *explicit* (based on a labor contract) or *implicit* (based on labor market practices). These explicit and implicit agreements are difficult to renegotiate while still in effect, even if the price level in the economy turns out to be higher or lower than expected.

Potential Output and the Natural Rate of Unemployment

Here's how resource owners and firms negotiate resource price agreements for a particular period, say, a year. Firms and resource suppliers expect a certain price level to prevail in the economy during the year. You could think of this as the *consensus* view for the upcoming year. Based on consensus expectations, firms and resource suppliers reach agreements on resource prices, such as wages. For example, firms and workers may expect the price level to increase 3 percent next year, so they agree on a nominal wage increase of 4 percent, which would increase the real wage by 1 percent. If these price-level expectations are realized, the agreed-on nominal wage translates into the expected real wage, so everyone is satisfied with the way things work out—after all, that's what they willingly negotiated. When the actual price level turns out as expected, we call the result the economy's potential output. *Potential output is the amount produced when there are no surprises about the price level.* So, at the agreed-on real wage, workers are supplying the quantity of labor they want and firms are hiring the quantity of labor they want. Both sides are content with the outcome.

We can think of **potential output** as the economy's maximum sustainable output, given the supply of resources, the state of technology, and the formal and informal production incentives offered by the rules of the game. Potential output is also referred to by other terms, including the *natural rate of output* and the *full-employment rate of output*.

potential output
The economy's maximum sustainable output, given the supply of resources, technology, and rules of the game; the output level when there are no surprises about the price level

The unemployment rate that occurs when the economy produces its potential GDP is called the **natural rate of unemployment**. That rate prevails when cyclical unemployment is zero. When the economy produces its potential output, the number of job openings equals the number of people unemployed for frictional, structural, and seasonal reasons. Widely accepted estimates of the natural rate of unemployment range from about 4 percent to about 6 percent of the labor force.

natural rate of unemployment
The unemployment rate when the economy produces its potential output

Potential output provides a reference point, an anchor, for the analysis in this chapter. *When the price-level expectations of both workers and firms are fulfilled, the economy produces its potential output.* Complications arise, however, when the actual price level differs from expectations, as we'll see next.

Actual Price Level Is Higher Than Expected

As you know, each firm's goal is to maximize profit. Profit equals total revenue minus total cost. Suppose workers and firms reach a wage agreement. What if the economy's price level turns out to be higher than expected? What happens *in the short run* to real GDP supplied? The **short run** in macroeconomics is a period during which some resource prices remain fixed by explicit or implicit agreements. Does output in the short run exceed the economy's potential, fall short of that potential, or equal that potential?

short run
In macroeconomics, a period during which some resource prices, especially those for labor, are fixed by explicit or implicit agreements

Because the prices of many resources are fixed for the duration of contracts, firms welcome a higher than expected price level. After all, the selling prices of their products, on average, are higher than expected, while the costs of at least some of the resources they employ remain constant. *A price level that is higher than expected results in a higher profit per unit, so firms have a profit incentive in the short run to increase production beyond the economy's potential level.*

At first it might appear odd to talk about producing beyond the economy's potential, but remember that potential output means not zero unemployment but the natural rate of unemployment. Even in an economy producing its potential output, there is some unemployed labor and some unused production capacity. If you think of potential GDP as the economy's *normal capacity,* you get a better idea of how production can temporarily exceed that capacity. For example, during World War II, the United States pulled out all the stops to win the war. Factories operated around the clock. Overtime was common. The unemployment rate dropped below 2 percent—well under its natural rate. People worked longer and harder for the war effort than they normally would have.

Think about your own study habits. During most of the term, you display your normal capacity for academic work. As the end of the term draws near, however, you may shift into high gear, finishing term papers, studying late into the night for final exams, and generally running yourself ragged trying to pull things together. During those final frenzied days of the term, you study beyond your normal capacity, beyond the schedule you follow on a regular or sustained basis. We often observe workers exceeding their normal capacity for short bursts: fireworks technicians around the Fourth of July, accountants during tax time, farmers during harvest time, and elected officials toward the end of a campaign or legislative session. Similarly, firms and their workers are able, *in the short run,* to push output beyond the economy's potential. But that higher rate of output is not normal and not sustainable.

Why Costs Rise When Output Exceeds Potential

The economy is flexible enough to expand output beyond potential GDP, but as output expands, the cost of additional output increases. Although many workers are bound by contracts, wage agreements may require overtime pay for extra hours or weekends. As the economy expands and the unemployment rate declines, additional workers are harder to find. Retirees, homemakers, and students may require extra pay to draw them into the labor force. If few additional workers are available or if workers require additional pay for overtime, the nominal cost of labor increases as output expands in the short run, even though most wages remain fixed by implicit or explicit agreements.

As production increases, the demand for nonlabor resources increases as well, so the prices of those resources in markets where prices are flexible—such as the market for oil—will increase, reflecting their greater scarcity. Also, as production increases, firms use their machines and trucks more intensively, so equipment wears out faster and is more prone to breakdowns. Thus, the nominal cost per unit of output rises when production is pushed beyond the economy's potential output. But *because some resource prices are fixed by contracts, the economy's price level rises faster than the per-unit production cost, so firms still find it profitable to increase the quantity supplied.*

When the economy's actual price level exceeds the expected price level, the real value of an agreed-on nominal wage declines. We might ask why workers would be willing to increase the quantity of labor they supply when the price level is higher than expected. One answer is that labor agreements require workers to do so, at least until workers have a chance to renegotiate.

In summary: If the price level is higher than expected, firms have a profit incentive to increase the quantity of goods and services supplied. At higher rates of output, however, the per-unit cost of additional output increases. Firms expand output as long as the revenue from additional production exceeds the cost of that production.

An Actual Price Level Lower Than Expected

We have learned that if the price level is greater than expected, firms expand output in the short run, but as they do, the marginal cost of production increases. Now let's look at the effects of a price level that turns out to be lower than expected. Again, suppose that firms and resource suppliers have reached an agreement based on an expected price level. If the price level turns out to be lower than expected, firms find production less profitable, as reflected in the recent headline, "Consumer Price Drop Squeezes Profits."[1] The prices firms receive for their output are on average lower than they expected, yet many of their production costs, such as nominal wages, do not fall.

1. Sudeep Reddy and Dana Mattioli, "Consumer Price Drop Squeezes Profits," *Wall Street Journal*, 18 June 2010.

Because production is less profitable when prices are lower than expected, firms reduce their quantity supplied, so the economy's output is below its potential. As a result, some workers are laid off, some work fewer hours, and unemployment exceeds the natural rate. Not only is less labor employed, but machines go unused, delivery trucks sit idle, and entire plants may shut down—for example, automakers sometimes halt production for weeks.

Just as some costs increase in the short run when output is pushed beyond the economy's potential, some costs decline when output falls below that potential. As resources become unemployed, resource prices decline in markets where prices are flexible.

To Review: If the economy's price level turns out to be higher than expected, firms maximize profit by increasing the quantity supplied beyond the economy's potential output. As output expands, the per-unit cost of additional production increases, but firms expand production as long as prices rise more than costs. If the economy's price level turns out to be lower than expected, firms produce less than the economy's potential output because prices fall more than costs. All of this is a long way of saying that *there is a direct relationship in the short run between the actual price level and real GDP supplied.*

The Short-Run Aggregate Supply Curve

What we have been describing so far traces out the **short-run aggregate supply** (SRAS) **curve**, which shows the relationship between the actual price level and real GDP supplied, other things constant. Again, the *short run* in this context is the period during which some resource prices, especially those for labor, are fixed by implicit or explicit agreements. For simplicity, we can think of the short run as the duration of labor contracts, which are based on the expected price level.

short-run aggregate supply (SRAS) curve
A curve that shows a direct relationship between the actual price level and real GDP supplied in the short run, other things constant, including the expected price level

Suppose the expected price level is 110. The short-run aggregate supply curve in Exhibit 1, $SRAS_{110}$, is based on that expected price level (hence the subscript 110). If the price level turns out as expected, producers supply the economy's *potential output*, which in Exhibit 1 is $14.0 trillion. Although not shown in the exhibit, the aggregate demand curve would intersect the aggregate supply curve at point *a*. If the economy produces its potential output, unemployment is at the *natural rate*. Nobody is surprised, and all are content with the outcome. There is no tendency to move away from point *a* even if workers and firms could renegotiate wages.

In Exhibit 1, output levels that fall short of the economy's potential are shaded red, and output levels that exceed the economy's potential are shaded blue. The slope of the short-run aggregate supply curve depends on how sharply the marginal cost of production rises as real GDP expands. If costs increase modestly as output expands, the supply curve is relatively flat. If these costs increase sharply as output expands, the supply curve is relatively steep. Much of the controversy about the short-run aggregate supply curve involves its shape. Shapes range from flat to steep. Notice that the short-run aggregate supply curve becomes steeper as output increases, because some resources become scarcer and thus more costly as output increases.

From the Short Run to the Long Run

This section begins with the price level exceeding expectations in the short run to see what happens in the long run. The long run is long enough that firms and resource suppliers can renegotiate all agreements based on knowledge of the actual price level. *So in the long run, there are no surprises about the price level.*

EXHIBIT 1 Short-Run Aggregate Supply Curve

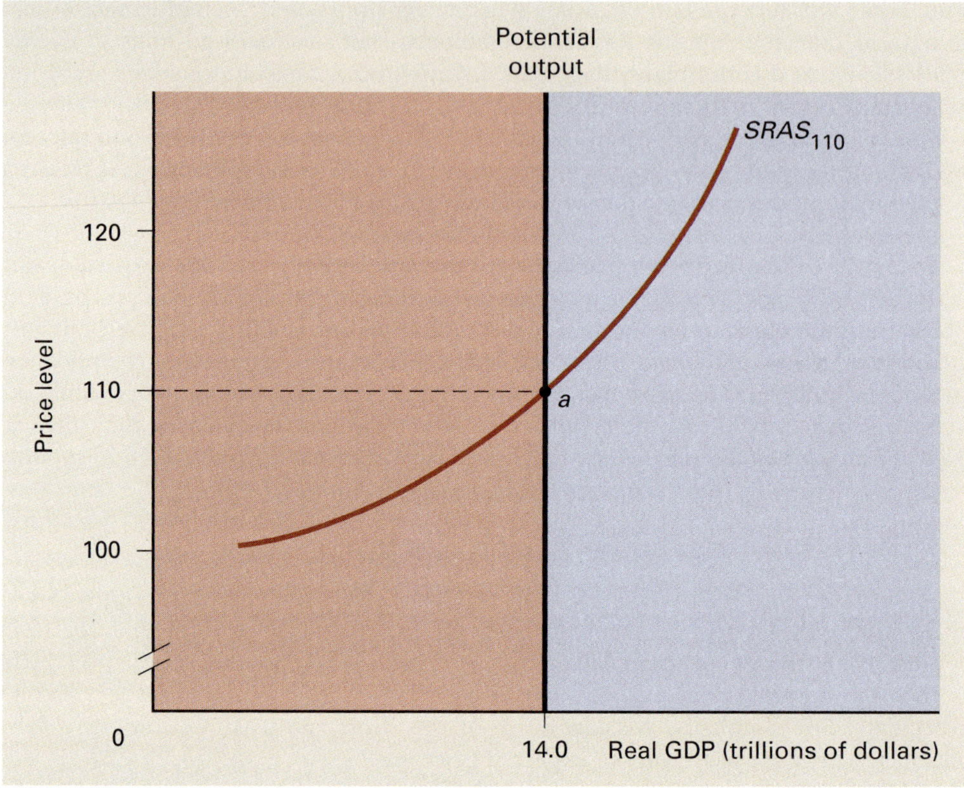

The short-run aggregate supply curve is based on a given expected price level, in this case, 110. Point *a* shows that if the actual price level equals the expected price level of 110, firms supply potential output. If the actual price level exceeds 110, firms supply more than potential. If the actual price level is below 110, firms supply less than potential. Output levels that fall short of the economy's potential are shaded red; output levels that exceed the economy's potential are shaded blue.

Closing an Expansionary Gap

Let's begin our look at the long-run adjustment in Exhibit 2 with an expected price level of 110. The short-run aggregate supply curve for that expected price level is $SRAS_{110}$. Given this short-run aggregate supply curve, the equilibrium price level and real GDP depend on the aggregate demand curve. The actual price level would equal the expected price level only if the aggregate demand curve intersects the aggregate supply curve at point *a*—that is, where the short-run quantity equals potential output. Point *a* reflects potential output of $14.0 trillion and a price level of 110, which is the expected price level.

short-run equilibrium
The price level and real GDP that result when the aggregate demand curve intersects the short-run aggregate supply curve

expansionary gap
The amount by which actual output in the short run exceeds the economy's potential output

But what if aggregate demand turns out to be greater than expected, such as *AD*, which intersects the short-run aggregate supply curve $SRAS_{110}$ at point *b*. Point *b* is the **short-run equilibrium**, reflecting a price level of 115 and a real GDP of $14.2 trillion. The actual price level in the short run is higher than expected, and output exceeds the economy's potential of $14.0 trillion.

The amount by which short-run output exceeds the economy's potential is called an **expansionary gap**. In Exhibit 2, that gap is the short-run output of $14.2 trillion minus potential output of $14.0 trillion, or $0.2 trillion. When real GDP exceeds its

EXHIBIT 2 Long-Run Adjustment When the Price Level Exceeds Expectations

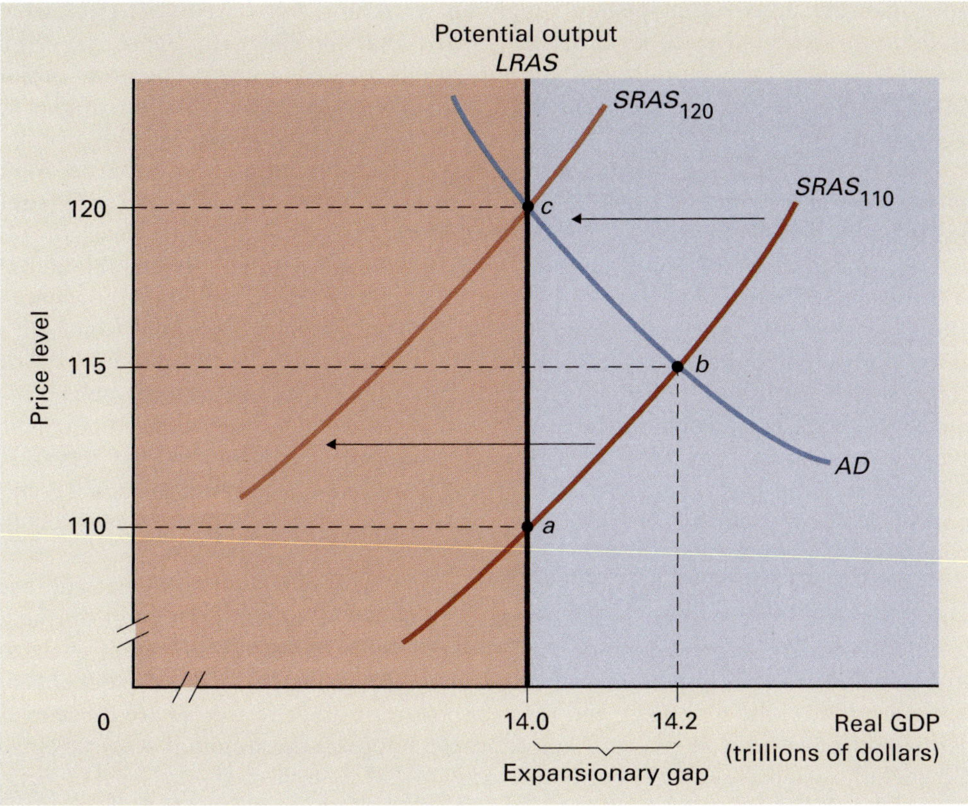

If the expected price level is 110, the short-run aggregate supply curve is $SRAS_{110}$. If the actual price level turns out as expected, the quantity supplied is the potential output of $14.0 trillion. But here the price level ends up higher than expected, and output exceeds potential, as shown by the short-run equilibrium at point *b*. The amount by which actual output exceeds the economy's potential output is called the expansionary gap. In the long run, price-level expectations and nominal wages will be revised upward. Costs will rise and the short-run aggregate supply curve will shift leftward to $SRAS_{120}$. Eventually, the economy will move to long-run equilibrium at point *c*, thus closing the expansionary gap.

potential, the unemployment rate is less than its natural rate. Employees are working overtime, machines are being pushed to their limits, and farmers are sandwiching extra crops between usual plantings. Remember that the nominal wage was negotiated based on an expected price level of 110; because the actual price level is higher, that nominal wage translates into a lower-than-expected real wage. As we will see, output exceeding the economy's potential creates inflationary pressure. *The more that short-run output exceeds the economy's potential, the larger the expansionary gap and the greater the upward pressure on the price level.*

What happens in the long run? The **long run** is a period during which firms and resource suppliers know about market conditions, particularly aggregate demand and the actual price level, and have the time to renegotiate resource payments based on that knowledge. Because the higher-than-expected price level cuts the real value of the nominal wage originally agreed to, workers try to negotiate a higher nominal wage at their earliest opportunity. Workers and other resource suppliers negotiate higher

long run
In macroeconomics, a period during which wage contracts and resource price agreements can be renegotiated; there are no surprises about the economy's actual price level

nominal payments, raising production costs for firms, so the short-run aggregate supply curve shifts leftward, resulting in cost-push inflation. In the long run, the expansionary gap causes the short-run aggregate supply curve to shift leftward to $SRAS_{120}$, which results in an expected price level of 120. Notice that the short-run aggregate supply curve shifts until the equilibrium output equals the economy's potential output. *Actual output can exceed the economy's potential in the short run but not in the long run.*

As shown in Exhibit 2, the expansionary gap is closed by long-run market forces that shift the short-run aggregate supply curve from $SRAS_{110}$ left to $SRAS_{120}$. Whereas $SRAS_{110}$ was based on resource contracts reflecting an expected price level of 110, $SRAS_{120}$ is based on resource contracts reflecting an expected price level of 120. At point *c* the expected price level and the actual price level are identical, so the economy is not only in short-run equilibrium but it's also in **long-run equilibrium**. Consider all the equalities that hold at point *c:* (1) the expected price level equals the actual price level; (2) the quantity supplied in the short run equals potential output, which also equals the quantity supplied in the long run; and (3) the quantity supplied equals the quantity demanded. Looked at another way, *long-run equilibrium occurs where the aggregate demand curve intersects the vertical line drawn at potential output.* Point *c* continues to be the equilibrium point unless there is some change in aggregate demand or in aggregate supply.

long-run equilibrium
The price level and real GDP that occurs when (1) the actual price level equals the expected price level, (2) real GDP supplied equals potential output, and (3) real GDP supplied equals real GDP demanded

Note that the situation at point *c* is no different *in real terms* from what had been expected at point *a*. At both points, firms supply the economy's potential output of \$14.0 trillion. The same amounts of labor and other resources are employed, and although the price level, the nominal wage, and other nominal resource payments are higher at point *c*, the real wage and the real return to other resources are the same as they would have been at point *a*. For example, suppose the nominal wage averaged \$22 per hour when the expected price level was 110. If the expected price level increased from 110 to 120, an increase of 9.1 percent, the nominal wage would also increase by that same percentage to an average of \$24 per hour, leaving the real wage unchanged. With no change in real wages between points *a* and *c*, firms demand enough labor and workers supply enough labor to produce \$14.0 trillion in real GDP.

Thus, if the price level turns out to be higher than expected, the short-run response is to increase quantity supplied. But production exceeding the economy's potential creates inflationary pressure. In the long run this causes the short-run aggregate supply curve to shift to the left, reducing output, increasing the price level, and closing the expansionary gap.

If an increase in the price level is predicted accurately year after year, firms and resource suppliers would build these expectations into their long-term agreements. The price level would move up each year by the expected amount, but the economy's output would remain at potential GDP, thereby skipping the round-trip beyond the economy's potential and back.

Closing a Recessionary Gap

Let's begin again with an expected price level of 110 as presented in Exhibit 3, where blue shading indicates output exceeding potential and red shading indicates output below potential. If the price level turned out as expected, the resulting equilibrium combination would occur at *a,* which would be both a short-run and a long-run equilibrium. Suppose this time that the aggregate demand curve intersects the short-run aggregate supply curve to the left of potential output, yielding a price level below that expected. The intersection of the aggregate demand curve, AD'', with $SRAS_{110}$ yields the short-run equilibrium at point *d*, where the price level is below expectations and

EXHIBIT 3 Long-Run Adjustment When the Price Level Is Below Expectations

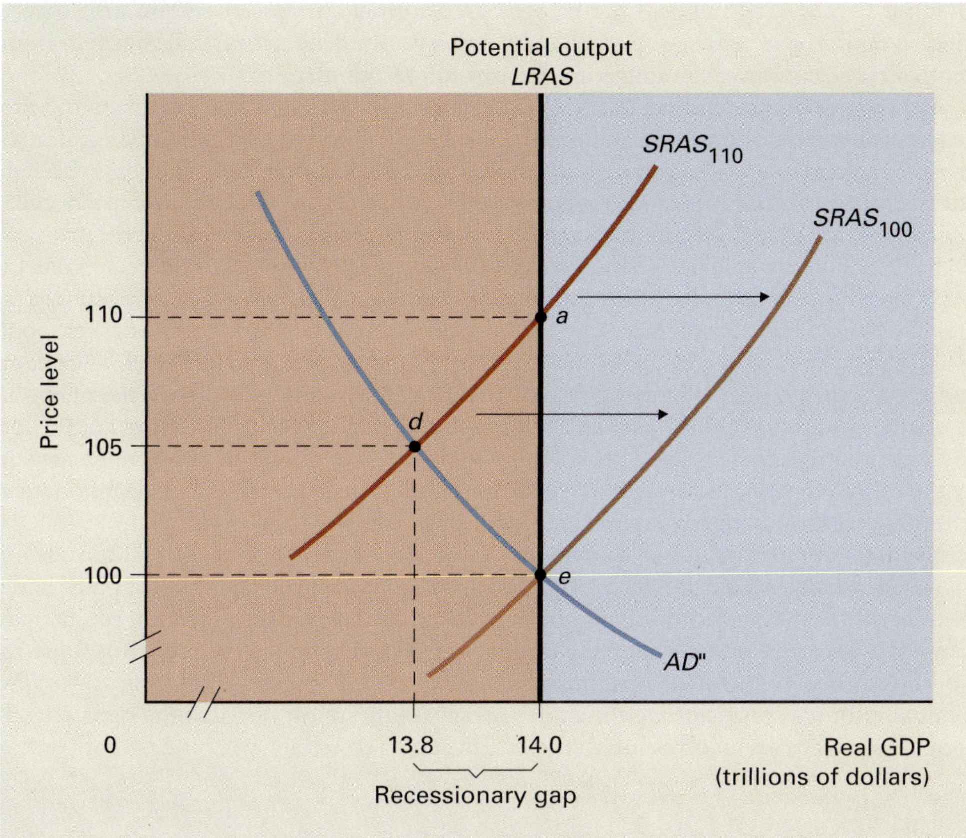

When the actual price level is below expectations, as indicated by the intersection of the aggregate demand curve *AD"* with the short-run aggregate supply curve $SRAS_{110}$, short-run equilibrium occurs at point *d*. Production below the economy's potential opens a recessionary gap. If prices and wages are flexible enough in the long run, nominal wages will be renegotiated lower. As resource costs fall, the short-run aggregate supply curve eventually shifts rightward to $SRAS_{100}$ and the economy moves to long-run equilibrium at point *e*, with output increasing to the potential level of $14.0 trillion.

production is less than the economy's potential. The amount by which actual output falls short of potential GDP is called a **recessionary gap**. In this case, the recessionary gap is $0.2 trillion, and unemployment exceeds its natural rate.

recessionary gap
The amount by which actual output in the short run falls short of the economy's potential output

Because the price level is less than expected, the nominal wage, which was based on the expected price level, translates into a higher real wage in the short run. What happens in the long run? With the price level lower than expected, employers are no longer willing to pay as high a nominal wage. And with the unemployment rate higher than the natural rate, more workers are competing for jobs, putting downward pressure on the nominal wage. If the price level and the nominal wage are flexible enough, the combination of a lower price level and a pool of unemployed workers competing for jobs should make workers more willing to accept lower nominal wages next time wage agreements are negotiated.

If firms and workers negotiate lower nominal wages, the cost of production decreases, shifting the short-run aggregate supply curve rightward, leading to deflation and greater output. The short-run supply curve continues to shift rightward until it intersects the aggregate demand curve where the economy produces its potential output. This is reflected in Exhibit 3 by a rightward shift of the short-run aggregate supply curve from $SRAS_{110}$ to $SRAS_{100}$. *If the price level and nominal wage are flexible enough, the short-run aggregate supply curve shifts rightward until the economy produces its potential output.* The new short-run aggregate supply curve is based on an expected price level of 100. Because the expected price level and the actual price level are now identical, the economy is in long-run equilibrium at point *e*.

Although the nominal wage is lower at point *e* than that originally agreed to when the expected price level was 110, the real wage is the same at point *e* as it was at point *a*. Because the real wage is the same, the amount of labor that workers supply is the same and real output is the same. All that has changed between points *a* and *e* are nominal measures—the price level, the nominal wage, and other nominal resource prices.

We conclude that when incorrect expectations cause firms and resource suppliers to overestimate the actual price level, output in the short run falls short of the economy's potential. As long as wages and prices are flexible enough, however, firms and workers should be able to renegotiate wage agreements based on a lower expected price level. The negotiated drop in the nominal wage shifts the short-run aggregate supply curve to the right until the economy once again produces its potential output. If wages and prices are not flexible, they will not adjust quickly to a recessionary gap, so shifts of the short-run aggregate supply curve may be slow to move the economy to its potential output. The economy can therefore get stuck at an output and employment level below its potential.

We are now in a position to provide an additional interpretation of the red- and blue-shaded areas of our exhibits. If a short-run equilibrium occurs in the blue-shaded area, that is, to the right of potential output, then market forces in the long run increase nominal resource costs, shifting the short-run aggregate supply to the left. If a short-run equilibrium occurs in the red-shaded area, then market forces in the long run reduce nominal resource costs, shifting the short-run aggregate supply curve to the right. Closing an expansionary gap involves inflation and closing a recessionary gap involves deflation.

Tracing Potential Output

If wages and prices are flexible enough, the economy produces its potential output in the long run, as indicated in Exhibit 4 by the vertical line drawn at the economy's potential GDP of $14.0 trillion. This vertical line is called the economy's **long-run aggregate supply (LRAS) curve**. *The long-run aggregate supply curve depends on the supply of resources in the economy, the level of technology, and the production incentives provided by the formal and informal institutions of the economic system.*

long-run aggregate supply (LRAS) curve
A vertical line at the economy's potential output; aggregate supply when there are no surprises about the price level and all resource contracts can be renegotiated

In Exhibit 4, the initial price level of 110 is determined by the intersection of *AD* with the long-run aggregate supply curve. If the aggregate demand curve shifts out to *AD′*, then in the long run, the equilibrium price level increases to 120 but equilibrium output remains at $14.0 trillion, the economy's potential GDP. Conversely, a decline in aggregate demand from *AD* to *AD″*, in the long run, leads only to a fall in the price level from 110 to 100, with no change in output. Note that these long-run movements are more like tendencies than smooth and timely adjustments. It may take a long time for resource prices to adjust, particularly when the economy faces a recessionary gap. But as long as wages and prices are flexible, the economy's potential GDP is consistent with any price level. *In the long run, equilibrium output equals long-run aggregate supply, which is also potential output. The equilibrium price level depends on the aggregate demand curve.*

Wage Flexibility and Employment

What evidence is there that a vertical line drawn at the economy's potential GDP depicts the long-run aggregate supply curve? Except during the Great Depression, unemployment over the last century has varied from year to year but typically has

EXHIBIT 4 Long-Run Aggregate Supply Curve

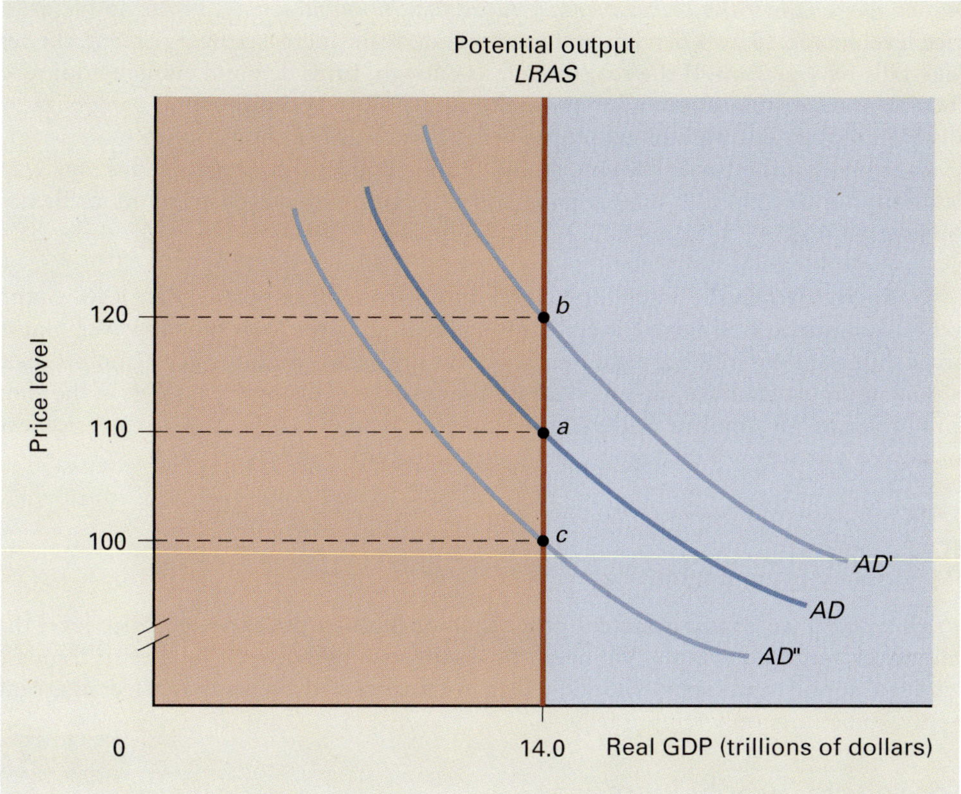

In the long run, when the actual price level equals the expected price level, the economy produces its potential. In the long run, $14.0 trillion in real GDP is supplied regardless of the actual price level. As long as wages and prices are flexible, the economy's potential GDP is consistent with any price level. Thus, shifts of the aggregate demand curve, in the long run, do not affect potential output. The long-run aggregate supply curve, *LRAS*, is a vertical line at potential GDP.

returned to what would be viewed as a natural rate of unemployment—again, estimates range from 4 percent to 6 percent.

An *expansionary* gap creates a labor shortage that eventually results in a higher nominal wage and a higher price level. But a *recessionary* gap does not necessarily generate enough downward pressure to lower the nominal wage. Studies indicate that nominal wages are slow to adjust to high unemployment. Nominal wages have declined in particular industries; during the 1980s, for example, nominal wages fell in airlines, steel, and trucking. But seldom have we observed actual declines in nominal wages across the economy, especially since World War II. Nominal wages do not adjust downward as quickly or as substantially as they adjust upward, and the downward response that does occur tends to be slow and modest. Consequently, we say that nominal wages tend to be "sticky" in the downward direction.[2] *Because nominal wages fall slowly, if at all, the supply-side adjustments needed to close a recessionary gap may take so long as to seem ineffective.* What, in fact, usually closes a recessionary gap is an increase in aggregate demand as the economy pulls out of its funk.

2. For evidence on sticky wages, see Alessandro Barattieri et al., "Some Evidence on the Importance of Sticky Wages," NBER Working Paper 16130 (June 2010).

Although the nominal wage seldom falls, an actual decline in the nominal wage is not necessary to close a recessionary gap. All that's needed is a fall in the real wage. And *the real wage falls if the prices increase more than nominal wages*. For example, if the price level increases by 4 percent and the nominal wage increases by 3 percent, the real wage falls by 1 percent. If the real wage falls enough, firms demand enough additional labor to produce the economy's potential output. More generally, total compensation falls if employers cut back on employee benefits such as health insurance.

At the end of the book, the case study, "Public Policy: U.S. Output Gaps and Wage Flexibility," looks more at output gaps and discusses why wages aren't more flexible downward.

To Review: When the actual price level differs from the expected price level, output in the short run departs from the economy's potential. In the long run, however, market forces shift the short-run aggregate supply curve until the economy once again produces its potential output. Thus, surprises about the price level change real GDP in the short run but not in the long run. Shifts of the aggregate demand curve change the price level but do not affect potential output, or long-run aggregate supply.

Shifts of the Aggregate Supply Curve

In this section, we consider factors other than changes in the expected price level that may affect aggregate supply. We begin by distinguishing between long-term trends in aggregate supply and **supply shocks**, which are unexpected events that affect aggregate supply, sometimes only temporarily.

supply shocks
Unexpected events that affect aggregate supply, sometimes only temporarily

Aggregate Supply Increases

The economy's potential output is based on the willingness and ability of households to supply resources to firms, the level of technology, and the institutional underpinnings of the economic system. Any change in these factors could affect the economy's potential output. Changes in the economy's potential output over time were introduced in the earlier chapter that focused on U.S. productivity and growth. The supply of labor may change over time because of a change in the size, composition, or quality of the labor force or a change in preferences for labor versus leisure. For example, the U.S. labor force has more than doubled since 1948 as a result of population growth and a growing labor force participation rate, especially among women with children. At the same time, job training, education, and on-the-job experience increased the quality of labor. Increases in the quantity and the quality of the labor force have increased the economy's potential GDP, or long-run aggregate supply.

The quantity and quality of other resources also change over time. The capital stock—machines, buildings, and trucks—increases when gross investment exceeds capital depreciation. And the capital stock improves with technological breakthroughs. Even the quantity and quality of land can be increased—for example, by claiming land from the sea, as is done in the Netherlands and Hong Kong, or by revitalizing soil that has lost its fertility. These increases in the quantity and quality of resources increase the economy's potential output.

Finally, institutional changes that define property rights more clearly or make contracts more enforceable, such as the introduction of clearer patent and copyright laws, will increase the incentives to undertake productive activity, thereby increasing potential output. *Changes in the labor force, in the quantity and quality of other resources, and in the institutional arrangements of the economic system tend to occur gradually.* Exhibit 5 depicts a gradual shift of the economy's potential output from \$14.0 trillion to \$14.5 trillion. The long-run aggregate supply curve shifts from *LRAS* out to *LRAS′*.

EXHIBIT 5 Effect of a Gradual Increase in Resources on Aggregate Supply

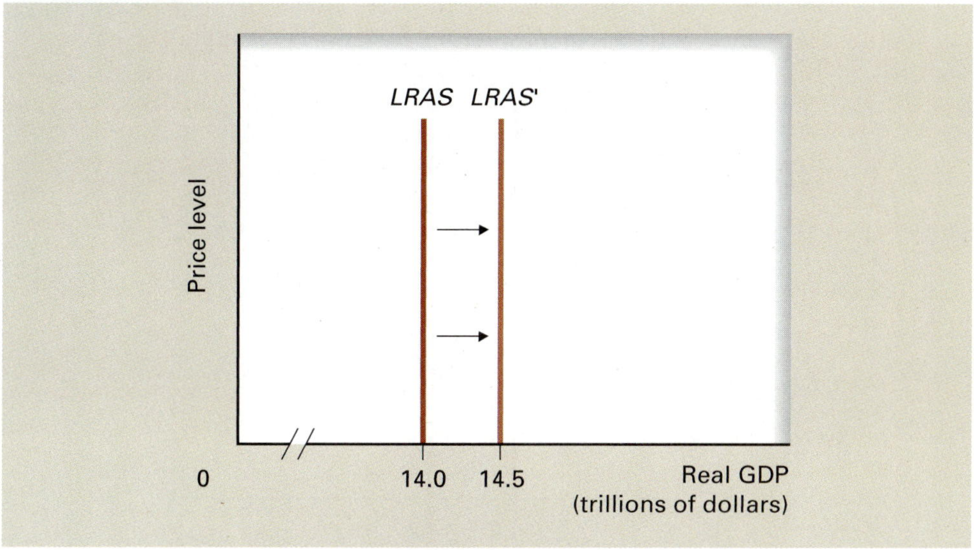

A gradual growth in the supply of resources increases the potential GDP—in this case, from $14.0 trillion to $14.5 trillion. The long-run aggregate supply curve shifts to the right.

In contrast to the gradual, or long-run, changes that often occur in the supply of resources, *supply shocks* are unexpected events that change aggregate supply, sometimes only temporarily. **Beneficial supply shocks** increase aggregate supply; examples include (1) abundant harvests that increase the food supply, (2) discoveries of natural resources, such as oil in Alaska or the North Sea, (3) technological breakthroughs that allow firms to combine resources more efficiently, such as faster computers or the Internet, and (4) sudden changes in the economic system that promote more production, such as tax cuts that stimulate production incentives or stricter limits on frivolous product liability suits.

beneficial supply shocks
Unexpected events that increase aggregate supply, sometimes only temporarily

Exhibit 6 shows the effect of a beneficial supply shock from a technological breakthrough. The beneficial supply shock shown here shifts the short-run and long-run aggregate supply curves rightward. Along the aggregate demand curve, *AD*, the equilibrium combination of price and output moves from point *a* to point *b*. *For a given aggregate demand curve, the happy outcome of a beneficial supply shock is an increase in output and a decrease in the price level.* The new equilibrium at point *b* is a short-run and a long-run equilibrium in the sense that there is no tendency to move from that point as long as whatever caused the beneficial effect continues, and a technological discovery usually has a lasting effect. Likewise, substantial new oil discoveries usually benefit the economy for a long time. On the other hand, an unusually favorable growing season won't last. When a normal growing season returns, the short-run and long-run aggregate supply curves return to their original equilibrium position—back to point *a* in Exhibit 6.

Decreases in Aggregate Supply

Adverse supply shocks are sudden, unexpected events that reduce aggregate supply, sometimes only temporarily. For example, a drought could reduce the supply of a variety of resources, such as food, building materials, and water-powered electricity. An overthrow of a government could destabilize the economy. Or terrorist attacks could

adverse supply shocks
Unexpected events that reduce aggregate supply, sometimes only temporarily

EXHIBIT 6 Effects of a Beneficial Supply Shock on Aggregate Supply

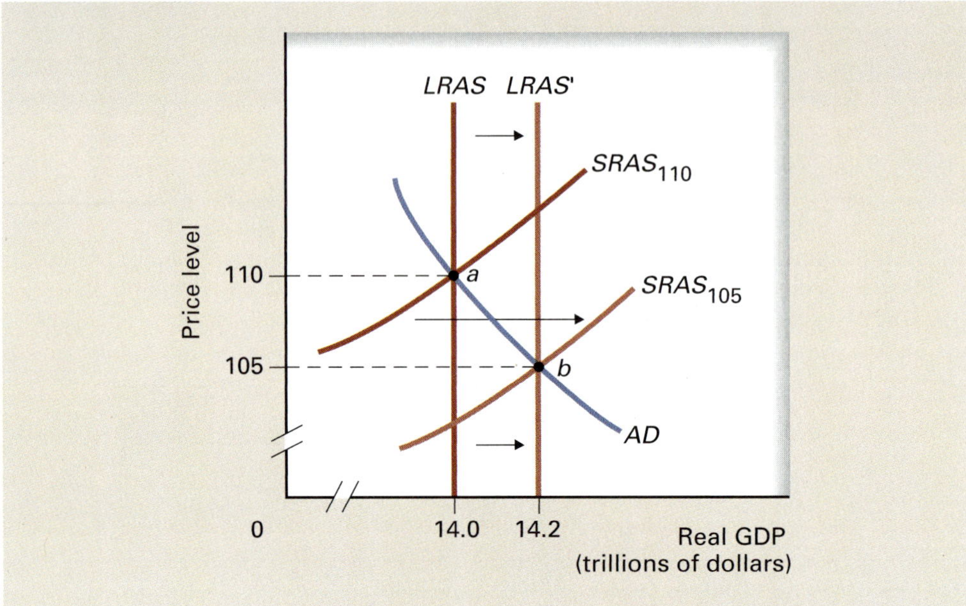

A beneficial supply shock that has a lasting effect, such as a breakthrough in technology, permanently shifts both the short-run and the long-run aggregate supply curves to the right. A beneficial supply shock lowers the price level and increases output, as reflected by the change in equilibrium from point *a* to point *b*. A temporary beneficial supply shock shifts the aggregate supply curves only temporarily.

shake the institutional underpinnings of the economy, as occurred in America, England, and Spain. Such attacks add to the cost of doing business—everything from airline screening to building security.

An **adverse supply shock** is depicted as a leftward shift of both the short-run and long-run aggregate supply curves, as shown in Exhibit 7, moving the equilibrium combination from point *a* to point *c* and reducing potential output from $14.0 trillion to $13.8 trillion. As mentioned earlier, the combination of reduced output and a higher price level is often referred to as stagflation. The United States encountered stagflation during the 1970s, when the economy was rocked by a series of adverse supply shocks, such as crop failures around the globe and the oil price hikes by OPEC in 1974 and 1979. If the effect of the adverse supply shock is temporary, such as a poor growing season, the aggregate supply curve returns to its original position once things return to normal. But some economists question an economy's ability to bounce back, as discussed in the case study, "Public Policy: Why Has Unemployment Been So High in Europe?" at the end of the book.

Conclusion

This chapter explains why the aggregate supply curve slopes upward in the short run and is vertical at the economy's potential output in the long run. Firms and resource suppliers negotiate contracts based on the economy's expected price level, which depend on expectations about aggregate demand. Unexpected changes in the price level can

EXHIBIT 7 Effects of an Adverse Supply Shock on Aggregate Supply

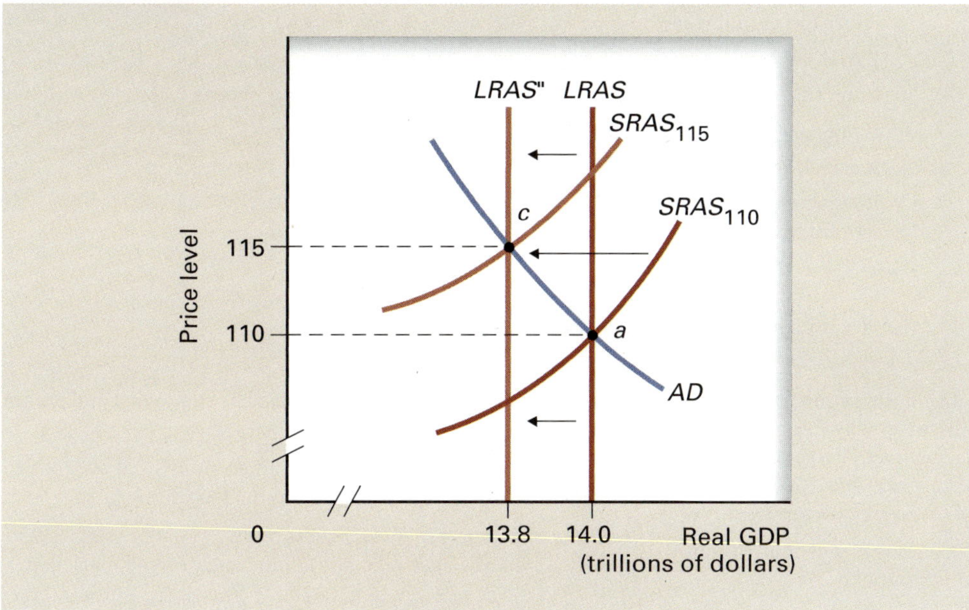

Given the aggregate demand curve, an adverse supply shock, such as a drought, shifts the short-run and long-run aggregate supply curves to the left, increasing the price level and reducing real GDP, a movement called stagflation. This change is shown by the move in equilibrium from point *a* to point *c*. If the shock is just temporary, the shift of the aggregate supply curves will be temporary.

move output in the short run away from its potential level. But if firms and resource suppliers fully adjust to price surprises, the economy in the long run moves toward its potential output. Potential output is the anchor for analyzing aggregate supply in the short run and long run.

Summary

1. Short-run aggregate supply is based on resource demand and supply decisions that reflect the expected price level. If the price level turns out as expected, the economy produces its potential output. If the price level exceeds expectations, short-run output exceeds the economy's potential, creating an expansionary gap. If the price level is below expectations, short-run output falls short of the economy's potential, creating a recessionary gap.
2. Output can exceed the economy's potential in the short run, but in the long run, higher nominal wages will be negotiated at the earliest opportunity. This increases the cost of production, shifting the short-run aggregate supply curve leftward along the aggregate demand curve until the economy produces its potential output.
3. If output in the short run is less than the economy's potential, and if wages and prices are flexible enough, lower nominal wages will reduce production costs in the long run. These lower costs shift the short-run aggregate supply curve rightward along the aggregate demand curve until the economy produces its potential output.
4. Evidence suggests that when output exceeds the economy's potential, nominal wages and the price level increase. But there is less evidence that nominal wages and the price level fall when output is below the economy's potential. Wages appear to be "sticky" in the downward direction. What usually closes a recessionary gap is an increase in aggregate demand.
5. The long-run aggregate supply curve, or the economy's potential output, depends on the amount and quality of resources available, the state of technology, and formal and informal institutions, such as patent laws and business practices, that shape production incentives. Increases in resource availability, improvements in technology, or institutional changes that provide more attractive production incentives increase aggregate supply and potential output.
6. Supply shocks are unexpected, often temporary changes in aggregate supply. Beneficial supply shocks increase output, sometimes only temporarily. Adverse supply shocks reduce output and increase the price level, a combination called stagflation. Adverse supply shocks may be temporary.

Key Concepts

Nominal wage 496
Real wage 496
Potential output 497
Natural rate of unemployment 497
Short run 497
Short-run aggregate supply (SRAS) curve 499
Short-run equilibrium 500
Expansionary gap 500
Long run 501
Long-run equilibrium 502
Recessionary gap 503
Long-run aggregate supply (LRAS) curve 504
Supply shocks 506
Beneficial supply shocks 507
Adverse supply shocks 507

Questions for Review

1. Short-Run Aggregate Supply In the short run, prices may rise faster than costs. This chapter discusses why this might happen. Suppose that labor and management agree to adjust wages continuously for any changes in the price level. How would such adjustments affect the slope of the aggregate supply curve?
2. Potential Output Define the economy's potential output. What factors help determine potential output?
3. Actual Price Level Higher than Expected Discuss some instances in your life when your actual production for short periods exceeded what you considered your potential production. Why does this occur only for brief periods?
4. Nominal and Real Wages Complete each of the following sentences:
   a. The _______ wage measures the wage rate in dollars of the year in question, while the _______ wage measures it in constant dollars.
   b. Wage agreements are based on the _______ price level and negotiated in _______ terms. Real wages are then determined by the _______ price level.
   c. The higher the actual price level, the _______ is the real wage for a given nominal wage.
   d. If nominal wages are growing at 2 percent per year while the annual inflation rate is 3 percent, then real wages change by _______.
5. Recessionary Gaps After reviewing Exhibit 3 in this chapter, explain why recessionary gaps occur only in the short run and only when the actual price level is below what was expected.
6. Short-Run Aggregate Supply In interpreting the short-run aggregate supply curve, what does the adjective *short-run* mean? Explain the role of labor contracts along the *SRAS* curve.
7. Recessionary Gap What does a recessionary gap imply about the actual rate of unemployment relative to the natural rate? What does it imply about the actual price level relative to the expected price level? What must happen to real and nominal wages in order to close a recessionary gap?
8. Expansionary Gap How does an economy that is experiencing an expansionary gap adjust in the long run?
9. Output Gaps and Wage Flexibility What are some reasons why nominal wages may not fall during a recessionary gap?
10. Case Study: U.S. Output Gaps and Wage Flexibility (See page 756.) Unemployment is costly to employers, employees, and the economy as a whole. What are some explanations for the *coordination failures* that prevent workers and employers from reaching agreements?
11. Long-Run Adjustment In the long run, why does an actual price level that exceeds the expected price level lead to changes in the nominal wage? Why do these changes cause shifts of the short-run aggregate supply curve?
12. Long-Run Aggregate Supply The long-run aggregate supply curve is vertical at the economy's potential output level. Why is the long-run aggregate supply curve located at this output rather than below or above potential output?
13. Long-Run Aggregate Supply Determine whether each of the following, other things held constant, would lead to an increase, a decrease, or no change in long-run aggregate supply:
   a. An improvement in technology
   b. A permanent decrease in the size of the capital stock
   c. An increase in the actual price level
   d. An increase in the expected price level
   e. A permanent increase in the size of the labor force
14. Changes in Aggregate Supply What are supply shocks? Distinguish between beneficial and adverse supply shocks. Do such shocks affect the short-run aggregate supply curve, the long-run aggregate supply curve, or both? What is the resulting impact on potential GDP?

Problems and Exercises

15. Real Wages In Exhibit 2 in this chapter, how does the real wage rate at point *c* compare with the real wage rate at point *a*? How do nominal wage rates compare at those two points? Explain your answers.

16. Natural Rate of Unemployment What is the relationship between potential output and the natural rate of unemployment?
    a. If the economy currently has a frictional unemployment rate of 2 percent, structural unemployment of 2 percent, seasonal unemployment of 0.5 percent, and cyclical unemployment of 2 percent, what is the natural rate of unemployment? Where is the economy operating relative to its potential GDP?
    b. What happens to the natural rate of unemployment and potential GDP if cyclical unemployment rises to 3 percent with other types of unemployment unchanged from part (a)?
    c. What happens to the natural rate of unemployment and potential GDP if structural unemployment falls to 1.5 percent with other types of unemployment unchanged from part (a)?

17. Expansionary and Recessionary Gaps Answer the following questions on the basis of the following graph:

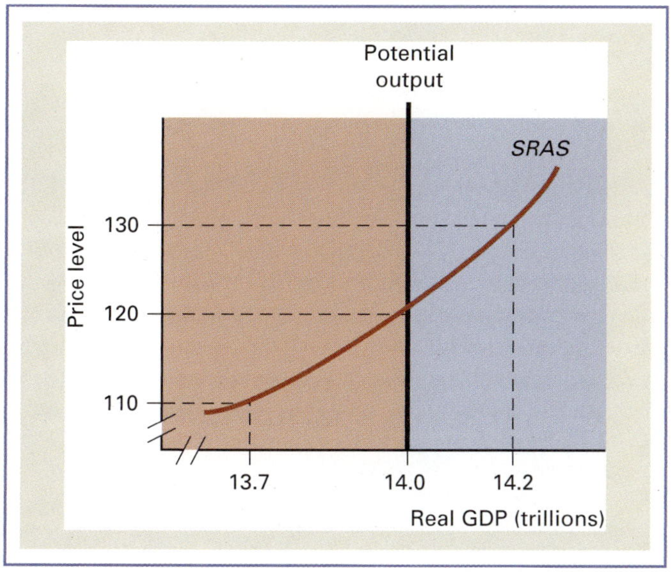

    a. If the actual price level exceeds the expected price level reflected in long-term contracts, real GDP equals _______ and the actual price level equals _______ in the short run.
    b. The situation described in part (a) results in a(n) _______ gap equal to _______.
    c. If the actual price level is lower than the expected price level reflected in long-term contracts, real GDP equals _______ and the actual price level equals _______ in the short run.
    d. The situation described in part (c) results in a(n) _______ gap equal to _______.
    e. If the actual price level equals the expected price level reflected in long-term contracts, real GDP equals _______ and the actual price level equals _______ in the short run.
    f. The situation described in part (e) results in _______ gap equal to _______.

18. Long-Run Adjustment The ability of the economy to eliminate any imbalances between actual and potential output is sometimes called self-correction. Using an aggregate supply and aggregate demand diagram, show why this self-correction process involves only temporary periods of inflation or deflation.

19. Changes in Aggregate Supply List three factors that can change the economy's potential output. What is the impact of shifts of the aggregate demand curve on potential output? Illustrate your answers with a diagram.

20. Supply Shocks Give an example of an adverse supply shock and illustrate graphically. Now do the same for a beneficial supply shock.

21. Case Study: Why Has Unemployment Been So High in Europe? (See page 758.) European unemployment is a hot topic. Use any Web browser to search for the words "European unemployment." Just by scanning the headlines, see how many possible explanations you can list. How do they compare to the explanations reviewed in this case study?

Global Economic Watch Exercises

Login to www.cengagebrain.com and access the Global Economic Watch to do these exercises.

22. Global Economic Watch Go to the Global Economic Crisis Resource Center. Select Global Issues in Context. In the Basic Search box at the top of the page, enter the phrase "output gap." On the Results page, go to the Global Viewpoints Section. Click on the link for the March 5, 2009, article "Inflation Should Be Lesser Worry for MPC." At the time of publication, what was the output gap in South Africa?

23. Global Economic Watch Go to the Global Economic Crisis Resource Center. Select Global Issues in Context. In the Basic Search box at the top of the page, enter the phrase "real wage." Using articles from the past two years, find one article about a country where real wages are growing and one where real wages are falling. Compare and contrast the economic situations in the countries.

Fiscal Policy

26

AP Photo/Damian Dovarganes

- President Barack Obama claimed on February 17, 2010, that "it is largely thanks to the Recovery Act that a second depression is no longer a possibility." The Japanese government cut taxes and increased spending to stimulate its troubled economy. These are examples of *fiscal policy,* which focuses on the effects of taxing and public spending on aggregate economic activity. What is the proper role of fiscal policy in the economy?
- Can fiscal policy reduce swings in the business cycle?
- Why did fiscal policy fall on hard times for a quarter century, and what brought it back to life?
- Does fiscal policy affect aggregate supply?
- And how did the cash-for-clunkers program work out?

Answers to these and other questions are addressed in this chapter, which examines the theory and practice of fiscal policy.

In this chapter, we first explore the effects of fiscal policy on aggregate demand. Next, we bring aggregate supply into the picture. Then, we examine the role of fiscal policy in moving the economy to its potential output. Finally, we review U.S. fiscal policy as it has been practiced since World War II. Throughout the chapter, we use simple tax and spending models to explain fiscal policy.

A more complex treatment, along with the algebra behind it, appears in the appendix to this chapter.

Topics discussed include:

- Theory of fiscal policy
- Discretionary fiscal policy
- Automatic stabilizers
- Lags in fiscal policy
- Limits of fiscal policy
- Deficits, surpluses, then more deficits
- Fiscal policy response to the 2007–2009 recession

Theory of Fiscal Policy

Our macroeconomic model so far has viewed government as passive. But government purchases and transfer payments at all levels in the United States total more than $5 trillion a year, making government an important player in the economy. From highway construction to unemployment compensation to income taxes to federal deficits, fiscal policy affects the economy in myriad ways. We now move fiscal policy to center stage. As introduced in Chapter 3, *fiscal policy* refers to government purchases, transfer payments, taxes, and borrowing as they affect macroeconomic variables such as real GDP, employment, the price level, and economic growth. When economists study fiscal policy, they usually focus on the federal government, although governments at all levels affect the economy.

Fiscal Policy Tools

automatic stabilizers
Structural features of government spending and taxation that reduce fluctuations in disposable income, and thus consumption, over the business cycle

discretionary fiscal policy
The deliberate manipulation of government purchases, taxation, and transfer payments to promote macroeconomic goals, such as full employment, price stability, and economic growth

The tools of fiscal policy sort into two broad categories: automatic stabilizers and discretionary fiscal policy. **Automatic stabilizers** are revenue and spending programs in the federal budget that automatically adjust with the ups and downs of the economy to stabilize disposable income and, consequently, consumption and real GDP. For example, the federal income tax is an automatic stabilizer because (1) once adopted, it requires no congressional action to operate year after year, so it's *automatic*, and (2) it reduces the drop in disposable income during recessions and reduces the jump in disposable income during expansions, so it's a *stabilizer*, a smoother. **Discretionary fiscal policy**, on the other hand, requires the deliberate manipulation of government purchases, transfer payments, and taxes to promote macroeconomic goals like full employment, price stability, and economic growth. President Obama's 2009 stimulus plan is an example of discretionary fiscal policy. Some discretionary policies are temporary, such as one-time tax cuts or government spending increases to fight a recession. President Bush's 2008 one-time tax rebate is an example.

Using the income-expenditure framework developed earlier, we initially focus on the demand side to consider the effect of changes in government purchases, transfer payments, and taxes on real GDP demanded. The short story is this: *At any given price level, an increase in government purchases or in transfer payments increases real GDP demanded, and an increase in net taxes decreases real GDP demanded, other things constant.* Next, we see how and why.

Changes in Government Purchases

Let's begin by looking at Exhibit 1, with real GDP demanded of $14.0 trillion, as reflected at point *a*, where the aggregate expenditure line crosses the 45-degree line. You may recall that this equilibrium was determined two chapters back, where government purchases and net taxes equaled $1.0 trillion each and did not vary with income—that is, they were autonomous, or independent of income. Because government purchases equal net taxes, the government budget is balanced.

Now suppose federal policy makers, believing that unemployment is too high, decide to stimulate aggregate demand by increasing government purchases $0.1 trillion, or by $100 billion. To consider the effect on aggregate demand, let's initially assume that nothing else changes, including the price level and net taxes. This additional spending shifts the aggregate expenditure line up by $0.1 trillion to $C + I + G' + (X - M)$. At real GDP of $14.0 trillion, spending now exceeds output, so production increases. This increase in production increases income, which in turn increases spending, and so it goes through the series of spending rounds.

EXHIBIT 1 **Effect of a $0.1 Trillion Increase in Government Purchases on Aggregate Expenditure and Real GDP Demanded**

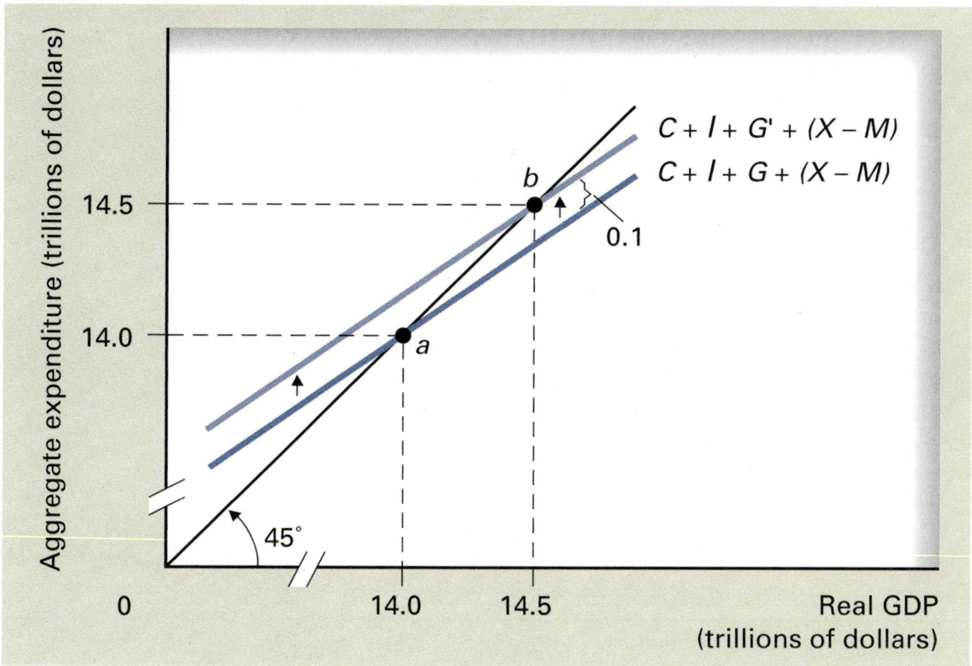

As a result of a $0.1 trillion increase in government purchases, the aggregate expenditure line shifts up by $0.1 trillion, increasing the level of real GDP demanded by $0.5 trillion. This model assumes the price level remains unchanged.

The initial increase of $0.1 trillion in government purchases eventually increases real GDP demanded at the given price level from $14.0 trillion to $14.5 trillion, shown as point *b* in Exhibit 1. Because output demanded increases by $0.5 trillion as a result of an increase of $0.1 trillion in government purchases, the multiplier in our example is equal to 5 (assuming, as in earlier chapters, that the marginal propensity to consume is 0.8). *As long as consumption is the only spending component that varies with income, the multiplier for a change in government purchases, other things constant, equals* $1/(1 - MPC)$, or $1/(1 - 0.8)$ in our example. Thus, we can say that for a given price level, and assuming that only consumption varies with income,

$$\Delta \text{ Real GDP demanded} = \Delta G \times \frac{1}{1 - MPC}$$

where, again, the delta symbol (Δ) means "change in." This same multiplier appeared two chapters back, when we discussed shifts of the consumption function, the investment function, and the net exports function.

Changes in Net Taxes

A change in net taxes also affects real GDP demanded, but the effect is less direct. A *decrease* in net taxes, other things constant, *increases* disposable income at each level of real GDP, so consumption increases. In Exhibit 2, we begin again at equilibrium point

EXHIBIT 2 Effect of a $0.1 Trillion Decrease in Net Taxes on Aggregate Expenditure and Real GDP Demanded

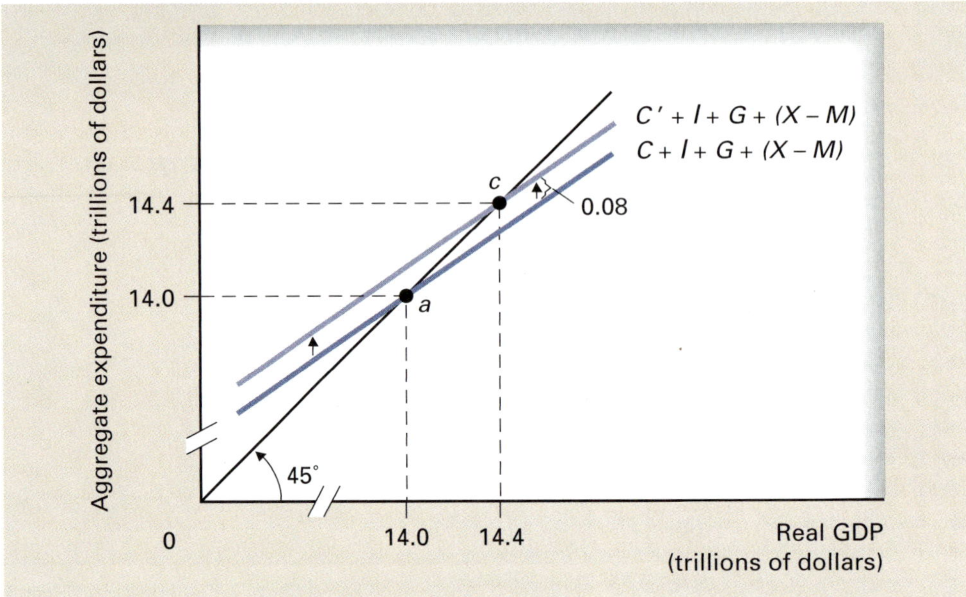

As a result of a decrease in net taxes of $0.1 trillion, or $100 billion, consumers, who are assumed to have a marginal propensity to consume of 0.8, spend $80 billion more and save $20 billion more at every level of real GDP. The consumption function shifts up by $80 billion, or $0.08 trillion, as does the aggregate expenditure line. An $80 billion increase of the aggregate expenditure line eventually increases real GDP demanded by $0.4 trillion. Keep in mind that the price level is assumed to remain constant during all this.

a, with real GDP demanded equal to $14.0 trillion. To stimulate aggregate demand, suppose federal policy makers cut net taxes by $0.1 trillion, or by $100 billion, other things constant. We continue to assume that net taxes are autonomous—that is, that they do not vary with income. A $100 billion reduction in net taxes could result from a tax cut, an increase in transfer payments, or some combination of the two. The $100 billion decrease in net taxes increases disposable income by $100 billion at each level of real GDP. Because households now have more disposable income, they spend more and save more at each level of real GDP.

Because households save some of the tax cut, consumption increases in the first round of spending by less than the full tax cut. Specifically, *consumption spending at each level of real GDP rises by the decrease in net taxes multiplied by the marginal propensity to consume.* In our example, consumption at each level of real GDP increases by $100 billion times 0.8, or $80 billion. Cutting net taxes by $100 billion causes the aggregate expenditure line to shift up by $80 billion, or $0.08 trillion, at all levels of real GDP, as shown in Exhibit 2. This initial increase in spending triggers subsequent rounds of spending, following a now-familiar pattern in the income-expenditure cycle based on the marginal propensities to consume and to save. For example, the $80 billion increase in consumption increases output and income by $80 billion, which in the second round leads to $64 billion in consumption and $16 billion in saving, and so on through successive rounds. As a result, real GDP demanded eventually increases from $14.0 trillion to $14.4 trillion per year, or by $400 billion.

The effect of a change in net taxes on real GDP demanded equals the resulting shift of the aggregate expenditure line times the simple spending multiplier. Thus, we can say that the effect of a change in net taxes is

$$\Delta \text{ Real GDP demanded} = (-\,MPC \times \Delta\, NT) \times \frac{1}{1 - MPC}$$

The simple spending multiplier is applied to the shift of the aggregate expenditure line that results from the change in net taxes. This equation can be rearranged as

$$\Delta \text{ Real GDP demanded} = \Delta\, NT \times \frac{-\,MPC}{1 - MPC}$$

where $-MPC/(1 - MPC)$ is the **simple tax multiplier**, which can be applied directly to the change in net taxes to yield the change in real GDP demanded at a given price level. This tax multiplier is called *simple* because, by assumption, only consumption varies with income (taxes do not vary with income). For example, with an MPC of 0.8, the simple tax multiplier equals −4. In our example, a *decrease* of $0.1 trillion in net taxes results in an *increase* in real GDP demanded of $0.4 trillion, assuming a given price level. As another example, an *increase* in net taxes of $0.2 trillion would, other things constant, *decrease* real GDP demanded by $0.8 trillion.

Simple tax multiplier
The ratio of a change in real GDP demanded to the initial change in autonomous net taxes that brought it about; the numerical value of the simple tax multiplier is −MPC/(1 − MPC)

Note two differences between the government purchase multiplier and the simple tax multiplier. First, the government purchase multiplier is positive, so an increase in government purchases leads to an increase in real GDP demanded. The simple tax multiplier is negative, so an increase in net taxes leads to a decrease in real GDP demanded. Second, the multiplier for a given change in government purchases is larger by 1 than the absolute value of the multiplier for an identical change in net taxes. In our example, the government purchase multiplier is 5, while the absolute value of the tax multiplier is 4. This holds because changes in government purchases affect aggregate spending directly—a $100 billion increase in government purchases increases spending in the first round by $100 billion. In contrast, a $100 billion decrease in net taxes increases consumption indirectly by way of a change in disposable income. Thus, each $100 billion decrease in net taxes increases disposable income by $100 billion, which, given an MPC of 0.8, increases consumption in the first round by $80 billion; people save the other $20 billion. In short, an increase in government purchases has a greater impact on real GDP demanded than does an identical tax cut because some of the tax cut gets saved, so it leaks from the spending flow.

To Review: An increase in government purchases or a decrease in net taxes, other things constant, increases real GDP demanded. Although not shown, the combined effect of changes in government purchases and in net taxes is found by summing their individual effects.

Including Aggregate Supply

To this point in the chapter, we have focused on the amount of real GDP demanded at a given price level. We are now in a position to bring aggregate supply into the picture. The previous chapter introduced the idea that natural market forces may take a long time to close a recessionary gap. Let's consider the possible effects of using discretionary fiscal policy in such a situation.

Discretionary Fiscal Policy to Close a Recessionary Gap

What if the economy produces less than its potential? Suppose the aggregate demand curve *AD* in Exhibit 3 intersects the aggregate supply curve at point *e*, yielding the short-run output of $13.5 trillion and price level of 105. Output falls short of the economy's potential, opening up a recessionary gap of $0.5 trillion. Unemployment exceeds the natural rate. If markets adjusted naturally to high unemployment, the short-run aggregate supply curve would shift rightward in the long run to achieve equilibrium at the economy's potential output, point *e*″. History suggests, however, that wages and other resource prices could be slow to respond to a recessionary gap.

expansionary fiscal policy
An increase in government purchases, decrease in net taxes, or some combination of the two aimed at increasing aggregate demand enough to reduce unemployment and return the economy to its potential output; fiscal policy used to close a recessionary gap

Suppose policy makers believe that natural market forces will take too long to return the economy to potential output. They also believe that the appropriate increase in government purchases, decrease in net taxes, or some combination of the two could increase aggregate demand just enough to return the economy to its potential output. A $0.2 trillion increase in government purchases reflects an **expansionary fiscal policy** that increases aggregate demand, as shown in Exhibit 3 by the rightward shift from

EXHIBIT 3 Discretionary Fiscal Policy to Close a Recessionary Gap

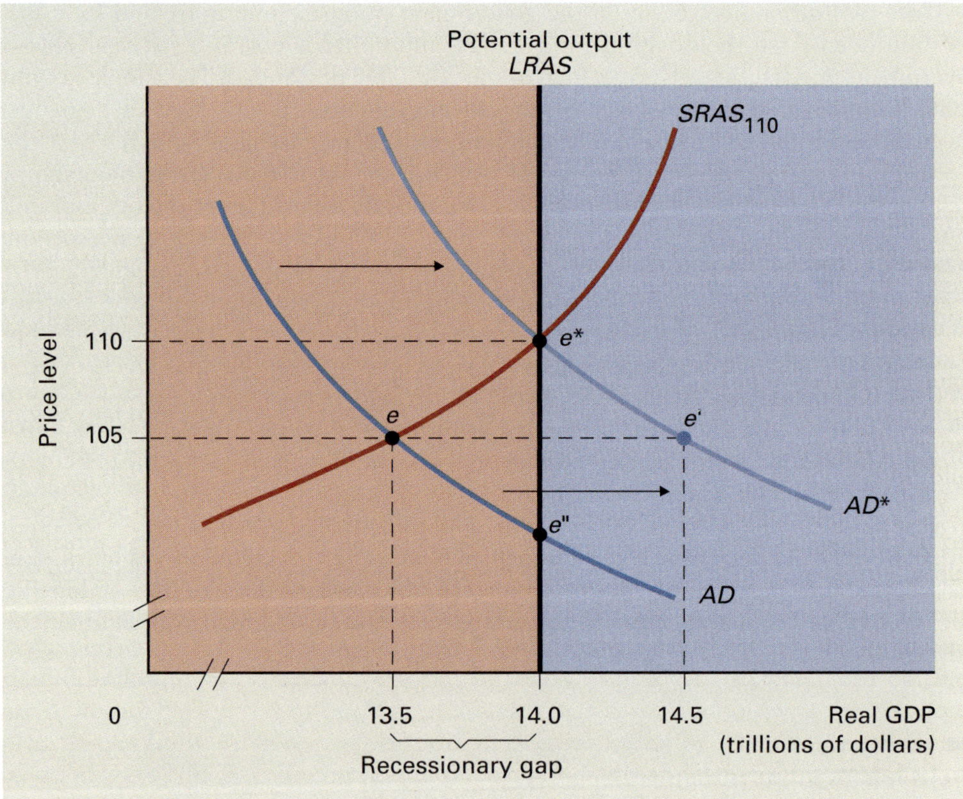

The aggregate demand curve *AD* and the short-run aggregate supply curve, $SRAS_{110}$, intersect at point *e*. Output falls short of the economy's potential. The resulting recessionary gap is $0.5 trillion. This gap could be closed by discretionary fiscal policy that increases aggregate demand by just the right amount. An increase in government purchases, a decrease in net taxes, or some combination could shift aggregate demand out to *AD**, moving the economy out to its potential output at *e**.

AD to AD^*. If the price level remained at 105, the additional spending would increase the quantity demanded from \$13.5 to \$14.5 trillion. This increase of \$1.0 trillion reflects the simple spending multiplier effect, given a constant price level.

At the original price level of 105, however, excess quantity demanded causes the price level to rise. As the price level rises, real GDP supplied increases, but real GDP demanded decreases along the new aggregate demand curve. The price level rises until quantity demanded equals quantity supplied. In Exhibit 3, the new aggregate demand curve intersects the aggregate supply curve at e^*, where the price level is 110, the one originally expected, and output equals potential GDP of \$14.0 trillion. Note that *an expansionary fiscal policy aims to close a recessionary gap.*

The intersection at point e^* is not only a short-run equilibrium but a long-run equilibrium. If fiscal policy makers are accurate enough (or lucky enough), the appropriate fiscal stimulus can close the recessionary gap and foster a long-run equilibrium at potential GDP. But the increase in output results in a higher price level. What's more, if the federal budget was in balance before the fiscal stimulus, the increase in government spending creates a budget deficit. In fact, the federal government has run deficits in all but 4 of the last 40 years.

What if policy makers overshoot the mark and stimulate aggregate demand more than necessary to achieve potential GDP? In the short run, real GDP exceeds potential output. In the long run, the short-run aggregate supply curve shifts back until it intersects the aggregate demand curve at potential output, increasing the price level further but reducing real GDP to \$14.0 trillion, the potential output.

Discretionary Fiscal Policy to Close an Expansionary Gap

Suppose output exceeds potential GDP. In Exhibit 4, the aggregate demand curve, AD', intersects the aggregate supply curve to yield short-run output of \$14.5 trillion, an amount exceeding the potential of \$14.0 trillion. The economy faces an expansionary gap of \$0.5 trillion. Ordinarily, this gap would be closed by a leftward shift of the short-run aggregate supply curve, which would return the economy to potential output but at a higher price level, as shown by point e''.

But the use of discretionary fiscal policy introduces another possibility. By reducing government purchases, increasing net taxes, or employing some combination of the two, the government can implement a **contractionary fiscal policy** to reduce aggregate demand. This could move the economy to potential output without the resulting inflation. If the policy succeeds, aggregate demand in Exhibit 4 shifts leftward from AD' to AD^*, establishing a new equilibrium at point e^*. Again, with just the right reduction in aggregate demand, output falls to \$14.0 trillion, the potential GDP. Closing an expansionary gap through fiscal policy rather than through natural market forces results in a lower price level, not a higher one. Increasing net taxes or reducing government purchases also reduces a government deficit or increases a surplus. So a contractionary fiscal policy could reduce inflation and reduce a federal deficit. Note that *a contractionary fiscal policy aims to close an expansionary gap.*

contractionary fiscal policy
A decrease in government purchases, increase in net taxes, or some combination of the two aimed at reducing aggregate demand enough to return the economy to potential output without worsening inflation; fiscal policy used to close an expansionary gap

Such precisely calculated expansionary and contractionary fiscal policies are difficult to achieve. Their proper execution assumes that (1) potential output is accurately gauged, (2) the relevant spending multiplier can be predicted accurately, (3) aggregate demand can be shifted by just the right amount, (4) various government entities can somehow coordinate their fiscal efforts, and (5) the shape of the short-run aggregate supply curve is known and remains unaffected by the fiscal policy itself.

EXHIBIT 4 Discretionary Fiscal Policy to Close an Expansionary Gap

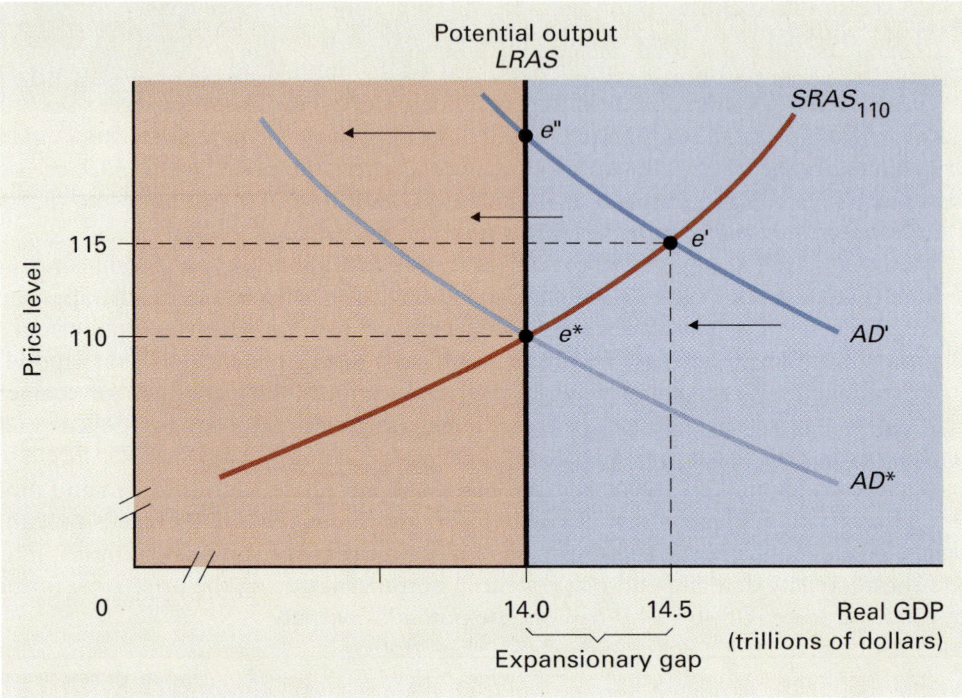

The aggregate demand curve *AD'* and the short-run aggregate supply curve, $SRAS_{110}$, intersect at point *e'*, resulting in an expansionary gap of \$0.5 trillion. Discretionary fiscal policy aimed at reducing aggregate demand by just the right amount could close this gap without inflation. An increase in net taxes, a decrease in government purchases, or some combination could shift the aggregate demand curve back to *AD** and move the economy back to potential output at point *e**.

The Multiplier and the Time Horizon

In the short run, the aggregate supply curve slopes upward, so a shift of aggregate demand changes both the price level and the level of output. When aggregate supply gets in the act, we find that the simple multiplier overstates the amount by which output changes. The exact change of equilibrium output in the short run depends on the steepness of the aggregate supply curve, which in turn depends on how sharply production costs increase as output expands. *The steeper the short-run aggregate supply curve, the less impact a given shift of the aggregate demand curve has on real GDP and the more impact it has on the price level, so the smaller the spending multiplier.*

If the economy is already producing its potential, then in the long run, any change in fiscal policy aimed at stimulating demand increases the price level but does not affect output. Thus, *if the economy is already producing its potential, the spending multiplier in the long run is zero.*

The Evolution of Fiscal Policy

Now that you have some idea of how fiscal policy can work in theory, let's take a look at fiscal policy in practice, beginning with the approach used before the Great Depression.

Prior to the Great Depression

Before the 1930s, discretionary fiscal policy was seldom used to influence the macroeconomy. Public policy was shaped by the views of **classical economists**, who advocated *laissez-faire,* the belief that free markets were the best way to achieve economic prosperity. Classical economists did not deny that depressions and high unemployment occurred from time to time, but they argued that the sources of such crises lay outside the market system, in the effects of wars, tax increases, poor growing seasons, natural disasters, changing tastes, and the like. Such external shocks could reduce output and employment, but classical economists also believed that natural market forces, such as changes in prices, wages, and interest rates, could correct these problems.

classical economists
A group of 18th- and 19th-century economists who believed that economic downturns corrected themselves through natural market forces; thus, they believed the economy was self-correcting and needed no government intervention

Simply put, classical economists argued that if the economy's price level was too high to sell all that was produced, prices would fall until the quantity supplied equaled the quantity demanded. If wages were too high to employ all who wanted to work, wages would fall until the quantity of labor supplied equaled the quantity demanded. And if the interest rate was too high to invest all that had been saved, interest rates would fall until the amount invested equaled the amount saved.

So the classical approach implied that natural market forces, through flexible prices, wages, and interest rates, would move the economy toward potential GDP. There appeared to be no need for government intervention. What's more, the government, like households, was expected to live within its means. The idea of government running a deficit year after year was considered immoral. Thus, before the onset of the Great Depression, most economists believed that discretionary fiscal policy could do more harm than good. Besides, the federal government itself was a bit player in the economy. At the onset of the Great Depression, for example, all federal outlays were less than 3 percent relative to GDP (compared to about 25 percent today).

The Great Depression and World War II

Although classical economists acknowledged that capitalistic, market-oriented economies could experience high unemployment from time to time, the depth and duration of the depression strained belief in the economy's ability to heal itself. The Great Depression was marked by four consecutive years of contraction during which unemployment reached 25 percent. Investment plunged 80 percent. Many factories sat idle. With vast unemployed resources, output and income fell well short of the economy's potential.

The stark contrast between the natural market adjustments predicted by classical economists and the years of high unemployment during the Great Depression represented a collision of theory and fact. In 1936, John Maynard Keynes of Cambridge University, England, published *The General Theory of Employment, Interest, and Money,* a book that challenged the classical view and touched off what would later be called the Keynesian revolution. *Keynesian theory and policy were developed in response to the problem of high unemployment during the Great Depression.* Keynes's main quarrel with the classical economists was that prices and wages did not seem to be flexible enough to ensure the full employment of resources. According to Keynes, prices and wages were relatively inflexible in the downward direction—they were "sticky"—so natural market forces would not return the economy to full employment in a timely fashion. Keynes also believed business expectations might at times become so grim that even very low interest rates would not spur firms to invest all that consumers might save.

Three developments in the years following the Great Depression bolstered the use of discretionary fiscal policy in the United States. The first was the influence of Keynes's

General Theory, in which he argued that natural forces would not necessarily close a recessionary gap. Keynes thought the economy could get stuck well below its potential, requiring the government to increase aggregate demand to boost output and employment. The second development was the impact of World War II on output and employment. The demands of war greatly increased production and erased cyclical unemployment during the war years, pulling the U.S. economy out of its depression. The third development, largely a consequence of the first two, was the passage of the **Employment Act of 1946**, which gave the federal government responsibility for promoting full employment and price stability.

Employment Act of 1946
Law that assigned to the federal government the responsibility for promoting full employment and price stability

Prior to the Great Depression, the dominant fiscal policy was a balanced budget. Indeed, to head off a modest deficit in 1932, federal tax rates were raised, which only deepened the depression. In the wake of Keynes's *General Theory* and World War II, however, policy makers grew more receptive to the idea that fiscal policy could improve economic stability. The objective of fiscal policy was no longer to balance the budget but to promote full employment with price stability even if budget deficits resulted.

Automatic Stabilizers

This chapter has focused mostly on discretionary fiscal policy—conscious decisions by public policy makers to change taxes and government spending to achieve the economy's potential output. Now let's get a clearer picture of automatic stabilizers. *Automatic stabilizers smooth out fluctuations in disposable income over the business cycle by stimulating aggregate demand during recessions and dampening aggregate demand during expansions.* Consider the federal income tax. For simplicity, we have assumed that net taxes are independent of income. In reality, the federal income tax system is progressive, meaning that the fraction of income paid in taxes increases as a taxpayer's income increases. During an economic expansion, employment and incomes rise, moving some taxpayers into higher tax brackets. As a result, taxes claim a growing fraction of income. This slows the growth in disposable income and, hence, slows the growth in consumption. Therefore, the progressive income tax relieves some of the inflationary pressure that might otherwise arise as output increases during an economic expansion. Conversely, when the economy is in recession, output declines, and employment and incomes fall, moving some people into lower tax brackets. As a result, taxes take a smaller bite out of income, so disposable income does not fall as much as GDP. Thus, the progressive income tax cushions declines in disposable income, in consumption, and in aggregate demand.

Another automatic stabilizer is unemployment insurance. During economic expansions, the system automatically increases the flow of unemployment insurance taxes from the income stream into the unemployment insurance fund, thereby moderating consumption and aggregate demand. During contractions, unemployment increases and the system reverses itself. Unemployment payments automatically flow from the insurance fund to the unemployed, increasing disposable income and propping up consumption and aggregate demand. Likewise, welfare payments automatically increase during hard times as more people become eligible. *Because of these automatic stabilizers, GDP fluctuates less than it otherwise would, and disposable income varies proportionately less than does GDP.* Because disposable income varies less than GDP does, consumption also fluctuates less than GDP does.

The progressive income tax, unemployment insurance, and welfare benefits were initially designed not so much as automatic stabilizers but as income redistribution programs. Their roles as automatic stabilizers were secondary effects of the legislation. Automatic stabilizers do not eliminate economic fluctuations, but they do reduce their magnitude. The stronger and more effective the automatic stabilizers are, the less need for discretionary fiscal policy. Because of the greater influence of automatic stabilizers, *the economy is more stable today than it was during the Great Depression and before.* As a measure of just how successful these automatic stabilizers have become in cushioning the impact of recessions, consider this: Since 1948, real GDP declined nine years, but real consumption fell only four years—by 0.8 percent in 1974, by 0.4 percent in 1980, by 0.3 percent in 2008, and by 1.2 percent in 2009. *Without much fanfare, automatic stabilizers have been quietly doing their work, keeping the economy on a more even keel.*

From the Golden Age to Stagflation

The 1960s was the Golden Age of fiscal policy. John F. Kennedy was the first president to propose a federal budget deficit to stimulate an economy experiencing a recessionary gap. Fiscal policy was also used on occasion to provide an extra kick to an expansion already under way, as in 1964, when Kennedy's successor, Lyndon B. Johnson, cut income tax rates to keep an expansion alive. *This tax cut, introduced to stimulate business investment, consumption, and employment, was perhaps the shining example of fiscal policy during the Golden Age.* The tax cut seemed to work wonders, increasing disposable income and consumption. The unemployment rate dropped under 5 percent for the first time in seven years, the inflation rate dipped under 2 percent, and the federal budget deficit in 1964 equaled only 0.9 percent of GDP (compared with an average of 3 percent between 1980 and 2010).

Discretionary fiscal policy is a demand-management policy; the objective is to increase or decrease aggregate demand to smooth economic fluctuations. But the 1970s brought a different problem—stagflation, the double trouble of higher inflation and higher unemployment resulting from a decrease in aggregate supply. The aggregate supply curve shifted left because of crop failures around the world, sharply higher OPEC-driven oil prices, and other adverse supply shocks. Demand-management policies are ill suited to cure stagflation because an increase of aggregate demand would increase inflation, whereas a decrease of aggregate demand would increase unemployment.

Other concerns also caused policy makers and economists to question the effectiveness of discretionary fiscal policy. These concerns included the difficulty of estimating the natural rate of unemployment, the time lags involved in implementing fiscal policy, the distinction between current income and permanent income, and the possible feedback effects of fiscal policy on aggregate supply. We consider each in turn.

Fiscal Policy and the Natural Rate of Unemployment

As we have seen, the unemployment that occurs when the economy is producing its potential GDP is called the *natural rate of unemployment.* Before adopting discretionary policies, public officials must correctly estimate this natural rate. Suppose the economy is producing its potential output of $14.0 trillion, as in Exhibit 5, where the natural rate of unemployment is 5.0 percent. Also suppose that public officials mistakenly believe the natural rate to be 4.0 percent, and they attempt to reduce unemployment and increase real GDP through discretionary fiscal policy. As a result of their policy, the aggregate demand curve shifts to the right, from *AD* to *AD'*. In the short run, this stimulation of aggregate demand expands output to $14.2 trillion and reduces unemployment to 4.0 percent, so the policy appears successful. But stimulating aggregate demand opens up an expansionary gap, which in the long run results in a leftward shift of the short-run aggregate supply curve. This reduction in aggregate supply pushes up prices and reduces real GDP to $14.0 trillion, the economy's potential. Thus, policy makers initially believe their plan worked, but pushing production beyond the economy's potential leads only to inflation in the long run.

EXHIBIT 5 When Discretionary Fiscal Policy Overshoots Potential Output

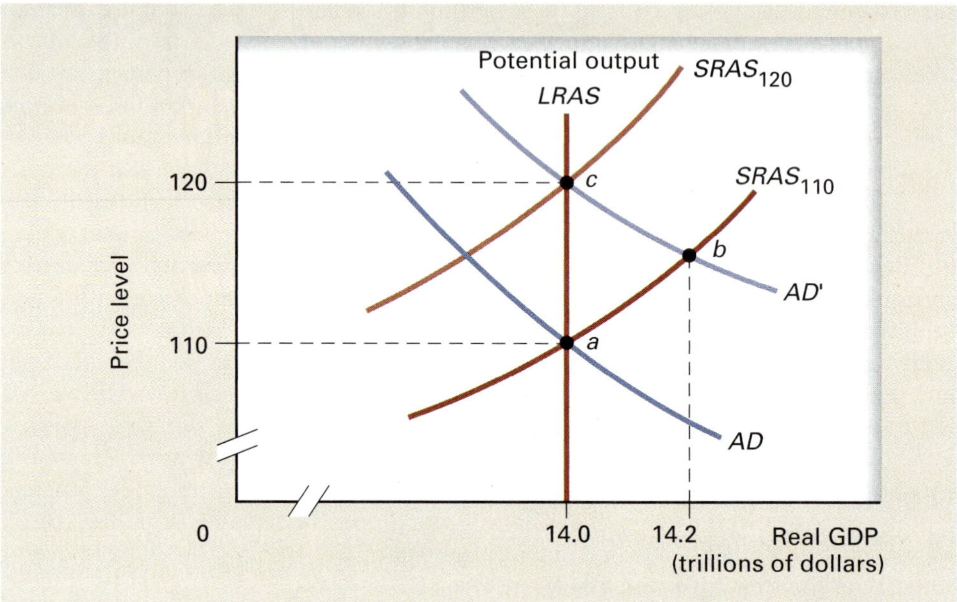

If public officials underestimate the natural rate of unemployment, they may attempt to stimulate aggregate demand even if the economy is already producing its potential output, as at point *a*. This expansionary policy yields a short-run equilibrium at point *b*, where the price level and output are higher and unemployment is lower, so the policy appears to succeed. But the resulting expansionary gap will, in the long run, reduce the short-run aggregate supply curve from $SRAS_{110}$ to $SRAS_{120}$, eventually reducing output to its potential level of $14.0 trillion while increasing the price level to 120. Thus, attempts to increase production beyond potential GDP lead only to inflation in the long run.

Given the effects of fiscal policy, particularly in the short run, we should not be surprised that elected officials might try to use it to get reelected. At the end of the book, the case study, "Public Policy: Fiscal Policy and Presidential Elections," looks at how political considerations could shape fiscal policies.

Lags in Fiscal Policy

The time required to approve and implement fiscal legislation may hamper its effectiveness and weaken discretionary fiscal policy as a tool of macroeconomic stabilization. Even if a fiscal prescription is appropriate for the economy when proposed, the months and sometimes years required to approve and implement legislation means the medicine could do more harm than good. The policy might kick in only after the economy has already turned itself around. Because a recession is not usually identified until at least six months after it begins, and because the 11 recessions since 1945 lasted only 11 months on average, discretionary fiscal policy allows little room for error (more later about timing problems).

Discretionary Fiscal Policy and Permanent Income

It was once believed that discretionary fiscal policy could be turned on and off like a water faucet, stimulating or dampening the economy at the right time by just the right amount. Given the marginal propensity to consume, tax changes could increase or decrease disposable income to bring about desired change in consumption. A more recent view suggests that people base their consumption decisions not merely on changes in their current income but on changes in their permanent income.

permanent income
Income that individuals expect to receive on average over the long term

Permanent income is the income a person expects to receive on average over the long term. Changing tax rates does not affect consumption much if people view the change as only temporary. For example, one-time tax rebates seem to have had little impact on consumption. The stimulative effects of the $117 billion tax-rebate program in early 2008 were disappointing. Surveys showed that only about 20 percent of households spent most of their rebate check. Other households saved most of it or paid down debt.[1] The *temporary* nature of the tax cuts meant that consumers faced only a small increase in their permanent income. Because permanent income changed little, consumption changed little. In short, *to the extent that consumers base spending decisions on their permanent income, attempts to fine-tune the economy with temporary tax changes are less effective.*

The Feedback Effects of Fiscal Policy on Aggregate Supply

So far we have limited the discussion of fiscal policy to its effect on aggregate demand. Fiscal policy may also affect aggregate supply, although this is usually unintentional. For example, suppose the government increases unemployment benefits, paid with higher taxes on earnings. If the marginal propensity to consume is the same for both groups, the increased spending by beneficiaries just offsets the reduced spending by workers. There would be no change in aggregate demand and thus no change in equilibrium real GDP, simply a redistribution of disposable income from the employed to the unemployed.

But could the program affect labor supply? Higher unemployment benefits reduce the opportunity cost of not working, so some job seekers may decide to search at a more leisurely pace. Meanwhile, higher tax rates reduce the opportunity cost of leisure, so some with jobs may decide to work fewer hours. In short, the supply of labor could decrease as a result of higher unemployment benefits funded by higher taxes on earnings. A decrease in the supply of labor would decrease aggregate supply, reducing the economy's potential GDP.

Both automatic stabilizers, such as unemployment insurance and the progressive income tax, and discretionary fiscal policies, such as changes in tax rates, may affect individual incentives to work, spend, save, and invest, although these effects are usually unintended consequences. We should keep these secondary effects in mind when we evaluate fiscal policies. It was concern about the effects of taxes on the supply of labor that motivated the tax cuts approved in 1981, when President Ronald Reagan and Congress agreed on a 23 percent reduction in average income tax rates to increase aggregate supply. But government spending grew faster than tax revenue, causing higher budget deficits, which stimulated aggregate demand. The incentive effects of the tax cuts on aggregate supply and the stimulus effects of deficit spending on aggregate demand both contributed to the longest peacetime expansion to that point in the nation's history.

1990 to 2007: From Deficits to Surpluses Back to Deficits

The large federal budget deficits of the 1980s and first half of the 1990s reduced the use of discretionary fiscal policy as a tool for economic stabilization. Because deficits were already high during economic expansions, it was hard to justify increasing deficits

1. See Matthew Shapiro and Joel Slemrod, "Did the 2008 Tax Rebated Simulate Spending," *American Economic Review*, 99 (May 2009): 374–379.

to stimulate the economy. For example, President Clinton proposed a modest stimulus package in early 1993 to help the recovery that was already under way. His opponents blocked the measure, arguing that it would increase the budget deficit. President George W. Bush's tax cuts during his first term were widely criticized by the opposition as budget-busting sources of a widening deficit.

Clinton did not get his way with his stimulus package, but in 1993, he did manage to substantially increase taxes on high-income households, a group that pays the lion's share of federal income taxes (the top 10 percent of earners pay about two-thirds of federal income taxes collected). The Republican Congress elected in 1994 imposed more discipline on federal spending as part of their plan to balance the budget. Meanwhile, the economy experienced a strong recovery fueled by growing consumer spending, rising business optimism based on technological innovation, market globalization, and the strongest stock market in history. The confluence of these events—higher taxes on the rich, more spending discipline, and a strengthening economy—changed the dynamic of the federal budget. Tax revenues gushed into Washington, growing an average of 8.3 percent per year between 1993 and 1998; meanwhile, federal outlays remained in check, growing only 3.2 percent per year. By 1998, that one-two punch knocked out the federal deficit, a deficit that only six years earlier reached a record at the time of $290 billion. The federal surplus grew from $69 billion in 1998 to $236 billion in 2000.

But in early 2001, the economy suffered a recession, so newly elected President George W. Bush pushed through an across-the-board $1.35 trillion, ten-year tax cut to "get the economy moving again." Then on September 11, 2001, 19 men in four hijacked airplanes ended thousands of lives and reduced the chances of a strong economic recovery. Although the recession lasted only eight months, the recovery was weak, and jobs did not start coming back until the second half of 2003, nearly two years after the recession officially ended. But, between 2003 and 2007, the economy added more than 8 million jobs. By late 2007, the economic expansion, which began in late 2001, had lasted six years, about average for expansions after World War II. The economy peaked in December 2007. The strengthening economy helped cut the federal deficit from $413 billion in 2004 to $161 billion in 2007. Then the world changed.

Fiscal Policy and the 2007–2009 Recession

After peaking in December 2007, the U.S. economy entered a recession, this time precipitated by declining home prices and rising foreclosure rates, as more borrowers failed to make their mortgage payments. The recession began quietly. Many economists doubted that one was even underway (the starting date of December 2007 would not be officially announced until a year later). But as a precaution, Congress and President Bush enacted a $168 billion plan in early 2008 to stimulate the softening economy. The money was borrowed, so it added to the federal deficit. The centerpiece was a $117 billion one-time tax rebate of up to $600 for individual filers and up to $1,200 for joint filers. Probably because the tax cuts were temporary, the results were disappointing and the stimulation minimal. As noted earlier in this chapter, surveys showed that most households saved the rebate or used it to pay down debt; the marginal propensity to consume from rebate money was estimated to be less than one-third.

After a quiet start, the recession gathered steam. Job losses jumped six-fold from an average of 31,000 a month during the first quarter of 2008 to an average of 191,000 a month in the second quarter. Then things got worse. In the third quarter, consumer spending fell 3.5 percent (at an annualized rate), the largest drop since 1980. Real GDP fell by 4.0 percent. And monthly job losses in the quarter averaged 334,000.

The Financial Crisis and Aftermath

The problem of falling home prices and rising default rates that simmered throughout 2007 and the first half of 2008 reached a boiling point in September 2008 when Lehman Brothers, the nation's fourth-largest investment bank with assets of over $600 billion and with 25,000 employees, filed for what became the largest bankruptcy in U.S. history. And AIG, a trillion dollar insurance giant, would have collapsed without a federal bailout. The financial crisis froze credit markets around the world. Nobody wanted to lend for fear that the borrower might go bankrupt. Facing financial chaos, public policy makers were emboldened to take some extraordinary measures. The first of these was the $700 billion Troubled Asset Relief Program, or TARP, passed in October 2008 and aimed at unfreezing financial flows by investing in financial institutions (these investments became known derisively as "bailouts"). TARP, to be discussed in a later chapter, helped calm credit markets, but the economy and the stock market continued to worsen. In the fourth quarter of 2008, real GDP fell 6.8 percent, the largest drop since 1980, and job losses averaged 662,000 a month, or 21 times the average for the first three months of the year. The unemployment rate climbed from 5.0 percent in January to 7.4 percent in December, the highest in nearly two decades.

The Stimulus Package

With the economy bleeding jobs, policy makers had a sense of urgency if not panic. On February 17, 2009, newly-elected President Barack Obama signed the **American Recovery and Reinvestment Act**, a $787 billion package of tax benefits and spending programs aimed at stimulating aggregate demand. The president called the measure "the most sweeping economic recovery package in our history." He predicted the measure would "create or save three and a half million jobs over the next two years." The projected cost would later rise to $862 billion, or about $7,500 per household.

American Recovery and Reinvestment Act
At an estimated cost of $862 billion, the largest stimulus measure in U.S history; enacted in February 2009 and projected to last two years

According to the White House Web site Recovery.gov, which was created to track the stimulus package and its consequences, 37 percent was for tax benefits, 28 percent was for entitlements (such as Medicaid), and 35 percent was for grants, contracts, and loans. Most of the tax benefits were one-time reductions for individuals. Grants, contracts, and loans included some "shovel ready" infrastructure projects, such as bridges and roads, but these projects were slow to get underway and they represented just a small fraction of stimulus spending (only 4 percent of the stimulus went to the Federal Highway Administration for highway and bridge projects).

The stimulus package was all deficit spending. The rationale for deficit spending is that unemployed labor and idle capital would be put to work. And if the spending multiplier exceeds one, a dollar of government spending produces more than a dollar of new output and income. Thus, the effectiveness of any stimulus program depends on the size of the tax and spending multipliers. During the debate on the measure, one group of economists argued that the multipliers were less than one and another group, including the president's economists, argued they were greater than one. Unfortunately, because of chronic deficits since the early 1980s, discretionary fiscal policies had not been used much, at least not explicitly, so few researchers have attempted to measure those effects, and not all those researchers tried to estimate multipliers.

Still, because the research question is so important, here are results from some fiscal studies published since 2009. Christina Romer and David Romer, both of the University of California, Berkeley, examined the impact of 54 legislated U.S. tax changes between 1945 and 2007 (so their research did not capture the recent recession). They concluded that a tax increase amounting to 1 percent of GDP would lower GDP by nearly 3 percent, suggesting a tax multiplier with an absolute value of nearly 3. Investment fell sharply in response to tax increases.[2] Alberto Alesina and Silvia Ardanga, both of Harvard, looked at 91 episodes of fiscal policy from 1970 to 2007 in 21 developed countries and found that tax cuts increased economic growth more than did increases in government spending. Also government spending cuts were more likely to reduce deficits than were tax increases.[3] Robert Barro, also of Harvard, studied wartime and defense spending, and estimated a spending multiplier of only 0.8.[4] Valerie Ramey of the University of California, San Diego, looked at government spending from 1939 to 2008 and found a multiplier in the range of 0.6 to 1.2.[5] Casey Mulligan of the University of Chicago observed labor markets during the 2008 to 2009 recession and drew the inference that government spending crowded out some private spending. He concluded the government spending multiplier was less than one.[6] And Daniel Wilson with the Federal Reserve Bank of San Francisco looked at the relationship between federal stimulus spending and state employment from February 2009 to May 2010. He found that spending on infrastructure and general purpose programs had a positive effect on employment, particularly during the first year of the stimulus. But spending on safety-net programs such as unemployment benefits and Medicaid had a negative effect on employment.[7] Overall, he concluded that the stimulus package created or saved about 0.8 million jobs during the period. Thus, the studies suggest that tax cuts seemed to have more of an impact on the economy than spending increases, and of those studies that estimated a spending multiplier, the average was less than one.

Government Spending and Real GDP

It may be too soon to isolate the impact of the largest stimulus program in history, first because some of the money had not yet been spent as of late 2010, and second because so much else was going on in the economy, such as the automatic stabilizers, other discretionary spending programs, and a massive intervention by the Federal Reserve, a topic covered in a later chapter. But just so you can get a rough idea what happened during the period, Exhibit 6 shows quarterly changes in real GDP and in government spending between the second quarter of 2008 and the first quarter of 2010 (all at annualized rates). First, notice the change in real GDP, which went from positive to negative, then back to positive over the eight quarters. The fourth quarter of 2008 showed the largest drop, with GDP falling 6.8 percent, the most since 1980. Government spending includes federal, state, and local spending; this total would reflect federal stimulus money to save state and local government jobs as well as spending for so-called "shovel-ready" projects (but not captured directly in government spending are tax cuts and transfer programs, though any effects should eventually be reflected in GDP).

2. See Christina Romer and David Romer, "The Macroeconomic Effects of Tax Changes: Estimates Based on a New Measure of Fiscal Shocks," *American Economic Review*, 100 (June 2010): 763–801. Christina Romer chaired President Obama's Council of Economic Advisers from January 2009 to September 2010.
3. Alberto Alesina and Silvia Ardanga, "Large Changes in Fiscal Policy: Taxes Versus Spending," *Tax Policy and the Economy*, 24 (2010): 35–68.
4. Robert J. Barro, "Government Spending Is No Free Lunch," *Wall Street Journal*, 22 January 2009.
5. Valerie Ramey, "Indentifying Government Spending Shocks: It's All in the Timing," *Quarterly Journal of Economics*, forthcoming.
6. Casey Mulligan, "Simple Analytics and Empirics of the Government Spending Multiplier and Other 'Keynesian Paradoxes,'" NBER Working Paper 15800, (March 2010).
7. Daniel J. Wilson, "Fiscal Spending Multipliers: Evidence from the 2009 American Recovery and Reinvestment Act," Federal Reserve Bank of San Francisco Working Paper, (June 2010).

EXHIBIT 6 Percent Change in Real GDP and Government Spending by Quarter (Annualized Rate)

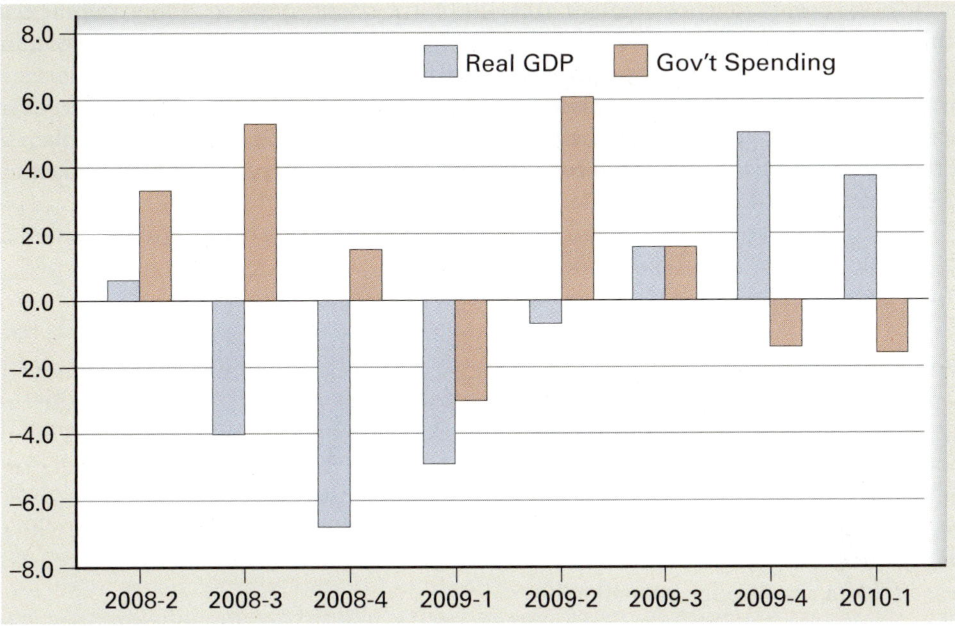

Source: National Economic Accounts, Bureau of Economic Analysis, at http://bea.gov/national/nipaweb/Index.asp.

Government spending declined the most in the first quarter of 2009, with a drop of 3.0 percent, the largest in a decade. That same quarter, President Obama signed the stimulus bill. Government spending grew the most, by 6.1 percent, the quarter following the enactment of the stimulus package. We should remember that association is not causation, but GDP fell only 0.7 percent the quarter after the stimulus was signed. Once GDP started growing again, government spending seemed to slow then turn negative for the final two quarters shown. Government spending during the four quarters following enactment of the stimulus package grew an average of 1.2 percent. By way of comparison, government spending the four prior quarters grew an average of 1.8 percent. So government spending grew less on average after the stimulus than before it. This was also true if we focus just on federal spending. Of course, the stimulus included tax cuts and increases in transfer payments, outlays not captured in government spending.

As of the middle of 2010, much of the stimulus money had not yet been spent. The White House claimed that the program was on track to create or save the 3.5 million jobs promised. The economy actually lost 3.2 million jobs during the nine months following passage of the stimulus measure. The White House argues that those losses would have been a lot worse without the stimulus. That's difficult to prove or disprove. We do know that the unemployment rate remained stubbornly high at about 9.5 percent deep into 2010. Altogether, employment fell by 8.4 million between December 2007 and December 2009, a decline of 6.1 percent. The federal deficit ballooned from $161 billion in 2007 to $459 billion in 2008 to $1.4 trillion in 2009, when 41 cents of each dollar spent by the federal government was borrowed. The White House projected deficits of $1.5 trillion in 2010 and $1.4 trillion in 2011. Those deficits add up to an awesome debt, to be discussed in the next chapter.

It is said that geologists learn more about the nature of the Earth's crust from one major upheaval, such as a huge earthquake or major volcanic eruption, than from a dozen lesser events. The recession of 2007–2009 traumatized the economy and the economics profession. Events will be dissected for years to develop a clearer understanding of how the economy works and what went wrong.

Congress and the president also adopted some more modest stimulus programs, such as tax incentives for home buyers and for car buyers. The case study at the end of the book, "Public Policy: Cash for Clunkers," looks at the program to stimulate car sales.

Conclusion

This chapter discussed fiscal policy in theory and in practice. It also examined several factors that reduce the size of the spending and taxing multipliers. In the short run, the aggregate supply curve slopes upward, so the impact on equilibrium output of any change in aggregate demand is blunted by a change in the price level. In the long run, aggregate supply is a vertical line, so if the economy is already producing at its potential, the spending multiplier is zero. To the extent that consumers respond primarily to changes in their permanent incomes, temporary changes in taxes affect consumption less, so the tax multiplier is smaller.

In the theory portion of this chapter, we assumed net taxes and net exports would remain unchanged with changes in income. In reality, income taxes increase with income and net exports decrease with income. The appendix introduces these more realistic assumptions. The resulting spending multipliers and tax multipliers are smaller than those developed to this point. In the next chapter, we look at the result of large federal deficits—mounting federal debt.

Summary

1. The tools of fiscal policy are automatic stabilizers and discretionary fiscal measures. Automatic stabilizers, such as the federal income tax, once implemented, operate year after year without congressional action. Discretionary fiscal policy results from specific legislation about government spending, taxation, and transfers. If that legislation becomes permanent, then discretionary fiscal policies often become automatic stabilizers.
2. The effect of an increase in government purchases on aggregate demand is the same as that of an increase in any other type of spending. Thus, the simple multiplier for a change in government purchases is $1/(1 - MPC)$.
3. A decrease in net taxes (taxes minus transfer payments) affects consumption by increasing disposable income. A decrease in net taxes does not increase spending as much as would an identical increase in government purchases because some of the tax cut is saved. The multiplier for a change in autonomous net taxes is $-MPC/(1 - MPC)$.
4. An expansionary fiscal policy can close a recessionary gap by increasing government purchases, reducing net taxes, or both. Because the short-run aggregate supply curve slopes upward, an increase in aggregate demand raises both output and the price level in the short run. A contractionary fiscal policy can close an expansionary gap by reducing government purchases, increasing net taxes, or both. Fiscal policy that reduces aggregate demand to close an expansionary gap reduces both output and the price level.
5. Fiscal policy focuses primarily on the demand side, not the supply side. The problems of the 1970s, however, resulted more from a decline of aggregate supply than from a decline of aggregate demand, so demand-side remedies seemed less effective.
6. After the "supply-side" tax cuts of the early 1980s, government spending grew faster than tax revenue, creating sizable budget deficits. The incentive effects of tax cuts on aggregate supply combined with the stimulative effects of deficit spending on aggregate demand, contributed to the longest peacetime expansion to that point in the nation's history. These large deficits discouraged additional discretionary fiscal policy as a way of stimulating aggregate demand further, but success in erasing deficits in the late 1990s spawned renewed interest in discretionary fiscal policy, as reflected by President Bush's tax cuts in the face of the 2001 recession.

7. Tax cuts and new spending increased deficits into 2004, but the economy added over 8 million jobs by 2007. The added output and income cut the federal deficit from about $400 billion in 2004 to about $160 billion in 2007.
8. After peaking in December 2007, the economy turned down, as consumers, firms, and financial markets were spooked by falling home prices and rising foreclosure rates. Job losses increased sharply after the financial crisis of September 2008. Government officials first tried to calm financial markets with TARP, then tried to stimulate the economy with the largest program in history. The economy lost 8.4 million jobs between December 2007 and December 2009. Jobs started coming back in 2010, but the unemployment rate remained high.

Key Concepts

Automatic stabilizers 514
Discretionary fiscal policy 514
Simple tax multiplier 517
Expansionary fiscal policy 518
Contractionary fiscal policy 519
Classical economists 521
Employment Act of 1946 522
Permanent income 525
American Recovery and Reinvestment Act 527

Questions for Review

1. Fiscal Policy Define *fiscal policy*. Determine whether each of the following, other factors held constant, would lead to an increase, a decrease, or no change in the level of real GDP demanded:
   a. A decrease in government purchases
   b. An increase in net taxes
   c. A reduction in transfer payments
   d. A decrease in the marginal propensity to consume
2. The Multiplier and the Time Horizon Explain how the steepness of the short-run aggregate supply curve affects the government's ability to use fiscal policy to change real GDP.
3. Evolution of Fiscal Policy What did classical economists assume about the flexibility of prices, wages, and interest rates? What did this assumption imply about the self-correcting tendencies in an economy in recession? What disagreements did Keynes have with classical economists?
4. Automatic Stabilizers Often during recessions, the number of young people who volunteer for military service increases. Could this rise be considered a type of automatic stabilizer? Why or why not?
5. Permanent Income "If the federal government wants to stimulate consumption by means of a tax cut, it should employ a permanent tax cut. If the government wants to stimulate saving in the short run, it should employ a temporary tax cut." Evaluate this statement.
6. Fiscal Policy Explain why effective discretionary fiscal policy requires information about each of the following:
   a. The slope of the short-run aggregate supply curve
   b. The natural rate of unemployment
   c. The size of the multiplier
   d. The speed with which self-correcting forces operate
7. Automatic Stabilizers Distinguish between discretionary fiscal policy and automatic stabilizers. Provide examples of automatic stabilizers. What is the impact of automatic stabilizers on disposable income as the economy moves through the business cycle?
8. Fiscal Policy Effectiveness Determine whether each of the following would make fiscal policy more effective or less effective:
   a. A decrease in the marginal propensity to consume
   b. Shorter lags in the effect of fiscal policy
   c. Consumers suddenly becoming more concerned about permanent income than about current income
   d. More accurate measurement of the natural rate of unemployment
9. Case Study: Fiscal Policy and Presidential Elections (See page 759.) Suppose that fiscal policy changes output faster than it changes the price level. How might such timing play a role in the theory of political business cycles?
10. From Deficits to Surpluses to Deficits What effect did the financial crisis of 2008 have on the federal budget deficit?
11. Case Study: Cash for Clunkers (See page 761.) Studies indicate that the Cash for Clunkers only shifted sales from later to earlier in 2009. Assuming that this is true, what was the spending multiplier for the Cash for Clunkers program?

Problems and Exercises

12. Changes in Government Purchases Assume that government purchases decrease by $10 billion, with other factors held constant, including the price level. Calculate the change in the level of real GDP demanded for each of the following values of the MPC. Then, calculate the change if the government, instead of reducing its purchases, increased autonomous net taxes by $10 billion.

    a. 0.9
    b. 0.8
    c. 0.75
    d. 0.6

13. Fiscal Multipliers Explain the difference between the government purchases multiplier and the net tax multiplier. If the MPC falls, what happens to the tax multiplier?

14. Changes in Net Taxes Using the income-expenditure model, graphically illustrate the impact of a $15 billion drop in government transfer payments on aggregate expenditure if the MPC equals 0.75. Explain why it has this impact. What is the impact on the level of real GDP demanded, assuming the price level remains unchanged?

15. Fiscal Policy with an Expansionary Gap Using the aggregate demand–aggregate supply model, illustrate an economy with an expansionary gap. If the government is to close the gap by changing government purchases, should it increase or decrease those purchases? In the long run, what happens to the level of real GDP as a result of government intervention? What happens to the price level? Illustrate this on an AD–AS diagram, assuming that the government changes its purchases by exactly the amount necessary to close the gap.

16. Fiscal Policy This chapter shows that increased government purchases, with taxes held constant, can eliminate a recessionary gap. How could a tax cut achieve the same result? Would the tax cut have to be larger than the increase in government purchases? Why or why not?

17. Multipliers Suppose investment, in addition to having an autonomous component, also has a component that varies directly with the level of real GDP. How would this affect the size of the government purchase and net tax multipliers?

Global Economic Watch Exercises

Login to www.cengagebrain.com and access the Global Economic Watch to do these exercises.

18. Global Economic Watch Go to the Global Economic Crisis Resource Center. Select Global Issues in Context. In the Basic Search box at the top of the page, enter the phrase "fiscal policy." On the Results page, go to the Global Viewpoints Section. Click on the link for the August 29, 2010, editorial "Why We Need a Second Stimulus." What are three reasons given for a second round of federal spending to follow the 2009 stimulus plan?

19. Global Economic Watch Go to the Global Economic Crisis Resource Center. Select Global Issues in Context. In the Basic Search box at the top of the page, enter the phrase "budget deficit." Use quotation marks before and after the phrase to ensure finding articles about the economic concept of the budget deficit. Choose one article from the past two years. Does the article express concern about the budget deficit in the country discussed?

Appendix

The Algebra of Demand-Side Equilibrium

In this appendix, we continue to focus on aggregate demand, using algebra. In Appendix B two chapters back, we solved for real GDP demanded at a particular price level, then derived the simple multiplier for changes in spending, including government purchases. The change in real GDP demanded, here denoted as ΔY, resulting from a change in government purchases, ΔG, is

$$\Delta Y = \Delta G \times \frac{1}{1 - MPC}$$

The government spending multiplier is $1/(1 - MPC)$. In this appendix, we first derive the multiplier for net taxes that do not vary with income. Then we incorporate proportional income taxes and variable net exports into the model. Note the simple multiplier assumes a shift of the aggregate demand curve at a given price level. By ignoring the effects of aggregate supply, we exaggerate the size of the multiplier.

Net Tax Multiplier

How does a \$1 increase in net taxes that do not vary with income affect real GDP demanded? We begin with Y, real GDP demanded, originally derived in Appendix B two chapters back:

$$Y = \frac{1}{1 - b}(a - bNT + I + G + X - M)$$

where b is the marginal propensity to consume and $a - bNT$ is that portion of consumption that is independent of the level of income (review Appendix B two chapters back if you need a refresher).

Now let's increase net taxes by \$1 to see what happens to the level of real GDP demanded. Increasing net taxes by \$1 yields

$$Y' = \frac{a - b(NT + \$1) + I + G + X - M}{1 - b}$$

The difference between Y' and Y is

$$Y - Y' = \frac{\$1(-b)}{1 - b}$$

Because b is the marginal propensity to consume, this difference can be expressed as $\$1 \times -MPC/(1 - MPC)$, which is the net tax multiplier discussed in this chapter. With the MPC equal to 0.8, the net tax multiplier equals $-0.8/0.2$, or -4, so the effect of increasing net taxes by \$1 is to decrease GDP demanded by \$4, with the price level assumed constant. For any change larger than \$1, we simply scale up the results. For example, the effect of increasing net taxes by \$10 billion is to decrease GDP demanded at a given price level by \$40 billion. A different marginal propensity to consume yields a different multiplier. For example, if the MPC equals 0.75, the net tax multiplier equals $-0.75/0.25$, or -3.

The Multiplier When Both *G* and *NT* Change

Although we did not discuss in the chapter the combined effects of changing both government purchases and net taxes, we can easily summarize these effects here. Suppose both increase by \$1. We can bring together the two changes in the following equation:

$$Y'' = \frac{a - b(NT - \$1) + I + G + \$1 + X - M}{1 - b}$$

The difference between this equilibrium and Y (the income level before introducing any changes in G or NT) is

$$Y'' - Y = \frac{\$1(-b) + \$1}{(1 - b)}$$

which simplifies to

$$Y'' - Y = \frac{\$1(1 - b)}{1 - b} = \$1$$

Equilibrium real GDP demanded increases by \$1 as a result of \$1 increases in both government purchases and net taxes. This result is referred to as the *balanced budget multiplier,* which is equal to 1.

More generally, we can say that if ΔG represents the change in government purchases and ΔNT represents the change in net taxes, the resulting change in aggregate output demanded, ΔY, can be expressed as

$$\Delta Y = \frac{\Delta G - b\Delta NT}{1 - b}$$

The Multiplier With a Proportional Income Tax

A net tax of a fixed amount has been useful to explain the fiscal impact of taxes, but this tax is not very realistic. Instead, suppose we introduce a *proportional income tax* rate equal to t, where t lies between 0 and 1. Incidentally, the proportional income tax is also the so-called *flat tax* discussed as an alternative to the existing progressive income tax. Tax collections under a proportional income tax equal the tax rate, t, times real GDP, Y. With tax collections of tY, disposable income equals

$$Y - tY = (1 - t)Y$$

We plug this value for disposable income into the equation for the consumption function to yield

$$C = a + b\,(1 - t)Y$$

To consumption, we add the other components of aggregate expenditure, I, G, and $X - M$, to get

$$Y = a + b\,(1 - t)Y + I + G + (X - M)$$

Moving the Y terms to the left side of the equation yields

$$Y - b\,(1 - t)Y = a + I + G + (X - M)$$

or

$$Y[1 - b\,(1 - t)] = a + I + G + (X - M)$$

By isolating Y on the left side of the equation, we get

$$Y = \frac{a + I + G + (X - M)}{1 - b(1 - t)}$$

The numerator on the right side consists of the autonomous spending components. A \$1 change in any of these components would change real GDP demanded by

$$\Delta Y = \frac{\$1}{1 - b(1 - t)}$$

Thus, the spending multiplier with a proportional income tax equals

$$\frac{1}{1 - b(1 - t)}$$

As the tax rate increases, the denominator increases, so the multiplier gets smaller. *The higher the proportional tax rate, other things constant, the smaller the spending multiplier.* A higher tax rate reduces consumption during each round of spending.

Including Variable Net Exports

The previous section assumed that net exports remained independent of disposable income. If you have been reading the appendixes along with the chapters, you already know how variable net exports fit into the picture. *The addition of variable net exports causes the aggregate expenditure line to flatten out because net exports decrease as real income increases.* Real GDP demanded with a proportional income tax and variable net exports is

$$Y = a + b\,(1 - t)Y + I + G + X - m\,(1 - t)Y$$

where $m(1 - t)Y$ shows that imports are an increasing function of disposable income. The above equation reduces to

$$Y = \frac{a + I + G + X}{1 - b + m + t(b - m)}$$

The higher the proportional tax rate, t, or the higher the marginal propensity to import, m, the larger the denominator, so the smaller the spending multiplier. If the marginal propensity to consume is 0.8, the marginal propensity to import is 0.1, and the proportional income tax rate is 0.2, the spending multiplier would be about 2.3, or less than half the simple spending multiplier of 5. And this still assumes the price level remains unchanged.

Since we first introduced the simple spending multiplier, we have examined several factors that reduce that multiplier: (1) a marginal propensity to consume that responds primarily to permanent changes in income, not transitory changes; (2) a marginal propensity to import; (3) a proportional income tax; and (4) the upward-sloping aggregate supply curve in the short run and a vertical aggregate supply curve in the long run. After we introduce money in later chapters, we consider still other factors that reduce the size of the spending multiplier.

Appendix Questions

1. THE ALGEBRA OF DEMAND-SIDE EQUILIBRIUM Suppose that the autonomous levels of consumption, investment, government purchases, and net exports are $500 billion, $300 billion, $100 billion, and $100 billion, respectively. Suppose further that the MPC is 0.85, that the marginal propensity to import is 0.05, and that income is taxed at a proportional rate of 0.25.
   a. What is the level of real GDP demanded?
   b. What is the size of the government deficit (or surplus) at this output level?
   c. What is the size of net exports at the level of real GDP demanded?
   d. What is the level of saving at this output?
   e. What change in autonomous spending is required to change equilibrium real GDP demanded by $500 billion?
2. SPENDING MULTIPLIER If the MPC is 0.8, the MPM is 0.1, and the proportional income tax rate is 0.2, what is the value of the spending multiplier? Determine whether each of the following would increase the value of the spending multiplier, decrease it, or leave it unchanged:
   a. An increase in the MPM
   b. An increase in the MPC
   c. An increase in the proportional tax rate
   d. An increase in autonomous net taxes
3. THE MULTIPLIER WITH A PROPORTIONAL INCOME TAX Answer the following questions using the following data, all in billions. Assume an MPC of 0.8.

Disposable Income	Consumption
$ 0	$ 500
500	900
1,000	1,300
1,500	1,700

   a. Assuming that net taxes are equal to $200 billion regardless of the level of income, graph consumption against income (as opposed to disposable income).
   b. How would an increase in net taxes to $300 billion affect the consumption function?
   c. If the level of taxes were related to the level of income (i.e., income taxes were proportional to income), how would this affect the consumption function?

Federal Budgets and Public Policy

27

AP Photo/Gerald Herbert

- How big is the federal budget, and where does the money go?
- Why is the federal budget process such a tangled web?
- In what sense is the federal budgeting process at odds with discretionary fiscal policy?
- How is a sluggish economy like an empty restaurant?
- Why has the federal budget been in deficit most years, and why did a surplus briefly materialize at the end of the 1990s?
- What is the federal debt, and who owes it to whom?
- Can a nation run deficits year after year and decade after decade?

Answers to these and other questions are examined in this chapter, which considers federal budgeting in theory and practice.

The word *budget* derives from the Old French word *bougette*, which means "little bag." The federal budget is now about \$3,700,000,000,000.00—\$3.7 trillion a year. That's big money! If this "little bag" held \$100 bills, it would weigh 40,000 *tons*! These \$100 bills could paper over a 24-lane highway stretching from northern Maine to southern California. A \$3.7 trillion stack of \$100 bills would tower 2,500 miles high. Here's another way to grasp the size of the federal budget: If all 4,600 tons of gold stored in Fort Knox were sold at about \$1,000 per ounce, the proceeds would run the federal government for only two weeks.

Government budgets have a tremendous impact on the economy. Government outlays at all levels amount to about 41 percent relative to GDP. Our focus in this chapter will be the federal budget, beginning with the budget process. We then look at the source of federal deficits and how they briefly became surpluses. We also examine the national debt and its impact on the economy.

Topics discussed include:

- The federal budget process
- Rationale for deficit spending
- Impact of federal deficits
- Crowding out and crowding in
- The short-lived budget surplus
- The burden of the federal debt

The Federal Budget Process

federal budget
A plan for federal government outlays and revenues for a specified period, usually a year

The **federal budget** is a plan of outlays and revenues for a specified period, usually a year. Federal *outlays* include both government purchases and transfer payments. Exhibit 1 shows U.S. federal outlays by major category since 1960. As you can see, the share of outlays going to national defense dropped from over half in 1960 to only 20 percent in 2011. Social Security's share has grown every decade. Medicare, medical care for the elderly, was introduced in 1965 and has also grown since then. In fact, Social Security and Medicare, programs aimed primarily at the elderly, combined for 32 percent of federal outlays in 2011. For the last two decades, welfare spending, which consists of cash and in-kind transfer payments, has remained relatively stable, and in 2011 accounted for 16 percent of federal outlays. And, thanks to record low interest rates, interest payments on the national debt were 6 percent of federal outlays in 2011, down from 15 percent as recently as 1996. So 49 percent, or nearly half the federal budget in 2011,

EXHIBIT 1 Defense's Share of Federal Outlays Declined Since 1960 and Redistribution Increased

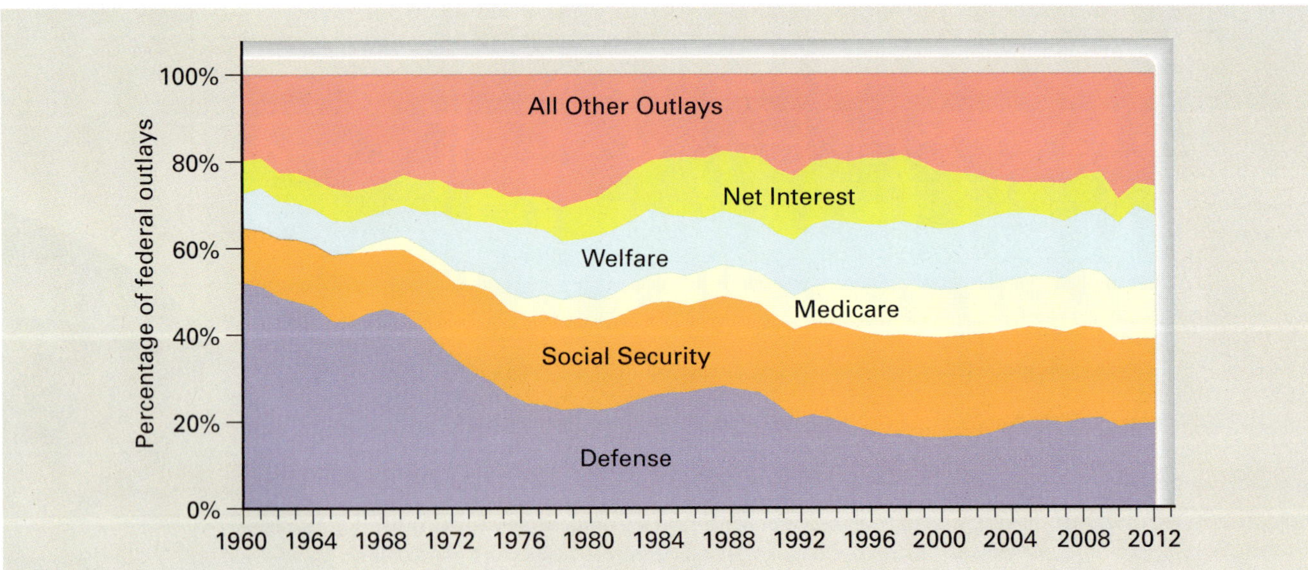

Source: Computed based on budget totals from *Economic Report of the President*, February 2010, Table B-80; and the Office of Management and Budget. For the most recent year, go to http://www.gpoaccess.gov/eop/. Percentage shares for 2010 and 2011 are estimates based on the president's budget.

redistributed income (Social Security, Medicare, and welfare); 20 percent went toward defense; 6 percent serviced the national debt; and the remaining 25 percent paid for everything else in the federal budget—from environmental protection to federal prisons to federal education aid. Since the 1960s, the federal government has shifted its focus from national defense to redistribution.

The Presidential and Congressional Roles

The president's budget proposal begins to take shape a year before it is submitted to Congress, with each agency preparing a budget request. In late January or early February, the president submits to Congress *The Budget of the United States Government,* a pile of books detailing spending and revenue proposals for the upcoming fiscal year, which begins October 1. At this stage, the president's budget is little more than detailed suggestions for congressional consideration. About the same time, the president's Council of Economic Advisors sends Congress the *Economic Report of the President*, which offers the president's take on the economy.

Budget committees in both the House and the Senate rework the president's budget until they agree on total outlays, spending by major category, and expected revenues. This agreement, called a **budget resolution**, guides spending and revenue decisions made by the many congressional committees and subcommittees. The budget cycle is supposed to end before October 1, the start of the new fiscal year. Before that date, Congress should have approved detailed plans for outlays along with revenue projections. Thus, the federal budget has a congressional gestation period of about nine months—though, as noted, the president's budget usually begins taking shape a year before it's submitted to Congress.

budget resolution
A congressional agreement about total outlays, spending by major category, and expected revenues; it guides spending and revenue decisions by the many congressional committees and subcommittees

The size and composition of the budget and the difference between outlays and revenues measure the budget's fiscal impact on the economy. *When outlays exceed revenues, the budget is in deficit. A deficit stimulates aggregate demand in the short run but reduces national saving, which in the long run could impede economic growth. Alternatively, when revenues exceed outlays, the federal budget is in surplus. A surplus dampens aggregate demand in the short run but boosts domestic saving, which in the long run could promote economic growth.*

Problems With the Federal Budget Process

The federal budget process sounds good on paper, but it does not work that well in practice. Here are several problems.

Continuing Resolutions Instead of Budget Decisions

Congress often ignores the timetable for developing and approving a budget. Because deadlines are frequently missed, budgets typically run from year to year based on **continuing resolutions,** which are agreements to allow agencies, in the absence of an approved budget, to spend at the rate of the previous year's budget. Poorly conceived programs continue through sheer inertia; successful programs cannot expand. On occasion, the president must temporarily shut down some agencies because not even the continuing resolution can be approved on time. For example, in late 1995 and early 1996, most federal offices closed for twenty seven days.

continuing resolutions
Budget agreements that allow agencies, in the absence of an approved budget, to spend at the rate of the previous year's budget

Lengthy Budget Process

You can imagine the difficulty of using the budget as a tool of discretionary fiscal policy when the budget process takes so long. Given that the average recession since World War II has lasted only eleven months and that budget preparations begin more than a year and a half before the budget takes effect, planning discretionary fiscal measures to reduce economic fluctuations is difficult if not impossible. That's one reason why attempts to stimulate an ailing economy often seem so halfhearted; by the time Congress and the president agree on a fiscal remedy, the economy has often recovered on its own.

Uncontrollable Budget Items

entitlement programs
Guaranteed benefits for those who qualify for government transfer programs such as Social Security and Medicare

Congress has only limited control over much of the budget. *About three-fourths of federal budget outlays are determined by existing laws.* For example, once Congress establishes eligibility criteria, **entitlement programs,** such as Social Security, Medicare, and Medicaid, take on lives of their own, with each annual appropriation simply reflecting the amount required to support the expected number of entitled beneficiaries. Health care reform introduced another major entitlement program, the cost of which has not yet been fully calculated. Congress has no say in such appropriations unless it chooses to change benefits or eligibility criteria. Most entitlement programs have such politically powerful constituencies that Congress is reluctant to mess with the structure.

No Separate Capital Budget

Congress approves a single budget that mixes *capital* expenditures, like new federal buildings and aircraft carriers, with *operating* expenditures, like employee payrolls and military meals. Budgets for businesses and for state and local governments usually distinguish between a *capital budget* and an *operating budget*. The federal government, by mixing the two, offers a fuzzier picture of what's going on.

Overly Detailed Budget

The federal budget is divided into thousands of accounts and subaccounts, which is why it fills volumes. To the extent that the budget is a way of making political payoffs, such micromanagement allows elected officials to reward friends and punish enemies with great precision. For example, a recent budget included $176,000 for the Reindeer Herders Association in Alaska, $400,000 for the Southside Sportsman Club in New York, and $5 million for an insect-rearing facility in Mississippi. By budgeting in such detail, Congress may lose sight of the big picture. When economic conditions change or when the demand for certain public goods shifts, the federal government cannot easily reallocate funds. Detailed budgeting is not only time consuming, it reduces the flexibility of discretionary fiscal policy and is subject to political abuse.

Possible Budget Reforms

Some reforms might improve the budget process. First, the annual budget could become a two-year budget, or *biennial budget*. As it is, Congress spends nearly all of the year working on the budget. The executive branch is always dealing with three budgets: administering an approved budget, defending a proposed budget before congressional committees, and preparing the next budget for submission to Congress. With a two-year budget, Congress would not be continually involved with budget deliberations, and cabinet members could focus more on running their agencies (many states have adopted two-year budgets). A two-year budget, however, would require longer-term economic forecasts and would be less useful than a one-year budget as a tool of discretionary fiscal policy.

Another possible reform would be to simplify the budget document by concentrating only on major groupings and eliminating line items. Each agency head would receive a total budget, along with the discretion to allocate that budget in a manner consistent with the perceived demands for agency services. The drawback is that agency heads may have different priorities than those of elected representatives. On the plus side, elected officials would be less able to insert favorite pork-barrel projects into the budget.

A final reform is to sort federal spending into a capital budget and an operating budget. A *capital budget* would include spending on physical capital such as buildings, highways, computers, military equipment, and other public infrastructure. An *operating budget* would include spending on the payroll, building maintenance, computer paper, transfer programs, and other ongoing outlays.

The Fiscal Impact of the Federal Budget

When government outlays—government purchases plus cash and in-kind transfer programs—exceed government revenue, the result is a *budget deficit*, a flow measure already introduced. Although the federal budget was in surplus from 1998 to 2001, before that it had been in deficit every year but one since 1960 and in all but eight years since 1930. After 2001 the budget slipped back into the red, where it remains. To place federal deficits in perspective, let's first examine the economic rationale for deficit financing.

The Rationale for Deficits

Deficit financing has been justified for outlays that increase the economy's productivity—capital outlays for investments such as highways, waterways, and dams. The cost of these capital projects should be borne in part by future taxpayers, who will also benefit from these investments. Thus, there is some justification for shifting some of the cost of capital projects to future taxpayers. State and local governments issue debt to fund capital projects, such as schools and infrastructure. But, as noted already, the federal government does not budget capital projects separately, so there is no explicit link between capital budgets and federal deficits.

Before the Great Depression, federal deficits occurred only during wartime. Because wars often involve great personal hardship, public officials are understandably reluctant to tax citizens much more to finance war-related spending. Deficits during wars were largely self-correcting, however, because military spending dropped after a war, but tax revenue did not.

The Great Depression led John Maynard Keynes to argue that public spending should offset any drop in private spending. As you know by now, Keynes argued that a federal budget deficit would stimulate aggregate demand. As a result of the Great Depression, automatic stabilizers were also introduced, which increased public outlays during recessions and decreased them during expansions. Deficits increase during recessions because tax revenues decline while spending programs such as unemployment benefits and welfare increase. For example, during the 1990–1991 recession, corporate tax revenue fell 10 percent but welfare spending jumped 25 percent. An economic expansion reverses these flows. As the economy picks up, so do personal income and corporate profits, boosting tax revenue. Unemployment compensation and welfare spending decline. Thus, federal deficits usually fall during the recovery stage of the business cycle.

Budget Philosophies and Deficits

Several budget philosophies have emerged over the years. Prior to the Great Depression, fiscal policy focused on maintaining an **annually balanced budget,** except during wartime. Because tax revenues rise during expansions and fall during recessions, an annually balanced budget means that spending increases during expansions and declines during

annually balanced budget
Budget philosophy prior to the Great Depression; aimed at matching annual revenues with outlays, except during times of war

recessions. But such a pattern magnifies fluctuations in the business cycle, overheating the economy during expansions and increasing unemployment during recessions.

cyclically balanced budget
A budget philosophy calling for budget deficits during recessions to be financed by budget surpluses during expansions

functional finance
A budget philosophy using fiscal policy to achieve the economy's potential GDP, rather than balancing budgets either annually or over the business cycle

A second budget philosophy calls for a **cyclically balanced budget,** meaning that budget deficits during recessions are covered by budget surpluses during expansions. Fiscal policy dampens swings in the business cycle without increasing the national debt. Nearly all states have established "rainy day" funds to build up budget surpluses during the good times for use during hard times.

A third budget philosophy is **functional finance,** which says that policy makers should be concerned less with balancing the budget annually, or even over the business cycle, and more with ensuring that the economy produces its potential output. If the budgets needed to keep the economy producing its potential involve chronic deficits, so be it. Since the Great Depression, budgets in this country have seldom balanced. *Although budget deficits have been larger during recessions than during expansions, the federal budget has been in deficit in all but a dozen years since 1930.*

Federal Deficits Since the Birth of the Nation

Between 1789, when the U.S. Constitution was adopted, and 1930, the first full year of the Great Depression, the federal budget was in deficit 33 percent of the years, primarily during war years. After a war, government spending dropped more than government revenue. Thus, deficits arising during wars were largely self-correcting once the wars ended.

Since the Great Depression, however, federal budgets have been in deficit 85 percent of the years. Exhibit 2 shows federal deficits and surpluses as a percentage of GDP since 1934. Unmistakable are the huge deficits during World War II, which dwarf deficits in other years. Turning now to the last quarter century, we see the relatively large deficits of the 1980s. These resulted from large tax cuts along with higher defense spending. Supply-side economists argued that tax cuts would stimulate enough economic activity to keep tax revenues from falling. Unspecified spending cuts were supposed to erase a

EXHIBIT 2 The Federal Deficit Relative to GDP Ballooned Recently

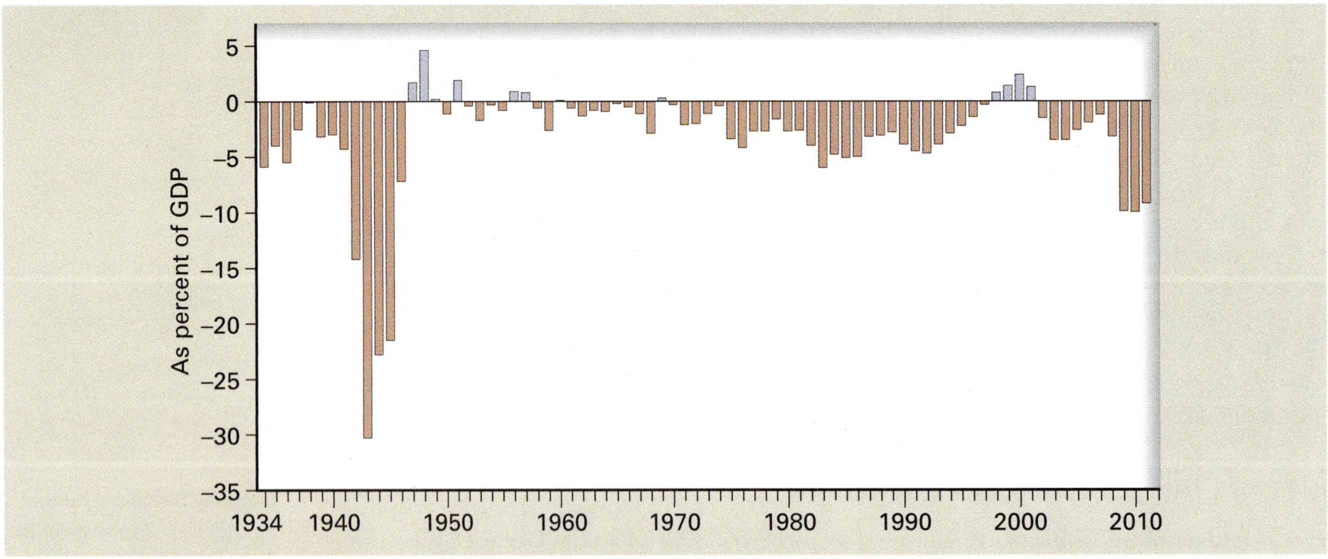

Source: *Economic Report of the President,* February 2010. Figures for 2010 and 2011 are based on the president's budget. For the latest data, go to http://www.gpoaccess.gov/eop/.

projected deficit, but Congress never made the promised cuts. In short, the president and Congress cut tax rates but not expenditures.

As the economy improved during the 1990s, the deficit decreased and then disappeared, turning into a surplus by 1998. But a recession in 2001, tax cuts, and higher federal spending turned surpluses into deficits. A weak recovery and the cost of fighting the war against terrorism worsened the deficits to 3.5 percent relative to GDP by 2003. But over the next four years, a stronger economy along with a rising stock market increased federal revenue enough to drop the deficit to about 1.2 percent relative to GDP in 2007. Because of the global financial crisis and the recession of 2007–2009, federal deficits relative to GDP swelled to levels not seen since World War II. The recession reduced revenues and expanded outlays, especially $862 billion for the American Reinvestment and Recovery Act, more popularly known as the stimulus program. The 2009 deficit was $1.4 trillion, or 9.9 percent relative to GDP, and the 2010 deficit was expected to reach $1.5 trillion, or 10 percent relative to GDP. Sizable deficits are projected for the next decade.

That's a short history of federal deficits. Now let's consider why the federal budget has been in deficit so long.

Why Deficits Persist

As we have seen, recent deficits climbed as the global financial crisis spilled into the wider economy, decreasing tax revenues and increasing government outlays. But why has the budget been in deficit for all but twelve years since 1934? The most obvious answer is that, unlike budgeters in 49 states, federal officials are not required to balance the budget. But why deficits rather than surpluses? One widely accepted model of the public sector assumes that elected officials try to maximize their political support, including votes and campaign contributions. Voters like spending programs but hate paying taxes, so public spending wins support and taxes lose it. Candidates try to maximize their chances of getting elected and reelected by offering budgets long on benefits but short on taxes. Moreover, members of Congress push their favorite programs with little concern about the overall budget. For example, a senator from Mississippi was able to include $1.5 billion in a budget for an amphibious assault ship to be built in his hometown of Pascagoula. The Navy never even asked for the ship.

Deficits, Surpluses, Crowding Out, and Crowding In

What effect do federal deficits and surpluses have on interest rates? Recall that interest rates affect investment, a critical component of economic growth. What's more, year-to-year fluctuations in investment are the primary source of shifts in the aggregate demand curve. Let's look at the impact of government deficits and surpluses on investment.

Suppose the federal government increases spending without raising taxes, thereby increasing the budget deficit. How will this affect national saving, interest rates, and investment? An increase in the federal deficit reduces the supply of national saving, leading to higher interest rates. Higher interest rates discourage, or *crowd out,* some private investment, reducing the stimulating effect of the government's deficit. The extent of **crowding out** is a matter of debate. Some economists argue that although government deficits may displace some private-sector borrowing, expansionary fiscal policy results in a net increase in aggregate demand, leading to greater output and employment in the short run. Others believe that the crowding out is more extensive, so borrowing from the public in this way results in little or no net increase in aggregate demand and output. Public spending merely substitutes for private spending.

crowding out
The displacement of interest-sensitive private investment that occurs when higher government deficits drive up market interest rates

Although crowding out is likely to occur to some degree, there is another possibility. If the economy is operating well below its potential, the additional fiscal stimulus provided by a higher government deficit could encourage some firms to invest more. Recall that an important determinant of investment is business expectations. Government stimulus of a weak economy could put a sunny face on the business outlook. As expectations grow more favorable, firms become more willing to invest. This ability of government deficits to stimulate private investment is sometimes called **crowding in**, to distinguish it from crowding out. Between 1993 and 2011, the Japanese government pursued deficit spending that averaged 6.0 percent relative to GDP as a way of getting that flat economy going, but with only limited success. Unfortunately, the global financial crisis and recession of 2007–2009 reversed those limited gains.

crowding in
The potential for government spending to stimulate private investment in an otherwise dead economy

Were you ever unwilling to patronize a restaurant because it was too crowded? You simply did not want to put up with the hassle and long wait and were thus "crowded out." Similarly, high government deficits may "crowd out" some investors by driving up interest rates. On the other hand, did you ever pass up an unfamiliar restaurant because the place seemed dead—it had no customers? Perhaps you wondered why? If you had seen just a few customers, you might have stopped in—you might have been willing to "crowd in." Similarly, businesses may be reluctant to invest in a seemingly lifeless economy. The economic stimulus resulting from deficit spending could encourage some investors to "crowd in."

The Twin Deficits

To finance the huge deficits, the U.S. Treasury must sell a lot of government IOUs. To get people to buy these Treasury securities, the government must offer higher interest rates, other things constant. So funding a higher deficit pushes up the market interest rates, other things constant. With U.S. interest rates higher, foreigners find Treasury securities more attractive. But to buy them, foreigners must first exchange their currencies for dollars. This greater demand for dollars causes the dollar to appreciate relative to foreign currencies. The rising value of the dollar makes foreign goods cheaper in the United States and U.S. goods more expensive abroad. Thus, U.S. imports increase and U.S. exports decrease, so the trade deficit increases.

Higher trade deficits mean that foreigners have dollars left over after they buy all the U.S. goods and services they want. With these accumulated dollars, foreigners buy U.S. assets, including U.S. government securities, and thereby help fund federal deficits. The increase in funds from abroad is both good news and bad news for the U.S. economy. The supply of foreign saving increases investment spending in the United States over what would have occurred in the absence of these funds. Ask people what they think of foreign investment in their town; they will likely say it's great. But foreign funds to some extent simply offset a decline in U.S. saving. Such a pattern could pose problems in the long run. The United States has surrendered a certain amount of control over its economy to foreign investors. And the return on foreign investments in the United States flows abroad. For example, a growing share of the federal government's debt is now owed to foreigners, as discussed later in the chapter.

America was once the world's leading creditor. Now it's the lead debtor nation, borrowing huge sums from abroad, helping in the process to fund the federal deficit. Some critics blame U.S. fiscal policy as reflected in the large federal deficits for the switch from creditor to debtor nation. Japan and China are big buyers of U.S. Treasury securities. A debtor country becomes more beholden to those countries that supply credit.

The Short-Lived Budget Surplus

Exhibit 3 summarizes the federal budget since 1970, showing outlays relative to GDP as the red line and revenues relative to GDP as the blue line. These percentages offer an overall look at the federal government's role in the economy. Between 1970 and 2011,

EXHIBIT 3 **The Sharp Recession of 2007–2009 Cut Federal Revenues and Increased Federal Outlays, Resulting in Huge Deficits**

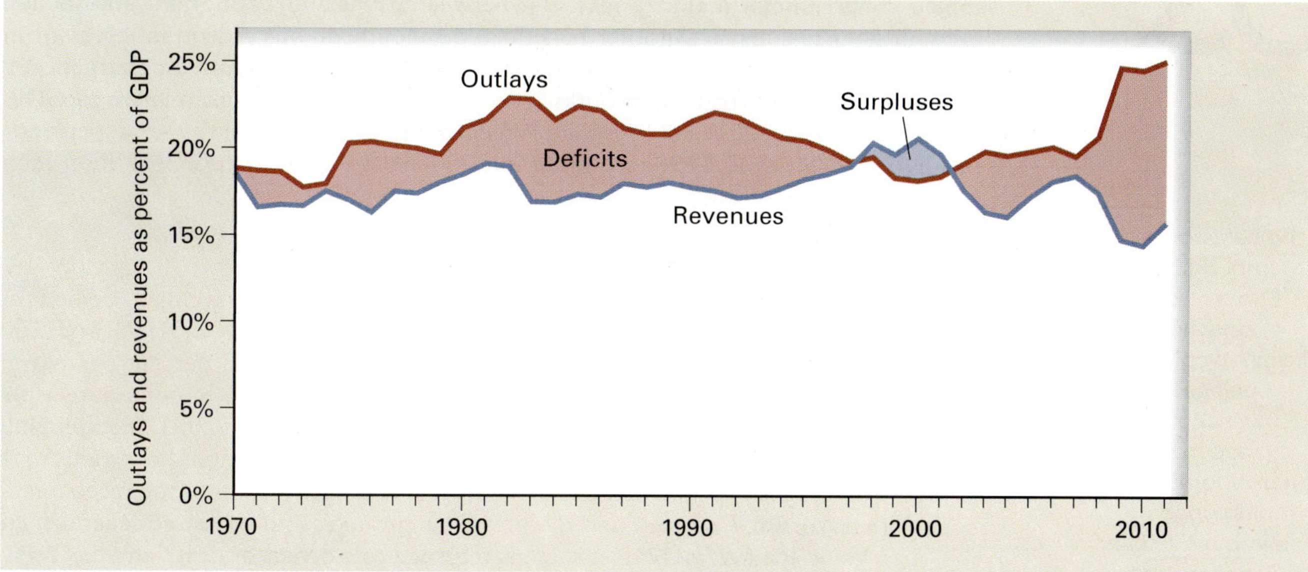

Source: *Economic Report of the President*, February 2010, Tables B-1 and B-78; and the Office of Management and Budget. Figures for 2010 and 2011 are based on the president's budget. For the latest data, go to http://www.gpoaccess.gov/eop/.

federal outlays averaged 20.6 percent and revenues averaged 17.7 percent relative to GDP. When outlays exceed revenues, the federal budget is in deficit, measured each year by the vertical distance between the blue and red lines. Thus, on average, the federal budget had a deficit of 2.9 percent relative to GDP. The pink shading shows the annual deficit as a percent of GDP. In the early 1990s, outlays started to decline relative to GDP, while revenues increased. This shrank the deficit and, by 1998, created a surplus, as indicated by the blue shading. Specifically, the deficit in 1990, which amounted to 3.8 percent relative to GDP, became a surplus by 1998, which lasted through 2001. What turned a hefty deficit into a surplus, and why has the surplus turned back into a deficit?

Tax Increases

With concern about the deficits of the 1980s growing, Congress and President George H. W. Bush agreed in 1990 to a package of spending cuts and tax increases aimed at trimming budget deficits. Ironically, those tax increases not only may have cost President Bush reelection in 1992 (because they violated his 1988 election promise of "no new taxes"), but they also began the groundwork for erasing the budget deficit, for which President Clinton was able to take credit. For his part, President Clinton increased taxes on high-income households in 1993, boosting the top marginal tax rate from 31 percent to 40 percent. The economy also enjoyed a vigorous recovery during the 1990s, fueled by rising worker productivity, growing consumer spending, globalization of markets, and a strong stock market. The combined effects of higher taxes on the rich and a strengthening economy raised federal revenue from 17.8 percent of GDP in 1990 to 20.6 percent in 2000. That may not seem like much of a difference, but it translated into an additional $275 billion in federal revenue in 2000.

Slower Growth in Federal Outlays

Because of spending discipline imposed by the 1990 legislation, growth in federal outlays slowed compared to the 1980s. What's more, the collapse of the Soviet Union reduced U.S. military commitments abroad. Between 1990 and 2000, military personnel dropped one-third and defense spending dropped 30 percent in real terms. An additional impetus for slower spending growth came from Republicans, who attained congressional majority in 1994. Between 1994 and 2000, domestic spending grew little in real terms. Another beneficial development was a drop in interest rates, which fell to their lowest level in thirty years, saving billions in interest charges on the national debt. In short, federal outlays dropped from 21.6 percent relative to GDP in 1990 to 18.2 percent in 2000. Again, if federal outlays remained the same percentage of GDP in 2000 as in 1990, spending in 2000 would have been \$330 billion higher than it was.

A Reversal of Fortune in 2001

Thanks to the tax-rate increases and the strong economy, revenues gushed into Washington, growing an average of 8.4 percent per year between 1993 and 2000. Meanwhile, federal outlays remained in check, growing only 3.5 percent per year. By 2000, that combination created a federal budget surplus of \$236 billion, quite a turnaround from a deficit that had topped \$290 billion in 1992. But in 2001 unemployment increased, the stock market sank, and terrorists crashed jets and spread anthrax. All this slowed federal revenues and accelerated federal spending. To counter the recession and cope with terrorism, Congress and the president cut taxes and increased federal spending. As a result, the federal budget surplus returned to a deficit by 2002 and has been in the red ever since. The era of federal budget surpluses was short-lived.

Trillion Dollar Deficits

The financial crisis of 2008 and the recession of 2007–2009 increased budget deficits for two reasons. On the revenue side, falling employment, income, and profits cut tax receipts. Discretionary tax cuts reduced revenue even more. On the spending side, automatic stabilizers such as unemployment benefits and welfare payments increased federal outlays, as did discretionary spending such as bailouts and the \$862 billion stimulus plan. The federal deficit climbed from \$161 billion in 2007 to \$459 billion in 2008 to \$1.4 billion in 2009. President Obama's budget projected deficits of \$1.5 trillion in 2010 and \$1.4 trillion in 2011. As if all that isn't problematic enough, two major programs spell more trouble for the federal budget in the long run, as discussed in the case study, "Public Policy: Reforming Social Security and Medicare" at the end of the book.

The Relative Size of the Public Sector

So far, we have focused on the federal budget, but a fuller picture includes state and local governments as well. For added context, we can look at government budgets over time compared to other major economies. Exhibit 4 shows government outlays at all levels relative to GDP in 10 industrial economies in 1992 and in 2011. Government outlays in the United States relative to GDP increased from 39 percent in 1992 to 41 percent in 2011. Despite the increase, the United States is projected to have a smaller public sector in 2011 than all but one of the other listed countries. Outlays relative to GDP increased in five of the major economies and decreased in five. The ten-country average remains at 46 percent. Government grew the most in Japan, rising from 33 percent relative to GDP in 1992 to 42 percent in 2011. Two decades of trying to stimulate the Japanese economy swelled the public sector. Government spending shrank the most in Canada, dropping from 53 percent to 43 percent relative to GDP.

Let's now turn our attention to a consequence of federal deficits—a sizable federal debt.

EXHIBIT 4 Government Outlays as a Percentage of GDP in 1992 and 2011

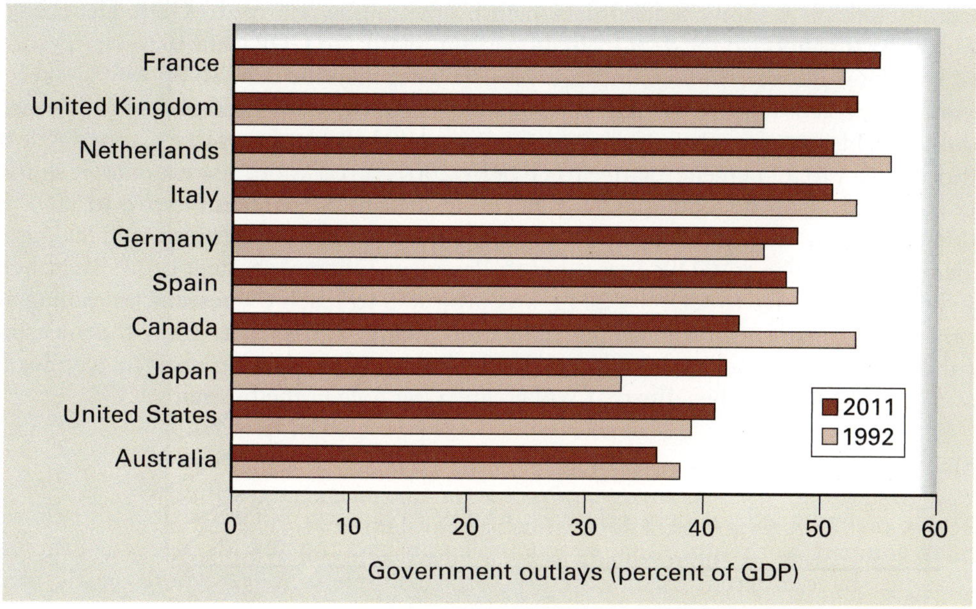

Government outlays relative to GDP increased in 5 of the 10 industrial economies between 1992 and 2010. The ten-country average remained unchanged at 46 percent. In the United States, the percentage increased from 39 to 41.

Source: Developed from figures available in *OECD Economic Outlook*, Vol. 87 (May 2011), Annex Table 25. Figures for 2011 are estimates. For the latest data, go to http://www.oecd.org/home/, click on "Statistics," then find the most recent issue of *OECD Economic Outlook*.

The National Debt

Federal deficits add up. It took 39 presidents, six wars, the Great Depression, and more than two hundred years for the federal debt to reach $1 trillion, as it did in 1981. It took only 5 presidents and another thirty years for that debt increase sevenfold in real terms, as it did by 2011. The federal deficit is a flow variable measuring the amount by which outlays exceed revenues in a particular year. The federal debt, or the **national debt**, is a stock variable measuring the net accumulation of past deficits, the amount owed by the federal government. This section puts the national debt in perspective by looking at (1) changes over time, (2) U.S. debt levels compared with those in other countries, (3) interest payments on the debt, (4) who bears the burden of the debt, and (5) what impact does the debt have on the nation's capital formation. Note that the national debt ignores the projected liabilities of Social Security, Medicare, other health-care entitlements or other federal retirement programs. If these liabilities were included, the national debt would easily double.

national debt
The net accumulation of federal budget deficits

Measuring the National Debt

In talking about the national debt, we should distinguish between the gross debt and debt held by the public. The *gross debt* includes U.S. Treasury securities purchased by various federal agencies. Because the federal government owes this debt to itself, analysts often focus instead on *debt held by the public*, which includes U.S. Treasury securities held by households, firms, banks (including Federal Reserve Banks), and foreign entities. As of 2011, the gross federal debt stood at $15.1 trillion, and the debt held by the public stood at $10.5 trillion.

One way to measure debt over time is relative to the economy's production and income, or GDP (just as a bank might compare the size of a mortgage to a borrower's income). Exhibit 5 shows federal debt held by the public relative to GDP. The cost of World War II ballooned the debt from 44 percent relative to GDP in 1940 to 109 percent in 1946. After the war, the economy grew much faster than the debt, so by 1980, debt fell to only 26 percent relative to GDP. But high deficits in the 1980s and early 1990s nearly doubled debt to 49 percent relative to GDP by 1993. Budget surpluses from 1998 to 2001 cut debt to 33 percent relative to GDP by 2001. A recession, a stock market slump, tax cuts, and higher federal spending increased debt to 37 percent relative to GDP in 2004, where it remained through 2007. Deficits from the 2007–2009 recession increased federal debt relative to GDP. According to President Obama's budget office, debt held by the public relative to GDP by 2011 was projected to reach 69 percent, exceeding all years except those during and immediately after World War II.[1] But, again, this measure of the debt ignores the fact that the federal government is on the hook to pay Social Security and Medicare benefits that will create a big hole in the budget.

International Perspective on Public Debt

Exhibit 5 shows federal debt relative to GDP over time, but how does the United States compare with other major economies around the world? Because different economies have different fiscal structures—for example some rely more on a central

EXHIBIT 5 Federal Debt Held by the Public as Percent of GDP Spiked Recently

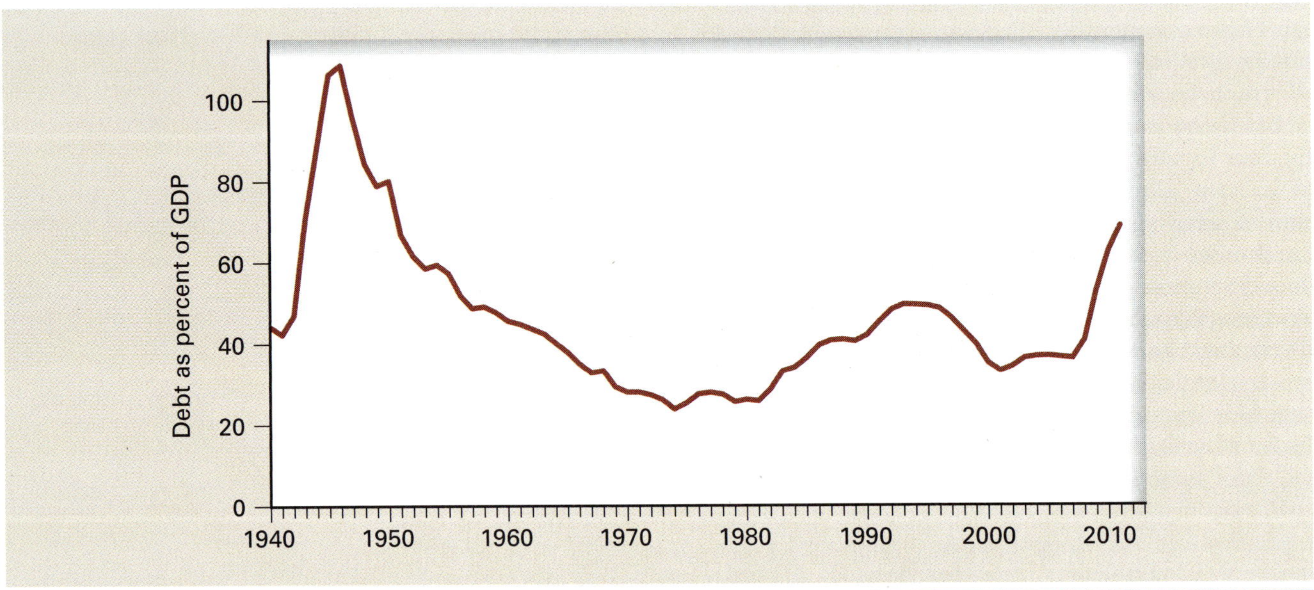

The huge cost of World War II rocketed federal debt from 44 percent of GDP in 1940 to over 100 percent by 1946. During the next few decades, GDP grew faster than federal debt so by 1980, federal debt had dropped to only 26 percent of GDP. But high deficits in recent years increased federal debt to 69 percent relative to GDP by 2011.

Source: Fiscal year figures from the *Economic Report of the President*, February 2010, Table 78, plus updates and projections for 2010 and 2011 from *Mid-Session Review: Budget of the U.S. Government Fiscal Year 2011*, Office of Management and Budget, July 2010, at http://www.whitehouse.gov/omb/assets/fy2011_msr/11msr.pdf. For the latest data go to http://www.gpoaccess.gov/eop/.

1. *Mid-Session Review: Budget of the U.S. Government Fiscal Year 2011*, Office of Management and Budget, July 2010, at http://www.whitehouse.gov/omb/assets/fy2011_msr/11msr.pdf.

EXHIBIT 6 Relative to GDP, U.S. Net Public Debt Above Average for Major Economies in 2011

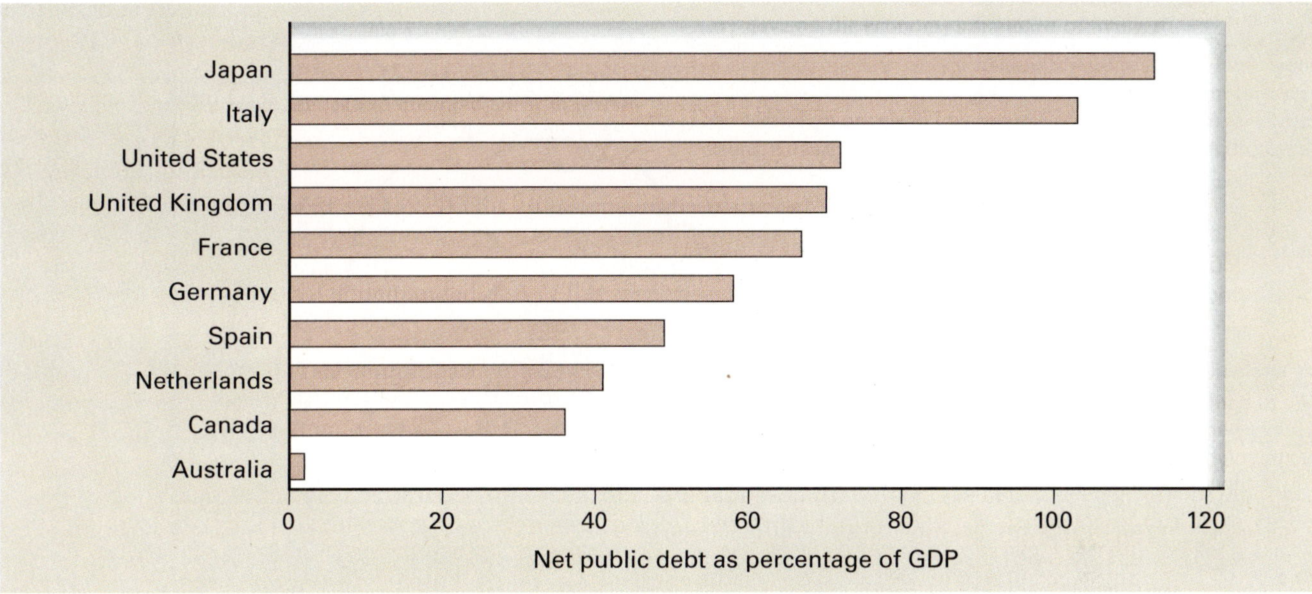

Source: *OECD Economic Outlook*, 87 (May 2010), Annex Table 33. Figures are projections for net debt at all levels of government in 2011. For the latest data, go to http://www.oecd.org/home/, click on "Statistics," then find the latest *OECD Economic Outlook*.

government—we should consider the debt at all government levels. Exhibit 6 compares the net government debt in the United States relative to GDP with those of nine other industrial countries. *Net debt* includes outstanding liabilities of federal, state, and local governments minus government financial assets, such as loans to students and farmers, securities, cash on hand, and foreign exchange on reserve. Net debt for the 10 nations was projected to average 61 percent in 2011 relative to GDP, somewhat below the United States figure of 72 percent (remember this is for all levels of government, not just the federal level). Australia was the lowest with only 2 percent net debt, and Japan was the highest at 113 percent relative to GDP. Much of Japan's debt was taken on during the "lost decade" of the 1990s as the government borrowed to fund efforts to stimulate the ailing economy. The United States ranked third among the 10 industrialized nations, up from fifth a decade ago. Thus, although the United States ranks low in public outlays relative to GDP, the country ranks high in public debt relative to GDP. That's because we have been running big deficits for decades, and really big ones lately.

Interest on the National Debt

Purchasers of federal securities range from individuals who buy $25 U.S. savings bonds to institutions that buy $1 million Treasury securities. Because most Treasury securities are short term, nearly half the debt is refinanced every year. Based on a $10.5 trillion debt held by the public in 2011, a 1 percentage point increase in the nominal interest rate ultimately increases interest costs by $105 billion a year.

Exhibit 7 shows interest on the federal debt held by the public as a percentage of federal outlays since 1960. After remaining relatively constant for two decades, interest payments climbed in the 1980s because growing deficits added to the debt and because of higher interest rates. Interest payments peaked at 15.4 percent of outlays in 1996,

EXHIBIT 7 Interest Payments on Federal Debt Held by the Public as Percentage of Federal Outlays Peaked in 1996

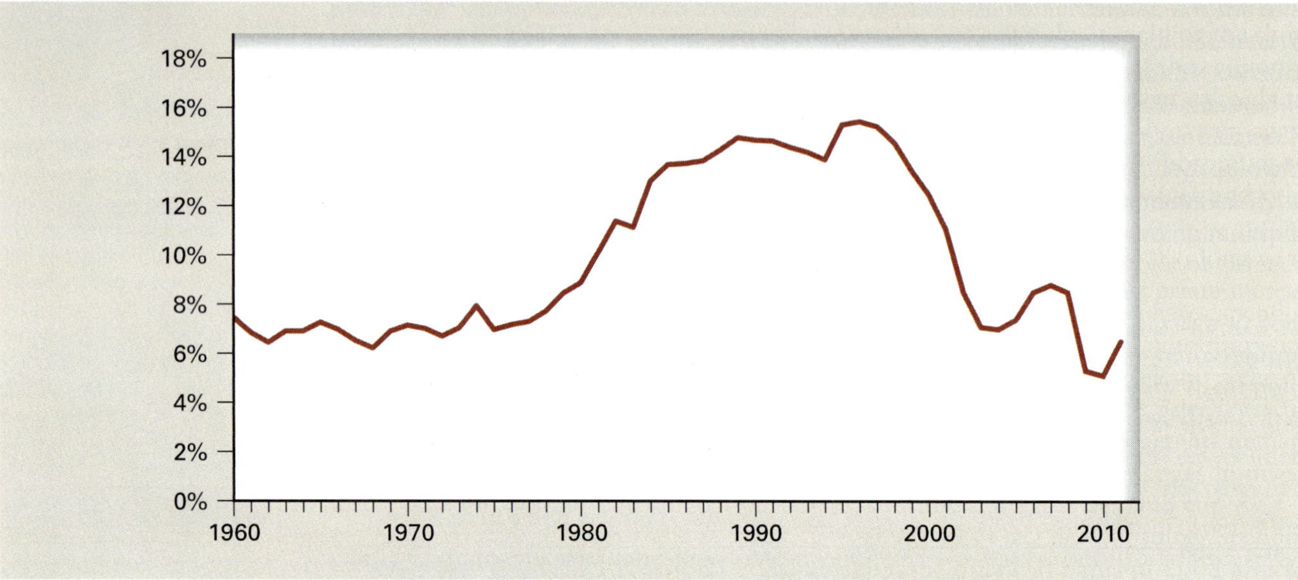

After remaining relatively constant during the 1960s and 1970s, interest payments as a share of federal outlays climbed during the 1980s and early 1990s because of growing deficits and higher interest rates. After peaking in 1996 at 15.4 percent of outlays, interest payments declined first because of budget surpluses and later because of declining interest rates.

Source: *Economic Report of the President*, February 2010. Figures for 2010 and 2011 are estimates based on the president's 2011 budget. For the latest figures, go to http://www.gpoaccess.gov/eop/.

then began falling first because of budget surpluses and later because of lower interest rates. By 2011, interest payments were expected to be 6.5 percent of outlays, the same as in 1972; the drop was due to record low interest rates. Interest's share of federal outlays will climb as debt grows and as interest rates rise from historic lows of recent years. For example, if the average interest rate paid by the federal government was 5 percent, instead of the record low rates actually paid, annual interest payments on a public debt of $10.5 trillion would be $525 billion, or 16.1 percent of federal outlays in 2011.

Are Persistent Deficits Sustainable?

Given that deficits have been with us so long, we might ask: How long can the country run a deficit? The short answer is: As long as lenders are willing to finance that deficit at reasonable interest rates. And that depends on the confidence that lenders have about getting repaid. At some point, chronic deficits may accumulate into such a debt that lenders demand an extremely high interest rate or refuse to lend at all. As interest rates rise, debt service costs could then overwhelm the budget.

U.S. government securities have been considered the safest in the world, and this has helped us finance our chronic deficits and rising debt. Ironically, the global financial panic encouraged investors around the globe to buy U.S. securities as they sought safety. This "flight to quality" drove down the interest rate the U.S. government had to pay, thus reducing the cost of servicing our debt. But that could change. Greece had little trouble borrowing until 2010, when the financial community decided the government debt there had become too high and therefore too risky.

Countries can continue to run deficits as long as the cost of servicing the resulting debt remains manageable. Suppose that debt service, which consists almost entirely of interest payments, remains at 10 percent or less of the federal budget. Something like that would appear to be sustainable (since 1960, U.S. debt service payments have averaged 9.8 percent of federal outlays). More generally, government could still run a deficit year after year, and the dollar amount of the deficit might even rise. As long as the economy is growing at least as fast as the debt service payments, those deficits should be manageable. But trillion dollar deficits are not sustainable.

Who Bears the Burden of the Debt?

Deficit spending is a way of billing future taxpayers for current spending. The national debt raises moral questions about the right of one generation to bequeath to the next generation the burden of its borrowing. To what extent do deficits and debt shift the burden to future generations? Let's examine two arguments about the burden of the federal debt.

We Owe It to Ourselves

It is often argued that the debt is not a burden to future generations because, although future generations must service the debt, those same generations receive the payments. It's true that if U.S. citizens forgo present consumption to buy bonds, they or their heirs will be repaid, so debt service payments stay in the country. Thus, future generations both service the debt and receive the payments. In that sense, the debt is not a burden on future generations. It's all in the family, so to speak.

Foreign Ownership of Debt

But the "we-owe-it-to-ourselves" argument does not apply to that portion of the national debt owed to foreigners. Foreigners who buy U.S. Treasury securities forgo present consumption and are paid back in the future. Foreign buyers reduce the amount of current consumption that Americans must sacrifice to finance a deficit. *A reliance on foreigners, however, increases the burden of the debt on future generations of Americans because future debt service payments no longer remain in the country.* Foreigners held 46 percent of all federal debt held by the public in 2010, triple the share of two decades ago. So the burden of the debt on future generations of Americans has increased both absolutely and relatively.

Exhibit 8 shows the major foreign holders of U.S. Treasury securities in April 2010, when foreigners held a total of $4.0 trillion of U.S. debt. China was the leader with $900 billion, or 23 percent of foreign-held U.S. debt. Japan ranks second, and the United Kingdom third. Together, Asian countries (including some not shown) had more than half of foreign-held federal debt. Despite the growth in federal debt, U.S. Treasury securities are considered the safest in the world because they are backed by the U.S. government. Whenever there is trouble around the world, investors flock to U.S. Treasury securities in a "flight to quality." Some other countries have proven to be less trustworthy borrowers. Argentina, Mexico, and Russia, for example, defaulted on some national debt.

Crowding Out and Capital Formation

As we have seen, government borrowing can drive up interest rates, crowding out some private investment. The long-run effect of deficit spending depends on how the government spends the borrowed funds. If the funds are invested in better highways and

EXHIBIT 8 Largest Foreign Holders of U.S. Treasury Securities as of April 2010 (in billions and as percent of foreign holdings)

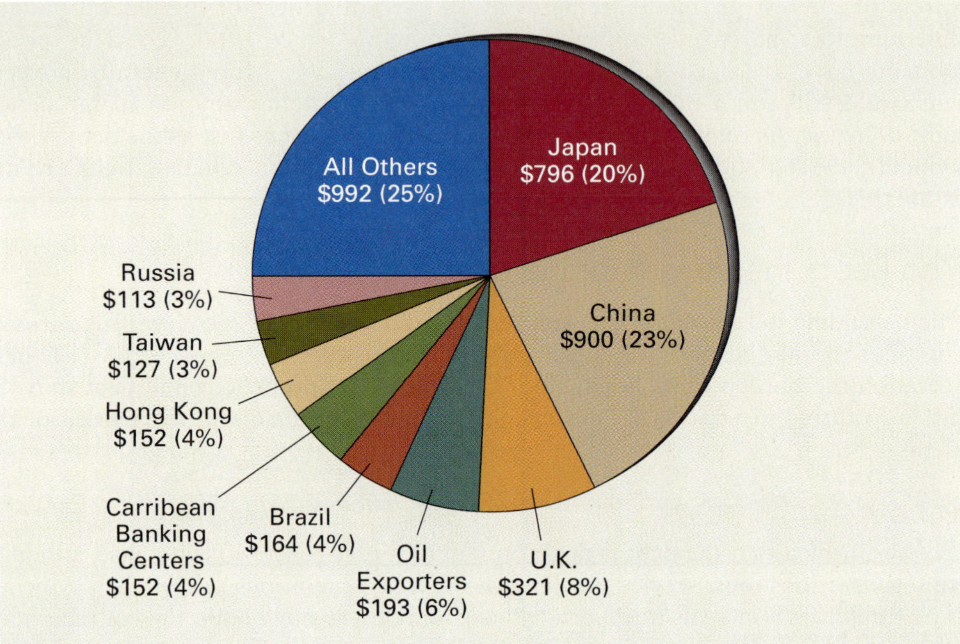

Source: Developed based on country totals from the U.S. Treasury Department at www.ustreas.gov/tic/mfh.txt. Caribbean Banks include the Bahamas, Bermuda, the Cayman Islands, and Panama.

a more educated workforce, this could enhance productivity in the long run. If, however, borrowed dollars go toward current expenditures such as more farm subsidies or higher retirement benefits, less capital formation results. With less investment today, there will be less capital in the future, thus hurting labor productivity and our future standard of living.

Ironically, despite the large federal deficits during the last few decades, public investments in roads, bridges, and airports—so-called *public capital*—declined, perhaps because a growing share of the federal budget goes toward income redistribution, especially for the elderly. The United States spent 3 percent of GDP building and maintaining the public infrastructure between 1950 and 1970. Since 1980 that share has averaged only 2 percent. Some argue that declining investment in the public infrastructure slows productivity growth. For example, the failure to invest sufficiently in airports and in the air traffic control system has led to congested air travel and flight delays, a problem compounded by the threat of terrorism. The $862 billion stimulus package approved in February 2009 was supposed to fund "shovel-ready" infrastructure improvements such as repairing crumbling roads and bridges. But surprisingly little went into such programs.

Government deficits of one generation can affect the standard of living of the next. Note again that our current measure of the national debt does not capture all burdens passed on to future generations. As mentioned earlier, if the unfunded liabilities of government retirement programs, especially Medicare, were included, this would more than double the national debt. A model that considers some intergenerational issues of public budgeting is discussed in the case study at the end of the book, "Public Policy: An Intergenerational View of Deficits and Debt."

Conclusion

John Maynard Keynes introduced the idea that federal deficit spending is an appropriate fiscal policy when private aggregate demand is insufficient to achieve potential output. The federal budget has not been the same since. Beginning in 1960, the federal budget was in deficit every year but one until 1998. And beginning in the early 1980s, large federal deficits dominated the fiscal policy debate, which put discretionary fiscal policy on hold. But after peaking at $290 billion in 1992, the deficit disappeared later in the decade because of higher tax rates on high-income households, lower growth in federal outlays, and a rip-roaring economy fueled by faster labor productivity growth and a dazzling stock market. The softening economy of 2001 and the terrorist attacks brought discretionary fiscal policy back in the picture. A recession and weak recovery, tax cuts, and spending increases swelled the federal deficit by 2004 to more than $400 billion, rivaling deficits of the 1980s and early 1990s. But the addition of 8 million more jobs helped cut the deficit more than half by 2007. After that, the economy went bad. The recession of 2007–2009 cut federal revenue and spurred federal spending, both of which increased the deficit to $1.4 trillion in 2009 and $1.5 trillion in 2010. Rising health care costs and the retirement of baby boomers will continue putting upward pressure on the deficit.

Monetary policy is the regulation of the money supply by the Federal Reserve. The next few chapters introduce money and financial institutions, review monetary policy, and discuss the impact of monetary and fiscal policy on economic stability and growth. Once we bring money into the picture, we consider yet another reason why the simple spending multiplier is overstated.

Summary

1. The federal budget process suffers from a variety of problems, including overlapping committee jurisdictions, lengthy budget deliberations, budgeting by continuing resolutions, budgeting in too much detail, failure to distinguish between operating costs and capital costs, and a lack of control over most of the budget. Suggested improvements include instituting a biennial budget, budgeting in less detail, and distinguishing between an operating budget and a capital budget.
2. Deficits increase during wars and severe recessions, but deficits remained high during the economic expansions of the 1980s. Those deficits arose from a combination of tax cuts during the early 1980s and growth in federal spending.
3. To the extent that deficits crowd out private capital formation, this decline in private investment reduces the economy's ability to grow. This is one cost of deficit spending. Foreign holdings of debt also impose a burden on future generations because debt payments go to foreigners. Thus, the deficits of one generation of Americans can reduce the standard of living of the next.
4. After peaking at $290 billion in 1992, the federal deficit turned into a surplus by 1998 because of higher tax rates, reduced outlays especially for defense, declining interest rates, and a strengthening economy fueled by growing labor productivity.
5. The recession of 2001 and terrorist attacks prompted tax cuts to "get the economy moving again." The weak recovery plus the tax cuts and federal spending increases all contributed to a growing federal deficit, which topped $400 billion in 2004. But by 2007 a growing economy helped cut the federal deficit by more than 50 percent. The recession of 2007–2009 cut federal revenue and spurred federal spending, both of which increased the deficit to $1.4 trillion in 2009 and $1.5 trillion in 2010. The longer term looks even bleaker as baby boomers begin retiring, prompting more spending for Social Security and Medicare.
6. Most recently the U.S. federal debt measured relative to GDP was above average for major industrial countries and was relatively high compared to U.S. historical levels stretching back to 1940. The recent recession and policy responses to it have rocketed the federal deficit above $1 trillion and sharply increased the national debt. Something has to give.

Key Concepts

Federal budget 538
Budget resolution 539
Continuing resolutions 539
Entitlement programs 540
Annually balanced budget 541
Cyclically balanced budget 542
Functional finance 542
Crowding out 543
Crowding in 544
National debt 547

Questions for Review

1. THE FEDERAL BUDGET PROCESS The federal budget passed by Congress and signed by the president shows the relationship between *budgeted* expenditures and *projected* revenues. Why does the budget require a forecast of the economy? Under what circumstances would actual government spending and tax revenue fail to match the budget as approved?
2. THE FEDERAL BUDGET PROCESS In what sense is the executive branch of the U.S. government always dealing with three budgets?
3. THE BUDGET PROCESS In terms of the policy lags described in the previous chapter, discuss the following issues associated with the budget process:
   a. Continuing resolutions
   b. Uncontrollable budget items
   c. Overly detailed budget
4. BUDGET PHILOSOPHIES Explain the differences among an annually balanced budget, a cyclically balanced budget, and functional finance. How does each affect economic fluctuations?
5. BUDGET PHILOSOPHIES One alternative to balancing the budget annually or cyclically is to produce a government budget that would be balanced if the economy were at potential output. Given the cyclical nature of government tax revenues and spending, how would the resulting budget deficit or surplus vary over the business cycle?
6. BUDGET PHILOSOPHIES The functional finance approach to budget deficits would set the federal budget to promote an economy operating at potential output. What problems would you expect if the country were to employ this kind of budgetary philosophy?
7. CROWDING OUT Is it possible for U.S. federal budget deficits to crowd out investment spending in other countries? How could German or British investment be hurt by large U.S. budget deficits?
8. CROWDING OUT How might federal deficits crowd out private domestic investment? How could this crowding out affect future living standards?
9. INTEREST ON THE DEBT Why did interest payments on the national debt fall from 15.4 percent of the federal budget in 1996 to 6.5 percent in 2011? Why is this percentage expected to increase in the future?
10. BURDEN OF THE DEBT Suppose that budget deficits are financed to a considerable extent by foreigners. How does this create a potential burden on future generations of Americans?
11. THE TWIN DEFICITS How is the U.S. budget deficit related to the foreign trade deficit?
12. THE SHORT-LIVED BUDGET SURPLUS Why did the federal budget go from a huge deficit in 1992 to a surplus in 1998? Explain the factors that contributed to the turnaround.
13. Case Study: Reforming Social Security and Medicare (See page 762.) Why are the Social Security and Medicare programs headed for trouble? When will the trouble begin? What solutions have been proposed?
14. CROWDING OUT AND CAPITAL FORMATION In earlier chapters, we've seen that the government can increase GDP in the short run by running a budget deficit. What are some long-term effects of deficit spending?
15. Case Study: An Intergenerational View of Deficits and Debt (See page 763.) Explain why Robert Barro argues that if parents are concerned enough about the future welfare of their children, the effects of deficit spending on the economy will be neutralized.
16. THE PRIVATE SECTOR Look at Exhibit 4. How have government outlays as a percent of GDP changed in the industrial countries depicted between 1992 and 2011? What explains the average trend in these economies?

Problems and Exercises

17. THE NATIONAL DEBT Try the following exercises to better understand how the national debt is related to the government's budget deficit.

    a. Assume that the gross national debt initially is equal to \$3 trillion and the federal government then runs a deficit of \$300 billion:
        i. What is the new level of gross national debt?
        ii. If 100 percent of the deficit is financed by the sale of securities to federal agencies, what happens to the amount of debt held by the public? What happens to the level of gross debt?
        iii. If GDP increased by 5 percent in the same year that the deficit is run, what happens to gross debt as a percentage of GDP? What happens to the level of debt held by the public as a percentage of GDP?

    b. Now suppose that the gross national debt initially is equal to \$2.5 trillion and the federal government then runs a deficit of \$100 billion:
        i. What is the new level of gross national debt?
        ii. If 100 percent of this deficit is financed by the sale of securities to the public, what happens to the level of debt held by the public? What happens to the level of gross debt?
        iii. If GDP increases by 6 percent in the same year as the deficit is run, what happens to gross debt as a percentage of GDP? What happens to the level of debt held by the public as a percentage of GDP?

Global Economic Watch Exercises

Login to www.cengagebrain.com and access the Global Economic Watch to do these exercises.

18. GLOBAL ECONOMIC WATCH Go to the Global Economic Crisis Resource Center. Select Global Issues in Context. In the Basic Search box at the top of the page, enter the phrase "in defense of debt." On the Results page, go to the Global Viewpoints Section. Click on the link for the March 15, 2010, editorial "In Defense of Debt." Why was the author not concerned about the high U.S. national debt?

19. GLOBAL ECONOMIC WATCH Go to the Global Economic Crisis Resource Center. Select Global Issues in Context. In the Basic Search box at the top of the page, enter the phrase "balanced budget." Choose one article from the past two years about your home country and one article from the past two years about a foreign country. Compare and contrast attitudes toward balanced national budgets.

Money and the Financial System

28

© Richard Wong/www.rwongphoto.com/Alamy

- Why are you willing to exchange a piece of paper bearing Alexander Hamilton's portrait and the number 10 in each corner for a pepperoni pizza with extra cheese?
- Has the penny outlived its usefulness?
- If Russia can't pay its bills, why don't they simply print more rubles?
- Because money is banned in federal prisons, what do inmates use instead?
- What's the difference between the *Fed* and the *Feds*?
- Why was someone able to cash a check written on a clean but frayed pair of underpants?

These and other questions are answered in this chapter, which introduces money and banking.

The word *money* comes from the name of the goddess (*Juno Moneta*) in whose temple Rome's money was coined. Money has come to symbolize all personal and business finance. You can read *Money* magazine and the "Money" section of *USA Today*, and visit Web sites such as money.cnn.com, moneycentral.msn.com/home.asp, and smartmoney.com (a Google search for "money" returned over a billion hits).

With money, you can articulate your preferences—after all, money talks. And when it talks, it says a lot, as in, "Put your money where your mouth is" and "Show me the money." Money is the grease that lubricates the wheels of market exchange (in fact, an old expression "grease the palm" means to pay someone). Just as grease makes for an easier fit among gears, money reduces the friction—the transaction costs—of exchange. Too little leaves some parts creaking; too much gums up the works.

This chapter is obviously about money. We begin with the evolution of money, tracing its use in broad strokes from primitive economies to our own. Then we turn to developments in the United States.

Topics discussed in this chapter include:

- Barter
- Functions of money
- Commodity and fiat money
- The Federal Reserve System
- Depository institutions
- U.S. banking structure
- Subprime mortgages
- Mortgage-backed securities

The Evolution of Money

In the beginning, there was no money. The earliest families were largely self-sufficient. Each produced all it consumed and consumed all it produced, so there was little need for exchange. Without exchange, there was no need for money. When specialization first emerged, as some people went hunting and others took up farming, hunters and farmers had to trade. Thus, the specialization of labor resulted in exchange, but the assortment of goods traded was limited enough that people could easily exchange their products directly for other products—a system called *barter.*

Barter and the Double Coincidence of Wants

double coincidence of wants
Two traders are willing to exchange their products directly

Barter depends on a **double coincidence of wants,** which occurs when one trader is willing to exchange his or her product for something another trader has to offer. If a hunter was willing to exchange hides for a farmer's corn, that was a coincidence. But if the farmer was also willing to exchange corn for the hunter's hides, that was a double coincidence—a *double coincidence of wants.* As long as specialization was limited, to, say, two or three goods, mutually beneficial trades were relatively easy to come by—that is, trade wasn't much of a coincidence. As specialization increased, however, finding the particular goods that each trader wanted became more difficult.

In a barter system, traders must not only discover a double coincidence of wants, they must also agree on an exchange rate. How many bushels of corn should the hunter get for a hide? If only two goods are traded, only one exchange rate needs to be worked out. As the variety of goods traded increases, however, exchange rates multiply. Specialization increased the transaction costs of barter. A huge difference in the values of the units to be exchanged also made barter difficult. For example, a hunter wanting to buy a home that exchanged for 1,000 hides would be hard-pressed finding a home seller needing that many. High transaction costs of barter gave birth to money.

The Earliest Money and Its Functions

Nobody actually recorded the emergence of money. We can only speculate about how it first came into use. Through experience with barter, traders may have found they could always find buyers for certain goods. If a trader could not find a good that he or she desired personally, some other good with a ready market could be accepted instead. So traders began to accept a certain good not for immediate consumption but because that good could be easily traded later. For example, corn might become acceptable because traders knew that it was always in demand. As one good became generally accepted in return for all other goods, that good began to function as **money**. *Any commodity that acquires a high degree of acceptability throughout an economy becomes money.*

money
Anything that is generally accepted in exchange for goods and services

Money fulfills three important functions: a *medium of exchange,* a *unit of account,* and a *store of value.* Let's consider each.

Medium of Exchange

Separating the sale of one good from the purchase of another requires an item acceptable to all involved in the transactions. If a society, by luck or by design, can find a commodity that everyone accepts in exchange for whatever is sold, traders can save time, disappointment, and sheer aggravation. Suppose corn takes on this role, a role that clearly goes beyond its role as food. We then call corn a medium of exchange because it is accepted in exchange by all buyers and sellers, whether or not they want corn to eat. A **medium of exchange** is anything that is generally accepted in payment for goods and services. The person who accepts corn in exchange for some product believes corn can be traded later for whatever is desired.

medium of exchange
Anything that facilitates trade by being generally accepted by all parties in payment for goods or services

commodity money
Anything that serves both as money and as a commodity; money that has intrinsic value such as gold or silver coins

In this example, corn is both a *commodity* and *money,* so we call it **commodity money**. The earliest money was commodity money. Gold and silver have been used as money for at least four thousand years. Cattle served as money, first for the Greeks, then for the Romans. In fact, the word *pecuniary* (meaning "of or relating to money") comes from the Latin word for cattle, *pecus*. Likewise, the word *fee* comes from the Old English word *feoh*, which also meant cattle. Roman soldiers received part of their pay in salt bricks; the salt portion was called the *salarium,* the origin of the word *salary*. Also used as money were wampum (strings of polished shells) and tobacco in colonial America, tea pressed into small cakes in Russia, rice in Japan, and palm dates in North Africa. Note that commodity money is a good, not a service; a service is intangible and cannot be held for later exchange.

Unit of Account

A commodity such as corn that grows to be widely accepted becomes a **unit of account**, a standard on which prices are based. The price of hides or shoes or pots is measured in bushels of corn. Thus, corn serves not only as a medium of exchange; it also becomes a common denominator, a yardstick, for *measuring the value* of each product exchanged in the economy. Rather than having to determine exchange rates among all products, as with a barter economy, people can price everything using a single measure, such as corn. For example, if a pair of shoes sells for 2 bushels of corn and a 5-gallon pot sells for 1 bushel of corn, then a pair of shoes has the same value in exchange as two 5-gallon pots.

unit of account
A common unit for measuring the value of each good or service

Store of Value

Because people do not want to buy something every time they sell something, the purchasing power acquired through a sale must somehow be preserved. Money serves as a **store of value** when it retains purchasing power over time. The better it preserves purchasing power, the better money serves as a store of value, and the more willing people are to hold it. Consider again the distinction between a stock and a flow. Recall that a *stock* is an amount measured at a particular point in time, such as the amount of food in your refrigerator, or the amount of money you have with you right now. In contrast, a *flow* is an amount per unit of time, such as the calories you consume per day, or the income you earn per week. *Money* is a stock and *income* is a flow. Don't confuse money with income. The role of money as a stock is best reflected by money's role as a store of value.

store of value
Anything that retains its purchasing power over time

Properties of the Ideal Money

The introduction of commodity money reduced the transaction costs of exchange compared with barter, but commodity money also involves some transaction costs. First, if the commodity money is perishable, as is corn, it must be properly stored or its quality deteriorates; even then, it won't maintain its quality for long. U.S. coins have a projected life of 30 years (a dollar note, only 18 months). So the ideal money should be *durable*. Second, if the commodity money is bulky, major purchases can become unwieldy. For example, truckloads of corn would be needed to purchase a home selling for 5,000 bushels of corn. So the ideal money should be *portable*, or easily carried. Dollar notes are easier to carry than dollar coins, which may explain why dollar coins never became popular in the United States. Third, some commodity money was not easily divisible into smaller units. For example, when cattle served as money, any price involving a fraction of a cow posed an exchange problem. So the ideal money should be *divisible*.

Fourth, if commodity money like corn is valued equally in exchange, regardless of its quality, people eat the best corn and trade away the rest. As a result, the quality remaining in circulation declines, reducing its acceptability. Sir Thomas Gresham wrote back in the 16th century that "bad money drives out good money"; this has come to be known as **Gresham's law**. People tend to trade away inferior money and hoard the best. Over time, the quality of money in circulation becomes less acceptable and, therefore, less useful as a medium of exchange. To avoid this problem, the ideal money should be of *uniform quality*.

Gresham's law
People tend to trade away inferior money and hoard the best

Fifth, commodity money usually ties up otherwise valuable resources, so it has a higher opportunity cost than, say, paper money. For example, corn that is used for money cannot at the same time be used for corn on the cob, corn flour, popcorn, corn chips, other food, corn oil, and biofuel. So the ideal money should have *a low opportunity cost*.

If the supply or demand for money fluctuates unpredictably, so will the economy's price level, and this is the final problem with commodity money. For example, if a bumper crop increases the supply of corn, more corn is required to purchase other goods. This we call *inflation*. Likewise, any change in the demand for corn *as food* from, say, the growing popularity of corn chips, would affect the exchange value of corn. Erratic fluctuations in the market for corn limit its usefulness as money, particularly as a unit of account and a store of value. So the ideal money *should maintain a relatively stable value over time*. Money supplied by a responsible issuing authority is likely to retain its value better over time than money whose supply depends on uncontrollable forces of nature such as good or bad growing seasons.

What all this boils down to is that the ideal money is durable, portable, divisible, of uniform quality, has a low opportunity cost, and is relatively stable in value. These qualities are reinforced in Exhibit 1, which also lists the rationale, good examples, and bad examples. Please spend a minute now reviewing the table. Read and consider the case study at the end of the book, "Bringing Theory to Life: Mackerel Economics in Federal Prisons," which shows how a commodity money emerged where currency was prohibited.

Coins

The division of commodity money into units was often natural, as in bushels of corn or heads of cattle. When rock salt was used as money, it was cut into uniform bricks. Because salt was usually of consistent quality, a trader had only to count the bricks to determine the amount of money. When silver and gold were used as money, both their quantity and quality were open to question. First, the amount had to be weighed, so transactions required scales. Second, because precious metals could be *debased* with cheaper metals, the quality of the metal had to be determined with each exchange. This was a nuisance.

EXHIBIT 1 Six Properties of Ideal Money

Quality	Rationale	Good Examples	Bad Examples
1. Durable	Money should not wear out quickly	Coins; sea shells	Strawberries; seafood
2. Portable	Money should be easy to carry, even relatively large sums	Diamonds; paper money	Lead bars; potatoes
3. Divisible	Market exchange is easier if denominations support a range of possible prices	Honey; paper money and coins	Cattle; diamonds
4. Uniform Quality	If money is not of uniform quality, people will hoard the best and spend the rest, reducing the quality in circulation	Salt bricks; paper money; coins	Diamonds
5. Low Opportunity Cost	The fewer resources tied up in creating money, the more available for other uses	Iron coins; paper money	Gold coins; diamonds
6. Stable Value	People are more willing to accept and and hold money if they believe it will keep its value over time	Anything whose supply can be limited by the issuing authority, such as paper money	Farm crops

This quantity and quality control problem was addressed by coining precious metals. *Coinage determined both the quantity and the quality of the metal.* Coins allowed payment by count rather than by weight. A flat surface on which this money was counted came to be called the *counter,* a term still used today. Initially, an image was stamped on only one side of a coin, leaving the other side blank. But people began shaving precious metal from the blank side. To prevent this, images were stamped on both sides. But another problem arose because bits of metal could still be clipped from the coin's edge. To prevent clipping, coins were bordered with a well-defined rim. If you have a dime or a quarter, notice the tiny serrations on the edge. These serrations, throwbacks from the time when these coins were silver, reduced the chances of "getting clipped."

The power to issue coins was vested in the *seignior,* or feudal lord. Counterfeiting was considered an act of treason. If the face value of the coin exceeded the cost of coinage, minting coins was profitable. **Seigniorage** (pronounced "seen'-your-edge") refers to the profit earned by the seignior from coinage. **Token money** is money whose face value exceeds its production cost. Coins and paper money now in circulation in the United States are token money. For example, the 25-cent coin costs the U.S. Mint only about 9 cents to make. Minting 25-cent coins nets the U.S. Treasury hundreds of millions of dollars a year in seigniorage. But the penny and even the nickel now cost more to mint than they are worth in exchange, a problem discussed in the case study, "Bringing Theory to Life: The Hassle of Small Change," at the end of the book.

seigniorage
The difference between the face value of money and the cost of supplying it; the "profit" from issuing money

token money
Money whose face value exceeds its cost of production

Money and Banking

The word *bank* comes from the Italian word *banca,* meaning "bench," which was a money changer's table. Banking spread from Italy to England, where London goldsmiths offered safekeeping for money and other valuables. The goldsmith gave depositors their money back on request, but because deposits by some tended to offset withdrawals by others, the amount of idle cash, or gold, in the vault changed little over time. Goldsmiths found that they could earn interest by lending from this pool of idle cash.

Goldsmiths offered depositors safekeeping, but visiting the goldsmith to get money to pay for each purchase became a nuisance. For example, a farmer might visit the goldsmith to withdraw enough money to buy a horse. The farmer would then pay the horse trader, who would promptly deposit the receipts with the goldsmith. Thus, money took a round-trip from goldsmith to farmer to horse trader and back to goldsmith. Because depositors soon grew tired of visiting the goldsmith every time they needed money, they began instructing the goldsmith to pay someone from their account. The payment amounted to moving gold from one stack (the farmer's) to another stack (the horse trader's). *These written instructions to the goldsmith were the first checks.* **Checks** have since become official looking, but they need not be, as evidenced by the actions of a Montana man who paid a speeding fine with instructions written on clean but frayed underpants. The Western Federal Savings and Loan of Missoula honored the check.

check
A written order instructing the bank to pay someone from an amount deposited

By combining the ideas of cash loans and checks, the goldsmith soon discovered how to make loans by check. Rather than lend idle cash, the goldsmith could simply create a checking balance for the borrower. *The goldsmith could extend a loan by creating an account against which the borrower could write checks. In this way goldsmiths, or banks, were able to create a medium of exchange, or to "create money."* This money, based only on an entry in the goldsmith's ledger, was accepted because of the public's confidence that these claims would be honored.

The total claims against the goldsmith consisted of claims by people who had deposited their money plus claims by borrowers for whom the goldsmith had created deposits. Because these claims exceeded the value of gold on reserve, this was the beginning of a **fractional reserve banking** system, a system in which bank reserves amounted to just a fraction of total deposits. The *reserve ratio* measured reserves as a percentage of total claims against the goldsmith, or total deposits. For example, if the goldsmith had reserves of $4,000 but deposits of $10,000, the reserve ratio would be 40 percent. The goldsmith was relying on the fact that not everyone would ask for their deposits at the same time.

fractional reserve banking system
Bank reserves amount to only a fraction of funds on deposit with the bank

Representative Money and Fiat Money

Another way a bank could create money was by issuing bank notes. **Bank notes** were pieces of paper promising the bearer specific amounts of gold or silver when the notes were presented to the issuing bank for redemption. In London, goldsmith bankers introduced bank notes about the same time they introduced checks. *Whereas checks could be redeemed only if endorsed by the payee, notes could be redeemed by anyone who presented them.* Paper money was often "as good as gold," because the bearer could redeem it for gold. In fact, paper money was more convenient than gold because it was less bulky and more portable. Bank notes that exchanged for a specific commodity, such as gold, were called **representative money**. The paper money *represented* gold in the bank's vault.

bank notes
Originally, pieces of paper promising a specific amount of gold or silver to anyone who presented them to issuing banks for redemption; today, Federal Reserve notes are mere paper money

representative money
Bank notes that exchange for a specific commodity, such as gold

The amount of paper money issued by a bank depended on that bank's estimate of the share of notes that would be redeemed. The higher the redemption rate, the fewer notes could be issued based on a given amount of reserves. Initially, these promises to pay were issued by private individuals or banks, but over time, governments took a larger role in printing and circulating notes. Once paper money became widely accepted, it was perhaps inevitable that governments would begin issuing **fiat money**, which derives its status as money from the power of the state, or by *fiat*. Fiat (pronounced "fee at") money is money because the government says so. The word *fiat* is from Latin and means "so be it." Fiat money is not redeemable for anything other than more fiat money; it is not backed by something of intrinsic value. You can think of fiat money as mere paper money. It is acceptable not because it is intrinsically useful or valuable—as is corn or gold—but because the government says it's money. Fiat money is declared **legal tender** by the government, meaning that you have made a valid and

fiat money
Money not redeemable for any commodity; its status as money is conferred initially by government decree but eventually by common experience

legal tender
U.S. currency that constitutes a valid and legal offer of payment of debt

legal offer of payment of your debt when you pay with such money. *Gradually, people came to accept fiat money because they believed that others would accept it as well.* The currency issued in the United States and throughout most of the world is fiat money.

A well-regulated system of fiat money is more efficient for an economy than commodity money. Fiat money uses only paper (a dollar note costs about 7 cents to make; the $100 note, about 10 cents), but commodity money ties up something intrinsically valuable. Paper money makes up only part of the money supply. Modern money also includes checking accounts, which are electronic entries in bank computers.

The Value of Money

Money has grown increasingly more abstract—from a physical commodity, to a piece of paper representing a claim on a physical commodity, to a piece of paper of no intrinsic value, to an electronic entry representing a claim on a piece of paper of no intrinsic value. So why does money have value? The commodity feature of early money bolstered confidence in its acceptability. Commodities such as corn, tobacco, and gold had value in use even if for some reason they became less acceptable in exchange. When paper money came into use, its acceptability was initially fostered by the promise to redeem it for gold or silver. But because most paper money throughout the world is now fiat money, there is no promise of redemption. So why can a piece of paper bearing the portrait of Alexander Hamilton and the number 10 in each corner be exchanged for a pizza or anything else selling for $10? *People accept these pieces of paper because, through experience, they believe that others will do the same.* The acceptability of money, which we now take for granted, is based on years of experience with the stability of its value and with the willingness of others to accept it as payment. As we will soon see, when money's value becomes questionable, so does its acceptability.

The *purchasing power* of money is the rate at which it exchanges for goods and services. The higher the price level in the economy, the less can be purchased with each dollar, so the less each dollar is worth. The purchasing power of each dollar over time varies inversely with the economy's price level. As the price level increases, the purchasing power of money falls. To measure the purchasing power of the dollar in a particular year, you first compute the price index for that year and then divide 100 by that price index. For example, relative to the base period of 1982 through 1984, the consumer price index for June 2010 was 217. The purchasing power of a dollar was therefore 100/217, or $0.46, measured in 1982–1984 dollars. Exhibit 2 shows the steady decline in the purchasing power of the dollar since 1960, when it was worth $3.38 in 1982–1984 dollars.

When Money Performs Poorly

One way to understand the functions of money is to look at instances where money did not perform well. In an earlier chapter, we examined hyperinflation in Zimbabwe. With prices growing by the hour, money no longer served as a reliable store of value, so workers couldn't wait to exchange their money for goods or for some "hard" currency—that is, a more stable currency. If inflation gets high enough, people no longer accept the nation's money and instead resort to some other means of exchange. On the other hand, if the supply of money dries up or if the price system is not allowed to function properly, barter may be the only alternative.

When the official currency fails to serve as a medium of exchange because of price controls or hyperinflation or when hoarding dries up money in circulation, some other means of exchange emerges. But this diverts more resources from production to exchange. A poorly functioning monetary system increases the transaction costs of

EXHIBIT 2 **Purchasing Power of $1.00 Measured in 1982–1984 Constant Dollars**

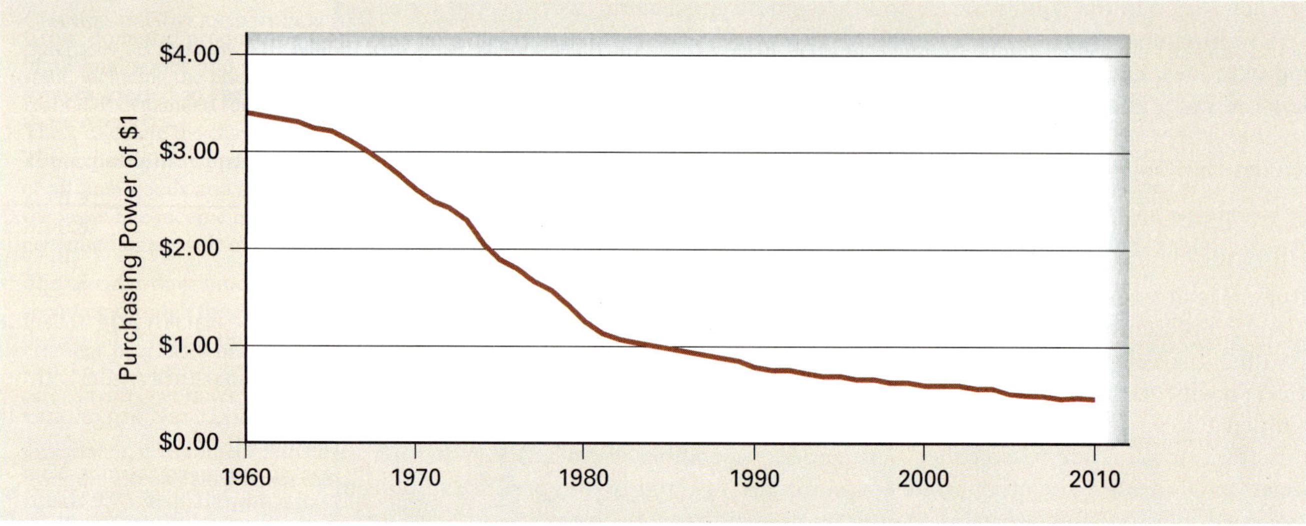

An increase in the price level over time reduces what $1.00 buys. Since 1960 the price level has risen every year except 2009, so the purchasing power of $1.00 (measured in 1982–1984 constant dollars) has fallen from $3.38 in 1960 to $0.46 in 2010.

Source: Developed using CPI figures from the U.S. Bureau of Labor Statistics. For the latest CPI, go to http://www.bls.gov/cpi/home.htm.

exchange. *No machine increases the economy's productivity as much as properly functioning money.* Indeed, it seems hard to overstate the value of a reliable monetary system. This is why we pay so much attention to money and banking.

Let's turn now to the development of money and banking in the United States.

Financial Institutions in the United States

financial intermediaries
Institutions such as banks, mortgage companies, and finance companies, that serve as go-betweens, borrowing from people who have saved to make loans to others

depository institutions
Commercial banks and thrift institutions; financial institutions that accept deposits from the public

commercial banks
Depository institutions that historically made short-term loans primarily to businesses

thrift institutions, or thrifts
Savings banks and credit unions; depository institutions that historically lent money to households

You have already learned about the origin of modern banks: Goldsmiths lent money from deposits held for safekeeping. So you already have some idea of how banks work. Recall from the circular-flow model that household saving flows into financial markets, where it is lent to investors. Financial institutions, such as banks, mortgage companies, and finance companies, accumulate funds from savers and lend them to borrowers. Financial institutions, or **financial intermediaries**, earn a profit by "buying low and selling high"—that is, by paying a lower interest rate to savers than they charge borrowers.

Commercial Banks and Thrifts

A wide variety of financial intermediaries respond to the economy's demand for financial services. **Depository institutions**—such as commercial banks, savings banks, and credit unions—obtain funds primarily by accepting customer *deposits*. Depository institutions play a key role in providing the nation's money supply. Depository institutions can be classified broadly into commercial banks and thrift institutions.

Commercial banks are the oldest, largest, and most diversified of depository institutions. They are called **commercial banks** because historically they made loans primarily to *commercial* ventures, or businesses, rather than to households. Commercial banks hold most deposits in the United States. **Thrift institutions**, or **thrifts**, include savings banks and credit unions. Historically, savings banks specialized in making home mortgage loans. Credit unions, which are more numerous but smaller than savings banks, extend loans only to their "members" to finance homes or other major consumer purchases, such as new cars. For the most part, this chapter will ignore credit unions, which are numerous but small and specialized.

Birth of the Fed

Before 1863, banks were chartered by the states in which they operated, so they were called *state banks*. These banks, like the English goldsmiths, issued bank notes. Notes from thousands of different banks circulated and most were redeemable for gold. The National Banking Act of 1863 and later amendments created a new system of federally chartered banks called *national banks*. National banks were authorized to issue notes and were regulated by the Office of the Comptroller of the Currency, part of the U.S. Treasury. State bank notes were taxed out of existence, but state banks survived by creating checking accounts for borrowers. To this day, the United States has a *dual banking system* consisting of state banks and national banks.

During the 19th century, the economy experienced a number of panic "runs" on banks by depositors seeking to withdraw their money. A panic was usually set off by the failure of some prominent financial institution. Fearful customers besieged their banks. Borrowers wanted additional loans and extensions of credit, and depositors wanted their money back. *As many depositors tried to withdraw their money, they couldn't because each bank held only a fraction of its deposits as cash reserves.* To reduce such panics, Congress created the **Federal Reserve System** in 1913 as the central bank and monetary authority of the United States.

Federal Reserve System, or the Fed
The central bank and monetary authority of the United States

Nearly all industrialized countries had formed central banks by 1900—such as the Bundesbank in Germany, the Bank of Japan, and the Bank of England, which has been around since 1694. But the American public's suspicion of monopoly power led to the establishment of not one central bank but separate banks in each of 12 Federal Reserve districts around the country. The new banks were named after the cities in which they were located—the Federal Reserve Banks of Boston, New York, Chicago, San Francisco, and so on, as shown in Exhibit 3 (which district are you in?). *Throughout most of its history, the United States had what is called a decentralized banking system. The Federal Reserve Act moved the country toward a system that was partly centralized and partly decentralized.* All national banks had to join the Federal Reserve System and thus were subject to new regulations issued by *the Fed*, as it came to be called (don't confuse *the Fed* with *the Feds*, shorthand for the FBI and other federal crime fighters). For state banks, membership was voluntary, and, to avoid the new regulations, most did not join.

Powers of the Federal Reserve System

The Federal Reserve was authorized to ensure sufficient money and credit in the banking system needed to support a growing economy. The power to issue bank notes was taken away from national banks and turned over to Federal Reserve Banks. (Take out a \$1 note and notice what it says across the top: "Federal Reserve Note." On the \$1 note, the seal to the left of George Washington's portrait identifies which Federal Reserve Bank issued the note.) The Federal Reserve was also granted other powers: *to buy and sell government securities, to extend loans to member banks, to clear checks in the banking system, and to require that member banks hold reserves equal to at least some specified fraction of their deposits.*

EXHIBIT 3 The Twelve Federal Reserve Districts

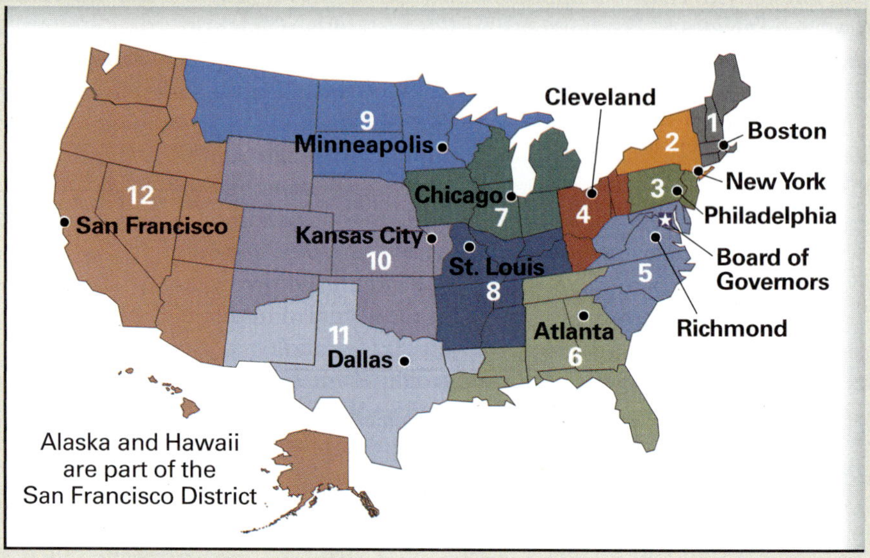

The map shows by color the area covered by each of the 12 Federal Reserve districts. Black dots note the locations of the Federal Reserve Bank in each district. Identified with a star is the Board of Governors headquarters in Washington, D.C.

Sources: Federal Reserve Board Web page at http://www.federalreserve.gov/otherfrb.htm.

Federal Reserve Banks do not deal with the public directly. Each may be thought of as a bankers' bank. Reserve banks hold deposits of member banks, just as depository institutions hold deposits of the public, and they extend loans to member banks, just as depository institutions extend loans to the public. The name *reserve bank* comes from the responsibility to hold member bank *reserves* on deposit.

reserves
Funds that banks use to satisfy the cash demands of their customers and the reserve requirements of the Fed; reserves consist of cash held by banks plus deposits at the Fed

Reserves are funds that banks have on hand or on deposit with the Fed to promote banking safety, to facilitate interbank transfers of funds, to satisfy the cash demands of their customers, and to comply with Federal Reserve regulations. By holding bank reserves, a reserve bank can clear a check written by a depositor at one bank and deposited at another bank, much like the goldsmith's moving of gold reserves from the farmer's account to the horse trader's account. Reserve banks are also authorized to lend to banks in need of reserves; the interest rate charged is called the *discount rate*.

A member bank is required to own stock in its district Federal Reserve Bank, and this entitles the bank to a 6 percent annual dividend. Any additional profit earned by the reserve banks is turned over to the U.S. Treasury. So, technically, the reserve banks are owned by the member banks in the district, but in practice the Fed is an independent agency of the federal government. When the Fed Chairman gets grilled, it's by Congress, not by member banks.

Banking Troubles During the Great Depression

From 1913 to 1929, both the Federal Reserve System and the national economy performed relatively well. But the stock market crash of 1929 was followed by the Great Depression, creating a new set of problems for the Fed, such as bank runs caused by panicked depositors. The Fed, however, dropped the ball by failing to act as a lender of last resort—that is, the Fed did not lend banks the money they needed to satisfy deposit withdrawals in cases of runs on otherwise sound banks. Many banks did not survive. Between 1930 and 1933, about 10,000 banks failed—about one-third of all U.S. banks. Most depositors at the failed banks lost everything.

In his first inaugural address in 1933, newly elected President Franklin D. Roosevelt said, "The only thing we have to fear is fear itself," a statement especially apt for a fractional reserve banking system. Most banks were sound as long as people had confidence in the safety of their deposits. But if many depositors tried to withdraw their money, they could not do so because each bank held only a fraction of deposits as reserves. Bank legislation passed during the Great Depression shored up the banking system and centralized power with the Fed in Washington. Here are some features of that legislation.

Board of Governors

The *Board of Governors*, which consists of seven members appointed by the president and confirmed by the Senate, became responsible for setting and implementing the nation's monetary policy. *Monetary policy,* a term introduced in Chapter 3, is the regulation of the economy's money supply and interest rates to promote macroeconomic objectives. The Board of Governors now oversees the 12 reserve banks, making the system more centralized. Each governor serves a fourteen-year nonrenewable term, with one term expiring every even-numbered year. *The long tenure is designed to insulate board members from political pressure.* A new U.S. president can be sure of appointing only two members during a presidential term, so a new president could not change monetary policy that much. One governor is also appointed to chair the Board for a four-year term, with no limit on reappointments.

Federal Open Market Committee

The **Federal Open Market Committee** (**FOMC**) makes decisions about the key tool of monetary policy, **open-market operations**—the Fed's buying and selling of government securities (tools of monetary policy are examined in the next chapter). The FOMC consists of the seven board governors plus five of the 12 presidents of the reserve banks; the chair of the Board of Governors heads the group. Because the New York Federal Reserve Bank carries out open-market operations, that bank's president always sits on the FOMC. The structure of the Federal Reserve System is presented in Exhibit 4. The FOMC and, less significantly, the Federal Advisory Committee (which consists of a banker from each of the 12 reserve bank districts) advise the board.

Federal Open Market Committee (FOMC)
The 12-member group that makes decisions about open-market operations—purchases and sales of U.S. government securities by the Fed that affect the money supply and interest rates; consists of the seven Board governors plus five of the 12 presidents of the Reserve Banks

Regulating the Money Supply

Because reserves amount to just a fraction of deposits, the United States has a *fractional reserve* banking system, as already noted. The Federal Reserve System has a variety of tools to regulate the money supply, including *(1) conducting open-market operations—buying and selling U.S. government securities; (2) setting the discount rate—the interest rate charged by reserve banks for loans to member banks; and (3) setting legal reserve requirements for member banks.* We explore these tools in greater detail in the next chapter.

open-market operations
Purchases and sales of government securities by the Fed in an effort to influence the money supply

Deposit Insurance

Panic runs on banks stemmed from fears about the safety of bank deposits. The *Federal Deposit Insurance Corporation (FDIC)* was established in 1933 to insure the first $2,500 of each deposit account. Today the insurance ceiling is $250,000 per depositor

EXHIBIT 4 Organization Chart of the Federal Reserve System

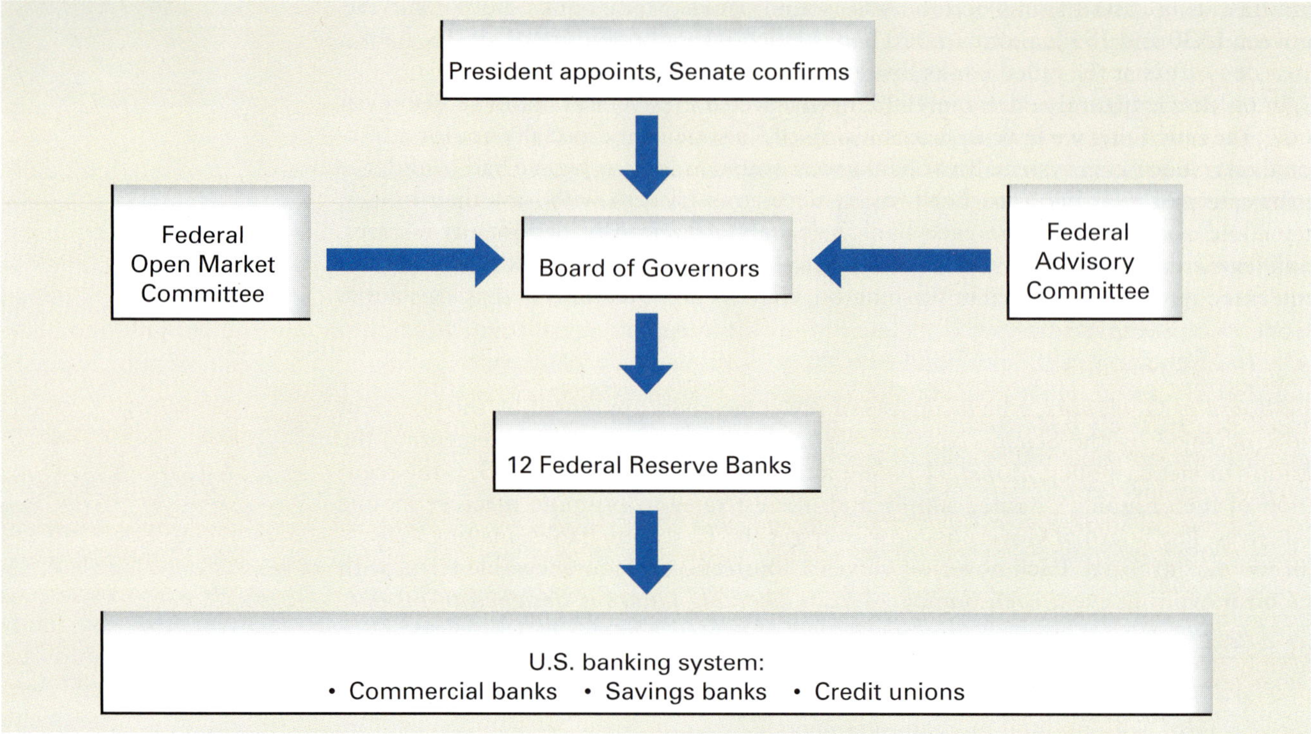

Members of the Board of Governors are appointed by the president and confirmed by the Senate. The seven board members also belong to the 12-member Federal Open Market Committee, which advises the board. The Board of Governors controls the Reserve Banks in each of the 12 districts, which in turn control the U.S. banking system.

per bank. Over 90 percent of all banks now purchase FDIC insurance, and in 2010, the FDIC insured $5.5 trillion in deposits. Other insurance programs take care of the rest. *Deposit insurance, by calming fears about the safety of bank deposits, worked wonders to reduce bank runs.*

Objectives of the Fed

Over the years, the Fed has accumulated additional responsibilities. Here are six frequently mentioned goals of the Fed: (1) a high level of employment in the economy, (2) economic growth, (3) price stability, (4) interest rate stability, (5) financial market stability, and (6) exchange rate stability. *These goals boil down to high employment; economic growth; and stability in prices, interest rates, financial markets, and exchange rates.* As we will see, not all of these objectives can be achieved simultaneously.

Banks Lost Deposits When Inflation Increased

Prior to the 1930s, banks could own corporate stocks and bonds, financial assets that fluctuated widely in value and contributed to instability of the banking system. Reforms enacted during the Great Depression limited bank assets primarily to loans and government securities—bonds issued by federal, state, and local governments. A *bond* is an IOU, so a government bond is an IOU from the government. Also, bank failures during the 1930s were thought to have resulted in part from fierce interest-rate competition among banks for customer deposits. To curb such competition, the Fed was empowered to set a ceiling on interest rates that banks could pay depositors.

These restrictions made banking a heavily regulated industry. Banks lost much of their freedom to wheel and deal, and the federal government insured most deposits. The assets banks could acquire were carefully limited, as were the interest rates they could offer depositors (checking deposits earned no interest). Banking thus became a highly regulated, even stuffy, industry. The term "banker's hours" was applied derisively to someone who had a short workday.

Ceilings on interest rates reduced interest-rate competition for deposits *among* banks. But a surge of inflation during the 1970s increased interest rates in the economy. When market interest rates rose above what banks could legally offer depositors, many withdrew their deposits and put them into higher-yielding alternatives. In 1972, Merrill Lynch, a major brokerage house, introduced an account combining a **money market mutual fund** with limited check-writing privileges. Money market mutual fund shares are claims on a portfolio, or collection, of short-term interest-earning assets. These mutual funds became stiff competition for bank deposits, especially checkable deposits, which at the time paid no interest at banks.

money market mutual fund
A collection of short-term interest-earning assets purchased with funds collected from many shareholders

Banking Deregulation

In response to the loss of deposits and other problems, Congress tried to ease regulations, giving banks greater discretion in their operations. For example, interest-rate ceilings for deposits were eliminated, and all depository institutions were allowed to offer money market deposit accounts. Such deposits jumped from only $8 billion in 1978 to $200 billion in 1982. Some states, like California and Texas, also deregulated state-chartered savings banks. The combination of deposit insurance, unregulated interest rates, and wider latitude in the kinds of assets that savings banks could purchase gave them a green light to compete for large deposits in national markets. Savings banks had been restricted to residential lending, but the 1982 legislation allowed them to make commercial loans. Once-staid financial institutions moved into the fast lane.

Banks could wheel and deal but with the benefit of deposit insurance. The combination of deregulation and deposit insurance encouraged some on the verge of failing to take bigger risks—to "bet the bank"—because their depositors would be protected by deposit insurance. This created a *moral hazard,* which in this case was the tendency of bankers to take unwarranted risks in making loans because deposits were insured. Banks that were virtually bankrupt—so-called zombie banks—were able to attract deposits because of deposit insurance. Zombie banks, by offering higher interest rates, also drew deposits away from healthier banks. Meanwhile, because deposits were insured, most depositors paid less attention to their banks' health. Thus, *deposit insurance, originally introduced during the Great Depression to prevent bank panics, caused depositors to become complacent about the safety of their deposits. Worse still, it caused those who ran troubled banks to take wild gambles to survive.*

Banks on the Ropes

Many of these gambles didn't pay off, particularly loans to real estate developers, and banks lost a ton of money. The insolvency and collapse of a growing number of banks prompted Congress in 1989 to approve what was then the largest financial bailout of any U.S. industry—a measure that would eventually cost about $180 billion in today's dollars. Taxpayers paid 80 percent of the total, and banks paid the remaining

20 percent through higher deposit insurance premiums. The money was spent to close down failing banks, pay off insured depositors, and find healthier banks to take over the deposit accounts.

Exhibit 5 shows the number of bank failures in the United States by year since 1980. From their 1989 peak of 608, annual failures dropped to none in 2005 or 2006. About 3,000 banks failed between the early 1980s and early 1990s.

U.S. Banking Developments

bank branches
A bank's additional offices that carry out banking operations

As failed banks disappeared or merged with stronger banks, the industry got healthier. Bank profits grew fourfold during the 1990s. Although the number of commercial banks fell by half since the mid-1980s, the United States, with over 6,500 FDIC insured commercial banks, still has more than any other country. Other major economies have fewer than 1,000 commercial banks (Japan and Canada, for example, have fewer than 100 banks each, though most banks have many branches). The large number of U.S. banks reflects past restrictions on **bank branches**, which are additional offices that carry out banking operations. Again, Americans, fearing monopoly power, did not want any one bank to become too large or powerful. The combination of intrastate and interstate restrictions on branching spawned the many commercial banks that exist today, most of which are relatively small. For example, the bottom 92 percent of U.S. commercial banks at the end of 2009 held just 12 percent of all deposits. Branching restrictions create inefficiencies, because banks cannot achieve optimal size and cannot easily diversify

EXHIBIT 5 Failures of U.S. Banks Peaked in 1989

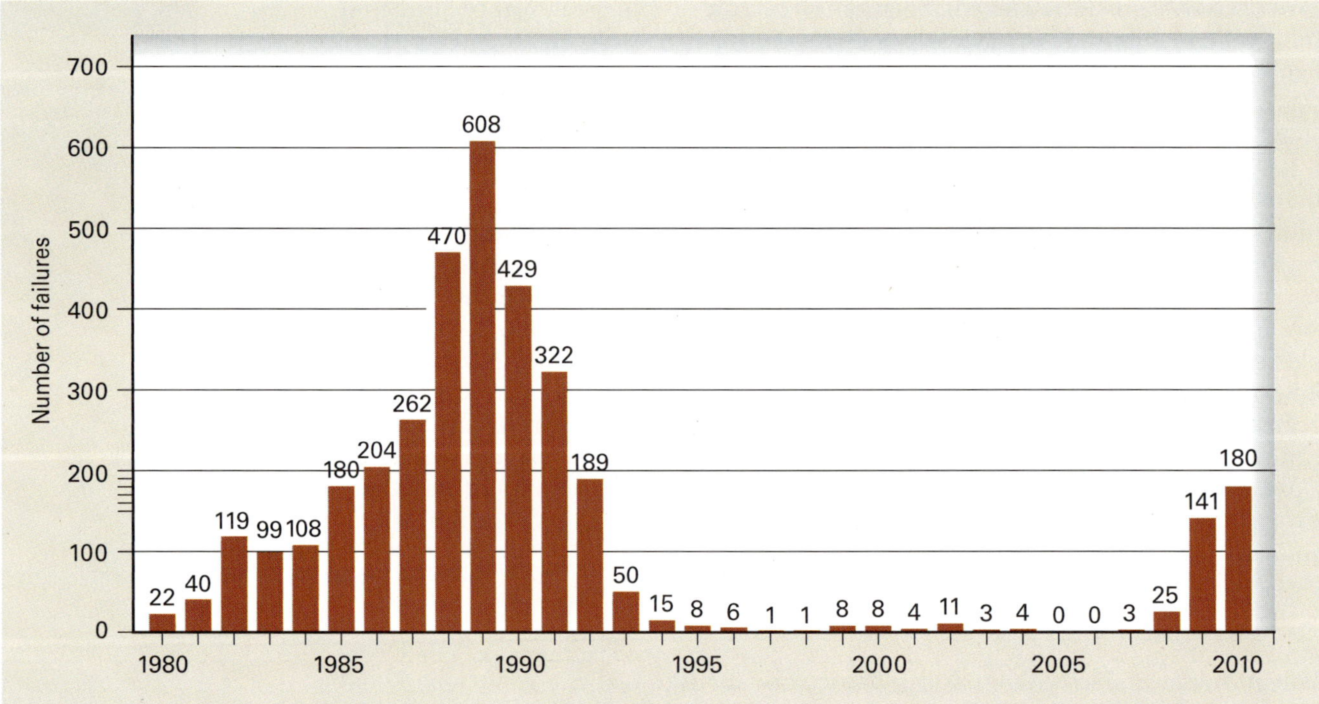

Source: Based on annual reports from the Federal Deposit Insurance Corporation. For the latest figures, go to http://www.fdic.gov/bank/individual/failed/banklist.html. Figure for 2010 is projected based on failures through August of that year.

their portfolios of loans across different regions. Branching restrictions were one reason for bank failures during the Depression. Such restrictions meant a bank made loans primarily in one community—it had all its eggs in that basket.

In recent years, federal legislation has lifted some restrictions on interstate branching and on the kinds of assets that banks can own. Two developments allowed banks to get around branching restrictions: bank holding companies and mergers. A **bank holding company** is a corporation that may own several different banks. The *Gramm-Leach-Bliley Act* of 1999 repealed some Depression-era restrictions on the kinds of assets a bank could own. A holding company can provide other services that banks are not authorized to offer, such as financial advising, leasing, insurance, credit cards, and securities trading. Thus, holding companies blossomed. Nearly 90 percent of the nation's checking deposits are in banks owned by holding companies. But in the aftermath of the financial crises, policy makers restricted the kinds of assets a bank can own and trade, as you'll soon see.

bank holding company
A corporation that owns banks

Another important development that allowed banks to expand their geographical reach is *bank mergers*, which have spread the presence of some banks across the country. Banks are merging because they want more customers and expect the higher volume of transactions to reduce operating costs per customer. Nationwide banking is also seen as a way of avoiding the concentration of bad loans that sometimes occur in one geographical area. The merger movement was initially fueled by a rising stock market and by federal legislation that facilitates consolidation of merged banks. More recently, some banks weakened by the financial crisis have been forced to merge with stronger banks to survive.

Bank holding companies and bank mergers have reduced the number of banks, but increased the number of branches. Exhibit 6 shows the number of commercial banks

EXHIBIT 6 **The Number of Commercial Banks Declined over the Last Three Decades, but the Number of Branches Continues to Grow**

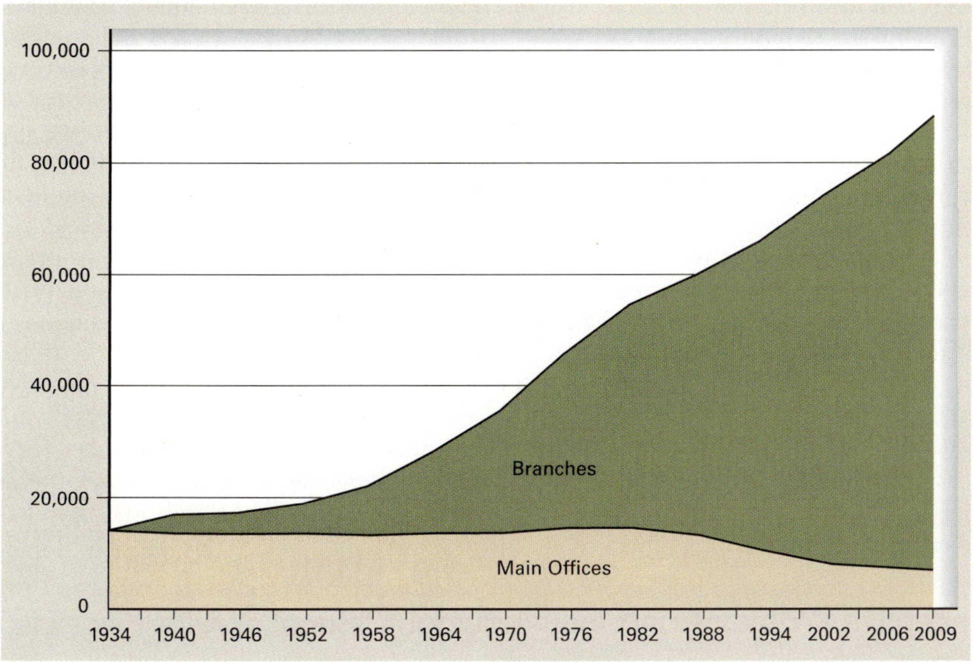

Source: Figures are for FDIC-insured commercial banks in the United States based on Federal Deposit Insurance Corporation data.

and bank branches in the United States since 1934. The number of banks, as indicated by "main offices," remained relatively constant between 1934 and 1982 but has since fallen by more than half as a result of failures, mergers, and holding companies. The number of bank branches increased steadily, however, more than doubling since 1982. So the number of branches per bank increased. In 1982, the average U.S. commercial bank had about three branches; by 2009, it had about 12 branches.

But the biggest financial development in recent years has been the introduction of the subprime mortgage, which contributed to the crisis of 2008 and the severe recession. Here's what happened.

Subprime Mortgages and Mortgage-Backed Securities

subprime mortgage
Mortgage for a borrower with a not-so-good credit rating

mortgage-backed security
A claim on payments made on the many mortgages bundled into this financial instrument

Prior to 2000, only a credit-worthy, or *prime*, borrower could get a home mortgage. But new statistical techniques and better computers increased a lender's ability to assess the risk of a **subprime mortgage,** which is a mortgage for a borrower with a not-so-good credit rating. Any household with a credit history could be assigned a numerical credit score, and this score could be used to predict how likely that borrower would be to default on mortgage payments. Borrowers more likely to default would pay a higher interest rate to compensate the lender for their higher risk. Hundreds of mortgages could then be bundled together based on credit scores into a **mortgage-backed security**, which represents a claim on the monthly payments made on those mortgages. The idea is that subprime mortgages could be blended with other mortgages in whatever proportion needed to arrive at a particular level of default risk for the security. And a securities-rating agency could look at the mix of mortgages and assign that security an overall credit rating. A higher proportion of subprime loans would result in a higher risk security, but would also yield a higher return for investors. Investors could choose securities based on their tolerance for risk. Mortgage-backed securities opened up new sources of financing for subprime borrowers.

After the U.S economy recovered from the recession of 2001, subprime mortgages grew in popularity. Fueled by cash flows coming into the United States from places like China, the subprime market became a trillion dollar business by 2007. This development was considered good for America because it gave more households access to mortgage credit. Subprime borrowers might pay higher interest rates than prime borrowers, but at least they could get mortgages. The availability of subprime mortgages turned some renters into homeowners, a group presumably more committed to the community. Indeed, federal regulators pressured financial institutions into lending to groups that before the advent of subprime mortgages had been underserved.

Subprime loans increased the demand for housing, which raised housing prices, which, in turn, fueled a boom in subprime loans in a reinforcing cycle. As home prices rose, many borrowers saw this as an opportunity to refinance. Based on the rising value of their homes, they would take out a bigger mortgage, use most of that money to pay off the old one, and still have money left over. Of course, monthly mortgage payments would increase too, but rising home prices meant that, in a pinch, the house could always be sold to pay off the mortgage. Home prices had been marching higher for at least two decades. Mortgage-backed securities were considered a safe investment offering an attractive return. They were sold around the world. Banks and other financial institutions bought a lot of them. What could go wrong?

Incentive Problems and the Financial Crisis of 2008

A subprime mortgage typically originated with a mortgage broker (two-thirds originated this way). The mortgage was then sold to an underwriter who bundled it with other mortgages and sold them as a mortgage-backed security to investors, the source of financing in the deal. Once the mortgage was originated, that mortgage broker earned a fee and soon lost interest in whether the borrower was good for the money. Research indicates that the riskier the loan, the higher the interest rate, and the more the broker made on that loan. Brokers had an incentive to encourage borrowers to apply for mortgages they could not afford, and some brokers falsified information on mortgage applications to make sure they would get approved. Some borrowers also exaggerated their income if there was no income verification (these became known as "liar's loans"). Making everything worse were lax regulations of mortgage originators, who were not required to tell borrowers whether or not they could afford the loans.

Meanwhile, banks and other financial institutions were earning attractive fees creating and selling mortgage-backed securities. Underwriters of mortgage-backed securities usually had little incentive to make sure that those who bought the securities would ultimately get paid. Worse yet, the credit-rating agencies that evaluated these securities also had a conflict of interest. They earned their fees by assessing the riskiness of these securities. But underwriters could shop around for the credit-rating agency that offered the highest rating. Thus, mortgage-backed securities tended to get better ratings than they deserved—that is, the securities were actually more risky than their credit ratings indicated.

As housing prices rose and the profitability of converting mortgages into securities increased, underlying credit standards fell. Riskier borrowers could get mortgages with little trouble. The size of the mortgage also increased as did the loan-to-value ratio, meaning that instead of borrowing up to 80 percent of a home's value, home buyers could borrow 90 or even 100 percent of its value. And borrowers could often take out a second mortgage to pay for the down payment, so they ended up needing little or no money down to buy a house. In 2001 half of all mortgages required down payments of 20 percent or less; by 2006 at least half required down payments of only 10 percent or less, and a quarter of mortgages had no down payment requirements at all.

Bundling hundreds of mortgages into a single mortgage-backed security made for a complicated investment, and this worsened the incentive problems. Yet as long as home prices rose, everyone was happy—the borrower, the mortgage originator, the banker who underwrote and sold the mortgage-backed security, the credit-rater, and the investor who found the yield attractive. But housing prices reached a level that in retrospect had gotten far out of whack with fundamentals of the housing market. After peaking in 2006, housing prices began to fall. Between 2006 and the middle of 2008, U.S. home prices plunged 22 percent on average. With housing prices tumbling, all the corners cut in the mortgage market soon became obvious. Many mortgages slipped "underwater," meaning that borrowers owed more than the house was worth. Such borrowers had an incentive to stop making payments. Many did, and defaults rose sharply, leading to millions of foreclosures.

Mortgage-backed securities quickly turned into "troubled assets." Because nobody wanted them, their value plummeted. Rising home foreclosures fed into the full-scale global financial panic in September 2008. The collapse of the major investment bank, Lehman Brothers, signaled that other financial institutions could soon follow. Nobody wanted to lend money they might not get back. Credit dried up. Panic spread to consumers, who cut consumption because of falling home prices, mounting job losses, and a collapsing stock market.

The Troubled Asset Relief Program

Policy makers had not seen anything like this in their lifetimes. By early October 2008, a consensus formed around a stopgap measure to help unfreeze credit markets and stabilize the banks. The **Troubled Asset Relief Program**, or **TARP**, authorized the

Troubled Asset Relief Program, or TARP
Government program that invested in financial institutions and automakers to help stabilize markets; in October 2008 budgeted at $700 billion but expected to cost much less

U.S. Treasury to purchase up to $700 billion in mortgage-backed securities. The idea was to buy these illiquid, difficult-to-value, assets and get them off the banks' books. Treasury officials soon decided that TARP money would not be used to buy troubled assets but instead to invest directly into financial institutions that were otherwise sound except for their troubled assets. The idea was to infuse new financial capital into these financial institutions to prevent more failures and to get banks lending again. The failure of Lehman Brothers was such a shock to financial markets that policy makers wanted to prevent other financial giants from collapsing. A trillion dollar institution such as AIG, with its financial ties to hundreds of other financial institutions, had become **too big to fail**—that is, its failure would have been such a disaster for the wider economy, that failure had to be prevented, even if it required a financial bailout.

too big to fail
A financial institution had become so large and so interconnected with other financial institutions that its failure would be a disaster for the wider economy; its collapse had to be prevented even if that required a bailout

TARP money was used to buy stakes in banks large and small (TARP money also bought government stakes in General Motors and Chrysler to keep the car makers operating). Once financial markets stabilized a bit and the stock market recovered some ground, the value of the Treasury's investment increased; these bailouts were expected to cost taxpayers about $100 billion. But housing prices continued to fall, homes continued to slip under water, and banks continued to suffer from mortgage defaults. As of 2010, underwater loans were greatest in Nevada, Arizona, Florida, Michigan, and California.

All these troubles contributed to a spike in bank failures. As was shown in Exhibit 5, failures increased from 25 in 2008 to 141 in 2009 to a projected 180 in 2010. Because of failures and mergers, the number of banks in the United States declined from about 18,000 in 1984 to about 8,000 in 2010. Eighty percent were commercial banks, and 20 percent savings banks. Commercial banks account for the overwhelming share of deposits. The troubles created by subprime mortgages, mortgage-backed securities, and other financial problems prompted regulatory reform in 2010. That's discussed next.

The Dodd-Frank Wall Street Reform and Consumer Protection Act

On July 21, 2010, President Obama signed into law the most sweeping overhaul of financial regulations since the Great Depression. The **Dodd-Frank Wall Street Reform and Consumer Protection Act,** named for its sponsors in the Senate and House, took eighteen months to develop and will take many years to implement. The legislation, which was 2,300 pages long, authorized 10 regulatory agencies to write and interpret hundreds of new rules governing financial markets.

Dodd-Frank Wall Street Reform and Consumer Protection Act
Sweeping regulatory changes aimed at preventing another financial crisis

Some provisions aim to remedy the incentive problems already discussed. To ensure that borrowers can repay a home loan, a mortgage originator must verify income, credit history, and job status. Mortgage originators cannot be paid more for funneling borrowers to riskier loans. To ensure that issuers of mortgage-backed securities are sensitive to the risk of these assets, issuers must retain at least 5 percent of the credit risk associated with the mortgages. And credit-rating agencies will be subject to new regulations.

For the first time, the law authorizes the Federal Reserve to regulate companies other than banks—such as insurance companies and investment firms—if they are mostly engaged in financial activities. The law imposes other regulations on banks, limiting their ability to trade on their own behalf and restricting their investments in hedge funds and private equity funds, which tend to be riskier.

The law establishes the *Financial Stability Oversight Council*, a super-regulator that will monitor Wall Street's largest firms and other market participants to spot and respond to emerging systemic risks. The nine-member panel, led by the Treasury Department, includes regulators from other agencies. Regulators get new authority to seize and liquidate troubled financial firms if their failure would jeopardize the nation's financial stability (such as with AIG). The idea is that reducing systemic risk and maintaining financial stability become regulatory objectives. A new *Bureau of Consumer Financial Protection* will have broad powers to write consumer-protection rules for banks and other firms that offer financial services.

Financial regulators get more funding, more information, and more power. Supporters say the law will reduce the likelihood of another financial crisis and will handle it better if one should occur. Others aren't so sure. Some economist argue that there are many ways a firm can take risks, and banning one form of risk-taking just shifts traders to other kinds of risk. For example, at a high enough interest rate, a bank may be willing to lend to extremely risky borrowers. What other unintended consequences will the new regulations create? Will regulations stifle financial innovation? Will U.S. financial institutions lose business to foreign competitors? Will the availability of credit be impaired by increased uncertainty and costs? Will new financial products be developed that make the regulations irrelevant? Will credit flows get choked by regulatory bureaucracy and politics? More generally, how will capitalism change if government regulators can seize and liquidate any financial institution? It's said that the military is often planning for the previous war. Are regulators, the same ones who allowed all this to happen in the first place, gearing up to prevent the previous financial crisis?

Top Banks in America and the World

The financial crisis of 2008 and the recession rattled the banking world. Let's take a look at the biggest banks in America and in the world. Exhibit 7 (a) shows the top 10 U.S. banks based on their U.S. deposits. Notice the wide range in size, with the top bank holding nearly 10 times the deposits as the bank ranked tenth. The top banks grew mostly through mergers and acquisitions. For example, BankAmerica and NationsBank merged to form Bank of America, which then acquired FleetBoston, a major bank in the Northeast, which itself was a product of several mergers. Bank of America now stretches from coast to coast with more than 6,200 branches.

Finally, because of the subprime mortgage and global financial crises of September 2008, some big banks that were on the ropes had to be taken over by healthier banks. For example, Wachovia, the nation's third largest bank, had to merge with Wells Fargo, then the nation's fourth largest. And Washington Mutual, at the time the sixth largest bank, was seized by the FDIC on September 25, 2008, after a ten-day bank run during which depositors withdrew $16 billion, or about 10 percent of all its deposits. The FDIC arranged for Washington Mutual to be acquired by JPMorgan Chase. You can see from panel (a) of Exhibit 7 that Wells Fargo most recently ranked second and JPMorgan Chase, third, among U.S. banks.

How big are U.S. banks on the world stage? Not very. Only one U.S. bank ranked among the top 10 based on worldwide assets. As shown by Exhibit 7 (b), JPMorgan Chase ranked eighth. Bank of America didn't make the top 10, but was eleventh. And Citibank ranked 21st. France and China placed four banks each in the top 25; the United Kingdom placed five in the top 25. Thus, the United States has the largest economy in the world by far, twice the size of second ranked China, but the United States is home to only three world-class banks. This partly reflects America's lingering fear of big banks. Some U.S. banks may be considered "too big to fail," but they are still too small to rank among the world's largest.

EXHIBIT 7 Top 10 Banks in America and the World

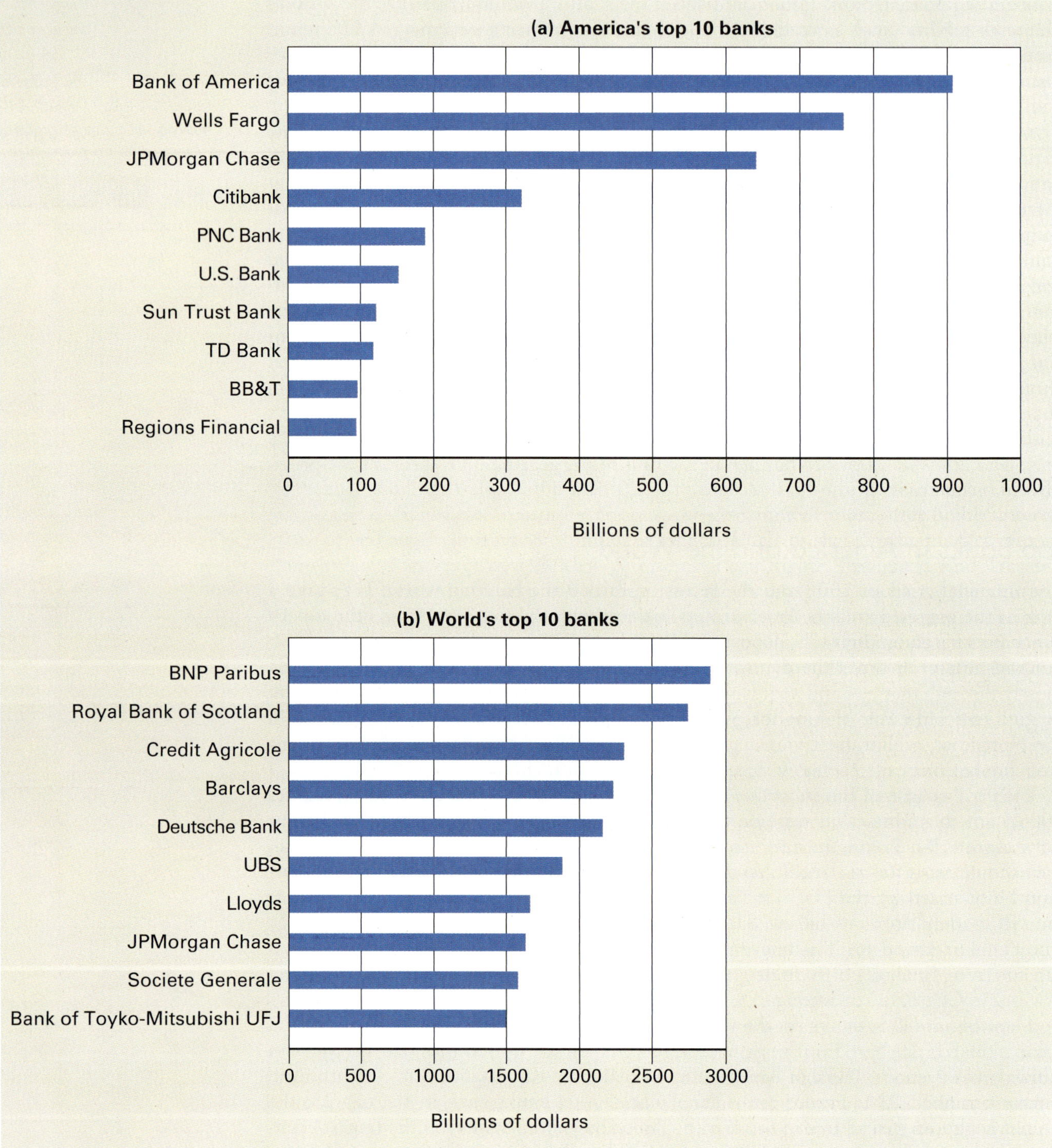

Among America's top 10 banks (based on U.S. deposits) in panel (a), size differs sharply, with the top bank nearly 10 times larger than the tenth ranked bank. Among the world's top 10 banks (based on worldwide assets) in panel (b), only one is American.

(a) Source: Federal Deposit Insurance Corporation as of 2009. Amounts of deposits based on holding companies.
(b) Source: "Top 50 Banks in the World," Bankers' Almanac. Available at http://www.bankersalmanac.com/addcon/infobank/bank-rankings.aspx. Figures are for 2010.

Conclusion

Money has grown increasingly more abstract over time, moving from commodity money to paper money that represented a claim on some commodity, such as gold, to paper money with no intrinsic value. As you will see, paper money constitutes only a fraction of the money supply. Modern money also consists of electronic entries in the banking system's computers. So money has changed from a physical commodity to an electronic entry. Money today does not so much change hands as change electronic accounts.

Money and banking have been intertwined ever since the early goldsmiths offered to hold customers' valuables for safekeeping. Banking has evolved from one of the most staid and regulated industries to one of the most competitive. Deregulation, branching innovations, and mergers have increased competition and have expanded the types of bank deposits. Reforms have given the Federal Reserve System more uniform control over depository institutions and have given the institutions greater access to the services provided by the Fed. Thus, all depository institutions can compete on more equal footing.

Deregulation provided greater freedom not only to prosper but also to fail. Failures of depository institutions create a special problem, however, because these institutions provide the financial underpinning of the nation's money supply, as you will see in the next chapter. There we examine more closely how banks operate and supply the nation's money.

Summary

1. Barter was the first form of exchange. As specialization grew, it became more difficult to discover the double coincidence of wants that barter required. The time and inconvenience of barter led even simple economies to use money.
2. Anything that acquires a high degree of acceptability throughout an economy thereby becomes money. The first moneys were commodities, such as gold. Eventually, what changed hands were pieces of paper that could be redeemed for something of value, such as gold. As paper money became widely accepted, governments introduced fiat money—pieces of paper not officially redeemable for anything other than more pieces of paper. Nearly all currencies throughout the world today are fiat money. People accept fiat money because, through experience, they believe that other people will do so as well. The ideal money is durable, portable, divisible, of uniform quality, has a low opportunity cost, and is relatively stable in value.
3. The value of money depends on what it buys. If money fails to serve as a medium of exchange, traders find other means of exchange, such as barter. If a monetary system breaks down, more time must be devoted to exchange, leaving less time for production, so efficiency suffers. No machine increases an economy's productivity as much as a properly functioning money.
4. The Federal Reserve System, or the Fed, was established in 1913 to regulate the banking system and issue the nation's currency. After a third of the nation's banks failed during the Great Depression, the Fed's powers were increased and centralized. The primary powers of the Fed became (a) to conduct open-market operations (buying and selling U.S. government securities), (b) to set the discount rate (the interest rate the Fed charges borrowing banks), and (c) to establish reserve requirements (the share of deposits banks must hold in reserve).
5. Regulations introduced during the Great Depression turned banking into a closely regulated industry. Reforms in the 1980s gave banks more flexibility to compete for deposits with other kinds of financial intermediaries. Some banks used this flexibility to make risky loans, but these gambles often failed, causing bank failures. By the mid-1990s, U.S. banks were thriving once again. Mergers and holding companies create larger banks that span the nation. But U.S. banks are still not that large by world standards.
6. A decades-long rise in home prices, the growth of subprime mortgages, and the spread of mortgage-backed securities created the financial crisis of September 2008. Credit dried up. The government first tried to stabilize markets by investing in financial institutions. Later, the Dodd-Frank Act of 2010, the most sweeping reform of financial markets since the Great Depression, authorized regulators to write and interpret hundreds of new financial rules. Banks are back to being more tightly regulated about the kinds of assets they can own and trade.

Key Concepts

Double coincidence of wants 558
Money 559
Medium of exchange 559
Commodity money 559
Unit of account 559
Store of value 559
Gresham's law 560
Seigniorage 561
Token money 561
Check 562
Fractional reserve banking system 562
Bank notes 562
Representative money 562
Fiat money 562
Legal tender 562
Financial intermediaries 564
Depository institutions 564
Commercial banks 564
Thrift institutions, or thrifts 564
Federal Reserve System, or the Fed 565
Reserves 566
Federal Open Market Committee (FOMC) 567
Open-market operations 567
Money market mutual fund 569
Bank branches 570
Bank holding company 571
Subprime mortgage 572
Mortgage-backed security 572
Troubled Asset Relief Program, or TARP 573
Too big to fail 574
Dodd-Frank Wall Street Reform and Consumer Protection Act 574

Questions for Review

1. Barter Define a double coincidence of wants and explain its role in a barter system.
2. Money Versus Barter "Without money, everything would be more expensive." Explain this statement. Then take a look at a Web page devoted to barter at http://www.ex.ac.uk/~RDavies/arian/barter.html. What are some current developments in barter exchange?
3. Functions of Money What are the three important functions of money? Define each of them.
4. Functions of Money "If an economy had only two goods (both *nondurable*), there would be no need for money because exchange would always be between those two goods." What important function of money does this statement disregard?
5. Characteristics of Money Why is universal acceptability such an important characteristic of money? What other characteristics can you think of that might be important to market participants?
6. Commodity Money Why do you think rice was chosen to serve as money in medieval Japan? What would happen to the price level if there was a particularly good rice harvest one year?
7. Commodity Money Early in U.S. history, tobacco was used as money. If you were a tobacco farmer and had two loads of tobacco that were of different qualities, which would you supply as money and which would you supply for smoking? Under what conditions would you use both types of tobacco for money?

Problems and Exercises

8. Origins of Banking Discuss the various ways in which London goldsmiths functioned as early banks.
9. Types of Money Complete each of the following sentences:
   a. If the face value of a coin exceeds the cost of coinage, the resulting revenue to the issuer of the coin is known as _______.
   b. A product that serves both as money and as a commodity is _______.
   c. Coins and paper money circulating in the United States have face values that exceed the value of the materials from which they are made. Therefore, they are forms of _______.
   d. If the government declares that creditors must accept a form of money as payment for debts, the money becomes _______.
   e. A common unit for measuring the value of every good or service in the economy is known as a(n) _______.
10. Fiat Money Most economists believe that the better fiat money serves as a store of value, the more acceptable it is. What does this statement mean? How could people lose faith in money?
11. The Value of Money When the value of money was based on its gold content, new discoveries of gold were frequently followed by periods of inflation. Explain.

12. Case Study: Mackerel Economics in Federal Prisons (See page 764.) How well do pouches of mackerel satisfy the six properties of ideal money listed in Exhibit 1?
13. Depository Institutions What is a depository institution, and what types of depository institutions are found in the United States? How do they act as intermediaries between savers and borrowers? Why do they play this role?
14. Federal Reserve System What are the main powers and responsibilities of the Federal Reserve System?
15. Bank Deregulation Some economists argue that deregulating the interest rates that could be paid on deposits combined with deposit insurance led to the insolvency of many depository institutions. On what basis do they make such an argument?
16. The Structure of U.S. Banking Discuss the impact of bank mergers on the structure of American banking. Why do banks merge?
17. Case Study: The Hassle of Small Change (See page 765.) What are three possible solutions to the problem that the penny now costs more to produce than it's worth in exchange?
18. Incentive Problems and the Financial Crisis of 2008 What incentives motivated the behaviors that caused the financial crisis of 2008?

Global Economic Watch Exercises

Login to www.cengagebrain.com and access the Global Economic Watch to do these exercises.

19. Global Economic Watch Go to the Global Economic Crisis Resource Center. Select Global Issues in Context. In the center of the page is the Global Economic Crisis Overview. Click on the link for View Full Overview. Though not discussed in the text, Fannie Mae and Freddie Mac played important roles in the 2008 financial crisis. What does the Overview says about these agencies?
20. Global Economic Watch Go to the Global Economic Crisis Resource Center. Select Global Issues in Context. In the Basic Search box at the top of the page, enter the phrase "TARP." Find one article in favor of the Troubled Asset Relief Program and one against. Compare and contrast the arguments.

Banking and the Money Supply

29

- How do banks create money?
- Why are banks called First Trust or Security National rather than Benny's Bank or Loadsamoney?
- How is the Fed both literally and figuratively a money machine?
- Why are we so interested in banks, anyway?
- After all, isn't banking a business like any other, such as dry cleaning, auto washing, or home remodeling?
- Why not devote a chapter to the home-remodeling business?

Answers to these and related questions are provided in this chapter, which examines banking and the money supply.

In this chapter, we take a closer look at the unique role banks play in the economy. Banks are special in macroeconomics because, like the London goldsmith, they can convert a borrower's IOU into money, one key to a healthy economy. Because regulatory reforms have eliminated many of the distinctions between commercial banks and thrift institutions, all depository institutions are usually referred to more simply as banks.

We begin by going over the definitions of money, from the narrow to the broad view. Then, we look at how banks work and how they create money. We also consider the Fed in more detail. As you will see, the Fed attempts to control the money supply directly by issuing currency and indirectly by regulating bank reserves.

Topics discussed include:

- Money aggregates
- Checkable deposits
- Balance sheets
- Money creation
- Money multiplier
- Tools of the Fed

Money Aggregates

When you think of money, what comes to mind is probably currency—dollar notes and coins. But as you learned in the last chapter, dollar notes and coins account for only part of the money supply. In this section, we consider two definitions of money.

Narrow Definition of Money: M1

checkable deposits
Bank deposits that allow the account owner to write checks to third parties; ATM or debit cards can also access these deposits and transmit them electronically

money aggregates
Measures of the economy's money supply

M1
The narrow measure of the money supply, consisting of currency and coins held by the nonbanking public, checkable deposits, and traveler's checks

Suppose you have some cash with you right now—dollar notes and coins. These are part of the money supply as narrowly defined. If you were to deposit this cash in your checking account, you could then write checks directing your bank to pay someone from your account. **Checkable deposits** are bank deposits that allow the account owner to write checks to third parties. Checkable deposits are included in the narrow definition of money and can also be tapped with an ATM card or a debit card. Banks hold a variety of checkable deposits. In recent years, financial institutions have developed other kinds of accounts that carry check-writing privileges but also earn interest.

Money aggregates are measures of the money supply defined by the Federal Reserve. The narrow definition, called **M1**, consists of currency (including coins) held by the nonbanking public, checkable deposits, and traveler's checks. Note that currency in bank vaults is not counted as part of the money supply because it is not being used as a medium of exchange—it's just sitting there out of circulation. But checkable deposits are money because their owners can write checks or use debit cards to tap them. Checkable deposits are the liabilities of the issuing banks, which stand ready to convert them into cash. But unlike cash, checks are not legal tender, as signs that say "No Checks!" attest.

The currency circulating in the United States consists mostly of Federal Reserve notes, which are produced by the U.S. Bureau of Engraving and Printing and are issued by and are liabilities of the 12 Federal Reserve Banks. About 40 percent of the Fed's liabilities consist of Federal Reserve notes. The Fed spends about $600 million a year printing, storing, and distributing notes. Because Federal Reserve notes are redeemable for nothing other than more Federal Reserve notes, U.S. currency is *fiat money*. The other component of currency is coins, manufactured by the U.S. Mint, which sells these coins to Federal Reserve Banks at face value. Like paper money, U.S. coins are token money because their metal value is usually less than their face value (though, as noted in the previous chapter, metal values of the penny and the nickel may soon exceed their face values). The U.S. Mint, a division of the U.S. Treasury, reaps any seigniorage from coin production (in 2009 this amounted to about $450 million, mostly from quarters).

As much as two-thirds of Federal Reserve notes now circulate abroad.[1] Some countries such as Panama, Ecuador, and El Salvador use U.S. dollars as their currency. In other countries, especially those that have experienced high inflation, U.S. dollars circulate alongside the local currency. In Vietnam, for example, some restaurants list prices in U.S. dollars, not in dong, the national currency. Dollars circulating abroad are actually a good deal for Americans because a $100 note that costs only about 10 cents to print can be "sold" to foreigners for $100 worth of goods and services. It's as if these countries were granting us an interest-free loan during the period the $100 note circulates abroad, usually several years. But having our currency used around the world poses special problems when it comes to counterfeiting, as discussed in the case study, "Public Policy: Faking It," at the end of the book.

1. Louise L. Roseman, "State of U.S. Coins and Currency," Testimony Before the Committee on Financial Services, U.S. House of Representatives, Washington, D.C., 20 July 2010 at http://www.federalreserve.gov/newsevents/testimony/roseman20100720a.htm.

Broader Definition of Money: M2

Economists regard currency and checkable deposits as money because each serves as a medium of exchange, a unit of account, and a store of value. Some other financial assets perform the store-of-value function and can be converted into currency or to checkable deposits. Because these are so close to money, they are called near-monies and are included under a broader definition.

Savings deposits earn interest but have no specific maturity date. Banks often allow depositors to shift funds from savings accounts to checking accounts by phone, ATM card, or online, so distinctions between narrow and broad definitions of money have become blurred. **Time deposits** (also called *certificates of deposit*, or *CDs*) earn a fixed rate of interest if held for a specified period, ranging from several months to several years. Premature withdrawals are penalized by forfeiture of some interest. Neither savings deposits nor time deposits serve directly as media of exchange, so they are not included in M1, the narrow definition of money.

Money market mutual fund accounts, mentioned in the previous chapter, are another component of money when defined more broadly. But, because of restrictions on the minimum balance, on the number of checks that can be written per month, and on the minimum amount of each check, these popular accounts are not viewed as money as narrowly defined.

Recall that M1 consists of currency (including coins) held by the nonbanking public, checkable deposits, and traveler's checks. **M2** includes M1 as well as savings deposits, small-denomination time deposits, money market mutual fund accounts, and other miscellaneous near-monies. Exhibit 1 shows the size and relative importance of

savings deposits
Deposits that earn interest but have no specific maturity date

time deposits
Deposits that earn a fixed interest rate if held for the specified period, which can range from several months to several years; also called certificates of deposit

M2
A money aggregate consisting of M1 plus savings deposits, small-denomination time deposits, money market mutual funds, and other miscellaneous near-monies

EXHIBIT 1 Measures of the Money Supply (Week of July 12, 2010)

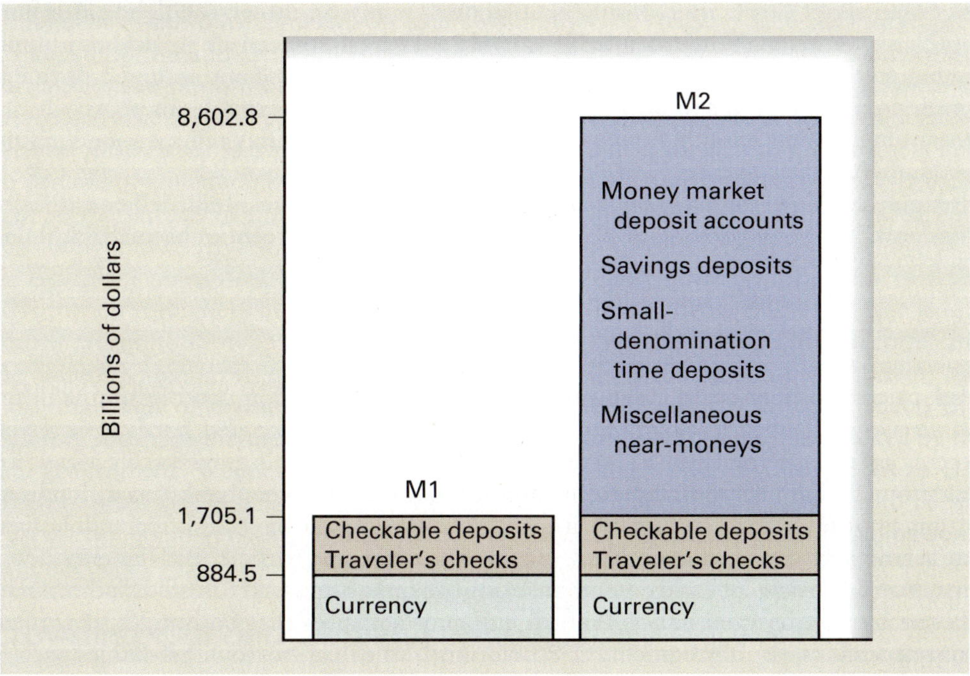

Source: Based on seasonally adjusted averages for the week from the Federal Reserve Board. For the latest data, go to http://www.federalreserve.gov/releases/h6/Current/.

each money aggregate. As you can see, compared to M1, M2 is about five times larger. Thus, the narrow definition of money is only a fraction of the broader aggregate. But distinctions between M1 and M2 become less meaningful as banks allow depositors to transfer funds from one account to another.

Credit Cards and Debit Cards: What's the Difference?

You may be curious why the narrow definition includes funds accessed by debit cards but not funds accessed by credit cards. After all, most sellers accept credit cards as readily as they accept cash, checks, or debit cards (online sellers even prefer credit cards), and credit cards finance more than 20 percent of all consumer purchases. Credit cards offer an easy way to get a loan from the card issuer. If you buy an airline ticket with a credit card, the card issuer lends you the money to pay for the ticket. You don't need money until you repay the credit card issuer. The credit card has not eliminated your use of money, merely delayed it. Three in four households have general purpose credit cards. About half of those with credit cards carry a balance from month to month, and that group's median balance is about $3,000.

On the other hand, when you use your debit card, you tap directly into your checking account, paying with electronic money—part of M1. Debit cards get their name because they *debit*, or draw down, your checking account immediately. A **debit card**, also called a check card or bank card, combines the functions of an ATM card and a check. Debit cards are issued by banks, sometimes jointly with Visa, MasterCard, or other major card issuers. Even though debit cards look like credit cards, and even may bear a name such as Visa, they are not credit cards.

debit card
Cards that tap directly into the depositor's bank account to fund purchases; also called a check card, and often doubles as an ATM card

Many people prefer debit cards to checks because no checkbook is required and payments are made directly and immediately. Transactions using debit cards and other electronic transfers now exceed payments by check. Like ATM cards, debit cards usually require a personal identification number, or PIN, to use. In that regard, debit cards are safer than credit cards, which could be used more easily by a thief. But debit cards have some disadvantages. Whereas a debit card draws down your checking account immediately, credit cards provide a grace period between a purchase and required payment. And some people prefer to borrow beyond the grace period—that is, they carry a balance from month to month. Also, because debit cards immediately reduce your checking account, you can't dispute a bill or withhold payment as you can after writing a credit card and you can't stop payment as you can after writing a check. Still, debit cards came from nowhere a few years ago to be used by more than 60 percent of households today.

How Banks Work

Banks attract deposits from savers to lend to borrowers, earning a profit on the difference between the interest paid depositors and the interest charged borrowers. Savers need a safe place for their money, and borrowers need credit; banks try to earn a profit by serving both groups. To inspire depositor confidence, banks usually present an image of trust and assurance with impressive offices, a big safe often visible from the lobby, and names that impress. Banks are more apt to be called Fidelity Trust, First National, or U.S. Bankcorp than Benny's Bank, Loans 'R' Us, or Loadsamoney. In contrast, *finance companies* are financial intermediaries that do not get their funds from depositors, so they can choose names aimed more at borrowers—names such as Household Finance or The Money Store. Likewise, mortgage companies do not rely on depositors, so they pick names aimed at home buyers, names such as Lender's Depot or Get Home Loans Fast.com.

Banks Are Financial Intermediaries

By bringing together both sides of the money market, banks serve as financial intermediaries, or as go-betweens. They gather various amounts from savers and repackage these funds into the amounts demanded by borrowers. Some savers need their money next week, some next year, some only after retirement. Likewise, borrowers need credit for different lengths of time. Banks, as intermediaries, offer desirable durations to both groups. In short, *banks reduce the transaction costs of channeling savings to creditworthy borrowers.* Here's how.

Coping with Asymmetric Information

Banks, as lenders, try to identify borrowers who are willing to pay interest and are able to repay the loan. But borrowers have more reliable information about their own credit history and financial plans than do lenders. Thus, in the market for loans, there is **asymmetric information**—an inequality in what's known by each party to the transaction. Asymmetric information is unequal information. This wouldn't be a problem if borrowers could be trusted to report relevant details to lenders. Some borrowers, however, have an incentive to suppress important information, such as other debts outstanding, a troubled financial history, or plans to use the borrowed money to fund a risky venture. Because of their experience and expertise in evaluating loan applicants, banks can better cope with asymmetric information than could an individual saver. Banks also know more about lending agreements than do individual savers. Thus, savers, rather than lending their money directly, are better off depositing their money in banks, and letting banks do the lending. *The economy is more efficient because banks develop expertise in evaluating creditworthiness, structuring loans, and enforcing loan contracts.*

asymmetric information
A situation in which one side of the market has more reliable information than the other side

Reducing Risk through Diversification

By developing a diversified portfolio of assets rather than lending funds to a single borrower, banks reduce the risk to each individual saver. A bank, in effect, lends a tiny fraction of each saver's deposits to each of its many borrowers. If one borrower fails to repay a loan, it hardly affects a large, diversified bank. Certainly such a default does not represent the personal disaster it would if one saver's entire nest egg was loaned directly to that defaulting borrower. But if a number of borrowers stop repaying their loans, as happened with subprime mortgage loans during the recent financial crisis, then some banks fail.

Starting a Bank

We could consider the operation of any type of depository institution (commercial bank, savings bank, or credit union), but let's focus on commercial banks because they are the most important in terms of total assets. What's more, the operating principles also apply to other depository institutions. Suppose some business leaders in your hometown want to open a commercial bank called Home Bank. To obtain a *charter*, or the right to operate, they must apply to the state banking authority in the case of a state bank or to the U.S. Comptroller of the Currency in the case of a national bank. The chartering agency reviewing the application judges the quality of management, the need for another bank in the region, the proposed bank's funding, and the likely success of the bank.

Suppose the founders plan to invest $500,000 in the bank, and they so indicate on their application for a national charter. If their application is approved, they

net worth
Assets minus liabilities; also called owners' equity

balance sheet
A financial statement at a given point in time that shows assets on one side and liabilities and net worth on the other side; because assets must equal liabilities plus net worth, the two sides of the statement must be in balance

asset
Anything of value that is owned

liability
Anything that is owed to other people or institutions

incorporate, issuing themselves shares of stock—certificates of ownership. Thus, they exchange $500,000 for shares of stock in the bank. These shares are called the *owners' equity*, or the **net worth**, of the bank. Part of the $500,000, say $50,000, is used to buy shares in their district Federal Reserve Bank. So Home Bank is now a member of the Federal Reserve System. With the remaining $450,000, the owners acquire and furnish the bank building.

To focus our discussion, we examine the bank's **balance sheet**, presented in Exhibit 2. As the name implies, a balance sheet shows a balance between the two sides of the bank's accounts. The left side lists the bank's assets. An **asset** is any physical property or financial claim owned by the bank. At this early stage, assets include the building and equipment owned by Home Bank plus its stock in the district Federal Reserve Bank. The right side lists the bank's liabilities and net worth. A **liability** is an amount the bank owes. So far the bank owes nothing, so the right side includes only the net worth of $500,000. The two sides of the ledger must always be equal, or in *balance*, which is why it's called a *balance sheet*. So assets must equal liabilities plus net worth:

$$\text{Assets} = \text{Liabilities} + \text{Net worth}$$

The bank is now ready for business. Opening day is the bank's lucky day, because the first customer carries in a briefcase full of $100 notes and deposits $1,000,000 into a new checking account. In accepting this cash, the bank promises to repay the depositor that amount. The deposit therefore is an amount the bank owes—it's a liability of the bank. As a result of this deposit, the bank's assets increase by $1,000,000 in cash and its liabilities increase by $1,000,000 in checkable deposits. Exhibit 3 shows the effects of this transaction on Home Bank's balance sheet. The right side now shows two claims on the bank's assets: claims by the owners, called net worth, and claims by nonowners, called liabilities, which at this point consist of checkable deposits.

EXHIBIT 2 Home Bank's Balance Sheet

Assets		Liabilities and Net Worth	
Building and furniture	$450,000	Net worth	$500,000
Stock in district Fed	50,000		
Total	$500,000	Total	$500,000

EXHIBIT 3 Home Bank's Balance Sheet after $1,000,000 Deposit into Checking Account

Assets		Liabilities and Net Worth	
Cash	$1,000,000	Checkable deposits	$1,000,000
Building and furniture	450,000	Net worth	500,000
Stock in district Fed	50,000		
Total	$1,500,000	Total	$1,500,000

Reserve Accounts

Where do we go from here? As mentioned in the previous chapter, banks are required by the Fed to set aside, or to hold in reserve, a percentage of their checkable deposits. The dollar amount that must be held in reserve is called **required reserves**—checkable deposits multiplied by the required reserve ratio. The **required reserve ratio** dictates the minimum proportion of deposits the bank must hold in reserve. The current reserve requirement is 10 percent on checkable deposits (other types of deposits have no reserve requirement). All depository institutions are subject to the Fed's reserve requirements. Reserves are held either as cash in the bank's vault, which earns the bank no interest, or as deposits at the Fed, which earn a small rate of interest. Home Bank must therefore hold $100,000 as reserves, or 10 percent times $1,000,000.

required reserves
The dollar amount of reserves a bank is obligated by regulation to hold as cash in the bank's vault or on account at the Fed

required reserve ratio
The ratio of reserves to deposits that banks are obligated by regulation to hold

Suppose Home Bank deposits $100,000 in a reserve account with its district Federal Reserve Bank. Home Bank's reserves now consist of $100,000 in required reserves on deposit with the Fed and $900,000 in **excess reserves** held as cash in the vault. Home Bank earns no interest on cash in its vault. Excess reserves, however, can be used to make loans or to purchase interest-bearing assets, such as government bonds. By law, the bank's interest-bearing assets are limited primarily to loans and to government securities (if a bank is owned by a holding company, the holding company has broader latitude in the kinds of assets it can own).

excess reserves
Bank reserves exceeding required reserves

Liquidity Versus Profitability

Like the early goldsmiths, modern banks must be prepared to satisfy depositors' requests for funds. A bank loses reserves whenever a depositor withdraws cash, writes a check that gets deposited in another bank, or uses a debit card that ultimately shifts deposits to another bank. The bank must be in a position to satisfy all depositor demands, even if many depositors ask for their money at the same time. Required reserves are not meant to be used to meet depositor requests for funds; therefore, banks often hold excess reserves or other assets, such as government bonds, that can be easily liquidated, or converted to cash, to satisfy any unexpected demand for cash. Banks may also want to hold excess reserves in case a valued customer needs immediate credit.

The bank manager must therefore structure the portfolio of assets with an eye toward liquidity but must not forget that survival also depends on profitability. **Liquidity** is the ease with which an asset can be converted into cash without a significant loss of value. *The objectives of liquidity and profitability are at odds*. For example, more liquid assets yield lower interest rates than less liquid assets do. The most liquid asset is cash in the bank's vault, but such reserves earn no interest.

liquidity
A measure of the ease with which an asset can be converted into money without a significant loss of value

At one extreme, suppose a bank is completely liquid, holding all its assets as cash in its vault. Such a bank would have no difficulty meeting depositors' demands for funds. This bank is playing it safe—too safe. The bank earns no interest and will fail. At the other extreme, suppose a bank uses all its excess reserves to acquire high-yielding but illiquid assets, such as long-term home loans. Such a bank runs into problems whenever withdrawals exceed new deposits. There is a trade-off between liquidity and profitability. The portfolio manager's task is to strike the right balance between liquidity, or safety, and profitability.

Because vault cash earns no interest, banks prefer to hold reserves at the Fed. Any bank short of required reserves at the end of the day can borrow from a bank that has excess reserves at the Fed. The **federal funds market** provides for day-to-day lending and borrowing among banks of excess reserves on account at the Fed. These funds usually do not leave the Fed—instead, they shift among accounts. For example, suppose that at the end of the business day, Home Bank has excess reserves of $100,000 on

federal funds market
A market for overnight lending and borrowing of reserves among banks; the interbank market for reserves on account at the Fed

federal funds rate
The interest rate charged in the federal funds market; the interest rate banks charge one another for overnight borrowing; the Fed's target interest rate

account with the Fed and wants to lend that amount to another bank that finished the day short $100,000 in required reserves. These two banks are brought together by a broker who specializes in the market for federal funds—that is, the market for reserves at the Fed. The interest rate paid on this loan is called the **federal funds rate**; this is the rate the Fed targets as a tool of monetary policy, but more on that later.

How Banks Create Money

Let's now discuss how the Fed, Home Bank, and the banking system as a whole can create fiat money. Excess reserves are the raw material the banking system uses to create money. Again, our discussion focuses on commercial banks because they are the largest and most important depository institutions, although thrifts operate the same way.

Creating Money through Excess Reserves

Suppose Home Bank has already used its $900,000 in excess reserves to make loans and buy government bonds and has no excess reserves left. In fact, let's assume there are no excess reserves in the banking system. With that as a point of departure, let's walk through the money creation process.

Round One

To start, suppose the Fed buys a $1,000 U.S. government bond from a securities dealer, with the transaction handled by the dealer's bank—Home Bank. The Fed pays the dealer by crediting Home Bank's reserve account with $1,000, so Home Bank can increase the dealer's checking account by $1,000. Where does the Fed get these reserves? It makes them up—creates them out of thin air, out of electronic ether! The securities dealer has exchanged one asset, a U.S. bond, for another asset, checkable deposits. A U.S. bond is not money, but checkable deposits are, so the money supply increases by $1,000 in this first round. Exhibit 4 shows changes in Home Bank's balance sheet as a result of the Fed's bond purchase. On the assets side, Home Bank's reserves at the Fed increase by $1,000. On the liabilities side, checkable deposits increase by $1,000. Of the dealer's $1,000 checkable deposit, Home Bank must set aside $100 in required reserves (based on a 10 percent required reserve ratio). The remaining $900 becomes excess reserves, which can fuel a further increase in the money supply.

Round Two

Suppose Home Bank is your regular bank, and you apply for a $900 loan to help pay student fees. Home Bank approves your loan and increases your checking account by $900. *Home Bank has converted your promise to repay, your IOU, into a $900 checkable deposit. Because checkable deposits are money, this action increases the money supply by $900.* The money supply has increased by a total of $1,900 to this point—the $1,000 increase in the securities dealer's checkable deposits and now the $900 increase

EXHIBIT 4 Changes in Home Bank's Balance Sheet after the Fed Buys a $1,000 Bond from Securities Dealer

Assets		Liabilities and Net Worth	
Reserves at Fed	+$1,000	Checkable deposits	+$1,000

in your checkable deposits. In the process, what had been $900 in Home Bank's excess reserves now back up its loan to you. As shown in Exhibit 5, Home Bank's loans increase by $900 on the assets side because your IOU becomes the bank's asset. On the bank's liabilities side, checkable deposits increase by $900 because the bank has increased your account by that amount. In short, Home Bank has created $900 in checkable deposits based on your promise to repay the loan.

When you write a $900 check for student fees, your college promptly deposits the check into its checking account at Merchants Trust, which increases the college's account by $900, and sends your check to the Fed. The Fed transfers $900 in reserves from Home Bank's account to Merchants Trust's account. The Fed then sends the check to Home Bank, which reduces your checkable deposits by $900. The Fed has thereby "cleared" your check by settling the claim that Merchants Trust had on Home Bank. Your $900 in checkable deposits at Home Bank has become your college's $900 in checkable deposits at Merchants Trust. The total increase in the money supply to this point is still $1,900.

Round Three

But Merchants Trust now has $900 more in reserves on deposit with the Fed. After setting aside $90 as required reserves, or 10 percent of your college's checkable deposit increase, the bank has $810 in excess reserves. Suppose Merchants Trust lends this $810 to an English major starting a new business called "Note This," an online note-taking service for students in large classes. Exhibit 6 shows assets at Merchants Trust are up by $810 in loans, and liabilities are up by $810 in checkable deposits. At this point, checkable deposits in the banking system, and the money supply in the economy, are up by a total of $2,710 (= $1,000 + $900 + $810), all springing from the Fed's original $1,000 bond purchase.

The $810 loan is spent at the college bookstore, which deposits the check in its account at Fidelity Bank. Fidelity credits the bookstore's checkable deposits with $810 and sends the check to the Fed for clearance. The Fed reduces Merchants Bank's reserves by $810 and increases Fidelity's by the same. The Fed then sends the check to Merchants, which reduces the English major's checkable deposits by $810. So checkable deposits are down by $810 at Merchants and up by the same amount at Fidelity. Checkable deposits are still up by $2,710, as the $810 in checkable deposits has simply shifted from Merchants Trust to Fidelity Bank.

EXHIBIT 5 Changes in Home Bank's Balance Sheet after Lending $900 to You

Assets		Liabilities and Net Worth	
Loans	+$900	Checkable deposits	+$900

EXHIBIT 6 Changes in Merchants Trust's Balance Sheet after Lending $810 to English Major

Assets		Liabilities and Net Worth	
Loans	+$810	Checkable deposits	+$810

Round Four and Beyond

We could continue the process with Fidelity Bank setting aside $81 in required reserves and lending $729 in excess reserves, but you get some idea of money creation by now. Notice the pattern of deposits and loans. Each time a bank gets a fresh deposit, 10 percent goes to required reserves. The rest becomes excess reserves, which fuel new loans or other asset acquisitions. The borrower writes a check, which the recipient deposits in a checking account, thereby generating excess reserves to support still more loans. Because this example began with the Fed, the Fed can rightfully claim, "The buck starts here"—a slogan that appears on a large plaque in the Federal Reserve chairman's office.

To Review: An individual bank can lend no more than its excess reserves. When the borrower spends those funds, reserves at one bank usually fall, but total reserves in the banking system do not. The recipient bank uses most of the new deposit to extend more loans, creating more checkable deposits. The potential expansion of checkable deposits in the banking system therefore equals some multiple of the initial increase in reserves. Note that our example assumes that banks do not allow excess reserves to sit idle, that borrowed funds do not idle in checking accounts, and that the public does not hold some of the newly created money as cash. If excess reserves remained just that or if borrowed funds idled in checking accounts, they would not fuel an expansion of the money supply. And if people chose to hold borrowed funds in cash rather than in checking accounts, that idle cash would not add to reserves in the banking system.

A Summary of the Rounds

Let's review the money creation process: *The initial and most important step is the Fed's injection of $1,000 in fresh reserves into the banking system.* By buying the bond from the securities dealer, the Fed immediately increased the money supply by $1,000. Home Bank set aside $100 as required reserves and lent you its $900 in excess reserves. You paid your college fees, and the $900 ended up in your college's checkable account. This fueled more money creation, as shown in a series of rounds of Exhibit 7. As you can see, during each round, the increase in checkable deposits (column 1) minus the increase in required reserves (column 2) equals the potential increase in loans (column 3). Checkable deposits in this example can potentially increase by as much as $10,000.

In our example, money creation results from the Fed's $1,000 bond purchase from the securities dealer, but excess reserves would also have increased if the Fed purchased a $1,000 bond from Home Bank, lent Home Bank $1,000, or freed up $1,000 in excess reserves by lowering the reserve requirement.

EXHIBIT 7 Summary of the Money Creation Resulting from the Fed's Purchase of $1,000 U.S. Government Bond

Bank	(1) Increase in Checkable Deposits	(2) Increase in Required Reserves	(3) Increase in Loans (3) = (1) − (2)
Round 1. Home Bank	$ 1,000	$ 100	$ 900
Round 2. Merchants Trust	900	90	810
Round 3. Fidelity Bank	810	81	729
All remaining rounds	7,290	729	6,561
Totals	$10,000	$1,000	$9,000

What if the Fed paid the securities dealer in cash? By exchanging Federal Reserve notes, which become part of the money supply in the hands of the public, for a U.S. bond, which is not part of the money supply, the Fed would have increased the money supply by $1,000. Once the securities dealer put this cash into a checking account—or spent the cash, so the money ended up in someone else's checking account—the banking system's money creation process would have been off and running.

Reserve Requirements and Money Expansion

The banking system as a whole eliminates excess reserves by expanding the money supply. With a 10 percent reserve requirement, the Fed's initial injection of $1,000 in fresh reserves could support up to $10,000 in new checkable deposits in the banking system as a whole, *assuming no bank holds excess reserves, borrowed funds don't sit idle, and people don't want to hold more cash.*

The multiple by which the money supply increases as a result of an increase in the banking system's reserves is called the **money multiplier**. The **simple money multiplier** equals the reciprocal of the required reserve ratio, or $1/r$, where r is the reserve ratio. In our example, the reserve ratio was 10 percent, or 0.1, so the reciprocal is 1/0.1, which equals 10. The formula for the multiple expansion of money supply can be written as:

money multiplier
The multiple by which the money supply changes as a result of a change in fresh reserves in the banking system

simple money multiplier
The reciprocal of the required reserve ratio, or $1/r$; the maximum multiple of fresh reserves by which the money supply can increase

$$\text{Change in the money supply} = \text{Change in fresh reserves} \times 1/r$$

Again, the simple money multiplier assumes that banks hold no excess reserves, that borrowers do not let the funds sit idle, and that people do not want to hold more cash. The higher the reserve requirement, the greater the fraction of deposits that must be held as reserves, so the smaller the money multiplier. A reserve requirement of 20 percent instead of 10 percent would mean each bank must set aside twice as much in required reserves. The simple money multiplier in this case would be 1/0.2, which equals 5. The maximum possible increase in checkable deposits resulting from an initial $1,000 increase in fresh reserves would therefore be $1,000 × 5, or $5,000. *Excess reserves fuel the deposit expansion process, and a higher reserve requirement drains this fuel from the banking system, thereby reducing the amount of new money that can be created.*

On the other hand, with a reserve requirement of only 5 percent, banks would set aside less for required reserves, leaving more excess reserves available for loans. The simple money multiplier in that case would be 1/0.05, or 20. With $1,000 in fresh reserves and a 5 percent reserve requirement, the banking system could increase the money supply by a maximum of $1,000 × 20, which equals $20,000. Thus, the change in the required reserve ratio affects the banking system's ability to create money.

In summary, money creation usually begins with the Fed injecting new reserves into the banking system. An individual bank lends an amount no greater than its excess reserves. The borrower's spending ends up in someone else's checking account, fueling additional loans. *The fractional reserve requirement is the key to the multiple expansion of checkable deposits.* If each $1 deposit had to be backed by $1 in required reserves, the money multiplier would be reduced to 1, which is no multiplier at all.

Limitations on Money Expansion

Various leakages from the multiple expansion process reduce the size of the money multiplier, which is why $1/r$ is called the *simple* money multiplier. You could think of "simple" as meaning maximum. To repeat, our example assumes (1) that banks do not let excess reserves sit idle, (2) that borrowers do something with the money, and (3) that people do not choose to increase their cash holdings. How realistic are these assumptions? With regard to the first, banks have a profit incentive to make loans or buy some higher interest-bearing asset with excess reserves. Granted, banks earn some interest on reserves deposited with the Fed, but the rate is typically less than could be earned on loans or on most other interest-bearing assets. The second assumption is also easy to defend. Why would people borrow money if they didn't need it for something? The third assumption is trickier. Cash may sometimes be preferable to checking accounts because cash is more versatile, so people may choose to hold some of the newly created money as cash. To the extent that people prefer to hold idle cash, this drains reserves from the banking system. With less excess reserves, banks are less able to make loans, reducing the money multiplier. Incidentally, for the money multiplier to operate, a particular bank need not use excess reserves in a specific way; it could use them to pay all its employees a Christmas bonus, for that matter. As long as the money ends up as checkable deposits in the banking system, away we go with the money expansion process.

Multiple Contraction of the Money Supply

We have already outlined the money creation process, so the story of how the Federal Reserve System can reduce bank reserves, thereby reducing the money supply, can be a brief one. Again, we begin by assuming there are no excess reserves in the system and the reserve requirement is 10 percent. Suppose the Fed *sells* a $1,000 U.S. bond to a securities dealer and gets paid with a check drawn on the security dealer's account at Home Bank. So the Fed gets paid by drawing down Home Bank's reserves at the Fed by $1,000. The Fed has thereby reduced the money supply by $1,000 in this first round.

Because the dealer's checking account was reduced by $1,000, Home Bank no longer needs to hold $100 in required reserves. But Home Bank is still short $900 in required reserves (remember, when we started, there were no excess reserves in the banking system). To replenish reserves, Home Bank must recall loans (ask for repayment before the due date), or sell some other asset. As the poet Robert Frost wryly observed, "A bank is a place where they lend you an umbrella in fair weather and ask for it back again when it begins to rain." Suppose the bank calls in $900 loaned to a local business, and the loan is repaid with a check written against Merchants Bank. When the check clears, Home Bank's reserves are up by $900, just enough to satisfy its reserve requirement, but Merchants Bank's reserves and checkable deposits are down by $900. Checkable deposits are now down $1,900 as a result of the Fed's purchase of a $1,000 bond. Because there were no excess reserves at the outset, the loss of $900 in reserves leaves Merchants $810 short of its required level of reserves, forcing that bank to get more reserves.

And so it goes down the line. The Fed's sale of government bonds reduces bank reserves, forcing banks to recall loans or to somehow replenish reserves. This reduces checkable deposits each additional round. *The maximum possible effect is to reduce the money supply by the original reduction in bank reserves times the simple money multiplier, which again equals 1 divided by the reserve requirement, or 1/r*. In our example, the Fed's sale of $1,000 in U.S. bonds could reduce the money supply by as much as $10,000.

For a change of pace, read the case study which looks at a relatively recent financial development, payday lenders.

Now that you have some idea how fractional reserve banking works, we are in a position to summarize the Federal Reserve's role in the economy.

The Fed's Tools of Monetary Control

As mentioned in the previous chapter, in its capacity as a bankers' bank, the Fed clears checks for, extends loans to, and holds deposits of banks. About half of the narrow definition of money (M1) consists of checkable deposits. The Fed's control over checkable deposits works indirectly through its control over reserves in the banking system. You are already familiar with the Fed's three tools for controlling reserves: (1) open-market operations, or the buying and selling of U.S. government bonds; (2) the discount rate, which is the interest rate the Fed charges for loans it makes to banks; and (3) the required reserve ratio, which is the minimum fraction of reserves that banks must hold against deposits. Let's examine each of these in more detail, then look at some other Fed matters.

Open-Market Operations and the Federal Funds Rate

The Fed carries out open-market operations whenever it buys or sells U.S. government bonds in the open market. Decisions about open-market operations are made by the Federal Open Market Committee, or FOMC, which meets every six weeks and during emergencies. To increase the money supply, the Fed directs the New York Fed to buy U.S. bonds. This is called an **open-market purchase.** To reduce the money supply, the New York Fed is directed to carry out an **open-market sale.** Open-market operations are relatively easy to carry out. They require no change in laws or regulations and can be executed in any amount—large or small—chosen by the Fed. Their simplicity and ease of use make them the tool of choice for the Fed.

open-market purchase
The purchase of U.S. government bonds by the Fed to increase the money supply

open-market sale
The sale of U.S. government bonds by the Fed to reduce the money supply

Through open-market operations, the Fed influences bank reserves and the *federal funds rate*, which is the interest rate banks charge one another for borrowing excess reserves at the Fed, typically just for a day or two. Banks that need reserves can borrow excess reserves from other banks, paying the federal funds rate of interest. The federal funds rate serves as a good indicator of the "tightness" of monetary policy. For example, suppose the Fed buys bonds in the open market and thereby increases reserves in the banking system. As a result, more banks have excess reserves. Demand for excess reserves in the federal funds market falls and supply increases, so the federal funds rate—the interest rate for borrowing reserves in this market—declines. We can expect this lower federal funds rate to spread quickly to the economy at large. The excess reserves that have created the lower federal funds rate prompt banks to lower short-term interest rates in general and this increases the quantity of loans demanded by the public.

The Discount Rate

The second monetary policy tool available to the Fed is the **discount rate,** which is the interest rate the Fed charges for loans it makes to banks. Banks borrow from the Fed to satisfy their reserve requirements. A lower discount rate reduces the cost of borrowing, encouraging banks to borrow reserves from the Fed. The Fed usually does not encourage banks to borrow, but the Fed considers itself as the "lender of last resort," and a lender during a financial crisis, as occurred between 2007 and 2010 when some homeowners defaulted on their mortgages.

discount rate
The interest rate the Fed charges banks that borrow reserves

There are actually two discount rates. The *primary discount rate* is usually one percentage point above the federal funds rate. Thus, discount borrowing is less attractive than borrowing through the federal funds market. But during a financial crisis, the Fed could lower the primary discount rate to supply liquidity to the banking system as it did

12 times between August 2007 and December 2008, a response to the financial crisis. The Fed charges more interest on loans to banks considered less sound than to other banks. This *secondary discount rate* is usually about one-half a percentage point higher than the primary discount rate.

The Fed uses the discount rate more as a signal to financial markets about its monetary policy than as a tool for increasing or decreasing the money supply. The discount rate might also be thought of as an emergency tool for injecting liquidity into the banking system in the event of some financial crisis, such as the global credit crisis of 2008. Discount loans outstanding jumped from only $2 billion in August 2007, before the trouble started, to more than $130 billion in April 2009, when the economy was in a sharp recession. Banks would prefer to borrow reserves from other banks in the federal funds market rather than borrow reserves directly from the Fed.

Reserve Requirements

The Fed also influences the money supply through reserve requirements, which are regulations regarding the minimum amount of reserves that banks must hold to back up deposits. Reserve requirements determine how much money the banking system can create with each dollar of fresh reserves. If the Fed increases the reserve requirement, then banks have less excess reserves to lend out. This reduces the banking system's ability to create money. On the other hand, a lower reserve requirement increases the banking system's ability to create money. Reserve requirements can be changed by a simple majority vote of the Board of Governors. But changes in the reserve requirement disrupt the banking system, so the Fed seldom makes such changes. As noted already, the current reserve requirement is 10 percent on checkable deposits and zero on other deposits. Some countries such as Australia, Canada, and the United Kingdom have no reserve requirement. Banks there still hold reserves to deal with everyday cash requirements and can borrow from their central banks (at relatively high rates) if necessary.

Coping with Financial Crises

The Fed, through its regulation of financial markets, also tries to prevent major disruptions and financial panics. For example, during the uncertain days following the terrorist attacks of September 11, 2001, people used their ATM cards to load up on cash. Some were hoarding it. To ensure the banking system had sufficient liquidity, the Fed bought all the government securities offered for sale, purchasing a record $150 billion worth in two days.[2] The Fed also eased some regulations to facilitate bank clearances, especially for banks struck during the attacks. Likewise, when financial crises threatened in1987, 1989, 1998, and 2008, the Fed worked to ensure the financial system had sufficient liquidity. For example, to calm fears during a rash of mortgage defaults in 2007, the Fed lowered the discount rate from 6.25 percent to only 0.5 percent and encouraged banks to borrow from the Fed. To help banks improve their balance sheets, the Fed also began paying interest on bank reserves held at the Fed. To keep mortgage rates low, the Fed invested more than a $1 trillion in mortgage-backed securities. And to help prevent the insurance giant AIG from collapsing, the Fed invested more than $90 billion in the company. As a general approach, Ben Bernanke, the Fed Chairman, announced that the Fed would provide sufficient liquidity to reduce the harm of mortgage defaults on the overall economy. To prevent cash shortages during a crisis, the Fed stockpiles extra cash in bank vaults around the country and around the world.

2. Anita Rachavan, Susan Pulliam, and Jeff Opdyke, "Banks and Regulators Drew Together to Calm Rattled Markets after Attack," *Wall Street Journal*, 18 October 2001.

The Fed Is a Money Machine

One way to get a better idea of the Fed is to review its balance sheet, shown as Exhibit 8, with assets on the left and liabilities and net worth on the right. Because of the mortgage crisis and global financial meltdown of 2008, investors were reluctant to buy mortgage-backed securities. So the Fed stepped in and began buying them in late 2008. These securities account for nearly half of the Fed's assets. U.S. government bonds are a third of Fed assets (during normal times these bonds might account for 90 percent of assets). These IOUs from the federal government result from open-market operations, and they earn the Fed interest. Other assets include foreign currencies, most of which the Fed acquired during the financial crisis as foreign central banks swapped their currencies for U.S. dollars. Another Fed asset, AIG investments, resulted from rescuing the insurance giant during the financial crisis. Nearly all the Fed's assets earn interest.

On the other side of the ledger, Federal Reserve notes outstanding account for about 40 percent of Fed liabilities. These notes—U.S. currency—are IOUs from the Fed and are therefore liabilities of the Fed, but the Fed pays no interest on these notes. Thus, nearly all the Fed's assets earn interest, whereas one of the Fed's primary liabilities—Federal Reserve notes—requires no interest payments by the Fed. The Fed does pay interest on reserves but that rate has been extremely low—just a fraction of 1 percent (still, that rate exceeds what banks have been paying most depositors). *The Fed is therefore both literally and figuratively a money machine. It is literally a money machine because it supplies the economy with Federal Reserve notes; it is figuratively a money machine because most assets earn interest, but a main liability requires no interest payments*. The Fed also earns revenue from discount lending to banks and from other services it provides banks. After covering its operating costs, paying a small amount of interest on bank reserves at the Fed, and paying a 6 percent dividend to the member banks, the Fed turns over any remaining income to the federal government. In 2009, the Fed sent the U.S. Treasury $45 billion, the most ever in a single year.

On the right side of the ledger, you can see that depository institutions' reserves at the Fed totaled $1,052.5 billion. This reflects a huge jump in recent years. One reason for the increase is that in late 2008, the Fed began paying interest on bank reserves held by the Fed, as noted already. Also, because of the financial crisis, banks grew reluctant to make loans, preferring instead to let their reserves collect interest at the Fed. You can also see that the Fed held deposits of the U.S. Treasury, a reminder that the Fed is the federal government's banker.

EXHIBIT 8 Federal Reserve Bank Balance Sheet as of July 21, 2010 (Billions)

Assets		Liabilities and Net Worth	
Mortgage-backed securities	$1,124.6	Federal Reserve notes outstanding	$902.3
U.S. Treasury securities	777.0	Depository institution reserves	1,052.5
AIG investments	92.8	U.S. Treasury balance	243.8
Foreign currencies	93.7	Other liabilities	56.8
Discount loans to depository institutions	65.6	Net worth	80.3
Bank buildings	2.2		
Other assets	179.8		
Total	$2,335.7	Total	$2,335.7

Sources: Federal Reserve Bank at http://www.federalreserve.gov/releases/h41/Current/.

Conclusion

Banks play a unique role in the economy because they can transform someone's IOU into a checkable deposit, and a checkable deposit is money. The banking system's ability to expand the money supply depends on the amount of excess reserves in that system. In our example, it was the purchase of a $1,000 U.S. bond that started the ball rolling. The Fed can also increase reserves by lowering the discount rate enough to stimulate bank borrowing from the Fed (although the Fed uses changes in the discount rate more to signal its policy than to alter the money supply). And, by reducing the required reserve ratio, the Fed not only instantly creates excess reserves in the banking system but also increases the money multiplier. In practice, the Fed rarely changes the reserve requirement because of the disruptive effect of such a change on the banking system. *To control the money supply, the Fed relies primarily on open-market operations.*

Open-market operations can have a direct effect on the money supply, as when the Fed buys bonds from the public. But the Fed also affects the money supply indirectly, as when the Fed's bond purchase increases bank reserves, which then serve as fuel for the money multiplier. In the next chapter, we consider how changes in the money supply affect the economy.

Summary

1. The money supply is narrowly defined as M1, which consists of currency held by the nonbanking public plus checkable deposits and traveler's checks. A broader money aggregate, M2, includes M1 plus savings deposits, small-denomination time deposits, money market mutual funds, and other miscellaneous near-monies.
2. Banks are unlike other financial intermediaries because they can turn a borrower's IOU into money—they can create money. Banks match the different desires of savers and borrowers. Banks also evaluate loan applications and try to diversify portfolios of assets to reduce the risk to any one saver.
3. In acquiring portfolios of assets, banks try to maximize profit while maintaining enough liquidity to satisfy depositors' requests for money. Assets that earn the bank more interest are usually less liquid.
4. Any single bank can expand the money supply by the amount of its excess reserves. For the banking system as a whole, however, the maximum expansion of the money supply equals a multiple of fresh bank reserves. The simple money multiplier is the reciprocal of the reserve ratio, or $1/r$. This multiplier is reduced to the extent that (a) banks allow excess reserves to remain idle, (b) borrowers sit on their proceeds, and (c) the public withdraws cash from the banking system and holds it.
5. The key to changes in the money supply is the Fed's impact on excess reserves in the banking system. To increase excess reserves and thus increase the money supply, the Fed can buy U.S. government bonds, reduce the discount rate, or lower the reserve requirement. To reduce excess reserves and thus reduce the money supply, the Fed can sell U.S. government bonds, increase the discount rate, or increase the reserve requirement. By far the most important monetary tool for the Fed is open-market operations—buying or selling U.S. bonds.
6. The Fed was quite active during the financial crisis of 2008, pursuing several efforts to stabilize financial markets and unfreeze the flow of credit. Fed actions included extending discount loans to banks, offering interest on bank reserves at the Fed, helping AIG stay in business, and spending more than $1 trillion buying mortgage-backed securities to keep mortgage rates low.

Key Concepts

Questions for Review

1. MONEY AGGREGATES What are the two measures of the money supply and how is each measure defined?
2. MONEY AGGREGATES What portion of U.S. Federal Reserve notes circulate outside the United States? How does this affect the United States?
3. Case Study: Faking It (See page 767.) Why did the U.S. government consider it important to redesign the $100 note in order to combat the effects of the "supernote"?
4. MONEY AGGREGATES Determine whether each of the following is included in the M1 or M2 measures of the money supply:
   a. Currency held by the nonbanking public
   b. Available credit on credit cards held by the nonbanking public
   c. Savings deposits
   d. Large-denomination time deposits
   e. Money market mutual fund accounts
5. BANKS ARE FINANCIAL INTERMEDIARIES In acting as financial intermediaries, what needs and desires of savers and borrowers must banks consider?
6. MONEY AGGREGATES Suppose that $1,000 is moved from a savings account at a commercial bank to a checking account at the same bank. Which of the following statements are true and which are false?
   a. The amount of currency in circulation will fall.
   b. M1 will increase.
   c. M2 will increase.
7. BANK DEPOSITS Explain the differences among checkable deposits, savings deposits, and time deposits. Explain whether each of these deposits represents a bank asset or a bank liability.
8. RESERVE ACCOUNTS Explain why a reduction in the required reserve ratio cannot, at least initially, increase total reserves in the banking system. Is the same true of lowering the discount rate? What would happen if the Fed bought U.S. bonds from, or sold them to, the banking system?
9. LIQUIDITY VERSUS PROFITABILITY Why must a bank manager strike a balance between liquidity and profitability on the bank's balance sheet?
10. CREATING MONEY Often it is claimed that banks create money by making loans. How can commercial banks create money? Is the government the only institution that can legally create money?
11. FED TOOLS OF MONETARY CONTROL What three tools can the Fed use to change the money supply? Which tool is used most frequently? What are three limitations on the money expansion process?
12. DISCOUNT RATE What is the difference between the federal funds rate and the discount rate? What is the ultimate impact on the money supply of an increase in the discount rate?
13. FEDERAL FUNDS MARKET What is the federal funds market? How does it help banks strike a balance between liquidity and profitability?
14. THE FED IS A MONEY MACHINE Why is the Fed both literally and figuratively a money machine?
15. Case Study: Banking for the Poor: Payday Loans (See page 768.) Give one reason in favor of payday loans and one reason against.

Problems and Exercises

16. MONETARY AGGREGATES Calculate M1 and M2 using the following information:

Large-denomination time deposits	$304 billion
Currency and coin held by the nonbanking public	$438 billion
Checkable deposits	$509 billion
Small-denomination time deposits	$198 billion
Traveler's checks	$18 billion
Savings deposits	$326 billion
Money market mutual fund accounts	$637 billion

17. MONEY CREATION Show how each of the following initially affects bank assets, liabilities, and reserves. Do not include the results of bank behavior resulting from the Fed's action. Assume a required reserve ratio of 0.05.
    a. The Fed purchases $10 million worth of U.S. government bonds from a bank.
    b. The Fed loans $5 million to a bank.
    c. The Fed raises the required reserve ratio to 0.10.
18. MONEY CREATION Show how each of the following would initially affect a bank's assets and liabilities.
    a. Someone makes a $10,000 deposit into a checking account.
    b. A bank makes a loan of $1,000 by establishing a checking account for $1,000.
    c. The loan described in part (b) is spent.
    d. A bank must write off a loan because the borrower defaults.
19. RESERVE ACCOUNTS Suppose that a bank's customer deposits $4,000 in her checking account. The required reserve ratio is 0.25. What are the required reserves on this new deposit? What is the largest loan that the bank can make on the basis of the new deposit? If the bank chooses to hold reserves of $3,000 on the new deposit, what are the excess reserves on the deposit?
20. MONEY MULTIPLIER Suppose that the Federal Reserve lowers the required reserve ratio from 0.10 to 0.05. How does

this affect the simple money multiplier, assuming that excess reserves are held to zero and there are no currency leakages? What are the money multipliers for required reserve ratios of 0.15 and 0.20?

21. MONEY CREATION Suppose Bank A, which faces a reserve requirement of 10 percent, receives a $1,000 checking deposit from a customer.
    a. Assuming that it wishes to hold no excess reserves, determine how much the bank should lend. Show your answer on Bank A's balance sheet.
    b. Assuming that the loan shown in Bank A's balance sheet is redeposited in Bank B, show the changes in Bank B's balance sheet if it lends out the maximum possible.
    c. Repeat this process for three additional banks: C, D, and E.
    d. Using the simple money multiplier, calculate the total change in the money supply resulting from the $1,000 initial deposit.
    e. Assume Banks A, B, C, D, and E each wish to hold 5 percent excess reserves. How would holding this level of excess reserves affect the total change in the money supply?

22. MONETARY CONTROL Suppose the money supply is currently $500 billion and the Fed wishes to increase it by $100 billion.
    a. Given a required reserve ratio of 0.25, what should it do?
    b. If it decided to change the money supply by changing the required reserve ratio, what change should it make?

Monetary Theory and Policy

30

Michael Matisse/Jupiter Images

- Why do people maintain checking accounts and have cash in their pockets, purses, wallets, desk drawers, coffee cans—wherever?
- In other words, why do people hold money?
- How does the stock of money in the economy affect your ability to find a job, get a student loan, buy a car, or pay credit card bills?
- What have economic theory and the historical record taught us about the relationship between the amount of money in the economy and other macroeconomic variables?

Answers to these and related questions are addressed in this chapter, which examines monetary theory and policy.

The amount of money in the economy affects you in a variety of ways, but to understand these effects, we must dig a little deeper. So far, we have focused on how banks create money. But a more fundamental question is how money affects the economy, a topic called *monetary theory.* Monetary theory explores the effect of the money supply on the economy's price level, employment, and growth. The Fed's control over the money supply is called *monetary policy*. In the short run, changes in the money supply affect the economy by working through changes in the interest rate. In the long run, changes in the money supply affect the price level.

In this chapter, we consider the theory behind each time frame.

Topics discussed include:

- Demand and supply of money
- Money in the short run
- Federal funds rate
- Money in the long run
- Velocity of money
- Monetary policy targets

The Demand and Supply of Money

Let's begin by reviewing the important distinction between the *stock of money* and the *flow of income*. How much money do you have with you right now? That amount is a *stock*—an amount measured at a point in time. Income, in contrast, is a *flow*—an amount measured per period of time. Income is a measure of how much money you receive per period. Income has no meaning unless the period is specified. You would not know whether to be impressed that a friend earned $400 unless you knew whether this was per month, per week, per day, or per hour.

demand for money
The relationship between the interest rate and how much money people want to hold

The **demand for money** is a relationship between the interest rate and how much money people want to hold. Keep in mind that the quantity of money held is a stock measure. It may seem odd at first to be talking about the demand for money. You might think people would demand all the money they could get their hands on. But remember that money, the stock, is not the same as income, the flow. People express their demand for income by selling their labor and other resources. People express their demand for money by holding some of their wealth as money rather than holding other assets that earn more interest.

But we are getting ahead of ourselves. The question is: Why do people demand money? Why do people have money with them, stash money around the house, and have money in checking accounts? The most obvious reason people demand money is that money is a convenient medium of exchange. *People demand money to make purchases.*

The Demand for Money

Because barter represents an insignificant portion of exchange in the modern industrialized economy, households, firms, governments, and foreigners need money to conduct their daily transactions. Consumers need money to buy products, and firms need money to buy resources. *Money allows people to carry out economic transactions more easily and more efficiently.* With credit cards, the short-term loan delays the payment of money, but all accounts must eventually be settled with money.

The greater the value of transactions to be financed in a given period, the greater the demand for money. So the more active the economy is—that is, the more goods and services exchanged, reflected by real output—the more money demanded. Obviously an economy with a real GDP of $14 trillion needs more money than an economy half that size. Also, the higher the economy's price level, the greater the demand for money. The more things cost on average, the more money is needed to buy them. Shoppers in economies suffering from hyperinflation need mountains of cash.

You demand the money needed to fund your normal spending in the course of the day or week, and you may need money for unexpected expenditures. If you plan to buy lunch tomorrow, you will carry enough money to pay for it. But you may also want to be able to pay for other possible contingencies. For example, you could have car trouble or you could come across a sale on a favorite item. You can use checks, debit cards, or credit cards, for some of these unexpected purchases, but you still feel safer with some extra cash. You may have a little extra money with you right now for who knows what. Even *you* don't know.

The demand for money is rooted in money's role as a medium of exchange. But as we have seen, money is more than a medium of exchange; it is also a store of value. People save for a new home, for college, for retirement. People can store their purchasing power as money or as some other financial assets, such as corporate and government bonds. When people buy bonds and other financial assets, they are lending their money and are paid interest for doing so.

The demand for any asset is based on the services it provides. The big advantage of money as a store of value is its liquidity: Money can be immediately exchanged for whatever is for sale. In contrast, other financial assets, such as corporate or government bonds, must first be *liquidated*, or exchanged for money, which can then be used to buy goods and services. Money, however, has one major disadvantage when compared to other financial assets. Money in the form of currency and traveler's checks earns no interest, and the rate earned on checkable deposits is well below that earned on other financial assets; in recent years that rate has been close to zero. So holding wealth as money means giving up some interest. For example, suppose a business could earn 3 percent more interest by holding financial assets other than money. The opportunity cost of holding $1 million as money rather than as some other financial asset would amount to $30,000 per year. *The interest forgone is the opportunity cost of holding money.*

Money Demand and Interest Rates

When the market interest rate is low, other things constant, the cost of holding money—the cost of maintaining liquidity—is low, so people hold more of their wealth in the form of money. When the interest rate is high, the cost of holding money is high, so people hold less of their wealth in money and more in other financial assets that pay higher interest. Thus, *other things constant, the quantity of money demanded varies inversely with the market interest rate.*

The money demand curve D_m in Exhibit 1 shows the quantity of money people demand at alternative interest rates, other things constant. Both the quantity of money and the interest rate are in nominal terms. *The money demand curve slopes downward because the lower the interest rate, the lower the opportunity cost of holding money.* Movements along the curve reflect the effects of changes in the interest rate on the quantity of money demanded, other things assumed constant. The quantity of money demanded is inversely related to the price of holding money, which is the interest

EXHIBIT 1 Demand for Money

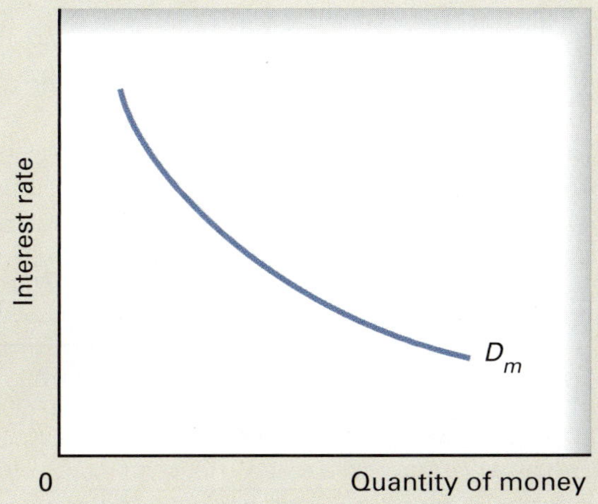

The money demand curve, D_m, slopes downward. As the interest rate falls, other things constant, so does the opportunity cost of holding money; the quantity of money demanded increases.

rate. Assumed constant along the curve are the price level and real GDP. If either increases, the demand for money increases, as reflected by a rightward shift of the money demand curve.

The Supply of Money and the Equilibrium Interest Rate

The supply of money—the stock of money available in the economy at a particular time—is determined primarily by the Fed through its control over currency and over excess reserves in the banking system. The supply of money S_m is depicted as a vertical line in Exhibit 2. *A vertical supply curve implies that the quantity of money supplied is independent of the interest rate.*

The intersection of the demand for money D_m with the supply of money S_m determines the equilibrium interest rate, *i*—the interest rate that equates the quantity of money demanded with the quantity supplied. At interest rates above the equilibrium level, the opportunity cost of holding money is higher, so the quantity of money people want to hold is less than the quantity supplied. At interest rates below the equilibrium level, the opportunity cost of holding money is lower, so the quantity of money people want to hold exceeds the quantity supplied.

If the Fed increases the money supply, the supply curve shifts to the right, as shown by the movement from S_m out to S'_m in Exhibit 2. At interest rate *i*, the quantity supplied now exceeds the quantity demanded. Because of the increased supply of money, people are *able* to hold more money. But at interest rate *i* they are *unwilling* to hold that much. Because people are now holding more of their wealth as money than they would like, they exchange some money for other financial assets, such as bonds. As the demand

EXHIBIT 2 Effect of an Increase in the Money Supply

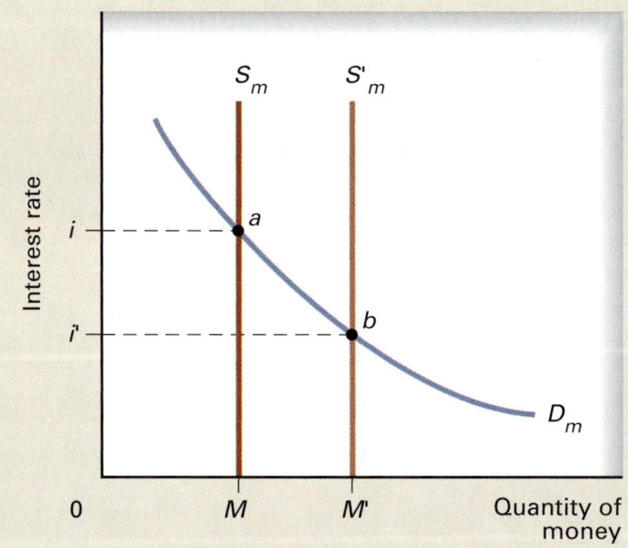

Because the money supply is determined by the Federal Reserve, it can be represented by a vertical line. At point *a*, the intersection of the money supply, S_m, and the money demand, D_m, determines the market interest rate, *i*. Following an increase in the money supply to S'_m, the quantity of money supplied exceeds the quantity demanded at the original interest rate, *i*. The new equilibrium occurs at point *b*.

for bonds increases, bond sellers can pay less interest yet still attract enough buyers. The interest rate falls until the quantity of money demanded just equals the quantity supplied. With the decline in the interest rate to i' in Exhibit 2, the opportunity cost of holding money falls enough that the public is willing to hold the now-larger stock of money. Equilibrium moves from point *a* to point *b*. *For a given money demand curve, an increase in the money supply drives down the interest rate, and a decrease in the money supply drives up the interest rate.*

Now that you have some idea how money demand and money supply determine the market interest rate, you are ready to see how money fits into our model of the economy. Specifically, let's see how changes in the money supply affect aggregate demand and equilibrium output.

Money and Aggregate Demand in the Short Run

In the short run, money affects the economy through changes in the interest rate. Monetary policy influences the market interest rate, which in turn affects investment, a component of aggregate demand. Let's work through the chain of causation.

Interest Rates and Investment

Suppose the Fed believes that the economy is producing less than its potential and decides to stimulate output and employment by increasing the money supply. Recall from the previous chapter that the Fed's primary tool for increasing the money supply is open-market purchases of U.S. government securities. The three panels of Exhibit 3 trace the links between changes in the money supply and changes in aggregate demand. We begin with equilibrium interest rate i, which is determined in panel (a) by the intersection of the money demand curve D_m with the money supply curve S_m. Suppose the

EXHIBIT 3 Effects of an Increase in the Money Supply on Interest Rates, Investment, and Aggregate Demand

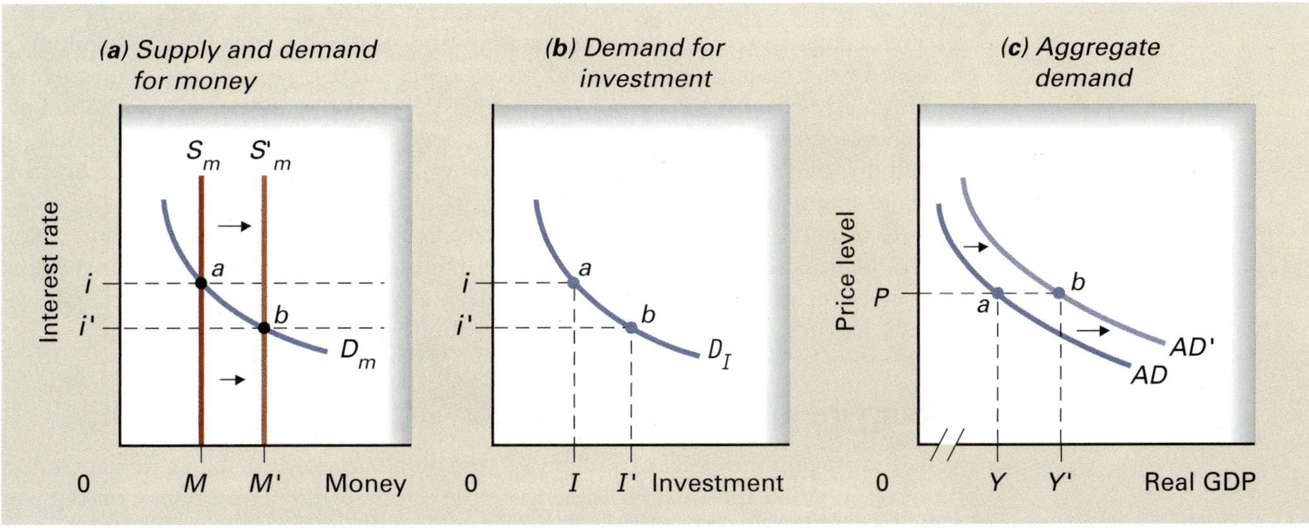

In panel (a), an increase in the money supply forces the interest rate down to i'. With the cost of borrowing lower, the amount invested increases from I to I', as shown in panel (b). This sets off the spending multiplier process, so the aggregate output demanded at price level P increases from Y to Y'. The increase is shown by the shift of the aggregate demand curve to the right in panel (c).

Fed purchases U.S. government bonds and thereby increases the money supply, as shown by a rightward shift of the money supply curve from S_m to S'_m. After the increase in the supply of money, people are holding more money than they would prefer at interest rate *i,* so they try to exchange one form of wealth, money, for other financial assets. Exchanging dollars for financial assets has no direct effect on aggregate demand, but it does reduce the market interest rate.

A decline in the interest rate to *i′*, other things constant, reduces the opportunity cost of financing new plants and equipment, thereby making new investment more profitable. Likewise, a lower interest rate reduces the cost of financing a new house. So a decline in the interest rate increases the amount of investment demanded. Panel (b) shows the demand for investment D_I first introduced several chapters back. When the interest rate falls from *i* to *i′*, the quantity of investment demanded increases from *I* to *I′*.

The spending multiplier magnifies this increase in investment, leading to a greater increase in aggregate demand, reflected in panel (c) by a rightward shift of the aggregate demand curve from *AD* to *AD′*. At the given price level *P*, real GDP increases from *Y* to *Y′*. The sequence of events can be summarized as follows:

$$M\uparrow \rightarrow i\downarrow \rightarrow I\uparrow \rightarrow AD\uparrow \rightarrow Y\uparrow$$

An increase in the money supply, *M*, reduces the interest rate, *i*. The lower interest rate stimulates investment, *I*, which increases aggregate demand from *AD* to *AD′*. At a given price level, real GDP demanded increases from *Y* to *Y′*. The entire sequence is also traced out in each panel by the movement from point *a* to point *b*.

Note that the graphs presented here ignore any feedback effects of changes in real GDP on the demand for money. Because the demand for money depends on the level of real GDP, an increase in real GDP would shift the money demand curve to the right in panel (a). If we had shifted the money demand curve, the equilibrium interest rate would still have fallen, but not by as much, so investment and aggregate demand would not have increased by as much. Thus, Exhibit 2 is a simplified view, but it still captures the essentials of how changes in the money supply affect the economy.

Now let's consider the effect of a Fed-orchestrated *increase* in interest rates. In Exhibit 3 such a policy could be traced by moving from point *b* to point *a* in each panel, but we dispense with a blow-by-blow discussion of the graphs. Suppose the Federal Reserve decides to reduce the money supply to cool down an overheated economy. A decrease in the money supply would increase the interest rate. At the higher interest rate, businesses find it more costly to finance plants and equipment, and households find it more costly to finance new homes. Hence, a higher interest rate reduces the amount invested. The resulting decline in investment is magnified by the spending multiplier, leading to a greater decline in aggregate demand.

As long as the interest rate is sensitive to changes in the money supply, and as long as investment is sensitive to changes in the interest rate, changes in the money supply affect investment. The extent to which a given change in investment affects aggregate demand depends on the size of the spending multiplier.

Adding the Short-Run Aggregate Supply Curve

Even after tracing the effect of a change in the money supply on aggregate demand, we still have only half the story. To determine the effects of monetary policy on the equilibrium real GDP in the economy, we need the supply side. An aggregate supply curve helps show how a given shift of the aggregate demand curve affects real GDP and the price level. In the short run, the aggregate supply curve slopes upward, so the quantity supplied increases only if the price level increases. *For a given shift of the aggregate demand curve, the steeper the short-run aggregate supply curve, the smaller the increase in real GDP and the larger the increase in the price level.*

Suppose the economy is producing at point *a* in Exhibit 4, where the aggregate demand curve *AD* intersects the short-run aggregate supply curve $SRAS_{110}$, yielding a short-run equilibrium output of $13.8 trillion and a price level of 105. As you can see, the actual price level of 105 is below the expected price level of 110, and the short-run equilibrium output of $13.8 trillion is below the economy's potential of $14.0 trillion, yielding a recessionary gap of $0.2 trillion.

At point *a*, real wages are higher than had been negotiated and many people are looking for jobs. The Fed can wait to see whether the economy recovers on its own. Market forces could cause employers and workers to renegotiate lower nominal wages. This would lower production costs, pushing the short-run aggregate supply curve rightward, thus closing the recessionary gap. But if Fed officials are impatient with natural market forces, they could try to close the gap using an expansionary monetary policy. For example, during 2007 and 2008, the Fed aggressively cut the federal funds rate from 5.25 percent to between 0 and 0.25 percent to stimulate aggregate demand. If the Fed lowers that rate by just the right amount, this stimulates investment, thus increasing the aggregate demand curve enough to achieve a new equilibrium at point *b*, where the economy produces its potential output. Given all the connections in the chain of causality between changes in the money supply and changes in equilibrium output,

EXHIBIT 4 Expansionary Monetary Policy to Close a Recessionary Gap

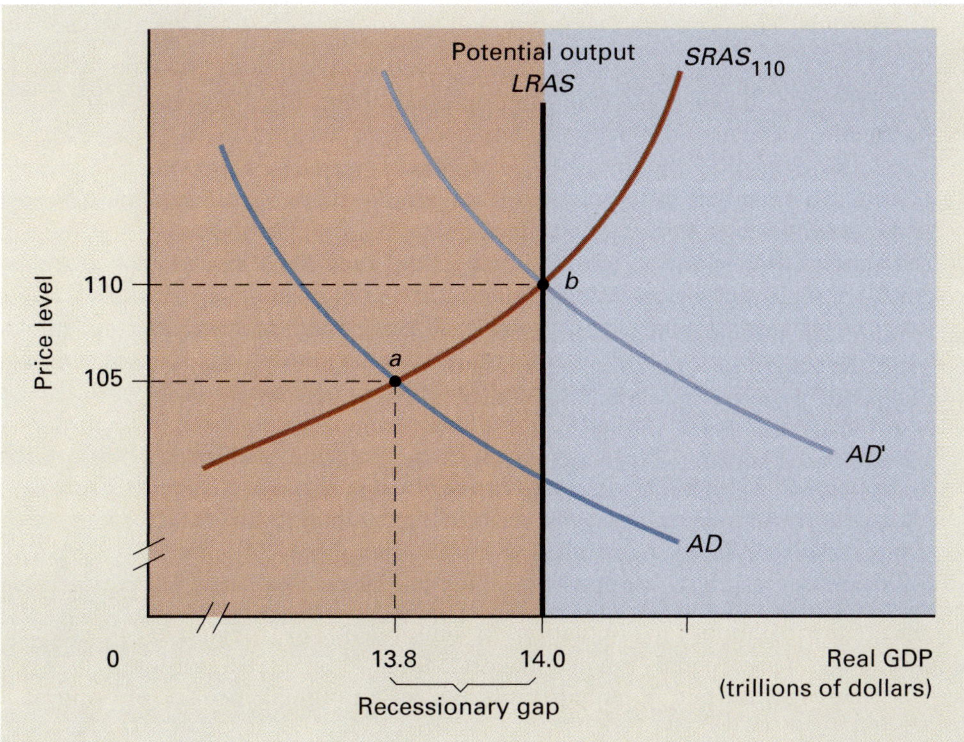

At point *a*, the economy is producing less than its potential in the short run, resulting in a recessionary gap of $0.2 trillion. If the Federal Reserve increases the money supply by just the right amount, the aggregate demand curve shifts rightward from *AD* to *AD'*. A short-run and long-run equilibrium is established at point b, with the price level at 110 and output at the potential level of $14.0 trillion.

however, it would actually be quite remarkable for the Fed to execute monetary policy so precisely. If the Fed overshoots the mark and stimulates aggregate demand too much, this would open up an expansionary gap, thus creating inflationary pressure in the economy.

To Review: As long as the money demand curve and the investment demand curve each slopes downward, an increase in the money supply reduces the market interest rate, increasing investment and consequently increasing aggregate demand. And as long as the short-run aggregate supply curve slopes upward, the short-run effect of an increase in the money supply is an increase in both real output and the price level. But here is one final qualification: Lowering the interest rate may not always stimulate investment. Economic prospects may become so glum that lower interest rates may fail to achieve the desired increase in aggregate demand. In response to the recent financial crisis, for example, the Fed cut the federal funds rate to near zero by the end of 2008, but investment in 2009 still dropped sharply.

That's the theory of monetary policy in the short run. The case study at the end of the book, "Public Policy: Targeting the Federal Funds Rate," looks at how the Fed executes that policy.

Money and Aggregate Demand in the Long Run

When we looked at the impact of money on the economy in the short run, we found that money influences aggregate demand and equilibrium output through its effect on the interest rate. Here we look at the long-run effects of changes in the money supply on the economy. *The long-run view of money is more direct: if the central bank supplies more money to the economy, sooner or later people spend more. But because the long-run aggregate supply curve is fixed at the economy's potential output, this greater spending simply increases the price level.* In short, more money is chasing the same output. Here are the details.

The Equation of Exchange

equation of exchange
The quantity of money, M, multiplied by its velocity, V, equals nominal GDP, which is the product of the price level, P, and real GDP, Y; or $M \times V = P \times Y$

velocity of money
The average number of times per year each dollar is used to purchase final goods and services

Every transaction in the economy involves a two-way swap: The buyer exchanges money for goods and the seller exchanges goods for money. One way of expressing this relationship among key variables in the economy is the **equation of exchange**, first developed by classical economists. Although this equation can be arranged in different ways, depending on the emphasis, the basic version is

$$M \times V = P \times Y$$

where M is the quantity of money in the economy; V is the **velocity of money**, or the average number of times per year each dollar is used to purchase final goods and services; P is the average price level; and Y is real GDP. The equation of exchange says that the quantity of money in circulation, M, multiplied by V, the number of times that money changes hands, equals the average price level, P, times real output, Y. The price level, P, times real output, Y, equals the economy's nominal income and output, or nominal GDP.

By rearranging the equation of exchange, we find that velocity equals nominal GDP divided by the money stock, or

$$V = \frac{P \times V}{M}$$

For example, nominal GDP in 2009 was \$14.12 trillion, and the money stock as measured by M1 averaged \$1.69 trillion. The velocity of money indicates how often each dollar is used on average to pay for final goods and services during the year. So in 2009, velocity was \$14.12 trillion divided by \$1.69 trillion, or 8.4. Given GDP and the money supply, each dollar in circulation must have been spent 8.4 times on average to pay for final goods and services. There is no other way these market transactions could have occurred. The value of velocity is implied by the values of the other variables. Incidentally, velocity measures spending only on final goods and services—not on intermediate products, secondhand goods, financial assets, or illegal activity, even though such spending also occurs. So velocity underestimates how hard the money supply works during the year.

The equation of exchange says that total spending ($M \times V$) always equals total receipts ($P \times Y$), as was the case in our circular-flow analysis. As described so far, however, the equation of exchange is simply an *identity*—a relationship expressed in such a way that it is true by definition. Another example of an identity would be a relationship equating miles per gallon to the distance driven divided by the gasoline required.

The Quantity Theory of Money

If velocity is relatively stable over time, or at least predictable, the equation of exchange turns from an identity into a theory—the quantity theory of money. The **quantity theory of money** states that if the velocity of money is stable, or at least predictable, then the equation of exchange can be used to predict the effects of changes in the money supply on *nominal* GDP, $P \times Y$. For example, if M increases by 5 percent and V remains constant, then $P \times Y$, or nominal GDP, must also increase by 5 percent. For a while, some economists believed they could use the equation of exchange to predict nominal output in the short run. Now it's used primarily as a guide in the long run.

quantity theory of money
If the velocity of money is stable, or at least predictable, changes in the money supply have predictable effects on nominal GDP

So an increase in the money supply results in more spending in the long run, meaning a higher nominal GDP. How is this increase in $P \times Y$ divided between changes in the price level and changes in real GDP? The answer does not lie in the quantity theory, for that theory is stated only in terms of nominal GDP. The answer lies in the shape of the aggregate supply curve.

The long-run aggregate supply curve is vertical at the economy's potential level of output. With real output, Y, fixed and the velocity of money, V, relatively stable, a change in the stock of money translates directly into a change in the price level. Exhibit 5 shows the effect of an increase in the money supply in the long run. An increase in the money supply causes a rightward shift of the aggregate demand curve, which increases the price level but leaves output unchanged at potential GDP. So the economy's potential output level is not affected by changes in the money supply. *In the long run, increases in the money supply, with velocity stable or at least not decreasing, result only in higher prices.* For example, an examination of 73 inflation periods across major economies since 1960 concludes that important triggers to inflation were expansionary monetary policies.[1]

To Review: If velocity is stable, or at least predictable, the quantity theory of money says that changes in the money supply will, in the long run, result in predictable effects on the economy's price level. Velocity's stability and predictability are key to the quantity theory of money. Let's consider some factors that might influence velocity.

1. John Boschen and Charles Weise, "What Starts Inflation: Evidence from OECD Countries," *Journal of Money, Credit and Banking*, 35 (June 2003): 323–349.

EXHIBIT 5 In the Long Run, an Increase in the Money Supply Results in a Higher Price Level, or Inflation

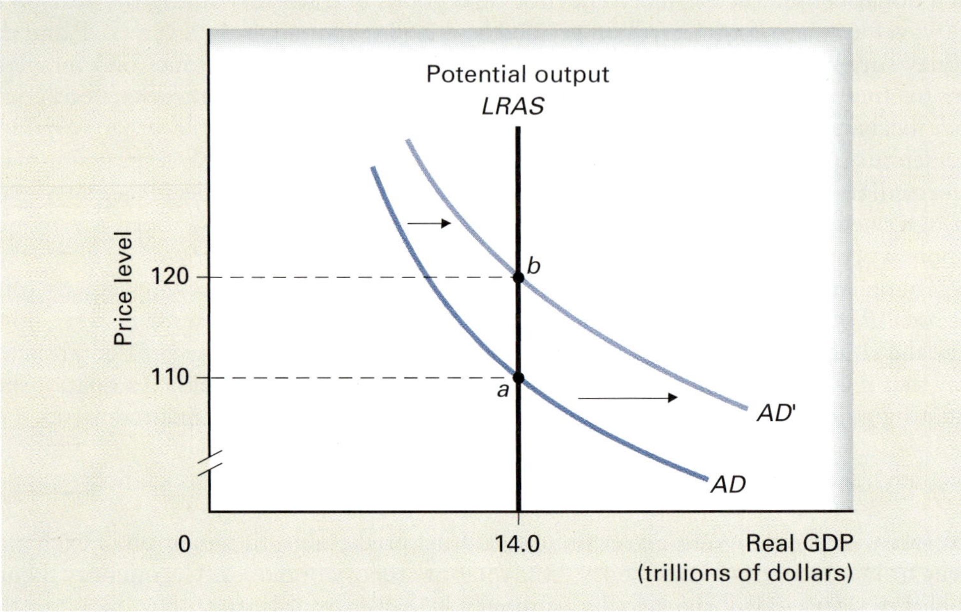

The quantity theory of money predicts that if velocity is stable, then an increase in the money supply in the long run results in a higher price level, or inflation. Because the long-run aggregate supply curve is fixed, increases in the money supply affect only the price level, not real output.

What Determines the Velocity of Money?

Velocity depends on the customs and conventions of commerce. In colonial times, money might be tied up in transit for days as a courier on horseback carried a payment from a merchant in Boston to one in Baltimore. Today, the electronic transmission of funds occurs in an instant, so the same stock of money can move around much more quickly to finance many more transactions. *The velocity of money has also increased because of a variety of commercial innovations that facilitate exchange.* For example, a wider use of charge accounts and credit cards has reduced the need for shoppers to carry cash. Likewise, automatic teller machines have made cash more accessible at more times and in more places. What's more, debit cards are used at a growing number of retail outlets, such as grocery stores and drug stores, so people need less "walking around" money.

Another institutional factor that determines velocity is the frequency with which workers get paid. Suppose a worker who earns $52,000 per year gets paid $2,000 every two weeks. Earnings are spent evenly during the two-week period and are gone by the end of the period. In that case, a worker's average money balance during the pay period is $1,000. If a worker earns the same $52,000 per year but, instead, gets paid $1,000 weekly, the average money balance during the pay period falls to $500. *Thus, the more often workers get paid, other things constant, the lower their average money balances, so the more active the money supply and the greater its velocity.* Payment practices change slowly over time, and the effects of these changes on velocity are predictable.

Another factor affecting velocity depends on how stable money is as a store of value. *The better money serves as a store of value, the more money people hold, so the lower its velocity.* For example, the introduction of interest-bearing checking accounts made money a better store of value, so people were more willing to hold money in checking accounts and this financial innovation reduced velocity. On the other hand, when inflation increases unexpectedly, money turns out to be a poorer store of value. People become reluctant to hold money and try to exchange it for some asset that retains its value better. This reduction in people's willingness to hold money during periods of high inflation increases the velocity of money. During hyperinflations, workers usually get paid daily, boosting velocity even more. Thus, *velocity increases with a rise in the inflation rate, other things constant.* Money becomes a hot potato—nobody wants to hold it for long.

Again, the usefulness of the quantity theory in predicting changes in the price level in the long run hinges on how stable and predictable the velocity of money is over time.

How Stable Is Velocity?

Exhibit 6 graphs velocity since 1960, measured both as nominal GDP divided by M1 in panel (a) and as nominal GDP divided by M2 in panel (b). Between 1960 and 1980, M1 velocity increased steadily and in that sense could be considered at least predictable. M1 velocity bounced around during the 1980s. But in the early 1990s, more and more banks began offering money market funds that included limited check-writing privileges, or what is considered M2. Deposits shifted from M1 to M2, which increased the velocity of M1. Also in recent years, more people began using their ATM and debit cards to pay directly at grocery stores, drugstores, and a growing number of outlets, and this too increased the velocity of M1 because people had less need for walking-around money (plus you can easily get cash back on debit-card transactions). M1 velocity increased from about 6.0 in 1993 to over 10.0 in 2007. M1 velocity dropped during the 2007–2009 recession. Because of anxiety about the economy, people hoarded more cash, which slowed velocity to 8.4 in 2009. M2 velocity appears more stable, as you can see by comparing the two panels in Exhibit 6.

For a few years, the Fed focused on changes in the money supply as a target for monetary policy in the short run. Because M1 velocity became so unstable during the 1980s, the Fed in 1987 switched from targeting M1 to targeting M2. But when M2 velocity became volatile in the early 1990s, the Fed announced that money aggregates, including M2, would no longer be considered reliable guides for monetary policy in the short run. *Since 1993, the equation of exchange has been considered more of a rough guide linking changes in the money supply to inflation in the long run.*

What is the long-run relationship between increases in the money supply and inflation? Since the Federal Reserve System was established in 1913, the United States has suffered three episodes of high inflation, and each was preceded and accompanied by sharp increases in the money supply. These occurred from 1913 to 1920, 1939 to 1948, and 1967 to 1980. At the end of the book, case study, "Public Policy: The Money Supply and Inflation Around the World" examines other evidence linking money growth with inflation in the long run worldwide.

Targets for Monetary Policy

In the short run, monetary policy affects the economy largely by influencing the interest rate. In the long run, changes in the money supply affect the price level, though with an uncertain lag. Should monetary authorities focus on the interest rates in the short run or the supply of money in the long run? As we will see, the Fed lacks the tools to focus on both at the same time.

EXHIBIT 6 The Velocity of Money

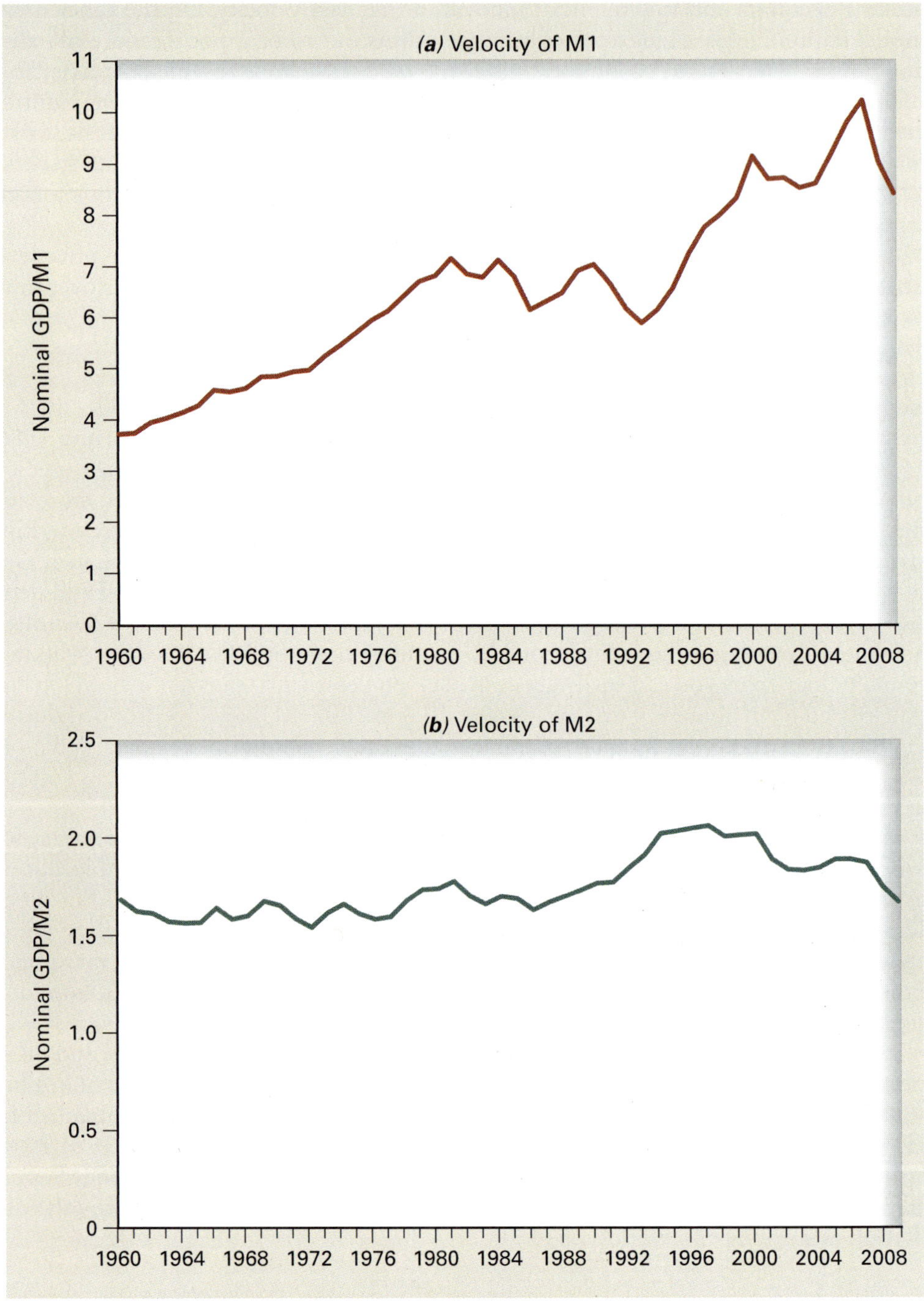

M1 velocity fluctuated so much during the 1980s that M1 growth was abandoned as a short-run policy target. M2 velocity appears more stable than M1 velocity, but both are now considered by the Fed as too unpredictable for short-run policy use.

Source: *Economic Report of the President*, February 2010. To compute the latest velocity, go to http://www.gpoaccess.gov/eop/, find the statistical tables in the appendix then divide nominal GDP by M1 and by M2.

Contrasting Policies

To demonstrate the effects of different policies, we begin with the money market in equilibrium at point *e* in Exhibit 7. The interest rate is *i* and the money stock is *M*, values the monetary authorities find appropriate. Suppose there is an increase in the demand for money in the economy, perhaps because of an increase in nominal GDP. The money demand curve shifts to the right, from D_m to D'_m.

When confronted with an increase in the demand for money, monetary authorities can choose to do nothing, thereby allowing the interest rate to rise, or they can increase the money supply enough to hold the interest rate constant. If monetary authorities do nothing, the quantity of money in the economy remains at *M*, but the interest rate rises because the greater demand for money increases the equilibrium combination from point *e* up to point *e′*. Alternatively, monetary authorities can try to keep the interest rate at its initial level by increasing the supply of money from S_m to S'_m. In terms of possible combinations of the money stock and the interest rate, monetary authorities must choose from points lying along the new money demand curve, D'_m.

A growing economy usually needs a growing money supply to pay for the increase in aggregate output. If monetary authorities maintain a constant growth in the money supply, and if velocity remains stable, the interest rate fluctuates unless the growth in the supply of money each period just happens to match the growth in the demand for money (as in the movement from *e* to *e*" in Exhibit 7). Alternatively, monetary authorities could try to adjust the money supply each period by the amount needed to

EXHIBIT 7 Targeting Interest Rates Versus Targeting the Money Supply

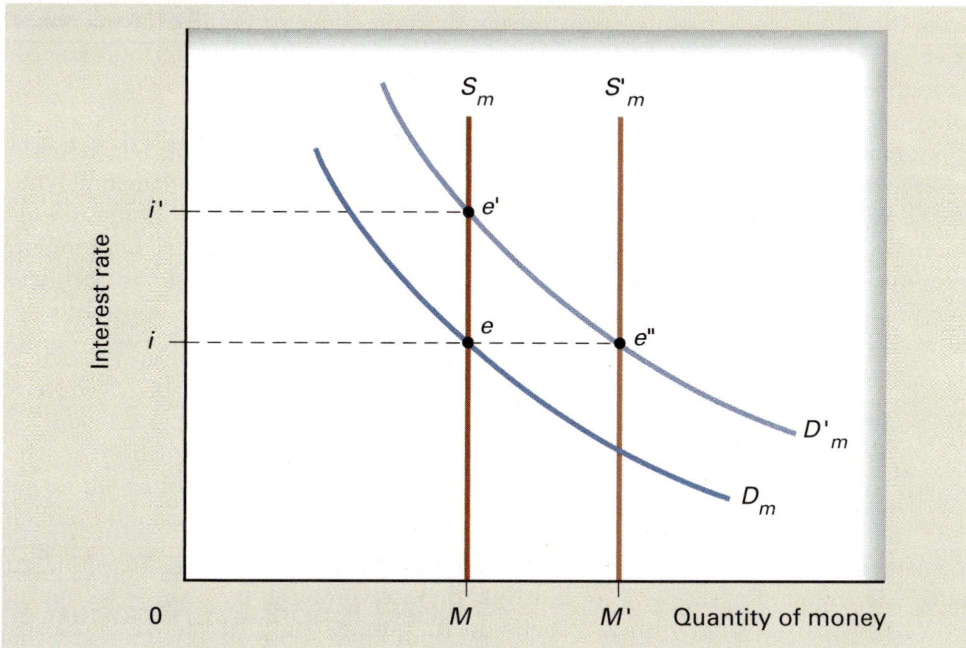

An increase in the price level or in real GDP, with velocity stable, shifts rightward the money demand curve from D_m to D'_m. If the Federal Reserve holds the money supply at S_m, the interest rate rises from *i* (at point *e*) to *i′* (at point *e′*). Alternatively, the Fed could hold the interest rate constant by increasing the money supply to S'_m. The Fed may choose any point along the money demand curve D'_m.

keep the interest rate stable. With this latter approach, changes in the money supply would have to offset any changes in the demand for money. This essentially is what the Fed does when it holds the federal funds target constant, as it did through 2009 and 2010.

Interest rate fluctuations could be harmful if they create undesirable fluctuations in investment. For interest rates to remain stable during economic expansions, the money supply would have to grow at the same rate as the demand for money. Likewise, for interest rates to remain stable during economic contractions, the money supply would have to shrink at the same rate as the demand for money. Hence, for monetary authorities to maintain the interest rate at some specified level, the money supply must increase during economic expansions and decrease during contractions. But an increase in the money supply during an expansion would increase aggregate demand even more, and a decrease in the money supply during a contraction would reduce aggregate demand even more. *Such changes in the money supply would thus tend to worsen fluctuations in economic activity, thereby adding more instability to the economy.* With this in mind, let's review monetary policy over the years.

Targets before 1982

Between World War II and October 1979, the Fed attempted to stabilize interest rates. Stable interest rates were viewed as a prerequisite for an attractive investment environment and, thus, for a stable economy. Milton Friedman, a Nobel Prize winner, argued that this exclusive attention to interest rates made monetary policy a source of instability in the economy because changes in the money supply reinforced fluctuations in the economy. He said that the Fed should pay less attention to interest rates and instead should focus on a steady and predictable growth in the money supply. The debate raged during the 1970s, and Friedman won some important converts. Amid growing concern about a rising inflation rate, the Fed, under a new chairman, Paul Volcker, announced in October 1979 that it would deemphasize interest rates and would instead target specific money aggregates. Not surprisingly, interest rates became much more volatile.

But many observers believe that a sharp reduction in money growth in the latter half of 1981 caused the recession of 1982. Inflation declined rapidly, but unemployment climbed to 10 percent. People were worried. As you might expect, the Fed was widely criticized. Farmers, politicians, and businesspeople denounced Volcker. Emotions ran high. Volcker was reportedly even given Secret Service protection. In October 1982, three years after the focus on interest rates was dropped, Volcker announced that the Fed would again pay some attention to interest rates.

Targets after 1982

The Fed is always feeling its way, looking for signs about the direction of the economy. The rapid pace of financial innovations and deregulation during the 1980s made the definition and measurement of the money supply more difficult. Alan Greenspan, who became the Fed chairman in 1987, said that, in the short run, changes in the money supply "are not linked closely enough with those of nominal income to justify a single-minded focus on the money supply."[2] In 1993, he testified in Congress that the Fed would no longer target money aggregates, such as M1 and M2, as a guide to monetary policy. As we've seen, the Fed in recent years has

2. Quoted in "Greenspan Asks That Fed Be Allowed to Pay Interest," *Wall Street Journal*, 11 March 1992.

targeted the federal funds rate. *No central bank in a major economy now makes significant use of money aggregates to guide policy in the short run. Still, most policy makers also agree that in the long run, changes in the money supply influence the price level and inflation.*

While monetary targets are important, also significant is what Fed officials have to say. For example, they might announce that they are following a problem closely and are prepared to stabilize financial markets as needed. Such reassurance is sometimes all that's required to calm market jitters.

Other Fed Actions and Concerns

As we have seen, the Fed shapes monetary policy in a variety of other ways, as it did during the recession of 2007–2009, when it (1) invested in AIG so the giant insurer would not fail and drag other companies down with it, (2) invested more than $1 trillion in mortgage-backed securities to keep mortgage rates low and offer liquidity in that troubled market, (3) worked with the U.S. Treasury and with other regulators to stabilize banks and thaw frozen credit lines, and (4) worked with the U.S. Treasury and other regulators to help conduct a **stress test** of the 19 largest banks to determine which ones needed more financial capital to weather a bad economy.

stress test
Bank regulators assessed the soundness of large banks to determine which ones needed more financial capital to weather a bad economy

All these efforts could be summed up as the *Fed trying to do whatever it takes to keep financial markets from freezing up.* Fed officials did not want a repeat of the Great Depression, when they dropped the ball by not supplying the liquidity that the banking system needed. The effects of some Fed actions are reflected in its balance sheet, and economists are paying more attention to that to understand monetary policy.[3]

At some point the Fed will have to unwind certain actions taken during the financial crisis, and it will have to do so in a way that's not inflationary. At the same time, the Fed must be mindful of the possibility of deflation, which is also bad news and can be self-reinforcing. For example, as home prices slide, few people want to buy because they expect prices to go lower; if enough people hold back, then, what do you know, prices drop even more.

International Considerations

As national economies grow more interdependent, the Fed has become more sensitive to the global implications of its action. What happens in the United States often affects markets overseas and vice versa. The Fed has tried to sooth troubled world markets in a variety of ways. When Mexico faced financial difficulties in 1982 and again in 1994, Fed officials helped arrange loans to prevent a financial crises. A worldwide financial panic in the fall of 1998 because of defaults on Russian bonds prompted the Fed to lower the federal funds rate to supply more liquidity here and abroad. And a worldwide shortage of credit in 2007–2009 caused by mortgage defaults in the United States prompted the Fed to supply additional liquidity to the banking system to ensure the orderly functioning of financial markets. Although not the main focus of monetary policy, international considerations are of growing importance to the Fed.

3. See, for example, Vasco Curdia and Michael Woodford, "The Central-Bank Balance Sheet as an Instrument of Monetary Policy," NBER Working Paper 16208, (July 2010).

Conclusion

This chapter has described two ways of viewing the effects of money on the economy's performance, but we should not overstate the differences. In the model that focuses on the short run, an increase in the money supply means that people are holding more money than they would like at the prevailing interest rate, so they exchange one form of wealth, money, for other financial assets, such as corporate or government bonds. This greater demand for other financial assets has no direct effect on aggregate demand, but it does reduce the interest rate, and thereby stimulates investment. The higher investment gets magnified by the spending multiplier, increasing aggregate demand. The effect of this increase in demand on real output and the price level depends on the shape of the short-run aggregate supply curve.

In the model that focuses on the long run, changes in the money supply act more directly on the price level. If velocity is relatively stable or at least predictable, then a change in the money supply has a predictable effect on the price level in the long run. As long as velocity is not declining, an increase in the money supply means that people eventually spend more, increasing aggregate demand. But because long-run aggregate supply is fixed at the economy's potential output, increased aggregate demand leads simply to a higher price level, or to inflation.

Summary

1. The opportunity cost of holding money is the higher interest forgone by not holding other financial assets instead. Along a given money demand curve, the quantity of money demanded relates inversely to the interest rate. The demand for money curve shifts rightward as a result of an increase in the price level, an increase in real GDP, or an increase in both.
2. The Fed determines the supply of money, which is assumed to be independent of the interest rate. The intersection of the supply and demand curves for money determines the market interest rate. In the short run, an increase in the supply of money reduces the interest rate, which increases investment. This boosts aggregate demand, which increases real output and the price level.
3. The long-run approach focuses on the role of money through the equation of exchange, which states that the quantity of money, M, multiplied by velocity, V, the average number of times each dollar gets spent on final goods and services, equals the price level, P, multiplied by real output, Y. So $M \times V = P \times Y$. Because the aggregate supply curve in the long run is a vertical line at the economy's potential output, a change in the money supply affects the price level but not real output.
4. Between World War II and October 1979, the Fed tried to maintain stable interest rates as a way of promoting a stable investment environment. During the 1980s and early 1990s, the Fed paid more attention to growth in money aggregates, first M1 and then M2. But the velocity of M1 and M2 became so unstable that the Fed shifted focus back to interest rates, particularly the federal funds rate. To pursue its main goals of price stability and sustainable economic growth, the Fed uses open-market operations to adjust the federal funds rate, raising the rate to prevent higher inflation and lowering the rate to stimulate economic growth.
5. As a result of the financial crisis of September 2008, the Fed broadened its scope of action to include offering interest on bank reserves at the Fed, bailing out a huge financial institution, lending more than $100 billion in discount loans to banks, investing more than $1 trillion in mortgage-backed securities to keep mortgage rates low, and helping financial regulators perform stress tests on the nation's largest banks. The Fed's actions during the crisis suggest that it would do whatever was required to ensure the survival of the banking system and the economy.

Key Concepts

Demand for money 600
Equation of exchange 606
Velocity of money 606
Quantity theory of money 607
Stress test 613

Questions for Review

1. DEMAND FOR MONEY Determine whether each of the following would lead to an increase, a decrease, or no change in the quantity of money people wish to hold. Also determine whether there is a shift of the money demand curve or a movement along a given money demand curve.
   a. A decrease in the price level
   b. An increase in real output
   c. An improvement in money's ability to act as a store of value
   d. An increase in the market interest rate
2. DEMAND FOR MONEY If money is so versatile and can buy anything, why don't people demand all the money they can get their hands on?
3. MONETARY POLICY What is the impact of a decrease in the required reserve ratio on aggregate demand?
4. Case Study: Targeting the Federal Funds Rate (See page 769.) Why has the Federal Reserve chosen to focus on the federal funds rate rather than some other interest rate as a tool of monetary policy?
5. EQUATION OF EXCHANGE Using the equation of exchange, show why fiscal policy alone cannot increase nominal GDP if the velocity of money is constant.
6. VELOCITY Why do some economists believe that higher expected inflation will lead to a rise in velocity?
7. VELOCITY OF MONEY Determine whether each of the following would lead to an increase or a decrease in the velocity of money:
   a. Increasing the speed of funds transfers
   b. Decreased use of credit cards
   c. Decreasing the frequency that workers are paid
   d. Increased customer use of ATM, or debit, cards at retailers
8. QUANTITY THEORY OF MONEY The quantity theory states that the impact of money on nominal GDP can be determined without details about the *AD* curve, so long as the velocity of money is predictable. Discuss the reasoning behind this claim.
9. Case Study: The Money Supply and Inflation Around the World (See page 771.) According to Exhibit 2 in this case, what is the relationship between the rate of money supply growth and the inflation rate? How does this explain the hyperinflation experienced in some economies?
10. HOW STABLE IS VELOCITY? What factors have led to changes in the velocity of M1 and M2 over the past three decades?
11. MONEY SUPPLY VERSUS INTEREST RATE TARGETS In recent years the Fed's monetary target has been the federal funds rate. How does the Fed raise or lower that rate, and how is that rate related to other interest rates in the economy such as the prime rate?
12. How did the Fed respond to the financial crisis of 2008? What unusual actions did the Fed undertake to calm troubled financial markets and stabilize banks?

Problems and Exercises

13. MONEY DEMAND Suppose that you never carry cash. Your paycheck of $1,000 per month is deposited directly into your checking account, and you spend your money at a constant rate so that at the end of each month your checking account balance is zero.
    a. What is your average money balance during the pay period?
    b. How would each of the following changes affect your average monthly balance?
       i. You are paid $500 twice monthly rather than $1,000 each month.
       ii. You are uncertain about your total spending each month.
       iii. You spend a lot at the beginning of the month (e.g., for rent) and little at the end of the month.
       iv. Your monthly income increases.
14. MONEY AND AGGREGATE DEMAND Would each of the following increase, decrease, or have no impact on the ability of open-market operations to affect aggregate demand? Explain your answer.
    a. Investment demand becomes less sensitive to changes in the interest rate.
    b. The marginal propensity to consume rises.
    c. The money multiplier rises.
    d. Banks decide to hold additional excess reserves.
    e. The demand for money becomes more sensitive to changes in the interest rate.
15. MONETARY POLICY AND AGGREGATE SUPPLY Assume that the economy is initially in long-run equilibrium. Using an *AD–AS* diagram, illustrate and explain the short-run and long-run impacts of an increase in the money supply.
16. MONETARY POLICY AND AN EXPANSIONARY GAP Suppose the Fed wishes to use monetary policy to close an expansionary gap.
    a. Should the Fed increase or decrease the money supply?
    b. If the Fed uses open-market operations, should it buy or sell government securities?
    c. Determine whether each of the following increases, decreases, or remains unchanged in the short run: the market interest rate, the quantity of money demanded, investment spending, aggregate demand, potential output, the price level, and equilibrium real GDP.
17. EQUATION OF EXCHANGE Calculate the velocity of money if real GDP is 3,000 units, the average price level is $4 per unit, and the quantity of money in the economy is $1,500. What happens to velocity if the average price level drops to $3 per unit? What happens to velocity if the average price level remains at $4 per unit but the money supply rises to $2,000? What happens to velocity if the average price level falls to $2 per unit, the money supply is $2,000, and real GDP is 4,000 units?

18. QUANTITY THEORY OF MONEY What basic assumption about the velocity of money transforms the equation of exchange into the quantity theory of money? Also:
    a. According to the quantity theory, what will happen to nominal GDP if the money supply increases by 5 percent and velocity does not change?
    b. What will happen to nominal GDP if, instead, the money supply decreases by 8 percent and velocity does not change?
    c. What will happen to nominal GDP if, instead, the money supply increases by 5 percent and velocity decreases by 5 percent?
    d. What happens to the price level in the short run in each of these three situations?

19. MONEY SUPPLY VERSUS INTEREST RATE TARGETS Assume that the economy's real GDP is growing.
    a. What will happen to money demand over time?
    b. If the Fed leaves the money supply unchanged, what will happen to the interest rate over time?
    c. If the Fed changes the money supply to match the change in money demand, what will happen to the interest rate over time?
    d. What would be the effect of the policy described in part (c) on the economy's stability over the business cycle?

Global Economic Watch Exercises

Login to www.cengagebrain.com and access the Global Economic Watch to do these exercises.

20. GLOBAL ECONOMIC WATCH Go to the Global Economic Crisis Resource Center. Select Global Issues in Context. In the Basic Search box at the top of the page, enter the phrase "Fed maintains status quo." On the Results page, go to the News Section. Click on the link for the June 23, 2010, article "Fed Maintains Status Quo." What does the article say about whether the Fed considers international economic conditions when setting U.S. monetary policy?

21. GLOBAL ECONOMIC WATCH Go to the Global Economic Crisis Resource Center. Select Global Issues in Context. Go to the menu at the top of the page and click on the tab for Browse Issues and Topics. Choose Business and Economy. Click on the link for Central Banks. Find an article about the central bank of a foreign country. Compare what you read in the article to what you learned about the Federal Reserve in the chapter.

Macro Policy Debate: Active or Passive?

31

Mia Foster/Photo Edit

- Does the economy work fairly well on its own, or does it require active government intervention?
- Does government intervention do more harm than good?
- If people expect government to intervene if the economy falters, does this expectation affect people's behavior?
- Does this expectation affect government's behavior?
- What is the relationship between unemployment and inflation in the short run and in the long run?

Answers to these and other questions are provided in this chapter, which discusses the appropriate role for government in economic stabilization.

You have studied both fiscal and monetary policy and are now in a position to consider the overall impact of public policy on the U.S. economy. This chapter distinguishes between two general approaches: the active approach and the passive approach. The active approach views the economy as relatively unstable and unable to recover from shocks when they occur. According to the active approach, economic fluctuations arise primarily from the private sector, particularly investment, and natural market forces may not help much or may be too slow once the economy gets off track.

To move the economy to its potential output, the active approach calls for government intervention and discretionary policy. The passive approach, on the other hand, views the economy as relatively stable and able to recover from shocks when they do occur. When the economy derails, natural market forces and automatic stabilizers nudge it back on track in a timely manner. According to the passive approach, not only is active discretionary policy unnecessary, but such activism may do more harm than good.

In this chapter, we consider the pros and cons of *active* intervention in the economy versus *passive* reliance on natural market forces and automatic stabilizers. We also examine the role that expectations play in stabilization policy. You will learn why unanticipated stabilization policies have more impact on employment and output than do anticipated ones. Finally, the chapter explores the trade-off between unemployment and inflation.

Topics discussed include:

- Active versus passive approach
- Self-correcting mechanisms
- Rational expectations
- Policy rules and policy credibility
- The time-inconsistency problem
- Short-run and long-run Phillips curves
- Natural rate hypothesis

Active Policy Versus Passive Policy

According to the *active approach,* discretionary fiscal or monetary policy can reduce the costs of an unstable economy, such as higher unemployment. According to the *passive approach,* discretionary policy may contribute to the instability of the economy and is therefore part of the problem, not part of the solution. The two approaches differ in their assumptions about the effectiveness of natural market forces compared with government intervention.

Closing a Recessionary Gap

Perhaps the best way to describe each approach is by examining a particular macroeconomic problem. Suppose the economy is in short-run equilibrium at point *a* in panel (a) of Exhibit 1, with real GDP at $13.8 trillion, which is below the economy's potential of $14.0 trillion. The recessionary gap of $0.2 trillion drives unemployment above its natural rate (the rate when the economy produces potential GDP). This gap could result from lower-than-expected aggregate demand. What should public officials do?

Those who subscribe to the passive approach, as did their classical predecessors, have more faith in the *self-correcting forces* of the economy than do those who favor the active approach. In what sense is the economy self-correcting? According to the passive approach, wages and prices are flexible enough to adjust within a reasonable period to labor shortages or surpluses. High unemployment causes wages to fall, which reduces production costs, which shifts the short-run aggregate supply curve rightward in panel (a) of Exhibit 1. (Money wages need not actually fall; money wage increases need only lag behind price increases, so that real wages fall. Or perhaps nonwage compensation is reduced, such as health care benefits.) The short-run aggregate supply curve, within a reasonable period, shifts from $SRAS_{110}$ to $SRAS_{100}$, moving the economy to its potential output at point *b*. *According to the passive approach, the economy is stable enough, gravitating in a reasonable time toward potential GDP. Automatic stabilizers also help move the economy toward potential GDP. Consequently, advocates of passive policy see little reason for discretionary policy.* The passive approach is to let natural market forces and automatic stabilizers close the recessionary gap. So the prescription of passive policy is to do nothing beyond the automatic stabilizers already built into taxes, transfers, and government purchases.

EXHIBIT 1 Closing a Recessionary Gap

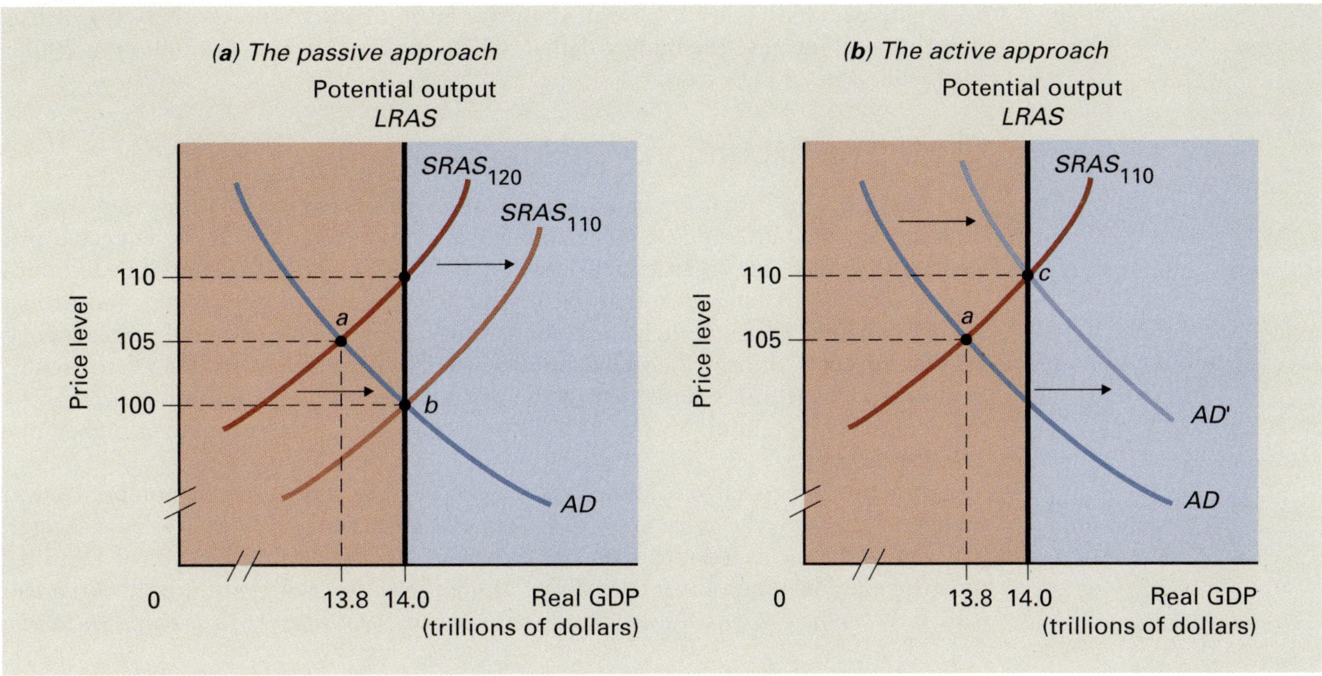

At point *a* in both panels, the economy is in short-run equilibrium, with unemployment exceeding its natural rate. According to the passive approach, shown in panel (a), high unemployment eventually causes wages to fall, reducing the cost of doing business. The decline in costs shifts the short-run aggregate supply curve rightward from $SRAS_{110}$ to $SRAS_{100}$, moving the economy to its potential output at point *b*. In panel (b), the government employs an active approach to shift the aggregate demand curve from *AD* to *AD′*. If the active policy works perfectly, the economy moves to its potential output at point *c*.

Advocates of an active approach, on the other hand, believe that prices and wages are not that flexible, particularly in the downward direction. They think that when adverse supply shocks or sagging demand push unemployment above its natural rate, market forces may be too slow to respond. The longer market forces take to reduce unemployment to the natural rate, the greater the output lost and the greater the economic and psychological cost to those unemployed. *Because advocates of an active policy associate a high cost with the passive approach, they favor an active stabilization policy to stimulate aggregate demand.*

A decision by public officials to intervene in the economy to achieve potential output—that is, a decision to use discretionary policy—reflects an active approach. In panel (b) of Exhibit 1, we begin at the same point *a* as in panel (a). At point *a*, short-run equilibrium output is below potential output, so the economy is experiencing a recessionary gap. Through discretionary monetary policy, discretionary fiscal policy, or some of both, as occurred in 2008 and 2009, active policy attempts to increase aggregate demand from *AD* to *AD′*, moving equilibrium from point *a* to point *c*, thus closing the recessionary gap.

In 2008 and 2009, policy makers tried to revive a troubled economy using both fiscal and monetary policy. President Barack Obama's $862 billion stimulus plan, the largest on record, was approved by Congress in February 2009 and was aimed at counteracting the deep recession triggered by the financial crisis. As noted in the previous chapter, the Fed had already cut its target interest rate a record amount. This combination of fiscal and monetary policy was the most concentrated attempt to boost aggregate demand ever. One possible cost of using discretionary policy to stimulate aggregate demand is an increase in the price level, or inflation. Another cost of fiscal stimulus is to increase the budget deficit, which rocketed from $459 billion in 2008 to $1.4 trillion in 2009.

Closing an Expansionary Gap

Let's consider the situation in which the short-run equilibrium output exceeds the economy's potential. Suppose the actual price level of 115 exceeds the expected price level of 110, resulting in an expansionary gap of $0.2 trillion, as shown in Exhibit 2. The passive approach argues that natural market forces prompt workers and firms to negotiate higher wages at their next opportunity. These higher nominal wages increase production costs, shifting the short-run supply curve leftward, from $SRAS_{110}$ to $SRAS_{120}$, as shown in panel (a). Consequently, the price level increases and output decreases to the economy's potential. So the natural adjustment process results in a higher price level, or inflation.

An active approach sees discretionary policy as a way to reach potential output without increasing the price level. Advocates of an active policy believe that if aggregate demand can be reduced from *AD*″ to *AD*′, as shown in panel (b) of Exhibit 2, then the equilibrium point moves down along the initial aggregate supply curve from *d* to *c*. *Whereas the passive approach relies on natural market forces and automatic*

EXHIBIT 2 Closing an Expansionary Gap

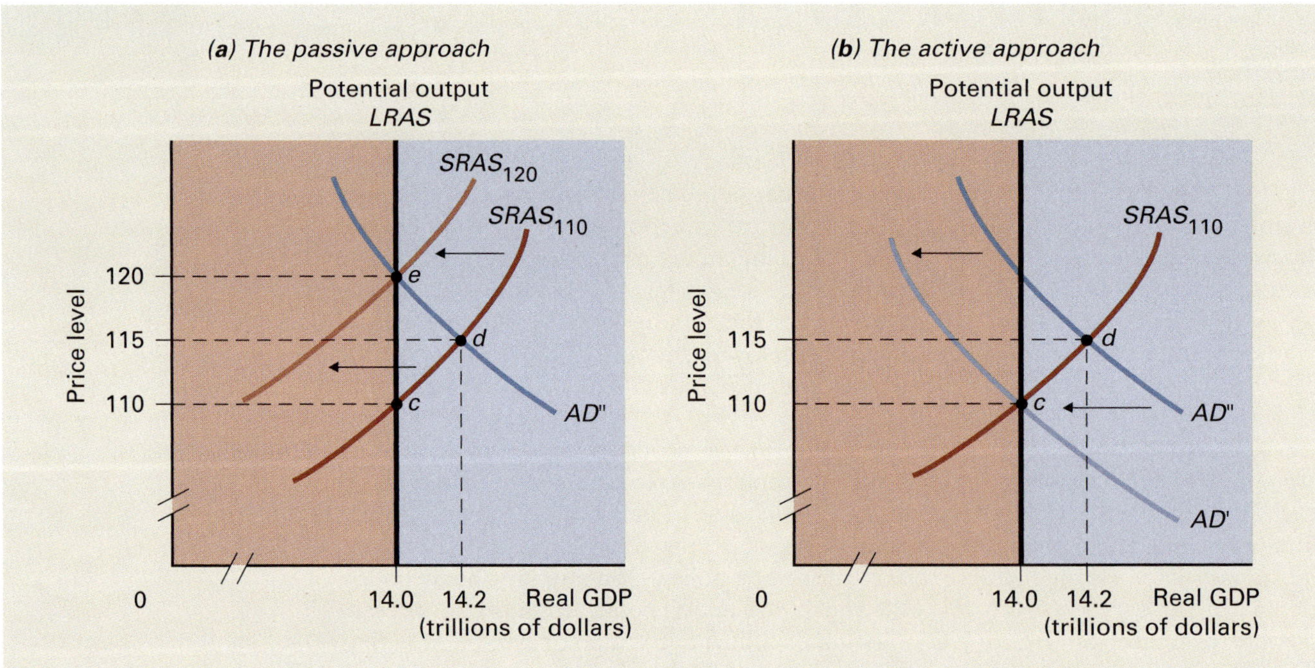

At point *d* in both panels, the economy is in short-run equilibrium, producing $14.2 trillion, which exceeds the economy's potential output. Unemployment is below its natural rate. In the passive approach reflected in panel (a), the government makes no change in policy, so natural market forces eventually bring about a higher negotiated wage, increasing firm costs and shifting the short-run supply curve leftward to $SRAS_{120}$. The new equilibrium at point *e* results in a higher price level and lower output and employment. An active policy reduces aggregate demand, shifting the equilibrium in panel (b) from point *d* to point *c*, thus closing the expansionary gap without increasing the price level.

stabilizers to close an expansionary gap through a decrease in the short-run aggregate supply curve, the active approach relies on just the right discretionary policy to close the gap through a decrease of the aggregate demand curve. In the long run, the passive approach results in a higher price level and the active approach results in a lower price level. Thus, the correct discretionary policy can relieve the inflationary pressure associated with an expansionary gap. Whenever the Fed attempts to cool down an overheated economy by increasing its target interest rate, as it did in 17 steps between mid-2004 and mid-2006, it employs an active monetary policy to close an expansionary gap. The Fed tried to orchestrate a so-called *soft landing* to gently slow the rate of growth before that growth triggered unacceptably high inflation.

Problems With Active Policy

The timely adoption and implementation of an active policy is not easy. One problem is identifying the economy's potential output and the natural rate of unemployment. Suppose the natural rate of unemployment is 5 percent, but policy makers mistakenly believe it's 4 percent. As they pursue their elusive goal of 4 percent, they push aggregate output beyond its potential, fueling higher prices in the long run but with no permanent reduction in unemployment. Recall that when output exceeds the economy's potential, this opens up an expansionary gap, causing a leftward shift of the short-run aggregate supply curve until the economy returns to its potential output at a higher price level.

Even if policy makers can accurately estimate the economy's potential output and the natural rate of unemployment, formulating an effective policy requires detailed knowledge of current and future economic conditions. To craft an effective strategy, policy makers must first be able to forecast aggregate demand and aggregate supply without active intervention. In other words, they must be able to predict what would happen with a passive approach. Second, they must have the tools needed to achieve the desired result relatively quickly. Third, they must be able to predict the effects of an active policy on the economy's key performance measures. Fourth, fiscal and monetary policy makers must work together, or at least not work at cross-purposes. Congress and the president pursue fiscal policy while the Fed pursues monetary policy; these groups often fail to coordinate their efforts. If an active policy requires coordination, the policy may not work as desired. In early 1995, for example, Congress was considering an expansionary tax cut while the Fed was pursuing a contractionary monetary policy. Fifth, policy makers must be able to implement the appropriate policy, even when this involves short-term political costs. For example, during inflationary times, the optimal policy may call for a tax increase, a reduction in government spending, or a tighter monetary policy—policies that are unpopular because they may increase unemployment. Finally, policy makers must be able to deal with a variety of timing lags. As we see next, these lags complicate the execution of an active policy.

The Problem of Lags

So far, we have ignored the time required to implement policy. That is, we have assumed that the desired policy is selected and implemented instantaneously. We have also assumed that, once implemented, the policy works as advertised—again, in no time. Actually, there may be long, sometimes unpredictable, lags at several stages in the process. These lags reduce the effectiveness and increase the uncertainty of active policies.

First, is a **recognition lag**—the time it takes to identify a problem and determine how serious it is. For example, time is required to accumulate evidence that the economy is indeed performing below its potential. Even if initial data look troubling, data are usually revised later. For example, the government releases three estimates of

recognition lag
The time needed to identify a macroeconomic problem and assess its seriousness

quarterly GDP growth coming a month apart—an *advanced* estimate, a *preliminary* estimate, and a *final* estimate. What's more, these estimates are often revised years later or even a decade later. Therefore, policy makers sometimes wait for more proof before responding to what may turn out to be a false alarm. Because a recession is not identified as such until more than 6 months after it begins and because the average recession since 1945 has lasted only about 11 months, a typical recession is nearly over before officially recognized as a recession. What's more, the average lag between a recession's end and the official announcement that it has ended is about 15 months. So for a year or more after a recession ends, policy makers don't know for sure that it has ended. For example, the recent recession ended in June 2009, but that ending date was not identified until September 2010.

decision-making lag
The time needed to decide what to do once a macroeconomic problem has been identified

Even after enough evidence accumulates, policy makers often need time to decide what to do, so there is a **decision-making lag**. In the case of discretionary fiscal policy, Congress and the president must agree on an appropriate course of action. Fiscal policy usually takes months to develop and approve; it could take more than a year. On the other hand, the Fed can implement monetary policy more quickly and does not even have to wait for regular meetings. For example, as the economy weakened in 2008, the Fed announced interest rate cuts twice between regular meetings. So the decision-making lag is shorter for monetary policy than for fiscal policy.

implementation lag
The time needed to introduce a change in monetary or fiscal policy

Once a decision has been made, the new policy must be introduced, which usually involves an **implementation lag**. Again, monetary policy has the advantage: After a policy has been adopted, the Fed can immediately begin buying or selling bonds to influence bank reserves and thereby change the federal funds rate. The implementation lag is longer for fiscal policy. If tax rates change, new tax forms must be printed and distributed advising employers of changes in tax withholding. If government spending changes, the appropriate government agencies must get involved. The implementation of fiscal policy can take more than a year. For example, in February 1983, the nation's unemployment rate reached 10.3 percent, with 11.5 million people unemployed. The following month, Congress passed the Emergency Jobs Appropriation Act providing $9 billion to create what supporters claimed would be hundreds of thousands of new jobs. Fifteen months later, only $3.1 billion had been spent and only 35,000 new jobs had been created, according to a U.S. General Accounting Office study. By that time, the economy was already recovering on its own, lowering the unemployment rate from 10.3 percent to 7.1 percent and adding 6.2 million new jobs. So this public spending program was implemented only after the recession had bottomed out and recovered. Likewise, in spring 1993, President Clinton proposed a $16 billion stimulus package to boost what appeared to be a sluggish recovery. The measure was defeated because it would have increased an already large federal deficit, yet the economy still added 5.6 million jobs over the next two years anyway. As a final example of an implementation lag, in February 2009, Congress approved a $862 billion stimulus plan, which President Obama said would create or save 3.5 million jobs over two years. The idea was to spend the money quickly by funding "shovel-ready" projects. But six months after passage, only 20 percent was spent, with little of that for "shovel-ready" projects. Meanwhile, the unemployment rate climbed.

effectiveness lag
The time needed for changes in monetary or fiscal policy to affect the economy

Once a policy has been implemented, there is an **effectiveness lag** before the full impact of the policy registers on the economy. With monetary policy, the lag between a change in the federal funds rate and the change in aggregate demand and output can take from months to a year or more. Fiscal policy, once enacted, usually requires 3 to 6 months to take effect and between 9 and 18 months to register its full effect. Because of the effectiveness lag, the economy may turn around on its own before the policy registers its full impact. A stimulus package may end up merely adding more inflationary pressure to a recovering economy.

These lags make active policy difficult to execute. The more variable the lags, the harder it is to predict when a particular policy will take hold and what the state of the economy will be at that time. To advocates of passive policy, these lags are reason enough to avoid active discretionary policy. *Advocates of a passive approach argue that an active stabilization policy imposes troubling fluctuations in the price level and real GDP because it often takes hold only after market forces have already returned the economy to its potential output level.*

Talk in the media about "jump-starting" the economy reflects the active approach, which views the economy as a sputtering machine that can be fixed by an expert mechanic. The passive approach views the economy as more like a supertanker on automatic pilot. The policy question then becomes whether to trust that automatic pilot (the self-correcting tendencies of the economy) or to try to override the mechanism with active discretionary policies.

A Review of Policy Perspectives

The active and passive approaches reflect different views about the stability and resiliency of the economy and the ability of Congress or the Fed to implement appropriate discretionary policies. As we have seen, advocates of an active approach think that the natural adjustments of wages and prices can be painfully slow, particularly when unemployment is high. Prolonged high unemployment means that much output must be sacrificed, and the unemployed must suffer personal hardship during the slow adjustment period. If high unemployment lasts a long time, labor skills may grow rusty, and some people may drop out of the labor force. Therefore, prolonged unemployment may cause the economy's potential GDP to fall.

Thus, active policy advocates see a high cost of not using discretionary policy. Despite the lags involved, they prefer action—through discretionary fiscal policy, discretionary monetary policy, or some combination of the two—to inaction. Passive policy advocates, on the other hand, believe that uncertain lags and ignorance about how the economy works undermine active policy. Rather than pursue a misguided activist policy, passivists prefer to sit back and rely on the economy's natural ability to correct itself just using automatic stabilizers. Consider active versus passive approaches during recent presidential campaigns, as discussed in the case study, "Public Policy: Active Versus Passive Presidential Candidates" at the end of the book.

The Role of Expectations

The effectiveness of a particular government policy depends in part on what people expect. As we saw in an earlier chapter, the short-run aggregate supply curve is drawn for a given expected price level reflected in long-term wage contracts. If workers and firms expect continuing inflation, their wage agreements reflect these inflationary expectations. One approach in macroeconomics, called **rational expectations**, argues that people form expectations on the basis of all available information, including information about the probable future actions of policy makers. Thus, aggregate supply depends on what sort of macroeconomic course policy makers are expected to pursue. For example, if people were to observe policy makers using discretionary policy to stimulate aggregate demand every time output falls below potential, people would come to anticipate the effects of this policy on the price level and output. Robert Lucas, of the University of Chicago, won the 1995 Nobel Prize for his studies of rational expectations. We consider the role of expectations in the context of monetary policy, but fiscal policy would have a similar effect.

rational expectations
A school of thought that argues people form expectations based on all available information, including the likely future actions of government policy makers

Discretionary Policy and Inflation Expectations

Monetary authorities must testify before Congress regularly to offer an assessment of the economy. As noted in the previous chapter, the Fed also announces, after each meeting of the FOMC, any changes in its interest rate targets and the likely direction, or "bias," of future changes. And Fed officials often deliver speeches around the country. Those interested in the economy sift through all this material to discover the likely path of monetary policy.

Let's examine the relationship between Fed policy pronouncements, Fed actions, and equilibrium output. Suppose the economy is producing potential output so unemployment is at its natural rate. At the beginning of the year, firms and employees must negotiate wage agreements. While negotiations are under way, the Fed announces that throughout the year, monetary policy will aim at sustaining potential output while keeping the price level stable. This policy seems appropriate because unemployment is already at the natural rate. Workers and firms understand that the Fed's stable price policy appears optimal under the circumstances because an expansionary monetary policy would lead only to higher inflation in the long run. Until the year is under way and monetary policy is actually implemented, however, the public can't know for sure what the Fed will do.

As long as wage increases do not exceed the growth in labor productivity, the Fed's plan of a stable price level should work. Alternatively, workers could try to negotiate a higher wage growth, but that would ultimately lead to inflation. Suppose workers and firms believe the Fed's pronouncements and reach wage settlements based on a constant price level. If the Fed follows through as promised, the price level should turn out as expected. Output remains at the economy's potential, and unemployment remains at the natural rate. The situation is depicted in Exhibit 3. The short-run aggregate supply curve, $SRAS_{110}$, is based on wage contracts reflecting an expected price level of 110. If the Fed follows the announced course, the aggregate demand curve will be *AD* and equilibrium will be at point *a*, where the price level is as expected and the economy is producing $14.0 trillion, the potential output.

Suppose, however, that after workers and firms have agreed on nominal wages—that is, after the short-run aggregate supply curve has been determined—public officials become dissatisfied with the unemployment rate. Perhaps election-year concerns with unemployment, a false alarm about a recession, or overestimating potential output convince the Fed to act. An expansionary monetary policy increases the aggregate demand curve from *AD*, the level anticipated by firms and employees, to *AD*'. This unexpected policy stimulates output and employment in the short run to equilibrium point *b*. Output increases to $14.2 trillion, and the price level increases to 115. This temporary boost in output and reduction in unemployment may last long enough to help public officials get reelected.

So the price level is now higher than workers expected, and their agreed-on wage buys less in real terms than workers bargained for. At their earliest opportunity, workers will negotiate higher wages. These higher wage agreements will eventually cause the short-run aggregate supply curve in Exhibit 3 to shift leftward, intersecting *AD*′ at point *c*, the economy's potential output (to reduce clutter, the shifted short-run aggregate supply curve is not shown). So output once again returns to the economy's potential GDP, but in the process the price level rises to 122.

Thus, the unexpected expansionary policy causes a short-run pop in output and employment. But in the long run, the increase in the aggregate demand curve yields only inflation. The **time-inconsistency problem** arises when policy makers have an incentive to announce one policy to shape expectations but then to pursue a different policy once those expectations have been formed and acted on.

time-inconsistency problem
When policy makers have an incentive to announce one policy to influence expectations but then pursue a different policy once those expectations have been formed and acted on

EXHIBIT 3 Short-Run Effects of an Unexpected Expansionary Policy

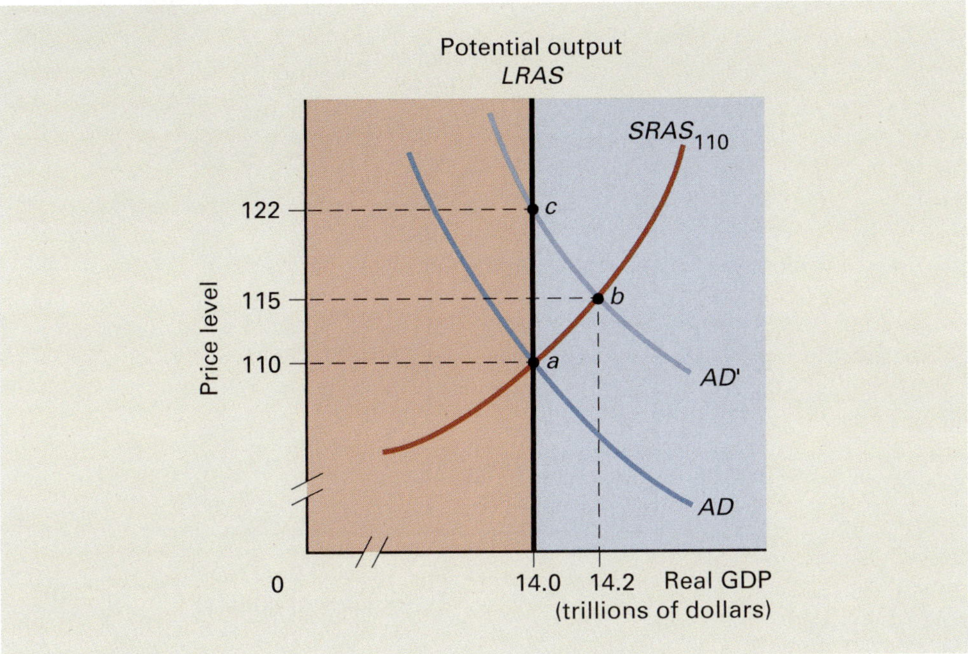

At point *a*, workers and firms expect a price level of 110; supply curve $SRAS_{110}$ reflects that expectation. But an unexpected expansionary policy shifts the aggregate demand curve out to *AD'*. Output in the short run (at point *b*) exceeds its potential. In the long run, costs increase, shifting *SRAS* leftward until the economy produces its potential output at point *c* (the resulting supply curve is not shown). The short-run effect of an unexpected expansion is greater output, but the long-run effect is just a higher price level.

Anticipating Policy

Suppose policy makers become alarmed by the high inflation. The next time around, the Fed once again announces a monetary policy aimed at producing potential output while keeping the price level stable at 122. Based on their previous experience, however, workers and firms have learned that the Fed is willing to accept higher inflation in exchange for a temporary boost in output. Workers may be fooled once by the Fed's actions, but they won't be fooled again. Workers and their employers take the Fed's announcement with a grain of salt. Workers, in particular, do not want to get caught again with their real wages down should the Fed implement a stimulative monetary policy. Workers and firms expect the Fed's actions will increase the price level. The bottom line is that workers and firms negotiate a high wage increase.

In effect, workers and firms are betting the Fed will pursue an expansionary policy regardless of pronouncements to the contrary. The short-run aggregate supply curve reflecting these higher wage agreements is depicted by $SRAS_{132}$ in Exhibit 4, where 132 is the expected price level. Note that *AD′* would result if the Fed followed its announced policy; that demand curve intersects the potential output line at point *c*, where the price level is 122. But *AD″* is the aggregate demand that workers and firms expect based on an expansionary monetary policy. They have agreed to wage settlements that will produce the economy's potential output if the Fed behaves as *expected*, not as *announced*. Thus, a price level of 132 is based on rational expectations. In effect, workers and firms expect the expansionary monetary policy to shift aggregate demand from *AD′* to *AD″*.

EXHIBIT 4 Short-Run Effects of a More Expansionary Policy Than Announced

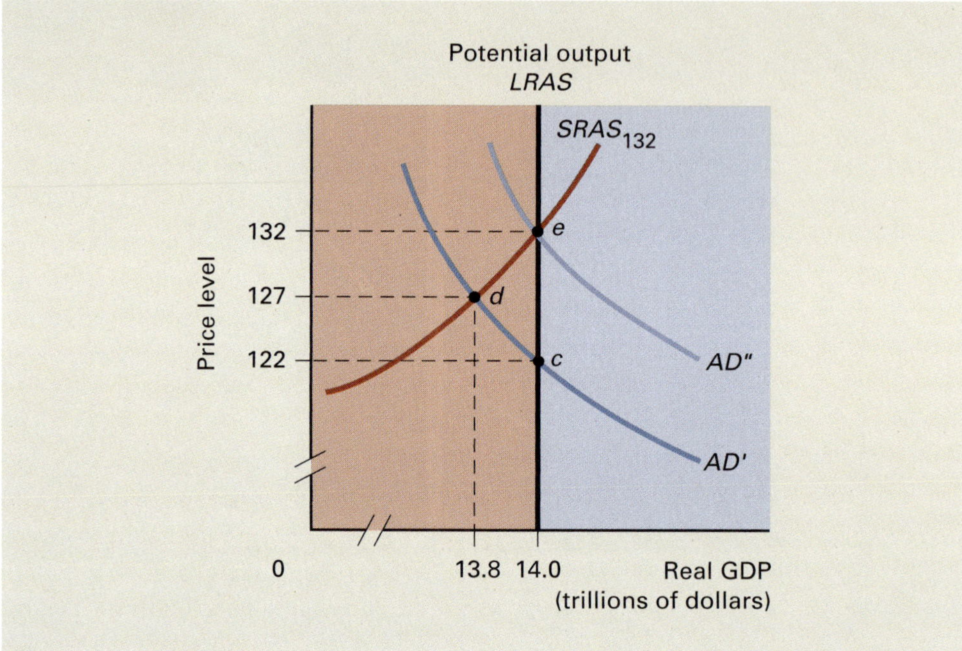

The Fed announces it plans to keep prices stable at 122. Workers and firms, however, expect monetary policy to be expansionary. The short-run aggregate supply curve, $SRAS_{132}$, reflects their expectations. If the Fed follows the announced stable-price policy, short-run output at point *d* is less than the economy's potential output of $14.0 trillion. To keep the economy at its potential, the Fed must stimulate aggregate demand as much as workers and firms expect (shown by point *e*), but this is inflationary.

Monetary authorities must now decide whether to stick with their announced plan of a stable price level or follow a more expansionary monetary policy. If they pursue the constant-price-level policy, aggregate demand turns out to be *AD′* and short-run equilibrium occurs at point *d*. Short-run output falls below the economy's potential, resulting in unemployment exceeding the natural rate. If monetary authorities want to keep output at its potential, they have only one alternative—to match public expectations. Monetary authorities will likely pursue an expansionary monetary policy, an action that increases inflation and reinforces public skepticism of policy announcements. This expansionary policy results in an aggregate demand of *AD″*, leading to equilibrium at point *e*, where the price level is 132 and output equals the economy's potential.

Thus, workers and firms enter negotiations realizing that the Fed has an incentive to pursue an expansionary monetary policy. So workers and firms agree to higher wage increases, and the Fed follows with an expansionary policy, one that results in more inflation. Once workers and firms come to expect an expansionary monetary policy and the resulting inflation, such a policy does not spur even a temporary increase in output beyond the economy's potential. *Economists of the rational expectations school believe that if the economy is already producing its potential, an expansionary policy, if fully anticipated, has no effect on output or employment, not even in the short run. Only unanticipated expansionary policy can temporarily push output beyond its potential.*

Policy Credibility

If the economy was already producing its potential, an unexpected expansionary policy would increase output and employment temporarily. The costs, however, include not only inflation in the long term but also a loss of credibility in Fed pronouncements the next time around. Is there any way out of this? For the Fed to pursue a policy consistent with a constant price level, its announcements must somehow be *credible*, or believable. Workers and firms must believe that when the time comes to make a hard decision, the Fed will follow through as promised. Perhaps the Fed could offer some sort of guarantee to convince people it will stay the course—for example, the Fed chairman could promise to resign if the Fed does not follow the announced policy. Ironically, policy makers are often more credible and therefore more effective if they have some of their discretion taken away. In this case, a hard-and-fast rule could be substituted for a policy maker's discretion. We examine policy rules in the next section.

Consider the problems facing central banks in countries that have experienced hyperinflation. For an anti-inflation policy to succeed at the least possible cost in forgone output, the public must believe central bankers. How can central bankers in an economy ripped by hyperinflation establish credibility? Some economists believe that the most efficient anti-inflation policy is **cold turkey**, which is to announce and execute tough measures to stop inflation, such as halting the growth in the money supply. For example, in 1985, the annual rate of inflation in Bolivia was running at 20,000 percent when the new government announced a stern policy. The restrictive measures worked, and inflation was stopped within a month, with little loss in output. Around the world, credible anti-inflation policies have been successful.[1] Drastic measures sometimes involve costs. For example, some economists argue that the Fed's dramatic efforts to curb high U.S. inflation in the early 1980s triggered what was then the worst recession since the Great Depression. Some say that the Fed's pronouncements were simply not credible and therefore resulted in a recession.

cold turkey
The announcement and execution of tough measures to reduce high inflation

Much depends on the Fed's time horizon. If policy makers take the long view, they will not risk their long-term policy effectiveness for a temporary reduction in unemployment. If Fed officials realize that their credibility is hard to develop but easy to undermine, they will be reluctant to pursue policies that ultimately just increase inflation.

Often Congress tries to pressure the Fed to stimulate the economy. By law, the Fed must "promote effectively the goals of maximum employment, stable prices, and moderate long-term interest rates." The law lets the Fed decide how best to do this. The Fed does not rely on congressional appropriations, so Congress can't threaten to withhold funds. Thus, although the U.S. president appoints the Board of Governors, and the Senate must approve these appointments, the Fed operates somewhat independently. Consider the link around the world between central bank independence and price stability in the case study, "Public Policy: Central Bank Independence and Price Stability," found at the end of the book.

Policy Rules Versus Discretion

Again, the active approach views the economy as unstable and in need of discretionary policy to cut cyclical unemployment when it arises. The passive approach views the economy as stable enough that discretionary policy is not only unnecessary but may

1. For a discussion about how four hyperinflations in the 1920s ended, see Thomas Sargent, "The Ends of Four Big Inflations," in *Inflation: Causes and Consequences*, edited by Robert Hall (University of Chicago Press, 1982): 41–98.

actually worsen economic fluctuations. In place of discretionary policy, the passive approach often calls for predetermined rules to guide policy makers. In the context of fiscal policy, these rules take the form of automatic stabilizers, such as unemployment insurance, a progressive income tax, and transfer payments, all of which aim to dampen economic fluctuations. In the context of monetary policy, passive rules might be the decision to allow the money supply to grow at a predetermined rate, to maintain interest rates at some predetermined level, or to keep inflation below a certain rate. For example, the European Central Bank announced a rule that it would not lower its target interest rate if inflation exceeded 2.0 percent a year. Most central banks have committed to achieving low **inflation targets**, usually specifying a particular rate for the next year or two. Advocates of inflation targets say such targets encourage workers, firms, and investors to plan on a low and stable inflation rate. Opponents of inflation targets worry that the Fed would pay less attention to jobs and economic growth. In this section, we examine the arguments for policy rules versus discretion mostly in the context of monetary policy, the policy focus in recent decades.

inflation target
Commitment of central bankers to keep inflation below a certain rate for the next year or two

Limitations on Discretion

The rationale for the passive approach rather than the use of active discretion arises from different views of how the economy works. One view holds that *the economy is so complex and economic aggregates interact in such obscure ways and with such varied lags that policy makers cannot comprehend what is going on well enough to pursue an active monetary or fiscal policy*. For example, if the Fed adopts a discretionary policy that is based on a misreading of the current economy or a poor understanding of the lag structure, the Fed may be lowering the target interest rate when a more appropriate course would be to leave the rate unchanged or even to raise it. As a case in point, during a meeting of the FOMC, one member lamented the difficulty of figuring out what was going on with the economy, noting, "As a lesson for the future, I'd like to remind us all that as recently as two meetings ago we couldn't see the strength that was unfolding in the second half [of the year].... It wasn't in our forecast; it wasn't in the other forecasts; and it wasn't in the anecdotal reports. We were standing right on top of it and we couldn't see it. That's just an important lesson to remember going forward."[2]

A comparison of economic forecasters and weather forecasters may shed light on the position of those who advocate the passive approach. Suppose you are in charge of the heating and cooling system at a major shopping mall. You realize that weather forecasts are unreliable, particularly in the early spring, when days can be warm or cold. Each day you must guess what the temperature will be and, based on that guess, decide whether to fire up the heater, turn on the air conditioner, or leave them both off. Because the mall is huge, you must start the system long before you know for sure what the weather will be. Once the system is turned on, it can't be turned off until much later in the day.

Suppose you guess the day will be cold, so you turn on the heat. If the day turns out to be cold, your policy is correct and the mall temperature will be just right. But if the day turns out to be warm, the heating system will make the mall unbearable. You would have been better off with nothing. In contrast, if you turn on the air conditioning system expecting a warm day but the day turns out to be cold, the mall will be freezing. The lesson is that if you are unable to predict the weather, you should use

2. FOMC board member Thomas Melzer, in a transcript of the 22 December 1992 meeting of the Federal Open Market Committee, p. 14. Meeting transcripts are published after a five-year lag and are available at http://www.federalreserve.gov/monetarypolicy/fomc_historical.htm.

neither system. Similarly, if policy makers cannot predict the course of the economy, they should not try to fine-tune monetary or fiscal policy. Complicating the prediction problem is the fact that policy officials are not sure about the lags involved with discretionary policy. The situation is comparable to your not knowing how long the system actually takes to come on once you flip the switch.

This analogy applies only if the cost of doing nothing—using neither heat nor air conditioning—is relatively low. In the early spring, you can assume that there is little risk of weather so cold that water pipes freeze or so hot that walls sweat. A similar assumption in the passive view is that the economy is fairly stable and periods of prolonged unemployment are unlikely. In such an economy, the costs of *not* intervening are relatively low. In contrast, advocates of active policy believe that wide and prolonged swings in the economy (analogous to wide and prolonged swings in the outside temperature) make doing nothing risky.

Rules and Rational Expectations

Another group of economists also advocates the passive approach, but not because they believe the economy is too complex. Proponents of the rational expectations approach, discussed earlier, claim that people have a pretty good idea how the economy works and what to expect from government policy makers. For example, people know enough about monetary policies pursued in the past to forecast, with reasonable accuracy, future policies and their effects on the economy. Some individual forecasts are too high and some too low, but on average, forecasts turn out to be about right. *To the extent that monetary policy is fully anticipated by workers and firms, it has no effect on the level of output; it affects only the price level.* Thus, only unexpected changes in policy can bring about short-run changes in output.

In the long run, changes in the money supply affect only inflation, not potential output, so followers of the rational expectations theory believe that the Fed should avoid discretionary monetary policy. Instead, the Fed should follow a predictable monetary rule. A monetary rule would reduce policy surprises and keep output near the natural rate. *Whereas some economists favor rules over discretion because of ignorance about the lag structure of the economy, rational expectations theorists advocate a predictable rule to avoid surprises, because surprises result in unnecessary departures from potential output.* For example, broad legislation to stimulate the economy, bail out the banks and automakers, require employer-provided health insurance, and regulate financial institutions extensively were said to create uncertainty in the economy about what might be next. And this uncertainty discouraged some firms from hiring and kept some consumers from spending.

Despite support by some economists for explicit rules rather than discretion, central bankers are reluctant to follow hard-and-fast rules about the course of future policy. Discretion has been used more than explicit rules since the early 1980s, though policy has become more predictable because the Fed now announces the probable trend of future target rate changes. As former Fed Chairman Paul Volcker argued nearly three decades ago:

> The appeal of a simple rule is obvious. It would simplify our job at the Federal Reserve, make monetary policy easy to understand, and facilitate monitoring of our performance. And if the rule worked, it would reduce uncertainty.... But unfortunately, I know of no rule that can be relied on with sufficient consistency in our complex and constantly evolving economy.[3]

3. Paul Volcker, before the Committee on Banking, Finance, and Urban Affairs, U.S. House of Representatives, August 1983.

Volcker's successor, Alan Greenspan, expressed similar sentiment:

> The Federal Reserve, should, some conclude, attempt to be more formal in its operations by tying its actions solely to the prescriptions of a formal policy rule. That any approach along these lines would lead to an improvement in economic performance, however, is highly doubtful.[4]

And, Ben Bernanke, who succeeded Greenspan as chairman, views the matter now mostly as a nonissue:

> [T]he argument that monetary policy should adhere mechanically to a strict rule, made by some economists in the past, has fallen out of favor in recent years. Today most monetary economists use the term "rule" more loosely to describe a general policy strategy, one that may include substantial scope for policymaker discretion and judgment.[5]

So far, we have looked at active stabilization policy, which focuses on shifts of the aggregate demand curve, and passive stabilization policy, which relies more on natural shifts of the short-run aggregate supply curve. In the final section, we focus on an additional model, the Phillips curve, to shed more light on the relationship between aggregate demand and aggregate supply in the short and long runs.

The Phillips Curve

At one time, policy makers thought they faced a long-run trade-off between inflation and unemployment. This view was suggested by the research of New Zealand economist A. W. Phillips, who in 1958 published an article that examined the historical relation between inflation and unemployment in the United Kingdom.[6] Based on about 100 years of evidence, his data traced an inverse relationship between the unemployment rate and the rate of change in nominal wages (serving as a measure of inflation). This relationship implied that the opportunity cost of reducing unemployment was higher inflation, and the opportunity cost of reducing inflation was higher unemployment.

The Phillips Framework

phillips curve
A curve showing possible combinations of the inflation rate and the unemployment rate

The possible options with respect to unemployment and inflation are illustrated by the hypothetical **Phillips curve** in Exhibit 5. The unemployment rate is measured along the horizontal axis and the inflation rate along the vertical axis. Let's begin at point *a*, which depicts one possible combination of unemployment and inflation. Fiscal or monetary policy could be used to stimulate output and thereby reduce unemployment, moving the economy from point *a* to point *b*. Notice, however, that the reduction in unemployment comes at the cost of higher inflation. A reduction in unemployment with no change in inflation would be represented by point *c*. But as you can see, this alternative is not available.

4. Alan Greenspan, "Monetary Policy Under Uncertainty," Remarks at a symposium sponsored by the Federal Reserve Bank of Kansas City, Jackson Hole, Wyoming, 29 August 2003, which can be found at http://www.federalreserve.gov/boarddocs/speeches/2003/20030829/default.htm.
5. Ben Bernanke, "The Logic of Monetary Policy," Remarks Before the National Economists Club, Washington D.C., 2 December 2004, which can be found at http://www.federalreserve.gov/boarddocs/Speeches/2004/20041202/default.htm.
6. A. W. Phillips, "Relation between Unemployment and the Rate of Change in Money Wage Rates in the United Kingdom, 1861–1957," *Economica*, 25 (November 1958): 283–299.

EXHIBIT 5 Hypothetical Phillips Curve

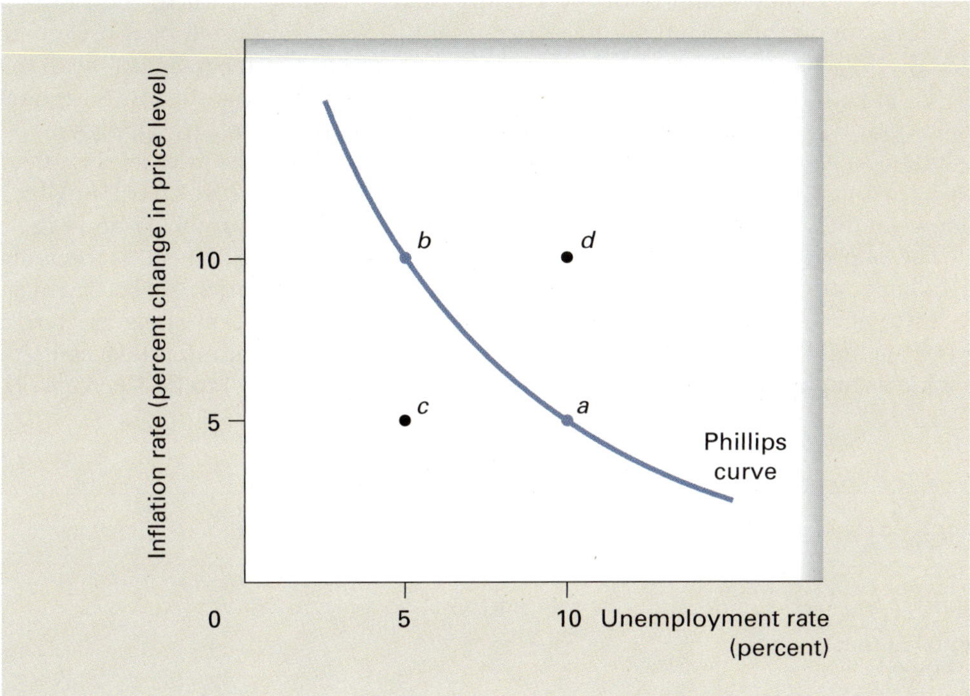

The Phillips curve shows an inverse relation between unemployment and inflation. Points *a* and *b* lie on the Phillips curve and represent alternative combinations of inflation and unemployment that are attainable as long as the curve itself does not shift. Points *c* and *d* are off the curve.

Most policy makers of the 1960s came to believe that they faced a stable, long-run trade-off between unemployment and inflation. The Phillips curve was based on an era when inflation was low and the primary disturbances in the economy were shocks to aggregate demand. The effect of changes in aggregate demand can be traced as movements along a given short-run aggregate supply curve. If aggregate demand increases, the price level rises but unemployment falls. If aggregate demand decreases, the price level falls but unemployment rises. With appropriate demand-management policies, policy makers believed they could choose any point along the Phillips curve. The 1970s proved this view wrong in two ways. First, some of the biggest disturbances were adverse *supply* shocks, such as those created by oil embargoes and worldwide crop failures. These shocks shifted the aggregate supply curve leftward. A reduction of the aggregate supply curve led to both higher inflation *and* higher unemployment. Stagflation was at odds with the Phillips curve. Second, economists learned that when short-run output exceeds potential, an expansionary gap opens. As this gap closes by a leftward shift of the short-run aggregate supply curve, greater inflation *and* higher unemployment result—again, an outcome inconsistent with a Phillips curve.

The increases in both inflation and unemployment caused by a decrease in aggregate supply can be represented by an outcome such as point *d* in Exhibit 5. By the end of the 1970s, increases in both inflation and unemployment suggested either that the Phillips curve had shifted outward or that it no longer described economic reality. The dilemma called for a reexamination of the Phillips curve, and this led to a distinction between the short-run Phillips curve and the long-run Phillips curve.

The Short-Run Phillips Curve

To discuss the underpinnings of the Phillips curve, we must return to the short-run aggregate supply curve. Suppose the price level this year is reflected by a price index of, say, 100, and that people expect prices to be about 3 percent higher next year. So the price level expected next year is 103. Workers and firms therefore negotiate wage contracts based on that expectation. As the short-run aggregate supply curve in Exhibit 6(a) indicates, if *AD* is the aggregate demand curve and the price level is 103, as expected, output equals the economy's potential, shown here to be $14.0 trillion. Recall that when the economy produces its potential, unemployment is at the natural rate.

The short-run relationship between inflation and unemployment is presented in Exhibit 6(b) under the assumption that people expect inflation to be 3 percent. Unemployment is measured along the horizontal axis and inflation along the vertical axis. Panel (a) shows that when inflation is 3 percent, the economy produces its potential. Unemployment is at the natural rate, assumed in panel (b) to be 5 percent. The

EXHIBIT 6 Aggregate Supply Curves and Phillips Curves in the Short Run and Long Run

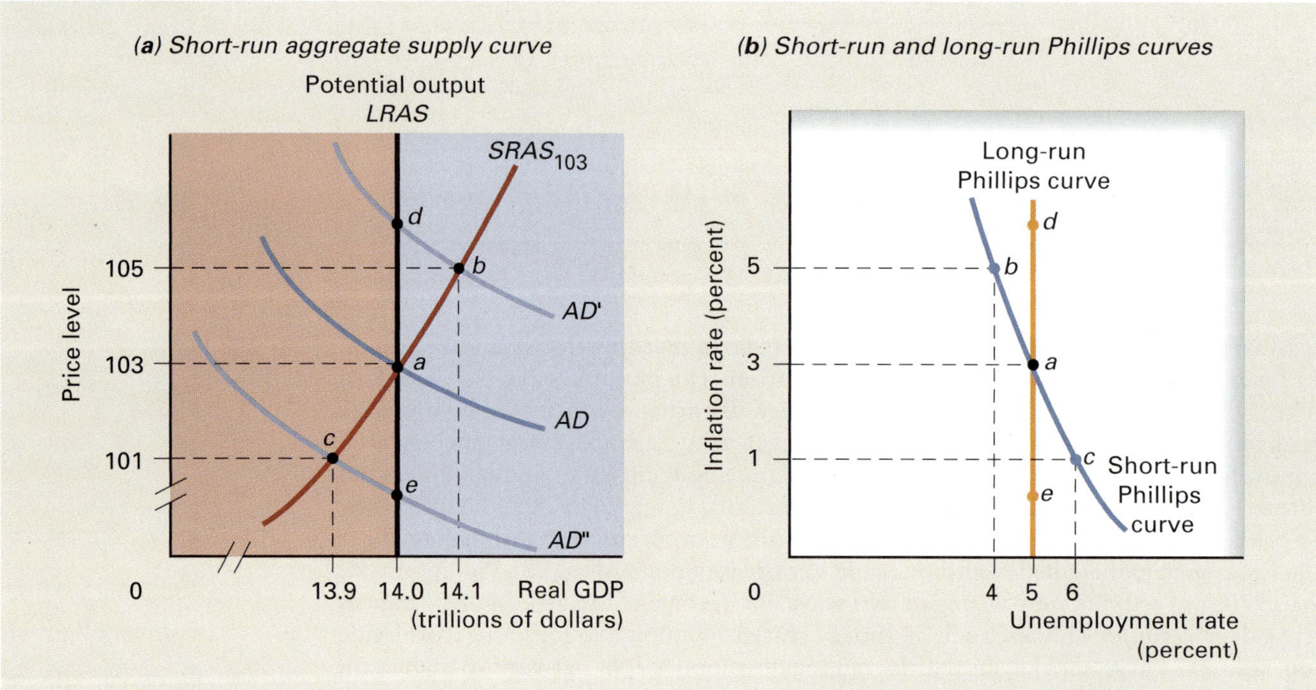

If people expect a price level of 103, which is 3 percent higher than the current level, and if *AD* turns out to be the aggregate demand curve, then the actual price level is 103 and output is at its potential. Point *a* in both panels represents this situation. Unemployment is the natural rate, assumed to be 5 percent in panel (b).

If aggregate demand turns out to be greater than expected (*AD′* instead of *AD*), the economy in the short run is at point *b* in panel (a), where the price level of 105 exceeds expectations and output exceeds its potential. The resulting higher inflation and lower unemployment are shown as point *b* in panel (b). If aggregate demand turns out to be less than expected (*AD"* instead of *AD*), short-run equilibrium is at point *c* in panel (a), where the price level of 101 is lower than expected and output falls short of potential. Lower inflation and higher unemployment are shown as point *c* in panel (b). In panel (b), points *a*, *b*, and *c* trace a short-run Phillips curve.

In the long run, the actual price level equals the expected price level. Output is at the potential level, $14.0 trillion, in panel (a). Unemployment is at the natural rate, 5 percent, in panel (b). Points *a*, *d*, and *e* depict long-run points in each panel. In panel (a) these points trace potential output, or long-run aggregate supply (*LRAS*). In panel (b), these points trace a long-run Phillips curve.

combination of 3 percent inflation and 5 percent unemployment is reflected by point *a* in panel (b), which corresponds to point *a* in panel (a).

What if aggregate demand turns out to be greater than expected, as indicated by *AD′*? In the short run, the greater demand results in point *b*, with a price level of 105 and output of $14.1 trillion. Because the price level exceeds that reflected in wage contracts, inflation also exceeds expectations. Specifically, inflation turns out to be 5 percent, not 3 percent. Because output exceeds potential, unemployment falls below the natural rate to 4 percent. The new combination of unemployment and inflation is depicted by point *b* in panel (b), which corresponds to point *b* in panel (a).

What if aggregate demand turns out to be lower than expected, as indicated by *AD″*? In the short run, the lower demand results in point *c*, where the price level of 101 is less than expected and output of $13.9 trillion is below potential. Inflation of 1 percent is less than the expected 3 percent, and unemployment of 6 percent exceeds the natural rate. This combination is reflected by point *c* in panel (b), which corresponds to point *c* in panel (a).

Note that the short-run aggregate supply curve in panel (a) can be used to develop the inverse relationship between inflation and unemployment shown in panel (b), called a **short-run Phillips curve.** This curve is created by the intersection of alternative aggregate demand curves along a given short-run aggregate supply curve. *The short-run Phillips curve is based on labor contracts that reflect a given expected price level, which implies a given expected rate of inflation.* The short-run Phillips curve in panel (b) is based on an expected inflation of 3 percent. If inflation turns out as expected, unemployment equals the natural rate. If inflation exceeds expectations, unemployment in the short run falls below the natural rate. If inflation is less than expected, unemployment in the short run exceeds the natural rate.

short-run Phillips curve
Based on an expected inflation rate, a curve that reflects an inverse relationship between the inflation rate and the unemployment rate

The Long-Run Phillips Curve

If inflation exceeds expectations, output exceeds the economy's potential in the short run but not in the long run. Labor shortages and shrinking real wages prompt higher wage agreements. The short-run aggregate supply curve shifts leftward until it passes through point *d* in panel (a) of Exhibit 6, returning the economy to its potential output. The unexpectedly higher aggregate demand curve has no lasting effect on output or unemployment. Point *d* corresponds to a higher price level, and thus higher inflation. Closing the expansionary gap generates both higher unemployment and higher inflation, a combination depicted by point *d* in panel (b). Note that whereas points *a*, *b*, and *c* are on the same short-run Phillips curve, point *d* is not.

To trace the long-run effects of a lower-than-expected price level, let's return to point *c* in panel (a), where the actual price level is below the expected level, so output is below its potential. If workers and firms negotiate lower money wages (or if the growth in nominal wages trails inflation), the short-run aggregate supply curve could shift rightward until it passes through point *e*, where the economy returns once again to its potential output. Both inflation and unemployment fall, as reflected by point *e* in panel (b).

Note that points *a*, *d*, and *e* in panel (a) depict long-run equilibrium points; the expected price level equals the actual price level. At those same points in panel (b), expected inflation equals actual inflation, so unemployment equals the natural rate. We can connect points *a*, *d*, and *e* in the right panel to form the **long-run Phillips curve.** *When workers and employers adjust fully to any unexpected change in aggregate demand, the long-run Phillips curve is a vertical line drawn at the economy's natural rate of unemployment.* As long as prices and wages are flexible enough, the rate of unemployment, in the long run, is independent of the rate of inflation. *Thus, according to proponents of this type of analysis, policy makers cannot, in the long run, choose between unemployment and inflation. They can choose only among alternative rates of inflation.*

long-run Phillips curve
A vertical line drawn at the economy's natural rate of unemployment that traces equilibrium points that can occur when workers and employers have the time to adjust fully to any unexpected change in aggregate demand

The Natural Rate Hypothesis

natural rate hypothesis
The natural rate of unemployment is largely independent of the stimulus provided by monetary or fiscal policy

The natural rate of unemployment occurs at the economy's potential output, discussed extensively already. An important idea that emerged from this reexamination of the Phillips curve is the **natural rate hypothesis**, which states that in the long run, the economy tends toward the natural rate of unemployment. This natural rate is largely independent of any *aggregate demand* stimulus provided by monetary or fiscal policy. Policy makers may be able to push output beyond its potential temporarily, but only if the policy surprises the public. The natural rate hypothesis implies that *the policy that results in low inflation is generally the optimal policy in the long run.*

Evidence of the Phillips Curve

What has been the actual relationship between unemployment and inflation in the United States? In Exhibit 7, each year since 1960 is represented by a point, with the unemployment rate measured along the horizontal axis and the inflation rate measured along the vertical axis. Superimposed on these points are short-run Phillips curves showing patterns of unemployment and inflation during what turns out to be five distinct periods since 1960. Remember, each short-run Phillips curve is drawn for a given *expected inflation rate*. An increase in inflationary expectations shifts the short-run Phillips curve away from the origin.

EXHIBIT 7 Short-Run Phillips Curves Since 1960

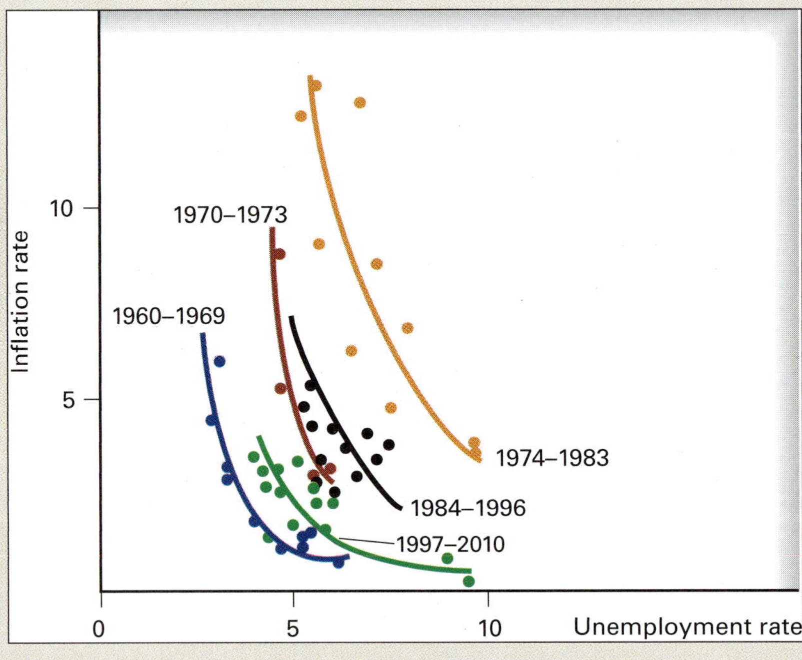

Each curve represents the U.S. unemployment-inflation combination for a given period, with colored points showing the years associated with each colored curve. Shifts of the short-run Phillips curve reflect changes in inflation expectations. Curves closer to the origin reflect lower expected inflation.

Source: Based on inflation and unemployment figures from the Economic Report of the President, February 2010, at http://www.gpoaccess.gov/eop/ and the U.S. Bureau of Labor Statistics at http://www.bls.gov/. Figures for 2010 are through June.

The clearest trade-off between unemployment and inflation occurred between 1960 and 1969; the blue points for those years fit neatly along the blue curve. In the early part of the decade, inflation was low but unemployment relatively high; as the 1960s progressed, unemployment declined but inflation increased. Inflation during the decade averaged only 2.5 percent, and unemployment averaged 4.8 percent.

The short-run Phillips curve shifted away from the origin for the period from 1970 to 1973 (in red), when inflation and unemployment each climbed to an average of 5.2 percent. In 1974, sharp increases in oil prices and crop failures around the world reduced aggregate supply, which sparked another outward shift of the Phillips curve. During the 1974–1983 period (in orange), inflation averaged 8.2 percent and unemployment 7.5 percent. After the Fed reduced inflationary expectations in the early 1980s, the short-run Phillips curve shifted inward. Average inflation for 1984–1996 (in black) fell to 3.7 percent and average unemployment fell to 6.1 percent. Finally, data for 1997 to 2010 (in green) suggest a new, lower short-run Phillips curve, with average inflation of only 2.2 percent and average unemployment of 5.6 percent. Thus, the Phillips curve shifted rightward between the 1960s and the early 1980s. Since then, the Fed has learned more about how to control inflation, thereby reducing inflation expectations and shifting the Phillips curve back nearly to where it started in the 1960s.

Conclusion

This chapter examined the implications of active and passive policy. The important question is whether the economy is stable and self-correcting when it gets off track or unstable and in need of active government intervention. Advocates of active policy believe that the Fed or Congress or both should reduce economic fluctuations by stimulating aggregate demand when output falls below its potential level and by dampening aggregate demand when output exceeds its potential level. Advocates of active policy argue that government attempts to reduce the ups and downs of the business cycle may not be perfect but are still better than nothing. Some activists also believe that high unemployment may be self-reinforcing, because some unemployed workers lose valuable job skills and grow to accept unemployment as a way of life, as may have happened in Europe.

Advocates of passive policy, on the other hand, believe that discretionary policy may worsen cyclical swings in the economy, leading to higher inflation in the long run with no permanent increase in potential output and no permanent reduction in the unemployment rate. This group favors passive rules for monetary policy and automatic stabilizers for fiscal policy.

The active-passive debate in this chapter has focused primarily on monetary policy because discretionary fiscal policy has been hampered by large federal deficits that ballooned the national debt. But the recession of 2007–2009 was so severe that most fiscal policy makers decided to worry later about deficits and debt.

Summary

1. Advocates of active policy view the private sector—particularly fluctuations in investment—as the primary source of economic instability in the economy. Activists argue that achieving potential output through natural market forces can be slow and painful, so the Fed or Congress or both should stimulate aggregate demand when actual output falls below potential.
2. Advocates of passive policy argue that the economy has enough natural resiliency to return to potential output within a reasonable period if upset by some shock. They point to the variable and uncertain lags associated with discretionary policy as reason enough to steer clear of active intervention.

3. The effect of particular government policies on the economy depends on what people come to expect. The theory of rational expectations holds that people form expectations based on all available information including past behavior by public officials. According to the rational expectations school, government policies are mostly anticipated by the public, and therefore have less effect than unexpected policies.
4. The passive approach suggests that the government should follow clear and predictable policies and avoid discretionary intervention to stimulate or dampen aggregate demand over the business cycle. Passive policies are reflected in automatic fiscal stabilizers and in explicit monetary rules, such as keeping inflation below a certain rate.
5. At one time, public officials thought they faced a stable trade-off between higher unemployment and higher inflation. More recent research suggests that if there is a trade-off, it exists only in the short run, not in the long run. Expansionary fiscal or monetary policies may stimulate output and employment in the short run. But if the economy was already at or near its potential output, these expansionary policies, in the long run, result only in more inflation.

Key Concepts

Questions for Review

1. Active Versus Passive Policy Contrast the active policy view of the behavior of wages and prices during a recessionary gap to the passive policy view.
2. Active Policy Why do proponents of active policy recommend government intervention to close an expansionary gap?
3. Active Versus Passive Policy According to advocates of passive policy, what variable naturally adjusts in the labor market, shifting the short-run aggregate supply curve to restore unemployment to the natural rate? Why does the active policy approach assume that the short-run aggregate supply curve shifts leftward more easily and quickly than it shifts rightward?
4. Review of Policy Perspectives Why might an active policy approach be more politically popular than a passive approach, especially during a recession?
5. The Role of Expectations Some economists argue that only unanticipated increases in the money supply can affect real GDP. Explain why this may be the case.
6. Anticipating Monetary Policy In 1995, the Fed began announcing its interest rate targets immediately following each meeting of the FOMC. Prior to that, observers were left to draw inferences about Fed policy based on the results of that policy. What is the value of this greater openness?
7. Policy Credibility What is policy credibility and how is it relevant to the problem of reducing high inflation? How is credibility related to the time-inconsistency problem?
8. Case Study: Central Bank Independence and Price Stability (See page 774.) One source of independence for the Fed is the term length for members of the Board of Governors. In the chapter before last, we learned that the Fed is a "money machine." Does this suggest another source of Fed independence from Congress?
9. Rationale for Rules Some economists call for predetermined rules to guide the actions of government policy makers. What are two contrasting rationales that have been given for such rules?
10. Rational Expectations Suppose that people in an election year believe that public officials are going to pursue expansionary policies to enhance their reelection prospects. How could such expectations put pressure on officials to pursue expansionary policies even if they hadn't planned to?
11. Potential GNP Why is it hard for policy makers to decide whether the economy is operating at its potential output level? Why is this uncertainty a problem?
12. Phillips Curves Describe the different policy trade-offs implied by the short-run Phillips curve and the long-run Phillips curve. What forces shift the long-run Phillips curve?

Problems and Exercises

13. ACTIVE VERSUS PASSIVE POLICY Discuss the role each of the following plays in the debate between the active and passive approaches:
    a. The speed of adjustment of the nominal wage
    b. The speed of adjustment of expectations about inflation
    c. The existence of lags in policy creation and implementation
    d. Variability in the natural rate of unemployment over time
14. Case Study: Active Versus Passive Presidential Candidates (See page 773.) What were the main differences between candidates Bush and Clinton in the 1992 presidential campaign? Illustrate their ideas using the aggregate supply and demand model.
15. PROBLEMS WITH ACTIVE POLICY Use an *AD–AS* diagram to illustrate and explain the short-run and long-run effects on the economy of the following situation: Both the natural rate of unemployment and the actual rate of unemployment are 5 percent. However, the government believes that the natural rate of unemployment is 6 percent and that the economy is overheating. Therefore, it introduces a policy to reduce aggregate demand.
16. POLICY LAGS What lag in discretionary policy is described in each of the following statements? Why do long lags make discretionary policy less effective?
    a. The time from when the government determines that the economy is in recession until a tax cut is approved to reduce unemployment
    b. The time from when the money supply is increased until the resulting effect on the economy is felt
    c. The time from the start of a recession until the government identifies the existence and severity of the recession
    d. The time from when the Fed decides to reduce the money supply until the money supply actually declines
17. RATIONAL EXPECTATIONS Using an *AD–AS* diagram, illustrate the short-run effects on prices, output, and employment of an increase in the money supply that is correctly anticipated by the public. Assume that the economy is initially at potential output.
18. LONG-RUN PHILLIPS CURVE Suppose the economy is at point *d* on the long-run Phillips curve shown in Exhibit 6. If that inflation rate is unacceptably high, how can policy makers get the inflation rate down? Would rational expectations help or hinder their efforts?

Global Economic Watch Exercises

Login to www.cengagebrain.com and access the Global Economic Watch to do these exercises.

19. GLOBAL ECONOMIC WATCH Go to the Global Economic Crisis Resource Center and select Global Issues in Context. In the Basic Search box at the top of the page, enter the phrase "policy credibility." On the Results page, go to the News Section. Click on the link for the September 24, 2010, article "Research Conducted at Chongqing University Has Provided New Information About Economic Psychology." Does the research described support the importance of policy credibility?
20. GLOBAL ECONOMIC WATCH Go to the Global Economic Crisis Resource Center and select Global Issues in Context. In the Basic Search box at the top of the page, enter the phrase "inflation target." Write a brief summary of one article published within the past three years.

International Trade

32

AP Photo/Reed Saxon

- This morning you pulled on your Levi's jeans from Mexico, pulled over your Benetton sweater from Italy, and laced up your Timberland boots from Thailand. After a breakfast that included bananas from Honduras and coffee from Brazil, you climbed into your Volvo from Sweden fueled by Venezuelan oil and headed for a lecture by a visiting professor from Hungary. If the United States is such a rich and productive country, why do we import so many goods and services?
- Why don't we produce everything ourselves?
- How can the U.S. economy grow if we import more goods and services?
- And why do some producers try to block imports?

Answers to these and other questions are addressed in this chapter.

The world is a giant shopping mall, and Americans are big spenders. For example, the U.S. population is less than 5 percent of the world's population, but Americans buy more than half the Rolls Royces and diamonds sold around the world. Americans also buy Japanese cars, French wine, European vacations, Chinese products galore, and thousands of other goods and services from around the globe. Foreigners buy U.S. products too—grain, aircraft, movies, software, trips to New York City, and thousands of other goods and services.

In this chapter, we examine the gains from international trade and the effects of trade restrictions on the allocation of resources. The analysis is based on the familiar tools of demand and supply.

Topics discussed include:

- Gains from trade
- Absolute and comparative advantage revisited
- Tariffs and quotas
- Cost of trade restrictions
- Arguments for trade restrictions
- Free trade agreements

The Gains From Trade

A family from Virginia that sits down for a meal of Kansas prime rib, Idaho potatoes, and California string beans, with Georgia peach cobbler for dessert, is benefiting from interstate trade. You already understand why the residents of one state trade with those of another. Back in Chapter 2, you learned about the gains arising from specialization and exchange. You may recall how you and your roommate could maximize output when you each specialized. The law of comparative advantage says that the individual with the lowest opportunity cost of producing a particular good should specialize in that good. Just as individuals benefit from specialization and exchange, so do states and, indeed, nations. To reap the gains that arise from specialization, countries engage in international trade. *Each country specializes in making goods with the lowest opportunity cost.*

A Profile of Exports and Imports

Just as some states are more involved in interstate trade than others, some nations are more involved in international trade than others. For example, exports account for about one-quarter of the gross domestic product (GDP) in Canada and the United Kingdom; about one-third of GDP in Germany, Sweden, and Switzerland; and about half of GDP in the Netherlands. Despite the perception that Japan has a huge export sector, exports make up only about one-sixth of its GDP.

U.S. Exports

U.S. exports of goods and services amounted to $1.6 trillion, or 11 percent of GDP in 2009. The left panel of Exhibit 1 shows the composition by major category. The largest category is services, which accounted for 32 percent of U.S. exports in 2009. U.S. service exports include transportation, insurance, banking, education, consulting, and tourism. Capital goods ranked second at 27 percent of exports, with aircraft the largest export industry (Boeing is the top U.S. exporter in any industry). Third most important are industrial supplies, at 19 percent of the total, with chemicals and plastics most important here. Capital goods and industrial supplies help foreign producers make stuff and together accounted for nearly half of U.S. exports. Consumer goods (except food, which appears separately) accounted for only 10 percent of exports (pharmaceuticals tops this group). Consumer goods include entertainment products, such as movies and recorded music.

U.S. Imports

U.S. imports of goods and services in 2009 totaled $1.9 trillion, or about 14 percent relative to GDP. The right panel of Exhibit 1 shows the composition of U.S. imports. The biggest category, at 25 percent, is industrial supplies, with oil-related products accounting for most of this. Whereas consumer goods accounted for only 10 percent of U.S. exports, they were 23 percent of U.S. imports, with pharmaceuticals the largest item. Ranked third in importance is capital goods, at 20 percent, with computers the largest item. Note that services, which accounted for 32 percent of U.S. exports, were only 19 percent of imports.

Trading Partners

To give you some feel for America's trading partners, here were the top 10 destinations for merchandise exports for 2009 in order of importance: Canada, Mexico, China, Japan, United Kingdom, Germany, Netherlands, South Korea, France, and Brazil. The

EXHIBIT 1 Composition of U.S. Exports and Imports in 2009

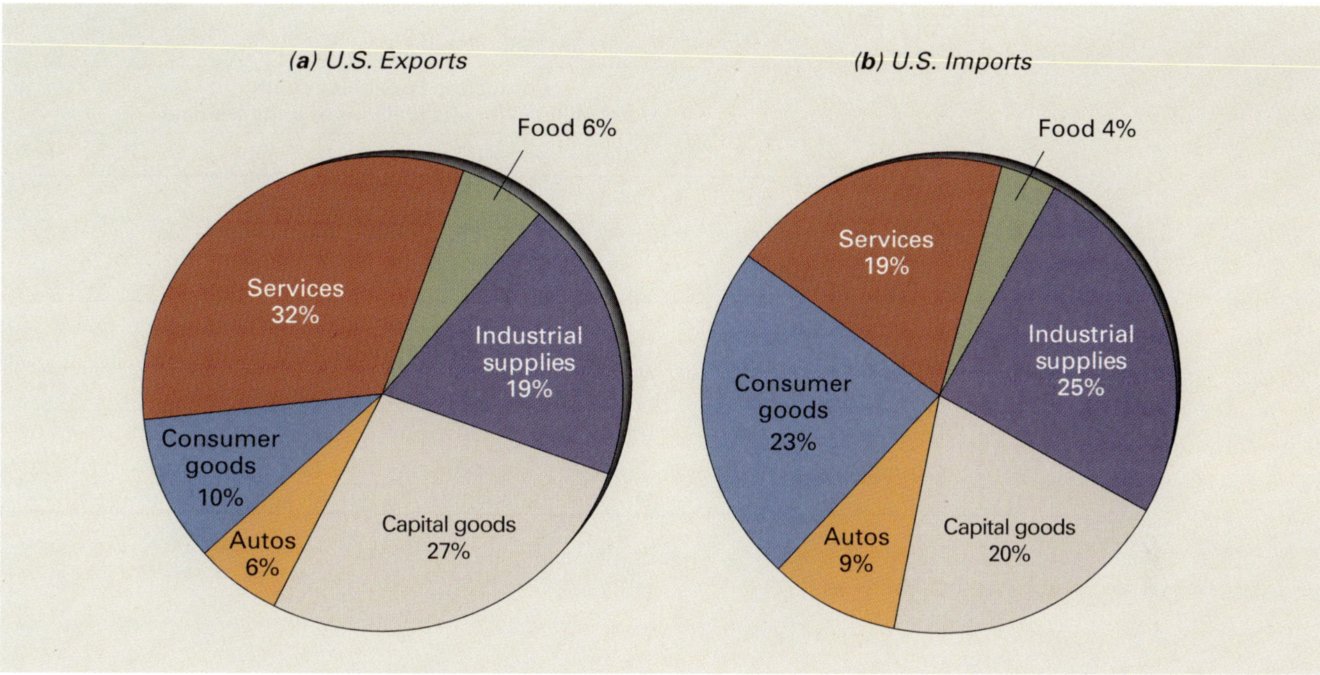

Sources: Based on government estimates in "International Data," *Survey of Current Business*, 90 (June 2010), Table F, p. D-60.

top 10 sources of merchandise imports in order of importance were China, Canada, Mexico, Japan, Germany, United Kingdom, South Korea, France, Taiwan, and Ireland.

Production Possibilities without Trade

The rationale behind most international trade is obvious. The United States grows little coffee because our climate is not suited to coffee. More revealing, however, are the gains from trade where the comparative advantage is not so obvious. Suppose that just two goods—food and clothing—are produced and consumed and that there are only two countries in the world—the United States, with a labor force of 100 million workers, and the mythical country of Izodia, with 200 million workers. The conclusions derived from this simple model have general relevance for international trade.

Exhibit 2 presents production possibilities tables for each country, based on the size of the labor force and the productivity of workers in each country. The exhibit assumes that each country has a given technology and that labor is efficiently employed. If no trade occurs between countries, Exhibit 2 also represents each country's *consumption possibilities* table. The production numbers imply that each worker in the United States can produce either 6 units of food or 3 units of clothing per day. If all 100 million U.S. workers produce food, they make 600 million units per day, as shown in column U_1 in panel (a). If all U.S. workers make clothing, they produce 300 million units per day, as shown in column U_6. The columns in between show some workers making food and some making clothing. Because a U.S. worker can produce either 6 units of food or 3 units of clothing, *the opportunity cost of 1 more unit of clothing is 2 units of food.*

EXHIBIT 2 Production Possibilities Schedules for the United States and Izodia

(a) United States

	Production Possibilities with 100 Million Workers (millions of units per day)					
	U_1	U_2	U_3	U_4	U_5	U_6
Food	600	480	360	240	120	0
Clothing	0	60	120	180	240	300

(b) Izodia

	Production Possibilities with 200 Million Workers (millions of units per day)					
	I_1	I_2	I_3	I_4	I_5	I_6
Food	200	160	120	80	40	0
Clothing	0	80	160	240	320	400

Suppose Izodian workers are less educated, work with less capital, and farm less fertile soil than U.S. workers, so each Izodian worker can produce only 1 unit of food or 2 units of clothing per day. If all 200 million Izodian workers specialize in food, they can make 200 million units per day, as shown in column I_1 in panel (b) of Exhibit 2. If they all make clothing, total output is 400 million units per day, as shown in column I_6. Some intermediate production possibilities are also listed in the exhibit. Because an Izodian worker can produce either 1 unit of food or 2 units of clothing, *the opportunity cost of 1 more unit of clothing is 1/2 unit of food.*

We can convert the data in Exhibit 2 to a production possibilities frontier for each country, as shown in Exhibit 3. In each diagram, the amount of food produced is measured on the vertical axis and the amount of clothing on the horizontal axis. U.S. combinations are shown in the left panel by U_1, U_2, and so on. Izodian combinations are shown in the right panel by I_1, I_2, and so on. Because we assume for simplicity that resources are perfectly adaptable to the production of each commodity, each production possibilities curve is a straight line. The slope of this line differs between countries because the opportunity cost of production differs between countries. The slope equals the opportunity cost of clothing—the amount of food a country must give up to produce another unit of clothing. The U.S. slope is -2, and the Izodian slope is $-1/2$. The U.S. slope is steeper because its opportunity cost of producing clothing is greater.

autarky
National self-sufficiency; no economic interaction with foreigners

Exhibit 3 illustrates possible combinations of food and clothing that residents of each country can produce and consume if all resources are efficiently employed and there is no trade between the two countries. **Autarky** is the situation of national self-sufficiency, in which there is no economic interaction with foreign producers or consumers. Suppose that U.S. producers maximize profit and U.S. consumers maximize utility with the combination of 240 million units of food and 180 million units of clothing—combination U_4. This is called the *autarky equilibrium.* Suppose also that Izodians are in autarky equilibrium, identified as combination I_3, of 120 million units of food and 160 million units of clothing.

EXHIBIT 3 Production Possibilities Frontiers for the United States and Izodia Without Trade (millions of units per day)

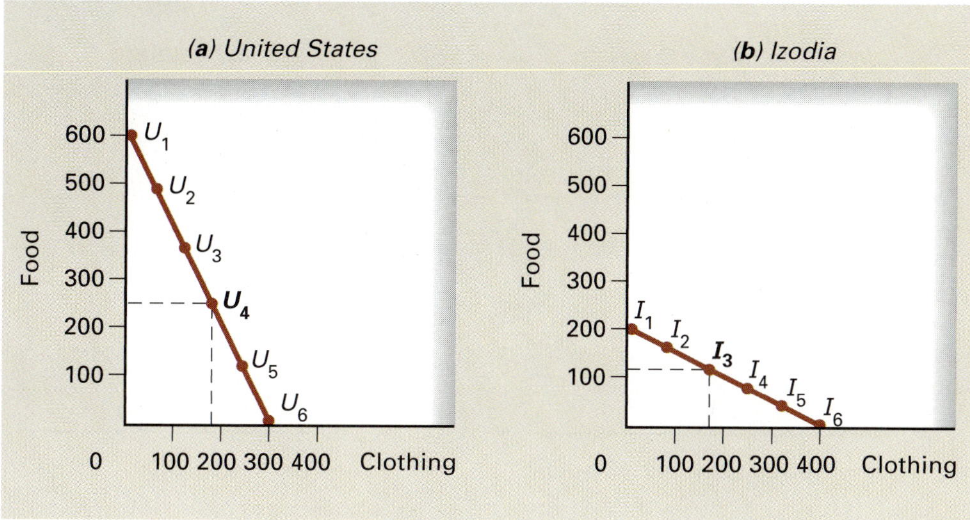

Panel (a) shows the U.S. production possibilities frontier; its slope indicates that the opportunity cost of an additional unit of clothing is 2 units of food. Panel (b) shows production possibilities for Izodia; an additional unit of clothing costs 1/2 unit of food. Clothing has a lower opportunity cost in Izodia.

Consumption Possibilities Based on Comparative Advantage

In our example, each U.S. worker can produce more clothing and more food per day than can each Izodian worker, so Americans have an *absolute advantage* in the production of both goods. Recall from Chapter 2 that having an absolute advantage means being able to produce something using fewer resources than other producers require. Should the U.S. economy remain in autarky—that is, self-sufficient in both food and clothing productions—or could there be gains from specialization and trade?

As long as the opportunity cost of production differs between the two countries, there are gains from specialization and trade. *According to the law of comparative advantage, each country should specialize in producing the good with the lower opportunity cost.* The opportunity cost of producing 1 more unit of clothing is 2 units of food in the United States compared with 1/2 unit of food in Izodia. Because the opportunity cost of producing clothing is lower in Izodia than in the United States, both countries gain if Izodia specializes in clothing and exports some to the United States, and the United States specializes in food and exports some to Izodia.

Before countries can trade, however, they must agree on how much of one good exchanges for another—that is, they must agree on the **terms of trade**. As long as Americans can get more than ½ a unit of clothing for each unit of food produced, and as long as Izodians can get more than ½ a unit of food for each unit of clothing produced, both countries will be better off specializing. Suppose that market forces shape the terms of trade so that 1 unit of clothing exchanges for 1 unit of food. Americans thus trade 1 unit of food to Izodians for 1 unit of clothing. To produce 1 unit of clothing themselves, Americans would have to sacrifice 2 units of food. Likewise, Izodians trade 1 unit of clothing to Americans for 1 unit of food, which is only half what Izodians would sacrifice to produce 1 unit of food themselves.

terms of trade
How much of one good exchanges for a unit of another good

Exhibit 4 shows that with 1 unit of food trading for 1 unit of clothing, Americans and Izodians can consume anywhere along their blue consumption possibilities frontiers.

EXHIBIT 4 **Production (and Consumption) Possibilities Frontiers With Trade (millions of units per day)**

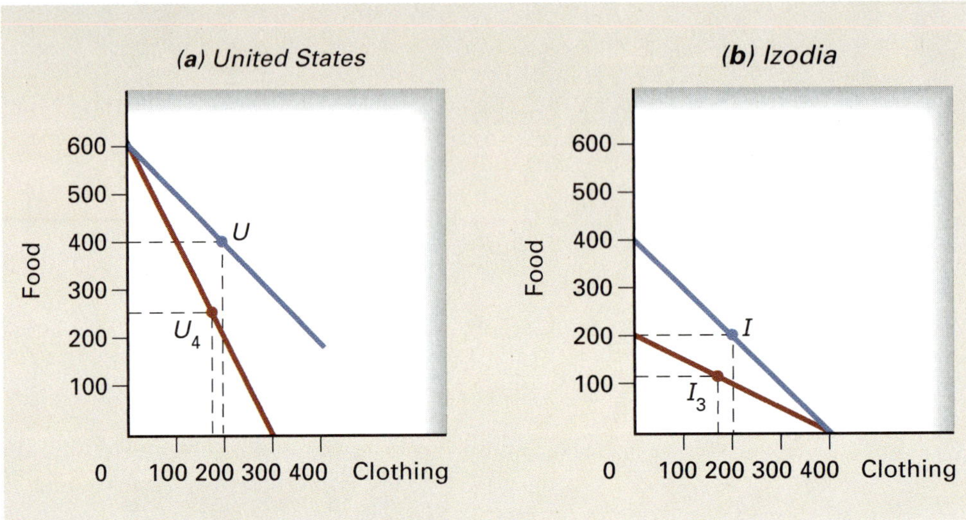

If Izodia and the United States can specialize and trade at the rate of 1 unit of clothing for 1 unit of food, both can benefit as shown by the blue lines. By trading with Izodia, the U.S. can produce only food and still consume combination *U*, which has more food and more clothing than U_4. Likewise, Izodia can attain preferred combination *I* by trading some clothing for U.S. food.

The consumption possibilities frontier shows a nation's possible combinations of goods available as a result of specialization and exchange. (Note that the U.S. consumption possibilities curve does not extend to the right of 400 million units of clothing, because Izodia could produce no more than that.) The amount each country actually consumes depends on the relative preferences for food and clothing. Suppose Americans select combination *U* in panel (a) and Izodians select point *I* in panel (b).

Without trade, the United States produces and consumes 240 million units of food and 180 million units of clothing. With trade, Americans specialize to produce 600 million units of food; they eat 400 million units and exchange the rest for 200 million units of Izodian clothing. This consumption combination is reflected by point *U*. Through exchange, Americans increase their consumption of both food and clothing.

Without trade, Izodians produce and consume 120 million units of food and 160 million units of clothing. With trade, Izodians specialize to produce 400 million units of clothing; they wear 200 million and exchange the rest for 200 million units of U.S. food. This consumption combination is shown by point *I*. Through trade, Izodians, like Americans, are able to increase their consumption of both goods. How is this possible?

Because Americans are more efficient in the production of food and Izodians more efficient in the production of clothing, total output increases when each specializes. Without specialization, world production was 360 million units of food and 340 million units of clothing. With specialization, food increases to 600 million units and clothing to 400 million units. Thus, both countries increase consumption with trade. *Although the United States has an absolute advantage in both goods, differences in the opportunity cost of production between the two nations ensure that specialization and exchange result in mutual gains.* Remember that comparative advantage, not absolute advantage, creates gains from specialization and trade. The only constraint on trade is that, for each good, *world production must equal world consumption.*

We simplified trade relations in our example to highlight the gains from specialization and exchange. We assumed that each country would completely specialize in producing a particular good, that resources were equally adaptable to the production of either good, that the costs of transporting goods from one country to another were inconsequential, and that there were no problems in arriving at the terms of trade. The world is not that simple. For example, we don't expect a country to produce just one good. Regardless, specialization based on the law of comparative advantage still leads to gains from trade.

Reasons for International Specialization

Countries trade with one another—or, more precisely, people and firms in one country trade with those in another—because each side expects to gain from exchange. How do we know what each country should produce and what each should trade?

Differences in Resource Endowments

Differences in resource endowments often create differences in the opportunity cost of production across countries. Some countries are blessed with an abundance of fertile land and favorable growing seasons. The United States, for example, has been called the "breadbasket of the world" because of its rich farmland ideal for growing wheat. Coffee grows best in the climate and elevation of Colombia, Brazil, and Jamaica. Honduras has the ideal climate for bananas. Thus, the United States exports wheat and imports coffee and bananas. Seasonal differences across countries also encourage trade. For example, in the winter, Americans import fruit from Chile, and Canadians travel to Florida for sun and fun. In the summer, Americans export fruit to Chile, and Americans travel to Canada for camping and hiking.

Resources are often concentrated in particular countries: crude oil in Saudi Arabia, fertile soil in the United States, copper ore in Chile, rough diamonds in South Africa. The United States grows abundant supplies of oil seeds such as soybeans and sunflowers, but does not have enough crude oil to satisfy domestic demand. Thus, the United States exports oil seeds and imports crude oil. More generally, *countries export products they can produce more cheaply in return for products that are unavailable domestically or are cheaper elsewhere.*

Exhibit 5 shows, for 12 key resources, U.S. production as a percentage of U.S. consumption. If production falls short of consumption, this means the United States imports the difference. For example, because America grows coffee only in Hawaii, U.S. production is only 1 percent of U.S. consumption, so nearly all coffee is imported. The exhibit also shows that U.S. production falls short of consumption for oil and for metals such as gold, zinc, copper, and aluminum. If production exceeds consumption, the United States exports the difference. For example, U.S.-grown cotton amounts to 417 percent of U.S. cotton consumption, so most U.S. grown cotton is exported. U.S. production also exceeds consumption for other crops, including wheat, oil seeds, and coarse grains (corn, barley, oats). In short, when it comes to basic resources, the United States is a net importer of oil and metals and a net exporter of crops.

Economies of Scale

If production is subject to *economies of scale*—that is, if the long-run average cost of production falls as a firm expands its scale of operation—countries can gain from trade if each nation specializes. Such specialization allows firms in each nation to produce

EXHIBIT 5 U.S. Production as a Percentage of U.S. Consumption for Various Resources

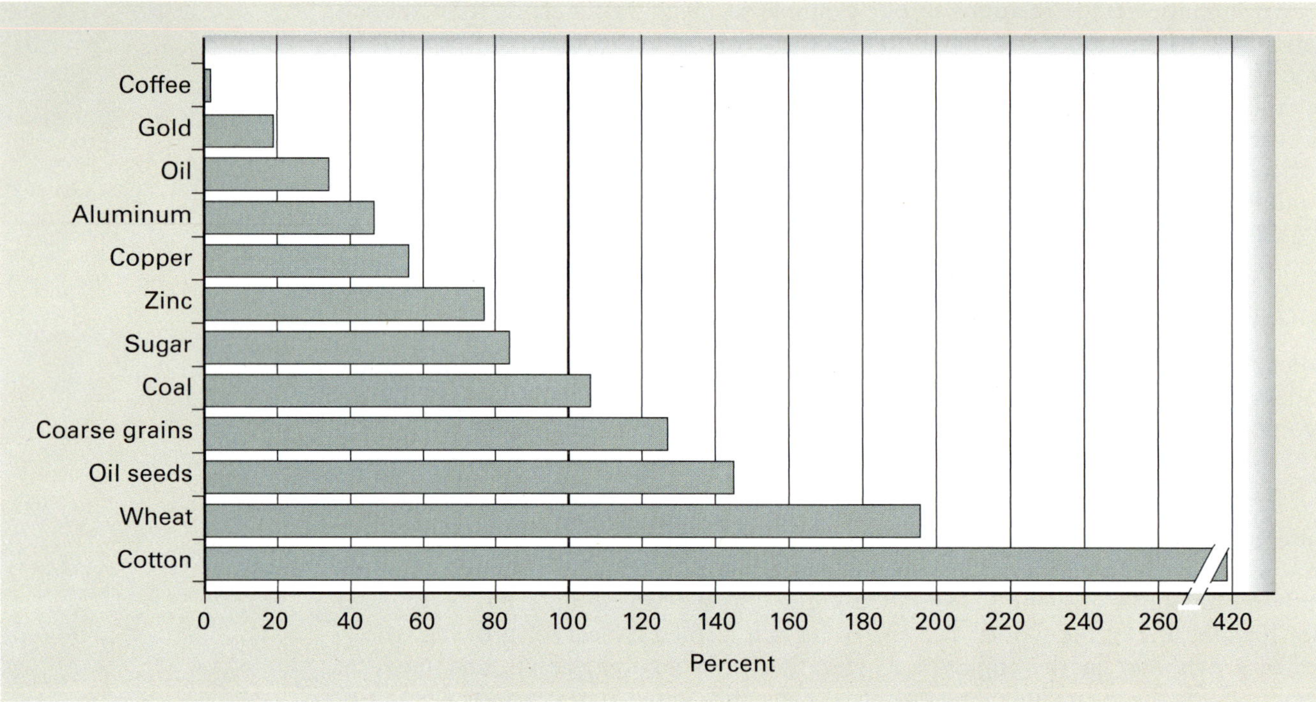

If U.S. production is less than 100 percent of U.S. consumption, then imports make up the difference. If U.S. production exceeds U.S. consumption, then the amount by which production exceeds 100 percent of consumption is exported.

Source: Based on annual figures selected from *The Economist Pocket World in Figures: 2010 Edition* (Profile Books, 2010).

more, which reduces average costs. The primary reason for establishing the single integrated market of the European Union was to offer producers there a large, open market of now more than 500 million consumers. Producers could thereby achieve economies of scale. Firms and countries producing at the lowest opportunity costs are most competitive in international markets. For example, 60 percent of the world's buttons come from a single Chinese city.

Differences in Tastes

Even if all countries had identical resource endowments and combined those resources with equal efficiency, each country would still gain from trade as long as tastes differed across countries. Consumption patterns differ across countries and some of this results from differences in tastes. For example, the Czechs and Irish drink three times as much beer per capita as do the Swiss and Swedes. The French drink three times as much wine as do Australians. The Danes eat twice as much pork as do Americans. Americans eat twice as much chicken as do Hungarians. Americans like chicken, but not all of it. The United States is the world's leading exporter of chicken feet, and China is the world's leading importer (Tyson Foods alone sends more than 2.8 billion chicken feet to China each year). Soft drinks are four times more popular in the United States than in Europe. The English like tea; Americans, coffee. Algeria has an ideal climate for growing grapes (vineyards there date back to Roman times). But Algeria's population is 99 percent Muslim, a religion that forbids alcohol consumption. Thus, Algeria exports wine.

Trade Restrictions and Welfare Loss

Despite the benefits of exchange, nearly all countries at one time or another erect trade barriers, which benefit some domestic producers but harm other domestic producers and all domestic consumers. In this section, we consider the effects of trade barriers and the reasons they are imposed.

Consumer Surplus and Producer Surplus From Market Exchange

Before we explore the net effects of world trade on social welfare, let's develop a framework showing the benefits that consumers and producers get from market exchange. Consider a hypothetical market for apples shown in Exhibit 6. The height of the demand curve shows what consumers are willing and able to pay for each additional pound of apples. In effect, the height of the demand curve shows the *marginal benefit* consumers expect from each pound of apples. For example, the demand curve indicates that some consumers in this market are willing to pay $3.00 or more per pound for the first few pounds of apples. But every consumer gets to buy apples at the market-clearing price,

EXHIBIT 6 Consumer Surplus and Producer Surplus

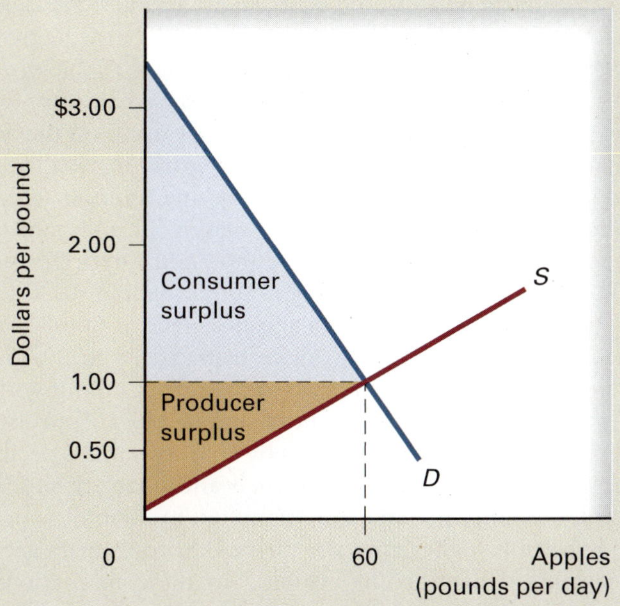

Consumer surplus, shown by the blue triangle, indicates the net benefits consumers reap from buying 60 pounds of apples at $1.00 per pound. Some consumers would have been willing to pay $3.00 or more per pound for the first few pounds. Consumer surplus measures the difference between the maximum sum of money consumers would pay for 60 pounds of apples and the actual sum they pay. Producer surplus, shown by the gold triangle, indicates the net benefits producers reap from selling 60 pounds at $1.00 per pound. Some producers would have supplied apples for $0.50 per pound or less. Producer surplus measures the difference between the actual sum of money producers receive for 60 pounds of apples and the minimum amount they would accept for this amount.

which here is $1.00 per pound. Most consumers thus get a bonus, or a surplus, from market exchange.

The blue-shaded triangle below the demand curve and above the market price reflects the *consumer surplus* in this market, which is the difference between the most that consumers would pay for 60 pounds of apples per day and the actual amount they do pay. We all enjoy a consumer surplus from most products we buy.

Producers usually derive a similar surplus. The height of the supply curve shows what producers are willing and able to accept for each additional pound of apples. That is, the height of the supply curve shows the expected *marginal cost* from producing each additional pound. For example, the supply curve indicates that some producers face a marginal cost of $0.50 or less per pound for supplying the first few pounds. But every producer gets to sell apples for the market-clearing price of $1.00 per pound. The gold-shaded triangle above the supply curve and below the market price reflects the *producer surplus*, which is the difference between the actual amount that producers receive for 60 pounds and what they would accept to supply that amount.

The point is that market exchange usually generates a surplus, or a bonus, for both consumers and producers. In the balance of this chapter, we look at the gains from international trade and how trade restrictions affect consumer and producer surplus.

Tariffs

A *tariff*, a term first introduced in Chapter 3, is a tax on imports. (Tariffs can apply to exports, too, but we will focus on import tariffs.) A tariff can be either *specific*, such as a tariff of $5 per barrel of oil, or *ad valorem*, such as 10 percent on the import price of jeans. Consider the effects of a specific tariff on a particular good. In Exhibit 7, *D* is the U.S. demand for sugar and *S* is the supply of sugar from U.S. growers (there were about 10,000 U.S. sugarcane growers in 2010). Suppose that the world price of sugar is $0.10 per pound. The **world price** is determined by the world supply and demand for a product. It is the price at which any supplier can sell output on the world market and at which any demander can purchase output on the world market.

world price
The price at which a good is traded on the world market; determined by the world demand and world supply for the good

With free trade, any U.S. consumers could buy any amount desired at the world price of $0.10 per pound, so the quantity demanded is 70 million pounds per month, of which U.S. producers supply 20 million pounds and importers supply 50 million pounds. Because U.S. buyers can purchase sugar at the world price, U.S. producers can't charge more than that. Now suppose that a specific tariff of $0.05 is imposed on each pound of imported sugar, raising the U.S. price from $0.10 to $0.15 per pound. U.S. producers can therefore raise their own price to $0.15 per pound without losing business to imports. At the higher price, the quantity supplied by U.S. producers increases to 30 million pounds, but the quantity demanded by U.S. consumers declines to 60 million pounds. Because quantity demanded has declined and quantity supplied by U.S. producers has increased, U.S. imports fall from 50 million to 30 million pounds per month.

Because the U.S. price is higher after the tariff, U.S. consumers are worse off. Their loss in consumer surplus is identified in Exhibit 7 by the combination of the blue- and pink-shaded areas. Because both the U.S. price and the quantity supplied by U.S. producers have increased, their total revenue increases by the areas *a* plus *b* plus *f*. But only area *a* represents an increase in producer surplus. Revenue represented by the areas *b* plus *f* merely offsets the higher marginal cost U.S. producers face in expanding sugar output from 20 million to 30 million pounds per month. Area *b* represents part of the net welfare loss to the domestic economy because those 10 million pounds could have been imported for $0.10 per pound rather than produced domestically at a higher marginal cost.

Government revenue from the tariff is identified by area *c*, which equals the tariff of $0.05 per pound multiplied by the 30 million pounds imported, for tariff revenue

EXHIBIT 7 Effect of a Tariff

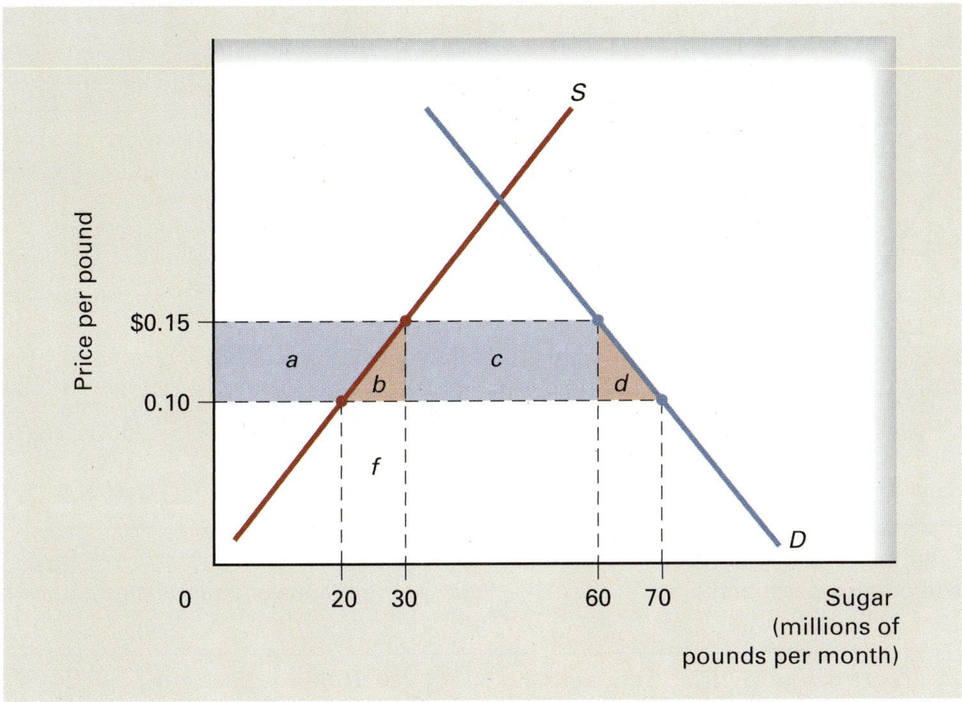

At a world price of $0.10 per pound, U.S. consumers demand 70 million pounds of sugar per month, and U.S. producers supply 20 million pounds per month; the difference is imported. After the imposition of a $0.05 per pound tariff, the U.S. price rises to $0.15 per pound. U.S. producers supply 30 million pounds, and U.S. consumers cut back to 60 million pounds. At the higher U.S. price, consumers are worse off; their loss of consumer surplus is the sum of areas *a*, *b*, *c*, and *d*. The net welfare loss to the U.S. economy consists of areas *b* and *d*.

of $1.5 million per month. Tariff revenue is a loss to consumers, but because the tariff goes to the government, it can be used to lower taxes or to increase public services, so it's not a loss to the U.S. economy. Area *d* shows a loss in consumer surplus because less sugar is consumed at the higher price. This loss is not redistributed to anyone else, so area *d* reflects part of the net welfare loss of the tariff. Therefore, areas *b* and *d* show the domestic economy's net welfare loss of the tariff; *the two triangles measure a loss in consumer surplus that is not offset by a gain to anyone in the domestic economy.*

In summary: Of the total loss in U.S. consumer surplus (areas *a*, *b*, *c*, and *d*) resulting from the tariff, area *a* goes to U.S producers, area *c* becomes government revenue, but areas *b* and *d* are net losses in domestic social welfare.

Import Quotas

An *import quota* is a legal limit on the amount of a commodity that can be imported. Quotas usually target imports from certain countries. For example, a quota may limit furniture from China or shoes from Brazil. To have an impact on the domestic market, a quota must be less than what would be imported with free trade. Consider a quota on the U.S. market for sugar. In panel (a) of Exhibit 8, *D* is the U.S. demand curve and *S* is the supply curve of U.S. sugar producers. Suppose again that the world price of sugar

EXHIBIT 8 Effect of a Quota

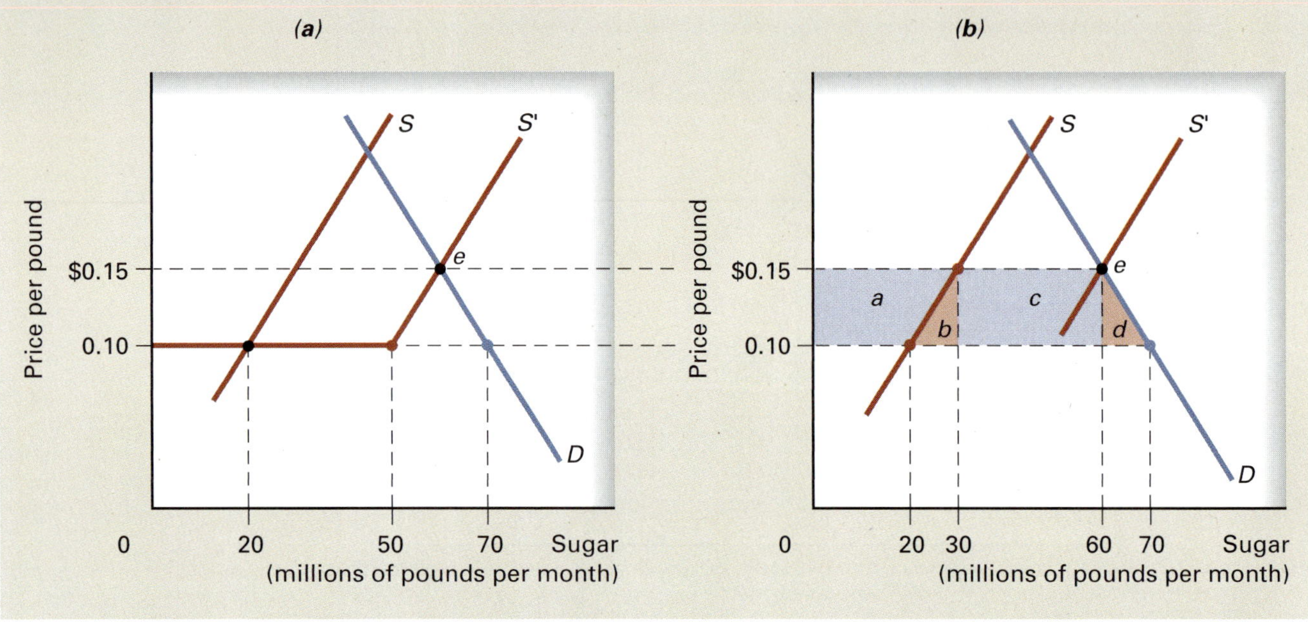

In panel (a), *D* is the U.S. demand curve and *S* is the supply curve of U.S. producers. If the government establishes a sugar quota of 30 million pounds per month, the supply curve combining U.S. production and imports becomes horizontal at the world price of $0.10 per pound and remains horizontal until the quantity supplied reaches 50 million pounds. For higher prices, the new supply curve equals the horizontal sum of the U.S. supply curve, *S*, plus the quota of 30 million pounds. The new U.S. price, $0.15 per pound, is determined by the intersection of the new supply curve, *S'*, with the U.S. demand curve, *D*. Panel (b) shows the welfare effect of the quota. As a result of the higher U.S. price, consumer surplus is cut by the shaded area. The blue-shaded areas illustrate the loss in consumer surplus that is captured by domestic producers and those who are permitted to fulfill the quota, and the pink-shaded triangles illustrate the net welfare cost of the quota on the U.S. economy.

is $0.10 per pound. With free trade, that price would prevail in the U.S. market as well, and a total of 70 million pounds would be demanded per month. U.S. producers would supply 20 million pounds and importers, 50 million pounds. With a quota of 50 million pounds or more per month, the U.S. price would remain the same as the world price of $0.10 per pound, and the U.S. quantity would be 70 million pounds per month. In short, a quota of at least 50 million pounds would not raise the U.S. price above the world price because 50 million pounds were imported without a quota. A more stringent quota, however, would cut imports, which, as we'll see, would raise the U.S. price.

Suppose U.S. trade officials impose an import quota of 30 million pounds per month. As long as the U.S. price is at or above the world price of $0.10 per pound, foreign producers will supply 30 million pounds. So at prices at or above $0.10 per pound, the total supply of sugar to the U.S. market is found by adding 30 million pounds of imported sugar to the amount supplied by U.S. producers. U.S. and foreign producers would never sell in the U.S. market for less than $0.10 per pound because they can always get that price on the world market. Thus, the supply curve that sums domestic production and imports is horizontal at the world price of $0.10 per pound and remains so until the quantity supplied reaches 50 million pounds.

Again, for prices above $0.10 per pound, the new supply curve, *S'*, adds horizontally the 30-million-pound quota to *S*, the supply curve of U.S. producers. The U.S. price is found where this new supply curve, *S'*, intersects the domestic demand curve, which in

Exhibit 8 occurs at point *e*. *By limiting imports, the quota raises the domestic price of sugar above the world price and reduces quantity below the free trade level.* (Note that to compare more easily the effects of tariffs and quotas, this quota is designed to yield the same equilibrium price and quantity as the tariff examined earlier.)

Panel (b) of Exhibit 8 shows the distribution and efficiency effects of the quota. As a result of the quota, U.S. consumer surplus declines by the combined blue and pink areas. Area *a* becomes U.S. producer surplus and thus involves no loss of U.S. welfare. Area *c* shows the increased economic profit to those permitted by the quota to sell Americans 30 million pounds for $0.15 per pound, or $0.05 above the world price. If foreign exporters rather than U.S. importers reap this profit, area *c* reflects a net loss in U.S. welfare.

Area *b* shows a welfare loss to the U.S. economy, because sugar could have been purchased abroad for $0.10 per pound, and the U.S. resources employed to increase sugar production could instead have been used more efficiently producing other goods. Area *d* is also a welfare loss because it reflects a reduction in consumer surplus with no offsetting gain to anyone. Thus, areas *b* and *d* in panel (b) of Exhibit 8 measure the minimum U.S. welfare loss from the quota. If the profit from quota rights (area *c*) accrues to foreign producers, this increases the U.S. welfare loss.

Quotas in Practice

The United States has granted quotas to specific countries. These countries, in turn, distribute these quota rights to their exporters through a variety of means. *By rewarding domestic and foreign producers with higher prices, the quota system creates two groups intent on securing and perpetuating these quotas.* Lobbyists for foreign producers work the halls of Congress, seeking the right to export to the United States. This strong support from producers, coupled with a lack of opposition from consumers (who remain rationally ignorant for the most part), has resulted in quotas that have lasted decades. For example, sugar quotas have been around more than 50 years. For the past three decades, U.S. sugar prices have been double the world price, on average, costing U.S. consumers billions. Sugar growers, who account for only 1 percent of U.S. farm sales, have accounted for 17 percent of political contributions from agriculture since 1990.[1]

Some economists have argued that if quotas are to be used, the United States should auction them off to foreign producers, thereby capturing at least some of the difference between the world price and the U.S. price. Auctioning off quotas would not only increase federal revenue at a time when it's desperately needed, but an auction would reduce the profitability of quotas, which would reduce pressure on Washington to perpetuate them. American consumers are not the only victims of sugar quotas. Thousands of poor farmers around the world miss out on an opportunity to earn a living by growing sugar cane for export to America.

Tariffs and Quotas Compared

Consider the similarities and differences between a tariff and a quota. Because both have identical effects on the price in our example, they both lead to the same change in quantity demanded. In both cases, U.S. consumers suffer the same loss of consumer surplus, and U.S. producers reap the same gain of producer surplus. The primary difference is that the revenue from the tariff goes to the U.S. government, whereas the revenue from the quota goes to whoever secures the right to sell foreign goods in the U.S. market. *If quota rights accrue to foreigners, then the domestic economy is worse*

1. Michael Schroeder, "Sugar Growers Hold Up Push for Free Trade," *Wall Street Journal*, 3 February 2004.

off with a quota than with a tariff. But even if quota rights go to domestic importers, quotas, like tariffs, still increase the domestic price, restrict quantity, and thereby reduce consumer surplus and economic welfare. Quotas and tariffs can also raise production costs. For example, U.S. candy manufacturers face higher production costs because of sugar quotas, making them less competitive on world markets. Finally, and most importantly, *quotas and tariffs encourage foreign governments to retaliate with quotas and tariffs of their own, thus shrinking U.S. export markets, so the welfare loss is greater than shown in Exhibits 7 and 8.*

Other Trade Restrictions

Besides tariffs and quotas, a variety of other measures limit free trade. A country may provide *export subsidies* to encourage exports and *low-interest loans* to foreign buyers. Some countries impose *domestic content requirements* specifying that a certain portion of a final good must be produced domestically. Other requirements masquerading as health, safety, or technical standards often discriminate against foreign goods. For example, European countries once prohibited beef from hormone-fed cattle, a measure aimed at U.S. beef. Purity laws in Germany bar many non-German beers. Until the European Community adopted uniform standards, differing technical requirements forced manufacturers to offer as many as seven different versions of the same TV for that market. Sometimes exporters will voluntarily limit exports, as when Japanese automakers agreed to cut exports to the United States. The point is that *tariffs and quotas are only two of many devices used to restrict foreign trade.*

Recent research on the cost of protectionism indicates that international trade barriers slow the introduction of new goods and better technologies. So, rather than simply raising domestic prices, trade restrictions slow economic progress.

Freer Trade by Multilateral Agreement

Mindful of how high tariffs cut world trade during the Great Depression, the United States, after World War II, invited its trading partners to negotiate lower tariffs and other trade barriers. The result was the **General Agreement on Tariffs and Trade (GATT)**, an international trade treaty adopted in 1947 by 23 countries, including the United States. Each GATT member agreed to (1) reduce tariffs through multinational negotiations, (2) reduce import quotas, and (3) treat all members equally with respect to trade.

General Agreement on Tariffs and Trade (GATT)
An international tariff-reduction treaty adopted in 1947 that resulted in a series of negotiated "rounds" aimed at freer trade; the Uruguay Round created GATT's successor, the World Trade Organization (WTO)

dumping
Selling a product abroad for less than charged in the home market or for less than the cost of production

Uruguay Round
The final multilateral trade negotiation under GATT; this 1994 agreement cut tariffs, formed the World Trade Organization (WTO), and will eventually eliminate quotas

Trade barriers have been reduced through trade negotiations among many countries, or "trade rounds," under the auspices of GATT. Trade rounds offer a package approach rather than an issue-by-issue approach to trade negotiations. Concessions that are necessary but otherwise difficult to defend in domestic political terms can be made more acceptable in the context of a larger package that also contains politically and economically attractive benefits. Most early GATT trade rounds were aimed at reducing tariffs. The Kennedy Round in the mid-1960s included new provisions against **dumping**, which is selling a commodity abroad for less than is charged in the home market or less than the cost of production. The Tokyo Round of the 1970s was a more sweeping attempt to extend and improve the system.

The most recently completed round was launched in Uruguay in September 1986 and ratified by 123 participating countries in 1994. The number of signing countries now exceeds 150. This so-called **Uruguay Round**, the most comprehensive of the eight postwar multilateral trade negotiations, included 550 pages of tariff reductions on 85 percent of world trade. The Uruguay Round also created the World Trade Organization (WTO) to succeed GATT.

The World Trade Organization

World Trade Organization (WTO)
The legal and institutional foundation of the multilateral trading system that succeeded GATT in 1995

The **World Trade Organization (WTO)** now provides the legal and institutional foundation for world trade. Whereas GATT was a multilateral agreement with no institutional foundation, the WTO is a permanent institution in Geneva, Switzerland. A staff of about 500 economists and lawyers helps shape policy and resolves trade disputes between member countries. Whereas GATT involved only merchandise trade, the WTO also covers services and trade-related aspects of intellectual property, such as books, movies, and computer programs. The WTO will eventually phase out quotas, but tariffs will remain legal. As a result of the Uruguay Round, average tariffs fell from 6 percent to 4 percent of the value of imports (when GATT began in 1947, tariffs averaged 40 percent).

Whereas GATT relied on voluntary cooperation, the WTO settles disputes in a way that is faster, more automatic, and less susceptible to blockage than the GATT system was. The WTO resolved more trade disputes in its first decade than GATT did in nearly 50 years. Since 2000, developing countries have filed 60 percent of the disputes. But the WTO has also become a lightning rod for globalization tensions, as discussed in the case study, "Bringing Theory to Life: Doha Round and Round," located at the end of the book.

Common Markets

Some countries looked to the success of the U.S. economy, which is essentially a free trade zone across 50 states, and have tried to develop free trade zones of their own. The largest and best known is the European Union, which began in 1958 with a half dozen countries and expanded by 2010 to 27 countries and over 500 million people. The idea was to create a barrier-free European market like the United States in which goods, services, people, and capital are free to flow to their highest-valued use. Sixteen members of the European Union have also adopted a common currency, the *euro*, which replaced national currencies in 2002.

The United States, Canada, and Mexico have developed a free trade pact called the North American Free Trade Agreement (NAFTA). Through NAFTA, Mexico hopes to attract more U.S. investment by guaranteeing companies that locate there duty-free access to U.S. markets, which is where over two-thirds of Mexico's exports go. Mexico's 115 million people represent an attractive export market for U.S. producers, and Mexico's oil reserves could ease U.S. energy problems. The United States would also like to support Mexico's efforts to become more market oriented, as is reflected, for example, by Mexico's privatization of its phone system and banks. Creating job opportunities in Mexico also reduces pressure for Mexicans to cross the U.S. border illegally to find work. After more than a decade of NAFTA, agricultural exports to Mexico have doubled, as has overall trade among the three nations, but Americans still buy much more from Mexicans and Canadians than the other way around.

Free trade areas are springing up around the world. The United States signed a free trade agreement with the Dominican Republic and five Central American countries, called DR-CAFTA. Ten Latin American countries form Mercosur. The association of Southeast Asian nations make up ASEAN. And South Africa and its four neighboring countries form the Southern African Customs Union. Regional trade agreements require an exception to WTO rules because bloc members can make special deals among themselves and thus discriminate against outsiders. Under WTO's requirements, any trade concession granted to one country must usually be granted to *all other* WTO members.

Arguments for Trade Restrictions

Trade restrictions are often little more than handouts for the domestic industries they protect. Given the loss in social welfare that results from these restrictions, it would be more efficient simply to transfer money from domestic consumers to domestic producers. But such a bald payoff would be politically unpopular. Arguments for trade restrictions avoid mention of transfers to domestic producers and instead cite loftier goals. As we shall now see, none of these goals makes a strong case for restrictions, but some make a little more sense than others.

National Defense Argument

Some industries claim they need protection from import competition because their output is vital for national defense. Products such as strategic metals and military hardware are often insulated from foreign competition by trade restrictions. Thus, national defense considerations outweigh concerns about efficiency and equity. How valid is this argument? Trade restrictions may shelter the defense industry, but other means, such as government subsidies, might be more efficient. Or the government could stockpile basic military hardware so that maintaining an ongoing productive capacity would become less critical. Still, technological change could make certain weapons obsolete. Because most industries can play some role in national defense, instituting trade restrictions on this basis can get out of hand. For example, many decades ago U.S. wool producers secured trade protection at a time when some military uniforms were still made of wool.

The national defense argument has also been used to discourage foreign ownership of U.S. companies in some industries. For example, in 2005 a Chinese state-owned company was prevented from buying Unocal Oil. And in 2010, the Congressional Steel Caucus tried to block a Chinese plan to buy a Mississippi steel plant, saying that such a deal "threatens American jobs and our national security."[2]

Infant Industry Argument

The infant industry argument was formulated as a rationale for protecting emerging domestic industries from foreign competition. In industries where a firm's average cost of production falls as output expands, new firms may need protection from imports until these firms grow enough to become competitive. Trade restrictions let new firms achieve the economies of scale necessary to compete with mature foreign producers.

But how do we identify industries that merit protection, and when do they become old enough to look after themselves? Protection often fosters inefficiencies. The immediate cost of such restrictions is the net welfare loss from higher domestic prices. These costs may become permanent if the industry never realizes the expected economies of scale and thus never becomes competitive. As with the national defense argument, policy makers should be careful in adopting trade restrictions based on the infant industry argument. Here again, temporary production subsidies may be more efficient than import restrictions.

Antidumping Argument

As we have noted already, *dumping* is selling a product abroad for less than in the home market or less than the cost of production. Exporters may be able to sell the good for less overseas because of export subsidies, or firms may simply find it profitable to sell for less

2. Yjun Zhang, "China Steel Group Accuses U.S. Lawmakers of Protectionism," *Wall Street Journal*, 5 July 2010.

in foreign markets where consumers are more sensitive to prices. But why shouldn't U.S. consumers pay as little as possible? If dumping is *persistent,* the increase in consumer surplus would more than offset losses to domestic producers. *There is no good reason why consumers should not be allowed to buy imports for a persistently lower price.*

An alternative form of dumping, termed *predatory dumping,* is the *temporary* sale abroad at prices below cost to eliminate competitors in that foreign market. Once the competition is gone, so the story goes, the exporting firm can raise the price in the foreign market. The trouble with this argument is that if dumpers try to take advantage of their monopoly position by sharply increasing the price, then other firms, either domestic or foreign, could enter the market and sell for less. There are few documented cases of predatory dumping.

Sometimes dumping may be *sporadic,* as firms occasionally try to unload excess inventories. Retailers hold periodic "sales" for the same reason. Sporadic dumping can be unsettling for domestic producers, but the economic impact is not a matter of great public concern. Regardless, all dumping is prohibited in the United States by the Trade Agreements Act of 1979, which calls for the imposition of tariffs when a good is sold for less in the United States than in its home market or less than the cost of production. In addition, WTO rules allow for offsetting tariffs when products are sold for "less than fair value" and when there is "material injury" to domestic producers. For example, U.S. producers of lumber and beer frequently accuse their Canadian counterparts of dumping.

Jobs and Income Argument

One rationale for trade restrictions that is commonly heard in the United States, and is voiced by WTO protestors, is that they protect U.S. jobs and wage levels. Using trade restrictions to protect domestic jobs is a strategy that dates back centuries. One problem with such a policy is that other countries usually retaliate by restricting *their* imports to save *their* jobs, so international trade is reduced, jobs are lost in export industries, and potential gains from trade fail to materialize. That happened big time during the Great Depression, as high tariffs choked trade and jobs.

Wages in other countries, especially developing countries, are often a fraction of wages in the United States. Looking simply at differences in wages, however, narrows the focus too much. Wages represent just one component of the total production cost and may not necessarily be the most important. Employers are interested in the labor cost per unit of output, which depends on both the wage and labor productivity. Wages are high in the United States partly because U.S. labor productivity remains the highest in the world. High productivity can be traced to better education and training and to the abundant computers, machines, and other physical capital that make workers more productive. U.S. workers also benefit greatly from a relatively stable business climate.

But what about the lower wages in many developing countries? Low wages are often linked to workers' lack of education and training, to the meager physical capital available to each worker, and to a business climate that is less stable and hence less attractive for producers. But once multinational firms build plants and provide technological know-how in developing countries, U.S. workers lose some of their competitive edge, and their relatively high wages could price some U.S. products out of the world market. This has already happened in the consumer electronics and toy industries. China makes 80 percent of the toys sold in the United States. Some U.S. toy sellers, such as the makers of Etch A Sketch, would no longer survive had they not outsourced manufacturing to China.

Domestic producers do not like to compete with foreign producers whose costs are lower, so they often push for trade restrictions. But if restrictions negate any cost advantage a foreign producer might have, the law of comparative advantage becomes inoperative and domestic consumers are denied access to the lower-priced goods.

Over time, as labor productivity in developing countries increases, wage differentials among countries will narrow, much as they narrowed between the northern and southern United States during the last century. As technology and capital spread, U.S. workers, particularly unskilled workers, cannot expect to maintain wage levels that are far above comparable workers in other countries. So far, research and development has kept U.S. producers on the cutting edge of technological developments, but staying ahead in the technological race is a constant battle.

Declining Industries Argument

Where an established domestic industry is in jeopardy of closing because of lower-priced imports, could there be a rationale for *temporary* import restrictions? After all, domestic producers employ many industry-specific resources—both specialized labor and specialized machines. This human and physical capital is worth less in its best alternative use. If the extinction of the domestic industry is forestalled through trade restrictions, specialized workers can retire voluntarily or can gradually pursue more promising careers. Specialized machines can be allowed to wear out naturally.

Thus, in the case of declining domestic industries, trade protection can help lessen shocks to the economy and can allow for an orderly transition to a new industrial mix. But the protection offered should not be so generous as to encourage continued investment in the industry. Protection should be of specific duration and should be phased out over that period.

The clothing industry is an example of a declining U.S. industry. The 22,000 U.S. jobs saved as a result of one trade restriction paid an average of less than $30,000 per year. But a Congressional Budget Office study estimated that the higher domestic clothing prices resulting from trade restrictions meant that U.S. consumers paid two to three times more than apparel workers earned. Trade restrictions in the U.S. clothing and textile industry started phasing out in 2005 under the Uruguay Round of trade agreements.

Free trade may displace some U.S. jobs through imports, but it also creates U.S. jobs through exports. When Americans celebrate a ribbon-cutting ceremony for a new software company, nobody credits free trade for those jobs, but when a steel plant closes here, everyone talks about how those jobs went overseas. What's more, many foreign companies have built plants in the United States and employ U.S. workers. For example, a dozen foreign television manufacturers and all major Japanese automakers now operate plants in the United States.

The number employed in the United States has nearly doubled in the last four decades. To recognize this job growth is not to deny the problems facing workers displaced by imports. Some displaced workers, particularly those in steel and other unionized, blue-collar industries, are not likely to find jobs that pay nearly as well as the ones they lost. As with infant industries, however, the problems posed by declining industries need not require trade restrictions. To support the affected industry, the government could offer wage subsidies or special tax breaks that decline over time. The government has also funded programs to retrain affected workers for jobs that are in greater demand.

Problems With Trade Protection

Trade restrictions raise a number of problems in addition to those already mentioned. First, protecting one stage of production usually requires protecting downstream stages of production as well. Protecting the U.S. textile industry from foreign competition, for example, raised the cost of cloth to U.S. apparel makers, reducing *their* competitiveness. Thus, when the government protected domestic textile manufacturers, the domestic garment industry also needed protection. Second, the cost of protection includes not only the welfare loss from the higher domestic price but also the cost of the resources used by domestic producer groups to secure the favored protection. The cost of *rent seeking*—lobbying fees, propaganda, and legal actions—can sometimes equal or exceed the direct welfare loss from restrictions. A third problem with trade restrictions is the transaction costs of enforcing the myriad quotas, tariffs, and other trade restrictions. These often lead to smuggling and black markets. A fourth problem is that economies insulated from foreign competition become less innovative and less efficient. The final and biggest problem with imposing trade restrictions is that other countries usually retaliate, thus shrinking the gains from trade. Retaliation can set off still greater trade restrictions, leading to an outright trade war.

Consider steel tariffs discussed in the case study, "Public Policy: Steel Tariffs," located at the back of the book.

Conclusion

International trade arises from voluntary exchange among buyers and sellers pursuing their self-interest. Since 1950 world output has risen eightfold, while world trade has increased nearly twentyfold. World trade offers many advantages to the trading countries: access to markets around the world, lower costs through economies of scale, the opportunity to utilize abundant resources, better access to information about markets and technology, improved quality honed by competitive pressure, and, most importantly, lower prices for consumers. Comparative advantage, specialization, and trade allow people to use their scarce resources efficiently to satisfy their unlimited wants.

Despite the clear gains from free trade, restrictions on international trade date back centuries, and pressure on public officials to impose trade restrictions continues today. Domestic producers (and their resource suppliers) benefit from trade restrictions in their markets because they can charge domestic consumers more. Trade restrictions insulate domestic producers from the rigors of global competition, in the process stifling innovation and leaving the industry vulnerable to technological change from abroad. With trade quotas, the winners also include those who have secured the right to import goods at the world prices and sell them at the domestic prices. Consumers, who must pay higher prices for protected goods, suffer from trade restrictions, as do the domestic producers who import resources. Other losers include U.S. exporters, who face higher trade barriers as foreigners retaliate with their own trade restrictions.

Producers have a laser-like focus on trade legislation, but consumers remain largely oblivious. Consumers purchase thousands of different goods and thus have no special interest in the effects of trade policy on any particular good. Congress tends to support the group that makes the most noise, so trade restrictions often persist, despite the clear and widespread gains from freer trade.

Summary

1. Even if a country has an absolute advantage in all goods, that country should specialize in producing the goods in which it has a comparative advantage. If each country specializes and trades according to the law of comparative advantage, all countries will benefit from greater consumption possibilities.
2. Quotas benefit those with the right to buy goods at the world price and sell them at the higher domestic price. Both tariffs and quotas harm domestic consumers more than they help domestic producers, although tariffs at least yield government revenue, which can be used to fund public programs or to cut taxes.
3. Despite the gains from free trade, restrictions have been imposed for centuries. The General Agreement on Tariffs and Trade (GATT) was an international treaty ratified in 1947 to reduce trade barriers. Subsequent negotiations lowered tariffs and reduced trade restrictions. The Uruguay Round, ratified in 1994, lowered tariffs, phases out quotas, and created the World Trade Organization (WTO) as the successor to GATT. The Doha Round was launched in 2001, but failed to reach an agreement as of 2010.
4. Arguments used by producer groups to support trade restrictions include promoting national defense, nurturing infant industries, preventing foreign producers from dumping goods in domestic markets, protecting domestic jobs, and allowing declining industries time to wind down and exit the market.
5. Trade restrictions impose a variety of strains on the economy besides the higher costs to consumers. These include (1) the need to protect downstream stages of production as well, (2) expenditures made by favored domestic industries to seek trade protection, (3) costs incurred by the government to enforce trade restrictions, (4) the inefficiency and lack of innovation that result when an industry is insulated from foreign competition, and (5), most important, the trade restrictions imposed by other countries in retaliation.

Key Concepts

Questions for Review

1. PROFILE OF IMPORTS AND EXPORTS What are the major U.S. exports and imports? How does international trade affect consumption possibilities?
2. REASONS FOR TRADE What are the primary reasons for international trade?
3. GAINS FROM TRADE Complete each of the following sentences:
   a. When a nation has no economic interaction with foreigners and produces everything it consumes, the nation is in a state of ________.
   b. According to the law of comparative advantage, each nation should specialize in producing the goods in which it has the lowest ________.
   c. The amount of one good that a nation can exchange for one unit of another good is known as the ________.
   d. Specializing according to comparative advantage and trading with other nations results in ________.
4. REASONS FOR INTERNATIONAL SPECIALIZATION What determines which goods a country should produce and export?
5. TARIFFS High tariffs usually lead to black markets and smuggling. How is government revenue reduced by such activity? Relate your answer to the graph in Exhibit 7 in this chapter. Does smuggling have any social benefits?
6. TRADE RESTRICTIONS Exhibits 7 and 8 show net losses to the economy of a country that imposes tariffs or quotas on imported sugar. What kinds of gains and losses would occur in the economies of countries that export sugar?
7. THE WORLD TRADE ORGANIZATION What is the World Trade Organization (WTO) and how does it help foster multilateral trade? (Check the WTO Web site at http://www.wto.org/.)
8. Case Study: The Doha Round and Round (See page 775.) What was the major sticking point holding up progress in the Doha Round?
9. ARGUMENTS FOR TRADE RESTRICTIONS Explain the national defense, declining industries, and infant industry arguments for protecting a domestic industry from international competition.
10. ARGUMENTS FOR TRADE RESTRICTIONS Firms hurt by cheap imports typically argue that restricting trade will save U.S. jobs. What's wrong with this argument? Are there ever any reasons to support such trade restrictions?
11. Case Study: Steel Tariffs (See page 776.) How did the steel tariff affect the domestic steel industry, the workers in the steel industry, workers in steel-use industries, and consumers?

Problems and Exercises

12. COMPARATIVE ADVANTAGE Suppose that each U.S. worker can produce 8 units of food or 2 units of clothing daily. In Fredonia, which has the same number of workers, each worker can produce 7 units of food or 1 unit of clothing daily. Why does the United States have an absolute advantage in both goods? Which country enjoys a comparative advantage in food? Why?

13. COMPARATIVE ADVANTAGE The consumption possibilities frontiers shown in Exhibit 4 assume terms of trade of 1 unit of clothing for 1 unit of food. What would the consumption possibilities frontiers look like if the terms of trade were 1 unit of clothing for 2 units of food?

14. IMPORT QUOTAS How low must a quota be in effect to have an impact? Using a demand-and-supply diagram, illustrate and explain the net welfare loss from imposing such a quota. Under what circumstances would the net welfare loss from an import quota exceed the net welfare loss from an equivalent tariff (one that results in the same price and import level as the quota)?

15. TRADE RESTRICTIONS Suppose that the world price for steel is below the U.S. domestic price, but the government requires that all steel used in the United States be domestically produced.
    a. Use a diagram like the one in Exhibit 7 to show the gains and losses from such a policy.
    b. How could you estimate the net welfare loss (deadweight loss) from such a diagram?
    c. What response to such a policy would you expect from industries (like automobile producers) that use U.S. steel?
    d. What government revenues are generated by this policy?

Global Economic Watch Exercises

Login to www.cengagebrain.com and access the Global Economic Watch to do these exercises.

18. GLOBAL ECONOMIC WATCH Go to the Global Economic Crisis Resource Center. Select Global Issues in Context. In the Basic Search box at the top of the page, enter the phrase "Doha Round." On the Results page, go to the News Section. Click on the link for the October 1, 2010, article "America Embraces Trade Discrimination." In what ways does the author criticize U.S. trade policy?

19. GLOBAL ECONOMIC WATCH Go to the Global Economic Crisis Resource Center. Select Global Issues in Context. Go to the menu at the top of the page and click on the tab for Browse Issues and Topics. Choose Business and Economy. Click on the link for Globalization. Find one article in favor of globalization and international trade and one article against. Compare and contrast the arguments in the articles.

International Finance

33

YOSHIKAZU TSUNO/AFP/Getty Images

- How can the United States export more than nearly any other country yet still have the world's highest trade deficit?
- Are high trade deficits a worry?
- What's the official "fudge factor" used to compute the balance of payments?
- What's meant by a "strong dollar"?
- Why does a nation try to influence the value of its currency?
- And what's up with China?

Answers to these and other questions are explored in this chapter, which focuses on international finance.

If Starbucks wants to buy 1,000 espresso machines from the German manufacturer, Krups, it will be quoted a price in euros. Suppose the machines cost a total of €1 million (euros). How much is that in dollars? The dollar cost will depend on the exchange rate. When trade takes place across international borders, two currencies are usually involved. Supporting the flows of goods and services are flows of currencies that fund international transactions. The exchange rate between currencies—the price of one in terms of the other—is how the price of a product in one country translates into the price facing a buyer in another country. Cross-border trade therefore depends on the exchange rate.

In this chapter we examine the market forces that affect the relative value of one currency in terms of another.

Topics discussed include:

- Balance of payments
- Trade deficits and surpluses
- Foreign exchange markets
- Purchasing power parity
- Flexible exchange rates
- Fixed exchange rates
- International monetary system
- Bretton Woods agreement
- Managed float

Balance of Payments

A country's gross domestic product, or GDP, measures the economy's income and output during a given period. To account for dealings abroad, countries must also keep track of international transactions. A country's *balance of payments,* as introduced in Chapter 3, summarizes all economic transactions during a given period between residents of that country and residents of other countries. *Residents* include people, firms, organizations, and governments.

International Economic Transactions

The balance of payments measures economic transactions between a country and the rest of the world, whether these transactions involve goods and services, real and financial assets, or transfer payments. The balance of payments measures a *flow* of transactions during a particular period, usually a year. Some transactions do not involve actual payments. For example, if *Time* magazine ships a new printing press to its Australian subsidiary, no payment is made, yet an economic transaction involving another country has occurred. Similarly, if CARE sends food to Africa or the Pentagon provides military assistance to the Middle East, these transactions must be captured in the balance of payments. So remember, although we speak of the *balance of payments,* a more descriptive phrase would be the *balance-of-economic transactions.*

Balance-of-payments accounts are maintained according to the principles of *double-entry bookkeeping.* Some entries are called *credits,* and others are called *debits.* As you will see, the balance of payments consists of several individual accounts. An individual account may not balance, but a deficit in one or more accounts must be offset by a surplus in the other accounts. Because total credits must equal total debits, there is a *balance* of payments—hence, the name. During a given period, such as a year, the inflow of receipts from the rest of the world, which are entered as credits, must equal the outflow of payments to the rest of the world, which are entered as debits.

The first of two major categories in the balance of payments is the current account. The current account records *current* flows of funds into and out of the country, including imports and exports of goods and services, net income earned by U.S. residents from foreign assets, and net transfer payments from abroad. These are discussed in turn.

The Merchandise Trade Balance

The *merchandise trade balance,* a term introduced in Chapter 3, equals the value of merchandise exports minus the value of merchandise imports. The merchandise account reflects trade in goods, or tangible products (stuff you can put in a box), like French wine or U.S. computers, and is often referred to simply as the *trade balance.* The value of U.S. merchandise exports is a credit in the U.S. balance-of-payments account because U.S. residents get *paid* for the exported goods. The value of U.S. merchandise imports is a debit in the balance-of-payments account because U.S. residents *pay* foreigners for imported goods.

If merchandise exports exceed merchandise imports, the trade balance is in *surplus.* If merchandise imports exceed merchandise exports, the trade balance is in *deficit.* The merchandise trade balance, which is reported monthly, influences foreign exchange markets, the stock market, and other financial markets. The trade balance depends on a variety of factors, including the relative strength and competitiveness of the domestic

EXHIBIT 1 U.S. Imports Have Topped Exports Since 1976, and the Trade Deficit Has Widened

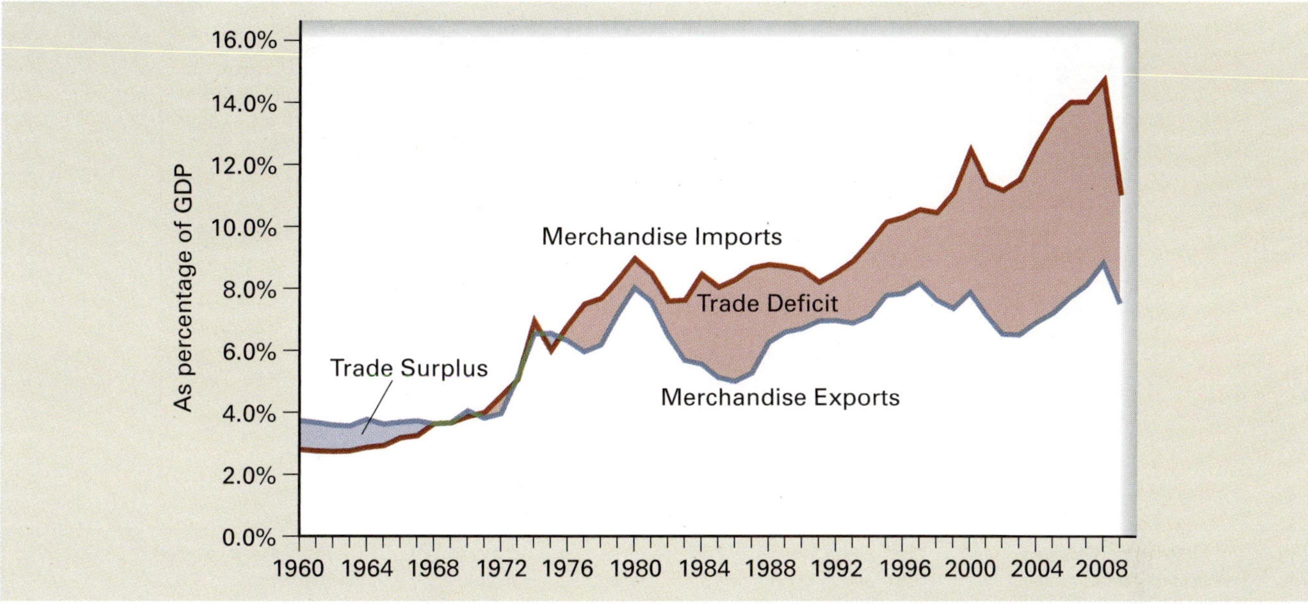

Note that since 1980, merchandise exports have remained in the range of about 5 percent to 8 percent of GDP. But merchandise imports have trended up from about 9 percent in 1980 to about 15 percent in 2008, before backing off to 11 percent in 2009, the year following the financial crisis.

Source: Developed from merchandise trade data from the *Economic Report of the President,* February 2010, and *Survey of Current Business*, 90 (June 2010), U.S. Department of Commerce. For the latest data, go to http://bea.gov.

economy compared with other economies and the relative value of the domestic currency compared with other currencies. Strong economies with growing incomes tend to buy more of everything, including imports.

U.S. merchandise trade since 1960 is depicted in Exhibit 1, where exports, the blue line, and imports, the red line, are expressed as a percentage of GDP. During the 1960s, exports exceeded imports, and the resulting trade surpluses are shaded blue. Since 1976, imports have exceeded exports, and the resulting trade deficits are shaded pink. Trade deficits as a percentage of GDP increased from 1.3 percent in 1991 to a peak of 6.3 percent in 2006. The recession of 2007–2009 slowed U.S. imports more than U.S. exports, so by 2009 the trade deficit relative to GDP fell to 3.5 percent, the lowest in more than a decade.

Because per capita income in the United States ranks among the highest in the world, the United States imports more goods from each of the world's major economies than it exports to them. Exhibit 2 shows the U.S. merchandise trade deficit with major economies or regions of the world in 2009. The $227 billion trade deficit with China was by far the largest, nearly four times that with Latin America, the European Union, or the OPEC nations. The Chinese bought $69 billion in U.S. goods in 2009, but Americans bought $296 billion in Chinese goods, or about $2,575 per U.S. household. So China sold America four times more than it bought from America. Chances are, most of the utensils in your kitchen were made in China; most toys are also Chinese made. The United States is the world's biggest importer and has a trade surplus with only a few major economies, including Australia, Brazil, and the Netherlands.

EXHIBIT 2 U.S. Merchandise Trade Deficits in 2009 by Country or Region

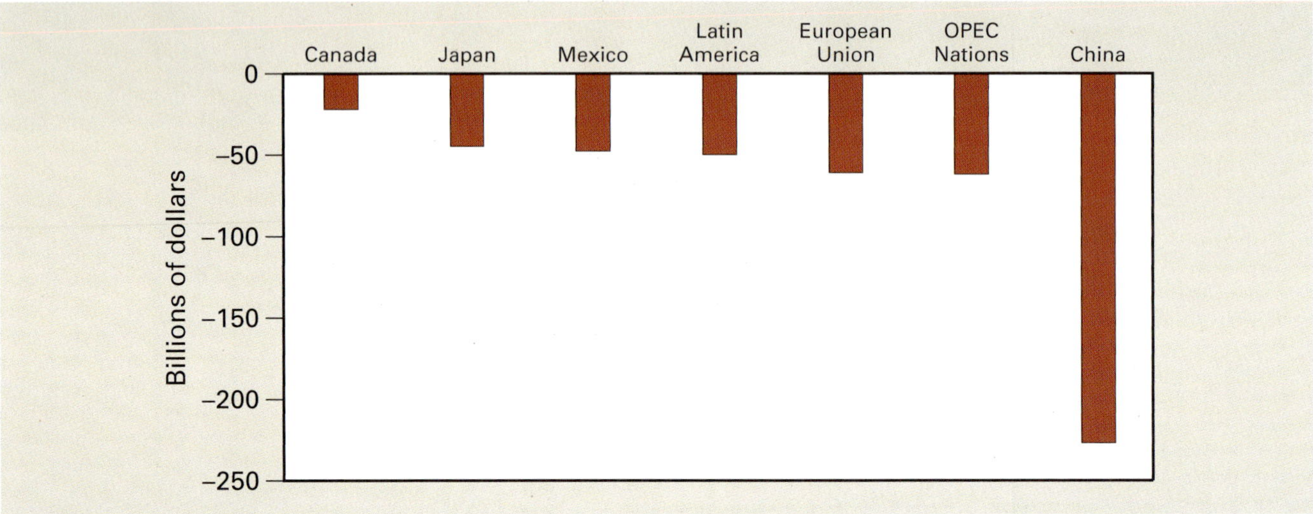

The United States imports more goods from each of the world's major economies than it exports to them. The largest U.S. trade deficit is with China, which exported four times more to the United States in 2009 than it imported from the United States.

Source: Developed from data in "Exports, Imports, and Trade Balance by Country and Area: 2009 Annual Totals," Exhibit 13, U.S. Bureau of Economic Analysis, 10 June 2010.

Balance on Goods and Services

The merchandise trade balance focuses on the flow of goods, but services are also traded internationally. *Services* are intangibles, such as transportation, insurance, banking, education, consulting, and tourism. Services are often called "invisibles" because they are not tangible. The value of U.S. service exports, as when an Irish tourist visits New York City, is listed as a credit in the U.S. balance-of-payments account because U.S. residents get paid for these services. The value of U.S. service imports, like computer programming outsourced to India, is listed as a debit in the balance-of-payments account because U.S. residents must pay for the imported services.

balance on goods and services
The portion of a country's balance-of-payments account that measures the value of a country's exports of goods and services minus the value of its imports of goods and services

Because the United States exports more services than it imports, services have been in surplus for the last three decades. The **balance on goods and services** is the export value of goods and services minus the import value of goods and services, or *net exports*, a component of GDP.

Net Investment Income

net investment income from abroad
Investment earnings by U.S. residents from their foreign assets minus investment earnings by foreigners from their assets in the United States

U.S. residents earn investment income, such as interest and dividends, from assets owned abroad. This investment income flows to the United States and is a credit in the balance-of-payments account. On the other side, foreigners earn investment income on assets owned in the United States, and this payment flows out of the country. This outflow is a debit in the balance-of-payments account. **Net investment income from abroad** is U.S. investment earnings from foreign assets minus foreigners' earnings from their U.S. assets. From year to year, this figure bounces around between a positive and a negative number. In 2009, net investment income from foreign holdings was $89 billion.

Unilateral Transfers and the Current Account Balance

Unilateral transfers consist of government transfers to foreign residents, foreign aid, money workers send to families abroad, personal gifts to friends and relatives abroad, charitable donations, and the like. Money sent out of the country is a debit in the balance-of-payments account. For example, immigrants in the United States often send money to families back home. **Net unilateral transfers abroad** equal the unilateral transfers received from abroad by U.S. residents minus unilateral transfers sent to foreign residents by U.S. residents. U.S. net unilateral transfers have been negative since World War II, except for 1991, when the U.S. government received sizable transfers from foreign governments to help pay their share of the Persian Gulf War. In 2009, net unilateral transfers were a negative $130.2 billion, with private transfers accounting for most of that (government grants and transfers made up the rest). Net unilateral transfers abroad averaged about $430 per U.S. resident in 2009.

net unilateral transfers abroad
The unilateral transfers (gifts and grants) received from abroad by U.S. residents minus the unilateral transfers U.S. residents send abroad

The United States places few restrictions on money sent out of the country. Other countries, particularly developing countries, strictly limit the amount that may be sent abroad. More generally, many developing countries, such as China, restrict the convertibility of their currency into other currencies.

When we add net unilateral transfers to net exports of goods and services and net income from assets owned abroad, we get the **balance on current account**, which is reported quarterly. Thus, *the current account includes all international transactions in currently produced goods and services, net income from foreign assets, and net unilateral transfers.* It can be negative, reflecting a current account deficit; positive, reflecting a current account surplus; or zero.

balance on current account
The portion of the balance-of-payments account that measures that country's balance on goods and services, net investment income from abroad, plus net unilateral transfers abroad

The Financial Account

The current account records international transactions in goods, services, asset income, and unilateral transfers. The **financial account** records international purchases of assets, including financial assets, such as stocks, bonds, and bank balances, and real assets such as land, housing, factories, and other physical assets. For example, U.S. residents purchase foreign securities to earn a higher return and to diversify their portfolios. Money flows out when Americans buy foreign assets or build factories overseas. Money flows in when foreigners buy U.S. assets or build factories here. The international purchase or sale of assets is recorded in the financial account.

financial account
The record of a country's international transactions involving purchases or sales of financial and real assets

Between 1917 and 1982, the United States ran a financial account deficit, meaning that U.S. residents purchased more foreign assets than foreigners purchased assets from the United States. The net income from these foreign assets improved our current account balance. But in 1983, for the first time in 65 years, foreigners bought more assets in the United States than U.S. residents purchased abroad. Since 1983, foreigners have continued to buy more U.S. assets most years than the other way around, meaning there has usually been a surplus in the financial account.

By the end of 2009, foreigners owned $21.1 trillion in U.S. assets and U.S. residents owned $18.4 trillion in foreign assets. Thus, foreigners owned $2.7 trillion more assets in the United States than U.S. residents owned abroad. This is not as bad as it sounds, because foreign purchases of assets in the United States add to America's productive capacity and promote employment and labor productivity here. But the income from these assets flows to their foreign owners, not to Americans. Remember, the investment income from these assets shows up in the current account.

Deficits and Surpluses

Nations, like households, operate under a budget constraint. Spending cannot exceed income plus cash on hand and borrowed funds. We have distinguished between *current* transactions, which include exports, imports, asset income, and unilateral transfers, and *financial* transactions, which reflect purchases of foreign real and financial assets. Any surplus or deficit in one account must be offset by deficits or surpluses in other balance-of-payments accounts.

Exhibit 3 presents the U.S. balance-of-payments statement for 2009. All transactions requiring payments from foreigners to U.S. residents are entered as credits, indicated by a plus sign (+), because they result in an inflow of funds from foreign residents to U.S. residents. All transactions requiring payments to foreigners from U.S. residents are entered as debits, indicated by a minus sign (–), because they result in an outflow of funds from U.S. residents to foreign residents. As you can see, a surplus in the financial account of $197.7 billion was more than offset by a current account deficit of $419.8 billion. A *statistical discrepancy* is required to balance the payments, and that amounts to $222.1 billion. Think of the statistical discrepancy as the official "fudge factor" that (1) measures the error in the balance-of-payments and (2) satisfies the double-entry bookkeeping requirement that total debits must equal total credits. The statistical discrepancy was especially large in 2009, because the global financial crisis created unusual gyrations in international accounts.

Foreign exchange is the currency of another country needed to carry out international transactions. A country runs a deficit in its current account when the amount of foreign exchange received from exports, from foreign assets, and from unilateral transfers falls short of the amount needed to pay for imports, pay foreign holders of U.S. assets, and make unilateral transfers. If the current account is in deficit, the necessary foreign exchange must come from a net inflow in the financial account. Such an inflow

EXHIBIT 3 U.S. Balance of Payments for 2009 (billions of dollars)

Current Account	
1. Merchandise exports	+1,045.5
2. Merchandise imports	−1,562.5
3. Merchandise trade balance (1 + 2)	−517.0
4. Service exports	+509.2
5. Service imports	−370.8
6. Goods and services balance (3 + 4 + 5)	−378.6
7. Net investment income from abroad	+89.0
8. Net unilateral transfers	−130.2
9. Current account balance (6 + 7 + 8)	−419.8
Financial Account	
10. Change in U.S. owned assets abroad	−237.5
11. Change in foreign-owned assets in United States	+435.2
12. Financial account balance (10 + 11)	+197.7
13. Statistical discrepancy	+222.1
TOTAL (9 + 12 + 13)	0.0

Source: Computed from estimates in "U.S. International Transactions," *Survey of Current Business,* 90 (June 2010), Table F.2., p. D-61.

in the financial account could stem from borrowing from foreigners, selling domestic stocks and bonds to foreigners, selling a steel plant in Pittsburgh or a ski lodge in Aspen to foreigners, and so forth.

If a country runs a current account surplus, the foreign exchange received from exports, from foreign assets, and from unilateral transfers from abroad exceeds the amount needed to pay for imports, to pay foreign holders of U.S. assets, and to make unilateral transfers abroad. If the current account is in surplus, this excess foreign exchange results in a net outflow in the financial account through lending abroad, buying foreign stocks and bonds, buying a shoe plant in Italy or a villa on the French Riviera, and so forth.

When all transactions are considered, accounts must balance, though specific accounts usually don't. The statistical discrepancy ensures that, in the aggregate, accounts sum to zero. A deficit in a particular account should not necessarily be viewed as a source of concern, nor should a surplus be a source of satisfaction. The deficit in the U.S. current account in recent years has usually been offset by a financial account surplus. As a result, foreigners have been acquiring more claims on U.S. assets.

Foreign Exchange Rates and Markets

Now that you have some idea about international flows, we can take a closer look at the forces that determine the underlying value of the currencies involved. Let's begin by looking at exchange rates and the market for foreign exchange.

Foreign Exchange

Foreign exchange, recall, is foreign money needed to carry out international transactions. The **exchange rate** is the price measured in one country's currency of buying one unit of another country's currency. Exchange rates are determined by the interaction of the households, firms, private financial institutions, governments, and central banks that buy and sell foreign exchange. The exchange rate fluctuates to equate the quantity of foreign exchange demanded with the quantity supplied. Typically, foreign exchange is made up of bank deposits denominated in the foreign currency. When foreign travel is involved, foreign exchange often consists of foreign paper money.

exchange rate
The price measured in one country's currency of purchasing one unit of another country's currency

The foreign exchange market incorporates all the arrangements used to buy and sell foreign exchange. This market is not so much a physical place as a network of telephones and computers connecting financial centers all over the world. Perhaps you have seen pictures of foreign exchange traders in New York, Frankfurt, London, or Tokyo in front of computer screens amid a tangle of phone lines. The foreign exchange market is like an all-night diner—it never closes. A trading center is always open somewhere in the world.

We will consider the market for the euro in terms of the dollar. But first, a little more about the euro. For decades the nations of Western Europe tried to increase their economic cooperation and trade. These countries believed they would be more productive and more competitive with the United States if they acted less like many separate economies and more like the 50 United States, with a single set of trade regulations and a single currency. Imagine the hassle involved if each of the 50 states had its own currency.

In 2002, euro notes and coins entered circulation in the 12 European countries adopting the common currency. The big advantage of a common currency is that Europeans no longer have to change money every time they cross a border or trade with another country in the group. Again, the inspiration for this is the United States, arguably the most successful economy in world history.

So the euro is the common currency of the *euro zone,* as the now 16-country region is usually called. The price, or exchange rate, of the euro in terms of the dollar is the number of dollars required to purchase one euro. An increase in the number of dollars needed to purchase a euro indicates weakening, or **depreciation**, of the dollar. A decrease in the number of dollars needed to purchase a euro indicates strengthening, or **appreciation**, of the dollar. Put another way, a decrease in the number of euros needed to purchase a dollar is a depreciation of the dollar, and an increase in the number of euros needed to purchase a dollar is an appreciation of the dollar.

currency depreciation
With respect to the dollar, an increase in the number of dollars needed to purchase one unit of foreign exchange in a flexible rate system

currency appreciation
With respect to the dollar, a decrease in the number of dollars needed to purchase one unit of foreign exchange in a flexible rate system

Because the exchange rate is usually a market price, it is determined by demand and supply: The equilibrium price is the one that equates quantity demanded with quantity supplied. To simplify the analysis, suppose that the United States and the euro zone make up the entire world, so the demand and supply for euros in international finance is the demand and supply for foreign exchange from the U.S. perspective.

The Demand for Foreign Exchange

Whenever U.S. residents need euros, they must buy them in the foreign exchange market, which could include your local bank, paying for them with dollars. Exhibit 4 depicts a market for foreign exchange—in this case, euros. The horizontal axis shows the quantity of foreign exchange, measured here in billions of euros per day. The vertical axis shows the price per unit of foreign exchange, measured here in dollars per euro. The demand curve *D* for foreign exchange shows the inverse relationship between the dollar price of the euro and the quantity of euros demanded, other things assumed constant. Assumed constant along the demand curve are the incomes and preferences of U.S. consumers, expected inflation in the United States and in the euro zone, the

EXHIBIT 4 The Foreign Exchange Market

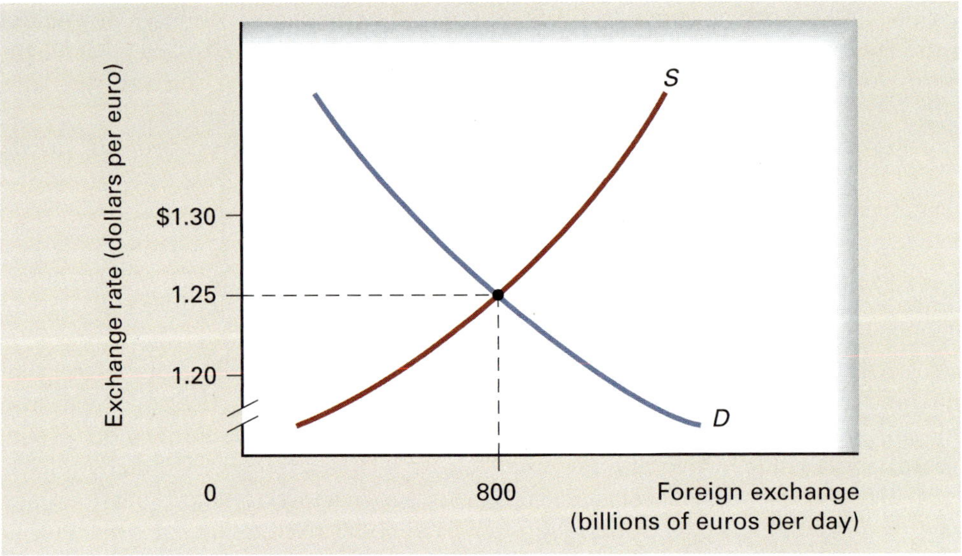

The fewer dollars needed to purchase one unit of foreign exchange, the lower the price of foreign goods and the greater the quantity of foreign goods demanded. Thus, the demand curve for foreign exchange slopes downward. An increase in the exchange rate makes U.S. products cheaper for foreigners. This implies an increase in the quantity of foreign exchange supplied. The supply curve of foreign exchange slopes upward.

euro price of goods in the euro zone, and interest rates in the United States and in the euro zone. U.S. residents have many reasons for demanding foreign exchange, but in the aggregate, the lower the dollar price of foreign exchange, other things constant, the greater the quantity of foreign exchange demanded.

A drop in the dollar price of foreign exchange, in this case the euro, means that fewer dollars are needed to purchase each euro, so the dollar prices of euro zone products (like German cars, Italian shoes, tickets to the Louvre, and euro zone securities), which list prices in euros, become cheaper. The cheaper it is to buy euros, the lower the dollar price of euro zone products to U.S. residents, so the greater the quantity of euros demanded by U.S. residents, other things constant. For example, a cheap enough euro might persuade you to tour Rome, climb the Austrian Alps, wander the museums of Paris, or crawl the pubs of Dublin.

The Supply of Foreign Exchange

The supply of foreign exchange is generated by the desire of foreign residents to acquire dollars—that is, to exchange euros for dollars. Euro zone residents want dollars to buy U.S. goods and services, acquire U.S. assets, make loans in dollars, or send dollars to their U.S. friends and relatives. Euros are supplied in the foreign exchange market to acquire the dollars people want. An increase in the dollar-per-euro exchange rate, other things constant, makes U.S. products cheaper for foreigners because foreign residents need fewer euros to get the same number of dollars. For example, suppose a Dell computer sells for $600. If the exchange rate is $1.20 per euro, that computer costs 500 euros; if the exchange rate is $1.25 per euro, it costs only 480 euros. The number of Dell computers demanded in the euro zone increases as the dollar-per-euro exchange rate increases, other things constant, so more euros will be supplied on the foreign exchange market to buy dollars.

The positive relationship between the dollar-per-euro exchange rate and the quantity of euros supplied on the foreign exchange market is expressed in Exhibit 4 by the upward-sloping supply curve for foreign exchange (again, euros in our example). The supply curve assumes that other things remain constant, including euro zone incomes and tastes, expectations about inflation in the euro zone and in the United States, and interest rates in the euro zone and in the United States.

Determining the Exchange Rate

Exhibit 4 brings together the demand and supply for foreign exchange to determine the exchange rate. At a rate of $1.25 per euro, the quantity of euros demanded equals the quantity supplied—in our example, 800 billion euros per day. Once achieved, this equilibrium rate will remain constant until a change occurs in one of the factors that affect supply or demand. If the exchange rate is allowed to adjust freely, or to *float,* in response to market forces, the market will clear continually, as the quantities of foreign exchange demanded and supplied are equated.

What if the initial equilibrium is upset by a change in one of the underlying forces that affect demand or supply? For example, suppose higher U.S. incomes increase American demand for all normal goods, including those from the euro zone. This shifts the U.S. demand curve for foreign exchange to the right, as Americans buy more Italian marble, Dutch chocolate, German machines, Parisian vacations, and euro zone securities.

This increased demand for euros is shown in Exhibit 5 by a rightward shift of the demand curve for foreign exchange. The demand increase from D to D' leads to an increase in the exchange rate per euro from $1.25 to $1.27. Thus, the euro increases in

EXHIBIT 5 **Effect on the Foreign Exchange Market of an Increased Demand for Euros**

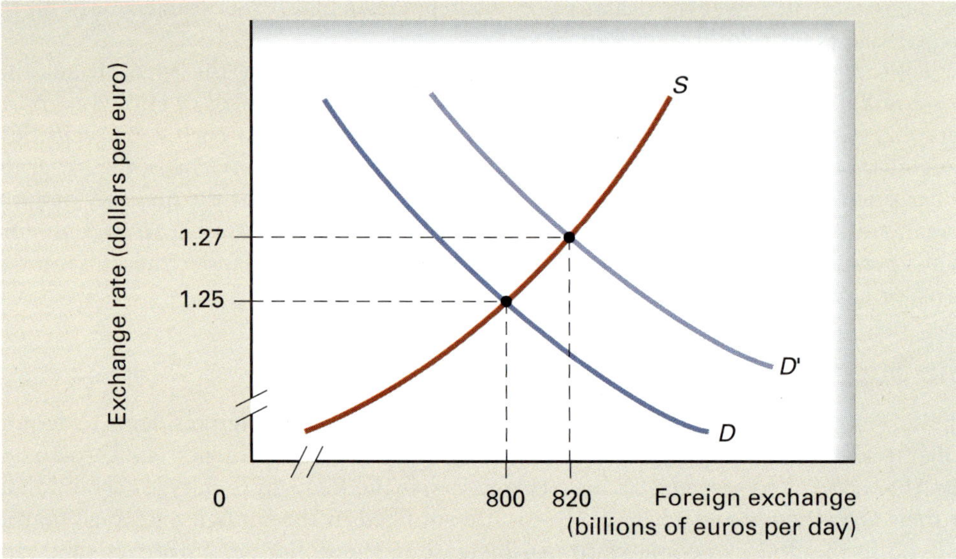

The intersection of the demand curve for foreign exchange, *D*, and the supply curve for foreign exchange, *S*, determines the exchange rate. At an exchange rate of $1.25 per euro, the quantity of euros demanded equals the quantity supplied. An increase in the demand for euros from *D* to *D*′ increases the exchange rate from $1.25 to $1.27 per euro.

value, or appreciates, while the dollar falls in value, or depreciates. An increase in U.S. income should not affect the euro supply curve, though it does increase the *quantity of euros supplied*. The higher exchange value of the euro prompts those in the euro zone to buy more American products and assets, which are now cheaper in terms of the euro.

To Review: Any increase in the demand for foreign exchange or any decrease in its supply, other things constant, increases the number of dollars required to purchase one unit of foreign exchange, which is a depreciation of the dollar. On the other hand, any decrease in the demand for foreign exchange or any increase in its supply, other things constant, reduces the number of dollars required to purchase one unit of foreign exchange, which is an appreciation of the dollar.

Arbitrageurs and Speculators

Exchange rates between two currencies are nearly identical at any given time in markets around the world. For example, the dollar price of a euro is the same in New York, Frankfurt, Tokyo, London, Zurich, Hong Kong, Istanbul, and other financial centers. **Arbitrageurs**—dealers who take advantage of any difference in exchange rates between markets by buying low and selling high—ensure this equality. Their actions help to equalize exchange rates across markets. For example, if one euro costs $1.24 in New York but $1.25 in Frankfurt, an arbitrageur could buy, say, $1,000,000 worth of euros in New York and at the same time sell them in Frankfurt for $1,008,065, thereby earning $8,065 minus the transaction costs of the trades.

arbitrageur
Someone who takes advantage of temporary geographic differences in the exchange rate by simultaneously purchasing a currency in one market and selling it in another market

Because an arbitrageur buys and sells simultaneously, little risk is involved. In our example, the arbitrageur increased the demand for euros in New York and increased the supply of euros in Frankfurt. These actions increased the dollar price of euros in New York and decreased it in Frankfurt, thereby squeezing down the difference in exchange rates. Exchange rates may still change because of market forces, but they tend to change in all markets simultaneously.

The demand and supply of foreign exchange arises from many sources—from importers and exporters, investors in foreign assets, central banks, tourists, arbitrageurs, and speculators. **Speculators** buy or sell foreign exchange in hopes of profiting by trading the currency at a more favorable exchange rate later. By taking risks, speculators aim to profit from market fluctuations—they try to buy low and sell high. In contrast, arbitrageurs take less risk, because they *simultaneously* buy currency in one market and sell it in another.

speculator
Someone who buys or sells foreign exchange in hopes of profiting from fluctuations in the exchange rate over time

Finally, people in countries suffering from economic and political turmoil, such as occurred in Russia, Indonesia, the Philippines, and Zimbabwe, may buy *hard* currency as a hedge against the depreciation and instability of their own currencies. The dollar has long been accepted as an international medium of exchange. It is also the currency of choice in the world markets for oil and illegal drugs. But the euro eventually may challenge that dominance, in part because the largest euro denomination, the 500 euro note, is worth about six times the largest U.S. denomination, the $100 note. So it would be six times easier to smuggle euro notes than U.S. notes of equal value.

Purchasing Power Parity

As long as trade across borders is unrestricted and as long as exchange rates are allowed to adjust freely, the **purchasing power parity (PPP) theory** predicts that the exchange rate between two currencies will adjust in the long run to reflect price differences between the two currency regions. *A given basket of internationally traded goods should therefore sell for about the same around the world (except for differences reflecting transportation costs and the like).* Suppose a basket of internationally traded goods that sells for $10,000 in the United States sells for €8,000 in the euro zone. According to the purchasing power parity theory, the equilibrium exchange rate should be $1.25 per euro. If this were not the case—if the exchange rate were, say, $1.20 per euro—then you could exchange $9,600 for €8,000, with which you buy the basket of commodities in the euro zone. You could then sell that basket of goods in the States for $10,000, yielding you a profit of $400 minus any transaction costs. Selling dollars and buying euros will also drive up the dollar price of euros.

purchasing power parity (PPP) theory
The idea that the exchange rate between two countries will adjust in the long run to equalize the cost between the countries of a basket of internationally traded goods

The purchasing power parity theory is more of a long-run predictor than a day-to-day indicator of the relationship between changes in the price level and the exchange rate. For example, a country's currency generally appreciates when inflation is low compared with other countries and depreciates when inflation is high. Likewise, a country's currency generally appreciates when its real interest rates are higher than those in the rest of the world, because foreigners are more willing to buy and hold investments denominated in that high-interest currency. As a case in point, the dollar appreciated during the first half of the 1980s, when real U.S. interest rates were relatively high, and depreciated during 2002 to 2004, when real U.S. interest rates were relatively low.

Because of trade barriers, central bank intervention in exchange markets, and the fact that many products are not traded or are not comparable across countries, the purchasing power parity theory usually does not explain exchange rates at a particular point in time that well. For example, if you went shopping in Switzerland tomorrow, you would soon notice a dollar does not buy as much there as it does in the United States. At the end of the book, the case study, "Bringing Theory to Life: The Big Mac Index" considers the purchasing power parity theory based on the price of Big Macs around the globe.

Flexible Exchange Rates

flexible exchange rate
Rate determined in foreign exchange markets by the forces of demand and supply without government intervention

For the most part, we have been discussing a system of **flexible exchange rates,** which are determined by demand and supply. Flexible, or *floating,* exchange rates adjust continually to the myriad forces that buffet foreign exchange markets. Consider how the exchange rate is linked to the balance-of-payments accounts. Debit entries in the current or financial accounts increase the demand for foreign exchange, resulting in a depreciation of the dollar. Credit entries in these accounts increase the supply of foreign exchange, resulting in an appreciation of the dollar.

Fixed Exchange Rates

fixed exchange rate
Rate of exchange between currencies pegged within a narrow range and maintained by the central bank's ongoing purchases and sales of currencies

When exchange rates are flexible, governments usually have little direct role in foreign exchange markets. But if governments try to set exchange rates, active and ongoing central bank intervention is often necessary to establish and maintain these **fixed exchange rates.** Suppose the European Central Bank selects what it thinks is an appropriate rate of exchange between the dollar and the euro. It attempts to *fix,* or to *peg,* the exchange rate within a narrow band around the particular value selected. If the euro threatens to climb above the maximum acceptable exchange rate, monetary authorities must sell euros and buy dollars, thereby keeping the dollar price of the euro down. Conversely, if the euro threatens to drop below the minimum acceptable exchange rate, monetary authorities must sell dollars and buy euros. This increased demand for the euro will keep its value up relative to the dollar. Through such intervention in the foreign exchange market, monetary authorities try to stabilize the exchange rate, keeping it within the specified band.

currency devaluation
An increase in the official pegged price of foreign exchange in terms of the domestic currency

currency revaluation
A reduction in the official pegged price of foreign exchange in terms of the domestic currency

If monetary officials must keep selling foreign exchange to keep the value of their domestic currency from falling, they risk running out of foreign exchange reserves. Faced with this threat, the government has several options for eliminating the exchange rate disequilibrium. First, the pegged exchange rate can be increased, meaning that foreign currency costs more in terms of the domestic currency. This is a **devaluation** of the domestic currency. (A decrease in the pegged exchange rate is called a **revaluation.**) Second, the government can reduce the domestic demand for foreign exchange directly by imposing restrictions on imports or on financial outflows. Many developing countries do this. Third, the government can adopt policies to slow the domestic economy, increase interest rates, or reduce inflation relative to that of the country's trading partners, thereby indirectly decreasing the demand for foreign exchange and increasing the supply of foreign exchange. Several Asian economies, such as South Korea and Indonesia, pursued such policies to stabilize their currencies. Finally, the government can allow the disequilibrium to persist and ration the available foreign reserves through some form of foreign exchange control.

This concludes our introduction to the theories of international finance. Let's examine international finance in practice.

Development of the International Monetary System

gold standard
An arrangement whereby the currencies of most countries are convertible into gold at a fixed rate

From 1879 to 1914, the international financial system operated under a **gold standard,** whereby the major currencies were convertible into gold at a fixed rate. For example, the U.S. dollar could be redeemed at the U.S. Treasury for one-twentieth of an ounce of gold. The British pound could be redeemed at the British Exchequer, or treasury, for one-fourth of an ounce of gold. Because each British pound could buy five times as much gold as each dollar, one British pound exchanged for $5.

The gold standard provided a predictable exchange rate, one that did not vary as long as currencies could be redeemed for gold at the announced rate. But the money supply in each country was determined in part by the flow of gold between countries, so each country's monetary policy was influenced by the supply of gold. A balance-of-payments deficit resulted in a loss of gold, which theoretically caused a country's money supply to shrink. A balance-of-payments surplus resulted in an influx of gold, which theoretically caused a country's money supply to expand. The supply of money throughout the world also depended on the vagaries of gold discoveries. When gold production did not keep pace with the growth in economic activity, the price level dropped. When gold production exceeded the growth in economic activity, the price level rose. For example, gold discoveries in Alaska and South Africa in the late 1890s expanded the U.S. money supply, leading to inflation.

The Bretton Woods Agreement

During World War I, many countries could no longer convert their currencies into gold, and the gold standard eventually collapsed, disrupting international trade during the 1920s and 1930s. Once an Allied victory in World War II appeared certain, the Allies met in Bretton Woods, New Hampshire, in July 1944 to formulate a new international monetary system. Because the United States had a strong economy and was not ravaged by the war, the dollar was selected as the key reserve currency in the new international monetary system. All exchange rates were fixed in terms of the dollar, and the United States, which held most of the world's gold reserves, stood ready to convert foreign holdings of dollars into gold at a rate of $35 per ounce. Even though the rate that dollars could be exchanged for gold was fixed by the Bretton Woods agreement, *other* countries could adjust *their* exchange rates relative to the U.S. dollar if they found a chronic disequilibrium in their balance of payments—that is, if a country faced a large and persistent deficit or surplus.

The Bretton Woods agreement also created the **International Monetary Fund (IMF)** to set rules for maintaining the international monetary system, to standardize financial reporting for international trade, and to make loans to countries with temporary balance-of-payments problems. The IMF lends a revolving fund of about $250 billion to economies in need of reserves; there are plans to double that. Headquartered in Washington, D.C., the IMF has 186 member countries and a staff of 2,400 drawn from around the world (half the staff members are economists).

International Monetary Fund (IMF)
An international organization that establishes rules for maintaining the international monetary system and makes loans to countries with temporary balance-of-payments problems

The Demise of the Bretton Woods System

During the latter part of the 1960s, inflation increased in the United States more than in other countries. Because of U.S. inflation, the dollar had become *overvalued* at the official exchange rate, meaning that the gold value of the dollar exceeded the exchange value of the dollar. In 1971, U.S. merchandise imports exceeded merchandise exports for the first time since World War II. Foreigners exchanged dollars for gold. To stem this gold outflow, the United States stopped exchanging gold for dollars, but this just made the dollar less attractive. In December 1971, the world's 10 richest countries met in Washington and devalued the dollar by 8 percent. They hoped this devaluation would put the dollar on firmer footing and would save the "dollar standard." With prices rising at different rates around the world, however, an international monetary system based on fixed exchange rates was doomed.

When the U.S. trade deficit tripled in 1972, it became clear that the dollar was still overvalued. In early 1973, the dollar was devalued another 10 percent, but this did not quiet foreign exchange markets. The dollar, for three decades the anchor of the international monetary system, suddenly looked vulnerable, and speculators began betting that the dollar would fall even more, so they sold dollars. Dollars were exchanged for German marks because the mark appeared to be the most stable currency. Bundesbank, Germany's central bank, tried to defend the dollar's official exchange rate by selling marks and buying dollars. Why didn't Germany want the mark to appreciate? Appreciation would make German goods more expensive abroad and foreign goods cheaper in Germany, thereby reducing German exports and increasing German imports. So the mark's appreciation would reduce German output and employment. But after selling $10 billion worth of marks, the Bundesbank gave up defending the dollar. As soon as the value of the dollar was allowed to float against the mark, the Bretton Woods system, already on shaky ground, collapsed.

The Current System: Managed Float

managed float system
An exchange rate system that combines features of freely floating rates with sporadic intervention by central banks

The Bretton Woods system has been replaced by a **managed float system**, which combines features of a freely floating exchange rate with sporadic intervention by central banks as a way of moderating exchange rate fluctuations among the world's major currencies. Most small countries, particularly developing countries, still peg their currencies to one of the major currencies (such as the U.S. dollar) or to a "basket" of major currencies. What's more, in developing countries, private international borrowing and lending are severely restricted; some governments allow residents to purchase foreign exchange only for certain purposes. In some countries, different exchange rates apply to different categories of transactions.

Critics of flexible exchange rates argue that they are inflationary, because they free monetary authorities to pursue expansionary policies; and flexible exchange rates have often been volatile. This volatility creates uncertainty and risk for importers and exporters, increasing the transaction costs of international trade. Furthermore, exchange rate volatility can lead to wrenching changes in the competitiveness of a country's export sector. These changes cause swings in employment, resulting in louder calls for import restrictions. For example, the exchange rate between the Japanese yen and the U.S. dollar has been relatively unstable, particularly because of international speculation.

Policy makers are always on the lookout for a system that will perform better than the current managed float system, with its fluctuating currency values. *Their ideal is a system that will foster international trade, lower inflation, and promote a more stable world economy.* International finance ministers have acknowledged that the world must find an international standard and establish greater exchange rate stability.

The current system also allows some countries to manipulate their currencies to stimulate exports and discourage imports, as discussed at the end of the book in the case study about China ("World of Business: What about China?").

Conclusion

The United States is very much a part of the world economy, not only as the largest exporter nation but also as the largest importer nation. Although the dollar remains the unit of transaction in many international settlements—OPEC, for example, still states oil prices in dollars—gyrations of exchange rates have made those involved in international finance wary of putting all their eggs in one basket. The international monetary system is now going through a difficult period as it gropes for a new source of stability four decades after the collapse of the Bretton Woods agreement.

Summary

1. The balance of payments reflects all economic transactions between one country and the rest of the world. The current account measures flows from (a) goods; (b) services, including consulting and tourism; (c) income from foreign assets; and (d) unilateral transfers, or public and private transfer payments to and from foreign residents. The financial account measures international transactions in real and financial assets.
2. Foreign exchange pays for transactions across international borders. In the absence of government intervention, the demand and supply of foreign exchange determines the market exchange rate. According to the theory of purchasing power parity (PPP), the exchange rate between two countries will adjust in the long run to equalize the cost between the countries of a basket of internationally traded goods.
3. Under a system of flexible, or floating, exchange rates, the value of the dollar relative to foreign exchange varies with market forces. An increase in the demand for foreign exchange or a decrease in its supply, other things constant, increases the value of foreign exchange relative to the dollar, which is a depreciation of the dollar. Conversely, a decrease in the demand for foreign exchange or an increase in its supply, other things constant, decreases the value of foreign exchange relative to the dollar, which is an appreciation of the dollar.
4. Under a system of fixed exchange rates, monetary authorities try to stabilize the exchange rate, keeping it between a specified ceiling and floor value. A country may try to hold down the value of its currency, so that exports will be cheaper to foreigners and imports will cost more to domestic consumers. One objective here is to increase domestic production and employment.
5. For much of the twentieth century, the international monetary system was based on fixed exchange rates. A managed float system has been in effect for the major currencies since the demise of the Bretton Woods system in the early 1970s. Although central banks often try to stabilize exchange rates, fluctuations in rates persist. These fluctuations usually reflect market forces but they still raise the transaction costs of international trade and finance.

Key Concepts

Balance on goods and services 664
Net investment income from abroad 664
Net unilateral transfers abroad 665
Balance on current account 665
Financial account 665
Exchange rate 667
Currency depreciation 668
Currency appreciation 668
Arbitrageur 670
Speculator 671
Purchasing power parity (PPP) theory 671
Flexible exchange rate 672
Fixed exchange rate 672
Currency devaluation 672
Currency revaluation 672
Gold standard 672
International Monetary Fund (IMF) 673
Managed float system 674

Questions for Review

1. Balance of Payments Suppose the United States ran a surplus in its balance on goods and services by exporting goods and services while importing nothing.
   a. How would such a surplus be offset elsewhere in the balance-of-payments accounts?
   b. If the level of U.S. production does not depend on the balance on goods and services, how would running this surplus affect our *current* standard of living?
   c. What is the relationship between total debits and total credits in the balance on goods and services?
   d. When all international economic transactions are considered, what must be true about the sum of debits and credits?
   e. What is the role of the statistical discrepancy?
2. Foreign Exchange What is the difference between a depreciation of the dollar and a devaluation of the dollar?
3. Arbitrageurs How do arbitrageurs help ensure that exchange rates are the same in markets around the world?
4. Purchasing Power Parity According to the theory of purchasing power parity, what will happen to the value of the dollar (against foreign currencies) if the U.S. price level doubles and price levels in other countries remain constant? Why is the theory more suitable for analyzing events in the long run?
5. Case Study: The Big Mac Index (See page 778.) The Big Mac Index computed by the *Economist* magazine has consistently found the U.S. dollar to be undervalued against some currencies and overvalued against others. This finding seems to call for a rejection of the purchasing power parity theory. Explain why this index may not be a valid test of the theory.
6. The Current System: Managed Float What is a managed float? What are the disadvantages of freely floating exchange rates that led countries to the managed float system?

7. **Merchandise Trade Balance** Explain why a U.S. recession that occurs as the rest of the world is expanding will tend to reduce the U.S. trade deficit.

8. Case Study: What about China? (See page 779.) Why would China want its own currency to be undervalued relative to the U.S. dollar? How does China maintain an undervalued currency?

Problems and Exercises

9. **Balance of Payments** The following are hypothetical data for the U.S. balance of payments. Use the data to calculate each of the following:
   a. Merchandise trade balance
   b. Balance on goods and services
   c. Balance on current account
   d. Financial account balance
   e. Statistical discrepancy

	Billions of Dollars
Merchandise exports	350.0
Merchandise imports	2,425.0
Service exports	2,145.0
Service imports	170.0
Net income and net transfers	221.5
Outflow of U.S. capital	245.0
Inflow of foreign capital	100.0

10. **Balance of Payments** Explain where in the U.S. balance of payments an entry would be recorded for each of the following:
    a. A Hong Kong financier buys some U.S. corporate stock.
    b. A U.S. tourist in Paris buys some perfume to take home.
    c. A Japanese company sells machinery to a pineapple company in Hawaii.
    d. U.S. farmers make a gift of food to starving children in Ethiopia.
    e. The U.S. Treasury sells a bond to a Saudi Arabian prince.
    f. A U.S. tourist flies to France on Air France.
    g. A U.S. company sells insurance to a foreign firm.

11. **Determining the Exchange Rate** Use these data to answer the following questions about the market for British pounds:

Pound Price (in $)	Quantity Demanded (of pounds)	Quantity Supplied (of pounds)
$4.00	50	100
3.00	75	75
2.00	100	50

   a. Draw the demand and supply curves for pounds, and determine the equilibrium exchange rate (dollars per pound).
   b. Suppose that the supply of pounds doubles. Draw the new supply curve.
   c. What is the new equilibrium exchange rate?
   d. Has the dollar appreciated or depreciated?
   e. What happens to U.S. imports of British goods?

Global Economic Watch Exercises

Login to www.cengagebrain.com and access the Global Economic Watch to do these exercises.

12. **Global Economic Watch** Go to the Global Economic Crisis Resource Center. Select Global Issues in Context. In the Basic Search box at the top of the page, enter the phrase "China's exchange rate reform." On the Results page, go to the News Section. Click on the link for the July 30, 2010, article "China's Exchange Rate Reform on Right Track." What is China's exchange rate policy?

13. **Global Economic Watch** Go to the Global Economic Crisis Resource Center. Select Global Issues in Context. In the Basic Search box at the top of the page, enter the phrase "foreign exchange." From the past two years, choose one article about a foreign country. What did you learn about international finance in that country?

34 Economic Development

AP Photo/Kamran Jebreili

- Why are some countries so poor while others are so rich?
- What determines the wealth of nations?
- Why do families in low-income countries have more children than those in higher-income countries?
- Why have abundant natural resources such as oil or diamonds turned out to be a curse for some countries?
- And how might programs that send subsidized food and used clothing to poor countries have the unintended consequence of retarding economic development there?

People around the world face the day under quite different circumstances. Even during a national recession, most Americans rise from a comfortable bed in a nice home, select the day's clothing from a wardrobe, choose from a variety of breakfast foods, and drive to school or to work in one of the family's personal automobiles. But some of the world's 6.9 billion people have little housing, clothing, or food. They have no automobile and no formal job. Their health is poor, as is their education. Many cannot read or write. A billion people need eyeglasses but can't afford them.

In this chapter, we sort out rich nations from poor ones and try to explain the difference. We discuss sources of economic development, and weigh the pros and cons of foreign aid.

Topics discussed in this chapter include:

- Developing countries
- The key to development
- Privatization
- The poorest billion
- Foreign trade and development
- Foreign aid and development

Worlds Apart

Differences in economic vitality among countries are huge. Countries are classified in a variety of ways based on their economic development. The yardstick most often used to compare living standards across nations is the amount an economy produces per capita, or *output per capita*. The World Bank, an economic development institution affiliated with the United Nations (UN), estimates income per capita to classify economies. The measure begins with *gross national income (GNI)*, which is the market value of all goods and services produced by resources supplied by the countries' residents and firms, regardless of the location of the resource. For example, U.S. GNI includes profit earned by an American factory in Great Britain but excludes profits earned by a Japanese factory in Kentucky.

GNI measures both the value of output produced and the income that output generates. The World Bank computes the GNI per capita, then adjusts figures across countries based on the purchasing power of that income in each country. Using this measure, the World Bank sorts countries around the world into three major groups: *high-income economies*, *middle-income economies*, and *low-income economies*.

developing countries
Nations typified by high rates of illiteracy, high unemployment, high fertility rates, and exports of primary products; also known as low-income and middle-income economies

industrial market countries
Economically advanced capitalist countries of Western Europe, North America, Australia, New Zealand, and Japan; also known as developed countries and high-income economies

Data on world population and world output are summarized in Exhibit 1. High-income economies in 2009 made up only 16 percent of the 6.9 billion people on Earth, but accounted for 73 percent of world output. So high-income economies, *with only about one-sixth of the world's population, produced nearly three-quarters of the world's output*. Middle-income economies made up 69 percent of the world's population, but accounted for 26 percent of the world output. And low-income countries made up 15 percent of the world's population, but account for only 1 percent of world output.

Developing and Industrial Economies

The low- and middle-income economies are usually referred to as **developing countries**. Most high-income economies are also referred to as **industrial market countries**. So low- and middle-income economies, what are called developing countries, made up

EXHIBIT 1 Share of World Population and World Output From High-, Middle-, and Low-Income Economies as of 2009

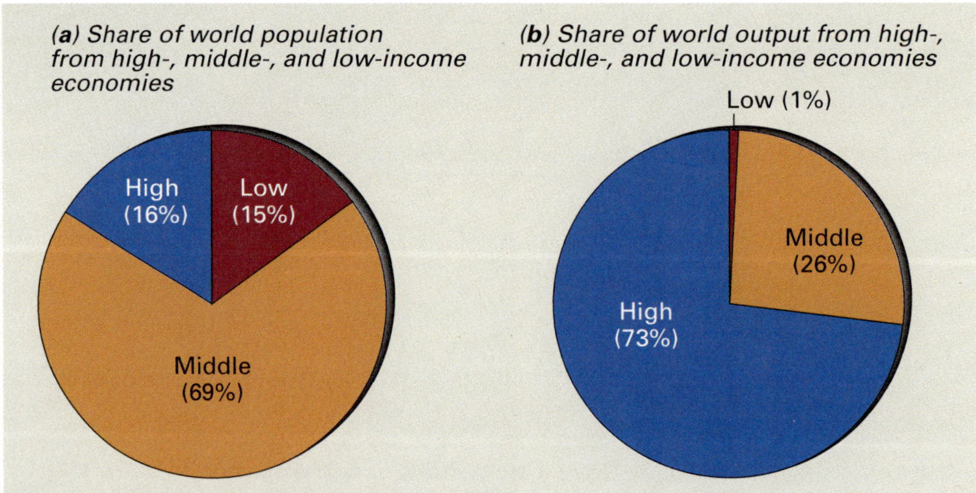

Source: Based on population and output estimated from the World Bank's *World Development Report: 2010*, Table 1 and Table 4 at http://siteresources.worldbank.org/INTWDR2010/Resources/5287678-1226014527953/Statistical-Annex.pdf. Find the World Bank at http://web.worldbank.org.

84 percent of the world's population in 2009 but produce only 27 percent of the output. Compared to industrial market countries, developing countries usually have higher rates of illiteracy, higher unemployment, faster population growth, and exports consisting mostly of agricultural products and raw materials.

On average, about half of the labor force in developing countries works in agriculture versus only about 3 percent in industrial market countries. Because farming methods are relatively primitive in developing countries, farm productivity is low and some households barely subsist. Industrial market countries or *developed countries* are primarily the economically advanced capitalist countries of Western Europe, North America, Australia, New Zealand, and Japan. They were the first to experience long-term economic growth during the 19th century.

Exhibit 2 presents income per capita in 2009 for a sample of high-, middle-, and low-income economies. Because most countries in the sample have large populations, together they account for 56 percent of the world population. Countries are listed from top to bottom in descending order based on income per capita. Again, figures have been adjusted to reflect the actual purchasing power of the local currency in its respective economy. The bars in the chart are color-coded, with high-income economies in blue, middle-income economies in orange, and low-income economies in red. Per capita income in the United States, the exhibit's top-ranked country, was seven times that of China, a middle-income economy. But per capita in China, in turn, was about seven

EXHIBIT 2 Per Capita Income for Selected Countries in 2009

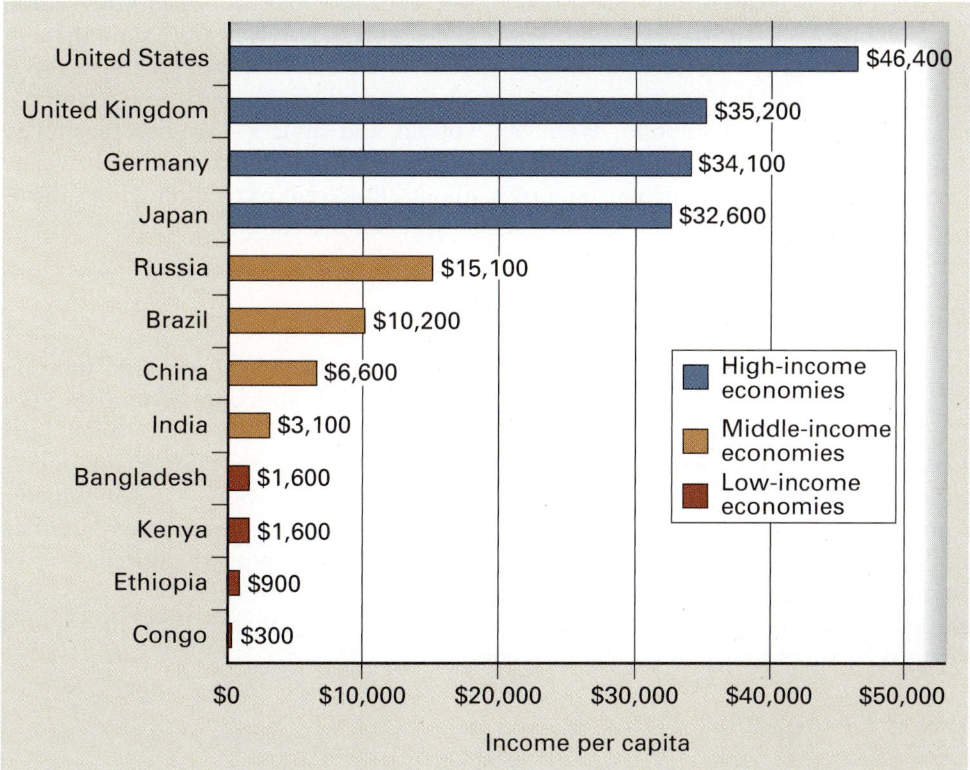

Source: Developed from estimates from the Central Intelligence Agency's *World Factbook: 2010* at www.cia.gov/library/publications/the-world-factbook/index.html. Figures are based on the purchasing power of each country's currency.

times that of Ethiopia and 22 times that of the Democratic Republic of the Congo, both, poor African nations. Residents of China likely feel poor relative to America, but they appear well off compared to the poorest nations. U.S per capita income was 51 times that of Ethiopia, and 155 times that of the Congo, one of the poorest nations on Earth. Thus, there is a tremendous range of per capita income around the world.

Exhibit 2 looks at income per capita, but neither income nor population is always measured accurately, especially in the poorest countries. Some economists have looked for simpler ways of measuring an economy, as discussed at the end of the book in the case study, "The Information Economy: Night Lights and Income."

Health and Nutrition

Differences in stages of development among countries are reflected in a number of ways besides per capita income. For example, many people in developing countries suffer from poor health as a result of malnutrition and disease. AIDS is devastating some developing countries, particularly those in sub-Saharan Africa. In 2007, about 150 of every 1,000 people ages 15 to 49 in South Africa, Zambia, and Zimbabwe had HIV, compared to only 3 of every 1,000 among those in high-income economies. In sub-Saharan Africa, life expectancy at birth averaged 52 years versus 80 years in high-income economies, 69 years in middle-income economies, and 59 years in all low-income economies.

Malnutrition

Those in the poorest countries consume only half the calories of those in high-income countries. Even if an infant survives the first year, malnutrition can turn normal childhood diseases, such as measles, into life-threatening events. The World Health Organization cites malnutrition as the biggest single threat to the world's public health. Malnutrition is a primary or contributing factor in more than half of the deaths of children under the age of 5 in low-income countries. Diseases that are well controlled in the industrial countries—malaria, whooping cough, polio, dysentery, typhoid, and cholera—can become epidemics in poor countries. Many of these diseases are water borne, as safe drinking water is often hard to find. In low-income countries, about 28 percent of children under the age of 5 suffered from malnutrition in 2007. Among middle-income countries the figure was 23 percent. Among high-income countries, it was 3 percent.

Infant Mortality

Health differences among countries are reflected in child mortality. Child mortality rates are much greater in low-income countries than in high-income countries. As of 2007, the mortality rate for children up to 5 years of age was 7 per 1,000 live births in high-income economies, 58 in middle-income economies, and 120 in low-income economies. Rates for our representative sample of high-, medium-, and low-income economies appear in Exhibit 3. Again, high-income economies appear as blue bars, middle-income as orange bars, and low-income as red bars. Among the dozen countries shown, child mortality was highest in the sub-Saharan African nations of Congo, Ethiopia, and Kenya. Child mortality among all 48 sub-Saharan African countries averaged 21 times that in high-income countries.

High Birth Rates

Developing countries are identified not only by their low-incomes and high mortality rates but also by their high birth rates. This year, more than 80 million of the 90 million people added to the world's population will be born in developing countries. In fact,

EXHIBIT 3 Child Mortality Rates per 1,000 Live Births as of 2007

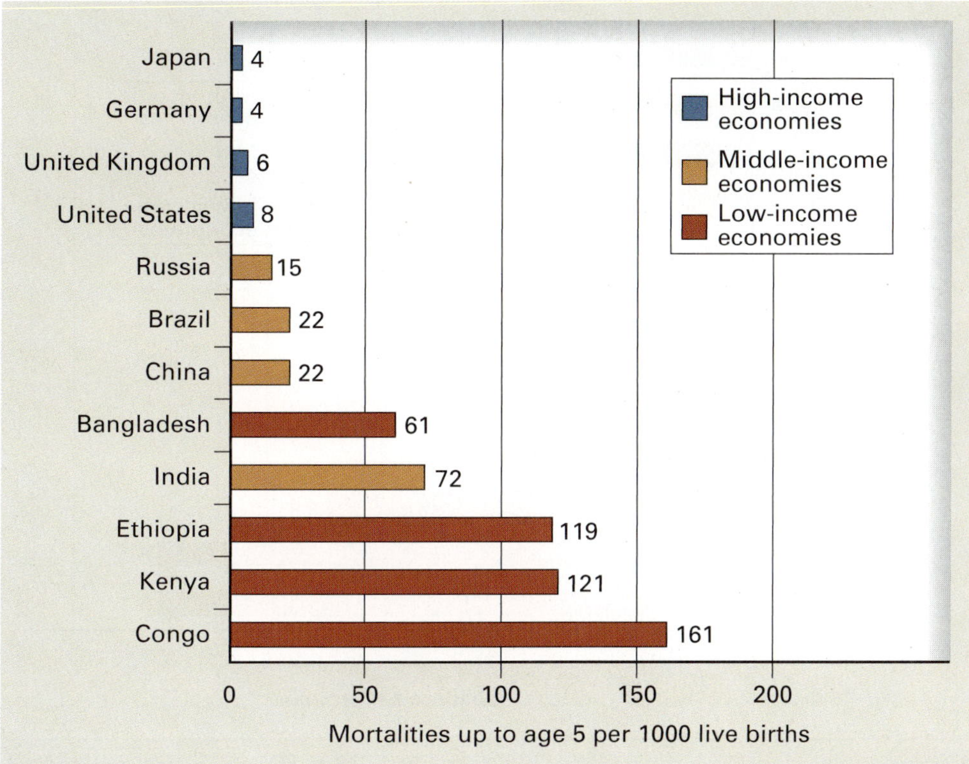

Source: Based on figures from the World Bank's *World Development Report: 2010*, Table 3. Find the World Bank at http://www.worldbank.org.

the birth rate is one of the clearest ways of distinguishing between industrial and developing countries. Very few low-income economies have a fertility rate below 2.2 births per woman, but none of the industrial market economies has a fertility rate above that level.

Exhibit 4 presents total fertility rates per woman for selected countries as of 2010. Ethiopia and the Congo, the two poorest nations on the list, each has among the world's highest fertility rates at 6.1. This means each woman on average gives birth to 6.1 children during her lifetime. Note that the four low-income economies, shown as red bars, have the highest fertility rates. Historically, families tend to be larger in poor countries because children are viewed as a source of farm labor and as economic and social security as the parents age. Most developing countries have no pension or social security system for the aged. The higher child mortality rates in poorer countries also engender higher birth rates, as parents strive to ensure a sufficiently large family.

Sub-Saharan African nations are the poorest in the world and have the fastest-growing populations. Because of high fertility rates in the poorest countries, children under 15 years old make up 43 percent of the population there. In high-income countries, children make up only 18 percent of the population. Italy, a high-income economy, became the first country in history with more people over the age of 65 than under the age of 15. Germany, Greece, Spain, Portugal, Japan, Hungary, Switzerland, and

EXHIBIT 4 **Average Number of Births During a Woman's Lifetime as of 2010**

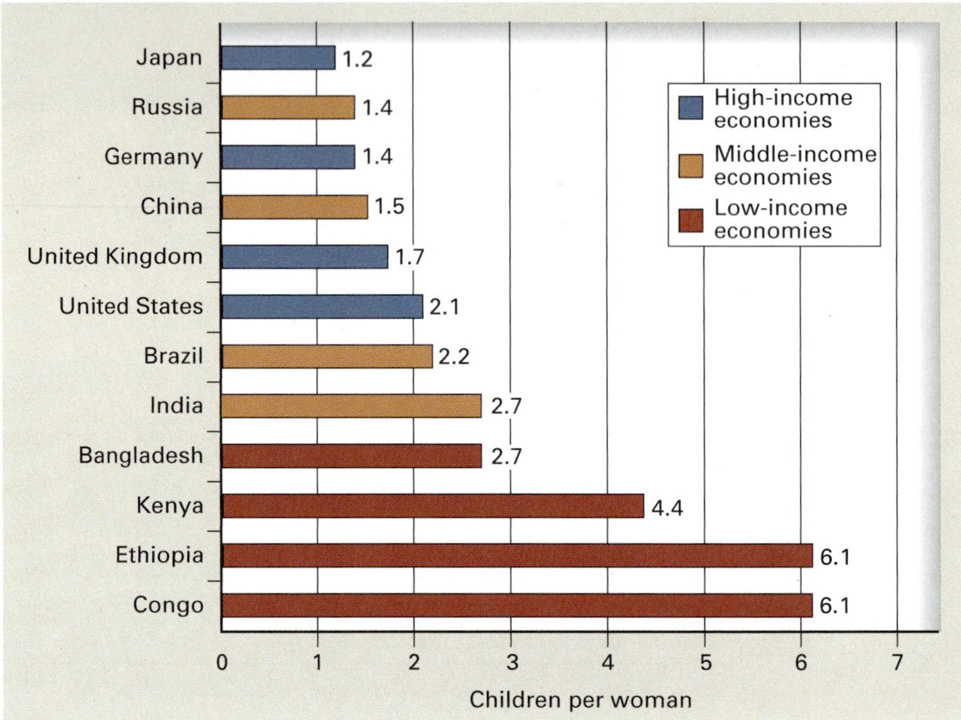

Source: Developed from estimates from the Central Intelligence Agency's *World Factbook: 2010* at www.cia.gov/library/publications/the-world-factbook/index.html.

the United Kingdom have since followed. An aging population poses fiscal problems, because these same countries typically offer generous health and pension benefits to the elderly.

In some developing countries, the population growth rate has exceeded the growth rate in total production, so the standard of living as measured by per capita output has declined. Still, even in the poorest of countries, attitudes about family size are changing. According to the United Nations, the birth rate during a typical woman's lifetime in a developing country has fallen from six children in 1965 to under three children today. Evidence from developing countries more generally indicates that when women have employment opportunities outside the home, fertility rates decline. And as women become better educated, they earn more and tend to have fewer children.

Women in Developing Countries

Throughout the world, the poverty rate is higher for women than men, particularly women who head households. The percentage of households headed by women varies from country to country, but nears 50 percent in some areas of Africa and the Caribbean. Because women often must work in the home as well as in the labor market, poverty can impose a special hardship on them. In many cultures, women's responsibilities include gathering firewood and carrying water, tasks that are especially burdensome if firewood is scarce and water is far from home.

Women in developing countries tend to be less educated than men. In the countries of sub-Saharan Africa and South Asia, for example, only half as many women as men complete high school. In Ethiopia, among those ages 15 and older, half the males can read and write, but only one third of females can. Women have fewer employment opportunities and earn lower wages than men do. For example, Sudan's Muslim fundamentalist government bans women from working in public places after 5:00 P.M. In Algeria, Egypt, Jordan, Libya, and Saudi Arabia, women account for only about one-quarter of the workforce. Women are often on the fringes of the labor market, working long hours in agriculture. They also have less access to other resources, such as land, capital, and technology.

Productivity: Key to Development

We have examined some signs of poverty in developing countries, but not why poor countries are poor. At the risk of appearing simplistic, we might say that poor countries are poor because they do not produce many goods and services. In this section, we examine why some developing countries experience such low productivity.

Low Labor Productivity

Labor productivity, measured in terms of output per worker, is by definition low in low-income countries. Why? Labor productivity depends on the quality of the labor and on the amount of capital, natural resources, and other inputs that combine with labor. For example, one certified public accountant with a computer and specialized software can sort out a company's finances more quickly and more accurately than can a thousand high school–educated file clerks with pencils and paper.

One way a nation raises its productivity is by investing more in human and physical capital. This investment must be financed by either domestic savings or foreign funds. Income per capita in the poorest countries is often too low to support much investment. In poor countries with unstable governments, the wealthy minority frequently invests in more stable foreign economies. This leaves less to invest domestically in either human or physical capital; without sufficient capital, workers remain less productive.

Technology and Education

What exactly is the contribution of education to the process of economic development? Education helps people make better use of resources. If knowledge is lacking, other resources may not be used efficiently. For example, a country may be endowed with fertile land, but farmers may lack knowledge of irrigation and fertilization techniques. Or farmers may not know how to rotate crops to avoid soil depletion. In low-income countries, 36 percent of those 15 and older were illiterate in 2007, compared to 17 percent in middle-income countries, and only 1 percent in high-income countries. Many in developing countries drop out of school because the family can't afford it or would rather put the child to work. Child labor in developing countries obviously limits educational opportunities.

Education also makes people more receptive to new ideas and methods. Countries with the most advanced educational systems were also the first to develop. In the 20th century, the leader in schooling and economic development was the United States. In Latin America, Argentina was the most educationally advanced nation 100 years ago, and it is one of the most developed Latin American nations today. The growth of education in Japan during the 19th century contributed to a ready acceptance of technology and thus to Japan's remarkable economic growth in the 20th century.

Inefficient Use of Labor

Another feature of developing countries is that they use labor less efficiently than do industrial nations. Unemployment and underemployment reflect inefficient uses of labor. *Underemployment* occurs when skilled workers are employed in low-skill jobs or when people are working less than they would like—a worker seeking full-time employment may find only a part-time job. *Unemployment* occurs when those willing and able to work can't find jobs.

Unemployment is measured primarily in urban areas, because in rural areas farm work is usually an outlet for labor even if many workers are underemployed there. The unemployment rate in developing nations on average is about 10 percent to 15 percent of the urban labor force. Unemployment among young workers—those aged 15 to 24—is typically twice that of older workers. In developing nations, about 30 percent of the combined urban and rural workforce is either unemployed or underemployed. In Zimbabwe, the unemployment rate was 95 percent in 2010; it's no surprise why Zimbabwe is the poorest nation in the world—even poorer than the Congo.

In some developing countries, the average farm is as small as two acres. Productivity is also low because few other inputs, such as capital and fertilizer, are used. *Although more than half the labor force in developing countries works in agriculture, only about one-third of output in these countries stems from agriculture.* In the United States, where farmers account for only 2 percent of the labor force, a farmer with modern equipment can farm hundreds or even thousands of acres (the average U.S. farm is about 500 acres). In developing countries, a farmer with a hand plow or an ox-drawn plow can farm maybe 10 to 20 acres. U.S. farmers, though only one-fiftieth of the labor force, grow enough to feed a nation and to lead the world in farm exports. The average value added per U.S. farm worker is about 75 times that of farm workers in low- and middle-income countries.

Low productivity obviously results in low income, but low income can, in turn, affect worker productivity. Low income means less saving and less saving means less investment in human and physical capital. Low income can also mean poor nutrition during the formative years, which can retard mental and physical development. These difficult beginnings may be aggravated by poor diet and insufficient health care in later life, making workers poorly suited for regular employment. Poverty can result in less saving, less education, less capital formation, a poor diet, and little health care—all of which can reduce a worker's productivity. Thus, *low income and low productivity may reinforce each other in a cycle of poverty.*

Natural Resources

Some countries are rich in natural resources. The difference is most striking when we compare countries with oil reserves and those without. The Middle East countries of Bahrain, Kuwait, Qatar, Saudi Arabia, and the United Arab Emirates are classified as high-income economies because they were lucky enough to be sitting atop huge oil reserves. But oil-rich countries are the exception. Many developing countries, such as Chad and Ethiopia, have little in the way of natural resources. Most developing countries without oil reserves are in trouble whenever oil prices rise. Since oil must be imported, higher oil prices drain oil-poor countries of precious foreign exchange.

Oil-rich countries also show us that an abundant supply of a natural resource is not in itself enough to create a modern industrial economy. On the other hand, Japan has one of the most developed economies in the world, yet has few natural resources. Connecticut is consistently the most productive of the United States measured in per capita income, but the state has little in the way of natural resources (its main natural resource is gravel). In fact, many researchers believe that reliance on resource wealth can be something of a curse for a nation.

Financial Institutions

Another requirement for development is an adequate and trusted system of financial institutions. An important source of funds for investment is the savings of households and firms. People in some developing countries have little confidence in their currency because some governments finance a large fraction of public outlays by printing money. This practice results in high inflation and sometimes very high inflation, or hyperinflation, as has occurred recently in Zimbabwe, where annual inflation was just about incalculable. High and unpredictable inflation discourages saving and hurts development.

Developing countries have special problems because banks are often viewed with suspicion. At the first sign of economic problems, many depositors withdraw their funds. Because banks cannot rely on a continuous supply of deposits, they cannot make loans for extended periods. If financial institutions fail to serve as intermediaries between savers and borrowers, the lack of funds for investment becomes an obstacle to growth. During the global financial crisis of 2008, banks in industrial market countries also suffered from depositors' sagging confidence. One measure of banking presence is the credit provided by banks as a percent of that nation's total output. This percentage is more than five times greater in high-income countries than in low-income countries.

Capital Infrastructure

Production and exchange depend on a reliable infrastructure of transportation, communication, sanitation, and electricity. Roads, bridges, airports, harbors, and other transportation facilities are vital to commercial activity. Reliable mail service, telephone communications, Internet connections, clean water, and electricity are also essential for advanced production techniques. Imagine how difficult it would be to run even a personal computer if the supply of electricity and access to the Internet were unavailable or continually interrupted, as is often the case in many developing countries.

Some developing countries have serious deficiencies in their physical infrastructures. As just one measure, Exhibit 5 shows the number of fixed and mobile telephone lines per 1,000 people in 2009 for the 12 countries examined earlier. The high-income economies have about 7 times more phones per 1,000 people than the bottom four countries, which are low-income economies. Germany, the top rated in this category, had 1,929 phone lines per 1,000 people. Bottom-ranked Ethiopia had just 46 phone lines per 1,000 people. Still, more than half the world's population had cell phones in 2009.[1]

Phone lines help knit together an economy's communications network. Countries without reliable phone service have difficulty not only communicating but reaping the benefits of other technology advances, such as the Internet. Exhibit 6 shows Internet users as a percent of the population in 2008 for our sample countries. There is an unmistakable digital divide between high-income and low-income economies. In the four high-income economies, an average 75 percent of the population used the Internet. In low-income economies, just 2 percent used the Internet on average. Even in India, which has a reputation as computer savvy, what with all the online support centers and software companies we read about, only 7 percent of the population were Internet users.

1. "Father of the Cell Phone," *The Economist*, 6 June 2009.

EXHIBIT 5 **Fixed and Mobile Phone Lines per 1,000 People for 2009**

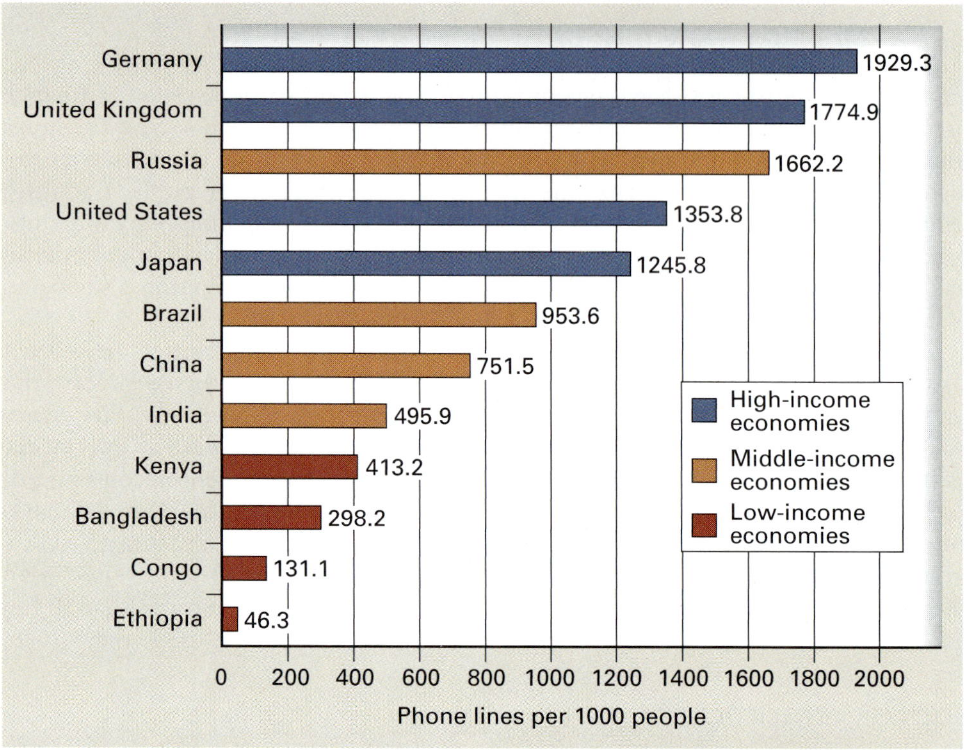

Source: Computed based on fixed and mobile line estimates from the Central Intelligence Agency's *World Factbook: 2010* at www.cia.gov/library/publications/the-world-factbook/index.html.

Entrepreneurship

An economy can have abundant supplies of labor, capital, and natural resources, but without entrepreneurship, the other resources will not be combined efficiently to produce goods and services. Unless a country has entrepreneurs who are able to bring together resources and take the risk of profit or loss, development may never get off the ground. Many developing countries were once under colonial rule, a system of government that offered the local population fewer opportunities to develop entrepreneurial skills.

One source of entrepreneurial experience for developing countries comes from McDonald's and other international franchises. For example, by providing management training, McDonald's stimulates entrepreneurship directly through its franchises and indirectly by showing competitors how a business is run. Such franchises also demonstrate to customers what they should come to expect in the way of service, cleanliness, quality, and the like.[2]

Government officials sometimes decide that entrepreneurs are unable to generate the kind of economic growth the country needs. State enterprises are therefore created to do what government believes the free market cannot do. But state-owned enterprises

2. Adrian Tschoegli, "McDonald's—Much Maligned, But an Engine of Economic Development," *Global Economy Journal*, 7(Issue 4 2007) at http://www.bepress.com/gej/vol7/iss4/5/.

EXHIBIT 6 **Internet Users as Percent of Population for 2008**

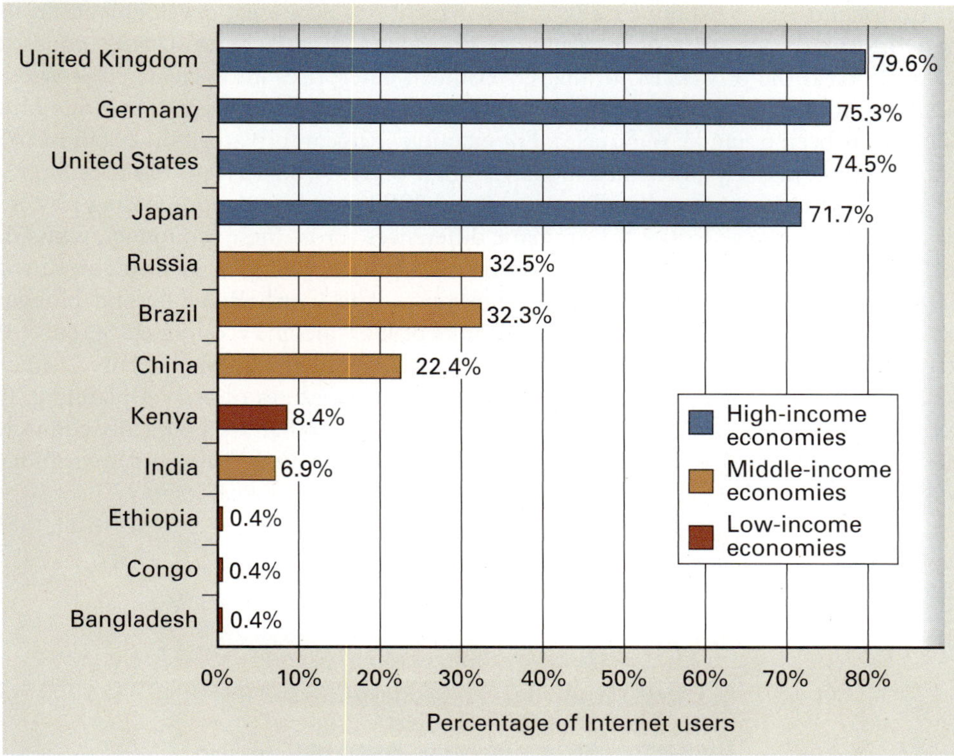

Source: Computed from user estimates in the Central Intelligence Agency's *World Factbook: 2010* at www.cia.gov/library/publications/the-world-factbook/index.html.

may have objectives other than producing goods efficiently—objectives that could include providing jobs for friends and relatives of government officials.

Rules of the Game

Finally, in addition to human capital, natural resources, financial institutions, capital infrastructure, and entrepreneurship, a successful economy needs reliable *rules of the game*. Perhaps the most elusive ingredients for development are the formal and informal institutions that promote production and exchange: the laws, customs, conventions, and other institutional elements that sustain an economy. A stable political environment with well-defined property rights is important. Little private-sector investment will occur if potential investors believe their capital might be appropriated by government, destroyed by civil unrest, blown up by terrorists, or stolen by thieves.

Under capitalism, the rules of the game include private ownership of most resources and the coordination of economic activity by the price signals generated by market forces. Market coordination answers the questions of what to produce, how to produce it, and for whom to produce it. Under socialism, the rules of the game include government ownership of most resources and the allocation of resources through central plans. For example, countries such as Cuba and North Korea carefully limit the private ownership of resources like land and capital. More generally, personal freedom

privatization
The process of turning government enterprises into private enterprises

is limited in centrally planned economies (for example, in North Korea, people need a government permit just to travel outside their own town).[3]

Although there is no universally accepted theory of economic development, around the world markets have been replacing central plans in many once-socialist countries. **Privatization** is the process of turning government enterprises into private enterprises in these transitional economies. Privatization is the opposite of *nationalization* (what Hugo Chávez has been doing in Venezuela). For example, Russian privatization began in 1992 with the sale of municipally owned shops. Exhibit 7 presents, for 10 transitional economies, the gross domestic product (GDP) per capita in 2009 based on the purchasing power of the domestic currency. Notice the dramatic differences across these economies, with GDP per capita in the Czech Republic nearly nine times greater than that in Vietnam. Russia's GDP per capita was midway between those two. The Czech Republic and Hungary, identified with blue bars, have joined the ranks of high-income economies. Seven of the 10 countries are middle-income economies, and are identified with orange bars. Vietnam, the red bar, is a low-income economy that still reflects vestiges of central planning. For example, banks there are more likely to lend to businesses that are politically connected than to those that are the most profitable. Thus, the most profitable Vietnamese firms tend to avoid banks and rely instead on reinvested earnings and informal loans.[4]

EXHIBIT 7 GDP per Capita for Transitional Economies in 2009

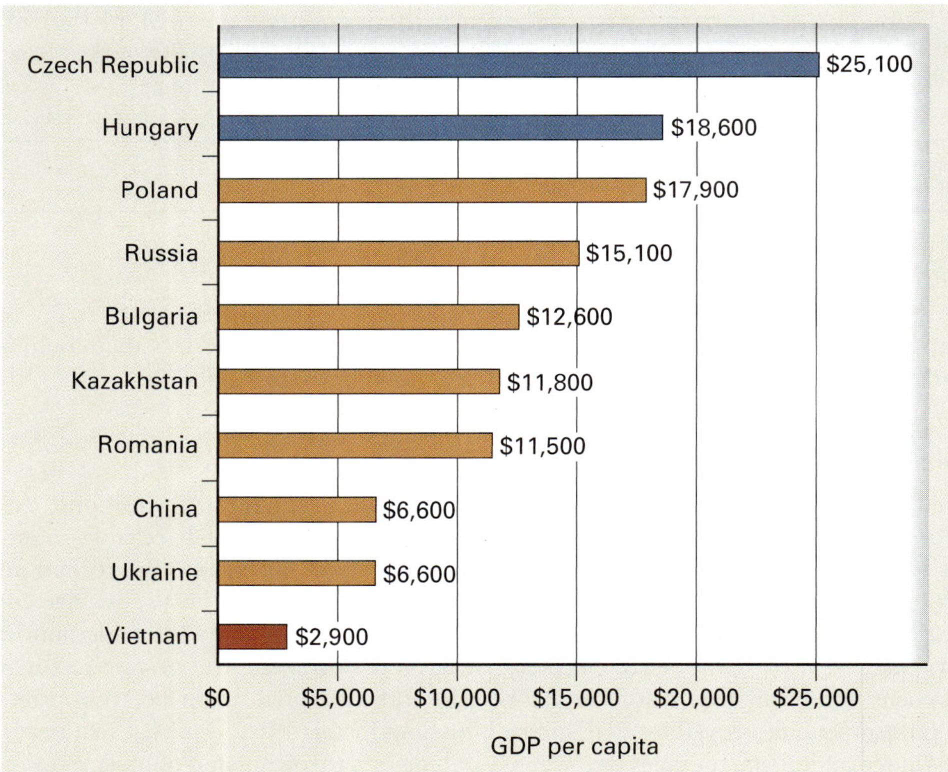

Sources: Computed from estimates in the Central Intelligence Agency's *World Factbook:* at www.cia.gov/library/publications/the-world-factbook/index.html. Figures are based on the purchasing power of the local currency.

3. Peter Wonacott, "The Mystery of North Korean Fans," *Wall Street Journal*, 26 June 2010.
4. Edmund J. Malesky and Markus Taussig, "Where Is Credit Due? Legal Institutions, Connections, and the Efficiency of Bank Lending in Vietnam," *Journal of Law, Economics, and Organization*, 25 (October 2009): 525–578.

High-income economies have developed a reliable and respected system of property rights and customs and conventions that nurture productive activity. These successful economies have also cultivated the social capital that helps the economy run more smoothly. **Social capital** consists of the shared values and trust that promotes cooperation in the economy. At the national level, social capital could be reflected in a sense of common purpose. For example, despite the troubling recession, polls show that Americans remain among the most patriotic people in the world. In a 2010 survey, 83 percent said they were "extremely" or "very" proud to be Americans.[5] At the local level, social capital could be expressed by a neighborhood crime watch, and there is evidence that such efforts help reduce property crime.[6] Low-income economies typically have poorly defined property rights, less social capital, and in the extreme, customs and conventions where bribery is commonplace and government corruption is an everyday practice. Worse still, civil wars have ravaged some of the poorest countries on Earth. Such violence and uncertainty make people less willing to invest in their own future or in the future of their country.

social capital
The shared values and trust that promote cooperation in the economy

Although it is common to sort countries into advanced industrial economies and developing economies, there are broad differences among developing economies, as discussed at the end of the book in the case study, "Bringing Theory to Life: The Poorest Billion," which looks at the billion people living in the poorest economies.

Income Distribution Within Countries

Thus far the focus has been on income differences across countries, and these differences can be vast. But what about income differences within a country? Are poor countries uniformly poor or are there sizable income differences among that nation's population? One way to measure inequality across households is to look at the share of national income going to the poorest fifth of the population. As a point of reference, in the unlikely event that income in an economy were evenly distributed across all households, then the poorest fifth would also receive exactly one fifth, or 20 percent, of national income. More realistically, the poorest fifth receives less than 20 percent of the income, but how much less? Is the percentage of income going to the poorest fifth higher for low-income countries than for high-income countries? In other words, is income more evenly distributed among poor countries than among rich countries? Not necessarily. Among our 12 nations, the poorest fifth of the population got an average of 7.7 percent of the income in the high-income countries, 5.8 percent in middle-income countries, and 7.2 percent in low-income countries. So, at least in this sample, income was less evenly distributed among middle-income countries than in high- or low-income countries.

International Trade and Development

Developing countries need to trade with developed countries to acquire the capital and technology that will increase labor productivity on the farm, in the factory, in the office, and in the home. To import capital and technology, developing countries must first acquire the funds, or foreign exchange, needed to pay for imports. Exports usually generate more than half of the annual flow of foreign exchange in developing countries. Foreign aid and private investment make up the rest.

5. Lexington, "Where Has All the Greatness Gone," *The Economist*, 17 July 2010.
6. Paolo Buonanno, "Does Social Capital Reduce Crime," *Journal of Law and Economics*, 52 (February 2009): 145–170.

Trade Problems for Developing Countries

Primary products, such as agricultural goods and other raw materials, make up the bulk of exports from developing countries, just as manufactured goods make up the bulk of exports from industrial countries. About half the merchandise exports from low-income countries consist of raw materials, compared to only 20 percent among high-income countries. A problem for developing countries is that the prices of primary products, such as coffee, cocoa, sugar, and rubber, fluctuate more widely than do the prices of finished goods, because crop supplies fluctuate with the weather.

When developing countries experience trade deficits, they often try to restrict imports. Because imported food is critical to survival, developing countries are more likely to cut imports of capital goods—the very items needed to promote long-term growth and productivity. Thus, many developing countries cannot afford the modern machinery that will help them become more productive. Developing countries must also confront industrial countries' trade restrictions, such as tariffs and quotas, which often discriminate against primary products. For example, the United States strictly limits sugar imports and has done so for more than half a century. Such restrictions are one reason the Doha Round of trade agreements has not gone smoothly.

Migration and the Brain Drain

Migration plays an important role in the economies of developing countries. A major source of foreign exchange in some countries is the money sent home by migrants who find jobs in industrial countries. According to the World Bank, migrants sent home about $450 billion in 2008. Thus migration provides a valuable safety valve for poor countries. But there is a downside. Often the best and the brightest professionals, such as doctors, nurses, and engineers, migrate to developed countries. For example, every year thousands of nurses migrate from countries such as Kenya and the Philippines to the United States, where half the world's nurses are employed. The financial attraction is powerful: A nurse in the Philippines would start there at less than $6,000 a year, compared with at least $36,000 in the United States.

The Philippines economy benefits from the billions sent home by overseas workers. So the upside of the brain drain for the poor country is the money sent home by overseas workers. Still, a nation is hurt when its best and brightest leave for opportunities elsewhere. Some African countries are demanding compensation for educating the doctors and nurses who move to high-income economies.

Import Substitution Versus Export Promotion

import substitution
A development strategy that emphasizes domestic manufacturing of products that were imported

An economy's progress usually involves moving up the production chain from agriculture and raw material to manufacturing then to services. If a country is fortunate, this transformation occurs gradually through natural market forces. For example, in 1850 most U.S. jobs were in agriculture. Now most jobs are in the service sector. Sometimes governments try to speed up the evolution. Many developing countries, including Argentina and India, pursued a strategy called **import substitution**, whereby domestic manufacturers would make products that until then had been imported. To insulate domestic manufacturers from foreign competition, the government imposed stiff tariffs and quotas. This development strategy became popular for several reasons. First, demand already existed for these products, so the "what to produce" question was easily answered. Second, import substitution provided infant industries a protected market. Finally, import substitution was popular with those who supplied resources to the favored domestic industries.

Like all trade protection, however, import substitution erased the gains from specialization and comparative advantage among countries. Often the developing country replaced low-cost foreign goods with high-cost domestic versions of those same goods. And domestic producers, shielded from foreign competition, usually failed to become efficient. Worse still, other countries often retaliated with their own trade restrictions.

Critics of import substitution claim that export promotion is a surer path to economic development. **Export promotion** concentrates on producing for the export market. This development strategy begins with relatively simple products, such as textiles. As a developing country builds its technological and educational base—that is, as the developing economy learns by doing—producers can then make more complex products for export. Economists favor export promotion over import substitution because the emphasis is on comparative advantage and trade expansion rather than on trade restriction. Export promotion also forces producers to grow more efficient in order to compete on world markets. Research shows that facing global competition boosts domestic efficiency.[7] What's more, export promotion requires less government intervention in the market than does import substitution.

export promotion
A development strategy that concentrates on producing for the export market

Of the two approaches, export promotion has been more successful around the world. For example, the newly industrialized countries of East Asia have successfully pursued export promotion, while Argentina, India, and Peru have failed with their import-substitution approach. In 1965, the newly industrialized economies of Hong Kong, South Korea, Singapore, and Taiwan had an average income only 20 percent that of high-income countries. Now these four are themselves high-income countries. Most Latin American nations, which for decades had favored import substitution, are now pursuing free trade agreements with each other and with the United States. Even India is dismantling trade barriers, with an emphasis on importing high-technology capital goods. One slogan of Indian trade officials is "Microchips, yes! Potato chips, no!"

Trade Liberalization and Special Interests

Although most people would benefit from freer international trade, some would be worse off. Consequently, governments in developing countries often have difficulty pursuing policies conducive to development. Often the gains from economic development are widespread, but the beneficiaries, such as consumers, do not recognize their potential gains. On the other hand, the losers tend to be concentrated, such as producers in an industry that had been sheltered from foreign competition, and they know quite well the source of their losses. So the government often lacks the political will and support to remove impediments to development, because the potential losers fight reforms that might harm their livelihood while the potential winners remain largely unaware of what's at stake. What's more, consumers have difficulty organizing even if they become aware of what's going on. A recent study by the World Bank suggests a strong link in Africa between governments that cater to special-interest groups and low rates of economic growth.

Nonetheless, many developing countries have been opening their borders to freer trade. People around the world have been exposed to information about the opportunities and products available on world markets. So consumers want the goods and firms want the technology and capital that are available abroad. Both groups want government to ease trade restrictions. Studies by the World Bank and others have underscored the successes of countries that have adopted trade liberalization policies.

7. See Martin Baily and Hans Gersbach, "Efficiency in Manufacturing and the Need for Global Competition," in *Brookings Papers on Economic Activity: Microeconomics*, M. Baily, P. Reiss, and C. Winston, eds. (Washington, D.C.: Brookings Institution, 1995): 307–347.

Foreign Aid and Economic Development

We have already seen that because poor countries do not generate enough savings to fund an adequate level of investment, these countries often rely on foreign financing. Private international borrowing and lending are heavily restricted by the governments of developing countries. Governments may allow residents to purchase foreign exchange only for certain purposes. In some developing countries, different exchange rates apply to different categories of transactions. Thus, the local currency is not easily convertible into other currencies. Some developing countries also require foreign investors to find a local partner who must be granted controlling interest. All these restrictions discourage foreign investment. In this section, we will look primarily at foreign aid and its link to economic development.

Foreign Aid

foreign aid
An international transfer made on especially favorable terms for the purpose of promoting economic development

Foreign aid is any international transfer made on *concessional* (that is, especially favorable) terms for the purposes of promoting economic development. Foreign aid includes grants, which need not be repaid, and loans extended on more favorable repayment terms than the recipient could normally secure. Concessional loans have lower interest rates, longer repayment periods, or grace periods during which repayments are reduced or even waived (similar to some student loans). Foreign aid can take the form of money, capital goods, technical assistance, food, and so forth.

Some foreign aid is granted by a specific country, such as the United States, to another specific country, such as the Philippines. Country-to-country aid is called *bilateral* assistance. Other foreign aid goes through international bodies such as the World Bank. Assistance provided by organizations that use funds from a number of countries is called *multilateral*. For example, the World Bank provides loans and grants to support activities that are viewed as prerequisites for development, such as health and education programs or basic development projects like dams, roads, and communications networks. And the International Monetary Fund extends loans to countries that have trouble with their balance of payments.

During the last four decades, the United States has provided the developing world with over $400 billion in aid. Since 1961, most U.S. aid has been coordinated by the U.S. Agency for International Development (USAID), which is part of the U.S. Department of State. This agency concentrates primarily on health, education, and agriculture, providing both technical assistance and loans. USAID emphasizes long-range plans to meet the basic needs of the poor and to promote self-sufficiency. Foreign aid is a controversial, though relatively small, part of the federal budget. Since 1993, official U.S. aid has been less than 0.2 percent of U.S. GDP, compared to an average of 0.3 percent from 21 other industrialized nations.

Does Foreign Aid Promote Economic Development?

In general, foreign aid provides additional purchasing power and thus the possibility of increased investment, capital imports, and consumption. But it remains unclear whether foreign aid *supplements* domestic saving, thus increasing investment, or simply *substitutes* for domestic saving, thereby increasing consumption rather than investment. What is clear is that foreign aid often becomes a source of discretionary funds that benefit not the poor but their leaders. Historically, more than 90 percent of the funds distributed by USAID have gone to governments, whose leaders assume responsibility for distributing these funds.

Much bilateral funding is tied to purchases of goods and services from the donor nation, and such programs can sometimes be counterproductive—they have unintended consequences. For example, in the 1950s, the United States began the Food for Peace program, which helped sell U.S. farm products abroad, but some recipient governments turned around and sold that food to finance poorly conceived projects. Worse yet, the availability of low-priced food from abroad drove down farm prices in the developing countries, hurting poor farmers there. The same holds for clothing. Used clothing donated to thrift shops and charitable organizations in industrialized countries typically winds up for sale in Africa, where the low price discourages local production of clothing.[8] Before used clothing swamped the continent, Africa had a textile industry, but no more. Textiles are often the first rung on the ladder to developing a broader manufacturing base.

Foreign aid may have raised the standard of living in some developing countries, but it has not necessarily increased their ability to become self-supporting at that higher standard of living. Many countries that receive aid are doing less of what they had done well. Their agricultural sectors have suffered. For example, though we should be careful when drawing conclusions about causality, per capita food production in Africa has fallen since 1960. Outside aid has often insulated government officials from their own incompetence and from the fundamental troubles of their own economies. No country receiving U.S. aid in the past 25 years has moved up in status from developing to industrial. And most countries today that have achieved industrial status did so without foreign aid. Development success typically takes time and involves gradual movements toward freer markets.

Because of disappointment with the results of government aid, the trend is toward channeling funds through private nonprofit agencies such as CARE. More than half of foreign aid now flows through private channels. The privatization of foreign aid follows a larger trend toward privatization in transitional economies around the world.

Conclusion

Because no single theory of economic development has become widely accepted, this chapter has been more descriptive than theoretical. We can readily identify the features that distinguish developing from industrial economies. Education is key to development, both because of its direct effect on productivity and because those who are more educated tend to be more receptive to new ideas. A physical infrastructure of transportation and communication systems and utilities is needed to link economic participants. And trusted financial institutions help link savers and borrowers. A country needs entrepreneurs with the vision to move the economy forward. Finally, the most elusive ingredients are the laws, manners, customs and ways of doing business that nurture economic development. Economic history is largely a story of economies that have failed to produce a set of economic rules of the game that lead to sustained economic growth. Some transitional economies and some newly emerging industrial countries in Asia show that economic development continues to be achievable.

8. Garth Frazer, "Used-Clothing Donations and Apparel Production in Africa," *Economic Journal*, 118 (October 2008): 1764-1784.

Summary

1. Developing countries are distinguished by low output per capita, poor health and nutrition, high fertility rates, poor education, and saving rates that are usually too low to finance sufficient investment in human and physical capital.
2. Worker productivity is low in developing countries because the stocks of human and physical capital are low, technological advances are not widely diffused throughout the economy, entrepreneurship is scarce, financial markets are not well developed, some talented professionals migrate to high-income countries, formal and informal institutions do not provide sufficient incentives for market activity, and governments may serve the interests of the group in power rather than the public interest.
3. The key to a rising standard of living is increased productivity. To foster productivity, developing nations must stimulate investment, support education and training programs, provide sufficient infrastructure, and foster supportive rules of the game.
4. Increases in productivity do not occur without prior saving, but low incomes in developing countries offer less opportunity to save. Even if some higher-income people in poor countries have the money to save, financial institutions are not well developed, and savings are often sent abroad, where there is a more stable investment climate.
5. Import substitution is a development strategy that emphasizes domestic production of goods that were imported. Export promotion concentrates on producing for the export market. Over the years, export promotion has been more successful than import substitution because it relies on specialization and comparative advantage.
6. Foreign aid has been a mixed blessing for most developing countries. In some cases, that aid has helped countries build the roads, bridges, schools, and other capital infrastructure necessary for development. In other cases, foreign aid has simply increased consumption and insulated government from painful but necessary reforms. Worse still, subsidized food and used clothing from abroad has undercut domestic production and economic development, particularly in Africa.

Key Concepts

Developing countries 678
Industrial market countries 678
Privatization 688
Social capital 689
Import substitution 690
Export promotion 691
Foreign aid 692

Questions for Review

1. DEVELOPING COUNTRIES Why is agricultural productivity in developing countries usually so low?
2. WORLDS APART Compare developing and industrial market economies on the basis of each of the following general economic characteristics, and relate the differences to the process of development:
   a. Diversity of the industrial base
   b. Child mortality rates
   c. Educational level of the labor force
3. Case Study: Night Lights and Income (See page 780.) Is the relationship between night lights and income an example of the association-is-causation fallacy? Why or why not?
4. PRODUCTIVITY AND DEVELOPMENT Among the problems that hinder growth in developing economies are poor infrastructure, lack of financial institutions and a sound money supply, a low saving rate, poor capital base, and lack of foreign exchange. Explain how these problems are interconnected.
5. How does privatization contribute to productivity?
6. CLASSIFICATION OF ECONOMIES What are the arguments for using real per capita GNI to compare living standards between countries? What weakness does this measure have?
7. Case Study: The Poorest Billion (See page 781.) What three poverty traps help explain the plight of nations comprising the poorest billion people?
8. FOREIGN AID AND ECONOMIC DEVELOPMENT Foreign aid, if it is to be successful in enhancing economic development, must lead to a more productive economy. Describe some of the problems in achieving such an objective through foreign aid.
9. INTERNATIONAL TRADE AND DEVELOPMENT From the perspective of citizens in a developing country, what are some of the benefits and drawbacks of international trade?
10. FOREIGN AID AND ECONOMIC DEVELOPMENT It is widely recognized that foreign aid that promotes productivity in developing economies is superior to merely shipping products like food to these countries. Yet the latter is the approach frequently taken. Why do you think this is the case?

Problems and Exercises

11. Worlds Apart GNI per capita income most recently was about 155 times greater in the United States than in the Congo. Suppose GNI per capita grows an average of 3 percent per year in the richer country and 6 percent per year in the poorer country. Assuming such growth rates continue indefinitely into the future, how many years would it take before per capita income in the Congo exceeds that of the United States? (To simplify the math, suppose at the outset per capita income is $155,000 in the richer country and $1,000 in the poorer country.)

12. Import Substitution Versus Export Promotion Explain why domestic producers who supply a good that competes with imports would prefer an import-substitution approach to trade policy rather than an export-promotion approach. Which policy would domestic consumers prefer and why?

Global Economic Watch Exercises

Login to www.cengagebrain.com and access the Global Economic Watch to do these exercises.

13. Global Economic Watch Go to the Global Economic Crisis Resource Center. Select Global Issues in Context. In the Basic Search box at the top of the page, enter the phrase "import substitution." On the Results page, go to the News Section. Click on the link for the September 17, 2010, article "Uzbekistan Aims at Import Substitution." What is limiting the success of Uzbekistan's import substitution strategy?

14. Global Economic Watch Go to the Global Economic Crisis Resource Center. Select Global Issues in Context. Go to the menu at the top of the page and click on the tab for Browse Issues and Topics. Choose Business and Economy. Click on the link for the World Bank. Find one article supporting the work of the World Bank and one article against. Compare and contrast the arguments in the articles.

Case Studies

Chapter 1

World of Business

A Yen for Vending Machines Japan faces a steady drop in the number of working-age people. Here are three reasons why: (1) Japan's birthrate has dropped to a record low, (2) Japan allows little immigration, and (3) Japan's population is aging. As a result, unemployment has usually been lower in Japan than in other countries. For example, Japan's unemployment rate in 2010 was only about half that of the United States and Europe. Because labor is relatively scarce in Japan, it is relatively costly. To sell products, Japanese retailers rely more on physical capital, particularly vending machines, which obviously eliminate the need for sales clerks.

Japan has more vending machines per capita than any other country on the planet—twice as many as the United States and nearly 10 times as many as Europe. And vending machines in Japan sell a wider range of products than elsewhere, including beer, sake, whiskey, rice, fresh eggs, beef, vegetables, pizza, entire meals, fried foods, fresh flowers, clothes, toilet paper, fishing supplies including bait, video games, software, ebooks, toys, DVDs, mobile phone recharging, and even X-rated comic books. Japan's vending machines are also more sophisticated. Newer models come with video monitors and touch-pad screens. Wireless chips alert vendors when supplies run low. Some cigarette and liquor machines have artificial vision that reportedly are better at estimating age than are nightclub bouncers. Sanyo makes a giant machine that sells up to 200 different items at three different temperatures. Some cold-drink dispensers automatically raise prices in hot weather. Thousands of machines allow cell phone users to pay by pressing a few buttons on their phones.

As noted earlier, it is common practice in the United States to shake down vending machines that malfunction. Such abuse increases the probability the machines will fail again, leading to a cycle of abuse. Vending machines in Japan are less abused, in part because they are more sophisticated and more reliable and in part because the Japanese generally have greater respect for private property and, consequently, a lower crime rate (e.g., Japan's theft rate is about half the U.S. rate).

Forty percent of all soft-drink sales in Japan are through vending machines, compared to only 12 percent of U.S. sales. Japanese sales per machine are double the U.S. rate. Research shows that most Japanese consumers prefer an anonymous machine to a salesperson. Despite the abundance of vending machines in Japan, more growth is forecast, spurred on by a shrinking labor pool, technological innovations, and wide acceptance of machines there.

Sources: "Machines That Can See," *The Economist*, 5 March 2009; Hiroko Tabuchi, "Beef Bowl Economics," *New York Times*, 30 January 2010; and Trends in Japan at http://web-japan.org/trends/lifestyle/lif060720.html. For a photo gallery of vending machines in Japan go to http://www.photomann.com/japan/machines/.

CASE STUDY

e activity
Do you want to see more pictures of unusual vending machines in Japan? Go to http://www.toxel.com/tech and scroll down to find the search box. Enter "14 Cool Vending Machines from Japan." In the search results, click on the link for Read Full Post.

CASE STUDY

e activity

The Federal Reserve Bank of Minneapolis asked some Nobel Prize winners how they became interested in economics. Their stories can be found at http://www.minneapolisfed.org/publications_papers/pub_display.cfm?id=3591.

The Information Economy

College Major and Annual Earnings Earlier in the chapter, you learned that economic choice involves comparing the expected marginal benefit and the expected marginal cost. Surveys show that students go to college because they believe a college diploma is the ticket to better jobs and higher pay. Put another way, for nearly two-thirds of U.S. high school graduates, the expected marginal benefit of college apparently exceeds the expected marginal cost. The cost of college will be discussed in the next chapter; the focus here is on the benefits of college, particularly expected earnings.

Among college graduates, all kinds of factors affect earnings, such as general ability, effort, occupation, college attended, college major, and highest degree earned. PayScale.com collected real time information on annual pay from its 10 million users. The site focused on the 20 popular college majors where most graduates go into the private sector (this excluded public sector majors such as education and social work, where pay is relatively low). To isolate the effects of a college major on earnings, only workers with a bachelor's as their highest degree were included in the results. Exhibit 1 shows the median earnings in 2008 by major for two groups of college graduates: (1) those with zero to five years of job experience and (2) those with 10 to 20 years of job experience. Majors are listed from the top down by the median annual pay of those with between zero and five years experience, indentified by the light green bars. The top pay of $60,500 went to those majoring in computer engineering; indeed, the top five slots went to engineering and computer graduates. Economics ranked sixth out of twenty majors with a median pay of $48,100, or 20 percent below the top pay. Criminal justice majors held the bottom spot of $34,200, which was 44 percent below the top pay.

The dark green bars show the median pay by major for those with 10 to 20 years of job experience. Those majoring in computer engineering still lead the field with $104,000, an increase of 72 percent over the pay of newer graduates with that degree. Economics majors with 10 to 20 years of job experience saw a 100 percent pay increase to $96,200. While economics majors with zero to five years experience were paid 20 percent less than the top paying major, among those with at least a decade of job experience, the median pay for economics majors moved up to within 7 percent of the top pay. In fact, economics majors saw their median pay grow more both in dollar terms and in percentage terms than did any other major. This suggests that those who study economics acquire skills that appreciate with experience. The bump in median pay based on experience for the 19 other majors averaged 67 percent. Criminal justice remained the lowest paying major among those with 10 to 20 years of experience. Note that the majors ranked toward the top of the list tend to be more quantitative and analytical. The selection of a relatively more challenging major such as economics may send a favorable signal to future employers.

© Amy Etra/Photo Edit

Remember, the survey was limited to those whose highest degree was the baccalaureate, so it excluded the many economics majors who went on to pursue graduate studies in law, business administration, economics, public administration, journalism, and other fields (a different study found that lawyers with undergraduate degrees in economics earned more on average than lawyers with other majors).

A number of world leaders majored in economics, including three of the last seven U.S. presidents, Chile's president and billionaire, Sabastian Pinera (who earned a Ph.D. in economics from Harvard), Turkey's first female prime minister, Tansu Ciller (who earned a Ph.D. in economics from the University of

EXHIBIT 1 Median Annual Pay by College Major

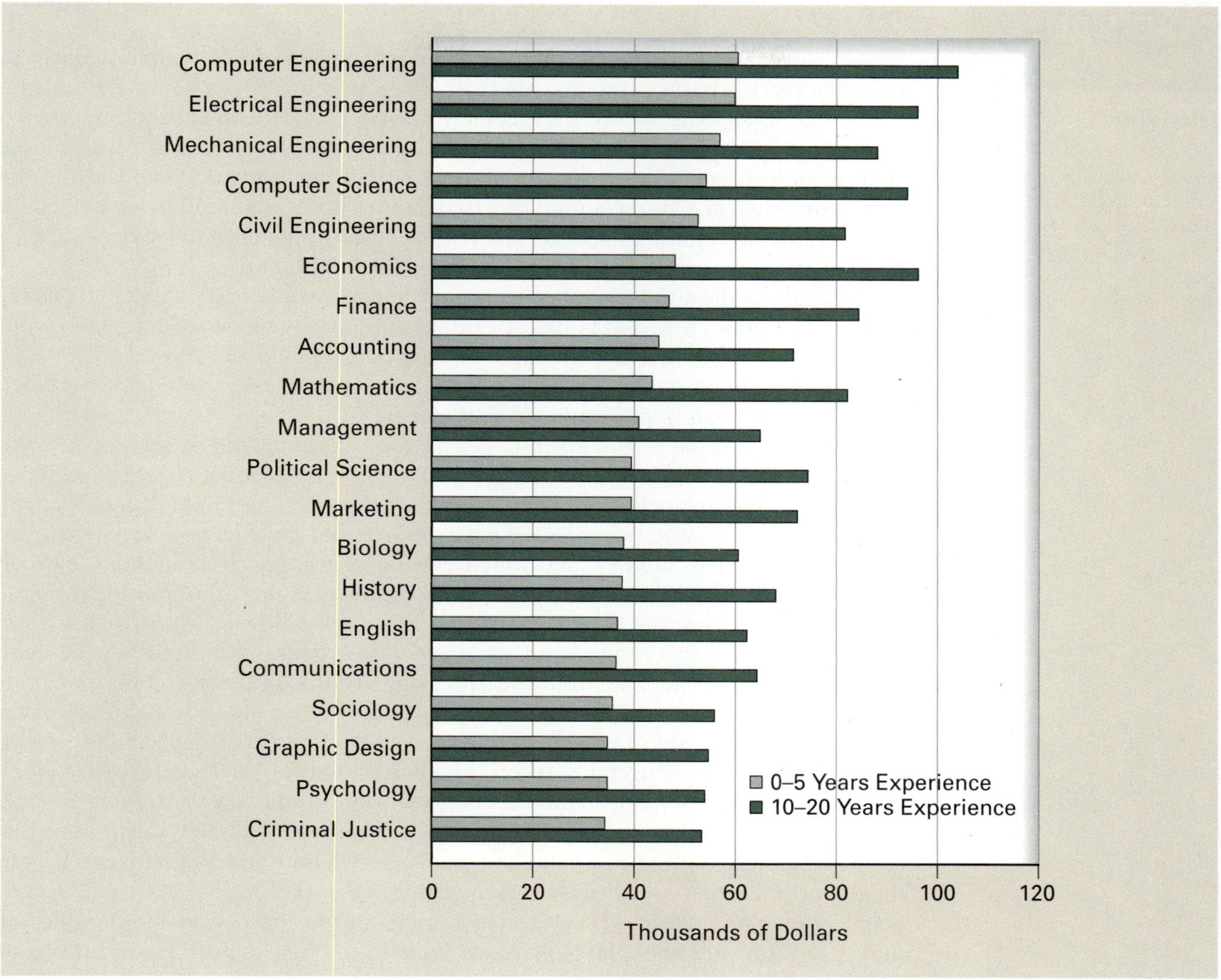

Connecticut), U.S. Supreme Court justices Steven Breyer and Anthony Kennedy, and former justice Sandra Day O'Connor. Other notable economics majors include billionaire Donald Trump, former eBay president (and billionaire) Meg Whitman, Microsoft chief executive officer (and billionaire) Steve Ballmer, CNN founder (and billionaire) Ted Turner, Intel president Paul Otellini, NFL Patriot's coach Bill Belichick, Governor Arnold Schwarzenegger, and Scott Adams, creator of Dilbert, the mouthless wonder.

Sources: Kurt Badenhausen, "Most Lucrative College Major," *Forbes.com*, 18 June 2008 at http://www.forbes.com/2008/06/18/college-majors-lucrative-lead-cx_kb_0618majors.html. "The World's Billionaires," *Forbes*, 11 March 2010; and R. Kim Craft and Joe Baker, "Do Economists Make Better Lawyers?, "*Journal of Economic Education*," 34 (Summer 2003): 263–281. For a survey of employment opportunities, go to the U.S. Labor Department's *Occupational Outlook Handbook* at http://www.bls.gov/oco/.

Chapter 2

CASE STUDY

e activity

Is college a sensible investment for you? Find out by reading "Sure You Should Go to College?" by Marty Nemko at http://www.martynemko.com/articles/sure-you-should-go-college_id1412.

Bringing Theory to Life

The Opportunity Cost of College What is your opportunity cost of attending college full time this year? What was the best alternative you gave up? If you held a full-time job, you would have some idea of the income you gave up to attend college. Suppose you expected to earn \$20,000 a year, after taxes, from a full-time job. As a full-time college student, you plan to work part time during the academic year and full time during the summer, earning a total of \$10,000 after taxes (about 40 percent of college students hold jobs during the academic year). Thus, by attending college this year, you gave up after-tax earnings of \$10,000 (= \$20,000 − \$10,000).

What about the direct cost of college itself? Suppose you are paying \$6,000 this year for in-state tuition, fees, and books at a public college (paying out-of-state rates would tack on \$6,000 to that, and attending a private college would add about \$15,000). *The opportunity cost of paying for tuition, fees, and books is what you and your family could otherwise have purchased with that money.*

How about room and board? Expenses for room and board are not necessarily an opportunity cost because, even if you were not attending college, you would still need to live somewhere and eat something, though these could differ from your college costs. Likewise, whether or not you attended college, you would still buy goods such as CDs, clothes, and toiletries, and services such as laundry, haircuts, and mobile service. Your spending for such products is not an opportunity cost of attending college but the personal cost that arises regardless of what you do. So for simplicity, assume that room, board, and personal expenses are the same whether or not you attend college. The forgone earnings of \$10,000 plus the \$6,000 for tuition, fees, and books yield an opportunity cost of \$16,000 this year for a student paying in-state rates at a public college. Opportunity cost jumps to about \$22,000 for students paying out-of-state rates and to about \$31,000 for those at private colleges. Scholarships, but not loans, would reduce your opportunity cost (why not loans?).

This analysis assumes that other things remain constant. But if, in your view, attending college is more of a pain than you expected your best alternative to be, then the opportunity cost of college is even higher. In other words, if you are one of those people who find college difficult, often boring, and in most ways more unpleasant than a full-time job, then the money cost understates your opportunity cost, because your best alternative offers a more enjoyable quality of life. If, on the other hand, you believe the wild and crazy life of a college student is more enjoyable than a full-time job would be, then the dollar figures overstate your opportunity cost, because your best alternative involves a less satisfying quality of life.

©iStockphoto.com/Oleg Prikhodko

Apparently, you view college as a good investment in your future, even though it's costly and perhaps even painful. College graduates on average earn about twice as much per year as high school graduates, a difference that exceeds \$1 million over a lifetime. These pay-gains from college prompt some college students to pile up debts to finance their education. Among those earning a bachelor's degrees at public four-year institutions in 2008, 38 percent graduated without education debt, but 6 percent were more than $40,000 in debt. One medical school graduate accumulated an education debt of $550,000 (counting unpaid interest and default charges).

Still, college is not for everyone. Some find the opportunity cost too high. For example, Bill Gates and Paul Allen dropped out of college to cofound Microsoft (both are now among the richest people on earth). Tiger Woods, once an economics major at Stanford, dropped out after two years to earn a fortune in professional golf. And Paula Creamer, who skipped college to play golf, won her first $1 million sooner than any LPGA player in tour history. High school basketball players who believed they were ready for the pros, such as Kobe Bryant and LeBron James, also skipped college (now players can't enter the pros until reaching 19 years of age and out of high school at least a year), as do most tennis pros. Many actors even dropped out of high school to follow their dreams, including Jim Carrey, Russell Crowe, Tom Cruise, Johnny Depp, Robert DeNiro, Cameron Diaz, Colin Farrell, Nicole Kidman, Jude Law, Lindsay Lohan, Demi Moore, Keanu Reeves, Kiefer Sutherland, Hilary Swank, Charlize Theron, and Kate Winslet.

Sources: Elyse Ashburn, "Why Do Students Drop Out? Because They Must Work at Jobs Too," *Chronicle of Higher Education*, 9 December 2009; Mary Pilon, "The $550,000 Student Loan Burden," *Wall Street Journal*, 13 February 2010; "The World's Billionaires," *Forbes*, 11 March 2010; and "College Board Connect to College Success" at http://www.collegeboard.com/.

CASE STUDY

Public Policy

Rules of the Game and Economic Development Rules of the game can affect the PPF by either nurturing or discouraging economic development. Businesses supply jobs, tax revenue, and consumer products, but owning and operating a business is risky even in the best of times. How hard is it for an entrepreneur to start a business, import products for sale, comply with tax laws, and settle business disputes? The World Bank, a nonprofit international organization, has developed a composite measure that rolls answers to all these questions into a single measure and ranks 183 countries from best to worst based on their ease of doing business. Exhibit 1 lists the best 10 and the worst 10 countries in terms of the ease of doing business. The countries with the friendliest business climate all have a high standard of living and a sophisticated economy. The United States ranks fourth best, behind Singapore, New Zealand, and Hong Kong. The 10 most difficult countries all have a low standard of living, a poor economy, and nine are in Africa.

e activity

You can see how difficult it is to do business in 183 countries by examining the rankings in the annual report on Doing Business. Find this and previous reports on other topics at the World Bank Group's Web site at http://www.doingbusiness.org.

Consider, for example, the burden facing a business that wants to sell an imported product. No business in the African country of Burundi makes bicycles, so a shop selling bicycles there must import them. Bicycles are shipped to Burundi via a port in Tanzania. In all, it takes the shop owner at least 10 documents and at least 71 days to get the bicycles from the port in Tanzania to the bicycle shop. Contrast this with 3 documents, and 5 days needed to import products in Denmark. Burundi is one of the poorest countries on earth, based on per capita income. Denmark is among the richest, with a per capita income about 120 times that of Burundi.

How does the burden imposed by business taxes differ across countries? In Burundi, businesses are subject to a tax rate totalling 279 percent of profit. So all business profits and much more are eaten up by taxes, in the process destroying the primary reason to even open a business. Meanwhile, a business in Hong Kong pays a tax rate amounting to only 24 percent of profit.

ALESSANDRO DELLA BELLA/KEYSTONE/Landov

Of course, some level of business regulation and taxation is necessary to ensure public health and safety and to nurture market competition. Few would argue, however, that the world's most prosperous economies have allowed businesses to go wild. But why would a country impose taxes and regulations so severe as to kill business development, thereby choking off the jobs, taxes, and consumer products that go with it? One possible explanation is that many countries with the worst business climate were once under colonial rule and have not yet developed the ability to operate government efficiently. Another possibility is that governments in poor countries usually offer the most attractive jobs around. Politicians create government jobs for friends, relatives, and supporters. Overseeing bureaucratic regulations gives all these people something to do, and high tax rates are needed to pay the salaries of all these political cronies.

EXHIBIT 1 Best 10 and Worst 10 Among 183 Countries Based on Ease of Doing Business

Best 10	Worst 10
1. Singapore	174. Niger
2. New Zealand	175. Eritrea
3. Hong Kong, China	176. Burundi
4. United States	177. Venezuela
5. United Kingdom	178. Chad
6. Denmark	179. Republic of Congo
7. Ireland	180. São Tomé and Principe
8. Canada	181. Guinea-Bissau
9. Australia	182. Democratic Republic of Congo
10. Norway	183. Central African Republic

Source: *Doing Business in 2010: Reforming Through Difficult Times,* (World Bank Publications, 2010) at http://www.doingbusiness.org/documents/fullreport/2010/DB10-full-report.pdf.

Perhaps the darkest explanation for the bad business climate in some countries is that business regulations and tax laws provide government bureaucrats with more opportunities for graft and corruption. For example, the more government documents needed to execute a business transaction, the more opportunities to seek bribes. In other words, obstacles are put in the way of business so that government bureaucrats can demand bribes to circumvent those obstacles. Even Irish rocker Bono, a long-time supporter of aid to Africa, has called for "advances in fighting the evils of corruption in Africa." Regardless of the explanation, poor countries are poor in part because they have not yet developed the rules of the game that nurture a prosperous economy.

Source: *Doing Business in 2010: Reforming Through Difficult Times,* (World Bank Publications, 2010) also available at http://www.doingbusiness.org/documents/fullreport/2010/DB10-full-report.pdf; and Bono, "A Time for Miracles," *Time,* 2 April 2007.

Chapter 3

The Information Economy

CASE STUDY

e activity

You can find more information and links about user-generated products—or user-generated content (UGC)—if you go to Wikipedia. Discover UGC characteristics and development, types, adoption by mass media, and criticisms at http://en.wikipedia.org/wiki/User-generated_content.

User-Generated Products In a market economy, new products and processes are usually developed by profit-seeking entrepreneurs, but sometimes sheer curiosity and the challenge of solving difficult problems lead to new and better ways of doing things. For example, loose communities of computer programmers have been collaborating for decades. By the early 1990s, they formed a grass roots movement known as "open source," which was fueled by the Internet. In 1991, Linus Torvalds, a student at the University of Helsinki in Finland, wrote the core program for what would become known as the Linux operating system. He posted his program online and invited anyone to tinker with the coding. Word spread, and computer aficionados around the world began spending their free time making Linux better.

Other software has developed in the open-source arena. For example, from the University of Illinois came web server software named Apache, and Swedish researchers developed database software called MySQL. The *Free Software Directory* lists more than 5,000 free software packages. The term *free* refers not only to the dollar cost of the software, which is zero, but to what you can do with the software—you can examine it, modify it, and redistribute it to anyone. Free user-generated software now includes the most widely used web server (Apache) and the second most popular desktop operating system (Linux), web browser (Firefox), and office suite (OpenOffice).

Other user-generated products include some familiar names—Wikipedia, MySpace, Facebook, YouTube, and Twitter. Wikipedia is a free online encyclopedia written and edited by volunteers. The idea is that collaboration over time will improve content much the way that open-source software has evolved. Wikipedia claims to be one of the most visited online sites. Founder Jimmy Wales says he spent a half million dollars getting Wikipedia going, but now the project relies on volunteers and donations.

MySpace and Facebook are social networking sites that allow users to post personal profiles, blogs, photos, music, videos, and more. The main attraction of these sites is material provided by users. The companies simply provide the software and hardware backbone to support the network. MySpace, founded in July 2003, was sold in July 2005 for about $330 million. Facebook was started by a college sophomore in 2004; the company had 500 million users by 2010 and an estimated market value of $10 billion.

YouTube is an online site that allows users to post their own videos and view those posted by others. Searching is easy. For example, "comparative advantage" turned up more than 150 videos, including "Econ Concepts in 60 Seconds." When sold to Google in 2006, YouTube had only 67 employees and no profit. Still, because visitors were viewing more than 100 million videos a day, all those eyeballs offered tremendous advertising potential. Google paid $1.7 billion for a company with no profit.

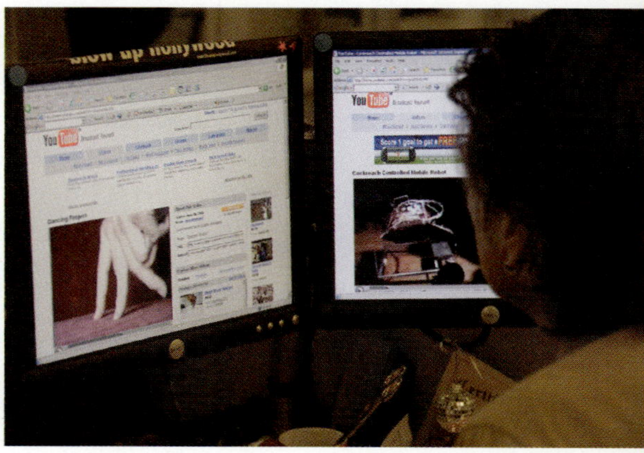

AP Photo/Cameron Bloch

Finally, Twitter is a social networking and microblogging service that allows users to send and receive "tweets," which are messages limited to 140 characters. Delivery can be online via the Twitter Web site, by cell phones, or by using other applications. The company had about 100 million users in 2010, but projects one billion users by 2013.

User-generated products are not new. Radio call-in shows have been making money off callers for decades. But the Internet has increased opportunities for users to create new products and to improve existing products. Most of the users are just having fun. The more users involved, the more attractive that product is to each user. That's why networking and video sites try to dominate their markets.

Sources: Jaron Lanier, *You Are Not a Gadget*, (Knopf, 2010); "A World of Connections," *The Economist*, 5 February 2010; and Jessica Vascellaro, "Facebook CEO in No Rush to 'Friend' Wall Street," *Wall Street Journal*, 3 March 2010. The *Free Software Directory* is found at http://directory.fsf.org/.

CASE STUDY

e activity

Economists have begun to study the economic implications of the virtual office and other virtual phenomena. Try visiting Google (http://www.google.com) and Yahoo (http://www.yahoo.com). Search for the words ***virtual*** and ***economics,*** and see what you find.

Information Revolution

Technological change spawned by the microchip and the Internet that enhanced the acquisition, analysis, and transmission of information

The Information Economy

The Electronic Cottage The Industrial Revolution shifted production from rural cottages to urban factories. But the **Information Revolution** spawned by the microchip and the Internet has decentralized the acquisition, analysis, and transmission of information. These days, someone who claims to work at a home office is not necessarily referring to corporate headquarters but to a spare bedroom. According to a recent survey, the number of telecommuters, or "remote workers," has more than doubled in the last decade. Pushing the trend are worsening traffic, higher gas prices, wider access to broadband, growing self-employment resulting from layoffs during the recession of 2007–2009, and even the threat of terrorism. The average commute is 23 miles, and eliminating that can save about $1,000 a year in gas and can avoid putting more than 6,000 pounds of carbon dioxide into the atmosphere. What's more, it often makes sense to try a new business at home before moving to a separate, more costly, location. Most small businesses are home-based, at least at the start.

From home, people can write a document with coworkers scattered throughout the world, then discuss the project online in real time or have a videoconference on Skype (McDonald's saves millions in travel costs by videoconferencing). Software allows thousands of employees to share electronic files. A 2010 survey found the majority of those who use computers for most of their work believe they could work at home. When Accenture moved headquarters from Boston to a suburb, the company replaced 120 tons of paper records with an online database accessible anytime from anywhere in the world.

To support those who work at home, an entire industry has sprung up, with magazines, newsletters, Web sites, and national conferences. In fact, an office need not even be in a specific place. Some people now work in virtual offices, which have no permanent locations. With iPhones, BlackBerries, or other links, remote workers, can conduct business on the road—literally, "deals on wheels."

B Busco/Getty Images

Chip technology is decentralizing production, shifting work from a central office either back to the household or to no place in particular. More generally, the Internet has reduced transaction costs, whether it's a market report authored jointly by researchers from around the world or a new computer system assembled from parts ordered over the Internet. Easier communication has even increased contact among distant research scholars. For example, economists living in distant cities are four times more likely to collaborate now than they were two decades ago.

Sources: Betty Beard, "Survey: Most Could Work from Home," *Arizona Republic*, 6 March 2010; Colleen DeBaise, "For More Workers, Home is Where the Office Is," *Wall Street Journal*, 3 January 2010; and Daniel Hamermesh and Sharon Oster, "Tools or Toys? The Impact of High Technology on Scholarly Productivity," *Economic Inquiry*, 40 (October 2002): 539–555. For information about how to run a business from home, go to http://www.ows.doleta.gov/unemploy/self.asp.

CHAPTER 4

WORLD OF BUSINESS

CASE STUDY

e activity

HoopsHype hosts a current salary list for top NBA players at http://hoopshype.com/salaries.htm.

The Market for Professional Basketball Toward the end of the 1970s, the NBA seemed on the brink of collapse. Attendance had sunk to little more than half the capacity. Some teams were nearly bankrupt. Championship games didn't even merit prime-time television coverage. But in the 1980s, three superstars turned things around. Michael Jordan, Larry Bird, and Magic Johnson added millions of fans and breathed new life into the sagging league. Successive generations of stars, including Dwayne Wade, Kevin Durant, and LeBron James, continue to fuel interest.

Since 1980 the league has expanded from 22 to 30 teams and attendance has more than doubled. More importantly, league revenue from broadcast rights jumped nearly *50-fold* from $19 million per year in the 1978–1982 contract to $930 million per year in the current contract, which runs to 2016. Popularity also increased around the world as international players, such as Dirk Nowitzki of Germany and Yao Ming of China, joined the league (basketball is now the most widely played team sport in China). NBA rosters now include more than 80 international players. The NBA formed marketing alliances with global companies such as Coca-Cola and McDonald's, and

EXHIBIT 1 NBA Pay Leaps

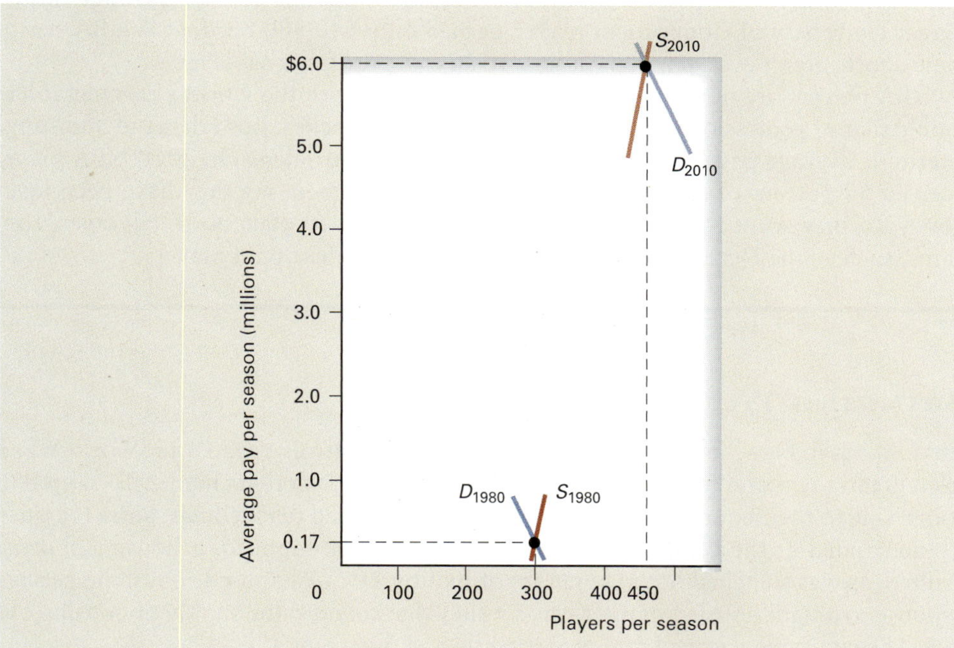

Because the supply of the world's top few hundred basketball players is relatively fixed by definition, the big jump in the demand for such talent caused average league pay to explode. Average pay increased from $170,000 in 1980 to $6,000,000 in 2010. Because the number of teams in the NBA increased, the number of players in the league grew from about 300 to about 450.

Sources: Howard Beck, "Falk Says NBA and Players Headed for Trouble," *New York Times*, 13 February 2010; Jonathan Abrams, "NBA's Shrinking Salary Cap Could Shake Up 2010 Free Agency," *New York Times*, 8 July 2010; and U.S. Census Bureau, *Statistical Abstract of the United States*: 2010 at http://www.census.gov/compendia/statab/.

BILL WAUGH/Reuters/Landov

league playoffs are now televised in more than 200 countries in 45 languages to a potential market of 3 billion people.

What's the key resource in the production of NBA games? Talented players. Exhibit 1 shows the market for NBA players, with demand and supply in 1980 as D_{1980} and S_{1980}. The intersection of these two curves generated an average pay in 1980 of $170,000, or $0.17 million, for the 300 or so players then in the league. Since 1980, the talent pool expanded somewhat, so the supply curve in 2010 was more like S_{2010} (almost by definition, the supply of the top few hundred players in the world is limited). But demand exploded from D_{1980} to D_{2010}. With supply relatively fixed, the greater demand boosted average pay to $6.0 million by 2010 for the 450 or so players in the league. Such pay attracts younger and younger players. Stars who entered the NBA right out of high school include Kobe Bryant, Kevin Garnett, and LeBron James. (After nine players entered the NBA draft right out of high school in 2005, the league, to stem the flow, required draft candidates to be at least 19 years old and out of high school at least one year. So talented players started turning pro after their first year of college; in 2008, for example, 12 college freshman were drafted including five of the top seven picks.)

But rare talent alone does not command high pay. Top rodeo riders, top bowlers, and top women basketball players also possess rare talent, but the demand for their talent is not sufficient to support pay anywhere near NBA levels. NBA players earn on average nearly 100 times more than WNBA players. For example, Diana Taurasi, a great University of Connecticut player, earned only $40,800 her first WNBA season. Some sports aren't even popular enough to support professional leagues.

NBA players are now the highest-paid team athletes in the world—earning at least double that of professionals in baseball, football, and hockey. Both demand *and* supply determine average pay. But the NBA is not without its problems. In 2010 NBA players received 57 percent of all team revenue. Some team owners say they have been losing money, so they want to cut the share of revenue going to players. To cut costs, some teams, such as the Detroit Pistons, have traded their highest paid players.

CASE STUDY

e activity

The New York State Division of Housing and Community Renewal features a number of fact sheets on rent control, stabilization, rent adjustments, special rights programs, and much more, at their Web site. Visit the site to see what kinds of problems exist with services, utilities, and other issues, at http://www.dhcr.state.ny.us/Rent/FactSheets/.

Bringing Theory to Life

Rent Ceilings in New York City New York City rent controls began after World War II, when greater demand for rental housing threatened to push rents higher. To keep rents from rising to their equilibrium level, city officials imposed rent ceilings. Since the quantity demanded at the ceiling rent exceeded the quantity supplied, a housing shortage resulted, as was sketched out in panel (b) of Exhibit 10 of Chapter 4. Thus, the perverse response to a tight housing market was a policy that reduced the supply of housing over time. The city-wide vacancy rate was recently just 3 percent.

Prior to rent controls, builders in New York City completed about 30,000 housing units a year and 90,000 units in the peak year. After rent controls, new construction dropped sharply. To stimulate supply, the city periodically promised rent-ceiling exemptions for new construction. But three times the city broke that promise after the housing was built. So builders remain understandably wary. During the peak year of the last decade only about 10,000 new housing units were built.

The excess demand for housing in the rent-controlled sector spilled into the free-market sector, increasing demand there. This greater demand raised rents in the free-market sector, making a rent-controlled apartment that much more attractive. New York City rent regulations now cover about 70 percent of the 2.1 million rental apartments in the city.

© Rudi Von Briel/Photo Edit

Tenants in rent-controlled apartments are entitled to stay until they die, and with a little planning, they can pass the apartment to their heirs. Rent control forces tenants into housing choices they would not otherwise make. After the kids have grown and one spouse has died, the last parent standing usually remains in an apartment too big for one person but too much of a bargain to give up. An heir will often stay for the same reason. Some people keep rent-controlled apartments as weekend retreats for decades after they have moved from New York. All this wastes valuable resources and worsens the city's housing shortage.

Since there is excess quantity demanded for rent-controlled apartments, landlords have less incentive to maintain apartments in good shape. A survey found that about 30 percent of rent-controlled housing in the United States was deteriorating versus only 8 percent of free-market housing. Similar results have been found for England and France. Sometimes the rent is so low that owners simply abandon their property. During one decade, owners abandoned a third of a million units in New York City. So rent controls reduce both the quality and the quantity of housing available.

You would think that rent control benefits the poor most, but it hasn't worked out that way. Henry Pollakowski, an MIT housing economist, concludes that tenants in low- and moderate-income areas get little or no benefit from rent control. But some rich people living in a rent-controlled apartment in the nicest part of town get a substantial windfall. Someone renting in upscale sections of Manhattan might pay only $1,000 a month for a three-bedroom apartment that would rent for $12,000 a month on the open market. According to a recent study, more than 87,000 New York City households with incomes exceeding $100,000 a year benefited from rent control by paying below-market rents.

Once a tenant leaves a rent-controlled apartment, landlords can raise the rent on the next tenant and under some circumstances can escape rent controls entirely. With so much at stake, landlords under rent control have a strong incentive to oust a tenant. Some landlords have been known to pay $5,000 bounties to doormen who report tenants violating their lease (for example, the apartment is not the tenant's primary residence or the tenant is illegally subletting). Landlords also hire private detectives to identify lease violators. And landlords use professional "facilitators" to negotiate with tenants about moving out. Many tenants end up getting paid hundreds of thousands of dollars for agreeing to move. Some have been paid more than $1 million. Facilitators can often find tenants a better apartment in the free-market sector along with enough cash to cover the higher rent for, say, 10 years. Since the rental market is in disequilibrium, other markets, such as the market for buying out tenants, kick in.

Sources: Edward Glaeser and Erzo Luttmer, "The Misallocation of Housing Under Rent Control," *American Economic Review*, 93 (September 1993): 1027–1046; Henry Pollakowski, "Who Really Benefits from New York City's Rent Regulation System?" Civic Report 34 (March 2003) at http://manhattan-institute.org/pdf/cr_34.pdf. Janny Scott, "Illegal Sublets Put Private Eyes on the Cast," *New York Times*, 27 January 2007; and Eileen Norcross, "Rent Control Is the Real New York Scandal," *Wall Street Journal*, September 13, 2008. The New York City Rent Guideline Board's Web site is at http://www.housingnyc.com/html/resources/dhcr/dhcr1.html.

Chapter 5

CASE STUDY

Behavioral Economics

e activity

The CDC stated that anti-smoking efforts targeting high school teens have been successful-including TV ads, school campaigns, and higher cost per pack. Read more at http://www.cdc.gov/tobacco/youth/index.htm. Find information about smoking cessation at http://www.lungusa.org/stop-smoking/.

Deterring Young Smokers As the U.S. Surgeon General warns on each pack of cigarettes, smoking can be hazardous to your health. Researchers estimate that cigarettes kill 440,000 Americans a year—10 times more than traffic accidents. Smoking is the overwhelming cause of lung cancer, the top cancer killer among women. Smoking is also the leading cause of heart disease, emphysema, and stroke.

According to the U.S. Centers for Disease Control and Prevention, each pack of cigarettes sold in the United States costs society more than $7 in higher health care costs and lost worker productivity. These costs exceed $150 billion a year, which works out to be about $3,400 per smoker per year.

Thus, smoking imposes major health and economic costs. Policy makers try to reduce these costs by discouraging smoking, especially among young people. About 80 percent of adult smokers began before the age of 18. Each day, about 3,500 U.S. teens under 18 try smoking for the first time, and about a third of those become regular smokers.

One way to reduce youth smoking is to prohibit cigarette sales to minors. A second way is to raise the price through higher cigarette taxes (the price now tops $9 per pack in New York City). The amount by which a given price hike reduces teen smoking depends on the price elasticity of demand. This elasticity is higher for teens than for adults. Why are teenagers more sensitive to price changes than adults? First, recall that one factor affecting elasticity is the importance of the item in the consumer's budget. Because teen income is relatively low, the share of income spent on cigarettes usually exceeds the share spent by adult smokers. Second, peer pressure shapes a young person's decision to smoke more than an adult's decision to continue smoking (if anything, adults face negative peer pressure for smoking). Teens often begin smoking by mooching cigarettes from peers. Thus, the effect of a higher price gets magnified among young smokers because that higher price also reduces smoking by peers. With fewer peers smoking, teens face less pressure and less opportunity to smoke. And, third, young people not yet addicted to nicotine are more sensitive to price increases than are adult smokers, who are more likely to be already hooked. The experience from other countries supports the effectiveness of higher cigarette taxes in reducing teen smoking. For example, a large tax increase on cigarettes in Canada cut youth smoking by two-thirds.

AP Photo/Bob Child

Another way to reduce smoking is to change consumer tastes through health warnings. In Canada, these warnings include photos showing how smoking can affect the brain, teeth, and gums, and a wilted cigarette depicts male impotence. In Australia, labels show gangrenous limbs, underweight babies, cancerous mouths, and blind eyes. Belgium adds corpses to the gallery of horrors. In California, a combination of higher cigarette taxes and an ambitious awareness program contributed to a 5 percent decline in lung cancer among women, even as the disease rose 13 percent in the rest of the country. (As of 2010, state taxes varied from a low of 7 cents per pack in South Carolina to a high of $3.46 in Rhode Island.)

But higher cigarette taxes can have unintended consequences. Researchers have found that smokers compensate for tax hikes by smoking each cigarette more intensively—that is, by sucking more smoke and nicotine from each cigarette. This poses an added health risk.

More generally, the message about the dangers of smoking, which seem to work, along with the higher cost of cigarettes has had an impact over time. Only about 20 percent of American adults now smoke, down from more than half in the 1960s.

Sources: Rosemary Avery et al., "Private Profits and Public Health: Does Advertising of Smoking Cessation Products Encourage Smokers to Quit?," *Journal of Political Economy*, 115 (June 2007): 447-481. Petter Lundborg and Henrik Andersson, "Gender, Risk Perceptions, and Smoking Behavior," *Journal of Health Economics*, 27 (September 2008): 1299–1311; Jerome Adda and Francesca Cornaglia, "Taxes, Cigarette Consumption, and Smoking Intensity," *American Economic Review*, 96 (September 2006): 1013–1028; and Deliana Kostova et al., "Prices and Cigarette Demand: Evidence from Youth Tobacco Use in Developing Countries," NBER Working Paper 15781, (February 2010).

CASE STUDY

Bringing Theory to Life

The Market for Food and the "Farm Problem" Despite decades of federal support and billions of tax dollars spent on various farm-assistance programs, the number of American farmers continues its long slide, dropping from 10 million in 1948 to under 3 million today. The demise of the family farm can be traced to the price and income elasticities of demand for farm products and to technological breakthroughs that increased supply.

Many of the forces that determine farm production are beyond a farmer's control. Temperature, rainfall, pests, and other natural forces affect crop size and quality. For example, favorable weather boosted crop production 16 percent in one recent year. Such increases create special problems for farmers because the demand for most farm crops, such as milk, eggs, corn, potatoes, oats, sugar, and beef, is price inelastic.

The effect of inelastic demand on farm revenue is illustrated in Exhibit 1. Suppose that in a normal year, farmers supply 10 billion bushels of grain at a market price of $5 a

e activity

What are the forces shaping U.S. agriculture today? The Economic Research Service of the U.S. Department of Agriculture provides some answers with its briefing book at http://www.ers.usda.gov/Emphases/Competitive/. Find out what the latest edition says about the current state of the American farm family. How have farm size and the number of family farms been changing? How does farm family income compare to average household income? What percent of farm income is a result of government farm support policies?

EXHIBIT 1 The Demand for Grain

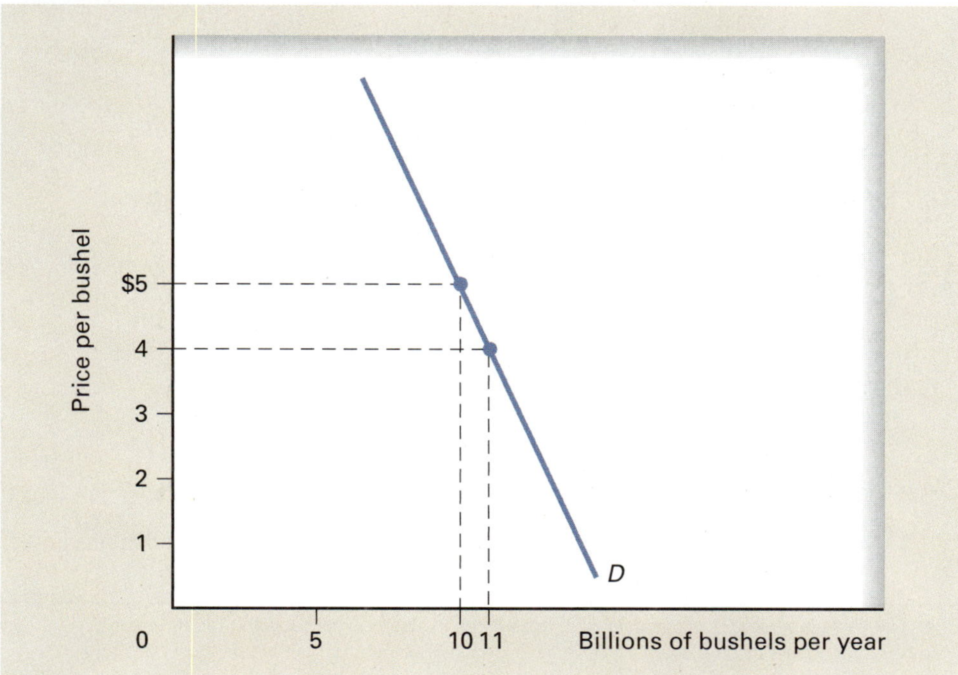

The demand for grain tends to be price inelastic. As the market price falls, so does total revenue.

bushel. Annual farm revenue, which is price times quantity, totals $50 billion in our example. What if favorable weather boosts grain production to 11 billion bushels, an increase of 10 percent? Because demand is price inelastic, the average price in our example must fall by more than 10 percent to, say, $4 per bushel to sell the extra billion bushels. Thus, the 10 percent increase in farm production gets sold only if the price drops from $5 to $4, or by 20 percent.

Total revenue declines from $50 billion to $44 billion. So, despite a 10 percent rise in production, total revenue drops. *Because demand is price inelastic, total revenue falls when the price falls.* Of course, for farmers, the upside of inelastic demand is that a lower-than-normal crop results in higher total revenue. For example, one recent drought sent corn prices up 50 percent, increasing farm revenue in the process. So weather-generated changes in farm production create year-to-year swings in farm revenue.

Fluctuations in farm revenue are compounded in the long run by the *income inelasticity* of demand for grain and, more generally, for food. As household incomes grow over time, spending on food may increase because consumers substitute prepared foods and restaurant meals for home cooking. But this move up the food chain has little effect on the total demand for farm products. Thus, as the economy grows over time and incomes rise, the demand for farm products tends to increase but by less than the increase in income. This modest increase in demand from *D* to *D'* is reflected in Exhibit 2.

EXHIBIT 2 The Effect of Increases in Demand and Supply on Farm Revenue

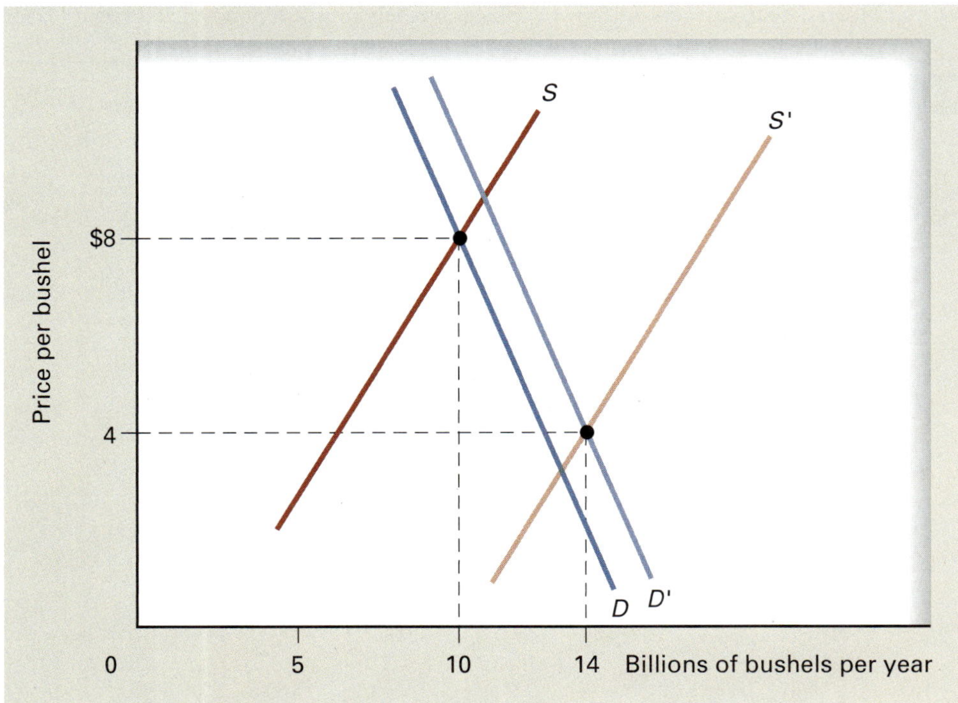

Over time, technological advances in farming have sharply increased the supply of grain. In addition, increases in consumer income over time have increased the demand for farm products. But because increases in the supply of grain exceed increases in demand, the combined effect is a drop in the market price and a fall in total farm revenue.

Because of technological improvements in production, however, the supply of farm products has increased sharply. Developments such as more sophisticated machines, better fertilizer, and healthier seeds have increased farm output per hour of labor 11-fold since 1950. For example, farmers can now seed at night using a 32-row planter and global positioning satellites. With new strains of pest-resistant plants, farmers have cut insecticide applications from seven per season to one or none.

Exhibit 2 shows a big increase in the supply of grain from *S* to *S'*. Because the supply increase exceeds the demand increase, the price declines. And because the demand for grain is price inelastic, the percentage drop in price exceeds the percentage increase in output. The combined effect in our example is lower total revenue. In the real world, the effect over time is not quite so bleak, but farmers have been getting a declining share of consumer spending for decades. Between 1960 and 2009, for example, total consumer spending on all goods and services (adjusted for inflation) in the United States increased more than 400 percent, but total farm revenue increased only 40 percent.

Sources: Scott Kilman and Lauren Etter, "Recession Finally Hits Down on the Farm," *Wall Street Journal*, 28 August 2009; Bruce L. Gardner, "Changing Economic Perspective on the Farm Problem," *Journal of Economic Literature*, 30 (March 1992): 62–105; and *Economic Report of the President*, February 2010, Tables B-99 at http://www.gpoaccess.gov/eop/2010/2010_erp.pdf; For current economic research at the U.S. Department of Agriculture, go to http://www.ers.usda.gov/.

Chapter 6

Bringing Theory to Life

CASE STUDY

e activity

Almost any question you might have about water supply and use in the United States can be answered by visiting the U.S. Geological Survey's Water Q&A Web page at http://ga.water.usgs.gov/edu/mqanda.html. Various terms are linked to pages with additional information. Another great source is the Environmental Protection Agency at http://www.epa.gov/ebtpages/water.html. This site includes links to many water issues such as the economic effects of pollution.

Water, Water, Everywhere Centuries ago, economists puzzled over the price of diamonds relative to the price of water. Diamonds are mere bling—certainly not a necessity of life in any sense. Water is essential to life and has hundreds of valuable uses. Yet diamonds are expensive, while water is cheap. For example, the $10,000 spent on a high-quality one-carat diamond could buy about 10,000 bottles of water or about 2.8 million gallons of municipally supplied water (which sells for about 35 cents per 100 gallons in New York City). However measured, diamonds are extremely expensive relative to water. For the price of a one-carat diamond, you could buy enough water to last two lifetimes.

How can something as useful as water cost so much less than something of such limited use as diamonds? In 1776, Adam Smith discussed what has come to be called the *diamonds-water paradox*. Because water is essential to life, the total utility derived from water greatly exceeds the total utility derived from diamonds. Yet the market value of a good is based not on its total utility but on what consumers are willing and able to pay for an additional unit—that is, on its *marginal utility*. Because water is so abundant in nature, we consume it to the point where the marginal utility of the last gallon purchased is relatively low. Because diamonds are relatively scarce compared to water, the marginal utility of the last diamond purchased is relatively high. Thus, water is cheap and diamonds expensive. As Ben Franklin said "We will only know the worth of water when the well is dry."

Speaking of water, sales of bottled water are growing faster than any other beverage category—creating a $15 billion U.S. industry, an average of 25 gallons per person in 2010. Bottled water ranks behind only soft drinks in sales, outselling coffee, milk, and beer. The United States offers the world's largest market for bottled water—importing water from places such as Italy, France, Sweden, Wales, even Fiji. "Water bars" in cities such as Newport, Rhode Island, and San Francisco feature bottled water as the main attraction. A 9-ounce bottle of Evian water costs $1.49. That amounts to $21.19

AP Photo/Doug Mills

per gallon, or nearly 10 times more than gasoline. You think that's pricey? Bling H_2O is available in bottles decorated with Swarovski crystals and sells for more than \$50 a bottle—that's about 100 times more than gasoline.

Why would consumers pay a premium for bottled water when water from the tap costs virtually nothing? After all, some bottled water comes from municipal taps (for example, New York City water is also bottled and sold under the brand name Tap'dNY). First, many people do not view the two as good substitutes. Some people have concerns about the safety of tap water, and they consider bottled water a healthy alternative (about half those surveyed in a Gallup Poll said they won't drink water straight from the tap). Second, even those who drink tap water find bottled water a convenient option away from home. And third, some bottled water is now lightly flavored or fortified with vitamins. People who buy bottled water apparently feel the additional benefit offsets the additional cost.

Fast-food restaurants now offer bottled water as a healthy alternative to soft drinks. Soft-drink sales have been declining for more than a decade as bottled water sales have climbed. But if you can't fight 'em, join 'em: Pepsi's Aquafina is the top-selling bottled water in America, and Coke's Dasani ranks second.

Sources: Dana Cimilluca et al., "Coke Near Deal for Bottler," *Wall Street Journal*, 25 February 2010; Jack Healy, "Five-cent Deposits Set for Bottled Water," *New York Times*, 24 October 2009; and Charles Duhigg, "That Tap Water Is Legal But May Be Unhealthy," *New York Times*, 16 December 2009. The Definitive Bottled Water site is http://www.bottledwaterweb.com/, and the New York City drinking water department is at http://www.nyc.gov/html/dep/html/drinking_water/index.shtml.

CASE STUDY

e activity

This case study points out that patients have little incentive to monitor physician behavior when they do not pay the bill. In an attempt to control costs, Medicare reduces the reimbursement rate for services provided by physicians. How do you suppose physicians respond? Auditors with the Centers for Medicare and Medicaid Services (CMS) examined physician behavior and found that they increase the volume and intensity of work in response to declining prices to maintain revenue. CMS's easy-to-read report on physician response, which includes several real examples, can be found at http://www.cms.gov/ActuarialStudies/. Under Actuarial Studies, click on Physician Response.

Public Policy

The Marginal Value of Free Medical Care Certain Americans, such as the elderly and those on welfare, receive government-subsidized medical care. State and federal taxpayers spend more than \$750 billion a year providing medical care to 94 million Medicare and Medicaid recipients, or more than \$8,000 per beneficiary. Medicaid is the largest and fastest growing spending category in most state budgets. Beneficiaries pay only a tiny share of Medicaid costs; most services are free.

The problem with giving something away is that a beneficiary consumes it to the point where the marginal value reaches zero, although the marginal cost to taxpayers can be sizable. This is not to say that people derive no benefit from these programs. Although beneficiaries may attach little or no value to the final unit consumed, they likely derive a substantial consumer surplus from all the other units they consume. For example, suppose that Exhibit 8 represents the demand for health care by Medicaid beneficiaries. If the price they face is zero, each beneficiary consumes health care to the point where the demand curve intersects the horizontal axis—that is, where his or her marginal valuation is zero. Although they attach little or no value to their final unit of Medicaid-funded health care, their consumer surplus is the entire area under the demand curve.

One way to reduce the cost to taxpayers without significantly harming beneficiaries is to charge a token amount—say, \$1 per doctor visit. Beneficiaries would eliminate visits they value less than \$1. This practice would yield significant savings to taxpayers but would still leave beneficiaries with abundant health care and a substantial consumer surplus (measured in Exhibit 8 as the area under the demand curve but above the \$1 price). As a case in point, one Medicaid experiment in California required some beneficiaries to pay $1 per visit for their first two office visits per month (after two visits, the price of additional visits reverted to zero). A control group continued to receive free medical care. The $1 charge reduced office visits by 8 percent compared to the control group. Medical care, like other goods and services, is also sensitive to its time cost (a topic discussed in the next section). For example, a 10 percent increase in the average travel time to a free outpatient clinic reduced visits by 10 percent. Similarly, when the relocation of a free health clinic at one college increased students' average walking time by 10 minutes, visits dropped 40 percent.

Ackerman Gruber Images

Another problem with giving something away is that beneficiaries are less vigilant about getting honest value, and this may increase the possibility of waste, fraud, and abuse. According to President Obama, "improper payments" for Medicaid and Medicare cost taxpayers nearly $100 billion in 2009. Medicaid fraud has replaced illegal drugs as the top crime in Florida. Crooks were charging the government for medical supplies that were not delivered or not needed (some supposed beneficiaries were dead). People won't tolerate padded bills and fake claims if they have to pay their own bills.

Finally, program beneficiaries have less incentive to pursue healthy behaviors themselves in their diet, their exercise, and the like. This doesn't necessarily mean certain groups don't deserve heavily subsidized medical care. The point is that when something is free, people consume it until their marginal value is zero, they pay less attention to getting honest value, and they take less personal responsibility for their own health.

Some Medicare beneficiaries visit one or more medical specialists most days of the week. Does all this medical attention improve their health care? Not according to a long-running Dartmouth Medical School study. Researchers there found no apparent medical benefit and even some harm from such overuse. As one doctor lamented, "The system is broken. I'm not being a mean ogre, but when you give something away for free, there is nothing to keep utilization down."[1] Even a modest money cost or time cost would reduce utilization, yet would still leave beneficiaries with quality health care and a substantial consumer surplus. Research suggests that up to 30 percent of all medical care is unnecessary.

Federal legislation in 2010 expanded the coverage of Medicaid and extended insurance coverage to many without it. Research by Michael Anderson and others suggests that one result will be a "substantial increase in care provided to currently uninsured individuals." No question, better health care can improve the quality of life, but overusing a service because the price is zero also wastes scarce resources.

Sources: Michael Anderson, Carlos Dobkin, and Tal Gross, "The Effects of Health Insurance Coverage on the Use of Medical Services," NBER Working Paper 15823 (March 2010); David Card, Carlos Dobkin, and Nicole Maestras, "The Impact of Nearly Universal Insurance Coverage on Health Care Utilization," *American Economic Review*, 98 (December 2008): 2242–2258; Elliot Fisher et al., "The Implications of Regional Variation in Medicare Spending," *Annals of Internal Medicine*, 18 February 2003; Gina Kolata, "Law May Do Little to Help Curb Unnecessary Care," *New York Times*, 29 March 2010; and Steven Rhoads, "Marginalism," in *The Fortune Encyclopedia of Economics*, edited by D. R. Henderson (New York: Warner, 1993): 31–33. A transcript of President Obama's remarks about 'improper payments' is at http://www.whitehouse.gov/the-press-office/remarks-president-health-insurance-reform-st-charles-mo. For more on Medicare and Medicaid, go to http://www.cms.hhs.gov/.

1. As reported by Gina Kolata, "Patients in Florida Lining Up for All That Medicare Covers," *New York Times*, 13 September 2003.

Chapter 7

CASE STUDY

e activity

Because of scale economies in the movie theater industry, a few large chains now operate thousands of screens. Regal Entertainment Group is one of the largest, with over 6,800 screens in over 550 theaters. Go to Regal's Web site at http://www.regmovies.com and click on "grand openings" to check out the average number of screens in each new theater. How does the number of screens in new theaters compare with the industry average, which is about 13?

Lanny Ziering/Jupiter Images

Bringing Theory to Life

Scale Economies and Diseconomies at the Movies Movie theaters experience both economies and diseconomies of scale. A theater with one screen needs someone to sell tickets, usually another to sell popcorn (concession stand sales account for well over half the profit at most theaters), and yet another to run the movie projector. If a second movie screen is added, the same staff can perform these tasks for both screens. Thus, by selling tickets to both movies, the ticket seller becomes more productive. Furthermore, construction costs per screen are reduced because only one lobby and one set of rest rooms are required. The theater may get a better deal from movie distributors, can run bigger, more noticeable newspaper ads, and can spread the cost over more films. This is why we see theater owners adding more and more screens; they are taking advantage of economies of scale. Since 1990, the number of movie screens in the United States has grown faster than the number of theaters, so the average number of screens per theater has increased. There are now an average of 13 screens per movie theater. Europe has experienced similar growth.

But why stop at, say, 10 or even 20 screens per theater? Why not 30 or 40 screens, particularly in thickly populated areas with sufficient demand? One problem with expanding the number of screens is that traffic congestion around the theater grows with the number of screens at that location. Public roads are a resource the theater cannot control. Also, the supply of popular films may not be large enough to fill so many screens (though some theaters have diversified beyond movies by broadcasting live baseball games, operas, rock concerts and other events). Finally, time itself is a resource that the firm cannot easily control. Only certain hours are popular with moviegoers. Scheduling becomes more difficult because the manager must space out starting and ending times to avoid the crush that occurs when too many customers come and go at the same time. No more "prime time" can be created. (To spread out the customers, theaters offer discounts for morning or early afternoon showings.) Thus, theater owners lack control over such inputs as the public roads, the supply of films, and the amount of "prime time" in the day. These factors contribute to diseconomies of scale.

Sources: Jeffrey McCracken and Lauren Schuker, "Movie Theaters Secure Financing for Digital Upgrade," *Wall Street Journal*, 25 February 2010; Brooks Barnes, "At Cineplexes, Sport, Opera, Maybe a Movie," *New York Times*, 23 March 2008; Sandy Cohen, "Movie Fans Prefer the Theater Experience," *Forbes*, 7 March 2007; and *Statistical Abstract of the United States: 2010*, U.S. Census Bureau, http://www.census.gov/compendia/statab/.

World of Business

CASE STUDY

Scale Economies and Diseconomies at McDonald's McDonald's experiences economies of scale at the plant, or restaurant, level because of its specialization of labor and machines, but it also benefits from economies of scale at the firm level. Experience gained from decades of selling hamburgers can be shared with new managers through centralized training programs. Costly research and efficient production techniques can also be shared across thousands of locations. For example, McDonald's took three years to decide on the exact temperature of the holding cabinets for its hamburger patties. What's more, the cost of advertising and promoting McDonald's through sponsorship of world events such as the Olympics can be spread across 32,000 restaurants in more than 120 countries.

Some diseconomies may also arise in such large-scale operations. The fact that the menu must be reasonably uniform across thousands of locations means that if customers in some parts of the country or the world do not like a product, it may not get on the menu, even though it might be popular elsewhere. Another problem with a uniform menu is that the ingredients must be available around the world and cannot be subject to droughts or sharp swings in price. For example, McDonald's considered adding a shrimp salad to the menu but decided not to when advised the move could deplete the nation's shrimp supply.

McDonald's has moved aggressively into overseas markets (about 10 percent of the beef sold in Japan goes into McDonald's hamburgers). Planning across so many markets has grown increasingly complex. For example, McDonald's is kosher in Israel, closes five times a day for Muslim prayer in Saudi Arabia, and serves mutton burgers in India, where cows are worshiped, not eaten. Running a worldwide operation also exposes the company to regional risks, such as environmental protests in Brazil, mad-cow disease in Europe, and terrorist bombings of outlets in France, Indonesia, Russia, and Turkey.

Change usually comes slowly in some large corporations, but the profit motive has forced McDonald's to reinvent itself. McDonald's has reorganized its U.S. operation into regions, allowing managers in each region more leeway in pricing and promotion. McDonald's has also become more flexible by putting mini-restaurants in airports, gas stations, and Walmarts. The company has been opening new stores and closing unprofitable ones. And McDonald's has reduced the time required to develop new products. For example, whereas Chicken McNuggets were seven years in the making, Chicken Wraps took less than a year to develop. This greater flexibility across countries and regions, the increased willingness to close unprofitable restaurants, and the reduction in product development time all reflect McDonald's effort to cope with diseconomies of scale.

Photo by Michael Lassman/Bloomberg via Getty Images

Sources: Daniel Gross, "Who Won the Recession? McDonald's," *Slate*, 11 August 2009, at http://www.slate.com/id/2224862/. Janet Adamy, "For McDonald's It's a Wrap," *Wall Street Journal*, 30 January 2007; Tess Stynes, "McDonald's Posts Robust Sales," *Wall Street Journal*, 8 March 2010; James L. Watson, ed., *Golden Arches East: McDonald's in East Asia* (Stanford University Press, 1998); and McDonald's Web site at http://www.mcdonalds.com/.

e activity

Surf the world of McDonald's at http://www.aboutmcdonalds.com/country/map.html. Because tastes vary, you can see that the McDonald's menu also varies. If you can read a foreign language, try to find a McDonald's page for a country where it is spoken.

Chapter 8

CASE STUDY

e activity

Visit http://www.ubid.com. uBid has registered almost 6 million customers and sold over $2 billion in merchandise since it started in 1997. Now go to http://www.eBay.com. Founded in 1995, eBay Inc. connects hundreds of millions of people around the world every day by providing the Internet platforms of choice for global commerce, payments, and communications. Which site would you prefer if you wanted to buy or sell something, and why? Are these companies part of a perfectly competitive market?

World of Business

Auction Markets Flower markets are global. About three-quarters of flowers purchased in the United States are imported. More than half the world's cut flowers move through the auction system in the Netherlands. Five days a week, in a huge building 10 miles outside Amsterdam, some 2,500 buyers gather to participate in FloraHolland Aalsmeer, the largest auction of its kind in the world. Every day over 20 million flowers and plants from thousands of growers around the globe are auctioned off in the world's largest roofed building, spread across the equivalent of 100 football fields. Flowers are grouped and auctioned off by type—long-stemmed roses, tulips, and so on. Hundreds of buyers sit in theater settings with their fingers on buttons. Nearly as many buyers bid online from remote locations. Once the flowers are presented, a clock-like instrument starts ticking off descending prices until a buyer pushes a button. The winning bidder gets to choose how many and which items to take. The clock starts again until another buyer stops it, and so on, until all flowers are sold. Auctions occur rapidly—on average a transaction takes place every 4 seconds.

This is an example of a *Dutch auction,* which starts at a high price and works down. Dutch auctions are more common when selling multiple lots of similar, though not identical, items, such as flowers in Amsterdam, tobacco in Canada, and fish in seaports around the world. Because there is some difference among the products for sale in a given market—for example, some flower lots are in better condition than others—this is not quite perfect competition because perfectly competitive markets sell identical products.

More common than the Dutch auction is the *English open outcry auction,* where bidding starts at a low price and moves up until only one buyer remains. Products sold this way include stocks, bonds, wine, art (think Sotheby's and Christie's), antiques, and livestock. On markets such as the Chicago Board of Trade, prices for commodities such as wheat, gold, and coffee beans are continuously determined in the trading pits using variations of an open outcry auction.

The birth of the Internet has breathed new life into auctions. Web sites such as eBay, uBid, and hundreds more hold online auctions for old maps, used computers, wine, airline tickets, antiques, military memorabilia, comic books, paperweights—you name it. The largest online site, eBay, offers over 2,000 categories in a forum that mimics a live auction. Internet auctions allow specialized sellers to reach a world of customers. A listing on eBay, for example, could reach millions of people in more than 100 countries.

© Sion Touhig/Sygma/Corbis

Computers are taking over markets in other ways. In New York, Chicago, Philadelphia, London, and Frankfurt, hand-waving traders in what seem like mosh pits are being replaced by electronic trading. The Nasdaq was the world's first virtual stock market. There is no Nasdaq trading floor as there is with the New York Stock Exchange. On the French futures exchange, after electronic trading was added as an option to the open-outcry system, electronic trading dominated within a matter of months. *Computers reduce the transaction costs of market exchange.*

Sources: Constance Cacey, "Petal Pushers," *New York Times*, 25 February 2007; Eric Felton, "The Flower, the Leaf and the Lobby: A Valentine's Tale," *Wall Street Journal*, 15 February 2010; and Lynette Evans, "Following the Flowers," *San Francisco Chronicle*, 3 March 2007. The FloraHolland Web site (in English) is at http://www.floraholland.com/en/Pages/default.aspx.

CASE STUDY

e activity

Market.Econ brings "experimental economics to the Internet" at http://market.econ.arizona.edu/. By supplying your email address, you can receive a password and play one of their games online. Be sure to read through any rules carefully. Charles Holt of the University of Virginia, an innovator in using games in the classroom, maintains a Web site with instructions and game sheets for some experiments at http://www.people.virginia.edu/~cah2k/programs.html.

INFORMATION ECONOMY

Experimental Economics Economists have limited opportunities to carry out the kind of controlled experiments available in the physical and biological sciences. But about four decades ago, Professor Vernon Smith began some experiments to see how quickly and efficiently a group of test subjects could achieve market equilibrium. His original experiment involved 22 students, 11 designated as "buyers" and 11 as "sellers." Each buyer was given a card indicating the value of purchasing one unit of a hypothetical commodity; these values ranged from $3.25 down to $0.75, forming a downward-sloping demand curve. Each seller was given a card indicating the cost of supplying one unit of that commodity; these costs ranged from $0.75 up to $3.25, forming an upward-sloping supply curve. Each buyer and seller knew only what was on his or her own card.

To provide incentives, participants were told they would get a cash bonus at the end of the experiment based on the difference between the price they negotiated in the market and their value (for buyers) or their cost (for sellers). For example, if a buyer assigned a $3.25 value was able to purchase the good for $1.50, that buyer would receive a cash bonus of $1.75 for that transaction. The point is that both buyers and sellers had a cash incentive to play the game for keeps. As a way of trading, Smith employed a system in which any buyer or seller could announce a bid or an offer to the entire group—a system called a *double-continuous auction*—based on rules similar to those governing stock markets and commodity exchanges. A transaction occurred whenever any buyer accepted an offer to sell or when any seller accepted an offer to buy. *Smith found that the price quickly moved to the market-clearing level,* which in his experiment was $2.00.

Economists have since carried out thousands of experiments to test the properties of markets. These show that under most circumstances, markets are extremely efficient in moving goods from producers with the lowest costs to consumers who place the highest value on the goods. This movement maximizes the sum of consumer and producer surplus and thus maximizes social welfare. One surprising finding is how few participants it takes to establish a market price. Market experiments sometimes use only four buyers and four sellers, each capable of trading several units. Some experiments use only two sellers, yet the competitive model performs well under double-continuous auction rules. Professor Smith won the Nobel Prize for his work in experimental economics.

Incidentally, most U.S. retail markets, such as supermarkets and department stores, use *posted-offer pricing*—that is, the price is marked, not negotiated. Experiments show that posted pricing does not adjust to changing market conditions as quickly as does a double-continuous auction. Despite their slow response time, posted prices may be the choice for large, relatively stable markets, because posted prices involve low transaction costs—that is, buyer and seller don't have to haggle over each transaction (imagine negotiating the price with a Walmart clerk for each item you wanted to buy). In contrast, double-continuous-auction pricing involves high transaction costs and, in the case of some stock and commodity markets, requires thousands of people in full-time negotiations to maintain prices at their equilibrium levels (although, as discussed in the previous case study, the Internet is reducing these transaction costs).

Experiments provide empirical support for economic theory and yield insights about how market rules affect market outcomes. Experiments also help create markets that did not exist before, such as the market for pollution rights or for broadcast spectrum rights—markets to be discussed in later chapters. Experiments also offer a safe and inexpensive way for people in emerging market and transitional economies to learn how markets work. The rapid development of online auctions has opened up a world of data for experimentalists.

Experimental economics is a hot topic for research and industry. For example, the number of papers published in the field jumped from fewer than 20 a year in the 1970s to more than ten times that today. The field also has its own research journals, including *Experimental Economics*. Most top U.S. business schools employ experimental economists. Some top corporations, such as Google, Hewlett-Packard, and IBM, as well as many universities created experimental-economics labs.

Sources: Vernon Smith, "Experimental Methods in Economics," *The New Palgrave Dictionary of Economics*, Vol. 2, edited by J. Eatwell et al. (Stockton, 1987), pp. 241–249; Vernon Smith, "Behavioral Economics and the Foundations of Economics," *Journal of Socio-Economics* (Issue 2, 2005), pp. 135–150; and Francesco Guala, *The Methodology of Experimental Economics* (Cambridge University Press, 2005). The academic journal *Experimental Economics* can be found at http://www.springer.com/economics/economic+theory/journal/10683.

CHAPTER 9

CASE STUDY

WORLD OF BUSINESS

Is a Diamond Forever? In 1866, a child walking along the Orange River in South Africa picked up an odd-looking pebble that turned out to be a 21-carat diamond. That discovery on a farm owned by Johannes De Beers sparked the largest diamond mine in history. When the Great Depression caused a slump in diamond prices, De Beers Consolidated Mines undertook efforts to control the world supply of diamonds and to increase consumer demand for them.

The company was able to increase consumer demand through a carefully tailored marketing program. De Beers spends about $200 million a year trying to convince people that diamonds are scarce, valuable, and perfect reflections of love. De Beers' slogan, "A diamond is forever," was recently acclaimed by the magazine *Advertising Age* as the most recognized and effective marketing slogan of the twentieth century. The phrase sends several messages, including (1) a diamond is so durable that it lasts forever, and so should love; (2) diamonds should remain in the family and not be sold; and (3) diamonds retain their value over time. This slogan is aimed at increasing the demand for diamonds and keeping secondhand diamonds, which are good substitutes for new ones, off the market, where they could otherwise increase supply and drive down the price. De Beers came up with the idea of a diamond engagement ring and more recently the "right-hand ring," a diamond worn by a woman as a sign of her independence.

To limit the supply of rough diamonds reaching the market, De Beers would invite about one hundred wholesalers to London, where each was offered a box of uncut diamonds for a set price—no negotiating. If De Beers needed to prop up the price of a certain size and quality of diamond, then few of those diamonds would show up in the boxes, thus limiting their supply. The company's actions violated U.S. antitrust laws (prior to a recent settlement, De Beers executives could have been arrested if they traveled to America). But there were no laws prohibiting U.S. wholesalers from buying from De Beers (as long as those transactions occurred outside U.S. borders).

e activity

At http://www.adiamondisforever.com, you can learn a lot about buying diamonds but nothing about the sponsoring firm—De Beers. For information about the company, check http://www.debeersgroup.com. What are the current prospects for De Beers' grip on the diamond market? De Beers is not standing idly by while Canadian diamonds come into the market. The company has set up operations in Canada. What have they accomplished there thus far? Find out at the De Beers Canada Web site at http://www.debeerscanada.com.

AP Photo/Saurabh Das

A monopoly that relies on the control of a key resource loses market power once that control slips away. In the mid-1990s, De Beers began losing control of some rough diamond supplies. Russian miners were selling half their diamonds to independent dealers. Australia's Argyle mine, now the world's largest, stopped selling to De Beers in 1996. And Yellowknife, a huge Canadian mine, began operations in 1998, but De Beers was guaranteed only about one-third of its output. As a result of all this erosion, De Beers' share of the world's uncut diamond supply slipped from nearly 90 percent in the mid-1980s to about 40 percent in 2010. Worse still for De Beers, newly developed synthetic diamonds are starting to appear on the jewelry market (they already account for 90 percent of industrial diamonds). To counter that threat, De Beers supplies precision equipment to help jewelers spot synthetics.

In a reversal of policy, De Beers has abandoned efforts to control the world diamond supply. In 2006, the company paid $300 million to settle a number of lawsuits charging anticompetitive practices in the United States and Europe. The company also agreed to comply with antitrust laws in the future. De Beers now hopes to become the "supplier of choice" by marketing the De Beers brand of diamonds at its own jewelry stores. De Beers had more than three dozen such stores worldwide as of 2010, including shops in New York and Beverly Hills. (Americans account for only 5 percent of the world's population but for nearly half the world's retail diamond purchases.) In an effort to differentiate its diamonds, De Beers has started etching its "Forevermark" on some stones, a microscopic engraving of authenticity. Some other diamond suppliers are starting to etch their own marks.

Another problem De Beers and other diamond suppliers face was dramatized by the Hollywood movie *Blood Diamond*, starring Leonardo DiCaprio. The terms *blood diamonds* and *conflict diamonds* refer to diamonds sold to fund civil wars that have killed or displaced millions of people in Africa, the source of much of the world's rough diamonds. Some customers are now asking for "conflict-free" diamonds. For its part, De Beers guarantees that its diamonds are "conflict free." Global economic turmoil in 2008 and 2009 also hurt diamond sales. Industrywide, revenue from diamond jewelry sales fell 16 percent in 2009 to $65 billion.

De Beers is an example of the legal and practical difficulties of maintaining a profitable monopoly. Once the company's control over uncut diamonds slipped away, so did its monopoly power. After losing that power, the company had less incentive to pursue its anticompetitive practices.

Sources: Vanessa O'Connell, "Diamond Industry Makeover Sends Fifth Avenue to Africa," *Wall Street Journal*, 26 October 2009; Tina Gooch, "Conflict Diamonds or Illicit Diamonds?" *Natural Resource Journal*, 48 (Winter 2008): 189–214; Robb Stewart, "Will Diamonds Sparkle Again for De Beers?" *Wall Street Journal*, 11 February 2010; and the De Beers home page at http://www.adiamondisforever.com/.

CASE STUDY

Public Policy

The Mail Monopoly The U.S. Post Office was granted a monopoly in 1775 and has operated under federal protection ever since. In 1971, Congress converted the Post Office Department into a semi-independent agency called the U.S. Postal Service, or USPS, which had total revenue of about $70 billion in 2009. Because of the national recession, revenue in 2009 was down 9 percent from 2008 and about the same as in 2006. More than 650,000 employees at 37,000 post offices deliver an average of 177 billion pieces of mail a year to 144 million home and business addresses. This amounts to about 40 percent of the world's total mail delivery. USPS pays no taxes and is exempt from local zoning laws. It has a legal monopoly in delivering regular, first-class letters and has the exclusive right to use the space inside your mailbox. Other delivery services such as FedEx or UPS cannot deliver to mail boxes or post office boxes.

The USPS monopoly has suffered in recent years because of rising costs and growing competition from new technologies. The price of a first-class stamp climbed from 6 cents in 1970 to 44 cents by 2010—a growth rate twice that of inflation. Long-distance phone service, one possible substitute for first-class mail, is much cheaper today than in 1970. New technologies such as email, ecards, online bill-payment, text messaging, and social-networking sites also displace USPS delivery services (email messages now greatly outnumber first-class letters). Because its monopoly applies only to regular first-class mail, USPS has lost chunks of other business to private firms offering lower rates and better service. The United Parcel Service (UPS), for example, is more mechanized and more containerized than the USPS and thus has lower costs and less breakage. The USPS has tried to emulate UPS but with only limited success. After Hurricane Katrina, it took seven months to reopen the USPS processing and distribution center in New Orleans. Rivals UPS, FedEx, and DHL all restored service within three weeks.

When the Postal Service raised third-class ("junk" mail) rates, businesses substituted other forms of advertising, including cable TV, telemarketing, and the Internet. UPS and other rivals now account for most ground-shipped packages. Even USPS's first-class monopoly is being threatened, because FedEx and others have captured 90 percent of the overnight mail business. Thus, USPS is losing business because of competition from overnight mail and from new technologies.

USPS has been fighting back, trying to leverage its monopoly power while increasing efficiency. On the electronic front, USPS tried to offer online postage purchases, online bill-paying service, and online document transmission service. But these new products were scrapped as failures. Changing technology and competition have been eroding USPS's government-granted monopoly. USPS lost about $4 billion in 2009 and said that without drastic changes, losses would total $238 billion over the next decade. Even a legal monopoly can lose money. Proposed changes include postage increases and dropping Saturday delivery.

© Bob Pardue-Lifestyle/Alamy

Sources: Corey Dade, "Post Office Renews Campaign to End Saturday Mail Service," *Wall Street Journal*, 3 March 2010; Liz Robbins, "Postal Service Revives Cutback Plans," *New York Times*, 2 March 2010; "The Trap: The Curse of Long-term Unemployment Will Bedevil the Economy," *The Economist*, 14 January 2010; and the USPS home page at http://www.usps.com.

e activity

How has the U.S. Postal Service dealt with competition and change? A chapter in its online history, at http://www.usps.com, describes the reforms made in the 1990s to compete with for-profit firms and email. What role do forces of competition play in rate setting? Online cost calculators are provided by both USPS at http://postcalc.usps.gov/ and UPS (United Parcel Service) at http://www.ups.com. Try finding the cost of sending a 2-lb. package to Fairbanks, Alaska (or to Miami, Florida, if you're in Alaska!). Which is cheaper—USPS or UPS? Why?

Chapter 10

World of Business

CASE STUDY

e activity

Check Blockbuster's website at http://www.blockbuster.com/. Is the company still operating? If yes, how is Blockbuster differentiating its product? If not, why do you think it shut down? Explain using economic concepts from this chapter.

Fast Forward to Creative Destruction The introduction in the 1970s of videocassette recorders, or VCRs, fueled demand for videotaped movies, which were originally so expensive ($75 to $100) that renting was the only way to go. The first wave of video rental stores required security deposits and imposed membership fees of up to $100. In those early days, most rental stores faced little competition so many outlets earned short-run economic profit. But because entry was relatively easy, this profit attracted competitors. Convenience stores, grocery stores, bookstores, even drugstores began renting videos as a sideline. Between 1982 and 1987, the number of rental outlets *quadrupled*, growing faster than VCR purchases.

Thus, the supply of video rentals increased faster than the demand. The 1990s brought more bad news for the industry, when hundreds of cable channels and pay-per-view options offered close substitutes for video rentals. The greater supply of rental outlets along with the increased availability of substitutes had the predictable effect on market prices. Rental rates crashed to as little as $0.99. Membership fees and tape deposits disappeared. So many outlets gave up on the business that a market developed to buy and resell their tape inventories.

The video rental business grew little during the 1990s. Even after the addition of DVDs and video games, the industry "shakeout" continued. One rental chain, Blockbuster, bought up weaker competitors and eventually accounted for more than a third of the U.S. market, with over 6,000 outlets. But Blockbuster faced its own growing pains, including an "excess inventory" of tapes and a failed effort to sell books, magazines, and snacks at its rental stores.

The latest threats to Blockbuster and other bricks-and-mortar rental stores are (1) on-demand movies delivered by broadband cable, (2) downloads from the Internet, (3) grab-and-go rental kiosks such as Redbox, and (4) online rental services that mail DVDs, such as QwikFliks and Netflix (Netflix offers 100,000 movie titles and mails out 2 million DVDs a day). In other developments, Walmart bought Vudu in 2010 to stream movies over the Internet in high definition using Vudu's compression technology. And Best Buy teamed up with Cinema Now to stream movies online. Other download competition came from Amazon.com's Unbox, Microsoft's Xbox, Apple TV, and Netflix (half of Netflix's 12 million subscribers stream movies).

Technological change has created powerful rivals to the bricks-and-mortar movie rental business. Competition is fierce. Blockbuster announced in 2010 that it planned to close 1,560 of its remaining 3,750 outlets and warned that it may be forced into bankruptcy. As a measure of how far Blockbuster's fortunes have fallen, in 2002 the company stock sold for about $30 per share. By September 2010, the price was less than 10 cents a share. Such is the dynamic nature of a market economy—out with the old and in with the new, in a competitive process that has been aptly called *creative destruction*. This destruction is no fun for producers on the losing end, but consumers benefit from a wider choice and more competitive prices.

Sources: James Jarman, "Video Stores Crippled by Online, Kiosk, Mail Services," *Arizona Republic*, 27 February 2010. Mary Ellen Lloyd, "Blockbuster Considers Bankruptcy Filing," *Wall Street Journal*, 17 March 2010; and Stephen Grocer, "Wal-Mart Pays Up for Vudu. Should It Have Bought NetFlix?," *Wall Street Journal*, 22 February 2010.

CASE STUDY

e activity

Zara is owned by the Intidex Group, one of the world's largest fashion distributors, with over 3,300 stores in 68 countries—and Zara having over 1,000 of them. Visit the Intidex Web site at http://www.inditex.com/en to read about their philosophy and their dimensions of corporate responsibility—including their model of sustainability, and the social, environmental, and economic dimensions of the organization.

World of Business

Timely Fashions Boost Profit for Zara One way a firm can increase market power is to offer a differentiated product. Zara, the largest fashion retailer in Europe, has been described as "possibly the most innovative and devastating retailer in the world." The company makes much of its clothing in its own workshops and factories, including designing, fabric dyeing, tailoring, and ironing. Zara also outsources some manufacturing to select suppliers that have developed the ability to make high-quality garments with the required flexibility and speed.

Zara's network of retail shops and clothing factories communicate through a sophisticated feedback mechanism for gathering market intelligence and putting it to work. Sales associates carry personal digital assistants to relay information on fashion trends and customer demand back to the company's team of 200 designers in Spain. Real-time sales data allow the factory to increase production of items that are selling and to bring out similar designs. Direct shipments from factory to shops also eliminate the need for costly warehouses.

Zara takes as little as two weeks to develop a new item and deliver it to one of its more than 1,000 retail stores. The industry average is six months. The company launches about 10,000 new designs a year, making new items in small batches at first so if something doesn't sell, there is not much left over. But if something catches on, stores can restock in a few days, so Zara doesn't miss out on a fashion wave. Thus, shops never have to wait long for fresh stock or to get an order filled. Whereas traditional stores such as the Gap may get new fashions twice a season, Zara distributes them twice a week. And in perhaps its most unusual of strategies, the company advertises little, relying instead on prime store location and word of mouth.

Digital Vision/Jupiter Images

In short, Zara believes that making most of its own apparel and selectively outsourcing the rest, reduces delays, exploits customer feedback, maintains flexibility, and ensures quality. This steady supply of new clothing lines and continuous supply of popular items help Zara differentiate its products. Amancio Ortega, Zara's founder, opened his first store in 1975. With a personal fortune of $25 billion in 2010, he became the richest person in Spain and the ninth richest on the planet. The market rewards successful innovators.

Sources: Nebahat Tokatli, "Insights from the Global Clothing Industry—The Case of Zara, A Fast Fashion Retailer," *Journal of Economic Geography*, 8 (January 2008): 21–38; Vanessa O'Connell, "How Fashion Makes Its Way from the Runway to the Rack," *Wall Street Journal*, 8 February 2007; "Supply-Chain Management," *The Economist*, 6 April 2009; and "The World's Billionaires," *Forbes*, 11 March 2010.

CHAPTER 11

WORLD OF BUSINESS

CASE STUDY

e activity

The National Association of Home Builders (NAHB) publishes the framing lumber prices for 1,000 board feet from *Random Lengths* and the Chicago Mercantile Exchange (CME) Futures Price each week. For current and historic lumber prices, visit http://www.nahb.org and search for "framing lumber prices." Note how prices change from 2005 through 2009. Why do you think this is so? Examine the CME futures prices. Does the future look better or worse?

Lumber Prices and Housing Markets The demand for lumber, like that for carpenters, is a derived demand—derived from lumber demand in its many uses, particularly housing. When the demand for new housing increases, so does the demand for lumber. For example, as the U.S. economy recovered from the 2001 recession, the demand for housing increased. Housing prices rose. This fueled the demand for lumber, a key resource in residential construction. The demand curve for lumber shifted rightward. Increased demand for housing boosted lumber prices between late 2001 and mid-2004. For example, the price per thousand board feet of framing lumber jumped from $281 in October 2001 to $473 in August 2004, a rise of 68 percent.

But in 2005, the U.S. housing market began to slump, and the slide stretched into 2009. The decline in housing demand reduced the demand for building products, shifting the demand curve for lumber to the left. All this had the expected effect on lumber prices, which fell sharply—for some types of lumber, to levels not seen in a decade. For example, the price per thousand board feet of framing lumber bottomed at $140 in 2009, a 70 percent drop from the high of 2004. As the price of lumber declined, so did lumber's profitability. Lumber mills cut production by 45 percent between 2005 and 2009. Weyerhaeuser Corporation, for example, suspended production indefinitely at two of its mills. Louisiana-Pacific Corporation closed its major mills. But as housing recovered in 2010, so did lumber prices, increasing to about $300 per thousand board feet by March of that year.

The demand for lumber is a prime example of derived demand.

Sources: Liam Pleven and Lester Aldrich, "High Lumber Prices Threaten Housing Market," *Wall Street Journal*, 16 February 2010; Dawn Wotapka, "Builders Get Back in Game," *Wall Street Journal*, 3 March 2010; and "Framing Lumber Prices," National Association of Home Builders, at http://www.nahb.org/generic.aspx?genericContentID=527.

PUBLIC POLICY

CASE STUDY

e activity

The U.S. Department of Labor maintains a Minimum Wage page at http://www.dol.gov/whd/minwage/q-a.htm with questions and answers about the legal aspects of the minimum wage. Also see the link on State Labor Law Topics. A continually updated

...continued

The McMinimum Wage In 2007, Congress and the president passed a law increasing the minimum wage from $5.15 to $7.25 an hour in three steps of 70 cents over two years. At the time, only about 4 percent of all workers earned less than $7.25 an hour. That group included mostly young workers, the majority part time, primarily in service and sales jobs. When the law was passed, 30 states plus the District of Columbia had their own minimum wages exceeding $5.15, with Washington State the highest at $7.93. In addition, more than 100 municipalities across the nation have introduced so-called *living-wage laws* that set minimum wages exceeding federal or state minimums. In Washington, D.C., for example, certain employers must pay at least $11.75 per hour.

Ever since a federal minimum wage of 25 cents was established in 1938, economists have been debating the benefits and costs of the law. The law initially covered only 43 percent of the workforce—primarily workers in large firms involved in interstate

***e* activity continued**

chart can be found at the Employment Policies Institute Web site at: http://www.epionline.org/mw_statistics_annual.cfm. The site also provides links to Questions and Answers about the economic impact of the minimum wage, living wage, and other labor issues. There are also links to several research reports on the impacts of minimum-wage laws. The liberal view can be found at the Economic Policy Institute's Web page on labor markets at http://epinet.org/subjectpages/labor.html.

commerce. Over the years, the minimum wage has been raised and the coverage has been broadened. By 2010, coverage more than doubled to about 90 percent of the workforce (groups still not covered include those working in small retail establishments and in small restaurants).

Advocates of minimum-wage legislation argue that it can increase the income of the poorest workers. Critics claim that it can cause employers either to cut nonwage compensation or to eliminate jobs. Dozens of studies have examined the effects of the minimum wage on employment. A few found a small positive effect on employment, but most found either no effect or a negative effect, particularly for teenage workers. One reason a higher minimum wage may not reduce total employment is that employers often respond by substituting part-time jobs for full-time jobs, by substituting more-qualified minimum-wage workers (such as college students) for less-qualified workers (such as high school dropouts), and by adjusting nonwage components of the job to reduce costs or increase worker productivity.

Here are some nonwage adjustments an employer could impose on workers in response to a higher minimum wage: reduced work hours, less convenient work hours, greater expected work effort, less on-the-job training, less time for meals and breaks, less extra pay for night shifts, fewer paid vacation days, fewer paid holidays, less sick leave, fewer health-care benefits, tighter limits on arriving late for work or leaving early, greater restrictions on personal phone calls or texting, and so on. For example, one researcher found that restaurants responded to a higher minimum wage by reducing vacation time and cutting night-shift premiums. Other researchers found that the imposition of a living-wage ordinance in Los Angeles caused employers to switch from untrained workers to those with formal training.

Of most concern to economists is a possible reduction in on-the-job training of young workers, especially those with little education. A higher minimum wage also raises the opportunity cost of staying in school. According to one study, a higher minimum wage encouraged some 16- to 19-year-olds to quit school and look for work, though many failed to find jobs. Thus, an increase in the minimum wage may have the unintended consequence of cutting school enrollment. And those who had already dropped out were more likely to become unemployed. By December 2009, more than half of African American males in their teens who wanted to work could not find jobs.

© Jim West/Alamy

A survey of 193 labor economists found that 87 percent believed "a minimum wage increases unemployment among young and unskilled workers." Minimum-wage increases, however, have broad public support. In one poll, the highest support, 81 percent, came from those aged 18 to 29, the group most likely to be affected by a hike in the minimum wage.

Sources: David Fairris and Leon Bujanda, "The Dissipation of Minimum Wage Gains for Workers Through Labor-Labor Substitution: Evidence from the Los Angeles Living Wage Ordinance," *Southern Economic Journal*, 75 (October 2008): 473–96; Robert Whaples, "Is There Consensus Among American Labor Economists?" *Journal of Labor Research* 27 (Fall 1996): 725–734; William Alpert, *The Minimum Wage in the Restaurant Industry* (Praeger, 1986); "Lost Wages of Youth," *Wall Street Journal*, 5 March 2010; and Joseph Sabia, "Identifying Minimum Wage Effects," *Industrial Relations*, 48 (April 2009): 311–328.

CHAPTER 12

WORLD OF BUSINESS

CASE STUDY

Winner-Take-All Labor Markets Each year *Forbes* magazine lists the multimillion-dollar earnings of top entertainers and professional athletes. Oprah Winfrey has made that list each year for more than two decades. Her annual income adds up. With wealth now in the billions, she ranks among the world's richest people. Entertainment and pro sports have come to be called **winner-take-all labor markets** because a few key people critical to the overall success of an enterprise are richly rewarded. For example, the credits at the end of a movie list a hundred or more people directly involved in the production. Hundreds, sometimes thousands, more work behind the scenes. Despite a huge cast and crew, the difference between a movie's financial success and failure usually depends on the performance of just a few critical people—the screenwriter, the director, and the lead actors. The same happens in sports. In professional golf tournaments, attendance and TV ratings are significantly higher with Tiger Woods in the mix. In professional basketball, LeBron James has been credited with filling once-empty seats and boosting the value of his team by $160 million. Thus, top performers generate a high marginal revenue product.

But high productivity alone is not enough to get paid a lot. To be paid anywhere near their marginal revenue product, there must be an open competition for top performers. This bids up pay, such as the $20 million per movie garnered by top stars—about 2,000 times the average annual acting earnings of Screen Actors Guild members. Simon Cowell reportedly earned $36 million judging *American Idol* in his final contract year; he was expected to leave that show to develop a new one that could earn him twice as much. In professional sports, before the free-agency rule was introduced (which allows players to seek the highest bidder), top players couldn't move on their own from team to team. They were stuck with the team that drafted them, earning only a fraction of their marginal revenue product.

Relatively high pay in entertainment and sports is not new. What is new is the spread of winner-take-all to other U.S. markets. The "star" treatment now extends to such fields as management, law, banking, finance, even academia. Consider, for example, corporate pay. In 1980, the chief executive officers (CEOs) of the 200 largest U.S. corporations earned about 42 times more than the average production worker. Now, this multiple tops 200. Comparable multiples are much lower in Germany and Japan. Why the big U.S. jump?

First, the U.S. economy has grown sharply in recent decades and is by far the largest in the world—with the value of total output equaling that of the next three economies combined. So U.S. businesses serve a wider market, making the CEO potentially more productive and more valuable. Second, breakthroughs in communications, production, and transportation mean that a well-run U.S. company can now usually sell a valued product around the world. Third, wider competition for the top people has increased their pay. For example, in the 1970s, U.S. businesses usually hired CEOs from company ranks, promoting mainly from within (a practice still common today in Germany and Japan). Because other firms were not trying to bid away the most talented executives, companies were able to retain them for just a fraction of the pay that now prevails in a more competitive market. Today top executives are often drawn from outside the firm—even

e activity

For current news stories about executive compensation, visit *Forbes* magazine's subsection about trends in this area at http://www.forbes.com/. Then search on "Special Report: CEO Compensation." What is the latest explanation for the pay differential? Who are the highest-paid CEOs? For a union's view on executive pay, go to http://www.aflcio.org/corporatewatch/paywatch/ and check the trends on executive pay. Do stock compensation for executives improve executives' performance?

winner-take-all labor markets

Markets in which a few key employees critical to the overall success of an enterprise are richly rewarded

outside the industry and the country. Fourth, although CEO pay has increased more than sixfold on average since 1980, so has the stock market value of the corporations they run. Fifth, a study of 732 firms in the United States, France, Germany, and the United Kingdom found that U.S. firms on average are more efficient than those in the other countries. One final reason why top CEO pay has increased in America is that high salaries are more socially acceptable here than they once were. High pay is still frowned on in some countries, such as Japan and Germany.

Some top executives are no doubt paid more than they are worth, but nobody claims the market for resources works perfectly. The claim is that an open competition for resources will tend to offer the most to those resources contributing the most. And in those cases where marginal productivity is huge, so is the pay.

Sources: Nicholas Bloom and John Van Reenan, "Measuring and Explaining Management Practices Across Firms and Countries," *Quarterly Journal of Economics*, 122 (November 2007): 1351–1408. Bill Livingston, "LeBron," *Cleveland Plain Dealer*, 6 May 2007; "Paula Abdul Stays Focussed on Her Craft," *The Los Angeles Times*, 5 May 2009. Urs Fischbacher and Christian Thoni, "Winner Take All Markets Are Inefficient," *Journal of Economic Behavior and Organization*," 67 (July 2008): 150–163; Xavier Gabaix and Augustin Landier, "Why Has CEO Pay Increased So Much," *Quarterly Journal of Economics*, 123 (February 2008): 49–100. *Economic Report of the President*, February 2010, at http://www.gpoaccess.gov/eop/.

CASE STUDY

e activity

Visit the United Auto Workers at http://www.uaw.org/ to view their history and newsfeed. If you select Where We Work, you will find a list of industries in which the UAW represents workers. Is the UAW a craft union, an industrial union, or some combination of the two?

Public Policy

Federal Bailout of GM, Chrysler, and the UAW In the 1970s, the United Auto Workers (UAW) negotiated what have been called "gold-plated benefits" for their workers and retirees. General Motors, Ford, and Chrysler, the so-called Big Three, believed that because they dominated the U.S. auto market and because they all faced the same labor costs, any higher costs could simply be passed along to car buyers. What could go wrong? Well, what went wrong was an onslaught of fierce competition from foreign automakers who would develop a reputation for high quality at competitive prices. These foreign automakers also began building plants in the United States operated by mostly nonunion workers. Pay and benefits for these nonunion workers, while still attractive, amounted to about three quarters of what UAW workers were getting (and UAW pay was double what average Americans earned).

Not only were UAW wages higher, but union work rules—some 5,000 pages detailing what each worker could and could not be asked to do—imposed expensive inefficiencies on production. If work rules were violated, a union representative could shut down the assembly line. General Motors, Ford, and Chrysler, were making costly vehicles that not enough people wanted to buy, and the companies were losing money by the truckload. GM, for example, lost over $60 billion between 2005 and 2008. Hard hit by fallout from the global financial crisis of 2008 and facing bankruptcy, the Big Three turned to the federal government for help. After some UAW pressure and political wrangling, federal officials agreed on a bailout of about $85 billion, with most of that going to GM (Ford ultimately decided not to accept federal aid).

Images by © Chris Rank/Corbis

The agreement called for GM and Chrysler to file for bankruptcy. By doing so, both companies were able to walk away from huge debt burdens built up from years of making costly products that didn't sell well enough. Those who had owned the companies, the stockholders, got wiped out in the bankruptcy—they got nothing. Bondholders and other creditors also took a beating—they would get back less than a third of what they had lent the automakers. Some suppliers were also left hanging and many dealerships were shut down. The group that benefited most from the bailout was UAW workers. They ended up owning 10 percent of the new GM and a majority of the new Chrysler. In years leading up to the bailout, many workers had taken buyouts, meaning that the company paid them a chunk of money to leave their jobs. The union also made some concessions, but mostly on the pay and benefits of workers hired in the future. Existing workers gave up little in the bailout agreement—certainly little compared to the drubbing suffered by company stockholders, creditors, suppliers, and car dealers.

The new GM emerged from bankruptcy with the federal government owning 61 percent in return for its $43 billion "investment." Much of the federal bailout money would be used to buy out existing workers and shore up the health care fund for union retirees. The Big Three are hoping to hire new workers at lower wages, but recently-laid-off workers still have first claim on any job openings, and they must be rehired at their previous high wages, not the lower wages to be paid new workers.

The Congressional Budget Office estimated that the government bailout would ultimately cost taxpayers $34 billion. That translates into $300 per U.S. household to support the pay and benefits of those making twice what average American workers earn. We can't necessarily blame the UAW for the demise of the American auto industry. Demanding higher pay, better benefits, and more restrictive work rules sounds like the job description of union representatives. But we can blame the managements for going along with these demands. Top auto executives lost their jobs in the bankruptcy. UAW workers gave up little in the bankruptcy.

In today's competitive marketplace, only an efficient, flexible work force will thrive. Technology advances too rapidly to drag along wages that exceed the market rate and featherbedding work rules that slow down production.

Sources: David Leonhardt, "$73 an Hour: Adding It Up," *New York Times*, 10 December 2008; Jonathan Welsh, "General Motors Says It Repaid Bailout. Not True, Says Watchdog Group," *Wall Street Journal*, 4 May 2010; Nick Bunkley, "Progress for Automakers After Losses," *New York Times*, 21 April 2010; and Bill Koenig, "Unions Resist Yielding More as GM, Ford, Chrysler Seek Aid," *Bloomberg*, 12 November 2009.

Chapter 13

The Information Economy

CASE STUDY

e activity

Wired News covers events in business and technology with daily updates at http://www.wired.com/, including many stories about conflicts over copyright. What are some of the current issues in protecting intellectual property rights that appear in the headlines? Do a search for "intellectual property" on the *Wired* site.

The Value of a Good Idea—Intellectual Property One potentially valuable capital resource is information, or so-called **intellectual property**, which is any intangible asset created by human knowledge and ideas. Intellectual property is costly to produce, but, once produced, it can be supplied at low cost. For example, the first copy of a new Windows operating system may cost Microsoft over $1 billion to develop, but each additional copy can be streamed over the Internet for virtually nothing. As soon as Microsoft sells a copy, that first customer becomes a potential supplier of that product.

Because of this special supply characteristic, the original producer often has difficulty controlling the distribution and may have trouble getting paid. To help with these problems, the U.S. Constitution granted Congress the power "to promote the Progress of Science and useful Arts, by securing for limited Times to Authors and Inventors the exclusive Right to use their respective Writings and Discoveries." This

AP Photo/EyePress

intellectual property
An intangible asset created by human knowledge and ideas

was the only "Right" spelled out in the U.S. Constitution as initially ratified by the states (the Bill of Rights, the first ten amendments to the Constitution, was ratified later). Originators are thereby better able to benefit from their creations. A *patent* establishes property rights to an invention or other technical advances. A *copyright* confers property rights to an original expression of an author, artist, composer, or computer programmer. And a *trademark* establishes property rights in unique commercial marks and symbols, such as McDonald's golden arches, Nike's swoosh, or Apple's apple with a bite out of it.

Granting property rights is one thing; enforcing them is another. (Do you have any pirated software, music, or DVDs?) Much of the software, music CDs, and DVDs sold around the world, particularly in Indonesia, Zimbabwe, Vietnam, China, India, and Russia, are pirated editions of products developed in the United States. For example, Windows 7, which retails for about $320 in the United States, was available in China in pirated form for as little as $3 even before its U.S. release date. Worldwide more than 40 percent of all software in use is pirated. The ready availability of pirated software stunts development of a homegrown software industry in countries where piracy thrives. And some movies are available on the black market as DVDs even before they open in U.S. theaters.

Enforcing property rights is costly, and this diminishes the incentive to create new products and new ideas. For example, in May 2010 makers of *The Hurt Locker*, the 2010 Oscar winner for best picture, filed copyright suits against 5,000 IP addresses that downloaded pirated copies of the movie. And the U.S. Copyright Group sued about 50,000 illegal downloaders of a dozen other movies. Pirated videos, music, computer games, and software bring no royalties to the artists, no wages to industry workers, no income to the producers or programmers, and no taxes to the government. Even within the United States, the music industry has been devastated by the ease with which music can be shared online. CD sales in 2010 were only half that of a decade earlier. Sharing music files is not a victimless crime: between 2000 and 2010, for example, more than one-fourth of music industry workers lost their jobs as sales declined. Most musicians now earn more from touring than from record sales.

Intellectual property is an intangible asset that fuels the digital economy. How society nurtures incentives to create new ideas, inventions, and artistic creations will affect economic development around the globe.

Sources: Jeff Leeds, "Plunge in CD Sales Shakes Up Big Labels," *New York Times*, 28 May 2007; Joel Mokyr, "Intellectual Property Rights, the Industrial Revolution, and the Beginning of Modern Economic Growth," *American Economic Review*, 99 (May 2009): 349–355. "Software Pirates in China Beat Microsoft to the Punch," Reuters, 18 October 2009; the World Intellectual Property Organization at http://www.wipo.int/; and Greg Sandoval, "*Hurt Locker* Downloaders, You've Been Sued," *CNET News*, 28 May 2010 at http://news.cnet.com/8301-31001_3-20006314-261.html.

Bringing Theory to Life

The Million-Dollar Lottery? Since 1963, when New Hampshire introduced the first modern state-run lottery, 43 states and the District of Columbia have followed suit, generating profits of about $20 billion a year. Publicity photos usually show the winner receiving an oversized check in the millions. But winners get paid in annual installments, so the present value of the prize is much less than advertised. For example, a million-dollar prizewinner usually gets $33,333 a year for 30 years. To put this in perspective, keep in mind that at an interest rate of 8 percent, the $33,333 received in the 30th year has a present value of only $3,313. If today you deposited $3,313 in an account earning 8 percent interest, you would wind up with $33,333 in 30 years (if we ignore taxes).

If the interest rate is 8 percent, the present value of a $33,333 annuity for the next 30 years is $375,256. Thus, the present value is much less than half of the promised million, which is why lottery officials pay in installments. Incidentally, we might consider the present value of receiving $33,333 a year forever. Using the formula for an annuity discussed earlier, the present value with an interest rate of 8 percent is $33,333/0.08 = $416,662. Because the present value of receiving $33,333 for 30 years is $375,256, continuing the $33,333 annual payment *forever* adds only $41,406 to the present value.

In most states, lottery winners have a choice of getting annual installments or taking a lump sum right away. For example, a $258 million Powerball winner in 2010 had a choice of getting 30 annual installments of $8.6 million each or taking a lump-sum payout of $125 million. The lump sum was less than half the advertised jackpot, and the implied discount rate was about 6 percent. After state and federal income taxes, the lump sum reduced to about $67 million—no question, still an awesome amount but only 26 percent of the headline prize of $258 million.

Among all the types of legal gambling, state lotteries offer the smallest payout—only about $0.55 of each dollar wagered goes to winners. Still, some people apparently view lotteries as good bets, especially the 5 percent of the population that buys half of all lottery tickets sold. To strengthen the state's monopoly grip over lotteries, private and foreign lotteries are outlawed in the United States. The value of one state's lottery monopoly was underscored when the governor of Texas proposed selling that state's lottery to a private firm—for $14 billion.

COREY LOWENSTEIN/MCT/Landov

Sources: "Missouri Store Clerk Wins $258 Million Powerball Jackpot," Associated Press, 22 April 2010; and an index of lottery sites found at http://www.state.wv.us/lottery/links.htm.

Case Study

e activity

Virginia has two big cash prize lotteries: Mega Millions and Lotto South. Winners in either can get a lump sum or payments over time. Visit the Web site at http://www.valottery.com to find out how each works. Note that the prizes are not awarded similarly. How is the value of the jackpot determined in each case? What interest rate is used?

Chapter 14

CASE STUDY

e activity

McDonald's maintains a Web site devoted to information about obtaining a U.S. franchise at http://www.aboutmcdonalds.com/mcd/franchising/us_franchising.html. Look over the FAQ file. How much cash does a potential franchisee currently need to qualify? How many partners can be involved in a franchise? Who selects the sites and who constructs the building?

World of Business

Reputation of a Big Mac McDonald's has 32,000 restaurants in more than 120 countries and employs more than a million people. The secret to their success is that customers around the world can count on product consistency whether in Phoenix, Anchorage, Moscow, or Hong Kong. *McDonald's has grown because it has attracted competent and reliable franchise owners and has provided them with appropriate incentives and constraints to offer a product of consistent quality.*

To avoid adverse selection, McDonald's seldom advertises for franchisees yet still has plenty of applicants. Even to be granted an interview, an applicant must show substantial financial resources and good business experience. An applicant who passes the initial screening must come up with a security deposit and complete the nine-month full-time training program. A franchise costs anywhere from $950,000 to $1,800,000, depending on the size and location, plus an opening fee of $45,000. Of that amount, the new franchisee must have "non-borrowed personal resources," of at least $500,000 in cash; this money can't come from friends or relatives. In effect, the applicant must have saved this amount or own assets such as property or stock that could be sold to raise the cash. Those with more savings have an edge in the selection process. McDonald's uses personal wealth as a signal of the individual's business sense and ability to manage money. The rest can be borrowed from a bank but must be paid back in no more than seven years. McDonald's is using the bank's loan officers to screen the applicant's creditworthiness. During the training period, the applicant is paid nothing, not even expenses. Some who complete training are rejected for a franchise. Once the restaurant opens, a franchisee must work full time. McDonald's does not offer franchises to partnerships or to groups of investors.

Thus, the franchisee has a deep financial stake in the success of the operation. As a further incentive, successful owners may get additional restaurants. If all goes well, the franchise is valid for 20 years and renewable after that, but it can be canceled at any time if the restaurant fails the company's standards of quality, pricing, cleanliness, hours of operation, and so on. The franchisee is bound to the company by highly specific investments of money and human capital, such as the time invested learning McDonald's operating system. The loss of a franchise would represent a huge financial blow. Through its franchise policies, McDonald's is trying to protect its most valuable asset—its reputation for "quality, service, cleanliness, and value." The golden arches are the second most recognized corporate symbol in the world (the stylized lettering of Coca-Cola ranks first). In selecting and monitoring franchisees, McDonald's has successfully addressed problems stemming from hidden characteristics and hidden actions.

McDonalds/Feature Photo Service/Newscom

Sources: Andrew Martin, "At McDonald's the Happiest Meal Is Hot Profits," *New York Times*, 10 January 2009; Esther Fung, "McDonald's to Double Restaurants in China," *Wall Street Journal*, 29 March 2010; D. L. Noren, "The Economics of the Golden Arches," *American Economist*, 34 (Fall 1990): 60–64; and "McDonald's Corporate Franchising" at http://www.aboutmcdonalds.com/mcd/franchising/us_franchising.html.

Behavioral Economics

Self-Control: Just Don't Do It! In the late 1960s, Walter Mischel, a psychologist at Stanford University, conducted an experiment to measure the self-control of children at a campus nursery school. A child was ushered into a small room and invited to choose a treat from a tray of marshmallows, cookies, and pretzel sticks. The child was then seated at a small table with the treat on a plate and made an offer: The child could eat the selected treat anytime, but a child who could wait 15 minutes before eating it would be rewarded with another of that same treat. After explaining the deal, the researcher left the room. These experiments were conducted with hundreds of children over several years. Films of the experiment show how each child struggled to delay gratification. Most held out no more than three minutes before eating the treat, but about 30 percent got the second treat by holding out the 15 minutes.

About a dozen years later, Professor Mischel surveyed the parents, teachers, and academic advisors of students involved in the experiment. He found that the children who were able to wait longer at age 4 or 5 grew into adolescents who were described as more academically and socially competent, more attentive, better planners, and more able to deal with frustration and stress. He and his colleagues continued to track these subjects into their late thirties and found that those who couldn't wait as children had a significantly higher body-mass index as adults and were more likely to have encountered problems with drug addiction.

A different experiment looking at the relationship between self-control and academic performance among 164 eighth-graders found that the ability to delay gratification—students were given a choice between a dollar right away or $2 the following week—was much more powerful at predicting academic performance than was I.Q. For decades, researchers viewed intelligence as a key variable in predicting success in life. But many researchers now believe that intelligence is at the mercy of self-control. After all, to succeed, even the smartest students still need to do their assignments.

What has come to be called "the marshmallow test" is a microcosm of many willpower issues, from watching TV instead of studying for a final exam to spending impulsively now rather than saving for something that really matters. From morning weigh-ins to New Year's resolutions, we all use devices to help boost our willpower. More generally, market and nonmarket solutions have evolved to help people overcome self-control problems. People who want to study more, save more, exercise more, quit smoking, lose weight, quit drinking, shop less impulsively, get off drugs, or stop gambling are often willing to pay time and money for help, as with tutors and enforced study hours, payroll-savings plans and excessive tax withholding (to ensure a refund later), fitness trainers and club memberships, nicotine gum and patches, diet plans and weight-loss surgery, Alcoholics Anonymous, Shopaholics Anonymous, rehab treatment, and Gamblers Anonymous. Some casinos allow problem gamblers to ban themselves from the premises; they will be turned away if they show up and can be denied any winnings if they do manage to gamble and win.

To pursue long-term goals, people must be able to postpone at least some immediate gratification. More economists are now looking at willpower issues. For example, Dean Karlan, a Yale economist, has developed a Web site at www. stickk.com to help people stick to their goals.

Sources: Walter Mischel et al., "The Nature of Adolescent Competencies Predicted by Preschool Delay of Gratification," *Journal of Personal and Social Psychology*, 54 (Winter 1988): 687–696; Angela Duckworth and Martin Seligman, "Self-Discipline Outdoes I.Q. in Predicting Academic Performance in Adolescents," *Psychological Science*, 16 (December 2005): 939–944; Tabea Bucher-Koenen and Carsten Schmidt, "Instant Gratification and Self-Control in Experiments with Children and Teenagers," American Economic Association Meetings, 5 January 2010; and Lex Borghans, Angela Duckworth, and James Heckman, "The Economics and Psychology of Personality Traits," *Journal of Human Resources*, 43 (Fall 2008): 972–1059.

CASE STUDY

e activity

Learn more about improving willpower from Alcoholics Anonymous (http://www.aa.org), Shopaholics Anonymous (http://www.shopaholicsanonymous.org), or Gamblers Anonymous (http://www.gamblersanonymous.org).

CHAPTER 15

CASE STUDY

e activity

The concerns of airline pilots about employment security and getting what they see as their fair share of industry revenues are presented through the Air Line Pilots' Association Web site at http://www.alpa.org/. What particular issues are of current concern to the pilots? A Report to Congressional Committees at the Government Accounting Office Web site—http://www.gao.gov/new.items/d06630.pdf—indicates that re-regulating the airline industry could reverse the consumer benefits of deregulation and would not necessarily save airline pensions. Read this report from the point of view of a pilot.

PUBLIC POLICY

Airline Regulation and Deregulation The Civil Aeronautics Board (CAB), established in 1938, once tightly regulated interstate airlines. Anyone trying to enter a particular airline market first had to persuade the CAB that the route needed another airline. During the 40 years prior to deregulation, potential entrants submitted more than 150 applications for long-distance routes, *but not a single new interstate airline was authorized*. The CAB also enforced strict compliance with regulated prices. In effect, the CAB created a cartel that fixed prices among the 10 major airlines and blocked new entry. Airlines reflected the capture theory of regulation.

Regulation insulated the industry from price competition, allowing labor unions to secure higher wages than they could in a more competitive setting. Working less than two weeks a month, airline pilots in 1978 earned more than $325,000 a year on average (in today's dollars). Some had so much free time they pursued second careers at the same time. The CAB had no regulatory power over airlines that flew only *intrastate* routes—flights between Los Angeles and San Francisco, for instance. Fares on intrastate airlines were only half those on identical routes flown by regulated airlines (Southwest Airlines sharpened its competitive skills as an intrastate operator in Texas).

Despite opposition from the existing airlines and labor unions, Congress deregulated airlines in 1978, thereby allowing price competition and new entry. Airfares in inflation-adjusted dollars are now more than one-quarter below regulated prices. Competition helps keep airfares lower. The airlines could also afford to lower fares because they became more efficient by filling a greater percentage of seats.

Deregulation in the United States spurred deregulation abroad. For example, after flights between Dublin and London were deregulated in 1986, that became the busiest international route in Europe, jumping from 2 million passengers a year before deregulation to 72 million passengers a year most recently.

Critics of deregulation worried that quality and safety would deteriorate. But the Federal Aviation Administration still regulates quality and safety. Since deregulation, accident rates have declined by anywhere from 10 to 45 percent, depending on the specific measure used (worldwide, donkeys and mules kill more people than plane crashes). Also, because of lower fares, more people fly rather than drive (air passenger miles have tripled), thereby saving thousands of lives that would have been lost driving (per passenger mile, flying is about 20 times safer than driving). Researchers found that during the three months following the 9/11 attacks, people drove more and flew less, resulting in about one thousand more driving deaths.

Some air passengers complain that service has declined in recent years, but that's because most people seem to prefer the lower fares of no-frills airlines. Most consumers view air travel as a commodity, and consider airlines as interchangeable. Thus, consumers seek the lowest fare. Low-cost, no-frills carriers such as Southwest Airlines and JetBlue are grabbing market share and forcing down fares wherever they fly. Competition is fierce. And even where they don't yet fly, just the threat of entry by the likes of Southwest Airlines reduces fares in that market. Many airlines have merged, disappeared, or gone bankrupt. Even with baggage fees and other new charges, major airlines still lost a total of $30 billion between 2005 and 2010. This has pushed down wages in the

Photo by George Frey/Getty Images

industry, making airline jobs across the board less attractive than during the regulated era. For example, pilot pay for major airlines now starts at about $40,000 per year, and the top pay in inflation-adjusted dollars is only half what it was prior to deregulation. Pay at regional airlines is even lower. But, on the whole, deregulation has benefited consumers by lowering fares, increasing the number of flights, and saving lives.

Sources: Austan Goolsbee and Chad Syverson, "How Do Incumbents Respond to Threats of Entry? Evidence from Major Airlines," *Quarterly Journal of Economics*, 123 (November 2008): 1611–1633; Sean Barrett, "Exporting Deregulation: Alfred Kahn and the Celtic Tiger," *Review of Network Economics*, 7 (December 2008): 573–602; Mike Esterl and Susan Carey, "Pressure Will Rise for Other Mergers," *Wall Street Journal*, 3 May 2010; Garrick Blalock et al., "Driving Fatalities After 9/11: A Hidden Cost of Terrorism," *Applied Economics*, 42 (Issue 14, 2009): 1717–1729; and Scott McCartney, "Pilot Pay: Want to Know How Much Your Captain Earns?" *Wall Street Journal*, 16 June 2009.

PUBLIC POLICY

CASE STUDY

Microsoft on Trial The U.S. Justice Department and 20 state attorneys general filed lawsuits in 1998 alleging that Microsoft tried to protect its operating-system monopoly and to extend that monopoly into Internet software. Windows software operated 90 percent of the nation's computers. The government charged that Microsoft's integration of its browser, Internet Explorer, into Windows 98 was not, as the company claimed, solely to make life easier for customers, but was aimed at boosting Explorer's market share. Government officials wanted Windows customers to have a choice of browsers. Microsoft disputed the charges and said the government was interfering with its right to create new products that benefit consumers.

The government argued during the trial that Microsoft engaged in predatory practices aimed at winning the browser war and harming competitors. The government, by focusing on why Microsoft did what it did and the impact on competition, was using a rule-of-reason approach. Microsoft, for its part, characterized itself as an aggressive but legal player in a fiercely competitive industry. Microsoft's lawyers said that the company would not hold such a huge market share if it failed to improve quality and value with each new version. They argued that the high market share "does not begin to reflect the intense competitive dynamic in the software industry." Even such a market share, they said, was "susceptible to rapid deterioration should the market leader fail to innovate at a rapid and competitive pace."

After 78 days of testimony and months of deliberation, the judge ruled that Microsoft maintained a monopoly in operating-system software by anticompetitive means and attempted to monopolize the browser market by unlawfully "tying" Internet Explorer with Windows. Microsoft appealed the ruling but eventually reached an out-of-court settlement with the Justice Department and with most of the state attorneys general. The settlement gave personal-computer makers greater freedom to install non-Microsoft software on new machines. It also banned retaliation against companies that take advantage of these freedoms, prohibited exclusive contracts, and required Microsoft to disclose design information to hardware and software makers so they can build competing products that run smoothly with Windows. The court approved this settlement. It was not until 2009, eleven years after the lawsuits began, that Microsoft had settled suits with all states and the District of Columbia.

Across the Atlantic, Microsoft had to defend itself against antitrust charges brought by the European Union. After years of litigation and fines topping a billion dollars, the company settled most charges there by 2010. Windows software still operates 90 percent of the world's computers, and Microsoft remains a powerful company, with

e activity

The New York Times maintains an archive of its articles about the lawsuit at http://www.nytimes.com/library/tech/reference/index-microsoft.html, and Microsoft maintains its own archive of articles at its Microsoft Legal News Center Web site at http://www.microsoft.com/presspass/legal/default.mspx. After the domestic suit was resolved came the European Union's antitrust suit. ITPRO in the UK provides a timeline of Microsoft's EU antitrust activities at http://www.itpro.co.uk/applications/news/125084/microsofts-eu-antitrust-timeline.html. The EU came to its decision in September 2007, largely rejecting the company's appeal of the landmark March 2004 antitrust ruling (http://blog.seattlepi.nwsource.com/microsoft/archives/121932.asp).

© George Frey/epa/Corbis

a stock market value of about $225 billion in May 2010. But when the U.S. antitrust suits were filed in 1998, Microsoft had a market value six times that of Apple. In May 2010, however, Apple topped Microsoft to become the most valuable technology company in the world. And Google, which in 1998 was still six years away from becoming a publicly traded company, was by May 2010 worth two-thirds as much as Microsoft. While Microsoft officials were tied down for more than a decade by antitrust suits here and abroad, the technology world changed around them. Antitrust scrutiny has now shifted to Apple and to Google, especially Apple's requirements for developing iPhone and iPad applications and Google's decisions about which search results to show first.

Sources: Thomas Catan and Yukari Kane, "Apple Draws Scrutiny from Regulators," *Wall Street Journal*, 4 May 2010; Miguel Helft, "Justice Dept. Criticizes Latest Google Book Deal," *New York Times*, 5 May 2010; R. Jai Krishna et al., "Ballmer Dismisses Microsoft Value Issue," *Wall Street Journal*, 27 May 2010; and Brad Stone, "Sure It's Big. But Is That Bad?," *New York Times*, 21 May 2010.

Chapter 16

CASE STUDY

e activity

Read an overview of the 2008 Farm Bill at http://www.ers.usda.gov/FarmBill/2008/Overview.htm. This site is hosted by the Economic Research Service (ERS) of the U.S. Department of Agriculture. Among many other resources, the ERS provides information about and analysis of the farm economy at http://www.ers.usda.gov/Browse/view.aspx?subject=FarmEconomy.

Public Policy

Farm Subsidies The Agricultural Marketing Agreement Act became law in 1937 to prevent what was viewed as "ruinous competition" among farmers. At the time, one in four Americans lived on a farm. In the years since, the government introduced a variety of policies that set floor prices for a wide range of farm products. Now, only one in fifty Americans lives on a farm, but this program is still with us. Subsidies in the 2008 Farm Act cost U.S. taxpayers $15.4 billion in 2009. Worse still, the U.S. government often sells surplus crops overseas for lower prices. That sounds altruistic, but U.S. exports put some poor farmers around the world out of business. U.S. farm subsidies continue to be a sticking point in negotiating freer international trade agreements.

Let's see how price supports have worked in the dairy industry, using a simplified example. Exhibit 1 presents the market for milk. Without government intervention, suppose the market price of milk would average $1.50 per gallon for a market quantity of 100 million gallons per month. In long-run equilibrium, dairy farmers would earn a normal profit in this competitive industry. Consumer surplus is shown by the blue-shaded area. Recall that consumer surplus is the difference between the most that consumers would be willing to pay for that quantity and the amount they actually pay.

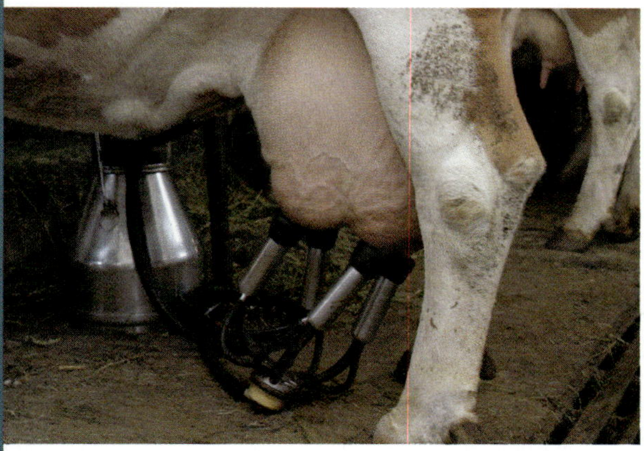

©iStockphoto.com/kickers

Now suppose the dairy lobby persuades Congress that milk should not sell for less than $2.50 per gallon. The higher price encourages farmers to increase their quantity supplied to 150 million gallons. Consumers, however, reduce their quantity demanded to 75 million gallons. To make the floor price of $2.50 stick, the government every month must buy the 75 million gallons of surplus milk generated by the floor price or somehow get dairy farmers to cut output to only 75 million gallons per month. For

EXHIBIT 1 Effects of Milk Price Supports

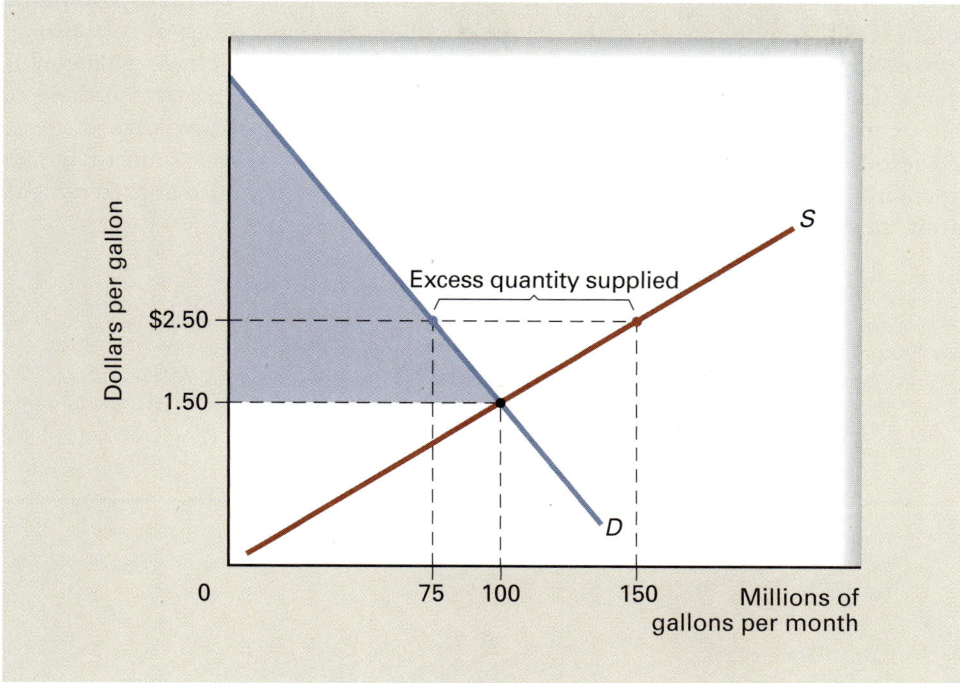

In the absence of government intervention in this simplified example, the market price of milk is $1.50 per gallon, and 100 million gallons are sold per month. If government establishes a floor price of $2.50 per gallon, then the quantity supplied increases and the quantity demanded decreases. To maintain the higher price, the government must buy the excess quantity supplied at $2.50 per gallon or must otherwise pay farmers to limit their quantity supplied to only 75 million gallons a month.

example, to reduce supply, the government spent about $1 billion on milk products in 2009 under one federal program.

Consumers end up paying dearly to subsidize farmers. First, the price consumers pay increases, in this example by $1 per gallon. Second, as taxpayers, consumers must also pay for the surplus milk or otherwise pay farmers not to produce that milk. So consumers pay $2.50 for each gallon they buy on the market and pay another $2.50 in higher taxes for each surplus gallon the government must buy. Instead of paying a free-market price of just $1.50 for each gallon consumed, the typical consumer-taxpayer in effect pays $5.00 for each gallon actually consumed.

How do farmers make out? Each receives an extra $1 per gallon in revenue compared to the free-market price. As farmers increase their quantity supplied in response to the higher price, however, their marginal cost of production increases. At the margin, the higher price just offsets the higher marginal cost of production. The government subsidy also bids up the price of specialized resources, such as cows and especially pasture land. Anyone who owned these resources when the subsidy was introduced would benefit. Farmers who purchased them after that (and, hence, after resource prices increased) earn only a normal rate of return on their investment. Because farm subsidies were originally introduced more than half a century ago, most farmers today earn just a normal return on their investment, despite the billions spent annually on subsidies.

If the extra $1 per gallon that farmers receive for milk were pure profit, farm profit would increase by $150 million per month under the government program. But total outlays by consumer-taxpayers jumped from $150 million per month for 100 million gallons to $375 million per month for just 75 million gallons. Thus, cost to consumer-taxpayers increases by $225 million, though they drink 25 million fewer gallons. Like other special-interest legislation, farm subsidies have a negative impact on the economy, as the losses outweigh the gains. The real winners are those who owned specialized resources when the subsidy was first introduced. Young farmers must pay more to get into a position to reap the subsidies. Ironically, subsidies aimed at preserving the family farm raise the costs of farming.

Sources: Barratt Kirwan, "The Incidence of U.S. Agricultural Subsidies on Farmland Rental Rates," *Journal of Political Economies*, 117 (February 2009): 138–164; Ani Katchova, "A Comparison of Economic Well-Being of Farm and Nonfarm Households," *American Journal of Agricultural Economics*, 90 (August 2008): 733–747; Bill Egbert, "Councilman Eric Gioia Having a Cow Over Milk Prices: $6 A Gallon Is Too High, He Says," *New York Daily News*, 5 July 2009; Calitza Jimenez, "USDA Pulls Plug on Some Farm Subsidy Data," Center for Public Integrity, 21 May 2010, at http://www.publicintegrity.org/data_mine/entry/2100/; and Joseph Glauber, "Statement Before the Senate Judiciary Committee," 19 September 2009, at http://www.usda.gov/oce/newsroom/archives/testimony/2009/VermontDairy.pdf.

CASE STUDY

e activity

Common Cause, a nonpartisan lobbying group promoting accountable government, tracks the role of money in politics at http://www.commoncause.org/moneyinpolitics. Read the report on campaign finance reform or click on the link to learn more about ending pay-to-play. In January 2010, the Supreme Court decided Citizens United v. Federal Election Commission, which affects political spending by corporations and unions. Read an analysis at http://www.scotuswiki.com/index.php?title=Citizens_United_v._Federal_Election_Commission and the official decision at http://www.supremecourt.gov/opinions/09pdf/08-205.pdf.

Public Policy

Campaign Finance Reform Critics have long argued that American politics is awash in special-interest money. Most Americans seem to agree. Two-thirds of those surveyed support public financing of campaigns if it eliminates funding from large private donations and organized interest groups. Since the 1970s, presidential campaigns have been in part publicly funded, but not congressional races. Candidates who accept public funds must abide by campaign spending limits. But, by rejecting public funds, candidates can ignore spending limits.

Senators John McCain and Russ Feingold proposed a ban on so-called soft-money contributions to national parties. *Soft money* allows political parties to raise unlimited amounts from individuals, corporations, and labor unions and to spend it freely on party-building activities, such as get-out-the-vote efforts, but not on direct support for candidates. *Hard money* is the cash parties raise under rules that limit individual contributions and require public disclosure of donors. The McCain-Feingold measure was approved as the Bipartisan Campaign Reform Act of 2002. The act bans the solicitation of soft money by federal candidates and prohibits political advertising by special interest groups in the weeks just before an election. The contribution limit to a presidential candidate is $2,300 for the primary and $2,300 for the general election, or a combined $4,600 for both.

Limits on special-interest contributions may reduce their influence in the political process, but such caps also increase the advantage of incumbents. Although there was anti-incumbent sentiment in the 2010 congressional election, historically about 95 percent of congressional incumbents usually get reelected. Incumbents benefit from a taxpayer-funded staff and free mailing privileges; these mailings often amount to campaign literature masquerading as official communications. Limits on campaign spending also magnify the advantages of incumbency by reducing a challenger's ability to appeal directly to voters. Some liberal *and* conservative thinkers agree that the supply of political money should be increased, not decreased. As Curtis Gans, director of the Committee for the Study of the American Electorate argued, "The overwhelming body of scholarly research . . . indicates that low spending limits will undermine political competition by enhancing the existing advantages of incumbency." *Money matters more to challengers* because the public knows less about them. Challengers must be able to spend enough to get their message out. One study found a positive relationship between spending by challengers and their election success but found no relationship between spending by incumbents and their reelection success. So campaign spending limits favor incumbents.

Image by © Brooks kraft/Corbis

The U.S. Supreme Court in 2010 ruled that the federal government may not ban certain types of political spending by corporations and labor unions, ruling that: "When governments seek to use its full power, including the criminal law, to command where a person may get his or her information, . . . it uses censorship to control thought."

Barack Obama and John McCain together spent a little more than $1 billion in the 2008 presidential race (with most of that spent by Obama). More than a billion dollars sounds like a lot of money, but Coke spends at least twice that on advertising each year. The point is that even well-meaning legislation often has unintended consequences. Efforts to limit campaign spending may or may not reduce the influence of special-interest groups, but *by reducing a challenger's ability to reach the voters, spending limits increase the advantage of incumbency, thus reducing political competition.*

Sources: Michael Ensley, "Individual Campaign Contributions and Candidate Ideology," *Public Choice*, 138 (January 2009): 229–238; Jess Bravin, "Supreme Court Reverses Limits on Campaign Spending," *Wall Street Journal*, 21 January 2010; Jonathan Salant, "Spending Doubled as Obama Led Billion-Dollar Campaign," *Bloomberg News*, 27 December 2008, at http://www.bloomberg.com/apps/news?pid=20601087&sid=apxzrZEHqU1o&refer=home#; the Federal Election Commission at http://www.fec.gov/; and Common Cause at http://www.commoncause.org.

Chapter 17

Public Policy

CASE STUDY

The Lungs of the Planet The tropical rainforests have been called the lungs of the planet because they naturally recycle carbon dioxide into oxygen and wood, thus eliminating heat-trapping gases and helping to maintain the world's atmospheric balance. These rainforests cover just 6 to 7 percent of the Earth's land surface but contain over half of the world's plant and animal species. The Amazon rainforest, for example, contains the largest collection of plant and animal life on Earth, along with 20 percent of the world's supply of fresh water.

The world's rainforests are located in countries that are relatively poor, such as Bolivia, Brazil, Colombia, Indonesia, Venezuela, and the Philippines. Landless peasants and settlers burn down these forests to create farmland and pastures. Worse yet, to meet the growing demand for timber, loggers strip rainforests. Because most of the rainforest amounts to an open-access resource, where property rights are not easily established, poor settlers and timber companies usually pursue a slash-and-burn approach. The world's tropical forests have been cut in half in the last 50 years.

Burning the world's rainforests spells trouble for the environment. The fires add greenhouse gases to the atmosphere. Destruction of tropical forests around the world is estimated to be responsible for about 20 percent of global greenhouse gas emissions. The loss of trees reduces the atmosphere's ability to cleanse itself and increases flash flooding and mud slides. Stripped of trees, the land contains huge amounts of carbon subject to oxidization. Soil gets eroded by rains and baked by the sun and runs out of nutrients after only two growing seasons. Such farming is unsustainable. With nutrients lost, the ecosystem is not very resilient—*it takes a century for a clear-cut forest to*

e activity

The Rainforest Alliance at http://www.rainforest-alliance.org/ is an international nonprofit organization dedicated to the conservation of tropical forests. Its goal is to promote economically viable alternatives to the destruction of this endangered natural resource. Look through this site to find examples of the role economics plays in the projects and research the group supports. The Rainforest Action Network is another group devoted to rainforest conservation but focuses more on citizen activism. Go to its site at http://www.ran.org/ and compare the approaches of these two groups.

Jason Edwards/Getty Images

return to its original state. The loss of the tropical forests involves other costs. A canopy of trees protects a rich, genetically diverse, ecosystem.

The tropical rainforests, by serving as the lungs of the planet, confer benefits around the globe. But these external benefits are usually ignored in the decision to clear the land. It's not the greed of peasants and timber companies that leads to inefficient, or wasteful, uses of resources. The problem is that the rainforests and the atmosphere are open-access resources that can be degraded with little immediate personal cost to those who clear the land. The costs of deforestation are imposed on people around the globe. As an example of how interrelated the global economy has become, the increased demand for biofuels to replace fossil fuels is a major driver of deforestations. Farmers clear rainforests to grow soybeans, one source of biodiesel fuel.

Poverty in the rainforest countries combined with the lack of legal title to the land encourage people to exploit that timber and soil rather than maximize the long-term value of these resources. For example, a secure property right to the land would reduce the need to clear it in order to claim some value. A farmer with title to the land could even leave a forest bequest to heirs. Research shows that people granted rights to the Amazon rainforest manage their land more conservatively. Property rights promote efficient harvesting of hardwoods and reforestation, allowing the forest to serve as an air filter. For example, the frequency of reforestation among those settlers granted land title was about 15 times greater than among those without title. Without title, the only way to capture some of the land's value is through a slash-and-burn approach. Thus, granting peasants and settlers property rights could help conserve the rainforests.

Sources: Alexai Barrionuevo, "Giants in Cattle Industry Agree to Help Fight Deforestation," *New York Times*, 6 October 2009; R. Godoy et al., "The Role of Tenure Security and Private Time Preference in Neotropical Deforestation," *Land Economics*, 74 (May 1998): 162–170; Charles Wood and Robert Walker, "Saving the Trees by Helping the Poor," *Resources for the Future* (Summer 1999): 14–17; and *State of the World's Forests: 2009*, Food and Agricultural Organization of the United Nations, at http://www.fao.org/docrep/011/i0350e/i0350e00.htm.

CASE STUDY

e activity

To get BP's perspective, go to http://www.bp.com and click on the tab for Gulf of Mexico response. For an analysis of the costs and maybe surprising benefits of an oil spill, go to http://www.alaskadispatch.com/dispatches/energy/5798-economics-of-an-oil-spill-cleanup. The *Alaska Dispatch* article discussed the aftermath of the 1989 Exxon Valdez spill.

Public Policy

BP's Oil Spill in the Gulf On April 20, 2010, the Deepwater Horizon oil rig exploded in the Gulf of Mexico in a drilling accident that killed 11 workers and hospitalized many. Both BP and the government initially underestimated the size of the spill, and neither had a response plan in place. Though the oil industry had experienced blowouts at shallower depths, an accident a mile down was new and devastating. Federal regulators seemed lax prior to the accident, perhaps captives of the industry. The size of the Gulf spill combined with live video of the gushing well and photos of oil-soaked birds marked this tragedy in the public's mind. President Obama called it the worst environmental disaster in U.S. history.

The explosion and resulting oil spill, accidental byproducts of BP's efforts to supply oil, threatened the livelihood of tens of thousands around the Gulf and could impose lasting damage on the habitat. BP spent billions on cleanup in the first three months, but that was peanuts compared to the costs company owners have and will face. More than 150 class-action lawsuits named BP as a defendant. Hoping to attract more clients, law firms purchased domain names such as offshoreinjuries.com and bigoilspills.com and advertised with billboards along the Gulf Coast. Environmental groups filed suits of their own. President Obama warned BP against "nickel and diming" the economic victims of the accident. And the Justice Department opened a criminal probe against BP for possible violations of the Clean Water Act and other environmental laws.

Here's a question: Was this oil spill a negative externality? Was this an unpriced byproduct that affected neither buyer nor seller but third parties? The buyers in this case were customers for BP gasoline and the seller was BP. Market competition may make it difficult for BP to pass along its spill-related costs, so BP consumers may not be much affected. How about BP?

If this were truly an externality, then the accident would have had little impact on the supplier, BP, or the company BP hired to drill the well, Transocean. But both have been profoundly affected. Because BP has been reviled by everyone from President Obama on down, the company's brand name will be tarnished for a generation, becoming the poster child of polluters in the public's mind, in the media, even in textbooks. Lawsuits will likely cost the company billions and may take years to settle (some Exxon-Valdez suits from the 1989 Alaska spill took more than two decades to resolve). For its part, Transocean, the owners of the rig, saw 11 workers die in the explosion and many more hospitalized. The drilling rig itself, which cost Transocean $375 million, sank two days after the explosion.

Although lawsuits may be in the courts for years, share owners of BP and Transocean didn't have to wait long to see their losses reflected in stock prices. Within six weeks of the accident, the share price of each company sank 50 percent. In BP's case, that meant a loss in the market value of the company of about $90 billion. Because Transocean was a smaller company, its market value fell about $15 billion. Although the exact amount of the spill may never be known, let's say the total turns out to be about 200 million gallons, a figure higher than any reported estimate. This would imply that BP and Transocean stockholders together lost more than $500 in market value for each of the 200 million gallons of crude oil spilled into the Gulf. There remained some question whether the companies will survive. For example, BP established a $20 billion fund to compensate those affected by the spill. The company was forced to sell rights to some oil fields to pay for the cleanup and was expected to issue bonds to raise more money. No question, many in the Gulf region have been harmed by the spill, and some of the damage could last for years. But many people will be compensated for their losses. The legal system, the government, the media, and the stock market have placed much of the cost of this accident squarely on BP and Transocean, and to that extent, most of what otherwise would have been external costs became internalized.

A.J. SISCO/UPI/Landov

Sources: Michael Shear and Steven Mufson, "Obama to BP: Take Care of Gulf Victims," *Washington Post*, 5 June 2010; Justin Gillis and Leslie Kaufman, "After Oil Spill, Hidden Damage Can Last for Years," *New York Times*, 17 July 2010; Dionne Searcey, "Attorneys Scramble to Gather the Most Plaintiffs for the Broadest Action Possible," *Wall Street Journal*, 2 June 2010; and Brian Baskins, "BP: 'No Evidence' of Problems with New Caps," *Wall Street Journal*, 17 July 2010.

Chapter 18

CASE STUDY

e activity

According to the U.S. Census Bureau, Connecticut, the District of Columbia, New Jersey, and Massachusetts had median earnings for men that were above $55,000 in 2008. Connecticut, New Jersey, and Maryland were the only states where median earnings for women were above $44,000, as was the District of Columbia. In each of the 50 states and the District of Columbia, median earnings were less for women than they were for men in 2008—in the District of Columbia, women earned about 88 cents for every dollar that men earned, higher than in any of the states. Go to the Census Bureau's site at http://pubdb3.census.gov/macro/032007/perinc/new10_000.htm and compare the wages by gender and race.

Public Policy

Marital Sorting and Income Inequality In the not too distant past, lawyers married secretaries and doctors married nurses. Now, Americans with increasing frequency are pairing off by education levels—lawyers marry lawyers, and doctors marry doctors. Why the change? Women have made huge inroads into the professions. In 1970, only about 10 percent of law or medical school enrollees were women. Now it's about 50 percent. More generally, women make up 54 percent of those ages 18 to 24 enrolled in college, graduate school, or professional school. Thus, men and women are now more likely to meet their future spouses in college, law school, medical school, graduate school, or some other advanced educational setting.

As a result of their educational strides, particularly in the professions, a growing number of women, for the first time in history, now have high-paying jobs and professional careers. The extent to which couples are educational equals has reached its highest point in decades. Choosing a marriage partner based on income is also on the rise. Studies find a growing similarity between women's wages before marriage and the future earnings of the men they marry.

So this power couple marries and has children, and these offspring benefit from the high income and any other advantages passed along from their well-educated parents, including better health. With this head start in life, many from that next generation, in turn, go to the best colleges, where they are likely to meet their future spouses. A study of the nation's top 147 colleges found that only 9 percent of admissions come from families in the bottom half of the income distribution. The whole cycle thereby gets reinforced and perpetuated.

The flip side of this is that someone with only a high school education is now less likely to marry a college graduate than was once the case. What's more, among women born after 1960, someone with only a high school education is less likely to ever marry than is someone with a college education. Only about 11 percent of all births in 1970 were to unmarried mothers; that share climbed to 41 percent by 2008. As you will see, children born to single mothers typically face special challenges, not the least of which is a higher rate of poverty. *A growth in power couples and in unmarried mothers anchors the top and bottom ends of the income distribution, contributing to the widening income gap observed in the U.S. economy.*

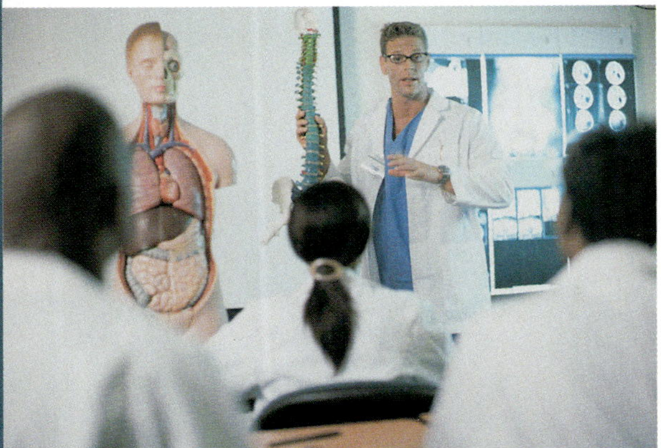

Comstock/Jupiter Images

Sources: Raquel Fernández and Richard Rogerson, "Sorting and Long-Term Inequality," *Quarterly Journal of Economics*, 116 (4, 2001): 1305–1341; Ashlesha Datar et al., "Endowments and Parental investment in Infancy and Early Childhood," *Demography*, 47 (February 2010): 145–162; and Chinhui Juhn and Kristin McCue, "Trends in Earnings Instability of Couples: How Important Is Marital Sorting?" NBER Working Paper, (September 2009).

CASE STUDY

e activity

To track dividends' contribution to personal income, go to http://www.bea.gov/national/nipaweb/index.asp. Click on "list of Selected NIPA Tables." In the new window, scroll down to Section 2 and click on Table 2.1. Personal Income and Its Disposition. Choose the years that you want to examine and look for Line 15: Personal dividend income.

PUBLIC POLICY

The Rich Got Poorer During the Recession The sharp and painful national recession of 2007–2009 was hard on many Americans. The unemployment rate doubled between 2007 and 2009. To help people through this rough patch, the social safety net was broadened. Extra months were added to unemployment benefits; in many states benefits were extended to nearly two years, or four times the usual duration. Spending targeted for the poor (see the programs identified in Exhibit 5) grew by 13 percent between 2007 and 2009, even after adjusting for inflation. The progressive income tax rate declined for all but those in the highest-income brackets, as falling incomes meant lower tax brackets. Indeed, an estimated 47 percent of households paid no federal personal income taxes in 2009. No question, some people were still having a rough time, but public programs softened the blow, particularly at the low end of the income distribution.

It may seem odd, but one of the hardest hit groups, at least on a relative basis, was high-income households, many of whom lost a ton with the double whammy of a stock market crash and a real-estate crash. High-income households also depend more on corporate dividends, which experienced their sharpest drop since the government began keeping records a half century ago.

Jonathan Parker and Annette Vissing-Jorgensen, economists at Northwestern University, found that incomes of the affluent tend to fall more, in both absolute dollars and in percentage terms, during a recession than do the incomes of the typical household. The exposure to economic fluctuations of households in the top 10 percent based on income is about five times greater than the exposure of the typical household. And the incomes of the super rich, defined as the top one-hundredth of 1 percent, fall the most in percentage terms. Along with the decline in income of the rich comes a decline in consumption. The two researchers expected that the recession of 2007–2009 would cause a sharp reduction in consumption inequality across income classes. In short, the rich were hit harder in relative terms by the recession than were other income groups, so they cut their consumption more.

How has the declining fortunes of the rich affected the economy more broadly? A drop in their income and wealth reduced contributions to universities, charities, museums, and other institutions that rely on their generosity. Federal and state tax revenues were also down sharply because these sources rely so much on the taxes paid by the affluent. For example, most recently the top 1 percent of tax filers based on income paid over 40 percent of all federal income taxes collected.

High-income households aren't just cash cows for tax collectors. The rich often get that way by starting successful businesses that create jobs. Consumption by the rich, including spending on luxuries, also helps create jobs in the economy. But a recession is a bad time for costly luxuries. In 2009, for example, 1,312 homes with mortgage balances in excess of $5 million were foreclosed on and went to public auction in the United States. That foreclosure rate more than doubled in early 2010, and included the 11,817 square-foot Tudor mansion of actor Nicolas Cage. Other luxuries also took a hit during the recession. Diamond sales worldwide fell 16 percent in 2009; thousands of U.S. jewelry stores closed their doors. The best seats at the new Yankee Stadium failed to sell until prices were cut in half. And hundreds of luxury boats, too costly to maintain, were abandoned or purposely run aground. Florida

Photo by James Aylott/Online USA

recently had to remove more than a hundred derelict boats from public waterways, up from only a handful the year before.

Troubles of the rich will never elicit much public sympathy, but high-income households represent a critical source of tax revenue, charitable giving, and job creation in the economy.

Sources: Jonathan Parker and Annette Vissing-Jorgensen, "Who Bears Aggregate Fluctuations and How," *American Economic Review*, 99 (May 2009): 399–405; David Leonhart and Geraldine Fabrikant, "Rise of Superrich Hits a Sobering Wall," *New York Times*, 21 August 2009; Craig Karmin and James Hagerty, "Foreclosures Hit Rich and Famous," *Wall Street Journal*, 9 April 2010; and David Streitfeld, "Boats Too Costly to Keep Are Littering Coastlines," *New York Times*, 1 April 2009.

CHAPTER 19

CASE STUDY

WORLD OF BUSINESS

The Global Economy Years ago what happened in other economies was not that important to Americans. But now many resources flow freely across borders. Technology has also spread around the globe. Though business cycles are not perfectly synchronized across countries, a link is usually apparent. Consider the experience of two leading economies—the United States and the United Kingdom, economies separated by the Atlantic Ocean. Exhibit 1 shows for each economy the year-to-year percentage change in real GDP since 1978. Again, *real* means that the effects of inflation have been erased, so remaining changes reflect *real* changes in the total amount of goods and services produced each year.

If you spend a little time following the annual changes in each economy, you can see the similarities. For example, both economies went into recession in the early 1980s, grew well for the rest of the decade, entered another recession in 1991, recovered for the rest of the decade, then slowed down in 2001. Both economies picked up steam in 2004, but the global financial crisis of 2008 caused sharply lower output by 2009.

One problem with the linkage across economies is that a slump in other major economies could worsen a recession in the United States and vice versa. For example, the financial crisis of 2008 affected economies around the world, increasing unemployment and cutting production. Trouble in seemingly minor economies, such as Greece, can spill over and drag other economies down with them. On the other hand, economic strength overseas can give the U.S. economy a lift. As the *Wall Street Journal* reported, "Many U.S. companies are finding strength in overseas profits, helping to offset a weak housing market and a credit crunch at home."

Source: Timothy Aeppel, "Overseas Profits Help U.S. Firms Through Tumult," *Wall Street Journal*, 9 August 2007; Bob Davis, "Geithner Plans to Press Germany on European Rescue," *Wall Street Journal*, 22 May 2010; "The Greek Crisis: The End of the Party," *The Economist*, 8 May 2010; *Economic Report of the President*, February 2010; and the Bureau of Economic Analysis at http://bea.gov/index.htm. Figures for 2010 and 2011 are projections found in *OECD Economic Outlook*, 87 (May 2010), Table 1.

e activity

Standard-of-living statistics for the United Kingdom are available from the Office of National Statistics at http://www.statistics.gov.uk/. This site includes data on the percentage of households owning appliances, autos, etc. Compare the availability of cars and telephones in the United Kingdom to the United States by viewing the U.S. Census reports at http://www.census.gov/.

EXHIBIT 1 U.S. and U.K. Annual Growth Rates in Output Are Similar

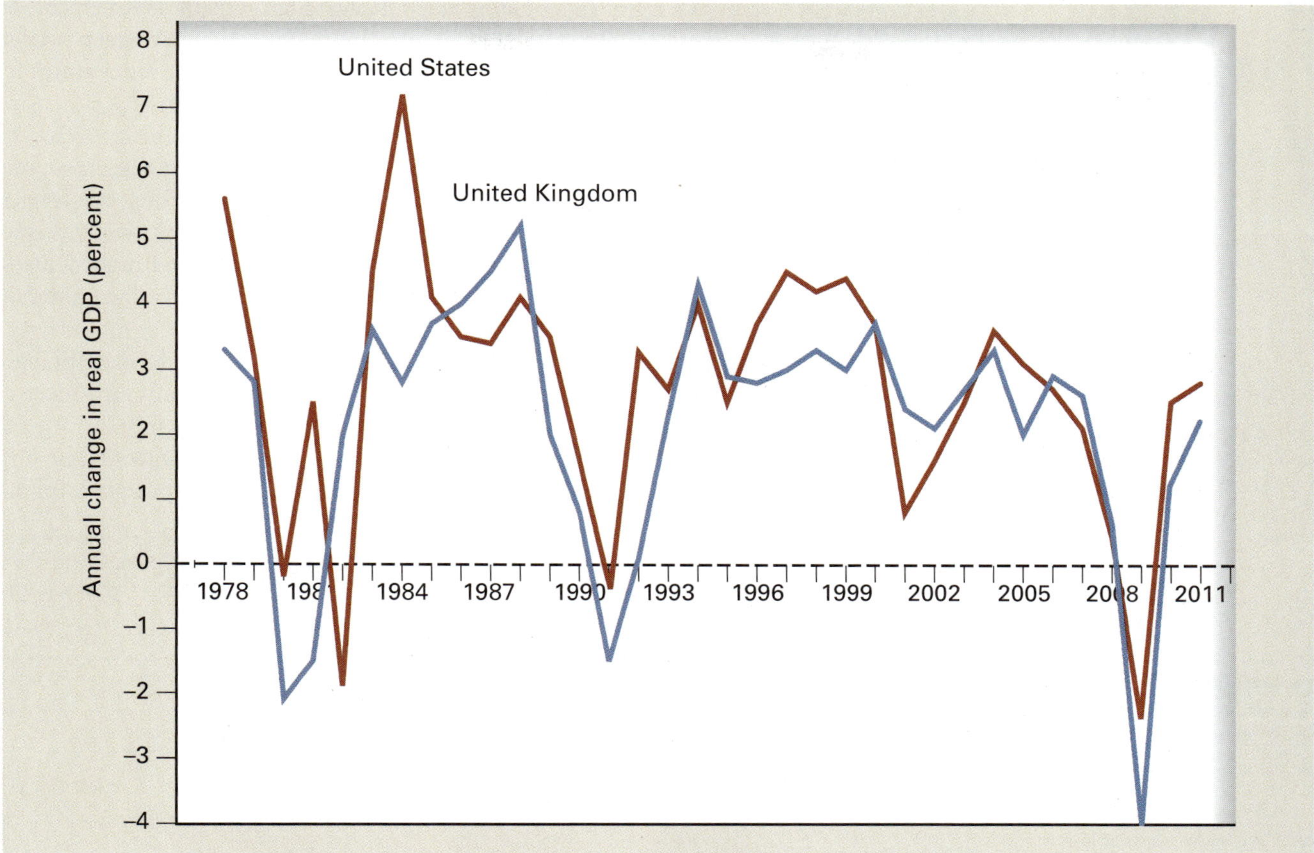

Though economic fluctuations are not perfectly synchronized across major economies, a link is usually apparent. For example, the United States and the United Kingdom are separated by the Atlantic Ocean, but their real GDPs changed from year to year by roughly similar percentages during the last quarter century.

Source: U.S. growth estimates from Bureau of Economic Analysis, U.S. Department of Commerce. For the latest, go to http://bea.gov/index.htm then click on Gross Domestic Product. U.K. growth estimates from *OECD Economic Outlook* 87 (May 2010), Annex Table 1. Growth rates for 2010 and 2011 are OECD projections.

Public Policy

U.S. Economic Growth Since 1929 Points in Exhibit 2 trace the U.S. real GDP and price level for each year since 1929. Aggregate demand and aggregate supply curves are shown for 2009, but all points in the series reflect such intersections. Years of growing GDP are indicated as blue points and years of declining GDP as red ones. Despite the Great Depression of the 1930s and the 11 recessions since World War II, the long-term growth in output is unmistakable. Real GDP, measured along the horizontal axis in 2005 constant dollars, grew from about $1.0 trillion in 1929 to about $13.0 trillion in 2009—a thirteenfold increase and an average annual growth rate of 3.3 percent. The price index also rose, but not quite as fast, rising from 10.6 in 1929 to 109.8 in 2009—more than a tenfold increase and an average inflation rate of 3.0 percent per year. Note that what matters here is the growth in real GDP, because that nets out the effects of inflation (inflation is mostly troublesome noise in the economy). Since 1983, annual output declined only twice—in 1991 and in 2009.

Because the U.S. population is growing, the economy must create more jobs just to employ the additional people entering the workforce. For example, the U.S. population grew from

CASE STUDY

e activity

Are you interested in learning more about the economic history of the past century? J. Bradford De Long's brief article, "Slouching Toward Utopia," provides one economist's evaluation of key developments. You can read it at http://www.bos.frb.org/economic/nerr/rr1998/q3/delo98_3.htm.

122 million in 1929 to 307 million in 2009, a rise of 152 percent. Fortunately, employment grew even faster, from 47 million in 1929 to 140 million in 2009, for a growth of 198 percent. So, since 1929, employment grew more than enough to keep up with a rising population. Despite the recessions, the United States has been an impressive job machine over the long run.

Not only did the number employed triple since 1929, the average education of workers increased as well. Other resources, especially capital, also rose sharply. What's more, the level of technology improved steadily, thanks to breakthroughs such as the personal computer and the Internet. The availability of more and higher-quality human capital and physical capital increased the productivity of each worker, contributing to the thirteenfold jump in real GDP since 1929.

real GDP per capita
Real GDP divided by the population; the best measure of an economy's standard of living

Real GDP is important, but the best measure of the average standard of living is an economy's **real GDP per capita**, which tells us how much an economy produces on average per resident. Because real GDP grew much faster than the population, real GDP *per capita* jumped sixfold between 1929 and 2009. The United States is the largest economy in the world and a leader among major economies in output per capita.

Sources: "GDP and the Economy," *Survey of Current Business* 90 (April 2010); 1–5; *Economic Report of the President*, February 2010; *Economic Report of the President*, January 1980; and *OECD Economic Outlook* 87 (May 2010). For the latest real GDP and price level data, go to http://bea.gov/. For the latest population data, go to http://www.census.gov. For the latest employment data, go to http:// www.bls.gov.

EXHIBIT 2 Tracking U.S. Real GDP and Price Level Since 1929

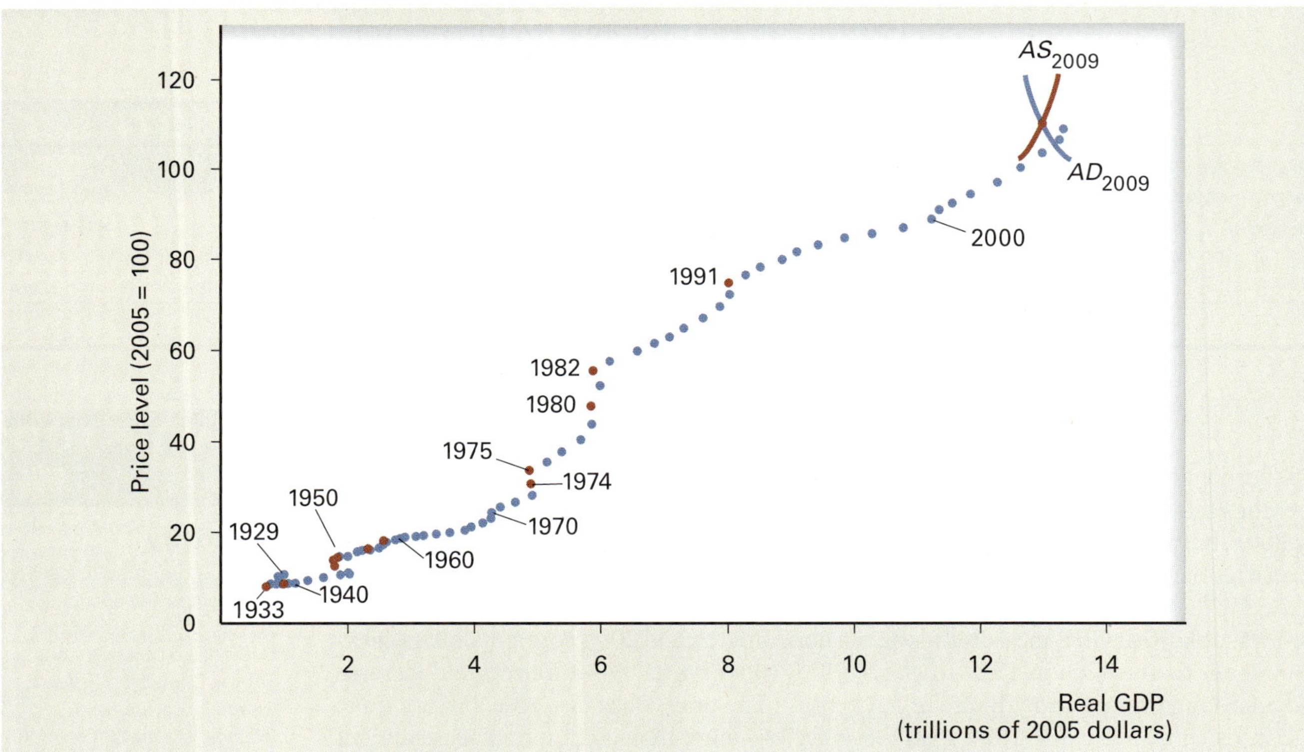

As you can see, both real GDP and the price level trended higher since 1929. Blue points indicate years of growing real GDP, and red points are years of declining real GDP. Real GDP in 2009 was 13 times greater than in 1929.

Chapter 20

Public Policy

CASE STUDY

e activity

The Bureau of Economic Analysis is charged with estimating GDP and its components. You can find selected National Income and Product Account tables at http://www.bea.gov/national/nipaweb/Index.asp. Choose "list of Selected NIPA Tables." Table 1.1.1 tells you by how much each component has grown. Table 1.1.2 shows the contribution of each component to GDP growth. Can you explain the difference between these two types of statistics? The BEA also produces the monthly report, *Survey of Current Business,* with articles describing and interpreting national income data. The current issue and back issues are accessible through http://www.bea.gov/scb/index.htm. Compare what you find at the BEA site to what you find at The State of the USA.

GDP and the State of the USA GDP estimates have been refined for decades and are arguably the most complex data aggregation effort in the world. But they have their limits, as discussed already, and they have their critics. One criticism is that GDP leaves out much of what's going on in the nation—with health care, the environment, the family, energy use, and so on. One challenge to GDP as the primary indicator of national progress is coming from a nonprofit group that has developed a Web site to bring together hundreds of indicators. The idea is to help Americans assess the progress of the United States by using quality data selected by experts.

First, a little background. In 2003, a team at the U.S. Government Accountability Office, the investigative arm of Congress, was looking for alternatives to GDP to assess national progress. The team became an independent nonprofit agency in 2007 and took the name "The State of the USA." With startup funding from the Gates, Hewlett, MacArthur, and Rockefeller foundations, the group set out to identify data that would amount to a report card on how the country is doing in specific areas—such as health care, education, the environment, safety, energy, transportation, the economy, the family, and so forth. The goal is to help citizens and leaders assess what progress has been made and where we need to improve.

The effort got a big boost from a small provision in the massive 2010 health care bill that requires Congress to help finance and oversee a "key national indicator system." State of the USA will become that system, overseen by the National Academy of Sciences, a group of preeminent scholars established by Abraham Lincoln in 1863 to "investigate, examine, experiment, and report upon any subject of science or art" whenever called upon to do so by any department of the government (half the 20 economists in the National Academy are Nobel laureates). Along with the federal authorization came federal funding totaling $70 million between 2010 and 2018.

The objective is not so much to replace GDP as the primary measure of economic performance, but to broaden the conversation and the debate by including many more data series. Instead of just having one gauge on the dashboard, GDP, there would be many gauges. The State of the USA Web site went live in 2010, and is accessible for free. Eventually, The State of the USA plans to offer about 300 indicators. Rather than develop original data, the site compiles and displays data gathered by others. Despite the number of data series, the group says the site will be selective, not encyclopedic. For example, in health care alone the government collects about 1,000 different measures. The State of the USA offers what they claim are the 20 most crucial health care measures. The group says its objective is not to interpret the data but to disseminate it in a strictly nonpartisan manner.

The idea is to offer data in a form that can be easily shared to promote as wide a distribution as possible. Data will be available on the national level, state level, and as far down the jurisdictional chain as possible. For example, one of the 20 health care measures reports smoking rates by state (West Virginia is the highest and Utah is the lowest). The State of the USA will also offer a variety of interactive features to encourage exploration, such as motion charts with audio tutorials focusing on health costs and outcomes for the developed world. Check out the site and see what you think.

Source: State of the USA

Sources: Jon Gertner, "The Rise and Fall of the G.D.P." *New York Times,* 10 May 2010; and The State of the USA site at http://www.stateoftheusa.org/.

CASE STUDY

e activity

At http://www.bls.gov/cpi/cpiqa.htm, the Bureau of Labor Statistics addresses common misconceptions about the Consumer Price Index. Find out how food, energy, and housing are incorporated into the index. You can also read about substitution effects and hedonic quality adjustments.

Public Policy

Price Check on Aisle 2 The U.S. economy is one of the most dynamic in the world, marked by rapid technological change. The Bureau of Labor Statistics (BLS), the government agency that calculates the CPI each month, employs dozens of economists to analyze the impact of any quality changes to products in the CPI market basket. Each month 400 data collectors visit stores to record about 85,000 prices for 211 item categories in the CPI basket. About a week before the CPI is released, the BLS office is locked down with bright red "restricted area" signs on all the doors. A total of 90 people, including product specialists and the other economists working on the CPI, compute the basic indexes in each category. Results are released at 8:30 A.M., Eastern Time, about two weeks after the end of the month in question. This release is a big deal.

Most price adjustments are straightforward. For example, if a candy bar shrinks but its price doesn't, the CPI shows this as a price increase. But sometimes a product changed in a more complicated way. Each economist at BLS specializes in particular products, such as televisions, automobiles, kitchen appliances, and so on. One of their greatest challenges is to identify substitutes for products that are no longer available. For example, data collectors find the model of TV they priced the previous month is missing about one-fifth of the time. When a particular product is missing, a four-page checklist of features such as screen size and the type of remote control guides the data collector to the nearest comparable model. That price is reported and the product specialist in Washington must then decide whether it's an acceptable substitute.

Digital Vision/Getty Images

For example, the TV specialist decided that the newer version of the 27-inch model had some important improvements, including a flat screen. A complex computer model estimated that the improvements alone would be valued by consumers as worth \$135 more. After factoring improvements into the price of the \$330 set, the analyst determined that the price of the TV had actually declined 29 percent [= 135/(330 + 135)]. In another example, the price of a 57-inch TV dropped from \$2,239 to \$1,910, for an apparent decline of 15 percent. But on closer inspection, the analyst found that the new model lacked an HDTV tuner that had been included in the model it replaced. This tuner would be valued by consumers at \$514. So, instead of declining 15 percent, the price of the 57-inch TV actually rose 11 percent [= 1,910/(2,239 − 514)].

The TV analyst is applying the *hedonic method*, which breaks down the item under consideration into its characteristics, and then estimates the dollar value of each characteristic. This is a way of capturing the impact of a change in product quality on any price change. Otherwise, price changes would not reflect the fact that consumers are getting more or less for their money as product features change over time.

Sources: Jon Hilsenrath, "A Deeper Look at the Fed's Inflation Debate," *Wall Street Journal*, 5 April 2010; Javier Hernandez, "Prices of Consumer Goods Hold Steady, Indicating That Inflation Is at Bay," *New York Times*, 18 March 2010; and Mary Kokoski, Keith Waehrer, and Patricia Rosaklis, "Using Hedonic Methods for Quality Adjustment in the CPI," U.S. Bureau of Labor Statistics Working Paper (2000) found at http://www.bls.gov/cpi/cpiaudio.htm.

CHAPTER 21

CASE STUDY

e activity

Data on workers marginally attached to the labor force are available at http://data.bls.gov/cgi-bin/surveymost?ln. Page down to check the box for Marginally Attached to Labor Force - LNU05026642. Click the Retrieve data button. Choose the years you want to examine and check the box to "include graphs." Select the GO button.

PUBLIC POLICY

"Hiring Picks Up, But Jobless Rate Rises" So reads the headline describing the April 2010 jobs report. In a burst of hiring, the U.S. economy added 290,000 jobs, for what was then the biggest monthly gain in four years. That sure sounds like good news—until you learn that the U.S. unemployment rate climbed too, from 9.7 percent to 9.9 percent. How could that rate rise when the economy was adding so many jobs?

Because of a severe recession, the number of unemployed increased by over 8 million between early 2008 and early 2010. But even that total understates the number who wanted jobs. Recall that to be counted as unemployed, those wanting work must have looked for a job in the prior four weeks. With 8 million people looking for work, and with firms more likely to be firing than hiring, the chances of finding a job diminished. In frustration, some gave up their search, and these people are called discouraged workers, a term already introduced. But the U.S. Labor Department identifies a second group of people who wanted a job but did not look for work in the prior four weeks. This group faced transportation problems, family problems, or some other snag that kept them from looking. It wasn't that they were frustrated with their search, they just got sidetracked with some personal issues. Discouraged workers and this group that got sidetracked are considered *marginally attached to the labor force*.

©iStockphoto.com/Arthur Kwiatkowski

At the beginning of 2010, an estimated 2.4 million people were marginally attached to the labor force. This was 1.1 million more than before the recession began. Thus, when the economy started showing signs of life, as it did in early 2010, some people who had been sidelined for one reason or another took notice and decided to look for work, thus joining or rejoining the labor force. In April 2010 the labor force increased by about 800,000 people from the month earlier. Most of those people didn't find jobs right away, so they swelled the ranks of the unemployed. Even though the economy created 290,000 jobs during the month, that was not enough to offset the spike in the labor force. Thus, we get the seeming paradox of healthy job growth but a rising unemployment rate.

The same happened during the recession of 2001; the unemployment rate did not start to decline until two years after the recession ended. That's why the unemployment rate is often considered a lagging indicator of economic activity. Even after the economy starts to recover from a recession, the unemployment rate continues to increase for reasons that are not all bad. Those who want a job are encouraged enough by the uptick in jobs to look for one.

Sources: Jeannine Aversa, "Hiring Picks Up, But Jobless Rate Rises," *Arizona Republic*, 8 May 2010; Sara Murray and Joe Light, "Job Gains Speed Up and More Seek Work," *Wall Street Journal*, 8 May 2008; "Ranks of Discouraged Workers and Others Marginally Attached to the Labor Force Rise During Recession," *Issues in Labor Statistics*, (April 2009); and figures from the U.S. Bureau of Labor Statistics at http://www.bls.gov/.

CASE STUDY

e activity

You can find economic information about many countries at The World Factbook published by the Central Intelligence Agency (https://www.cia.gov/library/publications/the-world-factbook/index.html). Above the map of the world, click the arrow for the drop-down list and scroll to Zimbabwe. In the menu below the map of the country, click on the plus sign to expand information about the economy. Can you find the latest inflation rate?

Bringing Theory to Life

Hyperinflation in Zimbabwe In the troubled nation of Zimbabwe in southern Africa, the Zimbabwean dollar was once worth about 1.59 U.S. dollars. But the collapse of the economy in the early 2000s severely devalued the Zimbabwean dollar. The government tried paying its bills by printing huge amounts of money, and the result was inflation on an epic scale—hyperinflation. Consider this: The price level at the end of 2008 was *150 million times* higher than at the beginning of that year. To put that in perspective, with such inflation in the United States, a gallon of gasoline that sold for $2.75 at the beginning of the year would cost $412.5 million by year-end. Jeans that sold for $25 would cost $3.8 billion at year-end. With the value of the Zimbabwean dollar cheapening by the hour, nobody wanted to hold any for long. Those fortunate enough to have jobs in this wreck of an economy wanted to get paid at least daily; they then immediately spent their pay before prices climbed more.

With such wild inflation, everyone, including merchants, had trouble keeping up with prices. Different price increases among sellers of the same product encouraged buyers to shop around more. Even though the government was printing money at an astounding rate, the huge spike in prices meant that it took mountains of cash to buy anything, an amount both difficult to round up and onerous to carry. For months, the maximum amount people could withdraw daily from their bank had the purchasing power of one U.S. dollar. Because carrying enough money for even small purchases became physically impossible, currency in Zimbabwe was issued in ever higher denominations, with the highest being a $100 trillion dollar note; that's $100,000,000,000,000. In addition to issuing these higher denominations, three times the central bank issued an entirely new series of notes, each a huge multiple of the previous one, while doing away with the old series. For example, the new Zimbabwean dollar issued in February 2009 exchanged for 1,000,000,000,000 of the dollars it replaced. Larger denominations and new series of notes facilitated transactions but fed inflation, which raged all the more.

Many merchants would accept only stable currencies such as the U.S. dollar or the South African rand, and would rather barter than accept Zimbabwean currency. No question, the country had all kinds of other problems, but hyperinflation made everything worse. For example, Zimbabwe's GDP plunged 75 percent between 2006 and 2009, and the unemployment rate reached 90 percent.

©iStockphoto.com/Kenny McLeish

As a way out of the mess, by mid-2009 the government allowed all transactions to be conducted in foreign currencies, something that was already happening. The local currency, already worthless (a $100 trillion note was worth only U.S. pennies), mostly disappeared. Thus, Zimbabwe is now under what it calls a "multiple currency system" and the country plans to operate that way until at least through 2012. Price inflation grew only five percent in 2009 under the multiple currency system. Although Zimbabwe ended its inflation nightmare, hyperinflation is usually flaring up somewhere in the world, as yet another country looks to print money as a "free lunch" solution to budget problems. For example, inflation in Venezuela reached 30 percent in 2010.

Sources: "Zimbabwe: Reaching Rock Bottom," *The Economist*, 8 December 2008; Douglas Rogers, "Zimbabwe's Accidental Triumph," *New York Times*, 14 April 2010; and Zimbabwe's Federal Reserve Bank at http://www.rbz.co.zw/. This case study also drew on the author's visit to Zimbabwe in September 2008.

Chapter 22

The Information Economy

CASE STUDY

e activity

While the application of computing technologies by U.S. firms has grown drastically, cost and technical issues have made warehouse management systems unapproachable for many small companies. But hosted warehouse systems are beginning to change this; do a search on Google at http://www.google.com for "warehouse management systems" and learn how they work. You can also visit http://www.upslogisticstech.com/pages/realstories/ for real world stories of UPS Logistics Technologies transportation management software being used to increase productivity in online grocery shopping, beverage delivery, medical supplies, and more.

Computers, the Internet, and Productivity Growth The first microprocessor, the Intel 4004, could perform about 400 computations per second when it hit the market in 1971. IBM's first personal computer, introduced a decade later, executed 330,000 computations per second. Today a $500 PC can handle over 6 billion computations per second, or *15 million* times what the 1971 Intel 4004 could do. Such advances in computing power have fueled a boom in computer use and made the United States a world leader. U.S. companies and universities are well ahead of other countries in high technology applications, ranging from software to biotechnology.

Computers help people work together. For example, design engineers in California can use the Web to test new ideas with marketers in New York, cutting development time in half. Sales representatives on the road can use laptops or other wireless devices to log orders and serve customers. U.S. insurance companies can coordinate data entry done as far away as India to handle claims more efficiently. An owner of multiple restaurants can use the Internet to track sales up to the minute, check the temperatures of freezers, refrigerators, and fryers, and observe each restaurant through a live video feed. New generations of machines monitor themselves and send messages detailing any problems as they arise. For example, General Electric uses the Internet to keep tabs on factory equipment thousands of miles away. Some home appliances, such as refrigerators and TVs, are also Internet compatible. Computers not only improve the quality and safety in many industries, including automobiles and airlines, but they increase the versatility of machines, which can be reprogrammed for different tasks.

Computers boost productivity through two channels: (1) efficiency gains in the production of computers and semiconductors and (2) greater computer use by industry. These two channels account for much of the gain in productivity growth since 1996. Although computer hardware manufacturers make up only a tiny fraction of the U.S. economy, their pace of innovation quickened enough since 1996 to boost overall U.S. productivity growth. For example, Intel's 3.1-gigahertz Pentium 4 processor sold for under $100, much less than the $990 for the 1.1-gigahertz Pentium 3 it ultimately replaced. What's more, efficiency in semiconductor production and price declines since 1996 advanced IT use by business more generally, which also enhanced labor productivity. America invested more and earlier in IT than did other major economies, so productivity benefits showed up here first. The jump in labor productivity that began in the 1990s resulted from greater investment in information and communication technology.

Finding the best way to use new technology takes time. There are usually lags between when a new technology is introduced and when the benefits show up—for example, cash registers tied to the inventory system in warehouses (think Wal-mart) and communications systems connected to offices in different buildings and even different countries (think General Electric). What really set the productivity gains in motion was the big drop in semiconductor prices during the late 1990s. Going digital became a no-brainer for business. Computers per worker increased, which boosted labor productivity throughout the entire economy but especially in the service sector.

© Jagadeesh/Reuters/Corbis

The question is how long can the productivity pop from computers and the Internet last? Northwestern University's Robert Gordon argues that the economy enjoyed a one-time boost from computers and the Internet. Other economists are more upbeat, but they acknowledge that it takes a steady stream of innovations to keep U.S. productivity growing.

Sources: Dale Jorgenson, Mun Ho, and Kevin Stiroh, "A Retrospective Look at the U.S. Productivity Growth Resurgence," *Journal of Economic Perspectives*, 22 (Winter 2008): 3–24; "Something Is Not Working," *The Economist*, 29 April 2010; and "U.S. Productivity Growth in Quarter Tops Forecast," *New York Times*, 6 May 2010. The federal government's labor productivity home page is http://www.bls.gov/lpc/home.htm.

CASE STUDY

e activity

Gross National Happiness (GNH) is the goal proclaimed by the King of Bhutan. Learn more about GNH at http://www.grossnationalhappiness.com/. Click on Questionnaire to learn how GNH is tabulated.

Public Policy

Income and Happiness The Declaration of Independence in 1776 identified "certain unalienable Rights, that among these are Life, Liberty, and the Pursuit of Happiness." This did not guarantee happiness but did establish the pursuit of happiness as an "unalienable" right, meaning that right cannot be taken away, given away, or sold. Eighteenth-century philosopher and social reformer Jeremy Bentham argued that government policy should promote the greatest happiness for the greatest number of people.

Many people today apparently agree. In recent polls, 77 percent of Australians and 81 percent of Brits believed that a government's prime objective should be promoting the greatest happiness rather than the greatest wealth. The United Nations sponsored an international conference on "Happiness and Public Policy." Thailand now compiles a monthly Gross Domestic Happiness Index. Even China has joined in the fun, reporting a happiness index based on polling results about living conditions, income, the environment, social welfare, and employment. Australia, Canada, Germany and the United Kingdom are also developing indexes of happiness or well being. For example, the Canadian Index of Well Being will contain a measure of social connectedness, among other things.

Economists have long shied away from asking people how they feel, preferring instead to observe their behavior. But more now see some value in asking questions. In the most extensive of polls, the Gallup organization asked people in 130 countries: "How satisfied are you with your life, on a scale of zero to ten?" The results, are not surprising. Most people in the high income areas, such as the United States, Europe, and Japan, said they are happy. Most people in the poor areas, especially in Africa, said they are not. Also, within a given country, income and happiness are positively related. After evaluating all the results of the Gallup world poll, Angus Deaton of Princeton concluded: "The very strong global relationship between per capita GDP and life satisfaction suggests that on average people have a good idea of how income, or the lack of it, affects their lives."[1]

So these results are no surprise. What does puzzle economists is that other surveys suggest that Americans on average do not seem any happier over time even though each generation became richer than the last. The proportion of Americans who say they are happy has stayed about the same despite 60 years of economic growth.

The United States is unusual in that regard. Surveys in Europe and Japan do find an increase in happiness with

1. Angus Deaton, "Income, Health, and Well-Being Around the World: Evidence from the Gallup World Poll," *Journal of Economic Perspectives*, 22 (Spring 2008): 69.

increases in income over time. Here's a possible explanation. Americans begin taking for granted those luxuries they most desired. For example, two generations ago color TVs, automobiles, and major appliances were luxuries, but now they are must-have items for most households. Computers and flat screen HDTVs will soon move from luxuries to necessities. As each generation attains a higher standard of living, people become less sensitive to the benefits, they take them for granted, and thus they say they are no happier.

Sources: Jon Gertner, "The Rise and Fall of the GDP," *New York Times*, 10 May 2010; Daniel Gilbert, *Stumbling On Happiness* (New York: Knopf, 2006); Guglielmo Caporale et al. "Income and Happiness Across Europe: Do Reference Values Matter?" *Journal of Economic Psychology*, 30 (February 2009): 42–51; Angus Deaton, "Income, Health, and Well-Being Around the World: Evidence from the Gallup World Poll," *Journal of Economic Perspectives*, 22 (Spring 2008): 53–72; and Betsey Stevenson and Justin Wolfers, "The Paradox of Declining Female Happiness," *American Economic Journal: Economic Policy*, 1 (August 2009): 190–225.

CHAPTER 23

BRINGING THEORY TO LIFE

CASE STUDY

The Life-Cycle Hypothesis Do people with high incomes save a larger fraction of their incomes than those with low incomes? Both theory and evidence suggest they do. The easier it is to make ends meet, the more income is left over to save. Does it follow from this that richer economies save more than poorer ones—that economies save a larger fraction of total disposable income as they grow? In his famous book, *The General Theory of Employment, Interest, and Money,* published in 1936, John Maynard Keynes drew that conclusion. But as later economists studied the data, it became clear that Keynes was wrong. *The fraction of disposable income saved in an economy seems to stay constant as the economy grows.*

So how can it be that richer people save more than poorer people, yet richer countries do not necessarily save more than poorer ones? Several answers have been proposed. One of the most important is the **life-cycle model of consumption and saving.** According to this model, young people tend to borrow to finance education and home purchases. In middle age, people pay off debts and save more. In old age, they draw down their savings, or dissave. Some still have substantial wealth at death, because they are not sure when death will occur and because some parents want to bequeath wealth to their children. And some people die in debt. But on average net savings over a person's lifetime tend to be small. The life-cycle hypothesis suggests that the saving rate for an economy as a whole depends on, among other things, the relative number of savers and dissavers in the population.

A problem with the life-cycle hypothesis is that the elderly do not seem to draw down their assets as much as the theory predicts. One reason, already mentioned, is that some want to leave bequests to children. Another reason is that the elderly seem particularly concerned about covering unpredictable expenses such as from divorce, health problems, or living much longer than the average life span. Because of such uncertainty, many elderly spend less and save more than the life-cycle theory predicts. Researchers have found that those elderly who have not experienced a divorce or health problems build their net wealth well into old age.

e activity

Until quite recently, the Japanese government had been trying to encourage more consumer spending, but the Japanese public often would put extra income into savings. How could they be persuaded to spend more? An innovative policy was to issue purchase vouchers (http://web-japan.org/trends98/honbun/ntj981201.html). To whom did the government intend to issue the coupons? Why? Would 20,000 yen in vouchers ensure that spending would increase by that amount?

life-cycle model of consumption and saving

Young people borrow, middle agers pay off debts and save, and older people draw down their savings; on average, net savings over a lifetime is usually little or nothing

Noel Hendrickson/Jupiter Images

Still, the life-cycle hypothesis offers a useful theory of consumption patterns over a lifetime.

Sources: Martin Browning and Thomas Crossley, "The Life-Cycle Model of Consumption and Saving," *Journal of Economic Perspective* 15 (Summer 2001): 3–22; *OECD Economic Outlook* 87 (May 2010); and James Poterba, Steven Venti, and David Wise, "Family Status Transitions, Latent Health, and the Post Retirement Evolution of Assets," NBER Working Paper 15789, (February 2010).

CASE STUDY

e activity

Visit the Web site for the Research Seminar in Quantitative Economics (RSQE) at the University of Michigan at http://rsqe.econ.lsa.umich.edu/. RSQE is "an economic modeling and forecasting unit which has been in operation at the University of Michigan since 1952. RSQE provides forecasts of the economic outlook for the U.S. and Michigan economies, based on quarterly econometric models." On the menu at the left, click on Forecasts. Read the executive summary for their latest U.S. forecast. What are the sources of the predicted trend? How, specifically, do the forecasters believe that the types of consumption and investment spending cited in the text will change and affect real GDP?

Public Policy

Investment Varies More than Consumption We already know that consumption averaged 70 percent of GDP during the most recent decade, and investment varied from year to year and averaged 16 percent of GDP during the most recent decade. Now let's compare the year-to-year variability of consumption and investment. Exhibit 1 shows the annual percentage changes in GDP, consumption, and investment, all measured in real terms.

EXHIBIT 1 Annual Percentage Change in U.S. Real GDP, Consumption, and Investment

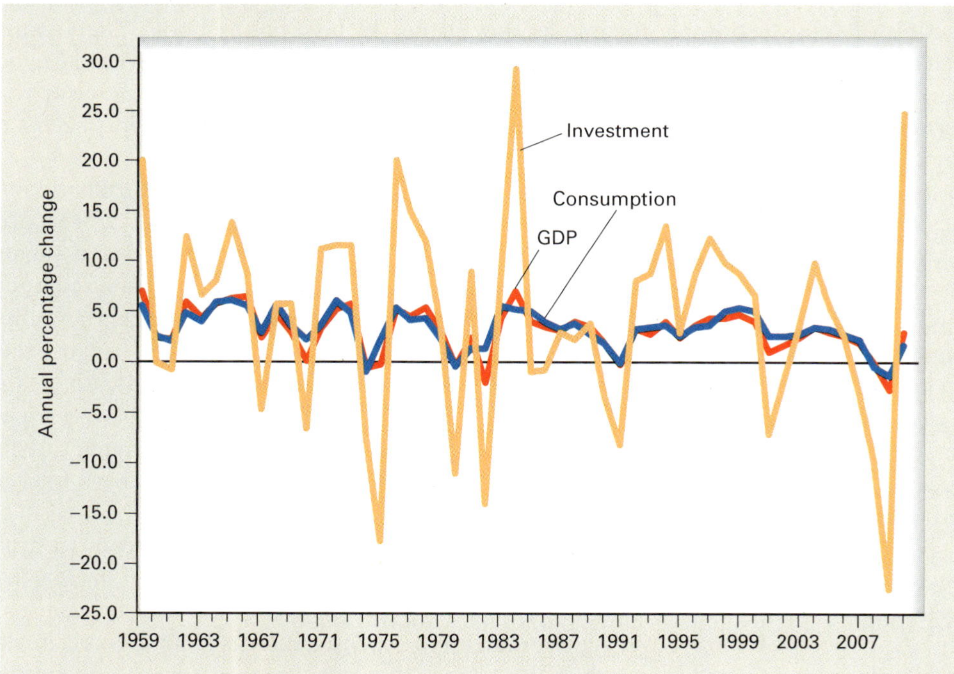

Investment varies much more year-to-year than consumption does and accounts for nearly all the variability in real GDP. This is why economic forecasters pay special attention to the business outlook and investment plans.

Source: Bureau of Economic Analysis, U.S. Department of Commerce. Figures for 2010 are projections based on annualized rates from the first half of the year. For the latest data, go to http://bea.gov/.

Digital Vision/Getty

Two points are obvious. First, investment fluctuates much more than either consumption or GDP. For example, in the recession year of 1982, GDP declined 1.9 percent but investment dropped 14.0 percent; consumption actually increased 1.4 percent. In 1984, GDP rose 7.2 percent, consumption increased 5.3 percent, but investment soared 29.5 percent. Second, fluctuations in consumption and in GDP appear to be entwined, although consumption varies a bit less than GDP. Consumption varies less than GDP because consumption depends on disposable income, which varies less than GDP.

During the six years of falling GDP over the last half century, the average decline in GDP was only 0.9 percent, but investment dropped an average of 13.6 percent. Consumption actually increased by an average of 0.3 percent. So *while consumption is the largest spending component, investment varies much more than consumption and accounts for nearly all the year-to-year variability in real GDP*. Note that GDP does not always fall during years in which a recession occurs. That's because the economy is not necessarily in recession for the entire year. For example, because the recession of 2001 lasted only eight months, GDP managed a small gain for the year of 1.1 percent and consumption grew 2.7 percent. It was the 7.0 percent fall in investment that caused the recession. That's why economic forecasters pay special attention to business expectations and investment plans.

Sources: *Economic Report of the President*, February 2010, *Survey of Current Business* 90, various months for 2010; and *OECD Economic Outlook* 87 (May 2010). For data and articles about economic aggregates, go to the Bureau of Economic Analysis site at http://bea.gov/.

CHAPTER 24

PUBLIC POLICY

CASE STUDY

The Ripple Effect on the Economy of 9/11 When hijacked planes hit the World Trade Center and the Pentagon, America's sense of domestic security changed. The thousands of lives lost and the billions of dollars of property destroyed were chronicled at length in the media. Let's look at the impact of the tragedy on just one industry—air travel—to see how slumping demand there affected aggregate expenditure.

Once aviation regulators became aware of the hijackings, they grounded all nonmilitary aircraft immediately. This cost the airlines hundreds of millions of dollars a day in lost business. During the days following the attack, video of the second plane crashing into the twin towers was shown again and again, freezing this image in people's minds and heightening public concerns about airline safety. These worries, coupled with the airport delays from added security (passengers were told to arrive up to three hours before flights), reduced the demand for air travel once planes were allowed to fly again. For short flights, it became quicker and easier to drive than to fly. Two weeks after the attacks, airlines were operating only 75 percent of their flights, and these flights were only 30 percent full instead of the usual 75 percent full. Airlines requested federal support, saying they would go bankrupt otherwise. Congress quickly approved a $15 billion aid package of loans and grants.

Despite the promise of federal aid, airlines laid off 85,000 workers, or about 20 percent of their workforce. Flight reductions meant that as many as 900 aircraft would

e activity

The World Travel and Tourism Council conducts economic research on the impact of the travel industry on GDP in the United States and around the world. Updated reports on the national and global impact of changes in the travel industry are available at http://www.wttc.travel/. Find the latest report for the United States. What is the current contribution of travel and tourism to U.S. GDP? What do you think is meant by direct versus indirect impacts? How did these change following the events of September 11, 2001?

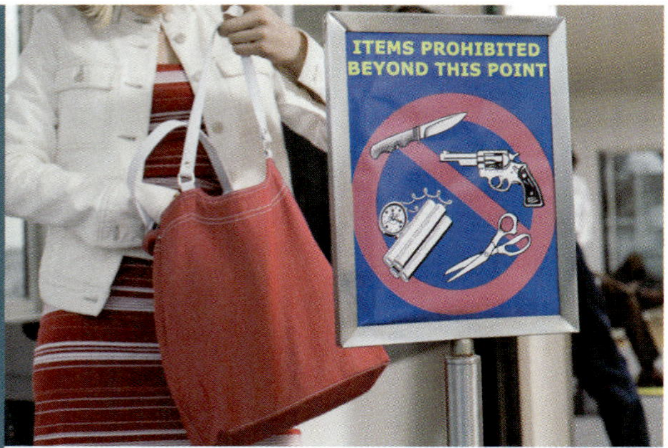

Creatas/Jupiter Images

be parked indefinitely, so investment in new planes collapsed. Boeing, the major supplier of new planes and America's leading exporter, announced layoffs of 30,000 workers. This triggered layoffs among suppliers of aircraft parts, such as jet engines and electronic components. For example, Rockwell Collins, an electronics supplier, said 15 percent of its workforce would lose jobs. Other suppliers in the airline service chain also cut jobs. Sky Chef, a major airline caterer, laid off 4,800 of its 16,000 employees.

Airports began rethinking their investment plans. Half the major U.S. airports said they were reevaluating capital improvement plans to see if these investments made sense in this new environment. Honolulu airport, for example, suspended plans to add extra gates and renovate its overseas terminals.

Within three weeks after the attacks, job cuts announced in the industry exceeded 150,000. These were part of only the first round of reduced consumption and investment. In an expanding economy, job losses in one sector can be made up by job expansions in other sectors. But the U.S. economy was already in a recession at the time of the attack, having lost about a million jobs between March 2001 and September 2001. People who lost jobs or who feared for their jobs reduced their demand for housing, clothing, entertainment, restaurant meals, and other goods and services. For example, unemployed flight attendants would be less likely to buy new cars, reducing the income of autoworkers and suppliers. People who lost jobs in the auto industry would reduce *their* demand for goods and services. So the reductions in airline jobs had a ripple effect.

Airlines are only one part of the travel industry. With fewer people traveling, fewer needed hotel rooms, rental cars, taxi rides, and restaurant meals. Each of those sectors generated a cascade of job losses. The terrorist attacks also shook consumer confidence, which in September 2001 suffered its largest monthly drop since October 1990, on the eve of the first Persian Gulf War. Within 10 days following the attacks, the number of people filing for unemployment benefits jumped to a nine-year high. Again, these early job losses could be viewed as just part of the first round of reduced aggregate expenditure. The second round would occur when people who lost jobs or who feared they would lose their jobs started spending less. The U.S. economy continued to shed jobs for nearly two years after the attacks, losing about 2 million more jobs. Researchers estimate that business interruptions resulting from the attacks cost the U.S. economy a little over $100 billion, or about 1 percent of GDP.

Sources: Adam Z. Rose et al., "The Economic Impacts of the September 11 Terrorist Attacks: A Computable General Equilibrium Analysis," *Peace Economics, Peace Science, and Public Policy*, 15 (Issue 2, 2009), Berkeley Electronic Press at http://www.bepress.com/peps/vol15/iss2/; Will Pinkston, "Airports Reconsider Expansion Plans as Future of Air Travel Gets Murkier," *Wall Street Journal*, 27 September 2001; Luke Timmerman, "Boeing Warns Bad May Get Worse," *Seattle Times*, 21 September 2001; U.S. Department of Labor at http://www.bls.gov/ and the Federal Aviation Administration at http://www.faa.gov/

Bringing Theory to Life

Case Study

e activity

The Bureau of Economic Analysis provides a useful glossary at http://www.bea.gov/glossary/glossary.cfm. Look up the definitions of *durable goods, nondurable goods,* and *services.*

Consumer Spending on Services During the Recession As noted earlier, consumption is the largest component of aggregate spending, averaging about 70 percent of the total during the past decade. And consumption depends primarily on income. But at any given level of income, consumption depends on other factors, such as net wealth. The biggest source of net wealth for most households is their home. Nationally, home prices increased steadily between 1987 and 2006, tripling on average during a long march upward. The rise in housing prices made homeowners feel flush and thus more inclined to spend at each income level. Consumption as a share of disposable income rose from 90 percent in 1987 to 94 percent in 2006.

But there is no economic law that says home prices can't fall. Let's look at what happened to consumption and real GDP when home prices turned down sharply. After peaking in 2006, average home prices in the United States dropped about 22 percent by the third quarter of 2008. That was the first sustained drop in at least two decades and it shook people up. In later chapters, we'll look at the wider fallout from the housing bust, but here the focus is on consumer spending. Percent changes in consumption, its components, and in real GDP are shown in Exhibit 1 for the four quarters in the heart of what some have called the *Great Recession*. Real GDP in the third quarter of 2008 fell 4.0 percent (at an annualized rate). Consumption fell 3.5 percent, the biggest drop since 1980. During the four quarters shown, the decline in GDP averaged 4.1 percent

EXHIBIT 1 Percentage Changes by Quarter in Real GDP and Consumption Categories During the Four Worst Quarters of the 2007–2009 Recession

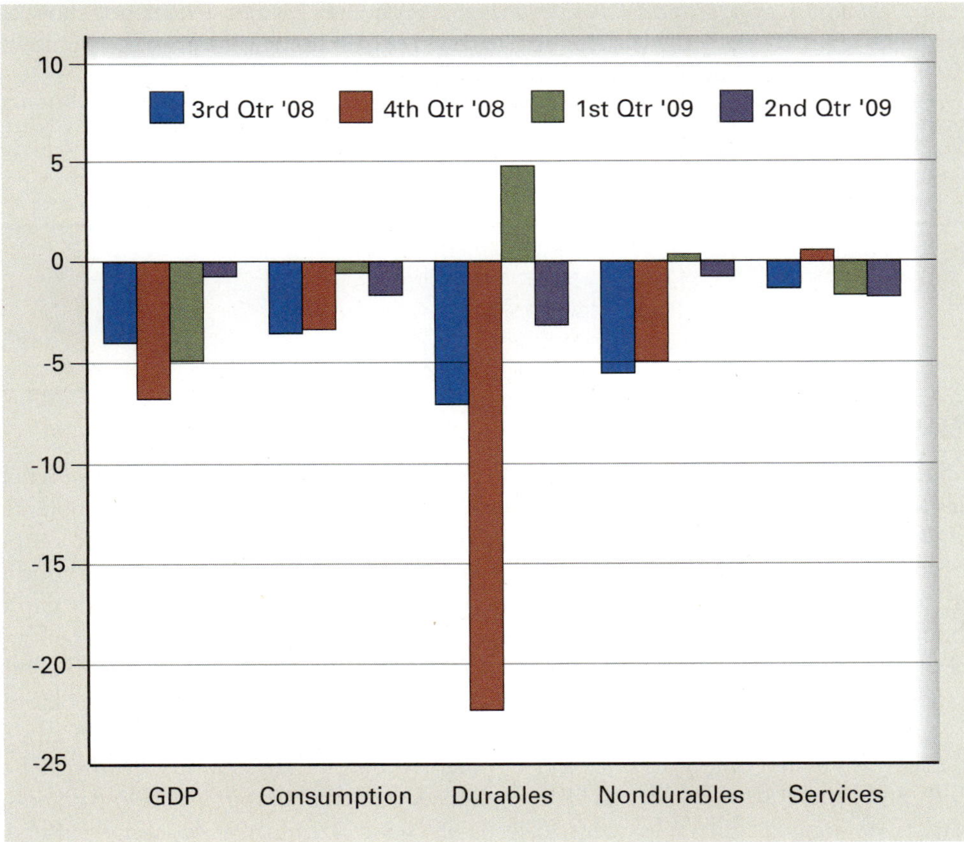

Source: National Economic Accounts, Bureau of Economic Analysis, U.S. Dept. of Commerce. Data are seasonally adjusted at annual rates.

and the decline in consumption averaged 2.2 percent. As usual, consumption varied less than GDP.

Let's sort consumption into its components. With the economy souring, with job prospects looking iffy, and with the stock market crashing, many households decided to put off buying new cars, new furniture, and other durable goods. Consumer spending on durable goods dropped 12.0 percent in the third quarter of 2008. That drop nearly doubled in the fourth quarter to 22.3 percent, the largest fall since 1981. For the four quarters, the decline averaged 8.2 percent. All this would be a big problem for the economy except for one fact: Durable goods account for a small share of all consumption, just 12 percent.

Let's look at nondurable goods. People still bought groceries, but they shifted to house brands and to cheaper cuts of meat. As a result, spending on nondurable goods fell 5.5 percent in the third quarter of 2008, the biggest drop in that category since 1974. The decline for the four quarters averaged 2.7 percent. Nondurable goods are 22 percent of consumption.

But even with a weak economy, spending on consumer services, such as housing, utilities, health care, and education, didn't change that much. This category fell 1.3 percent in the third quarter of 2008, and the decline for the four quarters averaged just 1.0 percent. Here's the good news: Services make up 66 percent of consumption, and about 50 percent of GDP. Thus, the biggest consumption category slipped the least. *The decline in GDP over the four quarters was bad enough, but without the relative stability of service spending, things could have been worse.* Although Exhibit 1 does not show the third quarter of 2009, by then GDP started growing again though the growth rate slowed 2010. The recession ended in June 2009.

Sources: "National Economic Accounts," Bureau of Economic Analysis, U.S. Dept. of Commerce at http://bea.gov/national/nipaweb/nipa_underlying/SelectTable.asp and http://bea.gov/national/nipaweb/SelectTable.asp. U.S. home prices are based on Standard & Poor's Case-Shiller Index at http://www.standardandpoors.com/home/en/us/.

Chapter 25

CASE STUDY

e activity

For the latest on output gaps among the world's leading economies, go to the OECD's Web site at http://www.oecd.org/home/. From there you can access Publications & Documents, which leads you to the latest OECD Outlook. Click on Complete Statistical Annex. What is the current output gap in the United States? How does the U.S. gap compare to that in the other leading economies?

Public Policy

U.S. Output Gaps and Wage Flexibility Let's look at estimates of actual and potential GDP. Exhibit 1 measures actual GDP minus potential GDP as a percentage of potential GDP for the United States. When actual output exceeds potential output, the output gap is positive and the economy has an expansionary gap. For example, actual output in 2000 was 1.7 percent above potential output, amounting to an expansionary gap of about \$190 billion (in 2005 dollars). When actual output falls short of potential output, the output gap is negative and the economy suffers a recessionary gap. For example, actual output in 2009 was 4.9 percent below potential output, amounting to a recessionary gap of about \$630 billion (in 2005 dollars). Note that the economy need not be in recession for actual output to fall short of potential output. For example, from 1991 to 1997, and from 2001 to 2003, real GDP expanded, yet actual output was below potential output. As long as unemployment exceeds its natural rate, the economy suffers a recessionary gap.

EXHIBIT 1 **The U.S. Output Gap Measures Actual Output Minus Potential Output as a Percentage of Potential Output**

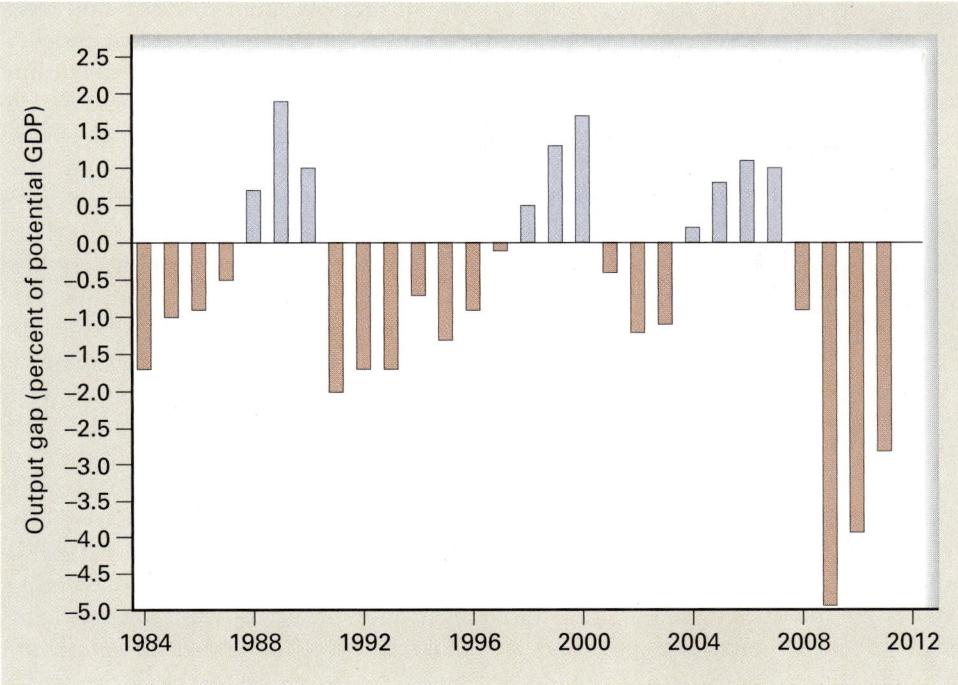

The output gap each year equals actual GDP minus potential GDP as a percentage of potential GDP. When actual output exceeds potential output, the output gap is positive and the economy has an expansionary gap, as shown by the blue bars. When actual output falls short of potential output, the output gap is negative and the economy suffers a recessionary gap, as shown by the pink bars. Note that the economy need not be in recession for actual output to fall below potential output.

Source: Developed from estimates by the *OECD Economic Outlook* 87 (May 2010), Annex Table 10. Figures for 2010 and 2011 are OECD projections. OECD data can be found at http://www.oecd.org/home/.

Employers and employees clearly would have been better off if these recessionary gaps had been reduced or eliminated. After all, more people would have jobs to produce more goods and services, thereby increasing the nation's standard of living. If workers and employers fail to reach an agreement that seems possible and that all would prefer, then they have failed to coordinate in some way. Recessionary gaps can thus be viewed as resulting from a **coordination failure**.

coordination failure
A situation in which workers and employers fail to achieve an outcome that all would prefer

If employers and workers can increase output and employment by agreeing to lower nominal wages, why don't they? As we have already seen, some workers are operating under long-term contracts, so wages aren't very flexible, particularly in the downward direction. But if long-term contracts are a problem, why not negotiate shorter ones? First, negotiating contracts is costly and time consuming (for example, airline union contracts take an average of 1.3 years to negotiate). Longer contracts reduce the frequency, and thus reduce the average annual cost, of negotiations. Second, long-term contracts reduce the frequency of strikes, lockouts, and other settlement disputes. Thus, both workers and employers gain from longer contracts, even though such contracts make wages more sticky and make recessionary gaps more likely to linger.

When demand is slack, why do employers lay off workers rather than cut nominal wages? Yale economist Truman Bewley interviewed over 300 managers, union officials, and employment recruiters and concluded that resistance to pay cuts comes, not from

Digital Vision/Jupiter Images

workers or unions, but from employers. Employers believe that pay cuts damage worker morale more than layoffs do. By lowering morale, pay cuts increase labor turnover and reduce productivity. In contrast, the damage from layoffs is brief and limited because laid off workers are soon gone and cannot disrupt the workplace, and remaining workers may be more grateful just to have jobs. What's more, even during severe recessions, such as the recent downturn, about nine in ten workers still have jobs, so most workers have little incentive to support a wage cut to maintain employment.

Another reason workers may be reluctant to accept lower nominal wages is unemployment benefits. When a worker is laid off, the incentive to accept a lower wage is reduced by the prospect of unemployment benefits. The greater these benefits and the longer they last, the less the pressure to accept a lower wage. For example, in the latter part of the 1920s, unemployment benefits nearly tripled in Great Britain and eligibility requirements were loosened. Despite record high unemployment during the Great Depression, money wages in Great Britain remained unchanged during the period. For some people, unemployment benefits had become a viable alternative to accepting a lower wage. Because of the high unemployment rates from 2008 to 2010, Congress extended benefits and some states added to that extension. In New York, for example, some unemployed workers were eligible for up to 99 weeks of benefits.

Sources: Truman Bewley, *Why Wages Don't Fall During a Recession* (Cambridge, Mass.: Harvard University Press, 2000); Laurence Ball and David Romer, "Sticky Prices and Coordination Failures," *American Economic Review*, 81 (June 1991): 539–552; Daniel Benjamin and Levis Kochin, "Searching for an Explanation of Unemployment in Interwar Britain," *Journal of Political Economy*, 87 (June 1979): 441–470; and *Survey of Current Business* 90 (June 2010).

CASE STUDY

e activity

Learn about unemployment rates in Europe by finding the most current press release from Eurostat at http://epp.eurostat.ec.europa.eu/. The OECD follows trends in market reforms in Europe designed to reduce the structural impediments to lowering the unemployment rate. You can access the latest reports and analyses at http://www.oecd.org/home/. Go to By Topic, then to Employment under the Society heading, and follow the link to Labour Markets.

...continued

Public Policy

Why Has Unemployment Been So High in Europe? Between World War II and the mid-1970s, unemployment in Western Europe was low. From 1960 to 1974, for example, the unemployment rate in France never got as high as 4 percent. The worldwide recession of the mid-1970s, however, jacked up unemployment rates. But unemployment continued to climb in Continental Europe long after the recession ended, topping 10 percent during the 1990s, and was still 8 percent to 9 percent in 2007, even before the recession (once the recession set in, rates returned to 10 percent in 2009). Some observers claim that the natural rate of unemployment has increased in these countries.

Some economists have borrowed a term from physics, **hysteresis** (pronounced *his-ter-eé-sis*), to argue that the natural rate of unemployment depends in part on the recent history of unemployment. *The longer the actual unemployment rate remains above what had been the natural rate, the more the natural rate itself increases.* For example, those unemployed can lose valuable job skills, such as the computer programmer who loses touch with the latest developments. As weeks of unemployment stretch into months and years, the shock and stigma may diminish, so the work ethic weakens. What's more, some European countries offer generous unemployment benefits indefinitely, reducing the hardship of unemployment. On average, unemployment benefits in Western Europe replace 60 to 80 percent of lost pay versus about 50 percent in the United States. Some Europeans have collected benefits *for more than a decade*. Unemployment benefits in Belgium have no time limit.

Still, no consensus exists regarding the validity of hysteresis. The theory has been less relevant in the United States and Great Britain, where unemployment fell from 10 percent in 1982 to 4.5 and 5.5, respectively, in 2007. It remains to be seen whether higher unemployment from 2008 to 2010 will increase the natural rate. About four in every ten Americans unemployed in 2010 had been out of work for 27 weeks or more. This was the highest in the six decades that such a measure has been reported.

An alternative explanation for high unemployment in Continental Europe is that legislation introduced there in the 1970s made it more difficult to lay off workers. In most European countries, job dismissals must be approved by worker councils, which consider such factors as the worker's health, marital status, and number of dependents. Severance pay has also become mandatory and can amount to a year's pay or more. With layoffs difficult and costly, hiring became almost an irreversible decision for an employer, so firms have become reluctant to add workers, particularly untested workers with little experience. Also, high minimum wages throughout Europe, high payroll taxes, and an expanded list of worker rights have increased labor costs. For example, in Sweden, parents are guaranteed between them a total of 16 months paid leave after the birth of a child, and the mother has the right to work no more than six hours a day until the child reaches grade school. In Austria, mothers are guaranteed two years of paid leave after a birth plus job protection. Swedish workers are also guaranteed at least five weeks of vacation a year; French workers get at least six weeks (American workers have no vacation guarantees).

AP Photo/Michel Euler

Regardless of the explanation, the result has been high unemployment in Continental Europe during normal times, particularly among young workers.

Sources: Francine Fontaine and Jagadeesh Sivadasan, "Do Labor Market Rigidities Have Microeconomic Effects? Evidence from Within the Firm," *American Economic Journal: Applied Economics*, 1 (April 2009): 88–129; Rafael Lalive and Josef Zweimuller, "How Does Parental Leave Affect Fertility and Return to Work?" *Quarterly Journal of Economics*, 124 (August 2009): 1363–1402; "The Trap: The Curse of Long-Term Unemployment Will Bedevil the Economy," *The Economist*, 14 January 2010; Katrin Bennhold, "In Sweden the Men Have It All," *New York Times*, 9 June 2010; and *OECD Economic Outlook*, 87 (May 2010).

e activity continued

What changes have been made in employment protection and other labor laws in the European countries to deal with high rates of unemployment? What types of liberalization and other changes can you find that have been made in labor and product markets to promote employment?

hysteresis
The theory that the natural rate of unemployment depends in part on the recent history of unemployment; high unemployment rates increase the natural rate of unemployment

Chapter 26

Public Policy

Fiscal Policy and Presidential Elections After the recession of 1990–1991, the economy was slow to recover. At the time of the 1992 presidential election, the unemployment rate still languished at 7.5 percent, up 2 percentage points from when President George H. W. Bush had taken office in 1989. The higher unemployment rate was too much of a hurdle to overcome, and Bush lost his reelection bid to challenger Bill Clinton. Clinton's campaign slogan was: "It's the economy, stupid."

The link between economic performance and reelection success has a long history. Ray Fair of Yale University examined presidential elections dating back to 1916 and found, not surprisingly, that the state of the economy during the election year affected

CASE STUDY

e activity

Visit http://www.cato.org, which is the Web site for the Cato Institute, a non-profit public policy research foundation in Washington, D.C. Search for

...continued

e activity continued

the Fiscal Policy Report Card on America's Governors. In the report, governors with the most fiscally conservative records—the tax and budget cutters—received the highest grades. Those who increased spending and taxes the most received the lowest grades. In the most recent report, find the grade for the governor of your state. Then check the previous report. Did your state's grade improve or become worse? Do you know why?

political business cycles
Economic fluctuations that occur when discretionary policy is manipulated for political gain

the outcome. Specifically, Fair found that a declining unemployment rate and strong growth rate in GDP per capita increased election prospects for the incumbent party. On the other hand, the financial crisis just weeks before the presidential election of 2008 helped Barack Obama defeat the incumbent party candidate, John McCain (before that crisis, the two were even in the polls). Another Yale economist, William Nordhaus, developed a theory of **political business cycles**, arguing that incumbent presidents, during an election year, use expansionary policies to stimulate the economy, often only temporarily. For example, evidence suggests that President Nixon used expansionary policies to increase his chances for reelection in 1972, even pressuring the Federal Reserve chairman to pursue an expansionary monetary policy. There is also evidence of a political business cycle of sorts at the municipal level, where, prior to an election, city officials spend more on those items most visible to the electorate, such as city parks.

The evidence to support the theory of political business cycles is not entirely convincing. One problem is that the theory limits presidential motives to reelection, when in fact presidents may have other objectives. For example, the first President Bush, in the election year of 1992, passed up an opportunity to sign a tax cut for the middle class because that measure would also have increased taxes on a much smaller group—upper-income taxpayers.

An alternative to the theory of political business cycles is that Democrats care more about unemployment and less about inflation than do Republicans. This view is supported by evidence indicating that during Democratic administrations, unemployment is more likely to fall and inflation is more likely to rise than during Republican administrations. Republican presidents tend to pursue contractionary policies soon after taking office and are more willing to endure a recession to reduce inflation. The country suffered a recession during the first term of the last six Republican presidents. Democratic presidents tend to pursue expansionary policies to reduce unemployment and are willing to put up with higher inflation and higher deficits to do so. President Barack Obama, for example, pushed through what would turn out to be an $862 billion stimulus package even though it worsened what was already a huge federal deficit.

© Istockphoto/Cosmonaut Creative Media, LLC

A final problem with the political-business-cycle theory is that other issues sometimes compete with the economy for voter attention, particularly when the economy is doing well. For example, in the 2004 election, President Bush's handling of the war on terror, especially the war in Iraq, became at least as much of a campaign issue as his handling of the economy.

Sources: Linda Veiga and Francisco Veiga, "Political Business Cycles at the Municipal Level," *Public Choice*, 131 (April 2007): 45–64; Burton Abrams, "How Richard Nixon Pressured Arthur Burns: Evidence from the Nixon Tapes," *Journal of Economic Perspectives* (Fall 2006): 177–188; *Economic Report of the President*, February 2010; Ray Fair, *Predicting Presidential Elections and Other Things* (Stanford University Press, 2002); and William Nordhaus, "Alternative Approaches to the Political Business Cycle," *Brookings Papers on Economic Activity*, No. 2 (1989): 1–49.

Public Policy

CASE STUDY

e activity

Using Canada as a control group, an academic study—"Evaluating 'Cash-for-Clunkers'"—raised the same concerns about the program as described in the case study. Read the paper at http://www.rff.org/documents/RFF-DP-10-39.pdf.

Cash for Clunkers On June 24, 2009, President Obama signed into law the Consumer Assistance to Recycle and Save (CARS) Act, better known as the "cash-for-clunkers" program. The measure appropriated $1 billion to pay from $3,500 to $4,500 to each car buyer who traded a "clunker," or an older car with gas mileage of 18 miles per gallon or less, for a new one with better gas mileage. The clunker had to be "drivable," and registered and insured by the same person for at least a year prior to the sale (to prevent someone from buying a junk just as a trade-in).

Once car dealers began submitting paperwork for government reimbursement, it became clear the program would soon burn through the $1 billion appropriation. So Congress put $2 billion more into the pot and limited the program to a month (the $1 billion was originally expected to last four months). The 135 pages of government rules were constantly changing, and the Web site dealers used often crashed. The 2,000 people needed to process paperwork had trouble reimbursing dealers, so some dealers had to drop out of the program.

Still, nearly 680,000 new vehicles were sold during the month of the program. That spike in sales, some argue, is clear evidence of the program's success. For example, the Transportation Secretary claimed this "is the one stimulus program that seems to be working better than just about any other program." And the program's Web site said it was "wildly successful." But evidence suggests that the overwhelming majority of those car sales would have occurred anyway during the last half of 2009. For example, according to analysis by the automotive Web site Edmunds.com, which tracks car sales, the net effect of the program was only 125,000 additional vehicle sales, implying a government cost of $24,000 per additional sale.

AP Photo/Damian Dovarganes

But even if the program was expensive on a per vehicle basis, didn't the economy in general and car makers in particular need a boost? First, the $3 billion spent on the program was money the government didn't have; the outlays increased the federal deficit, already at record levels. Ultimately, to pay for the program, taxes must be raised or other government spending must be cut. Second, at least some of the stimulus benefited other economies. Japanese manufacturers accounted for 41 percent of the program sales and the Big Three (General Motors, Ford, and Chrysler), 39 percent. Third, automakers already received the $83 billion in bailout funds (and at least $34 billion would not likely ever be repaid). What about helping other sectors hit hard by the recession such as furniture makers and the travel industry? Why not "cash for couches" or "cash for cruises"?

Proponents of cash for clunkers would point out that cars are a special case, because a second objective of the program was to clear the air by replacing clunkers with cars that would get maybe 10 more miles to the gallon. Christopher Knittel of the University of California, Davis, estimated that the government could have gotten 10 times more carbon reduction by spending the $3 billion in the market for carbon offsets.

For most buyers, the clunker money served as the down payment on a new car, so more people could afford one, and didn't that stimulate the economy? From that stimulus effect must be subtracted the housing, furniture, clothes, vacation trips, and other items that those consumers wouldn't be buying in the future, because they face additional monthly payments for car leases or car loans. Finally, by mandating the destruction of each trade-in vehicle (a disposal facility had to crush or shred each clunker with evidence of such supplied to the government), Congress removed up to 680,000 drivable cars from the used-car market, inevitably raising the prices of the used cars that low-income households tend to buy. The destruction also reduced the supply of salvageable used parts that are bought mostly by low-income drivers looking to keep their cars running. Cash for clunkers was never that popular with the public. Polls show that most Americans did not approve of the program.

Sources: Emily Maltby, "Used Car Dealers Feel Clunkers Pinch," *Wall Street Journal*, 6 October 2009; Irwin M. Stelzer, "Seven Lessons of Cash-for-Clunkers Failure," *Washington Examiner*, 28 August 2009; Christopher R. Knittel, "The Implied Cost of Carbon Dioxide Under the Cash for Clunkers Program," Working Paper (31 August 2009) at http://www.econ.ucdavis.edu/faculty/knittel/papers/CfC_final_latest.pdf; and the government program's site at http://www.cars.gov/.

Chapter 27

CASE STUDY

e activity

The National Academy of Social Insurance is a nonpartisan research organization formed to study Social Security and Medicare. Go to its Web site, at http://www.nasi.org, to access its publications. There you will find Briefs and Fact Sheets about the current status of and issues related to both Medicare and Social Security. Click on the Research menu and select Medicare and Health Policy to find information about the impact of health care reform.

Public Policy

Reforming Social Security and Medicare Social Security is a federal redistribution program established during the Great Depression that collects payroll taxes from current workers and their employers to pay pensions to current retirees. More than 47 million beneficiaries averaged about $1,070 per month from the program in 2010. For two-thirds of beneficiaries, these checks account for more than half of their income. Benefits increase each year to keep up with inflation as measured by the CPI. Medicare, established in 1965 to provide short-term medical care for the elderly, is an in-kind transfer program funded mostly by payroll taxes on current workers and their employers (beneficiaries also pay a small amount). Medicare in 2010 helped pay medical expenses for about 40 million Americans age 65 and older plus about 7 million other people with disabilities. Medicare costs averaged about $9,700 per beneficiary in 2010 and is growing much faster than inflation. Social Security and Medicare are credited with helping reduce poverty among the elderly from about 35 percent in 1960 to under 10 percent most recently—a poverty rate below other age groups.

In the early 1980s, policy makers recognized the huge impact that baby boomers would have on such a pay-as-you-go program. When 76 million baby boomers begin retiring in 2011, Social Security costs and, especially, Medicare costs are set to explode. Reforms adopted in 1983 raised the payroll tax rate, increased the tax base by the rate of inflation, gradually increased the retirement age from 65 to 67 by 2022, increased the penalty for early retirement, and offered incentives to delay retirement. These reforms were an attempt to make sure that revenues would exceed costs at least while baby boomers remain in the workforce. But these reforms were not enough to sustain the programs. Americans are living longer, fertility rates have declined, and health care costs are rising faster than inflation. The 65-and-older population will nearly double by 2030 to 72 million people, or about 20 percent of the U.S. population.

In 1940, there were 42 workers per retiree. Today, there are 3.3 workers per retiree. By 2030, only 2.1 workers will support each retiree. Based on current benefits levels, spending on Social Security and Medicare, now 8 percent relative to GDP and 32 percent of federal outlays, by 2030 will reach 12.5 percent relative to GDP and 50 percent of federal outlays. The huge sucking sound will be the federal deficit arising mostly from Social Security and Medicare. The Congressional Budget Office projects a 2030 deficit of 9 percent relative to GDP. All these numbers spell trouble ahead.

But you don't have to look into the future to find trouble. Because of the 2007–2009 recession, Social Security tax receipts declined as people lost jobs, and outlays increased as some of those out of work decided to retire early. As a result, in 2010 Social Security payouts exceeded pay-ins for the first time in history. That wasn't supposed to happen until 2016, and it put more pressure on the entire federal budget. Prior to 2010, Social Security pay-ins exceeded payouts. The idea was that this surplus would accumulate over time, so there would be funds available when baby boomers started to retire. But Congress never saved any of the surplus; instead they raked it off, put IOUs in the Social Security Trust Fund, then spent it. The Trust Fund is simply a box of government IOUs. Nothing's there.

©iStockphoto/Sally Llanes

What to do, what to do? Possible reforms include increasing taxes, reducing benefits, raising the eligibility age, using a more accurate index to calculate the annual cost-of-living increase in benefits (meaning smaller annual increases), reducing benefits to wealthy retirees (they are already taxed on up to 85 percent of Social Security income and pay up to three times more for one part of Medicare), and slowing the growth of Medicare costs.

In summary, Social Security and Medicare helped reduce poverty among the elderly, but the programs grow more costly as the elderly population swells and as the flow of young people into the workforce slows. When Social Security was created in the 1930s, life expectancy was 60 years, so only a minority would ever reach 65 to get benefits. Now people live 20 years longer on average, and they collect benefits for most of those added years. Something has to give if these programs are to be available when you retire. President Obama and the Congress raised Medicare payroll taxes on high income households, but these higher revenues will fund health care reform more generally, not Medicare in particular. The health care measure also cuts Medicare funding by about $150 billion over ten years. Social Security and Medicare remain in big trouble.

Sources: Susan Davis, "Public Faith in Social Security Drops," *Wall Street Journal*, 20 July 2010; Ben Bernanke, "Long-Term Fiscal Challenges Facing the United States," Testimony Before the Committee on the Budget, U.S. Senate, 18 January 2007, at http://www.federalreserve.gov/boarddocs/testimony/2007/20070118/default.htm; Mary Williams Walsh, "Social Security to See Payout Exceed Pay-In This Year," *New York Times*, 24 March 2010; and "Status of the Social Security and Medicare Programs: A Summary of the 2009 Annual Report," Social Security and Medicare Boards of Trustees, at http://www.ssa.gov/OACT/TRSUM/index.html.

PUBLIC POLICY

CASE STUDY

e activity

In the course of his research on intergenerational transfers, Robert Barro coined the now well-known phrase Ricardian Equivalence. See the definition at Investopedia: http://www.investopedia.com/terms/r/ricardianequivalence.asp.

An Intergenerational View of Deficits and Debt Harvard economist Robert Barro has developed a model that assumes parents are concerned about the welfare of their children who, in turn, are concerned about the welfare of *their* children, and so on for generations. Thus, the welfare of all generations is tied together. According to Barro, parents can reduce the burden of the federal debt on future generations. Here's his argument. When the government runs deficits, it keeps current taxes lower than they would otherwise be, but taxes in the future must increase to service the higher debt. If there is no regard for the welfare of future generations, then the older people get, the more attractive debt becomes relative to current taxes. Older people can enjoy the benefits of public spending now but will not live long enough to help finance the debt through higher taxes or reduced public benefits.

But parents can undo the harm that deficit financing imposes on their children by consuming less now and saving more. As governments substitute deficits for taxes, parents will consume less and save more to increase gifts and bequests to their children to help pay the higher taxes in the future. If greater saving offsets federal deficits, deficit spending will not increase aggregate demand because the decline in consumption will negate the fiscal stimulus provided by deficits. According to Barro, this intergenerational

Jane Veshkin/Photodisc/Getty Images

transfer offsets the future burden of higher debt and neutralizes the effect of deficit spending on aggregate demand, output, and employment.

The large budget deficits caused in part by tax cuts and spending increases of the 1980s would seem to provide a natural experiment for testing Barro's theory. The evidence fails to support his theory because the large federal deficits coincided with lower, not higher, saving rates. Yet defenders of Barro's view say that maybe the saving rate was low because people were optimistic about future economic growth, an optimism reflected by the strong performance of stock markets. Or maybe the saving rate was low because people believed tax cuts would result not in higher future taxes but in lower government spending, as President Reagan promised.

But there are other reasons to question Barro's theory. First, those with no children may be less concerned about the welfare of future generations. Second, his theory assumes that people are aware of federal spending and tax policies and about the future consequences of current policies. Until recently, most people seemed to know little about such matters. One survey found that few adults polled had any idea about the size of the federal deficit. In the poll, respondents were offered a range of choices, but only 1 in 10 said correctly that the deficit that year was between $100 billion and $400 billion.

But with federal deficits topping $1 trillion, people seem more aware and more concerned about deficits than ever. If Barro's view is correct, recent deficits should call forth an increase in saving. That rate did increase from 2.1 percent of disposable income in 2007 to 6.2 percent by the second quarter of 2010. That could offer support for Barro's view, or it could simply reflect how cautious people became about spending with jobs scarce and the economy seemingly adrift.

Sources: Robert J. Barro, "The Ricardian Approach to Budget Deficits," *Journal of Economic Perspectives* 3 (Spring 1989); Jesus Cueresma and Gerhard Reitschuler, "Is the Ricardian Equivalence Proposition and 'Aerie Fairy' Theory for Europe," *Economica*, 74 (November 2007): 682–694; and Gerald Seib, "A Plague Stalking America: The Deficit Addiction," *Wall Street Journal*, 27 April 2010. Saving rate figures are from the Bureau of Economic Analysis, U.S. Dept. of Commerce.

Chapter 28

CASE STUDY

e activity

See the Wikipedia article on tea bricks at http://en.wikipedia.org/wiki/Tea_brick. Click on "Use as currency" in the Contents box. It is another example of an unusual commodity used as money.

Bringing Theory to Life

Mackerel Economics in Federal Prisons The economist R.A Radford spent several years in prisoner-of-war camps in Italy and Germany during World War II, and he wrote about his experience. Although economic activity was sharply limited, many features of a normal economy were found in the prison life he observed. For example, in the absence of any official currency behind bars, cigarettes came to serve all three roles of money: medium of exchange, unit of account, and store of value. Cigarettes were of uniform quality, of limited supply (they came in rations from the International Red Cross), reasonably durable, and individually could support small transactions or, in packs, larger ones. Prices measured in cigarettes became fairly uniform and well known throughout a camp of up to 50,000 prisoners of many nationalities.

Now fast-forward half a century to the U.S. federal prison system. Prisoners are not allowed to hold cash. Whatever money sent by relatives or earned from prison jobs (at 40 cents an hour) goes into commissary accounts that allow inmates to buy items such as snacks and toiletries. In the absence of cash, to trade among themselves federal prisoners also came to settle on cigarettes as their commodity money (despite official prohibitions against trade of any kind among inmates). Cigarettes served as the informal money until 2004, when smoking was banned in all federal prisons.

© Image Source/Jupiter Images

Once the ban took effect, the urge to trade created incentives to come up with some other commodity money. Prisoners tried other items sold at the commissary including postage stamps, cans of tuna, and Power Bars, but none of that seemed to catch on. Eventually prisoners settled on cans of mackerel, a bony, oily fish. So inmates informally use "macks"—as the commodity money came to be called—to settle gambling debts, to buy services from other inmates (such as ironing, shoe shining, and cell cleaning), and to buy goods from other inmates (including special foods prepared with items from the commissary and illicit items such as home-brewed "prison hooch"). At those federal prisons where the commissary opens only one day a week, some prisoners fill the void by running mini-commissaries out of their lockers.

After wardens banned cans (because they could be refashioned into makeshift knives), the commodity money quickly shifted from cans of mackerel to plastic-and-foil pouches of mackerel. The mack is considered a good stand-in for the dollar because each pouch costs about $1 at the commissary, yet most prisoners, aside from weight-lifters seeking extra protein, would rather trade macks than eat them.

Wardens try to discourage the mackerel economy by limiting the amount of food prisoners can stockpile. Those caught using macks as money can lose commissary privileges, can be reassigned to a less desirable cell, or can even spend time in the "hole." Still, market forces are so strong that the mackerel economy survives in many federal prisons.

Sources: R. A. Radford, "The Economic Organization of a P.O.W. Camp," *Economica*, 12 (November 1945): 189–201: and Justin Scheck, "Mackerel Economics in Prisons Leads to Appreciation of the Oily Fillets," *Wall Street Journal*, 2 October 2008.

Bringing Theory to Life

CASE STUDY

The Hassle of Small Change About 2.4 billion U.S. pennies were minted in 2009, and about 150 billion pennies circulated. That's about 500 pennies per U.S. resident. Most pennies are resting in change jars, drawers, or other gathering places for the lowly coin. Pennies are abandoned in the tiny change bins and donation cans at store counters. Many people won't bother to pick one up on the sidewalk (as evidenced by the number you find there). The penny, like all U.S. currency, has over time been robbed of its exchange value by inflation. Today's penny buys only one-seventh as much as it did in the 1950s. Pennies can't be used in parking meters, vending machines, or pay telephones, and penny candy is long gone. To avoid the hassle of small change, some restaurants, such as the Vanilla Bean Café in Pomfret, Connecticut, charge prices exactly divisible by 25 cents (including sales taxes). That way, pennies, nickels, and dimes aren't needed for any transaction.

e activity

The average price for zinc shot up from $0.35 a pound in 2002 to $1.00 in 2010—driven in large part by increased demand from China—and pennies are 97.5 percent zinc. Visit the Web site of Citizens for Retiring the Penny at http://www.retirethepenny.org/index.html to read about the myths that surround retiring the penny, and to link to other relevant sites, including Americans for Common Cents, a pro-penny lobbying group funded by the zinc industry.

The exchange value of the penny has declined as the cost of minting it has risen. For more than a century, the penny was 95 percent copper. In 1982, copper prices reached record levels, so the U.S. Mint began making pennies from zinc, with just a thin copper finish. Then, the price of zinc rose, boosting the metal cost of a penny in 2009 to

© R.Alcorn

0.8 cents. Add to that the 0.8-cent minting cost per penny, and you get 1.6 cents per coin. So the government loses a 0.6 cents on each penny minted, or $14.4 million on pennies minted in 2009. Nickels, which are mostly copper, are also money losers; in 2009 they cost 6 cents to make.

Has the penny outlived its usefulness? In the face of rising metal prices, the government has some options. First option: mint them from a lower-cost alloy. This would buy some time, but inflation would eventually drive the metallic cost above the exchange value of the coin. Second option: abolish the penny. Take it out of circulation. Countries that have eliminated their smallest coins include Australia, Britain, Finland, Hong Kong, and the Netherlands. New Zealand eliminated its 5-cent coin, as well as its 2-cent and 1-cent coins. The United States abolished the half-cent coin in 1857, at a time when it was worth 8 cents in today's purchasing power.

Third option: decree that the penny is worth 5 cents, the same as a nickel. At the same time, the government could withdraw nickels from circulation. With pennies worth so much more, there would be no incentive to hoard them for their metallic value (a current problem), and it would likely be decades before the metallic value caught up with the exchange value. Rebasing the penny to 5 cents would create windfall profits for those now hoarding pennies, but would increase the money supply by about $6 billion, a drop in the bucket compared to a total money supply of $1.7 trillion, so the move would have virtually no effect on inflation.

If the penny gets so little respect, why did the Treasury mint 2.4 billion in 2009. As noted, some people are hoarding pennies, waiting for the day when the metallic value exceeds the exchange value. Another source of demand is the sales tax, which adds pennies to transactions in 44 states. Charities also collect millions from change cans located at check-out counters. And zinc producers lobby heavily to keep the penny around as a major user of the metal. Thus, the penny still has its boosters. That's why retailers continue to order pennies from their banks, these banks order pennies from the Fed, the Fed orders them from the U.S. Mint, and the Mint presses yet more pennies into idle service.

Sources: Austan Goolsbee, "Now that the Penny Isn't Worth Much, It's Time to Make It Worth 5 Cents," *New York Times*, 1 February 2007; Elizabeth Williamson, "Will Nickel-Free Nickels Make a Dime's Worth of Difference," *Wall Street Journal*, 10 May 2010; and Thomas Sargent and Francois Velde, *The Big Problem of Small Change* (Princeton, NJ: Princeton University Press, 2002). View the rounded prices on Vanilla Bean Café's menu at http://www.thevanillabeancafe.com/. .

Chapter 29

Public Policy

CASE STUDY

e activity

Visit the information page about the new $100 notes from the U.S. Treasury Department at http://newmoney.gov for a detailed explanation of the new design and security features of the $100 Franklin note. Take the interactive quiz.

Faking It As just noted, as much as two-thirds of U.S. currency is held abroad, mostly as a safe, liquid, and portable store of value. The foreign demand for U.S. currency spiked immediately following the financial crisis of September 2008 as people sought the world's most trusted currency; some people hoarded dollars. One possible threat to the integrity of U.S. currency is the so-called supernote—a counterfeit $100 note of extremely high quality that began circulating around 1990; the suspected origin is North Korea. It's a remarkable forgery, including sequential serial numbers and a polymer security thread that took Crane & Company, the supplier of paper for U.S. currency since 1879, years to develop. By perfectly emulating the ferrous oxide inked in Benjamin Franklin's portrait, the supernote sometimes fools currency-scanning machines at the nation's 12 Federal Reserve Banks.

Expert engravers produced the supernote, but technological improvements in copy machines, computers, and printers now allow even amateurs to make counterfeits. About half the fake notes found in a recent year were produced with computers, copiers, and printers, up from just 1 percent in 1995. On U.S. soil, the Secret Service seizes most counterfeit money before it circulates. But foreign counterfeiting poses a problem for the U.S. Secret Service, which is primarily a domestic police force (few of the 2,000 agents work abroad). Most counterfeit money seized here is printed abroad, and seizures abroad have been growing.

The $100 note was redesigned in 1996 for the first time since 1928. Other denominations have added extra colors other than green and black for the first time in modern American history. To help combat technological improvements in counterfeiting, the U.S. Treasury now redesigns U.S. currency every 7 to 15 years. The $100 note got the same colorful treatment for circulation in February 2011. New features include 3-D security images that change from bells to 100s as the note is tilted. The $1 note is not popular with counterfeiters and will not get a facelift. Vending machine owners also oppose any change in the $1 note.

The $20 note is most popular among domestic counterfeiters, and the $100 note most popular among foreign counterfeiters. Colombia is the world's largest source of bogus American currency. Colombia borders on Ecuador, which converted to the U.S. dollar in 2000 and thus offers a ready outlet for counterfeits. As noted earlier, in some countries the U.S. dollar circulates alongside the local currency, which offers more outlets for counterfeiters.

Most other countries that redesign their currency recall notes with the old design and impose a time limit on their validity. The United States has a policy of never recalling currency for fear that the world's hoarders of dollars might switch to other currencies, such as euros (remember, we want foreigners to keep hoarding their U.S. dollars). Over time, preference for the new currency and the replacement of old notes as they pass through the Fed will eventually eliminate old notes. But different designs of the same denomination will circulate side by side for some time, especially $100 notes. To give you some idea how long this could take, U.S. notes exceeding $100 were last printed in 1946, and the Fed began taking them out of circulation in 1969. Yet more than 100,000 notes of $1,000 or more are still hoarded by the public here and abroad and remain legal tender. Some still show up at Federal Reserve Banks, where they are destroyed. Every U.S. note issued since 1861 remains legal tender today. That's one reason U.S. dollars are prized around the world. They all come with a lifetime money-back guarantee, so to speak.

Sources: Darrella Hughes, "U.S. Unveils New $100 Bill," *Wall Street Journal*, 21 April 2010; Jim Dwyer, "Awash in $100 Bills that Add Up to Zero," *New York Times*, 23 April 2010; "'Supernote' Investigation," U.S. Secret Service, 25 April 2006, at http://cryptome.org/supernote-nk.pdf; and "The Use and Counterfeiting of U.S. Currency Abroad, Part 3," *A Final Report to the Congress by the Secretary of the Treasury*, September 2006. The U.S. Treasury also has a Web site about new notes at www.newmoney.gov.

CASE STUDY

e activity

The Missouri Attorney General's office provides an online payday loan calculator at http://ago.mo.gov/cgi-bin/ConsumerCorner/calculators/payday.cgi.

Behavioral Economics

Banking for the Poor: Payday Loans A "payday loan" is a relatively small amount of money—say, $300—borrowed for a short period, usually about two weeks, by lower-income people who have a checking account, a job, and direct deposit of their paycheck. For example, the borrower writes a post-dated check for $300 to the payday lender, and gets $255 in cash. The lender holds onto the check until the next payday, two weeks later, then cashes it, netting $45 on the transaction. Or the borrower can decide to rollover the loan by paying the lender another $45 to hold the check for two more weeks. Most borrowers roll over their loans more than once. The implied annual rate of interest is at least 400 percent.

Payday lending began in Arizona in 2000 and peaked at 715 stores there. Nationally, payday lender stores reached into the tens of thousands. Here are some questions: Do payday loans benefit an underserved population by providing ready access to short-term credit, albeit at a high cost? Or do payday loans trap customers into habitual borrowing at steep interest rates with no way out? Should government regulators protect borrowers from the bad consequences of their own choices? Or would a ban simply force such borrowers into even less attractive options?

Some earlier research using geographical differences in regulation across the country suggested that payday loans, despite their high interest rates, may provide benefits to borrowers and their communities. For example, although this may sound odd, according to one argument, some people may deliberately borrow at such costly rates so they will have more incentive to repay the loan quickly. But more recent research raises some troubling questions about payday loans. For example, Brian Melzer of Northwestern University finds no evidence that having access to payday loans alleviates economic hardship. On the contrary, access to payday lenders leads to more difficulty paying mortgages, rent, and utilities; a greater chance of losing one's home; and an increased tendency to put off needed medical care, dental care, and prescription drug purchases.

AP Photo/Matt York

Using a database of 145,000 payday loan applicants from a large lender in Texas, Paige Skiba of Vanderbilt and Jeremy Tobacman of the University of Pennsylvania compare payday borrowers with similarly situated applicants who were denied payday loans to determine whether payday borrowing affects the likelihood of bankruptcy. They find that, for first-time applicants with below average credit scores, access to payday loans doubles the chances of filing for bankruptcy during the following two years (compared to first-time applicants with below average credit scores who were denied payday loans). Seemingly small loans cause such a large effect because borrowers are already financially strapped when they begin with a payday loan. In addition, many payday borrowers take out multiple loans, so the interest burden piles up.

Finally, a study by the North Carolina bank commissioner analyzes how families fared after payday lenders were forced from that state in 2006. A survey of payday borrowers found that most knew the dollar cost per $100, but only one in six had any idea about the implied annual percentage rate. Some said they were glad they no longer were tempted by what they viewed as a costly product–easy to get into, but hard to get out of. About three quarters of the fees collected by payday lenders come from rollovers of existing loans. Many payday lenders offer half-off discounts to new customers.

Arizona, where it all started, imposed a 36 percent cap on payday loans effective July 2010, the same ceiling placed on other lenders, such as banks. Altogether 16 states have imposed interest rate caps. Payday lenders claim they can't survive at such low rates, and many leave those states. Some payday lenders switch to using auto titles as collateral, but interest caps still apply. Research into the impact of payday loans is ongoing, but recent evidence suggests this option could make borrowers worse off, not better off.

Sources: "North Carolina Consumers After Payday Lending," University of North Carolina, (November 2007); Paige Skiba and Jeremy Tobacman, "Do Payday Loans Cause Bankruptcy?" Unpublished manuscript, (November 9, 2009); Ryan Randazzo, "Payday Lender to Close 47 Stores, Leave State," *Arizona Republic*, 12 July 2010; and Brian T. Melzer, "The Real Cost of Credit Access: Evidence from Payday Lending," Northwestern University, (January 3, 2009) at http://www.kellogg.northwestern.edu/faculty/melzer/realcosts_melzer_01_03_09.pdf.

Chapter 30

Public Policy

CASE STUDY

e activity

The Federal Reserve Banks provide reports, surveys, speeches, and other information for Fed Watchers. At the Federal Reserve Bank of Philadelphia at http://www.phil.frb.org, click on Economic Research. Select a recent survey or report, such as the Survey of Professional Forecasters, and read the latest offering. What indications can you find about the future direction of interest rates?

Targeting the Federal Funds Rate At 2:15 P.M. on December 16, 2008, immediately following a regular meeting, the Federal Open Market Committee (FOMC) announced that it would lower its target for the federal funds rate to between 0 and 0.25 percent, the tenth reduction in 15 months. In cutting the target rate, the FOMC stated that "The Federal Reserve will employ all available tools to promote the resumption of sustainable economic growth and to preserve price stability. In particular, the Committee anticipates that weak economic conditions are likely to warrant exceptionally low levels of the federal funds rate for some time." True to its words, the FOMC kept the rate near zero for at least the next two years.

As you know by now, the federal funds rate is the interest rate banks charge one another for overnight lending of reserves at the Fed. Because lowering the rate reduces the cost of covering any reserve shortfall, banks are more willing to lend to the public. To execute this monetary policy, the FOMC authorized the New York Fed to make open-market purchases to increase bank reserves until the federal funds rate fell to the target level.

For four decades, the Fed has reflected its monetary policy in this interest rate. (For a few years, the Fed targeted money aggregates, but more on that later.) There are many interest rates in the economy—for credit cards, new cars, mortgages, home equity loans, personal loans, business loans, and more. Why focus on such an obscure rate? First, by changing bank reserves through open-market operations, the Fed has a direct lever on the federal funds rate, so the Fed's grip on this rate is tighter than on any other market rate. Second, the federal funds rate serves as a benchmark for determining other short-term interest rates in the economy. For example, after the Fed announces a rate change, major banks around the country usually change by the same amount their prime interest rate—the interest rate banks charge their best corporate customers. The federal funds rate affects monetary and financial conditions, which in turn affect employment, aggregate output, and the price level. The Fed uses the federal funds rate to pursue its primary goals of price stability and sustainable economic growth.

Exhibit 1 shows the federal funds rate since early 1996. As a lesson in monetary policy, let's walk through the Fed's rationale. Between early 1996 and late 1998, the economy grew nicely with low inflation, so the FOMC stabilized the rate in a range of

EXHIBIT 1 Recent Ups and Downs in the Federal Funds Rate

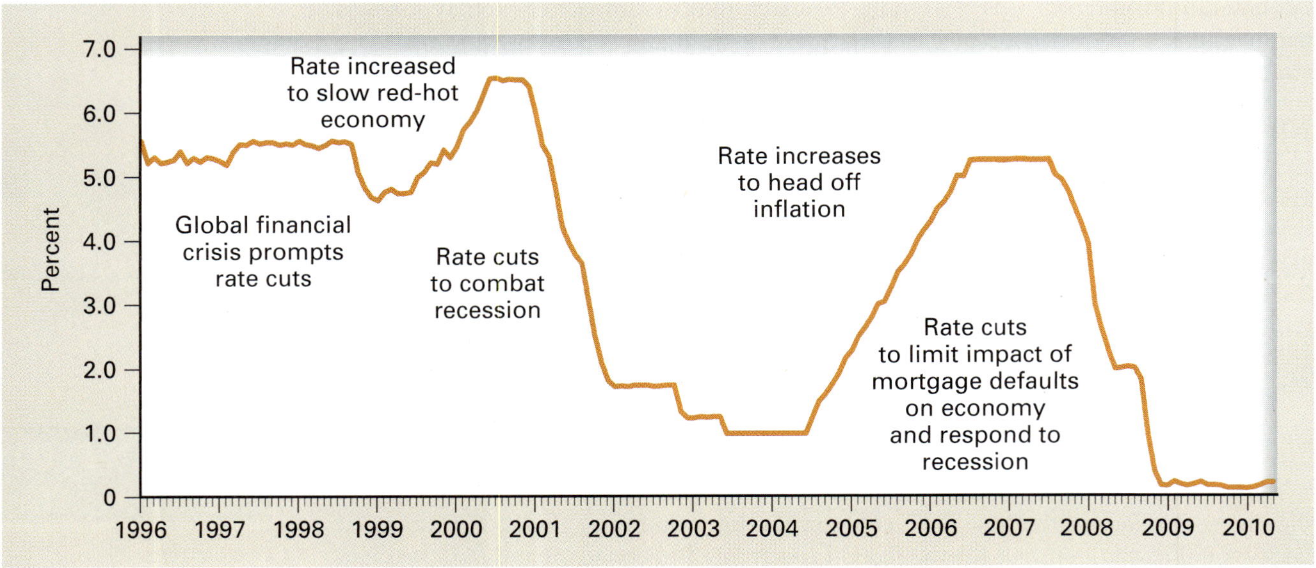

Since the early 1990s, the Fed has pursued monetary policy primarily through changes in the federal funds rate, the rate that banks charge one another for borrowing and lending excess reserves overnight.

Source: Based on monthly averages from the Federal Reserve Bank.

5.25 percent to 5.5 percent. But in late 1998, a Russian default on its bonds and the near collapse of a U.S. financial institution created economic havoc, prompting the FOMC to drop the target rate to 4.75 percent. By the summer of 1999, those fears abated, and instead the FOMC became concerned that robust economic growth would trigger higher inflation. In a series of steps, the federal funds target was raised from 4.75 percent to 6.5 percent. The FOMC announced at the time that the moves "should markedly diminish the risk of rising inflation going forward." Some critics argued that the Fed's rate hikes contributed to the 2001 recession. In 2001, concerns about waning consumer confidence, weaker capital spending, and the 9/11 terrorist attacks prompted the FOMC to reverse course. Between the beginning of 2001 and mid-2003, the FOMC cut the rate from 6.5 percent to 1.0 percent, reflecting at the time the most concentrated monetary stimulus on record. The rate remained at 1.0 percent for a year. Some economists criticized the Fed for keeping rates too low too long. They charged that this "easy money" policy overstimulated the housing sector, encouraging some to buy homes they really couldn't afford. These home purchases, critics argued, inflated the bubble in housing prices and sowed the seeds for mortgage defaults that hit years later.

Anyway, after leaving the rate at 1.0 percent for a year, the FOMC began worrying again about inflationary pressure. Between June 2004 and June 2006, the target federal funds rate was increased from 1.0 percent to 5.25 percent in 17 steps. The FOMC then hit the pause button, leaving the rate at 5.25 percent for more than a year. This takes us up to September 2007, when troubles in the housing sector, a rising mortgage default rate, and a softening economy prompted the first in a series of federal funds rate cuts. After 10 cuts over 15 months, the target rate in December 2008 stood between 0 and 0.25 percent, the lowest in history.

Over the years, the Fed has tried to signal its intentions more clearly to financial markets—to become more transparent. In 1995, the FOMC began announcing immediately after each meeting its target for the federal funds rate. Since 2000, the post-meeting statement also included the probable "bias" of policy in the near term—that is, whether or not its current level or direction of interest rate changes would continue. And in 2005, the FOMC began releasing the minutes three weeks after each meeting. By generating such concrete news, FOMC meetings became widely followed media events.

If the situation is serious enough, the FOMC may act between regular meetings, and this has a more dramatic impact, particularly on the stock market. The Fed held six unscheduled meetings in 2008. Still, in announcing rate changes, the FOMC must be careful not to appear too troubled about the economy, because those fears could harm business and consumer confidence further. Also, the FOMC must avoid overdoing rate cuts. As one member of the Board of Governors warned, the FOMC must not cut the rate so much that it "ends up adding to price pressure as the growth strengthens." Thus, the FOMC performs a delicate balancing act in pursuing its main goals of price stability and sustainable economic growth.

Sources: Sewell Chan, "Fed Study Suggests Rates Will Stay at Record Lows Until 2012," *New York Times*, 14 June 2010; Michael Derby, "Most Primary Dealers Agree Fed Rate Increases Won't Come Soon," *Wall Street Journal*, 3 June 2010; and "FOMC Statement on Interest Rates," "Minutes of the Federal Open Market Committee," and "Federal Open Market Committee Transcripts" for various meetings. Find the latest FOMC statements, minutes, and transcripts at http://www.federalreserve.gov/monetarypolicy/fomc.htm.

PUBLIC POLICY

CASE STUDY

e activity

You can read about the economies of other countries in the country profiles at the CIA World Factbook at https://www.cia.gov/library/publications/the-world-factbook/index.html. Other sources for international economic data are The World Bank (http://www.worldbank.org/), the International Monetary Fund (http://www.imf.org), and the Organization for Economic Co-operation and Development (www.oecd.org).

The Money Supply and Inflation Around the World If we view economies around the world as evidence, what's the link between inflation and changes in the money supply in the long run? According to the quantity theory, as long as the velocity of money is fairly stable, there should be a positive relation in the long run between the percentage change in the money supply and the percentage change in the price level. Panel (a) of Exhibit 2 illustrates the relationship between the average annual growth rate in M2 and the average annual inflation rate for 85 countries over a 10-year period. As you can see, the points fall rather neatly along the trend line, showing a positive relation between money growth and inflation. Because most countries are bunched below an inflation rate of 30 percent, let's break these points out in finer detail in panel (b). Although panel (a) shows a sharper link between money growth and inflation than does panel (b), in both panels, countries with higher rates of money growth experience higher rates of inflation.

In panel (a), Argentina, Bolivia, and Israel—countries with inflation of more than 100 percent per year—also experienced annual money growth exceeding 100 percent. Argentina, which had the highest inflation rate over the 10-year period in the sample, at 395 percent per year, also had the highest average annual money growth, at 369 percent. Hyperinflation first appeared about a century ago, and in every case it has been accompanied by rapid growth in the supply of money.

How does hyperinflation end? The central bank must somehow convince the public it is committed to halting the rapid growth in the money supply. The most famous hyperinflation was in Germany between August 1922 and November 1923, when inflation averaged 322 percent *per month*. Inflation was halted when the German government created an independent central bank that issued a new currency convertible into gold. Germany had a similar problem after World War II when currency became nearly useless because Allied victors imposed strict price controls on the country. Experts estimate that the lack of a viable currency cut German output in half. Germany's "economic miracle" of 1948 was due largely to the adoption of a reliable monetary system.

EXHIBIT 2 **A Decade of Annual Inflation and Money Growth in 85 Countries (average annual percent)**

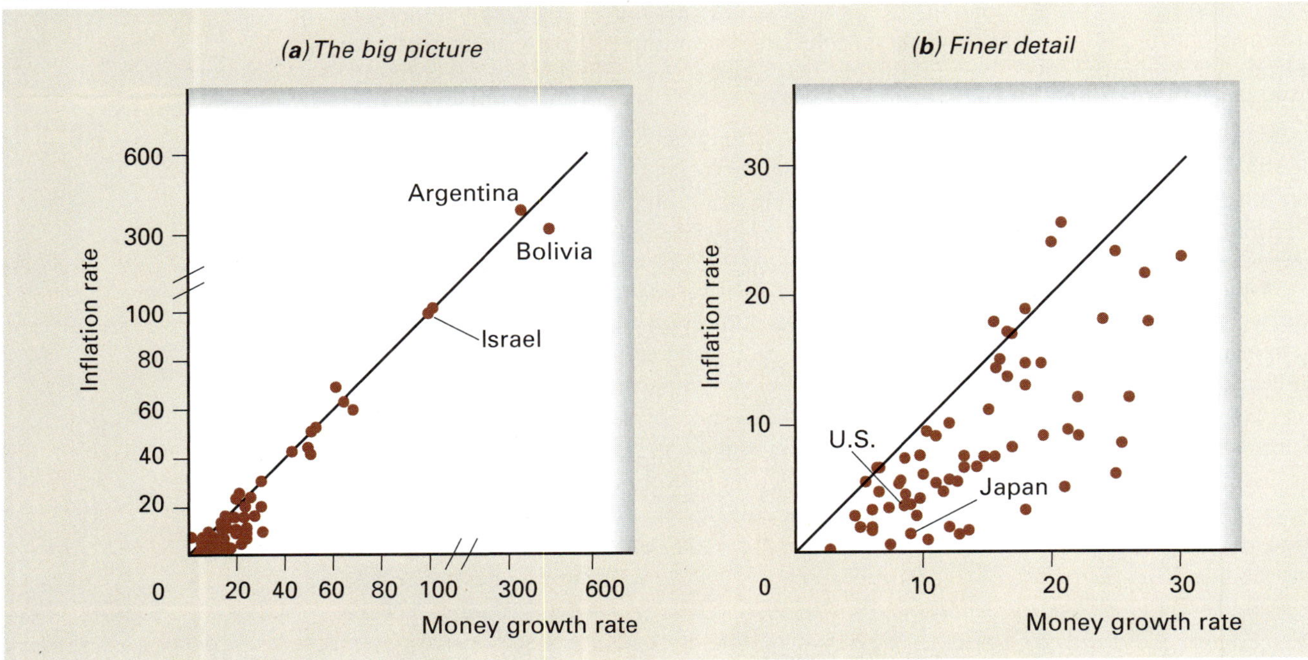

Panel (a) shows that money growth is clearly linked with inflation based on a sample of 85 countries over a 10-year period. In each country that experienced hyperinflation, the inflation rate matched the growth in the money supply. Panel (b) offers finer detail for the subset of countries with inflation and money growth below 30 percent. Again, money growth and inflation are positively related in the long run.

Source: The World Bank, *World Development Report* 1992 (New York: Oxford University Press, 1992), Table 13. Figures are annual averages for 1980 to 1990.

Argentina, Bolivia, and Israel all managed to tame the beast of hyperinflation, with inflation under 3 percent by 2000. Residents of all three countries, perhaps mindful of past hyperinflation, still hold lots of U.S. dollars as a store of value.

AP Photo/Dario Lopez-Mills

Exhibit 2 reflects averages from 1980 to 1990, but the relationship holds up if we focus on a more recent decade. From 1992 to 2002, for example, inflation, while generally lower around the world than in the 1980s, was still highest in countries with the highest money growth rates. Brazil, Belarus, Romania, and Russia experienced hyperinflation and also had extremely high rates of money growth. The highest was in Brazil, where the inflation and the money supply each grew an average of about 210 percent per year during the decade. In Venezuela, the money supply increased by 30 percent in 2009 and by July 2010 the annual rate of inflation was 33 percent, about the highest in the world at the time. As Nobel prize winner Milton Friedman famously put it, "Inflation is always and everywhere a monetary phenomenon, in the sense that it cannot occur without a more rapid increase in the quantity of money than in output."

Sources: *World Development Report 2010* at http://econ.worldbank.org; Greg Ip, "Taking the Measure of the World's Cash Hoard," *Wall Street Journal*, 3 November 2005; Gerald Dwyer and R. W. Hafer, "Are Money Growth and Inflation Still Related?" *Federal Reserve Bank of Atlanta Economic Review*, (Second Quarter 1999): 32–43; "Economic and Financial Indicators," *The Economist*, 17 July 2010.

CHAPTER 31

PUBLIC POLICY

Active Versus Passive Presidential Candidates During the third quarter of 1990, after what at the time had become the longest peacetime economic expansion of the century, the U.S. economy slipped into a recession, triggered by Iraq's invasion of oil-rich Kuwait. Because of large federal deficits at the time, policy makers were reluctant to adopt discretionary fiscal policy to revive the economy. That task was left to monetary policy. The recession lasted only eight months, but the recovery was sluggish—so sluggish that unemployment continued to edge up in what was derisively called a "jobless recovery."

That sluggish recovery was the economic backdrop for the presidential election of 1992 between Republican President George H. W. Bush and Democratic challenger Bill Clinton. Because monetary policy did not seem to be providing enough of a kick, was additional fiscal stimulus needed? With the federal budget deficit in 1992 already approaching $300 billion, a record amount to that point, would a higher deficit do more harm than good?

Bush's biggest political liabilities during the campaign were the sluggish recovery and growing federal deficits; these were Clinton's biggest political assets. Clinton argued that (1) Bush had not done enough to revive the economy; (2) Bush and his predecessor, Ronald Reagan, were responsible for the sizable federal deficits; and (3) Bush could not be trusted because he broke his 1988 campaign pledge of "no new taxes" by signing a tax increase in 1990 to help cut federal deficits. Clinton promised to raise tax rates on the rich and cut them for the middle class. He also promised to create jobs through government spending that would "invest in America."

Bush tried to remind voters that, technically, and the economy was growing again, so the recession was over. But that was a hard sell with unemployment averaging 7.6 percent during the six months leading up to the election (remember that the unemployment rate is a lagging indicator).

Clinton saw a stronger role for government, and Bush saw a stronger role for the private sector. Clinton's approach was more *active* and Bush's more *passive*. In the end, high unemployment rates during the campaign made people more willing to gamble on Clinton. Apparently, during troubled times, an active policy has more voter appeal than a passive one. Ironically, the economy at the time was stronger than conveyed by the media and by challenger Clinton ("It's the economy, stupid" became Clinton's rallying cry). Real GDP in 1992 grew 3.4 percent, which would turn out to exceed the average annual growth rate during Clinton's first term.

George W. Bush was not about to make the same mistake as his father. Shortly after taking office in 2001, he proposed the first of three tax cuts to stimulate a weak economy. These cuts, along with growth in government spending combined with the Fed's interest rate cuts for the greatest stimulus of aggregate demand to that point since World War II. Although the recession was over by the end of 2001, the unemployment rate continued to rise to a peak of 6.3 percent in June 2003. Then, as if on cue, in the final 12 months before the election of 2004, the economy added 2 million jobs. Despite an unpopular war in Iraq, the additional jobs helped Bush get reelected.

The 2008 presidential election was like no other in at least the last half century. President Bush was presiding over two unpopular wars, a financial crisis, and an economy sinking fast. But Bush was not on the ballot. Republican John McCain faced Democrat Barack Obama. Soon after the financial crisis of September 2008, the two candidates issued a joint statement supporting the

CASE STUDY

e activity

President George H. W. Bush's final State of the Union address was on January 28, 1992—a time when the country was recovering from a mild recession. The text of his speech—and the State of the Union speeches of other presidents—is available from the C-Span archives at http://www.c-span.org/executive/stateoftheunion.asp. Read it to determine whether he was in favor of an active or passive approach to dealing with the sluggish recovery. Next compare President Clinton's final address in 2000 to that of President George H. W. Bush. How activist did Clinton appear given economic conditions during his last year? What additional government programs and/or tax cuts was he proposing? Were these to stimulate the economy or for some other purpose? Also read President George W. Bush's final State of the Union address for January of 2008. How does his approach compare to that of the first President Bush's approach? What economic policies did President Barack Obama support in his latest State of the Union address?

AP Photo/Mark Lennihan

TARP measure, the most significant legislative action prior to the November election—so, no policy difference between the two candidates on that one.

But the candidates differed on other issues. For example, McCain favored extending the Bush tax cuts, which were set to expire in 2011. Obama would extend the Bush tax cuts but only for those making less than $250,000 a year. Obama proposed broad health care reform with more government regulations. McCain favored tax incentive to increase health coverage, saying he preferred "choices" to "mandates." Obama proposed creating millions of new jobs with "green energy" programs. Not McCain.

More generally, Obama blamed Bush and, by association, McCain, for the financial crisis, arguing that they had stripped away regulations that would have prevented it (though the critical 1999 bank deregulation act was signed by President Clinton).

A presidential poll taken a month before the election found that those whose top concern was the economy preferred Obama over McCain by 2 to 1. When the economy is in trouble, voters seem to support a more active approach. That's what they got.

Sources: "Obama, McCain Lay Out Contrasts Before Undecided Voters," CNN, 8 October 2008 at http://www.cnn.com/2008/POLITICS/10/07/presidential.debate/index.html; David Wessel, "Wanted: Fiscal Stimulus Without Higher Taxes," *Wall Street Journal*, 5 October 1992; *Economic Report of the President*, February 2010; Bob Woodward, *The Agenda* (New York, 1994); and the St. Louis Federal Reserve Bank's database at http://research.stlouisfed.org/fred2/.

CASE STUDY

e activity

Read an interview at the Centre for Economic Policy Research at http://www.cepr.org/press/audio/P135/. The report by the interviewees asks if central banks should respond to movements in stock markets, housing markets, and foreign exchange markets. What is the conclusion? You can also do a search on this site for discussion papers on price stability.

PUBLIC POLICY

Central Bank Independence and Price Stability Some economists argue that the Fed would do better in the long run if it committed to the single goal of price stability rather than also worry about achieving potential output. But to focus on price stability, a central bank should be insulated from political influence, because price stability may involve some painful remedies. When the Fed was established, several features insulated it from politics, such as the 14-year terms with staggered appointments of Board members. Also, the Fed has its own income source (interest earned from securities and fees earned from bank services), so it does not rely on Congress for a budget.

Does central bank independence affect performance? When central banks for 17 advanced industrial countries were ranked from least independent to most independent, inflation during the 15-year span examined turned out to be the lowest in countries with the most independent central banks and highest in countries with the least independent central banks. The least independent banks at the time were in Spain, New Zealand, Australia, and Italy. The most independent central banks were in Germany and Switzerland. Countries with the least independent central banks experienced inflation that averaged four times higher than countries with the most independent central banks. The U.S. central bank is considered relatively independent; U.S. inflation was double that of the most independent countries and half that of the least independent countries.

The trend around the world is toward greater central bank independence. For example, the Central Bank of New Zealand has adopted a monetary policy of inflation rate targeting, with price stability as the primary goal. Chile, Colombia, and Argentina—developing countries that suffered hyperinflation—have legislated more central bank independence. The Maastricht agreement, which defined the framework for a single European currency, the euro, identified price stability as the main objective of the new European Central Bank. That bank has a policy of not reducing the interest rate if inflation exceeds 2.0 percent. In fact, the European Central Bank came under criticism before the recent financial crisis for not cutting interest rates even though a recession loomed and unemployment topped 8 percent. The Bank of England and Swiss National Bank also have a inflation target of no higher than 2.0 percent. Many central banks have adopted low inflation targets. The Federal Reserve does not have an explicit inflation target, but Fed head Bernanke has favored one in the past. Some Fed watchers claim the Fed has an informal inflation target of 1.5% to 2.0%.

Sources: Natasha Brereton, "U.K. Inflation Eases in May," *Wall Street Journal*, 15 June 2010; Sarah Lynch and Tom Barkley, "Jobless Claims Decline," *Wall Street Journal*, 15 July 2010; Alberto Alesina and Lawrence Summers, "Central Bank Independence and Macroeconomic Performance: Some Comparative Evidence," *Journal of Money, Credit and Banking*, 25 (May 1993): 151–162; Ben Bernanke, "A Perspective on Inflation Targeting: Why It Seems to Work," *Business Economics*, 38 (July 2003): 7–15; Stefano Eusepi and Bruce Preston, "Central Bank Communication and Expectations Stabilization." *American Economic Journal: Macroeconomics*, 2 (July 2010): 235–271; and Ben Bernanke, "Inflation Targeting," *Federal Reserve Bank of St. Louis Review*, 86 (July/August 2004): 165–168. For online links to more than 160 central banks, including all those discussed in this case study, go to http://www.bis.org/cbanks.htm.

Chapter 32

Bringing Theory to Life

Doha Round and Round The trade-barrier reductions from the Uruguay Round were projected to boost world income by more than $500 billion when fully implemented, or about $72 per person. In poor countries around the world, any additional income from reduced trade barriers could be a lifesaver.

But when WTO members met in Seattle in November 1999 to set an agenda and timetable for the next round of trade talks (later to become known as the Doha Round), all hell broke loose, as 50,000 protesters disrupted the city. Most were peaceful, but police made more than 500 arrests over three days, and property damage reached $3 million. T-shirts sold the week before the meeting dubbed the event the "Battle in Seattle," and so it was.

Organizers used their objections to free trade as a recruiting and fund-raising tool for a variety of interest groups, including labor unions, environmentalists, and farmers. Union members feared losing jobs overseas, environmentalists feared that producers would seek out countries with lax regulations, farmers in Japan, South Korea, Europe, and the United States feared foreign competition, and other groups feared technological developments such as hormone-fed beef and genetically modified food. The Seattle protest was by far the largest demonstration against free trade in the United States.

Protestors would probably be surprised to learn that WTO members are not of one mind about trade issues. For example, the United States and Europe usually push to protect worker rights around the world, but developing countries, including Mexico, Egypt, India, and Pakistan, object strenuously to focusing on worker rights. These poorer nations are concerned that the clothing, shoes, and textiles they make have not gained access to rich nations quickly enough. Many developing countries view attempts to impose labor and environmental standards as just the latest effort to block goods coming from poor countries. For example, workers in China rioted when U.S. companies operating there proposed shortening the work week. Chinese workers wanted a longer work week, believing they could earn more.

Without international groups such as the WTO to provide a forum for discussing labor and environmental issues around the world, conditions in poor countries would

CASE STUDY

e activity

The World Trade Organization's Web site describes its role and functions and explains the value of reducing trade barriers. The basics on what the WTO is and how it operates can be found at http://www.wto.org/english/thewto_e/whatis_e/whatis_e.htm. What policies support the goal of nondiscriminatory trade? For an example of how one industry has been affected, read the WTO disputes involving textiles at http://www.wto.org/english/tratop_e/texti_e/texti_e.htm. For more on how Nike is responding to criticisms of its labor practices visit its Web site on the subject at http://www.nikebiz.com/responsibility/ (click on Workers/Factories, then on Audit Tools).

Imaginechina via AP Images

likely be worse. Working conditions in many poor countries have been slowly improving, thanks in part to trade opportunities along with pressure for labor rights from WTO and other international groups. For example, Cambodia is one of the poorest countries in the world, but the highest wages in the country are earned by those working in the export sector. Take, for example, Deth, a young mother who sewed T-shirts and shorts at the June Textile factory in Cambodia, mostly for Nike. She worked from 6:15 A.M. to 2:15 P.M. with a half hour for lunch, extra pay for overtime, and double pay for working holidays. Though her pay was low by U.S. standards, it supported her family and was more than twice what judges and doctors average in Cambodia. Factories tend to hire young women, a group otherwise offered few job opportunities. Factory jobs have provided women with status and social equality they never had. Still, protest groups in rich countries called the June Textile factory a "sweatshop" and wanted it shut down. In part because of media pressure, Nike ended its contract with the factory. Researchers have also found that freer trade with Mexico has increased job opportunities there for women.

Doha Round
The multilateral trade negotiation round launched in 2001, but still unsettled as of 2010; aims at lowering tariffs on a wide range of industrial and agricultural products; the first trade round under WTO

After failing to get off the ground in Seattle, the round of talks was launched two years later in Doha, Qatar. In setting the agenda for the **Doha Round**, members agreed to improve market access around the world, phase out export subsidies, and substantially reduce distorting government subsidies in agriculture. Reaching agreement proved easier said than done. Headed by Brazil and India, a group of developing countries demanded stronger commitments to reduce agricultural subsidies in the United States, Europe, and Japan. But farmers in these industrial economies wanted to keep their subsidies and protection from imports. For example, the average farm in Japan is about four acres, so farming there is inefficient and costly (rice in Japan is triple the world price). Talks in Cancun in 2003, Hong Kong in 2005, and Geneva in 2006 and 2008 ended bitterly as the Doha Round went round and round. By late 2010 the Doha Round was still spinning its wheels.

Even in the absence of a Doha agreement, some countries continue to reduce trade barriers through *bilateral* agreements, or agreements between two countries. For example, the United States abolished tariffs on Korean flat TV screens and cars.

Sources: David Wessel, "Free-Trade Winds May Be Blowing Again," *Wall Street Journal*, 1 July 2010; Sewell Chan and Jackie Calmes, "White House to Push Free Trade Deal with South Korea," *New York Times*, 27 June 2010; Ernesto Aguayo-Tellez et al., "Did Trade Liberalization Help Women? The Case of Mexico in the 1990s," NBER Working Paper 16195, (July 2010); Gina Chon, "Dropped Stitches," *Asiaweek*, 22 December 2000; and the Web site for the World Trade Organization at http://www.wto.org.

CASE STUDY

e activity
Read news feeds about the steel industry at http://www.steelonthenet.com/feeds/. You can follow the steel industry in different regions of the world.

Public Policy

Steel Tariffs The U.S. steel industry has been slow to adopt the latest technology and consequently has suffered a long, painful decline for decades—a death from a thousand cuts. Between 1997 and 2001, about 30 percent of U.S. steel producers filed for bankruptcy, including Bethlehem Steel and National Steel. During that stretch, 45,000 U.S. steel jobs disappeared, leaving about 180,000 jobs remaining. Imports accounted for 30 percent of the U.S. market, with most of that steel coming from Europe.

Steel leaders turned to the White House for help, arguing that the industry needed a technological tune-up to become more competitive but needed trade protection during the process. This is a variant of the infant-industry argument. Many of the jobs lost were in "rust-belt" states, such as Ohio, West Virginia, and Pennsylvania, states also critical in presidential elections. We can only speculate what role politics played in the decision, but in March 2002, President George W. Bush imposed tariffs on steel, claiming that imports caused "material injury" to the U.S. steel industry. The tariffs, which ranged from 8 percent to 30 percent on 10 steel categories, were scheduled to last three years.

As expected, the tariffs cut imports and boosted the U.S. price of steel. By 2003, steel imports slumped to their lowest level in a decade. The higher domestic price of steel helped U.S. steel makers but made steel-using industries here less competitive on world markets. For example, the tariffs added about $300 to the average cost of a U.S. automobile. According to one estimate, the tariffs cost 15,000 to 20,000 jobs in steel-user industries.

The European Union and other steel-exporting nations filed a complaint, and in November 2003, the WTO ruled that the tariffs violated trade agreements. The European Union, with about 300,000 of its own steel jobs at stake, announced that if the tariffs were not repealed, EU countries would retaliate with tariffs on U.S. exports. Japan and South Korea also threatened retaliatory tariffs.

After the negative WTO ruling and facing threats of retaliation, the White House repealed the steel tariffs in December 2003, claiming that they had served their purpose. Approximately $650 million in higher tariffs was collected during the 21 months they were imposed. The steelworkers union called the repeal "an affront to all workers." But union members should not have been surprised in light of the WTO ruling, threatened retaliation from abroad, and the fact that several months earlier, the steelworkers union endorsed a Democrat for president.

A big threat to the steel industry has come not from foreign competition but from the financial crisis. In August 2008, U.S. steel makers were operating at 90 percent of capacity. The global financial panic of 2008 temporarily cut U.S. steel production to only 40 percent of capacity by December 2008.

The only tariff threats in recent years have been against Chinese exporters. In 2009, the Obama White House imposed a 35 percent tariff on Chinese tires. Despite minor trade skirmishes, and despite clamors in Washington to insulate U.S. jobs from Chinese goods, and despite the rocky going for the Doha Round, the trend among industrial economies is toward lower tariffs, especially on raw materials. The United States, the European Union, and Japan have eliminated nearly all tariffs on raw materials.

Sources: Steven Greenhouse, "With a Receptive White House, Labor Begins to Line-Up Battles," *New York Times*, 22 September 2009; James Areddy, "U.S. Businesses Back More Trade Action Vs. China," *Wall Street Journal*, 24 May 2010; Robert Guy Matthews, "Industry Cuts Back as Steel Prices Fall," *Wall Street Journal*, 6 July 2010; and "Steel Industry Executive Summary: May 2010," International Trade Administration, U.S. Dept. of Commerce at http://hq-web03.ita.doc.gov/License/Surge.nsf/webfiles/SteelMillDevelopments/$file/exec%20summ.pdf?openelement.

CHAPTER 33

CASE STUDY

e activity

You will need a subscription to search The Economist's archive at http://www.economist.com/. But you can register for a complimentary 14-day pass and then search for the Big Mac Index. Read the article by Nicholas Vardy at http://seekingalpha.com/article/26635-burgernomics-profiting-from-the-bigmac-index. What weaknesses does Vardy say the Big Mac Index has, and why do economists still use it? Another article at http://www.comsec.com.au/public/news.aspx?id=809 states The Economist should replace the Big Mac Index with the iPod Index. Do you agree?

BRINGING THEORY TO LIFE

The Big Mac Index As you have already learned, the PPP theory predicts that in the long run the exchange rate between two currencies should move toward equalizing the cost in each country of an identical basket of internationally traded goods. A lighthearted test of the theory has been developed by *The Economist* magazine, which compares prices around the world for a "market basket" consisting simply of one McDonald's Big Mac—a product that, though not internationally traded, is essentially the same in more than 100 countries. *The Economist* begins with the price of a Big Mac in the local currency and then converts that price into dollars based on the exchange rate prevailing at the time. A comparison of the dollar price of Big Macs across countries offers a crude test of the PPP theory, which predicts that prices should be roughly equal in the long run.

Exhibit 1 lists the dollar price of a Big Mac in March 2010, in 22 surveyed countries plus the euro zone average. By comparing the price of a Big Mac in the United States (shown as the green bar) with prices in other countries, we can derive a crude measure of whether particular currencies, relative to the dollar, are overvalued (red bars) or undervalued (blue bars). For example, because the price of a Big Mac in Norway, at \$6.87, was 92 percent higher than the U.S. price of \$3.58, the Norwegian krone was the most overvalued relative to the dollar of the countries listed. But Big Macs were cheaper in most of the countries surveyed. The cheapest was in China, where \$1.83 was 49 percent below the U.S. price. Hence, the Chinese yuan was the most undervalued relative to the dollar.

EXHIBIT 1 In March 2010, A Big Mac Cost More in the United States Than in Most Other Countries

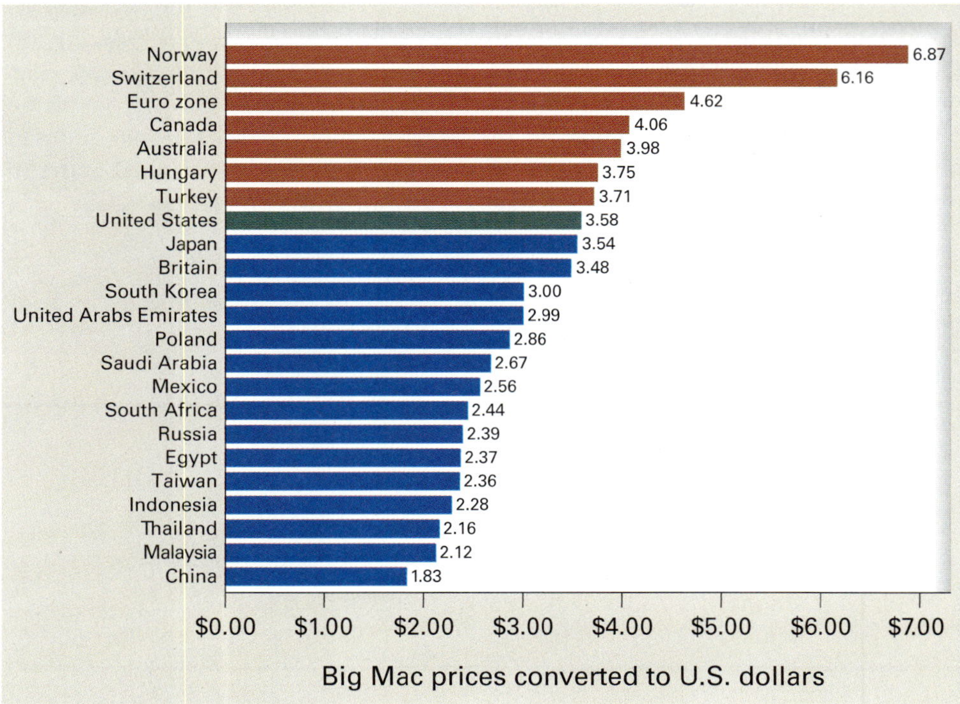

Source: Based on a survey in "The Big Mac Index: Exchanging Blows," *The Economist*, 17 March 2010. Local prices are converted into U.S. dollars using the prevailing exchange rate.

Thus, Big Mac prices in March 2010 ranged from 92 percent above to 49 percent below the U.S. price. The euro was 29 percent overvalued. The price range lends little support to the PPP theory, but that theory relates only to traded goods. The Big Mac is not traded internationally. Part of the price of a Big Mac must cover rent, which can vary substantially across countries. Taxes and trade barriers, such as tariffs and quotas on beef, may also distort local prices. And wages differ across countries, with a McDonald's worker averaging about $8 an hour in the United States versus more like $1 an hour in China. So there are understandable reasons why Big Mac prices differ across countries.

© Mark Richards/PhotoEdit Inc.

Sources: "The Big Mac Index: Exchanging Blows," *The Economist*, 17 March 2010; David Parsley and Shang-Jin Wei, "In Search of a Euro Effect: Big Lessons from a Big Mac Meal?" *Journal of International Money and Finance*, 27 (March 2008): 260–276; Ali Kutan et al., "Toward Solving the PPP Puzzle: Evidence from 113 Countries," *Applied Economics*, 41 (Issue 24, 2009): 3057–3066; and the McDonald's Corporation international Web site at http://www.mcdonalds.com.

WORLD OF BUSINESS

CASE STUDY

What about China? The U.S. trade deficit with China of $227 billion in 2009 exceeded America's combined deficits with the European Union, OPEC countries, and Latin America. The deficit with China grew about 15 percent annually between 2000 and 2009. Americans spend four times more on Chinese products than the Chinese spend on American products. Between 2007 and 2010, China's holdings of U.S. Treasury securities more than doubled from $400 billion to $900 billion.

e activity

The New York Times reviews the basics of the U.S.-China exchange rate at http://www.nytimes.com/2010/09/19/weekinreview/19chan.html. The Bank of China publishes up-to-date exchange rates at http://www.boc.cn/sourcedb/whpj/enindex.html.

Many economists, politicians, and union officials argue that China manipulates its currency, the yuan, to keep Chinese products cheaper abroad and foreign products more expensive at home. This stimulates Chinese exports and discourages imports, thereby boosting Chinese production and jobs. At the same time, the average Chinese consumer is poorer because the yuan buys fewer foreign products.

As we have seen, any country that establishes a fixed exchange rate that undervalues or overvalues the currency must intervene continuously to maintain that rate. Thus, if the official exchange rate has chronically undervalued the Chinese yuan relative to the dollar, as appears to be the case, then Chinese authorities must continuously exchange yuan for dollars in foreign exchange markets. The increased supply of yuan keeps the yuan down, and the increased demand for dollars keeps the dollar up.

But the charge that China manipulates its currency goes beyond simply depressing the yuan and boosting the dollar. China's trading partners increasingly feel they are being squeezed out by Chinese producers without gaining access to Chinese markets. China seeks every trade advantage, especially for the 125 state-owned enterprises run directly by the central government. For example, China offers some domestic producers tax rebates and subsidies to promote exports, while imposing quotas and tariffs to discourage imports, such as a 25 percent tariff on auto-parts imports.

© Annie Reynolds/PhotoLink/Getty Images

China has tried to soothe concerns about the trade deficit. Most importantly, Chinese authorities in 2005 began allowing the yuan to rise modestly against the dollar. As a result, the yuan rose a total of 20 percent against the dollar between July 2005 and July 2010. China also announced plans to cut tax rebates paid to its exporters and to lower some import duties. But these measures seem to have had little effect on America's monster deficit with China.

Prior to an international finance meeting in June 2010, a key European Central Bank official said "the rigidity of the Chinese monetary regime had slowed down the recovery in the developed world." Facing political pressure to do something, China announced that it would allow the exchange rate to become more flexible. We'll see.

Sources: Lee Branstetter and Nicholas Lardy, "China's Embrace of Globalization," NBER Working Paper 12373 (July 2006); Jason Dean and Shen Hong, "China Central Bank Tames Yuan Appreciation Hopes," *Wall Street Journal*, 22 June 2010; Yujan Zhang, "China Steel Group Accuses U.S. Lawmakers of Protectionism," *Wall Street Journal*, 5 July 2010; and Michael Casey, "Showdown Looms Over China's Currency at G-20," *Wall Street Journal*, 11 June 2010.

Chapter 34

CASE STUDY

e activity

To see city lights displayed across the earth, go to DaylightMap at http://www.daylightmap.com/?night=1.

The Information Economy

Night Lights and Income GDP and economic growth are measured poorly for many developing economies. J. Vernon Henderson and two colleagues from Brown University have proposed a different measure of economic activity that does not rely on any of the usual statistics, such as employment, income, or output. Their approach uses photos taken at night from outer space to measure the density of light on the ground. Consumption of most goods and services in the evening requires light. As personal income rises, so does consumption and night lights. Using U.S. Air Force weather satellite photos, the researchers observe changes in a region's light density over a 10-year period. They use this change in light to supplement existing income growth measures.

For example, the trio examine the differential effects of the economic transition on income and light in former Soviet republics versus neighboring Eastern Europe. In particular, they compare the former Soviet republics of Moldova and Ukraine, where per capita income fell in the wake of the USSR's breakup, with neighboring Hungary, Poland, and Romania, countries that experienced a much smoother and more successful transition from central planning. The two photos below show night lights in Hungary, Poland, and Romania in the left portion of each photo and Moldova and Ukraine in the right portion of each photo. The photo on the left was taken in 1992 and the one on the right in 2002. The photos show that the more brightly lit areas in 2002 are in the Eastern European countries (the left half portion of the right-hand photo), where light intensity increases from 1992 to 2002. Also noticeable is the dimming of lights for their neighbors on the right of the photo, who were formerly part of the Soviet Union. In Moldova and in Ukraine, income per capita fell by an average of 33 percent, and light intensity dropped by an average of 57 percent. In Hungary, Poland, and Romania, where income per capita rose by an average of 40 percent, light intensity rose an average of 64 percent.

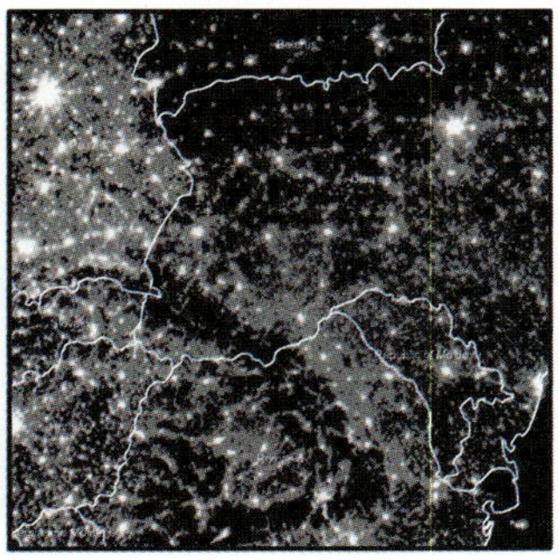

NOAA and USAF Weather Agency

When the researchers use their approach on countries with especially low-quality national income data, the night-light measure sometimes differs from the standard measure of income. For example, in the Congo, night lights suggest a 27 percent rise in GDP from 1992 to 2002, but official estimates of income indicate a 23 percent drop over the same time period. Thus, the Congo seems to be growing faster than official estimates suggest. On the other hand, although official data for Myanmar are limited, what's available suggests an income growth of 128 percent during the ten years, but the night-light data imply growth of only 40 percent.

The night-light approach is most valuable where the quality of other data are poor, such as in many African economies, or when data are simply not available, such as for Somalia, Liberia, and North Korea. The three economists don't expect their night-light measure to replace official estimates of income and growth, but, rather, to complement these data, especially where statistics are of poor quality or nonexistent.

Sources: J. Vernon Henderson, Adam Storeygard, and David Weil, "Measuring Economic Growth from Outer Space," NBER Working Paper, (July 2009).

NOAA, National Geophysical Data Center, Data 1992 F-10 and 2002 F-15, http://www.ngdc.noaa.gov/dmsp/downloadV4composites.html#AXP

CASE STUDY

e activity

Visit the site of the World Bank at http://www.worldbank.org/ and, under Data, read some of the recent reports on the World Development Indicators.

Bringing Theory to Life

The Poorest Billion Not long ago, the world was one-sixth rich and five-sixths poor. Now, thanks to impressive growth in places like China, the world is more like one-sixth rich, two-thirds not rich but improving, and one-sixth poor and going nowhere. Most developing economies are experiencing a rising standard of living. But that still leaves about a billion people trapped in economies that are not only extremely poor, but stagnant or getting worse. All told, about 45 countries fit into this poorest-billion category, including 30 countries in sub-Saharan Africa plus the likes of Cambodia, Haiti, Laos, Myanmar, North Korea, and Yemen.

Economist Paul Collier, of Oxford University in England, has examined what went wrong with these "trapped countries." Based on decades of research, he identifies some poverty traps. About 750 million people of the bottom billion have recently lived through, or are still in the midst of, a civil war. Such wars can drag on for years with economically disastrous consequences. For example, the ethnic conflict in Burundi between the Hutus and the Tutsis has lasted three decades, which helps explain why that country is among the poorest in the world. And war in the Congo over the last dozen years has killed more than five million people. Unfortunately, the poorer a country becomes, the more likely it is to succumb to civil war. And once a country goes through one civil war, more are likely. Ethnic conflict, or *civil war*, is Collier's first poverty trap.

But why, aside from poverty itself, are so many sub-Saharan countries mired in civil war? He finds that three factors heighten the risk of such conflicts: (1) a relatively high proportion of young, uneducated men with few job prospects (who, thus, have a low opportunity cost); (2) an imbalance between ethnic groups, with one tending to outnumber the rest; and (3) a supply of natural resources like diamonds or oil, which both creates an incentive to rebel and helps finance that rebellion. The presence of mineral wealth in an otherwise poor country can also undermine democracy itself. Government revenue from mineral sales reduces taxes, which dampens public debate about how taxes should be spent. For example, because of oil revenue, the Nigerian government relies less on taxes, so there is less pressure for government accountability, and hence

AP Photo/Pieter Malan

fewer checks and balances on a corrupt government. Thus, *misuse of natural resource wealth* is Collier's second poverty trap. About 300 million of the poorest billion live in countries that have fallen into this trap.

This leads us to the third poverty trap: *a dysfunctional or corrupt government*. Government officials who pursue self-glorification and self-enrichment do serious harm to the economy. Much of the public budget disappears through wasteful programs rife with graft and payoffs. For example, a recent survey that tracked government funds for rural health clinics in Chad found that less than 1 percent of the money reached the clinics. About 750 million of the poorest billion live in countries that pursue disastrous economic policies or where government corruption harms the economy.

Can these poorest billion be helped? It will take more than band concerts. Collier doubts that unconditional foreign aid makes much of a difference. He points to the ill effects of oil as an unconditional source of government revenue. International trade may help, but because these countries have difficulty competing with the likes of China or Vietnam, they may need special trade advantages. Another way the rest of the world could help is by requiring Western banks to report deposits by corrupt officials. The rest of the world could also assist these poor countries develop laws and regulations to ensure the transparent management of natural resources, to help detect fiscal fraud, and to promote a free press. But even with all that, what these countries need most, Collier argues, is about 10 years of domestic peace—backed by an outside force if necessary, such as the UN. All that is a tall order, but the stakes are high for the billion people trapped and going nowhere in these poor nations.

Sources: Paul Collier, *The Bottom Billion: Why the Poorest Countries Are Failing and What Can Be Done About It*, (Oxford University Press, 2007); and Paul Collier, *The Plundered Planet*, (Oxford University Press, 2010).

Glossary

ability-to-pay tax principle Those with a greater ability to pay, such as those earning higher incomes or those owning more property, should pay more taxes

absolute advantage The ability to make something using fewer resources than other producers use

accounting profit A firm's total revenue minus its explicit costs

adverse selection Those on the informed side of the market self-select in a way that harms those on the uninformed side of the market

adverse supply shocks Unexpected events that reduce aggregate supply, sometimes only temporarily

agent A person or firm who is supposed to act on behalf of the principal

aggregate demand curve A curve representing the relationship between the economy's price level and real GDP demanded per period, with other things constant

aggregate demand The relationship between the economy's price level and aggregate output demanded, with other things constant

aggregate expenditure line A relationship tracing, for a given price level, spending at each level of income, or real GDP; the total of C + I + G + (X − M) at each level of income, or real GDP

aggregate expenditure Total spending on final goods and services in an economy during a given period, usually a year

aggregate income All earnings of resource suppliers in an economy during a given period, usually a year

aggregate output A composite measure of all final goods and services produced in an economy during a given period; real GDP

aggregate supply curve A curve representing the relationship between the economy's price level and real GDP supplied per period, with other things constant

allocative efficiency The condition that exists when firms produce the output most preferred by consumers; marginal benefit equals marginal cost

American Recovery and Reinvestment Act At an estimated cost of $862 billion, the largest stimulus measure in U.S history; enacted in February 2009 and projected to last two years

annually balanced budget Budget philosophy prior to the Great Depression; aimed at matching annual revenues with outlays, except during times of war

annuity A given sum of money received each year for a specified number of years

antitrust policy Government regulation aimed at preventing monopoly and fostering competition in markets where competition is desirable

applied research Research that seeks answers to particular questions or to apply scientific discoveries to develop specific products

arbitrageur Someone who takes advantage of temporary geographic differences in the exchange rate by simultaneously purchasing a currency in one market and selling it in another market

asset Anything of value that is owned

association-is-causation fallacy The incorrect idea that if two variables are associated in time, one must necessarily cause the other

asymmetric information A situation in which one side of the market has more reliable information than the other side

asymmetric information One side of the market has better information about the product than does the other side

autarky National self-sufficiency; no economic interaction with foreigners

automatic stabilizers Structural features of government spending and taxation that reduce fluctuations in disposable income, and thus consumption, over the business cycle

autonomous A term that means "independent"; for example, autonomous investment is independent of income

average revenue Total revenue divided by quantity, or AR = TR/q; in all market structures, average revenue equals the market price

average total cost Total cost divided by output, or ATC = TC/q; the sum of average fixed cost and average variable cost, or ATC = AFC + AVC

average variable cost Variable cost divided by output, or AVC = VC/q

backward-bending supply curve of labor As the wage rises, the quantity of labor supplied may eventually decline; the income effect of a higher wage increases the demand for leisure, which reduces the quantity of labor supplied enough to more than offset the substitution effect of a higher wage

balance of payments A record of all economic transactions during a given period between residents of one country and residents of the rest of the world

balance on current account The portion of the balance-of-payments account that measures that country's balance on goods and services, net investment income from abroad, plus net unilateral transfers abroad

balance on goods and services The portion of a country's balance-of-payments account that measures the value of a country's exports of goods and services minus the value of its imports of goods and services

balance sheet A financial statement at a given point in time that shows assets on one side and liabilities and net worth on the other side;

because assets must equal liabilities plus net worth, the two sides of the statement must be in balance

bank branches A bank's additional offices that carry out banking operations

bank holding company A corporation that owns banks

bank notes Originally, pieces of paper promising a specific amount of gold or silver to anyone who presented them to issuing banks for redemption; today, Federal Reserve notes are mere paper money

barrier to entry Any impediment that prevents new firms from entering an industry and competing on an equal basis with existing firms

barter The direct exchange of one product for another without using money

base year The year with which other years are compared when constructing an index; the index equals 100 in the base year

basic research The search for knowledge without regard to how that knowledge will be used

behavioral assumption An assumption that describes the expected behavior of economic decision makers, what motivates them

behavioral economics An approach that borrows insights from psychology to help explain economic choices

beneficial supply shocks Unexpected events that increase aggregate supply, sometimes only temporarily

benefits-received tax principle Those who get more benefits from the government program should pay more taxes

binding arbitration Negotiation in which union and management must accept an impartial observer's resolution of a dispute

bond Certificate reflecting a firm's promise to pay the lender periodic interest and to repay the borrowed sum of money on the designated maturity date

bounded rationality The notion that there is a limit to the information that a firm's manager can comprehend and act on

budget resolution A congressional agreement about total outlays, spending by major category, and expected revenues; it guides spending and revenue decisions by the many congressional committees and subcommittees

bureaus Government agencies charged with implementing legislation and financed by appropriations from legislative bodies

capital deepening An increase in the amount of capital per worker; one source of rising labor productivity

capital The buildings, equipment, and human skills used to produce goods and services

capture theory of regulation Producers' political power and strong stake in the regulatory outcome lead them, in effect, to "capture" the regulating agency and prevail on it to serve producer interests

cartel A group of firms that agree to coordinate their production and pricing decisions to reap monopoly profit

chain-weighted system An inflation measure that adjusts the weights from year to year in calculating a price index, thereby reducing the bias caused by a fixed-price weighting system

check A written order instructing the bank to pay someone from an amount deposited

checkable deposits Bank deposits that allow the account owner to write checks to third parties; ATM or debit cards can also access these deposits and transmit them electronically

circular-flow model A diagram that traces the flow of resources, products, income, and revenue among economic decision makers

classical economists A group of 18th- and 19th-century economists who believed that economic downturns corrected themselves through natural market forces; thus, they believed the economy was self-correcting and needed no government intervention

Clayton Act of 1914 Beefed up the Sherman Act; outlawed certain anticompetitive practices not prohibited by the Sherman Act, including price discrimination, tying contracts, exclusive dealing, interlocking directorates, and buying the corporate stock of a competitor

Coase theorem As long as bargaining costs are low, an efficient solution to the problem of externalities is achieved by assigning property rights to one party or the other, it doesn't matter which

coincident economic indicators Variables that reflect peaks and troughs in economic activity as they occur; examples include employment, personal income, and industrial production

COLA Cost-of-living adjustment; an increase in a transfer payment or wage that is tied to the increase in the price level

cold turkey The announcement and execution of tough measures to reduce high inflation

collateral An asset pledged by the borrower that can be sold to pay off the loan in the event the borrower defaults

collective bargaining The process by which union and management negotiate a labor agreement

collusion An agreement among firms to increase economic profit by dividing the market and fixing the price

command-and-control environmental regulations An approach that required polluters to adopt particular technologies to reduce emissions by specific amounts; inflexible regulations based on engineering standards that ignore each firm's unique ways of reducing pollution

commercial banks Depository institutions that historically made short-term loans primarily to businesses

commodity A standardized product, a product that does not differ across producers, such as bushels of wheat or an ounce of gold

commodity money Anything that serves both as money and as a commodity; money that has intrinsic value such as gold or silver coins

common-pool problem Unrestricted access to a renewable resource results in overuse

comparative advantage The ability to make something at a lower opportunity cost than other producers face

competing-interest legislation Legislation that confers concentrated benefits on one group by imposing concentrated costs on another group

complements Goods, such as milk and cookies, that relate in such a way that an increase in the price of one shifts the demand for the other leftward

conglomerate merger A merger of firms in different industries

consent decree The accused party, without admitting guilt, agrees not to do whatever it was charged with if the government drops the charges

constant long-run average cost A cost that occurs when, over some range of output, long-run average cost neither increases nor decreases with changes in firm size

constant-cost industry An industry that can expand or contract without affecting the long-run per-unit cost of production; the long-run industry supply curve is horizontal

constant-elasticity demand curve The type of demand that exists when price elasticity is the same everywhere along the curve; the elasticity value is unchanged

consumer equilibrium The condition in which an individual consumer's budget is exhausted and the last dollar spent on each good yields the same marginal utility; therefore, utility is maximized

consumer price index, or CPI A measure of inflation based on the cost of a fixed market basket of goods and services

consumer surplus The difference between the most a consumer would pay for a given quantity of a good and what the consumer actually pays

consumption function The relationship in the economy between consumption and income, other things constant

consumption Household purchases of final goods and services, except for new residences, which count as investment

continuing resolutions Budget agreements that allow agencies, in the absence of an approved budget, to spend at the rate of the previous year's budget

contraction A period during which the economy declines as reflected by falling output, employment, income, and other aggregate measures

contractionary fiscal policy A decrease in government purchases, increase in net taxes, or some combination of the two aimed at reducing aggregate demand enough to return the economy to potential output without worsening inflation; fiscal policy used to close an expansionary gap

convergence A theory predicting that the standard of living in economies around the world will grow more similar over time, with poorer countries eventually catching up with richer ones

cooperative An organization consisting of people who pool their resources to buy and sell more efficiently than they could individually

coordination failure A situation in which workers and employers fail to achieve an outcome that all would prefer

coordination game A type of game in which a Nash equilibrium occurs when each player chooses the same strategy; neither player can do better than matching the other player's strategy

core competency Area of specialty; the product or phase of production a firm supplies with greatest efficiency

corporate stock Certificate reflecting part ownership of a corporation

corporation A legal entity owned by stockholders whose liability is limited to the value of their stock ownership

cost-push inflation A sustained rise in the price level caused by a leftward shift of the aggregate supply curve

craft union A union whose members have a particular skill or work at a particular craft, such as plumbers or carpenters

cross-price elasticity of demand The percentage change in the demand of one good divided by the percentage change in the price of another good; it's positive for substitutes, negative for complements, and zero for unrelated goods

crowding in The potential for government spending to stimulate private investment in an otherwise dead economy

crowding out The displacement of interest-sensitive private investment that occurs when higher government deficits drive up market interest rates

currency appreciation With respect to the dollar, a decrease in the number of dollars needed to purchase one unit of foreign exchange in a flexible rate system

currency depreciation With respect to the dollar, an increase in the number of dollars needed to purchase one unit of foreign exchange in a flexible rate system

currency devaluation An increase in the official pegged price of foreign exchange in terms of the domestic currency

currency revaluation A reduction in the official pegged price of foreign exchange in terms of the domestic currency

cyclical unemployment Unemployment that fluctuates with the business cycle, increasing during contractions and decreasing during expansions

cyclically balanced budget A budget philosophy calling for budget deficits during recessions to be financed by budget surpluses during expansions

deadweight loss of monopoly Net loss to society when a firm with market power restricts output and increases the price

debit card Cards that tap directly into the depositor's bank account to fund purchases; also called a check card, and often doubles as an ATM card

decision-making lag The time needed to decide what to do once a macroeconomic problem has been identified

deflation A sustained decrease in the price level

demand A relation between the price of a good and the quantity that consumers are willing and able to buy per period, other things constant

demand curve A curve showing the relation between the price of a good and the quantity consumers are willing and able to buy per period, other things constant

demand for loanable funds The negative relationship between the market interest rate and the quantity of loanable funds demanded, other things constant

demand for money The relationship between the interest rate and how much money people want to hold

demand-pull inflation A sustained rise in the price level caused by a rightward shift of the aggregate demand curve

demand-side economics Macroeconomic policy that focuses on shifting the aggregate demand curve as a way of promoting full employment and price stability

depository institutions Commercial banks and thrift institutions; financial institutions that accept deposits from the public

depreciation The value of capital stock used up to produce GDP or that becomes obsolete during the year

depression A severe and prolonged reduction in economic activity as occurred during the 1930s

derived demand Demand that arises from the demand for the product the resource produces

developing countries Countries with a low living standard because of less human and physical capital per worker

developing countries Nations typified by high rates of illiteracy, high unemployment, high fertility rates, and exports of primary products; also known as low-income and middle-income economies

differentiated oligopoly An oligopoly that sells products that differ across suppliers, such as automobiles or breakfast cereal

discount rate The interest rate the Fed charges banks that borrow reserves

discounting Converting future dollar amounts into present value

discouraged workers Those who drop out of the labor force in frustration because they can't find work

discretionary fiscal policy The deliberate manipulation of government purchases, taxation, and transfer payments to promote macroeconomic goals, such as full employment, price stability, and economic growth

diseconomies of scale Forces that may eventually increase a firm's average cost as the scale of operation increases in the long run

disequilibrium The condition that exists in a market when the plans of buyers do not match those of sellers; a temporary mismatch between quantity supplied and quantity demanded as the market seeks equilibrium

disinflation A reduction in the rate of inflation

disposable income (DI) The income households have available to spend or to save after paying taxes and receiving transfer payments

dividends After-tax corporate profit paid to stockholders rather than retained by the firm and reinvested

division of labor Breaking down the production of a good into separate tasks

Dodd-Frank Wall Street Reform and Consumer Protection Act Sweeping regulatory changes aimed at preventing another financial crisis

Doha Round The multilateral trade negotiation round launched in 2001, but still unsettled as of 2010; aims at lowering tariffs on a wide range of industrial and agricultural products; the first trade round under WTO

dominant-strategy equilibrium In game theory, the outcome achieved when each player's choice does not depend on what the other player does

double coincidence of wants Two traders are willing to exchange their products directly

double counting The mistake of including both the value of intermediate products and the value of final products in calculating gross domestic product; counting the same production more than once

dumping Selling a product abroad for less than charged in the home market or for less than the cost of production

duopoly A market with only two producers; a special type of oligopoly market structure

earned-income tax credit A federal program that supplements the wages of the working poor

economic efficiency approach An approach that offers each polluter the flexibility to reduce emissions as cost-effectively as possible, given its unique cost conditions; the market for pollution rights is an example

economic fluctuations The rise and fall of economic activity relative to the long-term growth trend of the economy; also called business cycles

economic growth An increase in the economy's ability to produce goods and services; reflected by an outward shift of the economy's production possibilities frontier

economic profit A firm's total revenue minus its explicit and implicit costs

economic regulation Government regulation of natural monopoly, where, because of economies of scale, average production cost is lowest when a single firm supplies the market

economic rent Portion of a resource's total earnings that exceeds its opportunity cost; earnings greater than the amount required to keep the resource in its present use

economic system The set of mechanisms and institutions that resolve the what, how, and for whom questions

economic theory, or economic model A simplification of reality used to make predictions about cause and effect in the real world

economics The study of how people use their scarce resources to satisfy their unlimited wants

economies of scale Forces that reduce a firm's average cost as the scale of operation increases in the long run

economies of scope Average costs decline as a firm makes a range of different products rather than specialize in just one product

economy The structure of economic activity in a community, a region, a country, a group of countries, or the world

efficiency The condition that exists when there is no way resources can be reallocated to increase the production of one good without decreasing the production of another; getting the most from available resources

efficiency wage theory The idea that offering high wages attracts a more talented labor pool and encourages those hired to perform well to keep their jobs

effectiveness lag The time needed for changes in monetary or fiscal policy to affect the economy

elastic demand A change in price has a relatively large effect on quantity demanded; the percentage change in quantity demanded exceeds the percentage change in price; the resulting price elasticity has an absolute value exceeding 1.0

elastic supply A change in price has a relatively large effect on quantity supplied; the percentage change in quantity supplied exceeds the percentage change in price; the price elasticity of supply exceeds 1.0

Employment Act of 1946 Law that assigned to the federal government the responsibility for promoting full employment and price stability

entitlement programs Guaranteed benefits for those who qualify for government transfer programs such as Social Security and Medicare

entrepreneur A profit-seeking decision maker who starts with an idea, organizes an enterprise to bring that idea to life, and assumes the risk of the operation

entrepreneurial ability The imagination required to develop a new product or process, the skill needed to organize production, and the willingness to take the risk of profit or loss

equation of exchange The quantity of money, M, multiplied by its velocity, V, equals nominal GDP, which is the product of the price level, P, and real GDP, Y; or $M \times V = P \times Y$

equilibrium The condition that exists in a market when the plans of buyers match those of sellers, so quantity demanded equals quantity supplied and the market clears

excess capacity The difference between a firm's profit-maximizing quantity and the quantity that minimizes average cost; firms with excess capacity could reduce average cost by increasing quantity

excess reserves Bank reserves exceeding required reserves

exchange rate The price measured in one country's currency of purchasing one unit of another country's currency

exclusive dealing A supplier prohibits its customers from buying from other suppliers of the product

exhaustible resource A resource in fixed supply, such as crude oil or coal

expansion A period during which the economy grows as reflected by rising output, employment, income, and other aggregate measures

expansionary fiscal policy An increase in government purchases, decrease in net taxes, or some combination of the two aimed at increasing aggregate demand enough to reduce unemployment and return the economy to its potential output; fiscal policy used to close a recessionary gap

expansionary gap The amount by which actual output in the short run exceeds the economy's potential output

expected rate of return on capital The expected annual earnings divided by capital's purchase price

expenditure approach to GDP Calculating GDP by adding up spending on all final goods and services produced in the nation during the year

explicit cost Opportunity cost of resources employed by a firm that takes the form of cash payments

export promotion A development strategy that concentrates on producing for the export market

externality A cost or a benefit that affects neither the buyer nor seller, but instead affects people not involved in the market transaction

fallacy of composition The incorrect belief that what is true for the individual, or part, must necessarily be true for the group, or the whole

featherbedding Union efforts to force employers to hire more workers than demanded at a particular wage

federal budget deficit A flow variable measuring the amount by which federal government outlays exceed federal government revenues in a particular period, usually a year

federal budget A plan for federal government outlays and revenues for a specified period, usually a year

federal debt A stock variable that measures the net accumulation of annual federal deficits

federal funds market A market for overnight lending and borrowing of reserves among banks; the interbank market for reserves on account at the Fed

federal funds rate The interest rate charged in the federal funds market; the interest rate banks charge one another for overnight borrowing; the Fed's target interest rate

federal Open Market Committee (FOMC) The 12-member group that makes decisions about open-market operations—purchases and sales of U.S. government securities by the Fed that affect the money supply and interest rates; consists of the seven Board governors plus five of the 12 presidents of the Reserve Banks

federal Reserve System, or the Fed The central bank and monetary authority of the United States

Federal Trade Commission (FTC) Act of 1914 Established a federal body to help enforce antitrust laws; run by commissioners assisted by economists and lawyers

fiat money Money not redeemable for any commodity; its status as money is conferred initially by government decree but eventually by common experience

final goods and services Goods and services sold to final, or end, users

financial account The record of a country's international transactions involving purchases or sales of financial and real assets

financial intermediaries Institutions such as banks, mortgage companies, and finance companies, that serve as go-betweens, borrowing from people who have saved to make loans to others

financial markets Banks and other financial institutions that facilitate the flow of funds from savers to borrowers

firms Economic units formed by profit-seeking entrepreneurs who employ resources to produce goods and services for sale

fiscal policy The use of government purchases, transfer payments, taxes, and borrowing to influence economy-wide variables such as inflation, employment, and economic growth

fixed cost Any production cost that is independent of the firm's rate of output

fixed exchange rate Rate of exchange between currencies pegged within a narrow range and maintained by the central bank's ongoing purchases and sales of currencies

fixed resource Any resource that cannot be varied in the short run

fixed-production technology Occurs when the relationship between the output rate and the generation of an externality is fixed; the only way to reduce the externality is to reduce the output

flexible exchange rate Rate determined in foreign exchange markets by the forces of demand and supply without government intervention

flow variable A measure of something over an interval of time, such as your income per week

foreign aid An international transfer made on especially favorable terms for the purpose of promoting economic development

foreign exchange Foreign money needed to carry out international transactions

fractional reserve banking system Bank reserves amount to only a fraction of funds on deposit with the bank

free-rider problem Because nobody can be easily excluded from consuming a public good, some people may try to reap the benefits of the good without paying for it

frictional unemployment Unemployment that occurs because job seekers and employers need time to find each other

full employment Employment level when there is no cyclical unemployment

functional finance A budget philosophy using fiscal policy to achieve the economy's potential GDP, rather than balancing budgets either annually or over the business cycle

game theory An approach that analyzes oligopolistic behavior as a series of strategic moves and countermoves by rival firms

GDP price index A comprehensive inflation measure of all goods and services included in the gross domestic product

General Agreement on Tariffs and Trade (GATT) An international tariff-reduction treaty adopted in 1947 that resulted in a series of negotiated "rounds" aimed at freer trade; the Uruguay Round created GATT's successor, the World Trade Organization (WTO)

gold standard An arrangement whereby the currencies of most countries are convertible into gold at a fixed rate

golden rule of profit maximization To maximize profit or minimize loss, a firm should produce the quantity at which marginal revenue equals marginal cost; this rule holds for all market structures

good A tangible product used to satisfy human wants

government purchase function The relationship between government purchases and the economy's income, other things constant

government purchases Spending for goods and services by all levels of government; government outlays minus transfer payments

Gresham's law People tend to trade away inferior money and hoard the best

gross domestic product (GDP) The market value of all final goods and services produced in the nation during a particular period, usually a year

gross world product The market value of all final goods and services produced in the world during a given period, usually a year

Herfindahl-Hirschman Index, or HHI A measure of market concentration that squares each firm's percentage share of the market then sums these squares

hidden actions One side of an economic relationship can do something that the other side cannot observe

hidden characteristics One side of the market knows more than the other side about product characteristics that are important to the other side

horizontal merger A merger in which one firm combines with another that produces the same type of product

hyperinflation A very high rate of inflation

hypothesis A theory about how key variables relate

hysteresis The theory that the natural rate of unemployment depends in part on the recent history of unemployment; high unemployment rates increase the natural rate of unemployment

implementation lag The time needed to introduce a change in monetary or fiscal policy

implicit cost A firm's opportunity cost of using its own resources or those provided by its owners without a corresponding cash payment

import substitution A development strategy that emphasizes domestic manufacturing of products that were imported

income approach to GDP Calculating GDP by adding up all earnings from resources used to produce output in the nation during the year

income assistance programs Welfare programs that provide money and in-kind assistance to the poor; benefits do not depend on prior contributions

income effect of a price change A fall in the price of a good increases consumers' real income, making consumers more able to purchase goods; for a normal good, the quantity demanded increases

income effect of a wage increase A higher wage raises a worker's income, increasing the demand for all normal goods, including leisure, so the quantity of labor supplied to market work decreases

income elasticity of demand The percentage change in demand divided by the percentage change in consumer income; the value is positive for normal goods and negative for inferior goods

income-expenditure model A relationship that shows how much people plan to spend at each income level; this model identifies, for a given price level, where the amount people plan to spend equals the amount produced in the economy

increasing marginal returns The marginal product of a variable resource increases as each additional unit of that resource is employed

increasing-cost industry An industry that faces higher per-unit production costs as industry output expands in the long run; the long-run industry supply curve slopes upward

individual demand The relation between the price of a good and the quantity purchased by an individual consumer per period, other things constant

individual supply The relation between the price of a good and the quantity an individual producer is willing and able to sell per period, other things constant

industrial market countries Economically advanced capitalist countries of Western Europe, North America, Australia, New Zealand, and Japan, plus the newly industrialized Asian economies of Taiwan, South Korea, Hong Kong, and Singapore

industrial market countries Economically advanced capitalist countries of Western Europe, North America, Australia, New Zealand, and Japan; also known as developed countries and high-income economies

industrial policy The view that government—using taxes, subsidies, and regulations—should nurture the industries and technologies of the future, thereby giving these domestic industries an advantage over foreign competition

Industrial Revolution Development of large-scale factory production that began in Great Britain around 1750 and spread to the rest of Europe, North America, and Australia

industrial union A union consisting of both skilled and unskilled workers from a particular industry, such as all autoworkers or all steelworkers

inelastic demand A change in price has relatively little effect on quantity demanded; the percentage change in quantity demanded is less than the percentage change in price; the resulting price elasticity has an absolute value less than 1.0

inelastic supply A change in price has relatively little effect on quantity supplied; the percentage change in quantity supplied is less than the percentage change in price; the price elasticity of supply is less than 1.0

inferior good A good, such as used clothes, for which demand decreases, or shifts leftward, as consumer income rises

inflation An increase in the economy's average price level

inflation target Commitment of central bankers to keep inflation below a certain rate for the next year or two

Information Revolution Technological change spawned by the microchip and the Internet that enhanced the acquisition, analysis, and transmission of information

initial public offering (IPO) The initial sale of corporate stock to the public

injection Any spending other than by households or any income other than from resource earnings; includes investment, government purchases, exports, and transfer payments

innovation The process of turning an invention into a marketable product

intellectual property An intangible asset created by human knowledge and ideas

interest rate Interest per year as a percentage of the amount loaned

interest rate Interest per year as a percentage of the amount saved or borrowed

interest Payment to resource owners for the use of their capital

interest The dollar amount paid by borrowers to lenders

interlocking directorate A person serves on the boards of directors of two or more competing firms

intermediate goods and services Goods and services purchased by firms for further reprocessing and resale

International Monetary Fund (IMF) An international organization that establishes rules for maintaining the international monetary system and makes loans to countries with temporary balance-of-payments problems

inventories Producers' stocks of finished and in-process goods

investment function The relationship between the amount businesses plan to invest and the economy's income, other things constant

investment The purchase of new plants, new equipment, new buildings, and new residences, plus net additions to inventories

labor force participation rate The labor force as a percentage of the adult population

labor force Those 16 years of age and older who are either working or looking for work

labor productivity Output per unit of labor; measured as real GDP divided by the hours of labor employed to produce that output

labor union A group of workers who organize to improve their terms of employment

labor The physical and mental effort used to produce goods and services

lagging economic indicators Variables that follow, or trail, changes in overall economic activity; examples include the interest rate and the average duration of unemployment

law of comparative advantage The individual, firm, region, or country with the lowest opportunity cost of producing a particular good should specialize in that good

law of demand The quantity of a good that consumers are willing and able to buy per period relates inversely, or negatively, to the price, other things constant

law of diminishing marginal returns As more of a variable resource is added to a given amount of another resource, marginal product eventually declines and could become negative

law of diminishing marginal utility The more of a good a person consumes per period, the smaller the increase in total utility from consuming one more unit, other things constant

law of increasing opportunity cost To produce more of one good, a successively larger amount of the other good must be sacrificed

law of supply The amount of a good that producers are willing and able to sell per period is usually directly related to its price, other things constant

leading economic indicators Variables that predict, or lead to, a recession or recovery; examples include consumer confidence, stock market prices, business investment, and big-ticket purchases, such as automobiles and homes

leakage Any diversion of income from the domestic spending stream; includes saving, taxes, and imports

legal tender U.S. currency that constitutes a valid and legal offer of payment of debt

leisure Time spent on nonwork activities

liability Anything that is owed to other people or institutions

life-cycle model of consumption and saving Young people borrow, middle agers pay off debts and save, and older people draw down their savings; on average, net savings over a lifetime is usually little or nothing

linear demand curve A straight-line demand curve; such a demand curve has a constant slope but usually has a varying price elasticity

liquidity A measure of the ease with which an asset can be converted into money without a significant loss of value

loanable funds market The market in which savers (suppliers of loanable funds) and borrowers (demanders of loanable funds) come together to determine the market interest rate and the quantity of loanable funds exchanged

long run A period during which all resources under the firm's control are variable

long run In macroeconomics, a period during which wage contracts and resource price agreements can be renegotiated; there are no surprises about the economy's actual price level

long-run aggregate supply (LRAS) curve A vertical line at the economy's potential output; aggregate supply when there are no surprises about the price level and all resource contracts can be renegotiated

long-run average cost curve A curve that indicates the lowest average cost of production at each rate of output when the size, or scale, of the firm varies; also called the planning curve

long-run equilibrium The price level and real GDP that occurs when (1) the actual price level equals the expected price level, (2) real GDP supplied equals potential output, and (3) real GDP supplied equals real GDP demanded

long-run industry supply curve A curve that shows the relationship between price and quantity supplied by the industry once firms adjust in the long run to any change in market demand

long-run Phillips curve A vertical line drawn at the economy's natural rate of unemployment that traces equilibrium points that can occur when workers and employers have the time to adjust fully to any unexpected change in aggregate demand

long-term unemployed Those out of work for 27 weeks or longer

lorenz curve A curve showing the percentage of total income received by a given percentage of recipients whose incomes are arrayed from smallest to largest

M1 The narrow measure of the money supply, consisting of currency and coins held by the nonbanking public, checkable deposits, and traveler's checks

M2 A money aggregate consisting of M1 plus savings deposits, small-denomination time deposits, money market mutual funds, and other miscellaneous near-monies

macroeconomics The study of the economic behavior of entire economies, as measured, for example, by total production and employment

managed float system An exchange rate system that combines features of freely floating rates with sporadic intervention by central banks

marginal Incremental, additional, or extra; used to describe a change in an economic variable

marginal cost The change in total cost resulting from a one-unit change in output; the change in total cost divided by the change in output, or $MC = \Delta TC/\Delta q$

marginal product The change in total product that occurs when the use of a particular resource increases by one unit, all other resources constant

marginal propensity to consume (MPC) The fraction of a change in income that is spent on consumption; the change in consumption divided by the change in income that caused it

marginal propensity to save (MPS) The fraction of a change in income that is saved; the change in saving divided by the change in income that caused it

marginal resource cost The change in total cost when an additional unit of a resource is hired, other things constant

marginal revenue (MR) The firm's change in total revenue from selling an additional unit; a perfectly competitive firm's marginal revenue is also the market price

marginal revenue product The change in total revenue when an additional unit of a resource is employed, other things constant

marginal social benefit The sum of the marginal private benefit and the marginal external benefit of production or consumption

marginal social cost The sum of the marginal private cost and the marginal external cost of production or consumption

marginal tax rate The percentage of each additional dollar of income that goes to the tax

marginal utility The change in your total utility from a one-unit change in your consumption of a good

Marginal valuation The dollar value of the marginal utility derived from consuming each additional unit of a good

market demand The relation between the price of a good and the quantity purchased by all consumers in the market during a given period, other things constant; sum of the individual demands in the market

market failure A condition that arises when the unregulated operation of markets yields socially undesirable results

market power The ability of a firm to raise its price without losing all its customers to rival firms

market structure Important features of a market, such as the number of firms, product uniformity across firms, firm's ease of entry and exit, and forms of competition

market supply The relation between the price of a good and the quantity all producers are willing and able to sell per period, other things constant

market work Time sold as labor

market A set of arrangements by which buyers and sellers carry out exchange at mutually agreeable terms

means-tested program A program in which, to be eligible, an individual's income and assets must not exceed specified levels

median income The middle income when all incomes are ranked from smallest to largest

median wage The middle wage when wages of all workers are ranked from lowest to highest

median-voter model Under certain conditions, the preferences of the median, or middle, voter will dominate the preferences of all other voters

mediator An impartial observer who helps resolve differences between union and management

Medicaid An in-kind transfer program that provides medical care for poor people; by far the most costly welfare program

Medicare Social insurance program providing health insurance for short-term medical care to older Americans, regardless of income

medium of exchange Anything that facilitates trade by being generally accepted by all parties in payment for goods or services

mercantilism The incorrect theory that a nation's economic objective should be to accumulate precious metals in the public treasury; this theory prompted trade barriers to cut imports, but other countries retaliated, reducing trade and the gains from specialization

merchandise trade balance The value during a given period of a country's exported goods minus the value of its imported goods

microeconomics The study of the economic behavior in particular markets, such as that for computers or unskilled labor

minimum efficient scale The lowest rate of output at which a firm takes full advantage of economies of scale

mixed system An economic system characterized by the private ownership of some resources and the public ownership of other resources; some markets are regulated by government

monetary policy Regulation of the money supply to influence economy-wide variables such as inflation, employment, and economic growth

money aggregates Measures of the economy's money supply

money income The number of dollars a person receives per period, such as $400 per week

money market mutual fund A collection of short-term interest-earning assets purchased with funds collected from many shareholders

money multiplier The multiple by which the money supply changes as a result of a change in fresh reserves in the banking system

money Anything that is generally accepted in exchange for goods and services

monopolistic competition A market structure with many firms selling products that are substitutes but different enough that each firm's demand curve slopes downward; firm entry is relatively easy

monopoly A sole supplier of a product with no close substitutes

moral hazard A situation in which one party, as a result of a contract, has an incentive to alter their behavior in a way that harms the other party to the contract

mortgage-backed security A claim on payments made on the many mortgages bundled into this financial instrument

movement along a demand curve Change in quantity demanded resulting from a change in the price of the good, other things constant

movement along a supply curve Change in quantity supplied resulting from a change in the price of the good, other things constant

Nash equilibrium A situation in which a firm, or a player in game theory, chooses the best strategy given the strategies chosen by others; no participant can improve his or her outcome by changing strategies even after learning of the strategies selected by other participants

national debt The net accumulation of federal budget deficits

natural monopoly One firm that can supply the entire market at a lower per-unit cost than could two or more firms

natural rate hypothesis The natural rate of unemployment is largely independent of the stimulus provided by monetary or fiscal policy

natural rate of unemployment The unemployment rate when the economy produces its potential output

natural resources All gifts of nature used to produce goods and services; includes renewable and exhaustible resources

net domestic product Gross domestic product minus depreciation

net export function The relationship between net exports and the economy's income, other things constant

net exports The value of a country's exports minus the value of its imports

net investment income from abroad Investment earnings by U.S. residents from their foreign assets minus investment earnings by foreigners from their assets in the United States

net taxes (NT) Taxes minus transfer payments

net unilateral transfers abroad The unilateral transfers (gifts and grants) received from abroad by U.S. residents minus the unilateral transfers U.S. residents send abroad

net wealth The value of assets minus liabilities

net worth Assets minus liabilities; also called owners' equity

nominal GDP GDP based on prices prevailing at the time of production

nominal interest rate The interest rate expressed in dollars of current value (that is, not adjusted for inflation) as a percentage of the amount loaned; the interest rate specified on the loan agreement

nominal wage The wage measured in dollars of the year in question; the dollar amount on a paycheck

nonmarket work Time spent getting an education or on do-it-yourself production for personal consumption

normal good A good, such as new clothes, for which demand increases, or shifts rightward, as consumer income rises

normal profit The accounting profit earned when all resources earn their opportunity cost

normative economic statement A statement that reflects an opinion, which cannot be proved or disproved by reference to the facts

not-for-profit organizations Groups that do not pursue profit as a goal; they engage in charitable, educational, humanitarian, cultural, professional, or other activities, often with a social purpose

oligopoly A market structure characterized by so few firms that each behaves interdependently

open-access good A good such as ocean fish that is rival in consumption but nonpayers cannot be excluded easily

open-market operations Purchases and sales of government securities by the Fed in an effort to influence the money supply

open-market purchase The purchase of U.S. government bonds by the Fed to increase the money supply

open-market sale The sale of U.S. government bonds by the Fed to reduce the money supply

opportunity cost The value of the best alternative forgone when an item or activity is chosen

other-things-constant assumption The assumption, when focusing on the relation among key economic variables, that other variables remain unchanged; in Latin, ceteris paribus

outsourcing A firm buys inputs from outside suppliers

partnership A firm with multiple owners who share the profits and bear unlimited liability for the firm's losses and debts

patent A legal barrier to entry that grants the holder the exclusive right to sell a product for 20 years from the date the patent application is filed

payoff matrix In game theory, a table listing the payoffs that each player can expect from each move based on the actions of the other player

per se illegal In antitrust law, business practices deemed illegal regardless of their economic rationale or their consequences

perfect competition A market structure with many fully informed buyers and sellers of a standardized product and no obstacles to entry or exit of firms in the long run

perfectly discriminating monopolist A monopolist who charges a different price for each unit sold; also called the monopolist's dream

perfectly elastic demand curve A horizontal line reflecting a situation in which any price increase would reduce quantity demanded to zero; the elasticity has an absolute value of infinity

perfectly elastic supply curve A horizontal line reflecting a situation in which any price decrease drops the quantity supplied to zero; the elasticity value is infinity

perfectly inelastic demand curve A vertical line reflecting a situation in which any price change has no effect on the quantity demanded; the elasticity value is zero

Perfectly inelastic supply curve A vertical line reflecting a situation in which a price change has no effect on the quantity supplied; the elasticity value is zero

permanent income Income that individuals expect to receive on average over the long term

per-worker production function The relationship between the amount of capital per worker in the economy and average output per worker

phillips curve A curve showing possible combinations of the inflation rate and the unemployment rate

physical capital Manufactured items used to produce goods and services; includes new plants and new equipment

political business cycles Economic fluctuations that occur when discretionary policy is manipulated for political gain

populist legislation Legislation with widespread benefits but concentrated costs

pork-barrel spending Special-interest legislation with narrow geographical benefits but funded by all taxpayers

positive economic statement A statement that can be proved or disproved by reference to facts

positive rate of time preference Consumers value present consumption more than future consumption

potential output The economy's maximum sustainable output, given the supply of resources, technology, and rules of the game; the output level when there are no surprises about the price level

predatory pricing Pricing tactics employed by a dominant firm to drive competitors out of business, such as temporarily selling below marginal cost or dropping the price only in certain markets

present value The value today of income to be received in the future

price ceiling A maximum legal price above which a product cannot be sold; to have an impact, a price ceiling must be set below the equilibrium price

price discrimination Increasing profit by charging different groups of consumers different prices for the same product

price elasticity formula Percentage change in quantity demanded divided by the percentage change in price; the average quantity and the average price are used as bases for computing percentage changes in quantity and in price

price elasticity of demand Measures how responsive quantity demanded is to a price change; the percentage change in quantity demanded divided by the percentage change in price

price elasticity of supply A measure of the responsiveness of quantity supplied to a price change; the percentage change in quantity supplied divided by the percentage change in price

price floor A minimum legal price below which a product cannot be sold; to have an impact, a price floor must be set above the equilibrium price

price index A number that shows the average price of products; changes in a price index over time show changes in the economy's average price level

price leader A firm whose price is matched by other firms in the market as a form of tacit collusion

price level A composite measure reflecting the prices of all goods and services in the economy relative to prices in a base year

price maker A firm with some power to set the price because the demand curve for its output slopes downward; a firm with market power

price taker A firm that faces a given market price and whose quantity supplied has no effect on that price; a perfectly competitive firm that decides to produce must accept, or "take," the market price

prime rate The interest rate lenders charge their most trustworthy business borrowers

principal A person or firm who hires an agent to act on behalf of that person or firm

principal-agent problem The agent's objectives differ from those of the principal's, and one side can pursue hidden actions

prisoner's dilemma A game that shows why players have difficulty cooperating even though they would benefit from cooperation

private good A good, such as pizza, that is both rival in consumption and exclusive

private property rights An owner's right to use, rent, or sell resources or property

privatization The process of turning government enterprises into private enterprises

producer surplus A bonus for producers in the short run; the amount by which total revenue from production exceeds variable cost

product market A market in which a good or service is bought and sold

production function The relationship between the amount of resources employed and a firm's total product

Production possibilities frontier (PPF) A curve showing alternative combinations of goods that can be produced when available resources are used efficiently; a boundary line between inefficient and unattainable combinations

productive efficiency The condition that exists when production uses the least-cost combination of inputs; minimum average cost in the long run

productivity The ratio of a specific measure of output, such as real GDP, to a specific measure of input, such as labor; in this case productivity measures real GDP per hour of labor

profit Reward for entrepreneurial ability; sales revenue minus resource cost

progressive taxation The tax as a percentage of income increases as income increases

proportional taxation The tax as a percentage of income remains constant as income increases; also called a flat tax

public good A good that, once produced, is available for all to consume, regardless of who pays and who doesn't; such a good is nonrival and nonexclusive, such as a safer community

public utilities Government-owned or government-regulated monopolies

purchasing power parity (PPP) theory The idea that the exchange rate between two countries will adjust in the long run to equalize the cost between the countries of a basket of internationally traded goods

pure capitalism An economic system characterized by the private ownership of resources and the use of prices to coordinate economic activity in unregulated markets

pure command system An economic system characterized by the public ownership of resources and centralized planning

quantity demanded The amount of a good consumers are willing and able to buy per period at a particular price, as reflected by a point on a demand curve

quantity supplied The amount offered for sale per period at a particular price, as reflected by a point on a given supply curve

quantity theory of money If the velocity of money is stable, or at least predictable, changes in the money supply have predictable effects on nominal GDP

quota A legal limit on the quantity of a particular product that can be imported or exported

rational expectations A school of thought that argues people form expectations based on all available information, including the likely future actions of government policy makers

rational ignorance A stance adopted by voters when they realize that the cost of understanding and voting on a particular issue exceeds the benefit expected from doing so

rational self-interest Each individual tries to maximize the expected benefit achieved with a given cost or to minimize the expected cost of achieving a given benefit

real GDP per capita Real GDP divided by the population; the best measure of an economy's standard of living

real gross domestic product (real GDP) The economy's aggregate output measured in dollars of constant purchasing power

real income Income measured in terms of the goods and services it can buy; real income changes when the price changes

real interest rate The interest rate expressed in dollars of constant purchasing power as a percentage of the amount loaned; the nominal interest rate minus the inflation rate

real wage The wage measured in dollars of constant purchasing power; the wage measured in terms of the quantity of goods and services it buys

recession A period of decline in economic activity lasting more than a few months, as reflected by falling output, employment, income, and other aggregate measures

recessionary gap The amount by which actual output in the short run falls short of the economy's potential output

recognition lag The time needed to identify a macroeconomic problem and assess its seriousness

recycling The process of converting waste products into reusable material

regressive taxation The tax as a percentage of income decreases as income increases

renewable resource A resource that regenerates itself and so can be used indefinitely if used conservatively, such as a properly managed forest

rent Payment to resource owners for the use of their natural resources

rent seeking Activities undertaken by individuals or firms to influence public policy in a way that increases their incomes

representative money Bank notes that exchange for a specific commodity, such as gold

required reserve ratio The ratio of reserves to deposits that banks are obligated by regulation to hold

required reserves The dollar amount of reserves a bank is obligated by regulation to hold as cash in the bank's vault or on account at the Fed

reserves Funds that banks use to satisfy the cash demands of their customers and the reserve requirements of the Fed; reserves consist of cash held by banks plus deposits at the Fed

residential construction Building new homes or dwelling places

resource complements Resources that enhance one another's productivity; a decrease in the price of one resource increases the demand for the other

resource market A market in which a resource is bought and sold

resource substitutes Resources that substitute in production; an increase in the price of one resource increases the demand for the other

retained earnings After-tax corporate profit reinvested in the firm rather than paid to stockholders as dividends

resources The inputs, or factors of production, used to produce the goods and services that people want; resources consist of labor, capital, natural resources, and entrepreneurial ability

right-to-work states States where workers in unionized companies do not have to join the union or pay union dues

rule of reason Before ruling on the legality of certain business practices, a court examines why they were undertaken and what effect they have on competition

rules of the game The formal and informal institutions that promote economic activity; the laws, customs, manners, conventions, and other institutional elements that determine transaction costs and thereby affect people's incentive to undertake production and exchange

saving function The relationship between saving and income, other things constant

savings deposits Deposits that earn interest but have no specific maturity date

scarcity Occurs when the amount people desire exceeds the amount available at a zero price

screening The process used by employers to select the most qualified workers based on observable characteristics, such as a job applicant's level of education and course grades

seasonal unemployment Unemployment caused by seasonal changes in the demand for certain kinds of labor

secondary effects Unintended consequences of economic actions that may develop slowly over time as people react to events

seigniorage The difference between the face value of money and the cost of supplying it; the "profit" from issuing money

service An activity, or intangible product, used to satisfy human wants

Sherman Antitrust Act of 1890 First national legislation in the world against monopoly; prohibited trusts, restraint of trade, and monopolization, but the law was vague and, by itself, ineffective

shift of a demand curve Movement of a demand curve right or left resulting from a change in one of the determinants of demand other than the price of the good

shift of a supply curve Movement of a supply curve left or right resulting from a change in one of the determinants of supply other than the price of the good

short run A period during which at least one of a firm's resources is fixed

short run In macroeconomics, a period during which some resource prices, especially those for labor, are fixed by explicit or implicit agreements

shortage At a given price, the amount by which quantity demanded exceeds quantity supplied; a shortage usually forces the price up

short-run aggregate supply (SRAS) curve A curve that shows a direct relationship between the actual price level and real GDP supplied in the short run, other things constant, including the expected price level

short-run equilibrium The price level and real GDP that result when the aggregate demand curve intersects the short-run aggregate supply curve

short-run firm supply curve A curve that shows how much a firm supplies at each price in the short run; in perfect competition, that portion of a firm's marginal cost curve that intersects and rises above the low point on its average variable cost curve

short-run industry supply curve A curve that indicates the quantity supplied by the industry at each price in the short run; in perfect competition, the horizontal sum of each firm's short-run supply curve

short-run Phillips curve Based on an expected inflation rate, a curve that reflects an inverse relationship between the inflation rate and the unemployment rate

signaling Using a proxy measure to communicate information about unobservable characteristics; the signal is more effective if more-productive workers find it easier to send than do less-productive workers

simple money multiplier The reciprocal of the required reserve ratio, or $1/r$; the maximum multiple of fresh reserves by which the money supply can increase

simple spending multiplier The ratio of a change in real GDP demanded to the initial change in spending that brought it about; the numerical value of the simple spending multiplier is $1/(1 - MPC)$; called "simple" because only consumption varies with income

Simple tax multiplier The ratio of a change in real GDP demanded to the initial change in autonomous net taxes that brought it about; the numerical value of the simple tax multiplier is $-MPC/(1 - MPC)$

SNAP An in-kind transfer program that offers low-income households vouchers redeemable for food; benefit levels vary inversely with household income

social capital The shared values and trust that promote cooperation in the economy

social insurance Government programs designed to help make up for lost income of people who worked but are now retired, unemployed, or unable to work because of disability or work-related injury

social regulation Government regulations aimed at improving health and safety

Social Security Supplements retirement income to those with a record of contributing to the program during their working years; by far the largest government redistribution program

social welfare The overall well-being of people in the economy; maximized when the marginal cost of production equals the marginal benefit to consumers

sole proprietorship A firm with a single owner who has the right to all profits but who also bears unlimited liability for the firm's losses and debts

special-interest legislation Legislation with concentrated benefits but widespread costs

specialization of labor Focusing work effort on a particular product or a single task

speculator Someone who buys or sells foreign exchange in hopes of profiting from fluctuations in the exchange rate over time

stagflation A contraction, or stagnation, of a nation's output accompanied by inflation in the price level

stock variable A measure of something at a particular point in time, such as the amount of money you have with you right now

store of value Anything that retains its purchasing power over time

strategy In game theory, the operational plan pursued by a player

stress test Bank regulators assessed the soundness of large banks to determine which ones needed more financial capital to weather a bad economy

strike A union's attempt to withhold labor from a firm to halt production

structural unemployment Unemployment because (1) the skills demanded by employers do not match those of the unemployed, or (2) the unemployed do not live where the jobs are

subprime mortgage Mortgage for a borrower with a not-so-good credit rating

substitutes Goods, such as Coke and Pepsi, that relate in such a way that an increase in the price of one shifts the demand for the other rightward

substitution effect of a price change When the price of a good falls, that good becomes cheaper compared to other goods so consumers tend to substitute that good for other goods

substitution effect of a wage increase A higher wage encourages more work because other activities now have a higher opportunity cost

sunk cost A cost that has already been incurred, cannot be recovered, and thus is irrelevant for present and future economic decisions

Supplemental Security Income (SSI) An income assistance program that provides cash transfers to the elderly poor and the disabled; a uniform federal payment is supplemented by transfers that vary across states

supply curve A curve showing the relation between price of a good and the quantity producers are willing and able to sell per period other things constant

supply of loanable funds The positive relationship between the market interest rate and the quantity of loanable funds supplied, other things constant

supply shocks Unexpected events that affect aggregate supply, sometimes only temporarily

supply A relation between the price of a good and the quantity that producers are willing and able to sell per period, other things constant

supply-side economics Macroeconomic policy that focuses on a rightward shift of the aggregate supply curve through tax cuts or other changes to increase production incentives

surplus At a given price, the amount by which quantity supplied exceeds quantity demanded; a surplus usually forces the price down

tariff A tax on imports

tastes Consumer preferences; likes and dislikes in consumption; assumed to remain constant along a given demand curve

tax incidence The distribution of tax burden among taxpayers; who ultimately pays the tax

Temporary Assistance for Needy Families (TANF) An income assistance program funded largely by the federal government but run by the states to provide cash transfer payments to poor families with dependent children

term structure of interest rates The relationship between the duration of a loan and the interest rate charged; typically interest rates increase with the duration of the loan, because longer loans are considered more risky

terms of trade How much of one good exchanges for a unit of another good

thrift institutions, or thrifts Savings banks and credit unions; depository institutions that historically lent money to households

time deposits Deposits that earn a fixed interest rate if held for the specified period, which can range from several months to several years; also called certificates of deposit

time-inconsistency problem When policy makers have an incentive to announce one policy to influence expectations but then pursue a different policy once those expectations have been formed and acted on

tit-for-tat In game theory, a strategy in repeated games when a player in one round of the game mimics the other player's behavior in the previous round; an optimal strategy for getting the other player to cooperate

token money Money whose face value exceeds its cost of production

too big to fail A financial institution had become so large and so interconnected with other financial institutions that its failure would be a disaster for the wider economy; its collapse had to be prevented even if that required a bailout

total cost The sum of fixed cost and variable cost, or TC = FC + VC

total product A firm's total output

total revenue Price multiplied by the quantity demanded at that price

total utility The total satisfaction you derive from consumption; this could refer to either your total utility of consuming a particular good or your total utility from all consumption

traditional public-goods legislation Legislation that involves widespread costs and widespread benefits—nearly everyone pays and nearly everyone benefits

transaction costs The costs of time and information required to carry out market exchange

transfer payments Cash or in-kind benefits given to individuals as outright grants from the government

Troubled Asset Relief Program, or TARP Government program that invested in financial institutions and automakers to help stabilize markets; in October 2008 budgeted at $700 billion but expected to cost much less

trust Any firm or group of firms that tries to monopolize a market

tying contract A seller of one good requires a buyer to purchase other goods as part of the deal

U.S. official poverty level Benchmark level of income computed by the federal government to track poverty over time; initially based on three times the cost of a nutritionally adequate diet

underemployment Workers are overqualified for their jobs or work fewer hours than they would prefer

underground economy An expression used to describe market activity that goes unreported either because it is illegal or because those involved want to evade taxes

underground economy Market transactions that go unreported either because they are illegal or because people involved want to evade taxes

undifferentiated oligopoly An oligopoly that sells a commodity, or a product that does not differ across suppliers, such as an ingot of steel or a barrel of oil

unemployment benefits Cash transfers to those who lose their jobs and actively seek employment

unemployment rate The number unemployed as a percentage of the labor force

unit of account A common unit for measuring the value of each good or service

unit-elastic demand curve Everywhere along the demand curve, the percentage change in price causes an equal but offsetting percentage change in quantity demanded, so total revenue remains the same; the elasticity has an absolute value of 1.0

unit-elastic demand The percentage change in quantity demanded equals the percentage change in price; the resulting price elasticity has an absolute value of 1.0

unit-elastic supply curve A percentage change in price causes an identical percentage change in quantity supplied; depicted by a supply curve that is a straight line from the origin; the elasticity value equals 1.0

unit-elastic supply The percentage change in quantity supplied equals the percentage change in price; the price elasticity of supply equals 1.0

Uruguay Round The final multilateral trade negotiation under GATT; this 1994 agreement cut tariffs, formed the World Trade Organization (WTO), and will eventually eliminate quotas

utility The satisfaction received from consumption; sense of well-being

value added At each stage of production, the selling price of a product minus the cost of intermediate goods purchased from other firms

variable cost Any production cost that changes as the rate of output changes

variable resource Any resource that can be varied in the short run to increase or decrease production

variable technology Occurs when the amount of externality generated at a given rate of output can be reduced by altering the production process

variable A measure, such as price or quantity, that can take on different values at different times

velocity of money The average number of times per year each dollar is used to purchase final goods and services

vertical integration The expansion of a firm into stages of production earlier or later than those in which it specializes, such as a steel maker that also mines iron ore

vertical merger A merger in which one firm combines with another from which it had purchased inputs or to which it had sold output

wages Payment to resource owners for their labor

winner's curse The plight of the winning bidder who overestimates an asset's true value

winner-take-all labor markets Markets in which a few key employees critical to the overall success of an enterprise are richly rewarded

world price The price at which a good is traded on the world market; determined by the world demand and world supply for the good

World Trade Organization (WTO) The legal and institutional foundation of the multilateral trading system that succeeded GATT in 1995

Index

C

Q

R

S

T